The Economics
of Adjustment and Growth

Pierre-Richard Agénor

The Economics
of Adjustment and Growth

Second Edition

Harvard University Press

Cambridge, Massachusetts, and London, England

2004

Library of Congress Cataloging-in-Publication Data

Agénor, Pierre-Richard.
   The economics of adjustment and growth / Pierre-Richard Agénor.—
2nd ed.
      p.   cm.
   Includes bibliographical references and index.
   ISBN 0-674-01578-9 (alk. paper)
      1. Structural adjustment (Economic policy)   2. Economic development.
I. Title.

   HD87.A364 2004
   338.9—dc22   2004046556

To my late mother, Rolande,
for her love, courage, and devotion

Contents

16   Aid, External Debt, and Growth 621

17   Sequencing, Gradualism, and the Political Economy of Adjustment 653

Acknowledgments

This book is the product of years of research on the analytical foundations of adjustment programs in developing countries. Much of the material presented here was first used in the lectures that I have given in universities and research centers all around the world on these topics; some of it also comes from the notes prepared for my graduate courses at Georgetown University and Yale University. I was fortunate, in the early days of my professional career, to engage in joint research with a number of highly talented economists; my intellectual debt to them (especially Joshua Aizenman, Bob Flood, Peter Montiel, and Mark Taylor) is immeasurable. I am also grateful to Joshua Aizenman (who derived the results presented in the appendix to Chapter 2), anonymous reviewers for Harvard University Press, and several readers of the first edition for their reactions and suggestions, which led to considerable improvements and corrections. I alone, of course, should be held responsible for the final product and its shortcomings. I am also very grateful to Brooks Calvo and Nihal Bayraktar for their research assistance. Finally, I would like to express my appreciation to the publishers of the *Handbook of International Macroeconomics,* the *Journal of Development Economics,* and the *IMF Staff Papers* for permission to dwell on material contained in some of my earlier publications.

Introduction and Overview

Understanding the process through which economic adjustment affects economic growth and standards of living remains a key issue for economists and policy-makers in the developing world. Among some of the lessons that have emerged during the past decades is the realization that macroeconomic and financial volatility may have large adverse effects on growth rates and the level of income. Instability in relative prices and overall inflation may have a negative effect on the expected return to capital and the decision to invest; in turn, the lack of investment may hamper economic growth and worsen the plight of the poor. It has also been recognized that microeconomic (or structural) rigidities may have sizable effects on macroeconomic imbalances. For instance, interest rate ceilings that result in negative real rates of return may lead to disequilibrium between domestic savings and investment and greater reliance on foreign capital, thereby contributing to balance-of-payments problems. Thus, attempts at macroeconomic stabilization may fail if they are not complemented with adequate microeconomic (and often institutional) reforms.

Although the intricate interactions between the micro and macro dimensions of adjustment policies are now better understood, there have been few attempts to integrate them in a systematic and coherent framework. By and large, most textbooks in the field of development economics have maintained their focus on long-term growth, and continue to treat macroeconomic issues as a sideshow. In my book with Peter Montiel, *Development Macroeconomics*, first published in 1996, I took the opposite position and focused almost exclusively on macro-economic policy issues. However, the advanced nature of that book makes it more suitable for graduate students and technically oriented professional macroeconomists.

This book fills a gap in the existing literature by providing a rigorous, but accessible, analysis of policy issues involved in both aspects of economic adjustment in developing countries—short-run macroeconomic management *and* structural adjustment policies aimed at fostering economic growth. As in my earlier work, the book emphasizes the need to take systematically into account important *structural features* of these countries for economic analysis. The underlying perspective is that structural (micro-) economic characteristics play an important role in both the transmission of policy shocks and the response of the economy to adjustment policies. It is therefore essential to take into account the behavioral implications of these characteristics in designing stabilization

1

and adjustment programs. As will become clear to the reader, an important analytical literature doing precisely that already exists; however, some of this literature has been available (often in compact form) only in professional economic journals. This book makes much of this material available in a coherent and, I hope, reader-friendly format.

The structure and contents of this book are likely to make it of interest to a variety of readers. A first group may consist of professional economists interested in a rigorous, but not overly mathematical, overview of recent developments in the principles of macroeconomic management and the economics of reform. It includes, in particular, economists in developing countries involved on a day-to-day basis with stabilization and structural adjustment issues, economists working in international organizations dealing with development, and economists in private financial institutions. A second group of readers includes advanced undergraduate students pursuing a degree in economic management, or students specializing in political science or public affairs, with a knowledge of intermediate microeconomics and macroeconomics. Although the material covered in the book is dense, the relatively self-contained nature of most of the chapters provides considerable discretion to teachers in choosing the exact list of topics to be covered during, say, a one-semester course. Finally, parts of the book can also be used as supplementary readings for advanced undergraduate courses in macroeconomics (Chapters 1 to 9), economic growth (Chapters 10 to 13), international economics (Chapters 7, 8, 14, and 16), and public economics (Chapters 3 and 15), quantitative techniques (Chapter 9), and political economy (Chapter 17).[1]

The book is organized as follows. Chapters 1 to 9 focus on policy issues related to short-run macroeconomic adjustment. Chapter 1 provides a brief review of aggregate accounts, and the specification of flow and stock budget constraints. The first three parts of the chapter discuss basic concepts of macroeconomic accounting, a summary format for current account and financial transactions, as well as various aggregate identities and key macroeconomic relationships, and show how they are related to the sectoral budget constraints. The fourth part presents the principles underlying the construction of a social accounting matrix—an extremely useful tool for summarizing micro and macro features of an economy (including the distribution of income among agents). Social accounting matrices have gained considerably in popularity in recent years, because they are often used as a basis for the construction of applied general equilibrium models.

Chapter 2 begins with a discussion of the determinants of consumption and saving in developing countries. It starts with standard theories (the Keynesian specification, the permanent income hypothesis, and the basic life-cycle

---

[1]It should be clear from this overview that there are a number of issues that normally figure prominently in textbooks in development economics but nevertheless are not addressed in this book. In particular, the rural economy is not discussed in any depth, despite its importance for the process of development. Basu (1997) provides a detailed discussion of many of the important topics in this area, including stagnation and backward agriculture, tenancy and efficiency, rural credit markets and interlinkages in rural markets.

model) and continues with various extensions aimed at capturing factors that have been shown empirically to play an important role in developing economies. These factors include income levels and income variability, intergenerational links, liquidity constraints, inflation and macroeconomic instability, government saving behavior, social security and pension systems, and changes in the terms of trade. The second part of the chapter focuses on the determinants of private investment and includes a brief review of standard models (which emphasize accelerator effects and the cost of capital), as well as a discussion of the role of uncertainty and irreversibility. As in the case of consumption and saving, several additional factors found to be important in empirical studies on developing countries are also discussed, including credit rationing, changes in relative prices, public investment, macroeconomic instability, and the debt overhang—a particularly important consideration for low-income countries. The recent empirical evidence is also systematically reviewed.

Chapter 3 examines various issues associated with fiscal policy in macroeconomic adjustment. It begins with a description of the composition of conventional sources of public revenue and expenditure in developing countries. Implicit sources of revenue and expenditure (such as seigniorage and the inflation tax, and contingent liabilities) are examined next, and their implications for the measurement of the fiscal deficit of the consolidated public sector and the stance of fiscal policy are discussed. The second part specifies the government budget constraint and describes various measures of the fiscal stance. The third part presents a simple, yet very useful, technique aimed at disentangling the short- and medium-term effects of fiscal policy. The next three parts examine the link between fiscal imbalances and current account deficits, and issues associated with public debt sustainability and public sector solvency. The chapter concludes with a discussion of the link between commodity price booms and the fiscal balance, and the link between fiscal adjustment, expectations, and economic activity.

Chapter 4 focuses on the structure of the financial system and its implications for monetary policy. It begins with a description of some of the main characteristics of the financial system in developing countries—most notably the pervasive nature of government restrictions and the role played by banks in the process of financial intermediation. The determinants of money demand, the nature and operation of indirect instruments of monetary policy, together with the sources of credit market imperfections and credit rationing, are taken up next. The discussion then focuses on the transmission process of monetary policy under fixed and flexible exchange rates, and the use of inflation targeting as an operational framework for monetary policy. As a policy regime, inflation targeting has gained considerable popularity in recent years, in both industrial and developing countries; however, its performance in cyclical downturns remains open to question. The last part discusses issues raised by dollarization (the simultaneous use of domestic and foreign currencies) for the conduct of monetary policy.

Chapter 5 discusses various issues related to exchange rate management. It begins by reviewing the recent evolution of exchange rate regimes in developing countries and discusses in detail the operation of currency board arrangements and exchange rate bands. The second part examines the various criteria that affect the choice of an exchange rate regime and identifies the potential trade-offs that may arise among them. Understanding the nature of these trade-offs is important because, as recent exchange rate crises have demonstrated, policy challenges do change over time; exchange rate arrangements must be adapted to changing circumstances. The third part explores the role of credibility factors, as well as the implications of inconsistencies between fiscal and exchange rate policies, for the viability of a fixed exchange rate regime. The links between exchange rates, competitiveness, and trade balance movements are examined in the fourth part, after a brief review of alternative measures of the real exchange rate. The last part of the chapter examines the channels through which exchange rate adjustment may induce contractionary effects on output—an issue that remains controversial in the developing world.

The focus of Chapter 6 is on inflation and disinflation policies. The first part of the chapter discusses the sources of chronic inflation and hyperinfla-tion. It begins with an examination of the link between fiscal deficits, seignior-age, and inflation, and continues with a discussion of various other sources of price increases, including wage inertia, exchange rate depreciations, terms-of-trade shocks, and the inflation bias associated with a lack of credibility. The second part examines the factors affecting the choice of nominal anchors in disinflation programs, focusing notably on the macroeconomic dynamics asso-ciated with monetary- and exchange-rate based stabilization programs. The third part focuses on the role of credibility in disinflation. It reviews sources of credibility problems and discusses ways through which policymakers can en-hance credibility—including, in particular, central bank independence and price controls. The last part reviews two experiences with alternative types of adjust-ment programs: Egypt (1992-97), where stabilization was based on a pegged exchange rate, and Uganda (1987-95), where a money supply anchor was used. A key lesson of these experiences is the role played by fiscal adjustment. Getting the government budget under control is essential to ensure a sustained reduction in inflation.

In recent years many developing countries have continued to globalize and integrate their economies through trade and international financial flows. In-deed, the share of trade (exports plus imports) in the gross domestic product of the developing world has risen from about one-third in the mid-1980s to al-most 45 percent in 1996; it could exceed 50 percent by the year 2005. This tendency marks a sharp break from past trends and reflects the adoption of outward-oriented reforms by a growing number of these countries. However, the trend toward globalization has not been without setbacks. The efficiency, consumption smoothing, and risk-diversification gains of financial integration have been mitigated by the high economic and social costs associated with large and abrupt reversals in capital flows. At the same time, the financial crises in Mexico, East Asia, Brazil, Turkey, and Argentina in recent years have raised concerns regarding the effects of capital inflows in an environment in which financial institutions are weak. These issues are discussed in Chapters 7 and 8.

Chapter 7 focuses on the surge in capital inflows to the developing world in the early 1990s and the policy responses they have elicited. The first part of the chapter reviews overall trends in the evolution and geographical distribution of capital flows. It highlights the high degree of concentration of private capital flows to a small group of countries in Asia and Latin America. The second part focuses on the factors underlying the surge in private capital flows. Both domestic and external factors appeared to have played a role, although their relative importance varied considerably across countries and regions. Examples of the first type of factors are the measures aimed at liberalizing capital movements taken in the late 1980s by a number of developing countries; an example of the second type is fluctuations in world interest rates. The third part reviews the recent evidence on the volatility of various components of capital inflows, whereas the fourth part discusses the macroeconomic effects of these flows—notably their effect on domestic liquidity and credit growth, the real exchange rate, and the balance of payments. The fifth part presents a static, three-good framework with imperfect capital mobility and a supply side-bank credit link, and examines the effects of a change in the world interest rate on the domestic economy. The last part examines the policy responses to large capital inflows, including sterilization, nominal exchange rate flexibility, fiscal adjustment, and capital controls, and gives a detailed discussion of the nature and effectiveness of the type of restrictions put in place by Chile until 1998. Market failures, as any sensible economist recognizes, abound in the real world; they do not necessarily, however, create a *prima facie* case for government intervention—nor do they guarantee that government intervention, if it occurs, will be successful. Nevertheless, the experience of countries like Chile suggests that capital controls can be an effective means of limiting short-term speculative pressures and can be justified when these pressures are not warranted by underlying fundamentals, but instead result from rumors, cross-country contagion effects, and herding behavior.

As noted earlier, the incidence of financial crises seems to have increased in recent years, at the same time that global financial integration has been increasing cross-border movements in capital. Chapter 8 focuses on the determinants of financial crises. The first part reviews two broad types of models of currency crises, those that emphasize the role of economic fundamentals, and those that highlight the interplay between fundamental and extraneous factors—such as changes in market sentiment. The second part reviews three recent currency crises, the Mexican peso crisis of December 1994, the Thai baht crisis of July 1997, and the Brazilian real crisis of January 1999. The third part examines the causes of banking crises and the empirical evidence on both banking and currency crises. The final part attempts to identify factors affecting financial volatility on world capital markets (particularly the role of contagion and herding behavior) and ways through which the adverse effects of such volatility can be mitigated.

Chapter 9 focuses on tools for macroeconomic policy analysis. It begins by looking at ways of assessing macroeconomic fluctuations using cross-correlation techniques. A simple method for decomposing the effects of external shocks on the domestic economy is presented next. The third part focuses on the analytical foundations of financial programming—the basic approach underlying stabilization programs designed by the International Monetary Fund (IMF). Both simplified and elaborate versions of the financial programming approach are presented. The fourth part considers the medium-term programming framework of the World Bank, while the fifth part discusses various attempts aimed at merging the IMF and World Bank models by integrating medium-term, supply-side considerations (as in the Bank approach) into a financial programming framework. The resulting model, however, remains subject to a number of limitations, and several of them are identified. The sixth part discusses three-gap models. The final part presents a simple applied general equilibrium model also developed at the World Bank that has proved to be quite useful to assess the long-run effects of fiscal and trade policies on relative prices and resource allocation.

The question of what determines the rate of growth and how it can be influenced by economic policy has always been a central preoccupation in development economics. The second part of the book, which consists of Chapters 10 to 13, reviews the recent literature on economic growth and its determinants. Chapter 10 begins by summarizing some of the facts related to economic growth, poverty, and income distribution. The evidence on growth focuses both on the long-run experience (over the period 1820-1992) of industrial and developing countries, and on the post-World War II experience. The sharp divergence, in the developing world, of the performance of East Asian countries and sub-Saharan African countries is discussed in detail. The chapter concludes with a summary of the basic facts that appear to characterize the process of economic growth in developing countries. It discusses, in particular, the links between growth, saving, and investment, as well as the link between poverty, inequality, and economic growth. This collection of facts serves as a useful background for interpreting and judging the ability of growth theories, both old and new, to explain the evidence.

Chapter 11 presents the standard neoclassical model of economic growth (the Solow-Swan model) and assesses its ability to answer some of the basic facts identified in Chapter 10.The inability of the basic model to explain the persistent divergence in growth rates across countries (except as a consequence of economies being on different transitional dynamic paths) is emphasized. Chapter 12 presents the new, so-called endogenous growth theories. The first part of the chapter explores the sources of knowledge accumulation and the resulting effects on growth. The second part analyzes the role of human capital accumulation in the growth process, and the impact of public policy on education. The last part examines the effects of various other factors on growth, including fiscal policy, inflation and macroeconomic instability, trade and financial openness, financial development, political factors, and income distribution. It also emphasizes the critical role played by institutions (such as a credible legal system for the enforcement of property rights, and proper checks and balances to avoid corruption and rent-seeking behavior in the public sector) for an efficient allocation of individual skills and talents. Establishing and maintaining the rule of law by improving the functioning of public institutions may indeed be one of the most important tasks of governments in the developing world today—although such reforms, by challenging vested interests, may face serious political resistance.

Developments in growth theory have been accompanied in the past few years by a flurry of empirical studies aimed at assessing the determinants of economic growth in industrial and developing countries alike. Chapter 13 reviews the recent evidence on both "old" and "new" theories and highlights in the process some of the (serious) methodological problems confronting many of the empirical studies. It first discusses growth accounting techniques and uses the methodology to analyze the controversy over the sources of growth in East Asia since the early 1950s. It then provides an overview of the cross-country growth literature. In doing so it focuses on recent studies, which provide a better treatment of issues such as measurement errors, time averaging, simultaneity bias, and omitted-variable problems than the early literature. In line with the presentation of endogenous growth models in Chapter 12, the review considers the evidence on the role of physical and human capital, fiscal policy, inflation and macroeconomic stability, the degree of trade and financial openness, political variables, and income distribution. The last part of the chapter assesses the evidence on the speed of convergence (or lack thereof) in income per capita across countries.

Since the early 1980s, numerous developing countries have implemented large-scale structural adjustment programs, involving fiscal, financial, and trade reforms. The third part of the book, Chapters 14 to 17, reviews the recent literature and evidence on these reforms, as well as the interaction between economic and political factors in the design of reform programs. Chapter 14 focuses on structural adjustment policies with a direct effect on the real sector—namely, trade reform (which may have a substantial impact on product and the labor markets), regional integration and the role of preferential trading areas, and labor market reforms—such as measures aimed at reducing labor costs and at curtailing the power of trade unions in the wage bargaining process. The effect of trade liberalization on wage inequality and the impact of labor market reforms on flexibility and economic growth have indeed attracted much attention in recent years, but the literature remains somewhat unsettled regarding the direction of these effects.

Chapter 15 focuses on fiscal and financial reforms. The first two parts of the chapter discuss the efficiency effects of tax reform and its links with trade liberalization, as well as measures aimed at enhancing control and management of public expenditure. Civil service downsizing, fiscal decentralization, and pension reform are discussed next. The third part studies the effects on saving, investment, and growth of a policy that has featured prominently in financial reform programs, namely, interest rate liberalization. Both the rationales for, and the risks associated with, this policy are reviewed, in light of the recent experience of developing countries. The chapter also discusses the links between financial liberalization and financial fragility, and measures aimed at reforming and strengthening weak banking systems—a phenomenon made manifest, in many countries, by domestic financial liberalization and increased openness to world capital markets. The key message of this analysis is that, as demonstrated for instance by the financial turmoil that accompanied the East Asia crisis, developing countries must proceed cautiously in opening their capital account. Capital account liberalization cannot take place in isolation, without appropriate macroeconomic, exchange rate, and financial sector policies. This may sound like a trivial statement nowadays, but it took in fact a long time for international institutions to recognize the importance of prerequisites and moderate their "over-zealous" advocacy of the benefits of financial liberalization.

At the same time that a small group of developing countries have been receiving massive inflows of capital, the debt burden of several low-income countries has become unsustainable. As noted earlier, private capital inflows have concentrated on a small group of (upper-income) developing countries; low-income countries, particularly those of sub-Saharan Africa, have by and large failed to attract private flows, in some cases despite significant market-based economic reforms—possibly because these reforms did little to reduce the perceived degree of investment risk. Chapter 16 begins by discussing the links between foreign aid, investment, and growth, and recent studies on the effectiveness of foreign assistance. It then analyzes the links between foreign borrowing and growth, and the effects of a large burden of debt on investment incentives and growth. The fourth part considers practical issues involved in measuring the debt burden, and the fifth part the various agreements under which debt relief has been provided to low-income countries. The last part examines recent attempts to reduce multilateral official debt, as well as their limitations. Many observers have taken a rather pessimistic view of existing efforts to provide debt relief to the poorest countries and have advocated a bolder approach than what the international community is currently contemplating.

Chapter 17 focuses on the sequencing of policy reforms and the role of political factors in the design of adjustment programs. The first part considers the various channels through which macroeconomic stabilization and structural reforms may interact during the liberalization process. The second discusses the sequencing and speed of reforms—an issue that has remained at the forefront of the policy agenda in many countries. Whether reform should be implemented overnight, and whether there exists an optimal sequencing of liberalization policies, are both subject to intense debate. Analytical arguments as well as the empirical evidence on these questions are reviewed. For instance, the existence of policy complementarities suggests that the implementation of a broad and consistent set of reforms may minimize the risks of policy reversals by enhancing their credibility and sustainability. At the same time, in a country where implementation capacity is weak, structural adjustment programs cannot have unrealistic expectations about how fast adjustment will occur; otherwise, they may underestimate the (economic and political) costs of more rapid implementation.

The last part of the chapter focuses on the political dimension of adjustment programs. The role of political feasibility in the design of these programs, and whether political sustainability can be ensured by an adequate sequencing of reforms, are both examined in detail. Other issues that are discussed in the chapter include poverty-reducing policies and social safety nets (a feature that is increasingly found in adjustment programs), and the link between corruption and foreign aid, that is, whether foreign assistance can play a signaling and credibility-enhancing role in an environment in which corruption is high.

Each chapter ends with a summary of the main issues covered. Many of them incorporate a technical appendix as well. Finally, two unpublished annexes, available by contacting me at the University of Manchester, treat a set of issues that were left out of the book because of its already imposing length. Annex A deals with intertemporal models of the current account, whereas Annex B deals with the structure, functioning, and macroeconomic implications of informal markets for credit and foreign exchange. In particular, Annex B explores analytically the short- and longer-run macro dynamics associated with exchange market unification.

Chapter 1

Budget Constraints and Aggregate Accounts

By organizing our data in the form of accounts we can obtain a coherent picture of the stocks and flows, incomings and outgoings of whatever variables we are interested in . . . Given [a coherent set of accounts], we can formulate some hypotheses, or *theories*, about the technical and behavioural relationships that connect them. By combining facts and theories we can construct a *model* which when translated into quantitative terms will give us an idea of how the system under investigation actually works.

J. Richard N. Stone, *The Accounts of Society*, Nobel Memorial Lecture, 1984.

An integrated and consistent set of economic accounts is a prerequisite for any modeling exercise in macroeconomic analysis. This chapter discusses the relationships between national accounting, stock and flow budget constraints, and the consistency requirements that macroeconomic models must satisfy. Section 1.1 discusses the basic accounting concepts upon which macroeconomic analysis dwells (production, income, and expenditure) and the national income accounting concepts derived from them. Section 1.2 presents a **consistency accounting matrix**, the purpose of which is to summarize in a convenient format all current and financial transactions in an economy during a given period of time. Section 1.3 derives various aggregate identities and some key macroeconomic relationships and shows how they relate to sectoral budget constraints. Section 1.4 presents the principles underlying the construction of **social accounting matrices**, which integrate both sectoral and aggregate data on production, expenditure, and income flows.

1.1   Production, Income, and Expenditure

Macroeconomic analysis is organized around three basic accounting concepts: production, income, and expenditure.

- **Production** of goods and services is carried out by domestic agents, including firms, self-employed workers (in the formal or informal sector), financial institutions (banks, insurance companies, mutual funds), and the government.

- **Income** consists of wages and salaries, firms' operating surpluses, property income (including interest and dividends), and imputed compensation (for self-employed workers or property owners, that is, rentiers).

- **Expenditure** consists of outlays on durable and nondurable final consumption goods and investment. In general, production and spending units are different—except for subsistence production by households (mostly in agriculture) and the production of government services.

The three concepts of production, income, and expenditure are linked by three basic macroeconomic relationships, which result from the *budget constraints* faced by each category of agents:

- **Production and income**. The value of production, for the economy as a whole, must equal the value of income (excluding transfers) generated domestically. Such income, however, may accrue to either *resident* economic agents or to *nonresident* agents. Similarly, resident agents may receive factor payments from abroad. Income accruing to residents, or **national income**, is thus defined as gross domestic product (GDP) plus net factor payments from abroad.

- **Income, expenditure, and savings**. For any economic agent, income earned (regardless of whether the source is domestic or foreign) plus transfers (from domestic sources or the rest of the world) must be equal to expenditure plus savings, the latter being either positive or negative.

- **Savings and asset accumulation**. Savings plus borrowing must equal asset acquisition for any economic agent. These assets may be **physical assets** (capital goods, for instance, but not consumer durables) or **financial assets** (such as bank deposits or government bonds). Borrowing, just like savings, may be either positive or negative.

1.2   A Consistency Accounting Matrix

This section sets out an integrated macroeconomic accounting framework that stresses two types of transactions between agents: transactions in goods and services, and financial transactions. Such a framework (which thus combines income and flow-of-funds accounts) is an important step in the design of a consistent macroeconomic model, such as the **RMSM-X model** of the World Bank described in Chapter 9.

This integrated accounting framework records all incoming and outgoing transactions for each category of agent. Thus, the balance of all transactions (real and financial) for each and every one of them is necessarily equal to zero, and the balance of income-expenditure transactions is equal and of opposite sign to the balance of financial transactions. As a result, several equivalence relationships, or *identities*, emerge among the various magnitudes recorded in the accounts.

Consider an economy in which the following four categories of agents operate:

- The *private nonfinancial sector*, which includes the household sector as well as the private corporate sector.

- The *financial sector*, which includes both the central bank and the commercial banks as well as other financial intermediaries (private savings banks, finance companies, and public savings institutions).[1]

- The *general government*, which comprises all levels of government (central, state, and local) as well as public sector corporations funded through the government budget.[2]

- The *external (nonresident) sector*, which includes all transactions of non-residents with residents.

Following Easterly (1989), Table 1.1 presents the transactions between these agents in the form of a **consistency matrix**, which essentially describes the sources and uses of funds in the economy. Five sets of accounts are incorporated in the consistency framework:

- the national accounts;

- the accounts of the nonfinancial private sector;

- the government accounts;

- the balance sheet of the financial sector;

- the balance of payments, which captures the consolidated accounts of the external sector—that is, transactions between residents and nonresidents.

---

[1]The analysis here focuses only on the role of the financial system as an intermediary for channeling savings across sectors. A high degree of aggregation is thus reasonable. A disaggregated financial structure would, of course, be more appropriate to analyze, for instance, how regulations imposed by the central bank on commercial banks—such as cash reserve ratios or statutory liquidity ratios—affect the money supply and the provision of loans to other agents.

[2]In general, whether public-owned enterprises are included in the government sector or in the private nonfinancial sector varies across countries; it depends on whether public enterprises are viewed as primarily *profit-seeking* entities (like private enterprises) or as primarily *government-controlled* entities. The share of assets under public control is often used to make the distinction, but this can be unreliable.

Table 1.1 A consistency accounting matrix

Sources (rows) and Uses (columns)	Current Account					Capital Account					Total
	A National Accounts	B Government	C Financial System	D Nonfinancial Private Sector	E External Sector	F Government	G Financial System	H Nonfinancial Private Sector	I External Sector	J Total Investment	
1 National Accounts		C^g		C^p	X	I^g		I^p		$I = I^p + I^g$	$Y = C^g + C^p + X - J + I$
2 Government	$T_I - SUB + OS^g$			T_D	NT^{gt}						$T^g = T_I - SUB + OS^g + T_D + NT^{gt}$
3 Financial System											
4 Nonfinancial Private Sector	$W + \Pi + Y_s$	$NT^{pg} + INT^{pg}$			$NT^{pt} + NFP^{pt}$						$Y^p = W + \Pi + Y_s + NT^{pg} + INT^{pg} + NT^{pt} + NFP^{pt}$
5 External sector	J	INT^{fg}		INT^{fp}							$J + INT^{fg} + INT^{fp}$

Savings and Borrowings

Sources (rows) and Uses (columns)	A National Accounts	B Government	C Financial System	D Nonfinancial Private Sector	E External Sector	F Government	G Financial System	H Nonfinancial Private Sector	I External Sector	J Total Investment	Total
6 Government		S^g					ΔL^{gb}	ΔB^p	ΔFB^g		$S^g + \Delta L^{gb} + \Delta B^p + \Delta FB^g$
7 Financial system								ΔM			ΔM
8 Nonfinancial private sector				S^p			ΔL^{pb}		ΔFB^p		$S^p + \Delta L^{pb} + \Delta FB^p$
9 External sector					CA		ΔR^*				$CA + \Delta R^*$
10 Total Savings (Sum of previous 4 rows)		S^g		S^p	CA						$S^g + S^p + CA = I$
Total	$Y + J = TI - SUB + OS^g + (W + \Pi + Y_s) + J$	$G + S^g = T^g$		$CC^p + S^p = Y^p$	$X + NT^{gt} + NT^{pt} + NFP^{pt} + CA$	I^g	$\Delta L + \Delta R^*$	$I^p + \Delta B^p + \Delta M$	$\Delta FB^g + \Delta FB^p$	$I = I^p + I^g$	

Notes: G in column B is defined as $G = C^g + NT^{pg} + (INT^{pg} + INT^{fg})$. CC^p in column D is defined as $CC^p = C^p + T_D + INT^{fp}$. ΔL in column G is defined as $\Delta L = \Delta L^{gb} + \Delta L^{pb}$.

Reading across rows (labeled 1, 2, etc.) in Table 1.1 provides the *sources* of finance for each sector, whereas reading down columns (labeled A, B, etc.) indicates the *uses* of finance. *Ex post*, each sector's deficit must be financed and, as such, the sum of the rows is always equal to the sum of the columns. *Ex ante*, these sectoral balances become *constraints* for modeling the behavior of each group of agents.

1.2.1 Current Account Transactions

Row 1 and column A, the **national accounts**, consolidate the current-period activities of *all production units* together, regardless of the type of good or service produced: incorporated enterprises (financial and nonfinancial), informal sector firms, producers of government services, and production by households for own consumption. Across row 1, the table describes how goods and services that are produced domestically, Y, or imported, J, are allocated between

- government final consumption, C^g;

- private final consumption, C^p;

- exports, X;

- the acquisition of *physical assets* by the government and the private sector, or investment, I^g and I^p, with $I = I^p + I^g$.

Column A decomposes the value of current domestic production, Y, defined as *GDP at current market prices*, into the various types of income that are generated through the sale (plus own consumption) of domestic output. Income consists of

- net indirect taxes, that is, indirect taxes, T_I, less subsidies, SUB;

- the operating surplus of government enterprises, OS^g;

- wages and salaries, W, and profits, Π;

- incomes of the self-employed and own-account producers, Y_s.

The sum of wages, salaries, and the incomes of own-account producers—referred to, in the United Nations System of National Accounts (SNA) as *employee compensation*—along with the operating surpluses of all enterprises (including funds set aside for depreciation by producing units), is value added at producers' prices and is referred to as *GDP at factor cost*, Y_{fc}. By convention, *value added at factor cost*, V_{fc}, accrues to households (and to the government, in the case of the operating surplus of state-owned enterprises) even though a fraction of these earnings might be retained by enterprises or the government to finance capital formation. Adding *net indirect taxes* to V_{fc} yields *value added at market prices*, that is, what purchasers actually pay for goods and services. The sum of value added at market prices and imports is equal to the *total amount of goods and services* available for final use.

Row 2 and column B account for the current transactions of the **government**. The sources of current government revenue, T^g, are identified across row 2 and consist of

- net indirect taxes, $T_I - SUB$;

- the operating surpluses of government-owned enterprises, OS^g;

- direct taxes levied on the nonfinancial private sector, T_D;

- net transfers to the government from the rest of the world, NT^{gf}.

Column B provides a decomposition of total current government *expenditures*, G, into

- government consumption of goods and services, C^g, which essentially represents the cost of producing government services;

- net transfers to the nonfinancial private sector, NT^{pg};

- interest paid to the private sector on domestic public debt, INT^{pg};

- interest payments on public foreign debt, INT^{fg}.

Government savings, S^g, shown at the bottom of column B, is thus the difference between current government revenue and expenditure, that is,

$$S^g = T^g - G,$$

with

$$T^g = T_I - SUB + OS^g + T_D + NT^{gf},$$
$$G = C^g + (NT^{pg} + INT^{pg}) + INT^{fg}.$$

Row 3 and column C describe the balance sheet of the consolidated **financial sector**. In the case considered here, again, the financial system operates as a *pure intermediary*; it has therefore no independent revenue and expenditure accounts. The revenues of financial institutions minus their costs represent the value added of these institutions to the economy. Because this value added is included in the production accounts of the domestic economy as income to the nonfinancial private sector or to the government, row 3 and column C are empty.

Row 4 and column D describe the accounts of the **nonfinancial private sector**. Row 4 identifies the *sources* of income of the private sector, Y^p, which consist of

- factor income, including wages and salaries, W, profits, Π, and incomes of the self-employed, Y_s;

- net transfers received from the government, NT^{pg};

- interest payments from the government on its domestic debt, INT^{pg};

- net transfers, NT^{pf}, plus net factor payments from abroad, NFP^{pf}.

Column D describes the *allocation* of the nonfinancial private sector income into

- private consumption, C^p;

- payment of direct taxes, T_D;

- interest payments on private external debt, INT^{fp}.

Private saving, S^p, shown at the bottom of column D, is the balancing item and is the difference between total private sector income, Y^p, and total current expenditures of the private sector, CC^p:

$$S^p = Y^p - CC^p,$$

where[3]

$$CC^p = C^p + T_D + INT^{fp}.$$

Row 5 and column E depict the **current account** of the **balance of payments.** Row 5 provides the sources of income accruing *to* foreign residents, which consist of

- the value of imports of goods and services, J;[4]

- public and private sector interest payments on their respective external debts, INT^{fg} and INT^{fp}.

Column E describes the sources of income accruing *from* foreign residents. These sources of income are

- exports of goods and services, X;

- net current (as opposed to capital) transfers to the government and private sectors, NT^{gf} and NT^{pf};

- net factor payments to the private sector, NFP^{pf}.

Savings by foreign residents, shown at the bottom of column E, is the balancing item between external receipts and payments, that is, the *current account balance*, CA:

$$CA = X + (NT^{gf} + NT^{pf}) + NFP^{pf} - J - INT^{fg} - INT^{fp}.$$

---

[3]Note that *property income* paid and received by resident households does not appear as separate entries in Table 1.1. Such incomes are accounted for in the operating surpluses of producing units and cancel each other out.

[4]Note that, following conventional practice, payments of *principal* on the external debt are recorded in net terms in the capital account (see rows 6 to 9 and columns F through I), not in the current account of the balance of payments.

1.2.2 Capital Account Transactions

While rows 1 to 5 and columns A through E describe the current accounts of the economy, rows 6 to 9 and columns F through J describe the corresponding capital account transactions, that is, the financing of *asset acquisition* by the government, the private nonfinancial sector, and the external sector.[5]

Row 6 describes the sources of financing of asset accumulation by the **government**, which consist of

- government savings, S^g;

- net borrowing from the financial system, ΔL^{gb};

- net borrowing from the private sector, in the form of placement of government bonds, ΔB^p;

- net foreign borrowing, ΔFB^g.

Column F contains only one item, gross fixed capital investment by the government, I^g.[6]

Row 7 and column G depict the accounts of the **financial sector**. Row 7 indicates that, as an intermediary, the financial system acquires liabilities principally in the form of new domestic currency issues, demand deposits and time deposits, ΔM.[7] Column G indicates that the assets of the financial system consist of loans to the government, ΔL^{gb}, loans to the private sector, ΔL^{pb}, and net foreign assets, ΔR^*.

Row 8 and column H describe the capital account transactions of the non-financial private sector. Row 8 indicates that asset acquisition by the private sector is financed by private sector savings, S^p, net borrowing from the financial system, ΔL^{pb}, and net borrowing from abroad, ΔFB^p. Asset acquisition is detailed in column H and consists of

- private investment, I^p, which includes physical assets, inventories and working capital, as well as intangible nonfinancial assets;

- net lending to the government (that is, acquisition of government securities), ΔB^p;

- increases in holdings of monetary assets, ΔM, that is, liabilities issued by the financial sector.

---

[5] The block consisting of rows 1 to 5 and columns A through E represent the *flows-of-funds matrix*, which can be used separately if the focus of analysis is on the determination of the economy's investment-savings balance.

[6] Asset acquisition by the government may also take the form of acquisition of financial assets in the form of loans to the private sector and acquisition of foreign assets. However, the last two items have been netted out from government borrowing from the private sector, ΔB^p, and foreign borrowing of the government, ΔFB^g, and therefore do not appear explicitly as separate entities in Table 1.1.

[7] For simplicity, it is assumed that the financial sector does not hold net government liabilities, such as treasury bills.

Row 9 and column I depict the capital account transactions of the external sector. Row 9 indicates that savings by foreign residents (that is, the current account deficit), CA, plus acquisition of net foreign exchange reserves by the financial system, ΔR^*, are the counterpart to net foreign borrowing of the government, ΔFB^g, and the private sector, ΔFB^p, as shown in column I.

Finally, row 10 and column J describe the overall **savings-investment balance** of the economy. Row 10 indicates that total domestic savings (the sum of government saving, S^g, private saving, S^p, and foreign saving, that is, the current account deficit, CA) must finance total investment (given by I in column J), that is, the sum of government investment, I^g, and private investment, I^p.

1.3   Identities and Budget Constraints

The current and capital account transactions of the four categories of agents that are summarized in the consistency accounting matrix of Table 1.1 can be used to show that standard national income identities are essentially *flow budget constraints*, that is, basic relationships that relate income and expenditure of each category of agents.

1.3.1   Gross Domestic Product and Absorption

Gross domestic product (GDP), or the value of goods and services that are produced by the domestic economy, can be derived from the basic macroeconomic relationship that relates the value of domestic production to the value of incomes that are domestically generated. From Table 1.1, two different approaches can be adopted for estimating GDP: the **expenditure approach** or the **value-added approach**.

- From row 1 and column A, we have

$$C^g + C^p + X + I^g + I^p = W + \Pi + Y_s + OS^g + (T_I - SUB) + J. \quad (1)$$

  GDP at market prices, $Y = W + \Pi + Y_s + OS^g + (T_I - SUB)$, is thus equal to the sum of private consumption, C^p, public consumption, C^g, private investment, I^p, public investment, I^g, and net exports of goods and services, $X - J$:

$$Y = C + I + X - J, \quad (2)$$

  where $C = C^p + C^g$ is total consumption, and $I = I^p + I^g$ is total investment.

- GDP at factor cost, Y_{fc}, is given by the sum of factor incomes, that is, wages, W, profits, Π, own-income of the self-employed, Y_s, augmented by the operating surplus of government enterprises, OS^g:

$$Y_{fc} = W + \Pi + Y_s + OS^g. \quad (3)$$

Substituting Equations (2) and (3) into Equation (1) yields

$$Y = Y_{fc} + (T_I - SUB),$$

which indicates that GDP at market prices is equal to GDP at factor cost plus indirect taxes net of subsidies.

Equation (2) can be rewritten as

$$Y + J - X = C + I = A, \tag{4}$$

which equates total supply of goods and services (that is, the sum of domestic output plus net imports) to **domestic absorption**, A, which consists of the sum of domestic consumption and investment. Equation (4) can also be rewritten as

$$J - X = A - Y = I - (Y - C) = I - S, \tag{5}$$

which relates net imports, $J - X$, to an excess of domestic absorption over output $(A - Y)$, or equivalently an excess of investment over savings, $I - S$. Thus, a reduction in the trade deficit requires either a reduction in absorption relative to output or, equivalently, an increase in net domestic savings.

1.3.2   The Government Budget Constraint

Equating the sum of the entries in row 2 and column B leads to

$$T_I - SUB + OS^g + T_D + NT^{gf} = C^g + NT^{pg} + (INT^{pg} + INT^{fg}) + S^g. \tag{6}$$

Given the definitions of T^g and G provided earlier, this equation can be rewritten as

$$T^g - G = S^g. \tag{7}$$

Equation (7) indicates that total current revenue of the government, T^g, must be equal to total current public expenditure, G, plus government savings, S^g.

Equating the sum of the entries in row 6 and column F yields

$$S^g + \Delta L^{gb} + \Delta B^p + \Delta F B^g = I^g, \tag{8}$$

which indicates that government savings plus net domestic and foreign borrowing must be equal to the flow of (physical) assets acquired by the government.[8] This constraint thus essentially relates government savings, borrowing, and asset acquisition.

Substituting Equation (7) into Equation (8) and rearranging the resulting expression reveals the sources of financing of the government budget deficit, as discussed in detail in Chapter 3:

$$G + I^g - T^g = \Delta L^{gb} + \Delta B^p + \Delta F B^g. \tag{9}$$

---

[8] Recall that the government acquisition of domestic financial assets (such as deposits in commercial banks or loans extended to the private sector) as well as foreign assets are netted out from domestic and from foreign borrowing, respectively.

The expression on the left-hand side of Equation (9) represents the overall fiscal deficit of the government (with G now defined to include interest payments on the public debt), whereas the expression on the right-hand side indicates the sources of deficit financing—direct borrowing from the banking system and the private sector, and borrowing from abroad.

1.3.3   The Private Sector Budget Constraint

The private sector budget constraint can be derived in a similar fashion. Equating the sum of the entries in row 4 and column D shows that

$$W + \Pi + Y_s + NT^{pg} + INT^{pg} + NT^{pf} + NFP^{pf} = C^p + T_D + INT^{fp} + S^p. \quad (10)$$

Defining total private sector income as

$$Y^p = W + \Pi + Y_s + NT^{pg} + INT^{pg} + NT^{pf} + NFP^{pf},$$

and private expenditure as

$$CC^p = C^p + T_D + INT^{fp},$$

expression (10) can be rewritten as

$$Y^p = CC^p + S^p, \quad (11)$$

as shown earlier. Equating the sum of the entries in row 8 and column H implies

$$S^p + \Delta L^{pb} + \Delta FB^p = I^p + \Delta B^p + \Delta M. \quad (12)$$

Substituting out for S^p in Equation (12) by using Equation (11) yields the private sector budget constraint:

$$Y^p - CC^p + \Delta L^{pb} + \Delta FB^p = I^p + \Delta B^p + \Delta M. \quad (13)$$

Equation (13) equates private sector income plus (domestic and foreign) borrowing, less total current expenditure, to private sector asset acquisition in the form of money (currency plus demand and time deposits), physical investment, and lending to the government.

1.3.4   The External Sector Budget Constraint

Equating the sum of the entries in row 5 and column E yields

$$J + INT^{fg} + INT^{fp} = X + NT^{gf} + NT^{pf} + NFP^{pf} + CA, \quad (14)$$

whereas equating the sum of all entries in row 9 and column I implies

$$CA = \Delta FB^g + \Delta FB^p - \Delta R^*. \quad (15)$$

Equation (15) indicates that a current account deficit (or positive savings by the external sector) must be financed either by an increase in net foreign borrowing by the private sector or the government and a capital inflow (implying an increase in the country's debt burden) or by drawing down the stock of reserves held by the financial sector.

Let **J** denote *gross payments* by the domestic economy, that is, the sum of imports and all interest payments on external debt, and let **X** be *gross receipts* to the domestic economy, obtained by adding to exports net transfers and net factor payments from abroad:

$$\mathbf{J} = J + INT^{fg} + INT^{fp},$$

$$\mathbf{X} = X + NT^{gf} + NT^{pf} + NFP^{pf}.$$

Using these definitions, and substituting Equation (14) into (15), yields the *external sector budget constraint*:

$$\mathbf{J} - \mathbf{X} = \Delta F - \Delta R^*, \qquad (16)$$

where $\Delta F = \Delta FB^g + \Delta FB^p$ denotes total capital inflows. The expression on the left-hand side of Equation (16) represents the *net resource inflow* in terms of goods and services, whereas the expression on the right-hand side is **net foreign asset acquisition**, or **net foreign borrowing** by domestic residents.

1.3.5   The Balance Sheet of the Financial System

As indicated earlier, the financial system in the present accounting framework is a pure intermediary. It does not, therefore, face a budget constraint *per se* but rather a balance sheet accounting identity that holds automatically *ex post*. Equating the sum of the entries in row 7 and column G yields

$$\Delta L + \Delta R^* = \Delta M, \qquad (17)$$

where $\Delta L = \Delta L^{gb} + \Delta L^{pb}$. Equation (17) states that assets of the financial system, which consist of credit to the government and private sectors and net foreign assets, must be equal to its liabilities, which consist of broad money.

Equation (17) can be rewritten as

$$\Delta R^* = \Delta M - \Delta L,$$

which indicates that the change in foreign exchange reserves is equal to the demand for money (assuming that the money market is in equilibrium) less the change in total domestic credit. This equation suggests that if the demand for money is held constant, then increases in domestic credit are offset by decreases in reserves on a one-to-one basis. Alternatively, it implies that given a desired level of reserves, and with the demand for money exogenously determined, the required change in domestic credit can be estimated. As discussed in Chapter 9, this basic relationship is at the heart of the International Monetary Fund's model of **financial programming**.

1.3.6   The Savings-Investment Balance

Adding the budget constraints of the government and private sectors, that is, Equations (9) and (13), and using Equation (7) and (11), yields

$$S + \Delta L + \Delta F = I + \Delta M, \tag{18}$$

that is, using Equation (16) to eliminate ΔF:

$$S + \Delta L + (\mathbf{J} - \mathbf{X}) + \Delta R^* = I + \Delta M.$$

Using Equation (17), the above equation yields the **savings-investment balance**:

$$I = S + (\mathbf{J} - \mathbf{X}), \tag{19}$$

which states that aggregate domestic investment, I, is financed by domestic savings, S, and foreign saving, $\mathbf{J} - \mathbf{X}$, the latter being synonymous to the current account deficit, CA. Equation (19) is identical to the result obtained by equating the sum of the entries in row 10 and column J, thereby indicating that the overall savings-investment balance is a *macroeconomic budget constraint* obtained by summing up the *sectoral budget constraints*.

Equation (19) can also be rewritten as

$$(S^g - I^g) + (S^p - I^p) = \mathbf{X} - \mathbf{J},$$

which implies, as discussed further in Chapter 3, that an improvement in the current account balance can occur only to the extent that government or private savings rise relative to government or private investment.

Similarly, Equation (18) can be rewritten as

$$S - I + \Delta F = \Delta M - \Delta L.$$

From Equation (5), $S - I = Y - A$. Substituting this result in the above equation yields

$$Y + \Delta F - A = \Delta M - \Delta L, \tag{20}$$

which links money, domestic credit, and absorption. The term $Y + \Delta F$ in the above expression can be viewed as representing *total resources available* for domestic consumption and investment. Equation (20) thus indicates that domestic absorption, A, will exceed total available resources by the amount by which domestic credit expansion, ΔL, exceeds the flow demand for money (assuming money market equilibrium), ΔM. The identity also shows that with available resources fixed and ΔM given, a reduction in domestic credit ΔL will improve the balance of payments, that is, increase reserves, ΔR^*, by reducing absorption.

1.4 Social Accounting Matrices

The consistency accounting matrix described earlier focuses only on aggregate macroeconomic data. By contrast, a **social accounting matrix** (or SAM, for short) provides a framework for combining these data with sectoral information on production, factor markets, and institutions (households, firms, and possibly different levels of government).[9] The general structure of a "typical" SAM is shown in Table 1.2. Just like the consistency framework presented earlier, a SAM is a square matrix in which each transactor or account has its own row and column. Payments (or expenditures) are listed in columns and the receipts in rows. Because each account must balance, the corresponding row and column totals are equal. There are six types of accounts in a typical SAM: the activities, commodities, and factor (labor and capital) accounts; the current (income and spending) accounts of the domestic institutions, often divided into households, firms, and the government; the savings-investment (or capital) account; and the rest-of-the-world (ROW) account.

1.4.1 Activity, Commodity, and Factor Accounts

Activity or *production accounts* are used to record purchases of raw materials and intermediate goods and hire factor services to produce marketed commodities or home-consumed output. Their expenditures (shown in column A) therefore include the purchase of intermediate commodities that are used as production inputs. The remainder is, by definition, value added (net of taxes on activities), of which a part may be payable to the government as a tax on the activity (such as an *ad valorem* producer tax). Value added is then distributed to factors of production in the form of wage payments and of rent to fixed factors. The receipts (row 1) of the activities derive from sales on the domestic market and (imputed) home consumption.

Commodity accounts show purchases of domestic products from the activity accounts and purchases of imports from the rest of the world. More specifically, commodity accounts (shown in column B) purchase imports as well as domestically produced (and marketed) commodities and pay indirect taxes on these commodities (including tariffs levied on imports). Their receipts (row 2) proceed from sales on the domestic market of intermediate products to activities, of final goods to households and government for consumption, of investment goods to domestic firms, and exports to the rest of the world. In general, because commodity accounts are defined separately from activities, they need not have the same sectoral definitions as activities. For instance, the same commodity (a food crop) may be produced by several types of activities (small- and large-scale farms in agriculture) with different production technologies. This illustrates the importance of distinguishing between the two sets of accounts.

---

[9] This section draws on Reinert and Roland-Holst (1997) and Löfgren, Harris, and Robinson (2001), who discuss the use of SAMs in applied general equilibrium modeling (see also Chapter 9).

Table 1.2 A social accounting matrix

	RECEIPTS	A Activities	B Commodities	C Factors	D (EXPENDITURES) Households	E Firms	F Government	G Savings-Investment	H Rest of the World	Total
1	Activities		Marketed output		Home-consumed output					Activity income (gross output)
2	Commodities	Intermediate inputs			Private consumption		Government consumption	Investment	Exports	Aggregate demand
3	Factors	Value added							Factor income from ROW	Factor income
4	Households			Factor income to households	Inter-household transfers	Distributed profits to households	Transfers to households		Transfers to households from ROW	Household income
5	Firms			Gross profits			Transfers to enterprises		Transfers to enterprises from ROW	Enterprise income
6	Government	Producer taxes, value added tax	Sales taxes and tariffs	Factor income to government, factor taxes	Transfers to government, direct household taxes	Distributed profits to government, payment of direct taxes			Transfers to government from ROW	Government income
7	Savings-Investment				Household savings	Retained earnings	Government savings		Foreign savings a/	Total savings
8	Rest of the World (ROW)		Imports	Factor income to ROW		Distributed profits to ROW	Government transfers to ROW	Capital transfers abroad		Foreign exchange payments
	Total	Activity expenditure	Aggregate supply	Factor expenditure	Household expenditure	Enterprise expenditure	Government expenditure	Total investment	Foreign exchange receipts	

a/ Includes changes in official reserves.

Factor accounts include labor and capital accounts. They receive payments (shown in row 3) from the sale of their services to activities in the form of wages and rent, and income from abroad as remittances and capital income. These revenues are distributed (column C) to households as labor income and distributed profits, to firms as retained earnings, to the government, and to the rest of the world. Corresponding factor taxes are also paid to the government.

1.4.2   Institutions and the Capital Account

Institutions include households, firms, and the government, with households usually disaggregated in different socioeconomic groups identified by physical location and sector of activity (such as rural and urban households, wage earners and profit earners, skilled and unskilled households in the urban formal sector, and so on).

Household income (shown in row 4) includes factor income (as described above) and various transfers coming from other households, the government, domestic firms (mostly dividends), or from abroad (such as worker remittances). Household expenditure (column D) consists of home consumption, consumption of marketed goods, and income taxes, with residual savings transferred to their capital account.

Firms retain a fraction of their profits and receive transfers from the government and the rest of the world (row 5), and spend on taxes and transfers to households, the government, and the rest of the world (column E). Their residual savings also go into their capital account. The government receives, on the income side (row 6), factor income, direct and indirect tax revenues, and current transfers from abroad.

The government expenditure account (column F) differs from the "administrative activities" account included in the activity accounts, which buys intermediate goods, pays wages, and delivers "administrative services." In column F, the government spends its current expenditures on directly buying the services provided by the activity account. The other items in the current budget are transfers to households, firms, and the rest of the world, with the remaining savings being transferred to the capital account.

The savings-investment (or capital) account collects savings from all institutions together with net foreign capital transfers (or foreign savings) from the rest of the world (row 7). Savings are used to finance domestic fixed capital formation (both private and public) and capital transfers abroad (column G).[10]

1.4.3   The Rest-of-the-World Account

Transactions between the domestic economy and the *rest of the world* are recorded in the last set of accounts. The economy receives income from the

---

[10]In principle, a separate savings-investment account could be identified for each of the institutions described above. In practice, however, adequate data are rarely available, and generally only the government capital account is separated from a consolidated capital account of the domestic private institutions.

rest of the world as factor payments, and payment for exports (row 8); it also pays for imports and transfers to the rest of the world (column H). The difference between receipts and payments represents net foreign capital transfers, or foreign savings.[11] Thus, as implied by the standard national accounting identities reviewed earlier, the deficit in the foreign capital account must exactly match the deficit in the domestic savings-investment account. Moreover, in a SAM framework, just as in the consistency matrix described earlier, if all accounts except one are balanced, then the last one will also be in equilibrium.

1.4.4   SAMs and Economy-wide Models

The accounts embedded in the SAM serve to delineate the overall structure of an economy-wide model (as suggested in the epigraph for this chapter), the specification of which requires that the behavioral and market equilibrium relationships that underlie each account be made explicit. The activity, commodity, and factor accounts all require the specification of market behavior (supply, demand, and market-clearing conditions), whereas the household and government accounts embody the budget constraints (income equals expenditure) faced by households and the public sector. The capital account and the rest-of-the-world account represent the macroeconomic requirement for internal (saving equals investment) and external (exports plus capital inflows equal imports). Chapter 9 will present examples of general equilibrium models that dwell on a SAM framework.

It is worth stressing that there is no unique way of disaggregating and organizing the data in a SAM; much depends on the needs of the user. In particular, the number of accounts in each category depends on the objectives of the study. For instance, the degree of disaggregation of the household account depends on how many separate economic groups the user wants to distinguish to analyze the distributional effects of policy shocks. Similarly, the government account could be disaggregated into several entities (to account for public enterprises and local governments). A SAM that emphasizes the role of agriculture may have many agricultural subsectors rather than only one or two, as is typical in most general-purpose SAMs.

In addition, SAMs may vary in the way transactions are recorded; remittances, for instance, can be received either by the labor factor or by the household. Imports are sometimes also split between intermediate goods and final goods, with the former being directly bought by the activities accounts, and the latter by institutions accounts.

Finally, there has been renewed interest in the development of **financial SAMs,** in the context of applied macro models emphasizing real-financial sector linkages, such as the Integrated Macroeconomic Model for Poverty Analysis developed by Agénor (2003) and Agénor, Izquierdo, and Fofack (2003) and briefly discussed in Chapter 9. Financial SAMs are related to the "real" SAMs

---

[11]If the SAM does not contain asset accumulation accounts, and if the foreign exchange used by the economy results in a decrease in reserves, the latter should be aggregated to net foreign savings.

described in Table 1.2 by showing how the net savings of different institutions are allocated to financial asset accumulation, in addition to physical capital. Here again, the structure and degree of disaggregation of the SAM depends very much on the purpose at hand.

1.5 Summary

- Macroeconomic analysis is organized around three basic accounting concepts: production, income, and expenditure. These concepts are linked by three *basic macroeconomic relationships*, which result from the *budget constraints* faced by each category of agents.

- A **consistency accounting matrix** integrates transactions in goods and services as well as financial transactions among agents. By imposing various *identities* among these magnitudes, it provides a useful accounting framework for designing consistent macroeconomic models.

- Standard *national income identities*, such as the ones relating the gross domestic product and absorption, and savings and investment, are essentially *flow budget constraints*, that is, basic relationships that relate income, expenditure, and saving of each category of agents.

- A **social accounting matrix** (SAM) is a framework that combines macroeconomic data with sectoral information on production, factor markets, and institutions (households, firms, and possibly different levels of government).

- There is no unique way of disaggregating and organizing the data in a SAM; the number of accounts depends on the objectives of the study. For instance, the degree of disaggregation of the household account depends on how many separate economic groups that the user feels is necessary to study changes in income distribution.

- **Financial SAMs** have regained some degree of popularity in recent years. This has resulted in part from the development of applied general equilibrium models emphasizing real-financial sector linkages, such as the Integrated Macroeconomic Model for Poverty Analysis developed by Agénor (2003) and Agénor, Izquierdo, and Fofack (2003).

Chapter 2

Consumption, Saving, and Investment

If people regarded future benefits as equally desirable with similar benefits at the present time, they would probably endeavour to distribute their pleasures and other satisfactions evenly throughout their lives. They would therefore generally be willing to give up a present pleasure for the sake of an equal pleasure in the future, provided they could be certain of having it. But in fact human nature is so constituted that in estimating the "present value" of a future benefit most people generally make a second deduction from its future value, in the form of what we may call a "discount," that increases with the period for which the benefit is deferred. One will reckon a distant benefit at nearly the same value which it would have for him if it were present; while another who has less power of realizing the future, less patience and self-control, will care comparatively little for any benefit that is not near at hand.

Alfred Marshall, *Principles of Economics*, Book 3, Chapter 5, 8th ed., 1920.

Consumption expenditure accounts for a large fraction of private spending in developing countries; understanding its determinants is thus important for short- and long-run economic analysis. The fraction of income that is not spent, domestic saving, plays an essential role as well: it continues to finance a large share of domestic investment in most developing countries. As discussed in Chapter 10, saving and investment rates are strongly correlated over time and across countries with rates of economic growth. From a policy perspective, understanding the patterns and determinants of consumption, saving, and investment may thus be a crucial step in designing programs aimed at raising standards of living.

Figure 2.1 shows the evolution of domestic saving and investment rates around the world during the period 1976-2001. The data suggest that gross domestic saving rates in East Asia have remained significantly higher than those

observed in industrial countries (with the exception of Japan during 1976-83)—
reaching almost 35 percent of GDP for the period 1992-2001. By contrast,
saving rates in South Asia, sub-Saharan Africa, and in heavily indebted poor
countries in general, saving rates remain very low. In sub-Saharan Africa, saving
rates have actually fallen during the past three decades. A similar pattern is observed for gross domestic investment; whereas investment rates have remained
high in East Asia (averaging about 30 percent of GDP), they have stagnated at
relatively lower levels in other developing regions and in heavily indebted poor
countries. The difference between domestic saving and domestic investment,
foreign saving, has been particularly large in sub-Saharan Africa.

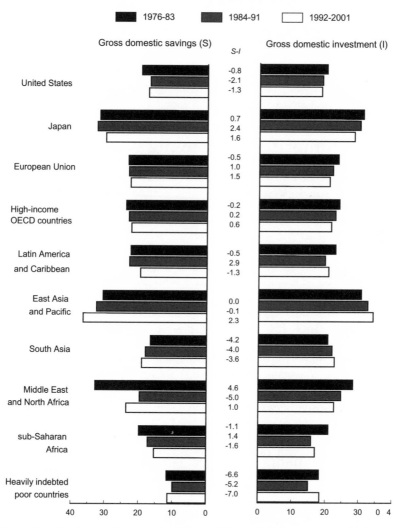

Figure 2.1. Saving and investment rates, 1976-2001 (in percent of GDP). Source:
World Bank.

The first part of this chapter, section 2.1, focuses on the determinants of consumption and saving in developing countries. It begins by reviewing the permanent income hypothesis, as well as the life-cycle model and some of its extensions. It then considers various factors that empirical studies have identified as playing an important role in developing economies: income levels and income variability, intergenerational links, liquidity constraints (which stem from credit market imperfections), inflation and macroeconomic instability, government saving behavior, the external debt burden, social security and pension systems, changes in the terms of trade, and the effect of financial development. The empirical evidence on these various effects is then analyzed.

Section 2.2 focuses on the determinants of private investment. Two standard effects are first reviewed: the flexible accelerator effect and the cost of capital. The more recent emphasis on the role of uncertainty and irreversibility is taken up next. As in the case of consumption and saving, several additional factors found to be important in empirical studies are discussed: credit rationing and foreign exchange constraints, the real exchange rate, public investment, macroeconomic instability, and the external debt burden. Several recent empirical studies are then reviewed.

2.1   Consumption and Saving

The simplest approach to consumption and saving behavior is the so-called **Keynesian approach**, which assumes that current consumption, c, is a function of *disposable income*, $y - T$, where y is current income and T the level of direct taxes:

$$c = (1 - \theta)(y - T), \tag{1}$$

with $0 < \theta < 1$ denoting the marginal propensity to save.

The simple (and somewhat mechanical) approach described by Equation (1) has some merit, both as a first approximation in empirical macroeconomic models and, as discussed later, as a reflection of the behavior of consumers subject to **liquidity constraints**. It is also a good description of consumption and saving behavior at very low levels of income, where subsistence is a predominant concern and intertemporal considerations (of the type discussed later) are absent. However, decades of evidence on consumption and saving patterns in industrial and developing countries alike have highlighted the role of **intertemporal factors**, that is, the role played by households' choices between the present and the future.

2.1.1   The Permanent Income Hypothesis

The permanent income hypothesis (PIH), like the life-cycle model discussed next, relates current consumption to a measure of **permanent** or **lifetime** disposable income. It was first proposed by Friedman (1957). To illustrate its implications, consider a simple framework in which consumers (or households) are identical and live for only two periods, 1 and 2. For simplicity, households are endowed with **perfect foresight**; thus, at period 1 they know with certainty the period-2 values of income, prices, and so on. Measured in nominal terms, the representative household's budget constraint for period 1 is given by

$$p_1 c_1 + p_1 A_1 = p_1(y_1 - T_1) + (1 + i_0)p_0 A_0, \tag{2}$$

where c_1 denotes consumption, A_0 the initial (end of previous period) stock of financial assets, A_1 assets at the end of period 1, y_1 factor income (or endowment), T_1 lump-sum taxes, i_0 the nominal rate of return on assets held at the end of the previous period, and p_0 (p_1) the price index for the initial period (period 1).

Equation (2) can be rewritten as

$$p_1 A_1 - p_0 A_0 = i_0 p_0 A_0 + p_1(y_1 - T_1) - p_1 c_1.$$

which essentially states that the change in assets, $p_1 A_1 - p_0 A_0$, is equal to the sum of interest and noninterest (disposable) income, $i_0 p_0 A_0 + p_1(y_1 - T_1)$, minus consumption spending, $p_1 c_1$.

Similarly, the budget constraint for period 2 is given by

$$p_2 c_2 + p_2 A_2 = p_2(y_2 - T_2) + (1 + i_1)p_1 A_1, \tag{3}$$

with y_2 in general different from y_1.

The household lives only two periods and leaves no net wealth to its heirs (that is, **no bequests**). Thus, $A_2 = 0$.[1] Suppose also that there is **no money illusion**; the period-by-period budget constraints of Equations (2) and (3) can thus be written in *real terms* by dividing, respectively, by p_1 and p_2. The first-period budget constraint becomes

$$c_1 + A_1 = y_1 - T_1 + (1 + r_0)A_0, \tag{4}$$

where r_0 is the real interest rate, defined as

$$1 + r_0 = \left(\frac{p_0}{p_1}\right)(1 + i_0).$$

Because $p_1/p_0 = (p_1 - p_0 + p_0)/p_0 = 1 + \pi_1$, where $\pi_1 \equiv \Delta p_1/p_0$ is the inflation rate between periods 0 and 1, this expression is also equal to

$$1 + r_0 = \frac{1 + i_0}{1 + \pi_1}.$$

Similarly, the budget constraint for period 2, given that $A_2 = 0$, becomes

$$c_2 = y_2 - T_2 + (1 + r_1)A_1, \tag{5}$$

---

[1] For the condition $A_2 = 0$ to be optimal from the point of view of the household, it must be assumed that the marginal utility of consumption (as defined later) in the second period is positive.

where now[2]

$$1 + r_1 = (\frac{p_1}{p_2})(1 + i_1) = \frac{1 + i_1}{1 + \pi_2}. \tag{6}$$

Eliminating A_1 from Equation (4) by using Equation (5) yields the household's **intertemporal** or **lifetime budget constraint**:

$$c_1 + \frac{c_2}{1 + r_1} = (1 + r_0)A_0 + (y_1 - T_1) + \frac{y_2 - T_2}{1 + r_1}. \tag{7}$$

In its simplest form, the PIH assumes that the household's objective is to maintain a *perfectly stable* (or *smooth*) consumption path ($c_1 = c_2$ in the present case) by dividing its lifetime resources equally among each period of life. The amount consumed by the household in each period is equal to its permanent income, y_P, which can be defined as the **annuity value** (in the sense of a regular, periodic payment) of the sum of assets held by the household and the discounted present value of (expected) future income. Formally, y_P is obtained as the level of income that gives the household the same present value of its lifetime resources as that implied by its actual intertemporal budget constraint, that is, using (7):

$$y_P + \frac{y_P}{1 + r_1} = (1 + r_0)A_0 + (y_1 - T_1) + \frac{y_2 - T_2}{1 + r_1}. \tag{8}$$

In the particular case in which $r_0 = r_1 = r$, permanent income is

$$y_P = (\frac{1 + r}{2 + r})\left\{(1 + r)A_0 + (y_1 - T_1) + \frac{y_2 - T_2}{1 + r}\right\}.$$

If, in addition, the initial stock of assets is zero ($A_0 = 0$) and the interest rate is zero ($r = 0$), permanent income becomes an *exact average* of the present and future values of disposable income:

$$y_P = [(y_1 - T_1) + (y_2 - T_2)]/2.$$

The difference between current and permanent income is generally defined as **transitory income**. Because $c_1 = y_P$, saving (which takes place only in period 1 in this simplified framework) is indeed nothing but the transitory component of current disposable income:

$$s_1 = (y_1 - T_1) - y_P. \tag{9}$$

The prediction that transitory income is entirely saved—or, more generally, that saving and borrowing are used solely for consumption-smoothing purposes—has formed the basis for a number of empirical tests of the PIH in developing countries, as discussed below.

---

[2]Taking natural logarithms of Equation (6) yields $\ln(1 + r_1) = \ln(1 + i_1) - \ln(1 + \pi_2)$. Using the approximation $\ln(1 + x) \simeq x$, for x small, yields $r_1 \simeq i_1 - \pi_2$; that is, the real interest rate is approximately equal to the nominal rate of return minus the one-period-ahead inflation rate.

2.1.2   The Life-Cycle Model

The life-cycle approach to consumption and saving behavior, first proposed by Modigliani and Brumberg (1954) and Ando and Modigliani (1963), postulates that individuals smooth consumption over time by taking into account anticipated changes in their **resources**, induced by **education** and **age**, as well as movements in the (expected) rate of return on savings. Figure 2.2, adapted from Deaton (1999a), illustrates the stylized pattern of income, consumption, and savings predicted by the standard life-cycle model for a representative individual, under the assumptions of perfect credit markets. During the first part of his (or her) life, a typical individual earns relatively little and consumes a lot; his consumption therefore exceeds his expenses, and he therefore borrows. Because income increases at first with education and age, as human capital is being built, the individual reaches a point where he no longer needs to borrow (point A); beyond that point, saving becomes positive. Income, however, begins to decline beyond a certain age; with consumption growing at a slower rate, saving continues to increase for a while but eventually also begins to fall. Once retirement is reached, income drops (by the distance BB') to a level below consumption. If the reduction in income is *unanticipated*, consumption falls abruptly upon retirement, from C to C'. If, on the contrary, the fall in resources is perfectly anticipated, consumption begins to decline smoothly before retirement age is reached with no discrete change at that point. In either case, the individual must continue to adjust expenditure downward and *dissave* until death, in order to maintain his consumption close to his ability to pay for it.

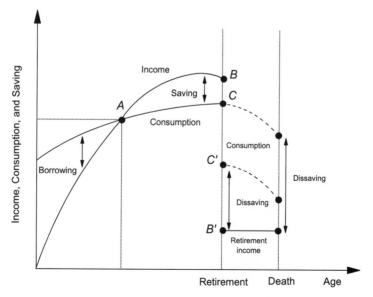

Figure 2.2. Income, consumption, and saving in the life-cycle model. Adapted from Deaton (1999, p. 42).

The Basic Framework

Analytically, the implications of the life-cycle approach can be illustrated in a two-period framework similar to the one presented earlier.[3] Suppose, as before, that the representative household leaves no bequests; thus, $A_2 = 0$. The household's **lifetime budget constraint**, Equation (7), can be rewritten as

$$c_1 + \frac{c_2}{1 + r_1} = W_1, \tag{10}$$

where W_1 can be defined as **lifetime wealth**. Note that W_1 depends directly on r_1; in particular, an increase in r_1 (for $y_2 - T_2$ given) lowers the present value of future income and therefore reduces W_1. Thus, $dW_1/dr_1 < 0$.

Suppose now that the household's preferences are **intertemporally additive**, that is, that its **lifetime utility**, U, is the sum of the utility of consumption derived in period 1, $u(c_1)$, plus the utility of consumption in period 2, $u(c_2)$, discounted at the subjective **rate of time preference**, $\rho > 0$. Formally,

$$U = u(c_1) + \frac{u(c_2)}{1 + \rho}, \tag{11}$$

where the **subutility function** $u(\cdot)$ is assumed to be increasing in c but at a decreasing rate—that is, $u' > 0$ and $u'' < 0$. The value of ρ measures the **degree of impatience**; the higher it is, the lower the utility provided by future consumption.

Maximizing (11) with respect to c_1 and c_2 subject to the lifetime budget constraint (10) can be performed by forming the **Lagrangian expression**

$$L = u(c_1) + \frac{u(c_2)}{1 + \rho} - \lambda \left\{ c_1 + \frac{c_2}{1 + r_1} - W_1 \right\},$$

where λ is the **Lagrange multiplier** (see, for instance, Chiang, 1984, pp. 372-75). The first-order optimality conditions are given by

$$u'(c_1) = \lambda,$$

$$u'(c_2)/(1 + \rho) = \lambda/(1 + r_1).$$

Combining these two equations yields

$$u'(c_1) = \frac{1 + r_1}{1 + \rho} u'(c_2), \tag{12}$$

which is known as the **Euler equation**. Essentially, this equation states that the marginal utility of consumption at the current period must be equal to the marginal utility of consumption in the next period, weighted by the ratio of the market and subjective discount terms.[4]

---

[3] The subsequent presentation draws in part on Muellbauer and Lattimore (1995).

[4] The derivation treats r_1 and $y_2 - T_2$ as deterministic terms. Under more general assumptions, the Euler equation continues to have the form shown in Equation (12), but with the term $u'(c_2)$ on the right-hand side appearing in *expected* value form.

In the special case in which the rate of time preference is equal to the real rate of return ($\rho = r_1$), Equation (12) becomes $u'(c_1) = u'(c_2)$, implying that

$$c_1 = c_2. \tag{13}$$

The household therefore maintains a completely smooth consumption path across periods, as in the simple form of the PIH discussed earlier. Substituting Equation (13) in the life-cycle budget constraint (Equation (10)) would then yield

$$\left\{ 1 + \frac{1}{1 + r_1} \right\} c_1 = W_1,$$

that is

$$c_1 = \frac{W_1}{\kappa_1}, \quad \kappa_1 \equiv 1 + \frac{1}{1 + r_1}, \tag{14}$$

where κ_1 is the inverse of the **marginal propensity to consume out of wealth**.[5]

For instance, with **logarithmic preferences**, lifetime utility is given by

$$U = \ln c_1 + \frac{\ln c_2}{1 + \rho},$$

and the Euler equation is

$$1/c_1 = \left(\frac{1 + r_1}{1 + \rho} \right)(1/c_2).$$

Another example is the case of preferences characterized by a **constant elasticity of substitution** (CES), in which lifetime utility is given by

$$U = \left\{ c_1^{-\alpha} + \frac{c_2^{-\alpha}}{1 + \rho} \right\}^{-1/\alpha}, \tag{15}$$

where $\alpha > -1$. The Lagrangian expression is now

$$L = \left\{ c_1^{-\alpha} + \frac{c_2^{-\alpha}}{1 + \rho} \right\}^{-1/\alpha} - \lambda \left\{ c_1 + \frac{c_2}{1 + r_1} - W_1 \right\}.$$

The first-order optimality conditions are now given by

$$U^{-(1+\alpha)/\alpha} c_1^{-(1+\alpha)} = \lambda,$$

$$U^{-(1+\alpha)/\alpha} \frac{c_2^{-(1+\alpha)}}{1 + \rho} = \frac{\lambda}{1 + r_1},$$

which can be rearranged to give the Euler equation as

---

[5] As shown in Equation (14), κ_1 depends only on the real interest rate; in the presence of bequests, the marginal propensity to consume out of wealth would generally be smaller.

$$c_1^{-1/\sigma} = \frac{(1+r_1)}{1+\rho} c_2^{-1/\sigma}. \tag{16}$$

Taking logarithms of both sides yields

$$\ln(\frac{c_2}{c_1}) = \ln\left[1 + \frac{(c_2 - c_1)}{c_1}\right] = \sigma \ln(\frac{1+r_1}{1+\rho}),$$

that is, using the approximation $\ln(1+x) \simeq x$:

$$\frac{(c_2 - c_1)}{c_1} \simeq \sigma(r_1 - \rho). \tag{17}$$

Let the **elasticity of substitution** between period-1 consumption c_1 and period-1 consumption c_2 be defined as the proportional change in the consumption ratio c_2/c_1 associated with a unit proportional change in the ratio of marginal utilities $u'(c_1)/u'(c_2)$, holding total utility constant. It can be shown that if preferences are given by (15), this elasticity, denoted σ, is given by

$$\sigma = \frac{1}{1+\alpha}.$$

Equation (17) therefore shows that the elasticity of substitution measures the responsiveness of the change in consumption between the two periods to changes in **intertemporal prices**, that is, the real interest rate. The greater the elasticity of substitution is, the greater will be the reduction in current consumption (relative to future consumption) induced by a rise in the real interest rate.

Taking both terms in expression (16) to the power $-\sigma$ yields

$$c_2 = \left\{\frac{1+r_1}{1+\rho}\right\}^\sigma c_1. \tag{18}$$

Combining this result with the lifetime budget constraint, Equation (10), yields

$$\left[1 + \left\{\frac{1+r_1}{1+\rho}\right\}^\sigma \div (\frac{1}{1+r_1})\right] c_1 = W_1,$$

which leads to an equation similar to (14),

$$c_1 = \frac{W_1}{\kappa_1},$$

but now with κ_1 given by

$$\kappa_1 = 1 + \frac{1}{(1+\rho)^\sigma(1+r_1)^{1-\sigma}}.$$

If the values of ρ and r_1 are sufficiently small, κ_1 can be approximated by[6]

$$\kappa_1 \simeq 1 + \frac{1}{1 + \sigma\rho + (1 - \sigma)r_1}. \qquad (19)$$

Given that $c_1 = W_1/\kappa_1$, the impact of r_1 on c_1 is given by

$$\frac{dc_1}{dr_1} = \frac{1}{\kappa_1} \left\{ \frac{dW_1}{dr_1} - (\frac{W_1}{\kappa_1})(\frac{d\kappa_1}{dr_1}) \right\}. \qquad (20)$$

Expressions (19) and (20) have several implications.

First, if the discount rate and the market interest rate are equal ($\rho = r_1$), changes in the elasticity of intertemporal substitution have *no effect* on κ_1, which is thus equal to its value given in Equation (14), $1 + 1/(1 + r_1)$.

Second, from (19), the sign of the effect of an increase in r_1 on κ_1 is

$$\text{sg}(d\kappa_1/dr_1) = -\text{sg}(1 - \sigma),$$

which indicates that, in general, $d\kappa_1/dr_1$ is *ambiguous*; the effect of a change in the interest rate on first-period consumption and saving is thus in general indeterminate because of conflicting **income** and **substitution effects**. A higher interest means that each additional unit of current-period saving will allow a greater increase in second-period consumption than was previously the case. At the margin, this will tend to reduce first-period consumption and increase savings (substitution effect). At the same time, the higher interest rate increases the level of second-period consumption that can be financed from the existing level of first-period savings, which tends to decrease the level of saving (the income effect).

- If σ is *less than unity*, $d\kappa_1/dr_1 < 0$. Because, as shown earlier, dW_1/dr_1 is also negative, (20) implies that an increase in the interest rate in this case has an *ambiguous* overall effect on consumption and saving (defined as $s_1 = y_1 - T_1 - c_1$) in the first period.

- If, on the contrary, σ is *greater than unity*, $d\kappa_1/dr_1 > 0$; and because $d\kappa_1/dW_1 < 0$, (20) implies that an increase in r_1 unambiguously lowers first-period consumption ($dc_1/dr_1 < 0$) and raises saving. The substitution effect dominates the income effect.

- A change in the interest rate has *no effect* on κ_1 ($d\kappa_1/dr_1 = 0$) if σ is *equal to unity*. The case where $\sigma = 1$ corresponds to the case where the utility function is logarithmic, and the propensity to consume out of wealth κ_1 is equal to $1 + 1/(1 + \rho)$. Income and substitution effects offset each

---

[6] Let $x = (1 + \rho)^\sigma (1 + r_1)^{1-\sigma} - 1$; the second term on the right-hand side of the first expression in (19) is therefore $1/(1 + x)$. Using the approximation $x \simeq \ln(1 + x)$, for x small, implies that

$$x \simeq \ln(1 + \rho)^\sigma (1 + r_1)^{1-\sigma} \simeq \sigma\rho + (1 - \sigma)r_1,$$

which can be substituted in the expression $1/(1 + x)$ to give the result shown in the second expression of (19).

other exactly and the household's propensity to consume (and to save) is *independent* of the rate of return, r_1. Because $d\kappa_1/dW_1 < 0$, (20) also implies that $dc_1/dr_1 < 0$ and $ds_1/dr_1 > 0$.

Third, the greater the degree of intertemporal substitution σ is, the larger will be the marginal effect on consumption and saving induced by a change in the interest rate $(\partial[d\kappa_1/dr_1]/\partial\sigma > 0)$. Fourth, if the degree of intertemporal substitution σ is *zero* and disposable income in period 2 is equal to the period-1 level $(y_2 - T_2 = y_1 - T_1)$, then $\kappa_1 = 1 + 1/(1 + r_1)$ and

$$c_1 = \frac{W_1}{\kappa_1} = \frac{(1 + r_0)A_0}{1 + 1/(1 + r_1)} + y_1 - T_1, \tag{21}$$

which shows that an increase in the real interest rate, r_1, by increasing the return on the existing level of assets, raises unambiguously period-1 consumption—because the substitution effect is absent.

Finally, if the elasticity of substitution σ is *positive* and the initial level of assets is zero $(A_0 = 0)$, and with disposable income in period 2 equal to the period-1 level, then

$$c_1 = \kappa_1^{-1} \frac{y_1 - T_1}{1 + 1/(1 + r_1)},$$

which implies that an increase in the interest rate has an unambiguously *negative* effect on consumption—because the income effect is absent. By implication, large movements in the level of assets over time may make it difficult to use time-series techniques to detect a stable aggregate effect of real interest rates on saving.[7]

Age and the Dependency Ratio

The life-cycle model predicts that, in any given population, the *young* will save relatively little as they anticipate increases in their future incomes. *Middle-aged individuals*, who are nearing the peak of their earnings, tend to save the most, in anticipation of relatively low incomes after retirement. The *elderly* tend to have a low, or even negative, saving rate, although the desire to *leave a bequest* or to cover the *contingency of living longer* than expected could provide a motivation for saving even after retirement. Thus, the *aggregate saving rate* will tend to fall in response to an increase in either the **youth-dependency ratio** (that is, the ratio of the under-20 age group to the 20-64 age group) or in the ratio of the elderly to the working age population.

To formally assess the influence of age in the life-cycle model described earlier, consider the case in which the household's horizon is $T > 2$. In addition to results similar to those derived earlier, it can be shown that the inverse marginal propensity to consume out of assets, κ_1, varies with the time horizon and therefore with age (Muellbauer and Lattimore, 1995). Suppose that the real

---

[7]As discussed later, a small and unstable real interest rate effect is consistent with the evidence for developing countries.

interest rate is constant over time at r, that the values of ρ and r are sufficiently small, and that preferences take the form of the **CES utility function** specified earlier. In such conditions, κ_1 is given not by Equation (19) but instead by

$$\kappa_1 = 1 + \mu + \mu^2 + \ldots + \mu^{T-1} = \frac{1 - \mu^T}{1 - \mu}, \tag{22}$$

where[8]

$$\mu = \frac{1}{(1+\rho)^\sigma (1+r)^{1-\sigma}} \simeq \frac{1}{1 + \sigma\rho + (1-\sigma)r} < 1. \tag{23}$$

If the household earns the same disposable income in all periods ($y_1 - T_1 = y_2 - T_2 = \ldots$), and if the rate of time preference and the interest rate are equal ($\rho = r$), consumption in period 1 will be given by

$$c_1 = \frac{W_1}{\kappa_1} = \frac{(1+r_0)A_0}{\kappa_1} + (y_1 - T_1).$$

In such conditions, the effect of age on consumption will operate entirely through κ_1. Suppose, for instance, that $\rho = r = 0.04$. Then, from Equation (23), $\mu = 1/(1+r) = 0.96$, and from Equation (22):

$$\kappa_1|_{T=10} = 8.5, \quad \kappa_1|_{T=20} = 14.2, \quad \kappa_1|_{T=40} = 20.7.$$

These results show that the inverse of the marginal propensity to consume out of wealth *increases* with the time horizon; put differently, younger agents, with their longer time horizons, have a lower propensity to consume out of assets than older generations.[9]

This result is important because it implies that, at the aggregate level, the distribution of assets between the young, the middle-aged, and the elderly matters for consumption and saving patterns. This issue is central to the question

---

[8] Consider, for instance, the case where $T = 3$. The CES utility function, Equation (15) can be written as

$$U = \left\{ c_1^{-\alpha} + \frac{c_2^{-\alpha}}{1+\rho} + \frac{c_3^{-\alpha}}{(1+\rho)^2} \right\}^{-1/\alpha},$$

and the lifetime budget constraint, Equation (10), becomes

$$c_1 + \frac{c_2}{1+r_1} + \frac{c_3}{(1+r_1)^2} = W_1.$$

The first-order conditions are given by Equation (18) together with

$$c_3 = [(1+r_1)/1 + \rho]^{2\sigma} c_1.$$

Combining these results with the lifetime budget constraint above yields $c_1 = W_1/\kappa_1$, with now

$$\kappa_1 = 1 + \mu + \mu^2,$$

where μ is defined in Equation (23). The last term in that expression is the approximation given before [see Equation (19)]. Generalizing the above expressions to the case where $T > 3$ is straightforward.

[9] Note that the difference between the marginal propensities to consume of the old and young *rises* as the average discount rate falls.

of the effects of per capita real income growth on aggregate saving behavior. Everything else equal, the larger the share of total wealth held by the middle-aged households (those whose income is the highest) in any given country, the higher the saving rate, and the higher the *growth rate* of income (see Chapter 12). However, as discussed below, everything else is *not* equal in the presence of **borrowing constraints**. In addition, demographic factors such as the share of the working population relative to that of retired persons are likely to explain only the *long-term trends* in saving, not the short-term fluctuations in the propensity to save.

2.1.3   Other Determinants

The analytical and empirical literature on consumption and saving behavior in developing countries has highlighted various limitations of the standard permanent income and life-cycle models described in the previous sections and has offered various extensions. This section reviews some of the most important additional factors that have been found to be relevant in understanding consumption and saving in these countries.

Income Levels and Income Uncertainty

Recent empirical research has highlighted the fact that at low or *subsistence levels of income*, the saving rate tends also to be low. As documented in Chapter 10, as the level of income increases, so does the saving rate. This result has two implications:

- In low-income countries the response of saving to changes in *real interest rates* is likely to be weak; a significant response of household saving tends to occur only at levels of income substantially above the subsistence level (Ogaki, Ostry, and Reinhart, 1996). This result has important implications for policies aimed at stimulating financial saving through interest rate liberalization (see Chapter 15).

- Changes in *income distribution*, induced for instance by redistributive tax policies, can have important effects on measured saving rates at the aggregate level.

Many households in developing countries derive their incomes from agriculture; but in that sector, incomes can be subject to relatively large fluctuations resulting from variations in climatic conditions or changes in domestic and world prices of agricultural commodities. These sources of **income uncertainty** are often compounded by **macroeconomic instability** and vulnerability to external shocks.[10] In general, increased uncertainty regarding future income will enhance the **precautionary motive** for saving (see the appendix to this chapter;

---

[10]The higher savings rates registered by the low-inflation countries in Asia, for instance, suggest the importance of a stable macroeconomic environment.

Caballero, 1990; and Deaton, 1992), although in a highly unstable macroeconomic environment, increased uncertainty may *reduce* saving through its effect on the variability of rates of return.

The effect of income uncertainty on consumption and savings may also vary at different points in the life cycle of individuals, while at the same time having a limited impact on *aggregate* savings. Irvine and Wang (2001), for instance, studied the effect of both income and lifespan uncertainty on patterns of wealth accumulation in a life-cycle model with a retirement phase—during which the (stochastic) process driving income changes. They found that greater income uncertainty (possibly resulting from adverse shocks during retirement years) induces individuals to save more in the early part of their life cycle, but that the reverse pattern may be observed later in their working life.

Intergenerational Links

Some authors, such as Gersovitz (1988), have argued that the greater importance of extended family arrangements may imply that **intergenerational links** are likely to be particularly strong in developing countries. There are two ways in which such links can affect consumption and saving behavior:

- They may affect **household preferences** by affecting, for instance, the degree to which the marginal utility of consumption declines with the level of consumption, or by increasing the **rate of time preference**.

- They may lengthen the **effective planning horizon** over which households make their consumption and saving decisions.

Liquidity Constraints

Intertemporal consumption smoothing requires well-functioning financial markets to allow agents to borrow and lend across periods. In many developing countries, however, well-developed financial markets either do not exist, or when they do, they do not function very well. In particular, households often have limited access to credit markets, and **credit rationing** may be pervasive (see Chapter 4). The existence of **liquidity constraints** affects the ability of households to transfer resources across time periods, as well as across uncertain states of nature, relative to income. As a result, consumption (and thus saving) tends to be highly correlated with *current* income, rather than permanent income or life-cycle wealth, as indicated earlier. Empirical evidence by Veidyanathan (1993) and Rossi (1988) suggests indeed that the incidence of liquidity constraints may be quite significant in a number of developing countries. There is also evidence for industrial countries suggesting that liquidity constraints (together with precautionary saving considerations, as discussed earlier) have an important impact on aggregage consumption (see Sarantis and Stewart, 2003).

Formally, liquidity constraints can be introduced in the simple two-period model presented earlier (in which $A_2 = 0$) by requiring that real financial assets in period 1 be nonnegative:

$$A_1 \geq 0.$$

This constraint implies that households are prevented from borrowing ($A_1 < 0$), but not from saving.[11] Assuming, in addition, that households are relatively impatient (that is, that the rate of time preference is greater than the real interest rate) and thus willing to consume today, Deaton (1992) showed that there are two possible outcomes in period 1:

- The household wants to borrow but cannot, in which case consumption is the sum of current holdings of assets and current income; there is no saving, and marginal utility is not equated across periods.

- The household does *not* want to borrow, in which case consumption is *less* than the sum of assets and income; saving is positive, and marginal utility is equated across periods—as predicted by the Euler equation, Equation (12).

As also shown by Deaton (1992), the exact form of the relationship between consumption and current resources (assets and income) depends on the parameters (mean and variance) characterizing the distribution of income, as well as the structure of the household's preferences. At low levels of resources, liquidity constraints are binding, and all resources are spent. Beyond a certain level of resources (which depends, in particular, on the parameters of the process driving income), liquidity constraints cease to bind, the marginal propensity to consume begins to fall, and saving becomes positive due to precautionary considerations (as discussed earlier). More generally, the behavior of a liquidty-constrained household may be similar to that of an agent who can borrow as much as desired but who has a significant precautionary motive (see Browning and Lusardi, 1996, pp. 1808-9, for a simple example); thus, distinguishing between the two types of effects may be difficult in practice.

In the presence of liquidity constraints, **financial liberalization** can have an adverse effect on saving rates. To the extent that the desire of households to smooth consumption over time is constrained by limited access to credit markets, increased access to these markets will allow individuals to bring forward their consumption (and thereby reduce saving) over their working life, through increased borrowing. For instance, greater availability of loans for purchases of *housing* and *consumer durables* may obviate the need for households to save in preparation for making large initial payments for such purchases. But the incidence of liquidity constraints may also respond *endogenously* to changes in

---

[11] Credit constraints have been modeled in various other ways in the literature. Chah, Ramey, and Starr (1997) assume that consumers can only borrow against their stock of durables. Ludvigson (1999) specifies the credit limit as a fraction of current income, implying that borrowing constraints vary stochastically over time with the level of income. Wirjanto (1995) studies the case where the lending rate is an increasing (and convex) function of the absolute amount borrowed, whereas Scott (1996) and Lawrance (1995) assume that it is a function of the debt-to-income ratio.

saving rates. Evans and Karras (1996) found indeed a negative relationship between these two variables. One possible explanation is that increases in savings (and wealth) raise the collateral that households can pledge in order to secure loans.

Inflation and Macroeconomic Stability

Consumption and saving may also respond to changes in the *level* of inflation. On the one hand, if households are net creditors, an increase in the inflation rate for instance will lower the real value of wealth if asset prices are not fully indexed. To offset this negative wealth effect, households may raise their saving rate. On the other, to the extent that agents anticipate that inflation will persist in the future, or even increase from current levels, they may choose to increase spending now (to take advantage of temporarily lower prices), and thus reduce their saving rate.

The *variability* of inflation, which is often used as a proxy for the degree of macroeconomic instability, may also affect saving, possibly in opposite directions:

- To the extent that it increases uncertainty about *future income*, a high degree of price variability may lead to an increase in the saving rate, as a result of the **precautionary motive** for saving discussed earlier.

- But to the extent that a highly variable rate of inflation is associated with higher uncertainty about the *expected real interest rate* (or the expected return to saving), it may reduce the propensity to save.

Government Saving

A key feature of the life-cycle model is that saving behavior is directly influenced by households' assessment of their *future pattern* of income and consumption. A key variable that affects this assessment is government policy, particularly *government saving* or *dissaving*.

The extent to which shifts in government saving induce offsetting changes in private saving has been a central issue in much of the modern literature in macroeconomics and public economics. Three major interpretations of this relationship have been offered in the literature.

- The **conventional view** assumes that a fall in government saving (resulting from a tax cut or a bond-financed increase in government spending) will tend to raise consumption and reduce saving by *myopic* households (that is, households who care solely about the present), by shifting the tax burden from present to *future* generations. As a result, a decline in government saving will lead to a decline in national saving.[12]

---

[12] The reduction in private saving may be dampened by a rise in the real interest rate—although, as discussed later, this effect is likely to be relatively small. In an open economy, the rise in domestic interest rates may also attract foreign capital and lead to an increase in *foreign* saving.

- The **Keynesian view** suggests that higher *temporary* government dissaving will raise consumption and income, in the presence of under-utilized production capacity, proportionally to the inverse of the marginal propensity to save, as predicted by the standard **multiplier effect**. In turn, higher income will raise private saving. Whether or not this increase in private saving is large enough to offset the initial decline in government saving (and thus lead to a rise in national saving) is *a priori ambiguous*.[13]

- The **Ricardian view** asserts that to the extent that individuals are rational and *far-sighted*, they will realize that a permanent rise in government spending today (or, equivalently, an increase in government dissaving) must be paid for either now or later. They will increase therefore saving by an equivalent amount—hence the term **Ricardian equivalence** (Barro, 1974, 1989).

To illustrate the principle of Ricardian equivalence, suppose that the government, just like the representative household, has a two-period horizon and finances its expenditures in periods 1 and 2, G_1 and G_2, with the lump-sum taxes that it collects, T_1 and T_2. Suppose also that the government faces the same interest rate as households, and let B denote government debt. Measured in nominal terms, the government's budget constraint for period 1 is given by

$$p_1(G_1 - T_1) + i_0 p_0 B_0 = p_1 B_1 - p_0 B_0,$$

where the left-hand side is the overall budget deficit (inclusive of interest payments), with B_0 denoting initial government liabilities. The right-hand side measures the change in debt, which is used to finance the overall deficit.

Assuming that all the debt is retired in period 2 (so that $B_2 = 0$), the government budget constraint for period 2 is given by

$$p_2(G_2 - T_2) + (1 + i_1)p_1 B_1 = 0.$$

Dividing the first equation by p_1 and the second by p_2 yields, after consolidation, the **government intertemporal budget constraint**:

$$G_1 + \frac{G_2}{1 + r_1} + (1 + r_0)B_0 = T_1 + \frac{T_2}{1 + r_1}, \tag{24}$$

where, as before, $1 + r_0 = (1 + i_0)(p_0/p_1)$, and similarly for r_1. This equation indicates that the present value of government spending, plus initial government liabilities (principal and interest), must equal the present value of taxes.

The economy is closed, so that public debt is held by the private sector only. As a result, the period-by-period budget constraints of the representative household, (2) and (3), must incorporate all interest payments on, and accumulation

---

[13]If the reduction in government saving is assumed to be *permanent* rather than temporary, the effect on private saving would be similar to the one predicted by the conventional view if households are short-sighted.

of, government bonds. Formally, these constraints are now given by, again with $A_2 = B_2 = 0$, and now with $A_0 = 0$ as well for simplicity:

$$p_1 A_1 + (p_1 B_1 - p_0 B_0) = p_1(y_1 - T_1) + i_0 p_0 B_0 - p_1 c_1,$$

$$p_2 c_2 = p_1(y_1 - T_1) + (1 + i_1)p_1(A_1 + B_1).$$

From these equations, the representative household's intertemporal budget constraint is now, instead of (7),

$$c_1 + \frac{c_2}{1 + r_1} = (1 + r_0)B_0 + y_1 - T_1 + \frac{y_2 - T_2}{1 + r_1}, \tag{25}$$

which indicates that the present value of consumption spending must be equal to initial government liabilities (inclusive of interest payments) plus the present value of after-tax income.

Combining (24) and (25) (by substituting out taxes) yields the intertemporal budget constraint of the private sector that holds when households fully internalize the intertemporal budget constraint of the public sector:

$$c_1 + \frac{c_2}{1 + r_1} = y_1 - G_1 + \frac{y_2 - G_2}{1 + r_1}.$$

This equation shows that the present value of consumption spending is equal to the present value of income *before taxes* minus the present value of government spending. It implies that, for a given pattern of government spending (G_1, G_2), any two debt-tax patterns (B_1, T_1, T_2) and (B_1', T_1', T_2') that satisfy the government budget constraint will have no effect on the optimal consumption path (c_1, c_2) chosen by the representative household; they are thus economically equivalent. Put differently, for a given present value of government expenditure, because agents "internalize" the government intertemporal budget constraint, the intertemporal distribution of debt and taxes does not matter. The *timing* of taxes and the *size* of government debt do not influence private sector behavior. A rise in the budget deficit (dissaving) resulting from a tax cut, for instance, will have no effect on the national saving rate because private saving will rise by an equivalent amount in anticipation of future tax liabilities. Thus, taken to its extreme form, the Ricardian approach implies that the choice between debt financing and tax financing of fiscal deficits is irrelevant.

The Ricardian view has been subject to a number of criticisms, at both the analytical and the empirical level. From an analytical point of view, it has been argued that it dwells on four unrealistically strict assumptions:

- consumers are *far-sighted*;

- successive generations are linked by *altruistically motivated bequests*;

- consumers do not face *liquidity constraints*; and

- taxes are *nondistortionary*.

The empirical evidence in favor of the hypothesis of full Ricardian equivalence appears mixed for industrial countries (see Seater, 1993). For developing countries, however, the bulk of the evidence is decisively against it (see Agénor and Montiel, 1999). A key reason is that although individuals in such countries may form expectations about their future tax liabilities in a systematic way, liquidity constraints (which play a pervasive role in these countries, as discussed earlier) may prevent them from acting on these expectations by adjusting their consumption-saving behavior as would be predicted by the Ricardian equivalence proposition. Another reason is that households in developing countries appear to have relatively *short planning horizons* (see Baffoe-Bonnie and Khayum, 1997), a phenomenon that can result from a relatively high degree of income uncertainty (as noted earlier) and the absence of markets to diversify risk. As a result, consumption tends to be highly correlated with *current* income (as opposed to *expected* lifetime income), and Ricardian equivalence may not hold.

Expectations, Taxation, and Debt

Government saving and dissaving behavior can also affect private saving indirectly through changes in *anticipations* of future spending and taxes. For instance, in the foregoing discussion of the Ricardian view, the time path of government spending was assumed to be given. In some circumstances, however, changes in taxes and debt may signal *future changes* in public expenditure, which may be internalized by private agents. If, say, a tax cut signals a decrease in future government spending, it may lead to an increase in the private sector's perceived wealth and a rise in consumption. In such conditions, the equivalence result would not hold.

As another example, in a situation in which the public sector's foreign debt burden suddenly deteriorates (as a result, say, of an increase in debt service resulting from a rise in world interest rates), the private sector may anticipate a significant increase in taxation in the future. The **substitution effect** associated with such expectations will tend to favor current consumption at the expense of saving, whereas the **income effect** would tend to reduce consumption in all periods. Thus, a high level of debt may reduce the national saving rate.[14]

Social Security, Pensions, and Insurance

As discussed in Chapter 15, the availability of formal public pension and social security schemes has increased significantly in many developing countries. As implied by the life-cycle framework, the potential effect of these schemes may be to lower the private saving rate through three channels:

- by *redistributing income* to the elderly;

---

[14]See Chapter 16 for a discussion of the longer-run effects of foreign indebtedness on saving and investment.

- by reducing the need to *save for retirement* (unless the introduction of these schemes is accompanied by a reduction of the retirement age);

- by curbing the need for *precautionary saving* to cover the contingency of living longer than expected.

The impact of increased social security benefits on national saving may thus depend on the effect that such changes have on *public saving*.[15] To the extent that the social security system is *unfunded*, public saving will not rise directly to offset any induced decline in private saving. In line with the Ricardian argument developed earlier, it could be argued that in this case private agents would not reduce their current saving because they would anticipate that taxes will eventually have to be raised to finance future pension outlays. Nevertheless, some of the empirical evidence suggests that increases in public pensions result in a decline in private and national savings, albeit by less than the full increase in pension benefits (Mackenzie, Gerson, and Cuervas, 1997).

Private pension plans have also been developed in many developing countries in recent years. In principle, individuals should view their contributions to *funded* private pensions as a perfect substitute for other forms of saving. But, in practice, individuals do not seem to fully take into account their pension contributions in determining their saving behavior. The result is that the introduction of private pension plans is often accompanied by an increase in national saving rates. This is for instance the conclusion reached by Corbo and Schmidt-Hebbel (2003) in the case of *Chile* (see Chapter 15).

Finally, the increased availability of various kinds of *insurance*, such as health, liability, unemployment, personal loss, and liability, may also influence saving behavior. To the extent that insurance plans limit expected outlays for contingencies and emergencies, they tend to reduce income uncertainty and therefore the need for precautionary saving.

Changes in the Terms of Trade

Another factor affecting saving in an open economy is **terms-of-trade shocks**, that is, large movements in the relative price of a country's exports in terms of its imports. A key channel through which such shocks are deemed to operate is the **Harberger-Laursen-Metzler** (HLM) effect, which posits a positive relationship between temporary changes in the terms of trade and saving, through their positive effect on *wealth* and *income*.[16] More specifically, the HLM effect predicts that an adverse *transitory* movement in the terms of trade will lead to a decrease in a country's current level of income that is larger than the decrease

---

[15] Strictly speaking, as pointed out by Edwards (1996c, p. 25), what matters is the relation between contributions and *expected* social security benefits in the future. Whether aggregate saving increases will depend, however, on what happens to government saving once the social security reform is implemented.

[16] The initial formulation of the argument by Harberger (1950) and Laursen and Metzler (1950) relied on a Keynesian-type open economy framework. Extensions to an intertemporal setting were provided notably by Obstfeld (1982) and Svensson and Razin (1983). These contributions also clarified the distinction between permanent and transitory shocks.

in its permanent income, causing, as discussed earlier, a fall in saving. On the contrary, a *permanent* deterioration in the terms of trade, to the extent that it leads to a concomitant reduction in both current income and permanent income, will have no effect on saving.

The consumption smoothing effect emphasized by the conventional HLM effect may be partly offset by two types of substitution effects: an **intertemporal substitution** (or **consumption-tilting**) effect, and an **intratemporal substitution** effect. To understand how these two effects operate, note first that the conventional HLM effect is usually derived in a static setting in which the domestic economy and the rest of the world produce the same tradable good. As in Ostry and Reinhart (1992) and Cashin and McDermott (2003), consider instead a small open economy where households consume both imported and nontraded goods.

Suppose for a moment that these two categories of goods are perfect substitutes, so that their relative price is constant. Movements in the terms of trade may nevertheless induce large changes in the *temporal pattern* of consumption. For instance, a temporary deterioration in the terms of trade (induced by, say, a rise in the price of imported goods) leads to a rise in the **cost of living**, that is, the price of current consumption relative to the price of future imports and future consumption. The increase in the overall price level leads to a rise in the *consumption rate of interest* (that is, the real rate of interest measured in terms of the price of the *consumption basket*), thereby increasing the cost of current consumption relative to future consumption and inducing agents to shift consumption into the future and to save more today. This is the **consumption-tilting** effect. The larger the **intertemporal elasticity of consumption** (as defined earlier) is, the larger the increase in current saving will be.

Suppose now that imported and nontraded goods are *not* perfect substitutes, as the evidence suggests. Movements in their relative price induced by changes in the terms of trade will therefore also affect saving decisions. The reason is that, in an economy where households consume both home and imported goods, changes in relative prices affect the cost of living and thus the consumption rate of interest. As a result, there is an **intratemporal substitution** effect associated with a terms-of-trade shock; this effect may be large enough to offset the conventional effect associated with consumption-smoothing considerations. For instance, to the extent that an adverse, transitory terms-of-trade shock leads to a temporary increase in the relative price of imported goods, the switch toward nontraded goods will raise their relative price and the consumption rate of interest; total expenditure will fall and saving will tend to increase. This effect may be large enough to offset the decline in private saving induced by consumption-smoothing considerations.

Overall, therefore, the net effect of terms-of-trade shocks on saving is theoretically ambiguous. The importance of the consumption-smoothing effect relative to the two types of substitution effects identified above can only be assessed empirically.

Financial Deepening

Financial development may affect saving both directly and indirectly. To the extent that improved financial intermediation leads to a reduction in the *cost* of intermediation, it will increase the return to saving. At the same time, to the extent that increased efficiency in the process of financial intermediation leads to an expansion of *investment* and stimulates the *rate of economic growth* (as discussed in Chapter 12), the increase in income will also lead to an increase in saving. As noted earlier, however, in cases where financial liberalization leads to an increase in the supply of credit to previously credit-constrained households, private saving may fall.

Household and Corporate Saving

Finally, it should be noted that the foregoing discussion focused only on saving by *households*. This focus is justified in many of those developing countries where private saving rates are essentially determined by household behavior. In some others, however, *corporate saving* (in the form of, say, retained earnings) may also be significant and may respond to different variables than those affecting the decisions of households. Whether or not this distinction matters for understanding movements in the *aggregate* private savings rate depends on households' responses to higher corporate saving: if firms retain more earnings, households may save less by a corresponding amount. In such conditions, households *pierce the corporate veil* and aggregate private saving behavior will largely reflect household behavior. López-Mejía and Ortega (1998) found indeed that in Colombia periods of high (low) corporate saving rates were accompanied by periods of low (high) household saving rates. A high degree of compensation (or offsetting effect) between household saving and corporate saving was also found by Bennett, Loayza, and Schmidt-Hebbel (2001) in the case of Chile. In such conditions, changes in dividends have no effect on private consumption (that is, they affect only saving), because agents realize that changes in their income are offset by a decline of the same amount in the value of the firms that they hold.

2.1.4   Empirical Evidence

It is important to note, at the outset, that data limitations make the empirical analysis of the determinants of consumption and saving behavior difficult in developing countries. In practice, saving is typically measured as a *residual* and is beset by classification, valuation, and measurement problems. For instance, *public saving* data for some countries include that of *public enterprises;* in other countries, public enterprise saving is included with that of the *private sector.* These problems may explain at least in part why, as suggested in Figure 2.1, saving rates tend to vary considerably across regions in the developing world.

As noted earlier, a key implication of the PIH is that transitory income changes are (dis-)saved and permanent changes consumed. As discussed by Agénor and Montiel (1999, chap. 3), there exists some evidence supporting this claim; several empirical studies found that the propensity to consume out of permanent income exceeds the propensity to consume out of current income. This is consistent with the PIH. At the same time, however, the elasticity of consumption with respect to permanent income is not typically found to be unity, nor is the propensity to consume out of transitory income found to be zero. The more recent study by Loayza, Schmidt-Hebbel, and Servén (2000) confirmed these results. In particular, the evidence for both industrial and developing countries suggests that there exists a close correlation between actual income and consumption; the strict form of the PIH cannot explain this relationship.

Other recent studies of the determinants of saving in developing countries, in addition to Loayza, Schmidt-Hebbel, and Servén (2000), include those by Masson, Bayoumi and Samiei (1998), Hadjimachael and Ghura (1995), Edwards (1996c), and Dayal-Gulati and Thimann (1997). The study by Masson, Bayoumi, and Samiei (1998) covered 64 developing countries over the period 1970-93. Their results indicated that

- an increase in *public saving* tends to be associated with *higher national saving*, suggesting that Ricardian equivalence does not hold;

- a decrease in the **age dependency ratio** (that is, the ratio of the young and the elderly to the working-age population) raises private saving substantially, as found earlier by Rossi (1989);

- increases in *per capita income* raise the private saving rate;

- changes in *real interest rates* have no significant effect on private or national saving;

- increases in *foreign saving* (as measured by the *current account deficit*) affect national saving negatively, but the offset was only partial (estimated to be between 40 and 50 percent), suggesting that an increased availability of external financing typically supports both higher consumption and higher investment;

- *terms-of-trade windfalls* have a positive, but transitory, effect on national saving.

Hadjimachael and Ghura (1995) used a panel of 41 sub-Saharan African countries over the period 1986-92 to investigate the effectiveness of *public policies* in stimulating private saving and investment. They found that policies that kept inflation low, reduced *macroeconomic uncertainty*, promoted financial development, and increased public saving led to higher national saving rates. They also found that a reduction in the **external debt burden** significantly increased national saving—possibly because of a reduction in expectations of future taxation, as indicated earlier.

Edwards (1996c) studied the determinants of saving in a group of 25 developing countries and 11 industrialized countries over the period 1970-92. His results showed a significant effect on private savings rates of the following variables:

- the rate of growth of per capita income,

- the **monetization ratio**, which is similar to the indicator of financial deepening defined earlier;

- *foreign saving* (measured again by the current account deficit), with a negative coefficient less than unity—suggesting that the crowding out effect of foreign saving is less than one to one, as found by Masson, Bayoumi, and Samiei (1998);

- *government saving*, with a negative effect that is less than one to one—in contrast to the Ricardian equivalence hypothesis;

- *social security* (as measured by the ratio of public expenditure on social security and welfare to total public spending), with a significantly negative coefficient.

The real interest rate (proxied by the ex post real bank deposit rate), the structure of the economy (as measured by the share of manufacturing, mining, and agriculture in output), and inflation variability were not significant. The age dependency ratio was also found to be insignificant for the group of developing countries as a whole, but results for Latin America only suggested that it had a significantly negative effect on saving.[17] Overall, the most important variables were the growth of per capita income, government saving, and the monetization ratio.

Dayal-Gulati and Thimann (1997) studied the determinants of private (personal and corporate) saving in a group of five Southeast Asian countries—Indonesia, Malaysia, Philippines, Singapore, and Thailand—and nine Latin American countries—Argentina, Brazil, Chile, Colombia, Mexico, Paraguay, Peru, Uruguay, and Venezuela—over the period 1975-95. They found evidence that terms-of-trade shocks have a positive effect on saving. Government saving only partially crowds out private saving, suggesting again a rejection of the strict form of the Ricardian equivalence proposition. Social security expenditures were associated with lower private saving, and fully funded pension schemes had a positive effect. Macroeconomic stability (as measured by the deviation of inflation from an underlying moving average) and financial deepening (as measured by the ratio of broad money to GDP) also affected positively private saving and played an important role in explaining differences in saving patterns across the two regions. Per capita income also had a positive effect.

The study by Loayza, Schmidt-Hebbel, and Servén (2000) used an extensive cross-country database to study the determinants of saving. A novelty of the analysis was also their attempt to distinguish between short- and long-term determinants of saving rates—a distinction that appeared to be highly significant in their empirical results. Their analysis showed, in particular, that *macroeconomic uncertainty* (as measured by the variance of inflation) had a positive

---

[17]A negative correlation between saving and the age dependency ratio was also found by Cárdenas and Escobar (1998) in the case of Colombia.

effect on private saving rates, consistent with the **precautionary motive** discussed earlier. *Public sector saving* had a negative but less than proportional effect on private saving, suggesting once again that Ricardian equivalence does not hold in strict terms. *Real interest rates* had no significant effect on saving, whereas *terms-of-trade improvements* were positively associated with private and national saving rates, although the effect was small.

Various other studies corroborated and complemented the findings described above. For instance, Ostry and Reinhart (1992) found that although intratemporal substitution between nontradables and importables may be a significant channel through which terms-of-trade shocks affect savings, overall their empirical results supported the view that transitory adverse movements in the terms of trade led to a reduction in private saving—as predicted by the HLM effect. In addition, Ghosh and Ostry (1994) found a positive correlation between the *variability* of the terms of trade and saving. Ogaki, Ostry, and Reinhart (1996), in a study covering a large number of developed and developing countries, found that saving rates tended to rise with per capita income levels, especially during the transition from low-income levels (where subsistence needs predominate) to middle-income levels. More specifically, the evidence suggested that saving rates tended to increase with the level of per capita income and to *level off* (or even decline) at very high levels of income. This **inverted U-shape** pattern has been documented in other studies as well. Finally, Ogaki, Ostry, and Reinhart also found the **intertemporal elasticity of substitution**, even in middle-income countries, to be quite low—less than unity in most cases. For Tanzania, for instance, the estimated elasticity was 0.2, whereas for Chile and Brazil, it reached 0.6. These results imply, as shown earlier, that a rise in interest rates will in general have an ambiguous (or even negative) effect on consumption and saving—thereby mitigating the benefits of financial liberalization (see Chapter 15). Indeed, Bandiera, Caprio, Honohan, and Schiantarelli (2000) found that financial liberalization—as measured by a composite index of financial reforms—had an adverse effect on saving in a group of eight developing countries.

At the same time, however, there are several issues that are either inadequately addressed in the current literature or remain unresolved. One problem, for instance, is the evidence on the effect of foreign saving (as measured by the current account deficit) on domestic saving rates. As indicated earlier, Masson, Bayoumi, and Samiei (1998) and Edwards (1996c) both found this effect to be significantly negative, with a coefficient of less than unity—a finding that suggests that foreign saving is a *substitute*, albeit a less than perfect one, for domestic saving. However, in the data that most researchers use, private saving is calculated *residually* as domestic investment plus the current account surplus minus public saving—a key national accounts *identity* that was explicitly derived in Chapter 1. The implication, however, is that the use of the current account balance along with public saving as explanatory variables brings the regression equation close to being *overidentified*: the high significance levels on the current account balance could therefore be nothing but a statistical artifact.

Another important problem is the lack of robust empirical evidence on the effect of interest rates on saving. As shown earlier, the effect of a change in the real interest rate on saving is *theoretically ambiguous* as a result of conflicting **income** and **substitution effects**. The evidence (or the lack thereof) may thus be consistent with the view that these effects tend to *offset* each other, implying that the net effect is small and often cannot be adequately detected by the data. What this implies, as noted earlier, is that the direct effect of policies aimed at raising rates of return offered to savers may be largely ineffective. It should be noted, however, that several studies have used sample periods during which *regulated interest rates*, exhibiting little variation over time, were in place. Another problem is that the effect of interest rates on saving may be *nonlinear*: not only can it depend on the *level of income*, as shown by Ogaki, Ostry, and Reinhart (1996), it may also be *stronger* at *positive real interest rates* than at the *negative real interest rates* often observed when nominal interest rates are subject to government controls (see Chapter 4). Along the same lines, it would be worth exploring to what extent terms-of-trade shocks tend to have *asymmetric effects* on aggregate saving rates, as a result, for instance, of the tendency of governments to increase spending excessively in good times. Agénor and Aizenman (2002) provide a more formal examination of these asymmetric effects as well as some empirical evidence for sub-Saharan Africa.

2.2 Investment

Investment typically represents a much smaller component of aggregate demand than does consumption. But because it determines the rate at which physical capital is accumulated, it plays an essential role in the expansion of the economy's production capacity (see Chapters 11 and 12). This section reviews various models of investment behavior, based on both scale and relative price variables. It begins by describing the basic **flexible accelerator** model in section 2.2.1 and then extends it to account for the **cost of capital** in section 2.2.2. Much of the recent analytical and empirical research on the determinants of investment has focused on the role of **uncertainty** and **irreversibility**; these issues are analyzed in section 2.2.3. Section 2.2.4 discusses various other factors that have been found to affect investment in developing countries.[18] Section 2.2.5 reviews some of the recent empirical evidence on the determinants of private investment in these countries.

2.2.1 The Flexible Accelerator

In its simplest form, the **flexible accelerator** model of investment is derived under the assumption that the production technology in the economy is characterized by a fixed relationship between the *desired* capital stock and the level of

---

[18] The *q-theory* of investment, which makes investment an increasing function of the ratio of the value of the firm to the cost of purchasing the firm's equipment and other capital goods, is not developed here because it has met with very limited empirical success in developing countries.

output. Formally, suppose that the desired stock of capital, $\tilde{K}$, is proportional to expected output, y^a:

$$\tilde{K} = \alpha y^a, \quad \alpha > 0. \tag{26}$$

Suppose that (because it takes time to build, plan, and install new equipment) the actual stock of capital adjusts to the difference between the desired stock at the current period and the actual stock in the previous period:

$$\Delta K = \kappa(\tilde{K} - K_{-1}), \quad 0 < \kappa < 1. \tag{27}$$

Equation (27) represents the simplest version of the flexible accelerator. To see its implications, note that, by definition, gross private investment, I^p, is given by

$$I^p = \Delta K + \delta K_{-1}, \quad 0 < \delta < 1, \tag{28}$$

where δ is the rate of depreciation. Using the **lag operator** L (defined by $Lx = x_{-1}$), this equation can be rewritten as

$$I^p = [1 - (1 - \delta)L]K, \tag{29}$$

which implies also that $K_{-1} = I^p_{-1}/[1 - (1 - \delta)L]$. Combining Equations (26) and (27) yields

$$K = \alpha\kappa y^a + (1 - \kappa)K_{-1},$$

that is, using (29),

$$I^p = \alpha\kappa[1 - (1 - \delta)L]y^a + (1 - \kappa)I^p_{-1}. \tag{30}$$

In the particular case where $\delta = 0$ (no depreciation), $\kappa = 1$ (adjustment to the desired capital stock is instantaneous), and expected future output is well approximated by current output, the investment function becomes

$$I^p = \alpha\Delta y. \tag{31}$$

Equation (31) has a particularly simple form: it relates investment linearly to changes in current output. Variables such as profitability, uncertainty, and the cost of capital play no role. However, despite its simplicity (or perhaps because of it), Equation (31) continues to be used in practical policy tools (see Chapter 9).

2.2.2 The User Cost of Capital

An alternative approach is to view investment as depending inversely on the **user cost of capital**, c_K, or equivalently the **flow price of capital services**, which consists of three components (Jorgenson, 1963):

- an *opportunity cost*, which is measured by the interest that the firm would receive if instead of investing in physical capital it used its resources to acquire an asset with a positive rate of return. If i denotes the interest rate on this alternative asset and P_K the price of one unit of capital (that is, the nominal market price of one unit of capital goods), this cost is iP_K;

- the cost resulting from the *depreciation* of the capital good; with δ denoting the rate of depreciation of capital, this cost (per unit time) is given by δP_K;

- the *capital loss* (or *gain*) resulting from the fact that the price of capital may be falling (rising), implying that the firm would obtain less (more) if it waits to sell the capital; this is measured by $-\Delta P_K$ per unit time.

Thus, the user cost of capital is given by

$$c_K = P_K \left\{ i + \delta - \frac{\Delta P_K}{P_K} \right\}, \tag{32}$$

where the quantity $i - \Delta P_K/P_K$ can be viewed as a real interest rate measured in terms of the price of capital goods. If capital goods are imported and subject to a tariff rate ι_M, and firms are subject to income taxation at the rate ι_Π, this expression becomes[19]

$$c_K = \frac{(1 + \iota_M)P_K}{1 - \iota_\Pi} \left\{ i + \delta - \frac{\Delta P_K}{P_K} \right\}. \tag{33}$$

In the above derivations, the user cost of capital is assumed to depend on the *opportunity cost* of investment, that is, the rate of return on an alternative asset that the firm would choose to acquire instead of investing in physical capital. This assumes implicitly that the firm carrying the investment has the resources to do so—in the form of retained earnings, for instance. However, if the firm must borrow from banks to finance capital outlays (as is often the case in developing countries), the cost of capital would depend directly on the bank lending rate, instead of the opportunity cost of investment.

In practical applications, the cost of capital is often combined with the flexible accelerator model described earlier. A simple way to do so is to write the *desired* capital stock as a function not only of desired output, as in Equation (26), but also as an inverse function of c_K:

$$\tilde{K} = \alpha y^a / c_K. \tag{34}$$

Using this specification simply leads to replacing y^a by y^a/c_K in Equation (30), implying therefore that investment is now inversely related to the cost of capital services. This extended model, however, continues to suffer from a major limitation: it does not account for the impact of uncertainty on the decision to invest.

---

[19] See Auerbach (1995) for a detailed discussion of how taxation affects the cost of capital and investment. As argued by Bustos, Engel and Galetovic (2004) in the case of Chile, if business taxes are offset by generous depreciation allowances (which reduce taxable profits) and tax-deductible interest payments, changes in the corporate tax rate ι_Π may have a limited impact on the user cost of capital—in contrast to what expression (33) would suggest.

2.2.3   Uncertainty and Irreversibility

An important insight of the recent literature on investment is that under uncertainty, private investment decisions may be significantly affected by **irreversibility effects** (Dixit and Pindyck, 1994). Such effects arise essentially from the fact that firm-specific investment typically involves **sunk costs**, which can only be partially recuperated because of the (generally large) discount that firms must face in valuing second-hand equipment. If the outcome of an irreversible investment turns out to be worse than expected, firms may get stuck with *excess capital* or *low returns*, whereas if prospects improve, new entrants may compete away part of the gains. Because *downside risk* may increase without corresponding upside gain, waiting has value as it gives firms the opportunity to process new information before the decision to invest is actually taken.

To examine in a more formal manner the effects of uncertainty and irreversibility on investment, consider the following simple example based on Servén (1997). Suppose that a *risk-neutral firm* must decide whether to invest in a project in which the initial cost is completely sunk at the purchase cost P_K at the beginning of period $t_0 = 0$.[20] It yields a known return of R_0 at the end of that period. But future demand for the good generated by the project is uncertain; as a result, the rate of return on the project in period $t = 1, 2, \ldots$ denoted R, is also uncertain.

Given the information available at period 0, the expected value of the future return is $E_0 R$. The *net present value* of the *anticipated return stream of cash flows* associated with the project, V_0, is thus

$$V_0 = -P_K + \frac{R_0}{1+i} + \frac{E_0 R_1}{(1+i)^2} + \ldots,$$

that is

$$V_0 = -P_K + \frac{R_0}{1+i} + \left[\frac{1}{1+i}\right]^2 \sum_{h=0}^{\infty} (1+i)^{-h} E_0 R_{h+1}, \tag{35}$$

where i is the discount rate, taken to be equal to the rate of return on an alternative investment, such as riskless government bonds. Assuming that the return at $t = 1$ and beyond is constant at R, the third term in this expression can be rewritten as

$$\frac{E_0 R}{(1+i)^2} \sum_{h=0}^{\infty} (1+i)^{-h} = \frac{E_0 R}{(1+i)^2} \left[1 + \frac{1}{1+i} + \frac{1}{(1+i)^2} + \ldots\right]$$

$$= \frac{E_0 R}{(1+i)^2} \left[\frac{1}{1 - 1/(1+i)}\right] = \frac{E_0 R}{i(1+i)}.$$

Using this result, Equation (35) can be rewritten as

$$V_0 \equiv -P_K + \frac{R_0 + E_0 R/i}{1+i}. \tag{36}$$

---

[20] Risk neutrality in the present context means that the firm's utility is linear in realized profits; maximizing utility and maximizing profits are thus basically the same.

The conventional **net present value criterion** suggests that the investment is profitable and thus should be made as long as $V_0 > 0$. Rearranging terms in Equation (36) yields

$$R_0 - iP_K + \frac{E_0 R - iP_K}{i} > 0, \tag{37}$$

where the term iP_K can be interpreted as the user cost of capital if the depreciation rate is zero and the price of capital is constant over time [see Equation (32)]. With **full reversibility** of investment, the *future would not matter*; the optimal decision rule would thus be to invest today as long as

$$R_0 - iP_K > 0, \tag{38}$$

that is, as long as the current return exceeds the user cost of capital. The presence of irreversibility requires taking into account also the difference between the *expected return* and the user cost of capital, as shown in the last term of Equation (37).

But although Equation (37) must hold in an *ex ante* sense, it may not *ex post;* the reason is that there is a *nonzero probability* that at some period t in the future, the inequality (38) may be reversed, that is, $R - iP_K < 0$. The firm may thus be "locked" in an unprofitable investment. There is, therefore, an *incentive to delay* investment in order to learn more about the factors affecting future return—in the present case, about the state of market demand for the good produced by the firm.

To determine how uncertainty affects the decision rule (37), consider first the case where the firm knows for sure that uncertainty will completely vanish at period $t = 1$ and beyond, and that the project's returns for $t = 2, ..., \infty$ will remain constant at the level realized in the first period, R. Suppose then that the firm decides not to invest at all today and to invest in the next period if and only if the *realized return exceeds the user cost of capital*. In that case, the net present value of the anticipated stream of cash flows, V_1, will be given by, noting that $\Pr(R \le iP_K) \cdot 0 = 0$,

$$V_1 \equiv \Pr(R > iP_K) \left\{ \frac{-P_k}{1+i} + \left[\frac{1}{1+i} \right]^2 \sum_{h=0}^{\infty} (1+i)^{-h} E_0(R \mid R > iP_K) \right\}$$

where

- $\Pr(R > iP_K)$ is the probability that the *project's return exceeds the cost of capital*;

- $E_0(R \mid R > iP_K)$ is the *expected value* of R, conditional on the project's return exceeding the cost of capital.

Thus, in the particular case where $\Pr(R > iP_K) = 0$, $V_1 = 0$ and the firm has no incentive to invest either. More generally, comparing the above strategy with the previous case can be done by calculating

$$V_1 - V_0 = \left(\frac{1}{1+i} \right) \left\{ \Pr(R \le iP_K) \frac{E_0(iP_K - R \mid R \le iP_K)}{i} - (R_0 - iP_K) \right\},$$

an expression that is obtained by using the following result from basic statistics to substitute for $E_0 R$ in (35):

$$E_0 R = \Pr(R > iP_K)E_0(R \mid R > iP_K) + \Pr(R \le iP_K)E_0(R \mid R \le iP_K).$$

The firm is *better off investing today* if

$$V_1 - V_0 < 0,$$

a condition that can be rewritten as

$$R_0 - iP_K > \Pr(R \le iP_K)\frac{E_0(iP_K - R \mid R \le iP_K)}{i}. \qquad (39)$$

Condition (39) compares two expressions:

- the **cost of waiting**, as given by the net return foregone in period 0 by not investing, $R_0 - iP_K$; and

- the **value of waiting**, given by the *irreversible mistake* that would be revealed tomorrow should future returns fall short of the user cost of capital ($R \le iP_K$). The *expected present value* of such a mistake is measured by the right-hand side of Equation (39):

  - the mistake is made with probability $\Pr(R \le iP_K)$;

  - its expected per-period size, given today's information, is

  $$E_0(iP_K - R \mid R \le iP_K);$$

  - because it accrues every period into the indefinite future, it has to be multiplied by $1/i$ to transform it to present value terms.

Thus, condition (39) indicates that it is profitable to invest *immediately* only if the first-period return exceeds the conventionally measured user cost of capital by a margin that is large enough to compensate for the possibility of an irreversible mistake—that is, *if the cost of waiting outweighs the value of waiting*.

An important implication of Equation (39) is that the possibility that in the future R may exceed iP_K has no effect on the investment threshold and thus no effect on the decision to invest today. Intuitively, the reason for this asymmetry is that the option to wait has no value in those good states of nature in which investing would have been the right decision anyway—it is only valuable in those states in which investing today would have been, *ex post*, a bad decision. This **option value of waiting**, δ, is given by

$$\delta = \max\left(V_1 - V_0, 0\right).$$

If $V_1 - V_0 < 0$, the option has no value, and the optimal decision is to invest today (at period 0). In general, however, the option value of waiting can be large, especially in a highly uncertain environment. As a consequence, uncertainty can become a powerful deterrent to investment *even under risk neutrality*.[21] Such uncertainty may result from various domestic and external sources, including a high degree of volatility in aggregate demand, large movements in the terms of trade and relative prices, and incomplete credibility of macroeconomic policies (see Chapter 6).[22]

In the simple example considered here, an increase in the *spread* of the distribution of future returns—as a result, for instance, of increased **macroeconomic volatility**—that increases the likelihood of "bad" outcomes (that is, $R \leq iP_K$) will raise the critical threshold that the marginal productivity of capital must reach, and thus tend to depress investment. This result, however, does not always hold. If the opportunity cost of waiting, R_0, is uncertain rather than known—as would be the case for investment projects subject to completion lags—and the firm can abandon the project at a cost in the future (that is, investment is **partly reversible**), then higher uncertainty could *hasten* investment, by making extreme favorable realizations of R_0 more likely—even if at the same time extreme adverse realizations also become more likely. The reason is that the firm can now avoid the impact of negative outcomes on profitability by shutting down the project (Bar-Ilan and Strange, 1996). Thus, although both the value and the cost of waiting rise with higher uncertainty, the latter rises by a greater amount. Nevertheless, the above setting implies that the higher the degree of irreversibility (that is, the higher the degree of asymmetry in investment adjustment costs), the more likely it is that uncertainty will have an adverse effect on capital formation.

Recent research on the relation between uncertainty and investment has emphasized the role of various other factors, including market structure, the degree of risk aversion, and capital market imperfections. Abel and Eberly (1999) showed that working in the opposite direction to the effect of irreversibility on the user cost of capital is a **hangover effect**, which arises because irreversibility prevents the firm from selling capital even when the marginal revenue product is low. As a result, irreversibility may either increase or decrease capital accumulation. As shown by Caballero (1991), if (risk-neutral) firms are subject to **asymmetric adjustment costs**, uncertainty and investment would tend to be positively related under perfect competition and constant returns to scale, whereas they would be negatively related under imperfect competition and decreasing returns to scale.[23] Zeira (1990) also showed that with **risk-averse**

---

[21] It is important to emphasize that these results do not depend on the existence of risk-averse firms or restrictions on the degree to which risks can be diversified. Even if firms are risk neutral, and even if risks are fully diversifiable, investment will still depend on the perceived degree of uncertainty.

[22] As noted for instance by Aizenman and Marion (1999), volatility and uncertainty are in principle two different phenomena. Volatility (or variability) exists when a variable tends to fluctuate over time, whereas uncertainty exists when these fluctuations are unpredictable. In practice, however, volatile variables tend also to be unpredictable as well.

[23] See Chapter 11 for a definition of constant, increasing, and decreasing returns to scale. Caballero's results clarified an early contribution by Abel (1983), who showed that in the absence of irreversibility and under risk neutrality, an increase in uncertainty (over the behavior

firms, uncertainty has an ambiguous impact on investment. The higher the degree of risk aversion, the more likely it is that uncertainty will reduce investment. Finally, as shown by Aizenman and Marion (1999), a negative link between uncertainty (or volatility) and investment can result from the existence of a **credit ceiling** (as discussed earlier in the context of consumption behavior). Such a ceiling typically leads to a *nonlinearity* in the investor's intertemporal budget constraint. It may therefore hamper the expansion of investment in good times (that is, states in which the firm faces high and growing demand for its products) without mitigating the fall in capital formation in bad times. This asymmetry may lead to a situation in which higher volatility reduces the average rate of investment.

The thrust of the foregoing discussion is thus that, on purely theoretical grounds, the effect of uncertainty on private investment is in general ambiguous. Fundamentally this is because uncertainty affects investment through a variety of channels and, depending in particular on the degree of risk aversion, market structure, and the nature of adjustment costs, the relation between these variables can be either positive or negative. Empirical evidence (as discussed below) is therefore necessary to assess in what direction the net effect operates.

2.2.4   Other Determinants

In addition to the variables considered earlier, the decision to invest in developing economies has been shown to depend on a variety of other factors. These factors include most notably the degree of credit rationing (alluded to above), the availability of foreign exchange, movements in the real exchange rate, the level of public investment, the degree of macroeconomic volatility, and the existence of a large external debt.[24]

Credit Rationing

As discussed in more detail in Chapter 4, the lack of development of *equity markets* makes firms highly dependent on *bank credit* not only for **working capital needs** (associated with the need to pay workers and buy raw materials prior to the sale of output) but also for the longer-term financing of capital accumulation. As also discussed in Chapter 4, in countries where interest rates are highly regulated (so that real interest rates are negative), excess demand for credit will typically exist, forcing banks to ration their loans. The fact that banks are imperfectly informed about the *quality* of the projects in which firms plan to invest may also lead to (endogenous) credit rationing, the degree of which may be related to the availability of collateral, and thus the existing capital stock (Demetriades and Devereux, 2000). Both cases suggest that it is the *quantity* of credit, rather than its price (the interest rate) that should be

---

of output prices) tends to increase the desired capital stock and thus investment.

[24]Income distribution, which is not discussed here, may also affect investment decisions through its effect on the profit rate, the level of aggregate demand, and social and political instability. Chapters 13 and 14 discuss the longer-run effects of income inequality.

considered as a determinant of investment. In addition, the second argument suggests that small firms (for which information is typically more difficult to acquire and process) may be more affected by credit constraints, as documented for instance by Fielding (2000) in the case of South Africa and Galindo and Schiantarelli (2003) for several countries in Latin America.

Foreign Exchange Constraint

Capital goods such as machines and equipment must often be imported in developing economies. In some of them, more than half of merchandise imports consist of capital goods and spare parts for these goods. Because the foreign exchange needed to pay for such imports may not be available—as a result of, say, balance-of-payments difficulties or because of higher-priority needs, such as servicing the external public debt—private investment may be subject to a *foreign exchange constraint*.

The Real Exchange Rate

The real exchange rate (as measured by the price of nontraded goods relative to the price of traded goods) affects private investment through both demand- and supply-side channels:

- On the *demand side*, a real exchange rate depreciation resulting from a nominal depreciation lowers private sector real wealth and expenditure through its effect on domestic prices; the fall in domestic absorption may lead firms to revise their expectations of future demand and to lower investment outlays, through the accelerator effect.

- On the *supply side*, because a real exchange rate depreciation raises the price of traded goods (measured in domestic-currency terms) relative to the price of home goods, it may stimulate investment in the tradable sector and depress capital formation in the nontradable sector.

- At the same time, however, a real depreciation may raise the real cost of **imported capital goods**—a likely outcome if the country is dependent on noncompetitive imported capital goods and intermediate goods, as is often the case in the developing world. It may have an adverse effect on private investment by raising the user cost of capital (Buffie, 1986).

Public Investment

Public investment has in general an *ambiguous effect* on private investment as a result of several opposing factors:

- Public investment may, by increasing the fiscal deficit, **crowd out** private capital formation by reducing credit available to the private sector or by raising interest rates.

- By contrast, public investment in infrastructure projects (such as capital outlays in power, telecommunications, transport, health, and education) may be *complementary* to private investment.

- By increasing aggregate demand, public investment may stimulate private investment through the accelerator effect.

How an increase in public investment is financed is crucial to determining the extent to which it may crowd out private capital formation. Even if public investment takes the form of increased outlays on infrastructure, the net effect may still be negative if, for instance, the increase in spending is financed through an increase in the corporate income tax. This is because such an increase would translate, as shown in Equation (33), into a rise in the cost of capital.

Macroeconomic Instability

As noted earlier, in the presence of irreversibility and asymmetric adjustment costs, macroeconomic instability may have large (and possibly negative) effects on private capital formation. There are several other channels through which macroeconomic instability may affect private investment:

- An unstable macroeconomic environment is often characterized by a high *level of inflation*; in turn, a high inflation rate may lower investment by *distorting price signals* and the information content of relative price changes.

- Macroeconomic instability also translates into *high inflation variability*; in turn, a highly variable inflation rate may have an adverse effect on **expected profitability**; if firms are risk averse, their level of investment will fall.

More generally, an increase in policy uncertainty may cause risk-averse firms to reallocate resources away from risky activities, thereby lowering the desired stock of capital.[25] Through the accelerator effect identified above, this fall may translate into a reduction in private investment.

Inflation may also affect private investment through two other channels. On the one hand, to the extent that higher (expected) inflation lowers the real interest rate, it may lead to a a portfolio shift away from real money balances and toward physical capital. This is the so-called **Tobin-Mundell effect**. On the other, however, if (expected) inflation raises the cost of acquiring capital, as a result of a **cash-in-advance constraint**, it could lower private investment. Thus, in general, the effect of inflation on private investment is ambiguous.

The Debt Burden Effect

A large ratio of foreign debt to output may have an adverse effect on private investment through various channels.

---

[25] Credit rationing may also intensify as uncertainty increases.

- Resources used to service the public debt may *crowd out* government investment in areas where complementarities exist between public and private capital outlays, as discussed earlier; this would tend to reduce private investment.

- A high debt-to-output ratio (and a concomitantly high debt service ratio) may lead domestic agents to transfer funds abroad, instead of saving domestically, because of the *fear of future tax liabilities* to service this debt; this is similar to the effect alluded to earlier in the context of saving. It tends to lower private investment both directly and indirectly—in the latter case, by raising the domestic cost of capital goods.[26]

- A high debt burden could discourage foreign direct investment by increasing the likelihood that the government may resort to the *imposition of restrictions* on external payment obligations—including on current payments on investment income. To the extent that foreign direct investment is complementary to domestic private investment, the latter will fall also.

- When firms hold a large stock of foreign-currency liabilities, they become highly vulnerable to exchange rate movements. A nominal depreciation, for instance, raises automatically the burden of debt and reduces the firm's net worth. The resulting increase in the risk of default may lead domestic banks to tighten credit restrictions (as discussed above) and may depress investment.

2.2.5 Empirical Evidence

The foregoing discussion suggests a general empirical formulation of a private investment function that encompasses many of the empirical specifications used in studies conducted in recent years for developing countries. With I^p/y denoting the ratio of private investment to output, this specification can be written as

$$\frac{I^p}{y} = H(\Delta y, c_K, \frac{L^p}{P}, R^*, I_G^I, I_G^O, z, \sigma_z, \pi, \sigma_\pi, \frac{D^*}{y}). \tag{40}$$

This specification includes

- the **accelerator effect**, as captured by changes in output, Δy;

- the **user cost of capital**, c_K, as defined in Equation (32);

- **credit rationing**, as captured by the real stock of bank credit to the private sector, L^p/P;

- the **foreign exchange constraint**, as measured by the country's (average) level of foreign reserves, R^*;

---

[26] In this sense, a large external debt burden constitutes an additional source of macroeconomic uncertainty.

- **public investment**, which consists of investment in infrastructure, I_G^I, and other investments, I_G^O, with the former variable expected to have a positive effect and the second an ambiguous effect;

- The **real exchange rate**, z, which has in general an ambiguous effect;

- **macroeconomic instability**, as captured by the variability of the real exchange rate, σ_z, and the variability of inflation, σ_π. All these variables are expected to have a negative effect;

- the **level of inflation**, π, which captures both macroeconomic instability and other effects, such as the *Tobin-Mundell effect* discussed earlier. This variable may therefore have an ambiguous impact on private investment;

- The **ratio of foreign debt to output**, as measured by D^*/y, which is likely to have a negative effect.

A detailed overview of the early empirical literature on investment in developing countries was provided by Rama (1993). Rama reviewed 31 studies of investment covering the period from the 1960s to the mid-1980s. Dynamics in many cases were captured by specifying a *partial adjustment process*, of the type shown in Equation (27). Such a process, however, does not account very well for the various lags that arise in practice between the moment the decision to invest is taken and actual investment—such as delays involved in choosing, receiving, and installing new capital goods. More importantly, most of these studies were plagued by **specification bias**, and possibly **spurious correlation** problems; the time-series properties of the endogenous and exogenous variables were often not properly assessed before estimation (see the appendix to Chapter 9).

Two other studies are those of Oshikoya (1994) and Hadjimichael and Ghura (1995) for sub-Saharan Africa. Oshikoya's investigation provided a detailed analysis of the determinants of private investment during the 1970s and 1980s in eight African countries: four middle-income countries (Cameroon, Morocco, Mauritius, and Tunisia) and four low-income countries (Malawi, Tanzania, Zimbabwe, and Kenya). For sub-Saharan Africa as a whole, real GDP per capita grew on average by only 0.4 percent per annum during 1973-80 and fell by 1.2 percent per annum during the period 1980-89. Investment also fell substantially during that period; the ratio of total domestic investment to GDP fell from 20.8 percent per annum during 1973-80 to 16.1 percent during 1980-89. In the sample of countries considered by Oshikoya, the private investment ratio fell in the early 1980s but increased in the late 1980s in middle-income countries; this ratio fell throughout the 1980s among the low-income countries. The share of private investment in total investment also fell, for the group as a whole, from 53 percent in 1970-79 to 51.4 percent during 1984-88. This overall result, however, reflects essentially the sharp increase in the public investment rate in low-income countries; middle-income countries were able to increase the share of private investment in total investment during the late 1980s.

Oshikoya estimated separate investment equations (with the lagged dependent variable as a regressor) on pooled data for the period 1970-88. His results indicated, in particular, the following points.

- *Changes in real output* (the accelerator effect) had a significant and positive impact on private investment only in low-income countries.

- *Public investment* was positively related to private investment in both groups, with a stronger complementarity effect in middle-income countries.

- The impacts of the real exchange rate and inflation differed markedly across the two groups. The *real exchange rate* had a positive and significant effect on middle-income countries, but a negative (albeit statistically insignificant) effect in low-income countries. The *inflation rate* had a strong and unambiguously negative impact in the low-income group but a positive and significant effect in the middle-income group.

- The *debt service ratio* had a strong, negative effect on private investment in both country groups.

- Measures of *macroeconomic uncertainty* and *instability* (the coefficients of variation of real output growth and the real exchange rate) had a negative effect on investment during the 1980s.

Standardized regression coefficients, which are unit-free and measure the relative importance of the independent variables on the private investment rate, suggested that the debt service ratio, the domestic inflation rate, the public investment rate, and the real exchange rate had the largest effect on private investment in middle-income countries. Credit to the private sector, domestic inflation, the growth rate of output, and the debt service ratio had the largest effect on private investment in low-income countries. The importance of the accelerator effect in the latter group may be due to investors having myopic expectations or short planning horizons.

Another empirical study focusing on sub-Saharan Africa by Hadjimichael and Ghura (1995) reaches very similar conclusions:

- Public and private investment appear to be complementary.

- Policies aimed at fostering macroeconomic stability (lower inflation and real exchange rate variability) tend to promote private investment.

- A high debt burden (measured as the ratio of external debt to exports) has an adverse effect on investment.

Pattillo, Poirson, and Ricci (2002) also provided some empirical evidence of a negative relationship between external debt and private capital formation for sub-Saharan Africa. Using a sample covering 93 developing countries over the period 1969-98, they found that on average external debt begins to have a negative impact on growth when it reaches about 160-170 percent of exports or 35-40 percent of GDP.

Four other studies, by Servén (1997, 1998), Pattillo (1998), and Aizenman and Marion (1999), provide further evidence on the adverse effect of uncertainty on private investment. Servén (1997) found evidence suggesting that uncertainty and macroeconomic volatility were key factors in explaining the low levels of investment observed in sub-Saharan Africa in the 1980s and 1990s. Pattillo (1998) pointed to the same phenomena in explaining the behavior of private investment in Ghana.

In a subsequent study, Servén (1998) focused on a dataset covering 94 developing countries over the period 1970-95. He first pointed out that simple measures of volatility (such as standard deviations of inflation or real exchange rates) may only *partially* capture the impact of policy uncertainty, and therefore make it quite difficult to test empirically its impact on capital formation. Instead, he constructed an alternative measure of uncertainty based on the dispersion of the **innovations** of macroeconomic variables—that is, the standard deviations of the *residuals* of an autoregressive forecasting equation for each variable. Specifically, five macroeconomic variables were considered in Servén's study: three related to the aggregate profitability of capital (output growth, inflation, and the relative price of investment goods, the latter representing a proxy for the user cost of capital) and two more closely related to the relative profitability of different economic sectors (the terms of trade and the real exchange rate). These variables were entered both individually and in a composite form in the regressions. He controlled for some of the other determinants of investment discussed earlier—such as changes in output, the cost of capital (captured by the relative price of capital), the real interest rate, and credit to the private sector—and used alternative econometric procedures to allow for simultaneity, country-specific effects, and parameter heterogeneity across countries. The results indicated a robust negative effect of macroeconomic uncertainty on investment, particularly when such uncertainty was measured by the real exchange rate.

Finally, Aizenman and Marion (1999) also considered a large sample of developing countries (46 in all) over the period 1970-92. They measured macroeconomic volatility in several ways, including—like Servén (1998)—a specification based on the innovations of a set of aggregate variables (government consumption as a share of output, nominal money growth, and the real exchange rate). Their formal econometric tests confirmed a significant negative correlation between the alternative volatility measures that they constructed and private investment—even after allowing for various control variables suggested by the recent empirical literature on economic growth (see Chapter 13).[27]

Overall, therefore, most recent *macro*economic studies provide significant evidence of a negative link between uncertainty and private investment in develop-

---

[27] It should be noted that Aizenman and Marion also found evidence that volatility negatively affected the rate of economic growth; this relationship provides an indirect channel (operating via the accelerator effect) through which uncertainty can affect private investment. They did not, however, include output growth as a regressor in their investment equations.

ing countries—possibly reflecting, as noted previously, the role of irreversibility factors. As argued by Gunning and Mengistae (2001), however, most of the *micro*economic evidence for sub-Saharan Africa (based on industrial surveys), although supportive of the view that risk and uncertainty have a detrimental effect on private investment, is largely indirect; what is needed to corroborate this view is more direct evidence of firms' perceptions of the risks that they face.

2.3   Summary

- Because of their ultimate effects on growth, understanding the patterns and determinants of consumption, saving, and investment is a crucial step in designing policies aimed at raising standards of living.

- The **Keynesian consumption function** postulates a linear relation between consumption and current disposable income. It a good description of consumption and saving behavior at very low levels of income (where subsistence is a predominant concern) and in the presence of *liquidity constraints*.

- The **permanent income hypothesis** postulates that individuals (or households) set consumption equal to their **permanent income**, defined as the annuity value of the sum of assets and the discounted present value of expected future disposable income. A key implication of this assumption is that transitory income changes are (dis-)saved and permanent changes consumed.

- The **life-cycle approach** to consumption and saving assumes that individuals have a finite horizon and attempt to smooth their consumption path on the basis of their (expected) life-cycle wealth or anticipated lifetime income. Saving is seen as providing for retirement and changes systematically over the individual's lifetime.

- Specifically, the life-cycle model predicts that the saving rate should decline as the *retired proportion* of the population increases; this result extends to those *below labor-force age* as well. Thus, the higher the **age dependency ratio**, the lower the saving rate will be.

Analytical and empirical studies have identified various other factors affecting consumption and saving in developing economies:

- **Income levels** and **income variability**: saving rates are low at low levels of income. Changes in **income distribution** therefore affect aggregate saving rates. High income variability tends to raise saving as a result of a **precautionary motive**.

- **Intergenerational links**, which affect the effective planning horizon for consumption and saving decisions, as well as household preferences.

- **Liquidity constraints**, or restricted access to capital markets, which limit opportunities for households to borrow and lend and therefore the ability to smooth consumption intertemporally.

- **Inflation**, which may either increase the saving rate (as a result of a negative wealth effect) or reduce it (because agents expect inflation to persist in the future).

- **macroeconomic instability** (as captured by inflation variability), which may either raise the saving rate (if it increases income uncertainty) or reduce it (if it increases uncertainty on the rate of return).

- **Government saving** behavior, which may have an ambiguous effect on private saving. **Ricardian equivalence**, in particular, postulates that deficits and taxes are equivalent in their effect on private consumption. Households regard public debt simply as taxes delayed. This view, however, is subject to a number of criticisms at the analytical level and is not supported by the evidence for developing countries.

- The **debt burden**: a high level of debt may, through *anticipations of future taxes*, lower saving rates.

- **Social security**, **pension systems**, and **insurance**: the desire to accumulate assets for retirement or bequests depends on anticipated changes in income and wealth and the availability of pensions. The need to save for **contingencies** depends on the extent of insurance coverage.

- **Terms-of-trade** shocks: the **Harberger-Laursen-Metzler** effect predicts a positive relationship between *transitory* changes in the terms of trade and saving. However, if households consume both nontradables and importables, changes in their *relative price* induced by terms-of-trade shocks will also affect saving decisions through an **intratemporal substitution** effect, which may offset the conventional HLM effect.

- The degree of **financial development**: the need to save for large purchases of consumer goods depends on the extent to which households can borrow or not for these purposes. There is also an indirect effect through income, to the extent that increased efficiency in the financial intermediation process raises investment and the economy's growth rate.

Investment plays an important macroeconomic role because it determines the rate of growth of the physical capital stock and ultimately the growth rate of output. Models of investment behavior emphasize both quantity and relative price variables:

- The **flexible accelerator** assumes the existence of a fixed relationship between the desired capital stock and the *level* of output. In its simplest form, it generates a positive relationship between investment and *changes* in current output.

- The **user cost of capital,** which consists of an *opportunity cost,* a measure of the *depreciation rate of capital,* and the *capital loss* (or *gain*) induced by changes in the price of capital, has an adverse effect on investment.

- **Uncertainty** and **irreversibility** affect investment decisions because

  - most investments in fixed capital are partly or completely sunk; they cannot be fully recovered by selling the purchased capital goods once they have been put in place, and they cannot be used in a different activity without incurring a substantial cost;

  - investment decisions face uncertainty about their *future rewards.* Investors must consider various possible outcomes and attach probabilities to them.

- Because investors can control the *timing* of investment, they may postpone it in order to acquire more information about the future.

- Investment can thus be viewed as an *option* to purchase an asset at different points in time. The loss of this option, which is part of the opportunity cost of investment, is ignored in conventional net present-value calculations.

- The optimal investment policy is to balance the *value of waiting* for new information with the *cost of postponing* the investment in terms of foregone returns.

- The standard net present-value investment rule (invest when the anticipated return on the additional capital equals its purchase and installation costs) must therefore be modified: the anticipated return must *exceed* the purchase and installation cost by an amount equal to the value of keeping the option open.

- The volatile economic environment that characterizes most developing countries implies that uncertainty can have a strong effect on aggregate investment.

Other variables that have been found to affect investment in developing economies include:

- The degree of **credit rationing,** which results from the fact that, with limited or no equity financing, firms are highly dependent on bank credit not only for their working capital needs but also for the longer-term financing of capital outlays.

- **Foreign exchange constraints**, because capital goods are often imported.

- The **real exchange rate**, which affects private investment through both the accelerator effect (as a result of wealth and income effects) and the domestic price of *imported capital goods.*

- **Public investment**, which can either **crowd out** private capital formation (for instance, by reducing credit available to the private sector) or increase it if it has a *complementary* nature, such as investment in **infrastructure** projects. The composition of public investment and how it is financed are thus important.

- **Macroeconomic instability**, as measured by a high and variable rate of inflation, lowers investment by *(a) distorting price signals* and the *information content* of relative price changes, and *(b)* reducing *expected profitability*.

- The **debt burden**, which lowers private capital formation by reducing complementary public investment, by raising the *fear of future tax liabilities* to cover the country's debt service payments, and by discouraging complementary foreign direct investment.

Appendix to Chapter 2
Income Uncertainty and Precautionary Saving

The effects of income uncertainty on saving can be illustrated in a simple two-period framework.[28] In general, precautionary saving arises when individuals consume less (and therefore save more) while young to guard against a possible fall in income later in life. Thus, the analysis of precautionary saving must begin with the analysis of how uncertain income affects consumption. Consider the case of an economy in which the representative household lives two periods and faces the following budget constraints, in the absence of taxes $(T_1 = T_2 = 0)$:

$$c_1 = y_1 - s_1, \quad c_2 = y_2 + (1+r)s_1, \tag{A1}$$

where c_h, y_h denote consumption and income, respectively, in period h, s_1 saving (in period 1), and r is the real interest rate. For simplicity, the household possesses no initial endowment. Income in the second period, y_2, is supposed to be stochastic; specifically, it is given by

$$y_2 = (1+\varepsilon)y_1, \tag{A2}$$

where ε is a random shock with zero mean and constant variance σ_ε^2.

The household determines saving by maximizing the following intertemporal, time-additive utility function:

$$U = u(c_1) + \frac{Eu(c_2)}{1+\rho},$$

where ρ is the rate of time preference, and E the mathematical expectations operator. Using (A1) and (A2) yields

$$U = u(y_1 - s_1) + E\left\{\frac{u[(1+\varepsilon)y_1 + (1+r)s_1]}{1+\rho}\right\}. \tag{A3}$$

Let $r = \rho$; it can be established that saving is *proportional* to the variance of the shock ε:

$$s_1 = \frac{y_1}{2+r}\phi\sigma_\varepsilon^2, \quad \phi \equiv -\frac{u'''(y_1)y_1}{2u''(y_1)}. \tag{A4}$$

The above expression implies that saving is positively related to income uncertainty only if ϕ is positive. In turn, because $u'' < 0$, ϕ is positive only if $u''' > 0$, that is, only if **decreasing absolute risk aversion** prevails.[29] In general, for a utility function $u(\cdot)$, the degree of absolute risk aversion, θ, is measured by (minus) the ratio of the second-order derivative to the first, that

---

[28] The basic results of this appendix were derived by Joshua Aizenman. Skinner (1988) developed a multi-period life-cycle model of consumption with uncertain interest rates and income, and solves explicitly for the optimal consumption by using a second-order approximation to the Euler equation.

[29] Models that assume quadratic utility functions rule out by assumption precautionary savings against income risk, because the third-order derivative is zero.

is, $-u''/u'$ (see Varian, 1992, pp. 177-78). Decreasing absolute risk aversion requires θ to fall as consumption increases, and this indeed requires the third-order derivative u''' to be positive. The term ϕ can be interpreted as (half) the elasticity measuring the household's prudence—positive and higher values of that elasticity imply that an increase in uncertainty raises expected marginal utility, leading consumers to defer consumption, thereby increasing saving in the current period (see Leland, 1968, and Sandmo, 1970).

To establish the above result, note that the first-order condition from Equation (A3) yields

$$u'(y_1 - s_1) = E\{u'[y_1 + \varepsilon y_1 + (1+r)s_1]\}.$$

It can be noted that, by approximation,

$$u'(y_1 - s_1) \simeq u'(y_1) - s_1 u''(y_1),$$

and that

$$u'[y_1 + \varepsilon y_1 + (1+r)s_1] \simeq u'(y_1) + u''(y_1)[\varepsilon y_1 + (1+r)s_1] + \frac{u'''(y_1)}{2}[\varepsilon y_1 + (1+r)s_1]^2,$$

which implies that

$$E\{u'[y_1 + \varepsilon y_1 + (1+r)s_1]\} \simeq u'(y_1) + u''(y_1)(1+r)s_1 + \frac{u'''(y_1)}{2}E(\varepsilon y_1)^2.$$

Using these results yields

$$-s_1 u''(y_1) \simeq u''(y_1)(1+r)s_1 + \frac{u'''(y_1)}{2}E(\varepsilon)^2 y_1^2,$$

which implies that

$$s_1(2+r) \simeq \sigma_\varepsilon^2 \frac{y_1^2}{2}\left(-\frac{u'''}{u''}\right).$$

This expression is simply Equation (A4), given the definition of ϕ. An implication of this result is that the elasticity of saving with respect to the (gross) interest rate, is negative and approximately equal to minus one-half:

$$\frac{d\ln s_1}{d\ln(1+r)} = -\frac{1+r}{2+r} \simeq -0.5.$$

Chapter 3

Fiscal Deficits, Public Debt, and the Current Account

> It is common to speak as though, when a Government pays its way by way of inflation, the people of the country avoid taxation . . . this is not so. What is raised by printing notes is just as much taken from the public as is a beer-duty or an income tax. What a Government spends the public pays for. There is no such a thing as an uncovered deficit.

> John Maynard Keynes, *A Tract on Monetary Reform*, 1923 (p. 62).

Key constraints on fiscal policy and macroeconomic management in developing countries are an inadequate tax base, a limited ability to collect taxes, reliance on money financing, and (in some cases) high levels of public debt. Administrative (and sometimes political) constraints on the ability of tax authorities to collect revenue have often led to the imposition of high tax rates on a narrow tax base. The consequences have often been endemic tax evasion and unbridled expansion of the informal economy. At times the high degree of reliance on monetary financing of fiscal deficits in some countries has also resulted in macroeconomic instability, capital flight, and currency crises (see Chapter 8). High and growing levels of public debt exert pressure on real interest rates and have also led to financial volatility and macroeconomic instability.

This chapter provides an overview of fiscal policy issues in developing countries. Section 3.1 reviews the structure of public finances in these countries, focusing first on conventional (or explicit) sources of revenue and expenditure and subsequently on seigniorage and the inflation tax, as well as on quasi-fiscal activities. Section 3.2 examines the government budget constraint and the various ways in which fiscal deficits can be measured. Section 3.3 discusses a simple technique that has proved useful for assessing the medium-term stance of fiscal policy. The role of budget ceilings and fiscal transparency is examined in section 3.4. The link between fiscal deficits and current account deficits is studied in section 3.5. Issues of public debt sustainability and public sector solvency are examined in sections 3.6 and 3.7. Sections 3.8 and 3.9 focus on two important policy issues: the link between commodity price booms and fiscal deficits, and the link between fiscal adjustment, expectations, and economic activity.

3.1 Structure of Public Finances

Three aspects of public finances in developing countries are discussed in this section. The first is the composition of conventional sources of revenue and expenditure, and differences between industrial and developing countries. The second is the revenue from money creation, seigniorage. The third is the importance of quasi-fiscal activities and the role of contingent liabilities.

3.1.1 Conventional Sources of Revenue and Expenditure

Public revenue and expenditure patterns vary considerably across developing countries. Figure 3.1 shows the ratios of revenue and expenditure of the *central government* during the period 1990-2000 by regions. In Madagascar, for instance, these ratios barely exceeded 11 percent of GDP, whereas they were almost twice as high in countries like India, Kenya, and Sri Lanka. And in Singapore, revenue (at 26.6 percent of GDP) exceeded expenditure (18.7 percent) by almost eight percentage points. These numbers should be viewed with some caution, because they refer to the central government only. A more comprehensive analysis would refer to the *general* government, which includes central, state, provincial, and local government institutions, as well as agencies such as social security boards (but excluding state-owned enterprises). A comprehensive view of the government is essential to understand notions such as public sector borrowing, fiscal deficits, and solvency conditions, as discussed later. Available data, however, often relate to the central government; comparability problems tend to force cross-country studies to limit themselves to a narrow definition of government.

The general structure of conventional sources of revenue and expenditure differs significantly between industrial and developing countries. As discussed by Burgess and Stern (1993), the main differences are the following.

- The shares of *total tax revenue* and *total central government expenditure* in output are larger in industrial than in developing countries. As shown in Figure 3.2, which covers averages over the period 1990-2000, both ratios tend to increase with the level of real income per capita.[1] Data for industrial countries show that the ratio of government expenditure to GDP increased almost continuously during the past century—now exceeding 50 percent in countries like France and Italy. One possible explanation

---

[1] Stotsky and WoldeMariam (1997) studied the determinants of the tax revenue-to-GDP ratio in a group of 43 sub-Saharan African countries during the period 1990-95. Their analysis showed that the share of agriculture in output had a negative effect, and that the export-to-GDP ratio and import-to-GDP ratio both had a positive effect on the tax revenue-to-GDP ratio. The level of per capita income, by contrast, was not significant.

for this (secular) rise in the size of government is the increased need for *risk insurance* as the degree of openness and exposure to external shocks increase (Rodrik, 1998*b*).

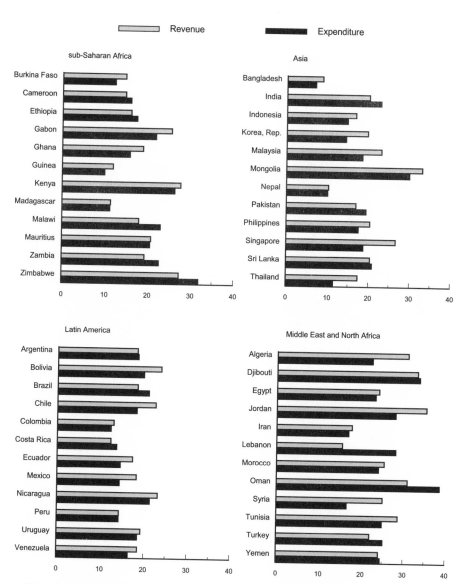

Figure 3.1. Central government: Revenue and Expenditure (in percent of GDP, average over 1990-2000). Source: World Bank.

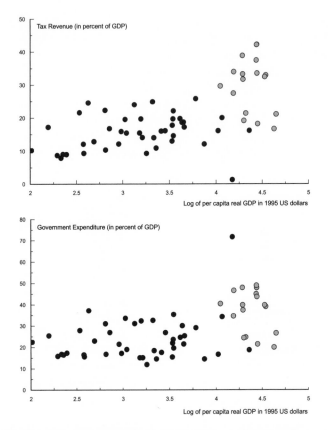

Figure 3.2. Tax revenue, government expenditure, and per capita real GDP (average over 1990-2000). Forty-four developing countries and 17 industrialized countries are included. A dark circle refers to developing countries and a lighter circle to industrial countries. Source: World Bank.

- The *composition* of spending also differs between the two groups of countries. Developing countries devote a substantially larger fraction of expenditures to *general public services, defense, education,* and other economic services (reflecting the role of government in production) than do industrial countries, whereas the latter spend somewhat more on *health,* and substantially more on *social security.*

- The main source of *central government revenue* in both groups is taxation; however, the share of *nontax revenue* in total revenue (consisting, for instance, of transfers from public enterprises) is much higher in developing than in industrial countries.

- Within *direct taxes*, the share of tax revenue raised from *individual incomes* is much larger than that from *corporations* in developing countries, while the reverse is true in industrial countries.

- Within total tax revenue, the relative shares of *direct taxes, taxes on domestic goods and services*, and *taxes on foreign trade* vary considerably across developing countries and over time, as illustrated in Figure 3.3.[2] In industrial countries, income taxes account for the largest share of tax revenue, and taxes on foreign trade are negligible. There has been a gradual move away from trade taxes to taxes on domestic sales as economies develop and their domestic production and consumption bases expand.

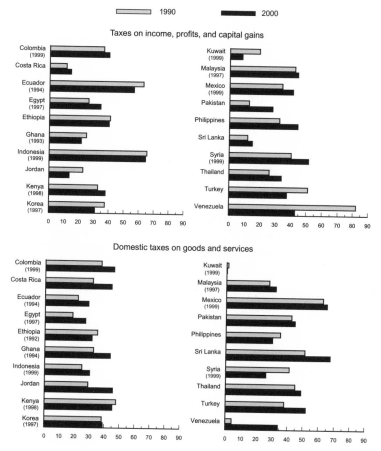

Figure 3.3. Direct and indirect taxes (in percent of total tax revenue). Source: World Bank.

The need for revenue in developing countries is large. One reason, of course, is the need for the government to invest in infrastructure, foster the development of market institutions, and encourage employment creation in order to reduce poverty. Another reason may be related to a *deficit bias*, which is due to

---

[2] Trade taxes consist now primarily of import duties in most developing countries, and continue to be used quite extensively in some cases—although in recent years trade liberalization has led to a significant reduction in tariffs in many cases (see Chapter 14).

the fact that although fiscal policy is decided collectively, the parties involved (the different pressure groups and their representatives) do not fully recognize the full social cost of the programs they support. This is known as the *commons problem*, and has been well studied in recent years in the context of Latin America (see Grisanti, Stein, and Talvi, 1998).

Despite high revenue needs, however, taxation systems in many developing countries remain highly inefficient. A key reason has been the severe (administrative and sometimes political) constraints on the ability of tax authorities to collect revenue. The consequences are that *direct taxation* plays a much more limited role in developing than in industrial countries and *high tax rates* tend to be levied on a *narrow base*—a policy that has encouraged tax evasion and led to a high degree of reliance on monetary financing.

3.1.2 Seigniorage and Inflationary Finance

Because, as indicated earlier, limited administrative capacity and political constraints hinder the collection of tax revenue in developing countries, and because many countries continue to have a limited scope for issuing domestic debt (as a result of insufficiently developed capital markets, as discussed in Chapter 4), developing countries tend to rely more on **seigniorage** than do industrial countries. Generally speaking, seigniorage consists of the amount of real resources extracted by the government by means of *base money creation*. Denoting by M the nominal base money stock and P the price level, seigniorage revenue can be formally defined as the change in the nominal base money stock divided by the price level, $\Delta M/P$.[3] Equivalently, this expression can be rewritten as

$$\frac{\Delta M}{P} = \frac{M}{P} - (\frac{P_{-1}}{P})(\frac{M_{-1}}{P_{-1}}) = \Delta(\frac{M}{P}) + (1 - \frac{P_{-1}}{P})(\frac{M_{-1}}{P_{-1}}),$$

or

$$\frac{\Delta M}{P} = \Delta(\frac{M}{P}) + (\frac{P - P_{-1}}{P_{-1}})(\frac{M_{-1}}{P}),$$

that is, with $m \equiv M/P$ denoting real cash balances and $\pi \equiv \Delta P/P_{-1}$ the inflation rate:

$$\frac{\Delta M}{P} = \Delta m + \pi(\frac{P_{-1}}{P})m_{-1} = \Delta m + (\frac{\pi}{1+\pi})m_{-1}. \tag{1}$$

Equation (1) shows that seigniorage can also be defined as the sum of the *increase in the real stock of money*, Δm, and the change in the real money stock that would have occurred with a constant nominal stock because of inflation, $\pi m_{-1}/(1+\pi)$. The second term in that expression represents the **inflation tax**,

---

[3]The reason why the appropriate base for the inflation tax is not *broad money* but only *base money* is because the government extracts net resources from agents in the economy only to the extent that the erosion of the money stock resulting from inflation is not offset by inflationary gains that accrue to domestic borrowers. Only base money represents (central bank) liabilities that are not offset by private-sector debt owed to commercial banks.

with $\pi/(1 + \pi)$ denoting the *tax rate* and m_{-1} the *tax base*. The determination of the *optimal* inflation tax is discussed in Chapter 6.

The above definitions also lead to the following observations.

- The last expression in Equation (1) implies that in a stationary state, with real balances constant ($\Delta m = 0$), seigniorage is equal to the inflation tax.

- The monetary base in the above setting is implicitly treated as bearing no interest. This is not always the case; *required reserves* of commercial banks held with the central bank sometimes earn interest. In such conditions, the formulas in Equation (1) *overstate* seigniorage revenue and a correction must be made to obtain an appropriate measure.

A related concept to the conventional definition given above, also referred to as seigniorage, is the **interest burden foregone** (or interest savings) by the government through its ability to issue *non-interest-bearing liabilities*. The view here is that the private sector's revenue loss from foregone interest earnings (that is, the *opportunity cost of money*) corresponds to an equivalent revenue gain for the government from issuing money. It is measured in flow terms by iM/P, where i is the nominal short-term interest rate on, say, government bonds. As shown by Buiter (1997), the conventional measure of seigniorage, $\Delta M/P$, and the opportunity cost measure are related by the identity that equates the present discounted value of current and future seigniorage to the present discounted value of the current and future interest burden foregone (which corresponds approximately to the *operating profits* of the central bank), minus the initial base money stock. In practice, however, this concept is seldom used, because the choice of the relevant opportunity cost i is somewhat arbitrary.

During the 1980s a number of developing countries, such as Zambia, relied heavily on seigniorage as a source of revenue to finance their budget deficits (see Adam, 1995). Figure 3.4 presents data on seigniorage (measured as the change in the base money stock divided by nominal GDP) for the period 1995-2001 for a group of 30 developing economies. The figure shows considerable differences across countries in the use of seigniorage—from more than 5 percent in Lebanon to less than 1 percent in Brazil, Colombia, Kenya, Korea, and Singapore. Reliance on seigniorage also tends to be associated with large fiscal deficits—an issue that will be explored further in Chapter 6.

3.1.3   Quasi-Fiscal Activities and Contingent Liabilities

Quasi-fiscal activities can be defined as operations whose effect can in principle be duplicated by budgetary measures in the form of an *explicit* tax, subsidy, or direct expenditure (Mackenzie and Stella, 1996, p. 3). They are often carried out by the country's central bank, but sometimes also by state-owned commercial banks and other public financial institutions, such as development banks. They are motivated most of the time by the desire to hide what are essentially budgetary activities for political or other reasons.

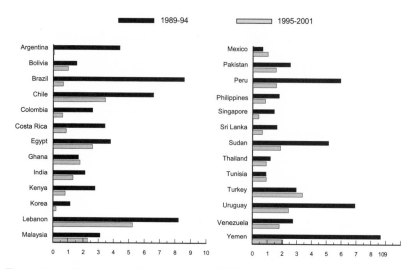

Figure 3.4. Seigniorage (in percent of GDP, average 1989-2001). Seignorage is measured as the change in the base money stock divided by nominal GDP. Source: World Bank.

Main examples of quasi-fiscal activities include:

- **Subsidized credit**, which involves most commonly lending at preferential rates by the central bank to the government or other public entities, or subsidized lending by specialized state-owned financial institutions (such as agricultural or mortgage banks) to groups of borrowers from the private sector—often with inadequate collateral requirements.

- Manipulation of **reserve** and **statutory liquidity requirements**, for instance through central bank regulations requiring commercial banks to hold large reserves (which then serve as a base for lending to the government at below-market rates) or a large share of their liquid assets in the form of government securities paying below-market interest rates. Both policies provide the government with captive sources of financing for its budget deficit.[4]

- **Multiple exchange rate practices**. This may take the form, for instance, of the central bank allowing access by the government to its foreign reserves at a more appreciated exchange rate to service its foreign debt or finance the purchase of imported goods by state-owned enterprises. Or it may be a *surrender requirement* on export proceeds at a rate that is more appreciated than the market rate. This implicit tax on exports may have potentially large distortionary effects on trade flows and production

---

[4]Note that if the central bank is at the same time required to remunerate liquid reserves at market-related rates, lending to the government at lower rates creates a quasi-fiscal expenditure.

patterns. Removing it—by unifying foreign exchange markets—also has potentially important implications for inflation (see Annex B).[5]

- **Exchange rate guarantees** given by the central bank on the repayment of principal and interest on foreign-currency denominated debt of other public sector or private sector entities. For instance, the central bank may guarantee to some privileged borrowers that the exchange rate at which debt service payments are converted is the rate at which the loan was initially contracted. Such guarantees can entail a fairly sizable subsidy element.

- **Bailout** of **troubled commercial banks**, which occurs when the central bank provides an infusion of capital in banks under stress, or directly takes control of some of the nonperforming assets of problem banks and issues interest-paying bonds in return.

- **Sterilization operations**, which essentially result from the central bank paying interest on its liabilities at a rate higher than the one earned on the foreign exchange reserves that it chose to accumulate, often as a counterpart to sustained capital inflows (see Chapter 7).

Exchange rate guarantees, in particular, are common operations for central banks; essentially, they imply that the *cost of borrowing* on a claim denominated in domestic currency is the rate of interest prevailing on world capital markets. If domestic interest rates are significantly higher than foreign rates, the implicit subsidy can be large and may lead to *overborrowing*. As long as the exchange rate remains at the level prevailing when the loan was contracted, the guarantee remains indeed implicit and has no effect on the profit-and-loss account of the central bank. However, if the nominal exchange rate *depreciates*, the Central Bank may face sizable losses. In Jamaica, central bank losses from exchange rate guarantees exceeded 5 percent of GDP in the early 1990s.

By shifting what are essentially taxes and subsidies from government accounts to the accounts of the central bank, quasi-fiscal activities can severely distort the measurement of revenues and expenditure not only of the government but of other public sector entities as well.[6] They may also render attempts to assess the stance of fiscal policy (on the basis, for instance, of an analysis of public debt sustainability, as discussed below) meaningless.

Examples of the importance of quasi-fiscal deficits (and how misleading conventional measures of fiscal deficits are as indicators of the fiscal policy stance) are provided by the experiences of Chile and Argentina. In the early 1980s, the monetary authorities in both countries extended emergency loans to financial institutions and suffered large losses from exchange rate guarantee programs. The central bank of Chile, in particular, suffered from large quasi-fiscal losses in

---

[5] On Annex B, see Introduction and Overview.

[6] The existence of large quasi-fiscal activities (as discussed later) may explain why, as shown in Figure 3.2, the ratio of government expenditure to GDP appears to be significantly lower in developing economies compared with industrial countries.

the mid-1980s as a result of a guarantee on a foreign exchange resale scheme that it implemented during the period 1982-85 (Mackenzie and Stella, 1996, p. 25). During that period, according to estimates provided by Easterly and Schmidt-Hebbel (1994), consolidated quasi-fiscal deficits averaged more than 10 percent of GDP a year in that country—more than double the size of conventionally measured deficits.

The foregoing discussion suggests that many quasi-fiscal activities lead to the creation of **contingent implicit liabilities**, which in general can be defined as obligations that the government is *expected* to fulfill, although the required outlays are typically uncertain before a failure (or some event) occurs. Important examples, as noted earlier, are the liabilities created by the need to support the financial system (when its stability appears to be at risk) and large enterprises (both private and state owned).

Governments in developing countries are also faced with various types of **contingent explicit fiscal liabilities**, which can be broadly defined as obligations that the government is legally compelled to honor if the entity that incurred them in the first place cannot (or chooses not to) do so; examples are state guarantees of borrowing by parastatal enterprises or local government entities (Polackova, 1998).

Contingent liabilities, together with direct liabilities—both explicit and implicit, such as those assumed under pay-as-you-go social security schemes, and future recurrent costs of public investment projects)—have grown at a rapid pace in many developing countries in recent years and have created significant fiscal risks in many countries, as argued by Polackova and Mody (2002). Because conventional measures of the fiscal stance (as discussed later) do not account properly for the expected future cost of all the contingent liabilities incurred by the government, they provide misleading indicators of its ability to pay and the sustainability of budget deficits.

Because of their potentially severe distortionary effects on the allocation of resources, eliminating or at least reducing the scope of quasi-fiscal activities has become a key objective of macroeconomic management. The elimination of the implicit tax on exports, for instance, can be achieved through exchange market unification (see Annex B). For political and other reasons, however, the first-best solution may be difficult to achieve in the short term. It then becomes important to bring such operations into the budget, by first identifying and quantifying them and subsequently by transforming them into *explicit* taxes and expenditures. Appropriate accounting of explicit and implicit contingent liabilities is essential for assessing the stance of fiscal policy.

However, this may be a very difficult task; as noted by Blejer and Cheasty (1991, p. 1667), the calculation of the expected cost of contingent liabilities may be complicated by **moral hazard** problems. The very fact that the government chooses to assume explicitly these liabilities may lead to changes in private sector behavior that may make the realization of the events against which liabilities are created more likely. Moreover, increasing fiscal transparency may encounter strong political resistance.

3.2 The Government Budget Constraint

In general, the budget constraint of the government can be written as

$$G - (T_T + T_N) + iB_{-1} + i^* EB_{g-1}^* = \Delta L^g + \Delta B + E\Delta B_g^*, \qquad (2)$$

where

- G is *public spending* on goods and services (including current and capital expenditure);

- T_T is *tax revenue* (net of transfer payments) and T_N nontax revenue,

- B is the end-of-period stock of *domestic public debt*, which bears interest at the market-determined rate i;

- B_g^* is the end-of-period stock of *foreign currency-denominated public debt*, which bears interest at the rate i^*;

- E is the *nominal exchange rate*;

- L^g is the nominal *stock of credit* allocated by the central bank.

The left-hand side of Equation (2) captures the components of the budget deficit: spending on goods and services and debt service, net of taxes. The right-hand side shows that the government can finance its budget deficit by either issuing domestic bonds, borrowing abroad, or borrowing from the central bank. For simplicity, the central bank is assumed not to charge interest on its loans to the government (this has often been the case in practice).

There are several points worth noting regarding Equation (2).

- It does not consider explicitly *foreign grants* or revenues derived from assets such as *natural resources* and *publicly owned capital*—components that may, in practice, be important in some countries. For simplicity, these items are subsumed in T_N.

- It does not account explicitly for the cash income derived from the *sale of public sector assets*, such as receipts from the privatization of public enterprises. Such income is often counted as revenue and included in T_N. However, because the resulting increase in public resources is only temporary, this practice may lead observers to *underestimate* the underlying level of the fiscal deficit. The proceeds from the sale of public assets are best treated as a *financing item*, which reduces net borrowing.[7]

---

[7]Sales of public assets also affect the government's *net worth*; for instance, if the sale value of a public enterprise plus the present value of future taxes from the privatized entity exceeds the sum of the present value of future subsidies and future losses that the government would occur if it were to keep the enterprise, then the government's net worth will increase. In turn, changes in the government's net worth may affect the risk premium that bond holders demand on public debt and thus interest payments on that debt.

- It does not explicitly account for *extrabudgetary activities*. Yet many countries continue to have special funds (some of them quite large) not included in the general government budget. Despite considerable progress in some cases toward greater fiscal transparency (as discussed later), the existence of these funds continues to make measuring the stance of fiscal policy very difficult.

The left-hand side of Equation (2) defines the **conventional fiscal deficit**. Let $T = T_T + T_N$ denote total government revenue; the **primary** (or noninterest) **fiscal deficit** can be defined as[8]

$$D = G - T.$$

Substituting this definition in Equation (2) yields

$$D + iB_{-1} + i^* EB^*_{g-1} = \Delta L^g + \Delta B + E\Delta B^*_g. \tag{3}$$

The conventional fiscal deficit can be very sensitive to *inflation*. The key reason is the effect of inflation on *nominal interest payments* on the public debt. Illustrative calculations by Tanzi, Blejer, and Teijeiro (1993) show indeed that inflation can have a sizable effect on the conventional deficit when the domestic public debt (and thus the interest rate bill) is high. In such conditions, the conventional deficit does not provide a reliable measure of the increase in the government's real indebtedness. The inflation-induced part of the nominal interest bill is, in a sense, an **amortization payment** that compensates holders of government debt for the erosion of the real value of the debt stock; put differently, some of the deficit does not increase *real debt*, but effectively maintains it at its previous level. As a consequence, the conventional deficit suffers from two limitations.

- It is no longer a reliable indicator of the extent to which the fiscal stance is *sustainable*, in the sense that the issuance of public debt is occurring at a rate in excess of the growth rate of the resources available for eventual debt service (see below). For instance, the conventional deficit may increase sharply as a result of a sudden rise in inflation, without necessarily implying a deterioration in the longer-run sustainability of the fiscal stance.

- Changes in the conventional deficit no longer provide an adequate measure of *fiscal effort* by policymakers. The primary deficit is in this case a more reliable measure—despite inadequately reflecting the financing implications of the policy stance.

Economists therefore often use an alternative concept to the conventional deficit, the **operational deficit**, which is calculated by netting out the inflationary component in nominal interest payments (and receipts) from the conventional deficit, defined in real terms. To show the importance of this adjustment,

[8]In practice, as noted by Blejer and Cheasty (1991, p. 1655), the primary deficit is often calculated by subtracting *gross* interest payments from government expenditure; conceptually, however, only the *net* interest paid by the government should be taken out.

suppose for simplicity that the government holds no external debt ($B^* = 0$). The government budget constraint, Equation (3), then becomes

$$D + iB_{-1} = \Delta L^g + \Delta B.$$

Dividing both sides of this expression by the price level, P, yields

$$d + i(\frac{P_{-1}}{P})b_{-1} = \frac{\Delta L^g}{P} + (\frac{P_{-1}}{P})\frac{\Delta B}{P_{-1}}, \tag{4}$$

where d is the real primary deficit and b the real stock of government bonds. The last term in this expression can be rewritten as

$$(\frac{P_{-1}}{P})\frac{\Delta B}{P_{-1}} = b - (\frac{P_{-1}}{P})b_{-1} = \Delta b + (1 - \frac{P_{-1}}{P})b_{-1},$$

or

$$(\frac{P_{-1}}{P})\frac{\Delta B}{P_{-1}} = \Delta b + \pi(\frac{P_{-1}}{P})b_{-1}.$$

Substituting this result in the government budget constraint gives

$$d + (i - \pi)(\frac{P_{-1}}{P})b_{-1} = \frac{\Delta L^g}{P} + \Delta b.$$

Because $P_{-1}/P = 1/(1 + \pi)$, the above expression can be rewritten as

$$d + (\frac{i - \pi}{1 + \pi})b_{-1} = \frac{\Delta L^g}{P} + \Delta b,$$

or equivalently

$$d + rb_{-1} = \frac{\Delta L^g}{P} + \Delta b, \tag{5}$$

where r is the real interest rate, defined by

$$r = \frac{1 + i}{1 + \pi} - 1.$$

The expression $d + rb_{-1}$ in Equation (5) measures the total fiscal deficit in real terms. It differs from the nominal fiscal deficit deflated by the price level P, which is given by the left-hand side of Equation (4), that is, $d + i(P_{-1}/P)b_{-1}$. Using the previous result $P_{-1}/P = 1/(1 + \pi)$, this expression can be rewritten as

$$d + i(\frac{P_{-1}}{P})b_{-1} = d + (\frac{i}{1 + \pi})b_{-1} = d + (r + \frac{\pi}{1 + \pi})b_{-1}.$$

Comparing the last expression to (5) shows that simply deflating the conventional fiscal deficit by current prices leads to an *overestimation* of the real operational deficit, by the quantity

$$\frac{\pi}{1 + \pi}b_{-1}, \tag{6}$$

which essentially represents the compensation to creditors for the falling real value of their claims on the government caused by inflation. Subtracting the quantity (6) from the conventional fiscal deficit deflated by current prices can lead to dramatically different measures of the fiscal stance when inflation is high. In Brazil, for instance, in 1988 the conventional deficit (or total borrowing requirement) of the general government (covering the federal government and states and municipalities) amounted to 27.3 percent of GDP, the operational deficit to 4.5 percent, and the primary deficit to 0.5 percent. Figure 3.5 shows the evolution of the operational and primary fiscal deficits (together with interest payments) between 1985 and 1996; indeed, sharp differences between these two measures persisted throughout the period—particularly during the years of high inflation preceding the implementation of the **Real Plan** in July 1994 (see Agénor and Montiel, 1999).

The operational deficit becomes a problematic concept when inflation is *highly variable*, because of difficulties in measuring and interpreting real interest payments. Specifically, because interest rates are a function of *expected* inflation, the use of *actual* inflation rates (as shown in the formula above) to calculate the operational deficit can be misleading if large, unanticipated inflationary shocks occur during the period. For instance, expansionary fiscal policy (say, a rise in spending) could push actual inflation above the rate implied by the nominal interest rate (a scenario that is more likely to occur when debt is not recontracted very frequently), leading to *negative ex post real interest rates*, and thus a negative real interest bill. Thus, the operational deficit may fall if this effect is large enough—even if at the same time the primary deficit is deteriorating.

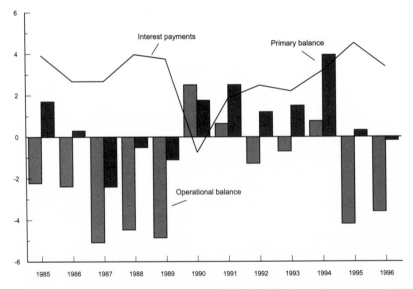

Figure 3.5. Brazil: Alternative measures of the fiscal balance (percentage of GDP). General government only. Source: Bevilaqua and Werneck (1997).

Finally, it should be noted that inflation may also affect *noninterest expenditure* and *revenue*—and thus all three measures of the fiscal deficit. For instance, inflation may increase spending on entitlement programs (such as *subsidies* and *transfers*) or lead to an increase in tax revenue if tax rates are progressive. It can also reduce real revenue in the presence of **collection lags**—an effect known as the **Olivera-Tanzi effect** (see Olivera, 1967, and Tanzi, 1978). The reason is that there is typically a lag between the time tax payments are *assessed* and the time they are *collected* by the fiscal authorities. In the case of indirect, *domestically based taxes* (such as turnover or sales taxes), the collection lag is generally four to six weeks; for *direct taxes*, the lag is much longer and may reach well over a year for personal income taxes. Even in the case of *customs duties*, where the assessed base is denominated in foreign currency, taxpayers are generally allowed several weeks to make payments to the tax administration. If n is the collection lag expressed in months, and π the monthly inflation rate, the amount by which real revenue drops is given by $(1+\pi)^{-n} - 1$. For instance, with inflation running at 10 percent a month, real revenue collection would drop (relative to the case of zero inflation) by 9.1 percent if the collection lag is one month, 17.4 percent if the lag is two months, and 24.9 percent if the lag is three months. The converse of the Olivera-Tanzi effect is the **Patinkin effect**, which arises if nominal government spending is fixed and its real value is reduced by inflation. Thus, the net effect of (high) inflation on the budget is in general ambiguous, and depends on whether the real value of government expenditure falls by more than real tax revenues.

3.3   Assessing the Stance of Fiscal Policy

Useful tools for assessing the medium-term stance of fiscal policy are the **structural budget balance** and the **fiscal impulse measure**. The key idea is that a proper assessment of medium-term fiscal strategies requires determining the extent to which changes in actual budget deficits reflect *structural* factors, in particular *discretionary* fiscal policy action*s*, rather than *cyclical* movements.[9] This distinction is important because movements of the budget deficit attributable to the business cycle (or short-term fluctuations in aggregate demand) can be viewed as essentially *self-correcting*, whereas changes in deficits owing to structural factors can be offset only through discretionary policy measures. Removing the self-correcting cyclical component from the observed budget deficit, therefore, provides a more accurate indication of medium-term fiscal positions. The resulting indicator is the *structural budget deficit*.

Calculations of structural budget deficits are typically based on the use of budget elasticities to adjust revenues, T_S, and total expenditures, G_S, for movements in the cyclical *output gap*, GAP, defined as the ratio of *potential* (or

---

[9] Cyclical adjustments to the fiscal stance are also important to assess the dynamics associated with stabilization programs. Talvi (1997), for instance, estimates that in Uruguay during 1991-93 the cyclically adjusted budget deficit exceeded the actual deficit by a cumulative value of nine percentage points of GDP.

capacity) GDP to actual GDP, in order to generate directly an estimate of the
level of the structural budget deficit, D_S:[10]

$$D_S = G_S - T_S = G \cdot GAP^{\eta_G} - T \cdot GAP^{\eta_T}, \tag{7}$$

where η_T and η_G are, respectively, the elasticities applied to revenue and expenditure to correct for cyclical effects. Two remarks are worth making about
η_T and η_G:

- The cyclical adjustment of tax revenues is done in practice on *disaggregated
  estimates*. An aggregate revenue elasticity η_T can then be formed as a
  weighted average of the disaggregated revenue component elasticities, by
  using as weights the average shares of the revenue component in total
  revenue during a given period.

- In typical calculations, only some components of noninterest government
  expenditure are adjusted; net interest payments are almost never corrected.

- Once the structural budget deficit is known, the cyclical budget deficit,
  D_C, can be estimated as the difference between the observed budget deficit
  and the structural budget deficit:

$$D_C = (G - G_S) - (T - T_S) = G(1 - GAP^{\eta_G}) - T(1 - GAP^{\eta_T}).$$

If G excludes interest payments, then D_S is the **primary structural deficit**.
The overall structural deficit is then obtained by adding these payments to D_S.

Both the OECD and the IMF publish estimates of structural deficits on
a regular basis. In the OECD approach (see Suyker, 1999), tax revenues are
normally decomposed into business taxes, direct taxes on households, social
security contributions, indirect taxes, and other revenues. Spending is usually decomposed into current primary expenditure and net interest payments
plus capital spending. In most cases only unemployment-related benefits under the first component are adjusted. η_G is thus a composite of the elasticity
of unemployment-related expenditure with respect to output and the share of
unemployment-related expenditure in total current primary expenditure.

The IMF approach follows a similar logic to calculate structural revenue and
expenditure components (see Hagemann, 1999). In the IMF approach, however,
unemployment benefits are adjusted not for cyclical movements in output but for
deviations of unemployment from the "natural" rate. To the extent that these
variable behave differently, IMF and OECD estimates may differ significantly—
in addition, of course, to differences that may result from different elasticity
assumptions. For developing countries, where unemployment benefits are limited or nonexistent (see Chapter 14), cyclical movements in output would have
typically a relatively weak effect on general government expenditures, implying

---

[10]To simplify the exposition, lagged effects of the cyclical output gap on the budget are
ignored.

that in most practical cases η_G is likely to be small. Thus, for these countries, both the OECD and the IMF approaches boil down to an adjustment of tax revenues.

A key step in calculating structural budget balances is the estimation of potential output. For industrial countries, a common approach is first to estimate a production function linking output to capital, labor, and total factor productivity. Potential output is then estimated as the level of output that is consistent with what is considered *normal capital utilization*, and with the *natural rate of unemployment*—the unemployment rate deemed consistent with stable nominal wage growth and inflation. These, in turn, are estimated by removing cyclical variations in labor market participation rates, total factor productivity, and unemployment. In developing countries, however, this approach is generally not feasible because of the lack of adequate and reliable data on variables such as the capital stock. Potential output is often approximated by trend output, which can be estimated for instance by the **Hodrick-Prescott filter** or the modified **band pass filter** (see Chapter 9).

Once the structural budget balance is known, a **fiscal impulse measure** can be calculated, as the annual change in the primary structural budget balance, expressed as a share of (actual or potential) output. A negative value indicates a *contractionary* demand impulse emanating from fiscal policy, and a positive value an *expansionary* demand impulse.[11] An application of this methodology to developing economies is by Bevilaqua and Werneck (1997), who focused on Brazil's experience during the period 1989-96. They corrected revenue and expenditure not only for changes in cyclical output but also for changes in inflation. Among other results, they found that the fiscal stance was significantly more expansionary in Brazil than what conventional indicators (such as the primary deficit) indicated. Another example is provided by Perry and Servén (2003) for Argentina.

It is important to note, however, that there are several limitations associated with structural budget deficit and fiscal impulse measures. One limitation is that movements in the structural components of revenues and expenditures cannot be viewed only as directly related either to discretionary fiscal policy measures or to the business cycle; other factors may matter as well.

- On the *revenue side*, such factors include changes in natural resource revenues, nonneutralities of the tax system with respect to inflation, and changes in the composition of the economy's tax base induced by economic growth.

- On the *expenditure side*, they include changes in pension benefits due to changes in the demographic composition of the population, and contingencies that lead to nondiscretionary expenditures.

---

[11] See Blejer and Chu (1988) and Heller, Haas, and Mansur (1986) for details. Their description is based on a simpler procedure for calculating the fiscal stance, that is, the structural budget balance.

Moreover, as noted by Chand (1993), these measures do not account for the effects of fiscal policy on long-term interest rates and the distortions associated with tax and transfer programs on the *supply side* of the economy. Finally, structural changes in the economy, or tax or expenditure reforms, may change the sensitivity of the budget to cyclical output in the future; thus, the assumption of constant elasticities may not be appropriate over the medium term.

3.4   Deficit Rules, Budget Ceilings, and Fiscal Transparency

Measures aimed at reducing fiscal deficits (such as cuts in expenditure on the wage bill or transfers to households) do not always guarantee a sustained improvement of public finances. Although some attempts at fiscal consolidation do result in a lasting improvement in the fiscal balance and a reduction of the public debt, others are reversed after a while, often as a result of political resistance to austerity. In recent years much effort has been devoted to understanding how institutional reforms and explicit fiscal frameworks may help to achieve and maintain fiscal consolidation—in part by reinforcing the political commitment to fiscal restraint in the face of pressures for expansion—while at the same time leaving some room for fiscal policy to dampen business cycle fluctuations through automatic stabilizers and, if necessary, discretionary actions.

Recent institutional reforms can be classified into three groups:

- Formal **deficit and debt rules**, which involve maintaining the deficit and the public debt ratios to GDP at a fixed value, often irrespective of the cyclical position of the economy. In practice, the definition of an appropriate ceiling has proved difficult; debt ceilings have been set not on the basis of theoretical calculations but rather by concerns about reducing high debt levels, and have thus generally been chosen on the basis of the circumstances of individual countries. However, if debt is well below the ceiling, there may be significant room for maneuver in the short run and little restraint on policy.[12]

- **Expenditure limits**, which consist of imposing ceilings on specific areas of expenditure (for instance, discretionary as opposed to nondiscretionary) or particular programs. The principal advantages of capping expenditure are that this process is well understood by players in budget negotiations and by the wider public, and it tackles deficit bias by addressing the principal source of rising deficits, namely political and institutional pressures to increase expenditure. Governments are also made accountable for what they can control most directly, which is not the case with deficits, given that they are highly dependent on economic developments.

---

[12] How to measure the debt measure is also an issue. Gross debt can be easily measured and compared across countries, but net debt is the best indicator to assess fiscal sustainability, although it presents substantial measurement difficulties in terms of which assets to consider and how to value them.

- **Fiscal transparency**, which aims to alter the trade-off between the need for flexibility and discipline in fiscal policy. In general, a commitment to transparency should improve credibility and increase the chances that a government can retain credibility in the event that it needs to temporarily deviate from, or substantively change, its fiscal rules or targets.

Both fiscal rules and transparency serve to strengthen *fiscal discipline*, thus helping governments maintain their commitment to improve public finances. Ceilings on specific expenditure items, for instance, can impose fiscal discipline while allowing the operation of automatic stabilizers on both the revenue and the expenditure side, and can therefore operate, in effect, like a cyclically adjusted deficit rule. In contrast, caps on overall spending could force unwarranted cuts in discretionary spending items during a cyclical downturn in order to support higher transfer spending. But whereas rules aim to limit the influence of contingent events on fiscal outcomes, transparency aims to increase accountability for the design and implementation of fiscal policy.

Institutional reforms emphasizing transparency, deficit and debt rules, or expenditure rules have occurred in many industrial countries in recent years, particularly in the euro area, the United States, Canada, New Zealand, Australia, Switzerland, the United Kingdom, and Sweden. In the euro area, the commitment was made under the Stability and Growth Pact to limit the deficit to 3 percent of GDP. The United Kingdom adopted the *golden rule* of borrowing only to finance capital spending, and accompanied it by the *sustainable investment rule*, which limits net debt to 40 percent of GDP over the cycle. Expenditure limits have been implemented in the United States, Sweden, Finland, and the Netherlands, and are supported by procedural requirements whereby proposals resulting in overruns in certain expenditure areas must be accompanied by offsetting expenditure cuts elsewhere or by revenue increases. New Zealand pioneered an approach to fiscal management that places primary and explicit emphasis on transparency (generally defined as being open to the public about the structure and functions of government, public sector accounts, and fiscal policy intentions and projections), with the Fiscal Responsibility Act of 1994. Australia and the United Kingdom have adopted similar arrangements.[13] The key elements that these frameworks share are an explicit legal basis, an elaboration of guiding principles for fiscal policy, a requirement that objectives are clearly stated, an emphasis on the need for a longer-term focus to fiscal policy, and demanding requirements for fiscal reporting to the public.

Some developing countries have also adopted improvements in their fiscal frameworks recently. Peru introduced a Fiscal Transparency Law in 1999, which sets limits on the deficit and the growth of government expenditure. It also established a **fiscal stabilization fund** to ensure that fiscal savings in good years can be used during recessions and contains measures to encourage transparency. Brazil introduced a Fiscal Responsibility Law in May 2000 that prohibits finan-

---

[13] Legislation, however, is not the only means to achieve fiscal transparency; in other advanced economies such as Canada Sweden and the United States, transparency is associated with a long tradition of open governments.

cial support operations among different levels of government (that is, a prohibition on the federal government from financing state and local governments), sets limits on personnel expenditure, and requires that limits on the indebtedness of each level of government be set by the senate. It also includes measures to improve transparency and accountability. Similar fiscal responsibility legislation is being considered in several other countries, including Colombia and India.

The advantage of fiscal rules is that, compared with other approaches, they are clear and focus on a generally well understood macroeconomic aggregate (Kopits, 2001). The main criticism of *deficit rules* in general, and balanced budget rules in particular, is that they are inflexible and tend to be *pro-cyclical*— with fiscal imbalances rising in good times, and vice versa. In response, deficit rules have been refined and now generally apply either to a cyclically adjusted deficit measure (such as the **structural budget deficit** defined earlier) or an average over the economic cycle. By doing so, these rules may allow the operation of automatic stabilizers and possibly provide some room for discretionary policy within the cycle. However, this increased flexibility comes at a cost, because the benchmark against which fiscal performance is to be judged is made more complicated—especially if estimates of potential output are revised. This increases the scope to bypass the rules, making them potentially harder to enforce, which in turn may undermine their credibility. In countries with a poor record of policy consistency over time, this may be particularly costly. In fact, the experience so far with fiscal policy rules has been mixed; although there have been some successful cases, a number of rules have been ineffective, suspended, or abandoned (see Kopits, 2001). To be effective, a rules-based fiscal policy has to address two potential drawbacks:

- Achieving fiscal sustainability under a fiscal rule should not come at the expense of macroeconomic stability, by impairing the short-run stabilization role of fiscal policy. Fiscal rules must be flexible enough to accommodate exogenous shocks, beyond the control of the government.

- Application of fiscal rules in a framework that does not ensure budgetary transparency would likely be self-defeating, by leading to circumventions and the proliferation of nontransparent, off-budget practices, or "creative accounting" (see Milesi-Ferretti, 2004). Thus, an integrated fiscal framework that promotes fiscal transparency would be a prerequisite for the implementation of a rules-based fiscal policy.

Avoiding the excessive rigidity of fiscal rules thus remains a key issue in their design. Well-designed **escape clauses** may be necessary to avoid obviating entirely any *countercyclical* role to fiscal policy. An alternative approach, as suggested by Wyplosz (2002), might be the creation of an independent Fiscal Policy Committee, as an increasing number of countries have done after adopting inflation targeting as their operational framework for monetary policy (see Chapter 4). Political resistance may well prove to be, however, an insurmountable obstacle.

3.5   Fiscal Imbalances and External Deficits

As derived in Chapter 1, the link between fiscal and external accounts stems from the aggregate balance between saving and investment:

$$(I^p - S^p) + (G - T) = J - X - N_T, \tag{8}$$

where I^p is private investment, S^p private saving, G current government spending, T current government revenue, J (X) imports (exports) of goods and services, and N_T net current transfers from abroad. This equation is obtained by rearranging the accounting identities relating gross national income on an expenditure basis and an income basis. It indicates that the counterpart to the current account balance (or foreign saving) is government dissaving or an excess of private investment over private saving.

The implication of Equation (8) is that, as long as $I^p - S^p$ remains stable, changes in fiscal deficits will be closely associated with movements in current account deficits. There is some empirical evidence suggesting that this is indeed the case (see Chinn and Prasad, 2003). In general, however, this may not always be the case. As discussed in Chapter 2, an increase in public expenditure may lead to a concomitant reduction of private investment (as a result of a **crowding-out effect** through the credit market) with all other components unchanged; or, private saving may increase, as individuals anticipate the rise in *future taxes* that they may incur as a result of the need to service the higher level of public debt occurring today. Thus, the correlation between fiscal and external deficits depends on the effect of fiscal policy on the private sector's investment and saving decisions. In addition, fiscal deficits may *respond to*, rather than *cause*, changes in the current account. Both effects also suggest that the so-called **Lawson doctrine**—according to which large current account deficits resulting from an excess of private investment over saving should not be a cause for concern—is in general misleading.

3.6   Consistency and Sustainability

An integrated framework for assessing empirically the consistency between fiscal policy and macroeconomic targets (such as inflation, output growth, and real interest rates) was proposed by Anand and van Wijnbergen (1989). This section begins by presenting a discrete-time version of their model and discusses its limitations. The analysis is then extended to consider *jointly* the issues of fiscal and external sustainability.

3.6.1   A Consistency Framework

The consistency framework for fiscal and macroeconomic policy analysis proposed by Anand and van Wijnbergen (1989) essentially dwells on the government budget constraint presented above [Equation (2)]. It can be operated in two modes:

- the **deficit mode**, which allows the analyst to calculate a *financeable fiscal deficit*, given targets for inflation and other macroeconomic variables;

- the **inflation mode**, which allows the calculation of the *rate of inflation* consistent with given targets for the fiscal deficit and other macroeconomic variables.

As shown earlier, the government budget constraint states that the fiscal deficit (the sum of the primary deficit plus interest payments on domestic and external debt) must be financed by issuing either monetary liabilities or interest-bearing domestic bonds or by foreign borrowing. In the presence of multiple macroeconomic targets (such as a given rate of inflation or a target rate of output growth), such sources of financing may become *interdependent* and determine the level of the primary deficit that can be financed from *below the line*. To the extent that the actual deficit exceeds the level that can be financed (given the other policy targets), policymakers must either adjust their fiscal stance and/or revise their other objectives.

Consider the specification of the government budget constraint given in Equation (3), which is rewritten here for convenience:

$$D + iB_{-1} + i^*EB^*_{g-1} = \Delta B + E\Delta B^*_g + \Delta L^g, \tag{9}$$

where D is again the noninterest primary deficit, B (B^*_g) the end-of-period stock of domestic (foreign) debt of the government, i (i^*) the interest rate on domestic (foreign) debt, L^g net credit from the central bank to the government, and E the nominal exchange rate.

The first step is to consolidate the balance sheets of the government and the central bank, to obtain a more comprehensive definition of the public sector and a more accurate measure of public sector expenditure and revenue.[14] Adding and subtracting on the right-hand side of Equation (9) the quantity $E\Delta R^*$, the change in official reserves held by the central bank (measured in domestic-currency terms), yields

$$D + iB_{-1} + i^*EB^*_{g-1} = \Delta B + E(\Delta B^*_g - \Delta R^*) + (\Delta L^g + E\Delta R^*). \tag{10}$$

As before, suppose that the central bank extends credit only to the government. Its balance sheet is given by

Assets	Liabilities	
L^g	C_U	
ER^*	RR	$\}M,$
	NW^{cb}	

where C_U is currency in circulation, RR reserves held at the central bank by commercial banks against their deposit liabilities, and NW^{cb} the central bank's

---

[14]See Robinson and Stella (1993) for a general discussion of the practical issues that may arise in this consolidation process.

accumulated profits or net worth. For simplicity, it is assumed that no interest is paid on required reserves.

The *monetary base*, M, is defined as the sum of currency in circulation and required reserves held by commercial banks at the central bank:

$$M = C_U + RR. \tag{11}$$

The central bank's balance sheet and the above definition imply that the change in the monetary base, ΔM, is equal to the change in credit to the government, ΔL^g, plus the change in official reserves, $E\Delta R^*$, minus the change in the central bank's net worth, ΔNW^{cb}:

$$\Delta M = \Delta L^g + E\Delta R^* - \Delta NW^{cb}. \tag{12}$$

From the profit-and-loss account of the central bank, and abstracting from other sources of revenue and expenditure, net profits consist of interest earnings on official reserves, $i^* ER^*_{-1}$, which are used by the central bank only to increase its net worth:

$$i^* ER^*_{-1} = \Delta NW^{cb}.$$

Subtracting central bank profits, $i^* ER^*_{-1}$, from the fiscal deficit on the left-hand side of Equation (10), and the central bank's increase in net worth, ΔNW^{cb}, from the public sector's increase in liabilities on the right-hand side and denoting by $B^* = B^*_g - R^*$ the public sector's net foreign debt yields

$$D + iB_{-1} + i^* EB^*_{-1} = \Delta B + E\Delta B^* + \Delta L^g + E\Delta R^* - \Delta NW^{cb},$$

where $\Delta B^* = \Delta B^*_g - \Delta R^*$. From the above definition of the change in the monetary base [Equation (12)], the last three terms on the right-hand side of this expression are simply ΔM. Thus,

$$D + iB_{-1} + i^* EB^*_{-1} = \Delta B + E\Delta B^* + \Delta M. \tag{13}$$

Equation (13) consolidates the accounts of the government and the central bank. Two observations are useful at this stage.

- Because base money is considered a liability of the public sector, net foreign assets held by the central bank must also be subtracted from the government's foreign debt to calculate the net external liabilities of the public sector.

- The above derivations remain almost identical if the central bank lends to commercial banks and to the private sector. In that case the definition of the base money stock would need to be adjusted to correspond to the central bank's net liabilities to the private sector. This would be done by defining the *adjusted monetary base* as the sum of (a) currency in circulation minus central bank credit to the private sector; and (b) required reserves minus central bank loans to commercial banks.

To make explicit the links between fiscal deficits, money creation, and inflation, Equation (13) can be rewritten in real terms. Dividing each term by P, the domestic price level, yields

$$d + i(\frac{P_{-1}}{P})b_{-1} + i^* z(\frac{P^*_{-1}}{P^*})b^*_{-1} = \Delta B/P + E\Delta B^*/P + \Delta M/P, \quad (14)$$

where

- $d = D/P$ is the *real primary deficit*;
- $b = B/P$ the real value of the stock of domestic debt in terms of *domestic goods*;
- $b^* = B^*/P^*$ the real value of the *stock of foreign debt* in terms of *foreign goods*, with P^* denoting the foreign price level;
- $z = EP^*/P$ is the *real exchange rate*.

By definition,

$$\frac{\Delta B}{P} = b - (\frac{P_{-1}}{P})b_{-1} = \Delta b - \left[(\frac{P_{-1}}{P}) - 1\right]b_{-1}.$$

Again, let $\pi \equiv \Delta P/P_{-1}$ be the domestic inflation rate. As shown earlier, the above expression can be rewritten as

$$\frac{\Delta B}{P} = \Delta b + \pi(\frac{P_{-1}}{P})b_{-1}.$$

Similarly,

$$\frac{\Delta B^*}{P} = (\frac{P^*}{P})b^* - (\frac{P^*_{-1}}{P})b^*_{-1} = (\frac{P^*}{P})\Delta b^* - \left[(\frac{P^*_{-1}}{P}) - (\frac{P^*}{P})\right]b^*_{-1},$$

that is, with π^* denoting the foreign rate of inflation:

$$\frac{\Delta B^*}{P} = (\frac{P^*}{P})\Delta b^* + (\frac{P^*}{P})(\frac{P^*_{-1}}{P^*})\pi^* b^*_{-1}.$$

Consequently,

$$\frac{E\Delta B^*}{P} = z\Delta b^* + z(\frac{P^*_{-1}}{P^*})\pi^* b^*_{-1}.$$

Substituting these results in Equation (14) yields

$$d + (\frac{P_{-1}}{P})(i - \pi)b_{-1} + z(\frac{P^*_{-1}}{P^*})(i^* - \pi^*)b^*_{-1} = \Delta b + z\Delta b^* + \Delta M/P.$$

As noted earlier, $P_{-1}/P = 1/(1 + \pi)$; thus

$$(\frac{P_{-1}}{P})(i - \pi) = \frac{i - \pi}{1 + \pi} = \frac{1 + i}{1 + \pi} - 1, \quad (\frac{P^*_{-1}}{P^*})(i^* - \pi^*) = \frac{1 + i^*}{1 + \pi^*} - 1,$$

implying that

$$d + rb_{-1} + r^* z b^*_{-1} = \Delta b + z \Delta b^* + \Delta M/P, \tag{15}$$

where r and r^* denote *real interest rates* in terms of domestic and foreign goods, respectively, given by

$$1 + r = \frac{1+i}{1+\pi}, \quad 1 + r^* = \frac{1+i^*}{1+\pi^*}.$$

Equation (15) can be further rearranged to explicitly account for the effect of changes in the real exchange rate on the cost of servicing public debt. By definition,

$$\begin{aligned} \Delta(zb^*) &= zb^* - z_{-1}b^*_{-1} = zb^* + z_{-1}(\Delta b^* - b^*), \\ &= zb^* + z_{-1}\Delta b^* - z_{-1}b^*, \end{aligned}$$

that is,

$$\begin{aligned} \Delta(zb^*) &= \Delta zb^* + z_{-1}\Delta b^* = \Delta z(\Delta b^* + b^*_{-1}) + z_{-1}\Delta b^* \\ &= \Delta zb^*_{-1} + z_{-1}\Delta b^* + \Delta z \Delta b^*. \end{aligned}$$

Assuming that Δz and Δb^* are small implies that the last term in the above expression can be ignored, so that

$$\Delta(zb^*) \simeq \Delta zb^*_{-1} + z_{-1}\Delta b^* = \hat{z}(\frac{z_{-1}}{z})zb^*_{-1} + (\frac{z_{-1}}{z})z\Delta b^*, \tag{16}$$

where $\hat{z} = \Delta z/z_{-1}$ is the *rate of depreciation* of the real exchange rate. Using this result to substitute for $z\Delta b^*$ in Equation (15) and rearranging yields

$$d + rb_{-1} + (r^* + \hat{z})zb^*_{-1} = \Delta b + (\frac{z}{z_{-1}})\Delta(zb^*) + \Delta M/P. \tag{17}$$

Equation (17) indicates that the real fiscal deficit of the consolidated public sector must be equal to changes in the real values of domestic and foreign debt plus revenue from seigniorage.

From Equation (1), seigniorage revenue $\Delta M/P$ is given by $\Delta m + \pi m_{-1}/(1+\pi)$. The above equation can also be written as

$$d + rb_{-1} + (r^* + \hat{z})zb^*_{-1} = \Delta b + (\frac{z}{z_{-1}})\Delta(zb^*) + \Delta m + \frac{\pi}{1+\pi}m_{-1}. \tag{18}$$

Equation (18) can be used in various ways to ensure the consistency between fiscal policy and macroeconomic targets. Most importantly, it can generate two types of values for a given money demand function:

- the value of the *primary fiscal deficit*, $\tilde{d}$, that is consistent with a given total debt-to-output ratio (for both domestic and foreign debt) and an inflation target;

- the value of the *inflation rate* (and thus seigniorage revenue), $\tilde{\pi}$, that is consistent with a given total debt-to-output ratio and a target for the primary fiscal deficit.

Consider the first mode. Suppose that both domestic and foreign debt ratios are targeted to grow at the constant rate of growth of output, θ:

$$\Delta b/b_{-1} = \theta, \quad \Delta(zb^*)/z_{-1}b^*_{-1} = \theta.$$

Measuring all variables in proportion of output, y, therefore yields

$$\Delta b/y = \theta(b_{-1}/y),$$

$$\frac{\Delta(zb^*)}{y} = \theta(\frac{z_{-1}b^*_{-1}}{y}) = \theta(\frac{zb^*_{-1}}{y})(\frac{z_{-1}}{z}).$$

Note that in the above expressions, to ensure consistency between real and nominal values, it is necessary to assume that nominal output is defined as $Y = Py$. Thus, P in the foregoing discussion should be interpreted as the GDP deflator, rather than the consumer price index.

Dividing each term in Equation (18) by real output, and using the preceding results to substitute for $\Delta(zb^*)/y$ yields

$$\frac{d}{y} + \frac{rb_{-1}}{y} + (r^* + \hat{z})(\frac{zb^*_{-1}}{y}) = \theta(\frac{b_{-1}}{y}) + \theta(\frac{zb^*_{-1}}{y}) + \frac{\Delta m}{y} + (\frac{\tilde{\pi}}{1+\tilde{\pi}})\frac{m_{-1}}{y},$$

or equivalently, noting that $y = (1+\theta)y_{-1}$,

$$\frac{d}{y} + (\frac{r-\theta}{1+\theta})\frac{b_{-1}}{y_{-1}} + (\frac{r^* + \hat{z} - \theta}{1+\theta})(\frac{zb^*_{-1}}{y_{-1}}) = s, \tag{19}$$

where s is seigniorage as a proportion of output, given by:

$$s = \frac{\Delta m}{(1+\theta)y_{-1}} + \frac{\tilde{\pi}}{(1+\tilde{\pi})(1+\theta)}(\frac{m_{-1}}{y_{-1}}).$$

For given values of the real domestic and foreign interest rate (r and r^*), the rate of depreciation of the real exchange rate, $\hat{z}$, a target rate of output growth, θ, an inflation target, $\tilde{\pi}$, and a properly specified money demand function (which is required to calculate revenue from the inflation tax at the target rate of inflation, $\tilde{\pi} m_{-1}(\tilde{\pi})/(1+\tilde{\pi})$, as well as the change in real money balances, Δm), Equation (19) allows the analyst to determine the **financeable primary deficit** (in proportion of output), $d/y|_f$. This value is given by

$$\frac{d}{y}\Big|_f = -(\frac{r-\theta}{1+\theta})\frac{b_{-1}}{y_{-1}} - (\frac{r^* + \hat{z} - \theta}{1+\theta})\frac{zb^*_{-1}}{y_{-1}} + s.$$

Given the value of the financeable primary fiscal deficit, the reduction in the *actual* fiscal deficit-to-output ratio, $d/y|_a$, required to achieve consistency can be calculated as

$$\frac{d}{y}\Big|_\Delta = \frac{d}{y}\Big|_a - \frac{d}{y}\Big|_f.$$

Alternatively, and this is the second mode, Equation (19) allows one to calculate the *consistent* (or *sustainable*) *rate of inflation* for a given target value of d/y. In this case, however, *multiple solutions* for the sustainable inflation rate may arise if the money demand function is nonlinearly related to inflation and/or nominal interest rates—as occurs in the logarithmic example discussed below.[15]

In practice, estimates of base money demand can be derived from single equations (as discussed in the next chapter) or from a complete *model of portfolio choice* that includes not only the demand for currency but also the demand for sight deposits, time deposits, and (in countries where this is relevant) foreign-currency deposits, all as a function of income, inflation, and interest rates (see, for instance, Anand and van Wijnbergen, 1989). The demand for reserves by commercial banks may also be estimated by using a simple portfolio model, taking into account existing legislation on reserve requirements. A major advantage of this extended approach is that it allows the investigator to assess the effects of *changes in financial regulations*—such as changes in reserve requirement rates or administered interest rates—on the financeable fiscal deficit or the sustainable rate of inflation.

It is also common in practical applications to use a two- or three-year moving average of actual real output growth rates and interest rates, and a constant real exchange rate ($\hat{z} = 0$), to calculate sustainable measures of inflation or the primary deficit. In addition, care is needed with respect to two other considerations:

- Assessing the magnitude and likelihood of realization of **contingent liabilities**, such as foreign exchange guarantees (as discussed earlier), may be critical to adequately assess the fiscal stance and its sustainability (Towe, 1990). As much as possible, measures of the primary deficit should include **quasi-fiscal losses**.

- The degree of *concessionality of foreign debt* must be accounted for in assessing sustainability (see Cuddington, 1997). For many developing countries, foreign financing often contains a sizable *grant element*; the larger that element is, the higher will be the level of foreign indebtedness consistent with fiscal sustainability.[16] In effect, concessionality reduces the *effective* real interest rate on foreign borrowing.

To illustrate the functioning of the consistency framework described above, suppose that there are no commercial banks in the economy and thus no required reserves ($RR = 0$); the monetary base consists therefore only of currency in circulation, so that $M = C_U$. Suppose also that the demand for currency (or money, for short) takes the form $\ln(C_U/y) = 0.1 - 1.5\ln(1+\pi) - 2.1\ln(1+i)$.[17]

---

[15] In practice, analysts would then tend to choose the lower of the two inflation rates.

[16] Foreign grants contain a 100 percent element of concessionality; they are, however, generally treated as an addition to *revenue*, not as a financing item.

[17] Alternatively, if the demand for broad money is known, the demand for base money can be obtained by assuming a constant multiplier. In practice, however, the money multiplier can display a high degree of variability and/or a significant trend.

Suppose also that there is no foreign debt to begin with ($b^* = 0$, and therefore the path of the real exchange rate does not need to be specified), that $\theta = 0.02$, $\tilde{\pi} = 0.63$, $r = r^* = 0.04$, d/y is 0.04 initially, and that the targeted (domestic) debt-to-output ratio is 0.1. The financeable primary deficit, as calculated from Equation (19), is $d/y = 0.027$ for $t = 1$, 0.028 for $t = 2, ...$, and 0.030 for $t = 10$. If alternatively, the policymaker's objective is to find the inflation rate that is consistent with a primary deficit-output ratio constant at 0.03, similar calculations would yield $\pi = 73\%$ for $t = 1$, 71% for $t = 2$, and 58% for $t = 10$.

The framework described above cannot, of course, guarantee that all the objectives of macroeconomic policy will be achieved—it only ensures that the fiscal stance is consistent with these objectives. It remains, however, subject to two major limitations.

- It lacks a *simultaneous determination* of the primary deficit, output growth rates, and the real interest rate. A permanent reduction, say, in the primary deficit required for debt sustainability, brought about through a cut in government expenditure for instance, would tend to lower real interest rates (by reducing the degree of **crowding out** in domestic capital markets or the perceived risk of default on government debt), raise the rate of growth of output (by increasing private investment), and increase money demand (by reducing inflationary expectations).[18]

- To ensure a constant debt-to-output ratio, the sustainable primary deficit is calculated under the assumption that liabilities grow at the economy's rate of output growth. Of course, it could be assumed alternatively that the debt is constant (or even falls) in absolute terms. But regardless of the assumption made, however, *lenders play no role*. By contrast, as discussed later, the role of lenders is at the heart of the **solvency constraint**.

Accounting for the simultaneous determination of output growth, real interest rates, inflation, and the fiscal deficit requires extending the analysis to a *general equilibrium* setting. Without a general equilibrium framework, it is possible that changes in macroeconomic policy that are intended to eliminate an *ex ante* inconsistency between the inflation target and the primary fiscal deficit will do so at the cost of increasing the degree of inconsistency between the inflation and deficit projections, on the one hand, and the assumed path of real output, the real interest rate, and the real exchange rate, on the other. From an operational standpoint, there is of course a trade-off between analytical rigor and the type of applied models that are routinely used for practical policy purposes. But greater effort to develop macroeconomic models that embed the analysis of fiscal sustainability issues in a more comprehensive, but yet tractable, framework is clearly an important task for economists.

---

[18]It may also be empirically important to allow for the feedback effect of inflation on the primary deficit—the Olivera-Tanzi effect discussed earlier. Different rates of inflation may affect not only the primary deficit but also the real interest rate and the rate of depreciation of the real exchange rate.

3.6.2 Fiscal and External Sustainability

The foregoing discussion focused on the sustainability of the government fiscal stance, taking into account the restrictions imposed by domestic and foreign borrowing. However, fiscal sustainability is neither necessary nor sufficient for **external sustainability**. The behavior of the *private sector* is a crucial link in explaining any divergence between fiscal and external sustainability.

From the savings-investment identity given earlier [Equation (8)], any increase in government dissavings (the excess of government expenditure over revenue), given private savings and investment behavior, will translate automatically into an increase in the current account deficit. However, a sustainable fiscal stance need not be sufficient for external sustainability if private sector behavior is such that its *net savings* (that is, gross savings minus gross investment) are highly negative and/or falling. Conversely, an unsustainable fiscal stance does not necessarily imply an unsustainable external position if net savings by the private sector are positive and/or growing.

An extension of the Anand-van Wijnbergen framework to consider the links between fiscal and external sustainability was proposed by Parker and Kastner (1993).

- A key feature of their model is that net private savings, projected on the basis of estimated equations for consumption and investment, are added to net public savings to determine the current account balance.

- Real interest rates are also determined endogenously, and are specified as depending in part on the debt-output ratio. This specification captures the existence of a **risk premium**; the higher the level of public debt, the lower the probability that debt will be sustainable, the higher the **risk of default**, and the higher the real interest rate—relative to the risk-free rate.

- Taxes are exogenous, but linking them to the growth rate of output is straightforward.

For given targets for output growth (and thus fiscal revenue), inflation, and domestic and foreign borrowing, the model generates consistent estimates of *public spending*. The difference between *financeable* expenditure and *actual* expenditure defines the fiscal adjustment required to meet both fiscal and external targets. Conversely, given targets for output growth, domestic and foreign borrowing, and government spending, the model can generate consistent levels of inflation and interest rates. Thus, not only does the model attempt to capture explicitly the role of the private sector in assessing external sustainability, it also addresses another limitation of the basic consistency framework presented above—the need to account for general equilibrium interactions among macroeconomic variables.

By introducing a risk premium in the determination of interest rates, the model also improves over the basic framework in which lenders play a completely passive role. It remains, however, far from complete, given the insufficient attention paid to the financial system and the specification of the supply side (a crucial aspect for medium-term projections).

3.7   Sustainability and Solvency Constraints

The analysis of fiscal (and external) sustainability developed in the context of a consistency framework focuses generally on the *flow* budget constraint of the government and tends to be essentially *static* in nature. It is now well recognized, however, that the government budget constraint has an *intertemporal* dimension as well. Associated with it is an **intertemporal solvency condition**, which is central to an evaluation of the medium- and long-run sustainability of fiscal deficits and public debt.

To derive the intertemporal budget constraint and the solvency condition that it implies, consider the flow budget constraint of the government, as given by Equation (2), and suppose for simplicity that there is *no foreign financing* of the deficit—an assumption that may accord particularly well with the situation of some of the smaller developing countries, for which access to world capital markets tends to be severely limited. It is straightforward to show that the budget constraint can be written in a form that represents a simplification of Equation (17),

$$d + rb_{-1} = \Delta b + \Delta M/P, \tag{20}$$

where d, b, and r are as defined above. Now, define

- $\mathbf{d} = d/y$ as the primary deficit measured as a fraction of GDP;

- $\mathbf{b} = b/y$ as the ratio of (end-of-period) government debt to GDP;

- $s = \Delta M/Py$ as seigniorage revenue as a fraction of GDP;

- θ the rate of growth of real GDP.

Thus, noting that $y = (1 + \theta)y_{-1}$, Equation (20) can be rewritten as[19]

$$\mathbf{b} = \left(\frac{1+r}{1+\theta}\right)\mathbf{b}_{-1} + \mathbf{d} - s. \tag{21}$$

Equation (21) indicates that if the domestic real interest rate, r, exceeds the rate of growth of output $(r > \theta)$, the term $(1 + r)/(1 + \theta)$ will exceed unity, and the debt-output ratio will increase *explosively* over time—unless seigniorage revenue minus the primary deficit grows sufficiently rapidly.

---

[19] As shown by Buiter (1997), in the general case in which the country borrows abroad and purchasing power parity does not hold, an equation similar to (21) can be derived by defining **d** as the *adjusted* primary deficit.

Assuming constant values of r and θ, Equation (21) can be solved *recursively forward* in time from period $t = 0$ to period N. If $t = 0$ is the current period, applying (21) for $t = 1$ yields

$$\mathbf{b}_1 = \left(\frac{1+r}{1+\theta}\right)\mathbf{b}_0 + \mathbf{d}_1 - s_1.$$

For period $t = 2$, the result is

$$\mathbf{b}_2 = \left(\frac{1+r}{1+\theta}\right)\mathbf{b}_1 + \mathbf{d}_2 - s_2 = \left(\frac{1+r}{1+\theta}\right)^2\mathbf{b}_0 + \left(\frac{1+r}{1+\theta}\right)(\mathbf{d}_1 - s_1) + \mathbf{d}_2 - s_2.$$

Repeating the same procedure yields, for $t = N + 1$:

$$\mathbf{b}_{N+1} = \left(\frac{1+r}{1+\theta}\right)^{N+1}\mathbf{b}_0 + \sum_{j=0}^{N}\left(\frac{1+r}{1+\theta}\right)^{N-j}(\mathbf{d}_{j+1} - s_{j+1}). \qquad (22)$$

Assuming for simplicity perfect foresight (which obviates the need to use *expected* values), this expression can be rewritten as

$$\mathbf{b}_0 = \sum_{j=0}^{N}\left(\frac{1+\theta}{1+r}\right)^{j+1}(s_{j+1} - \mathbf{d}_{j+1}) + \left(\frac{1+\theta}{1+r}\right)^{N+1}\mathbf{b}_{N+1}. \qquad (23)$$

Equation (23) indicates that today's outstanding stock of domestic debt (measured in proportion of output) must be equal to the *present discounted value* of the future stream of seigniorage revenue, adjusted for the primary fiscal balance, between the current date and some terminal date $N + 1$, plus the present discounted value of the debt held at that terminal future date.

Suppose that $N + 1$ is indeed the relevant terminal date for the government. The **solvency constraint** in this case requires that the outstanding level of debt at that date be *nonpositive*:

$$\mathbf{b}_{N+1} \leq 0. \qquad (24)$$

Imposing this constraint to Equation (23) implies that the outstanding level of debt cannot exceed, for a solvent government whose horizon is $N + 1$, the present discounted value of future seigniorage revenue, adjusted for future primary fiscal deficits:

$$\mathbf{b}_0 \leq \sum_{h=1}^{N+1}\left(\frac{1+\theta}{1+r}\right)^{h}(s_h - \mathbf{d}_h), \qquad h = j + 1. \qquad (25)$$

The current stance of fiscal policy is then deemed sustainable if its continuation through period $N + 1$ does not violate the solvency constraint (25).

In general, of course, although actual governments may have a limited term, they are not bound to repay debts contracted during their tenure at the end of their term. Thus, to the extent that future governments will honor the debts incurred today, the solvency constraint (24) is overly restrictive. All that is required to ensure solvency is that, eventually, the present discounted value of the *terminal debt* of the government goes to zero. Formally, the solvency constraint then takes the form of the **No-Ponzi scheme (NPS) condition**, given by

$$\lim_{N \to \infty} \left(\frac{1+\theta}{1+r}\right)^{N+1} \mathbf{b}_{N+1} \leq 0. \tag{26}$$

Given the NPS condition, as before, the value of the initial stock of debt cannot exceed the present discounted value of the infinite flow of future seigniorage revenue adjusted for primary deficits:[20]

$$\mathbf{b}_0 \leq \sum_{h=1}^{\infty} \left(\frac{1+\theta}{1+r}\right)^h (s_h - \mathbf{d}_h). \tag{27}$$

Clearly the NPS condition matters only if the real interest rate on the public debt exceeds the long-run growth rate of GDP ($r > \theta$); otherwise, as implied by Equation (22), the debt will eventually tend to a constant value if the horizon N is sufficiently long. Indeed, suppose that $r < \theta$, and that both s and $\mathbf{d}$ are constant over time; then, for $N \to \infty$, the first term in (22) vanishes, and the second becomes

$$(\mathbf{d} - s) \left\{ \left(\frac{1+r}{1+\theta}\right) + \left(\frac{1+r}{1+\theta}\right)^2 + \cdots \right\}.$$

The sum of the geometric progression in brackets is $1/[1 - (1+r)/(1+\theta)]$, so that the debt will converge to

$$\mathbf{b}_\infty = \left(\frac{1+\theta}{\theta - r}\right) (\mathbf{d} - s),$$

which is positive as long as $\mathbf{d} > s$.

The above framework can be used for various policy exercises. For instance, it can be used to calculate the magnitude of the (constant) primary deficit-output ratio that would be needed to get from an initial debt-output ratio $\mathbf{b}_0$, to a target future value of that ratio (say) H periods later, $\mathbf{b}_H$. This quantity, following Buiter (1997), can be called the *required* primary deficit-output ratio. By comparing the required ratio to the actual ratio (obtained by assuming, say, that current policies will remain unchanged) the **primary fiscal gap** can be obtained. Along similar lines, the sustainability index proposed by Blanchard (1993) is based on the difference between the actual tax rate and the *sustainable tax rate*, defined as the tax rate that is required to restore (for a given path of

---

[20] With variable output growth rates and interest rates, the NPS condition given by Equation (26) becomes $\lim_{N \to \infty} \Pi_{i=1}^{N+1}[(1+\theta_i)/(1+r_i)]\mathbf{b}_{N+1} \leq 0$, whereas condition (27) becomes $\mathbf{b}_0 \leq \sum_{h=1}^{\infty} \Pi_{i=1}^{h}[(1+\theta_i)/(1+r_i)](s_h - \mathbf{d}_h)$.

public spending and transfers) the level of the debt-output ratio to its initial level after a given number of years H.

Analyzing intertemporal solvency requirements is important to assess the stance of fiscal policy and its sustainability.[21] What the foregoing discussion implies, however, is that solvency is not *sufficient* to identify a unique fiscal stance. Suppose that for a given path of output growth and real interest rates there exists a given path of seigniorage, taxes, and recurrent spending that ensures solvency. Then, under the same assumptions, an increase in spending *today*, coupled with a sufficiently large reduction in spending *tomorrow*, will also ensure solvency. Similarly, a reduction in taxes today, associated with a sufficiently large increase tomorrow, will guarantee that the government is solvent. The reason is that what matters is the *present value* of government outlays and receipts, not what happens on a "day-to-day" basis. This *lack of uniqueness* implies that governments possess some degrees of freedom in the selection of fiscal policy instruments that they can manipulate to ensure solvency, as well as the timing of use of these instruments.

Governments also possess some degrees of freedom when current and expected policies imply that the solvency constraint is violated. The following are the main policy options that they may consider (individually or jointly) to close the solvency gap.

- Reduce current and future primary deficits, either by cutting spending or by raising tax and nontax revenues.

- Increase current and future seigniorage revenues. However, the scope for seigniorage to close the solvency gap is limited. If the economy is on the decreasing-yield segment of the **seigniorage Laffer curve**, an attempt to raise seigniorage revenue by increasing the growth rate of the base money stock will lead to higher inflation and a sharp fall in money demand, thereby *reducing* revenue (see Chapter 6).

- Declare an *outright default* or impose a *unilateral moratorium* on debt payments on the domestic and external public debt. However, by cutting access to capital markets and/or raising the **risk premium** embedded in domestic interest rates, such an option can *increase* the solvency gap.

In practice, solvency analysis is fraught with difficulties.[22] Estimating the present values of seigniorage revenues and future primary deficits is difficult. Estimating the real rate of interest and the rate of output growth (in the more realistic case in which they vary over time) is also problematic if the horizon is relatively long; the reason is that interactions (as discussed earlier) between

---

[21] As discussed in Chapter 16, *external* solvency can be analyzed in a manner that is similar to the procedure used to assess fiscal solvency.

[22] See, for instance, Buiter and Patel (1992) for an application to India, Tanner (1995) to Brazil, Koo (2002) to Korea, as well as Bravo and Silvestre (2002) and Uctum and Wickens ((2000) for several European countries. An econometric assessment of the solvency constraint often takes the form of testing the stationarity of the debt-to-output ratio. See the discussion by Cuddington (1997).

these variables and the primary fiscal deficit must be taken into account to avoid biasing the results. Calculating the primary fiscal balance that ensures solvency does not address the question of whether the fiscal policy stance is consistent with growth and other policy targets. As pointed out by Zee (1988), once the endogeneity and interdependence of the primary fiscal balance, private savings and investment, interest rates, and output growth is recognized, government solvency as defined earlier is *not sufficient* for fiscal policies to be *sustainable*—in the sense that the level of public debt converges to a stable long-run equilibrium path consistent with the steady state of the economy.

Equally important, the solvency constraint [given as either Equation (24) or (26)] imposes only *weak restrictions* on fiscal policy. As shown earlier, it has no meaning in an economy in which the real interest rate is lower than the growth rate of output. Put differently, if $r < \theta$, a primary surplus is not necessary to achieve solvency—the government can run a primary deficit of *any size*, and this would be consistent with a sustainable debt-to-output ratio. In fact, the debt-to-output ratio may rise *without bound*, as long as the growth rate of the debt does not equal or exceed the real interest rate.

In practice, however, the size of the debt-to-output ratio may have an important influence on the private sector's *perception* of the government's *commitment* to meet its intertemporal budget constraint, as well as its *ability* to do so. As long as the private sector expects the government to generate a sequence of primary budget surpluses at some future period, the constraint imposed by either Equation (25) or (27) will be met. However, as the debt ratio continues to grow, private agents may become *skeptical* about the government's ability to meet its budget constraint; this *loss of credibility* may translate into *higher interest rates*, as discussed in more detail later. Moreover, the larger the outstanding debt-to-output ratio is, and the longer appropriate policy actions are *postponed*, the greater will be the magnitude of the primary surplus needed to satisfy the solvency constraint. Because governments typically face a *limit* to the tax burden that they can impose on their citizens (notably because of adverse effects on incentives and income distribution), they face a **feasibility constraint** on the amount of revenue that they can raise (Spaventa, 1987). The result may be that a set of fiscal policies that initially met the solvency constraint may become inadequate over time.

3.8   Commodity Price Shocks and Deficits

The root causes of fiscal deficits in developing countries are often found in the biases generated by inadequate political structures, such as those resulting from the *commons problem* discussed earlier, and political conflict (see Chapter 17). In addition, and particularly in the short run, *commodity price shocks* may also play a role. Many developing economies continue to depend heavily on primary commodities for the bulk of their export receipts. In sub-Saharan Africa, for instance, the share of primary commodities in total exports accounted on average for about three-fourths in 1997; in some cases it exceeded 90 percent (see

Deaton, 1999*b*). In many countries that are dependent on primary commodity exports, tax revenues are strongly affected by movements in commodity prices.[23] And indeed, prices of *nonoil commodities* tend to fluctuate quite dramatically, in both nominal and real terms.

When commodity prices increase, for instance, government revenues are boosted both directly, in countries where commodity-producing sectors are state owned, and indirectly, through increased revenues from trade and income taxes. As documented by Collier and Gunning (1996), governments in a number of commodity-exporting countries have often used these windfall gains to finance *pro-cyclical expenditures* (instead of imposing a tax on export earnings) with the result that when commodity prices have declined, these countries have been left with large and unsustainable fiscal deficits. The reason, as noted by Cooper (1991, p. 87), is that "Governments typically behave as if positive shocks are permanent, and negative shocks are temporary."

For instance, in coffee-producing countries such as Kenya and Tanzania, expansions induced by the coffee price booms of the late 1970s and early 1980s led to sharp increases in domestic and external debt burdens, largely because the windfall gains were used to fund public sector expenditures that yielded little or no return. The experience in many oil-exporting countries (such as Mexico, Nigeria, and Venezuela) was similar following the sharp rises in oil prices during the late 1970s. In many cases, the expansion of government spending induced by a transitory improvement in the terms of trade was accompanied not only by growing fiscal deficits but also by a sustained *real exchange rate appreciation*—a phenomenon known as the **Dutch disease** (see Corden, 1984)—which exerted an adverse effect on exports and sometimes led to severe balance-of-payments difficulties.

Designing contingency mechanisms and institutional structures that are capable of ensuring that governments engage more in *expenditure smoothing* (by saving in good times in order to dissave in bad times) in response to movements in primary commodity prices and the terms of trade remains a key policy issue in many developing countries.

3.9   Can Fiscal Austerity Be Expansionary?

The conventional view of fiscal austerity (typically referred to as the **Keynesian view**) is that a cut in government spending will typically lower aggregate demand and reduce output.

Some economists have argued, however, that the conventional view does not necessarily hold in countries where, to begin with, budgetary imbalances and the public debt are large. On the contrary, it has been suggested that fiscal austerity may be *expansionary*. This possibility was referred to by Bertola and Drazen (1993), in particular, as the case of the **negative fiscal multiplier**. Barry and Devereux (1995, 2003) and Perotti (1999) also explored analytically

---

[23]For a discussion of the sources of volatility in primary commodity prices, see Bleaney and Greenaway (1993), Cuddington (1992), and Cashin, McDermott, and Scott (2002).

the implications of this view and considered some of the empirical evidence for industrial countries. Giavazzi, Jappelli, and Pagano (2000) provided evidence on expansionary fiscal contractions for both industrial and developing countries.

The idea of a negative fiscal multiplier rests essentially on the view that *expectations* about *future policy actions* may have a major effect on interest rates, depending on their *degree of credibility*—a notion that will receive more attention in the next two chapters. Consider, for instance, a country with a large and growing budget deficit and a high level of government debt. Suppose that the government announces its commitment to reduce the deficit within a given time frame, and begins its austerity program with an immediate cut in expenditure. To the extent that operators on financial markets regard the (actual and future) policy measures as fully credible, interest rates may fall immediately. The reason is that a credible policy announcement may be viewed as reducing the risk of higher inflation (or indirect default), currency overvaluation, and possibly future financial instability (see Chapter 8). As a result of the gain in credibility, the **risk premium** in interest rates is likely to decline. In the model of Miller, Skidelsky, and Weller (1990), for instance, there is a debt threshold above which the government is forced to impose a tax on bond holders. With random shocks to the level of debt, the risk premium tends to increase as the outstanding level of debt approaches the threshold, leading to a fall in private demand. A fiscal adjustment that reduces public debt well below the threshold would tend to reduce the risk premium, and thus interest rates.

In turn, the fall in interest rates and the associated reduction in the debt service burden of households and firms may have expansionary effects on output through various channels:

- Via the *demand side*, by lowering the cost of capital (as discussed in Chapter 2) and thereby increasing investment, by stimulating consumption of durables, and by increasing the market value of stocks, bonds, and real estate (thereby inducing a wealth effect).

- Via the *supply side*, by reducing the cost of financing working capital needs for credit-dependent firms (see Chapters 4 and 7).

Reduced uncertainty about the sustainability of the budgetary situation may also help directly to improve confidence among firms and households. By reducing the **option value of waiting** (as discussed in Chapter 2), lower uncertainty may stimulate investment. Consumption and investment may also be stimulated if the reduction in public debt service payments translates into lower budgetary pressures and, at least to some extent, lower expected future tax rates. The credibility and signaling effects of fiscal adjustment also depend on the *composition* of spending reductions; cuts in the wage bill, or welfare programs, may have a greater signaling effect about the government's commitment to fiscal austerity, precisely because they are more difficult to implement. Similarly, if fiscal adjustment takes the form of a cut in public investment in *infrastructure*, private agents may anticipate an adverse effect on private investment (given the complementarity effect noted in Chapter 2), growth, and income in the longer run, and the signaling effect may be muted.

Nevertheless, in any particular setting, expansionary effects may well outweigh the conventional, negative short-term output effects associated with cuts in government spending or increases in tax rates. Although there is not much evidence on the importance of negative fiscal multiplier effects in developing countries, it is an idea that has potentially important implications for the design of adjustment programs. Testing whether fiscal austerity can have positive output effects is not a trivial matter; the critical issue in this context is to measure the effect of current policies on the public's expectations about future policy changes, but these expectations are not observable. One could argue, for instance, that any behavior of private consumption following any type of fiscal adjustment can be rationalized by some assumption about what the current fiscal stance signals about unobservable future policies. But some progress has been made in identifying expansionary effects in the recent empirical literature. Giavazzi, Jappelli, and Pagano (2000) found that expansionary fiscal contractions tend to occur mostly in countries where *large* and *persistent* fiscal impulses are maintained; they argued that only such actions (which may be potentially costly, from a political standpoint) are capable of signaling a change in regime and thus exert a nonlinear effect on private sector expectations and behavior.

3.10 Summary

- The structure of conventional sources of revenue and expenditure differs significantly between industrial and developing countries.

- Shares of *tax revenue* and *government expenditure* in output are larger in industrial countries. Developing countries spend more on general public services, defense, and education; industrial countries spend somewhat more on social security and health.

- Although the relative shares of *direct taxes, taxes on domestic goods and services*, and *taxes on foreign trade* vary considerably across developing countries, there has been a gradual move away from trade taxes to taxes on domestic sales. In industrial countries, income taxes account for the largest share of tax revenue, and taxes on foreign trade are negligible.

- Within *direct taxes*, the share of tax revenue raised from individual incomes is much larger than that from corporations in developing countries, while the reverse is true in industrial countries.

- The collection of **seigniorage** and **quasi-fiscal operations** are two important features of public finances in developing countries.

- **Seigniorage** consists of the **inflation tax** (the reduction in the purchasing power of private holdings of cash money balances due to inflation) and autonomous changes in the level of real money balances. To the extent that money creation causes inflation, thereby affecting the real value of (nonindexed) nominal assets, seigniorage can be viewed as a tax on private agents' holdings of these assets.

- Although there are considerable differences across countries in the use of inflationary finance, the evidence suggests that reliance on seigniorage is higher in countries with larger fiscal deficits.

- **Quasi-fiscal outlays** and **receipts** are operations (generally of the central bank) that are functionally equivalent to subsidies and taxes imposed by the government. Difficulties in raising tax revenue through conventional means often explain the importance of these operations.

- Examples of quasi-fiscal operations are central bank loans at subsidized rates of interest (equivalent to interest subsidies), losses associated with the purchase and sale of foreign exchange in a multiple exchange rate system (equivalent to foreign exchange subsidies), and the imposition on commercial banks of reserve requirements obliging them to hold central bank liabilities earning below-market rates of interest (equivalent to a tax on deposits).

- These quasi-fiscal operations are **contingent** (or **unfunded**) **fiscal liabilities** that should be recognized, estimated, and converted into their subsidy or tax equivalents in order to add them to the fiscal accounts, conventionally measured, of the consolidated public sector. Otherwise, changes in the government's fiscal balance may provide a misleading picture of the true situation of the public sector's overall financial position.

- Reductions in central government expenditures may simply reflect a shift to quasi-fiscal activities and implicit government liabilities, rather than real fiscal adjustment. In particular, when expenditure data do not account for the contingent or unfunded liabilities created by quasi-fiscal activities—such as the implicit subsidies provided in the form of government guarantees to public enterprises engaged in borrowing—the ratio of actual government expenditure to output may significantly understate the extent of public sector intervention in the economy.

- The **problem of the commons** arises due to an important characteristic of many government programs: whereas they tend to generate benefits that are concentrated sectorally and or geographically, they are often financed from a common pool of resources. Under some institutional arrangements regarding the process of fiscal decision making, this can lead to overutilization of the common pool of resources, fiscal deficits, and overborrowing, because those who benefit from the programs fail to internalize their full cost.

- The conventional measure of the fiscal deficit derived from the **flow budget constraint** of the government can be very sensitive to inflation. A key reason is the effect of inflation on nominal interest payments on the public debt. Another reason is the **Olivera-Tanzi effect**, which refers to the erosion of the tax base by inflation due to the lag between the assessment and collection of taxes.

- When inflation is high and variable, changes in the nominal interest bill can affect the usefulness of the conventional fiscal balance as a guide for policy assessment. More useful concepts are the **primary balance**, which excludes interest payments from expenditure, and the **operational balance**, calculated by netting out the inflationary component in interest payments from the conventional balance.

- The **structural budget balance** measures what tax revenue and expenditure would be if actual GDP was equal to potential GDP. It is based on the view that changes in deficit attributable to the business cycle are self-correcting, whereas changes in deficits attributable to structural factors can be offset only through discretionary measures.

- In both the IMF and the OECD approaches, elasticities are used to adjust revenues and expenditures for movements in the cyclical output gap. Tax categories that are cyclically adjusted typically include business taxes, household direct taxes, social security contributions, and indirect taxes. Unemployment insurance benefits are the main item of government spending that are usually adjusted for cyclical movements.

- The **fiscal impulse measure** aims at capturing the effect of automatic stabilizers and discretionary changes in fiscal policy. It is calculated by first estimating the *cyclically neutral* component of the budget deficit (often under the assumption that government expenditures increase proportionately to *potential* output and that government revenues increase proportionately to *actual* output). The difference between the cyclically neutral and the actual budget deficits is the *fiscal stance*. The fiscal impulse is the annual change in the fiscal stance, expressed as a share of output. Such measures, however, are subject to a number of limitations, due in part to their partial equilibrium nature.

- Institutional reforms in fiscal management have taken the form of formal **deficit and debt rules**, **expenditure limits**, and improved **fiscal transparency**. All these frameworks share an explicit legal basis, an emphasis on the need for a longer-term focus to fiscal policy, and tougher requirements for fiscal reporting to the public.

- The advantage of fiscal rules is that they are clear and focus on a generally well understood macroeconomic aggregate. The main criticism of these rules is that they are inflexible and may be *pro-cyclical*. This problem can be addressed by focusing on a cyclically adjusted deficit measure, such as the **structural budget deficit**. By allowing the operation of automatic stabilizers, rules based on structural deficits can provide some room for discretionary policy within the cycle. However, the benchmark against which fiscal performance is to be judged is made more complicated; this may increase the opportunity to bypass the rules, making them potentially harder to enforce and undermining their credibility.

- Macroeconomically, aggregate domestic investment must be financed by domestic savings, public and private, and foreign saving (the current account deficit). This identity is sometimes used to argue that if policies do not have any effect in improving either government or private sector savings, the external balance cannot be expected to improve.

- As long as the *net investment position* of the private sector remains stable, changes in fiscal deficits will be closely associated with movements in current account deficits. In general, however, because fiscal deficits also affect the private sector's investment-saving balance, the correlation between fiscal and external deficits may be weak.

- A **consistency framework** aims at ensuring that fiscal objectives are consistent with other macroeconomic policy targets, such as growth, inflation, real interest rates, and the external current account.

- The framework proposed by Anand and van Wijnbergen (1989) dwells on the flow budget constraint of the government and can be operated in two modes: the **deficit mode**, which gives the **financeable deficit**, given targets for inflation and other macroeconomic variables; and the **inflation mode**, which gives the rate of inflation consistent with given targets for the fiscal deficit and other variables. In both cases, to ensure a constant debt-to-output ratio, the sustainable primary deficit is calculated under the assumption that liabilities grow at the economy's rate of output growth.

- The Anand-van Wijnbergen framework remains, however, subject to two major limitations. First, it lacks a *simultaneous determination* of the fiscal balance and other macroeconomic variables; more complex models may be useful and may allow the analyst to assess the role of the investment-saving balance of the private sector in assessing external sustainability.

- Second, lenders, or holders of government liabilities, *play no direct role* in determining the sustainable debt-to-output ratio. Applications also rarely account properly for contingent liabilities; these may be important in assessing debt sustainability in the medium term.

- Assessing the sustainability of fiscal policy on the basis of aggregate public debt dynamics does not ensure a sustainable external current account. To do so requires taking into account also changes in *private* saving and investment behavior induced by predicted movements in output, public debt, and interest rates.

- The government's **solvency** (or **intertemporal**) **constraint** indicates that the *discounted present value* of primary surpluses and seigniorage revenue (both in proportion of output) must be equal to the initial stock of the government debt-to-output ratio. The current stance of fiscal policy is deemed sustainable if its continuation into the indefinite future does not violate the solvency constraint.

- As long as the real interest rate is *lower* than the rate of growth of real output, this constraint does not bind. But if the real interest rate *exceeds* the rate of growth of real output, a policy aimed at maintaining a primary deficit that is expected to continue indefinitely may eventually lead to a violation of the solvency constraint *ex ante*. Satisfying the constraint *ex post* requires either a cut in the primary deficit, increased seigniorage revenue, or debt repudiation or restructuring.

- Solvency analysis, in practice, also lacks a *simultaneous determination* of macroeconomic aggregates.

- **Commodity price shocks** may have a significant impact on fiscal deficits. For countries that are heavily dependent on commodity exports, a rise in the price of these goods increases government revenues both directly, if commodity-producing sectors are state owned, and indirectly, through increased revenues from trade and income taxes.

- Governments in a number of commodity-exporting countries have often used windfall gains to finance *pro-cyclical expenditures* with the result that once commodity prices started to decline, these countries were left with large and unsustainable fiscal deficits. Terms-of-trade shocks have also led to significant real appreciation (the **Dutch disease** phenomenon). Managing commodity price shocks remains a key issue in fiscal policy.

- A cut in government spending is conventionally viewed as reducing aggregate demand and output. But fiscal austerity may also be expansionary if expectations about *future policy actions* affect interest rates. A credible commitment to reduce a large fiscal deficit may lead to an immediate fall in interest rates (because of the perceived reduction in the risk of inflation), which may stimulate aggregate demand and output. There is, however, limited evidence on these effects in developing countries.

Chapter 4

The Financial System and Monetary Policy

> The legal rate, it is to be observed, . . . ought not to be much above the lowest market rate . . . If the legal rate of interest [is fixed too high,] . . . the greater part of the money which was to be lent, would be lent to prodigals and projectors, who alone would be willing to give this high interest. Sober people, who will give for the use of money no more than a part of what they are likely to make by the use of it, would not venture into the competition.
>
> Adam Smith, *The Wealth of Nations*, Chapter 4, 1776.

Key features of the financial system in many developing countries are the relatively low degree of institutional diversification, the limited availability of financial assets, and the importance of government intervention. Although informal finance continues to play a significant role in some countries (particularly in sub-Saharan Africa), commercial banks remain the dominant financial institutions. Assets available to savers are often limited to bank deposits and money market instruments. In some countries governments have attempted for years to control the flow of funds to various categories of agents, either directly through forced allocation of bank lending or by imposing various price and quantity restrictions on bank activities. Almost invariably, the result of these policies has been to limit credit availability and to create severe distortions and inefficiencies in the financial intermediation process, with adverse effects on saving, investment, and growth. Although financial liberalization has proceeded at a rapid pace in some countries (creating problems of its own, as discussed in Chapter 15), government intervention remains pervasive in many cases.

This chapter begins with a description of some of the main features of the financial system in developing countries, with particular attention to the impact of government restrictions and the role of banks in the process of financial intermediation. Section 4.2 reviews the determinants of the demand for money in developing countries—a key building block of IMF-type financial programming models, as discussed in Chapter 9. Section 4.3 examines the nature and operation of indirect instruments of monetary policy in countries where the financial structure is relatively diversified, a well-functioning secondary market for government securities exists, and asset prices tend to be market-determined. Factors leading to endogenous forms of credit rationing are examined in section 4.4. Section 4.5 discusses the transmission process of monetary policy under fixed and flexible exchange rates, whereas section 4.6 examines the scope and functioning of inflation-targeting regimes—an operational framework for monetary policy that has gained considerable popularity in recent years. Section 4.7 focuses on issues raised by a high degree of dollarization (the simultaneous use of domestic and foreign currencies) for the conduct of monetary policy.

In most developing countries, the financial system was for many years subject to a variety of government-imposed restrictions. Although financial deregulation has proceeded rapidly in the past decade or so, these restrictions remain pervasive in many countries. The first part of this section examines the sources, and implications, of government restrictions on the functioning of the financial sector. The second discusses the role of commercial banks in the process of financial intermediation.

4.1   The Financial System

There is great diversity in the degree of development of the financial system among developing countries. Figure 4.1 shows average values over the period 1990-2001 for 44 developing countries and 14 industrial countries of two indicators of financial development: the ratio of narrow money to GDP, and the ratio of broad money to GDP. The latter measure can be viewed as indicative of the use of money and its close substitutes as means of payment. The second panel of the figure suggests that the depth of financial markets, as proxied by the broad money-to-output ratio, is higher in countries with relatively high income per capita.[1] At the same time, the evidence also suggests that means of payment and stores of wealth other than those included in the definition of broad money may be actively used in more developed financial systems (see Mishkin, 1998).

4.1.1   Financial Repression

In many developing countries, central banks continue to impose restrictions on the activity of commercial banks. In some cases, government intervention has the effect of keeping the interest rate that domestic banks can offer to savers at very low (and often negative) levels. In others, commercial banks have been compelled to hold short-term government securities at below-market rates, as

---

[1]Some studies have found, however, that this relationship may be *nonlinear* and may depend on the level of inflation—or, more generally, on the stability of the macroeconomic environment.

a result of statutory **liquidity requirements**.[2] At the same time, **required reserves** held by commercial banks at the central bank may be receiving below-market (or even zero) interest rates. All these restrictions are essentially *taxes* on the banking system and represent what McKinnon (1973) called early on, in a seminal contribution, **financial repression**.

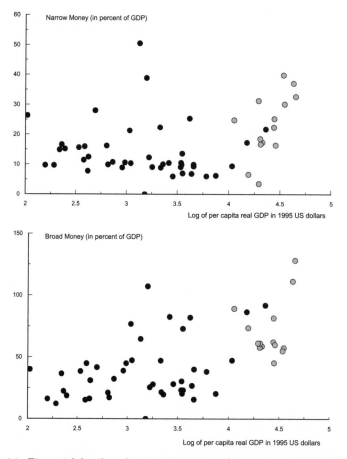

Figure 4.1. Financial depth and per capita income (average over 1990-2001). Forty-four developing countries and 14 industrialized countries are included. A dark circle refers to developing countries and a lighter circle to industrial countries. Source: World Bank.

In general, a state of financial repression can be defined as a situation characterized by

- *ceilings on nominal interest rates*, which typically lead to negative real rates, with an adverse effect on financial savings and investment decisions;

---

[2] In principle, liquidity requirements have a prudential goal—which is to discourage banks from taking large positions in assets that can be sold only at a significant loss (thereby undermining the solvency of the institution) in the event of a liquidity crisis.

- *quantitative controls* and *selective credit allocation* across production sectors, regions, or activities considered by the government to be a "priority," with lending often occurring at preferential interest rates;

- high *minimum reserve requirements* on bank deposits, which may vary across financial instruments and financial institutions;

- *direct control by the state* of part of the banking system, with loan decisions guided more by political factors than by standard efficiency considerations;

- *forced allocation of assets* or loans to the public sector by private commercial banks. A common example, as noted earlier, is the use of **statutory liquidity ratios**, which require commercial banks to hold a given proportion of their assets in the form of government debt.

To a large extent, the motivation for financial repression is the *inability to raise taxes* through conventional means—either because of **administrative inefficiencies** (as discussed in the previous chapter) or because of **political constraints**. By forcing commercial banks to lend to priority sectors, and by imposing large reserve and liquidity requirements on banks—thereby creating a captive demand for its own debt instruments—the government manipulates the financial system to promote its goals.

Financial repression can yield substantial revenue to the government. One source of revenue from financial repression is the *implicit tax on financial intermediation* generated by high reserve requirement rates. A second source is the *implicit subsidy* from which the government benefits by obtaining access to central bank financing at below-market (if not zero) interest rates. Giovannini and De Melo (1993) estimated that during the period 1984-87, for instance, the Mexican government extracted about 6 percent of GDP (or about 40 percent of total conventional tax revenue) from controls on financial markets. On average, during the period that these authors considered, governments in their sample of developing countries extracted about 2 percent of GDP in revenue from financial repression. The estimates provided by Fry, Goodhart, and Almeida (1996) are of the same order of magnitude.[3]

At the same time, however, financial repression entails significant costs, both real and financial. Interest rate ceilings that force rates to fall below market-clearing rates, in particular, may distort the economy through at least four channels (Fry, 1997, p. 755):

- Low interest rates tend to increase the preference of individuals for current consumption as opposed to future consumption (see Chapter 2); they tend therefore to *reduce savings* below the level that would be optimal from the point of view of society as a whole. This, in turn, may have an adverse effect on growth.

---

[3]See Easterly and Schmidt-Hebbel (1994) for another set of estimates of government revenue from financial repression in a group of developing countries during the late 1970s and 1980s.

- Low interest rates on bank deposits relative to interest rates on informal financial markets may reduce the supply of funds through the banking system and promote *disintermediation*. In turn, the development of *informal modes of financial intermediation* may alter substantially the transmission process of monetary policy, as discussed by Agénor and Haque (1996).

- Bank borrowers who are able to obtain the funds they require at low rates of interest will tend to choose relatively more *capital-intensive projects*. The implicit subsidy to physical capital may therefore translate into higher unemployment.

- The pool of potential borrowers typically contains entrepreneurs with *low-yielding projects*, who would not want to borrow at the higher market-clearing rate. To the extent that banks' selection processes contain an element of randomness, some investment projects that are financed will have yields below the threshold that would be self-imposed with market-clearing interest rates.

More generally, financial repression creates *severe inefficiencies*, which tend to restrict the development of financial intermediation, increase the spread between deposit and lending rates, and reduce saving and investment in the economy. Although the acceleration of the process of financial liberalization in recent years has led to a sharp reduction in revenue from financial repression in many countries, commercial banking sectors continue to be heavily regulated in several cases.

4.1.2   Banks and Financial Intermediation

Whether or not they are subject to excessive government regulations, banks continue to dominate the financial system in most developing countries—low- and middle-income countries alike. Of course, other specialized institutions exist in many cases, but they typically account for only a very small portion of total financial intermediation in the economy. Bank deposits remain the most important form of household savings, and banks loans (together with retained earnings) are the most important source of finance for firms, both for working capital needs and for investment in fixed capital. The overwhelming proportion of bank loans is, in fact, allocated to firms in many developing countries and is short term in nature.

As documented, for instance, by Rojas-Suárez and Weisbrod (1995), in the early 1990s banks accounted for between 50 and 90 percent of the financing needs of firms in Latin American countries. In 1992, the share of commercial banks in total net credit to private sector allocated by banks and other financial institutions represented about 99 percent in Argentina, 94 percent in Bolivia, 62 percent in Brazil, 79 percent in Chile, 49 percent in Colombia, 67 percent in Ecuador, 91 percent in Mexico, 76 percent in Peru, and 85 percent in Venezuela (Rojas-Suárez and Weisbrod, 1995, p. 5). Similar figures can be found in Asia.

Figure 4.2 shows the share of domestic credit provided by the banking sector in proportion to GDP for 1990 and 2001 for a group of developing economies.

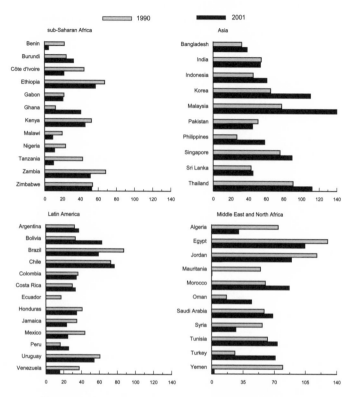

Figure 4.2. Domestic credit provided by banking sector (in percent of GDP). Source: World Bank.

Although the ratio fell in several countries (most notably in sub-Saharan Africa), it increased in many others—particularly in Asia. In Malaysia, for instance, the credit ratio increased dramatically and reached almost 140 percent in 2001. These figures are still low compared with those of Japan (260 percent in 1990 and 309 percent in 2001), but are similar in magnitude to those of Germany (103 in 1990 and 145 in 2001) and the United States (110 in 1990 and 161 in 2001).

Equity markets have increased in size in several developing countries in recent years. Figure 4.3 shows the dramatic increase in stock market capitalization (the value of all stocks quoted on the exchanges) in proportion of GDP in countries like Chile, Ghana, India, the Philippines, and Tunisia between 1990 and 2001. In addition, capital market alternatives to bank loans have also become available on a wider scale. In Chile, for instance, a significant *corporate bond market* has developed since the early 1990s; and some of the larger and better-known firms are now able to raise capital directly in the United States through *American depository receipts* (ADRs) and on euromarkets through *global depository receipts* (GDRs).[4] Bond markets allow greater dispersion of risk and a more efficient allocation of resources (thereby lowering the cost of capital), as well as greater mobilization of savings—particularly the long-term resources needed to finance investments with long gestation periods. Active secondary markets in government debt are also necessary to conduct monetary policy through indirect instruments, as discussed below.

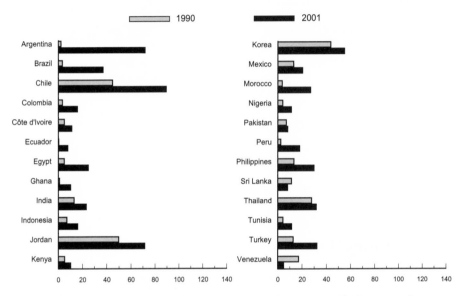

Figure 4.3. Stock market capitalization (in percent of GDP). Stock market capitalization is the share price multiplied by the number of shares outstanding for all listed domestic companies. Source: World Bank.

Nevertheless, the role of equity markets and other sources of finance in the process of financial intermediation between households and firms remains limited in the developing world. Stock market capitalization remains low compared with advanced industrial countries. In Japan, for instance, numbers comparable to those shown in Figure 4.3 are 96 percent for 1990 and 92 percent for 2001; for the United States, these numbers are 53 percent for 1990 and 137 percent in 2001. Equity finance in many countries remains confined to the largest firms and has not yet become a significant competitor as an alternative to bank loans and retained earnings. In countries where corporate bond markets have developed (as in Chile), they remain quite narrow, concentrated, and relatively illiquid.

It is thus essential to understand the central role that banks play in the economy. In general, banks have three main functions:

---

[4] Foreign firms use ADRs to become listed on a U.S. stock exchange without being subject to the U.S. Security and Exchange Commission's disclosure requirements. To issue ADRs, however, foreign firms must hold a deposit with a U.S. chartered bank to guarantee payment of dividends. Receipts verifying the existence of these deposits are the instruments that are actually traded.

- **transformation**—they transform the short-term, liquid deposits held by households (or asset holders) into illiquid liabilities issued by firms;

- **delegated screening and monitoring**—they screen potential borrowers and monitor actual borrowers on behalf of depositors;

- they **facilitate transactions** between agents (firms and workers, buyers and sellers) by providing *payment services.*

The legal, regulatory, and accounting structures within which banks operate in many developing countries remain weak and lack transparency. Inadequate **prudential supervision**, for instance, creates systemic fragility and may precipitate (or compound) bank runs and currency crises, as discussed in Chapters 8 and 15. The persistence of prudential problems also complicates the conduct of monetary policy. As discussed later, weaknesses in the banking system distort the transmission process of monetary policy because banks that are less able to control their balance sheets will be less responsive to changes in interest rates. Moreover, banking problems may lead to pressure on the central bank to extend credit to *bail out* troubled banks, thereby reducing the scope for tightening liquidity and raising interest rates to fend off speculative attacks (see Chapter 8).[5]

4.2   Money Demand

The demand for money plays an important macroeconomic role. As discussed in Chapter 9, it is at the heart of several operational approaches to macroeconomic analysis, in particular the **financial programming** framework used by the International Monetary Fund. In general, of course, the stability of money demand is essential for the conduct of monetary policy.

Numerous studies of the determinants of money demand in developing countries have been conducted in recent years. Let m^d denote real money balances; a general expression that captures the variables most often used in empirical applications can be written as follows:

$$m^d = m^d(y, i, \pi, \varepsilon^a, \sigma_\pi), \tag{1}$$

where

- y is the **level of transactions** in the economy (measured by either real income or consumption expenditure) and is expected to have a positive effect;

- i, π, and ε^a are, respectively, the domestic nominal rate of interest, the domestic inflation rate, and the rate of depreciation of the nominal exchange rate; these variables represent alternative measures of the **opportunity**

---

[5]Information problems can prevent interest rates in the credit market itself from responding to changes in credit demand or central bank lending rates, as discussed later.

cost of holding money, and are expected to have a negative effect on the demand for real money balances:

- The interest rate captures substitution between domestic *interest-bearing assets* and money holdings;

- the inflation rate captures substitution between *real assets* (such as durable goods and other valuables) and money holdings;

- the rate of depreciation of the nominal exchange rate captures substitution between domestic money and foreign currency, that is, the degree of **dollarization** or **currency substitution**, as discussed earlier.

- σ_π is the variability of inflation, which is often used as a proxy for *macroeconomic instability*; it tends to have a negative effect on holdings of money balances.

Empirical studies of money demand include Choudhry (1995), who focuses on Argentina, Israel, and Mexico. As documented by Agénor and Montiel (1999, chap. 9), all three countries experienced high inflation, large current account imbalances, and drastic devaluations during the sample periods. Choudhry included both the inflation rate and the rate of currency depreciation to measure the opportunity cost of holding domestic money. He found evidence of a stable long-run money demand function in all three cases for both narrow and broad definitions of the money supply. Thus the evidence suggests significant currency substitution during the sample period. However, elasticity estimates indicated that the currency substitution effect, despite being statistically significant, is relatively small compared with the direct effect of inflation on money demand. Other studies include Hoffman and Tahiri (1994) for Morocco, Ghartey (1998) for Ghana, Price (1994) for Indonesia, Thornton (1996) for Mexico, Fielding (1994) for four African countries, Cheong (2003) for Korea, as well as Phylaktis and Taylor (1993) and Feliz and Welch (1997) for several Latin American countries. All of these studies use *cointegration techniques* to distinguish between the short- and long-run determinants of money demand.[6]

Various other variables have also been included as determinants of money demand in empirical studies. These include measures of *financial innovation* and *financial development*. As noted earlier, financial liberalization—interest rate deregulation and greater competition in banking markets, as well as the liberalization of restrictions on cross-border capital flows, as discussed in Chapters 7 and 15—may affect significantly the relation between money demand and its determinants and complicate the conduct of monetary policy, as discussed below.

---

[6] See the appendix to Chapter 9 for a brief description of the methodology.

4.3 Indirect Instruments of Monetary Policy

As indicated earlier, under financial repression central banks use **direct instruments** of monetary policy (such as controls on interest rates, credit ceilings, and directed lending) to regulate the price, quantity, or composition of credit in an attempt to generate the resources that governments cannot obtain through conventional taxation. The evidence suggests, however, that financial repression has often created severe inefficiencies in credit allocation and the financial intermediation process. Moreover, direct instruments tend to lose their effectiveness because agents find ways to circumvent them—by relying, for instance, on informal credit channels (see Agénor and Haque, 1996). As a result, many countries have in the past few years liberalized their financial systems and adopted indirect instruments of monetary management.

Indirect instruments of monetary policy are market based and operate essentially through interest rates. Their main purpose is to affect overall monetary and credit conditions through changes in the supply and demand for liquidity.[7] They include, first, **open-market operations**, which consist of the following elements:

- The direct sale or purchase of financial instruments (treasury bills or central bank paper), generally in the **secondary market** for securities. In countries where financial markets are not sufficiently developed, open-market type operations take place through central bank intervention in **primary markets** for securities. For instance, the central bank may hold regular **auctions** of treasury bills (or central bank credit) and vary the amount offered in order to influence the level of liquid reserves held by commercial banks.[8]

- **Repurchase agreements** (which entail the acquisition of financial instruments by the central bank under a contract stipulating an agreed date and a specified price for the resale of these instruments) and **reverse repurchase agreements** (the sale of financial instruments by the central bank under a contract stipulating an agreed date and a specified price for their repurchase), which are used to alter liquid reserves of commercial banks. In contrast with direct operations, such agreements are aimed at providing *temporary* financing of cash shortages and surpluses, but do not directly influence supply and demand in the instrument used as collateral.[9]

---

[7] For an analysis of the process of transition from direct to indirect instruments of monetary policy in developing countries, see Alexander, Baliño, and Enoch (1995). They emphasize the need to improve in parallel other features of the financial system, including bank supervision and the legal framework—a key issue in the debate on financial liberalization (see Chapter 15).

[8] Feldman and Mehra (1993) provide a general discussion of the applications of auction markets (including auctions of government securities, central bank credit, and foreign exchange) and bidding techniques.

[9] Short-term repurchase and reverse repurchase agreements are also useful instruments for offsetting large shifts in liquidity caused by a surge in capital inflows or sudden outflows, as discussed in Chapter 6.

A second set of indirect instruments consists of **refinance** and **discount facilities** of the central bank, which are short-term lending operations that typically involve rediscounting high-quality financial assets (such as treasury bills). A third set consists of **reserve requirements**, which stipulate that commercial banks must hold a specified part of their assets in the form of reserves at the central bank. Despite their lack of flexibility as a policy instrument, reserve requirements can be an effective, one-off way of mopping up liquidity in the economy, particularly in periods of large capital inflows (see Chapter 7). However, *unremunerated* reserve requirements can be viewed as an implicit tax and may also lead to financial disintermediation.

The use of indirect instruments allows policymakers to exercise *greater flexibility* in implementing monetary policy. As documented for instance by Borio (1997), almost all industrial countries rely now on this type of instruments to control the behavior of monetary aggregates. Repurchase and reverse repurchase agreements, in particular, are often preferred to outright open-market operations because they do not require a liquid secondary market for securities, they have only an indirect impact on the price of the securities that are being temporarily transferred, and they require no link between the maturity date of these securities and that of the transaction (Borio, 1997, p. 40). Indirect instruments (particularly repurchase and reverse repurchase operations) are also becoming more widely used in the more advanced developing countries. In *Brazil*, for instance, the monetary authorities use both outright purchases and sales of treasury bills in the secondary market, as well as repurchase agreements through informal auctions (typically with overnight maturities), as instruments of monetary control. In the *Philippines*, reverse repurchase agreements are used to absorb excess liquid reserves; their maturities range from one week to a month, with a maximum of one year. More generally, as discussed in Chapter 15, the process of financial liberalization has been accompanied by increased reliance on the use of indirect instruments of monetary policy, particularly open-market operations (repurchase and reverse repurchase agreements). In *sub-Saharan Africa*, despite the embryonic nature of secondary markets for government debt in many countries, progress in that area has been notable during the early 1990s (Mehran et al., 1998).

Nevertheless, the transition away from a regime of direct instruments may create a variety of problems. In particular, the conduct of *open-market operations* may lead to two types of difficulties.

- The volume of central bank transactions may be large relative to the total volume of transactions in the secondary market. In such conditions, sales of government securities by the central bank to reduce liquidity may lead to a rise in interest rates on these securities—thereby raising the domestic *debt burden* of the government. Repurchase operations, based on the central bank's own securities, may in this case be preferable.

- A conflict may also arise between monetary management objectives and debt management objectives when monetary policy relies on **primary** market sales of government securities. For instance, the Treasury may be tempted to manipulate auctions in order to keep funding costs below market. More generally, when monetary management relies on primary market sales of government paper, a high frequency of auctions may hamper the development of an active secondary market.

4.4 Credit Rationing

A key feature that distinguishes the credit market from other markets for goods or financial assets is that the interest rate charged by a given bank on a loan contract to a given borrower typically differs from the return the bank *expects* to realize on the loan, which is equal to the product of the contractual interest rate and the *probability* that the borrower will actually repay the loan. Because of **imperfect** or **asymmetric information** between banks and their borrowers— that is, a situation in which borrowers have greater information about their own default risk than do banks—this probability is almost always less than unity. A seminal analysis by Stiglitz and Weiss (1981) showed that in the presence of asymmetric information **credit rationing** may emerge *endogenously*, instead of resulting from government-imposed restrictions.

The key idea that underlies this result is that the probability of repayment may be negatively related to the contractual interest rate; that is, as the interest rate on the loan increases, the probability of repayment may decline. The repayment probability for some borrowers may actually fall by more than the increase in the contractual interest rate if the latter rises beyond a certain level—implying that the **expected return** to the bank on loans to these borrowers may actually diminish as a result of further increases in the contractual rate. Because the bank has no incentive to lend in such conditions, it will stop lending completely to these borrowers—even if they are willing to accept higher contractual interest rates. There is, therefore, credit rationing. This result is one of the key insights of the Stiglitz-Weiss analysis.

The Stiglitz-Weiss model can be described as follows. Consider an economy populated by a bank and a group of borrowers, each of whom has a single, one-period project in which he (or she) can invest. Each project requires a fixed amount of funds, L; in the absence of any endowment, L is also the amount that each borrower must obtain to implement the project.[10] Each borrower i must pledge **collateral** in value $C_i < L$. All agents are risk-neutral profit maximizers.

Assume also that each project i requiring funding has a distribution of *gross payoffs*, $F(R_i, \theta_i)$, where R_i is the project's return (assumed constant across projects) and θ_i a parameter that measures the **riskiness** of the project. All projects yield either R_i (if they succeed) or 0 (if they fail); the borrower cannot, in any case, affect R_i. Although projects differ in risk, they all have the same mean return, R; thus, if p_i denotes the probability that the project yields R_i,

---

[10]The absence of endowment rules out the possibility for the borrower to invest his or her own funds or to raise funds by other means—such as equity issues or promissory notes.

then

$$p_i(\theta_i)R_i + [1 - p_i(\theta_i)] \cdot 0 = R, \tag{2}$$

for all i, where $p_i' < 0$. A higher value of θ is taken to represent an increase in risk. More precisely, an increase in θ captures an increase in the *variance* of the project's return, while leaving its mean constant. Shifts in θ are thus assumed to be *mean preserving*.[11] The assumption $p_i' < 0$ captures the idea that riskier projects are less likely to succeed.

Borrower i receives the fixed amount of loans, L, at the contractual interest rate r and defaults on the loan if the project's return R_i plus the value of the collateral C_i are insufficient to repay the loan (that is, $R_i + C_i < (1+r)L_i$). The bank therefore receives either the full contractual amount $(1+r)L_i$ or the maximum possible, $R_i + C_i$, in case of default. Assuming that lenders face no **collection** or **enforcement costs**—an assumption that will be further discussed below—the return to the bank, is given by the smaller of these two values:

$$\min\{R_i + C_i; (1+r)L\}.$$

Because the project yields a zero return if it fails, the return to the borrower is given by

$$\max\{R_i - (1+r)L; -C_i\}.$$

Stiglitz and Weiss show that for a given contractual interest rate, r, there is a *critical value* of θ, say $\tilde{\theta}$, such that an agent will borrow to invest if, and only if, $\theta > \tilde{\theta}$; that is, the interest rate serves as a **screening device**. They also show that an increase in the interest rate triggers two types of effects:

- an **adverse selection effect** (which translates into a rise in the threshold value $\tilde{\theta}$), resulting from the fact that by increasing the riskiness of the pool of applicants, less risky borrowers drop out of the market; and

- an **adverse incentive effect**, or **moral hazard effect**, which occurs because other borrowers are induced to choose projects for which the probability of default is higher—in turn because riskier projects are associated with higher expected returns. This has a negative effect on the lender's expected profit, which may dominate the positive effect of an increase in the contractual interest rate.[12]

The first result, $\partial\tilde{\theta}/\partial r > 0$, implies that the direct, positive effect of an increase in the contractual interest rate on the bank's expected (mean) rate of return on its loans, ρ (defined as the product of the contractual interest rate and the probability of repayment), may be partly offset by the negative effect due to the increase in the riskiness of the pool of borrowers. If the latter effect indeed

---

[11] See Varian (1992, p. 186) for a simple example of a mean-preserving distribution.

[12] More generally, moral hazard problems in the financial system arise whenever the owners, creditors, and depositors lack either the incentive (for instance, if there is deposit insurance, as discussed in Chapter 15) or the ability (because of poor disclosure requirements) to control the risk-taking activities of banks' managers.

dominates, the mean return to the lender ρ will not be monotonically related to r and credit rationing may occur in equilibrium. Note that the difference between the moral hazard effect and the adverse selection effect is simply that in the former case lenders choose the contractual interest rate to affect the actions of their borrowers (to get them to avoid riskier projects), whereas in the latter they do so to affect the quality of the pool of borrowers (to avoid causing borrowers with less risky projects to leave the market). Otherwise, the reasoning is essentially the same—in each case lenders are trying to channel funds into safer projects.

The above results can be illustrated with the help of Figure 4.4. The northeast panel in the figure shows the demand for loans, L^d, and the supply of loanable funds, L^s, both as functions of the contractual loan rate, r. The demand for loans is depicted, in a standard fashion, as a downward-sloping function of the loan interest rate. By contrast, the supply of funds is taken to be positively related to the loan interest rate *only up to* a certain interest rate level, $\tilde{r}$. As indicated earlier, increases in the interest rate beyond the bank-optimal rate $\tilde{r}$ trigger adverse selection and adverse incentive effects, which, by reducing the expected rate of return to the bank, lead to decreasing amounts of credit offered to borrowers. Thus, the relationship between the interest rate and the supply of loanable funds turns negative, and the value of L^s decreases to the right of $\tilde{r}$. Put differently, the supply curve of loans has a concave shape.

As noted earlier, the expected rate of return to the bank, ρ, is the product of the contractual interest rate and the probability of repayment. Owing to the adverse selection and adverse incentive effects associated with a rise in the interest rate, the repayment probability declines *by more* than the increase in the interest rate beyond the threshold level of the contractual rate, $\tilde{r}$. The relationship between ρ and the contractual rate of interest is thus non-monotonic, as illustrated by curve RR in the southeast panel of Figure 4.4. Moreover, RR has a more pronounced concave shape than L^s.

A higher expected rate of return raises the incentive to lend; there is, therefore, a positive relationship between ρ and the supply of loanable funds, as depicted in the southwest panel of Figure 4.4. The northwest panel shows a 45-degree line mapping of the equilibrium loan amount and the supply curve of loans, L^s. The value of the contractual interest rate that ensures equality between demand and supply of loans is obtained at point A in the northeast panel; however, the **credit-rationing equilibrium** (characterized by an excess demand for loans) occurs at the interest rate $\tilde{r}$, where the expected return to the bank, ρ, is at its maximum level. Again, the market-clearing interest rate is *not optimal* for the bank, because at that level bank profits are less than at $\tilde{r}$. It is also *inefficient*, because borrowers with high repayment probabilities drop out and are replaced by those with high default risk. By contrast, the non-market-clearing rate $\tilde{r}$ is both optimal and efficient, because bank profits are at a maximum level and risky borrowers are rationed out.[13]

---

[13] Stiglitz and Weiss also show that it is possible to have, in a situation in which there are several groups of observationally distinguishable borrowers, complete exclusion of some groups

Thus, under imperfect information, lending rates that are below market-clearing levels can be observed even in competitive credit markets. Such non-market-clearing lending rates reflect an *efficient response* to profit opportunities. The implication of this analysis is that increases in official interest rates, beyond a certain level, can be counterproductive. Even in a situation where there exists an excess demand for loans, and even if there is some degree of competition among banks, borrowers may face limits on their ability to borrow and banks may charge an interest rate below the level that would clear the market. It may be neither optimal nor efficient for the bank to raise interest rates to the market-clearing level, because at that rate the bank's expected profit is less than that achieved at the credit-rationing level, and borrowers with high repayment probabilities tend to drop out and are replaced by those with high default risks.

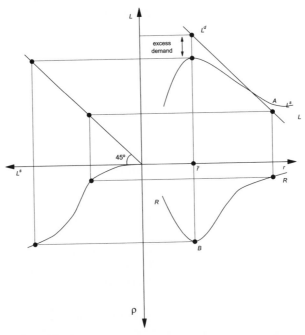

Figure 4.4. Interest rate determination in the Stiglitz-Weiss credit rationing model. Source: Adapted from Stiglitz and Weiss (1981, p. 397).

The Stiglitz-Weiss hypothesis of equilibrium credit rationing is helpful to understand why in some developing countries bank credit is severely rationed (in addition to the distortions in credit allocation induced by government regulations), with bank lending rates unresponsive to excess demand for credit. Kaufman (1996), for instance, used the Stiglitz-Weiss model to explain some of the aspects of Argentina's economic crisis of 1995-96 (see Chapter 8). Kaufman suggested that the degree of riskiness of projects (as measured by the coefficient

---

from the credit market—despite the fact that the expected productivity of their investments may be higher than those of the groups that actually receive credit.

θ above) may be *endogenously* related to the level of economic activity—which itself depends on the amount of loans available. This link creates a channel through which credit rationing can be exacerbated and may display persistence over time.

The Stiglitz-Weiss model suffers, however, from several limitations. The first is the assumption that lenders are completely unable to assess the degree of riskiness of potential borrowers. If interest rate increases do indeed lead to riskier projects being funded, banks have incentives to invest in **screening technologies** in order to acquire information about the risk characteristics of their customers. This is particularly plausible in a *dynamic* context, even though screening may be hampered somewhat by high-risk borrowers attempting to mimic low-risk borrowers.

A second issue relates to the assumption that all projects have the same mean return [see Equation (2)]. As shown by De Meza and Webb (1987), if on the contrary projects differ in expected return, rationing would not emerge in equilibrium. The reasoning is as follows. Suppose in the above framework that all projects have the same payoff R if successful, but that they differ in terms of their probability of success, which is assumed to be private information for the borrowers.

As before, suppose that unsuccessful projects have a zero return. Thus, projects with a higher probability of success have a higher mean expected return than those with a lower success probability. Banks prefer to lend to borrowers whose projects have a higher probability of success; but now, as the contractual lending rate is increased, it is projects with the lower success probabilities that are withdrawn from the market. Hence, there is a "favorable" selection effect, as opposed to an adverse selection effect, and the quality of the pool of loan applications actually increases as a result of the rise in interest rates. The relationship between the expected return to the bank, ρ, and the contractual rate is now monotonic; banks gain from *both* the higher debt repayments on successful projects and the improvement in the quality of potential applications as r rises. They will therefore set the contractual interest rate at the market-clearing level and rationing will not occur.

A third issue relates to the role of collateral, C, in the model. Wette (1983) showed that adverse selection effects similar to those emphasized by Stiglitz and Weiss may result if lenders attempt to raise mean returns by increasing the collateral required from borrowers. Higher collateral requirements may thus reduce the bank's expected profit and lead to equilibrium rationing. Bester (1985) argued, however, that if lenders can vary *both* collateral requirements and the contractual loan rate to screen loan applicants, the possibility of a rationing equilibrium disappears. The reason is that by manipulating both instruments, lenders can induce borrowers (whose willingness to pledge collateral tends to vary inversely with the degree of riskiness of their project) to *self-select* themselves into low- and high-risk groups. In a subsequent contribution, Stiglitz and Weiss (1992) argued that even if banks are able to manipulate interest rates and collateral, rationing may still emerge in equilibrium if borrowers are subject to **decreasing absolute risk aversion**. In such conditions, collateral and the degree of riskiness of borrowers will be positively correlated.[14]

A fourth, and perhaps more important, issue relates to the role of **collection** and **verification costs**. As noted earlier, such costs are absent in the Stiglitz-Weiss model. The asymmetry of information is purely *ex ante*: although projects differ in their distributions of return before implementation, lenders can observe (costlessly) *actual* (or *ex post*) outcomes. An alternative approach, developed notably by S. Williamson (1986), is to assume that projects are *ex ante* identical but only borrowers are able to observe the project returns costlessly. This *ex post* asymmetry of information also gives rise to a moral hazard problem, in the sense that borrowers have an incentive to declare a project return that is low enough to default on the loan, although the return may in fact be higher than needed to pay off the debt. To prevent this, lenders must commit themselves to incur *ex post* **monitoring** and **enforcement costs** to (*a*) verify the outcome of all the projects for which borrowers declare themselves bankrupt, and (*b*) legally enforce the terms of the loan contract (notably seizure of collateral) if the borrower chooses to default. As shown by S. Williamson (1986), in such conditions it is the positive relationship between the contractual interest rate and *expected* monitoring and enforcement costs that may generate a nonmonotonic relationship between the expected return to the lender ρ and the contractual lending rate r, thereby creating the possibility of credit rationing. The reason is that the higher the contractual lending rate, the more likely is any borrower to genuinely suffer bankruptcy and the more likely is the the lender to incur monitoring and enforcement costs. By raising contractual interest rates to the market-clearing level, the bank might incur a rise in these costs that may offset the direct benefits of the higher price on credit and actually lead to a *reduction* in expected returns to lending, as in the Stiglitz-Weiss framework. Again, because banks have no incentive to lend in such conditions, credit rationing will emerge in equilibrium. This alternative approach to credit market imperfections may be particularly relevant for developing countries, where enforcement of loan contracts can be very difficult due to the severe weaknesses in the legal system. It has been extended in a variety of directions and has proved fruitful to analyze, in particular, the role of the credit market in the transmission of external shocks to an economy's supply side (See Agénor and Aizenman (1999)).

4.5   The Transmission of Monetary Policy

In part because of the shift toward more flexible exchange rate regimes (as discussed in the next chapter), quantitative research on the transmission mechanism of monetary policy in developing countries has attracted renewed attention

---

[14]See the appendix to Chapter 2 for a definition of decreasing absolute risk aversion. It should be noted, however, that Stiglitz and Weiss (1992) considered only the case of a fixed collateral value. The extent to which their results carry over to the case in which the value of the collateral itself depends on whether the project succeeds or not *ex post* is not entirely clear.

in recent years. This section provides a review of the main channels through which monetary policy decisions are transmitted to aggregate demand and the supply side in a small open developing economy.[15] The discussion throughout focuses on the case of a country with a sufficiently developed financial system, where the operational target for monetary policy is an **overnight interest rate**, which the central bank controls by affecting commercial banks' liquid reserves through repurchase and reverse repurchase agreements (see the previous discussion).

If the pass-through of policy rates to short-term market interest rates is complete and rapid, then a representative market rate (for instance, the overnight interbank rate, the money market rate, or the three-month treasury bill rate) can be conveniently regarded as the policy instrument itself. In developing countries, however, due to various types of market imperfections, the pass-through is not always complete and may not occur very quickly. In addition, the level of short-term interest rates affects only a fraction of the financing of aggregate spending by households and firms. The private sector may also finance expenditure through retained earnings (as is often the case in developing countries) and, to a lesser extent, at longer-term rates through the banking system or the capital market. The cost of borrowing from these sources is only indirectly influenced by short-term interest rates.

The impact of changes in policy rates on the cost of finance thus depends on the degree of substitutability between different forms of finance, the pass-through of changes in these rates to short-term market interest rates (including bank lending and deposit rates), and the impact of changes in short-term interest rates on long-term rates. In turn, the degree of substitutability between different forms of finance depends on the structure and functioning of financial markets.

In practice, the relative importance of these different channels is not well known in developing countries. There is limited evidence on the extent to which policy rates affect short-term market interest rates, including bank lending rates. Borio and Fritz (1995) studied the response of interest rates on short-term bank loans to changes in policy-controlled rates in industrial countries, whereas Cottarelli and Kourelis (1994) focused on a broader sample that included several developing countries. They argued that stickiness in bank lending rates in any given economy depends on the country's financial structure, which in turn depends on factors such as the degree of development of financial markets, the degree of competition within the banking system, and the ownership structure of financial intermediaries. For instance, interest rate changes may entail significant *adjustment costs*. If the elasticity of the demand for bank loans is relatively low (as can be expected in the short term), the existence of these costs may lead to significant inertia in lending rates.

In general, the lower the degree of competition in the credit market is, the more limited alternative source of finance are, the lower the elasticity of the

---

[15] For a more detailed overview of the transmission channels of monetary policy, see Mishkin (1996, 1998) for industrial countries and Kamin, Turner and Van't dack (1995) for developing countries. Borio (1997) discusses the actual process of monetary policy implementation in several industrial countries.

demand for loans is, the more limited will be the response of lending rates to changes in policy and money market rates. Moreover, the more transitory the change in the money market rate is perceived to be, the less responsive will lending rates be. In developing countries where the banking system is dominated by state-owned banks, political pressure (or sheer inefficiency) may also delay adjustments in lending rates. The response of the money market rate itself may be limited as well if the interbank market for loans is not sufficiently competitive or if the adjustment in the policy rate is perceived as temporary in nature. Cottarelli and Kourelis (1994) estimated the degree of stickiness of bank lending rates in 31 industrial and developing countries, using both time-series and cross-country regressions. They found that the degree of inertia in lending rates varies considerably across countries in the short run; the impact effect (the contemporaneous change in the lending rate associated with a change in the money market rate, viewed as a proxy for the policy rate) is close to unity in some cases, zero in others.

This result clearly reflects the heterogeneity of the loan market across countries. For instance, in some countries rates charged to large companies ("prime" rates) respond faster than those applicable to smaller businesses or individuals. Another factor is the possible large differences in the degree of responsiveness of *funding costs* to market rates. Indeed, Cottarelli and Kourelis found that the degree of stickiness depends significantly on the structure of the financial system, as measured by factors such as barriers to competition, and the extent of state intervention in the banking system.

This finding is important for assessing the role and impact of monetary policy; it indicates that the transmission mechanism of monetary policy decisions may be enhanced by structural measures aimed at strengthening competition among financial intermediaries and promoting greater efficiency through private ownership (see Chapter 15). Nevertheless, it will be assumed in what follows that changes in the policy interest rate are transmitted to a significant extent (even after some delay) to market interest rates.

A synoptic view of the transmission channels of monetary policy for a small open developing country operating under fixed and flexible exchange rates is provided in Figures 4.5 and 4.6. These channels can be classified into **interest rate effects**, nominal **exchange rate effects** (under a flexible exchange rate regime), **asset price** and **balance sheet effects**, **credit availability effects**, and **expectations effects**.

Balance sheet effects and credit availability effects are often referred to as the **credit channel** (see Bernanke and Gertler, 1995). This essentially dwells on the view that the functioning of the credit market is hindered by asymmetries in information between borrowers and lenders, as discussed earlier. As a result of these credit market imperfections, banks play a key role in the transmission process of monetary policy. In a dynamic perspective, there are also, of course, *feedback effects* from the behavior of key macroeconomic aggregates (output and inflation) to policy decisions and expectations, which are shown as dotted lines in the figures.

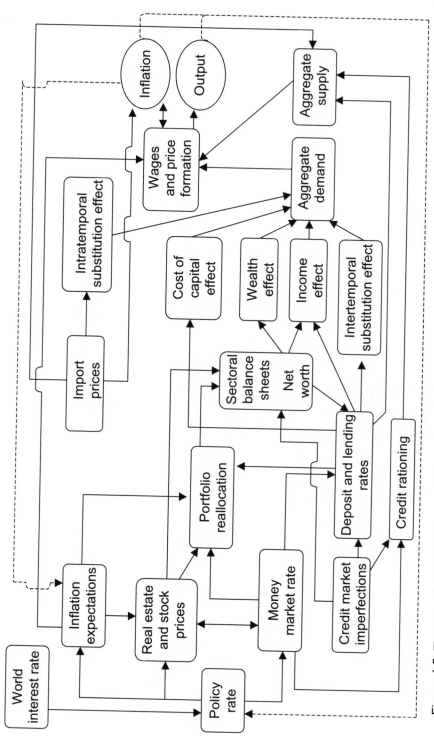

Figure 4.5. The transmission process of monetary policy under fixed exchange rates.

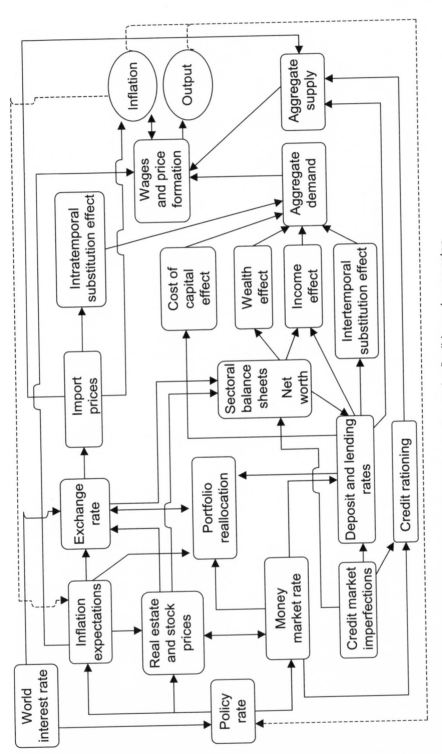

Figure 4.6. The transmission process of monetary policy under flexible exchange rates.

4.5.1   Interest Rate Effects

Changes in interest rates initiated by monetary policy decisions affect both aggregate demand and aggregate supply. With respect to aggregate demand, four channels of transmission can be distinguished:

- A **cost of capital effect**, on purchases of durable consumption goods, investment in housing, business investment on plant and equipment, as well as inventories. If firms must borrow to finance capital formation, a rise in real bank lending rates induced by an increase in nominal policy rates would raise the cost of capital and tend to lower investment and output.[16]

- A **wealth effect** on household expenditure. An increase in official rates that translates into higher interest rates on domestic financial assets (such as bank deposits) would tend to increase the demand for these assets and reduce *ceteris paribus* the demand for other assets, such as real estate. This, in turn, would tend to lower their price and reduce the value of these assets in households' portfolios. The net effect of this portfolio reallocation on private expenditure would depend on whether real wealth rises or falls.[17]

- An **income effect**, which can be positive or negative depending on whether households are net debtors or creditors toward the banking system. If households are net creditors, an increase in official interest rates that translates into higher bank (deposit) rates would lead to higher disposable income and higher spending. The greater the degree of substitutability between bank deposits and central bank loans as sources of funds for commercial banks is, the larger will be the effect of changes in official rates on deposit rates.

- An **intertemporal substitution effect** on consumer spending; a rise in real interest rates, for instance, lowers the present value of expected future income flows (including labor income), thereby reducing present consumption and lowering current output (see Chapter 2). Because a rise in interest rates also exerts a positive income effect (as noted previously) which tends to offset the adverse effect of intertemporal substitution on spending, the net impact on private expenditure is in general ambiguous.[18]

---

[16]Note that the user cost of capital, as defined in Chapter 2, accounts for the opportunity cost of investment, assuming that resources (in the form of retained earnings, for instance) are readily available to do so. If firms must borrow from banks to finance investment, the cost of capital is essentially the real bank lending rate.

[17]As discussed subsequently, the impact of a change in short-term real interest rates on spending and wealth will depend, of course, also on the expected duration of the change. To the extent that these effects are spread over time, they may be amplified by induced multiplier and accelerator effects.

[18]In addition, it should be noted that if the positive effect on private disposable income results from higher interest payments on government debt, the impact on private expenditure would be mitigated if individuals expect an increase in the deficit due to an increase in interest

To the extent that the rise in interest rates leads households to lower the demand for leisure and increase their supply of labor, a temporary rise in *potential* output may also result.

With respect to aggregate supply, there is a **production cost effect**, which may be particularly important in developing countries. If firms are net debtors with respect to the banking system, higher lending rates induced by higher refinancing costs for the banks will raise production costs. This would be the case, for instance, if firms must pay their workers prior to the sale of output and therefore borrow from the banking system. In such conditions, the effective cost of labor would include the lending rate (see Chapter 7).

The net, direct effect of changes in policy interest rates on output will thus in general depend on how much the contractionary supply-side effect is mitigated or exacerbated by aggregate demand effects.[19] If, for instance, the wealth effect is expansionary but takes some time to operate, an increase in interest rates may well induce a recession. In addition, the effect on inflation would depend on the process of wage and price formation. If wages and prices are sticky in the short run, and therefore do not respond rapidly to excess supply of labor and excess demand for goods and services, changes in policy interest rates will affect inflation only gradually, thereby increasing the risk of destabilizing effects.

4.5.2   Exchange Rate Effects

Under flexible exchange rates, policy-induced changes in the nominal exchange rate are an important transmission channel through which monetary policy affects both inflation and output (see Figure 4.6). Typically, for a given expected inflation rate, the immediate impact of an increase in domestic interest rates is an inflow of capital and an appreciation of the nominal exchange rate. In turn, the exchange rate has both direct and indirect macroeconomic effects:

- A direct effect on inflation via the *cost of imported goods*. This is usually the most rapid transmission channel from monetary policy to inflation in an open economy. An appreciation of the real exchange rate, for instance, lowers the domestic price of imports and has a direct downward effect on the price of import-competing goods. The pass-through of lower import prices to final demand prices, by contrast, may be spread over time.[20]

- An indirect effect on inflation via changes in *aggregate demand* and *expenditure*, themselves resulting from movements in the relative prices of tradable and nontradable goods. This is an **intratemporal substitution**

---

rates to be fully compensated by higher taxes in the future, as would be the case under (partial) Ricardian equivalence.

[19] As discussed later, under flexible exchange rates there are also indirect effects associated with changes in the nominal exchange rate.

[20] Lower consumer prices will tend to moderate wage demands and would thus also affect inflation gradually. For estimates of the pass-through of exchange rate changes into domestic inflation, see Agénor (2002a), Gagnon and Ihrig (2002), Goldfajn and Werlang (2000), Holmes (2002), McCarthy (1999), Schmidt-Hebbel and Werner (2002), and Ho and McCauley (2003).

effect.[21] For instance, an increase in the relative price of nontradable goods (a real appreciation) would tend to lower demand for these goods and put downward pressure on inflation. However, in countries that are net importers of capital goods (as is often the case in the developing world), the real appreciation may also stimulate private investment by lowering the domestic price of investment goods. This transmission channel may eventually have an impact on inflation and economic activity, although it may occur more gradually.

- A direct supply-side effect resulting from the impact of changes in the domestic-currency price of *imported inputs* (such as oil) on the production of tradables and nontradables. A depreciation of the nominal exchange rate, for instance, raises the domestic-currency price of imported intermediate products and may lead to a contraction in domestic output in both sectors if perfect substitutes for these inputs do not exist at home.

4.5.3   Asset Prices and Balance Sheet Effects

As noted earlier, changes in asset prices—mainly the price of land and the exchange rate, given the relatively low degree of development in equity markets in developing countries—can have large effects on the value of assets such as housing and holdings of foreign bonds, which in turn may affect spending by changing the perceived value of wealth.[22] For instance, exchange rate movements induced by policy changes in interest rates may have large valuation effects, depending on the structure of indebtedness of agents in the economy. A depreciation would reduce wealth in a country with a net foreign-currency liability position. The balance sheet effects of exchange rates fluctuations can in fact be far more significant than their effect on consumption expenditure and aggregate demand induced by perceived changes in wealth.

Changes in the value of real assets tend to occur early in the transmission process, both because asset prices tend to adjust faster than prices of goods and services, and because asset prices are inherently more sensitive to changes in interest rates and to changes in expectations; assets are generally held for the purpose of substituting consumption across periods or as hedges against anticipated movements in prices. As a result, they may carry considerable information about how agents perceive future economic developments. Asset prices, however, are also influenced by a variety of factors other than monetary policy in the short run. This raises the issue of whether, and to what extent, monetary policy should respond to short-term changes in asset prices—a particularly important topic in the context of industrial countries, where changes in equity prices tend to have large wealth effects (see Cecchetti, Genberg, Lipsky, and Wadhwani, 2000).

---

[21]Of course, the intratemporal substitution effect could result from a change in import prices measured in foreign currency (as opposed to a change in the nominal exchange rate), as shown in Figure 4.5.

[22]This wealth effect may also influence the ability to borrow and the willingness to lend.

Deteriorating balance sheets operate primarily on spending and aggregate demand in the short run, although in the longer run they may affect aggregate supply as well by inhibiting capital formation. Significant feedback and magnification effects are also likely. First, there may be feedback to asset prices, as declining spending and income, together with forced asset sales, lead to further decreases in asset values. Second, declining sales and employment imply continuing weakening of cash flows and, hence, further declines in spending. Alternatively, the magnification effect may operate through the external finance premium.

Net Worth and the Finance Premium

The **external finance premium** can be defined as the wedge between the cost of funds raised externally (the bank lending rate for most firms in developing countries) and the opportunity cost of internal funds (or retained earnings), which could be an interest rate on government bonds, the bank deposit rate, or the foreign rate of interest. This premium depends inversely on the borrower's **collateralizable net worth** relative to the obligation on the loan. Collateralizable net worth includes net financial assets and also any tangible physical assets (such as buildings or machinery) that may be pledged as collateral.

The Financial Accelerator

Because the premium for external funds affects the overall price of funds that the borrower faces (the lending rate), credit market imperfections affect consumption and investment decisions—regardless of whether rationing prevails or not (see again Figures 4.5 and 4.6). Changes in firms' net worth have an additional impact on the financing premium and hence the cost of capital. Rising asset prices, for instance, will improve firms' balance sheets, inducing banks to charge a lower finance premium on loans, hence lowering the cost of capital and stimulating investment. Thus balance sheet effects are propagated through a **financial accelerator** mechanism.

Models incorporating a mechanism of this type include Greenwald and Stiglitz (1993), Bernanke and Gertler (1989), Bernanke, Gertler, and Gilchrist (2000), Gertler (1992), Kiyotaki and Moore (1997), and Aghion, Banerjee, and Piketty (1999). In all of these models, procyclical movements in borrowers' financial positions lead to countercyclical movements of the premium for external funds. The net effect is a financial accelerator, which amplifies the cyclical fluctuations in borrowers' spending.[23] For instance, in the model of Bernanke and Gertler (1989), the agency costs of financial intermediation drive a wedge between the internal cost of funds and the cost of external (monitored) financing. Single-period exogenous shocks, by increasing these agency costs, can lead to declines in

---

[23]Fountas and Papagapitos (2001) provided indirect evidence that the financial accelerator matters for predicting output fluctuations in some European countries (France, Germany, Italy, and the United Kingdom) by using, as a measure of the external (finance) premium, the interest rate spread between corporate bonds and government securities.

investment and therefore in future output. Similarly, in the model of Bernanke, Gertler, and Gilchrist (2000), the effects of asset price changes are transmitted to a very significant extent through their effects on the balance sheets of households, firms, and financial intermediaries. Firms or households may use assets they hold as collateral when borrowing, in order to mitigate information and incentive problems that would otherwise limit their ability to obatin credit extension. Under such circumstances, a decline in asset values (for instance, a fall in home equity values) reduces available collateral and impedes potential borrowers' access to credit. Financial intermediaries, which must maintain an adequate ratio of capital to assets, can be deterred from lending, or induced to shift the composition of loans away from bank-dependent sectors (such as small business) by declines in the values of the assets they hold. In Kiyotaki and Moore (1997), collateralizable net worth also plays a key role in lowering the costs of lending; and by restricting the aggregate supply of credit, negative shocks to net worth also lower production. In their model land is used as collateral for working capital loans (which are intermediate inputs in the production process). A negative shock to the economy that lowers output will also result in a fall in the price of land, thereby reducing the value of collateral and magnifying the initial negative shock as banks restrict their loans for working capital.

The financial accelerator mechanism is more applicable to *small borrowers* because it is this group that may face a particularly high premium for external funds. There are a variety of reasons why this may be true. One possibility is that bankruptcy costs are proportionately greater for small borrowers, due to the existence of fixed costs in evaluation and monitoring.[24] Another possibility is that large borrowers have proportionately greater collateralizable net worth.[25] Moreover, unobservable idiosyncratic risk, which is a key determinant of the severity of the incentive problem, is likely to be proportionately greater for small borrowers, who are on average less well diversified.

The propagation mechanism that characterizes the financial accelerator is useful to understand why exchange rate devaluations can be contractionary in some of the developing countries that have experienced financial crises. A devaluation (or a sharp initial depreciation) of the currency has a direct effect on the balance sheets of firms. If firms are indebted in foreign currency, a devaluation raises the debt burden measured in domestic-currency terms. At the same time, because assets are typically denominated in domestic currency, there is no concomitant increase in the value of firms' assets. A devaluation therefore leads to a deterioration in firms' balance sheets and a decline in net worth, which, in turn, worsens the adverse selection problem because effective collateral has fallen, thereby providing less incentives to lend.[26] In turn, the

---

[24] See Gertler and Gilchrist (1994) for an example of how scale economies in bankruptcy costs can introduce a "small firm" effect.

[25] In Gertler (1992), net worth is a function of the borrower's discounted future earnings. To the extent that small firms have shorter expected horizons, their net worth is likely smaller in proportion to their current investments.

[26] The decline in net worth may also increase moral hazard incentives for firms to take on

decline in lending tends to affect negatively investment and economic activity. A case in point is the East Asia crisis (see Chapter 8). As a result of large interest differentials between domestic- and foreign-currency loans, banks and corporations in these countries accumulated a significant volume of unhedged foreign-currency denominated debt in the early 1990s. The large devaluations that occurred in the region after the Thai baht crisis of mid-1997 raised the domestic-currency value of these debts, weakening bank and corporate balance sheets, and inducing a collapse in credit and output.

4.5.4   Credit Availability Effects

The bank lending channel of monetary policy dwells on the fact that bank loans and funds raised in capital markets are not perfect substitutes. Certain types of borrowers, particularly small firms, lack or do not have access to capital markets and rely on banks, which have the capability to monitor and screen these borrowers' activities. But this capability is imperfect—borrowers have more information on their ability to repay a loan than do banks, as noted previously—so that banks also use nonprice rationing devices, such as security checks, credit risk evaluation, and collateral requirements, as part of the loan approval process. When monetary policy is tightened and bank liquid reserves fall, the supply of bank lending is reduced partly through these devices, because banks internalize the fact that raising lending rates alone may have adverse selection effects, as illustrated earlier by the Stiglitz-Weiss model. Borrowers who are dependent on banks will then be particularly affected. The balance sheet effects described earlier can reinforce this result, through their effect on collateralizable net worth.

Evidence on the credit channel of monetary policy in European countries is provided by Favero, Giavazzi, and Flabbi (1999), in a study based on micro data on banks' balance sheets. They found evidence suggesting that "small" and less liquid banks indeed tend to react more significantly than "larger" and more liquid banks to a squeeze in liquidity initiated by the central bank. There is also some evidence that credit constraints may be significant for some categories of borrowers (in particular, small and medium-sized firms). Along the same line, Huang (2003) found that, in the United Kingdom, small firms bear most of the reductions in the supply of banks, and because they do not have many alternatives to bank finance, they suffer more from monetary tightening than big firms. For developing countries, few studies are available; Disyatat and Vongsinsirikul (2003) provide evidence on the importance of the credit channel in Thailand. More generally, however, it has not yet conclusively been established (at the very least for developing countries) that credit availability effects are an important channel for monetary policy. In practice, there are important identification problems that arise in doing so. In particular, it is empirically difficult to distinguish between tight credit conditions caused by, on the one hand, a reduction in bank liquid reserves, and, on the other, by a decline in the

---

greater risk because they have less to lose if the loans do not perform.

creditworthiness of potential borrowers—that is, to discriminate between the bank lending channel and balance sheet effects.

4.5.5   The Role of Expectations

Changes in expectations (most importantly of inflation and movements in nominal exchange rates) may magnify the transmission channels described earlier, depending on the *degree of credibility* of the policy change and its *perceived duration*. For instance, a rise in interest rates that is perceived to be only temporary (due mostly to transitory pressures on the nominal exchange rate) may have no effect on private behavior. Similarly, an interest rate hike may have no impact on private spending because activity is low and unemployment is high, and agents expect the monetary authorities to eventually reverse their course of action to avoid compounding the effects of a recession on employment (see Chapter 6). But to the extent that a policy change is perceived as credible, its impact on the economy may be magnified by a change in expectations. Again, suppose that higher interest rates do indeed lower investment and consumption, and that agents understand that the fall in aggregate demand will eventually reduce inflation. With forward-looking price expectations, the policy change may lead to an immediate fall in inflation, as a result for instance of lower wage demands in today's labor contracts.

4.6   Monetary Policy: Inflation Targeting

The renewed impetus to efforts aimed at understanding and quantifying the transmission process of monetary policy in developing countries has in part been related to the transition to flexible exchange rates and the adoption of inflation targeting as a monetary policy framework in several of these countries.[27] In turn, the decision to target inflation directly was related to the growing recognition that inflation, as discussed by Driffill, Mizon, and Ulph (1990), entails severe social and economic costs—such as price distortions, lower savings and investment (which inhibits growth), and increased propensity to engage in hedging activities and capital flight—and that the use of monetary policy to achieve other goals (higher output or lower unemployment) may conflict with price stability.

   The first step in understanding the nature of an inflation-targeting framework is to analyze the relation between explicit policy goals, policy instruments, and preferences of the central bank, which affect the form of its reaction function. This section begins by examining the link between inflation targets and the nominal interest rate, viewed as the main instrument of monetary policy, when the central bank is concerned only about deviations of actual inflation

---

[27]This section draws to a large extent on Agénor (2002a), who provides a detailed discussion of the process leading to the adoption of inflation targeting in developing countries in recent years.

from its target value.[28] The analysis is then extended to consider the case in which both output and inflation enter the central bank's loss function. In both cases the analysis focuses on a closed economy; open-economy considerations are discussed later on.

4.6.1 Strict Inflation Targeting

Following Svensson (1997) and Agénor (2002a), consider a closed economy producing one (composite) good. The economy's structure is characterized by the following two equations, where all parameters are defined as positive:

$$\pi_t - \pi_{t-1} = \alpha_1 y_{t-1} + \varepsilon_t, \tag{3}$$

$$y_t = \beta_1 y_{t-1} - \beta_2 (i_{t-1} - \pi_{t-1}) + \eta_t, \quad \beta_1 < 1, \tag{4}$$

where $\pi_t \equiv p_t - p_{t-1}$ is the inflation rate at t (with p_t denoting the logarithm of the price level), y_t the **output gap** (defined as the logarithm of actual to potential output), and i_t the nominal interest rate, taken to be under the direct control of the central bank. ε_t and η_t are independently and identically distributed (i.i.d.) random shocks. The output gap can be viewed as measuring the cyclical component of output.

Equation (3) indicates that changes in inflation are positively related to the output gap, with a lag of one period. Equation (4) relates the output gap positively to its value in the previous period and negatively to the *ex post* real interest rate, again with a one-period lag. The appendix to this chapter considers the case in which both output and inflation expectations are **forward-looking**.

In this model, policy actions (changes in the nominal interest rate) affect output with a one-period lag and, as implied by (3), inflation with a two-period lag.[29] The lag between a change in the policy instrument and inflation will be referred to in what follows as the **control lag** or **control horizon**.

The assumption that the central bank directly controls the interest rate that affects aggregate demand warrants some discussion. In principle, what affects private consumption and investment decisions is the *cost of borrowing*, that is, given the characteristics of the financial structure that prevails in many developing countries, the bank lending rate. In general, bank lending rates depend on banks' funding costs, a key component of which being either the

---

[28] In what follows the term "instrument" is used in a broad sense to refer both to the operational target of monetary policy (such as the money market rate, as discussed earlier) and to the actual instrument(s) available to achieve this target (such as the interest rate on repurchase agreements).

[29] Note that introducing a forward-looking element in equation (3) would imply that monetary policy has some effect on contemporaneous inflation; this would make the solution of the model more complicated but would not affect some of the key results discussed below. See the appendix to this chapter, which dwells on Clarida, Galí, and Gertler (1999), for a discussion. Nevertheless, it should be kept in mind that the assumption of model-consistent expectations also has drawbacks; in particular, it downplays the role of model uncertainty—which, as discussed later, may be very important in practice.

deposit rate or the money market rate. In turn, both of these rates depend on the cost of short-term financing from the central bank.[30] Thus, to the extent that bank lending rates (and other market rates) respond quickly and in a stable manner to changes in policy rates, the assumption that the central bank controls directly the cost of borrowing faced by private agents can be viewed simply as a convenient shortcut.[31]

The central bank's period-by-period policy **loss function**, L_t, is taken for the moment to be a function only of inflation and is given by

$$L_t = \frac{(\pi_t - \tilde{\pi})^2}{2}, \tag{5}$$

where $\tilde{\pi}$ is the inflation target. An alternative assumption would be to assume that the the price target is specified in terms of the *price level*, as opposed to the inflation rate. The conventional view is that a price level target entails, on the one hand, a major benefit in that it reduces uncertainty about the future level of prices. On the other, if the economy is subject to (supply) shocks that alter the *equilibrium* price level, attempts to disinflate and lower the price level back to its pre-shock value may generate significant real costs and increased volatility in inflation and output.[32] In practice, however, all inflation-targeting central banks have opted to define their price objective in terms of the inflation rate.

The central bank's policy objective in period t is to choose a sequence of current and future interest rates $\{i_h\}_{h=t}^{\infty}$ so as to minimize, subject to (3) and (4), the expected sum of discounted squared deviations of actual inflation from its target value, U_t:

$$\min U_t = \mathrm{E}_t \sum_{h=t}^{\infty} \delta^{h-t} L_h = \mathrm{E}_t \left\{ \sum_{h=t}^{\infty} \delta^{h-t} \frac{(\pi_h - \tilde{\pi})^2}{2} \right\}, \qquad 0 < \delta < 1, \tag{6}$$

where δ denotes a discount factor and E_t the expectations operator conditional upon the central bank's information set at period t.

This optimization problem can be recast in a simpler form, which allows a more intuitive derivation of the optimal path of the policy instrument. To begin with, writing Equation (3) for $t + 2$ yields

$$\pi_{t+2} = \pi_{t+1} + \alpha_1 y_{t+1} + \varepsilon_{t+2}.$$

---

[30] Bank lending rates also depend on the perceived probability of default of potential borrowers and, in an open economy, the cost of funding on world capital markets. See Agénor and Aizenman (1998) for a model that captures these features of bank behavior.

[31] See Agénor (2002a) for a discussion of the empirical evidence. Note that if aggregate demand depends on longer-term interest rates, a similar effect would arise. This is because longer-term rates are driven in part by expected future movements in short-term interest rates, which are, in turn, influenced by current and expected future policy decisions of the central bank.

[32] This argument, however, has been challenged by Svensson (1999), who showed that under certain conditions price-level targeting may deliver a more favorable trade-off between inflation and output variability than does inflation targeting.

Updating (4) in a similar manner and substituting the result in the above expression for y_{t+1} yields

$$\pi_{t+2} = (\pi_t + \alpha_1 y_t + \varepsilon_{t+1}) + \alpha_1[\beta_1 y_t - \beta_2(i_t - \pi_t) + \eta_{t+1}] + \varepsilon_{t+2},$$

that is

$$\pi_{t+2} = a_1\pi_t + a_2 y_t - a_3 i_t + z_{t+2}, \tag{7}$$

where

$$z_{t+2} = \varepsilon_{t+2} + \varepsilon_{t+1} + \alpha_1\eta_{t+1},$$

$$a_1 = 1 + \alpha_1\beta_2, \quad a_2 = \alpha_1(1 + \beta_1), \quad a_3 = \alpha_1\beta_2.$$

Equation (7) indicates that inflation in period $t + 2$ can be expressed in terms of period t variables and shocks occurring at periods $t + 1$ and $t + 2$. Put differently, it implies that the interest rate set at period t by the central bank will affect inflation in year $t + 2$ and beyond, but not in years t and $t + 1$; similarly, the interest rate set in period $t + 1$ will affect inflation in periods $t + 3$ and beyond, but not in periods $t + 1$ and $t + 2$; and so on. The solution to the optimization problem described earlier can therefore be viewed as consisting of setting the nominal interest rate in period t (and then $t + 1$, $t + 2$, ...) so that the expected inflation in period $t + 2$ (and then $t + 3$, $t + 4$, ...) is equal to the target rate. Thus, because from (7) π_{t+2} is affected only by i_t and not by i_{t+1}, i_{t+2},..., the problem of minimizing the objective function U_t in (6) boils down to a sequence of one-period problems,

$$\min_{i_t} \frac{\delta^2}{2} E_t(\pi_{t+2} - \tilde{\pi})^2 + x_t, \tag{8}$$

subject to (7), with

$$x_t = E_t \left\{ \sum_{h=t+1}^{\infty} \min_{i_h} \delta^{h-t} E_t \left[\frac{(\pi_{h+2} - \tilde{\pi})^2}{2} \right] \right\}.$$

Because x_t in (8) does not depend on i_t, the central bank's optimization problem at period t consists simply of minimizing the expected, discounted squared value of $(\pi_{t+2} - \tilde{\pi})$ with respect to i_t:

$$\min_{i_t} \frac{\delta^2}{2} E_t(\pi_{t+2} - \tilde{\pi})^2. \tag{9}$$

From standard statistical results,[33]

$$E_t(\pi_{t+2} - \tilde{\pi})^2 = (\pi_{t+2|t} - \tilde{\pi})^2 + V_t(\pi_{t+2}), \tag{10}$$

where $\pi_{t+2|t} = E_t\pi_{t+2}$. This expression indicates that the central bank's optimization problem can be equivalently viewed as minimizing the sum of expected future squared deviations of inflation from target (the squared bias in

---

[33] This standard result is $E(x - x^*)^2 = (Ex - x^*)^2 + V(x)$, that is, the expected squared value of a random variable equals the square of the bias plus the conditional variance.

future inflation, $(\pi_{t+2|t} - \tilde{\pi})^2)$ and the variability of future inflation conditional on information available at t, $V_t(\pi_{t+2})$. Because $V_t(\pi_{t+2})$ is independent of the policy choice, the problem is thus simply to minimize the squared bias in future inflation.

Using (7), the first-order condition of problem (9) is given by

$$\delta^2 E_t \left\{ (\pi_{t+2} - \tilde{\pi}) \frac{\partial \pi_{t+2}}{\partial i_t} \right\} = -\delta^2 a_3 (\pi_{t+2|t} - \tilde{\pi}) = 0,$$

implying that

$$\pi_{t+2|t} = \tilde{\pi}. \tag{11}$$

Equation (11) shows that, given the two-period control lag, the optimal policy for the central bank is to set the nominal interest rate such that the expected rate of inflation for period $t + 2$ (relative to period $t + 1$) based on information available at period t be equal to the inflation target.

To derive explicitly the interest rate rule, note that from (7), because $E_t z_{t+2} = 0$, $\pi_{t+2|t}$ is given by

$$\pi_{t+2|t} = a_1 \pi_t + a_2 y_t - a_3 i_t, \tag{12}$$

which implies that, given the definition of a_1,

$$i_t = \frac{-(\pi_{t+2|t} - \pi_t) + \alpha_1 \beta_2 \pi_t + a_2 y_t}{a_3}.$$

This result shows that because interest rate changes affect inflation with a lag, monetary policy must be conducted in part on the basis of *forecasts*; the larger the amount by which the current inflation rate (which is predetermined up to a random shock, as implied by (3)) exceeds the forecast, the higher the interest rate. The fact that the inflation forecast can be considered an *intermediate policy target* is the reason why Svensson (1997) refers to inflation targeting as inflation *forecast* targeting.

The inflation forecast can readily be related to current, observable variables. To do so requires setting expression (12) equal to $\tilde{\pi}$ and solving for i_t:

$$i_t = \frac{-\tilde{\pi} + a_1 \pi_t + a_2 y_t}{a_3}.$$

Given the definitions of the a_h coefficients given above, this expression can be rewritten to give the following explicit form of the central bank's **reaction function**:

$$i_t = \pi_t + b_1 (\pi_t - \tilde{\pi}) + b_2 y_t, \tag{13}$$

where

$$b_1 = \frac{1}{\alpha_1 \beta_2}, \quad b_2 = \frac{1 + \beta_1}{\beta_2}.$$

Equation (13) indicates that it is optimal for the central bank to adjust the nominal interest rate upward to reflect current inflation (to a full extent), the difference between current and desired inflation rates, as well as increases in the output gap. As emphasized by Svensson (1997, p. 1119), the reason why current inflation appears in the optimal policy rule is *not* because it is a policy target but rather because it helps (together with the contemporaneous output gap) predict *future* inflation, as implied by (12).

In equilibrium, *actual* inflation in year $t + 2$ will deviate from the inflation forecast $\pi_{t+2|t}$ and the inflation target, $\tilde{\pi}$, only by the forecast error z_{t+2}, due to shocks occurring within the control lag, after the central bank has set the interest rate to its optimal value:

$$\pi_{t+2} = \pi_{t+2|t} + z_{t+2},$$

or

$$\pi_{t+2} - \tilde{\pi} = z_{t+2}. \tag{14}$$

The fact that even by following an optimal instrument-setting rule the central bank cannot prevent deviations from the inflation target due to shocks occurring within the control lag, is important in assessing the performance of inflation-targeting regimes in practice.

4.6.2 Policy Trade-offs and Flexible Inflation Targeting

Consider now the case in which the central bank is concerned not only about inflation but also about the size of the output gap. Specifically, suppose that the instantaneous policy loss function (5) is now given by

$$L_t = \frac{(\pi_t - \tilde{\pi})^2}{2} + \frac{\lambda y_t^2}{2}, \quad \lambda > 0, \tag{15}$$

where λ measures the relative weight attached to cyclical movements in output. The expected sum of discounted policy losses is now given by

$$U_t = \mathrm{E}_t \left\{ \sum_{h=t}^{\infty} \delta^{h-t} \left[\frac{(\pi_h - \tilde{\pi})^2 + \lambda y_h^2}{2} \right] \right\}. \tag{16}$$

Deriving the optimal interest rate rule when both inflation and output enter the objective function is now more involved. Essentially, the problem of minimizing (16) cannot be "broken down" into a series of one-period problems because of the dependence of current inflation on lagged output and the dependence of current output on lagged inflation. Using more advanced techniques, Svensson (1997, pp. 1140-43) showed that the first-order condition for minimizing (16) with respect to the nominal interest rate can be written as

$$\pi_{t+2|t} = \tilde{\pi} - \frac{\lambda}{\delta \alpha_1 \kappa} y_{t+1|t}, \tag{17}$$

where $\kappa > 0$ is given by

$$\kappa = \frac{1}{2} \left\{ 1 - \mu + \sqrt{(1 + \mu)^2 + 4\lambda / \alpha_1^2} \right\},$$

and

$$\mu = \frac{\lambda(1-\delta)}{\delta\alpha_1^2}.$$

Condition (17) implies that the inflation forecast $\pi_{t+2|t}$ will be equal to the inflation target $\tilde{\pi}$ only if the one-period ahead expected output gap is zero ($y_{t+1|t} = 0$). In general, as long as $\lambda > 0$, $\pi_{t+2|t}$ will exceed (fall short of) $\tilde{\pi}$ if the output gap is negative (positive). The reason is that if the output gap is expected to be negative for instance at $t+1$, the central bank will attempt to mitigate the fall in activity by lowering interest rates at t (given the one-period lag); this policy will therefore lead to higher inflation than otherwise at $t+2$, thereby raising the inflation forecast made at t for $t+2$. The higher λ is, the larger the impact of the expected output gap on the inflation forecast will be.

An alternative formulation of the optimality condition (17) can be obtained by noting that, from (3), with $E_t\varepsilon_{t+1} = 0$,

$$y_{t+1|t} = \frac{\pi_{t+2|t} - \pi_{t+1|t}}{\alpha_1}.$$

Substituting this result in (17) and rearranging terms yields

$$\pi_{t+2|t} - \tilde{\pi} = c(\pi_{t+1|t} - \tilde{\pi}), \qquad 0 \le c = \frac{\lambda}{\lambda + \delta\alpha_1^2\kappa} < 1. \tag{18}$$

This expression indicates that the deviation of the two-year inflation forecast from the inflation target is proportional to the deviation of the one-year forecast from the target; when $\lambda = 0$, then $c = 0$ and the previous result (Equation (11)) holds. The implication of this analysis is that, when cyclical movements in output matter for the central bank, it is optimal to adjust *gradually* the inflation forecast to the inflation target. By doing so, the central bank reduces fluctuations in output. As shown by Svensson (1997, pp. 1143-44), the higher the weight on output in the policy loss function is (the higher λ is), the more gradual the adjustment process will be (the larger c will be).

The interest rate rule can be derived explicitly by noting that, from (3) and (4),

$$\pi_{t+1|t} = \pi_t + \alpha_1 y_t, \qquad \pi_{t+2|t} = \pi_{t+1|t} + \alpha_1 y_{t+1|t},$$

$$y_{t+1|t} = \beta_1 y_t - \beta_2(i_t - \pi_t).$$

Substituting the first and third expressions in the second yields

$$\pi_{t+2|t} = \pi_t + \alpha_1(1 + \beta_1)y_t - \alpha_1\beta_2(i_t - \pi_t). \tag{19}$$

Equating (18) and (19) yield

$$i_t = \pi_t + b_1'(\pi_t - \tilde{\pi}) + b_2' y_t, \tag{20}$$

where

$$b_1' = \frac{1-c}{\alpha_1\beta_2}, \qquad b_2' = \frac{1-c+\beta_1}{\beta_2},$$

from which it can be verified that $b'_1 = b_1$ and $b'_2 = b_2$ when $\lambda = 0$ (and thus $c = 0$). Equation (20) indicates that the optimal instrument rule requires, as before, the nominal interest rate to respond positively to current inflation and the output gap, as well as the excess of current inflation over the target. However, an important difference between reaction functions (13) and (20) is that the coefficients of (20) are *smaller*, due to the positive weight attached to cyclical movements in output in the policy loss function. This more gradual response implies that the (expected) length of adjustment of current inflation to its target value, following a disturbance, will take longer than the minimum two periods given by the control horizon. The time it takes for expected inflation to return to target following a (permanent) unexpected shock is known as the **implicit targeting horizon** or simply as the **target horizon**. Naturally, the length of the implicit target horizon is positively related not only to the magnitude of the shock and its degree of persistence but also to the relative importance of output fluctuations in the central bank's objective function. It also depends on the *origin* of the shock—whether it is, for instance, an aggregate demand shock or a supply-side shock. This is because the transmission lag of policy adjustments depends in general on the type of shocks that the economy is subject to and on the channels through which these shocks influence the behavior of private agents.

A simple illustration of the concepts of control lag and target horizon is provided in Figure 4.7. Suppose that initially the rate of inflation is on target at $\tilde{\pi}$ and the output gap is zero. From (13) and (20), under either form of inflation targeting, the initial nominal interest rate is thus equal to $\tilde{\pi}$. Assume now that the economy is subject to an unexpected random shock to output at $t = 0$ (a sudden increase in, say, government spending) that leads to an increase in the inflation rate to $\pi_0 > \tilde{\pi}$. As implied by the reaction function under both strict and flexible inflation targeting, the central bank will immediately raise the nominal interest rate; but, because inflation is predetermined (monetary policy affects inflation with a two-period lag), actual inflation remains at π_0 in period $t = 1$.

The behavior of inflation for $t > 1$ depends on the value of λ. If $\lambda = 0$ (the central bank attaches no weight to movements in the output gap), inflation will return to its target value at exactly the control horizon, that is, in period $t = 2$. The nominal interest rate increases initially to $i_0 = \pi_0 + b_1(\pi_0 - \tilde{\pi})$ and returns to $\tilde{\pi}$ at period $t = 1$ and beyond; the output gap does not change at $t = 0$ but falls to $y_1 < 0$ in period $t = 1$, before returning to its initial value of 0 at period $t = 2$ and beyond. By contrast, with $\lambda > 0$, convergence of inflation to its target value may take considerably longer; the figure assumes, to fix ideas, that convergence occurs at $t = 8$.[34] The interest rate increases initially to $i'_0 = \pi_0 + b'_1(\pi_0 - \tilde{\pi}) < i_0$, which limits the fall in the output gap to $y'_1 < y_1$.

Although falling over time, the interest rate remains above its equilibrium value $\tilde{\pi}$ until period $t = 6$ (given the two-period control lag) whereas the output

---

[34]Strictly speaking, convergence of actual inflation to target when $\lambda > 0$ occurs only asymptotically, for $t \to \infty$.

gap remains negative until period $t = 7$. In general, the higher λ is, the flatter
will be the path of inflation, interest rates, and the output gap for $t > 1$. Thus,
the central bank's output stabilization goal has a crucial effect not only on the
determination of short-term interest rates but also on the *speed* at which the
inflation rate adjusts toward its target after a shock.

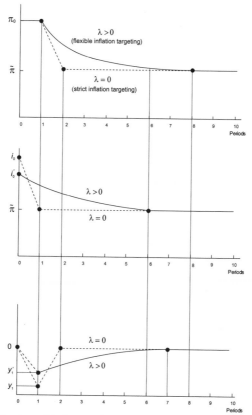

Figure 4.7. Behavior of inflation following a shock (in percent).

4.6.3   Comparison with Intermediate Target Strategies

Price stability as a medium- to long-term goal can be achieved, in principle,
not only by focusing directly on the final objective itself, inflation, but also by
adopting either a pegged nominal exchange rate or a monetary target as an
intermediate goal. This section reviews these two alternative frameworks for
monetary policy and compares them with inflation targeting.

Monetary vs. Inflation Targeting

Monetary targeting presumes the existence of a stable relationship between
one or more monetary aggregates and the general level of prices. When this

is the case, monetary policy can be directed at a particular rate of growth in the monetary aggregate (the intermediate objective) compatible with low inflation. Specifically, monetary targeting requires adequate knowledge of the parameters characterizing the demand for money. In an economy undergoing rapid financial liberalization, however, these parameters (notably the interest elasticity of money demand) may be *highly unstable*.[35] In such conditions money ceases to be a good predictor of future inflation; that is, the relation between the intermediate target and the final .objective becomes unstable. Similarly, in a context of disinflation, the demand for money may be subject to large and unpredictable shifts, because credibility of the program is lacking (see Chapter 6); as a consequence, the information content of money for future inflation will be very low. Both arguments suggest that relying on monetary aggregates can be potentially risky.

Exchange Rate vs. Inflation Targeting

Many countries in the developing world have viewed pegging their nominal exchange rate to a stable low-inflation foreign currency as a means to achieve domestic price stability, through a "disciplining mechanism" with two dimensions. First, to the extent that higher domestic inflation, relative to foreign inflation, results in a real exchange rate appreciation, the demand for domestic goods would fall and induce a cyclical downswing that would put downward pressure on domestic prices. Second, to the extent that wage- and price-setting decisions anticipate the consequences of wage and price increases being too large, they would make higher domestic inflation less likely to occur in the first place. In a sense, countries that target their exchange rates (against an anchor currency) attempt to "borrow" the foreign country's monetary policy credibility.

However, the experience of recent years has shown that in a world of high capital mobility and unstable capital movements, conventional pegged exchange rates have proved fragile (see Chapter 8). Most importantly, simply pegging the exchange rate did not prove to be a substitute for maintaining monetary stability and credibility at home. In fact, recent experiences suggest that exchange rate pegs can be sustainable only when they are credible, and credibility is to a large extent determined by domestic macroeconomic policies. To the extent that the adoption of inflation targeting signals a clear commitment to macroeconomic stability and a freely floating exchange rate, it may lead to a more stable currency.

It is worth emphasizing that a key characteristic of inflation-targeting regimes compared with other approaches to controlling inflation is that the adjustment of policy instruments relies on a systematic assessment of *future* (rather than past or current) inflation, as opposed to an arbitrary forecast. Under this regime, the central bank must explicitly quantify an inflation target and establish precise mechanisms to achieve this target. This implies that there is an important

---

[35] See for instance Pradhan and Subramanian (2003) for a study of how financial deregulation and innovation affected the empirical stability of the demand for money in India.

operational difference between an inflation-targeting regime, on the one hand, and monetary and exchange rate targeting, on the other.[36] Changes in monetary policy instruments usually affect the money supply and the exchange rate faster than inflation itself; as discussed earlier, this leads to the existence of a control lag and a reaction function that relates the policy instrument to an inflation forecast. The implication is that the credibility of an inflation-targeting regime depends not on achieving a publicly observable, intermediate target that is viewed as a leading indicator of future inflation (as is the case under monetary or exchange rate targeting), but rather on the credibility of a *promise* to reach the inflation target in the future. This in turn depends on whether the public believes that the central bank will stick resolutely to the objective of price stability. Credibility and reputation of the monetary authorities (as discussed in Chapter 6) may therefore play an even more crucial role in dampening inflation expectations under inflation targeting. At the same time, because performance can only be observed *ex post*, the need for transparency and accountability becomes more acute under this regime, in order to help the public assess the stance of monetary policy and determine whether deviations from target are due to unpredictable shocks rather than to policy mistakes.

4.6.4 Requirements for Inflation Targeting

There are three basic requirements for implementing an inflation-targeting regime:

- A high degree of **central bank independence** (see Chapter 6). The central bank must be endowed by the political authorities with a clear mandate to pursue the objective of price stability and most importantly a large degree of independence in the *conduct* of monetary policy—namely, in choosing the instruments necessary to achieve the target rate of inflation. This implies, in particular, the ability to resist political pressures to stimulate the economy during recessions and the absence of **fiscal dominance**, that is, a situation in which fiscal policy considerations play an overwhelming role in monetary policy decisions.

- The absence of an **implicit nominal exchange rate target**. When limiting (or preventing) nominal exchange rate movements is a policy target (perhaps because of a quick *pass-through effect*, as discussed in Chapter 5), it will be difficult for the central bank to convey to the public, in a credible and transparent manner, its intention to give priority to price stability over other objectives of monetary policy. Private agents would then be likely to discount heavily public pronouncements, and the lack of credibility will translate into higher inflation expectations.

---

[36]Note also that there is an important difference between exchange rate targeting and monetary targeting, in the sense that while it is possible to deviate temporarily from monetary targets if the underlying relationships appear to have changed, it is generally not possible to depart temporarily from an exchange rate peg (or a target band, for that matter) without there being a loss of credibility and possibly a currency crisis.

- Increased **transparency** and **accountability**. By making the central bank publicly accountable for its decisions, both increased transparency and increased accountability raise the incentive to achieve the inflation target—thereby enhancing the public's confidence in the ability of the monetary authorities to do so. And by exposing to public scrutiny the process through which monetary policy decisions are taken, they may lead to improved decision making by the central bank and therefore enhance its credibility.

In practice, such conditions have proved difficult to satisfy in many developing countries. For instance, accountability in an inflation-targeting framework is related to the difficulty of assessing performance only on the basis of inflation outcomes. The reason is that (as indicated earlier) there is a lag between policy actions and their impact on the economy; it is thus possible (or tempting) for the central bank to blame "unforeseen" or totally unpredictable events for inadequate performance, instead of taking responsibility for policy mistakes. To mitigate this risk, the central bank in inflation-targeting countries is usually required to justify its policy decisions and explain publicly differences between actual outcomes and inflation targets. Specifically, accountability has been promoted by providing public explanations (in the form of a public letter from the governor of the central bank to the government) of the reason(s) why the rate of inflation deviated from the target by more than a given percentage on either side, how long these deviations are expected to persist, and what policies the central bank intends to implement to bring inflation back to target.

Establishing an *operational* framework for implementing an inflation-targeting regime also requires a number of steps. The monetary authorities must

- specify a price index to target (such as the headline consumer price index, the GDP deflator, or a measure of **core inflation**), establish an explicit quantitative target for inflation (either as a point or as a band), and choose a *time horizon* over which the target will be achieved;[37]

- determine under what circumstances **escape clauses** or **exemptions** to the inflation target are warranted (such as large changes in world oil prices, or weather-related spikes in food prices), taking into account the potential *credibility loss* that the discretionary nature of such clauses and exemptions may involve;

- set up a methodology for *inflation forecasting* that uses indicators (or formal quantitative models) containing information or predictions on future inflation. This, in turn, requires a good understanding of the monetary transmission mechanism (as described earlier), and estimates of the time lag between the adjustment of monetary instruments and their effect on output and prices;

---

[37] See Wynne (1999) for a discussion of alternative ways of measuring core inflation.

- decide ways through which they can convince the public that achieving the inflation target takes precedence over all other objectives of monetary policy and devise a **forward-looking operating procedure** in which monetary policy instruments are adjusted (in line with the assessment of future inflation) to achieve the target.

Some of these operational requirements are far from trivial (see Agénor, 2002a) and may prevent rapid adoption of inflation targeting in some countries. Indeed, so far only a few of these countries have adopted inflation targeting as a monetary policy framework (see Schmidt-Hebbel and Tapia, 2002). They include Chile (which started to announce inflation targets in the early 1990s), Brazil (since June 1999, following the real crisis discussed in Chapter 8), South Africa (since February 2000), Thailand (since May 2000), and the Philippines (since January 2002).

In the Philippines, for instance, official reasons for the shift are evidence of instability in the relation between money and prices (resulting from financial deregulation), a growing focus on the goal of price stability, and the need to promote transparency. The overall consumer price index is used to measure inflation, although the central bank also calculates a measure of "core inflation." The target has a two-year horizon and is set jointly by the government and the central bank. Escape clauses can be triggered as a result of excessive volatility in the prices of unprocessed food (due to natural shocks affecting food supply) or the price of oil products, changes in government policy that directly affect prices (such as changes in the tax structure, incentives, and subsidies), and other natural shocks. The central bank publishes a quarterly inflation report; if actual inflation deviates from the target level, the governor of the central bank must explain in an open letter to the president the reason why it happened and what measures will be adopted to bring inflation back to target.

Several recent studies have attempted to provide an early assessment of the performance of inflation-targeting regimes. In one study, Johnson (2002) focused on the experience during the 1990s of five industrial countries (Australia, Canada, New Zealand, Sweden, and the United Kingdom) and a control group of six countries (France, Germany, Italy, the Netherlands, Japan, and the United States). He found that after the announcement of targets the *level* of expected inflation fell in all inflation-targeting countries (relative to the control group), but that neither the *variability* of expected inflation nor the *average absolute forecast error* changed significantly (controlling for the level and variability of past inflation).

In another study, Corbo, Landerretche, and Schmidt-Hebbel (2001) used a sample of 15 industrial and developing countries and data covering the 1990s. They used two control groups, "potential" targeters and nontargeters. They found that inflation-targeting countries were successful in meeting their targets, and that the **output sacrifice ratio** (the percentage fall in output resulting from a one-percentage-point reduction in inflation) was lower after the adoption of inflation targeting in these countries compared with other groups. Inflation persistence also declined strongly in inflation-targeting countries—a phenomenon that is consistent with the view that inflation targeting has played a role in strengthening the effect of forward-looking expectations on inflation, hence weakening the degree of inflation inertia (see Chapter 6). However, a broader assessment of the performance of inflation targeting in developing countries remains to be done, given that many of these countries have only recently adopted such a framework for monetary policy.

4.7   Monetary Policy in a Dollarized Economy

Dollarization refers to a situation in which a foreign currency is used as a unit of account, store of value, and a medium of exchange, concurrently with the domestic currency (Giovannini and Turtelboom, 1994).[38] A common measure of the degree of dollarization, the share of foreign-currency deposits in total domestic bank deposits, shows that dollarization has been at times pervasive in many countries, including Egypt and Turkey.[39] Moreover, dollarization seems to be associated with periods of economic instability and high inflation; Figure 4.8, which displays a variety of macroeconomic indicators for Turkey during the period 1987-2001, shows indeed that dollarization grew significantly during the period, in line with the increase in inflation rates. Dollarization can thus be viewed as an endogenous response by domestic agents attempting to avoid the **inflation tax** and capital losses on assets denominated in domestic currency (see Chapter 3).[40] At the same time, of course, it responds to *portfolio diversification* needs—which may exist even at relatively low inflation rates.

4.7.1   Persistence of Dollarization

The evidence also suggests that, even after sharp reductions in inflation, dollarization can remain relatively high. This is what apparently occurred in countries like Bolivia and Peru (see Savastano, 1996) and Argentina (Kamin and Ericsson, 2003).Several explanations have been offered to explain the persistence of a high degree of dollarization in a low-inflation environment. Guidotti and Rodríguez (1992) suggested that **transaction costs** incurred in switching from one currency to the other—justified by the assumption of economies of scale in the use of a single currency—imply that there is a range of inflation rates within which the degree of dollarization is likely to remain unchanged. Put differently, a reversal of dollarization after stabilization would tend to be slow if there are

---

[38] Calvo and Végh (1996) suggested the use of the term "dollarization" (or "asset substitution") to refer to the use of foreign currency as a store of value, and the term "currency substitution" to refer to a stage where, beyond dollarization, foreign money is also used as a medium of exchange or a unit of account. In practice, however, the terms currency substitution and dollarization are often used interchangeably.

[39] Using foreign-currency deposits to measure the degree of dollarization can seriously underestimate the pervasiveness of the problem; if the *risk of confiscation* of foreign-currency assets held in domestic banks is high, agents may hold their cash outside banks, literally "under the mattress." Foreign-currency deposits may also be held abroad.

[40] In some countries, like Brazil, macroeconomic instability has led not to dollarization but rather to the development of a variety of indexed financial assets.

no significant benefits associated with switching back to the domestic currency as a means of payment.

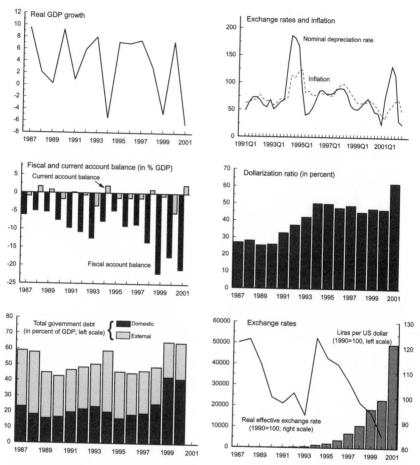

Figure 4.8. Turkey: Macroeconomic indicators, 1987-2001 (in percent per annum, unless otherwise indicated). Dollarization ratio is share of foreign currency deposits in total bank deposits. Note that in the panel on exchange rates, a rise represents a depreciation. Source: International Monetary Fund and official estimates.

Along the same line, Uribe (1997*b*) argued that transactions costs incurred in switching currencies may themselves depend on the degree of dollarization in the economy; this may occur because, from an individual's point of view, it may be more costly to switch from the domestic currency to the foreign currency if the incidence of dollarization is low. Reducing the propensity to hold foreign-currency balances therefore requires a very low inflation rate to induce individuals to regain skills in the use of the domestic currency. Kamin and Ericsson (2003) found evidence of this "ratchet" effect on money demand in the case of Argentina, a country where inflation declined rapidly during the early 1990s (see Chapter 8).

An alternative explanation of the persistence of dollarization that does not rely on the existence of transactions costs was offered by McNelis and Rojas-Suárez (1996). They emphasized the fact that the degree of dollarization depends not only on expectations of inflation and exchange rate depreciation, but also on the **risk** (or **volatility**) associated with these variables. Whereas during periods of high inflation the risk component tends to be dominated by the level of inflation itself, in periods of low inflation (or *post-stabilization* episodes) risk factors become more important. Everything else equal, increased risk (or volatility) of prices and exchange rates would induce asset holders to switch away from domestic currency and toward foreign currency. Thus, reducing the degree of dollarization requires not only a reduction in the levels of expected inflation and exchange rate depreciation, but also a reduction in the volatility of these variables. The empirical evidence for Bolivia and Peru (countries where, as indicated earlier, the degree of dollarization remained high even after inflation stabilization was achieved) provided by McNelis and Rojas-Suárez supports the view that **depreciation risk** is indeed an important factor in explaining the persistence of dollarization.

4.7.2   Implications of Dollarization

Dollarization may be beneficial to the extent that it leads to an increase in the flow of funds into the banking system, thereby promoting financial intermediation. Moreover, a low degree of dollarization (as measured by the share of foreign-currency accounts in domestic banks) may merely reflect "normal" portfolio diversification needs. However, high degrees of dollarization may significantly complicate the conduct of monetary and exchange rate policies.

First, dollarization involves a **loss of seigniorage revenue**, because the demand for domestic base money is lower than otherwise. This loss in revenue can lead to increased monetary financing and thus high inflation—which may in turn lead to a further reduction in holdings of domestic money balances (see Chapter 6). The outcome may be an **inflationary spiral**, with **full dollarization** as the ultimate outcome. Evidence provided by Edwards and Magendzo (2003), however, suggests that in fact inflation has been significantly lower in dollarized economies compared with nondollarized countries.

Second, dollarization affects the choice of assets that should be included in the *monetary aggregates* that are used by policymakers as indicators of monetary conditions or target variables. Aggregates including foreign currency cash and deposits are relevant if the use of foreign currency as a medium of exchange tends to distort the link between domestic money and inflation. There may be less reason to consider comprehensive measures if dollarization represents *asset diversification*, with no implications for aggregate demand and inflation.[41] In any case, recent empirical evidence for Latin America suggests that the greater

---

[41] The difficulty of interpreting the behavior of monetary aggregates including and excluding foreign-currency deposits is one of the reasons that has driven some countries to adopt inflation targeting, as discussed earlier.

the degree of currency substitution, the more sensitive a country's monetary aggregates are likely to be to sudden shifts in interest rates and exchange rates (see Prock, Soydemir, and Abugri, 2003).

Third, dollarization (in the form of foreign-currency deposits in domestic banks) essentially index bank deposits to the exchange rate. Because the domestic-currency value of foreign-currency deposits rises proportionately with exchange rate depreciation, monetary aggregates tend to *accommodate inflationary pressures.* To the extent that loans extended against foreign-currency deposits are denominated in domestic currency, the ensuing **currency mismatch** may weaken banks' balance sheets if the exchange rate depreciates and if lending rates cannot be adjusted to absorb the loss on loan principal measured in foreign-currency terms. These weaknesses can force the central bank to intervene, and the increase in liquidity can exacerbate inflationary pressures.

Fourth, dollarization affects the choice of an *exchange rate regime* (as discussed in Chapter 5), because it may lead to short-term foreign-currency liabilities that are high relative to foreign exchange reserves of the banking system. In such conditions, an increase in foreign-currency deposits held in domestic banks may increase the vulnerability of the banking system and the official exchange rate to abrupt reversals in market sentiment and capital flows (see Chapters 7 and 8). At the same time, dollarization may entail a high degree of volatility in a floating exchange rate, as a result of large and unpredictable shifts in the use of domestic and foreign currencies for transaction purposes.

Although the foregoing discussion suggests that dollarization may have adverse consequences for macroeconomic management, outright restrictions aimed at reducing holdings of foreign assets are likely to prove ineffective due to the ability of asset holders to evade them through informal currency markets (see Agénor and Haque, 1996). In addition, as argued by Chang and Velasco (2002), if policymakers have low credibility and dollarization can serve as an effective discipline device, it can actually improve welfare. More importantly, high degrees of dollarization are generally *not a cause,* but rather a *symptom,* of underlying financial imbalances and weaknesses. Thus, measures aimed at reducing dollarization—such as, for instance, the creation of an interest rate wedge in favor of domestic-currency deposits, the imposition of higher reserve requirement rates on foreign-currency deposits, or legal and institutional measures to foster the use of domestic currency over foreign means of payment in domestic transactions, particularly those involving the public sector—are unlikely to be effective in an unstable macroeconomic environment.

4.8   Summary

- **Financial repression** refers to a situation in which the financial system is subject to *ceilings on interest rates, quantitative controls* and *selective credit allocation, high minimum reserve requirements* on bank deposits, *direct control* by the state of part of the banking system, and *forced allo-*

cation of loans to the public sector by private commercial banks.

- The source of financial repression is often the inability of governments to raise taxes through conventional means.

- Financial repression can yield substantial revenue to the government, notably through the *implicit tax* on financial intermediation generated by high reserve requirement rates. However, it also entails *severe inefficiencies* which tend to restrict the development of formal financial intermediation (and to encourage **informal modes of financial intermediation**), increase the spread between deposit and lending rates, and reduce saving and investment.

- Banks remain the dominant channel of financial intermediation in the developing world, despite the expansion of capital markets observed in recent years. In many countries, banks still account for more than 80 percent of financial intermediation. With few exceptions, *equity markets* play a relatively insignificant role. Market capitalization is usually much lower than in industrial countries, and turnover is generally low.

- A key function of banks as financial intermediaries is to alleviate the imperfections arising from the **maturity mismatch** between relatively liquid deposits and longer-term loans. Weaknesses in the legal and supervisory structure, however, make banks vulnerable to abrupt macroeconomic shocks and complicate the conduct of monetary policy.

- The **demand for money** plays an important macroeconomic role. In addition to conventional transactions and opportunity cost variables, the substitution with real assets and foreign currency may be important. The degree of *inflation variability* and the pace of *financial innovation* may also play a significant role.

- *Direct instruments* of monetary policy aim at regulating the price, quantity, or composition of domestic credit. However, they tend to generate inefficiencies in the intermediation process. *Indirect instruments*, by contrast, encourage intermediation through the formal financial system. They also permit greater flexibility in implementing monetary policy.

- **Credit rationing** in the Stiglitz-Weiss model arises *endogenously*, as a result of **imperfect** or **asymmetric information** between lenders and borrowers.

- Whereas moderate increases in the contractual lending rate tend to increase bank loans in the model, rate increases beyond a certain level tend to lower the amount of credit by affecting adversely the *quality* of the pool of borrowers as a result of two effects: safe—that is, the more creditworthy—borrowers are discouraged and drop out of the market (the **adverse selection effect**); and other borrowers are induced to choose projects with a higher probability of default, because riskier projects are associated with higher expected profits (the **adverse incentive** or **moral hazard effect**).

- Thus, even in the presence of an *excess demand for loans*, the optimal response is to limit lending to potential borrowers and to charge an interest rate that maximizes the bank's expected profits, net of the cost of default. Raising the interest rate beyond this level would only lower the bank's overall return.

- A key implication of the existence of credit-market frictions is that cash flows and the conditions of balance sheets are important determinants of agents' ability to borrow and lend.

- The transmission channels of monetary policy can be classified into **interest rate effects, exchange rate effects, asset price** and **balance sheet effects, credit availability effects**, and **expectations effects**. Balance sheet effects and credit availability effects are often referred to as the **credit channel**, according to which the functioning of the credit market is hindered by asymmetries in information. As a result, banks play a key role in the transmission process of monetary policy.

- The impact of changes in policy interest rates depends on the financial structure, the substitutability between different forms of finance, the pass-through of changes in market interest rates to bank lending and deposit rates, and the impact of changes in short-term interest rates on long-term interest rates.

- Changes in interest rates affect aggregate demand through a **cost of capital effect** (which affects investment), a **wealth effect** (through the impact of changes in official rates on asset prices), an **income effect** (which can be positive or negative depending on whether households are net debtors or creditors toward the banking system), and an **intertemporal substitution effect** (because changes in real interest rates affect the present value of expected future income flows). Changes in interest rates also affect the supply side, by raising **production costs** for firms that are net debtors with respect to the banking system.

- Exchange rate changes induced by a change in policy interest rates have a direct effect on inflation via the **cost of imported goods**, an indirect effect on inflation via changes in aggregate demand and expenditure induced by an **intratemporal substitution effect**, and a direct supply-side effect operating through changes in the production of tradables and nontradables resulting from changes in the domestic-currency price of **imported inputs**.

- Changes in **asset prices** (such as land prices and the exchange rate) can have large effects on financial wealth. These changes affect activity not only through wealth effects on spending, but also through changes in borrowers' **net worth**, which in turn is inversely related to the **external finance premium** that firms face, defined as the wedge between the costs of funds raised externally (often the bank lending rate) and the opportunity cost of internal funds.

• **Balance sheet effects** operate through changes in firms' **collateralizable net worth**. When policy interest rates rise, and asset prices decline, the net worth of firms is reduced, and this tends to reduce the value of their collateral for loans. Increases in interest rates also reduce the cash flow of firms, thereby increasing their risk of default. Lenders therefore lend less and investment declines.

• Balance sheet effects can be propagated by the **financial accelerator mechanism**. The key idea underlying the financial accelerator mechanism is that economic disturbances influence borrowers' net worth, and hence the premium for external funds, in a way that likely enhances the overall impact of the shock. Procyclical movements in borrowers' financial positions lead to countercyclical movements of the premium for external funds; as a result, output and employment fluctuations over the course of the business cycle are exacerbated through the credit market.

• Changes in **expectations** may magnify the transmission channels indicated above, depending on the *degree of credibility* of the policy change and its *perceived duration*. With forward-looking price expectations, policy changes may lead to an immediate fall in inflation.

• **Inflation targeting** is a policy regime in which the monetary authorities' goal is to achieve directly an inflation objective. It has gained appeal in recent years as an operational framework for monetary policy, in part because of the growing difficulties associated with **monetary targeting** (because of instability in money demand) as well as **exchange rate targeting** (due to higher capital mobility and unstable short-term capital flows).

• If interest rate changes affect inflation with a lag, monetary policy must be conducted in part on the basis of an inflation forecast, which can be considered an *intermediate policy target*.

• Under **strict inflation targeting**, the authorities are concerned only with deviations of actual inflation from target, whereas under **flexible inflation targeting** deviations of output from trend (and possibly other variables) matter also. In both cases, the optimal rule relates the policy interest rate to current inflation, the difference between current and desired inflation rates, and increases in the output gap; under flexible targeting, however, adjustment of interest rates tends to be *more gradual*.

• Basic requirements for implementing an inflation-targeting regime include a high degree of **central bank independence** (particularly in the *con-*

duct of monetary policy), the absence of an **implicit nominal exchange rate target**, and increased **transparency** and **accountability**.

- To establish an *operational* framework for implementing a regime of inflation targeting, monetary authorities must specify a price index to target (such as the headline consumer price index, the GDP deflator, or a measure of **core inflation**); establish an explicit quantitative target for inflation (either as a point or as a band); choose a *time horizon* over which the target will be achieved; determine under what circumstances **escape clauses** or **exemptions** to the inflation target are warranted; set up a methodology for *inflation forecasting*; and devise a **forward-looking operating procedure** through which monetary policy instruments are adjusted to achieve the target.

- **Dollarization** (or **currency substitution**) refers to a situation in which a foreign currency is used, concurrently with the domestic currency, as a unit of account, store of value, and a medium of exchange. It reflects *portfolio diversification* needs and, in high-inflation countries, an attempt by domestic agents to protect themselves from bouts of inflation and capital losses on assets denominated in domestic-currency terms.

- Dollarization tends to be *asymmetric*—it tends to remain high even after a reduction in inflation. This may reflect either large **transaction costs** incurred in switching from one currency to the other—costs that may themselves depend on the initial degree of dollarization. Alternatively, it may reflect the persistence of **depreciation risk**.

- A high degree of dollarization may complicate the conduct of monetary policy and exchange rate management because it involves a loss of **seigniorage revenue**, affects the definition of monetary aggregates, distorts the link between money and inflation, and increases the vulnerability of commercial banks to *currency depreciation*.

- Outright restrictions aimed at reducing the degree of dollarization are unlikely to be effective because agents would typically *evade* them through informal currency markets. High degrees of dollarization are generally a *symptom* rather than *a cause* of underlying financial imbalances.

Appendix to Chapter 4
Inflation Targeting with Forward-Looking Expectations

This appendix follows Clarida, Galí, and Gertler (1999) and presents an analysis of inflation-targeting rules in a model with forward-looking inflation expectations.[42] Let q_t denote current output and z_t trend output (both in logs). Let y_t denote the output gap, and π_t inflation, as defined in the text. Aggregate demand is now assumed to depend positively on expected *future* output and negatively on the *ex ante* expected real interest rate:

$$y_t = \mathrm{E}_t y_{t+1} - \beta(i_t - \mathrm{E}_t \pi_{t+1}) + \eta_t, \qquad (A1)$$

where i_t is the nominal interest rate (the policy instrument) and η_t a disturbance term obeying:

$$\eta_t = \rho_\eta \eta_{t-1} + \zeta_t, \qquad (A2)$$

where $0 \leq \rho_\eta \leq 1$ and ζ_t is an i.i.d. random variable with zero mean and constant variance σ_ζ^2. Iterating Equation (A1) forward yields

$$y_t = \mathrm{E}_t \sum_{h=0}^{\infty} \left[-\beta(i_{t+h} - \pi_{t+h+1}) + \eta_{t+h} \right],$$

which shows that the current output gap depends on all the future values of the real interest rate and the demand shock. Thus, in general, both current and future monetary policy decisions (that is, changes in the nominal interest rate) will affect current output.

Inflation is positively related to the output gap, as before, but also on expected *future* inflation:

$$\pi_t = \alpha_1 y_t + \alpha_2 \mathrm{E}_t \pi_{t+1} + \varepsilon_t. \qquad (A3)$$

ε_t is a random disturbance obeying:

$$\varepsilon_t = \rho_\varepsilon \varepsilon_{t-1} + \nu_t, \qquad (A4)$$

where $0 \leq \rho_\varepsilon \leq 1$ and ν_t is an i.i.d. random variable with zero mean and constant variance σ_ν^2. The price equation (A3) implies that there is no inertia in inflation. Iterating forward yields again

$$\pi_t = \mathrm{E}_t \sum_{h=0}^{\infty} \alpha_2^h (\alpha_1 y_{t+h} + \varepsilon_{t+h}),$$

which shows that current inflation depends on all the future values of the output gap. It can be derived from a model with staggered nominal wage and price-setting decisions by monopolistically competitive firms (see Roberts, 1995).

---

[42] See also Svensson (2003) for a derivation of interest rate rules under forward-looking expectations.

The central bank's policy objective is, as in (16):

$$\min U_t = \mathrm{E}_t \left\{ \sum_{h=t}^{\infty} \delta^{h-t} \left[\frac{(\pi_h - \tilde{\pi})^2 + \lambda y_h^2}{2} \right] \right\}, \tag{A5}$$

where δ is a discount factor, π^* the inflation target, and λ measures the relative weight on the output gap. The central bank chooses $\{i_t\}_{t=0}^{\infty}$ to minimize (A5), subject to constraints (A1) and (A3). This problem differs from the one discussed in the text because both the output gap and inflation depend on their *future* values, and thus on expectations about future policy.

Under discretion, the central bank takes expectations as given in solving its optimization problem. To derive the optimal policy rule proceeds in two stages:

- The objective function (A5) is minimized by choosing y_t and π_t, given the inflation equation (A3). This is possible because no endogenous state variable appears in the objective function; thus future inflation and output are not affected by today's policy decisions and the central bank cannot directly affect private expectations.

- Conditional on the optimal values of y_t and π_t, the value of i_t implied by the aggregate demand equation (A1) is determined.

The first stage thus consists in choosing y_t and π_t to minimize

$$\frac{(\pi_t - \tilde{\pi})^2 + \lambda y_t^2}{2} + x_t,$$

where

$$x_t = \mathrm{E}_t \left\{ \sum_{h=t+1}^{\infty} \delta^{h-t} \left[\frac{(\pi_h - \tilde{\pi})^2 + \lambda y_h^2}{2} \right] \right\},$$

subject to

$$\pi_t = \alpha_1 y_t + z_t,$$

where $z_t = \alpha_2 \mathrm{E}_t \pi_{t+1} + \varepsilon_t$. The first-order conditions for the first-stage problem are

$$\pi_t - \tilde{\pi} + \mu_t = 0, \quad \lambda y_t - \mu_t \alpha_1 = 0,$$

where μ_t is a Lagrange multiplier. Combining these conditions gives

$$\pi_t = \tilde{\pi} - \left(\frac{\lambda}{\alpha_1}\right) y_t. \tag{A6}$$

Substituting this expression in (A3) for y_t yields

$$\pi_t = -\frac{\alpha_1^2}{\lambda}(\pi_t - \tilde{\pi}) + \alpha_2 \mathrm{E}_t \pi_{t+1} + \varepsilon_t,$$

that is

$$\pi_t = \frac{\alpha_1^2 \tilde{\pi}}{\lambda + \alpha_1^2} + \frac{\alpha_2 \lambda \mathrm{E}_t \pi_{t+1}}{\lambda + \alpha_1^2} + \frac{\lambda \varepsilon_t}{\lambda + \alpha_1^2}. \tag{A7}$$

This equation can be solved by using the **method of undetermined co-efficients** (see Minford and Peel, 2002). Conjecturing a solution of the form

$$\pi_t = \kappa_1 \tilde{\pi} + \kappa_2 \varepsilon_t, \tag{A8}$$

implies that $\pi_{t+1} = \kappa_1 \tilde{\pi} + \kappa_2 \varepsilon_{t+1}$, so that, using (A4):

$$E_t \pi_{t+1} = \kappa_1 \tilde{\pi} + \kappa_2 E_t \varepsilon_{t+1} = \kappa_1 \tilde{\pi} + \kappa_2 \rho_\varepsilon \varepsilon_t.$$

Substituting this expression in (A7) and rearranging terms yields

$$\pi_t = \frac{(\alpha_1^2 + \alpha_2 \lambda \kappa_1)}{\lambda + \alpha_1^2} \tilde{\pi} + \frac{\lambda(1 + \alpha_2 \kappa_2 \rho_\varepsilon)}{\lambda + \alpha_1^2} \varepsilon_t. \tag{A9}$$

Equating coefficients in (A8) and (A9) yields

$$\kappa_1 = \frac{\alpha_1^2 + \alpha_2 \lambda \kappa_1}{\lambda + \alpha_1^2}, \quad \kappa_2 = \frac{\lambda(1 + \alpha_2 \kappa_2 \rho_\varepsilon)}{\lambda + \alpha_1^2},$$

which can be rearranged to give

$$\kappa_1 = \frac{\alpha_1^2}{\lambda(1 - \alpha_2) + \alpha_1^2} < 1, \quad \kappa_2 = \frac{\lambda}{\lambda(1 - \alpha_2 \rho_\varepsilon) + \alpha_1^2}.$$

Thus, the solution for π_t is

$$\pi_t = \kappa_1 \tilde{\pi} + \lambda \theta \varepsilon_t, \tag{A10}$$

where

$$\theta = \frac{1}{\lambda(1 - \alpha_2 \rho_\varepsilon) + \alpha_1^2}.$$

Substituting (A10) in (A6) yields

$$y_t = -(\frac{\alpha_1}{\lambda})(\pi_t - \tilde{\pi}) = -(\frac{\alpha_1}{\lambda})\{(\kappa_1 - 1)\tilde{\pi} + \lambda \theta \varepsilon_t\},$$

that is

$$y_t = \Lambda \tilde{\pi} - \alpha_1 \theta \varepsilon_t, \quad \Lambda = \frac{\alpha_1(1 - \kappa_1)}{\lambda}. \tag{A11}$$

The second stage of the solution procedure consists in rewriting (A1) as

$$i_t = \frac{1}{\beta}\{(E_t y_{t+1} - y_t) + \eta_t\} + E_t \pi_{t+1}, \tag{A12}$$

and substituting for $E_t y_{t+1} - y_t$ and $E_t \pi_{t+1}$. From (A4) and (A10), $E_t \pi_{t+1}$ is given by

$$E_t \pi_{t+1} = \kappa_1 \tilde{\pi} + \lambda \theta E_t \varepsilon_{t+1} = \kappa_1 \tilde{\pi} + \lambda \theta \rho_\varepsilon \varepsilon_t, \tag{A13}$$

whereas from (A4) and (A11):

$$E_t y_{t+1} = \Lambda \tilde{\pi} - \alpha_1 \theta \rho_\varepsilon \varepsilon_t.$$

Using this expression together with (A11) yields

$$E_t y_{t+1} - y_t = \alpha_1 (1 - \rho_\varepsilon) \theta \varepsilon_t. \tag{A14}$$

Equation (A13) can be rewritten as

$$\theta \varepsilon_t = \frac{E_t \pi_{t+1}}{\lambda \rho_\varepsilon} - \frac{\kappa_1 \tilde{\pi}}{\lambda \rho_\varepsilon}.$$

Substituting this result in (A14) yields

$$E_t y_{t+1} - y_t = \left\{ \frac{\alpha_1 (1 - \rho_\varepsilon)}{\lambda \rho_\varepsilon} \right\} E_t \pi_{t+1} - \frac{\alpha_1 \kappa_1 (1 - \rho_\varepsilon)}{\lambda \rho_\varepsilon} \tilde{\pi}. \tag{A15}$$

Substituting (A15) in (A12) and rearranging terms yields the optimal interest rate rule:

$$i_t = \frac{\alpha_1 (1 - \rho_\varepsilon)}{\beta \lambda \rho_\varepsilon} E_t \pi_{t+1} - \frac{\alpha_1 \kappa_1 (1 - \rho_\varepsilon)}{\beta \lambda \rho_\varepsilon} \tilde{\pi} + \frac{\eta_t}{\beta} + E_t \pi_{t+1},$$

or equivalently

$$i_t = \delta E_t \pi_{t+1} - \Omega \tilde{\pi} + \frac{\eta_t}{\beta}, \tag{A16}$$

where

$$\Omega = \frac{\alpha_1 \kappa_1 (1 - \rho_\varepsilon)}{\beta \lambda \rho_\varepsilon}, \quad \delta = 1 + \frac{\alpha_1 (1 - \rho_\varepsilon)}{\lambda \beta \rho_\varepsilon} > 1.$$

Thus, the optimal policy rule (A16) also calls for inflation forecast targeting. Because $\delta > 1$, an expected increase in future inflation calls for a *more than proportional* increase in the current nominal interest rate, in order to raise the real interest rate today and reduce aggregate demand. Rewriting (A16) as

$$E_t \pi_{t+1} = \frac{i_t - \beta^{-1} \eta_t}{\delta} + \frac{\Omega}{\delta} \tilde{\pi}$$

implies that, if $\lambda \to 0$ (strict inflation targeting), because $1/\delta \to 0$ and $\Omega/\delta \to \kappa_1 \to 1$,

$$E_t \pi_{t+1} \simeq \tilde{\pi},$$

which is analogous to what Svensson's (1997) model would predict in the absence of a lag between changes in the output gap and inflation (see (11) in the text). Put differently, strict inflation targeting is optimal—in the sense of equating the inflation target and the one-period ahead expected value of inflation—only if the central bank has no concern for output fluctuations. Otherwise convergence to inflation back to target following a shock will be gradual, as implied by the discussion of flexible inflation targeting in the text. The optimal rule also calls for completely offsetting aggregate demand shocks, because they do not imply a short-run trade-off between output and inflation.

Chapter 5

Exchange Rate Regimes

Increased global financial integration and the growing incidence of currency crises in the developing world (both topics that will be covered in subsequent chapters) have led to renewed controversy over the role and performance of exchange rate regimes. The credibility and signaling effects of various types of exchange rate arrangements, and their resilience to abrupt reversals in capital flows, have become important considerations in choosing a particular regime. At the same time, issues such as the effect of exchange rate changes on trade flows, and the potential contractionary effects of these changes in the presence of imported intermediate inputs, have remained at the forefront of the policy debate.

Sections 5.1 and 5.2 provide a typology of exchange rate regimes and an overview of the evolution of exchange rate regimes in developing countries. Section 5.3 reviews the various factors that may affect the choice of an exchange rate regime and highlights the potential conflicts that may arise among them. Section 5.4 uses a simple illustrative model to emphasize the importance of *policy trade-offs* in affecting the degree of credibility of pegged exchange rate arrangements. Section 5.5 focuses on the effects of exchange rate changes on competitiveness and the trade balance. It begins by reviewing basic measures of competitiveness, and then considers the partial equilibrium approach to analyzing the effect of exchange rate changes on external accounts. Section 5.6 extends the analysis to consider a fully specified macroeconomic model that captures the role of imported inputs in the production process. The effects of exchange rate changes on both output and the trade balance are studied, and the limitations of the partial equilibrium approach are discussed.

5.1   The Nature of Exchange Rate Regimes

The array of exchange rate arrangements currently in operation in developing countries is wide and covers almost all types of regimes. A basic typology involves classifying them as pegged regimes, flexible regimes, band regimes, and multiple exchange rate regimes.

5.1.1   Pegged Exchange Rate Regimes

Pegged regimes come in several forms: **currency boards**, whereby the currency is irrevocably fixed against a foreign currency (see below); **adjustable pegs**, in which the currency is fixed against a foreign currency and is seldom changed; and **crawling pegs**, whereby the currency is initially fixed but policymakers subsequently adjust the exchange rate at regular intervals to take into account changes in inflation differentials or the state of the trade balance.

Currency boards were a popular exchange rate arrangement during the colonial era.[1] Under a *pure currency board*, the base money stock is fully backed by foreign reserves; the currency board only prints money against the reserve currency at a fixed exchange rate. Money issued by the currency board is also fully convertible on demand (at the fixed exchange rate) into the reserve currency, and vice versa. By definition, the ratio of the base money stock to the stock of foreign currency reserves is given by the exchange rate between the domestic currency and the reserve currency. By contrast, deposits in private domestic banks are not backed by the currency board's foreign exchange reserves; these are liabilities of private banks.

The case for a currency board is, first, similar to the case for a fixed exchange rate regime: by pegging the exchange rate, it constrains the scope for excessive monetary expansion.[2] This *monetary discipline* effect is likely to enhance confidence in the domestic currency and lead to lower inflation for a given rate of monetary expansion. Two additional arguments, however, are put forward in favor of adopting currency boards.

- They may help solve the **devaluation bias** inherent in discretionary exchange rate policy induced by **time inconsistency problems**, as discussed later. By removing—or at least severely limiting—the scope for discretionary monetary policy, a currency board should result in even greater discipline and confidence than simply pegging the exchange rate.

- The additional credibility gain that a currency board provides may help deter speculative attacks and currency crises, as discussed in Chapter 8.

---

[1] Malaysia, for instance, established a currency board in 1897 and dismantled it in 1967. The first currency board was introduced in Mauritius, in 1849. See Hanke and Schuler (1994) for a discussion of currency boards during the colonial period. Prior to the recent experience with a currency board (1991-2001), Argentina had gold-backed currency boards during 1902-14 and 1927-29.

[2] It is sometimes argued that adopting a currency board entails foregoing *seigniorage revenues*. As pointed out by Baliño and Enoch (1997), this is not quite correct, because the central bank continues to earn interest on its foreign assets while paying none on all or most of its domestic liabilities (the monetary base). Moreover, a central bank operating a conventional pegged exchange rate regime will also be limited in its ability to expand domestic credit, at least if it wants to sustain the peg for a sufficient duration. Thus seigniorage arguments are largely irrelevant in any comparison within the set of pegged exchange rate systems.

Of course, the difference between a currency board and a conventional fixed exchange rate regime is largely one of *degree*: a currency board can be abandoned just as a pegged exchange rate can. Institutional arrangements, however, typically make the abolition of a currency board considerably more difficult; this is precisely what provides the additional credibility of such regimes in the first place.

The additional credibility provided by a currency board, however, may come at a price.

- Compared with other pegged exchange rate regimes, currency boards are more constraining on monetary policy and on the ability of the authorities to alter the exchange rate peg. The cost associated with the *loss of flexibility* depends in general on how vulnerable the economy is to aggregate (domestic and external) shocks, and the availability of alternative policy instruments to offset the impact of these shocks.

- The credibility gain provided by a currency board to a country's economic policies may not be complete, because agents realize that such regimes can also be abandoned—even if doing so may be difficult. As a consequence, monetary authorities may not be able to completely eliminate the risk of devaluation and its impact on the **risk premium** faced by domestic borrowers on world capital markets.

- A currency board reduces the ability of the central bank to act as **lender of last resort** in the face of systemwide liquidity crunches. Because there is, in principle, no discount window, the central bank cannot offer lines of credit to private financial institutions experiencing short-term liquidity problems. Thus, countries with currency boards are more prone to bank runs and financial panics than countries with full-fledged central banks (see Chapter 8).

At the heart of this problem is the fact that private commercial banks usually hold just enough domestic currency to cover a *fraction* of their deposit liabilities. Under a currency board regime, commercial banks cannot rely on short-term borrowing from the central bank to finance transitory liquidity problems. As a result, a sudden loss of confidence by depositors can quickly turn into panic. The belief that a bank has become insolvent may trigger a run against that bank, as depositors try to withdraw funds before the bank runs out of cash. The bank's failure may create or exacerbate fears of other bank failures; this may lead, through a **domino effect**, to a full-blown financial crisis. The *credit crunch* that may follow the crisis may have a large, adverse effect on output and employment, putting pressure on policymakers to abandon the currency board regime. By contrast, with a full-fledged central bank, an essentially *solvent* bank with short-term liquidity problems will not automatically go under because it can have recourse to the discount window to cover the temporary cash shortage. Thus, currency boards are subject to the same type of trade-off (discussed later) between credibility and flexibility that any other type of pegged exchange rate regime may face.

5.1.2 Flexible Exchange Rate Regimes

In flexible regimes, the exchange rate is allowed to fluctuate in response to changes in demand and supply of foreign exchange. If the central bank does not intervene in the market for foreign exchange, the regime is a **free float**; otherwise, it is a **managed float**.

Floating exchange rate systems may be either an **interbank system** or an **auction system**, or a combination of these two systems.

- Under the *interbank system*, the exchange rate is negotiated in a market of commercial banks and authorized foreign exchange dealers. In theory, the exchange rate is allowed to fluctuate at any time. But, in practice, minimum and maximum limits are often imposed by the central bank on the commercial banks and dealers in order to prevent "cornering" of all the foreign exchange by any single member or group of dealers. This also prevents excessive exposure by commercial banks to exchange rate risk.

- In the *auction system*, export receipts are surrendered to the central bank at the prevailing exchange rate and the central bank, in turn, decides what amount of foreign exchange must be auctioned.

In practice, the two main variants of auction systems are the *Dutch auction system* and the *marginal price system* (see Feldman and Mehra, 1993). Under the former, each bidder whose bid is accepted must pay his or her bid price; a bidder may thus end up paying a significantly higher price if he or she incorrectly assesses the demand for foreign exchange. In the latter, a single rate called the *market-clearing price* is applicable to all bidders whose bids are accepted. All bidders above the market-clearing price are then allocated foreign exchange.

5.1.3 Band Regimes

Band regimes involve the announcement of a *central exchange rate* together with a **fluctuation band** (which may or may not be *symmetric*) around that rate. The central exchange rate is itself managed in some fashion—being, for instance, fixed or crawling. The implicit commitment of the central bank is to intervene actively at the margins of the band to prevent the exchange rate from moving outside the band. The implementation of a band also requires the adoption of a set of rules to guide foreign exchange market intervention, if any, within the band.

Band regimes aim to preserve some degree of exchange rate flexibility to promote relative price adjustment while retaining the role of the exchange rate as a **nominal anchor**. More specifically,

- relative to pegged exchange rate regimes, bands allow the exchange rate to adjust to *temporary* movements in relative prices and preserve some degree of **monetary autonomy**—the extent of which depends positively on the width of the band;

- relative to flexible exchange rate regimes, exchange rate bands, by constraining the range of fluctuation of the nominal exchange rate, continue to provide some nominal anchor for the domestic price level, depending now negatively on the width of the band (see Chapter 6).[3]

The extent to which a band regime succeeds in stabilizing the nominal exchange rate depends on its credibility. As formally demonstrated by Krugman (1991), in a perfectly credible band in which intervention takes place systematically and only at the upper and lower margins, the nominal exchange rate will be close to the central rate, even without intervention. Thus, the mere presence of the announced band may be stabilizing. However, the extent to which the other alleged benefits will materialize or not depends crucially on how the band is managed.

- If the central bank intervenes so as to keep the exchange rate very close to the central rate, or allows it to remain continuously at the top or bottom of the band, the band regime will behave like a fixed exchange rate—providing therefore no scope for relative price adjustments and no monetary autonomy.

- If the central rate parity is determined so as to maintain the *real exchange rate* constant, for instance, the economy's nominal anchor will have to be provided either by the money supply or an inflation target (see Chapters 4 and 6).

5.1.4   Multiple Exchange Rate Regimes

Multiple exchange rate regimes often take the form of a dual exchange rate system, in which commercial transactions take place at a fixed rate and financial transactions at a (generally more depreciated) floating rate.[4] In practice, such regimes have not worked well because of leakages among the various segments of the foreign exchange market. They are often adopted as transitory arrangements prior to fixing the exchange rate to an equilibrium value.

5.2   Evidence on Exchange Rate Regimes

This section begins by reviewing the broad evolution of exchange rate regimes in developing countries since the early 1980s. It then focuses on the recent experience of some particular countries (including Brazil, Chile, Indonesia, and Israel) with exchange rate bands.

---

[3] Another benefit of a band regime is that, as shown by Coles and Philippopoulos (1997), it would tend to stabilize the domestic inflation rate relative to what would happen under fixed exchange rates if inflation in partner countries is highly unstable.

[4] Dual exchange rate regimes may be informal in nature, as happens when governments impose foreign exchange restrictions in an attempt to defend an overvalued pegged exchange rate. As discussed in Annex B, this typically leads to the emergence of a parallel market for foreign exchange.

5.2.1   General Trends

In practice, a commonly used system to classify exchange rate regimes is the one introduced by the International Monetary Fund in 1982, which was revised in early 1999. Currently, the classification involves eight categories:

- **Exchange arrangements with no separate legal tender**. The currency of another country circulates as the sole legal tender (as is the case under dollarization) or the member belongs to a monetary or currency union in which the same legal tender is shared by the members of the union.

- **Currency board arrangements**. A monetary regime based on an implicit legislative commitment to exchange domestic currency for a specified foreign currency at a fixed exchange rate, combined with restrictions on the issuing authority to ensure the fulfillment of its legal obligation.

- **Other conventional fixed peg arrangements**. The country pegs its currency (formally or *de facto*) at a fixed rate to a major currency, or a basket of currencies, where the exchange rate fluctuates within a narrow margin of at most ±1 percent around a central rate.

- **Pegged exchange rates within horizontal bands**. The value of the currency is maintained within margins of fluctuation around a formal or *de facto* fixed peg that are wider than ±1 percent around a central rate.

- **Crawling pegs**. The currency is adjusted periodically in small amounts at a fixed, preannounced rate or in response to changes in selective quantitative indicators.

- **Exchange rates within crawling bands**. The currency is maintained within certain fluctuation margins around a central rate that is adjusted periodically at a fixed preannounced rate or in response to changes in selective quantitative indicators.

- **Managed floating with no preannounced path for the exchange rate**. The monetary authority influences the movements of the exchange rate through active intervention in the foreign exchange market without specifying, or precommitting to, a preannounced path for the exchange rate.

- **Independent floating**. The exchange rate is market determined, with any foreign exchange intervention aimed mainly at moderating the rate of change and preventing undue fluctuations in the exchange rate, rather than at establishing a level for it.

Figure 5.1, based on data compiled by Bubula and Otker-Robe (2002), shows the evolution of these regimes around the world between 1990 and 2001. The figure illustrates the shift toward either greater fixity or greater flexibility between

1990 and 2001, and the concomitant reduction in the proportion of intermediate regimes (such as conventional pegged exchange rate systems or band regimes with narrow margins). For the IMF membership as a whole, the share of hard pegs (which include formal dollarization, currency unions, both of them referred to earlier as "exchange arrangements with no separate legal tender," and currency boards) increased from 15.7 to 25.8 percent, whereas the share of floating regimes rose from 15.1 to 41.7 percent. For the group of developing countries only, the share of hard pegs (respectively, floating regimes) rose from 18.4 to 21.6 percent (respectively, 13.2 to 34.6 percent). In fact, the number of pegged arrangements has fallen continuously since the collapse of the Bretton Woods system of fixed but adjustable parities in the early 1970s. In the mid-1970s, 86 percent of developing countries had some type of pegged exchange rate regime. In the late 1990s, fewer than half did. Many of the countries that continue to peg their exchange rate are either small, highly open Caribbean islands or located in sub-Saharan Africa and belong to the **CFA franc Zone**.[5] More than one-third of developing countries now claim to have independently floating rates.

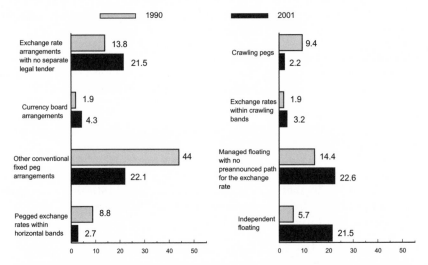

Figure 5.1. Exchange rate regimes (in percent of total IMF membership for each year shown). Source: Bubula and Otker-Robe (2002).

In practice, however, exchange rate regimes are difficult to classify, for various reasons.

---

[5] The CFA franc Zone consists of two separate groups of sub-Saharan African countries and the Comoros. The first group includes the seven members of the West African Monetary Union (Benin, Burkina Faso, Côte d'Ivoire, Mali, Niger, Senegal, and Togo), whose central bank (the BCEAO) has responsibility for conducting a common monetary policy. The second group consists of the six members of another common central bank, the BEAC (Cameroon, the Central African Republic, Chad, the Congo, Equatorial Guinea, and Gabon). Each of the two groups and the Comoros maintain separate currencies, but these currencies are commonly referred to as the CFA franc, which was maintained at a fixed parity against the French franc from 1948 to January 1994.

- The central bank may manage the exchange with considerable flexibility but set it daily or weekly on the basis of certain indicators—for instance, inflation differentials, the current account or the overall balance of payments, or projected supply and demand conditions in the market for foreign exchange. In such conditions, however, the exchange rate cannot be deemed market determined or freely floating.

- In particular, **real exchange rate targeting** implies fluctuations in the nominal exchange rate to offset inflation differentials.[6] It is not clear whether an inflation-adjusted peg qualifies as a form of fixed exchange rate, or a form of arrangement whereby the exchange rate is flexibly managed.

- The very notion of a freely floating exchange rate regime may have little empirical content. Determining how much foreign exchange market intervention is consistent with the category of *independently floating* regimes, for instance, requires assessing the degree to which intervention aims only at *smoothing* exchange rate movements—a difficult task in practice.

This last point is particularly important. It suggests that classification systems such as the one used by the International Monetary Fund are inadequate because they do not provide information that is sufficiently detailed to determine the *actual* degree of flexibility (that is, the extent of central bank intervention) among countries adopting the more flexible regimes. In particular, many of the countries that now claim to have independently floating rates use official intervention to alter the exchange rate path and should be classified as managed floaters or *de facto* peggers. Indeed, the recent evidence provided by Calvo and Reinhart (2002) suggests that many countries claiming to float their exchange rate actually do not. Rogoff and Reinhart (2002) have argued that the reverse is also true—countries that often declare themselves as peggers have in fact pursued a floating rate regime. These findings obviously call into question the validity of the empirical literature on the performance of exchange rate regimes, as discussed later.

5.2.2   Exchange Rate Bands

In practice, and in line with the description provided earlier, the choice of an exchange rate band covers four dimensions:

- The definition of the *central rate*, which can be in reference to either a single currency or a basket of currencies.

- Whether the central rate should be *fixed, crawling*, or *realigned irregularly* by discrete amounts. The choice among these options depends in part on the differential between domestic inflation and the rate of inflation of major trading partners, and the extent to which permanent shocks to the real exchange rate should be accommodated or not.

---

[6] For a discussion of real exchange rate targeting, see Lizondo (1993) and Montiel and Ostry (1991, 1992).

- The *width* of the band, that is, the permitted range of fluctuation of the exchange rate around the central rate.

- The rules governing *foreign exchange market intervention* by the central bank inside the bands.

During the late 1980s and the 1990s several developing countries adopted exchange rate band regimes, including Brazil (1995-99), Chile (1985), Colombia (1991), Ecuador (1994-99), Indonesia (1994-97), Israel (1989), and Mexico (1989-94).[7] The experience of these countries with respect to the four dimensions of implementation identified earlier varied widely, and several of these experiences eventually proved unsuccessful. Brazil is a case in point, and so is Indonesia.

- Exchange rate bands were introduced in Brazil in March 1995, in the aftermath of the Mexican peso crisis (see Chapter 8). The initial band was set at R$0.86-R$0.90 per U.S. dollar and was to be effective through May 1, 1995. However, because of the uncertainty about the exchange rate policy that would be adopted after that date, severe exchange market pressures developed. On March 10, 1995, the authorities set the band at R$0.88-R$0.93 per U.S. dollar and announced that it would be effective for an indefinite period. The band was subsequently modified on June 22, 1995, January 30, 1996, and February 18, 1997 (see Figure 5.2). The currency remained nevertheless subject to heavy speculative pressures. The central bank effectively used a *narrow trading band* of R$1.1975-R$1.2115 within a *maxi-band* of R$1.12-R$1.22 until January 13, 1999, at which point it decided to use only a maxi-band of R$1.20-R$1.32. On January 14, however, under renewed speculative pressures, the authorities abandoned the band regime, with the currency depreciating immediately from R$1.32 a day earlier to R$1.50.

- A band regime was introduced in January 1994 in Indonesia, with an initial width of about 1 percent on either side of the central rate. The central rate of the rupiah was set with regard to an unannounced currency basket, and continued to be depreciated in accordance with inflation differentials, thereby continuing the policy of stabilizing the real effective exchange rate.[8] The intervention band was widened progressively over time. After the collapse of Thailand's currency on July 2, 1997 (see Chapter 8), the central bank further widened the trading band on July 11, 1997, but the currency depreciated to near the ceiling of the new band by July 21. Continued exchange market pressures forced the authorities to abandon the band altogether in August 1997.

---

[7] The experience of Chile, Colombia, Indonesia, and Mexico is discussed by Agénor and Montiel (1999, chap. 7).

[8] Between 1988 and 1994, Indonesia operated a crawling peg regime, whose main objective was to depreciate the nominal exchange rate in order to offset the inflation differential with the country's major trading partners and maintain a competitive real exchange rate.

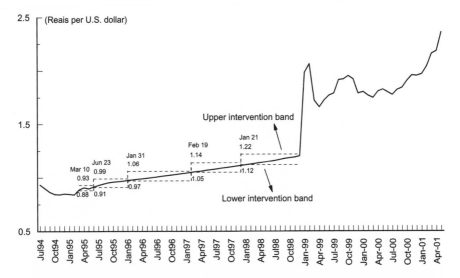

Figure 5.2. Brazil: Nominal exchange rate and intervention bands (July 1994-May 2001). Source: International Monetary Fund.

From the case of Brazil, the review of the experience with exchange rate bands of Chile, Colombia, Indonesia, and Mexico provided by Agénor and Montiel (1999, chap. 7), and the studies of Helpman, Leiderman, and Bufman (1994) and Leiderman and Bufman (1996), four major lessons appear to emerge:

- A band is a commitment to limited nominal exchange rate flexibility, not to a specific choice of nominal anchor. Bands are thus compatible with a variety of different weights that may be attached by the authorities to competitiveness and price stability objectives. Differences in such weights will be reflected in differences in the management of the *central rate*.

- There is no evidence suggesting that moving from a fixed rate to a band regime was associated with a significant increase in inflation. Thus, the greater flexibility that a band regime provides does not necessarily come at the expense of price stability. This finding suggests that some degree of flexibility can indeed enhance credibility.[9]

- The adoption of a band regime, however, does not resolve credibility problems. The Brazilian, Chilean, Colombian, Mexican, and Israeli bands were all characterized by periods of high **expectations of realignment**, reflecting perceived misalignment of the real exchange rate.

- Active management of the central rate to keep the real exchange rate in line with its equilibrium level may thus be indispensable to ensure the viability of a band regime under high capital mobility. If such adjustments

[9]See Cukierman, Spiegel, and Leiderman (2004) for a formal analysis of the roles of credibility and flexibility (as well as the distribution of external shocks) in the determination of the optimal width of an exchange rate band.

are not implemented in a timely fashion, recurrent speculative pressures may lead to a regime collapse.

5.3   Choosing an Exchange Rate Regime

In part because of the increased incidence of currency crises during the past few years (see Chapter 8), the issue of exchange rate regime choice remains one of the most debated questions in macroeconomic management. This section begins with a review of the conceptual issues involved in choosing an exchange rate arrangement. It then examines some of the empirical evidence on the determinants of regime choice.

5.3.1   Some Conceptual Issues

Conventional arguments in favor of a fixed exchange rate are that it provides a **nominal anchor** to prices, has often been instrumental in helping to bring down inflation (as discussed in the next chapter), and that it may help *promote fiscal discipline* or contribute to maintaining it once achieved. Because the exchange rate is a highly visible price, it can be monitored more easily than other variables—such as the money supply—and may allow rapid gains in credibility (see Canavan and Tommasi, 1997). Pegging to a low-inflation country can also help to signal the government's commitment to price stability and generate credibility gains, in the form of lower expectations of inflation and devaluation (Agénor, 1994). Indeed, Fielding and Bleaney (2000) found that the discipline effect on *inflation* has been significant in developing countries. However, there are also several arguments against choosing a fixed exchange rate.

- The evidence on the disciplinary effect of a fixed exchange rate on *fiscal policy* appears inconclusive, as argued by Tornell and Velasco (1998, 2000), and Stasavage (1997) in the context of the CFA franc Zone.

- The credibility gain associated with pegging to a low-inflation country tends to be, in practice, limited (Svensson, 1994). Building credibility and establishing a firm commitment to price stability often requires significant *domestic* policy and institutional reforms, such as granting independence to the central bank (see Chapter 6).

- While nominal exchange rate stability is important, some degree of flexibility in the exchange rate is also necessary to avoid excessive real appreciation and offset the impact of destabilizing shocks.[10] Pegging may in

---

[10] An extensive analytical literature has analyzed the links between the type of disturbances that an economy is subject to (real and nominal shocks, for instance) and the optimal choice of an exchange rate system, as well as the optimal degree of exchange rate flexibility (or foreign exchange market intervention). However, as pointed out by Van Gompel (1994) in his extensive overview, there are very few robust results that emerge from it—in contrast to the claims made in the early literature. A key problem in that regard is the possibility of conflicts among various policy objectives (minimization of either the variance of real output, the price

fact prevent real exchange rate adjustment in response to large domestic and external shocks. Glick, Hutchison, and Moreno (1997), for instance, argued that the pegged exchange rate regimes in place until 1997 were not the explanation for low inflation in East Asia. On the contrary, pegging prevented real exchange rate adjustment in response to large external nominal shocks—most notably the sharp depreciation of the U.S. dollar against the yen and the Deutsche mark during 1985-87 and the fall in U.S. interest rates during 1989-93—and therefore complicated macroeconomic management.[11]

- A pegged exchange rate creates a **moral hazard problem**. By eliminating (or reducing the propensity to hedge) foreign **currency risk**, a credibly fixed exchange rate provides an *implicit guarantee* and encourages domestic firms and banks to borrow on world capital markets at rates of interest that are lower than those charged on the domestic market.[12] This overborrowing (particularly when it is short term in nature) increases the vulnerability of the economy to adverse shocks.

- In countries prone to large random shocks, monetary aggregates may fluctuate erratically. In turn, changes in liquidity may translate into sharp movements in interest rates, which may have adverse effects on the supply side (as noted in Chapter 4) by affecting the cost of borrowing for working capital needs.

The arguments in favor of a flexible exchange rate are essentially symmetric to those against a fixed exchange rate. It gives national monetary authorities greater independence in choosing their inflation objective, and it provides a (partial) solution to the moral hazard problem posed by a fixed exchange rate. By purposely leaving some scope for unexpected exchange rate movements and avoiding implicit exchange rate guarantees, policymakers can induce domestic borrowers to internalize (at least some of) the costs of failing to hedge appropriately their foreign-currency liabilities. Arguments against choosing a flexible exchange rate are that they may not prevent a real exchange rate appreciation (in periods of surges in capital inflows in particular, as discussed in Chapter 7) and they may be characterized by excessive volatility (possibly exacerbated by a high degree of **dollarization**, as noted in Chapter 4) with possibly adverse effects on trade flows.

---

level, or real expenditure). Moreover, it is difficult in practice to discern the sources of shocks and identify relevant structural characteristics.

[11] In their view, low inflation in the region until the mid-1990s was the result of the large degree of insulation of fiscal policy from the political system.

[12] Moreover, with a pegged rate, agents know that the implicit guarantee of convertibility is limited by the availability of international reserves and the country's capacity to borrow abroad. Thus, when doubts arise as to the sustainability of its exchange rate arrangement, a country will attract mainly short-term, speculative capital inflows (see Chapter 7).

5.3.2 The Evidence

Several studies have attempted to shed light on the determinants of exchange rate regime choice and economic performance under the various regimes. Collins (1996) studied the determinants of regime choice in Latin America and the Caribbean, using a group of 24 countries over the period 1978-92. Macroeconomic imbalances, as measured by current account deficits and moderate to high inflation, were found to be significantly associated with a move to more flexible exchange rate arrangements during the period 1978-86; these indicators, however, appeared to have mattered less during 1987-92. In both periods, smaller and less open economies appeared less likely to select a flexible rate arrangement. Collins also argued that the endogeneity of regime choice introduces **sample selection bias** and makes any attempt to associate exchange rate regimes and economic performance (as proxied by the rate of output growth) hazardous.

Ghosh, Gulde, Ostry, and Wolf (1997), using a sample consisting of a large group of industrial and developing countries covering the period 1960 to 1990, found that countries with some form of fixed exchange rate experienced generally lower and less variable inflation than countries with flexible exchange rate arrangements. The superior inflation performance, however, was found mainly in countries that adjusted their exchange rate peg infrequently or not at all. Countries that frequently changed their exchange rate parity did not derive anti-inflationary benefits from the peg: indeed, they experienced higher and more volatile inflation rates than countries with freely floating exchange rates. This evidence supports the argument that simply pegging the exchange rate does not necessarily deliver low inflation. Rather, it is the overall macroeconomic policy framework that is important, whether in enabling an exchange rate peg to be maintained or, in the case of flexible exchange rates, in ensuring adherence to a nominal anchor such as the money supply.

Along the same lines, a study by Ghosh, Gulde, and Wolf (1997) examined the inflation performance of countries operating a currency board during the period 1970-96. To avoid biasing the results of their study, they controlled for regime choice endogeneity, because countries with a lower inclination to tolerate high inflation may be more likely to adopt a currency board in the first place. They found that, on average, inflation under currency board arrangements was substantially lower than under other pegged exchange rate regimes. They argued that lower inflation was achieved in part through a *discipline effect*, which led to lower growth in the money supply. But the difference in money growth rates is not sufficient to explain fully the inflation differential, suggesting an additional *confidence effect* whereby higher money demand results in lower inflation, for a given money growth rate. The last effect appeared to be the main factor explaining the size of the differential. In addition, fiscal deficits and the volatility of inflation were also lower under currency board arrangements.

Finally, Broda (2001) used a sample of 74 developing countries for the period 1973-96 to assess whether the response of real output, real exchange rates, and inflation to terms of trade shocks differ systematically across exchange rate regimes. He found that the behavior of both output and the real exchange rate differed significantly. Under fixed exchange rate regimes, negative terms-of-trade shocks are followed by large and significant losses in terms of growth, whereas the real exchange rate begins to depreciate only after two years. By contrast, under flexible regimes, output losses are smaller and real depreciations are large and immediate. These results seem to confirm the conventional view that flexible exchange rate regimes are able to "buffer" real shocks better than fixed regimes.

5.3.3   A Practical Guide

The foregoing discussion suggests that there are a number of factors that policy-makers should consider in choosing an exchange rate regime. As pointed out by Argy (1990) and Eichengreen and Masson (1998), these factors may be difficult to measure and may conflict with each other; the ultimate decision may thus depend on the *relative weight* attached to each of them in policymakers' prefer-ences. In addition, these weights may change over time. Nevertheless, relevant factors to ponder in selecting an exchange rate arrangement in practice include:

- The **size** and **degree of openness** of the economy. The higher the share of trade in output (as measured, for instance, by the share of exports and imports in GDP), the higher the costs of exchange rate volatility. Thus, small, highly open economies should opt for a pegged exchange rate regime.

- The level of **inflation**. A country that maintains a rate of inflation that is higher than that of its trading partners needs to maintain a flexible exchange rate to prevent a loss in competitiveness.

- The degree of **price** and **wage flexibility**. The more rigid real wages are, the greater the need for exchange rate flexibility to respond to external shocks. In the absence of flexible labor and product markets, asymmetric real shocks that require real exchange rate adjustments may cause large drops in output.

- The degree of **financial development**. In countries with thin and poorly developed financial markets, a flexible exchange rate regime may lead to large fluctuations in the exchange rate because of a limited number of transactions in the foreign exchange market.

- The degree of **credibility of policymakers**. The weaker the anti-inflation reputation of the central bank, the stronger the case for pegging the ex-change rate in order to build confidence that inflation will be controlled. Fixed exchange rates in many countries in Latin America and others like Egypt (as discussed in the next chapter) have helped economies to reduce inflation. In countries with a history of failed stabilization attempts, ex-treme forms of pegged exchange rate regimes (such as currency boards) may be the appropriate choice. However, the initial credibility gain may come at a high price subsequently, because of the loss in flexibility that such regimes entail. Argentina is a case in point (see Chapter 8).

- The degree of **capital mobility**. The more open the economy is to capital movements, the more difficult it is to defend and maintain a fixed exchange rate regime. A fixed exchange rate, in a world of high capital mobility, is a target for speculators because it offers a one-sided bet. As noted earlier, it leads to overborrowing on world capital markets and to increases in spending and **speculative bubbles**—increases in asset prices (stock and property prices) that are unwarranted by the evolution of fundamentals. This weakens the financial sector, which may in turn lower confidence in the capacity of the authorities to defend the pegged rate regime.

The increase in the degree of capital mobility around the world (as discussed in Chapter 7) has indeed made pegged exchange rate regimes less credible and more difficult to sustain—even with sound economic fundamentals and a consistent policy mix. The vulnerability of such systems to abrupt changes in investor sentiment has been well illustrated by the currency crises of the 1990s (see Chapter 8). As a result, economists like Obstfeld and Rogoff (1995) have argued that nowadays it may be preferable for countries to adopt either permanently fixed exchange rates (as in a monetary union) or fully flexible exchange rates.

More generally, the limitations that open capital markets and high capital mobility place on exchange rate management and monetary policy are well summed up by the notion of the **open-economy trilemma** emphasized by Obstfeld (1998): a country cannot simultaneously maintain fixed exchange rates and an open capital market while pursuing a monetary policy geared toward domestic economic objectives. Policymakers may choose only two of the above. If monetary policy is determined by domestic economic goals, either capital mobility or the exchange rate target must go. If a fixed exchange rate regime and a highly open capital account are the primary policy goals, the goal of maintaining an autonomous monetary policy (in the sense of being able to set domestic interest rates that differ from world rates) must be abandoned. Thus, the more important the exchange rate is as a policy goal, the more constrained monetary policy is in pursuing other (domestic) policy objectives.

Finally, it is also important to emphasize that considerations affecting the choice of exchange rate regime (as well as policymakers' preferences) *may change over time*. When inflation is high, a pegged exchange rate may prove more effective at reducing it, at least in the short run (see Chapter 6). But when stabilization is achieved, countries should shift toward a more flexible regime. Israel's exchange rate policy, for instance, entailed moving from a fixed exchange rate (imposed in the mid-1980s to stabilize from high inflation) to a currency band that was subsequently widened to prevent a loss of competitiveness. This **exit strategy** is particularly relevant when the resumption in economic activity is associated with inflationary pressures and in cases where large capital inflows are occurring. Under these circumstances, a more flexible exchange rate may help to alleviate inflationary pressures and prevent an overvaluation of the real exchange rate (Eichengreen and Masson, 1998, and Agénor, 2004b).

An exit strategy that may prove attractive is that of a **crawling band regime** (as discussed earlier) where the exchange rate is allowed to float within certain limits, and the band itself is devalued according to a predefined path based on, say, the inflation differential between the domestic economy and its major trade partners. The aim of this regime is, as noted earlier, to get the best of both worlds: to give some anchor against inflationary expectations, but also to avoid overvaluation and restore the two-way bet for speculators by using sufficiently wide margins. Inflation is thus reduced more slowly, but as long as fiscal discipline is maintained, the bands can be preserved. Without fiscal consolidation, however, this regime is no more successful than any other, as illustrated by the Brazilian real crisis (see Chapter 8). Sustained fiscal imbalances lead to high domestic interest rates, which attract short-term speculative capital inflows; an abrupt change in market sentiment may lead to unsustainable outflows—forcing the central bank to let the exchange rate float. From that perspective, the issue, then, is not one of *fixed versus floating rates*, but rather one of *good versus bad policies*. As argued by Calvo and Mishkin (2003), the choice of a particular exchange rate regime may matter less than the development of adequate fiscal and monetary institutions to conduct macroeconomic policy.

5.4   Trade-offs and Exchange Rate Credibility

The underlying theme of some of the foregoing discussion is the notion that the use of the exchange rate as a policy instrument typically entails a *trade-off* among policy objectives. For instance, attempts to maintain a fixed exchange rate and a high level of official reserves (in order to signal the central bank's commitment to defend the currency and fend off speculative attacks) is usually not viable if the ability to borrow on world capital markets is limited and if domestic inflation is high, because the resulting loss in competitiveness leads to a growing current account deficit and downward pressure on reserves. Similarly, although a devaluation of the nominal exchange rate can lead to a depreciation of the real exchange rate and improve the trade balance (as discussed in the next section), it may lead to a rise in domestic prices—ultimately eroding the initial positive effect on competitiveness.

A key argument of the recent literature on exchange rate management is that a fixed exchange rate can lend *credibility* to a government's commitment to a stable monetary policy. Herrendorf (1997), for instance, argued that if policymakers cannot control inflation perfectly under a floating exchange rate regime, and if by contrast agents can perfectly monitor the behavior of the nominal exchange rate under pegging, then fixing the exchange rate to a low-inflation currency may bring large credibility gains. In turn, by lowering inflationary expectations, and thus interest rates, increased credibility can lead to higher output. The problem, however, is that the government's commitment itself to fixing the exchange rate may lack credibility. The reason is that, as indicated above, governments face **policy trade-offs** in choosing whether or not to fix the exchange rate. In particular, the government may be *tempted to renege* on its promise to keep the exchange rate fixed because of potentially high returns to an unexpected devaluation. Thus, unless the **cost of devaluation** (economic or political) is sufficiently high, a fixed exchange rate will almost never achieve full credibility.

A simple model that describes the type of policy trade-offs that governments face when choosing to fix the exchange rate was developed by Welch and McLeod (1993) and is presented here. The authorities face a trade-off in the following situation.

- On the one hand, a depreciation of the real exchange rate lowers imports and stimulates exports, thereby leading to the accumulation of foreign exchange. Foreign reserves, in turn, improve the supply of liquidity services for external transactions.[13]

- On the other hand, however, a nominal devaluation raises domestic prices through its effect on the price of imported (intermediate and final) goods.

To capture this policy trade-off between inflation and the accumulation of foreign reserves, suppose first that *unanticipated* depreciations of the domestic currency improve the balance of payments, that is, the change in the central bank's foreign reserves, ΔR:

$$\Delta R = \alpha(\varepsilon - \varepsilon^a) + u, \quad \alpha > 0, \tag{1}$$

where ε (ε^a) is the actual (anticipated) rate of depreciation of the nominal exchange rate, and u a random external shock with zero mean and variance σ_u^2. This equation can be viewed as a quasi-reduced form derived from a model in which output itself depends on unanticipated movements in prices. Indeed, suppose that the economy produces only a tradable good, that purchasing power parity holds continuously, and that world inflation is zero; the actual rate of inflation, π, is then equal to the rate of depreciation, ε. Suppose also that the *expected* inflation rate (or devaluation rate) by the private sector, π^a, is set *before* the government decides whether or not to alter the path of the prevailing exchange rate. π^a and π may in general differ; the private sector's loss function is thus a function of the difference $\pi - \pi^a$. But on average, inflation expectations must be correct. Thus, to minimize losses due to incorrect predictions, private agents will act so as to ensure that, *ex post*,

$$\pi^a = E\pi, \text{ or } \varepsilon^a = E\varepsilon. \tag{2}$$

The central bank's **loss function**, L, is assumed to be quadratic and is given by

$$L = \frac{\varepsilon^2}{2} + \frac{\beta}{2}(\Delta R - \Delta\tilde{R})^2, \quad \beta > 0, \tag{3}$$

---

[13] As noted by Welch and McLeod (1993), foreign reserves also have an *insurance value* that may be particularly high for those countries that do not have access to trade-contingent debt instruments issued on international capital markets.

where $\Delta\tilde{R}$ denotes the desired change in reserves (assumed constant), and β a coefficient that measures the trade-off between inflation and international reserves; the higher β is, the higher the weight policymakers will attach to deviations of reserves from their target value.

Suppose that the central bank can react to shocks faster than the public, because prices are set before the shock is revealed. The central bank will then be able to cause *temporary deviations* from purchasing power parity by unexpectedly changing the nominal exchange rate. More specifically, suppose that the *timing of events* is as follows:

- The private sector sets its devaluation (or inflation) expectations and enters into contracts based on these expectations.

- The economy is hit by a random external shock (to, say, the terms of trade or the world interest rate), u.

- The central bank sets the devaluation rate on the basis of the observed value of the shock.

Given this sequence, the equilibrium solutions are given as follows. Under **discretion**, that is, a flexible exchange rate regime, the central bank chooses the rate of devaluation so as to minimize its policy loss. Formally, substituting Equation (1) in Equation (3) yields

$$L = \frac{\varepsilon^2}{2} + \frac{\beta}{2}[\alpha(\varepsilon - \varepsilon^a) + u - \Delta\tilde{R}]^2. \tag{4}$$

Minimizing this expression with respect to ε requires setting $\partial L/\partial\varepsilon = 0$, which yields

$$\varepsilon + \alpha\beta[\alpha(\varepsilon - \varepsilon^a) + u - \Delta\tilde{R}] = 0,$$

that is, with $\Omega = 1 + \alpha^2\beta$:

$$\varepsilon = \alpha\beta\frac{(\alpha\varepsilon^a - u + \Delta\tilde{R})}{1 + \alpha^2\beta} = \frac{\alpha^2\beta}{\Omega}\varepsilon^a + \frac{\alpha\beta(\Delta\tilde{R} - u)}{\Omega}. \tag{5}$$

Equation (5) represents the policymaker's **reaction function**, which takes the expected inflation-devaluation rate, ε^a, as given. In equilibrium, however, the value of ε^a must be consistent with the (expected) value of the devaluation rate set by the central bank, as given by its reaction function. Setting $\varepsilon^a = E\varepsilon$ in Equation (5), and noting that $Eu = 0$, this condition implies that

$$\varepsilon^a = \alpha\beta\Delta\tilde{R}. \tag{6}$$

Substituting this result back in Equation (5) yields

$$\varepsilon = \frac{\alpha\beta}{\Omega}(\Omega\Delta\tilde{R} - u) = \alpha\beta\Delta\tilde{R} - \frac{\alpha\beta}{\Omega}u, \tag{7}$$

which implies that

$$\varepsilon - \varepsilon^a = -\frac{\alpha\beta}{\Omega}u. \tag{8}$$

Substituting Equation (8) in Equation (1) implies that the actual change in reserves is

$$\Delta R = \alpha(-\frac{\alpha\beta}{\Omega})u + u = \frac{u}{\Omega}. \tag{9}$$

Because $\varepsilon^a = E\varepsilon$, the private sector's expected loss is zero. Substituting Equations (6), (8), and (9) in (3) implies that

$$L = \frac{1}{2}\left\{\alpha\beta\Delta\tilde{R} - \frac{\alpha\beta}{\Omega}u\right\}^2 + \frac{\beta}{2}(\frac{u}{\Omega} - \Delta\tilde{R})^2.$$

Because u is uncorrelated with $\Delta\tilde{R}$, the *expected* loss of the central bank is

$$EL^D = \frac{(\alpha\beta)^2}{2}\Delta\tilde{R}^2 + (\frac{\alpha\beta}{\Omega})^2\frac{\sigma_u^2}{2} + \frac{\beta}{2}(\frac{\sigma_u^2}{\Omega^2} + \Delta\tilde{R}^2),$$

or equivalently

$$EL^D = \frac{\beta}{2}\left[\Omega\Delta\tilde{R}^2 + \frac{\sigma_u^2}{\Omega}\right]. \tag{10}$$

Under a **credible precommitment**, the central bank irrevocably fixes the exchange rate; the devaluation rate will thus be zero ($\varepsilon = 0$) and the private sector will also expect $\varepsilon^a = 0$. Setting $\varepsilon = \varepsilon^a = 0$ in Equation (1) implies that *actual* movements in reserves are given by

$$\Delta R = u. \tag{11}$$

Substituting this result in Equation (3), together with $\varepsilon = 0$, yields

$$L^F = \beta(u - \Delta\tilde{R})^2/2.$$

Again, because $\varepsilon = \varepsilon^a$, the private sector's expected loss is zero. With u uncorrelated with $\Delta\tilde{R}$, the expected loss for the policymaker is now

$$EL^F = \frac{\beta}{2}(\Delta\tilde{R}^2 + \sigma_u^2). \tag{12}$$

In the absence of a commitment mechanism that forces the central bank to maintain the fixed exchange rate, the best option (or *dominant strategy*) for the government is discretion, or a flexible exchange rate. The reason is that the payoff to the central bank when $\varepsilon > 0$ is unambiguously larger than when $\varepsilon = 0$. Suppose indeed that the policymaker announces $\varepsilon = 0$ but that agents do not believe the policy at all. On the contrary, they expect the policymaker to act discretionarily, as indicated by its reaction function (5). They would therefore form their expectations according to (6). Substituting $\varepsilon = 0$ and (6) in (4) yields

$$L = \frac{\beta}{2}[-\alpha\varepsilon^a + u - \Delta\tilde{R}]^2 = \frac{\beta}{2}[u - (1 + \alpha^2\beta)\Delta\tilde{R}]^2,$$

so that $EL = \beta(\Omega \Delta \tilde{R}^2 + \sigma_u^2)/2$, which is greater than (10) because $\Omega > 1$. Knowing this, the private sector will always expect the central bank to opt for a flexible exchange rate regime, and the equilibrium outcome will always be the discretionary one.

Suppose now that there exists such a mechanism (such as membership in a currency union) that allows the central bank to precommit credibly to a fixed exchange rate. Is commitment always preferable? Consider first the case in which there are no random shocks to the economy, or equivalently here $\sigma_u^2 = 0$. From Equations (10) and (12),

$$EL^D = \frac{\beta \Omega \Delta \tilde{R}^2}{2}, \quad EL^F = \frac{\beta \Delta \tilde{R}^2}{2}, \tag{13}$$

which implies that, because $\Omega > 1$:

$$EL^D > EL^F.$$

Thus, the loss under discretion always exceeds the loss under commitment; a fixed exchange rate regime is always preferable.

Does this result continue to hold in the presence of random shocks, that is, $\sigma_u^2 \neq 0$? Subtracting the expression for EL^F given in Equation (12) from the expression for EL^D given in (10) yields

$$EL^D - EL^F = \frac{(\alpha \beta)^2}{2} \left[\Delta \tilde{R}^2 - \frac{\sigma_u^2}{\Omega} \right], \tag{14}$$

the sign of which is in general ambiguous. What this means is that even if there is indeed a commitment technology that allows the central bank to establish an irrevocably and fully credible fixed exchange rate, discretion may be preferable to precommitment. Specifically, as long as $EL^D - EL^F < 0$, the central bank is better off choosing discretion. It can be established that the effect of an increase in $\Delta \tilde{R}$ on the quantity $EL^D - EL^F$ is positive, that of σ_u^2 negative, and that of α and β ambiguous. For instance, the higher the degree of volatility of external shocks (the higher σ_u^2 is), the more likely it is that the central bank will choose a discretionary regime.

The foregoing analysis also indicates that fixed and flexible exchange rate regimes have different implications for inflation and reserves. If the central bank can credibly commit to the exchange rate rule that sets $\varepsilon = 0$, the equilibrium rates of exchange rate depreciation and inflation, ε, will be zero, whereas actual reserve fluctuations will completely accommodate external shocks [Equation (11)]. However, the higher the variance of the external shock u, or the larger the central bank's desired level of reserve accumulation, the higher will be its welfare loss. One apparent possibility for the central bank to improve on the outcome associated with a policy of setting $\varepsilon = 0$ might involve **cheating**: the central bank may begin by announcing a fixed exchange rate and then choose to devalue. The reason is that *expected* inflation, as a result of a credible announcement, drops to zero. Formally, maximizing Equation (4) with respect to ε with $\varepsilon^a = 0$ [or directly setting $\varepsilon^a = 0$ in the reaction function (5)] yields

$$\varepsilon = \frac{\alpha\beta(\Delta\tilde{R} - u)}{\Omega}. \tag{15}$$

Substituting this result in Equation (1) with $\varepsilon^a = 0$ implies that *actual* reserve accumulation under cheating will be

$$\Delta R = \alpha\varepsilon + u = \frac{\alpha^2\beta\Delta\tilde{R}}{\Omega} + \frac{u}{\Omega}. \tag{16}$$

Substituting Equations (15) and (16) in (3) yields

$$L = \frac{1}{2}\left\{\frac{\alpha\beta(\Delta\tilde{R} - u)}{\Omega}\right\}^2 + \frac{\beta}{2}[\frac{u}{\Omega} - (1 - \frac{\alpha^2\beta}{\Omega})\Delta\tilde{R}]^2.$$

The *expected* loss of the central bank is now

$$EL^C = (\frac{\alpha\beta}{\Omega})^2(\frac{\Delta\tilde{R}^2}{2} + \frac{\sigma_u^2}{2}) + \frac{\beta}{2}(\frac{\sigma_u^2}{\Omega^2} + \frac{\Delta\tilde{R}^2}{\Omega^2}),$$

that is

$$EL^C = \left\{(\frac{\alpha\beta}{\Omega})^2 + \frac{\beta}{\Omega^2}\right\}\left\{\frac{\Delta\tilde{R}^2 + \sigma_u^2}{2}\right\}.$$

Because

$$(\frac{\alpha\beta}{\Omega})^2 + \frac{\beta}{\Omega^2} = \beta\frac{(1 + \alpha^2\beta)}{\Omega^2} = \frac{\beta}{\Omega},$$

EL^C can also be written as

$$EL^C = \frac{\beta(\Delta\tilde{R}^2 + \sigma_u^2)}{2\Omega}. \tag{17}$$

Suppose that $\sigma_u^2 = 0$. Using Equations (13) and (17), it can be shown that

$$EL^D > EL^F > EL^C.$$

Thus, although all three regimes generate positive expected losses, the expected loss under cheating is lower than the expected loss obtained under commitment and discretion. Such a situation, however, is *not consistent*. The public would recognize the central bank's incentive to cheat, and the equilibrium outcome would revert to the discretionary flexible exchange rate case.[14] Rational individuals will recognize the policymaker's incentive to renege on its exchange rate announcement and will set expectations and prices to ensure that the marginal cost of devaluing is equal to the marginal benefit to the central bank.

The thrust of the foregoing analysis is that, in a setting in which both low inflation and accumulation of foreign exchange reserves are policy objectives, the

---

[14] Also, once the public realizes that the government has cheated, it will lose *reputation*, which may be difficult to regain and will increase the policy loss over time. See Agénor (1994) and Cukierman (1992).

possibility that the central bank can increase reserves by devaluing will hamper the credibility of a fixed exchange rate regime and lead to a **devaluation** or **inflation bias**—as long as the desired change in reserves is positive ($\Delta \tilde{R} > 0$), the central bank values reserve accumulation ($\beta > 0$), and exchange rate changes affect the balance of payments ($\alpha > 0$).

Private agents, knowing that the central bank has an incentive to devalue to accumulate reserves, will expect a devaluation to occur. They will set prices accordingly, generating positive inflation regardless of the central bank's announced policy stance. Even if the central bank does not actually devalue when private agents expect it to happen, the economy will suffer from positive inflation.

Because $\Omega > 1$, the coefficient of the random variable u in the solution for reserves under discretion [Equation (9)] is lower than the corresponding coefficient under fixed exchange rates [Equation (11)]. The flexible exchange rate regime is thus better able to dampen fluctuations in foreign exchange reserves resulting from unexpected external shocks. Again, however, as in the case of a credibly fixed exchange rate, in equilibrium the central bank cannot affect the *expected* change (or *average* change) in foreign reserves.

The foregoing discussion is a useful illustration of how policy trade-offs affect the choice of an exchange rate regime. Although a credible commitment to a fixed exchange rate regime may eliminate the inflationary bias associated with the flexible rate regime, it also increases the economy's *vulnerability to external shocks*—as discussed above in relation to Equation (14).

The choice of regime, therefore, depends on the relative importance policymakers attach to each of these two policy objectives. More generally, whether a country should opt for a fixed exchange rate regime also depends on how much the central bank values reserves relative to inflation, β, how sensitive changes in reserve are to unexpected movements in the exchange rate, α, and the targeted change in reserves, $\Delta \tilde{R}$.

Other models that emphasize the trade-off that the use of the exchange rate as a policy instrument entails include those of Agénor (1994), Agénor and Masson (1999), and Devarajan and Rodrik (1992). Agénor (1994) emphasized the trade-off between the **competitiveness effect** (the fact that a nominal devaluation may lead to a real depreciation and an expansion of exports) and the **inflationary effect**, whereas Agénor and Masson focused on the trade-off between the **interest rate effect** and the **inflationary effect** in the presence of external shocks to the balance of payments and imperfect capital mobility. The interest rate effect results from the fact that an adverse shock to, say, capital flows lowers official reserves. In the absence of complete sterilization (as defined in Chapter 7), the fall in reserves translates into a fall in the money supply—which in turn puts upward pressure on domestic interest rates. Such movements in interest rates may have adverse effects on output—or, as discussed in more detail in Chapter 8, may exacerbate weaknesses in the banking system.

Devarajan and Rodrik (1992) considered a model in which the trade-off that policymakers face in managing the exchange rate involves the inflationary bias associated with exchange rate flexibility, as in the models discussed above, and the fact that exchange rate changes can be used to reduce *output variability* by smoothing the consequences of terms-of-trade shocks on output. In their model, as in the framework described earlier, it is not possible to rank *a priori* fixed and flexible (or discretionary) exchange rate regimes. For large terms-of-trade shocks, flexible exchange rates are likely to be superior. Likewise, the more vulnerable the real economy is to these shocks, the more desirable are flexible arrangements. The greater the policymaker's built-in inflationary (devaluation) bias, the greater is the temptation to implement a surprise devaluation, and the less desirable will a fixed arrangement be.

Finally, an important point conveyed by Agell, Calmfors, and Jonsson (1996) is the need to take into account not only the credibility problems that arise when the exchange rate *alone* is used as a policy instrument, but also the problems that may surface when other instruments are used at the same time by policymakers.

Specifically, Agell, Calmfors and Jonsson (1996) considered the interdependence between exchange rate and *fiscal policies* in a small open economy, and its implications for the credibility of a currency peg. Their analysis is based on a model in which the policymaker can use both exchange rate and fiscal policies to affect output and employment. They showed that the equilibrium under discretion involves both inflation (that is, a *devaluation bias*, as in the model described earlier) and *accumulation of public debt*. Under the commitment regime in which the exchange rate is credibly fixed, inflation is lower; but this does not unambiguously improve welfare. The reason is that in the absence of adequate restrictions on fiscal policy, the reduction in inflation is achieved at the expense of increased government deficits.

Fiscal rules can, of course, be criticized (see Chapter 3). They often carry an arbitrary nature. More importantly, policymakers may need fiscal flexibility in the case of adverse shocks facing the economy. Nevertheless, the analysis by Agell, Calmfors, and Jonsson provides a healthy reminder of the importance of understanding the interactions between different policy instruments in the analysis of credibility issues.

5.5   Exchange Rates and the Trade Balance

Exchange rate adjustment has often figured prominently in adjustment programs implemented in countries suffering from chronically high current account deficits. The reason is that changes in nominal exchange rates can have significant effects on international competitiveness and trade flows, despite the fact that these effects can take a substantial amount of time to materialize. It is thus important to understand the mechanisms through which changes in nominal exchange rates affect imports and exports, and more generally economic activity.

This section begins by describing some of the most commonly used measures of competitiveness. It then examines, using a partial equilibrium approach, the effect of devaluation on the trade balance. The next section will extend the analysis to consider a complete macroeconomic model and will study the effect of exchange rate changes not only on trade flows but also on real output.

5.5.1 Measuring Competitiveness

Measures of international competitiveness attempt to capture changes in the relative price of foreign tradable goods relative to domestic tradable goods; they are generally based on real exchange rate indicators.[15] As discussed by Marsh and Tokarick (1996), there are three widely used measures of international competitiveness: those based, respectively, on *consumer prices, export unit values,* and *unit labor costs.*

The most frequently used measure of competitiveness is the real exchange rate based on consumer prices, z_C. This index is given by

$$z_C = E \cdot P_C^*/P_C, \tag{18}$$

where E is the nominal exchange rate (measured in units of domestic currency for one unit of foreign currency), and P_C (P_C^*) the domestic (foreign) consumer price index.[16] A rise in the domestic consumer price index relative to the foreign consumer price index would thus translate into an appreciation of the real exchange rate (a fall in z_C).

A major reason why the real exchange rate based on consumer prices is often used in practice to assess competitiveness is because consumer price indices are readily available and published at regular intervals. However, there are also several drawbacks associated with the use of such indices in a developing-country context.

- Consumer price indices tend to exhibit *significant volatility* (due for instance to sharp changes in the price of nontraded agricultural goods), which may be unrelated to competitiveness.

- The domestic price index may be influenced by various types of *government interventions* (including *price controls* and *excise taxes*), which may affect its reliability.

- Changes in prices of *intermediate goods* (which account for a significant portion of foreign trade for many developing countries) are generally excluded from consumer price indices, thereby reducing their usefulness for measuring changes in competitiveness.

- Because consumer price indices include prices of *imported final goods*, they tend to reflect movements in the *nominal exchange rate*; as a result, they

---

[15] Note that the real exchange rate here does not correspond to the relative price of tradable and nontradable goods within the country (that is, a measure of the terms of trade across production sectors), as used elsewhere in this book.

[16] For simplicity of exposition, the discussion assumes that the rest of the world consists of a single foreign country. In practice, all trading partners are weighted together to form a composite foreign country; the real exchange rate thus becomes a real effective exchange rate. For details, see, for instance, Bahmani-Oskooee (1995).

may understate changes in competitiveness. For instance, if the country's nominal exchange rate depreciates, the domestic-currency price of its imports will rise; and by automatically raising consumer prices, the extent of the country's real depreciation will be reduced.

• Such indices often do not accurately reflect underlying developments in *factor costs*, notably the cost of labor.

Another commonly used indicator of competitiveness is the real exchange rate index based on *export unit values* of manufacturing products, defined as

$$z_X = E \cdot P^*_{XV}/P_{XV}, \tag{19}$$

where P_{XV} is an index of export unit values of the home country, and P^*_{XV} a similar index for foreign competitors. This index, of course, is particularly relevant to explain the behavior of a country's exports. Although it does not contain any information relevant for assessing the performance of imports, it may be more appropriate than the index based on consumer prices (which includes the price of nontraded goods) to explain the behavior of the trade balance. A major drawback of this measure is that export unit values, being computed by dividing the nominal value of exports by the quantity exported, measure only the *average value* of exports per physical unit. They are thus proxies for the prices of exports, not the actual prices at which transactions take place. Changes in the index (19) are thus sensitive to changes in the composition of exports across countries—which can be themselves unrelated to changes in competitiveness *per se*.[17]

The third commonly used indicator of competitiveness is based on *relative unit labor costs* in the manufacturing sector. For each country, these unit labor costs are defined as the ratio of an index of *hourly compensation per worker* in the manufacturing sector (obtained as total earnings of labor divided by employment) to an index of *value added per man-hour*.[18] Formally, this indicator is defined as

$$z_L = \frac{EI^*_{ULC}}{I_{ULC}} = \frac{Ew^*_M L^*_M/V^*_M}{w_M L_M/V_M}, \tag{20}$$

where w_M, L_M, and V_M (respectively, w^*_M, L^*_M, and V^*_M) are the wage rate, employment, and real value added in the domestic (respectively foreign) manufacturing sector. This index is particularly useful as an indicator of competitiveness (and profitability) in manufacturing for countries where wage costs are an important component of production costs. However, it also has its limitations (Marsh and Tokarick, 1996):

• It becomes less useful where (as is the case in many developing countries) a variety of *intermediate inputs* are used in the production process and where *nonwage labor compensation* or capital costs are high.

---

[17] Export prices may also be heavily influenced by price strategies in the short run, such as pricing to market. See Marsh and Tokarick (1996).

[18] The index is also often calculated by using normalized unit labor costs, which are obtained by removing the cyclical movement in costs—using, for instance, the Hodrick-Prescott filter discussed in Chapter 9.

- Unit labor costs are not always reliable and can be highly sensitive to *cyclical movements* in labor productivity.

- Changes in unit labor costs may also reflect *substitution* among production factors rather than changes in competitiveness. For instance, an increase in *capital intensity* may raise the productivity of labor and lower unit labor costs without improving competitiveness, because capital now represents a higher share of unit production costs.

Cost- and price-based measures of competitiveness are related in a number of ways. To the extent, for instance, that the consumer price index is a (linear) function of the price of value added of each good produced in the economy (including manufacturing goods), and if each value-added price can be written as a function of labor costs and capital costs (profits), the real exchange rate indices based on consumer prices and unit labor costs would be clearly related. However, to the extent that prices of intermediate goods or capital change over time, and to the extent that such changes are reflected in consumer prices, the behavior of the two indices would be markedly different.

Figure 5.3 compares, for a group of 20 developing countries, the coefficient of variation—the ratio of the standard error to the mean—of the real effective exchange rate based on consumer prices and on unit labor costs, for the period 1979-95. Very few observations are actually located on or near the 45-degree line—a result that suggests that the two indices may provide very different pictures of real exchange rate fluctuations and thus changes in competitiveness. Thus that although the consumer price-based real effective exchange rate remains the main index used for exchange rate analysis for the large majority of developing countries (principally because of data availability and comprehensiveness of coverage), it does not necessarily provide an accurate measure of trade competitiveness.

5.5.2   Devaluation and the Trade Balance

The conventional analysis of the effect of exchange rate changes on trade flows and the trade balance suggests that a nominal devaluation affects the economy through two types of channels (see Södersten, 1980):

- as an **expenditure-reducing** policy, it reduces private spending and aggregate demand by raising the price level and lowering real money balances—or, more generally, the real value of financial assets;

- as an **expenditure-switching** policy, it influences the composition of output and domestic absorption between traded goods (importables and exportables) and nontraded goods.

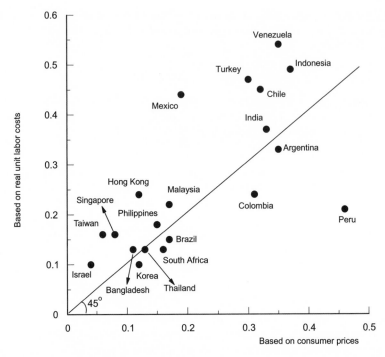

Figure 5.3. Coefficient of variation of real effective exchange rates (averages over 1979-95). Source: International Monetary Fund.

These supply- and demand-side effects of a nominal devaluation operate through its impact on relative prices and depend on various structural characteristics, including price and wage formation mechanisms in the nontradable sector. To the extent that prices of production inputs (labor and capital, say) rise *less than proportionately* to the increase in the domestic-currency price of output, a devaluation may lead to an expansion in activity—at least in the short run. The increase in the relative price of importables also tends to lower the demand for them and to increase demand for nontradables; this also tends to stimulate domestic output in the short run.

Analysis of the effects of exchange rate changes on the trade balance is often performed in a *partial equilibrium* framework, that is, by analyzing solely the effects of parity changes on trade flows. For simplicity, suppose that the country considered produces only one good, which is used for both exports and domestic consumption. The price of the good, P, is fixed on domestic markets.[19] Let X and J denote the nominal values of exports and imports, respectively, defined as $X = PQ_X$ and $J = P_J Q_J$, where Q_X and Q_J are real exports and real imports. P_J is the price of imported goods measured in domestic-currency terms, that is, $P_J = EP_J^*$, with E the nominal exchange rate and P_J^* the world price. The

---

[19]This assumption is not valid for most developing economies (export prices for these countries are usually set on world markets), but it will be adopted here, again, to simplify the presentation.

trade balance in real terms (that is, in terms of the price of domestic goods) can be written as $b = Q_X - zQ_J$, where $z = P_J/P$ measures the relative price of imports in terms of domestic goods. The change in b is given by

$$\Delta b = \Delta Q_X - z\Delta Q_J - Q_J\Delta z,$$

which implies that

$$\frac{\Delta b}{\Delta z} = \frac{\Delta Q_X}{\Delta z} - z(\frac{\Delta Q_J}{\Delta z}) - Q_J,$$

or equivalently

$$\frac{\Delta b}{\Delta z} = (\frac{Q_X}{z})\left\{(\frac{\Delta Q_X}{Q_X})(\frac{z}{\Delta z}) - z(\frac{\Delta Q_J}{\Delta z})(\frac{z}{Q_X}) - \frac{zQ_J}{Q_X}\right\}.$$

Suppose that trade is balanced initially, so that $Q_X = zQ_J$. The above expression can be rewritten as

$$\frac{\Delta b}{\Delta z} = (\frac{Q_X}{z})\left\{(\frac{\Delta Q_X}{Q_X})(\frac{z}{\Delta z}) - (\frac{\Delta Q_J}{\Delta z})(\frac{z}{Q_J}) - 1\right\}. \tag{21}$$

Let $\eta_X \equiv (\Delta Q_X/Q_X)(z/\Delta z)$ be the relative price elasticity of the foreign demand for exports, and let $\eta_J \equiv -(\Delta Q_J/Q_J)(z/\Delta z)$ be (the absolute value of) the elasticity of the domestic demand for imports. Equation (21) then becomes

$$\frac{\Delta b}{\Delta z} = (\frac{Q_X}{z})(\eta_X + \eta_J - 1),$$

or equivalently

$$\Delta b = (\frac{\Delta z}{z})Q_X(\eta_X + \eta_J - 1). \tag{22}$$

With given levels of domestic prices and the foreign-currency price of imports, $\Delta z/z = \Delta E/E$; an increase in the relative price z therefore reflects solely a nominal depreciation. Thus, Equation (22) requires, for the trade balance to improve ($\Delta b > 0$) following a devaluation, that

$$\eta_X + \eta_J > 1, \tag{23}$$

which is known as the **Marshall-Lerner condition**: the sum of the elasticities of export supply and import demand must exceed unity for the trade balance to improve.[20]

The Marshall-Lerner condition suggests that a key step in assessing the effect of exchange rate changes on the trade balance is to assess the sensitivity of trade flows to changes in relative prices. In practice, such attempts take the form of estimating econometrically equations in which volumes of exports and imports, or ratios to GDP, are related to changes in relative prices and to

---

[20] The derivations given here assume that the supply elasticities of exports and imports are infinite. For a more detailed derivation of the Marshall-Lerner condition, see Södersten (1980, pp. 363-366).

changes in real activity either at home (for imports) or abroad (for exports).[21] Such equations have consistently been used in policy work and macroeconomic models (see Chapter 9), although much of the early empirical work in this area lacked precision in the determination of real exchange rate elasticities. This lack of precision was associated with several factors.

- The use of *aggregate data* on trade flows, as is often the case in practice, may obscure differences in behavior across different *types of goods*, such as manufactured products and commodities. The relative importance of food items, for instance, varies significantly across developing countries; price elasticities may also be very different, depending on whether domestic substitutes are available or not.

- Real exchange rate measures based on consumer prices have often been used in empirical studies because of their availability. As discussed earlier, however, such measures may not reflect adequately movements in the *price of tradable goods* because they also include prices of nontraded goods.

- Changes in the *trade policy regime* or shifts in the type of goods being traded over time may be important and are often inadequately captured in estimated regressions.

More recent studies continue to face some of these problems but have relied increasingly on **cointegration analysis** (as briefly described in the appendix to Chapter 9) to achieve greater precision and determine short- and long-run elasticities. For instance, the empirical estimates of elasticities derived by Reinhart (1995) indicated a long-run price elasticity of import demand of -0.7 for Kenya, and a long-run price elasticity of export supply of 0.2, suggesting that the Marshall-Lerner condition is not satisfied. By contrast, for Colombia she found a price elasticity of import demand of -1.4 and a price elasticity of export supply of 0.5, which ensured that a real depreciation would improve the trade balance. The econometric results provided by Senhadji (1998, p. 264)—again using cointegration techniques—indicated that the short-term price elasticity for the real imports of goods and services of Nigeria was -0.3, whereas the long-term elasticity was -0.8.

Various other empirical studies confirm that there is a significant difference in the timing of the responses of trade volumes to activity and relative prices. Although the real activity effect occurs almost immediately, the response of trade volumes to changes in real exchange rates builds more gradually over time. Because a devaluation produces an unfavorable terms-of-trade response, with the domestic-currency value of import prices rising relative to export prices, the initial impact of a fall in the exchange rate on the nominal trade balance can be small or perverse. The expected effects of the exchange rate on the nominal trade balance may become apparent only in the medium term.

---

[21]See, for instance, Sekkat and Varoudakis (2000) for some panel data estimates for sub-Saharan Africa.

A possible explanation for this evidence is that apart from the price effects induced by a devaluation on the value of imports and exports, the response of quantities to these price changes may involve considerable time delays. If exports are invoiced in *local currency*, whereas imports are invoiced in *foreign currency*, the initial effect of the devaluation is to worsen the trade balance as the value of exports in foreign currency falls, whereas the dollar value of imports increases. Thus, as a result of a devaluation, the trade balance may get worse initially before it gets better. This particular phenomenon gives rise to the so-called **J-curve effect**.[22]

More generally, the literature focusing on the links between the exchange rate and the prices of internationally traded goods characterizes the **exchange rate pass-through**, or the degree to which exchange rate changes are reflected in the destination-country currency prices of traded goods, as consisting of the following phases (see Menon, 1995):

- An initial phase, the *currency contract* period, in which capital gains or losses on outstanding contracts are observed.

- A *pass-through* period, in which prices respond to the new exchange rate but quantities of trade are not yet affected.

- A *quantity adjustment* period, in which quantities and prices move toward a new equilibrium.

The trade balance can move in almost any direction in each of these sub-periods, and the duration of the lags that are involved in the second and third phases—which depend, in particular, on product characteristics and whether **pricing-to-market behavior** (see Krugman, 1987; and Marsh and Tokarick, 1996) is present or not—bears significantly on the overall outcome of the adjustment process. Put differently, a low pass-through would make it possible for trade flows to remain relatively insensitive to exchange rate changes, despite demand being highly elastic. Furthermore, if significant lags exist in the transmission of exchange rate changes to prices, and the subsequent lag in the response of trade volumes to the relative price change is also sizable, then the overall balance-of-payments adjustment process could be severely hampered.

Another important empirical issue is whether or not *supply terms* should also be included in export equations. Standard export volume equations only take account of *demand factors*, such as the growth of foreign income and relative prices, as indicated earlier. In a traditional demand and supply framework, the addition of a supply term involves relaxing the assumption that supply is perfectly elastic, which is used to identify the export equation. An alternative explanation, however, is the following. Suppose that all economies have the same underlying elasticities with respect to income. Then, with stable real exchange rates, high-growth economies should show a tendency for imports to grow faster than exports, whereas slow-growing economies should exhibit the opposite characteristic. Two factors may account for this pattern.

---

[22] For empirical evidence on the J-curve effect, see, for instance, Wilson (2001).

- As output expands, so does the *number of brands* produced by a country. Because consumers desire diversity, this increase in brands generates an increase in demand for exports (see Krugman, 1989*a*).

- The expansion of output supply may be correlated with the development of *higher-quality products* at prices that lead to an increase in the demand for exports.

This differential in the growth of exports and imports should be offset by an appreciation of the real exchange rate of faster-growing economies, as consumers are compensated for accepting more goods from these economies.[23] In practice, however, as discussed in Chapter 10, economies with high output growth rates also tend to have high growth rates of exports, with no significant evidence of real appreciation. Instead there appears to be a one-to-one relationship between estimated foreign income elasticities of export demand and growth in domestic home output—a result that Krugman (1989*a*) referred to as the **45-degree rule**. Accounting for supply factors may thus be important in estimating export equations, in order to avoid misspecification bias. Export equations that include supply terms were estimated, for instance, by Muscatelli and Stevenson (1995) for a group of Asian countries, with generally significant results.

Two other issues are worth highlighting in assessing the effects of exchange rate changes on trade flows and the trade balance.

- Changes in the exchange rate may have permanent effects on the trade balance through the fixed costs of entering or leaving a market, as emphasized by Dixit (1989) and Baldwin and Krugman (1989)—the so-called **beachhead effect**.

- Several studies suggest that although the day-to-day volatility of exchange rates in flexible exchange rate regimes does not appear to affect trade flows, year-to-year fluctuations do seem to have a significant impact on these flows—although it may become apparent only after a year or two. Grobar (1993) provided some evidence along these lines.

A more general problem relates to the *partial equilibrium* nature of the analysis on which the Marshall-Lerner condition is derived. In principle, a complete macroeconomic model must be used to assess the *general equilibrium effects* of exchange rate changes on output, inflation, relative prices, the government budget, and the trade balance. The next section provides a simple setting of this type in which *imported intermediated goods* play a role in the production process, as is often the case in developing countries. This model illustrates the inadequacy of the partial equilibrium approach, and the importance of accounting for general equilibrium interactions.

---

[23]This discussion ignores the impact of differential productivity growth between traded and nontraded goods on the real exchange rate, the so-called Balassa-Samuelson effect. See DeLoach (2001), Faria and León-Ledesma (2003), and the references therein, for a discussion of this effect and some recent evidence.

5.6 Devaluation with Imported Inputs

Imported intermediate goods play an important role in economic activity in developing countries. In some countries, the share of energy and nonenergy intermediate imports can exceed three-fifths of total imports. Through the cost of imported intermediates, the nominal exchange rate may thus have important short-run *supply-side effects*, in addition to its standard demand-side effects. Intuitively, therefore, the real effects of devaluation will depend in general on the relative strength of the supply and demand responses.

A simple model highlighting the mechanisms through which a nominal devaluation influences output both through the cost of imported inputs, on the supply side, and through trade flows and expenditure, on the demand side, is the static framework developed by Gylfason and Schmidt (1983). To begin with, consider a small open economy operating a fixed exchange rate regime. Gross domestic output, q, is produced from two inputs, *labor*, n, and *imported oil*, v, so that[24]

$$q = q(n, v). \tag{24}$$

Assuming that the production function is *linearly homogeneous*, it may be expressed in terms of rates of change as[25]

$$\hat{q} = \theta \hat{v} + (1 - \theta)\hat{n}, \quad 0 < \theta < 1, \tag{25}$$

where $\hat{x} \equiv \dot{x}/x$, and θ and $1 - \theta$ are, respectively, the shares of oil and labor in output.

Suppose that the foreign-currency price of oil is fixed on world markets and normalized to unity. The domestic price of oil is thus equal to the nominal exchange rate, E. The **elasticity of substitution** between the two production factors, σ, is defined as the percentage change in the ratio v/n, relative to the percentage change in the rate of technical substitution, q_n/q_v, which is equal to w/E if factor markets are competitive (see Varian, 1992). Thus

$$\sigma = \frac{\hat{v} - \hat{n}}{\hat{w} - \varepsilon}, \tag{26}$$

where $\varepsilon \equiv \dot{E}/E$ is the exogenous rate of devaluation of the nominal exchange rate and $\hat{w}$ is the rate of change of the nominal wage, taken as given.

Substituting (26) in (25) yields

$$\hat{q} = \theta \hat{v} + (1 - \theta)[\sigma(\varepsilon - \hat{w}) + \hat{v}],$$

so that the derived demand for oil (in rate-of-change form) may be expressed as

$$\hat{v} = \hat{q} - (1 - \theta)\sigma(\varepsilon - \hat{w}). \tag{27}$$

---

[24] The analysis can be extended to the case in which output is also a function of capital; see Gylfason and Schmidt (1983).

[25] A function $f(x_1, ..., x_n)$ is linearly homogeneous if, for a constant α, $f(\alpha x_1, ..., \alpha x_n) = \alpha f(x_1, ..., x_n)$. See Chiang (1984, pp. 411-14).

Real national income, y, differs from gross output by the amount of oil imports:

$$y = q - (E/P)v, \tag{28}$$

where P is the price of domestic output. This equation can be rewritten as[26]

$$\hat{y} = \frac{\hat{q}}{1-\theta} - \frac{\theta}{1-\theta}(\varepsilon - \pi + \hat{v}), \tag{29}$$

where $\pi \equiv \dot{P}/P$. Assuming **marginal cost pricing** implies that

$$\pi = \theta\varepsilon + (1-\theta)\hat{w}. \tag{30}$$

Combining Equations (27), (29), and (30) yields

$$\hat{y} = \hat{q} - \theta(1-\sigma)(\varepsilon - \hat{w}). \tag{31}$$

Equation (31) shows that if the degree of substitutability between oil and labor is sufficiently small ($\sigma < 1$), a devaluation (an increase in ε) will reduce real income for a given level of domestic output and nominal wages.

Consider now the demand side. By definition, national income, y, equals the sum of real domestic expenditure, c, and exports, x, less imports of oil, v, and final goods, h, all measured in terms of the price of domestic output:

$$y = c + x - h - (E/P)v. \tag{32}$$

Assuming that the trade balance is initially in equilibrium, that is,

$$x - h - (E/P)v = 0,$$

implies that Equation (32) can be rewritten as

$$\hat{y} = \hat{c} + \left\{\lambda + \frac{\theta}{1-\theta}\right\}[\hat{x} - (1-\beta)\hat{h} - \beta(\varepsilon - \pi + \hat{v})], \tag{33}$$

where $0 < \lambda < 1$ and $\theta/(1-\theta)$ are the shares of final goods imports and oil imports, respectively, in national income and

$$\beta = \frac{\theta}{\lambda(1-\theta) + \theta}, \quad 0 < \beta < 1, \tag{34}$$

with β and $1 - \beta$ being the shares of oil and final goods, respectively, in total imports.

---

[26] To derive (29), note first that, from (28) $\dot{y} = \dot{q} - (\dot{E}v/P + E\dot{v}/P - Ev\dot{P}/P^2)$, that is, dividing by y, and noting that $\hat{x} \equiv \dot{x}/x$,

$$\hat{y} = \hat{q}(q/y) - (Ev/Pq)(\varepsilon + \hat{v} + \pi)(q/y).$$

As defined earlier, $\theta \equiv Ev/Pq$ and from (28) $y/q + Ev/Pq = 1$, so that $y/q = 1 - \theta$, or equivalently $q/y = 1/(1 - \theta)$. Substituting these results in the previous equation yields equation (29).

Domestic absorption (in rate-of-change form) is assumed to be a linearly homogeneous function of (the rate of change of) income and real money balances:

$$\hat{c} = \gamma\hat{y} + (1-\gamma)(\mu - \pi), \quad 0 < \gamma < 1, \tag{35}$$

where $\mu \equiv \dot{M}/M$ is the growth rate of the nominal money stock, M, and γ the short-run elasticity of expenditure with respect to income.

Exports are assumed to depend on the relative price of foreign goods (or the real exchange rate), E/P, so that, in rate-of-change form:

$$\hat{x} = \eta(\varepsilon - \pi), \tag{36}$$

where $\eta > 0$ is the absolute value of the price elasticity of export demand.

Imports of final goods, measured in terms of the price of domestic output, are assumed to depend on domestic spending and on the real exchange rate:

$$\hat{h} = \hat{c} - (1-\delta)(\varepsilon - \pi), \tag{37}$$

where $\delta > 0$ is the absolute value of the price elasticity of the demand for imports of final goods. For simplicity, the elasticity of the demand for final imports with respect to total expenditure is assumed to be unity.

Finally, the demand for oil (measured in units of domestic output) can be expressed as a function of income and the factor price ratio using Equations (27), (30), and (31):

$$\varepsilon + \hat{v} - \pi = \hat{y} + (1-\sigma)(\varepsilon - \hat{w}). \tag{38}$$

Substituting Equations (35) to (38) into (33) yields the following expression for the effect of a devaluation (a rise in ε) on national income, for a given rate of growth of the money supply and nominal wages:

$$\hat{y}/\varepsilon = \{[\lambda(1-\theta) + \theta]\Omega - \theta\Gamma\}/\Delta, \tag{39}$$

where

$$\Omega = \eta + (1-\beta)\delta + \beta\sigma - 1,$$

$$\Delta = 1 - \gamma(1-\theta)(1-\lambda), \quad 0 < \Delta < 1,$$

$$\Gamma = \lambda(1-\theta)(\eta + \delta - 1) + \theta\eta + (1-\theta)(1-\lambda)(1-\gamma).$$

In the above expressions, the composite term Ω can be viewed as extending the traditional **Marshall-Lerner condition** [given earlier in Equation (23)] to the case of an oil-importing economy. Indeed, in the particular case in which $\beta = 0$, the term Ω becomes

$$\Omega = \eta + \delta - 1,$$

which is the standard Marshall-Lerner elasticity condition. The composite term Δ is the reciprocal of the multiplier of the model, and Γ/Δ can be viewed as representing the absolute value of the elasticity of y with respect to P in the income-expenditure Equation (33).

Thus, Equation (39) shows that, with μ and $\hat{w}$ given, the sign of $\hat{y}/\varepsilon$ cannot in general be ascertained *a priori*. In the general case, $\hat{y}/\varepsilon$ is, for instance, positive if the numerator of the expression on the left-hand side of Equation (39) is positive, that is

$$[\lambda(1 - \theta) + \theta]\Omega - \theta\Gamma > 0,$$

or equivalently, given the definition of β provided earlier [Equation (34)]:

$$\Omega - \beta\Gamma > 0.$$

More specifically, Equation (39) decomposes the effect of devaluation on real income into

- a **demand effect**, which is positive as long as the *extended* Marshall-Lerner condition is met, that is, $\Omega > 0$;

- a cost or **supply effect**, which is negative as long as the *traditional* Marshall-Lerner condition is met $(\eta + \delta > 1)$.

In more explicit terms, Equation (39) can be rewritten as

$$\frac{\hat{y}}{\varepsilon} = \{(1 - \theta)[(1 - \theta)\lambda(\eta + \delta - 1) + \theta\eta - \theta(1 - \lambda)(1 - \gamma)] - \theta(1 - \sigma)\}/\Delta.$$

In the above expression, the term $\theta(1 - \sigma)$ captures the **factor substitution effect** of the devaluation. The higher (lower) the elasticity of substitution between oil and labor inputs, σ, the more likely it is that a devaluation will increase (reduce) real income. When, for instance, the domestic price of imported oil increases, firms would reduce their demand for oil and increase their demand for labor, thereby dampening the reduction in output and income, to an extent that depends on σ. The remaining terms represent the conventional effects occurring through the export and import price elasticities η and δ and the **real balance effect**, $1 - \gamma$. In particular, the higher (lower) the price elasticities of the demand for exports and final goods imports, the more likely it is that a devaluation will increase (reduce) real income.

The above equation also suggests additional results.

- Everything else equal, the smaller the real balance effect on domestic absorption (the higher γ), the more likely it is that the devaluation will raise income.

- In the particular case in which there is no imported oil, $\theta = \beta = 0$ and the above expression becomes

$$\frac{\hat{y}}{\varepsilon} = \frac{\lambda(\eta + \delta - 1)}{1 - \gamma(1 - \lambda)},$$

which shows that a devaluation raises real income ($\hat{y}/\varepsilon > 0$) as long as the conventional Marshall-Lerner condition is met.

In addition, the effect of a higher share of oil imports in gross output—or, equivalently, the weight of the exchange rate in the domestic price index—is in general ambiguous.

- On the one hand, an increase in θ raises both the import cost effect (provided that $\sigma < 1$) and the real balance effect of the devaluation. It also lowers the multiplier. Through both channels, a higher value of θ tends to increase the likelihood of a negative income effect.

- On the other hand, the interaction of θ with η and δ has an ambiguous effect on $\hat{y}/\varepsilon$.

Thus, to summarize, the smaller the degree of dependence of the economy on imported inputs (as reflected by a high value of σ), and the greater the expenditure-switching and expenditure-reducing effects (as captured by high values of η, δ, and γ), the less likely it is that the devaluation will exert a contractionary effect on income.

As shown in (28), because of the presence of imported inputs, income and gross output differ. It is thus useful to examine also the effect of the devaluation on gross output. Setting $\hat{w} = 0$ in (31) yields

$$\hat{q}/\varepsilon = \hat{y}/\varepsilon + \theta(1 - \sigma),$$

which differs from the expression for $\hat{y}/\varepsilon$ given above by the term $\theta(1-\sigma)$. Thus, a devaluation raises gross output more (or lowers it less) than real income as long as $\sigma < 1$, that is, as long as the real import bill for oil cannot be reduced proportionately in response to the exchange rate devaluation, owing to a low degree of substitutability between labor and oil in the production process.

The foregoing discussion has taken the rates of growth of both nominal money balances and nominal wages as given. Suppose, for instance, that both variables grow at the same rate as the rate of depreciation of the exchange rate ($\mu = \hat{w} = \varepsilon$). It can then be shown that

$$\hat{q}/\varepsilon = \hat{y}/\varepsilon = 0,$$

which essentially states that a devaluation has no real effects if it does not succeed in lowering real wages and the real money stock. More generally, suppose that nominal wages are *partially indexed* on the cost of living, so that

$$\hat{w} = \phi[(1 - \lambda)\pi + \lambda\varepsilon], \quad 0 < \phi \leq 1.$$

Substituting for π from (30) yields

$$\hat{w} = \frac{\phi[\lambda + (1 - \lambda)\theta]}{1 - \phi(1 - \lambda)(1 - \theta)}\varepsilon,$$

which implies that $0 < \hat{w}/\varepsilon \leq 1$. It can be shown that, for given μ,

$$\left.\frac{\hat{y}}{\varepsilon}\right|_{\phi>0} = \left.\frac{\hat{y}}{\varepsilon}\right|_{\phi=0} + \left\{\frac{\theta(1 - \sigma) - (1 - \theta)\Gamma}{\Delta}\right\}\frac{\hat{w}}{\varepsilon},$$

where the first term on the right-hand side corresponds to Equation (39). It can be established that the expression in braces on the right-hand side of this equation is negative and larger, in absolute value, than the first term on the same side. Thus, if nominal wages adjust fully to the devaluation (so that $\hat{w}/\varepsilon = 1$), then a devaluation will have a **contractionary effect** on output if wages are (even partially) indexed. The magnitude of this effect depends, of course, on the degree of indexation, ϕ.

To establish the effects of a devaluation on external accounts, define first the trade balance in real terms as

$$b = y - c.$$

Using Equation (35), and noting that $dx = \hat{x}x$ for any variable x, a change in b may be written, using (35) and setting $\mu = 0$, as

$$db = dy - dc = (1 - \gamma)\hat{y}y + (1 - \gamma)\pi = (1 - \gamma)y(\hat{y} + \pi).$$

Assuming also that $\hat{w} = 0$ implies from (30) that $\pi/\varepsilon = \theta$, and thus

$$\frac{db}{\varepsilon} = (1 - \gamma)y(\frac{\hat{y}}{\varepsilon} + \theta). \tag{40}$$

Thus, a *sufficient* condition for the devaluation to improve the trade balance is that it raises real income ($\hat{y}/\varepsilon > 0$). For the trade balance to deteriorate following a devaluation requires not only a negative income effect but also that the effect be *sufficiently large* to outweigh the unambiguously positive effect through θ—which reflects the expenditure-reducing effect of the devaluation through the inflation-induced drop in real balances. Equation (40) also shows that in the special case where $\theta = 0$ (that is, there are no imported inputs), and provided that $\gamma < 1$ (the normal case), a devaluation affects in the same direction income and the trade balance. In particular, as indicated earlier, both effects are *positive* if the conventional Marshall-Lerner condition holds ($\eta + \delta > 1$).

Two numerical examples considered by Gylfason and Schmidt (1983) are useful to illustrate the above results. Suppose that nominal wage growth and nominal money growth are both zero and that $\sigma = 0.3$, $\eta = 0.1$, $\delta = 1.7$, $\gamma = 0.7$, $\theta = 0.06$, $\lambda = 0.03$, and $\beta = 0.7$. In this case, the extended Marshall-Lerner condition is *not satisfied*, and a 10 percent devaluation has the following effects:

- a reduction in gross output by -0.5 percent;

- a reduction in income by -0.9 percent;

- a **deterioration** of the **trade balance** equivalent to -0.1 percent of GNP.

Thus, a devaluation has negative output and income effects and leads to a worsening of external accounts. Suppose, by contrast, that σ, γ, and λ remain the same but that now $\eta = 0.5$, $\delta = 2.2$, $\theta = 0.03$, and $\beta = 0.5$. In this case, the extended Marshall-Lerner condition is satisfied and a 10 percent devaluation will raise gross output by 1.1 percent and income by 0.9 percent and improve the trade balance by 0.4 percent of GNP. The important lesson of these experiments is that, once the supply-side effects of exchange rate changes are taken into account, whether or not a devaluation is contractionary can be fairly sensitive to some of the economy's structural parameters. Indeed, as shown by Buffie (1989) in a more general framework, patterns of substitution between inputs (domestic and imported) are key in determining whether a devaluation is contractionary or not. In particular, Buffie showed that with rigid real wages, aggregate employment may rise (and not fall) following a devaluation, depending on whether labor and intermediate inputs are better or worse substitutes than capital and intermediate inputs.

The literature on exchange rate management has identified various other channels through which a devaluation may affect the supply side. In particular, whereas the previous analysis was developed in a *static* context, authors such as Risager (1988) emphasized the links between devaluation, nominal wage inertia, profitability, and investment in a *dynamic* setting. In Risager's model, firms produce one single good by means of labor and capital. The domestic good is an imperfect substitute for foreign goods; its price is thus determined endogenously by equating aggregate supply and demand. Nominal wages adjust to changes in the exchange rate only with a lag. Firms are forward looking, and investment is driven not only by the current levels of profits and interest rates but also by the *expected future rate of return* on capital. In this setting, and provided that the Marshall-Lerner condition is met, a devaluation (a decline in the relative price of the domestic good relative to foreign goods) leads to an increase in net exports, a rise in aggregate demand, and thus an increase in the price of the domestic good. Because nominal wages do not change in the short run, the *product wage* (the nominal wage divided by the price of the domestic good) and real labor costs fall—thereby raising profitability and investment. In the long run, however, nominal wages and domestic prices adjust fully to the devaluation (thereby returning the product wage to its original level), and both the capital stock and domestic output follow a downward path. Of course, because firms are forward looking, the faster nominal wages are expected to adjust to the increase in prices, the lower the perceived increase in profitability—and thus the lower the initial increase in investment and output.

A nominal devaluation can have an adverse effect on output through various other channels, including through changes in interest rates, taxation, or the effect of the nominal depreciation on the domestic-currency value of external debt—as discussed by Gylfason and Risager (1984) in an extension of the Gylfason-Schmid model, and by van Wijnbergen (1986).[27] The key lesson of the literature is that, far from being a curiosity, contractionary effects induced by nominal exchange rate changes can be significant; accounting for these effects may be important to ensure the sustainability of adjustment programs.

---

[27] Agénor and Montiel (1999, chap. 8) provide an extensive discussion of these various channels.

5.7 Summary

- Exchange rate arrangements in operation in developing countries cover **pegged exchange rate regimes** (including fixed rates, adjustable and crawling pegs, and currency boards), **flexible exchange rate regimes** (which include free floats and managed floats), **band regimes**, and **multiple exchange rate regimes**. A band regime involves the announcement of a *central exchange rate* together with a *fluctuation band* around that rate; the central exchange rate is itself managed in some fashion—being, for instance, fixed or crawling. The central bank intervenes at the margins of the band, to prevent the exchange rate from moving outside it.

- Pegged exchange rate regimes can cause distortions in the financial system. To the extent that the peg is considered an *implicit guarantee* that there will be no changes in the value of the currency, it is an incentive to borrow in foreign currencies and encourages the financial and business sectors to incur *excessive exchange risk*. A fixed exchange rate in a world of high capital mobility is a target for speculators because it offers a *one-sided bet*.

- The additional credibility gain provided by a currency board, compared with other pegged exchange rate regimes, results from the difficulty of altering the peg and may be important for countries with a history of macroeconomic instability.

- However, currency boards are more constraining on monetary policy. The cost associated with the *loss of flexibility* depends in general on the susceptibility of the economy to aggregate shocks, and whether alternative policy instruments are available. Because it reduces the ability of the central bank to act as **lender of last resort** in the face of economy-wide liquidity crunches, countries with currency boards are *more prone to bank runs* and *financial panics* than countries with full-fledged central banks.

- A *band regime* combines the advantages of both fixed and floating exchange rate regimes: it helps impose discipline on monetary policy, provides some degree of flexibility in response to external shocks (such as abrupt changes in capital flows, a rise in oil prices, or increase in world interest rates), helps limit exchange rate volatility, helps prevent overvaluation, and introduces some uncertainty about the path of the exchange rate—thereby lowering the incentives for foreign borrowing.

- The implementation of a credible band will, in and of itself, tend to have a stabilizing effect on exchange rate movements. However, in the presence of *fundamental policy inconsistencies*, a band regime is no more viable than a pegged rate regime.

- Although classifying exchange rate regimes can be difficult in practice, the evidence suggests that the number of pegged exchange rate arrangements has fallen considerably since the early 1970s. At the same time, however, very few developing countries operate floating exchange rate regimes that are completely free from central bank intervention.

- The evidence suggests that countries with pegged exchange rate regimes have experienced lower and less variable inflation than countries with flexible exchange rate arrangements. However, simply pegging the exchange rate does not necessarily lead to low inflation; overall consistency of the macroeconomic policy stance, and in particular coordination between fiscal and monetary policies, is needed for that purpose.

- In practice, factors that policymakers must take into account in choosing an exchange rate arrangement include the *size* and *degree of openness* of the economy, the level of *inflation*, the degree of *labor market flexibility*, the degree of *financial development*, the degree of *credibility of policymakers*, and the degree of *capital mobility*.

- The ability of a fixed exchange rate to lend credibility to a commitment to a stable monetary policy is limited by the fact that the commitment to fixing the exchange rate may, itself, lack credibility. The reason is that governments face **policy trade-offs** in choosing whether or not to fix the exchange rate. In particular, the government may be tempted to renege on its promise to keep the exchange rate fixed because of potentially high returns (in output terms) to an unexpected devaluation. Thus, unless the *cost of devaluation* (economic or political) is sufficiently high, a fixed exchange rate will almost never achieve full credibility.

- Measures of *international competitiveness* attempt to capture changes in the relative price of foreign tradable goods relative to domestic tradable goods; they are generally based on *real exchange rate indicators*. The three most widely used indicators for developing countries are those based on *consumer prices*, *export unit values*, and *unit labor costs*. These indicators may, however, provide conflicting signals in practice.

- A nominal devaluation affects the economy through an **expenditure-reducing** effect (a reduction in aggregate demand stemming from a rise in prices and a fall in real wealth) and an **expenditure-switching** effect (changes in the composition of output and domestic absorption between traded goods and nontraded goods, induced by the increase in the relative price of tradables).

- In a *partial equilibrium* framework, the condition for the trade balance to improve following a devaluation is the **Marshall-Lerner condition**, which requires the sum of the elasticities of export supply and import demand to exceed unity. However, even if the Marshall-Lerner condition is satisfied in the *long run*, *short-term* elasticities may be small enough to imply that an exchange rate adjustment will not lead immediately to an improvement in the trade balance.

- The **45-degree rule** refers to the fact that estimates of the elasticity of export demand to foreign income are high for high-growth economies and low for low-growth economies. The close correspondence between estimated activity elasticities for exports and real domestic growth suggests that terms measuring domestic supply should be incorporated in export equations to avoid mispecification.

- A nominal devaluation may have a short-run **contractionary effect** on output through its impact on the cost of *imported inputs*. Various other channels (operating through both the supply and the demand sides) may also lead to an adverse output effect of exchange rate adjustment, particularly in the short run where trade elasticities are low and the degree of substitution between production factors is limited. Accounting for these adverse effects may be important in the design of adjustment programs.

Chapter 6

Inflation and Disinflation Programs

Assessing the sources of inflation and evaluating alternative strategies to disinflate have for many years been the main focus of research on stabilization issues in developing countries, particularly in Latin America. In part, of course, this stems from the recognition of the substantial social costs imposed by high inflation, particularly on those who do not benefit from indexation. Although the days of very high inflation gave way during the 1990s to more moderate inflation rates in Latin America and elsewhere, it is important to draw on the lessons of these experiences for macroeconomic management.

Section 6.1 focuses on the sources of inflation. It begins by drawing a distinction between chronic inflation and hyperinflation, and discusses the sources of both phenomena: often large fiscal deficits that are monetized, but also other factors that may be particularly important in the short run—such as wage inflation, exchange rate depreciation and terms-of-trade shocks, changes in the frequency of price adjustment, supply-induced movements in food prices, and lack of credibility. Section 6.2 examines the factors affecting the choice of nominal anchors in disinflation programs, focusing notably on the macroeconomic dynamics associated with money- and exchange-rate-based stabilization programs. Section 6.3 examines the role of credibility in disinflation attempts. It begins by reviewing the various sources of credibility problems and considers alternative options that have been suggested to alleviate them—central bank independence, price and wage controls, and foreign assistance. Section 6.4 reviews two recent experiences with alternative types of adjustment programs: those of Egypt (1992-97) and Uganda (1987-95).

6.1 Sources of Inflation

In understanding the sources of inflation, a key distinction is between **hyperinflation** and **chronic inflation**. Both phenomena are often driven by large fiscal deficits and the need for seigniorage revenue; the dynamics involved are highlighted in the context of a simple model that yields multiple equilibria. Other factors that can affect the inflationary process, such as the degree of nominal wage rigidity and exchange rate depreciation, are examined next.

6.1.1   Hyperinflation and Chronic Inflation

Hyperinflation is generally defined on the basis of **Cagan's criterion** as an inflation rate of at least 50 percent per month, or 12,975 percent per annum.[1] As argued by Végh (1992), there are three main features of hyperinflation:

- It typically has its origin in **large fiscal imbalances** that are fully monetized by a passive central bank.

- **Nominal inertia** tends to disappear. In the face of extreme rates of inflation, workers, for instance, tend to refuse to engage in multi-period, nominal wage contracts. Most wages and prices become indexed to a foreign currency—and many transactions are actually *conducted* in a foreign currency. As noted in Chapter 4, the **dollarization** of the economy tends to be difficult to reverse once inflation falls.

- It brings about such a chaotic social and economic environment that the public becomes convinced that the situation is untenable—eventually creating the political conditions for drastic policies aimed at attacking it at its roots.

A typical example of hyperinflation in the 1990s is the former Zaire.[2] A deep and worsening political crisis during the period 1991-94 led to a drastic increase in government expenditure (including large rises in government wages). This increase, compounded by a drop in tax revenue, led to a worsening of the fiscal deficit, which was financed by money creation.[3] Inflation averaged 60 percent per annum during the 1980s, and surged to 4,500 percent in 1993 and 9,800 percent in 1994. For the 12-month period ending in September 1994 alone, currency in circulation grew at very high rates and inflation reached an annual rate of 12,850 percent. At the peak of the hyperinflation process, in December 1993, the inflation rate reached almost 240 percent a month (Figure 6.1). Although monthly inflation fell substantially in 1995-96, it was not brought completely under control—in large part because of the inability of the government to reduce public expenditure and increase conventional tax revenue, in order to reduce its reliance on monetary financing of its fiscal deficit. During the whole period, domestic prices were increasingly set in foreign currency (U.S. dollars or Belgian francs). As shown in the lower panel in Figure 6.1, during the whole episode

---

[1] A more modest threshold would be 20 percent per month, or 892 percent per annum.

[2] See Beaugrand (1997) for a discussion of Zaire's experience. On the basis of Cagan's criterion, Zaire's hyperinflation began in October 1991 and ended in September 1994.

[3] As argued by Beaugrand (1997), inflationary pressures were compounded by the Olivera-Tanzi effect (discussed in Chapter 3), which lowered government revenue in real terms and led to further increases in the real fiscal deficit.

the monthly rate of depreciation of the parallel exchange rate (a better measure of the marginal cost of foreign exchange than the official rate) remained closely correlated with the inflation rate.

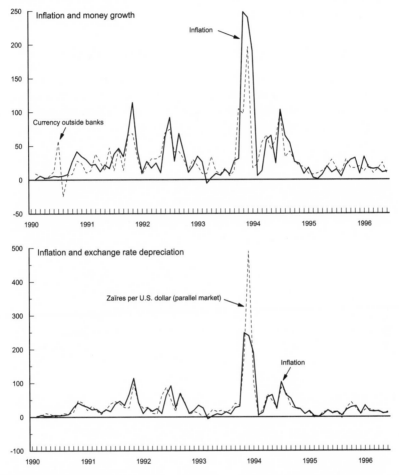

Figure 6.1. Zaire: Money growth, inflation, and exchange rate depreciation, 1990-96. Top: monthly rate of change of the stock of currency outside banks; bottom: parallel exchange rate in terms of old zaïres (the new zaïre was introduced in October 1993 at a parity of NZ = Z3,000,000; later data have been rescaled accordingly). Source: Beaugrand (1997).

The distinguishing features of **chronic inflation** stand in sharp contrast to those of hyperinflation.

- **Fiscal imbalances** are often *less acute* in the short run than those observed during episodes of hyperinflation. Consequently it is often more difficult to mobilize political support for reform.

- There is a high degree of **inflation inertia** resulting from widespread indexation of wages and financial assets.

- The public is often skeptical of new attempts to stop inflation, particularly when there is a history of failed stabilization efforts. This **lack of credibility** (discussed later) can be a powerful source of inertia.

6.1.2   Fiscal Deficits, Seigniorage, and Inflation

The foregoing discussion suggests that, in countries where the tax collection system, capital markets, and institutions are underdeveloped, fiscal imbalances are often at the root of hyperinflation and chronic inflation; governments often have no other option but to monetize their budget deficits.

To analyze how monetary growth and fiscal deficits affect inflation, consider the following simple model, adapted from Bruno and Fischer (1990), which focuses on the money market and its dynamic adjustment process. Suppose that real money demand, m^d, is a function of the *expected* inflation rate, π^a. Under *perfect foresight* (that is, rational expectations in an environment with no uncertainty) expected and actual inflation rates are equal, so that $\pi^a = \pi$. Using a semi-logarithmic form, money demand is thus

$$m^d = m_0 \exp(-\alpha\pi), \tag{1}$$

where $\alpha > 0$.

Equilibrium of the money market requires equality between money supply and money demand, $m^d = m^s = m$, which in turn implies that

$$\pi = -\frac{\ln(m/m_0)}{\alpha}. \tag{2}$$

Equation (2) shows that, along an equilibrium path, inflation and real money balances are negatively related. It defines a downward-sloping curve in the π-m space, denoted MM (for money market equilibrium) in the upper panel of Figure 6.2. When $\pi \to 0$, m tends to m_0. At any given moment in time, the economy must be located along MM.

To examine the dynamics of the inflationary process, suppose that the real fiscal deficit, d, is given by

$$d = d_A + \phi\pi, \quad \phi > 0, \tag{3}$$

where d_A can be defined as the *autonomous* component of the deficit, and $\phi\pi$ is a term measuring the **Olivera-Tanzi effect**—which, as discussed in Chapter 3, captures the fact that a rise in the inflation rate lowers the real value of tax revenue as a result of the lag involved in collecting taxes, thereby increasing the fiscal deficit.[4]

---

[4] As noted in Chapter 3, the Patinkin effect implies that inflation would tend to lower the deficit. For simplicity, government expenditure is assumed to be fully indexed to prices.

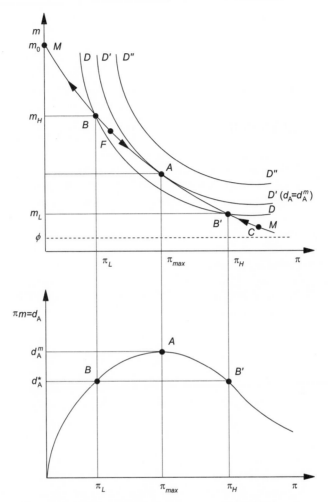

Figure 6.2. The seigniorage Laffer curve and the high-inflation trap.

The deficit must be financed by **seigniorage revenue**, that is

$$d = \mu m, \tag{4}$$

where $\mu \equiv \dot{M}/M$ is the rate of growth of the nominal money stock.[5]

The rate of change of real money balances is, by definition:

$$\dot{m}/m = \mu - \pi,$$

which can be written as, using Equation (4):

$$\dot{m}/m = d/m - \pi. \tag{5}$$

___
[5] This definition differs from the one given in Chapter 3 because of the continuous time nature of the present model. Defining seigniorage again as the change in the money base divided by the price level implies that $\dot{M}/P = (\dot{M}/M)m$, which is the definition given in the text.

Substituting Equation (3) in (5) therefore implies that in the steady state, with $\dot{m}/m = 0$, $\mu = \pi$ and

$$\pi = \frac{d_A}{m - \phi}, \tag{6}$$

which implies that inflation is related positively to the autonomous component of the fiscal deficit and negatively to real money balances in the long run.[6] Equation (6) is shown as curve DD in the upper panel of Figure 6.2. When $\pi \to \infty$, m tends to ϕ, and when $m \to \infty$, π tends to zero. DD approaches therefore the horizontal axis asymptotically. Note that DD depicts only a *steady-state* relationship between m and π. The economy moves continuously along MM in the short run; MM must intersect DD only when the economy reaches its *long-run equilibrium* position, characterized by a constant level of real money balances.

In general, depending on the size of the autonomous component of the fiscal deficit, d_A, curves MM and DD may or may not intersect. The upper panel of Figure 6.2 illustrates three cases:

- the case in which there is *no equilibrium* at all, corresponding to curve $D''D''$;

- the case in which there is *one equilibrium*, corresponding to curve $D'D'$ and depicted by point A;

- the case in which there are *two equilibria*, corresponding to curve DD and depicted by points B and B'.

Thus, whether the long-run equilibrium is unique depends on the size of the autonomous component of the fiscal deficit. Suppose, for simplicity, that $\phi = 0$. The steady-state relationship (6) is thus now given by $\pi m = d_A$. As noted earlier, when the rate of inflation approaches zero, real money balances tend to a finite value m_0; thus, the autonomous deficit must also be close to zero when inflation is very low. As the autonomous component of the deficit increases, steady-state seigniorage revenue (which is equal to the **inflation tax**, because real money balances are constant) must increase as well.[7] But the relationship is *nonlinear* because as inflation rises, real money demand falls [see Equation (1)]. More specifically, the exponential form of the money demand function implies that when inflation begins to rise, real money balances fall by relatively little, and revenue from the inflation tax increases at first. However, as inflation continues to rise, real money balances begin to fall at an accelerating rate, that is, at a rate *faster* than the rate at which inflation rises. Thus, after a

---

[6] To ensure that the equilibrium inflation given by Equation (6) is positive requires $m > \phi$. This condition can be rewritten in the form $\pi m/d > \eta_{d/\pi}$, where $\eta_{d/\pi}$ measures the inflation elasticity of the fiscal deficit. From Equation (4), with $\mu = \pi$, $\pi m/d = 1$. The inflation elasticity of the deficit must therefore be less than unity to ensure that $m > \phi$ in the steady state.

[7] Again, note that the definition of the inflation tax given in Chapter 3, $\pi m/(1+\pi)$, becomes in continuous time πm, because $\dot{M}/P = \dot{m} + \pi m$, and $\dot{m} = 0$ in the steady state.

phase during which πm increases (at a decreasing rate), it starts falling (at an increasing rate) and eventually tends to zero as π goes to infinity.

These results define a concave relationship, called the **seigniorage Laffer curve,** associating the (steady-state) inflation rate, π, and (steady-state) revenue from the inflation tax, $\pi m = d_A$. The curve is depicted in the lower panel of Figure 6.2. It shows that for a level of the autonomous deficit equal to, say, d_A^*, there are *two* corresponding rates of inflation, π_L and π_H, at points B and B'.[8] From the upper panel of Figure 6.2, the MM and DD curves in that case must intersect twice, at points B and B', corresponding again to π_L and π_H.

Uniqueness occurs only at the *optimal inflation rate,* π_{max}, which maximizes steady-state seigniorage; it is obtained by setting the derivative of πm with respect to π equal to zero:

$$\frac{d(\pi m)}{d\pi} = m + \pi \frac{dm}{d\pi} = 0, \tag{7}$$

which can be rewritten as

$$-\frac{dm/m}{d\pi/\pi} = \eta_{m/\pi} = 1.$$

This expression shows that the revenue-maximizing rate of inflation is reached when the elasticity of real money demand with respect to inflation, $\eta_{m/\pi}$, is exactly equal to unity. Beyond that point, increases in inflation yield less than proportional increases in the tax base.

Substituting Equation (1) in (7) yields

$$d(\pi m)/d\pi = d\left[\pi \exp(-\alpha\pi)\right]/d\pi = 0,$$

which implies that

$$\exp(-\alpha\pi) - \alpha\pi \exp(-\alpha\pi) = 0.$$

Thus

$$\pi_{max} = 1/\alpha, \tag{8}$$

which indicates that the optimal inflation rate is inversely related to the inflation elasticity of money demand.[9]

Substituting Equation (8) in (1) and using Equation (6), the level of the autonomous deficit corresponding to π_{max}, d_A^m, is given by, with $\phi = 0$:

$$d_A^m = \frac{m_0 \exp(-1)}{\alpha}.$$

[8] The same conclusion can be reached by depicting the inflation rate, π, against the *logarithm* of real money balances, $\ln m$. From Equation (2), MM would now be a *straight line* with a negative slope, whereas from Equation (6), given that $m = \exp(\ln m)$, DD would be a downward-sloping curve, convex toward the origin. Provided that the autonomous fiscal deficit is not too large, the model would again generate two equilibria.

[9] As shown by Végh (1989), if conventional taxes are subject to increasing marginal collection costs, the optimal inflation tax would be also an increasing function of government spending.

Both π_{max} and d_A^m are shown in the lower panel of Figure 6.2. Before point A, increases in inflation raise revenue from the inflation tax, so that $d(\pi m)/d\pi > 0$. Equivalently, the elasticity of money demand, $\eta_{m/\pi}$, is less than unity for $\pi < \pi_{max}$. Beyond point A, by contrast, increases in inflation reduce revenue $(d(\pi m)/d\pi < 0)$ and $\eta_{m/\pi}$ is greater than unity.

The next issue is to determine if the equilibrium, whether it is unique or not, is stable. This requires examining the *local stability* properties of the model. As noted above, the dynamic path of the economy must always be along the MM curve, because money market equilibrium must hold continuously. Assuming that the level of the autonomous deficit is d_A^*, there are two possible long-run equilibrium inflation rates, as noted earlier. The issue, then, is whether the economy, starting from an arbitrary initial position on MM, will converge toward B or B' in the upper panel of Figure 6.2. Two cases must be considered.

- Suppose first that the economy's initial position is at point F on MM, with F located *above* DD. For a given level of inflation, real money balances are therefore *higher* than their steady-state level, given by π/d_A^* (see Equation (6) with $\phi = 0$). From Equation (5), $\dot{m}/m$ must then be *negative*. Thus, the adjustment process entails a *reduction* in m, an increase in inflation, and hence a move toward B', away from B.

- Suppose now that, on the contrary, the economy starts from an initial point on MM located *below* DD, at, say, C. In this case, for a given inflation rate, real money balances are *lower* than their steady-state value; and from (5), $\dot{m}/m$ must then be *positive*. Thus, the transitional dynamics entail now a *rise* in m and hence also a move toward B'.

The foregoing discussion suggests that point B, which is associated with a *lower* inflation rate than what is optimal $(\pi_L < \pi_{max})$, is *unstable*. Any disturbance or exogenous shock—such as a sudden increase in government spending, leading to a rise in the autonomous component of the fiscal deficit—will lead the economy away from B. On the contrary, point B', which exhibits *higher* inflation than optimal $(\pi_H > \pi_{max})$, is a stable equilibrium.[10] Put differently, given the nature of the adjustment process under perfect foresight, a country can be stuck in a situation in which inflation is persistently high—a situation characterized by Bruno and Fischer (1990) as being akin to an **inflation trap**.

Clearly, any equilibrium characterized by $\pi > \pi_{max}$ is *inefficient*: the same amount of revenue could be collected at a lower inflation rate. What can governments do to move the economy away from an inefficient position? The obvious answer is to change either the autonomous component of the fiscal deficit, d_A, or the rate of growth of the nominal money supply, μ, because both affect the position of the economy along the seigniorage Laffer curve. For instance, a *credible reduction* in the money growth rate may shift MM and DD in such a way

---

[10]However, as shown by Evans and Yarrow (1981), with adaptive (or backward-looking) expectations, point B would be stable whereas point B' would be unstable. See also Bruno (1991), Bruno and Fischer (1990), Dornbusch and Fischer (1986), and Lee and Ratti (1993) for a more detailed discussion of the various cases.

that the MM curve will intersect the DD curve only once, at point A, as shown in the upper panel of Figure 6.2.

The view that countries can be stuck in an inflation trap is quite appealing, because it appears to be consistent with a number of episodes of high and chronic inflation that were observed in Latin America during the 1970s and 1980s, as discussed for instance by Agénor and Montiel (1999, chap. 9).[11] It is also of relevance for studying the dynamics of inflation in other developing countries where (as noted in Chapter 3) seigniorage accounts for a significant portion of fiscal revenues. However, in general the evidence suggests that the relationship between fiscal deficits, money growth, and inflation is relatively weak, particularly in the *short run*. De Haan and Zelhorst (1990) and Karras (1994*b*), for instance, investigated the link between monetary growth and budget deficits in developing countries. Both studies concluded that only in a small number of cases does a close, positive relationship exist between fiscal deficits and money growth. One possible explanation is that *expectations* about *future policy changes* play an important role, as emphasized by Kawai and Maccini (1990). A large budget deficit today, for instance, may be expected to be closed in the future through monetary or bond financing, which may raise expected and actual inflation immediately, or through a cut in government spending—which may lead to an immediate fall in the expected inflation rate. Because of the difficulty involved in measuring the stance of expectations, empirical studies of the links between fiscal deficits, money growth, and inflation often suffer from misspecification problems. Nevertheless, in a more recent study covering the period 1960-2001, Catao and Terrones (2003) were able to detect a robust relationship between fiscal deficits and inflation in high-inflation countries. So did Fischer, Sahay, and Végh (2002) in a study of 45 episodes of very high inflation in 25 countries.

The conceptual basis for the public finance approach to inflation has also been subject to criticism. In an early contribution, Bailey (1956) questioned the use of the seigniorage approach as a positive theory of extreme inflation. Because taxation is an alternative to money creation and because the marginal cost of taxation is moderate relative to the welfare costs of extreme inflation, high money growth (and therefore high inflation) is not optimal. More recently, Ashworth and Evans (1998), in an empirical study for 32 developing countries, found little evidence that the decision to raise revenue from inflation was guided by any kind of "optimal" taxation considerations. More generally, the idea of a stable inflation trap may be of limited usefulness to understand episodes of very high inflation or hyperinflation. As aptly noted by Dornbusch, Sturzenegger, and Wolf (1990, p. 9), in such cases "Inflation . . . reflects a state of fiscal chaos, rather than optimal public finance."

---

[11] A problem with the above model, however, is that (as pointed out by Dornbusch, Sturzenegger, and Wolf, 1990) it is not entirely consistent with the evidence. An increase in the nominal money growth rate generally tends to raise real balances initially; only later does inflation increase and overshoot for a while.

6.1.3   Other Sources of Chronic Inflation

In addition to fiscal deficits and money growth, there are several factors that
can affect the inflationary process in the *short run*. These factors include wage
inertia, exchange rate depreciation and changes in the terms of trade, the frequency of price adjustment, changes in food prices, and the inflation bias of
monetary policy under imperfect credibility.

Wage Inertia

Backward-looking wage formation mechanisms—such as **wage indexation** on
past inflation rates—can play an important role in inflation persistence, both
directly and indirectly—in transmitting, as discussed later, exchange rate movements to domestic prices.[12]

Consider, for instance, the following simple model of an economy producing
home goods and tradable goods. The inflation rate, π, is given by a weighted
average of changes in prices of both categories of goods:

$$\pi = \delta\pi_N + (1 - \delta)(\varepsilon + \pi_T^*), \quad 0 < \delta < 1, \tag{9}$$

where δ is the share of home goods in the price index, π_N the rate of change in
prices of home goods, π_T^* the rate of change in prices of tradables (measured in
foreign-currency terms), and ε the devaluation rate. Changes in prices of home
goods are set as a **markup** over nominal *wage growth*, $\hat{w}$, and the level of *excess
demand* for home goods, d_N:

$$\pi_N = \hat{w} + \alpha d_N, \tag{10}$$

which implies that, in equilibrium (with $d_N = 0$), $\pi_N = \hat{w}$.

Nominal wage growth is determined through indexation on past inflation as
follows:

$$\hat{w} = \gamma\pi_{-1}, \quad 0 < \gamma \leq 1, \tag{11}$$

with $\gamma = 1$ denoting full indexation. Combining Equations (9), (10), and (11)
yields

$$\pi = \delta\gamma\pi_{-1} + \alpha\delta d_N + (1 - \delta)(\varepsilon + \pi_T^*), \tag{12}$$

which shows that the larger the degree of wage indexation is, the greater the
degree of inflation persistence. Empirical research on the experience of countries
like Chile in the early 1980s and more recently Brazil has shown that backward-
looking wage indexation can indeed contribute to inflation inertia (see Agénor
and Montiel, 1999).

In addition, it has been observed in some countries that the *frequency* at
which nominal wages are adjusted tends to increase with the level of past inflation and contemporaneous inflationary pressures (generated for instance by large

---

[12] As noted by van Gompel (1994, p. 273), the absence, in practice, of instantaneous indexation is often the result of large costs associated with (*a*) gathering and processing information
on current movements in prices; (*b*) renegotiating wage agreements; and (*c*) increasing the
frequency of wage payments.

exchange rate depreciations), thereby raising inflation itself. Exogenous shocks in the **wage bargaining process** could also exert independent impulse effects on inflation (see Chapter 14), which could persist over time in the presence of an accommodative monetary policy.

Exchange Rates and the Terms of Trade

A nominal exchange rate depreciation (resulting from, say, a devaluation) can exert direct effects on the fiscal deficit through two channels:

- by affecting the domestic-currency value of *foreign exchange receipts* by the government (resulting, for instance, from surrender requirements on exports) and foreign exchange outlays, such as those associated with external debt service;

- by affecting the revenue derived from *ad valorem* taxes on *imports*. As discussed in Chapter 3, import taxes continue to represent an important source of revenue in many developing countries.

As a result, changes in the nominal exchange rate may affect the money supply and inflation. In addition, because exchange rate depreciation raises the prices of *import-competing goods* and *exportables*, it may exert pressure on wages as a result of its effect on the *cost of living*. This is particularly likely to occur in a setting in which (formal and informal) indexation mechanisms are pervasive, as indicated earlier.

Consider, for instance, a country facing a large current account deficit, and suppose that policymakers decide to devalue the official exchange rate to improve competitiveness and boost exports. The devaluation will increase directly the domestic-currency prices of both imported *final goods* and *imported inputs* (such as oil, as noted in Chapter 5), thereby putting upward pressure on domestic prices. The increase in prices can be large enough to outweigh the effect of the initial devaluation on competitiveness—thereby prompting policymakers to devalue again. The process can therefore turn into a **devaluation-inflation spiral**. In addition, if wages are indexed on the cost of living, they will increase also, putting further pressure on prices of domestic goods. The rise in domestic prices will in turn lead to further increases in wages and contribute to inflation inertia. There is indeed evidence showing that exchange rate changes have a significant effect on inflation in some developing countries, as documented for instance by Önis and Ozmucur (1990) for Turkey and Alba and Papell (1998) for Malaysia, the Philippines, and Singapore.

A similar process may be at play in countries where the official exchange rate is fixed but the *parallel market for foreign exchange* is large. A deterioration in external accounts may lead agents to expect a devaluation of the official exchange rate to restore competitiveness; such expectations will typically translate immediately into a depreciation of the parallel exchange rate. Because the parallel rate is a more adequate measure of the *marginal cost* of foreign exchange than the (fixed) official rate, domestic prices will tend to increase. In turn, this increase in prices will further erode competitiveness, leading agents to expect an even larger devaluation of the official exchange rate—an expectation that may translate into a further depreciation of the parallel exchange rate, and so on.[13] The evidence suggests indeed a strong correlation between parallel exchange rate depreciation and inflation in many cases. This was the case for Zaire during the hyperinflationary episode discussed earlier (see Figure 6.1).

In countries where the government is directly involved in controlling exports of a major primary commodity (as, for instance, with oil in Nigeria), there may be a direct effect of changes in the *terms of trade* on the budget as well as an indirect effect through taxes on corporate profits and domestic sales—which may be significant even if the government does not directly control exports. In such conditions, a deterioration in the terms of trade, for instance, would directly reduce government revenue and increase pressure for monetizing the fiscal deficit. Moreover, even an improvement in the terms of trade may lead to higher inflation in the future: as noted in Chapter 3, government spending has sometimes increased sharply in response to temporary *commodity price booms*; to the extent that such increases are difficult to reverse when commodity prices fall, the budget deficit may increase and inflationary finance may result.

The Frequency of Price Adjustment

In an environment in which high inflation is associated with highly variable inflation and uncertainty over the pricing horizon of price setters, the frequency of price adjustment becomes endogenous and tends to accelerate.[14] In turn, the shortening of the adjustment interval raises inflation, leading to a further shortening of the adjustment interval, and so on—with price setters more and more opting to denominate their prices in a foreign currency. Dornbusch, Sturzenegger, and Wolf (1990), in their analysis of inflationary episodes in Bolivia, Israel, Argentina, and Brazil, suggested indeed that there appears to be *increased synchronization* between domestic prices and the nominal exchange rate as inflation rises. Thus the shortening of price adjustment intervals may become another source of inflationary pressure, if the stance of monetary policy remains accommodative.

Food Prices

In many developing countries (particularly in sub-Saharan Africa) food items comprise the bulk of the goods included in the consumer price index. In Nigeria, for instance, the share of food items in the basket of goods accounted for in the

---

[13] Again, wage indexation mechanisms may exacerbate the problem. Note that the increasing differential between the parallel and official exchange rates will typically lead to a diversion of exports from official channels and reserve losses, which may eventually force the authorities to abandon the official exchange rate. See Agénor (1992).

[14] The existence of a positive relationship between the level and the variability of inflation is well documented in both developed and developing countries (see Dornbusch, Sturzenegger, and Wolf, 1990). Of course high variability is not synonymous with uncertainty.

index is 69 percent. Consequently, supply-side factors affecting *food prices*—notably agro-climatic conditions—have an important effect on the behavior of prices. In an econometric analysis of inflation in Nigeria over the period 1960-93, Moser (1995) found that rainfall had a significant effect on the rate of price increases—in addition to money growth and exchange rate changes. More generally, there is a close correlation between inflation in food prices and inflation in consumer prices in developing countries (see Agénor, 2002a). However, precisely because of the importance of food items in the cost-of-living indices in these countries, caution must be exercised in interpreting such a correlation as a causal relationship.

Time Inconsistency and the Inflation Bias

The discussion in the previous chapter suggested that imperfect credibility in the presence of policy trade-offs can generate a **devaluation bias** in exchange rate management. In a similar manner, lack of credibility may impart an **inflation bias** to monetary policy. Lack of credibility may result again from the **time inconsistency** problem faced by policy announcements: a policy that is optimal *ex ante* may no longer be optimal *ex post*. The reason is that policymakers are typically concerned not only about inflation as a policy goal (even when it is initially high) but also with the fact that inflation (at least to the extent that it is unexpected) may carry benefits as well. Knowing this, agents will discount announcements of a policy of low inflation and will expect the policymaker to act discretionarily—which is indeed what happens in equilibrium.

For instance, in the model first proposed by Barro and Gordon (1983), policymakers are concerned about both inflation and output (or unemployment), with a **loss function** given by

$$L = \frac{1}{2}(y - \tilde{y})^2 + \frac{\theta}{2}(\pi - \tilde{\pi})^2, \quad \theta > 0, \tag{13}$$

where y is current output, $\tilde{y}$ its desired level, π actual inflation, and $\tilde{\pi}$ the desired inflation rate—which may be related to the need for revenue from the inflation tax.[15] The coefficient θ measures the relative importance of deviations of inflation from its target value in the loss function.

The economy is characterized by an **expectations-augmented Phillips curve** given by

$$y = y_L + \alpha(\pi - \pi^a) + u, \quad \alpha > 0, \ y_L < \tilde{y}, \tag{14}$$

where y_L is the long-term (or capacity) level of output, π^a expected inflation, and u a disturbance term with zero mean and constant variance. The restriction $y_L < \tilde{y}$ ensures that the policymakers have an incentive to raise output above its long-run value.

---

[15] The idea that the policymakers' incentive to keep inflation high may be related to the need to maintain the revenue from seigniorage at high levels was emphasized by Barro (1983). Another reason may be the desire to reduce the real value of the nominal public debt.

Policymakers want private agents to expect low inflation, in order to exploit a favorable trade-off between inflation and output.[16] But the mere announcement of a policy of low inflation is not credible. This is because once expectations are formed, policymakers have an incentive to renege on the announcement in order to increase output toward the desired level $\tilde{y}$ and reduce unemployment. Private agents understand the incentive to renege and therefore do not believe the policy announcement in the first place. As a result, inflation will in equilibrium be higher than it would be otherwise. Monetary policy (viewed here as consisting of direct control over the actual inflation rate) suffers therefore from an inflation bias.

Formally, substituting Equation (14) in (13) yields

$$L = \frac{1}{2} \{y_L + \alpha(\pi - \pi^a) - \tilde{y} + u\}^2 + \frac{\theta}{2}(\pi - \tilde{\pi})^2. \tag{15}$$

With a binding commitment to low inflation, expected and actual inflation rates are equal ($\pi = \pi^a$); the loss function becomes

$$L = \frac{1}{2}(y_L - \tilde{y} + u)^2 + \frac{\theta}{2}(\pi - \tilde{\pi})^2,$$

and the value of π that minimizes the expected value of L is simply

$$\pi = \tilde{\pi}. \tag{16}$$

Under discretion, policymakers take expected inflation as given; the first-order condition for minimizing the expected value of Equation (15) with respect to π is thus

$$\alpha \left[y_L + \alpha(\pi - \pi^a) - \tilde{y} \right] + \theta(\pi - \tilde{\pi}) = 0,$$

which yields

$$\pi = \frac{\alpha^2 \pi^a + \theta \tilde{\pi} + \alpha(\tilde{y} - y_L)}{\theta + \alpha^2},$$

or equivalently

$$\pi = \tilde{\pi} + \frac{\alpha(\tilde{y} - y_L)}{\theta + \alpha^2} + \frac{\alpha^2(\pi^a - \tilde{\pi})}{\theta + \alpha^2}.$$

In equilibrium, expected and actual inflation must again be equal; setting $\pi = \pi^a$ in the above expression yields

$$\pi = \tilde{\pi} + \frac{\alpha(\tilde{y} - y_L)}{\theta}. \tag{17}$$

In either case, because $\pi = \pi^a$, in equilibrium output can deviate from its capacity level only as a result of random shocks:

$$y = y_L + u. \tag{18}$$

---

[16] See McCallum (1997) for a critical discussion of this view of monetary policy.

But under discretion the equilibrium inflation rate is higher than desired inflation (as shown in Equation (17)) because agents understand the policymakers' incentive to depart from a policy of low inflation once expectations are formed. The higher the difference between desired output and its capacity level $(\tilde{y} - y_L)$ is, the higher the slope of the Phillips curve α is, and the lower the relative importance of inflation in the policymaner's loss function θ is, the higher inflation will be in equilibrium.

As discussed earlier in the context of exchange rate management (Chapter 5), under most circumstances a **credible commitment** to a policy rule is welfare enhancing compared with a discretionary policy. In the above model, for instance, to the extent that policymakers can credibly commit themselves to low (or no) inflation, the economy will be better off: output will be the same as in the discretionary policy case [as shown by Equation (18), but inflation will be lower [$\pi = \tilde{\pi}$, as shown in (16)]. The difficulty with this argument, again, is that it is not easy for policymakers to announce credible commitments to noninflationary policies. Institutional mechanisms or arrangements through which policymakers can make credible commitments to noninflationary policies are discussed later. But in the absence of mechanisms that are capable of constraining policymakers' hands, announcements of a low-inflation policy will not be credible and the inflationary bias will persist.[17]

6.2   Nominal Anchors in Disinflation

One of the most debated issues in the analysis of disinflation policies is the relative merits of exchange-rate-based stabilization versus the targeting of money (or credit) growth in conjunction with exchange rate flexibility. This section reviews the main arguments for and against these two alternative approaches to inflation stabilization.

At the outset, it is worth noting that in an economy in which information is complete and no distortions or rigidities are present, exchange rate targets or monetary targets are *equivalent* policies under perfect capital mobility. However, this equivalence need not hold in the presence of incomplete information, market distortions and rigidities, or imperfect capital mobility. Fischer (1986), for instance, showed that in an economy with **multi-period nominal contracts**, in which policy fundamentals have been adjusted for disinflation purposes, exchange rate targets dominate monetary targets under *some* configurations of the underlying parameters, but are dominated under other configurations.[18] Agénor and Montiel (1999, chap. 11) showed that, under imperfect capital mobility, disinflation through a reduction in the nominal devaluation rate and disinflation through a fall in the rate of growth of domestic credit are not equivalent; in the

---

[17]As shown by Green (1996), a credible commitment to an explicit inflation target (as discussed in Chapter 4) can mitigate the inflationary bias, but possibly at the expense of higher variability in output.

[18]Although the robustness of Fischer's results remains an open issue (given the particular nature of the model that was used), his analysis illustrates a general point.

former case, the economy adjusts gradually to its long-run equilibrium position, whereas in the latter case there are no transitional dynamics.

In general, the choice between the exchange rate and the money supply as a nominal anchor can be viewed as depending on three main considerations:

- the *degree of controllability* and the effectiveness of the instrument in bringing down inflation;

- the *adjustment path* of the economy and the *relative costs* (measured in terms of output losses and lower employment) associated with each instrument;

- the *degree of credibility* that each instrument commands, and its relationship with fiscal policy.

6.2.1   Controllability and Effectiveness

In general, policymakers cannot directly control the money supply, whereas fixing the exchange rate can be done relatively quickly and without substantial costs. In addition, in an environment in which money demand is subject to large random shocks and velocity is unstable, the effectiveness of the money supply as an anchor is reduced, whereas an exchange rate peg will continue to anchor the price level through its direct impact on prices of tradables and inflation expectations. On such grounds, then, fixing the exchange rate rather than the money stock may appear preferable. Moreover, because it is a clear, *monitorable target*, a pegged rate may strengthen the government's commitment to the stabilization effort and help price- and wage-setters coordinate their price-setting decisions and expectations on a new, low-inflation equilibrium (Bruno, 1991). However, policymakers must also be able to convince private agents that they are willing and able to *defend* the fixed exchange rate. The discussion in the previous chapter of the policy trade-offs that arise in managing the exchange rate suggests that this may be difficult to achieve if the current account deficit is large or if official reserves are low. If agents lack confidence in the authorities' ability to defend a fixed exchange rate, **speculative attacks** will occur, eventually forcing the abandonment of the fixed exchange rate (see Chapter 8).

6.2.2   Adjustment Paths and Relative Costs

In general, the dynamic adjustment paths of the economy associated with money-based and exchange-rate-based stabilization programs (and thus the relative output costs associated with each approach) tend to differ significantly. In the model of Calvo and Végh (1993), for instance, exchange-rate-based stabilization programs lead to an initial expansion and a recession later on, whereas money-based programs are characterized by an initial contraction in output.

The former pattern has been dubbed the **boom-recession cycle** and is particularly marked in settings where the credibility of the stabilization program is low—in the sense that it is perceived as *temporary*. Agents, in an attempt to take advantage of temporarily low prices of tradable goods, increase spending. The resulting current account deficit and real exchange rate appreciation (which is particularly marked if nominal wage contracts are *backward-looking* and prices are set as a markup over production costs) eventually undermine the program and validate expectations—by forcing the authorities eventually to abandon the attempt to fix the exchange rate. By contrast, an expected collapse of a money-based program does not lead to **intertemporal expenditure switching** because the central bank does not commit its reserves to support the exchange rate; there is, therefore, no anticipation of a currency crisis.

The evidence in favor of large intertemporal substitution effects is, however, relatively weak. In particular, the econometric study by Reinhart and Végh (1995) suggested that although such effects can explain the behavior of consumption for some of the programs implemented in the 1980s, this is not the case for the *tablita* experiments of the 1970s in Argentina, Chile, and Uruguay (see Agénor and Montiel, 1999). Essentially, the low intertemporal substitution parameters estimated for these countries suggest that nominal interest rates would have had to fall substantially more than they did to account for a sizable fraction of the consumption boom recorded in the data.

In a more detailed review of the empirical evidence, Agénor and Montiel (1999) also concluded that intertemporal effects were not large enough to explain the pattern of output and consumption in exchange-rate-based stabilization programs, suggesting that other mechanisms may be at play.

One such mechanism emphasizes the interactions between monetary and *supply-side factors*. These factors were analyzed, in particular, by Roldós (1995), in a dependent-economy model with physical capital (which plays a dual role as a financial asset and a production input), endogenous labor supply, and a **cash-in-advance constraint** on purchases of both consumption and capital goods. Roldós showed that, as a result of the cash-in-advance constraint, inflation creates a wedge between the real rate of return on foreign-currency-denominated assets and that of domestic-currency-denominated assets—which include money and capital. Thus, a stabilization program based on a permanent—and thus fully credible, in the Calvo-Végh sense—reduction in the devaluation rate (and ultimately the inflation rate) reduces the wedge and leads to an increase in the desired capital stock in the long run. In the short run, consumption and investment increase, causing a real appreciation, a current account deficit, and an increase in output of home goods. During the transition period, firms increase gradually their purchases of capital goods and their capital stock (which is constant on impact), drawing labor into the (capital-intensive) tradable sector, raising wages, and leading to further appreciation of the real exchange rate. Over time, the increase in output of tradable goods lowers the initial current account deficit generated on impact by the increase in aggregate demand.

In a related contribution, Roldós (1997a) showed that a gradual and permanent reduction in the nominal devaluation rate leads to an initial boom when the intertemporal elasticity of substitution in labor supply is larger than that in consumption. The expansion in output occurs in both the tradable and the nontradable production sectors, as a result of a reduction in real wages. The reduction in the devaluation rate lowers inflation and raises the marginal value of wealth, thereby raising the opportunity cost of leisure and inducing an increase in labor supply in the initial phase of the program. The continued reduction over time in the rate of devaluation and the rate of inflation leads to further increases in the supply of labor and downward pressure on wages.

By contrast, Roldós (1995) found that real wages increase during the transition (after falling on impact), whereas the long-run effect on labor supply is ambiguous. The models developed by Roldós do not predict a recession at a later stage; nevertheless, a comprehensive analysis of alternative models (based on simulation techniques) by Rebelo and Végh (1997) also emphasized the importance of supply-side factors (notably the role of real wages) in explaining the boom-recession cycle in exchange-rate-based programs.

Another important consideration is assessing how the relative costs of money-based and exchange-rate-based programs relate to their implications for *remonetization*. A pegged exchange rate system provides a convenient way for households and enterprises to rebuild their real money balances after a period of high inflation.[19] The fall in inflationary expectations that a credible stabilization program generates at the outset may lead agents to increase their desired holdings of real money balances. Under a pegged exchange rate, this increase is satisfied automatically through the balance of payments, as agents repatriate their capital held abroad and convert it into domestic currency. By contrast, under a money supply anchor (that is, a floating-rate regime), there is no automatic mechanism for agents to rebuild their real money balances, because the central bank does not have to purchase repatriated capital in return for domestic money—notwithstanding operations aimed at smoothing exchange rate movements.

In principle, the central bank could support remonetization of the banking system by expanding domestic credit in line with rising demand for real money balances, but such a course of action is difficult to carry out, because domestic credit expansion by itself may undermine the credibility of the stabilization program. Therefore, many central banks refrain from domestic credit expansion, and the economy remains under-monetized, suffering from excessively high real interest rates and an overvalued currency.

The result is that successful anti-inflation programs under a money supply target (and floating exchange rates) tend to be more contractionary than those carried out under pegged exchange rates. Fischer, Sahay, and Végh (2002) provide evidence suggesting that money-based stabilization tend to be contractionary on impact (with output and consumption recovering after about two years), whereas exchange-rate based stabilization tend to be characterized by an initial expansion.[20]

---

[19]There exists considerable evidence showing a dramatic rise in velocity or demonetization in high-inflation economies.

[20]However, it should be noted that research by Easterly (1995) and Gould (1996) suggested that some money-based programs have also been characterized by an initial expansion of output.

6.2.3 Credibility, Fiscal Commitment, and Flexibility

The degree of credibility of the money supply and the exchange rate is an important consideration in choosing a nominal anchor. Credibility depends not only on the policymakers' ability to convey clear signals about their *policy preferences* (as discussed in more detail later) but also on the degree of controllability of policy instruments and the dynamic adjustment path of the economy, as argued earlier.

In particular, the ability of the public to observe the exchange rate at any point in time—as opposed to monetary and credit aggregates, which are only observable at substantial intervals, based on data that are usually supplied by the government—enhances the credibility of an exchange rate anchor. A money-based stabilization that is accompanied by an immediate recession, for instance, may lose credibility rapidly, if the short-term output and employment cost is high.

Likewise, when the exchange rate is used as a nominal anchor, residual inflation in home goods prices may remain high, as a result of backward-looking indexation of wages. Combined with the expansion of aggregate demand that often accompanies these programs, this may lead to a real appreciation that may immediately weaken the credibility of a policy aimed at fixing the exchange rate, because agents will anticipate future nominal devaluations aimed at realigning relative prices and prevent growing external imbalances.

In general, when lack of credibility is pervasive, the choice between money and the exchange rate may not matter a great deal; inflation will remain high regardless of the anchor.[21] An exchange-rate rule is, however, more successful in reducing inflation if there is *some* degree of credibility in the program; in that case, the initial expansion and the upward pressure on the real exchange rate will be dampened.

It has also been argued that an exchange rate anchor may induce a higher commitment to undertake the necessary accompanying stabilization measures, most importantly *fiscal adjustment*. The reason is that a loss in confidence (inducing large private capital outflows) threatens directly the program's anchor only in an exchange-rate-based stabilization plan. Because avoiding such a risk requires a high degree of confidence in the government's program, it may act as an incentive to stick to the targeted path of fiscal adjustment.[22] Thus, an exchange rate anchor is preferable whenever the underlying commitment of policymakers to fiscal discipline is presumed high.[23] Conversely, if there are

---

[21] The appendix to this chapter shows that, in a setting in which wage contracts are staggered over time, the lower the degree of credibility, the higher will be the degree of inflation persistence.

[22] This argument does not necessarily apply if the exchange-rate-based stabilization is based on a crawling peg, because under such a regime a less stringent path of fiscal adjustment could be accommodated by designing appropriately the preannounced exchange rate depreciation schedule. However, the credibility of the depreciation schedule itself may well depend on the perceived commitment to fiscal adjustment.

[23] The "underlying commitment of policymakers to fiscal discipline" refers to the exogenous preferences of policymakers, as opposed to their actual behavior, which is likely be endogenous to the choice of nominal anchor.

doubts about the government's commitment to fiscal restraint, an exchange rate peg would also lack credibility and would be impossible to defend.

A good illustration of this last point is provided by Végh's (1992) review of ten exchange-rate-based programs (all of them in Latin America, except for the 1985 Israeli stabilization) aimed at stopping high chronic inflation. Seven of these programs were classified as failures, in the sense that the peg could not be sustained and initial reductions in inflation were subsequently reversed. In two cases the failure was attributed to a real appreciation of the currency following slow convergence of inflation, in spite of achieving fiscal balance (Chile and Uruguay, 1978). In the remaining five, however, *failure to implement a lasting fiscal adjustment* was the main factor. This evidence suggests therefore that the discipline induced by an exchange rate anchor may not, in itself, be sufficient to ensure the fiscal adjustment necessary to sustain the peg.

6.2.4   The Flexibilization Stage

The foregoing discussion suggests that although a pegged exchange rate can be beneficial in stopping high inflation, maintaining it for too long can become problematic once inflation has stabilized at moderate (but not low) rates, with nominal rigidities (in price and wage formation) slowing further declines in inflation.

With a fixed nominal exchange rate, continued inflation higher than that prevailing in trading partners implies an appreciation of the real exchange rate, which eventually erodes external competitiveness and—unless matched by productivity gains in the traded goods sector—hinders export expansion.[24] In turn, a deteriorating trade performance may force the authorities to depreciate the exchange rate and reignite inflationary pressures. Several studies have indeed identified real appreciation as one of the causes of failure of inflation stabilization plans (see, for instance, Veiga, 1999).

More generally, a shift toward a more flexible exchange rate regime (such as a *crawling peg* or a *band regime*, as discussed in the previous chapter), once macroeconomic stability is achieved, provides an important mechanism through which adjustment to internal and external shocks can occur.[25]   At the same time, because switching away from a pegged rate may be perceived as a reduced commitment to low inflation, emphasis on fiscal and monetary discipline must be strengthened through transparent signals (such as the adoption of an explicit limit on the size of the structural budget deficit relative to GDP) to avoid any damage in credibility and an increase in inflation expectations.

---

[24]Note that a large devaluation at the outset of stabilization may lead to a large initial undervaluation of the real exchange rate. This strategy may provide a cushion to the system by allowing it, at least for a while, to absorb the real appreciation that may result from imposing a fixed exchange rate.

[25]As discussed in the next chapter, exchange rate flexibility may also be useful to facilitate the management of capital inflows. A relatively wide band of permissible currency fluctuations around a central rate, in particular, may help to deter short-term speculative movements.

6.3   Disinflation: The Role of Credibility

6.3.1   Sources of Credibility Problems

The current literature distinguishes among four different sources of credibility problems in disinflation programs:

- **Inconsistency** between the objective of disinflation and the policy instruments to achieve this objective, or the **sequencing** of policy measures in an overall reform program. For instance, if the main source of inflation is a large fiscal deficit and an expansion in money supply, a program that does not specify how fiscal discipline is to be restored will lack credibility.

- **Uncertainty** associated with the policy environment and exogenous shocks, which arises from the fact that the economy may be hit by shocks that are large enough to render the assumptions underlying even a well-designed (or internally consistent) program inadequate. If the probability of an adverse shock of this type is high, convincing private agents of the viability of the program targets (in the absence of **contingency mechanisms**) will be difficult and will adversely affect the degree of credibility of the stabilization effort. Examples of adverse shocks include external shocks, such as a deterioration in the country's terms of trade, or a rise in interest rates on world capital markets.[26]

- **Time inconsistency** of policy announcements, which results from the fact that a program that is optimal *ex ante* may not be optimal *ex post*, given possible trade-offs between disinflation and other economic goals. As noted earlier, time inconsistency leads to an **inflation bias** in monetary policy.

- **Incomplete** or **asymmetric information** about policymakers' preferences, which results from the fact that private agents may not know for sure how strong the commitment to low inflation is, particularly at the inception of a stabilization program.

In fact, it is only over time that private agents will come to believe that policymakers are serious about the policy goal of low inflation. This learning process will be slow in settings in which policymakers have a long tradition of **stop-and-go policies**, and the rotation of policymakers in office tends to be high—a situation that tends to create some degree of confusion regarding the true policy objectives and preferences of policymakers. **Imperfect monitoring capabilities** may also hamper the ability of private agents to detect policymakers' preferences. In particular, private agents may learn only gradually, through

---

[26]Political uncertainty may also affect credibility; the possibility that the government's majority base may collapse (because, for instance, it is built on a coalition of parties with different ideological orientations) may lead private agents to have doubts about the political feasibility of the stabilization program and to expect policy reversals—an issue that will be examined further in Chapter 17.

a **backward-induction process** (see, for instance, Cukierman, 1992). Under these conditions, policymakers can, in order to generate a temporary output gain, attempt to exploit their informational advantage. Nevertheless, imperfect monitoring capability makes building reputation by policymakers more difficult; and without a reputation for seriousness, policymakers will find it difficult to dampen inflationary expectations and reduce actual inflation.

Direct and robust quantitative techniques for assessing the relative importance of these various sources of lack of credibility remain limited. As discussed by Agénor and Taylor (1992), two methods that can be used are as follows:

- Specify a model of the inflationary process in which lagged inflation appears, such as Equation (12), and estimate it with *recursive least-squares techniques*. Changes over time in the behavior of the coefficient of the lagged inflation rate (a measure of inertia or persistence) can then be used to assess changes in the degree of credibility. Increased credibility will translate into a lower coefficient over time. Edwards (1995), for instance, used this method to assess the credibility of macroeconomic policy in Venezuela during the mid-1970s and the 1980s.[27]

- Study changes over time (possibly with recursive least-squares techniques as well) in the behavior of the coefficient of a variable measuring the opportunity cost of holding domestic money, such as the expected inflation rate (taken from household or business surveys, or proxied by the lagged actual inflation rate), the domestic interest rate, or the rate of depreciation of the (official or parallel) exchange rate, in a regression model of money demand. The assumption is that increased credibility will translate into not only a lower degree of persistence in the inflationary process (as argued earlier) but also in a shift toward domestic-currency-denominated assets— and thus a lower coefficient attached to the opportunity cost of holding domestic money balances.

6.3.2   Enhancing Credibility

Enhancing the degree of credibility of a disinflation program is important because it raises its probability of success. This subsection discusses four possible ways of doing so: the adoption of a drastic (big bang) program as a way to signal the policymaker's commitment to disinflation, greater central bank independence, the imposition of price controls, and recourse to conditional foreign assistance. The discussion throughout focuses on countries where policymakers must deal with high inflation, rather than hyperinflation. Kiguel and Liviatan (1992*b*) have argued that credibility is easier to establish in the latter case. In

---

[27] In Edwards's model of inflation, persistence is associated with both backward wage indexation and an exchange rate rule that relates the nominal devaluation rate to the (lagged) inflation differential between the domestic economy and the rest of the world. Under full wage indexation and full exchange rate indexation, inflation will exhibit a unit root and be nonstationary (see the appendix to Chapter 9).

chronic-inflation countries, where inertial mechanisms—such as staggered contracts and implicit or explicit indexation—are well developed, the public tends to view disinflation programs as postponable, thus reducing their credibility. By contrast, as noted earlier, the very nature of hyperinflation often leads agents to believe that it is not sustainable.

Big Bang and Gradualism

A number of economists have advocated an early phase of *overadjustment* (that is, more stringent fiscal and monetary policies than would be otherwise necessary to attain the inflation objective) as a means to signal to skeptical agents the policymakers' commitment to inflation stabilization. Such measures may be easier to implement in countries where a new government with a broad anti-inflation mandate is just being put in place, because in such circumstances the public is often more willing to bear the costs that are entailed. It has also been argued that the initial costs of a big bang program that brings inflation down quickly, though high, may be less than the costs associated with inflation continuing at a higher level for a longer period of time.

However, instead of helping to alleviate the credibility problem, adopting an overly tight policy stance may exacerbate it—and lead to a complete abandonment of the stabilization program—because it may create expectations of *future policy reversals.* Such expectations may result from the conjunction of two factors:

- large short-run output and employment costs and a consequent loss of *political support*—particularly if only a fragile political consensus was established at the outset of the program;

- the fact that the future benefits of disinflation (in terms of a lower inflation tax and higher output) are heavily discounted by the public.

In such conditions, enhancing the credibility of a disinflation program may require not so much shock therapy but rather the implementation of measures that are regarded as politically and economically *sustainable* and viewed as difficult to reverse by future governments.

Central Bank Independence

An institutional mechanism through which the credibility of policymakers can be enhanced is to grant the central bank full independence in the conduct of monetary and exchange rate policies, with a clear mandate to maintain price stability. Such independence may be critical in countries where central bank financing of government budget deficits is often the main source of inflation. Countries where such reforms have been implemented in recent years include Chile and Mexico.

There are various factors, however, that may mitigate the credibility gain to monetary policy that central bank independence may provide.

- *Legal independence* does not guarantee the absence of *political interference* and *political pressure* on the central bank's policy decisions. In practice, most governments in developing countries retain some degree of influence on these decisions.

- Moreover, as pointed out by Blackburn and Christensen (1989), the government (which established the central bank's independence in the first place) often retains the ability to restructure (or abolish) independence should the central bank refuse to compromise its position (at least partly) on matters over which the government fundamentally disagrees. As a result, even an independent central bank may be willing to make concessions to the government in order to retain its autonomy.

- Adhering to a rigid anti-inflation policy stance implemented by an independent central bank may be suboptimal (compared with some degree of discretion or **contingent rules**) in an economy subject to adverse economic shocks.

- The credibility of monetary policy may depend on the *overall stance* of macroeconomic policy, rather than on the degree of central bank independence *per se*. For instance, if the fiscal policy targets adopted by the Treasury are inconsistent with the low-inflation target of the monetary authorities, and are perceived as such by the public, credibility will be impossible to achieve—even with a highly independent central bank.

More generally, independent monetary and fiscal authorities may adopt policies that generate *coordination problems* and generate costs that may outweigh the gain resulting from central bank autonomy alone. This point is well illustrated in the game-theoretic model of monetary and fiscal management developed by Alesina and Tabellini (1990), in which inflation, public spending, and the level of distortionary taxation are all determined simultaneously from the strategic interactions between policymakers who possess conflicting objectives regarding inflation, employment, and public expenditure levels. The main insight of their analysis is the ambiguity of the net benefits from central bank precommitment to low inflation. The reason is that lower inflation reduces the revenue from inflationary finance (as discussed earlier) and forces the fiscal authority, in the presence of downward rigidity on public spending, to resort to a higher level of distortionary taxation.

Some early empirical studies focusing mostly on industrial countries and reviewed by Cukierman (1992) concluded that countries where central banks had the highest degree of autonomy also had the lowest levels of inflation. Central bank independence in these studies was measured in terms of a variety of factors, including the appointment mechanisms for the governor and the board of directors, the turnover of central bank governors, the approval mechanism for conducting monetary policy (the extent to which the central bank's policy decisions are immune from government or parliament interference), statutory requirements of the central bank regarding its basic aim and financing of the budget deficit (including whether or not interest rates are levied on deficit financing), and the existence of a ceiling on total government borrowing from the central bank.

However, another review of the empirical literature by Forder (1998) found no robust association between central bank independence and inflation performance in industrial countries and highlighted several methodological problems in many of the early studies. The studies by Sikken and De Haan (1998) and De Haan and Kooi (2000) for developing countries were also inconclusive. Sikken and De Haan, for instance, measured central bank independence using three indicators:

- The **synthetic legal measure** reported by Cukierman (1992), which incorporates four sets of variables: those related to the appointment, dismissal, and term of office of the governor of the central bank; variables related to the resolution of conflicts between the executive branch and the central bank over monetary policy and the participation of the central bank in the budgetary process; final objectives of the central bank, as stated in its charter; and legal restrictions on the ability of the public sector to borrow from the central bank.

- The **turnover rate** of central bank governors, which attempts to capture *actual* (as opposed to legal) independence. In developing countries measures of central bank independence based on legal statutes may be inadequate because political instability often means that the status of the central bank can be uncertain and/or subject to rapid changes.

- A **political vulnerability index**, defined as the fraction of political transitions that are followed within six months by a replacement of the central bank governor.

Using all three indicators and data for 30 developing countries for the period 1950-94, Sikken and De Haan found no evidence that central bank independence creates an incentive for governments to maintain low fiscal deficits. They also found that measures of independence are not clearly related to the degree of monetization of government budget deficits by the central bank. Thus, both analytical arguments and empirical evidence suggest that central bank independence may not have all the benefits that advocates tend to emphasize. The debate is certainly not over; the overview by Berger, De Haan, and Eijffinger (2001) is quite supportive, and another study by Brumm (2002) found a strong negative relationship between central bank independence and inflation. In any case, as pointed out by Hayo and Hefeker (2002), the existence of this relationship should not necessarily be interpreted as an indication of causality running from independence to inflation.

Price Controls

The case for using price controls has traditionally been viewed as resting on the argument that the inflationary process is characterized by substantial inertia, stemming from explicit or implicit indexation—a common feature, as discussed earlier, of economies suffering from chronically high inflation. Various economists have argued that, in such conditions, restrictive demand policies may be incapable of yielding a rapid fall in inflation.

There are also several arguments in favor of the *temporary* use of price controls, viewing them, as noted by Dornbusch, Sturzenegger, and Wolf (1990, pp. 51-52), as playing the following roles:

- **A realignment device**. In economies in which pricing decisions are not instantaneous (as a result, for instance, of the existence of multi-period contracts), price controls may help realign prices quickly and correct price distortions.

- **A coordination device**. Adjusting to a new, low-inflation environment requires price setters to reset their prices. This resetting brings into play expectations about what other agents think; price controls help to coordinate expectations toward a low-inflation path.

- **A fiscal device**. The reverse *Olivera-Tanzi effect* discussed earlier implied that the transition from high to low inflation yields an immediate gain in real revenue from taxation. This may lower the borrowing needs of the government from the central bank, helping to slow monetary expansion and thus overall inflation.

It has also been argued that price controls—despite the well-known microeconomic distortions that they entail—may help enhance credibility by serving as an *additional nominal anchor*. Blejer and Liviatan (1987), for instance, considered a situation in which lack of credibility stems from **asymmetric information** between the public and policymakers. In such conditions, as indicated earlier, the mere announcement of a low-inflation objective will not be fully believed. Private agents will adjust their expectations only gradually, after observing policy decisions. Price controls may give policymakers some *breathing room*—a period during which they can convince the public, by adopting and sticking to appropriate monetary and fiscal policies, of their commitment to disinflate. By allowing a rapid reduction in inflation, the reverse Olivera-Tanzi effect will also lead to an improvement in fiscal accounts (as mentioned earlier), adding credibility to the fiscal component of the program. Along the same lines, Persson and van Wijnbergen (1993) argued that price controls may help policymakers to reduce the **cost of signaling** their commitment to low inflation.

The most frequently cited example of a successful temporary application of price controls occurred in the context of the Israeli stabilization program of 1985, during which all nominal variables, including the exchange rate, were frozen (see Bruno, 1991, and Kiguel and Liviatan, 1992a). Combined with a sharp fiscal contraction and a restrictive monetary policy, the temporary application of price controls led to a quick reduction in inflation and enhanced government credibility, without a severe economic contraction.

However, the use of price controls as a credibility-enhancing device has been criticized from various perspectives. At the conceptual level, at least two arguments make the argument in favor of such controls less than convincing.

- The use of price controls may actually be *counterproductive*—in contrast to the view adopted by Blejer and Liviatan (1987)—because they do not enable the public to learn whether sufficient fiscal restraint has been achieved, that is, whether inflation has really been stopped or has only been temporarily repressed. In fact, controls may *lengthen* the time required for expectations to adjust to a new equilibrium.

- The credibility-enhancing effect of price controls may vanish if policymakers are unwilling or unable to control all prices in the economy, and if forward-looking price setters in the *uncontrolled sector* understand the incentives to depart from a preannounced price control policy in an attempt to reduce the macroeconomic costs associated with a price freeze (see Agénor, 1995). Paradoxically, the imposition of price controls in such a framework may lead to inflation inertia.

At the practical level, there are also a number of problems associated with the use of price controls. The imposition, enforcement, and phasing out of such controls are often difficult from an administrative point of view. Most importantly, by suppressing some of the symptoms of inflation, price controls have often undermined governments' willingness to attack the disease at its roots. In fact, such controls have often been used as a *substitute*, rather than as a *complement*, to fiscal and monetary adjustment. A case in point is Brazil, where three programs implemented in the late 1980s relied on price controls: the Cruzado Plan in 1986, the Bresser Plan in 1987, and the Verano Plan in 1989 (see Agénor and Montiel, 1999). However, because the price freeze was not accompanied by appropriate fiscal and monetary policies, inflation jumped to an even higher level in each case after a brief period of abatement. The repeated use of price controls diminished their effectiveness, as economic agents anticipated the price increases that would follow the flexibilization stage. Other experiences with price controls, as reviewed by Kiguel and Liviatan (1992a), lead to similar conclusions.

Aid as a Commitment Mechanism

It has recently been argued that countries engaged in disinflation programs may enhance their credibility and the probability of program success by subjecting themselves to an external enforcement agency whose commitment to low inflation is well established—such as a multilateral institution like the International Monetary Fund. Such an agency, in turn, provides foreign assistance *conditional* on attaining specific macroeconomic (and possibly structural) policy targets. Conditionality therefore turns the commitment mechanism into a *carrot-and-stick* one, which may strengthen the determination of the policymakers to enforce the terms of the agreement.

However, a variety of difficulties may arise in judging the credibility-enhancing effect of foreign assistance.

- Political considerations often play a role in deciding whether particular countries should receive external financial assistance. As a result, the public may be unwilling to accept an externally enforced program as a signal of the policymakers' commitment to low inflation.

- Conditionality is a double-edged sword. A right dose of it may serve as an incentive to stick to the terms of the agreed program. However, if the degree of conditionality attached to foreign aid is perceived to be excessive (in the sense of being based on unreasonably tight policy targets), uncertainty about external support may rise, leading to a loss in political support, delays in stabilization, and a higher possibility that the program will collapse, as argued by Orphanides (1996).

6.4 Two Stabilization Experiments

Episodes of chronically high inflation or outright hyperinflation have been common in the developing world for at least the past three decades.[28] A considerable literature (much of it summarized by Agénor and Montiel, 1999) has been devoted to the inflationary episodes of the 1980s and early 1990s, particularly those that brought chaos to several countries in Latin America. Instead of providing a detailed overview of this literature, this section focuses on two experiences: Egypt (1992-97) and Uganda (1987-95). These two cases illustrate the main approaches to stabilization reviewed earlier. The Egyptian program is more akin to an exchange-rate-based stabilization, whereas the Ugandan case is representative of a money-based approach. Both cases also provide useful illustrations of the role of fiscal adjustment in stabilization programs.

6.4.1 Egypt, 1992-97

In the second half of the 1980s and the early 1990s, Egypt faced large macroeconomic imbalances (see Figure 6.3).

- Although inflation, at an average rate of about 20 percent during the period 1985/86 to 1990/91, was not excessively high, the fiscal deficit reached an average of 15 percent of GDP during the same period, and annual rates of money growth averaged 18 percent.[29]

- The *dollarization ratio*, as measured by the share of foreign currency (U.S. dollar) deposits in total bank deposits, grew to about 40 percent in 1988 and 46 percent in 1990.

---

[28]There have also been episodes of chronic but moderate inflation; see Dornbusch and Fischer (1993) for a discussion of some of these cases.

[29]The fiscal year in Egypt starts in July of the first year noted and ends in June of the following year.

- Although a series of nominal devaluations, beginning in 1986, led to a depreciation of about 30 percent between 1986 and 1991 of the real effective exchange rate, the current account deficit reached nearly 8 percent of GDP in 1988/89 and almost 10 percent in 1990/91.

- Gross external debt increased substantially, amounting to 147 percent of GDP during the period 1988/89-1990/91. Debt service, in proportion of exports of goods and services, exceeded 25 percent in 1989/90.

Following several unsuccessful attempts at tackling these imbalances, a program of macroeconomic stabilization and structural reform was implemented in 1991. Key features of the program were a combination of fiscal, monetary, and credit policies together with an exchange rate anchor policy which was viewed as a way to

- signal the government's commitment to disinflate;

- limit *pass-through effects* of nominal exchange rate changes to prices.

The program led to a substantial adjustment in fiscal accounts, through both increases in revenue and reductions in expenditure.

- A general sales tax was introduced in 1991, and a global income tax reform was implemented in 1993, with significant effects on revenue.

- Oil revenues and Suez Canal receipts as well as taxes on imports increased substantially in early 1991.

- Cuts in public expenditure amounted to about 7.5 percent of GDP. These cuts were largely concentrated on investment outlays; cuts in current expenditure affected mostly subsidies and transfers rather than wages.

- The debt forgiveness and rescheduling agreement that Egypt reached with its official creditors through the **Paris Club** in 1991 also led to a substantial reduction in interest payments on its external debt.[30] Interest payments as a percentage of GDP fell from a peak of 9.5 percent in 1993/94, to 6.2 percent in 1996/97 (Handy et al., 1998, p. 16).

As a result of these measures, the overall budget deficit of the government declined sharply from about 8.6 percent of GDP in 1987/88 to 3.5 percent in 1992/93 and 1.3 in 1994/95. At the same time, the primary fiscal balance of the government improved from a deficit of about 9 percent of GDP in 1987/88 to a surplus of 5 percent in 1992/93 and 6.1 percent in 1994/95. Most of this adjustment took place during the first two years of the program. Gross domestic public debt fell from 70.5 percent of GDP in 1990/91 to 52 percent in 1996/97.[31]

---

[30] The Paris Club is an association of bilateral creditor countries (mostly industrial countries). See Chapter 16 for a discussion of its role in the context of debt rescheduling arrangements.

[31] During the same period Egypt also implemented a number of structural reforms aimed at liberalizing the trade system, eliminating input and consumer goods subsidies, and privatizing public sector enterprises.

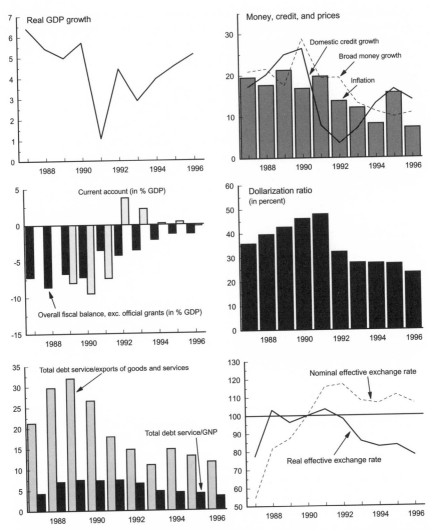

Figure 6.3. Egypt: Macroeconomic indicators, 1987-96 (in percent per annum, unless otherwise indicated). Data refer to the fiscal year (July 1-June 30), except for exchange rates. The year 1988, for instance refers to 1987/88. Dollarization ratio = U.S. dollar deposits in percent of total deposits. For nominal and real effective exchange rates, 1990 = 100; a rise is a depreciation. Source: International Monetary Fund.

Fiscal adjustment led to a sharp reduction in broad money growth, which fell from 28.7 percent in 1989/90 to 11.2 percent in 1993/94 and 10.5 percent in 1996/97. The rate of inflation declined from 16.8 percent in 1989/90 to 8.2 percent in 1993/94 and 6.2 percent in 1996/97. The adjustment effort, combined with debt relief and a surge in capital inflows, also resulted in an improvement in external accounts and a substantial accumulation of foreign reserves. The current account improved from a deficit of about 9.5 percent in 1989/90 to a surplus of 1.1 percent on average for the period 1991/92-1996/97. Official reserves reached US$28 billion in 1995/96. The ratio of gross foreign debt to GDP fell from 83 percent in 1990/91 to 39 percent in 1996/97; the ratio of debt service to exports of goods and services fell from a peak of 26.6 percent in 1989/90 to 14.8 percent in 1993/94 and less than 13 percent in 1996/97. The improvement in external accounts occurred despite a significant appreciation of the real effective exchange rate (based on consumer prices) by about 30 percent between July 1991 and December 1996.[32]

The dollarization ratio fell from about 46 percent in 1989/90 to nearly 32 percent in 1991/92, 23 percent in 1995/96, and 20 percent in 1996/97. The de-dollarization process gathered pace as a result of the large differential between interest rates on domestic assets and U.S. dollar deposits, which fell to 5 percent in 1994/95, compared with about 14 percent in 1991/92. In addition, the disinflation program appears to have gained credibility fairly rapidly, leading to a reduction in expectations of inflation and currency devaluation. Large capital inflows (a cumulative value of about US$5 billion, or 10.6 percent of GDP, between 1991/92 and 1993/94 alone) and the buildup of foreign reserves (which increased the central bank's ability to fend off speculative attacks) also enhanced the credibility of the exchange rate peg.[33]

The output cost of disinflation was a short-lived recession: real GDP growth dropped to 1.1 percent in 1990/91 (compared with 5.7 during the previous fiscal year) but rebounded rapidly to 4.6 percent in 1994/95 and 5 percent on average for 1995/96-1996/97. This reflected two factors:

- Real credit growth to the nongovernment sector remained positive throughout the stabilization program, averaging 11 percent between 1992/93 and 1996/97. The share of domestic bank credit to the private sector reached 43 percent in January 1996, compared with 29 percent in 1990/91.

- Although interest rates were liberalized in early 1991 and jumped to relatively high levels at the inception of the program, they went down very quickly. Nominal interest rates on deposits reached 16 percent in 1991/92 but declined to 10 percent in 1995/96; during the same period, lending rates dropped from 19 percent to 14 percent. Real interest rates on deposits fell from 4.7 percent in 1991/92 to 2.9 percent in 1994/95 (Subramanian, 1997). This rapid decline reflected the fall in inflation and the credibility gain, which dampened inflationary expectations; it avoided

[32]The dollar wage index computed by Subramanian (1997) suggests a real appreciation of about 25 percent between 1990/91 and 1995/96. The extent to which this appreciation did or did not reflect an equilibrium phenomenon, induced by productivity gains in the tradables sector, remains a matter of debate.

[33]During the period 1991/92 to 1993/94, Egypt conducted massive sterilization operations to neutralize the effect of capital inflows on the monetary base (see Chapter 7). The fiscal cost of sterilization—calculated as the change in net domestic assets of the Central Bank of Egypt, which can be viewed as the counterpart to the capital inflows, multiplied by the interest rate differential between domestic and foreign assets—is estimated by Subramanian (1997) to have reached a cumulative value of 4 percent of GDP. See also Handy et al. (1998, pp. 26-33).

excessive financial pressure on weak firms and dampened incentives to default.

Key lessons of Egypt's stabilization experience are the importance of fiscal adjustment and a favorable (or supportive) external environment. Debt reduction and write-offs (through their effect on debt service payments) contributed in significant ways to fiscal adjustment and improvements in the country's external accounts—despite an appreciating real exchange rate. Tighter policies, with a potentially higher output cost, would have been needed otherwise if the external constraint had been more severe. External assistance played an essential role in helping the program gain credibility, corroborating, to some extent, the potentially positive role of foreign aid highlighted earlier.

6.4.2   Uganda, 1987-95

Uganda faced a difficult economic situation in the mid-1980s, in part as a result of a civil war that started early in the decade and the economic devastation (notably in the transportation, power, and water facilities) that was associated with it. In 1986 per capita GDP was estimated to be at about 50 percent below the level of 1970, and inflation had risen to a yearly rate of 240 percent, from about 70 percent on average between 1978 and 1980. Domestic inflation, combined with a fixed exchange rate, led to a significant real appreciation and a loss of competitiveness. Foreign exchange shortages (despite increasing external payments arrears) led to a large spread between the official exchange rate and the parallel market exchange rate, thereby raising incentives to divert foreign exchange from the official market. The country also suffered from a significant and sustained deterioration in its terms of trade during the second half of the 1980s and early 1990s; in part as a consequence of the collapse of the International Coffee Agreement, the price of coffee (Uganda's main export) declined steadily between 1985 and 1993.

In 1987 the authorities launched a major stabilization effort in the context of a broad structural adjustment package, the Economic Recovery Program.[34] Stabilization took place through a tightening of monetary and fiscal policies. The Uganda shilling was devalued in May 1987 by 77 percent, with several smaller step devaluations initiated subsequently. The currency depreciation was accompanied by a substantial increase in producer prices, including a large rise in the coffee price paid to farmers. Import restrictions were also progressively removed.

GDP growth responded quickly to the adjustment measures, increasing in the first year of the program by about 8 percent over the previous year (Figure 6.4). But there was less success in achieving the program's stabilization objectives in the early years. Inflation remained high, at almost 200 percent in

---

[34] Other objectives of the program included substantial structural reforms in the areas of price liberalization, exchange and payment liberalization, public enterprise reform, financial sector reform, civil service reform, and army demobilization. See Sharer, De Zoysa, and McDonald (1995).

1987/88.[35] The main factors behind this result were the insufficient effort to tighten fiscal policy and the excessive growth of bank credit to the government.

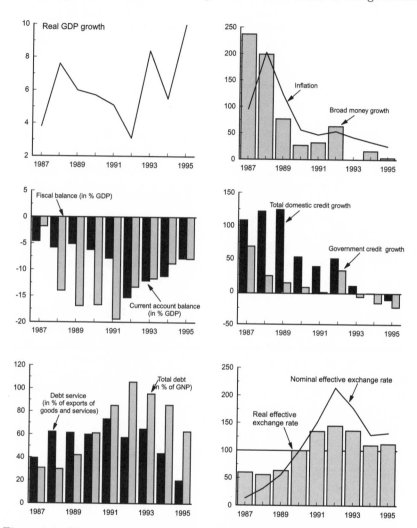

Figure 6.4. Uganda: Macroeconomic indicators, 1987-95 (in percent per annum, unless otherwise indicated). Data refer to the fiscal year (July 1-June 30), except for exchange rates. The year 1988, for instance, refers to 1987/88. For nominal and real effective exchange rates, 1990 = 100; a rise is a depreciation. Source: Sharer et al. (1995), International Monetary Fund, and World Bank.

During the same period, broad money also increased by about 200 percent. Although both inflation and money supply growth fell significantly in 1988/89 (to about 100 percent and 75 percent, respectively) insufficient efforts to curb

---

[35] The fiscal year in Uganda starts in July of the first year noted and ends in June of the following year.

government spending led to a further increase in the fiscal deficit.

In addition to a lack of fiscal adjustment, the difficulties in achieving early price stabilization and an improvement in external accounts also reflected the lingering effects on trade flows of an *overvalued official exchange rate* and a difficult external environment. Indeed, as noted earlier, Uganda faced a major deterioration in its terms of trade during the period 1987/88 to 1992/93. From a price of $2.05 per kilogram, coffee export prices fell steadily, reaching a low of $0.82 per kilogram in 1992/93—a decline of 60 percent. Accordingly, the value of export earnings dropped from $384 million in 1986/87 to $157 million in 1992/93. The lack of foreign exchange led to an accumulation of external arrears and an expansion of parallel currency markets.

New measures were implemented during 1989/90 and 1990/91. The Uganda shilling was devalued by about 41 percent in late 1989, with further adjustments taking place in the ensuing periods. Government spending was cut and tax revenues increased. The improvement in the fiscal position led to a reduction in credit expansion and money supply growth. As a result, inflation dropped to slightly below 30 percent in 1990/91 (Figure 6.4). Continued efforts to liberalize domestic prices and the exchange system (notably through the adoption of a bureau market for foreign exchange receipts for noncoffee exports and private transfers) provided favorable incentives to domestic producers and exporters of noncoffee products. Partly as result of these measures, the current account improved somewhat in 1991/92. However, because of weather-related supply factors and renewed pressure on domestic credit growth to the government (resulting from an increase in public sector spending), inflation rose to about 63 percent in that same year.

Fiscal and monetary discipline returned during the period 1992/93 to 1994/95.

- Greater expenditure control was accompanied with revenue measures and improved tax administration. Recurrent government expenditure dropped from 22.6 percent in 1991/92 to 18.7 percent in 1994/95, whereas total tax revenue rose to about 8 percent of GDP in 1992/93 and 10.5 percent in 1994/95, compared with 5.6 percent in 1988/89. The fiscal deficit dropped significantly from the peak reached in 1990/91.

- In November 1993, the foreign exchange market was unified with the introduction of an interbank market; all restrictions on current international transactions were also eliminated at the same time.[36] The removal of these restrictions not only provided strong investment incentives to exporters but also led to large private capital inflows.

After falling in 1992/93 by 0.6 percent, prices rose by 16 percent in 1993/94—in part as a result of adverse supply-side shocks—and by only 3.4 percent in 1994/95. At the same time, real output growth reached 8.4 percent in 1992/93, 5.5 percent in 1993/94, and 10 percent in 1994/95. Broad money growth dropped to about 25 percent in 1994/95. The external current account deficit

---

[36] Annex B discusses policy issues associated with exchange market unification.

(including official grants) fell to 12.1 percent, 11.2 percent and 7.8 percent during the same period, compared with 15.3 percent in 1991/92. The reduction in the external deficit in 1993/94 and 1994/95 was partly due to an improvement in the terms of trade, resulting from a recovery of world coffee prices and a substantial depreciation of the real effective exchange rate. However, foreign debt and the external debt service ratio remained stubbornly high (see Chapter 16).

The experience of Egypt and Uganda shows that *fiscal adjustment* played a key role in stabilization. In Uganda such adjustment took not only the form of a reduction and reallocation of government expenditure (toward a rehabilitation of an infrastructure devastated by the civil war) but also a rise in revenue and a strengthening of tax administration. The improvement in fiscal accounts allowed the authorities to regain control over the money supply and ultimately to tame inflation. The key lesson here is that the choice of a nominal anchor is by no means inconsequential, as discussed earlier, but without a significant reduction in fiscal imbalances, stabilization often ends in failure—regardless of the anchor chosen. A similar conclusion is reached by Ter-Minassian and Schwartz (1997) in a review of various stabilization programs implemented in Latin America since the early 1980s.[37]

Of course, fiscal reforms may differ significantly in terms of their (actual and perceived) degree of sustainability and can thus be associated with different patterns of behavior. Fiscal measures that are not perceived, for instance, as being politically sustainable (such as a drastic cut in public sector wages) may lack credibility and may create expectations of future fiscal expansion and monetization. It is also important to emphasize that the *composition* of fiscal adjustment, or the way fiscal imbalances are reduced for stabilization purposes, also has important implications for growth that should be taken into account. The evidence for Latin America, in particular, suggests that the initial brunt of expenditure cuts in stabilization programs often fell on public investment and/or operation and maintenance spending, as expenditures on wages and entitlement programs (such as social security payments, pensions, and transfers to various levels of government) proved to be relatively inflexible in the short run (Ter-Minassian and Schwartz, 1997). It is also worth emphasizing that it does make a difference whether the fiscal deficit is reduced by cutting unproductive expenditure or by raising taxes that have strong disincentive effects—even though from the point of view of macroeconomic adjustment the result would appear to be similar. In particular, as noted in Chapter 15, high rates of taxation levied on a narrow tax base foster tax evasion and may lead to an expansion of the informal economy, exacerbating fiscal constraints in the longer run.

6.5   Summary

- **Hyperinflation** (defined as an inflation rate of 50 percent per month or higher) is generally characterized by *large fiscal imbalances*, the dis-

---

[37] See also Agénor and Montiel (1999, chap. 9).

appearance of *nominal inertia* (with price setting and even transactions occurring in a foreign currency), and the perception that the process is unsustainable.

- **Chronic inflation** is characterized by less acute fiscal imbalances (which often makes it more difficult to mobilize political support for reform), a high degree of inertia resulting from widespread indexation of wages and financial assets, and *lack of credibility* in the policymakers' ability (or willingness) to stabilize.

- Fiscal imbalances and pressures to monetize budget deficits may lead the economy to a stable inflation equilibrium or **high inflation trap**.

- Other sources of chronic inflation include nominal wage inertia (through implicit or explicit indexation), exchange rate depreciation and changes in the terms of trade (which may have direct and indirect effects on the budget), the frequency of price adjustment, changes in food prices, and the **inflation bias** of monetary policy, which results from the **time inconsistency** problem faced by **policy announcements**.

The choice between the exchange rate and the money supply as a **nominal anchor** depends on the *degree of controllability* and the effectiveness of the instrument in bringing down inflation, the *adjustment path* of the economy and the *relative costs* associated with each instrument, and the *degree of credibility* that each instrument commands.

- Whereas the money supply cannot be controlled directly, fixing the exchange rate entails essentially no costs. In addition, *instability in money demand* may preclude the adoption of a monetary target. Because it is an easily monitorable target, a pegged rate is an attractive option in that it establishes an immediate focal point for coordinating price expectations and price setting.

- However, policymakers must also be able to convince agents of their ability to defend the pegged rate; this may be difficult if the current account deficit is large or if official reserves are deemed insufficient. In such conditions, **speculative attacks** may precipitate a currency collapse.

- The *adjustment paths* associated with money- and exchange-rate-based stabilization program (and thus the relative output costs associated with each instrument) tend to differ significantly. Exchange-rate-based stabilization programs are often characterized by a **boom-recession cycle**: an initial expansion in output and aggregate demand, and later on a recession.

- One explanation for the initial boom is related to the *lack of confidence* in the program's success: the perception that the program is likely to be temporary induces a boom in demand in anticipation of a collapse. The evidence on intertemporal substitution effects, however, does not suggest that such effects are large enough to explain the pattern of output. Another explanation focuses on the *supply-side effects* of stabilization.

- The *degree of credibility* of the money supply and the exchange rate as nominal anchors depends in part on the policymakers' ability to signal its *policy preferences*, and in part also on the degree of controllability of policy instruments and the dynamic adjustment path that they impart to the economy. An exchange rate anchor may induce a higher commitment to undertake necessary fiscal adjustment measures.

- The main risk associated with a fixed exchange rate anchor comes from the side of inflation. Because prices often do not stop rising immediately after the nominal exchange rate is fixed, the *real* exchange rate becomes progressively overvalued. In turn, overvaluation creates expectations of devaluation.

- To avoid this problem, the exchange rate should be fixed at the outset, but once a significant reduction in inflation is achieved, a more flexible arrangement (such as a crawling peg or a band regime) should be adopted, in order to maintain competitiveness.

- To the extent that the regime switch may increase inflationary pressures, fiscal policy may need to play a greater role in ensuring and maintaining macroeconomic stability.

Sources of *credibility problems* in disinflation programs include

- **inconsistency** between the disinflation goal and the policy instruments used to achieve this goal;

- **uncertainty,** in the absence of *contingency mechanisms*, associated with the policy environment and exogenous shocks;

- the **time-inconsistency** problem of policy announcements, which leads to an **inflation bias** in monetary policy;

- **incomplete** or **asymmetric information** about policymakers, which results from the fact that private agents may not know for sure how strong the commitment to low inflation is.

The literature suggests four ways of enhancing the degree of credibility of a disinflation program:

- The adoption of a *drastic (big bang) program* as a way to signal the policymaker's commitment to disinflation. However, an overly tight policy stance may exacerbate the credibility problem if it creates expectations of *future policy reversals*.

- Granting the central bank *full independence* in the conduct of monetary and exchange rate policies, with a clear mandate to maintain price stability. However, *legal* independence does not guarantee the absence of political interference and political pressure on the central bank's policy decisions. Moreover, adhering to a rigid anti-inflation policy may be suboptimal (compared with some degree of discretion) in an economy subject to adverse economic shocks. The credibility of monetary policy may depend more on the overall stance of macroeconomic policy, rather than on the degree of central bank independence.

- The temporary imposition of *price controls* as an additional nominal anchor, to help realign prices quickly and correct price distortions, coordinate expectations toward a low-inflation path, and increase real tax revenue (through a reverse Olivera-Tanzi effect). However, price controls may actually *lengthen* the time required for expectations to adjust to a new equilibrium, and may paradoxically lead to *inflation inertia*—if policymakers are unable to control all prices in the economy, and if price setters in the uncontrolled sector are forward looking. There are also a number of practical problems associated with the use of price controls.

- Recourse to *conditional foreign assistance* by an external enforcement agency whose commitment to low inflation is well established. However, an externally enforced program may be a noisy signal of the policymakers' commitment to low inflation due to political factors. Conditionality is also a double-edged sword. If the degree of conditionality attached to foreign aid is perceived to be excessive, it may increase uncertainty about its availability and lead to delays in stabilization.

- The experience of many developing countries (including Egypt and Uganda) suggests that, although the choice of a nominal anchor does matter, successful and lasting stabilization requires fiscal adjustment.

- But the *composition* of fiscal adjustment matters also. To the extent that fiscal imbalances are reduced by cutting public expenditure on physical capital, or by raising distortionary taxes, these imbalances may be exacerbated in the longer run as a result of adverse effects on growth and the propensity to evade taxation.

Appendix to Chapter 6
Inflation Persistence and Policy Credibility

This appendix presents a simple open-economy model, based on Agénor and Taylor (1992), with overlapping wage contracts. The model demonstrates the link between the perceived degree of policy credibility and the degree of inflation persistence.

Let y_t, p_t, and e_t denote the logarithms of domestic output, prices, and the exchange rate (the domestic price of foreign currency), respectively. Output is demand determined and capacity output is normalized to zero. Foreign prices are held constant and also normalized to zero. Aggregate demand is assumed to be given by

$$y_t = \alpha(m_t - p_t) + \beta(e_t - p_t) + u_t, \tag{A1}$$

where u_t is a stochastic demand shock.

As in Taylor's (1980) model, wage setting is staggered. Wage contracts are set for half the labor force each period and last for two periods. Current prices are thus an average of wages set in the current and the previous period, w_t and w_{t-1}, less any productivity shocks, s_t:

$$p_t = 0.5(w_t + w_{t-1}) - s_t. \tag{A2}$$

Wage negotiators are assumed to attempt to maintain a constant real wage for the duration of the contract. If δ denotes the share of domestic goods in the consumption basket of workers, then the target wage is given by

$$w_t = 0.5[\delta p_t + (1 - \delta)e_t] \tag{A3}$$

$$+ 0.5[\delta E_t p_{t+1} + (1 - \delta)E_t e_{t+1}] + 0.5\gamma(y_t + E_t y_{t+1}),$$

where $\gamma > 0$ and E_t denotes the mathematical expectation operator conditional on information available to wage contract negotiators in period t. Equation (A3) thus represents both cost-push inflationary factors (the first two terms), as well as demand-pull factors (the last term).

Suppose that the exchange rate is fixed at $\bar{e}$ and that the monetary policy rule is such that

$$m_t = \phi p_t + v_t, \tag{A4}$$

where $0 \leq \phi \leq 1$ and v_t represents money supply shocks. The parameter ϕ measures the degree of monetary accommodation.

Solving Equations(A1) through (A4) for domestic prices, and setting $\bar{e} = 0$ for simplicity, yields the following difference equation:

$$p_t = \frac{\mu}{4}(p_t + E_t p_{t+1} + p_{t-1} + E_{t-1}p_t + \lambda_t - s_t), \tag{A5}$$

where

$$\mu = \delta + \alpha\gamma(1 - \phi) - \beta\gamma,$$

and

$$\lambda_t = \frac{\gamma}{4} \left[\alpha \{ u_t + E_t u_{t+1} + u_{t-1} + E_{t-1} u_t \} + v_t + E_t v_{t+1} + v_{t-1} + E_{t-1} v_t \right].$$

Solving Equation (A5) forward yields

$$E_{t-1} p_t = \kappa_1 p_{t-1} + \left(\frac{4}{\mu \kappa_2} \right) \sum_{i=0}^{\infty} \kappa_2^{-i} E_{t-1} (\lambda_{t+i} - s_{t+i}), \tag{A6}$$

where κ_1 and κ_2 are the roots of the system, $0 < \kappa_1 < 1 < \kappa_2$, and κ_1 is given by

$$\kappa_1 = \frac{2 - \mu}{\mu} - \frac{(2 - \mu)^2 - \mu^2}{\mu}.$$

If all stochastic shocks affecting aggregate demand, the money supply, and productivity are assumed to be simple **random walks** (so that, for instance, $E_{t-1} v_t = v_{t-1}$) then a closed-form solution for inflation may be derived from Equations (A5)and (A6):

$$\Delta p_t = \kappa_1 \Delta p_{t-1} + \psi_t, \tag{A7}$$

where ψ_t is a composite shock with $E_{t-1} \psi_t = 0$.

Thus, from (A7), inflation will follow an **autoregressive process** of order 1, with an autoregressive parameter κ_1 (see Greene, 2000, chap. 17). Moreover, from the above definitions of μ and κ_1, it can be shown that $\partial \kappa_1 / \partial \phi > 0$; the degree of inflation persistence rises with the degree of monetary accommodation. Indeed, with full monetary accommodation ($\phi = 1$), then $\kappa_1 = 1$, the inflation process contains a **unit root**, and the system is unstable.

To examine the effect of a lack of policy credibility on inflation persistence in the above framework, suppose that the authorities announce a nonaccommodative policy of the type $m_t = \bar{m}$, but agents attach only a probability $0 < \rho < 1$ to the possibility of the policy being actually implemented. The probability that the accommodative policy rule (A4) will be followed instead is therefore $1 - \rho$. Solving the model as before, it is straightforward to verify that $\partial \kappa_1 / \partial \rho < 0$; the higher the credibility of the announced low inflation policy, the lower will be the degree of inflation persistence.

Chapter 7

Capital Inflows: Causes and Policy Responses

The degree of integration of financial markets around the world has increased dramatically in recent years. Measured in absolute terms, net capital flows to developing countries reached during 1993-96 their highest level since the debt crisis of the early 1980s. Private capital flows, in particular, have increased sharply since the early 1990s and have shifted from bank to nonbank sources, such as direct investment flows and portfolio investment (equities, bonds, and certificates of deposit). Such flows provide important potential benefits; in particular, they expand investors' opportunities for portfolio diversification and provide a potential for achieving higher risk-adjusted rates of return. The potential welfare gains resulting from international risk sharing can be large (Obstfeld, 1994). At the same time, however, the risk of abrupt reversals in capital flows has raised concerns among policymakers around the world. Such concerns were heightened by several financial crises—including (as discussed in the next chapter) the Mexican peso crisis of December 1994, the Asian crisis triggered by the collapse of the Thai baht in July 1997, and the Brazilian real crisis of January 1999. A key issue has been to identify the policy prerequisites that allow countries to exploit the gains, and minimize the risks, associated with financial integration.

This chapter provides an overview of the evidence on the determinants of, and policy issues associated with, the surge in capital flows. Section 7.1 discusses the recent behavior of capital flows, looking at both aggregate and individual-country data. Section 7.2 examines the factors (domestic and external) that account for the process of globalization of capital markets and the dramatic expansion of private capital flows since the early 1990s. Section 7.3 reviews the recent evidence on the volatility of various components of capital flows. The links between capital inflows, liquidity expansion, and movements in the real exchange rate are discussed in the section 7.4.

Section 7.5 presents a static, three-good framework with imperfect capital mobility—an adequate characterization for many developing countries, as noted in the appendix to this chapter. Another important feature of the model (which is also consistent with the evidence for developing countries) is the assumption that banks play a key role in the transmission process of macroeconomic shocks, because firms' working capital needs are financed by domestic credit. A graphical solution is provided and the effects of an external shock (a rise in the world interest rate) are examined. Section 7.6 examines the policy options that policymakers may have to limit the adverse short-term effects of capital flows on the economy. The analysis focuses, in particular, on sterilization policies, exchange rate flexibility, fiscal adjustment, as well as non-market-based approaches—including capital controls and changes in statutory reserve requirements.

7.1   Capital Flows: Recent Evidence

Figure 7.1 shows the evolution of capital flows to developing countries during the period 1984-2001. The figure shows that net capital flows (particularly to Asia and Latin America) increased dramatically between 1989 and the mid-1990s. Annual inflows averaged more than $150 billion a year between 1990 and 1995, and exceeded $200 billion in 1996—an amount well above 2 percent of the combined GDP of developing countries.[1]

The increase in *gross* flows since the mid-1980s has, in fact, been almost seven times as large as the increase in net flows. Figure 7.2 displays the behavior of total private capital flows in proportion of output for six countries in Asia and Latin America that accounted for a significant proportion of total inflows to developing countries during the period 1982-97: Chile, Indonesia, Korea, Malaysia, Mexico, and Thailand. Again, the figure shows the dramatic increase in inflows in the early 1990s. Net inflows to some of these countries averaged 5 to 8 percent of GDP over the period.[2] At the same time, Africa as a whole—with the exception of Nigeria and countries in North Africa (such as Tunisia and Morocco)—has attracted very little capital flows. This has reflected various factors, including most notably low growth prospects, political instability, and a volatile macroeconomic environment—all of which make returns on investments in many African countries highly uncertain (see Bhattacharya, Montiel, and Sharma, 1997).

The data shown in Figure 7.1 also reveal a major change in the *composition* of capital flows. Indeed, much of the increase in capital inflows to developing countries since the early 1990s has taken the form of **portfolio investment** (including bonds, equities, and short-term instruments such as certificates of deposits and commercial paper) and **net direct investment**—particularly in Asia. *Short-term flows* (which include mostly interbank lending) have also increased significantly.

---

[1] As a percentage of exports, however, total aggregate resource flows to developing countries during the early 1990s, though much above their level in the mid-1980s, remained below their level in the mid- to late 1970s.

[2] As noted by Calvo and Reinhart (1996), several smaller countries in Latin America and elsewhere have also experienced large increases in capital inflows; when measured in proportion of GDP, these flows almost match those recorded by the larger countries.

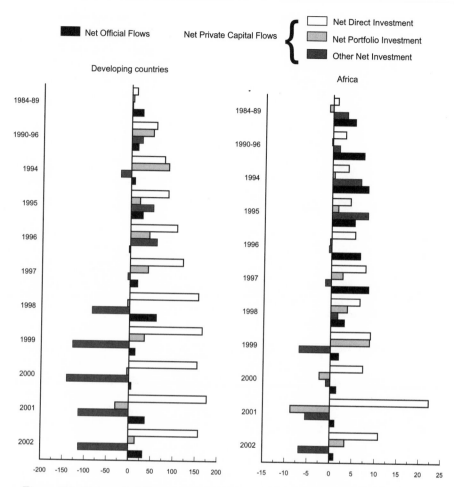

Figure 7.1. Net capital flows to developing countries, 1984-2001 (in billions of U.S. dollars). Source: International Monetary Fund.

By contrast, net *official flows* have fallen quite dramatically compared with the early 1980s in all regions. During the 1970s and early 1980s, most financing was indeed from commercial banks (to governments), and equity investment (both portfolio and direct) was a much smaller percentage than it is now. Following a series of currency crises in developing countries in the mid- to late 1990s (as discussed in the next chapter), portfolio flows dropped sharply, but foreign direct investment flows have remained resilient.

Figure 7.3 shows the behavior of total **foreign direct investment** (FDI) and **portfolio flows**, also in proportion of output, for the six Asian and Latin American countries shown in Figure 7.2. The data indicate that during the 1990s the composition of capital inflows to Asia shifted significantly toward portfolio investment. Equity flows to these countries, in particular, took the following forms:

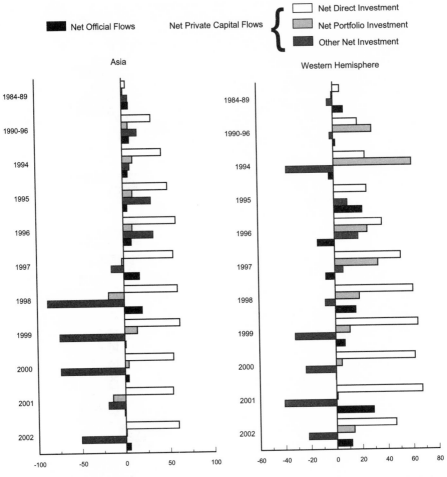

Figure 7.1 (*continued*)

- **direct equity purchases** by foreign investors in domestic stock markets;

- investments through **open-end** (or **closed-end**) **country funds**, that is, mutual funds that allow (or prevent) shareholders to redeem (or from redeeming) their shares at any moment in time, at the prevailing market prices;

- **direct equity offerings**, that is, sales of new equity issues by direct placement with specific institutional investors;

- issues of rights on equities held by depository institutions in the form of **American Depository Receipts** (ADRs) and **Global Depository Receipts** (GDRs). ADRs and GDRs are receipts issued by financial intermediaries in industrial countries against shares held in custody by these intermediaries in the developing countries.

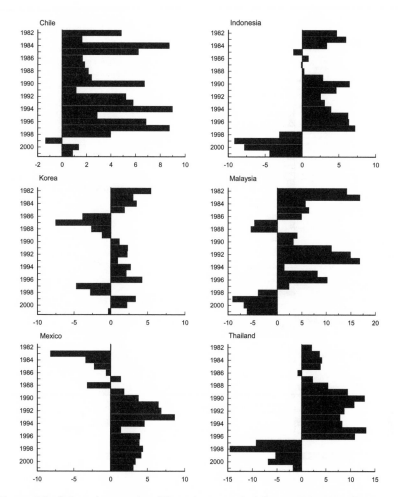

Figure 7.2. Selected countries: Net private capital flows, 1982-2001 (in percent of GDP). Source: International Monetary Fund.

The rising share of FDI has generally been considered to be one of the positive aspects of the surge in capital flows—in particular because it is generally taken to be determined by long-term profitability considerations (which makes these flows less subject to sudden shifts in market sentiment, as discussed in the next chapter) and often leads to the transfer of state-of-the-art technology. This latter aspect, as discussed in Chapter 12, is particularly important as a mechanism to foster economic growth.[3] However, there are several reasons why estimates of foreign direct investment flows, as measured by conventional balance-of-payments statistics, may *overstate* the actual importance of these flows (International Monetary Fund, 1997*a*, p. 64):

---

[3] However, recent evidence also suggests that there is a threshold level of *income per capita* and *human capital* that needs to be crossed before FDI can make a significant contribution to overall growth performance. See Borensztein, De Gregorio, and Lee (1998).

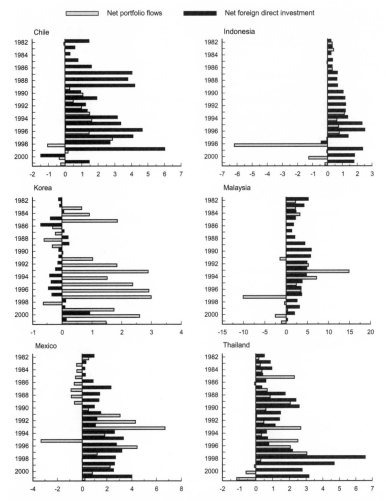

Figure 7.3. Selected countries: Net foreign direct investment and net portfolio flows, 1982-2001 (in percent of GDP). Source: International Monetary Fund.

- FDI flows reported in Figure 7.3 include among other items new equity, retained earnings, intrafirm debt, and valuation adjustments. However, valuation adjustments largely reflect *currency fluctuations*; adding them to reported FDI flows distorts the data.

- The distinction between FDI flows and portfolio flows in statistics compiled for the balance of payments is *arbitrary*. Foreign investment in the equity of a company above a critical proportion (usually 10 percent) of outstanding equity is classified as FDI, whereas that below the critical threshold is classified as portfolio investment. However, small differences above (below) the critical level do not necessarily represent any significant difference in the intentions of investors.

- If the foreign company undertaking the FDI borrows locally (from, say, a local bank) to finance its investment, depending on the form of incorporation of the company locally, setting up the plant may count as FDI while the bank lending could show up as a capital outflow, reducing the proportion of net bank lending in overall flows and raising the proportion of reported FDI flows.

- In some countries there may be tax or regulatory benefits from rechanneling domestic investment outlays through offshore instruments. As a result, FDI flows to the domestic economy may be overstated.

7.2   How Volatile Are Capital Flows?

In 1996 five Asian countries—Indonesia, Malaysia, the Philippines, South Korea, and Thailand—received net private capital *inflows* of about $93 billion. In 1997, in the wake of the Thai baht crisis and its contagion effects (as discussed in the next chapter), they recorded an *outflow* of $12 billion—a turnaround of $105 billion (most of it in the second half of 1997), which was equivalent to about 10 percent of their combined GDP. Three of these countries (Indonesia, South Korea, and Thailand) experienced a deep recession and a sharp increase in unemployment.

Most of the reversal that occurred between 1996 and 1997 was accounted for by changes in bank lending and to a lesser extent by portfolio flows; foreign direct investment remained essentially unchanged. Interbank lending to the crisis-stricken countries shifted in the second half of 1997 from an inflow of $40 billion to a net outflow of $30 billion. This evidence appears to be consistent with the conventional view on the degree of volatility of capital flows, which suggests that *short-term* flows (including again both portfolio investment and short-term bank lending) are inherently *more unstable* than longer-term flows (such as FDI and long-term bank lending). A study by Claessens, Dooley, and Warner (1995), however, using data for five developing countries and five industrial countries, found no significant differences between the time-series properties of short-term flows and long-term flows.[4] Portfolio flows, in particular, appeared to be no more volatile than other types of capital flows. They also found that because there is some substitution between the various flows, only an analysis of the aggregate capital account was meaningful. The implication of these results is that a program of capital controls aimed at discouraging a particular type of flow because of its (alleged) volatile behavior would not necessarily lead to more stable movements of capital (see below).

The findings of Claessens, Dooley, and Warner (1995) were confirmed in a subsequent study on six developing countries (Argentina, Brazil, Indonesia, Korea, Mexico, and Pakistan) by Chuhan, Perez-Quiros, and Popper (1996)—based on quarterly data covering the period 1985-94—but only in a *univariate*

---

[4]For both individual and aggregate flows, they measured volatility by coefficients of variation, persistence by measures of serial dependence (autocorrelation functions), and predictability by time-series measures of forecasting performance.

context. They found that short-term investment flows are sensitive to changes in all the other types of capital flows (including FDI), but that FDI is relatively insensitive to other flows—thereby supporting the conventional view that short-term capital flows are *hot money* whereas direct investment is not. They concluded that the composition of capital flows does matter; FDI may play a more prominent role in the determination of subsequent capital flows.

7.3   Domestic and External Factors

The process of globalization of capital markets and the surge in capital flows to developing countries have been the result of a variety of factors. Advances in *financial technology, information processing,* and *communications* have played an important role in explaining the increase in the speed of capital mobility. The dismantling of *capital controls* and other barriers to financial transactions in many developing countries have also had a significant impact on the process of global financial integration. In particular, the removal of restrictions on the repatriation of profits, and foreign ownership and participation in domestic stock markets, contributed to the expansion of equity flows to several developing countries.

In addition, as shown in several econometric studies, low interest rates prevailing in the United States and some other industrial countries in the early 1990s played an important role in explaining capital flows to developing countries during that period. Frankel and Okongwu (1996), for instance, in an analysis of the determinants of portfolio capital flows to six Latin American and East Asian countries (Argentina, Chile, Mexico, the Philippines, Korea, and Taiwan) using quarterly data covering the period 1987-94, found that U.S. interest rates had a major influence on these flows. As pointed out by Fernández-Arias (1996) and Fernández-Arias and Montiel (1996), this effect (also referred to as a **push factor**) may have been an *indirect* one: in addition to improving the relative rate of returns in favor of developing economies, low world interest rates improved the *creditworthiness* of some debtor countries.

However, the evidence also suggests that, in addition to world interest rates, domestic or **pull factors** (macroeconomic stabilization and structural reforms) have also played an important role in several countries. As noted earlier, capital account liberalization was an important component of structural adjustment in several developing countries. In many cases, *fiscal adjustment* (entailing large cuts in budget deficits) played a key stabilizing role and was instrumental in attracting capital flows. In countries like Argentina, Thailand, Mexico, and Chile, significant reductions in fiscal deficits preceded the surge in capital inflows and were associated with important changes in public expenditure policies, reductions in government subsidies, and tax reform (see Corbo and Hernández, 1996).

In Chile, the nonfinancial public sector balance was -0.4 percent of GDP three years prior to the inflow episode (which started in 1990), 3.6 percent two years before, and 5.3 percent a year before. In Thailand (where the inflow episode started in 1988), corresponding numbers are -6.3 percent, -4.8 percent, and -1.6 percent. Improved fiscal balances helped to lower inflationary expectations and signaled to markets a greater commitment to achieving and maintaining macroeconomic stability. It should also be noted, however, that there are instances where it is large fiscal *imbalances* themselves, coupled with a relatively tight monetary policy stance (and consequent upward pressures on domestic real interest rates), that led to large inflows of short-term capital, defined broadly to include also portfolio flows. Notable examples are Brazil and Turkey (see Agénor, McDermott, and Ucer, 1997).

A possible way to reconcile the results of the various econometric studies cited above is to view the evolution of fundamentals and growing financial integration as determining the *long-term trend* in recent private capital flows, whereas cyclical movements in interest rates in industrial countries represent one of the main factors affecting short-term movements in capital flows around their long-term trend. At the regional or individual country level, however, another important factor in the short term may be **herding behavior** or **contagion effects**, as discussed in more detail in the next chapter.

Contagion effects, in particular, may arise because investors decide to temporarily withdraw from a country (or a group of countries) in order to reevaluate risks and returns following a crisis in a neighboring country. Contagion effects may also arise as a result of technical factors—for instance, because institutional investors (such as *open-end mutual funds*) must sell off some of their assets to meet their obligations toward their clients. These effects tend to be short lived but they may also persist sufficiently to lead to a permanent reassessment of a country's fundamentals, thereby affecting longer-term flows of capital to that country as well. As shown by Fiess (2003) for Argentina, Brazil, Mexico, and Venezuela, there is evidence suggesting that indeed country risk and global factors have a strong impact on capital flows, whereas country risk appears to be determined by domestic variables (the primary balance to GDP ratio, and the public debt to GDP ratio).

The importance of distinguishing between the determinants of long- and short-term capital movements is well illustrated by the study by Larraín, Labán, and Chumacero (1997), which focused on private capital inflows to Chile during the period 1985-94. They found that each category of flows responds to different determinants.

- *Long-term* flows tended to respond to changes in economic fundamentals, such as the investment-output ratio and the external debt-output ratio (a proxy for **country risk**); short-term arbitrage conditions had no discernible impact.

- The behavior of *short-term* flows varied depending on whether they were or were not subject to **capital controls**—essentially an **unremunerated reserve requirement** introduced in June 1991, as discussed later.[5] Both

---

[5] Inflows that are subject to capital controls consisted essentially of short-term loans to the Chilean private banking and nonbanking sectors and (after 1991) changes in the stock of

categories of flows responded very significantly to interest rate differentials and arbitrage opportunities; in addition, short-term inflows that were subject to capital controls were significantly (and negatively) affected by changes in the reserve requirement rate.

Finally, among domestic factors, it is worth noting that there is evidence that the removal of capital controls on *outflows* may have led to an increase in *net inflows* of capital in several countries in the early 1990s, including Chile, Colombia, Egypt, and Thailand.[6] An analytical explanation of this apparent paradox was provided by Labán and Larraín (1997). They considered a model in which a policy aimed at liberalizing capital outflows takes the form of a reduction in the minimum period during which foreign investors must wait to repatriate the capital invested in the domestic country. This reduction is viewed as reducing the **degree of irreversibility** of the decision to invest domestically (see Chapter 2). This, in turn, lowers the **option value of waiting** until uncertainty about a possible change in the legislation that affects investment in domestic assets is resolved, because in this case nonresidents investing in the domestic economy will be stuck with the low-return asset for a shorter period of time. Thus, a reduction in the minimum repatriation period is likely to *increase*, not decrease, net capital inflows. Another explanation was offered by Drazen and Bartolini (1997); they argued that because controls on outflows are often imposed for fiscal purposes (namely, to maintain the base of the inflation tax, as discussed in Chapter 3), their removal can be interpreted by foreign investors as a signal that *future* capital taxation is less likely. This effect may be large enough to stimulate capital inflows.

7.4   Macroeconomic Effects of Capital Inflows

The surge in capital flows has led in a number of countries to a **credit boom** and an expansion of domestic liquidity. The reason is that these flows (particularly those taking the form of short-term foreign-currency deposits) have often been intermediated directly by the banking system. Even in cases where capital has flown into an economy through channels other than directly through banks, it could still lead to an increase in the capacity of the banking system to lend. For instance, if foreign investors decide to acquire equity on domestic stock markets, they must exchange a foreign-currency deposit for a domestic-currency deposit to pay for their purchase. As a result, the local bank obtains foreign-currency funds that can be used to expand domestic lending. Figure 7.4 shows the ratio of credit to GDP in periods before and during episodes of capital inflows in a group of countries since the late 1970s. The data indicate that episodes of inflows were, in almost all cases, associated with a higher rate of credit expansion.

---

foreign currency deposits in the domestic banking system.

[6] Chile started to lift restrictions on capital outflows in February 1991, Colombia in January 1992, and Thailand in April 1991. See Corbo and Hernández (1996).

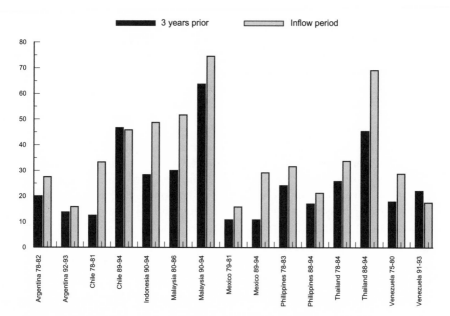

Figure 7.4. Capital inflow episodes and bank lending to the private sector (in percent of GDP). Source: World Bank.

Another effect of capital inflows has been a real exchange rate appreciation, brought about through higher domestic inflation.[7] In general, whether capital inflows are inflationary or not depends on various factors. A key issue in this context is the nature of the exchange rate regime.

- Under *flexible* exchange rates, a capital inflow (regardless of its sources) will lead to an appreciation of the nominal exchange rate, a fall in the relative price of imported goods and a shift away from consumption of nontradables—all of which will reduce inflationary pressures. The higher the degree of exchange rate flexibility, the less likely it is that capital inflows will have an inflationary effect.

- Under *fixed* exchange rates, whether capital inflows increase inflationary pressures depends on whether they are driven by autonomous factors (such as changes in world interest rates) or are brought about by an increase in domestic money demand, resulting, for instance, from lower inflation expectations (as often occurs in the immediate aftermath of a successful stabilization). In the latter case, there will be no inflationary effect.

The impact of capital inflows on inflation under fixed exchange rates also depends on the *policy response* to these inflows, namely, whether intervention is sterilized or unsterilized.

---

[7] This effect has in some cases reflected the relatively limited scope for market-based sterilization (as discussed later), itself resulting from the absence of well-developed financial markets and indirect monetary instruments.

- Under a regime of **unsterilized intervention** (in which the central bank exchanges domestic money for foreign-currency inflows), if capital inflows are an equilibrium response to an increase in money demand, they will not be inflationary because domestic interest rates are likely to rise. If capital inflows increase autonomously (as a result, say, of lower world interest rates), domestic interest rates will generally fall and inflationary pressures will increase.

- Under a regime of **sterilized intervention** (in which, for instance, the central bank exchanges directly bonds for inflows of foreign currency) an exogenous shift in money demand will lead to a larger increase in domestic interest rates than under unsterilized intervention, thus magnifying the downward pressure on prices exerted by capital inflows. By contrast, with an autonomous increase in capital inflows, domestic interest rates will not generally be affected: with a constant real money stock, agents would merely substitute interest-bearing domestic assets for foreign assets. Thus, autonomous capital inflows under sterilized intervention will have little inflationary effect.

In practice, estimating the potential inflationary effect of capital inflows is difficult. The reason is that it is almost always impossible to attribute capital inflows solely to one type of shocks—movements in, say, world interest rates—at any particular moment in time. A common approach is to examine the sources of the macroeconomic imbalances that underlie the current account deficits that are being financed by capital inflows.

The evidence provided by Calvo, Leiderman, and Reinhart (1996) and Corbo and Hernández (1996) suggests that during the early 1990s such deficits resulted mostly from increases in private *consumption* in Latin America, whereas in Asia they resulted mainly from a rise in *investment*.[8] To the extent that consumption falls relatively more on nontraded goods, capital inflows will tend to raise inflationary pressures, generating exchange rate overvaluation and growing external deficits. A study by the World Bank (1997a) found significant positive cross-country correlations during the inflow episode of the early 1990s between the extent of real appreciation and both increases in the current account deficit and in the share of consumption in domestic absorption. In countries like Argentina and Brazil, as discussed in the next chapter, these phenomena were particularly marked.[9]

An expansion in domestic liquidity and a real appreciation also characterized the experiences of India and Turkey. In India, the increase in capital inflows in the early 1990s led to a rapid increase in domestic liquidity. The counterpart was an accumulation of international reserves as the central bank intervened

---

[8] Corbo and Hernández (1996) compared the experiences of four Latin American countries (Argentina, Chile, Colombia, and Mexico) and five East Asian countries (Indonesia, Korea, Malaysia, the Philippines, and Thailand) with capital inflows.

[9] In addition, however, the lack of nominal exchange rate flexibility in both countries (Argentina after April 1991 and Brazil after February 1995) may have been a significant factor as well.

to avoid an exchange rate appreciation. Reductions in domestic interest rates contributed to increased consumption, rising inflation, and an appreciation of the real exchange rate. In Turkey, as noted earlier, the surge in capital inflows in the early 1990s occurred in the context of an inconsistent macroeconomic policy mix (a large and growing fiscal deficit coupled with a tight monetary policy), which resulted in high domestic interest rates. Finally, as documented by S. Calvo and Reinhart (1996), a real appreciation also characterized the experience of some smaller Latin American countries (the Dominican Republic, Ecuador, El Salvador, and Uruguay) in the early 1990s with capital inflows, with the notable exception of Costa Rica.

The impact of capital inflows on aggregate demand and the real exchange rate depends also on the *composition* of these flows. As discussed earlier, a large proportion of capital inflows to Latin America in the past few years has taken the form of portfolio investment rather than foreign direct investment, in contrast with what occurred in some Asian countries. Because flows of foreign direct investment may involve less financial intermediation than portfolio investment, their impact on the real exchange rate may be more limited. It should be emphasized, however, that there is limited evidence on this particular conjecture.

It is also important to note that capital inflows (as well as the policy responses that they may elicit, as discussed below) may imply contingent or **quasi-fiscal costs** because of their impact on the portfolio of assets held by the banking system. Intermediation of a surge in capital flows may weaken the quality of the banks' portfolios, increasing the vulnerability of the system to a sudden outflow of capital. This may be because of a **currency mismatch** (bank liabilities associated with capital inflows may be denominated in foreign currency, whereas loans are denominated in domestic currency) and a **maturity mismatch** (foreign-currency deposits by foreign investors may be short term, whereas loans are medium or long term).

In such conditions, an exogenous shock (an abrupt change in foreign investors' sentiment) can force the central bank to intervene and bail out ailing banks in order to avoid contagious runs and further capital outflows. In addition, the increase in liquid liabilities may induce banks to engage in more risky lending behavior—possibly exacerbating the vulnerability created by the maturity mismatch. The cost of these contingent liabilities should be taken into account in any analysis of the macroeconomic effects of capital flows.

At the same time, the risk of a systemic banking crisis also suggests that responding to a surge in inflows may require not only the implementation of short-term macroeconomic measures but also more fundamental improvements in **bank regulations** and **prudential requirements** (see Chapter 15).

7.5 External Shocks and Capital Flows

To analyze the impact of external shocks (namely, changes in world interest rates) on capital flows and the domestic economy, this section presents a three-good, open-economy macroeconomic model.

The economy considered has five types of agents: households, producers, commercial banks, the government, and the central bank. All households are identical in their endowments and behavior; in particular, they possess identical ownership shares of firms' profits. Similarly, all firms and banks are identical. The choices made by a representative firm in each sector, a representative household, and a representative bank are therefore the focus of the analysis.

The nominal exchange rate E is fixed. The economy produces two goods: a home good, which is used only for final domestic consumption, and an exportable good, the price of which is fixed on world markets. In addition, households consume an imported good which is not produced domestically. The capital stock in each sector is fixed within the time frame of the analysis, and workers are perfectly mobile across sectors.

Given the small country assumption, the demand for domestically produced exportables is perfectly elastic at the exogenous world currency price, so that output of these goods is supply determined. For simplicity, it will be assumed that output of exportable goods is entirely sold abroad.

7.5.1   Households

Households supply labor inelastically, consume both home and imported goods, and hold four categories of financial assets in their portfolios: domestic money (which bears no interest), deposits with the banking system, domestic bonds, and foreign bonds. In line with the discussion in the appendix to this chapter, all assets are taken to be **imperfect substitutes**. Foreigners do not hold domestic assets. Total domestic financial wealth is constant during the time frame of the analysis.

Consumption decisions follow a *two-stage process*. The representative household first determines *total* consumption, and then allocates that amount between consumption of the two goods. Total consumption expenditure C is assumed to depend positively on disposable income:[10]

$$C = (1 - s)(Y - T), \quad 0 < s < 1, \tag{1}$$

where Y denotes net factor income (defined below), T lump-sum taxes levied by the government, and s the marginal propensity to save.[11] C, Y, and T are all measured in terms of the domestic price of exportables—that is, the nominal exchange rate, assuming that the world price of exportables is normalized to unity.

---

[10] As noted in Chapter 2, the life-cycle model would predict a relationship between wealth and consumption, rather than income and consumption. However, as also noted in that chapter, in the presence of liquidity constraints, current income may have large effect on expenditure.

[11] For simplicity, the value of output and income are assumed equal. As noted in Chapter 1, the value of output generally exceeds that of income as a result of indirect taxes, net factor payments to nonresidents, and net unrequited transfers from the rest of the world.

In the second stage of the consumption process, the representative household determines consumption of imported goods (in quantity C_I) and home goods (in quantity C_N). Suppose, for simplicity, that the world price of imported goods, P_I^*, is constant and normalized to unity. The domestic-currency price of these goods is thus also equal to the nominal exchange rate, E. The allocation of total consumption expenditure is given by[12]

$$C_I = (1 - \delta)C, \quad 0 < \delta < 1, \tag{2}$$

$$P_N C_N = \delta E C, \tag{3}$$

where δ measures the share of home goods in total private expenditure.

Let $z \equiv E/P_N$ be the relative price of imported goods in terms of home goods; z will be referred to in what follows as the *real exchange rate*.[13] Equation (3) can thus be rewritten, using Equation (1), as

$$C_N = \delta z C = \delta z (1 - s)(Y - T). \tag{4}$$

Asset demand equations are given as follows. First, the demand for money is assumed to be related negatively to the opportunity cost of holding cash (measured by the interest rate on domestic bonds, i_b) and positively to income:[14]

$$M^d = M^d(\overset{-}{i_b}, \overset{+}{Y}). \tag{5}$$

Second, the demand for bank deposits is taken to depend positively on income and the bank deposit rate, i_d, and negatively on the rate of interest on domestic bonds:

$$D^p = D^p(\overset{+}{i_d}, \overset{-}{i_b}, \overset{+}{Y}). \tag{6}$$

Third, the (flow) demand for foreign bonds, ΔB^*, is assumed to be increasing in the spread between the interest rate on domestic bonds and the rate of interest on foreign bonds, i^*, augmented by the expected rate of devaluation of the nominal exchange rate, ε^a:

$$\Delta B^* = \gamma(i^* + \varepsilon^a - i_b), \quad \gamma > 0, \tag{7}$$

where γ can be viewed as a measure of the **degree of substitutability** between domestic and foreign bonds, or what amounts to the same thing here, the degree of capital mobility. In the particular case in which $\gamma \to \infty$, domestic and foreign

---

[12] It can be shown that the allocation rule given in (2)-(3) is optimal if utility is a Cobb-Douglas function of the quantities of home and imported goods.

[13] For the economy as a whole, a more conventional definition of the real exchange rate would imply defining z in terms of a weighted average of both categories of goods produced and traded in the economy—exportables and imported goods. Howver, because the terms of trade are constant in the present setting, the result is the same.

[14] Assuming that the opportunity cost of holding cash also depends on the interest rates on bank deposits and foreign bonds would not qualitatively affect the implications of the analysis.

bonds are perfect substitutes, capital is perfectly mobile, and the **uncovered interest parity condition** will hold:

$$i_b = i^* + \varepsilon^a.$$

Finally, because total financial wealth, W, is given, the demand function for domestic bonds, B, can be readily derived from Equations (5), (6), and (7) as

$$B = W - M^d - D^p - B^*.$$

7.5.2 Firms and the Labor Market

The economy considered possesses a concave transformation frontier between traded and nontraded goods. It operates at the point of tangency between the frontier and a straight line with slope equal to (minus) the reciprocal of the real exchange rate, defined earlier. Firms in each sector must finance their **working capital needs** prior to the sale of output, and therefore borrow from commercial banks. For simplicity, it is assumed that there is no substitute for bank loans, so that firms cannot issue and trade equities or bonds (claims on their capital stock) to finance their borrowing needs. This assumption is consistent with much of the evidence on the structure of financial markets in developing countries (see Chapter 4).[15] Working capital needs are assumed to consist solely of **labor costs**. Total production costs faced by the representative firm in each sector are thus equal to the wage bill plus **interest payments** made on bank loans needed to pay labor in advance.

The maximization problem faced by the representative firm in each production sector can be written as

$$\max_{Y_h} Y_h - \omega_h N_h - i_L L_h, \tag{8}$$

where the subscript h is used to denote the exportable ($h = X$) and nontradable goods ($h = N$) sector. Y_h denotes output of good h, N_h the quantity of labor employed in sector h, ω_h the **product wage** in sector h, L_h the real amount of bank loans obtained by the firm operating in sector h, and i_L the nominal bank lending rate.

The output-employment relationship in each sector takes the form

$$N_h = Y_h^\alpha, \quad \alpha > 1, \tag{9}$$

which implies that, because $\alpha > 1$, technology for the production of both categories of goods is characterized by decreasing returns to labor.

The typical firm's financial constraint is given by

$$L_h \geq \omega_h N_h, \tag{10}$$

---

[15] In addition, firms producing exportables and nontradables are modeled symmetrically, although in practice their behavior can differ substantially given differences in factor intensities.

which requires the amount of bank loans to be at least as large as real wage costs. In what follows constraint (10) will be assumed to be continuously binding, because the only reason for firms to demand loans is to finance labor costs.

Maximizing Equation (8) subject to (9) and (10) yields the output supply equation in sector h:

$$Y_h^s = \left\{ \frac{1}{\alpha \omega_h (1 + i_L)} \right\}^{1/(\alpha - 1)}, \tag{11}$$

which shows that output supply in h is inversely related to the **effective product wage** in that sector, $\omega_h (1 + i_L)$. Substituting Equation (11) in (9) yields labor demand in sector h as

$$N_h^d = \left\{ \frac{1}{\alpha \omega_h (1 + i_L)} \right\}^{\alpha/(\alpha - 1)} = N_h^d [\omega_h (1 + i_L)], \qquad N_h^{d\prime} < 0. \tag{12}$$

Using Equations (10)—holding with equality—and (12), the representative firm's demand for credit can be written as

$$L_h^d = \omega_h N_h^d \equiv L_h^d (\overset{?}{\omega_h}, \overset{-}{i_L}), \tag{13}$$

which shows that, in general, an increase in the product wage has an ambiguous effect on the demand for credit. On the one hand, it directly raises labor costs; on the other, it lowers the demand for labor. If the elasticity of the demand for labor is greater than unity in absolute terms, the net effect will be negative.[16] This is the case assumed in what follows.

Nominal wages are perfectly flexible and adjust to equilibrate supply and demand for labor. Thus, given perfect labor mobility across sectors, unemployment cannot emerge. Moreover, nominal wage flexibility implies that the product wage in the nontradable sector is equal to the real exchange rate times the product wage in the exportable sector:

$$\omega_N = z \omega_X. \tag{14}$$

Using Equations (13) and (14), the equilibrium condition between supply and demand for labor can thus be solved for the product wage in the exportable sector, ω_X:

$$N_X^d [\omega_X (1 + i_L)] + N_N^d [z \omega_X (1 + i_L)] = N^s,$$

where N^s denotes the constant supply of labor. Solving this equation yields

$$\omega_X = \omega_X (\overset{-}{z}, \overset{-}{i_L}), \tag{15}$$

which implies that the equilibrium product wage is negatively related to the real exchange rate and the bank lending rate. Moreover, $|\partial \omega_X / \partial z| < 1$, because

$$\frac{\partial \omega_X}{\partial z} \equiv -\frac{N_N^{d\prime}(1 + i_L)}{N_X^{d\prime}(1 + i_L) + N_N^{d\prime}(1 + i_L)} = -\frac{N_N^{d\prime}}{N_X^{d\prime} + N_N^{d\prime}}.$$

---

[16] By definition $dL_h^d/d\omega_h = \tilde{N}_h^d + \tilde{\omega}_h (\partial N_h^d/\partial \omega_h)$. Multiplying both sides by $\tilde{\omega}_h / \tilde{L}_h^d$ yields $\eta_{L_h^d/\omega_h} = 1 + \eta_{N_h^d/\omega_h}$, which therefore requires $\left| \eta_{N_h^d/\omega_h} \right| > 1$ for $dL_h^d/d\omega_h$ to be negative.

Substituting Equations (14) and (15) in Equation (11) yields the sectoral supply equations:[17]

$$Y_X^s = Y_X^s(\overset{+}{z}, \overset{-}{i_L}), \quad Y_N^s = Y_N^s(\overset{-}{z}, \overset{-}{i_L}). \tag{16}$$

These equations show that output of exportables (home goods) is positively (negatively) related to the real exchange rate, and that an increase in the bank lending rate has a negative effect on activity in both sectors.

Net factor income is given by

$$Y = Y_X^s + z^{-1}Y_N^s.$$

To determine the sign of Y_z note that

$$Y_z = \frac{\partial Y_X^s}{\partial z} + \tilde{z}^{-1}\frac{\partial Y_N^s}{\partial z} - \tilde{z}^{-2}\tilde{Y}_N^s,$$

where a '~' is used to denoted an initial equilibrium value. Assuming that firms operate along the economy's production possibility frontier, profit maximization yields (see, for instance, Buiter, 1988, pp. 225-26):

$$\frac{\partial Y_X^s}{\partial z} + \tilde{z}^{-1}\frac{\partial Y_N^s}{\partial z} = 0,$$

so that $Y_z < 0$. A depreciation of the real exchange rate lowers aggregate income because it reduces the value of output of nontradables measured in terms of the price of exportables. Thus, using Equations (16):

$$Y = Y(\overset{-}{z}, \overset{-}{i_L}). \tag{17}$$

Using (13) and (14), total demand for credit, L^d, measured in terms of the price of exportables, is given by

$$L^d = L_X^d(\omega_X, i_L) + z^{-1}L_N^d(z\omega_X, i_L),$$

that is, using (15),

$$L^d = L^d(\overset{?}{z}, \overset{-}{i_L}), \tag{18}$$

which shows that in general a real exchange rate depreciation (an increase in z) has an ambiguous effect on the total demand for credit. It will be assumed in what follows that $\partial L^d/\partial z > 0$, which corresponds to the case where the exportable sector accounts for a large initial share of the total demand for bank loans.

---

[17]Note that, after normalizing all initial prices and wages to unity, $\partial\omega_N/\partial z = \partial(z\omega_X)/\partial z = 1 + \partial\omega_X/\partial z > 0$, given that $|\partial\omega_X/\partial z| < 1$.

7.5.3 Commercial Banks

Assets of the representative commercial bank consist of credit extended to firms, L^s, and reserves held at the central bank, RR; for simplicity, banks hold no excess reserves. Bank liabilities consist of deposits held by households. The balance sheet of the representative commercial bank can therefore be written as

$$D^p = L^s + RR, \tag{19}$$

where all variables are measured in terms of the price of exportables.

Reserves held at the central bank do not pay interest and are determined by

$$RR = \mu D^p, \quad 0 < \mu < 1, \tag{20}$$

where μ is the coefficient of reserve requirements.

The actual level of deposits held by the private sector is demand determined and, from Equations (19) and (20), the supply of credit is

$$L^s = (1 - \mu)D^p. \tag{21}$$

Banks have no operating costs. Under a **zero-profit condition**, the relationship between the lending rate and the deposit rate is given by

$$i_L = \frac{i_d}{1 - \mu}. \tag{22}$$

This condition requires the marginal revenue per unit of currency lent to equal the bank's net interest payment per unit of currency deposited, which is in turn equal to the deposit rate adjusted for the reserve requirement tax.

Using Equations (6), (21), and (22), the supply of credit is thus given by

$$L^s = (1 - \mu)D^p[(1 - \mu)i_L, i_b, Y], \tag{23}$$

which shows, in particular, that L^s is increasing in the lending rate, i_L.

7.5.4 Government and the Central Bank

The government, as noted earlier, levies lump-sum taxes on households. It also consumes home goods, in quantity G_N.

The central bank lends to the government and ensures the costless conversion of domestic currency holdings into foreign currency at the prevailing fixed exchange rate, E. The real money supply, M^s, measured in terms of the price of exportables, is thus given by

$$M^s = L^g + R^*, \tag{24}$$

where R^* is the central bank's stock of net foreign assets (measured in foreign-currency terms) and L^g real credit to the government, which is assumed exogenous.

Changes in official reserves are determined by the behavior of the balance of payments, that is, the sum of the current account and the capital account. Ignoring interest payments on net foreign assets for simplicity, the balance of payments is

$$\Delta R^* = Y_X^s - C_I - \Delta B^*,$$

that is, using Equations (2), (7) and (16):

$$\Delta R^* = Y_X^s - (1 - \delta)C + \gamma(i_b - i^* - \varepsilon^a). \tag{25}$$

Thus, changes in official foreign reserves translate into one-to-one changes in the domestic money supply. Put differently, the central bank does not engage in **sterilized intervention** (see the discussion in section 7.6).

7.5.5   Equilibrium Conditions

To close the model requires specifying the equilibrium conditions of the markets for domestic bonds, domestic money, credit, and nontradable goods. By **Walras' law**, the first three conditions are not independent; one of them can be eliminated. The analysis here will focus on the equilibrium conditions of the markets for money and credit.

The Money Market

Using Equation (5), the equilibrium condition of the money market is given by

$$M^s = M^d(i_b, Y). \tag{26}$$

For a given level of the money supply, M^s (that is, for a given level of official reserves, R^*), and using Equation (17) to eliminate Y, Equation (26) defines the combinations of the real exchange rate and the interest rate on domestic bonds for which the money market is in equilibrium. Solving this equation for i_b yields

$$i_b = i_b(\bar{z}, \bar{i}_L; \bar{M}^s). \tag{27}$$

A real depreciation, for instance, lowers aggregate income and the transactions demand for money, requiring a fall in the bond rate to maintain money market equilibrium.

The Credit Market

The equilibrium condition of the credit market is given by

$$L^s = L^d,$$

so that, using Equations (18) and (23):

$$D^p[(1 - \mu)i_L, i_b, Y] = \frac{L^d(z, i_L)}{1 - \mu}, \tag{28}$$

Using Equation (17) again to eliminate Y, and assuming that $\partial L^d/\partial z > 0$ and the effect of income on the demand for bank deposits (given by $\partial D^p/\partial Y$) is not too large, the above equation can be solved for the equilibrium bank lending rate:

$$i_L = i_L(\overset{+}{z}, \overset{+}{i_b}).\tag{29}$$

Equation (29) shows that an increase in the interest rate on domestic bonds, by lowering the demand for bank deposits by households, creates an excess demand for loans—thereby requiring an increase in the lending rate. A real depreciation lowers the supply of credit (by reducing income and thus deposits) while raising the demand for loans, leading therefore to an increase in the equilibrium lending rate.

The Market for Home Goods

The equilibrium condition of the market for home goods is given by

$$C_N + G_N - Y_N^s = 0,\tag{30}$$

which can be rewritten as, using Equations (4), (16), and (17):

$$\delta z(1 - s)[Y(z, i_L) - T] + G_N - Y_N^s(z, i_L) = 0.$$

Solving this condition for the real exchange rate yields

$$z = \Omega(\overset{?}{i_L}; \overset{+}{T}, \overset{-}{G_N}).\tag{31}$$

Equation (31) shows that an increase in government spending on home goods requires an appreciation of the real exchange rate (a fall in z) to eliminate excess demand and maintain market equilibrium. An increase in taxes, by lowering private expenditure, creates an excess supply of nontraded goods and therefore requires a depreciation of the equilibrium real exchange rate. An increase in the bank lending rate has in general an ambiguous effect, because it reduces both income (and thus consumption) and the supply of nontraded goods. If the marginal propensity to save, s, is small then $\partial z/\partial i_L < 0$.

The logical structure of the model is illustrated in Figure 7.5.

7.5.6   Graphical Solution

A compact formulation of the equilibrium solution can be derived and illustrated in a simple diagram, involving the bank lending rate and the real exchange rate. To do so, the first step is to combine the money market and credit market equilibrium conditions by substituting out i_b, using Equation (27), in (29). Assuming that $\partial D^p/\partial i_b$ is not too large, the resulting equation is

$$i_L = \phi(\overset{+}{z}; \overset{-}{M^s}),\tag{32}$$

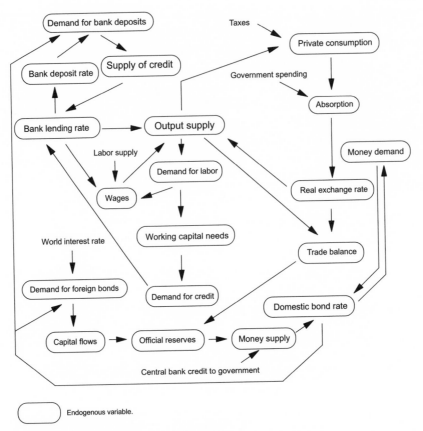

Figure 7.5. Logical structure of the model.

which will be referred to as the MM curve. It is upward sloping, because, for given M^s,

$$\left.\frac{di_L}{dz}\right|_{MM} = \phi_z > 0.$$

The equilibrium condition of the market for nontraded goods, Equation (31), gives a relationship between z and i_L that will be referred to as the NN curve. This curve is downward sloping, because

$$\left.\frac{di_L}{dz}\right|_{NN} = \Omega_{i_L}^{-1} < 0.$$

Finally, using Equation (29) to substitute out for i_L in Equation (27) yields the following alternative expression for the market-clearing interest rate on domestic bonds:

$$i_b = i_b[z, i_L(z, i_b), M^s] = \eta(\overset{-}{z}; \overset{-}{M^s}). \tag{33}$$

Using this result to substitute out for i_b, and using the supply equation of traded goods, Equation (16), then changes in official reserves [Equation (25)] are given by

$$\Delta R^* = Y_X^s(z, i_L) - (1 - \delta)(1 - s)[Y(z, i_L) - T] + \gamma[\eta(z; M^s) - i^* - \varepsilon^a].$$

Setting $\Delta R^* = 0$ in the above equation yields the combinations of z and i_L that ensure equilibrium of the balance of payments, that is, equality between the sum of the current and capital accounts. In the present setting, because credit to the government by the central bank is constant, external equilibrium implies a constant money supply, because from Equation (24) $\Delta M^s = \Delta R^*$. The balance-of-payments equilibrium condition can be written as[18]

$$z = \kappa(\overset{+}{i_L}; \overset{+}{i^*}, \overset{+}{M^s}). \tag{34}$$

For a given expected rate of depreciation, Equation (34) defines a curve in the z-i_L space, called the BB curve, which is upward sloping because

$$\left. \frac{di_L}{dz} \right|_{BB} = \kappa_{i_L}^{-1} > 0.$$

Curves MM, NN, and BB are illustrated in Figure 7.6.[19] Points located to the right (left) of MM represent combinations of the lending rate and the real exchange rate for which both the money and credit markets are characterized by excess supply (demand). Points located to the left (right) of NN represent combinations of z and i_L for which the market for nontraded goods is characterized by excess demand (supply). Finally, points located to the right (left) of BB represent situations in which the balance of payments is in deficit (surplus).

Suppose, for instance, that the initial position of the economy is at point A, characterized by equilibrium of the market for nontraded goods, and the credit and money markets. The short-run equilibrium, being to the left of the BB locus, corresponds to a balance-of-payments surplus; the lending rate is low, and the bond rate is high (see (27)], implying that the economy is recording both current and capital account surpluses. These surpluses (and the concomitant increase in official reserves and the money supply) tend to fall over time, until the balance of payments is in equilibrium ($\Delta R^* = 0$). The curve MM therefore continuously shifts to the right, until point E is reached. The external deficit at that point is eliminated, the money supply is constant, and all three curves intersect. Equilibrium values of the lending rate and the real exchange rate are given by $\tilde{z}$ and $\tilde{i}_L$.

The adjustment process operates as follows. The initial increase in the money supply tends to reduce the bond rate [as implied by (33)], which induces an outflow of capital and lowers the demand for bank deposits [see Equation (6)]. In turn, the fall in bank deposits tends to lower the supply of credit and to put

---

[18] To sign the partial derivatives in (34), note that $\partial Y_X^s / \partial i_L - (1 - \delta)(1 - s) Y_{i_L} < 0$. It is also assumed that $\partial Y_X^s / \partial z - (1 - \delta)(1 - s) Y_z + \gamma \eta_z > 0$.

[19] Although the figure assumes that MM is steeper than BB, in general it cannot be determined a priori whether ϕ_z is larger than $\kappa_{i_L}^{-1}$ in absolute terms without a formal dynamic analysis.

upward pressure on the lending rate [see Equation (29)], which further reduces i_b. At the same time, the increase in i_L tends to lower output of nontraded goods, and the incipient excess demand leads to an appreciation of the real exchange rate [see Equation (31)]. The real appreciation, by reducing aggregate income and the demand for credit, leads to further upward pressure on the equilibrium lending rate, and to lower exports, whereas the fall in the bond rate increases capital outflows, reducing reserves and the money supply. The adjustment process continues until the economy reaches its equilibrium position at point E.

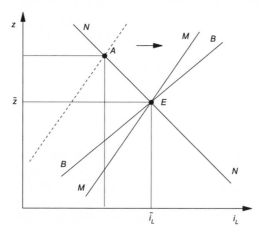

Figure 7.6. Macroeconomic equilibrium.

7.5.7 Rise in the World Interest Rate

Consider now a rise in the rate of return on foreign bonds, i^*. The immediate impact of this shock, as can be inferred from Equation (7), is to raise the demand for foreign bonds and reduce net capital inflows. At the initial levels of the bank lending rate and the real exchange rate, official reserves fall, reducing therefore the domestic money supply [see Equation (24)]. From Equation (27), maintaining equilibrium of the domestic money market requires an increase in the rate of return on domestic bonds, i_b. The increase in i_b, in turn, tends to reduce the demand for bank deposits by households and thus the supply of credit—requiring therefore an increase in the bank lending rate to maintain equilibrium of the credit market. At the same time, however, the incipient increase in i_L puts downward pressure on supply of (traded and) nontraded goods. To eliminate excess demand for nontraded goods and restore market equilibrium requires an appreciation of the real exchange rate. Although the real appreciation tends to lower the supply of exportables and to increase imports, the initial deficit in the balance of payments falls as a result of the increase in the domestic bond rate.

Graphically, as shown in Figure 7.7, the rise in i^* entails a rightward shift of the BB curve to $B'B'$. The adjustment process is similar to the one described earlier; the monetary contraction is associated with a rightward shift of the MM curve, until the general equilibrium point E' is reached. Adjustment entails an increase in domestic bank rates and an appreciation of the real exchange rate.

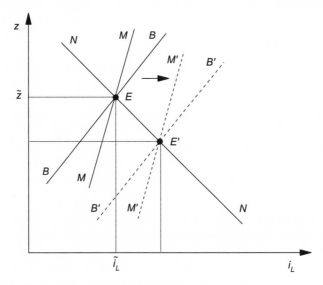

Figure 7.7. Increase in the world interest rate.

7.6 Policy Responses to Capital Inflows

Countries facing a surge in capital inflows have used various market-based instruments, such as sterilization, and some types of capital controls, as well as nonmarket-based instruments, such as reserve and liquidity requirements. This section discusses the pros and cons of these instruments, and reviews some of the experiences in implementing them. At the outset, it should be emphasized that determining appropriate policy responses to capital inflows depends importantly on what motivates these inflows—in particular whether or not they are perceived as *temporary* or *permanent*. For instance, a capital inflow induced by a permanent increase in money demand (as a result of a remonetization phenomenon induced by lower inflation, as discussed in Chapter 6) is not a great source of concern from a macroeconomic point of view. It essentially generates an accommodating increase in the money supply (through an expansion of the supply of credit intermediated by domestic banks), with limited inflationary pressures, as noted earlier.

In practice, however, determining to what extent capital inflows represent an endogenous response of this type is difficult. Data on income velocity as an indicator of money demand developments are not very reliable, because accurate estimates of movements in income are generally not available on a timely basis; they may, in any case, be hard to interpret because of the lags involved in the response of prices to changes in the money supply. The potential for shifts in money demand under unstable financial conditions or following financial reform makes an assessment of the monetary stance even more difficult. As a consequence, policymakers have often erred on the side of caution in responding to large capital inflows.

7.6.1   Sterilization

Central bank intervention in the foreign exchange market consists of any official sale or purchase of foreign assets against domestic assets. Intervention operations are typically financed using reserves, swaps, or official borrowing. As indicated earlier, there are essentially two types of interventions:

- **nonsterilized** operations, which involve a change in the domestic monetary base. They are analogous to conventional *open-market operations* (see Chapter 4) except that foreign, rather than domestic, assets are bought or sold;

- **sterilized operations**, which involve an offsetting domestic asset transaction that restores the original size of the monetary base.[20] For instance, an official nonsterilized purchase of foreign currency on the market for foreign exchange would result in an increase in the central bank's holdings of net foreign assets, R^*, and an expansion of the domestic monetary base, M. This operation can be sterilized by an offsetting sale of domestic bonds that reduces the central bank's net domestic assets, L, and returns the monetary base to its original level, that is

$$\Delta R^* + \Delta L = \Delta M = 0.$$

Sterilization was the first line of defense used by many countries facing large inflows in the early 1990s. The absorption of foreign exchange reserves by the central bank was viewed as a way to resist any tendency toward nominal appreciation under flexible exchange rate arrangements; and the simultaneous reduction in domestic credit was viewed as a way to resist the inflationary pressures associated with an expansion of the money supply.

For sterilization to be effective, capital mobility must be less than perfect; this is indeed what most of the evidence for developing countries suggests (see the appendix to this chapter). More generally, the ability to sterilize depends on the range of instruments available to do so and the absorptive capacity of domestic financial markets. The *maturity* of the sterilization instruments is also important. To discourage speculative short-term capital flows, medium-term sterilization bonds are generally preferable to short-term securities. The reason is that they limit the vulnerability of the central bank to capital outflows

---

[20]Some economists use a broader definition of sterilization that encompasses also changes in statutory reserve requirements and other measures that affect not only the monetary base but also the money multiplier. However, as discussed later, these alternative ways of limiting the expansion of monetary and credit aggregates have very different implications for variables such as the quasi-fiscal deficit and interest rates; a narrow definition is thus preferable.

when there is no guarantee (due to limited amounts of foreign exchange) that these bonds will be repaid on short notice—as might be necessary in case of a sudden shift in confidence. However, interest rates on longer-term bonds could increase commercial banks' exposure to capital outflows if they are required (as a result of central bank regulations) to hold a sizable share of their assets in such instruments. Thus, the maturity mix of the bonds can be chosen to reflect, in addition to fiscal considerations, factors such as the availability of foreign exchange, the need to strengthen the banking system, the duration of the inflows, and other factors affecting banks' reserves.

An important advantage of sterilization is that it can be implemented relatively quickly. It also provides some *breathing space* to policymakers, thereby allowing them to assess whether inflows are transitory or more likely to be permanent in nature. This may be particularly relevant in periods of unstable market conditions, during which policymakers may need to send clear signals about their monetary policy intentions. Moreover, the accumulation of reserves can provide some degree of cushion against a sudden reversal of inflows. In countries where the authorities do not have adequate prudential controls to ensure that banks maintain adequate quality of their asset portfolios (see Chapter 15), sterilization may help to insulate the domestic banking system from sudden reversals in inflows.

The sharp increases in official reserves recorded by several countries that have received large capital inflows since the early 1990s suggests that central banks intervened strongly in foreign exchange markets.[21] In almost all cases the objectives were to prevent an expansion of liquidity and a nominal appreciation of the domestic currency. In the first few years of the capital inflow episode that began in 1988 in Thailand, for instance, the associated increases in net foreign assets were accompanied by declines in domestic credit (Glick, Hutchison, and Moreno, 1997). In general, East Asian countries were better able than Latin American countries to sterilize capital inflows and limit the impact of foreign reserve accumulation on monetary expansion in the early years of the inflow episode (Corbo and Hernández, 1996).[22]

The extent to which changes in net foreign assets held by the central bank are neutralized by changes in net domestic credit is measured by the **offset coefficient**. This coefficient can be estimated empirically by regressing the change in the central bank's net domestic assets, ΔL, on the change in the central bank's net foreign assets, ΔR^*, taking into account the causality problem of whether the decline in domestic credit is the cause of subsequent capital inflows, or an

---

[21] The increase in official reserves may have been related also to a precautionary response by policymakers concerned by the volatility of capital flows and a heightened perception of instability in a more deregulated financial environment. See Aizenman and Marion (2003).

[22] Part of the reason is that central banks in East Asia, unlike those in Latin America, were able to force public institutions, such as social security funds, state banks, and public enterprises, to hold government bonds. Thus because of the greater (or stricter) control that they exerted over their financial markets and institutions, they were able to reduce liquidity without having to pay a large interest premium.

offset of previous inflows.[23] An alternative and indirect approach to assess the degree to which a country sterilizes is to study the evolution over time of the ratio of foreign reserves to the money supply. This indicator captures the *intent* of sterilization intervention, which is to control fluctuations in the supply of money by altering movements in domestic credit in response to purchases of foreign-currency assets by the central bank. In practice, such ratios are calculated by dividing official foreign reserves by various definitions of the money supply—the monetary base or narrow and broad money stocks.[24]

The experience of several developing countries in recent years shows, however, that sterilization can be difficult and may carry substantial costs.

- In countries where domestic markets in government securities are relatively *thin* and *illiquid*, the central bank's ability to sterilize may be limited because of the lack of adequate market-based instruments.

- Sterilization can lead to *higher* domestic interest rates if the bonds issued by the central bank for sterilization purposes are very imperfect substitutes for the domestic assets (say, equities) that attracted capital inflows in the first place. In turn, high domestic interest rates make domestic assets *more attractive* to world investors than they would otherwise be, and may thus lead to higher and more persistent capital inflows. This is what occurred in Brazil, Chile, Colombia, and Malaysia in the early 1990s.

- When the central bank must offer interest rates on its sterilization bonds that are higher than the rates that it earns on the foreign reserve assets that it accumulates, sterilization becomes costly and may burden an already weak fiscal position (Calvo, 1991). It increases public debt or **quasi-fiscal deficits** (as defined in Chapter 3) by preventing a downward adjustment in domestic interest rates.

- In Chile, for instance, capital inflows averaged about 6-7 percent of GDP a year during the early to mid-1990s. The Central Bank initially tried to insulate domestic liquidity from the effects of these inflows by purchasing large quantities of foreign exchange, sterilized by issuing central bank paper. This policy, however, increased the central bank's already high quasi-fiscal losses. Net costs to the central bank were estimated to be around 0.8 percent of GDP in Chile and Colombia in 1991 (Kiguel and

---

[23] See Kamas (1985) for a more elaborate application. Because perfect substitution between domestic and foreign assets implies a coefficient of minus unity in the regression, the regression framework suggested in the text has also been used to assess the degree of capital mobility; see the appendix to this chapter.

[24] The indicator based on the monetary base can be sensitive to whether sterilization operations are accompanied or not by changes in statutory reserve requirements. Because reserve requirements are part of the monetary base, increases in statutory reserve ratios that occur at the same time that sterilization is being implemented through the direct issuance to the public of central bank liabilities (which are not part of the monetary base) may bias the indicator downward.

Leiderman, 1993) and 1.2 percent in Colombia in 1993 (Cárdenas and Barrera, 1997, p. 35).[25]

- The use of sterilization policies is constrained by the **maturity structure** of the public debt. The shorter the maturity of the liabilities issued by the central bank to conduct sterilization operations, the easier it is for investors to exchange the debt for foreign currency. Thus, the use of short-term domestic assets may facilitate a run on the banking system. It may also create roll-over difficulties for the central bank in the event of an abrupt reversal in capital flows.

Finally, whether the accumulation of foreign exchange reserves induced by sterilization operations is beneficial or not from the point of view of macroeconomic management is open to question. On the one hand, large official reserves create **moral hazard** because policymakers may be tempted to delay needed (and often more painful) adjustments, such as spending cuts aimed at reducing fiscal deficits and external imbalances. On the other, low reserves can undermine the credibility of an exchange rate target, leading to speculative pressures and, as discussed in the next chapter, to a currency crisis.

7.6.2   Exchange Rate Flexibility

Several countries have allowed their nominal exchange rate to appreciate in response to large capital inflows. This appreciation has taken place in the context of both flexible and pegged exchange rate arrangements—in the latter case through either a revaluation or a reduced rate of crawl of the central rate. Greater exchange rate flexibility, by introducing uncertainty or *exchange rate risk*, can discourage speculative short-term cross-border flows. Further, as discussed in Chapter 5, increased exchange rate flexibility provides a greater degree of independence in the conduct of monetary policy and allows more control over the behavior of monetary aggregates. Under a completely flexible exchange rate, capital inflows lead to an appreciation of the nominal exchange rate and no change in official reserves or the money supply. Similarly, capital outflows translate into a nominal depreciation, with no effect on domestic liquidity.

In Chile, for instance, a series of revaluations and changes in the width of the exchange rate band occurred during the period of large inflows, 1991-94 (see Corbo and Hernández, 1996). Specifically, the reference rate within the band was revalued by 0.7 percent in both April and May 1991, by 2 percent in June 1991, by 5 percent on January 23, 1992, and by 9.5 percent on November 30, 1994. In January 1992, the band itself was widened from 5 percent to 10 percent in either direction. In June 1998, in the face of large capital *outflows*, Chile narrowed the width of its exchange rate from ±12.5 percent to ±2.25 percent, in order to reduce exchange rate uncertainty. The band was widened

---

[25] Cárdenas and Barrera also noted that interest rates in Colombia reached very high levels in December 1991—deposit rates stood at 38.5 percent, nearly 9 percentage points higher than in March of the same year. This is consistent with the argument mentioned earlier, which suggested that sterilization can lead to higher domestic interest rates.

again in September 1998 to ±3.5 percent. Chile effectively introduced a floating exchange rate system in September 1999, when it suspended the trading bands around the peso (see Morandé and Tapia, 2002).

To the extent that controlling inflation is the main objective of macroeconomic management (as is the case for instance in the context of a disinflation program), allowing the nominal exchange rate to appreciate may be the optimal response to capital inflows. In the long run, movements in inflation induced by nominal exchange rate adjustments will depend on the extent to which a real appreciation leads to shifts in resource allocation from the tradable to the nontradable sector, and on the response of prices of nontraded goods to such shifts. A positive supply response will exert downward pressure on prices of nontraded goods, thereby reducing inflationary pressures. As discussed in Chapter 4, in the short run a nominal exchange rate appreciation may affect inflation through three types of effects:

- A direct **price effect**, which stems from the impact of exchange rate movements on the domestic price of traded goods (prices of importable consumption goods and imported inputs) and indirect effects on the price of nontraded goods. In general, the extent to which a nominal exchange rate appreciation translates into lower domestic prices depends on the share of traded goods in total expenditure; the relative price elasticities of the demand and supply of nontradable goods; the price formation mechanism; and the existence of (implicit or explicit) wage indexation schemes.[26]

- A **wealth effect**, which results from the fact that a nominal exchange rate appreciation may put downward pressure on the overall price level. The increase in private agents' real wealth will raise aggregate demand; with a relatively inelastic supply of goods in the short run, inflationary pressures may increase, thus partly offsetting the downward effects of the initial appreciation on prices. If foreign-currency holdings represent a large fraction of assets held by households, an appreciation would tend to reduce real wealth and reinforce downward pressures on prices.

- An **expectations effect**, which depends on two related factors: the perceived structure of policy preferences, and the degree of credibility that agents attach to exchange rate appreciation. For instance, a real appreciation brought about by a revaluation of the nominal rate may dampen expectations of devaluation and inflation, thereby leading to a fall in domestic interest rates and an increase in money demand. The fall in interest rates may raise aggregate demand and increase inflationary pressures.

Policymakers, however, are generally concerned not only with inflation but also with the size of the current account deficit. When both objectives affect

---

[26] The short-run effect of a nominal exchange rate appreciation will also depend on the current phase of the economy's business cycle. Inflation response can be significantly influenced by the size of the output gap and the sensitivity of markups to excess demand.

policy preferences, the benefits of real appreciation are less clear-cut and **trade-offs** in the use of the nominal exchange rate are likely to emerge, as discussed in Chapter 5. In general, whether a nominal appreciation has potentially adverse effects on exports or not depends on three factors:

- The extent to which the nominal appreciation translates into a real appreciation. To the extent that a nominal appreciation tends to lower overall inflation, the associated real appreciation will be smaller than the nominal appreciation. The empirical evidence for developing countries suggests nevertheless that the real exchange rate responds significantly in the short run to nominal exchange rate adjustments (Reinhart, 1995). In the long run, a nominal appreciation has no effect on the real exchange rate—unless it is accompanied by permanent measures in the areas of fiscal, monetary, trade, and wage policies.

- The extent to which the real exchange rate has an impact on the supply of exports. This requires evaluating the short- and long-run price elasticities of exports. If the short-run elasticity is small and the exchange rate appreciation is perceived to be *temporary*, the impact will also be small.[27] The evidence reviewed in Chapter 5 suggests that long-run trade elasticities are often well below unity, implying that it would require large changes in relative prices to produce a sizable effect on exports.[28] Moreover, rather than the *level* of the real exchange rate, it may be its *volatility* that may have an adverse effect on exports, as some evidence for developing countries appears to suggest (Grobar, 1993).

- The extent to which the initial situation is one in which the real exchange rate is *undervalued* or not—as for instance at the inception of a disinflation program in which the nominal exchange rate is depreciated by a large amount before being fixed. A key consideration in this context is the rate of *productivity increases* in the exportables sector, relative to the rate of productivity increase in the nontradable sector. If the former is high—as a result of, say, ongoing structural reforms—then some real appreciation may be an equilibrium outcome of the adjustment process, as suggested by the Balassa-Samuelson effect (see DeLoach, 2001).

In practice, determining the degree of initial undervaluation and therefore the *margin of flexibility* in letting the exchange rate appreciate can be a complicated process. To calculate the effects of a devaluation on the real exchange rate requires information on substitution elasticities between tradable and nontradable goods in consumption and production, and on the share of tradable

---

[27] If the exportables sector uses large quantities of imported inputs, an appreciation of the exchange rate may have a net positive effect on output (see Chapter 5).

[28] If countries possess some market power in their export markets, pricing-to-market behavior predicts that upward movements in the nominal exchange rate that are perceived to be temporary will have little effect on relative export prices, as producers absorb them by reducing their profit margins.

goods in total expenditure. This is the *first-round* or *impact* effect, which will be sustained (as noted earlier) only if appropriate monetary, fiscal and other structural policies are implemented concurrently. To determine the equilibrium level of the real exchange rate in the long run requires detailed information on these other policies; without such information, the path of the real exchange rate, following a nominal devaluation, cannot be predicted with any reasonable degree of accuracy. This source of uncertainty can significantly constrain the ability of policymakers to use nominal appreciation as a response to large capital inflows.

7.6.3   Fiscal Adjustment

By implementing cuts in government spending on nontradables, governments can lower aggregate demand and dampen the inflationary impact of capital inflows—thereby mitigating their effect on the real exchange rate. In addition, to the extent that it reduces the government's borrowing needs, a tighter fiscal stance can also lead to lower domestic interest rates and thus reduce incentives for short-term capital to flow into the country. In Thailand, for instance, current public expenditure was reduced from an average of 16.3 percent of GDP during the period 1985-87 to 15.3 percent in 1988 (the first year of the inflow episode), 13.6 percent in 1989, 12.9 percent in 1990, 12.3 percent in 1991, and 11.9 percent in 1992. Other countries where fiscal policy was tightened in response to capital inflows include Chile, Indonesia (1990-94), Malaysia (1988-92), and the Philippines during 1990-92 (World Bank, 1997a). Corbo and Hernández (1996), in their evaluation of the various instruments used to manage capital inflows in nine Asian and Latin American countries, concluded that aggregate demand measures (essentially fiscal contractions) were the most effective.

However, two possible difficulties may arise when using fiscal adjustment as a response to capital inflows:

- Cuts in government spending do not necessarily translate into lower fiscal deficits. They may lead, for instance, to a slowdown in activity in the nontradable sector, and a concomitant reduction in tax revenue. To the extent that the fiscal deficit remains high, persistent interest rate differentials may lead to continued inflows of short-term capital.

- Cuts in government expenditure often cannot be implemented on short notice. Fiscal policy is usually set on the basis of medium- or long-term considerations (for instance, the need to ensure public debt sustainability, as discussed in Chapter 3), rather than in response to what may turn out to be short-term fluctuations in international capital flows. Fiscal discipline thus lacks flexibility as a policy instrument to respond to capital movements.

7.6.4   Capital Controls

During the early 1990s, several countries introduced restrictions aimed at preventing or alleviating the disruptive effects of surges in capital inflows. This
subsection begins by examining the various forms that capital controls can take,
and then turns to a discussion of the pros and cons of imposing them.

Forms of Capital Controls

In general, capital controls take the following forms (Mathieson and Rojas-
Suárez, 1993):

- **Exchange controls**, or **quantitative restrictions**, on capital movements, comprising controls on external asset and liability positions of domestic financial institutions, especially banks;[29] domestic operations of
  foreign financial institutions; and external portfolio, real estate, and direct investments of nonbank residents.

- **Dual** or **multiple exchange rate arrangements**, that is, separate exchange rates for commercial and financial transactions. The commercial
  exchange rate is typically more depreciated than the financial exchange
  rate, in order to avoid adverse effects on competitiveness.

- **Taxes** on financial transactions and income to discourage or control capital flows. These include *interest equalization taxes* to ensure that domestic
  (foreign) residents do not earn higher yields on foreign (domestic) financial instruments, and *transactions taxes* to discourage short-term capital
  movements.

An example of the last form of capital controls is the requirement that a
sum related to a foreign-currency transaction be deposited at the central bank,
interest free, for a specific period of time, thereby raising the *effective cost* of
the transaction. This is the scheme that Chile and other countries used, in
the form of a reserve requirement on all new foreign loans (see below). Firms
receiving foreign loans had to deposit a fraction of the loan, interest free, at the
central bank. This reserve requirement operates *de facto* like an implicit tax
on short-term foreign loans because borrowers had to pay interest on the full
amount of the foreign credit but could use only part of it.

The implicit tax associated with this scheme can be derived in the following
way.[30] Consider a situation where a domestic agent wants to borrow on world
capital markets. In the absence of any tax, the total cost of borrowing from the

---

[29] Such measures include limits on the share of foreign-currency liabilities of domestic commercial banks in their total liabilities. Although they are often presented as prudential regulations (see Chapter 15), these measures are tantamount to capital controls.

[30] The following derivations follow an unpublished appendix by Hernández and Schmidt-
Hebbel (1999). A more complete derivation of formula (37) below is provided by De Gregorio,
Edwards, and Valdés (1999).

point of view of the domestic agent, θ_N, is

$$\theta_N = i^* D L, \tag{35}$$

where i^* is the foreign nominal interest rate (corresponding to the currency in which the reserve requirement is constituted, as discussed below), L the principal of the loan, and D its duration or maturity.

Suppose that the authorities impose a **nonremunerated reserve requirement** (which may or may not be a function of the maturity of the deposit), at the rate r, with a holding period of the required deposit at the central bank equal to T; the cost of borrowing is now

$$\theta_T = \left\{ \frac{i^* D}{1 - r} - \frac{r}{1 - r} i^*(D - T) \right\} L. \tag{36}$$

The first term on the right-hand side of this equation is the direct cost of lending applied to the quantity $L/(1 - r)$, which is the fraction of the principal exempt from the reserve requirement. The second term is the implicit benefit (or cost) of the tax on lending, applied again to the fraction $L/(1 - r)$, for the residual period by which maturity exceeds (falls short of) the holding period of the reserve requirement. As long as $T > D$, this second term represents an additional cost to domestic borrowers.

The additional cost associated with the reserve requirement is thus given by subtracting Equation (36) from (35), which gives

$$\theta_N - \theta_T = \frac{rTi^*}{1 - r} L.$$

Measured per unit of foreign currency borrowed (that is, dividing by L) and per unit of time (that is, taking into account the duration of the loan, D), the implicit tax, ι, is therefore given by

$$\iota = \left(\frac{r}{1 - r}\right)\left(\frac{T}{D}\right)i^*. \tag{37}$$

The amount by which the reserve requirement increases the cost of foreign borrowing for a domestic agent (or, conversely, reduces the rate of return for a foreign investor) depends on the level of international interest rates, the reserve requirement rate, the duration of the investment, and the duration of the deposit. For instance, with a reserve requirement rate $r = 30$ percent, a cost of funds i^* equal to 7 percent, and a required holding period for the deposit of one year ($T = 1$), the tax rate is equal to 36 percent if the investment is for a duration of one month, 12 percent if the investment is for three months, 3 percent if the investment is for one year, 1 percent if the investment is for three years, 0.6 percent if the investment is for five years, and 0.3 percent if the investment has a ten-year maturity period.

Pros and Cons of Capital Controls

In general, as noted by Dooley (1996), the use of capital controls has been justified on four grounds:

- to help limit fluctuations in foreign reserves (under a fixed-exchange rate regime) or exchange rates (under a floating rate regime) generated by volatile short-run capital flows;

- to ensure that domestic savings are used to finance domestic investment (by reducing the rate of return on foreign assets) and to limit foreign ownership of domestic factors of production and natural resources;

- to maintain the government's ability to tax domestic financial activities and income through both explicit and implicit tax instruments (such as the inflation tax, as discussed in Chapters 3 and 6);[31]

- to prevent capital flows from disrupting stabilization programs.

In a second-best world, the possibility that some capital account restrictions could be beneficial (because they help to offset the effect of preexisting distortions) cannot be excluded *a priori*. A classic example is the analysis of the effects of capital flows in the presence of trade distortions by Brecher and Díaz-Alejandro (1977). They considered the case of a small open economy with a relatively abundant labor endowment but nevertheless chooses to protect its capital-intensive industries. Because protection raises the rate of return to capital invested domestically, foreign capital will flow in, leading to an expansion of capital-intensive industries and a contraction of labor-intensive sectors. The misallocation of resources between production sectors is thus magnified, leading to a reduction in the value of domestic production at world prices. The free movement of capital is thus welfare-reducing in the presence of trade barriers on capital-intensive activities.

Another second-best argument for capital controls is that *implicit* or *explicit government guarantees* may distort capital flows. For instance, the perception that the government would assist private borrowers to service external debts during a crisis (in effect, bailing them out) creates **moral hazard** and can induce agents to borrow more than they would otherwise (McKinnon and Pill, 1996). In such conditions, imposing capital controls may be welfare improving if doing so reduces the risk that adverse shocks (such as a shift in market sentiment that leads investors to reduce abruptly their holdings of domestic assets) may translate into a full-blown financial crisis.

The first-best argument *against* capital controls is, of course, that instead of introducing additional distortions in the economy by restricting the movement of capital, a country may be better off eliminating the distortion that led to

---

[31] Razin and Sadka (1991), for instance, argued that empirical estimates of capital flight from developing countries suggest that governments cannot tax residents' income from foreign capital at the same rate at which they tax domestic capital income. As a result, it is optimal in their model for the government to restrict capital outflows.

the inflows in the first place—in the two cases discussed above, by eliminating protection to capital-intensive industries (a sensible policy in a labor-abundant economy, even in the absence of capital flows), and by getting rid of implicit or explicit government guarantees. Moreover, there are several practical difficulties associated with the implementation and enforcement of capital controls:

- By limiting access to world capital markets, capital controls may restrict competition in domestic financial markets. They may also actually encourage **capital flight** through informal markets (see Agénor, 1992). As a result, they create inefficiencies in the domestic financial system and inhibit risk diversification.

- Because they are inherently discriminatory, capital controls create rents that agents may try to capture through bribery, corruption, and abuse of political influence. Such **rent-seeking activities** may be an important source of efficiency losses and resource misallocation (Alesina, Grilli, and Milesi-Ferretti, 1994).

- Capital controls are often used as a *substitute* for fundamental adjustments in the macroeconomic policy stance. Because the effectiveness of capital controls tends to deteriorate rather quickly, attempts to sustain inappropriate macroeconomic policies over a long horizon require tightening these controls over time, thus leading to further distortions (Ariyoshi et al., 2000).

- The imposition of capital controls, even on a temporary basis, can reduce the credibility of a financial liberalization program, because agents may be led to believe that the government is backtracking. As noted in the previous chapter, the risk of *future policy reversals* can be a major impediment to credibility.

- The extent to which capital controls can be enforced effectively remains a matter of debate. There is some evidence suggesting that controls on capital *outflows* have had little effectiveness.[32] While controls may be able to drive a wedge between domestic and foreign interest rates, the incentives to circumvent regulations (through informal currency markets, as discussed by Agénor, 1992) may be larger than the limited yield differential that controls generate. This is likely to be the case in situations of financial instability, induced by large macroeconomic imbalances.

Nevertheless, capital controls on *inflows* have received considerable attention over the past few years, most notably in light of Chile's experience. In June 1991,

---

[32] The econometric study of Johnston and Ryan (1994), for instance, showed that capital controls in developing countries during the 1980s and early 1990s were not effective in insulating the capital account of their balance of payments from domestic and external shocks. However, the measurement of controls in that study (through the use of dummy variables) is problematic because it does not capture changes in the *intensity* of controls over time. Many other existing studies of the effectiveness of capital controls suffer from the same limitation.

the Central Bank of Chile established a mandatory 20 percent nonremunerated reserve requirement on new foreign borrowing (excluding trade credits). This reserve requirement—which, as noted earlier, acts like an implicit tax on foreign borrowing—was later increased to 30 percent and extended to all liabilities to foreigners, including foreign-currency bank deposits, as well as to foreign investment in certain equities. The interest-free reserve requirement had to be kept at the central bank for one year, irrespective of the maturity of the loan or deposit, so that short-term inflows were taxed at a higher rate—thereby reducing their volume. The requirement rate was cut to 10 percent in June 1998 and set to zero in September 1998, largely as a result of the contagion effects of the Asian crisis (see Chapter 8).

Other controls and regulations on foreign capital inflows imposed early on in Chile included a minimum one-year holding period for all foreign investment flows; minimum amount and minimum rating requirements for American Depository Receipts (as defined earlier) and bond issues; and some limitations on foreign investment abroad by Chilean banks and other domestic financial institutions such as pension funds and insurance companies. These limitations were progressively relaxed, and institutional investors (including pension funds) were subsequently authorized to invest part of their portfolio abroad.

How successful was Chile's program of capital controls? As noted earlier, Larraín, Labán, and Chumacero (1997) found that the short-term inflows subject to capital controls were significantly (and negatively) affected by changes in the reserve requirement rate. Controls were also effective in increasing the *maturity* of inflows. Other studies attempting to assess the extent to which nonremunerated reserve requirements on short-term borrowing was successful in altering the level and the composition of capital inflows have reached different conclusions. Hernández and Schmidt-Hebbel (1999) provided a detailed overview of the literature. Their analysis indicated that significant data problems and methodological shortcomings suggest caution in assessing the results of existing studies. Their own results indicated that the nonremunerated reserve requirement affected both the level and composition of capital inflows in the desired direction; these effects, however, were *temporary*.[33] By contrast, Edwards (1999) concluded that capital controls in Chile were largely ineffective.

Other countries where capital controls have been used in recent years to regulate capital flows include Malaysia, Brazil, and Colombia. Malaysia introduced quantitative limits on capital inflows in January 1994; in particular, domestic residents were prohibited from selling short-term market instruments to foreigners, and controls were imposed on offshore borrowing and net foreign exchange positions of commercial banks (see World Bank, 1997a). Sweeping new controls were introduced in September 1998 to limit the large outflows of capital induced by the regional financial crisis that started in mid-1997 (see Chapter 8). Brazil and Colombia used various types of implicit and explicit controls, including, as in Chile, unremunerated reserve requirements. Colombia, in particular, adopted

---

[33] There is also some evidence suggesting that capital controls helped Chile to avoid the contagion effects of the Mexican peso crisis (reviewed in the next chapter), by limiting and smoothing out the impact of large and potentially destabilizing capital inflows on the economy.

in September 1993 a one-year, 47 percent nonremunerated reserve requirement on all foreign loans with maturities inferior to 18 months; the reserve requirement was extended in March 1994 to loans with maturities of up to three years subject to differentiated rates—93 percent for one-year deposits, 64 percent for 18-month deposits, and 53 percent for two-year deposits, regardless of the maturity of the loan. Borrowers were given the option to choose the desired holding period. In August 1994, the maximum maturity subject to the deposit requirement was extended to five years, and a new schedule of deposit rates (ranging from 140 percent for loans with a 30-day maturity, to 43 percent for loans with a five-year maturity period) was adopted.

Empirical studies of the effectiveness of controls in these three countries were provided by Kaplan and Rodrik (2001), Cardoso and Goldfajn (1998), and Cárdenas and Barrera (1997). Kaplan and Rodrik (2001) argued that capital controls in Malaysia were largely successful, in the sense that they helped to restrain capital outflows and promote faster economic recovery. Cardoso and Goldfajn (1998) found that capital controls in Brazil were temporarily effective in altering both the level and the composition of capital flows. By contrast, Cárdenas and Barrera (1997) concluded that although withholding taxes was temporarily effective in reducing short-term capital flows to Colombia, they had no discernible effect on the total volume of capital inflows. These conclusions were by and large corroborated in a study by Montiel and Reinhart (1999), which analyzed (on the basis of panel data techniques) the effectiveness of capital controls in a group of ten countries that experienced large capital inflows during the 1990s: Argentina, Brazil, Chile, Colombia, Costa Rica, Indonesia, Malaysia, Mexico, the Philippines, and Thailand. Montiel and Reinhart's analysis suggested that restrictions on capital inflows tended to reduce significantly the relative importance of short-term flows but had no discernible effect on the overall volume of capital flows.

In sum, the recent experience of countries like Brazil, Chile, and Colombia suggests that, while not a substitute for fundamental adjustments in the macroeconomic policy stance in cases of large imbalances, controls on capital *inflows* may be a useful supplement, particularly if used on a temporary basis, to other policy measures aimed at discouraging short-term, speculative inflows. The evidence on these controls suggests also that they may be subject to leakages over time (like controls on outflows) and that their extended use produces important allocative distortions; unremunerated reserve requirements, for instance, were imposed in some countries not only on short-term inflows but also on foreign direct investment, in order to limit the scope for diverting inflows through alternative channels.[34] Nevertheless, in periods of significant market turmoil, such controls may provide policymakers with additional time to react and implement more fundamental policy adjustments. The experience of Malaysia indeed appears to suggest that the imposition of capital controls in a crisis context can be successful. However, Malaysia's experience cannot necessarily be generalized

---

[34] Garber (1996) discussed ways by which reserve requirements aimed at penalizing short-term inflows in favor of longer-term investments can be evaded through the use of derivative instruments in the absence of tight controls on capital outflows.

to other countries. As discussed in the next chapter, the imposition of capital controls can actually precipitate a crisis, instead of preventing it.

7.6.5   Changes in Statutory Reserve Requirements

Increases in unremunerated reserve requirements on (resident and nonresident) deposits in domestic banks have been used as a complement to market-based instruments in various countries—including Chile, Korea (1988-90), Malaysia (1989-94), and the Philippines (1990)—particularly in cases where capital inflows were intermediated directly by the banking system. The main effect of higher, across-the-board statutory reserve requirement rates is to lower the **money supply multiplier**, reduce domestic credit and money supply expansion, and dampen inflationary pressures associated with large inflows of capital.[35]

However, increases in unremunerated reserve requirements are not necessarily without costs.

- They can undermine the *profitability* and *soundness* of the banking system. In cases where banks are faced with solvency problems, unremunerated reserve requirements may worsen banks' financial positions by encouraging excessive risk taking.

- They may reduce the *efficiency* of bank intermediation and promote alternative domestic channels of intermediation (such as nonbank financial intermediaries), thereby complicating supervision of the financial sector and the conduct of monetary policy.

- They may increase the fragility of banks that are under financial stress, without fully absorbing the excess liquidity held by healthy banks, particularly when liquidity is not evenly distributed among banks (as a result of an uneven distribution of the increase in the deposit base associated with the inflow of capital) and the interbank market for short-term funds does not operate efficiently.

7.6.6   Other Policy Responses

In attempting to cope with large capital flows, countries have responded in ways other than those reviewed earlier. Some countries have required commercial banks to hold *liquid deposits* abroad. Foreign liquidity requirements may be preferable to reserve requirements because they force commercial banks to be more cautious and address the **currency mismatch** that may characterize their balance sheets. However, they may not be sufficient to satisfy the demand for foreign exchange resulting from an abrupt outflow of capital taking the form of a

---

[35] Higher reserve requirements on foreign-currency deposits only (as imposed by Chile, Peru, and Sri Lanka, in particular) are best viewed as a form of capital controls, which aim at discouraging the accumulation of a particular type of financial liabilities in the banking system, as opposed to restraining overall lending.

reduction in foreign-currency deposits from a segment of the banking system. In such conditions, a perceived shortage of official reserves may well be sufficient to transform a bank run into a full-blown financial crisis. Moreover, unless they are only applied to foreign exchange deposits, foreign liquidity requirements expose commercial banks to **currency risk**. If the exchange rate is not credibly fixed, this risk (and the cost of hedging against it) can be substantial.

In some, mostly Asian countries, the transfer of **public sector deposits** from commercial banks to the central bank (or an increase in reserve requirement rates on deposits of the public sector held in commercial banks) has also been used to offset the liquidity effects of capital inflows. Malaysia and the Philippines, for instance, adopted this policy during 1992-94 (World Bank, 1997*a*). This measure can be more flexible and easier to implement than an increase in reserve requirements and less costly to the central bank than a sterilization operation. However, it may also penalize excessively those banks whose deposit base consists mostly of public sector deposits. Moreover, if used aggressively, it can hamper the development of an active interbank market.

7.7   Summary

- The surge in capital flows to developing countries in the early 1990s contrasts sharply with the experience of the mid-1980s, when most of these countries attracted very little foreign capital or recorded large net outflows. It also contrasts with the experience of the 1970s and the 1980s in that a substantial part of these flows now consists of *private, non-debt-creating flows*—such as **foreign direct investment** and acquisitions of **equity** in local stock markets. They have also been highly concentrated, with about ten countries receiving almost 80 percent of total net private capital flows.

- Foreign direct investment is in general less prone to abrupt reversals than portfolio investment; the determinants of its growth, location, and sectoral composition are longer term and more dependent on structural factors than the short-term risk-return considerations that influence portfolio flows.

- Foreign direct investment also has more direct effects on economic growth than other cross-border flows, because it facilitates **technology transfers** and generates spillovers into other sectors.

- Empirical studies have found that capital inflows respond to both external and internal factors, the relative importance of which varies across countries. **External** or **push factors** include changes in international interest rates and rates of return on foreign assets, the business cycle in industrial countries, and institutional changes affecting the propensity of investors in major industrial countries to diversify their portfolios internationally.

- **Internal** or **pull factors** are related to the domestic macroeconomic policy stance and the process of liberalization of foreign trade and opening of financial markets. The evidence suggests that capital inflows have occurred not only where fiscal adjustment took place in the preceding years (as in Thailand) but also in countries where it did not (as in Turkey). In the latter case, the combination of a lax fiscal policy and a tight monetary stance led to high interest rates, stimulating short-term speculative capital inflows.

- Liberalization of capital *outflows* may also cause an increase in capital *inflows*, because granting more freedom to foreign investors to repatriate their capital reduces the implicit cost of foreign investment in the country.

- The recent evidence suggests that *short-term* investment flows are more volatile (and thus more susceptible to large and abrupt reversals) than other types of capital flows, including direct investment.

- The *level* and *composition* of capital inflows have important macroeconomic effects. Large surges in inflows in the early stages of financial integration may lead to an unsustainable **credit boom** (which may increase the vulnerability of the domestic financial system), a *real appreciation*, and higher *macroeconomic volatility*.

- The fact that capital flows to Latin America were associated mostly with an increase in consumption (with a large component consisting of expenditure on nontradable goods), rather than investment, and the fact that countries like Argentina, Brazil, and Peru were pursuing exchange-rate-based stabilization programs during the first part of the 1990s, explains the large real appreciations observed in these countries.

- External shocks, through their impact on capital flows, can have large effects on the domestic economy in the short term. This is well illustrated in a static, three-good model with a credit-supply side link and imperfect capital mobility—both of which are key macroeconomic features of developing countries.

Policy responses to capital inflows have included a combination of market-based and non-market-based instruments.

- **Sterilization**, narrowly defined, is the offsetting of reserve inflows so as to leave the *monetary base* unaffected, through sales of government interest-bearing debt or central bank paper. Broadly defined, sterilization is the offsetting of inflows so as to leave the *broad money supply* unaffected, for instance, through increases in reserve requirements placed on commercial banks.

- Sterilization can be effective in the short term to dampen the effects of surges in inflows, but its effectiveness is more limited in the medium term, notably because of its impact on **quasi-fiscal deficits**. Sterilization conducted through open market operations may lead to central bank losses because the government bonds or central bank liabilities used for sterilization operations may carry higher interest rates than those earned by the central bank on its holdings of foreign-currency assets. Moreover, because sterilization through open-market operations tends to raise domestic interest rates, capital inflows may be exacerbated.

- A more flexible exchange rate policy (in the context, for instance, of an exchange rate band with an adjustable central rate) may be an effective way to insulate domestic liquidity from highly volatile capital flows. By increasing uncertainty in the behavior of the exchange rate, it may reduce speculative movements of capital. However, to the extent that nominal appreciations translate into real appreciations, it may have an adverse effect on the current account.

- *Cuts in government spending* can alleviate upward pressures on domestic prices and dampen the real appreciation that may be associated with capital inflows. However, fiscal policy is generally geared to long-term objectives and may not be flexible enough (as a result of various institutional constraints) to deal with surges in capital flows.

- Restrictions on international capital flows take a variety of forms, including multiple exchange rate arrangements, taxes or quantitative limits on capital movements, minimum reserve requirements on foreign loans or credits, ceilings on foreign borrowing, interest rate equalization taxes, limits on the share of foreign-currency liabilities in total liabilities of domestic commercial banks, and prohibitions on residents from selling short-term monetary instruments to nonresidents.

- Experience in several countries has shown that capital controls (on both *inflows* and *outflows*) tend to lose effectiveness over time as financial markets find ways to bypass existing regulations. However, the evidence also suggests that controls in some countries appeared to have been effective in limiting short-term capital inflows and that they may have induced a change in the composition of aggregate flows, increasing long-term flows relative to short-term flows. Although controls on short-term capital inflows impose costs (in terms of foregone access to capital and efficiency losses), they also provide important benefits to the extent that they allow countries to insulate themselves from potentially unstable capital movements and to put in place more fundamental policy measures. These benefits can be significant in periods of market turbulences.

- Increases in **statutory reserve requirements**, by limiting banks' capacity to lend, may dampen the liquidity effects and inflationary pressures associated with surges in capital inflows. However, changes in requirement rates lack flexibility and may promote financial disintermediation.

- Two common methods of estimating the degree of capital mobility are **tests of monetary autonomy**, which examine the extent to which the effect of changes in the central bank's net domestic assets on the monetary base is offset by changes in official net foreign assets, and tests of **uncovered interest parity**, which examine whether the nominal rates of return (adjusted for the expected rate of change in the nominal exchange rate) on comparable domestic and external financial instruments are equalized. Empirical studies suggest that, although capital mobility has increased significantly in recent years, it remains imperfect in most cases.

Appendix to Chapter 7
Measuring the Degree of Capital Mobility

Among the methods that have been used in the literature to measure the degree of capital mobility (or more generally the degree of integration of domestic and foreign financial markets) in developing countries, tests of **monetary autonomy** and tests based on the **uncovered interest parity** (UIP) **condition** have played an important role.[36]

Tests of monetary autonomy examine the extent to which the effect of changes in the central bank's net domestic assets on the monetary base are offset by changes in official net foreign assets through the balance of payments. Under perfect capital mobility, the **offset coefficient** should be equal to minus unity. Most of the early work in this area (see, for instance, Cumby and Obstfeld, 1983, and Kamas, 1985) concluded that developing countries retained significant amounts of monetary autonomy in the sense that the effect of changes in net domestic credit on the monetary base were offset only partially by changes in official reserves. More recent work (see Fry, 1995), however, has suggested higher coefficients in absolute value and thus an increase in the degree of capital mobility.

The UIP condition implies that the nominal rates of return (adjusted for the *expected* rate of change in the nominal exchange rate) on comparable domestic and external financial instruments should be equalized if the degree of capital mobility is high.[37] Early studies massively rejected the UIP condition for developing countries, often arguing that this was a consequence of the existence of various barriers that made domestic and foreign assets imperfect substitutes. These barriers to capital mobility included existing capital controls, high transaction costs, high information costs, discriminatory tax laws (based on the country of residence), high premia related to default risk, and the risk of *future* capital controls.

More recent analyses have used a more direct approach to estimate the degree of capital mobility, and allowed this measure to *vary over time*. This is particularly important because, as noted in the introduction to this chapter, many developing countries in recent years relaxed the controls imposed during the 1970s and early 1980s on capital movements. Moreover, even in countries where the *legislation* on capital controls has not been changed, it is possible that the *cost* of evading them may have changed significantly over time; as a result the degree of capital mobility may also have changed significantly. Faruqee

---

[36] Other methods that have been used in the literature are reviewed by Agénor and Montiel (1999, chap. 5); see also Maloney (1997) for a recent application. The evidence on capital mobility for industrial countries is reviewed by Obstfeld (1995b).

[37] Note that for *real* interest parity to hold, one must have not only uncovered interest parity, as defined in the text, but also *ex ante* relative purchasing power parity, that is, the expected rate of depreciation of the nominal exchange rate must be equal to the difference between expected domestic and foreign inflation rates. However, in practice, goods markets are *not* perfectly integrated; purchasing power parity is thus unlikely to hold. The possibility of an expected real depreciation implies that real interest parity may fail even if the nominal interest parity condition holds.

(1992), in particular, found evidence that the correlation between interest rates in the money markets in Korea, Malaysia, Singapore, and Thailand and the offshore three-month Japanese yen LIBOR rate increased during the 1980s.

In general, the existing evidence for developing countries suggests that the degree of capital mobility, despite increasing in recent years (in some cases quite dramatically), remains *imperfect*. This has important analytical implications, as illustrated in the model of section 7.5: domestic interest rates become determined through general equilibrium interactions rather than solely by foreign interest rates and exchange rate expectations.

Chapter 8

Financial Crises and Financial Volatility

> All economic events, by their very nature, are motivated by crowd psychology
> . . . Men think in herds; . . . they go mad in herds, while they only recover
> their senses slowly, and one by one.
>
> Preface to the second edition of Charles Mackay's *Memoirs of Extraordinary*
> *Popular Delusions and the Madness of Crowds*, 1852.

The increase in the degree of capital mobility across borders that accompanied the programs of domestic and external financial liberalization that many developing countries implemented during the 1980s and 1990s has brought tangible benefits to these countries, as documented in the previous chapter. The disturbing fact, however, is that the incidence of financial crises has grown in parallel (as documented by Glick and Hutchison, 1999, and Kaminsky and Reinhart, 1999), and the sheer economic and social costs of these crises have led many observers to question the desirability of greater international financial integration. This chapter analyzes the sources of financial crises, reviews several experiences with currency crises, examines the sources and effects of financial volatility, and considers various policy responses that can be implemented to mitigate these effects.

Section 8.1 presents the main analytical approaches that economists have developed to understand currency crises. Section 8.2 reviews three cases of exchange rate collapse: the Mexican peso crisis of December 1994, the Thai baht crisis of July 1997, and the Brazilian real crisis of January 1999. The links between banking and currency crises are examined in sections 8.3 and 8.4, from an analytical as well as empirical standpoint. Sections 8.5 and 8.6 focus on the determinants and effects of financial volatility on world capital markets (particularly the role of cross-country contagion and herding behavior) and on ways to limit the adverse effects of such volatility. Among the measures that can be implemented are the introduction of taxes on capital flows transactions, and foreign debt management. The appendix discusses practical aspects of speculative attacks, involving borrowing from the domestic bank system and the use of interest rates to fend off speculative pressures.

8.1   Sources of Exchange Rate Crises

The analytical literature on exchange rate crises is dominated by three types of models. Conventional or first-generation models tend to emphasize *inconsistencies* between fiscal, monetary, and exchange rate policies and the role of speculative attacks in "forcing" the abandonment of a currency peg. Second-generation models, by contrast, emphasize the vulnerability of exchange rate systems even in the presence of consistent macroeconomic policies and sound market fundamentals. They explicitly account for **policymakers' preferences** and the **trade-offs** that they face in their policy objectives, as discussed in Chapters 4, 5 and 6. In these models, an exchange rate "crisis" (a devaluation or a switch to a floating rate regime) is viewed as an *ex ante* optimal decision for the policymaker. These models also highlight the role of **self-fulfilling mechanisms**, **multiple equilibria**, and **credibility factors**. Third-generation models dwell on both first- and second-generation approaches to currency crises. They focus on balance sheet factors and emphasize the role of financial sector weaknesses and credit market imperfections (resulting from the type of asymmetric information problems discussed in Chapter 4) in triggering speculative attacks. They also pay particular attention to the role of monetary policy in these crises, aside from the decision to abandon the exchange rate parity.

8.1.1   Inconsistent Fundamentals

The canonical first-generation model of currency crises was formulated by Krugman (1979) and Flood and Garber (1984). The main features of their analysis can be presented in the context of a single (tradable) good, full-employment, small open economy model with exogenous output. The basic assumptions of the model can be summarized as follows.

- The foreign-currency price of the good is fixed (at, say, unity). The domestic price level is equal, as a result of **purchasing power parity**, to the nominal exchange rate.

- Agents are endowed with **perfect foresight** and hold three categories of assets: domestic money (which is not held abroad), and domestic and foreign bonds, which are **perfect substitutes**.

- The *demand for money* depends positively on output and negatively on the domestic interest rate.

- **Uncovered interest parity** equates the domestic interest rate to the foreign rate plus the expected (and actual, under perfect foresight) rate of depreciation of the nominal exchange rate.

- There are no private banks, so that the money stock (the *monetary base*) is equal to the sum of domestic credit issued by the central bank and the domestic-currency value of foreign reserves held by the central bank. The central bank pegs the exchange rate through **unsterilized intervention**.

- *Domestic credit* expands at a constant growth rate to finance the government budget deficit.

Formally, the conventional model can be defined by the following set of equations:

$$m^d = p + y - \alpha i, \quad \alpha > 0, \tag{1}$$

$$h^s = \gamma d + (1 - \gamma)R, \quad 0 < \gamma < 1, \tag{2}$$

$$\dot{d} = \mu > 0, \tag{3}$$

$$p = e, \tag{4}$$

$$i = i^* + \dot{e}, \tag{5}$$

where m^d denotes nominal money demand, p the price level, y real output (assumed exogenous), h^s the nominal supply of base money, d domestic credit, R the domestic-currency value of the foreign reserves held by the central bank, e the spot exchange rate, i^* the constant foreign interest rate, and i the domestic interest rate. All variables except i and i^* are measured in logarithms, and $\dot{x} \equiv dx/dt$.

Equation (1) shows that money demand is homogeneous in prices, positively related to income (with a unit elasticity) and negatively to the domestic interest rate. Equation (2) is a log-linear approximation to the identity defining the monetary base as a weighted average of the sum of domestic credit and the stock of foreign reserves held by the central bank; the coefficient γ reflects the proportion of domestic credit in the money stock at the point of linearization. Equation (3) indicates that domestic credit grows at the rate μ. Equations (4) and (5) define, respectively, purchasing power parity and uncovered interest parity.

To simplify the notation, suppose that $\gamma = 0.5$, and let $m^s = 2h^s$; Equation (2) therefore becomes

$$m^s = d + R. \tag{6}$$

For convenience, m^s will be referred to in what follows as the money supply. Similarly, interpreting m^d as twice the demand for base money implies that the money market equilibrium condition is

$$m^s = m^d = m.$$

Setting for simplicity $i^* = 0$ and using Equations (1), (4), and (5), money market equilibrium implies that

$$m - e = y - \alpha \dot{e}. \tag{7}$$

As long as the exchange rate is credibly fixed at $e = \bar{e}$, devaluation expectations will be zero and $\dot{e} = 0$; the above equation therefore becomes

$$m = \bar{e} + y, \tag{8}$$

which indicates that, with nominal money demand fixed at $\bar{e} + y$, the *nominal supply* of money by the central bank must also remain *fixed over time*. Put differently, under a fixed exchange rate regime, the rate of depreciation is zero and (because output is constant) real money balances are also constant. Thus, the central bank must accommodate any change in domestic money demand induced by, say, a change in output, through the purchase or sale of foreign reserves to the public (given that the rate of growth of domestic credit is exogenous).

To see what the above condition implies for the behavior of official reserves in a setting in which credit is growing over time, note that substituting Equation (6) in (8) yields

$$R = y + \bar{e} - d. \tag{9}$$

Differentiating this equation with respect to time, noting that output is constant, and using Equation (3) implies

$$\dot{R} = -\mu. \tag{10}$$

Equation (10) shows that, in order for the nominal money supply to remain constant and ensure equilibrium of the money market, *official reserves must fall at the same rate as the rate of credit expansion*.

This result has an important implication: in a setting in which the nominal credit stock is growing exogenously, *any finite stock of official reserves will be exhausted in a finite period of time*. Once foreign reserves reach a *lower bound* (say, R_{min}), the central bank will be unable to defend the prevailing parity and will be forced (unless credit policy can be altered to ensure that $\mu = 0$) to abandon the pegged rate regime. This is, in a sense, a **natural collapse**. Of course, when domestic credit is not growing ($\mu = 0$), there is no policy inconsistency and the fixed exchange rate regime can in principle survive indefinitely.

Suppose, however, that the central bank cannot credibly commit to setting $\mu = 0$ when the lower bound R_{min} is reached. Instead, it announces that it will abandon the prevailing fixed exchange rate once $R = R_{min}$ and adopt a *permanently floating exchange rate regime* thereafter.

With a positive rate of domestic credit growth, rational agents will anticipate that, without speculation, reserves will eventually fall to the lower bound, and will therefore foresee the ultimate collapse of the system. At that point, the rate of depreciation of the nominal exchange rate will jump from zero to a positive value; through the interest parity condition (5) the domestic interest rate will also jump upward, and from Equation (1) the demand for money will fall. To maintain money market equilibrium, the *real* money supply must also fall; and because the *nominal* money stock cannot change in a discrete manner (reserves are constant after the collapse and credit continues to grow smoothly), the nominal exchange rate must undergo a *step depreciation*. The rise in prices therefore imposes a **capital loss** on agents holding domestic-currency assets.

However, speculators endowed with perfect foresight will not wait passively to suffer the capital loss arising from an abrupt depreciation of the exchange rate at the time of collapse; they will attempt to reduce their holdings of domestic assets and in the process will force a crisis *before* the lower bound on reserves is reached—that is, before the regime collapses naturally. The issue is thus to determine the exact moment at which the fixed exchange rate regime is abandoned or, equivalently, the **transition time** to a floating rate regime.

As first shown by Flood and Garber (1984), this transition time can be calculated through a **backward-induction process**, which can be characterized as follows.

- In equilibrium, under perfect foresight, agents can never expect a *discrete jump* in the level of the exchange rate, because a jump would provide them with profitable arbitrage opportunities.

- As a consequence, **arbitrage** in the foreign exchange market requires the exchange rate that prevails immediately after the attack to be *equal* to the fixed rate prevailing at the time of the attack.

Formally, the time of collapse is found at the point where the **shadow floating rate**, the exchange rate that would prevail if reserves had fallen to the minimum level and the exchange rate were allowed to float freely, is *equal* to the prevailing fixed rate. The reason is that if the shadow floating rate falls below the prevailing fixed rate, speculators would not profit from driving the government's stock of reserves to its lower bound and precipitating the adoption of a floating-rate regime, because they would experience an instantaneous capital loss on their purchases of foreign exchange. On the contrary, if the shadow floating rate is above the fixed rate, speculators would experience an instantaneous capital gain. Neither anticipated capital gains nor losses at an infinite rate are compatible with a perfect-foresight equilibrium. Speculators will compete against each other to eliminate such opportunities.

A first step in calculating the time of the speculative attack is thus to solve for the shadow floating exchange rate. A simple method to do so is the **method of undetermined coefficients**, used also in the appendix to Chapter 4, which consists here of postulating that the (floating) exchange rate is a linear function of the money supply:

$$e = \kappa_0 + \kappa_1 m, \tag{11}$$

where κ_0 and κ_1 are coefficients that must be solved for given structural parameters of the model. In the above equation, m is the postattack value of the money supply, given by [using Equation (2)]

$$m = d + R_{min}. \tag{12}$$

Taking the rate of change of Equation (11), noting that κ_0 is constant and that from Equation (12) $\dot{m} = \dot{d}$ under a floating rate regime yields

$$\dot{e} = \kappa_1 \mu,$$

which can be substituted in (7) to yield, with $y = 0$ for simplicity,

$$e = m + \alpha \kappa_1 \mu. \tag{13}$$

Comparing Equations (13) and (11) yields

$$\kappa_0 = \alpha \mu, \quad \kappa_1 = 1,$$

which implies that the shadow exchange rate, in the **postcollapse regime**, depreciates at the same rate as the rate of growth of domestic credit:

$$\dot{e} = \mu.$$

From Equation (3), $d = d_0 + \mu t$. Using the definition of m given in Equation (12) and substituting in Equation (13) yields

$$e = d_0 + \alpha \mu + R_{min} + \mu t. \tag{14}$$

The fixed exchange rate regime collapses when the prevailing parity, $\bar{e}$, equals the shadow floating rate, e. From Equation (14) the exact time of collapse, t_c, is obtained by setting $\bar{e} = e$, so that

$$t_c = (\bar{e} - d_0 - R_{min})/\mu - \alpha,$$

or, because from Equations (2) and (8) $\bar{e} = d_0 + R_0$,

$$t_c = (R_0 - R_{min})/\mu - \alpha, \tag{15}$$

where R_0 denotes the initial stock of reserves.

Equation (15) has the following implications.

- The higher the initial stock of reserves, the lower the critical level, or the lower the rate of credit expansion, the longer it takes before the collapse occurs.

- With no speculative demand for money, that is, with $\alpha = 0$, the **natural collapse** occurs when reserves are run down to the minimum level; the time of collapse, t_n, is thus

$$t_n = (R_0 - R_{min})/\mu.$$

- The interest rate (semi-)elasticity of money demand determines the size of the downward shift in money balances and reserves that takes place when the fixed exchange rate regime collapses and the nominal interest rate jumps to reflect a positive (expected) rate of depreciation of the domestic currency. The larger α is, the earlier the crisis.

The analysis implies, therefore, that the speculative attack *always* occurs before the central bank would have reached the minimum level of reserves in the absence of speculation. Using Equation (9) with $y = 0$ yields the stock of reserves just before the attack (that is, at t_c^-):

$$R_{t_c^-} \equiv \lim_{t \to t^-} R_{t_c} = \bar{e} - d_{t_c^-},$$

where $d_{t_c^-} = d_0 + \mu t_c^-$, so that

$$R_{t_c^-} = \bar{e} - d_0 - \mu t_c^-. \tag{16}$$

Setting $t = t_c^-$ in Equation (14) yields

$$\bar{e} - d_0 = \mu(t_c^- + \alpha) + R_{min}. \tag{17}$$

Finally, combining Equations (16) and (17) yields

$$R_{t_c^-} = R_{min} + \alpha\mu. \tag{18}$$

The two panels of Figure 8.1 illustrate the behavior of all variables before and after the crisis. The path continuing through point A in the upper panel corresponds to the **natural collapse** scenario ($\alpha = 0$), which occurs at t_n. As shown in the lower panel, at that point the rate of depreciation of the exchange rate jumps from zero to μ and the domestic interest jumps from i^* to $i^* + \mu$ (that is, from G to G'), requiring a discrete depreciation of the nominal exchange rate from B' to C. The expected capital loss leads to a speculative attack that brings the regime down at $t_c < t_n$. The exchange rate remains constant at $\bar{e}$ until the collapse occurs and begins depreciating smoothly at point B in the lower panel. The domestic interest rate, as a result of the interest parity condition (5), jumps by μ at the moment the attack takes place (from point F to F'). Prior to the collapse at t_c, the money stock is constant, but its composition varies because domestic credit rises at the rate μ and reserves decline at the rate μ. In the postcollapse regime, the money stock is equal to R_{min} plus domestic credit, and grows also at the rate μ. An instant before the regime shift, a speculative attack occurs, and both reserves and the supply of money fall by $\alpha\mu$. The size of the attack, $\alpha\mu$, corresponds exactly to the reduction in money demand induced by the upward jump in the domestic interest rate.

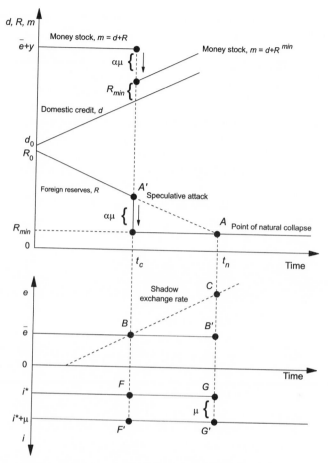

Figure 8.1. The "conventional" model of an exchange rate crisis. Source: Adapted from Agénor and Flood (1994, p. 230).

This canonical framework has been extended in a variety of directions (see Agénor and Flood, 1994). Important extensions include

- the nature of the *fiscal constraint* that underlies the assumption of an exogenous rate of credit growth and the factors that may prevent policy-makers from adjusting their fiscal and credit policies to prevent a crisis;[1]

- the nature of the **postcollapse exchange rate regime**;

- the *output, real exchange rate*, and *current account* implications of an anticipated exchange rate crisis;

- the role of *external borrowing* and **capital controls**; and

---

[1] As noted earlier, the central bank could choose, before reserves are exhausted, to change its credit policy rule to make it consistent with a fixed exchange rate—that is, set $\mu = 0$.

- *uncertainty* over the critical threshold of reserves and the credit policy rule.

Ozkan and Sutherland (1995), for instance, suggested that a fixed exchange rate system can survive longer with capital controls. However, it has also been shown that the *anticipation* of controls may have exactly the opposite effects. In general, the anticipation of capital controls has the same effect as the anticipation of a devaluation, because both reduce the future value of domestic assets for foreign investors. It follows that, paradoxically, the threat of capital controls may generate the very problem that they are supposed to remedy. Dellas and Stockman (1993) modeled the vicious circle that may result in this setting. They showed that the mere suspicion that policymakers may introduce capital controls may generate **self-fulfilling crises**, as discussed later.

The introduction of *uncertainty* on domestic credit growth in the canonical first-generation model of currency crises collapse models has the following implications.

- The transition to a floating rate regime becomes **stochastic**. As a result, the collapse time becomes a random variable that cannot be determined explicitly, as before.

- There will, in general, always be a *nonzero probability* of a speculative attack in the next period, a possibility that in turn leads to a **forward discount** on the domestic currency—the so-called **peso problem**—and higher domestic interest rates.

- The degree of uncertainty about the central bank's credit policy plays an important role in the speed at which reserves are depleted. In a stochastic setting, reserve losses tend to exceed increases in domestic credit because of a rising probability of regime collapse. Reserve depletion tends therefore to *accelerate* prior to the regime change. Such a pattern has often been observed in actual crises.

A key assumption of the model described earlier is that the money supply falls, in line with money demand, at the moment the currency attack takes place. However, if reserve losses are completely *sterilized* (as discussed in the previous chapter), there will be no discrete jump in the money supply.[2] Flood, Garber, and Kramer (1996) argued that in such conditions a fixed exchange rate regime *cannot be viable*; as long as agents understand that the central bank plans to sterilize an eventual speculative attack, they will attack *immediately*. To see this, consider again the money market equilibrium condition, Equation (7), with $y = i^* = 0$. If the money stock is constant as a result of sterilized intervention (at, say, $m = m^s$) and the exchange rate is fixed, this condition is

$$m^s - \bar{e} = 0,$$

---

[2] As discussed later, during the periods preceding the Mexican peso crisis of December 1994, policymakers engaged in sterilized intervention to mitigate the impact of speculative capital flows on domestic liquidity.

whereas in the postattack floating rate regime, with $\dot{e} = \mu$:

$$m^s - e = -\alpha\mu.$$

Subtracting the second expression from the first yields

$$e - \bar{e} = \alpha\mu > 0.$$

Thus, if the money supply is not allowed to change when the attack takes place, the shadow exchange rate (consistent with money market equilibrium) will always exceed the prevailing fixed exchange rate—thereby provoking an immediate attack. By adding a **risk premium** to the above model, Flood, Garber, and Kramer (1996) showed that it remains useful to understand currency crises under sterilized intervention. Essentially, the risk premium adjusts to keep the demand for money *constant* when the attack occurs, just as sterilization maintains the money supply constant.

There is considerable evidence suggesting that currency crises (or financial crises in general, as discussed later) tend to be preceded by a real exchange rate appreciation and growing current account deficits. A simple extension of the standard model to account for these facts is to assume that the economy produces two goods, one tradable, the other nontradable (see for instance Veiga, 1999). Suppose also that in the nontradable sector prices are set as a markup over wage costs; and suppose that nominal wages are *forward looking*, that is, set on the basis of the expected *future* evolution of the cost of living (Willman, 1988). If the cost of living is a weighted average of prices of tradables and nontradables, an anticipated future depreciation of the nominal exchange rate (due, as in the canonical first-generation model, to an expansionary fiscal policy accompanied by reserve losses) will translate into higher nominal wages today and higher prices of nontradables today. Because prices of tradables remain fixed until the actual regime change, the real exchange rate appreciates. In turn, the real appreciation reduces the relative price of importables and thus leads to increased imports and a growing current account deficit prior to the collapse.

8.1.2 Rational Policymakers and Self-Fulfilling Crises

A problem with first-generation models is that the exact timing of an exchange rate crisis may be difficult to pin down if, as first emphasized by Obstfeld (1986), the inconsistency between fiscal and exchange rate policies is *conditional* or *contingent* on the occurrence of a speculative attack. Suppose that the foreign exchange market is atomistic, so that no single speculator can, individually, launch an attack that drives international reserves to their minimum level and force the central bank to abandon the peg. Then, no agent will attack the currency unless he or she expects that a sufficient number of other agents will do so at the same time. In this case, the timing of a speculative attack becomes *indeterminate*, as it depends on *strategic uncertainty* regarding the coordination of private agents on one particular regime of expectations. In every period during which the official parity is enforced, *two equilibria* are possible: one characterized by a run on international reserves and the abandonment of the peg, and another in which no attack occurs and the official parity is maintained. **Self-fulfilling speculative attacks** are thus possible if private agents expect an easing of monetary policy after the abandonment of the fixed rate regime. Put differently, the mere expectation that monetary policy will become more accommodative following an attack may be sufficient to generate the anticipation of capital losses on domestic-currency assets resulting from a more depreciated exchange rate—thereby validating the attack in the first place. The attack itself brings about the crisis, which may or may not be preceded by a drop in reserves, a real exchange rate appreciation, and growing current account deficits, as emphasized in the canonical first-generation model and its various extensions.

A key feature of the second-generation literature on currency crises has also been an explicit modeling of *policymakers' preferences* and policy rules. In this setting, and as discussed in Chapter 5, policymakers are viewed as deriving benefits from pegging the currency—by, say, importing the **anti-inflation reputation** of a foreign central bank—but as also facing other policy targets, such as the accumulation of foreign reserves, a high level of output, low unemployment, and low domestic interest rates. Thus, depending on the circumstances that they face, policymakers may find it optimal to abandon the official parity. According to this approach, the occurrence of an exchange rate "crisis" (or, to use a more neutral expression, a discrete change in the exchange rate) is not necessarily related to central bank reserves reaching a lower limit. Rather, the abandonment of the peg is the result of the implementation of a **contingent rule** for setting the exchange rate. Each period, the policymaker considers the *costs* and *benefits* associated with maintaining the peg for another period, and must decide—given the relative weights attached to each objective in its policy loss function—whether or not to abandon it. This decision typically is viewed as depending on the realization of a particular set of domestic or external shock(s). For a given cost associated with abandoning the currency peg, there exists a *range of values* for the shock(s) that makes maintaining the peg optimal. However, for sufficiently large realizations of the shock(s), the *loss in flexibility* associated with the discretionary use of the exchange rate may exceed the loss incurred by abandoning the peg; in such circumstances, it is optimal for the policymaker to operate a regime change.

Another implication of such models—as emphasized early on by Obstfeld (1986)—is the existence of **multiple equilibria** and the possibility that shifts across these equilibria may be **self-fulfilling**: the economy may switch from an equilibrium in which devaluation expectations are low and the peg is sustainable to an equilibrium in which devaluation expectations are high and the peg becomes impossible to defend.

Obstfeld (1995*a*) provides a simple model that illustrates self-fulfilling crises and multiple equilibria. The model extends the Barro-Gordon framework discussed in Chapter 6 to account for labor market rigidities and aggregate demand shocks. The existence of such shocks creates a role for stabilization policy. For instance, an adverse shock to aggregate demand at the initial real wage will lead to a fall in output; in order to offset this effect, the policymaker can devalue the nominal exchange rate and thus lower real wages—but at the cost of higher inflation. The extent to which adverse shocks are accommodated by exchange rate adjustment will depend, in particular, on the form of the policy loss function.

Specifically, Obstfeld's model assumes purchasing power parity, so that (with the foreign-currency price level constant and normalized to zero) the logarithm of the domestic price level, p, is equal to the logarithm of the nominal exchange rate, e. The logarithm of output, y, depends negatively on the logarithm of the real wage, $w - e$ (with w denoting the logarithm of the nominal wage) and a serially independent shock, u, which captures shifts in aggregate demand:

$$y = -\alpha(w - e) - u, \quad \alpha > 0. \tag{19}$$

In this equation α measures the responsiveness of output to changes in the real wage, $w - e$. In what follows it will be assumed that u can take only nonnegative values in the interval $(0, u_m)$, where $u_m > 0$.

Nominal wages are set on the labor market *before* the demand shock is observed, so as to maintain a constant *expected* real wage:

$$w = \mathrm{E}_{-1}e, \tag{20}$$

where E_{-1} is the expectations operator conditional on information available at period $t - 1$.

As in the framework used in Chapter 6 to discuss time inconsistency and inflation bias, the policymaker's loss function, L, is quadratic in output deviations and in inflation:

$$L = \frac{1}{2}(y - \tilde{y})^2 + \theta\frac{\pi^2}{2}, \quad \theta > 0, \tag{21}$$

where $\tilde{y}$ is the desired level of output, π is inflation, and θ the weight attached to inflation in the loss function. The first term on the right-hand side reflects the cost of deviations from the desired level of output, whereas the second captures the cost of deviating from zero inflation.

Using Equation (19) and noting that inflation is simply $\pi = \Delta e$, Equation (21) can be rewritten as

$$L = \frac{1}{2}[-\alpha(w - e) - u - \tilde{y}]^2 + \theta\frac{(\Delta e)^2}{2}. \tag{22}$$

Suppose that the policymaker cannot precommit to a fixed exchange rate, and that it chooses discretionarily the nominal exchange rate e to minimize L given the nominal wage set at period $t - 1$. Minimizing Equation (22) over e yields the first-order condition

$$\frac{\partial L}{\partial e} = \alpha[-\alpha(w - e) - u - \tilde{y}] + \theta\Delta e = 0,$$

which yields the following reaction function:

$$e = e_{-1} + \lambda(w - e_{-1}) + \frac{\lambda}{\alpha}(u + \tilde{y}), \tag{23}$$

where

$$\lambda = \frac{\alpha^2}{\theta + \alpha^2}.$$

Equation (23) indicates that high nominal wages (relative to prices in the previous period) and a negative shock to aggregate demand (an increase in u) bring a partially offsetting devaluation of the nominal exchange rate. The coefficient $0 \le \lambda < 1$ can be viewed as measuring the extent to which the policymaker accommodates wage movements and demand shocks; λ is higher the greater the adverse impact of changes in the real wage on output are (as measured by α), and is smaller the greater the weight attached to inflation (measured by θ) in the policymaker's loss function is. Thus $\lambda \to 0$ in two particular cases:

- $\alpha \to 0$, so that output is independent of movements in real wages;

- $\theta \to \infty$, in which case the policymaker is only concerned about maintaining a zero rate of inflation.

In either case, Equation (23) implies that $e = e_{-1}$; when the policy loss from nonzero inflation, in particular, is infinitely large, a fixed exchange rate is optimal.

Firms and wage setters know the policymaker's reaction function and set wages (as indicated earlier) so as to take the policymaker's expected response into account. Equations (20) and (23) therefore imply that, in equilibrium:

$$w = e_{-1} + \lambda(w - e_{-1}) + \frac{\lambda}{\alpha}(\mathrm{E}_{-1}u + \tilde{y}),$$

or, setting $\mathrm{E}_{-1}u = \bar{u}$,

$$w = e_{-1} + \frac{\lambda(\bar{u} + \tilde{y})}{\alpha(1 - \lambda)}. \tag{24}$$

Combining Equations (23) and (24), the equilibrium level of the exchange rate is given by

$$e = e_{-1} + \frac{\lambda^2(\bar{u} + \tilde{y})}{\alpha(1 - \lambda)} + \frac{\lambda}{\alpha}(u + \tilde{y}),$$

that is

$$e = e_{-1} + \frac{\lambda}{\alpha}u + \frac{\lambda^2\bar{u} + \lambda\tilde{y}}{\alpha(1 - \lambda)}. \tag{25}$$

Equation (25) indicates that, under a discretionary policy regime, a fixed exchange rate ($e = e_{-1}$) prevails in equilibrium only if inflation is infinitely costly ($\theta \to \infty$, so $\lambda \to 0$). It also shows that the economy is characterized by a systematic **devaluation bias**, as measured by $\alpha^{-1}(\lambda^2\bar{u} + \lambda\tilde{y})/(1 - \lambda)$, which depends on the level of desired output and the mean value of the aggregate shock. It reflects the policymaker's attempt to exploit the potential short-run trade-off between output and inflation created by predetermined nominal wages. But although a precommitment to a fixed exchange rate would eliminate the devaluation bias, it would also prevent the policymaker from responding to unpredictable shocks to aggregate demand, u. Put differently, there is a trade-off, as discussed in Chapter 5, between *credibility* and *flexibility*. In choosing whether or not to maintain a fixed exchange rate or to devalue, the policymaker will select the alternative that minimizes its loss.

Describing the nature of the choice facing the policymaker proceeds as follows. Because the policymaker faces a predetermined nominal wage when deciding the value of the nominal exchange rate at period t, the (predetermined) expected rate of inflation, π^e, is given by the expected change in the exchange rate. Specifically, Equation (20) implies that nominal wage growth, $w - e_{-1}$, is equal to the expected inflation rate, so that

$$\pi^e = w - e_{-1} = \mathrm{E}_{-1}e - e_{-1}. \tag{26}$$

Under a fixed exchange rate, $e = e_{-1}$. Inflation is thus zero and the second term on the right-hand side of Equation (22) vanishes. Noting that $w - e = w - e_{-1}$ and using Equation (26), the policy loss derived from (22) is

$$L^F = \frac{1}{2}(\alpha\pi^e + u + \tilde{y})^2. \tag{27}$$

If the policymaker decides, instead, to devalue according to the reaction function described in Equation (23), it incurs a **fixed cost** c (measured in terms of, say, units of domestic output), in addition to the policy loss. To calculate this loss, note that, from (23),

$$w - e = (1 - \lambda)(w - e_{-1}) - \frac{\lambda}{\alpha}(u + \tilde{y}),$$

so that, using (26),

$$w - e = (1 - \lambda)\pi^e - \frac{\lambda}{\alpha}(u + \tilde{y}).$$

Because $w - e = w - e_{-1} - \Delta e$, using the preceding equation and (26) again yields

$$\Delta e = \pi^e - (w - e) = \lambda\pi^e + \frac{\lambda}{\alpha}(u + \tilde{y}). \tag{28}$$

Substituting these results in (22) yields

$$L^D = \frac{(1 - \lambda)^2}{2}[-\alpha\pi^e - (u + \tilde{y})]^2 + \frac{\theta\lambda^2}{2}[\pi^e + \frac{(u + \tilde{y})}{\alpha}]^2,$$

which can be re-arranged as

$$L^D = \frac{1}{2}\left[(1 - \lambda)^2 + \frac{\theta\lambda^2}{\alpha^2}\right][\alpha\pi^e + (u + \tilde{y})]^2.$$

From the definition of λ, $\theta = \alpha^2/\lambda - \alpha^2$. Thus,

$$(1 - \lambda)^2 + \frac{\theta\lambda^2}{\alpha^2} = 1 - 2\lambda + \lambda^2 + \lambda - \lambda^2 = 1 - \lambda,$$

so that

$$L^D = (\frac{1-\lambda}{2})(\alpha\pi^e + u + \tilde{y})^2. \tag{29}$$

The decision to devalue will thus take place whenever the policy loss associated with maintaining the exchange rate fixed exceeds the total loss associated with a discretionary adjustment:

$$L^F > L^D + c,$$

that is, using Equations (27) and (29), when

$$\frac{\lambda}{2}(\alpha\pi^e + u + \tilde{y})^2 > c.$$

This expression must be turned into an equality in order to determine the threshold value(s) of u. Rearranging terms yields

$$u^2 + 2(\alpha\pi^e + \tilde{y})u - \{2c/\lambda - (\alpha\pi^e + \tilde{y})^2\} = 0.$$

Assuming that the last term in brackets is positive, **Descartes' rule of signs** implies that this quadratic equation in u has two solutions, one negative and one positive (see Gandolfo, 1996, p. 54). By assumption, u cannot take negative values; the (unique) threshold value of u, denoted U, is thus equal to the positive root

$$U = \frac{-2(\alpha\pi^e + \tilde{y}) + \sqrt{4(\alpha\pi^e + \tilde{y})^2 - 4\{2c/\lambda - (\alpha\pi^e + \tilde{y})^2\}}}{2},$$

that is,

$$U = \sqrt{2c/\lambda} - \alpha\pi^e - \tilde{y} > 0. \tag{30}$$

Thus the policymaker devalues whenever $u > U$. The *ex post* optimal level of the exchange rate is given by Equation (23). Intuitively, when the adverse demand shock is large, the cost associated with low output (or high unemployment) is so high that the benefits of a stimulus (a fall in real wages) outweighs the inflationary and fixed costs induced by a devaluation.

From the definition of U, it is clear that a shift in market expectations, π^e, or in the cost of realignment, c, can lead to a change in the position of the threshold point and to a currency crisis—although none might have occurred in the absence of this shift. More precisely, the potential for a self-fulfilling exchange rate crisis arises in the above setting from a **circularity problem**.

- The threshold point U, which determines whether the policymaker devalues or not, depends on prior expectations of inflation and depreciation, π^e, as shown by Equation (30).

- In turn, these expectations depend on market perceptions of where the point U (that is, the value of u beyond which the policymaker finds it suboptimal to defend the prevailing exchange rate) lies. As shown in (26), π^e depends on nominal wages, which are fixed on the basis of the expected exchange rate. In turn, $E_{-1}e$ depends on the expected value of u, which is affected by U.

To illustrate how inflation expectations depend on the position of U, suppose that the shock u follows a **uniform distribution**, $g(u)$, in the interval $(0, u_m)$. Agents, again, anticipate a devaluation whenever $u > U$. To solve for π^e requires

- calculating the expected rate of depreciation given an anticipated trigger point U;

- calculating the actual threshold given the expected depreciation rate.

The expected depreciation rate can be written as the weighted average of two possible outcomes: either $u \leq U$ and the fixed exchange rate is maintained, or $u > U$, and it is devalued by a given amount Δe. Thus, in probabilistic terms,

$$\pi^e = \Pr(u \leq U) \cdot 0 + \Pr(u > U) \cdot E(\Delta e \mid u > U), \tag{31}$$

where $E(\Delta e \mid u > U)$ measures the expected size of the devaluation, given that $u > U$. With a uniform distribution,

$$\Pr(u > U) = \frac{u_m - U}{u_m} > 0. \tag{32}$$

From Equation (28),

$$E(\Delta e \mid u > U) = \frac{\lambda}{\alpha} E(u \mid u > U) + \frac{\lambda}{\alpha}(\alpha \pi^e + \tilde{y}),$$

where $E(u \mid u > U)$, the conditional expectation of u given that $u > U$, is equal to the mean of the conditional distribution of u, given that $u > U$:

$$E(u \mid u > U) = \int_U^{u_m} u g(u \mid u > U) du.$$

Again, from the properties of the uniform distribution,

$$E(u \mid u > U) = \int_U^{u_m} \frac{u}{u_m - U} du = \frac{[u^2/2]_U^{u_m}}{u_m - U} = \frac{u_m^2 - U^2}{2(u_m - U)} = \frac{u_m + U}{2},$$

which implies that

$$E(\Delta e \mid u > U) = \frac{\lambda}{\alpha}\left(\frac{u_m + U}{2}\right) + \frac{\lambda}{\alpha}(\alpha \pi^e + \tilde{y}). \tag{33}$$

Substituting Equations (32) and (33) in (31) yields therefore

$$\pi^e = \left(\frac{u_m - U}{u_m}\right)\left[\frac{\lambda}{\alpha}\left(\frac{u_m + U}{2}\right) + \frac{\lambda}{\alpha}(\alpha \pi^e + \tilde{y})\right],$$

which can be rewritten as

$$\pi^e = F(U) = \frac{\lambda}{\alpha}\left(\frac{u_m - U}{u_m}\right)\left[\left(\frac{u_m + U}{2}\right) + \tilde{y}\right] \div \left[1 - \lambda\left(\frac{u_m - U}{u_m}\right)\right]. \tag{34}$$

Substituting this solution in Equation (30) implies that the largest value of the aggregate demand shock consistent with maintaining the prevailing exchange rate fixed is a positive value u^* that solves the quadratic equation

$$\frac{\lambda}{2}[\alpha F(U) + u^* + \tilde{y}]^2 - c = 0,$$

or, because equilibrium requires setting $U = u^*$:

$$\alpha F(u^*) + u^* + \tilde{y} = \sqrt{2c/\lambda}.$$

Figure 8.2 illustrates the possibility of multiple devaluation trigger points in the above setting. The curve $\alpha F(u^*) + u^* + \tilde{y}$ is convex with respect to the origin and may intersect the horizontal line corresponding to the quantity $\sqrt{2c/\lambda}$ (which depends on the devaluation cost, c) only once, as is the case at point A. In general, however, the two curves will intersect twice at, say, points B and B'. It can be inferred from Equation (34) that $F'(U) < 0$, so that at the high value u_H^*, the expected rate of depreciation is relatively low, whereas at the low value u_L^* (corresponding to point A), devaluation expectations are relatively high. At that level of the expected depreciation rate, wages are so high and output so low that even a small adverse shock to output will lead to a devaluation. Again, a shift in market expectations, or in the (perceived) cost of realignment can lead to a change in the position of the threshold point u^* and to a currency crisis—although none might have occurred in the absence of this shift. If the private sector adopts the high value u_H^* as the value that will trigger the abandonment of the fixed exchange rate rule, then u_H^* will also solve the policymaker's optimization problem. Consequently, this value of the disturbance will indeed be the one that leads the policymaker to abandon the peg and devalue the currency. Similarly, if the private sector adopts the low value u_L^* as the value that it believes will induce an exchange rate regime switch, then it will also be optimal for the policymaker to adopt it as well. Thus, the economy can jump from one equilibrium to another; the shift in perceptions that triggers the jump can be completely unrelated to the behavior of macroeconomic fundamentals.

Figure 8.2 also shows that, as pointed out by Flood and Marion (1999), an increase in the cost of abandoning the peg may increase the likelihood of a crisis. Suppose for instance that the initial position of the economy is at point B, corresponding to the lower threshold u_L^*. An increase in c translates into an upward shift of the horizontal curve $\sqrt{2c/\lambda}$, thereby reducing the lower threshold value (from B to C) of the disturbance that makes a devaluation more likely.

The importance of market perceptions in determining the timing of a currency crisis suggests that a reputation for "toughness" may help policymakers to fend off speculative attacks and preserve a peg (see Chapter 5). However, as pointed out by Drazen and Masson (1994), toughness can be counterproductive. Speculators may infer that a policymaker resisting a speculative attack (through, for instance, high interest rates) is indeed "tough," thus deterring them from future attacks, or they may instead infer that the defense against the first speculative attack was so costly (in terms of low output and high unemployment) that the policymaker cannot possibly resist a future attack. A good example is the case of Sweden, as noted by Obstfeld (1995a) and Obstfeld and Rogoff (1995). In September 1992, Sweden's central bank successfully resisted an attack on the krona by raising the domestic interbank rate up to an annualized value of 500 percent. However, it responded to a second attack in November 1992 by floating the krona. The cost of defending the peg, given high unemployment, was just too high.

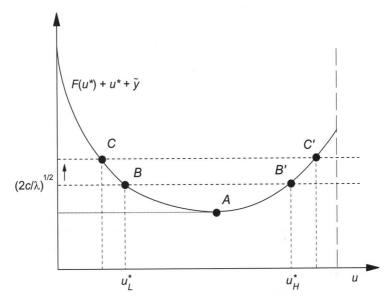

Figure 8.2. Multiple equilibrium in Obstfeld's model. Source: Adapted from Obstfeld (1995).

As discussed by Obstfeld (1996), various other sources of policy trade-offs, and thus trigger mechanisms, have been suggested in the recent literature on self-fulfilling crises. A particular channel, as discussed by Agénor and Masson (1999), focuses on the adverse effects of high interest rates, as discussed in the appendix to this chapter. For instance, banks may come under pressure if market interest rates rise unexpectedly, because borrowers may be unable to repay their debts as a result. To avoid a costly bailout, policymakers may want to implement a devaluation to boost output and firms' cash flows—although the incentive to devalue may be curtailed, as discussed later, if banks face a high burden of unhedged, foreign-currency debt. Or, with sticky prices in the short run, an increase in nominal interest rates may translate into a rise in *real* interest rates, which may generate self-fulfilling devaluation pressures. In models such as those of Calvo (1998) and Sachs, Tornell, and Velasco (1996a), it is a large volume of **short-term debt**, denominated in either domestic or foreign currency, that puts a country's exchange rate peg in a vulnerable position, where a self-fulfilling panic can lead to a sudden and massive speculative attack.

- A large stock of *domestic-currency* short-term debt may create doubts about public sector solvency, raise fears that the authorities may inflate to reduce the real value of public debt, and impose constraints on the ability of policymakers to use high interest rates to fend off speculative attacks (see the appendix to this chapter). These factors may lead creditors to refuse to roll over the maturing stock of debt, thereby compounding initial fears and increasing the currency's vulnerability.

- A large stock of *foreign-currency* short-term debt (which cannot be reduced by domestic inflation) may also raise concerns about external solvency and precipitate a speculative attack (see for instance Velasco, 1997*a*). These concerns may be heightened if, again, currency depreciation has an immediate impact on the local-currency value of foreign debt obligations, as discussed later in the context of the Asia crisis. In general, when the ratio of short-term foreign debt relative to official reserves is high, the risk of short-term liquidity problems may increase the vulnerability of the exchange rate to a sudden shift in expectations or perceptions.

An important implication of this analysis is that *flow measures* of the adequacy of reserves (such as the ratio of imports to official reserves) and vulnerability (such as the ratio of the current account deficit to output), as well as long-term solvency indicators (such as the ratio of total foreign debt to output), have limited usefulness as indicators of exchange rate vulnerability relative to *stock measures* such as the ratio of short-term external debt to official reserves, or the ratio of total (domestic and foreign) short-term debt to reserves. An alternative indicator of short-term vulnerability, as proposed by Calvo (1998), is the ratio of *broad money* to official reserves—on the ground that these components of money holdings represent contingent liabilities for the authorities in case of a currency crisis. However, even an indicator based on broad money may understate potential exchange market pressures if, for instance, holders of short-term domestic public debt become concerned about the sustainability of the exchange rate or about the government's ability to service its debt (as noted earlier). In such conditions, an aggregate consisting of all short-term government liabilities would be more appropriate. Judging which indicator is best in a particular set of circumstances is an empirical matter; the point, nevertheless, is that flow measures can be misleading indicators of exchange rate viability.

A more general message of the second-generation models of currency crises is that the possibility of self-fulfilling crises makes any pegged rate regime precarious. In most of the models discussed earlier, fundamentals, viewed as reflecting the policymaker's preferences and the economy's structure, affect the multiplicity of equilibria. But the policymaker is incapable of enforcing its preferred equilibrium should market expectations focus on an inferior one. Furthermore, **sunspots**—seemingly minor random events, such as the resignation of some government minister—could shift the exchange rate from a position where it is vulnerable to only very bad realizations of domestic and external shocks—a phenomenon with very low *ex ante* probability—to one where output is so low absent a devaluation and a fall in real wages that even relatively small shocks will induce policymakers to devalue.

The trouble with the above models is that, as noted by Obstfeld (1995*a*), if currency crises are viewed as a manifestation of possible multiple equilibria, there are no convincing explanations of the mechanisms through which market expectations coordinate (at a given moment in time) on a particular self-fulfilling set of expectations. In addition, the evidence on the role of self-fulfilling factors in exchange rate crises remains limited. The approach followed by Eichengreen, Rose, and Wyplosz (1996) for instance is to compare, using nonparametric statistical tests, the behavior of macroeconomic variables during periods of speculative pressure with their behavior during more "tranquil" periods. Significant differences in the behavior of these variables across periods are deemed to provide support for the view that speculative pressures are triggered by inconsistencies in the macroeconomic policy stance. If no differences are found, episodes of speculative pressures are viewed as the result of arbitrary shifts in expectations. Such tests, however, have limited power, and more robust methods remain to be devised, perhaps along the lines proposed by Ratti and Seo (2003).[3]

8.1.3   Third-Generation Models

Third-generation models of currency crises, proposed most notably by Krugman (1999), emphasize balance sheet factors and the role of financial sector weaknesses in triggering speculative attacks. They also pay particular attention to the role of monetary policy in this context. In the first- and second-generation models described above, monetary policy cannot avoid a crisis. Indeed, in the models emphasizing inconsistent fundamentals, monetary policy is passive, and once a devaluation is expected, it becomes inevitable. By contrast, third-generation models, such as Aghion, Bacchetta, and Banerjee (2001), have provided a role for monetary policy in a currency crisis—aside from the decision to abandon the exchange rate peg. These models assume that credit is necessary for production (as in the three-good model developed in Chapter 7) and that asymmetric information problems in the credit market may lead lenders to restrain the amount of loans available to firms—as opposed to complete rationing of the Stiglitz-Weiss type (see Chapter 4). Because tighter credit constraints may have an adverse impact on expected output, they also increase the likelihood of an exchange rate collapse.

Formally, these models assume that firms' ability to borrow on the domestic market for loans is limited to only a fraction of their net worth, as for instance in the model of Bernanke, Gertler, and Gilchrist (2000) discussed in Chapter 4. Lending operations are thus partially collateralized. As a result, loan rates incorporate a premium that reflects the perceived risk of default by borrowers. In part, the risk of default is related to moral hazard, that is, the incentive

---

[3] Section 8.4 discusses other general issues that arise in predicting financial crises.

for the firm to claim a "bad" outcome (low output) and avoid repaying its debt. If this effect is large enough, an increase in the lending rate due to some exogenous impulse (say, an increase in the cost of funds from the central bank) would tend to *reduce* the supply of loans (instead of increasing it), because banks internalize the fact that higher interest rates (and thus higher debt repayments) may increase the firms' incentive to default.

Indeed, suppose that because of the borrowing constraints imposed by their collateralizable net worth, domestic firms have accumulated a large amount of foreign-currency-denominated debt. Suppose also that there are speculative pressures on the exchange rate, and to fend them off the central bank raises its policy rate (a typical response, as discussed in the appendix to this chapter). In the framework considered here, this policy may lead to both higher lending rates and a reduction in the supply of loans (as the risk of default increases), which translates into a fall in current output. Because investors may anticipate repayment problems on foreign debt as a result of lower profits, the (actual or perceived) drop in output may put additional pressure on the exchange rate. In such conditions, the central bank should *lower* interest rates, instead of increasing them. Of course, higher domestic interest rates may also lead households to repatriate capital, or reduce the rate of capital outflows, which would tend to dampen pressures on the exchange rate and official reserves. The net effect of higher interest rates is thus, in general, ambiguous. This type of reasoning is useful to interpret the controversy over the role of monetary policy in the first stages of the Asia crisis (see Furman and Stiglitz, 1998, and Radelet and Sachs, 1998).

8.2   Currency Crises: Three Case Studies

Exchange rate crises have been a recurrent feature of the macroeconomic experience of developing countries, particularly in Latin America. Argentina and Brazil, for instance, experienced several such episodes during the 1980s (see Agénor and Montiel, 1999, chap. 16). This section discusses three crises that occurred during the 1990s: the Mexican peso crisis of December 1994, the Thai baht crisis of July 1997, and the Brazilian real crisis of January 1999. In all three cases, a much debated issue has been the role of economic fundamentals relative to self-fulfilling factors in causing these crises. In addition, the first two crises had significant repercussions on world capital markets.[4]

8.2.1   The 1994 Crisis of the Mexican Peso

Between 1988 and 1993, macroeconomic stabilization and economic reform in Mexico led to a sharp reduction in inflation and a significant improvement in the

---

[4]Other recent crises include the collapse of Argentina's peso (discussed by Perry and Servén, 2003) and the Turkish lira crisis (discussed by Yilmaz and Boratav, 2003).

operational balance of the public sector (Figure 8.3).[5] A key factor in bringing inflation down to single-digit levels was the exchange rate policy, which involved the fixing of the Mexican peso-U.S. dollar exchange rate from December 1987 until January 1989, followed by a preannounced narrow margin crawling peg and the adoption in November 1991 of a crawling peg with adjustable bands. The floor of the band was kept constant while its ceiling was allowed to depreciate relative to the U.S. dollar at a predetermined rate. As a result, the intervention band widened from 1 percent in November 1991 to 9 percent at the end of 1993. Between January 1990 and December 1993, the peso depreciated in nominal terms by about 17 percent; it continued to depreciate, albeit at a slower rate, between January and early December 1994 (Figure 8.4).

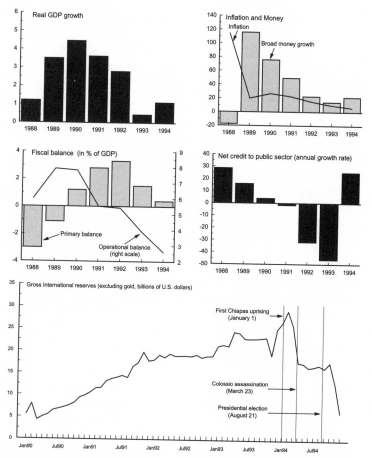

Figure 8.3. Mexico: Macroeconomic indicators, 1988-94. Source: International Monetary Fund.

---

[5]See Aspe (1993) for a comprehensive overview of Mexico's reform and stabilization during that period.

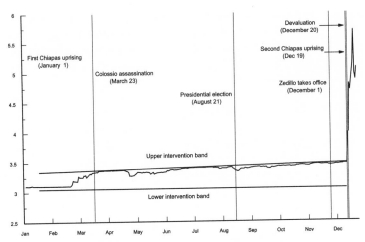

Figure 8.4. Mexico: Nominal exchange rate and intervention bands, 1994 (pesos per U.S. dollar). Source: Bank of Mexico and Bloomberg, Inc.

However, nominal depreciation over the period did not prove sufficiently large to prevent a sharp appreciation of the real exchange rate. Between January 1990 and December 1993, the real effective exchange rate based on consumer prices appreciated by almost 35 percent; the index based on unit labor costs appreciated by an even larger amount (Figure 8.5). At the same time, the current account deficit widened from 3.2 percent of GDP in 1990 to 4.8 percent in 1991 and 6.6 percent in 1992-93, averaging $24 billion in these two years (Figure 8.5). Despite the growing external deficit, a surge in capital inflows led to a significant increase in gross international reserves, which stood at $19.4 billion at the end of 1992 and $25.4 billion at the end of 1993, compared with $6.5 billion in 1989 (Figure 8.3). In order to sterilize these inflows, the authorities issued large amounts of short-term treasury bills (*Certificados de Tesorería*, or *Cetes* bonds) denominated in pesos.

Large capital inflows continued during the first quarter of 1994, after the approval of the North American Free Trade Agreement (NAFTA) by the U.S. Congress in November 1993. As a result, the interest rate differential between Cetes bonds and interest rates in the United States declined significantly. Figure 8.6 decomposes this differential into two components:

- the interest rate differential between Cetes and *Tesobonos* (short-term U.S. dollar liabilities repayable in pesos), which represents an indicator of **currency risk**;

- the Tesobono-U.S. certificate of deposit (CD) rate differential, which represents an indicator of country or **default risk**.[6]

The figures show that both components of the Cetes-U.S. interest rate differential narrowed in early 1994. The Cetes-Tesobono differential fell from a

---

[6] Using the yield on U.S. Treasury bills instead of the interest rate on CDs to calculate the risk of default does not make much difference.

peak of about 10 percent in early November 1993 to about 3 percent in early April 1994, whereas the Tesobono-U.S. CD rate differential dropped from about 2 percent in December 1993 to less than half a percentage point in early March 1994.

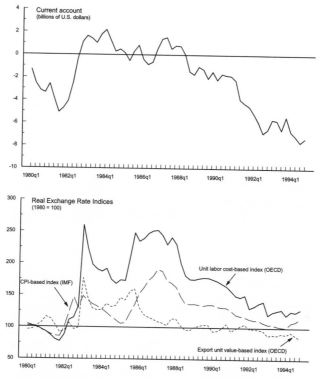

Figure 8.5. Mexico: Current account and real exchange rate indices, 1980-84. In real exchange rate indices, an increase is a depreciation. Source: International Monetary Fund and OECD.

However, the macroeconomic policy stance weakened considerably in 1994. Fiscal policy became more expansionary, as the government increased expenditure financed through state-controlled development banks.

- Credit to the financial system expanded sharply between March and June 1994, from 15.7 to 33.5 billion pesos. It rose further by about 10 percent (to 36.5 billion pesos) in September 1994.

- Net credit to the public sector also expanded, from -12.5 billion pesos in March to -2.1 billion pesos and -1.6 billion pesos in June and September, respectively (Figure 8.3).

- Credit extended by official or state-owned development banks (such as *Nacional Financiera*) grew at an annual rate of more than 40 percent in the first three quarters of the year.

The overall expansion in credit largely offset the effect on liquidity of the fall in net foreign assets of the Bank of Mexico. The monetary base fell only slightly, from 47.1 billion pesos in March 1994 to 45.3 billion in June and 45.8 billion in September 1994. Overall, the supply of base money expanded in 1994 at the same rate as in 1993 (about 18 percent), but credit extended by the banking system to the private sector expanded at a rate of 32 percent.

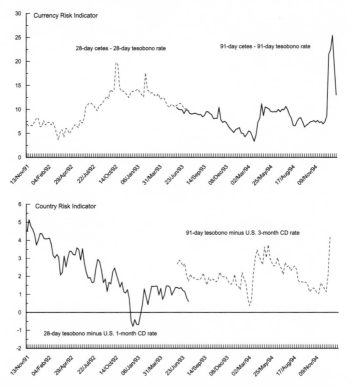

Figure 8.6. Mexico: Currency risk and country risk indicators, 1991-94 (in percent). Currency risk indicator based on monthly averages of weekly auction rates; country risk indicator based on monthly averages of weekly auction rates of Tesobonos. Source: Bank of Mexico and Bloomberg, Inc.

The expansion in domestic credit and relaxation of the fiscal stance (which appear to have been related to electoral considerations) and a series of adverse political events (unrest in Chiapas in January and the assassination of presidential candidate Luis D. Colosio in March), brought the Mexican peso under severe pressure in the second quarter of 1994. The Cetes-Tesobono interest rate differential rose above 10 percentage points in April (Figure 8.6). The stock of international reserves fell from $26.8 billion at the end of March to $16.9 billion by the end of June 1994.

To stem capital outflows, the authorities raised domestic interest rates and allowed the peso to move to the upper limit of the exchange rate band. Reserves then remained relatively stable through the period of the presidential election in August, as negotiations continued on the social-economic pact (the *Pacto*) into September. During that period, the exchange rate remained at or near the ceiling of the authorities' intervention bands (Figure 8.4). The authorities also substituted short-term debt denominated in foreign currency for peso-denominated debt.

As a result of these swap operations, the outstanding stock of Tesobonos more than doubled between March and April 1994, from 14.0 billion to 36.4 billion pesos, reaching 47.5 billion pesos in June and 64.9 billion pesos in July. The share of Tesobonos in proportion of the total stock of Cetes and Tesobonos held by the private sector rose from less than 10 percent in January-February 1994 to more than 40 percent in April and almost 60 percent in July (Figure 8.7).

The current account deficit continued to deteriorate in the third quarter of 1994 (reaching 7.6 percent of GDP on average for the year as a whole), heightening concerns about the sustainability of Mexico's external position. Political unrest in Chiapas intensified after the Zedillo administration took office on December 1, 1994. These developments were accompanied by increased exchange rate pressures and large capital outflows. Despite relative stability from the end of April until August and a slight improvement between September and October (Figure 8.3), official reserves fell further to $10 billion in mid-December.

The stock of Tesobonos continued to increase, from 78.4 billion pesos in September to 85.2 billion pesos in November. As a proportion of the privately held stock of Cetes and Tesobonos, the share of Tesobonos reached 80 percent in that month (Figure 8.7).

The continued accumulation of short-term U.S. dollar liabilities offset to some extent movements in reserves but exposed the authorities' debt servicing operations to greater exchange rate risk. Although currency risk and default risk indicators did not deteriorate significantly during that period (Figure 8.6), the Cetes-Tesobono interest rate differential remained significantly above its first quarter level—indicating that investors' devaluation expectations were somewhat higher toward the end of the year.[7] On December 20, the exchange rate band was widened by 15.3 percent and the Mexican authorities announced their intention to support the currency at about 4 pesos to the U.S. dollar. But the Bank of Mexico was unable to hold the exchange rate there. Widespread investor fears put further pressure on foreign exchange and financial markets (leading to a loss of reserves of about $4 billion in two days) and forced the adoption of a floating exchange rate regime on December 22.

The peso, which had closed at 3.47 to the U.S. dollar on December 19, quickly depreciated in the ensuing days to around 5.5 to the U.S. dollar. It recovered slightly afterward, but between December 20, 1994, and January 3, 1995, the peso depreciated by about 30 percent from its pre-devaluation rate. Domestic interest rates rose sharply, with the 28-day Cetes rate increasing nearly

---

[7]See Agénor and Masson (1999) for a more detailed discussion of the behavior of exchange rate expectations prior to the Mexican peso crisis.

threefold to an annualized level of 45 percent by January 10, 1995. At the end of December 1994, the value of the outstanding stock of Tesobonos amounted to about 29 billion U.S. dollars, or approximately 156 billion pesos, at the prevailing exchange rate.

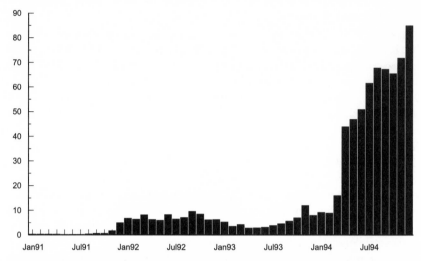

Figure 8.7. Mexico: Share of Tesobonos held by commercial banks and the nonfinancial private sector, 1991-94 (in proportion of total stock of Cetes and Tesobonos). Nonfinancial private sector includes both residents and nonresidents. Source: Bank of Mexico.

8.2.2   The 1997 Thai Baht Crisis

As noted in the previous chapter, Thailand experienced a surge in capital inflows beginning in 1988. To a large extent, these inflows were a response to improved economic prospects. Between 1986 and 1988, in particular, Thailand turned an overall fiscal deficit of 4.3 percent of GDP into a surplus of 2.6 percent.

Various other economic reforms were also initiated during that period; these reforms included a reduction or elimination of government controls over economic activity, the privatization of state-owned firms, a reduction in tariffs and quantitative import barriers, and a removal of capital controls. Capital inflows were associated with a sharp increase in investment; the ratio of gross capital formation to GDP increased from an average of 21.8 percent a year in 1984-88 to 28.4 percent in 1989-93. During the same period, public consumption spending fell sharply, from 13.6 percent of GDP to 9.9 percent.

Beginning in 1984 and until the 1997 crisis, the Thai baht was pegged to a weighted basket of currencies of Thailand's major trading partners. But in practice, the U.S. dollar remained the most important currency in the basket.[8]

---

[8] Glick, Hutchison, and Moreno (1997) estimated that over the period 1979-92, the weight of the U.S. dollar in Thailand's currency basket amounted to about 92 percent, compared with

Because inflation in Thailand in the early 1990s exceeded the levels recorded by its trading partners (including the United States), the pegged exchange rate regime led to a significant real appreciation.

The *de facto* peg to the U.S. dollar also implied that swings in the nominal and real values of the U.S. dollar relative to the Japanese yen and European currencies had significant effects on Thailand's real exchange rate. In particular, as a result of the nominal depreciation of the U.S. dollar relative to the yen and the Deutsche mark between 1991 and 1995 (with the U.S. currency reaching a low of 80 yen per U.S. dollar in the spring of 1995), the baht depreciated in real terms.

After the spring of 1995, however, the dollar started to appreciate (from 80 yen per U.S. dollar to over 125 in the summer of 1997, a 56 percent appreciation) taking the baht in its wake. Using 1990 as a base year, Thailand's real exchange rate had appreciated by 12 percent by the spring of 1997. Taking spring 1995 as a base period, the real appreciation of the baht was larger, and amounted to 17-18 percent.

The appreciation of the real exchange rate led, in turn, to a worsening of external accounts. Thailand's current account deficit grew significantly during the 1990s, reaching about 8 percent of GDP in late 1996 (Figure 8.8). For quite some time, Thailand's external deficits were viewed as relatively harmless, because they did not result from large imbalances in the public sector and because foreign borrowing was being used mainly to increase domestic investment— rather than domestic consumption, as occurred, for instance, in Mexico during the years preceding the peso crisis.[9]

The public sector fiscal balance, in fact, remained in surplus throughout the 1990s.[10] But in 1996 and early 1997, markets grew increasingly concerned about Thailand's macroeconomic problems and financial sector vulnerability.

Several factors led to questions about the vulnerability to sudden reversals in capital inflows and the *sustainability* of Thailand's external deficits.

- Real output growth dropped to 6.4 percent in 1996, compared with 8.6 percent in 1995.

---

5 percent for the yen and 3 percent for the Deutsche mark, whereas Esaka (2003) estimated the weight of the U.S. dollar to be about 82 percent during 1987-97. The exchange rate was also adjusted discretionarily at times between 1984 and mid-1997—with, for instance, a 15 percent devaluation in November 1984.

[9] The logic of the argument here relies on the saving-investment identity discussed in Chapters 1 and 3. If net government saving is close to zero or positive, external deficits merely indicate that, from a macroeconomic accounting point of view, the country is investing more than it is saving. From that perspective, external deficits are not symptomatic of a "problem."

[10] Part of the reason for the fiscal performance is the budgetary legislation in effect in Thailand. As noted by Glick, Hutchison, and Moreno (1997), deficits are limited to a small percentage of the year's total outlays, and there is an upper limit on the proportion of public expenditure that can be allocated to servicing the foreign public debt. The preparation and formulation of the budget is also the primary responsibility of technocrats in the civil service, and the parliament has, by law, limited ability to alter their decisions.

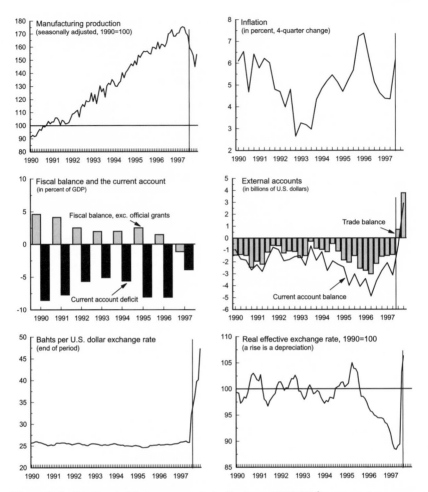

Figure 8.8. Thailand: Macroeconomic indicators, 1990-97 (in percent per annum, unless otherwise indicated). The vertical line corresponds to the date of flotation of the baht (July 2, 1997). Source: International Monetary Fund and Bank of Thailand.

- Net private capital inflows into Thailand averaged more than 10 percent of GDP during the 1990s and reached 13 percent of GDP in 1995 alone (see Chapter 7). However, 46 percent of the flows recorded during 1990-96 were in the form of short-term borrowing (excluding portfolio equity and international bonds). The existence of an offshore banking center provided an important channel for raising short-term capital by domestic firms and financial institutions.

- Merchandise exports slowed down sharply in 1996 and early 1997, reflecting in part the real appreciation of the baht and the loss in competitiveness.[11] In volume terms, exports fell by -0.7 percent in 1996, after growing

---

[11] The slowdown in exports in 1996 was also partly related to continued economic weakness

by 14.2 percent in 1995 (Radelet and Sachs, 1998, p. 31).[12]

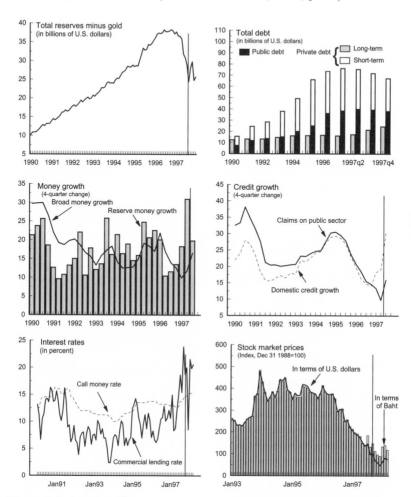

Figure 8.8. (*continued*)

- There was also a perceived shift in regional comparative advantage in some industries (such as telecommunications, semiconductors, and garments) to

in Japan (which accounts for about 14 or 15 percent of Thailand's exports) and the slack in the world semiconductor market.

[12] Some analysts have argued that the devaluation in China's official exchange rate in January 1994 also worsened competitiveness in Thailand and other countries of the region. However, the actual nominal exchange rate devaluation in China was much smaller than implied by the official devaluation, because it served essentially to unify the dual exchange rate regime then prevailing. Most external trade transactions were already being conducted at a more depreciated exchange rate (the swap market rate) prior to 1994. The weighted net devaluation for all exporters is estimated by the World Bank as being only in the range of 7-8 percent. In addition, as a result of high domestic inflation, China's *real* exchange rate *appreciated* between 1994 and 1997—by about 31 percent between January 1994 and June 1997, according to IMF estimates.

lower-wage countries such as China, India, and Vietnam.[13]

At the same time, the early favorable perception of the high levels of invest-ment (relative to domestic savings) as a sign of economic strength gave way to questions and concerns about the *allocation* of capital outlays and their sources of financing. It became apparent that much of the investment was risky and of low quality, going to low-productivity and speculative activities—overambitious infrastructure projects, inefficient government monopolies, and real estate de-velopment.[14]

Weaknesses in the banking system (in a context of inadequate prudential regulation and supervision) also began to emerge. In particular, banks were saddled with a large proportion of nonperforming loans, particularly in the real estate and property sectors. Between 1993 and 1996, domestic credit to the private sector grew at annual rates exceeding 20 percent, and the ratio of total credit to output almost doubled. As documented by Jansen (2003), foreign capital inflows also contributed to the credit boom of the early 1990s and to the ensuing overvaluation of asset prices.

Finally, there were growing concerns that financial institutions had exposed themselves to significant risk by relying heavily on *short-term borrowing in for-eign currency*, combined with *long-term loans in bahts*. This created a *mismatch* in terms of both *maturity* and *currency* on commercial banks' balance sheets.

Speculative pressures on the Thai baht started to build up around December 1996. During that month alone, the Central Bank lost about 2.3 percent of its foreign exchange reserves in defense of the currency.[15] On February 14, 1997, a massive attack led to a drop in the value of the baht by almost 1 percent against the U.S. dollar. The authorities responded to these pressures through *sterilized intervention* (a strategy that proved largely ineffective), increases in interest rates,[16] and restrictions on foreign exchange movements. On May 14-15, 1997, renewed speculative pressures on the baht led to heavy intervention by the Thai Central Bank, with assistance from the monetary authorities of Singapore.

---

[13]During the 1990s, China, with wage levels much lower than those in other countries of the region, started to produce and compete in many manufacturing sectors that had been the source of export growth for East Asia. As noted earlier, however, the 1994 devaluation of the Chinese currency did not have a significant *de facto* effect on competitiveness throughout the region.

[14]A crude macroeconomic indicator of the quality of investment is ICOR, the incremental capital output ratio (as measured by the ratio of the investment rate to the growth rate of output; see Chapter 9). In Thailand, ICOR increased from 2.9 in 1987-89 to 4.6 in 1990-92 and 5.2 in 1993-95, indeed suggesting a reduction in the productivity of investment. See Radelet and Sachs (1998, p. 40).

[15]Growing signs of tensions were evident before that date. In September 1996, Thailand's short-term debt rating was downgraded by Moody's, which cited the country's overreliance on short-term debt to finance the growing current account deficit. Between February 1996 and May 1997, stock market prices fell by about 60 percent (Figure 8.8).

[16]The interbank overnight interest rate rose from 10 percent to 12 percent in the first two months of 1997. The authorities, nevertheless, resisted further increases in interest rates as a response to speculative pressures, in order to avoid a negative effect on economic activity and a further weakening of banks' balance sheets. This perceived trade-off is consistent with the model of Agénor and Masson (1999); see section 8.1.2.

The Bank of Thailand also attempted to strengthen controls on capital transactions by imposing restrictions on the ability of domestic banks to extend credit in baht to offshore banks and sell baht for U.S. dollars in the spot market to nonresidents (speculators) in the offshore market, as well as restrictions on the ability of domestic banks to engage in foreign exchange swaps involving baht for U.S. dollars.[17] However, sustained speculative pressures continued in June, forcing the central bank to intervene to defend the exchange rate. In June alone, the Bank of Thailand lost about $4 billion defending the baht and incurred a $23 billion forward position. But the accelerated rate at which reserves were being lost forced the bank, on July 2, to move to a managed float regime.

The baht was effectively devalued by about 15 percent (relative to its level of the previous two months), ending the day at 28.8 to the U.S. dollar. The ratio of the country's gross short-term liabilities to reserves (taking into account forward contracts) was in the range of 6 to 8 prior to the July 2 devaluation—clearly a potential source of vulnerability, as emphasized in second-generation models of self-fulfilling currency crises.[18]

During the months that followed the flotation of the baht, the financial difficulties faced by financial and nonfinancial firms emerged as being far worse than originally thought. This generated uncertainty about the possibility of a full-blown financial crisis developing. In turn, this uncertainty led to a further weakening of the baht—which worsened further the situation of highly indebted domestic firms and validated initial expectations. Between the end of 1996 and September 1997, the baht depreciated relative to the U.S. dollar by 42 percent. The currency depreciation worsened the real burden of external debt faced by public sector entities, private financial institutions, and nonfinancial firms that had borrowed heavily in foreign currency.

The Bank of Thailand significantly tightened its monetary policy stance and increased interest rates only after the currency had collapsed and after a continuing period of depreciation. Unfortunately, the timing of the policy change did nothing but aggravate the financial situation of domestic firms, because the depreciation had already increased sharply the domestic-currency value of their foreign-currency liabilities. A sharp fall in domestic credit was accompanied by a fall in output, as well as by an increase in the bankruptcy rate and the proportion of nonperforming loans (from about 15 percent to 25 percent)—which further weakened an already fragile banking system.

In conclusion, Thailand's growing external deficits and a weak and poorly supervised financial system were the two main factors triggering the baht crisis. Because the corporate sector in Thailand—and in other fast-growing Asian countries as well, as discussed later—had accumulated large stocks of U.S. dollar liabilities in place of local currency debt in an attempt to reduce borrowing costs, the devaluation of the baht led to a full-blown financial and economic

---

[17]The appendix to this chapter discusses the various channels through which restrictions on foreign exchange transactions can be implemented, in order to limit access to local funds by speculators trying to establish a net short domestic currency position.

[18]As shown in Figure 8.8, Thailand's total external debt was about US$90 billion in mid-1997. See also Figure 8.13 and the discussion of the sources of the Asia crisis.

crisis. The stability of (and the high degree of confidence in) the fixed exchange rate had a perverse effect: most borrowers did not hedge their foreign-currency liabilities; as a result, they felt the brunt of the devaluation. The inability of domestic firms to service their foreign-currency debt was compounded by the continuing depreciation of the baht and the deepening economic recession, which led to a sharp increase in nonperforming loans and a rise in the bankruptcy rate. But the delayed policy response to the mounting problems faced in 1996 (with warning signs such as slowing export growth, real appreciation, a growing current account deficit increasingly financed by short-term private capital inflows, rapid domestic credit growth, and a dramatic fall in stock prices), and the authorities' resistance to an early adjustment of the exchange rate, also exacerbated the crisis.

8.2.3   The 1999 Brazilian Real Crisis

Faced with triple-digit inflation in the early 1990s, Brazil launched in mid-1994 an ambitious stabilization program, the Real Plan (see Agénor and Montiel, 1999). The plan was successful in rapidly achieving single-digit inflation. However, stabilization was accompanied by strong domestic demand growth and an appreciation of the real exchange rate, which forced the authorities to keep real interest rates at relatively high levels.

In turn, by increasing debt service payments, high interest rates contributed to a sharp deterioration in fiscal accounts. The conventional fiscal deficit increased from about 6 percent of GDP in 1994 to more than 10 percent in 1998 (see Figure 8.9). The operational deficit (that is, the deficit excluding the impact of inflation on interest payments, as discussed in Chapter 3) rose from an average of 2.4 percent of GDP in 1994-96 to nearly 8 percent in 1998, whereas the primary surplus fell from 2 percent of GDP in 1994-96 to approximate balance in 1998. As a result, the stock of domestic public debt grew rapidly between 1995 and 1998.[19] At the same time, the significant appreciation of the real exchange rate in the initial stages of the plan contributed to a widening current account deficit (Figure 8.9).

Growing fiscal and external imbalances led to a first wave of speculative pressures in late 1997, following the Asia crisis. The authorities responded with a sharp tightening of monetary policy and the announcement of fiscal measures aimed at reducing the deficit by the equivalent of 2 percent of GDP in 1998. High interest rates and a relaxation of capital account restrictions led to renewed inflows of capital in early to mid-1998, which helped rebuild international reserves (Figure 8.9).

However, fiscal adjustment proved difficult to achieve, because the key measures that were to be implemented required congressional approval. In December 1997, the government suffered a damaging political defeat when its civil service

---

[19] As noted by Bevilaqua and Garcia (2000), although much of the surge in debt was the combined result of the government's deficit and the high interest rates needed to defend the (overvalued) exchange rate, part of it was also due to government's previously hidden liabilities—some of which came to light when state enterprises were privatized.

pension reform proposals were defeated in Congress. The persistence of fiscal weaknesses and growing perceptions of external vulnerability, together with the general adverse effects of the Russian default in August 1998 on private capital flows to developing countries, led to renewed speculative pressures on the exchange rate in the second half of 1998. The authorities responded by intervening heavily in the foreign exchange market and by increasing interest rates sharply.

After the October 1998 presidential elections, a support package of about $44.5 billion (led by the International Monetary Fund) was announced. Financial support was made conditional on extensive fiscal adjustment. But the agreement with the IMF and the first disbursement in early December improved the outlook only marginally. Spreads on Brazil's international debt remained high and capital outflows continued. Congress refused to approve a number of crucial fiscal measures, casting doubt on the effectiveness of fiscal restraint and the ability of the authorities to achieve the fiscal targets.

The practical debt moratorium announced by the state of Minas Gerais in early 1999 increased pressure on the exchange rate regime.[20] In the first week of 1999, the country lost 0.5 billion U.S. dollars, reducing total reserves to around 38 billion U.S. dollars, compared with 70 billion U.S. dollars at the end of July 1998. The weakening of reserves made the position of central bank governor Gustavo Franco untenable, and he resigned on January 13, 1999. That same day, net capital outflows reached 0.7-0.8 billion U.S. dollars, following an outflow of 1.2 billion U.S. dollars the day before.

In an attempt to lessen pressure on reserves and prepare the ground for a loosening of monetary policy, the government attempted to implement a limited and controlled devaluation. The real, which had been allowed to fluctuate between a band of 1.12 to 1.22 to the U.S. dollar, was allowed on January 13 to trade between 1.20 and 1.32, with greater scope for fluctuation within the new band. Markets responded immediately to the revised arrangements, with the real trading near the floor of its new band at 1.31 to the U.S. dollar. This amounted to a 9 percent nominal devaluation of the currency in relation to its closing value on January 12.

However, this did little to calm speculative pressures, as fears about a possible debt default grew. Public debt prior to the crisis had a relatively short maturity (about 11 months), and consisted to a large extent of floating-rate instruments, thereby creating significant exposure to abrupt changes in short-term interest rates.

---

[20] In Brazil, state governors are responsible for a large proportion of total government spending. In early January, Itamar Franco—the governor of the state of Minas Gerais and then a staunch opponent of President Cardoso—announced a 90-day moratorium on the servicing of his state's debts to the federal government. Following Franco's lead, a number of other state governors, including those of Rio de Janeiro and Rio Grande do Sul, announced that they intended to renegotiate their debts with the federal government. Although some state governors expressed their support for Cardoso's administration, the confrontation weakened confidence.

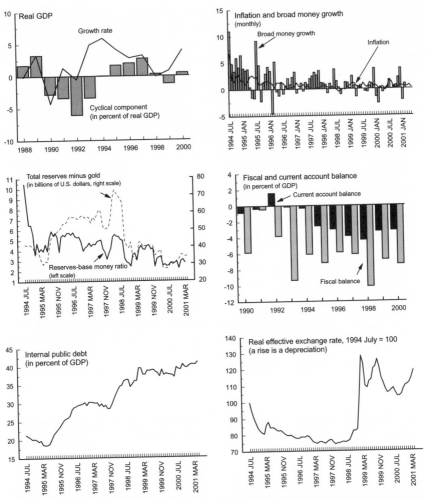

Figure 8.9. Brazil: Macroeconomic and financial indicators, 1990-2001 (in percent, unless otherwise indicated). Source: International Monetary Fund.

Moreover, at the end of 1998, the U.S. dollar-denominated and U.S. dollar-indexed federal debt represented about 28 percent of total debt (Bevilaqua and Garcia, 2000). The large stock of foreign-exchange denominated bonds and floating rate treasury bills led to the perception of vulnerability of the government deficit to devaluation and high interest rates, and the fear of potentially explosive dynamics of the domestic public debt-to-GDP ratio, should interest rates and debt servicing requirements fail to come down.

Sustained capital outflows continued, and on January 15 the real was floated. Fears of unstable debt dynamics and a vicious circle of continuing downward pressure on the currency and upward pressure on interest rates led to a sustained weakening of the currency, and the real depreciated by about 40 percent in the two ensuing months.

8.3   Banking and Currency Crises

As argued earlier, one of the key aspects of the Mexican peso crisis of December 1994 was the reluctance of the authorities to raise domestic interest rates in order to avoid further weakening the position of bank debtors and thus the overall situation of the banking system. Similar considerations appear to have played a role in Thailand in early 1997. More generally, the recent evidence on financial crises reveals the existence of close links between currency crises and banking crises. This section and the next review some of the recent analytical and empirical literature on these issues.

A first step in this analysis is to define what constitutes a **banking crisis**. Unlike currency crises, definitions vary among economists because banking crises have several dimensions. Caprio and Klingebiel (1996) defined a banking crisis as a situation in which either

- the capital of the banking system is practically exhausted; or

- nonperforming loans amount to or exceed 15 to 20 percent of total bank loans; or

- the cost of resolving these problems (through bank recapitalization, for instance) amounts to at least 3 to 5 percent of GDP.

Kaminsky and Reinhart (1999), by contrast, identified banking crises by an *event*, corresponding to either

- a **bank run**, associated with the closure, merging, or takeover by the public sector of at least one large financial institution; or,

- in the absence of a bank run, the closure, merging, or takeover of, or large-scale government assistance to, at least one important financial institution.

These definitions raise, of course, a number of problems. The last two characteristics of the Caprio-Klingebiel definition, in particular, relate to the *consequences* of banking crises and may be subject to wide margins of uncertainty. Differences in estimates can have a significant impact in comparing alternative methods for predicting crises (see below).

8.3.1   Causes of Banking Crises

Leaving these definitional issues aside, the recent literature has emphasized a variety of causes of banking crises. More generally, according to Goldstein and Turner (1996), the primary causes of banking crises in these countries are related to the following factors:

- *external* and *domestic macroeconomic volatility*, the main elements of which are often sudden adverse movements in the country's terms of trade and sharp fluctuations in world interest rates, real exchange rates, and inflation rates;

- *lending booms*, characterized by rapid increases in bank credit growth to the private sector during economic expansions;

- rapidly increasing *bank liabilities*, with large mismatches with respect to liquidity, maturity, and currency denomination (as noted earlier, for instance, in the context of the Thai baht crisis);

- insufficient strengthening of *bank supervision* and *regulation* prior to financial liberalization, which leaves bank supervisors ill prepared to prevent banks from engaging in overly risky lending activities (see Chapter 15);

- heavy *government involvement* in the banking system and loose controls on **connected lending**, that is, loans extended to banks' owners or managers and to their related businesses;

- weaknesses in the *accounting, disclosure*, and *legal infrastructure*, which hinder the operation of market discipline and effective banking supervision;

- *distorted incentives*, such as pressures for *regulatory forbearance* created by insufficient political protection of bank supervisors and the absence of suitable financial incentives for bank owners, managers, and depositors to avoid excessive risk and monitor lending activities;

- a *rigid exchange rate regime*, such as a currency board (as discussed in Chapter 5), which severely constrains the lender-of-last-resort function of the central bank and thus prevents it from reacting quickly to stop a bank run, for instance, by injecting liquidity.

One branch of the literature, dwelling on the seminal work of Diamond and Dybvig (1983), argues that banking crises may be purely **self-fulfilling**. The next sub-section provides a brief presentation of the Diamond-Dybvig model.

8.3.2   Self-Fulfilling Bank Runs

Consider an economy in which there are two categories of agents in the economy: households (whose preferences are identical *ex ante*) and a financial intermediary (a bank). The number of households is large and there is no aggregate uncertainty. There are three periods, $h = 0, 1$, and 2, and a single consumption good available to agents in each period. Each household has an initial endowment of one unit of the consumption good at period 0 and none in subsequent periods. They all deposit their endowment, E_0, with the bank at period 0 in return for consumption in periods 1 or 2. They observe in period 1 an idiosyncratic preference shock that is not observed by the bank; depending on the value of the shock, they decide to either withdraw their deposit and consume now (in period 1) or keep their deposit at the bank and consume later (in period 2). Households are also able to store at no cost the consumption good between periods 1 and 2, if they so choose.

Let u be a differentiable, strictly increasing and strictly concave utility function, and C_h consumption at period h. Households who consume in period 1 (respectively, period 2) obtain utility $u(C_1)$ [respectively, $u(C_2)$] and are called type-E (respectively, type-L) agents; E standing for *early* and L for *late* consumers. Let θ be the probability that a household will indeed choose to withdraw its period-0 endowment from the bank and consume now. Given the assumptions described above, the cross-sectional distribution of preference shocks realized at period 1 is the same as the probability distribution of these shocks for an individual household at period 0. Thus, θ is also the realized proportion of type-E households in period 1, and $1 - \theta$ the proportion of type-L households.

Assuming logarithmic preferences, the representative household's preferences are given by

$$U(C_1, C_2) = \begin{cases} u(C_1) = \ln C_1 & \text{with probability } \theta, \\[2mm] u(C_2) = \ln C_2 & \text{with probability } 1 - \theta. \end{cases}$$

The bank accepts a deposit of one unit from each household and knows that a fraction θ of them will be type-E agents. In exchange for the deposit, the bank offers each household a contract that allows it to withdraw either C_1 units of consumption at period 1 or C_2 units at period 2. The bank has access to two investment technologies. The first technology, corresponding to investment in a short-term asset, yields one unit of consumption at period 1 for every unit of investment made at the beginning of that period. The second technology, corresponding to investment in the long-term asset, yields $R > 1$ units of consumption at period 2 for every unit of investment made in period 1. In case of withdrawals in period 1, the bank must finance them by liquidating L units (per capita) invested in the long-term asset in period 1, receiving only $R(1 - L)$ in period 2.

The bank chooses (C_1, C_2, L) to maximize the *ex ante* expected utility of individual agents. It thus solves the problem

$$\max_{C_1, C_2, L} [\theta u(C_1) + (1 - \theta)u(C_2)],$$

subject to

$$\theta C_1 = L,$$

$$(1 - \theta)C_2 = R(1 - L).$$

Given the restrictions imposed on u, the first-order conditions for an interior solution are given by

$$\theta u'(\tilde{C}_1) + \mu_1 \theta = 0,$$

$$(1 - \theta)u'(\tilde{C}_2) + \mu_2(1 - \theta) = 0,$$

$$-\mu_1 + \mu_2 R = 0,$$

which can be combined to give

$$u'(\tilde{C}_1) = Ru'(\tilde{C}_2),$$

together with the constraints defined above:

$$\tilde{C}_1 = \frac{L}{\theta}, \quad \tilde{C}_2 = \frac{R(1-L)}{1-\theta}. \tag{35}$$

Given the logarithmic specification, the first equation implies that $1/\tilde{C}_1 = R/\tilde{C}_2$, or equivalently that $\tilde{C}_2 = R\tilde{C}_1$. This result, together with $R > 1$, implies that

$$\tilde{C}_2 > \tilde{C}_1.$$

A sufficient condition for $\tilde{C}_2/\tilde{C}_1$ to be less than R is to have $Cu'(C)$ decreasing in C. Thus, if u has a coefficient of **relative risk aversion** greater than unity (as assumed in what follows), type-E households will share in the higher returns of illiquid assets.

Is the first-best allocation $(\tilde{C}_1, \tilde{C}_2, \tilde{L})$ defined by Equation (35) achievable? A key insight of the Diamond-Dybvig analysis is that in attempting to implement Equation (35) the bank faces a **coordination problem**. In defining the first-best allocation problem above, it was assumed that only type-E households consumed C_1 and only type-L households consumed C_2. However, because preference shocks are privately observed, the bank is not able to guarantee this. In fact, the type-L household's decision whether to withdraw C_1 at period 1 and store it for later consumption or to withdraw C_2 at period 2 is a strategic one, which depends on what other households do. Diamond and Dybvig found, with **fractional reserves** and a **first-come first-served rule**, that there are two equilibrium outcomes in this setting:

- In the first, only those households with a true preference for early consumption choose to make an early withdrawal.

- In the second equilibrium, agents who actually prefer late consumption, fearing withdrawals by others of the same type, also choose to withdraw early—there is therefore a *bank run*. This run is costly and inefficient because the bank is forced to liquidate prematurely some of its higher-yielding investments.

Essentially, fractional reserves mean that banks do not hold all the liquidity necessary to repay deposits at par. And the first-come first-served rule implies that, should a large number of agents decide to withdraw early, depositors at the end of the sequential service line may be unable to get their money back, because banks suffer losses in liquidating assets. To avoid finding themselves in that situation, all depositors try to place themselves at the head of the line, causing a panic in the process. In practice, however, bank runs seldom have a purely self-fulfilling character. In developing countries, in particular, runs are often triggered by a noisy signal that nonetheless contains some information about the bank's ultimate solvency.

8.3.3   Links between Currency and Banking Crises

Links between currency and banking crises operate in both directions. There are two major channels through which a currency crisis can lead to a banking crisis.

- In the absence of *sterilization*, the large loss in international reserves that results from the speculative attack that precedes the abandonment of a fixed-exchange-rate regime may translate into a sharp decline in the base money stock and the supply of credit. In turn, the fall in credit may have an adverse effect on output and lead to a rise in nonperforming loans, and consequently to a banking crisis.[21]

- The exchange rate depreciation that often accompanies a currency crisis can create *solvency problems* among banks that are subject to large, un-hedged foreign exchange exposure.[22] Even if the foreign exchange position of the banks themselves is small, borrowers in sectors producing nontradables (such as real estate) may be highly indebted in foreign currency. To the extent that such borrowers face solvency problems and that a large proportion of bank loans are made to that sector, the depreciation of the exchange rate could also lead to a weakening of the banking system's position as well.

There are also two major channels through which a banking crisis can lead to a currency crisis; both relate to a situation in which the central bank must inject liquidity to bail out ailing banks or depositors, because of an explicit or implicit **deposit insurance** scheme. The difference between the two channels stems from the two options that the central bank has to finance the bailout.

- The central bank may allow an excessive expansion of domestic credit to provide liquidity. As emphasized in the conventional model of currency crises, the expansionary credit stance will eventually lead to an equilibrium speculative attack that forces the central bank to abandon the exchange rate peg.

- The central bank may finance the bailout by issuing large amounts of *domestic debt* as the counterpart to taking over a fraction of banks' nonperforming loans. As a result, market participants may perceive that the authorities have an incentive to reduce their debt burden through inflation or currency devaluation (as noted in Chapter 6) and this may lead to a

---

[21] Moreover, to the extent that depositors attempt to switch away from domestic-currency assets and acquire foreign exchange instead, they may force the commercial banks to reduce lending abruptly and liquidate existing loans to raise cash. Alternatively, the government may impose an outright suspension of the convertibility of deposits into cash.

[22] As argued by Garber and Lall (1998) in the context of the Mexican peso crisis, the degree of sophistication of financial instruments available on world capital markets nowadys is such that prudential bank regulations—in particular with respect to foreign exchange exposure—can easily be circumvented.

self-fulfilling crisis, as discussed earlier. Burnside, Eichenbaum, and Rebelo (2001) developed a model in which expectations of future contingent liabilities associated with financial distress (or the potential fiscal cost of a banking crisis) can lead to a currency crisis, well before the government starts to run fiscal deficits or print money.[23]

It is also possible, of course, that both currency and banking crises may result from *common macroeconomic shocks*. In particular, an unexpected sharp increase in world interest rates may be accompanied by abrupt capital outflows. To the extent that the capital inflows, to begin with, were intermediated by the banking system (a possibility that was discussed in the previous chapter), the outcome may well be a weakening of the banking system (as a result of a sharp reduction in banks' domestic deposits) and severe pressures on official reserves (as capita leaves the country), which would eventually prevent the central bank from defending the official exchange rate. This outcome is particularly likely in countries where the monetary and exchange rate regime is such that the authorities have limited capacity to act promptly and inject liquidity into the banking system, as for instance in a conventional currency board.

8.3.4   Liquidity Crises in an Open Economy

Chang and Velasco (1999) extended the Diamond-Dybvig framework to introduce a world capital market. Their analysis is useful for examining the implications of greater financial openness for banks' vulnerability to runs as well as the link between financial fragility and the fixed exchange rate system. One unit of a good can be invested in the world capital market at date $t = 0$ to yield one unit in either time $t = 1$ or $t = 2$. The investment technology retains the same characteristics as in Diamond-Dybvig; investment yields a return of $R > 1$ if it is held for two periods, but only $L < 1$ if it is liquidated after one period. Only domestic residents have access to this technology.

Demand deposit contracts require agents to surrender their endowment, E_0, and their rights to invest or borrow abroad to the bank at $t = 0$. Agents have the option of withdrawing C_1^* units of consumption from the bank in period 1 or C_2^* units of consumption in period 2, where consumption is greater if deposits are held for two periods, $C_2^* > C_1^*$. The bank can borrow B_0 from abroad at time $t = 0$ and B_1 at time $t = 1$. The bank faces an overall international credit ceiling of $\bar{B} = B_0 + B_1$. The bank invests the endowment and funds initially borrowed from abroad in the long-term illiquid technology ($I = E_0 + B_0$).

Chang and Velasco make two assumptions about foreign debt (that are later relaxed):

- the bank always repays its foreign debt;

---

[23] Moreover, such crises can be self-fulfilling: if markets decide that banks are weak and attack the currency, banks with direct (on-balance-sheet) or indirect foreign exchange exposure (through their clients' balance sheets) can be rendered insolvent.

- any foreign debt of one-period maturity acquired at time $t = 0$ can be automatically renewed at time $t = 1$ on the same conditions as before.

The model possesses two possible equilibrium outcomes. In one equilibrium, which corresponds to the optimal allocation, only agents who find out they must consume early withdraw deposits in period 1, and the bank can fully cover the withdrawals by borrowing from abroad at $t = 1$. The bank does not have to liquidate its long-term assets nor hold any liquid assets between $t = 0$ and $t = 1$. Alternatively, all domestic agents may attempt to withdraw their deposits at time $t = 1$ because they believe everyone else will be doing the same. In that case, the uninsured bank will fail, because its obligations to domestic depositors exceed the value of available assets.

The reason is as follows. If at $t = 1$ all agents try to withdraw their deposits, total withdrawals will be C_1^*. The value of bank assets at $t = 1$ is $B_1 + L(I - \bar{B}/R)$ because the bank borrows B_1 and liquidates $L(I - \bar{B}/R)$ of the long-term investment at a return of L. Liquidation is only partial because Chang and Velasco assume the bank honors its commitment to repay all its foreign debts at $t = 2$. As a result, the bank keeps a fraction γ of the investment illiquid to pay off the foreign debt at $t = 2$. Repayment of the foreign debt at $t = 2$ requires $R\gamma I = \bar{B}$. Because only $(I - \gamma I)$ of the long-term investment is liquidated early and $\gamma I = \bar{B}/R$, then $L(I - \gamma I) = L(I - \bar{B}/R)$. To show that at period 1 potential bank liabilities C_1^* exceed the liquidated value of bank assets $B_1 + L(I - \bar{B}/R)$, define θ_1 as the probability of consuming early and θ_2 as the probability of consuming late and use the solution for the optimal allocation

$$I = E_0 + B_0, \quad \theta_1 C_1^* = B_1, \quad \theta_2 C_2^* = RI - \bar{B}, \quad \bar{B} = B_0 + B_1,$$

to write

$$R\theta_1 C_1^* + \theta_2 C_2^* = RB_1 + (RI - \bar{B}) = RB_1 + R(E_0 + B_0) - (B_0 + B_1),$$

or equivalently,

$$R\theta_1 C_1^* + \theta_2 C_2^* = RE_0 + (R - 1)\bar{B}.$$

With a little bit of algebra, it can then be shown that bank assets at period 1 are

$$B_1 + L(I - \frac{\bar{B}}{R}) = LC_1^* - L[(\bar{B} - B_0)(1 + \frac{1}{L})] < C_1^*.$$

As in the Diamond-Dybvig model, this model version is silent on what causes the economy to jump from the no-run equilibrium to the run equilibrium. Here, a shift to more pessimistic expectations by foreign creditors increases the vulnerability of banks by reducing the amount of liquidity banks have available in the short run. The shift in expectations induces foreign creditors to stop lending and makes them unwilling to roll over the short-term debts banks previously incurred. As a result, the value of assets available to the bank at period 1 is reduced, increasing its vulnerability to a run.[24] Note how banks that previously had the greatest access to the international capital markets now face the largest drop in available assets when the adverse shift in expectations occurs. The reason is that banks with greater access to external funding initially faced a higher credit ceiling and acquired more short-term debt, B_0. When this debt cannot be rolled over, the drop in available resources, $(1 - L/R)B_0$, is greater. Without these resources, banks are more fragile. Indeed, greater fragility may increase the chance of a run.[25]

A key insight of the model is that, in the event of a run, in an open-economy setting the central bank can try to save banks or preserve the fixed exchange rate regime, but it cannot do both. If there is a bank run and the central bank is unable to inject liquidity rapidly (that is, act as a *lender of last resort*), the banking system may collapse. That would be the case under a currency board for instance, as discussed in Chapter 5. If the central bank can issue domestic liquidity to keep banks solvent, depositors could convert the domestic-currency denominated deposits withdrawn from the banks into foreign currency—in the amount C_1^* if the exchange rate equals one. The fixed exchange rate collapses because the foreign-currency assets available to meet this demand are only $B_1 + L(I - \bar{B}/R)$. The central bank can borrow from abroad and it can liquidate the assets it takes over from the private banks, but the total amount of foreign-currency assets it can acquire in this manner would still fall short of demand because $B_1 + L(I - \bar{B}/R) < C_1^*$. Thus, the fixed exchange-rate regime will collapse.

Several other important results emerge from the model. First, as noted earlier, in a newly liberalized financial environment with weak supervision and regulation, domestic banks may be vulnerable to *currency mismatch*—as a result of an increase in their foreign-currency liabilities (in the form of either direct borrowing from abroad or higher foreign-currency denominated deposits) and lending in domestic currency. These banks can become illiquid when their short-term liabilities in foreign currency exceed the amount of foreign currency they can gain access to on short notice. This is consistent with the empirical literature, discussed later, which points out that financial deregulation combined with explicit or implicit guarantees for poorly supervised banks can generate overlending, excessive risk taking, and an eventual crisis.

Second, the model shows that the accumulation of short-term external lia-

---

[24] If foreign creditors refuse to lend more at time $t = 1$, $B_1 = 0$ and the value of assets available to the bank at $t = 1$ falls to $L(I - \bar{B}/R)$. Note that if foreign creditors also refuse to roll over the initial debt, B_0 must be paid back at $t = 1$ and bank assets fall further, to $L \cdot I - B_0$.

[25] Chang and Velasco also discuss the effects of financial liberalization, achieved through lower reserve requirements or reduced monopoly power of banks, on the availability of bank assets at period 1. In addition, they analyze the effects on bank assets of asset price booms and busts, an unexpected increase in world interest rates at $t = 1$, and a government subsidy for the long-term investment project. They show that the coefficient of risk aversion for the consumer has to be greater than one to ensure the possibility of the bank-run equilibrium. As noted earlier, the Diamond-Dybvig model assumes a risk aversion parameter greater than one.

bilities by banks can be risky. If, as a result of an abrupt change in sentiment or contagion (as discussed later) foreign creditors refuse to roll over bank debts, banks would have less foreign-currency assets to draw on and would be more vulnerable to a run. Thus, the short maturity of capital inflows can contribute to bank fragility—and possibly to a collapse of the exchange rate regime, as noted earlier in the context of second-generation models of currency crises. A related point is that while a crisis can still be triggered by a shift in expectations of domestic depositors, as in the closed-economy version of the Diamond-Dybvig model, an adverse change in sentiment by foreign creditors may also contribute to precipitating a crisis. Indeed, the distinction between a pessimistic change in foreign creditors' views and a domestic bank run may be blurred, or both may occur at the same time and reinforce each other.

Finally, the model suggests that in the presence of illiquid banks, a fixed exchange rate regime may be doomed to failure. If the central bank does not (or cannot, in the case of a currency board) act as a lender of last resort, then bank runs can occur. If the monetary authority does act as a lender of last resort in domestic currency, then bank runs can be avoided but only at the cost of undermining the fixed exchange rate, because private agents will try to convert the newly issued domestic currency into foreign exchange. If the monetary authority tries to act as a lender of last resort in foreign currency, then it is drawing on the same reserve assets needed to support the fixed exchange rate commitment. Consequently, when there is a fixed exchange rate and domestic banks are illiquid, there will be either a banking crisis or a currency crisis should expectations turn pessimistic.

8.4   Predicting Financial Crises

A flurry of recent studies have attempted to devise indicator systems, or **early warning indicators**, aimed at predicting currency and banking crises. Among those that have attempted to study *jointly* the empirical determinants of these crises, the study of Kaminsky and Reinhart (1999) is one of the most representative. Their analysis covered the period 1970-95 and was based on a group of 20 countries, 13 of which belong to the developing world: Argentina, Bolivia, Brazil, Chile, Colombia, Indonesia, Malaysia, Peru, the Philippines, Thailand, Turkey, Uruguay, and Venezuela. Kaminsky and Reinhart examined a total of 76 episodes of currency crises and 26 episodes of banking crises. The data indicated that the *incidence* of both types of crises increased sharply between the early 1980s and the end of their sample period: the average number per year of currency crises in the sample rose from 2.6 during the period 1970-79 to 3.1 in 1980-95; for banking crises, the numbers are 0.3 and 1.4 for the same period. These data are corroborated by those of Glick and Hutchison (1999).

Kaminsky and Reinhart identified currency crises by calculating an index of *currency market turbulence*, defined as a weighted average of exchange rate changes and reserve changes.[26] Values of the index that were at least three

---

[26]Interest rates were excluded from the index, because the authors were unable to obtain

standard deviations above the mean were identified as crises. In practice, this definition appeared to coincide with some major events, such as devaluations, a change in the exchange rate regime, and the suspension of external convertibility of the domestic currency. As noted earlier, Kaminsky and Reinhart identified a banking crisis by either a bank run or (in the absence of a run) the closure, merging, takeover, or large-scale government assistance to at least one important financial institution.

Kaminsky and Reinhart used a large series of indicators to assess the extent to which they help predict banking and balance-of-payments crises. These variables included output and stock prices, financial sector variables (in particular the broad money multiplier, the domestic credit-to-GDP ratio, real deposit interest rates, the lending-deposit interest rate spread, and the broad money-official reserves ratio), and external sector variables (including exports, imports, the terms of trade, the real exchange rate, changes in net foreign assets, and interest rate differentials). As noted earlier, the use of the ratio of broad money to official reserves as an indicator of currency crises was first suggested by Calvo (1998). It captures the extent to which a central bank has sufficient foreign exchange reserves readily available to absorb a run by holders of domestic currency assets. If the ratio is relatively high, the currency can be viewed as vulnerable to speculative attacks.

The main conclusions of the study were the following:

- **Banking crises** are often *preceded* by *financial liberalization*, that is, periods during which interest rates were deregulated and other restrictions on the financial system removed.

- Banking and currency crises appear to share *common causes*. Long before a crisis episode, several of the indicators begin to send *stress signals*.

- The best predictors of currency crises are the degree of overvaluation of the real exchange rate, adverse movements in exports, an increasing ratio of broad money over official reserves, falling stock prices, and output.[27]

- The best predictors of banking crises are real exchange rate overvaluation, the broad money multiplier, the stock market, output, and real interest rates. A real exchange rate appreciation lowers the profitability of exports, and often precedes losses on unmatched currency positions (as discussed earlier). Reductions in equity prices have a negative effect on firms' net worth and the collateral on which bank loans are based. Increases in the broad money multiplier are associated with reductions in required reserve ratios, which often result from financial liberalization. Rises in domestic real interest rates, and adverse movements in output, often lead to an increase in the rate of default on bank loans.

---

reliable data on market-oriented rates for several of the developing countries included in their sample.

[27]By contrast, interest rate differentials, imports, bank deposits, and bank lending-deposit spreads were found to have no predictive power.

- On average, the earliest signals provided by the best predictors are between 17 months and a year before a currency crisis occurs, and between 18 months and as late as 6 months prior to the occurrence of a banking crisis.

- Both currency and banking crises appear to be more severe in Latin America than in other regions. Devaluations are in general larger, and the cost of bailing out troubled banks is greater.

- The pre- and post-crisis behavior of most of the indicators show very similar patterns across regions, for both currency and banking crises. In Latin America, however, nearly all of the indicators show larger deviations from their behavior during precrisis periods; these deviations (such as the degree of real exchange rate overvaluation) also tend to be more persistent. Another important peculiarity in the case of Latin America is a large drop in bank deposits following a banking crisis.

Some other recent studies have either corroborated or questioned the findings of Kaminsky and Reinhart (1999). Demirgüç-Kunt and Detragiache (1998), for instance, found that banking crises during the period 1980-94 tended to erupt when growth is low and inflation and real interest rates are high. Vulnerability to currency crises (as measured by a high ratio of the broad money stock to official reserves) and the existence of an explicit deposit insurance scheme also played a role. In a subsequent study they also found that banking crises are more likely to occur in liberalized financial systems (Demirgüç-Kunt and Detragiache, 2001) and in countries with explicit deposit insurance (Demirgüç-Kunt and Detragiache, 2002).[28] The latter effect is all the more important in countries where bank interest rates are deregulated and the institutional environment is weak. Kamin, Schindler, and Samuel (2001), in a study of 26 currency crises over the period 1981-1999, found that whereas domestic factors (such as credit expansion and fiscal deficits) were on average the main source of underlying vulnerability in most individual cases, adverse movements in external factors (such as world interest rates or the terms of trade) and external imbalances (as measured by the current account deficit) contributed to a larger extent to increases in crisis probabilities estimated during actual crisis years.

Berg and Pattillo (1999) assessed the ability of several empirical models of currency crises—including those of Kaminsky, Lizondo, and Reinhart (1998) and Sachs, Tornell, and Velasco (1996b)—to predict the Asian exchange rate crises that started with the collapse of the Thai baht reviewed earlier. They concluded that although none of the models reliably predicted the timing of the crises, they did have some value in the sense that variables such as a high credit growth rate, an overvalued exchange rate, and a high ratio of broad money to reserves did positively affect the probability of a crisis. They concluded that although accurately predicting currency crises remains a difficult (if not

---

[28] This, of course, is an argument not against financial liberalization *per se*, but rather against premature liberalization, because it is conducive to instability. See Chapter 15.

impossible) task, there are some indicators that policymakers should monitor closely—most notably movements in the real exchange rate. Edison (2003) also found that although early warning systems tend to provide many false alarms, some variables do merit more scrutiny—namely real exchange rate overvaluation, a high ratio of short-term debt to official reserves, a high ratio of broad money to reserves, substantial losses of foreign assets, and sharply declining equity prices. However, given the lack of robustness across existing studies, what should constitute the critical set of indicators remains a matter of debate. Moreover, some of the measures used in the literature are fairly crude and need to be refined. For instance, real exchange rate overvaluation is calculated in almost all of these studies as deviations of the actual real exchange rate from trend, but in principle it is the deviation of the actual rate from an *equilibrium* value that would be appropriate.

8.5 Financial Volatility: Sources and Effects

As noted in the previous chapter, the growing integration of world capital markets in recent years has increased the opportunities for investors to diversify risks. At the same time, however, the volatility of capital flows in the new global economy has created substantial risks. This section begins by examining the sources of volatility of capital flows and the role of herding behavior and cross-country contagion. It then discusses the contagion effects of the Mexican peso and the Thai baht crises reviewed earlier.

8.5.1 Volatility of Capital Flows

In general, the degree of volatility of capital flows is related to both actual or perceived movements in economic fundamentals, as well as external factors—which include not only movements in world interest rates (as documented in Chapter 7) but also investor herding and contagion across countries (as discussed later). Volatility can also be magnified by actual or expected *policy responses*. As noted in the previous chapter, private capital flows have often been channeled to the domestic economy through commercial banks. Credit market inefficiencies can magnify the effect of changes in, for instance, external interest rates, and lead to fluctuations in domestic output that may have feedback effects on capital flows (Agénor and Aizenman, 1998). More generally, the fact that investor sentiment (particularly that of highly leveraged, speculative trading institutions, such as *hedge funds*) is constantly changing in response to new information creates the potential for markets to overshoot on a scale that can generate financial crises with unacceptably large costs.[29]

---

[29]The Bank for International Settlements (BIS) estimated average daily turnover in the global foreign exchange market at about $1,200 billion in April 1995. By comparison, during the same period, average daily turnover in the world's ten largest stock markets was around $40 billion. The gap is much greater today.

The evidence suggests that volatility in capital inflows has tended to translate into exchange rate instability (under flexible exchange rates) and large fluctuations in official reserves (under a pegged exchange rate regime) and (in the absence of full sterilization) the money supply. There is also evidence that instability has also increased in domestic equity markets, although the evidence there is less clear-cut. Financial volatility may have adverse effects on the real side as well: in the absence of markets that would allow traders to hedge against foreign exchange risk, exchange rate volatility may hamper the expansion of exports (Grobar, 1993).

8.5.2   Herding Behavior and Contagion

More than long-term capital flows, portfolio flows tend to be particularly sensitive to herding behavior and contagion effects. Many economists view herding among investors—large movements into certain types of assets, followed by equally large movements out, with no apparent reason—as evidence of *irrational behavior*, as the epigraph at the beginning of this chapter would appear to indicate. Some recent literature, however, suggests differently; as noted by Devenow and Welch (1996), herding can also be a rational outcome resulting from the following effects:

- **payoff externalities**, which are related to the fact that the payoff to an agent (investor) adopting a specific action may be positively related to the number of other agents adopting the same action;

- **principal-agent considerations**, which result from the fact that a manager, in order to maintain or improve his or her reputation when markets are imperfectly informed, may prefer either to *hide in the herd* to avoid evaluation and criticism, or to *ride the herd* to generate reputational gains;

- **information cascades**, which are due to the fact that (small) agents that are only beginning to invest in a country may find it optimal to ignore their own information and follow the behavior of larger and more established investors.

Consider, for instance, the model of Calvo and Mendoza (2000), which assumes a global market with many identical investors forming decisions simultaneously. Investors determine (for given means and variances of asset returns) the optimal trade-off between diversification and costly information collection. They showed that with *informational frictions*, rational herding behavior may become more prevalent as the world capital market grows. The reason is that globalization reduces the incentives to collect country-specific information to discredit rumors and increases the likelihood that fund managers who worry about their relative performance will each select the same portfolio. Consequently, *small rumors* can induce herding behavior and lead to large capital outflows that are seemingly unrelated to a country's economic fundamentals—

and possibly to a self-fulfilling speculative attack on the domestic currency, as discussed earlier.[30]

Volatility of capital flows can also result directly from contagion effects (see Pritsker, 2001, and Pericoli and Sbracia, 2003). **Financial contagion** occurs when a country suffers massive capital outflows triggered by a perceived increase by international investors in the vulnerability of a country's currency or, more generally, a loss of confidence in the country's economic prospects, as a result of developments elsewhere.[31] Examples of financial contagion (or cross-border spillover effects) are the **Tequila effect** and the Asia crisis discussed in the next section.

It should be noted also that contagion can occur through two other channels, with indirect effects on the volatility of capital flows.

- Contagious shocks may take the form of *terms-of-trade shocks*. The Asia crisis led to a sharp reduction in demand for imports and a sharp drop in world commodity prices. Between June 1997 and April 1998,

  - oil prices dropped by almost 30 percent; this had adverse consequences on oil producers and exporters such as Saudi Arabia, Nigeria, and Mexico;

  - coffee prices dropped by 21 percent, affecting Brazil and Colombia;

  - Copper prices fell by 27 percent, affecting Chile and Zambia.

  By increasing the degree of uncertainty regarding the short-term economic prospects of a country, terms-of-trade shocks may translate into financial contagion—as appeared to have happened in the case of Brazil and Chile in late 1997 and early 1998.

- Contagion can also occur through a *competitiveness effect*. The sharp depreciation of the Thai baht that began in July 1997 put pressure on the currencies of neighboring countries that maintained a fixed exchange rate (as discussed later), in part because it implied a loss of competitiveness.

8.5.3   The Tequila Effect and the Asia Crisis

An example of contagion is the so-called **Tequila effect**, which followed the collapse of the Mexican peso on December 20, 1994 (see section 8.2.1). The Mexican crisis triggered exchange market pressures and increased financial market volatility in a number of developing countries. In Latin America, two economies were hit particularly hard: Argentina (a country that had been operating a currency board regime since its **Convertibility Plan** was introduced in April

---

[30] An alternative framework in which inadequate information may lead to herding and crises was developed by Huang and Xu (1999). In their model, poorly informed depositors overinvest in good times, and herd to panic in bad times (that is, when bad loans by banks become excessive).

[31] Such phenomena may be compounded by perceived changes in the country's policy stance.

1991) and Brazil (a country that had also been operating a pegged exchange rate regime). External interest rate spreads faced by Argentina rose sharply, reflecting an adverse shift in sentiment on world capital markets. In both countries, gyrations in market sentiment led in early 1995 to a sharp reduction in net capital inflows, a fall in official reserves, and intense pressure on asset prices. Between December 1994 and February 1995, the cumulative decline in stock market prices (measured in terms of U.S. dollars) reached 24.8 percent in Argentina and 22.6 percent in Brazil.

Whereas in subsequent months most countries that initially suffered from market turbulences regained financial and exchange market stability, a full-fledged economic crisis developed in Argentina. As illustrated in Figure 8.10, output contracted significantly in 1995, whereas bank deposits and domestic credit (as measured by bank claims on the private sector) fell dramatically. For 1995 as a whole, industrial output fell by 6.7 percent, real GDP by 4.6 percent, real private consumption by 6.1 percent, real domestic investment by 16 percent, and bank credit to the private sector by 5.5 percent in real terms.[32] The unemployment rate increased sharply, peaking at 18.5 percent in May 1995.[33]

The liquidity crunch led to a sharp rise in bank lending rates, on both peso- and U.S. dollar-denominated loans. The spread between the lending rates on these two categories of loans widened significantly between February and May 1995 (as shown in Figure 8.10), reflecting an increase in the perceived risk of a collapse of the currency board regime and a subsequent large exchange rate depreciation. Although the contraction in output and the expansion of merchandise exports (by 27 percent in volume terms for 1995 as a whole) led to an improvement in the trade balance, the massive shift away from peso deposits, capital flight and the reduction in new borrowing led to a collapse of foreign reserves and a dramatic fall in the monetary base.

Of course, whether a crisis would have occurred anyway in 1995, given the large appreciation of the real exchange rate and the consumption-induced deterioration in the external accounts recorded after the adoption of the Convertibility Plan in April 1991, is difficult to say. The logic of the **boom-recession cycle** (as discussed in Chapter 6) that often characterizes exchange-rate-based stabilization programs would have indeed predicted an eventual recession.

In part due to high residual inflation (an average of 24.9 percent in 1992 and 10.6 percent in 1993 compared with 171.7 percent in 1991), Argentina's real effective exchange rate based on consumer prices appreciated by nearly 27

---

[32] The decline in bank credit to the private sector in 1995 may have been exacerbated by the process of concentration in the banking industry, which is widely perceived to have entailed a loss of information about borrowers' net worth, thereby making banks more cautious in their lending decisions. It should also be noted that total credit (including credit to the public sector) actually increased between end-1994 and end-1995.

[33] The recession compounded the already unfavorable trends in the labor market. Unemployment rose steadily from around 6 percent in the immediate aftermath of the introduction of the Convertibility Plan to 12.5 percent in October 1994, despite an average rate of real output growth of more than 7 percent during the same period. The low output-employment elasticity has been attributed by some observers to a rise in the *participation rate* and increased substitution of capital for labor.

percent between April 1991 and December 1994.[34] At the same time, the current account deficit increased from 0.1 percent of GDP in 1991 to 2.8 percent in 1992, 3.1 percent in 1993, and 3.7 percent in 1994—reflecting a sharp increase in consumption and gross domestic investment, the latter rising by more than 5 percentage points of GDP between 1991 and 1994.

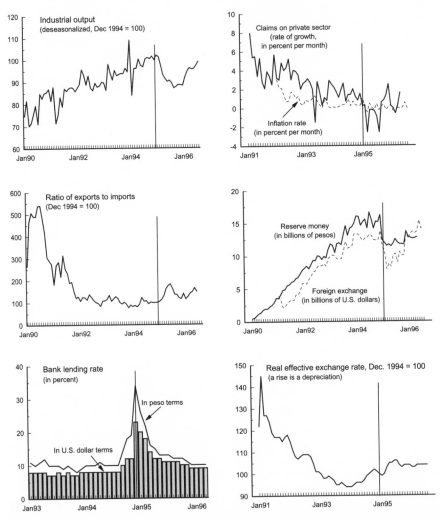

Figure 8.10. Argentina: Macroeconomic indicators, 1990-96. The vertical line corresponds to the Mexican peso crisis (December 1994). Source: FIEL and International Monetary Fund.

---

[34]This estimate is based on calculations made by the International Monetary Fund. It should be noted, however, that (as could be expected from the discussion in Chapter 5) estimates of the real effective exchange rate based on wholesale prices and unit labor costs show a significantly lower cumulative appreciation during the same period.

Nevertheless, the timing and severity of the economic downturn in Argentina suggest a contagion effect—massive capital outflows triggered by a loss of confidence by international investors in the country's economic prospects, and the perception that the exchange rate regime was about to suffer the same fate as Mexico's.

Following the Thai baht crisis described earlier, currencies of several other Asian countries (most notably Hong Kong, Korea, Malaysia, the Philippines, Singapore, and Taiwan) came under severe speculative pressures. Several of these countries were eventually forced to abandoned their exchange rate regime: the Philippines floated its currency on July 12, Indonesia widened its currency band from 8 percent to 12 percent and then floated the exchange rate on August 14, and Malaysia stopped defending its exchange rate peg in mid-July.

Despite some positive developments on the macroeconomic side (including low inflation, relatively high output growth rates, and the absence of significant fiscal imbalances), all of these countries were suddenly viewed by investors as suffering from similar weaknesses in economic fundamentals: overvalued exchange rates pegged to the U.S. dollar, growing current account deficits (particularly Korea and Malaysia), declining equity prices, and weak banking systems.[35] Nominal exchange rates depreciated significantly and equity prices fell dramatically after the collapse of the Thai baht in all of these countries.[36]

Two factors interacted to transform the initial market turbulences into a vicious circle of currency depreciation and deteriorating confidence in the region's economic prospects:

- *Overborrowing* on world capital markets at short maturities and excessive exposure to *foreign exchange risk* in the financial and corporate sectors, both encouraged by the implicit guarantee provided by pegged exchange rate regimes and the moral hazard created by expectations of a government bail-out in case of inadequate returns on (overly risky) investment projects.

- *Weak asset portfolios* of domestic banks (as measured by high ratios of nonperforming loans), caused in part by inadequate prudential regulations and lax supervision and in part by distorted incentives for project selection and monitoring—which resulted from the moral hazard created by the belief that the government would intervene to bail out lenders or borrowers and thus prevent bankruptcy.

---

[35] It should be noted that the evidence regarding the degree of overvaluation (as opposed to the degree of real appreciation) of Asian currencies prior to the crisis is somewhat ambiguous. Chinn (1998), for instance, estimated a model that determines the degree of overvaluation as the difference between actual and equilibrium values of the real exchange rate. Using consumer price indices to measure real exchange rate, Chinn found that in May 1997, the degree of overvaluation was 30 percent for Indonesia, 17 percent for Malaysia, 24 percent for the Philippines, and 13 percent for Thailand. However, using producer price indices, the results were -5 percent, 8 percent, 19 percent, and 7 percent, respectively—relatively small numbers, compared with the subsequent nominal depreciations that these countries experienced.

[36] The impact of the Asian crisis was not confined to Asia. Currencies in Latin America and South Africa, in particular, also came under severe pressure.

Figure 8.11 shows the sharp increase in foreign borrowing by bank and non-bank private sector entities in East Asia during 1995-97. Most of this borrowing was short term in nature.

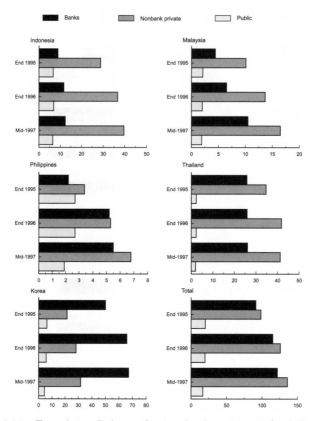

Figure 8.11. East Asia: Debt to foreign banks, 1995-97 (in billions of dollars). Source: Radelet and Sachs (1998, p. 26).

As shown in Figure 8.12, in the periods preceding the crisis, short-term external debt exceeded by a large amount the level of official reserves held by countries in the region. In particular, the ratio of short-term foreign liabilities to official reserves exceeded 170 percent in Indonesia and 210 percent in Korea in June 1997.

The perception of these financial fragilities may have led speculators to believe that pegged exchange rate regimes in several countries of the region could not be defended very long with high interest rates—because of their adverse effect on bankruptcy rates and nonperforming loans, as noted earlier—and thus led to persistent pressures on foreign exchange markets.[37]

[37] During the first stages of the crisis, political uncertainties in some countries and doubts about the resolve of policymakers to implement appropriate adjustment measures exacerbated pressures on currencies throughout the region.

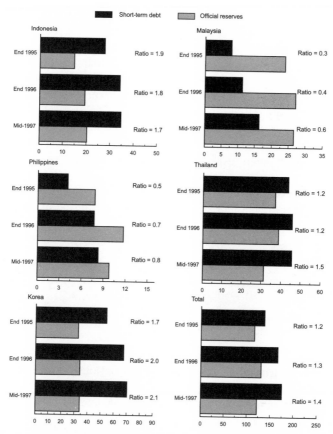

Figure 8.12. East Asia: Short-term debt and foreign exchange reserves, 1995-97 (in billions of dollars). Ratio is short-term debt over official reserves. For Mexico it reached $33.2/6.4 = 5.2$ at the end of 1994. Source: Radelet and Sachs (1998, p. 26).

The currency depreciations, in turn, led to a deterioration of the financial positions of banks and nonfinancial corporations (many of them, as in Thailand, carrying large unhedged positions in foreign currency) and an increase in the proportion of nonperforming loans. This, in turn, heightened concerns about the viability of domestic banking systems and created doubts about the extent to which corporate and financial sector foreign liabilities were effectively "insured" by implicit government guarantees. Both factors further undermined confidence—leading to renewed pressure on foreign exchange markets.[38]

8.6 Coping with Financial Volatility

As noted in the previous chapter, an alleged potential benefit of financial integration is that it allows countries to use international capital markets to diversify

---

[38]For a detailed analysis of the causes, propagation, and policy responses to the Asian crisis, see Alba et al. (1999) and Radelet and Sachs (1998).

and hedge against both idiosyncratic and global risks. But if those same markets are prone to *overexuberance* in good times and *excess pessimism* (leading to sudden withdrawals of capital) in bad times, then the benefits of portfolio diversification and risk insurance can easily be overwhelmed. Financial integration in this case *increases risks* instead of reducing them. The potential benefits of capital inflows can be completely offset by large and sudden outflows. The foregoing discussion suggested indeed that international capital markets can be prone to sharp shifts in sentiment regarding a country's short- and longer-term economic prospects. The discipline that they exercise over government policies, although beneficial in some respects, can be abrupt, excessive, and indiscriminate.

The type of preventive measures that policymakers can or should put in place before markets force a more costly resolution of (actual or perceived) policy inconsistencies has been an issue to which much thinking has been devoted in recent years. Among the suggestions that have emerged are a renewed emphasis on macroeconomic discipline, information disclosure, and the possibility of throwing *sand in the wheels* of capital markets by imposing a tax on foreign exchange transactions.

8.6.1 Macroeconomic Discipline

Various economists have argued that the constraints imposed by financial globalization are best addressed not by imposing restrictions on capital movements (whose effectiveness tends to be eroded over time, as discussed in the previous chapter), but by following transparent, disciplined, and sustainable macroeconomic policies. Monitoring exchange rate levels to ensure consistency with underlying fundamentals, implementing appropriate policy adjustments to correct fiscal imbalances and prevent an excessive buildup of domestic debt, maintaining a monetary policy consistent with low inflation, and ensuring that the ratio of unhedged foreign debt over official reserves remains sufficiently low are all preventive measures that are likely to reduce the risk of sudden changes in market sentiment. The better the economic fundamentals, the longer the track record of macroeconomic discipline, and the less susceptible the country is likely to be to potentially volatile flows or contagion effects—and thus the lower the probability of a financial crisis.

Adequate management of the public foreign-currency debt, in particular, has been viewed as an important component of a strategy aimed at reducing the volatility of capital flows and ensuring the viability of a fixed exchange rate.[39] As indicated earlier, some recent theories of currency crises have emphasized the fact that a large ratio of short-term (public and private) foreign-currency debt relative to official reserves may put a country in a vulnerable position

---

[39]It should also be noted that financial markets in many developing countries are using more and more sophisticated hedging techniques and financial instruments. These allow both domestic and foreign investors to manage their exposure to foreign exchange and interest rate risk, thereby dampening the impact on domestic markets of volatility on world financial markets.

where a self-fulfilling speculative attack may occur. In addition, a large stock of foreign-currency debt may magnify the impact of adverse external shocks on the economy (particularly when these shocks translate into a depreciation of the nominal exchange rate) and may constrain the policy options available to policymakers during a financial crisis.

More generally, a large, unhedged foreign-currency debt carries risks resulting not only from its *maturity profile* but also from its *currency composition*. To the extent that the ratio of foreign-currency debt (held or guaranteed) to international reserves exceeds unity, governments would be exposed to a large degree of *currency risk*. Suppose that a country pegging to the U.S. dollar attempts to take advantage of relatively low interest rates in Japan relative to the United States, by increasing its borrowing in Japanese yen. Suppose also that the country does not hedge its yen exposure. An appreciation of the yen vis-à-vis the U.S. dollar (and thus the domestic currency) would lead consequently to a rise in the dollar value of its external liabilities. In addition, a short-term foreign-currency debt at floating rates—indexed for instance on the London Interbank Offer Rate, LIBOR—exposes countries to *interest rate risk* resulting from abrupt changes in world interest rates.

However, macroeconomic discipline and improved management of foreign debt are by no means *sufficient* to prevent speculative attacks and highly volatile capital flows.

- Unwarranted changes in expectations can and do occur, even when underlying economic fundamentals appear strong. A case in point is Chile in the immediate aftermath of the Asia crisis; severe exchange market pressures developed despite apparently solid fundamentals—high growth rates, high saving rates, small fiscal deficits, and low inflation (see Morandé and Tapia, 2002).

- The strengthening of the financial system (including improved supervision and accounting standards) *takes time*. During the transition to a more efficient financial system, distortions in domestic capital markets may continue to exacerbate the adverse effects of external volatility.

For both reasons, policymakers may need during a transitory period to resort to additional instruments to prevent excessive volatility from adversely affecting domestic stability. As discussed in the previous chapter, short-term controls on capital flows may be part of the arsenal that they need to consider, although one should not lose sight of the fact that the effectiveness of most types of controls tends to erode rather quickly.

8.6.2 Information Disclosure

As noted earlier, when international investors can allocate their wealth over many risky foreign investments and face a fixed cost of information about each country, it may pay for individuals to diversify widely without waiting to become informed. In such conditions, capital flows can be volatile and subject to herding effects (Calvo and Mendoza, 2000). It has been argued that in such conditions a mechanism aimed at providing appropriate and timely information to markets (such as data on official foreign reserves, the maturity of public and private foreign borrowing, and the quality and composition of bank loans) may be beneficial in reducing volatility. However, the argument faces two problems: countries have limited incentives to provide *bad news* quickly to markets, and markets have limited ability to *verify* (at least in the very short run) the information that is provided. Knowing this, countries may be tempted to exploit this advantage by falsifying the information—particularly in bad times. There is therefore a need for a principal to *certify* in some way the information provided. In that regard, current efforts by multilateral institutions such as the International Monetary Fund and the World Bank to encourage countries to provide more timely data on their economies and at the same time impose quality standards are important. At the same time, however, it is not obvious that any of these institutions possesses clear incentives to play an explicit monitoring role in that area; the reason is that such a role (in addition to being unpopular) may create the very problem that it is aimed at avoiding—overreaction by markets to what may be perceived, incorrectly, as a potential deterioration of economic fundamentals.

8.6.3 The Tobin Tax

Several economists have revived the idea, first advanced by James Tobin in the late 1960s, of uniformly taxing spot transactions in foreign exchange—that is, all transactions involving the conversion of one currency into another in foreign exchange markets—as a way to reduce volatility on world financial markets (see Tobin, 1978). A key feature of the tax, according to its proponents, is that it would reduce *noise* from market trading while allowing traders to react to changes in economic fundamentals. It would therefore be superior to various forms of capital controls (see Chapter 7). By making currency trading more costly, it would *discourage speculation*—thereby reducing the volume of destabilizing short-term capital flows and leading to greater stability in exchange rates and movements in official reserves.

An extension of the Tobin tax to a **two-tier tax** was also proposed by Spahn (1995) for countries operating flexible exchange rate or band regimes. The proposal consists in imposing a **minimal rate transaction tax** (of, say, 0.02 percent) that would not impair market efficiency under normal market conditions, and an **exchange surcharge** that would be activated only in periods of *heavy speculative trading*—which are defined by Spahn as periods during which the trading price for a currency crosses an admissible band, consisting of a +/- x percent margin around a target, such as a moving average of the exchange rate. The idea is that in periods during which the surcharge is triggered, transactions costs would rise sufficiently to cause some traders to delay transactions, thus smoothing out fluctuations in exchange rates. The surcharge is thus a *variable tax* on (cash) transactions in foreign exchange. The exchange rate would thus be kept within a target range through taxation rather than central bank intervention.

There are, however, several potential difficulties that may considerably limit the effectiveness of the Tobin tax and most of its variants, such as Spahn's proposal. These difficulties lie in four areas (see Garber, 1996, and Garber and Taylor, 1995):

- establishing the tax base;

- identifying taxable transactions;

- setting the tax rate; and

- implementing the tax across borders.

To limit financial market distortions, the base for any tax on international financial transactions would have to be relatively broad. However, there are strong economic arguments for exempting certain types of trades from the tax—for instance, transactions made by regular market participants and those that increase market liquidity. Trading by financial intermediaries, in particular, generally plays a stabilizing role. The difficulty is that in practice it is hard to distinguish, on an institutional basis, between normal trading that ensures the efficiency and stability of financial markets and destabilizing noise trading, which should be the sole target of the tax. By reducing trading, it may lead to less liquid markets and paradoxically generate greater volatility.

Applying the Tobin tax only to *spot transactions* involving foreign currencies is likely to be ineffective, because market operators would eventually avoid the tax by trading in more sophisticated financial instruments such as over-the-counter **derivatives**.[40] The high degree of substitutability between financial instruments may thus hamper the application of the Tobin tax. Moreover, financial derivatives such as forward transactions, futures, and financial swaps allow market participants to transform *long-trading* into *short-trading* activities, with important repercussions on spot markets (see Garber and Lall, 1998). The volume of such transactions has grown at a very high pace over the past few years and now accounts for a significant share of all foreign exchange transactions.

Tobin's initial proposal called for a *low*, uniform tax rate. Given the small margins that traders realize on foreign exchange market transactions, even a 0.02 percent tax (as proposed by Spahn) may represent a significant tax on

---

[40] Derivatives are synthetic financial instruments derived from underlying assets. *Futures* and *options* are commonly traded derivative contracts. A futures contract is an agreement between two parties to buy or sell a specific quantity of a financial instrument at a specific price. The buyer and seller agree on a price (exchange rate) for the product to be delivered, or paid for at a specified time in the future known as the *settlement date*. An option on a financial instrument futures contract is a binding agreement between two parties that confers on the buyer or seller the right (but not the obligation) to buy or sell the underlying asset at or up to a specified point in the future. The buyer and seller agree on a price known as a *premium*. *Calls* confer the right to buy, whereas *puts* confer the right to sell at a predetermined price. The option (call or put) terms determine the time period within which the buyer can exercise the option.

trading activities in normal times. In addition, because some financial transactions are undertaken by several intermediaries, taxes on these transactions may have a **cascading effect**—implying that the *effective* tax rate may be significantly higher than the nominal rate applied to a single transaction. However, during periods of heavy speculation, even a tax of, say, 3 percent on round-trip transactions (sale and repurchase of foreign currencies) is unlikely to deter speculators who expect a *significant short-term change* in the exchange rate (a devaluation of, say, 15 percent). And a tax rate that is high enough to deter speculation even in such periods would hamper the functioning of financial markets. The possible (or uncertain) benefits in terms of reducing short-term speculative trading would thus be outweighed by the possible costs associated with impairing the efficiency of financial intermediation.

Finally, the *mobility* of financial transactions would make the tax easy to avoid—unless it is implemented and enforced around the world (Shome and Stotsky, 1996). However, the likelihood of a universal tax can only be viewed as a remote possibility, in part because of the difficult political and economic issues that the distribution of proceeds raises. For this reason, Eichengreen, Tobin, and Wyplosz (1995) favored a more indirect means to tax foreign exchange transactions, which is a *tax on lending to nonresidents*. This tax can be applied in one country because it applies to resident lenders. Although it would not be universal, it would reduce loans of domestic banks to foreign speculators, which constitutes an important channel of speculation (see the appendix to this chapter).

8.7 Summary

- Conventional or **first-generation** models of currency crises predict that a fixed exchange rate regime is not viable without long-run consistency between monetary, fiscal, and exchange rate policies. Excessive domestic credit growth leads to a gradual loss of foreign reserves and ultimately to a **natural collapse** of the regime, once the *minimum level of reserves* is reached and the central bank can no longer defend the pegged rate.

- Speculators, knowing that the system is doomed to a natural collapse, and willing to avoid *capital losses* that would result from a discrete change in the exchange rate, will attack the currency and force the central bank to abandon the pegged rate *before* the minimum level of reserves is reached.

- The speculative attack takes place at the point in time when the **shadow floating exchange rate** equals the prevailing fixed rate. This also corresponds to the moment in time when remaining international reserves at the central bank, which are gradually being depleted, precisely match the portfolio reallocation indicated by the postattack interest rate shift.

- **Second-generation** models of currency crises explicitly account for **policymakers' preferences** and the **trade-offs** that they face in their policy objectives. In this setting, an exchange rate "crisis" (a devaluation or a switch to a floating rate regime) is viewed as an *ex ante* optimal decision for the policymaker. These models also highlight the role of **self-fulfilling mechanisms**, **multiple equilibria**, and **credibility factors**.

- For instance, an arbitrary increase in inflation expectations (induced by a perceived incentive to relax monetary and fiscal policies in the face of persistent unemployment) may raise interest rates to such an extent that the cost of preserving the peg (that is, foregoing the possibility to stimulate output by raising prices and lowering real wages) becomes so large that the authorities may find it optimal to devalue or to abandon altogether the pegged rate.

- As a result, market expectations may take on the characteristics of **self-fulfilling prophecies**—crises arising without obvious policy inconsistencies. A speculative attack undermining the viability of a peg can be viewed as a *sudden switch* from one regime of expectations to the other. Thus, the exact timing of an exchange rate crisis becomes *indeterminate* and difficult to predict.

- These theories suggest that, in examining the determinants of currency crises, it may be necessary to consider a broader set of fundamentals than simply credit growth or the real exchange rate. In particular, the *ratio of short-term foreign currency liabilities to official reserves* appears to be an important indicator of exchange rate vulnerability. Heavy reliance on short-term foreign borrowing increases the economy's exposure to foreign exchange risk and to a potential reversal in capital flows.

- The fact that macroeconomic policies are not regarded as predetermined but are taken as responding to agents' expectations creates the possibility of self-fulfilling crises. However, models of self-fulfilling crises based on an arbitrary selection among multiple equilibria by financial market operators can only *rationalize* speculative attacks; they cannot truly *explain* them, despite being consistent with some of the events that may surround these attacks. They do not explain why the shift between equilibria occurs.

- Some of the second-generation models do not assert that exchange rates can be attacked irrespective of economic fundamentals. Rather, they suggest that the ability of a sudden change in expectations to trigger an attack is *bounded* by the position of fundamentals, such as the amount of short-term debt that the government has to roll over.

- **Third-generation** models of currency crises emphasize the role of balance sheet factors and financial sector weaknesses in triggering speculative attacks. They also provide a role for monetary policy in a currency crisis—aside from the decision to abandon the exchange rate parity. These models assume that credit is necessary for production and that asymmetric information problems in the credit market may lead lenders to restrain credit. Because tighter credit constraints may have an adverse impact on expected output, they also increase the likelihood of an exchange rate collapse. Multiple equilibria may also arise in these models.

- A combination of adverse political shocks, a large and growing current account deficit, and policy shortcomings led to increasing reserve losses and growing dependence on short-term external borrowing in 1994 in Mexico. A devaluation on December 20, 1994, triggered a loss of confidence that led to a full-blown financial and economic crisis. Events in Mexico led to serious pressures and increased volatility in financial and exchange markets in a number of Asian and Latin American countries, particularly in Argentina (the **Tequila effect**).

- Thailand's growing external deficits and a weak and poorly supervised financial system were the two main factors triggering the crisis of the Thai baht in July 1997. Large, unhedged stocks of U.S. dollar liabilities held by the banks and the corporate sector compounded the effects of the initial devaluation of the baht and led to a full-blown financial and economic crisis. Delayed policy response (despite various warning signs in the previous months) and the authorities' resistance to an early adjustment of the exchange rate may also have exacerbated the crisis.

- Banking crises result from various factors, including external and domestic macroeconomic volatility (including terms-of-trade shocks and sharp fluctuations in world interest rates), excessive **lending booms**, *large mismatches* with respect to *liquidity, maturity,* and *currency denomination* of assets and liabilities), inadequate preparation for financial liberalization, heavy government involvement in the banking system, and loose controls on insider lending.

- Exchange rate crises and banking crises are related in various ways. A currency crisis can lead to a banking crisis because an unsterilized, large loss in international reserves that results from the speculative attack that precedes the abandonment of a fixed exchange rate regime may translate into a sharp decline in the base money stock and credit availability. In turn, the credit crunch may lead to a rise in nonperforming loans and an increased incidence of bankruptcies by nonfinancial firms. Or, the sharp exchange rate depreciation that often accompanies a currency crisis can create **solvency problems** among banks that are (directly or indirectly, through their customers) exposed to large foreign exchange liabilities.

- A banking crisis can lead to a currency crisis if the central bank allows an excessive expansion of domestic credit to finance the bailout of ailing banks, depositors, or both under an explicit or implicit **deposit insurance scheme**. Both currency and banking crises may also result from common macroeconomic shocks—such as an unexpected sharp increase in world interest rates, which may lead to a bank run and large capital outflows.

- Recent empirical studies of the determinants of currency and banking crises suggest that banking crises are often preceded by financial liberalization. In the study by Kaminsky and Reinhart (1999), the best predictors of currency crises are the real exchange rate, exports, the ratio of broad money over official reserves, stock prices, and output. The best predictors of banking crises are the real exchange rate, the broad money multiplier, the stock market, output, and real interest rates. However, the possibility of predicting the actual *timing* of currency and banking crises appears very limited—in part because of the existence of self-fulfilling factors.

- Financial markets are prone to herding, panics, contagion, and boom-bust cycles. However, herding behavior is not necessarily a reflection of irrationality. Portfolio allocation to any given country can be subject to abrupt changes in response to very small changes in perceived expected returns. In addition, the benefits of collecting country-specific information to corroborate the investor's prior expectations regarding the rate of return on the country's assets tends to diminish. Thus, diversification reduces incentives to acquire information; uncorroborated rumors may trigger large capital flows.

- Volatility in capital inflows translates into exchange rate instability (under flexible exchange rates) or large fluctuations in official reserves (under a pegged exchange rate regime) and (without sterilization) the money supply.

- Macroeconomic policy discipline, improved prudential rules on banks, information disclosure, and improved management of foreign-currency debt (to avoid, in particular, excessive reliance on short-maturity debt) can reduce the risks associated with a high degree of financial openness but cannot eliminate them.

- The **Tobin tax** is a proposal to tax uniformly spot transactions in foreign exchange in an attempt to reduce exchange rate volatility induced by large capital flows. However, there is no evidence suggesting a close relationship between transactions costs and volatility on asset markets, and thus no evidence that the Tobin tax would, in fact, reduce market volatility.

- On the contrary, by increasing transactions costs, the tax may hinder (at a sufficiently high level) the operation of financial markets. It may create a disincentive to trade assets, and may raise the cost of capital—thereby exerting an adverse effect on investment and growth. There are also serious practical difficulties in implementing it, because it would penalize both stabilizing and destabilizing traders, because these two groups are difficult to identify in practice.

- To fend off speculative attacks, a first line of defense for the central bank is to raise interest rates to impose a squeeze on short sellers of the domestic currency. This interest rate defense is designed to raise the finance cost to speculators, prior to a possible devaluation, above their anticipated capital gains in the event the devaluation indeed takes place—a situation that might force an eventual closing of the short positions.

- However, the interest rate defense may not be effective if sophisticated financial instruments are used by speculators. Moreover, the potential costs of maintaining high interest rates in periods of heavy speculative currency pressures can also be high. In particular, the interest costs of a squeeze are imposed both on speculators and on agents who are short in the currency for commercial reasons; thus high interest rates will over time affect economic activity. If these costs are large, the central bank may not be able to convince agents of its commitment to defend the fixed exchange rate.

Appendix to Chapter 8
The Mechanics of Speculative Attacks
and Interest Rate Defense

The main focus of the first part of this chapter was a discussion of the *economics* of speculative attacks. This appendix describes the practical aspects or *mechanics* of speculative attacks, particularly the role of bank lending. It also discusses the use of high interest rates to fend off speculative pressures.[41]

Suppose that a speculator wants to initiate an attack on a given currency (say, the peso). To do so he must create a **short peso position**. This is often done by short-selling pesos through a **forward contract**, whose maturity is sufficiently long (say, one month) to a financial intermediary (say, a domestic bank). The first panel of Table 8.1 describes how this transaction takes place. Suppose that the *spot exchange rate* is 25 pesos per U.S. dollar and that the speculator short-sells 2,500 pesos. The bank thus commits to providing a payment of U.S. 100 dollars in one month to the speculator, in exchange for 2,500 pesos—money that the speculator may need to borrow, at a cost influenced by central bank policy (as discussed later).

Table 8.1. The mechanics of forward contract operations

Step 1. Forward contract: creates a currency mismatch			
Receipts		Payment	
Pesos in 1 month	2,500	Dollars in 1 month	100

Step 2. Forward contract + spot sale: creates a maturity mismatch			
Pesos in 1 month	2,500	Pesos in two days (spot)	2,500
Dollars in two days (spot)	100	Dollars in 1 month (forward)	100

Step 3. Forward + spot + swap = balanced position			
Pesos in 1 month (forward)	2,500	Pesos in 1 month (swap)	2,500
Pesos in two days (swap)	2,500	Pesos in two days (spot)	2,500
Dollars in 1 month (swap)	100	Dollars in 1 month (forward)	100
Dollars in two days (spot)	100	Dollars in two days (swap)	100

Source: International Monetary Fund (1997*a*, p. 38) and Garber (1998, p. 23).

Note: The assumed spot exchange rate is 25 pesos per U.S. dollar.

The bank engaged in the operation now has a **long peso position** as a result of this transaction. The **currency mismatch**, in turn, creates a **currency risk**. If, for instance, a depreciation of the currency takes place (from, say, 25 to 50 pesos per U.S. dollar) before the settlement date (that is, within a month), the bank will need 5,000 pesos to make the scheduled payment of U.S. 100 dollars. In order to balance its domestic-currency position, the bank will immediately sell pesos on the **spot market** for foreign exchange for the conventional settlement period—say, two days. Thus, the bank will pay 2,500

---

[41] The first part of this section draws largely on the International Monetary Fund (1997*a*, pp. 37-38) and Garber (1998).

pesos in two days, and receive in exchange U.S. 100 dollars. The second panel
of Table 8.1 summarizes this transaction.

However, although the bank has now eliminated its currency mismatch, it
still faces a **maturity mismatch** in both pesos and U.S. dollars:

- it must borrow 2,500 pesos overnight to cover settlement of the spot sale
  but it will receive pesos only in 30 days, once the U.S. dollars are actually
  sold to the speculator in exchange for pesos;

- in the opposite direction, it buys 100 U.S. dollars on the spot market today,
  but will need them only in 30 days from now; so it will lend overnight U.S.
  dollars and effectively has borrowed 30-day U.S. dollars.

In order to close this maturity mismatch, the bank can engage in a **foreign exchange swap**—that is, an agreement to exchange a specified payment
obligation denominated in one currency for a specified payment obligation denominated in a different currency. In this particular case, the swap entails

- a delivery of 100 U.S. dollars for 2,500 pesos in 2 days;

- a delivery of 2,500 pesos for 100 U.S. dollars 30 days forward.

The third panel in Table 8.1 summarizes the complete set of transactions
performed by the speculator and the bank.

What happens if the central bank intervenes in the forward market for foreign
exchange? Suppose that it purchases pesos forward by an amount that exactly
matches the forward sale of the speculator (that is, 2,500 pesos). The forward
intervention in that case will absorb the spot sale of pesos by the lending bank,
without any need for the central bank to intervene directly in the spot market.
Thus, intervention in the forward market by the central bank is tantamount to
supplying implicitly domestic-currency credit directly to short sellers of pesos.

In a period of market turbulence in which the probability of a devaluation is
high, net suppliers of domestic credit are likely to be difficult to find. Nevertheless, as can be inferred from the first part of Table 8.1, the banking system as
a whole (commercial banks and the central bank) must provide credit to short
sellers of pesos to finance a speculative attack. The previous example shows
clearly that the bank's domestic currency receipts from the forward contract
correspond to a *one-month loan* to the short seller. If the central bank does not
supply the credit implicitly through forward intervention (as in the case considered earlier), the credit must come through either its money market operations
or its loan facilities. In either case, the pesos provided by the banking system are
essentially a pass-through of credit from the central bank, which is the ultimate
counterparty in both segments of the position-balancing transactions initiated
by domestic lenders.

In periods of large capital outflows, exchange market pressures, and losses in
official reserves, one line of defense for policymakers is to increase interest rates.
In particular, by raising its lending rate (and thus, indirectly, rates charged by

commercial banks), the central bank can impose losses on speculators—that is, short sellers of pesos. As shown in the previous example, short sellers need to borrow in order to deliver pesos for U.S. dollars under the forward contract; raising interest rates increases the cost of domestic funds and thus reduces the expected return from speculation.[42]

However, hikes in interest rates may not always have their intended effect on speculators or on the exchange rate. If short sellers of the domestic currency have secured sufficient financing *before* the increase in interest rates is implemented, they will not suffer from it—unless the central bank maintains rates high for a sufficiently long period. The increased degree of sophistication of **derivative markets** may also have weakened the ability of a policy of high interest rates to fend off speculative attacks (Garber, 1998). Specifically, Garber and Spencer (1996) showed that the interest rate defense, which aims to squeeze speculators of liquidity, may not work because of **dynamic hedging strategies** that may trigger massive sales of the domestic currency. A dynamic hedging strategy requires asset holders to adjust the structure of their portfolios continuously according to a certain rule, so as to achieve a *risk exposure target*; in some of these strategies, a rise in the spread between foreign and domestic interest rates automatically triggers a forward or spot sale of the domestic currency. How widespread such dynamic trading strategies are is not entirely clear; nevertheless, their existence suggests that an interest rate hike by the central bank could have the perverse effect of inducing sales of the domestic currency—and thus exacerbate exchange market pressures.

In addition to these limitations, increases in interest rates aimed at defending an exchange rate target may entail various costs.

- The increase in lending rates raises the cost of borrowing not only for speculators but also for other financial intermediaries (particularly those involved in securities markets), which often finance their positions through short-term lines of credit. This creates a potential constraint on how high the central bank can let interest rates rise without creating financial stress.[43] Such considerations are particularly important if commercial banks are already suffering from heavy losses on their loan portfolio; the rise in interest rates may exacerbate these problems. It could also increase the expected fiscal deficit if these banks are insolvent and benefit from explicit or implicit government insurance of their liabilities (see Chapter 15). This, in turn, may reinforce exchange market pressures.

---

[42] More generally, to the extent that the increase in lending rates translates into higher interest rates on other domestic-currency assets, the attractiveness of these assets will increase.

[43] To mitigate this cost, a central bank can charge higher interest rates only to those identified as speculators and maintain low (or normal) rates to financial intermediaries through credit controls. In practice, countries have tended to identify as speculators foreign residents who engage in foreign exchange swaps with domestic banks, and either ban such swaps or ensure that heavy forward discounts be imposed on the forward segments of these operations. Similarly, domestic banks may be forbidden to provide on-balance-sheet overnight or longer maturity credit to foreign residents. However, experience suggests that such controls are difficult to enforce and generate a spread between onshore and offshore interest rates on domestic-currency loans (as was the case in Thailand).

- If total debt and debt service ratios of the nonfinancial private sector are already high, a rise in interest rates may bring these ratios to unsustainably high levels and lead to insolvencies and outright default—thereby weakening an already fragile banking system. The reduction in aggregate demand and output that high interest rates may entail could also exacerbate the position of firms and other debtors.

- In countries where fiscal imbalances are large and public debt is to a significant extent short-term and contracted at floating rates, a large increase in interest rates can feed back quickly into higher interest payments and an increase in the government's fiscal deficit (see Chapter 3). Increases in interest rates may have a perverse effect and actually weaken the attractiveness of the domestic currency if markets believe that the increase in debt service may be monetized, or if interest rate volatility rises sufficiently beyond what is considered to be an acceptable level of risk.

- A high interest rate defense against speculative attacks may be viewed as having a high opportunity cost in terms of domestic economic activity, particularly if the economy is slowing down, the unemployment rate is high or increasing, and inflation is low or falling. In such a situation, as discussed in Chapter 6, even a highly independent central bank may be reluctant to maintain this policy for a long period of time.

Several researchers have attempted to gauge the extent to which high interest rates can help prevent speculative attacks or sustain the value of a currency in the immediate aftermath of a financial crisis. Kraay (2003), for instance, used a sample of monthly data from 75 countries over the period 1960-99. He identified 105 successful attacks in his sample (episodes in which a nominal depreciation of at least 10 percent was preceded by a period of relatively stable exchange rates) and 117 failed attacks (episodes in which official reserves declined by a large amount, interest rate spreads rose above a given threshold, or both). He found that high interest rates were essentially unrelated with the probability that an attack is successful. In a comprehensive review of the empirical literature, much of which focuses on the immediate aftermath of currency crises, Montiel (2003) concluded that much of the evidence on the links between interest rates and the exchange rate is weak.

Chapter 9

Policy Tools for Macroeconomic Analysis

Since the early 1950s a variety of empirical techniques and quantitative models have been developed and used in the formulation of macroeconomic and structural adjustment programs in the developing world. This chapter focuses on the analytical foundations of some of these operational models and assesses their usefulness from a variety of perspectives—most notably, their ability to capture some of the key macroeconomic features identified in the previous chapters, their data requirements, and the ease with which they can be implemented.

Section 9.1 describes a simple empirical method for assessing business cycle regularities, based on cross correlation among macroeconomic variables. Analyzing these correlations is an important first step in identifying the key relationships that must be accounted for in a quantitative macroeconomic model. Section 9.2 presents the analytical framework (in both its basic and its extended forms) that has been at the heart of stabilization programs designed by (or prepared with the assistance of) the International Monetary Fund (IMF), the financial programming approach. Section 9.3 presents the World Bank's basic model, which focuses on medium-term growth. In contrast to financial programming models, productive capacity and the rate of capital accumulation are endogenously determined; however, the demand and financial sides of the economy are ignored. Section 9.4 shows how the two models can be integrated to analyze jointly stabilization and medium-term growth issues. Section 9.5 discusses the three-gap model developed by Bacha (1990). Section 9.6 presents a static, computable general equilibrium model that has proved useful in assessing the medium- and longer-term effects of fiscal adjustment and tariff reform in developing countries. The last part discusses the role of various types of lags in the transmission process of policy shocks and their impact on short-term macroeconomic projections.

9.1   Assessing Business Cycle Regularities

Understanding and distinguishing among the various factors affecting the short-
and long-run behavior of macroeconomic time series has been one of the main
areas of research in quantitative macroeconomic analysis in recent years. However, much of the research on these issues has focused on industrial countries,
with relatively limited attention paid to developing economies. At least two
factors may help account for this.

- Limitations on *data quality* and *frequency* continue to be constraining
  factors in some cases. For instance, quarterly data on national accounts
  are available for only a handful of developing countries; even when they
  are available, they are considered to be of significantly lower quality than
  annual estimates.

- Developing countries tend to be prone to *sudden crises* and marked gyrations in macroeconomic variables, often making it difficult to discern any
  type of cycle or economic regularities.

At the same time, there are at least three reasons why more attention to
the analysis of the stylized facts of macroeconomic fluctuations in developing
countries could be useful.

- Determining the regular features of economic cycles in an economy helps
  to specify *applied macroeconomic models* that may capture some of the
  most important correlations.

- The sign and magnitude of unconditional correlations can provide some
  indication of the *type of shocks* that have dominated fluctuations in some
  macroeconomic aggregates over a particular period of time.

- Assessing the pattern of *leads* and *lags* between aggregate time series
  and economic activity can be important for the design of stabilization
  programs. For instance, as discussed later, the cross correlation between
  changes in private credit and domestic output may play an important
  role in deciding how much credit to allocate to the private sector and the
  government.

To characterize short-run fluctuations (measured as deviations of a variable from its long-run trend) in macroeconomic time series, and to analyze
unconditional correlations between them and detrended output, the first step
involves choosing a measure of real activity. Real GDP is often chosen in annual studies, whereas an index of industrial output is often selected in quarterly
studies—usually because few developing countries produce consistent and reliable national accounts data at that frequency, as already noted. However, it
is important to note that using total GDP as a measure of output may not
always be appropriate. The reason is that agricultural output, which depends
on factors that may be unrelated to other macroeconomic variables (such as

weather conditions) may represent a large fraction of GDP. In such conditions, using *nonagricultural GDP* may be preferable.

The second step in the analysis consists in decomposing all macroeconomic series into nonstationary (trend) and stationary (cyclical) components, because most of the techniques that are commonly used to characterize the data empirically (including cross correlations) are valid only if the data are stationary. A common procedure to test for **unit roots** is to use the **Augmented Dickey-Fuller (ADF) test**, by running the following regression:

$$\Delta x_t = \alpha + \beta t + (\rho - 1)x_{t-1} + \sum_{h=1}^{k} \Phi_h \Delta x_{t-h} + u_t,$$

where u_t is an error term and $k \geq 0$. The null hypothesis of nonstationarity (that is, that the series contains a unit root) is H_0: $\rho = 1$. For x_t to be stationary, $\rho - 1$ should be negative and significantly different from zero.

Suppose that the observed variable x_t has no seasonal component and can be expressed as the sum of a trend x_t^* component and a cyclical component, x_t^c:

$$x_t = x_t^* + x_t^c. \tag{1}$$

At period t, the econometrician can observe x_t but cannot measure either x_t^* or x_t^c. The second step is thus to estimate the trend component of x_t. A possible option is to use the **Hodrick-Prescott (HP) filter** (see Hodrick and Prescott, 1997). It consists essentially in specifying an adjustment rule whereby the trend component of the series x_t moves continuously and adjusts gradually. Formally, the unobserved component x_t^* is extracted by solving the following minimization problem:

$$\min_{x_t^*} \left[\sum_{t=1}^{T} (x_t - x_t^*)^2 + \lambda \sum_{t=2}^{T} [(x_{t+1}^* - x_t^*) - (x_t^* - x_{t-1}^*)]^2 \right]. \tag{2}$$

Thus, the objective is to select the trend component that minimizes the sum of the squared deviations from the observed series, subject to the constraint that changes in x_t^* vary gradually over time. The coefficient λ is a positive number that penalizes changes in the trend component. The larger the value of λ, the smoother the resulting trend series.[1] It can be shown that the trend component x_t^* can be represented by a **two-sided symmetric moving average** expression of the observed series:

$$x_t^* = \sum_{h=-n}^{n} \alpha_{|h|} x_{t+h}, \tag{3}$$

where the parameters $\alpha_{|h|}$ depend on the value of λ.

---

[1] In general, the choice of the value of λ depends on the degree of the assumed stickiness in the series under consideration. The usual practice is to set, for instance, λ to 100 with annual time series, and 1,600 with quarterly time series. However, this choice is somewhat arbitrary; a more appropriate procedure would be to choose an "optimal" value of λ, using a data-dependent method. See Agénor, McDermott, and Prasad (2000).

The third step is to assess the degree of co-movement of each series, y_t, with output, x_t. This is done by measuring the magnitude of the **contemporaneous correlation coefficient**, $\rho(0)$, between the filtered components of y_t and x_t. A series y_t is said to be

- *procyclical* if $\rho(0)$ is positive;

- *countercyclical* if $\rho(0)$ is negative;

- *acyclical* if $\rho(0)$ is zero.

To establish which correlations are significantly different from zero, it can be noted that the statistic

$$\ln[\frac{1 + \rho(0)}{1 - \rho(0)}]/2$$

has an asymptotically normal distribution with a variance equal to $1/(T - 3)$, where T is the number of observations (see Kendall and Stuart, 1967, pp. 419-20). With 30 observations, this implies that positive correlations of 0.32 or larger are significantly different from zero at the 10 percent level, and of 0.48 or greater are significant at the 1 percent level. Using for instance a 10 percent significance threshold, the series y_t can be said to be

- *strongly contemporaneously correlated* with output if $0.32 \leq |\rho(0)| < 1$;

- *weakly contemporaneously correlated* with output if $0.1 \leq |\rho(0)| < 0.32$;

- *contemporaneously uncorrelated* with output if $0 \leq |\rho(0)| < 0.1$.

The last step is to determine the **phase shift** of y_t relative to output, by studying the **cross-correlation coefficients** $\rho(j)$, $j \in \{\pm 1, \pm 2, ...\}$. Specifically, y_t is said to

- *lead the cycle* by j period(s) if $|\rho(j)|$ is maximum for a negative j;

- *lag the cycle* if $|\rho(j)|$ is maximum for a positive j;

- be *synchronous* if $|\rho(j)|$ is maximum for $j = 0$.

The pattern of lead-lag correlations (in particular, the lag at which the peak positive correlation occurs) can be interpreted as indicating the speed at which innovations in variable y_t are transmitted to real activity x_t.

A comprehensive analysis of macroeconomic fluctuations in 12 developing countries based on the above approach and using quarterly data is provided by Agénor, McDermott, and Prasad (2000). Among other results, they found that private consumption, investment, and credit to the private sector tend to be procyclical. Consumption also tends to be less volatile than output (as would be expected from **consumption smoothing** behavior, discussed in Chapter 2) and tend to move synchronously with it.

The fiscal stance, measured by the ratio of government spending to tax revenue, is countercyclical in some countries—as found for instance by Calderón and Schmidt-Hebbel (2003) for many countries in Latin America—and procyclical in others, suggesting in the latter case that fiscal policy may exacerbate output fluctuations. Broad money does not appear to have a significant correlation with output, and often seems to lag movements in activity. The terms of trade (the ratio of export prices to import prices) tend in general to have a procyclical effect.[2]

Finally, in a number of countries, both prices and their rate of change (inflation) tend to be countercyclical. A negative cross correlation between (detrended) prices and (detrended) output is generally viewed as indicating the predominance of *demand shocks*, whereas a positive cross correlation is indicative of *supply shocks*.[3]

The HP filter described earlier remains the subject of much criticism. In particular, it has been argued that it removes potentially valuable information from time series and that it may impart *spurious cyclical patterns* to the data (see Cogley and Nason, 1995). It also assumes, as indicated in Equation (1), that the trend and cyclical components are independent. In reality, the choice of the relationship between the trend and cyclical components is arbitrary.

Nevertheless, the HP filter remains widely used. One reason might be that *any* detrending filter is, to some extent at least, arbitrary and is bound to introduce distortions that may affect the robustness of reported business cycle regularities or so-called *stylized facts*. A sensible approach is to use, in addition to the HP filter, other detrending techniques for robustness checking. Some of these techniques include the modified **band pass filter** proposed by Christiano and Fitzgerald (2003).

9.2   Financial Programming

Financial programming is at the core of macroeconomic policy exercises conducted by the International Monetary Fund. The first model of financial programming was developed by Polak (1957); essentially, the model can be viewed as a systematic attempt to integrate *monetary* and *credit* factors in discussions of balance-of-payments issues. The first part of this section presents the Polak model, whereas the second considers a more elaborate financial programming framework.

---

[2] The importance of terms-of-trade shocks on output fluctuations is emphasized by Kose and Riezman (2001). They do so in the context of a general equilibrium model of a small open economy calibrated with data for sub-Saharan Africa.

[3] Supply shocks are usually defined as those shocks that have permanent effects on output (and possibly other real variables), while demand shocks are those that have only temporary, but often persistent, effects on output. This teminology is somewhat misleading because most shocks perturb both demand and supply. More sophisticated methods, based on structural vector autoregression techniques, have been used to identify demand and supply shocks; see, for instance, Ahmed (2003), Fielding and Shields (2001), Fung (2002), Hoffmaister and Roldós (2001), Hoffmaister, Roldós, and Wickham (1998), and Rogers and Wang (1995).

9.2.1 The Polak Model

The Polak model considers a small open economy operating a fixed exchange rate regime. It is specified in *nominal terms* and consists of two identities, one behavioral equation, and an equilibrium condition.

- The first equation defines changes in the *nominal money supply*, M^s. Suppose, for simplicity, that all foreign assets are held by the central bank.[4] M^s is thus the sum of *domestic credit*, L, and *official foreign exchange reserves*, R:[5]

$$\Delta M^s = \Delta L + \Delta R. \tag{4}$$

- The second equation relates changes in official reserves to the *current account* (which is identical to the trade balance, assuming that there are no interest payments on foreign debt), and *capital inflows*, ΔF, which are treated as exogenous:

$$\Delta R = X - \alpha Y + \Delta F, \quad 0 < \alpha < 1, \tag{5}$$

where *exports*, X, are taken as exogenous, and *imports* are a constant fraction, α, of nominal income, Y. Given the assumption that all net foreign assets are held by the central bank, the change in net official reserves is identical to the balance of payments.

- The third equation specifies changes in the nominal demand for money, ΔM^d, as a function of changes in nominal income, ΔY:

$$\Delta M^d = \nu^{-1} \Delta Y, \quad \nu > 0, \tag{6}$$

where ν, the *income velocity of money*, is assumed to be constant over time.

- The fourth and last equation assumes that the money market is in *flow equilibrium*:

$$\Delta M^s = \Delta M^d. \tag{7}$$

The structure of the Polak model is summarized in Table 9.1. The change in net official reserves, ΔR, is the *target* variable. The change in the nominal money stock and nominal output, ΔM and ΔY, as well as imports, $J = \alpha Y$, are *endogenous* variables. Exports and capital inflows, X and ΔF, are *exogenous* variables. ΔL is the *policy instrument*. It is important to note that in the model there is no explicit decomposition of changes in nominal output into changes in prices and changes in real activity.

---

[4] This assumption can be rationalized by either assuming that there are no commercial banks operating in the economy, or that commercial banks are required to surrender all their foreign exchange receipts to the central bank. Accounting explicitly for net foreign assets held by commercial banks can be done by straightforward modifications to Eqs. (4) and (5).

[5] More precisely, R is the book value, in domestic currency terms, of official reserves. Of course, with a fixed exchange rate normalized to unity, the foreign- and domestic-currency values of official reserves are the same.

Table 9.1. Structure of the Polak model

Variables	Definition
Target	
ΔR	Change in official foreign reserves
Endogenous	
$J = \alpha Y$	Imports
ΔM	Change in nominal money balances
ΔY	Change in nominal output
Exogenous	
X	Exports
ΔF	Change in net capital flows
Policy instrument	
ΔL	Change in domestic credit
Parameters	
ν	Income velocity of money
α	Marginal propensity to import

The main use of the Polak model is to assess the effects of *changes in domestic credit* on the balance of payments—or, more precisely here, official reserves in foreign exchange. Using Equations (4), (6), and (7) yields

$$\Delta R = \nu^{-1}\Delta Y - \Delta L, \tag{8}$$

which indicates that the change in net official reserves will be positive only to the extent that the desired increase in nominal money balances exceeds the change in domestic credit. The *structure* of the balance of payments (that is, the relative importance of trade flows and capital movements) plays no direct role in this relationship; it matters only for the *adjustment process* to credit shocks.

To illustrate this result and analyze how credit shocks are transmitted in this setting, consider a once-and-for-all increase in L at period $t = 0$ by ΔL_0. The adjustment process operates as follows.

- The increase in ΔL_0 expands on impact the nominal supply of money by the same amount [Equation (4)]. This brings about an identical increase in the demand for money, as implied by Equation (7). Because velocity is constant, this increase in money demand requires a rise in nominal income by $\nu\Delta L_0$ [Equation (6)], which in turn raises imports by $\alpha\Delta Y_0 = \alpha\nu\Delta L_0$. Official reserves therefore fall by $-\alpha\nu\Delta L_0$ on impact.

- Because the initial increase in domestic credit remains fixed at ΔL_0, the money supply, at the beginning of period $t = 1$, increases by only $(1 - \alpha\nu)\Delta L_0$. Nominal income therefore increases by $\nu(1 - \alpha\nu)\Delta L_0$ and the first-period increase in imports is $\alpha\nu(1 - \alpha\nu)\Delta L_0$. The cumulated change in reserves at the end of the first period is consequently

$$\Delta R|_{t=1} = -\alpha\nu\Delta L_0 - \alpha\nu(1 - \alpha\nu)\Delta L_0,$$

whereas the cumulated change in the money supply at the end of the first period is

$$\Delta M^s|_{t=1} = \Delta L_0 - \alpha\nu\left[1 + (1 - \alpha\nu)\right]\Delta L_0 = (1 - \alpha\nu)^2\Delta L_0,$$

which is also equal to the increase in the money supply at the beginning of period $t = 2$.

With the same reasoning, the cumulated fall of reserves over an infinite horizon $(t \to \infty)$ is given by

$$\Delta R|_{t\to\infty} = -\left[\alpha\nu + \alpha\nu(1 - \alpha\nu) + \alpha\nu(1 - \alpha\nu)^2 + \ ...\right]\Delta L_0.$$

The term in brackets in the above expression can be written as

$$\alpha\nu\left[1 + (1 - \alpha\nu) + (1 - \alpha\nu)^2 + \ ...\right].$$

For the geometric series in brackets to converge, the term $1 - \alpha\nu$ must be less than unity; because $\alpha\nu > 0$, this condition is always satisfied. Thus, the above expression can be written as

$$\alpha\nu\frac{1}{1 - (1 - \alpha\nu)} = 1,$$

so that

$$\Delta R|_{t\to\infty} = -\Delta L_0.$$

The cumulative fall in official reserves, over an infinite horizon, is thus equal to the initial increase in domestic credit. Equation (4) therefore implies that

$$\Delta M^s|_{t\to\infty} = 0.$$

In the long run, the initial expansion in money supply through an increase in domestic credit is *completely offset* by the reduction in official reserves. Thus, nominal income and imports also return to their original levels after increasing initially. Put differently, in order to have $\Delta M^s = 0$, one also needs $\Delta Y = 0$.

Because the only long-run effect of a change in domestic credit is on foreign reserves, establishing a given target level of ΔR (given a projected path for money demand) allows the policymaker to estimate the *maximum allowable increase* in domestic credit, that is, a **credit ceiling**. Specifically, if $\Delta\tilde{R}$ denotes the reserve target, and ΔY^p the projected level of nominal income, the required change in credit is given by, using Equation (8):

$$\Delta L = \nu^{-1}\Delta Y^p - \Delta\tilde{R}.$$

Thus, controlling domestic credit expansion (in a setting in which exports, the income velocity of money, and capital flows can be treated as exogenous) is sufficient to attain a balance-of-payments objective. This implication of the model has been at the heart of the stabilization programs advocated by (or put in place with the support of) the IMF. The money demand function, as shown in the foregoing example, plays a critical role in the analysis. The particular form used here is actually not essential for the main implication of the model; a more general function (involving, for instance, interest rates or inflation, as discussed in Chapter 4) can readily be specified—as long as it is assumed stable and independent of changes in domestic credit (International Monetary Fund, 1987, p. 14).

The importance of controlling domestic credit expansion for balance-of-payments performance is also the key message of the **Monetary Approach to the Balance of Payments** (MABP), which in its most popular form relies on the assumptions of a stable demand for money, purchasing power parity, and continuous *stock equilibrium* of the money market (Kreinin and Officer, 1978). However, in addition to the nature of the concept used to characterize money market equilibrium, there is a key difference between the Polak model and the MABP: in the latter, any increase in domestic credit expansion (everything else equal) instantly crowds out official reserves by an equivalent amount.[6] In the Polak model, complete crowding out also occurs but only *in the long run*, and takes place through a series of adjustments in nominal income, imports, and the money supply. This adjustment process may be viewed as more realistic than the assumption underlying the MABP.

A key limitation of the Polak model is the assumption that changes in domestic credit have no effect (even in the short run) on the determinants of money demand, such as income or domestic interest rates. As noted in previous chapters, in many developing countries the bank credit-supply side link is often a critical feature of the economy. Another problem with the model (as well as with many of its extensions) is that it assumes a stable money demand function. In practice, especially over short horizons, the demand for money balances tends to be unstable—often as a result of volatile inflation expectations. In such conditions, it may provide an unreliable tool for macroeconomic projections. Finally, because the model is specified in purely nominal terms, it has nothing to say about the real effects of adjustment policies.

9.2.2 An Extended Framework

The Polak model has been modified and extended in several directions, and the flexibility that this has brought to practitioners explains in part why it remains, in one form or another, at the core of the financial programming exercises that underly IMF stabilization programs designed for economies operating under a fixed exchange rate. This subsection examines one of these extentions, due to Khan, Haque, and Montiel (1990), which distinguishes explicitly between

---

[6] Specifically, an excess supply of real money balances brought about by an increase in domestic credit gives rise to an excess demand for other financial assets as well as goods and services. In an open economy, this excess demand translates immediately into changes in net foreign reserves.

changes in real and nominal output and the sources of credit growth.[7]

Consider an economy producing one good, which is an imperfect substitute for imported goods. Let nominal income, Y, be defined as

$$Y = Py, \tag{9}$$

where P denotes the overall price index and y real output, which is assumed exogenous. The change in nominal income is given by

$$\Delta Y = Py - P_{-1}y_{-1} = Py + P_{-1}(\Delta y - y) = Py + P_{-1}\Delta y - P_{-1}y,$$

that is,

$$\Delta Y = \Delta Py + P_{-1}\Delta y = \Delta P(\Delta y + y_{-1}) + P_{-1}\Delta y = \Delta Py_{-1} + P_{-1}\Delta y + \Delta y\Delta P.$$

Assuming that both ΔP and Δy are small, the last term on the right-hand side in the above expression can be ignored and so

$$\Delta Y = \Delta Py_{-1} + P_{-1}\Delta y. \tag{10}$$

Changes in the overall price index are a function of changes in domestic prices, ΔP_D, and changes in foreign prices measured in domestic-currency terms, $\Delta E + \Delta P^*$:

$$\Delta P = \delta \Delta P_D + (1 - \delta)(\Delta E + \Delta P^*), \quad 0 < \delta < 1 \tag{11}$$

where E is the nominal exchange rate, P^* the price index of foreign goods measured in foreign-currency terms, and δ (respectively $1 - \delta$) a parameter that measures the relative weight of domestic goods (respectively imported goods) in the overall price index.

Domestic credit, L, consists now of credit to the *private sector*, L^p, and credit to the *government*, L^g:[8]

$$\Delta L = \Delta L^p + \Delta L^g. \tag{12}$$

Changes in credit to the private sector reflect demand for working capital (as discussed in Chapter 7) and, as such, are assumed proportional to changes in nominal output:

$$\Delta L^p = \theta \Delta Y, \quad \theta > 0. \tag{13}$$

The *money supply identity* is given, as in the Polak model, by

$$\Delta M^s = \Delta L + \Delta R, \tag{14}$$

---

[7] Other examples of extended IMF-type financial programming models include, for instance, Mikkelsen (1998).

[8] L^g is defined net of government deposits at the central bank. In practice, the definition of government used for programming exercises varies across countries. In what follows government and public sector are used as synonymous.

where ΔR is equal to $E\Delta R^*$, that is, the change in the foreign-currency value of official reserves ΔR^*, valued at the current exchange rate.[9]

Changes in official reserves are again related to the trade balance and capital inflows, ΔF, assumed exogenous:

$$\Delta R = X - J + \Delta F. \tag{15}$$

X, J, and ΔF are all measured in domestic-currency terms. ΔF consists now of private as well as public capital flows, ΔF^p and ΔF^g, which are both assumed to be given in foreign-currency terms, so that $\Delta F = E\Delta F^*$, or equivalently, assuming that $E_{-1} = 1$, $\Delta F = (1 + \Delta E)\Delta F^*$.

Exports are again exogenous. Imports in nominal terms are given by $J = EQ_J$, where Q_J is the volume of imports. Consequently, assuming that $\Delta E\Delta Q_J$ is small,

$$J = J_{-1} + \Delta E Q_{J-1} + E_{-1}\Delta Q_J.$$

Changes in the volume of imports are assumed to depend on changes in real output and changes in the price of domestic goods relative to the price of foreign goods:

$$\Delta Q_J = \alpha\Delta y + \eta[\Delta P_D - (\Delta E + \Delta P^*)],$$

where $\eta > 0$ measures the sensitivity of (the change in) imports to (changes in) relative prices. Substituting this result in the previous equation yields, noting that

$$J = J_{-1} + (Q_{J-1} - \eta E_{-1})\Delta E + E_{-1}[\alpha\Delta y + \eta(\Delta P_D - \Delta P^*)], \tag{16}$$

which shows that, as long as η is sufficiently large, a devaluation of the nominal exchange rate ($\Delta E > 0$) will lower imports, improve the trade balance, and increase official reserves. In the particular case where Q_{J-1} and E_{-1} are normalized to unity, the condition on η is $\eta > 1$.[10]

As in the Polak model, the income velocity of money is taken to be constant, implying that

$$\Delta M^d = \nu^{-1}\Delta Y, \quad \nu > 0. \tag{17}$$

The money market is again assumed to be in flow equilibrium:

$$\Delta M^s = \Delta M^d. \tag{18}$$

Finally, the *government budget constraint* relates the budget deficit $G - T$, where G is total expenditure and T is total tax revenue, to changes in foreign borrowing, ΔF^g (which is exogenous), and changes in central bank credit:[11]

$$G - T = \Delta L^g + \Delta F^g. \tag{19}$$

---

[9] Equation (14) assumes that capital gains and losses on foreign exchange reserves associated with changes in the nominal exchange rate are not monetized, but rather are treated as off-balance-sheet items. These effects can be introduced by adding the term $R_{-1}^*\Delta E$ on the right-hand side of (14), as in Khan, Haque, and Montiel (1990).

[10] The model can be modified to endogenize exports as a function also of relative prices; see Khan, Haque, and Montiel (1990).

[11] It is assumed that the government cannot borrow directly from the domestic private sector by issuing bonds. As noted in Chapter 4, this assumption has become particularly restrictive for a number of middle-income developing countries.

With ΔL^g and ΔF^g given, the government budget deficit is thus given from "below the line" and must be met by adjusting either spending or tax revenue.

Table 9.2 summarizes the structure of the extended Polak model. The change in domestic prices, ΔP_D, and the change in net official reserves, ΔR, are the *target* variables. Changes in the nominal money stock, ΔM, nominal output, ΔY, credit to the private sector, ΔL^p, the overall price index, ΔP, and imports, J, and the budget deficit, $G - T$, are all *endogenous* variables. Changes in real output, Δy, foreign prices, ΔP^*, and exports and capital inflows, X and ΔF, are *exogenous* variables. The variables y_{-1}, P_{-1}, $Q_{J,-1}$, and E_{-1} are *predetermined*. Changes in domestic credit to the government ΔL^g and the nominal exchange rate ΔE are the *policy instruments*. It is worth emphasizing that in this setting it is the government budget deficit as a whole that is considered endogenous. As discussed below, whether the adjustment occurs through movements in government spending (changes in G) or in taxes (changes in T) is left unspecified at this stage.

To relate targets, exogenous variables, and policy instruments in this setup, first substitute Equations (12), (13), (14), and (17) in (18) to give

$$\Delta R = (\nu^{-1} - \theta)\Delta Y - \Delta L^g,$$

where it is assumed that $\nu\theta < 1$, so that $\nu^{-1} - \theta > 0$.

Using Equation (10) to eliminate ΔY, and (11) to eliminate ΔP, yields

$$\Delta R - (\nu^{-1} - \theta)y_{-1}\delta\Delta P_D = \Lambda, \tag{20}$$

where

$$\Lambda = (\nu^{-1} - \theta)[y_{-1}(1 - \delta)(\Delta E + \Delta P^*) + P_{-1}\Delta y] - \Delta L^g.$$

Similarly, substituting Equation (16) in (15) yields

$$\Delta R + \eta E_{-1}\Delta P_D = X + \Delta F - J_{-1} - (Q_{J-1} - \eta E_{-1})\Delta E + \eta\Delta P^* - \alpha E_{-1}\Delta y. \tag{21}$$

These two equations can be solved in two different modes.

- In the **positive** or **policy mode**, Equations (20) and (21) are used to determine *simultaneously* ΔR and ΔP_D, for given values of X, ΔF, ΔP^*, Δy, the predetermined variables, and the policy instruments, ΔE and ΔL^g. Given the solution for ΔP, Equations (11), (10), (13), and (12) then determine, respectively, ΔP, ΔY, ΔL^p, and ΔL. $G - T$ is determined independently, because it depends only on ΔL^g and ΔF^g, which are both exogenous.

- In the **programming mode**, ΔR and ΔP_D are policy targets, denoted $\Delta\tilde{R}$ and $\Delta\tilde{P}_D$, in (20) and (21). These two equations are now solved for the two policy instruments, ΔE and ΔL^g. Given the solved value of the instrument ΔL^g, and given ΔF^g, Equation (19) determines residually the government fiscal deficit, $G - T$. This *programmed deficit* is achieved by adjusting either tax revenue, T, or public expenditure, G. The target for domestic prices (given the assumption that real output is exogenous), together with the solved value of ΔE, generate a programmed value for the change in the overall price index, ΔP, the change in nominal output, ΔY, and thus private sector credit, ΔL^p, through (10), (11), and (13).

Table 9.2. Structure of the extended financial programming model

Variables	Definition
Targets	
ΔR	Change in official foreign reserves
ΔP_D	Change in domestic prices
Endogenous	
ΔY	Change in nominal output
ΔL^p	Change in private sector credit
ΔM	Change in nominal money balances
ΔP	Change in the overall price index
ΔJ	Change in imports
$G - T$	Fiscal deficit
Exogenous	
Δy	Change in real output
ΔP^*	Change in foreign prices
X	Exports
$\Delta F = \Delta F^p + \Delta F^g$	Change in net capital flows
Policy instruments	
ΔL^g	Change in domestic credit to government
ΔE	Change in the nominal exchange rate
Predetermined	
y_{-1}	Real output in previous period
P_{-1}, E_{-1}	Price level and exchange rate in previous period
Q_{J-1}	Volume of imports in previous period
Parameters	
ν	Income velocity of money
δ	Share of domestic goods in the price index
α	Marginal propensity to import
θ	Response of private sector credit to output
η	Response of imports to relative prices

Actually, in the programming mode, the solution values for ΔE and ΔL^g can be calculated *recursively*, given the structure of the model. Because ΔL^g does not appear in (21), that equation can be used to obtain the appropriate level of ΔE, for given values of $\Delta \tilde{R}$ and $\Delta \tilde{P}_D$. Substituting the solution for ΔE in Equation (20) then yields the required value of ΔL^g.

The solution of the extended model is illustrated in Figure 9.1, in the ΔR-ΔP_D space. Curve MM is given by Equation (20) and has a positive slope. Curve BB is derived from Equation (21) and has a negative slope. The intersection of the two curves (at point E) defines the solution values for ΔR and

ΔP_D in the **positive mode** (that is, for given values of the exogenous variables and the policy instruments). To see how the model operates in **programming mode**, suppose, for instance, that the policymaker's objectives are to lower inflation and increase official reserves, by moving from the initial position at E to a point such as E'. This outcome can be achieved through a combination of two policy actions:

- a reduction in domestic credit to the government, ΔL^g, which implies a leftward shift in MM, with no change in BB, thereby moving the economy to point A;

- a depreciation of the nominal exchange rate, ΔE, which implies a rightward shift in both MM and BB, thereby moving the economy to point E'.

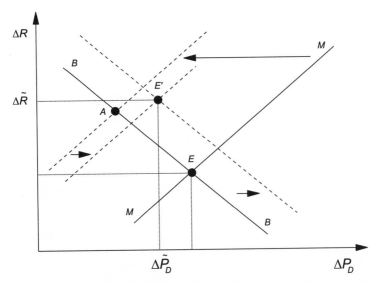

Figure 9.1. The extended financial programming model. Source: Adapted from Khan, Montiel, and Haque (1990, p. 161).

Graphically, the new equilibrium is obtained at point E' in Figure 9.1, where MM and BB intersect. By adjusting only L^g the economy could be moved to point A, at which inflation has fallen to the desired level, but reserves would remain below target. What this experiment suggests, therefore, is that it is necessary to use *two policy instruments* to achieve *two policy targets*, as suggested by the **Meade-Tinbergen principle**.

9.3 The World Bank RMSM Model

The World Bank uses for the macroeconomic projections that underlie some of its loan operations the RMSM-X model, which is discussed in the next section.

The present section focuses on the precursor to that model, the **Revised Minimum Standard Model** (RMSM), which was developed in the early 1970s.

The main objective of the model is to make explicit the link between *medium-term growth* and its *financing*. The basic model takes prices as given. It consists of five relationships.

- The first relationship relates the desired level of investment, I, to the change in real output, Δy:

$$I = \Delta y/\sigma, \quad \sigma > 0, \tag{22}$$

  where σ is the inverse of the **incremental capital-output ratio** (ICOR).

- The second relationship relates imports, J, and real output:

$$J = \alpha y, \quad 0 < \alpha < 1. \tag{23}$$

- The third relationship makes (as in the three-good model of Chapter 7) private consumption, C^p, proportional to disposable income, defined as income, y, minus taxes, T:

$$C^p = (1 - s)(y - T), \tag{24}$$

  where $0 < s < 1$ is the marginal propensity to save.

- The fourth relationship is the balance-of-payments identity defined earlier:

$$\Delta R = X - J + \Delta F, \tag{25}$$

  where X again denotes exports (assumed exogenous) and ΔF net capital inflows or net foreign borrowing.

- The last relationship is the national income identity, which is given by

$$y = C^p + G + I + (X - J), \tag{26}$$

  where G is again government expenditure.

The structure of the RMSM model is summarized in Table 9.3. Changes in real output, Δy, and the change in net official reserves, ΔR, are *the target* variables. Investment, I, imports, J, and private consumption, C^p, are all *endogenous* variables. Exports, X, are *exogenous*. Government spending, G, tax revenue, T, and the change in foreign borrowing, ΔF, are the *policy instruments*.

To see how targets, exogenous variables, and policy instruments are related in this setup, substitute Equations (23), (24) in (26) to give

$$I = (s + \alpha)y + (1 - s)T - (X + G),$$

that is, using (22) and noting that $y = y_{-1} + \Delta y$:

$$\Delta y = \frac{(s + \alpha)y_{-1} + (1 - s)T - (X + G)}{\sigma^{-1} - (s + \alpha)}, \tag{27}$$

where it is assumed that $\sigma^{-1} - (s + \alpha)$. Given that $0 < s, \alpha < 1$, and that ICORs typically exceed unity, this condition is always satisfied in practice.

Substituting (23) in (25) yields

$$\Delta R = X - \alpha(y_{-1} + \Delta y) + \Delta F. \tag{28}$$

The system consisting of Equations (27) and (28) can be solved in two different modes.

- In the **positive** or **policy mode**, Equations (27) and (28) are used to solve for Δy and ΔR. The system is in fact **recursive**: Equation (27) can first be used to determine Δy, for given values of X and the policy instruments, T and G, and the predetermined variable y_{-1}. Given this solution, Equation (28) is then used to determine ΔR, for given values of X, ΔF, and y_{-1}.

- In the **programming mode**, the solution can again be obtained recursively: Equation (27) can be used to determine either the value of G or T (with the other treated as exogenous) for a given target value of Δy; and for given target values of Δy and ΔR, Equation (28) can be used to determine the value of net capital inflows, ΔF. With $\Delta \tilde{y}$ and $\Delta \tilde{R}$ denoting the target levels of output and reserves, this solution is

$$\Delta F = \alpha(y_{-1} + \Delta \tilde{y}) - X + \Delta \tilde{R}. \tag{29}$$

The solution of the RMSM model in the positive mode is illustrated in Figure 9.2, in the Δy-ΔR space. The horizontal curve YY is given by Equation (27). Curve BB is derived from Equation (28) and has a negative slope. The intersection of the two curves (at point E) defines the equilibrium values of Δy and ΔR, for given values of the exogenous variables and the policy instruments.

Because setting a target level of output is tantamount to fixing imports and thus the trade balance (recall that exports are exogenous), the programming mode of the RMSM model described above is often described as the **trade-gap mode**: for $X - J$ given, the model calculates the appropriate level of external financing, ΔF, that satisfies the balance-of-payments identity, Equation (25).

Ignoring the trade gap and assuming that policymakers exert sufficient control over capital inflows to determine ΔF as in Equation (29) may not, of course, be warranted in all circumstances. In practice, countries do face *limits on foreign borrowing*. By treating external financing ΔF as given, the RMSM model—just as the RMSM-X model described later—can alternatively be closed by fixing, instead, the level of saving that is consistent with the programmed level of investment corresponding to the targeted level of output, $\Delta \tilde{y}$.

Specifically, using Equation (22), the required level of saving is $\Delta \tilde{y}/\sigma$. This is what is referred to as the **saving-gap** mode. In this case, it is often assumed that total consumption ($C = G + C^p$) is determined *residually* from the national income identity, Equation (26).

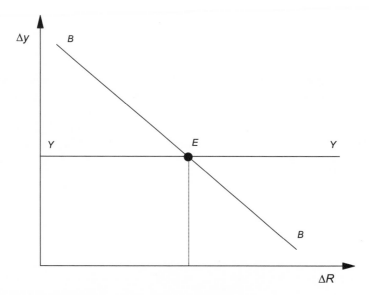

Figure 9.2. The RMSM model in the positive mode.

Assuming further that public consumption expenditure is policy determined yields private consumption as the residual variable, that is, using Equations (22) and (23):

$$C^p = y_{-1} + \Delta\tilde{y} - \Delta\tilde{y}/\sigma - X - \alpha(y_{-1} + \Delta\tilde{y}) - G.$$

The trouble with this functioning mode, of course, is that there is no reason *a priori* to expect the level of private consumption derived from the above equation to be equal to the level consistent with (24). Effectively, that equation is dropped from the system.

In general, of course, both the trade gap and the saving gap may represent binding constraints on the determination of output and changes in official reserves, implying that either one or both of these targets may need to be adjusted to accommodate a shortage in foreign exchange restrictions. The version of the RMSM model in which a (possibly binding) foreign exchange constraint is added is the **two-gap mode**.[12] Neither constraint is suppressed *a priori* so that either one of the two gaps might be binding. In such a two-gap situation, depending on which constraint is binding, observed domestic saving (imports) may be different from desired or required saving (imports).

The main use of the two-gap version of the RMSM model in the programming mode is to determine the financing requirements for alternative target rates of output growth (given also a target for official reserves) or, equivalently, to determine the feasibility of a particular rate of output growth given alternative foreign financing scenarios. To illustrate, rewrite the national income accounting

---

[12]The two-gap model, with its focus on foreign exchange and domestic saving as alternative constraints on growth, was developed by Chenery and Strout (1966). See Taylor (1994) for a more recent treatment.

identity (26) as

$$I = (y - T - C^p) + (T - G) + (J - X). \tag{30}$$

This formulation now equates domestic investment, I, to the sum of private sector savings, $y - T - C^p$, public sector savings, $T - G$, and foreign savings (or the trade surplus), $J - X$. This saving-investment balance was discussed in Chapter 1. Using Equation (24) to substitute out for C^p and (25) to substitute out for $J - X$ in (30), and with target levels of output and reserves given by $\Delta \tilde{y}$ and $\Delta \tilde{R}$, Equation (30) implies that investment is constrained by total saving, that is,

$$I \leq \kappa_S + \Delta F, \tag{31}$$

where

$$\kappa_S = s(y_{-1} + \Delta \tilde{y}) + [(1 - s)T - G] - \Delta \tilde{R}.$$

Equation (31) is the **saving constraint**. It is depicted (in equality form) in Figure 9.3 as curve SS in the I-ΔF space.

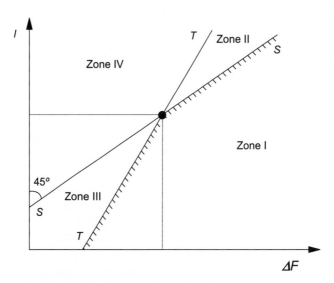

Figure 9.3. The RMSM model in two-gap mode.

The figure assumes that κ_S, which is in general ambiguous, is positive. Below curve SS the inequality (31) is satisfied, whereas above SS it is not. The constraint $I = \kappa_S + \Delta F$ is thus binding above SS. Changes in the policy instruments, T and G, and changes in the policy targets, $\Delta \tilde{y}$ and $\Delta \tilde{R}$, imply horizontal shifts in SS because they affect κ_S.

To derive the second constraint that operates in the two-gap version of the RMSM model requires rewriting the balance-of-payments constraint (25) in the form

$$J - X = \Delta F - \Delta \tilde{R}, \tag{32}$$

which gives the level of the trade account (or, again, imports) consistent with a given value of ΔF and a target level for reserves.

Substituting the import demand function, Equation (23), in the above equation and rearranging yields

$$\Delta y = (\Delta F - \Delta \tilde{R} + X)/\alpha - y_{-1}. \tag{33}$$

From Equation (22), $\Delta y = \sigma I$. Substituting Equation (33) for Δy in this expression implies that investment is also constrained by

$$I \leq \kappa_T + \Delta F/\alpha\sigma, \tag{34}$$

where

$$\kappa_T = (X - \Delta \tilde{R})/\alpha\sigma - y_{-1}/\sigma.$$

Table 9.3. Structure of the World Bank's RMSM framework

Variables	Definition
Targets	
Δy	Change in output
ΔR	Change in official foreign reserves
Endogenous	
I	Investment
C^p	Private consumption
J	Imports
Exogenous	ΔF
X	Exports
Policy instruments	
G	Government expenditure
T	Tax revenues
ΔF	Change in net foreign borrowing
Predetermined	
y_{-1}	Real output in previous period
Parameters	
σ	Inverse of the incremental capital-output ratio
s	Marginal propensity to save
α	Marginal propensity to import

Equation (34) is the **trade constraint**. It is represented in (equality form) in Figure 9.3 as curve TT, which is drawn under the assumption that $\kappa_T < 0$. In practice, the ICOR coefficient, $1/\sigma$, usually varies between 2 and 5; in general, therefore, given that $0 < \alpha < 1$, $\alpha\sigma < 1$. Curve TT (whose slope is $1/\alpha\sigma$) is thus typically steeper than SS, whose slope is unity. As before, the position of TT depends also on $\Delta \tilde{R}$. In addition, here, it also depends on the (exogenous) value of exports, X. But with X given, the only way to generate a shift in TT is through a revised target level for official reserves.

Both constraints, (31) and (34), provide an estimate of the level of investment. The constraint that yields the lowest level of the two is called the **binding constraint**. Curves SS and TT separate Figure 9.3 into four zones:

- Zone I, in which *no constraint is binding*;

- Zone II, in which only the *saving constraint is binding*;

- Zone III, in which only the *trade constraint is binding*;

- Zone IV, in which *both constraints are binding.*

Clearly, because TT is steeper than SS, the impact of foreign borrowing on investment, and thus on output and growth, will be larger if the trade constraint is binding, as opposed to the saving constraint.

To see how the two-gap version of the RMSM model operates in the programming mode (that is, with target levels for both official reserves and output), suppose that foreign financing is the constraining factor. The values of investment, changes in output, imports, and official reserves that are mutually consistent with each other (as well as with the policy instruments and the exogenous variables) are then determined through an *iterative process* which involves the following steps.

- Step *1*. Specify values for (a) the parameters σ, s, and α; (b) the predetermined variable, y_{-1}; (c) the exogenous variables, X and ΔF; (d) the policy instruments, T and G; and (e) the policy targets, $\Delta\tilde{y}$ and $\Delta\tilde{R}$.

- Step *2*. Given the policy target $\Delta\tilde{y}$, and using (22), determine the **required level of investment** as

$$I_R = \Delta\tilde{y}/\sigma.$$

- Step *3*. Determine the levels of investment, I_S and I_T, implied by the saving constraint [Equation (31)] and the trade constraint [Equation (34)]. Determine the **binding level of investment** given by the hatched area in Figure 9.3, as
$$I_{min} = \min(I_S, I_T). \tag{35}$$

- Step *4*. If the required level of investment does not exceed the minimum level, that is, if $I_{min} \geq I_R$, no constraint is binding, and the intersection of ΔF and I_R occurs in Zone I in Figure 9.3. Then proceed to step 6. If not, proceed to either step 4a, 4b, or 4c:

  - Step *4a*. If $I_{min} \leq I_R$, and the saving constraint is binding, the intersection of ΔF and I_R will occur in Zone II in Figure 9.3. Either increase taxes, T, and/or reduce public expenditure, G, and/or reduce the desired change in official reserves, $\Delta\tilde{R}$, until the constraint is relaxed or until further changes in the policy or target variables are ruled out as unfeasible.[13] If the constraint is relaxed so that the required investment level can be achieved, proceed to step 6. If not, proceed to step 5.

- Step 4b. If $I_{min} \leq I_R$, and the trade constraint is binding, the intersection of ΔF and I_R will occur in Zone III in Figure 9.3. Reduce the desired change in official reserves, $\Delta \tilde{R}$, until the constraint is relaxed or until further changes in the policy or target variables are ruled out as unfeasible.[14] If the constraint is relaxed so that the required investment level can be achieved, proceed to step 6. If not, proceed to step 5.

- Step 4c. If $I_{min} \leq I_R$, and both constraints are binding, the intersection of ΔF and I_R will occur in Zone IV in Figure 9.3. Reduce the desired change in official reserves, $\Delta \tilde{R}$ and/or adjust policy instruments T and G, until both constraints are relaxed or until further changes in the policy or target variables are ruled out as unfeasible.[15] If both constraints are relaxed so that the required investment level can be achieved, proceed to step 6. If not, proceed to step 5.

• Step 5. If step 4 does not yield the required level of investment needed to achieve the desired level of increase in output, then the targeted change in output must be revised and a new (lower) value must be set according to

$$\Delta \tilde{y} = \sigma I_{min},$$

which by definition is consistent with the binding(s) constraint(s).

• Step 6. Determine the required level of imports, J_R, as

$$J_R = \alpha(y_{-1} + \Delta \tilde{y}).$$

• Step 7. Given the required level of imports and the exogenous levels of X and ΔF, reestimate the targeted change in official reserves as follows:

$$\Delta \tilde{R}[1] = X - J_R + \Delta F.$$

---

[13] From Equations. (31) and (34), an increase in T or a reduction in G (by raising κ_S) shifts only SS to the left, increasing the feasibility region (zone I). A reduction in $\Delta \tilde{R}$, by contrast, shifts *both* SS and TT to the left. The shift in TT, however, is inconsequential, because the trade constraint was satisfied in the first place.

[14] From Equations (31) and (34), an increase in T or a reduction in G (by raising κ_S) would shift SS to the left. This, however, would be inconsequential, because the saving constraint was satisfied in the first place. There must therefore be a leftward shift in TT in order to increase the feasibility region. In turn, this can occur only through a reduction in $\Delta \tilde{R}$ (because X is given), which shifts *both* SS and TT to the left.

[15] As indicated earlier, a change in $\Delta \tilde{R}$ is necessary to shift the TT curve. Because as a result of a reduction in $\Delta \tilde{R}$ both SS and TT shift to the left, there may be no need to adjust T or G to expand sufficiently the feasibility region.

For consistency reasons, this revised targeted change in reserves must be compared to the original target value used in the saving and trade constraints. If both estimates $\Delta \tilde{R}[1]$ and $\Delta \tilde{R}$ are identical (a very unlikely outcome after only one iteration), go to step 8. If not, go back to step 3 and re-solve the model again with the revised target $\Delta \tilde{R}[1]$. Continue iterations until the estimate of $\Delta \tilde{R}$ used in step 3 is (almost) identical to the one provided by step 7, that is, until the values obtained between iterations h and $h-1$, $\Delta \tilde{R}[h]$ and $\Delta \tilde{R}[h-1]$, are very close. Once convergence has been achieved, the model yields interrelated consistent values of the levels of investment, the change in output, imports, and the change in official reserves.

- Step 8. Use Equation (24), along with the new value of output (given by $y = y_{-1} + \Delta \tilde{y}$) and the (possibly modified) value of taxes to estimate private consumption, C^p.

Various criticisms have been offered of the two-gap version of the RMSM model. Two of the most important ones are the following.

- It is often difficult, in practice, to decide *a priori* which constraint is binding. The RMSM framework assumes that imports are essential for investment and that the availability of foreign exchange, by allowing such imports, raises the growth rate of output. However, the saving gap can also in principle be closed by *reducing imports* or *increasing exports* (or both), thereby freeing foreign exchange necessary for investment.

- The RMSM model is incomplete because it is essentially a growth-oriented model with emphasis on a small number of real variables and no financial side. For instance, relative prices and induced substitution effects among production factors (and their possible impact on exports, for instance) are neglected.

9.4   The Merged Model and RMSM-X

The original RMSM model evolved into the **RMSM-X** framework, also developed at the World Bank. Essentially, RMSM-X integrates into RMSM the financial programming approach of the IMF, described earlier. The first part of this section describes the analytical structure of the merged IMF-World Bank model, which is at the core of RMSM-X; the RMSM-X framework itself is presented in the second part.

9.4.1   The Merged IMF-World Bank Model

The merged IMF-World Bank model combines the extended financial programming model described earlier and the World Bank's RMSM model. As in the extended IMF model, which assumes imperfect substitutability between domestic and imported goods, relative prices (and thus the nominal exchange rate) affect the demand for imports and domestic absorption.

Again, following Khan, Haque, and Montiel (1990), the merged model can be described as consisting of the following equations:

- The investment-real output link is given by an equation similar to (22):

$$I/P = \Delta y/\sigma,$$

where I is now *nominal* investment expenditure deflated by the price level, P. Assuming that $P_{-1} = 1$ in the above specification yields

$$\Delta y = \sigma I/(1 + \Delta P). \tag{36}$$

- The change in nominal output is given, as in Equation (10), by

$$\Delta Y = \Delta P y_{-1} + P_{-1} \Delta y. \tag{37}$$

- Changes in the overall price index are given by an equation similar to (11):

$$\Delta P = \delta \Delta P_D + (1 - \delta)\Delta E, \tag{38}$$

where, for simplicity, foreign prices are taken as constant ($\Delta P^* = 0$).

- Domestic credit consists again of credit to the private sector and credit to the government, as in Equation (12):

$$\Delta L = \Delta L^p + \Delta L^g, \tag{39}$$

with changes in private sector credit given by a relation similar to Equation (13),

$$\Delta L^p = \theta \Delta Y. \tag{40}$$

- The money supply identity, ignoring again capital gains and losses on official reserves due to exchange rate fluctuations, is given by an equation similar to (14):

$$\Delta M = \Delta L + \Delta R, \tag{41}$$

where ΔR is equal to $E\Delta R^*$.

- Changes in official reserves are given by an equation similar to (15):

$$\Delta R = X - J + \Delta F, \tag{42}$$

where X, J, and ΔF are all measured in domestic-currency terms, with ΔF consisting of private and public flows, ΔF^p and ΔF^g. Again, ΔF is assumed given in foreign currency terms, so that, with E_{-1} normalized to unity, $\Delta F = (1 + \Delta E)\Delta F^*$.

- Exports are exogenous and changes in nominal imports are determined by a relation similar to Equation (16), with $\Delta P^* = 0$:

$$J = J_{-1} + (Q_{J-1} - \eta E_{-1})\Delta E + E_{-1}(\alpha \Delta y + \eta \Delta P_D). \tag{43}$$

- Money demand is given by a relation identical to Equation (17), which assumes constant income velocity:

$$\Delta M^d = \nu^{-1} \Delta Y. \tag{44}$$

- The money market is assumed as before to be in flow equilibrium, as in Equation (18):

$$\Delta M^s = \Delta M^d. \tag{45}$$

- The government budget constraint is given again by Equation (19):

$$G - T = \Delta L^g + \Delta F^g. \tag{46}$$

To close the model requires an equation linking private investment and private saving. To do so requires specifying the *private sector budget constraint*. This is given by

$$Y - C^p - T = I + \Delta M^d - \Delta L^p - \Delta F^p,$$

which indicates that saving, $Y - C^p - T$, is allocated to investment and net accumulation of financial assets, given by the change in money balances, minus changes in liabilities (bank loans and foreign borrowing). Assuming, as in (24), that $C^p = (1 - s)(Y - T)$, this constraint implies that

$$I = s(Y_{-1} + \Delta Y - T) + \Delta L^p + \Delta F^p - \Delta M^d. \tag{47}$$

Combining the budget constraints (46) and (47) gives the economy's overall budget constraint, or saving-investment balance, which relates total domestic saving (private and public) and investment to foreign saving (that is, capital inflows) and asset accumulation net of borrowing from the domestic banking system (see Chapter 1).

Table 9.4 summarizes the structure of the merged model. The change in real output, Δy, domestic prices, ΔP_D, and the change in net official reserves, ΔR, are the *target* variables. Changes in the nominal money stock, ΔM, nominal output, ΔY, credit to the private sector, ΔL^p, the overall price index, ΔP, imports, J, the budget deficit, $G - T$, and investment, I, are *endogenous* variables. Exports, X, and changes in foreign borrowing, ΔF, are *exogenous* variables. Changes in domestic credit to the government, ΔL^g, taxes or government spending (T or G), and the nominal exchange rate, ΔE, are the *policy instruments*.

As before, a condensed form of the system can be derived. First, substitute Equation (44) in (47), and then both (46) and (47) in (36), together with (39), to give

$$\Delta y = \sigma (1 + \Delta P)^{-1} [s(Y_{-1} + \Delta Y) + (1 - s)T - G + \Delta L + \Delta F - \nu^{-1} \Delta Y],$$

so that, using Equation (40):

$$\Delta y = \sigma (1 + \Delta P)^{-1} [sY_{-1} + \tau \Delta Y + (1 - s)T - G + \Delta L^g + \Delta F],$$

where $\tau = s + \theta - \nu^{-1}$ is assumed positive, that is,

$$\nu(s + \theta) > 1.$$

Table 9.4. Structure of the merged IMF-World Bank model

Variables	Definition
Targets	
ΔR	Change in official foreign reserves
ΔP_D	Change in domestic prices
Δy	Change in real output
Endogenous	
ΔY	Change in nominal output
ΔL^p	Change in private sector credit
ΔM	Change in nominal money balances
ΔP	Change in the overall price index
ΔJ	Change in imports
$G - T$	Fiscal deficit
Exogenous	
X	Exports
$\Delta F = \Delta F^p + \Delta F^g$	Change in net capital flows
Policy instruments	
ΔD^g	Change in domestic credit to government
ΔE	Change in the nominal exchange rate
G or T	Government spending or taxes
Predetermined	
y_{-1}	Real output in previous period
P_{-1}, E_{-1}	Price level and exchange rate in previous period
Parameters	
ν	Income velocity of money
δ	Share of domestic goods in consumer prices
s	Marginal propensity to save
α	Marginal propensity to import
θ	Response of private sector credit to output
η	Response of imports to relative prices

Using Equation (37) to substitute for ΔY in the above expression, and multiplying both sides by $1 + \Delta P$ yields, assuming that $\Delta P \Delta y \simeq 0$ and setting $P_{-1} = 1$,

$$\Delta y = \frac{\kappa + \tau y_{-1} \Delta P}{\sigma^{-1} - \tau}, \qquad (48)$$

where

$$\kappa = sY_{-1} + (1 - s)T - G + \Delta L^g + \Delta F, \qquad (49)$$

and it is assumed that $\sigma^{-1} - \tau > 0$, that is,

$$\sigma \tau < 1.$$

Substituting Equation (38) for ΔP yields

$$\Delta y = \frac{\kappa + \tau y_{-1}[\delta \Delta P_D + (1-\delta)\Delta E]}{\sigma^{-1} - \tau},$$

which can be rewritten as

$$\Delta P_D = \frac{-\kappa + (\sigma^{-1} - \tau)\Delta y}{\delta \tau y_{-1}} - (1-\delta)\delta^{-1}\Delta E. \tag{50}$$

Second, as in the extended financial programming model, substituting Equations (39), (40), (41), and (44) in (45) yields

$$\Delta R + (\tau - s)\Delta Y = -\Delta L^g.$$

Using Equation (37) to eliminate ΔY, and (38) to eliminate ΔP yields, with $P_{-1} = 1$,

$$\Delta R + (\tau - s)(y_{-1}\delta \Delta P_D + \Delta y) = \Phi, \tag{51}$$

where

$$\Phi = -(\tau - s)y_{-1}(1-\delta)\Delta E - \Delta L^g.$$

Third, substituting Equation (43) in the balance-of-payments Equation (42) implies

$$\Delta R = X - J_{-1} - (Q_{J-1} - \eta E_{-1})\Delta E - E_{-1}(\alpha \Delta y + \eta \Delta P_D) + \Delta F. \tag{52}$$

Equations (50), (51), and (52) represent the condensed form of the model. Equation (50) can be rewritten as

$$\Delta P_D = \chi_{10} + \chi_{11}\Delta y, \tag{53}$$

with

$$\chi_{10} = \frac{-\kappa}{\delta \tau y_{-1}} - (1-\delta)\delta^{-1}\Delta E, \quad \chi_{11} = \frac{\sigma^{-1} - \tau}{\delta \tau y_{-1}},$$

which can be substituted in (51) to give

$$\Delta R = [\Phi + (\tau - s)y_{-1}\delta \chi_{10}] - \chi_{21}\Delta y, \tag{54}$$

and in (52) to give

$$\Delta R = \chi_{30} - \chi_{31}\Delta y, \tag{55}$$

where

$$\chi_{21} = (\tau - s)(y_{-1}\delta \chi_{11} + 1),$$
$$\chi_{30} = X - J_{-1} - (Q_{J-1} - \eta E_{-1})\Delta E - E_{-1}\eta \chi_{10} + \Delta F,$$
$$\chi_{31} = E_{-1}(\alpha + \eta \chi_{11}).$$

Equations (53), (54), and (55) can be solved, as before, in two different modes.

- In the **positive mode**, the system is *recursive*: Equations (54) and (55) jointly determine Δy and ΔR, for given values of the policy instruments and the exogenous variables. Given the solution value for Δy, Equation (53) determines ΔP_D, again for given values of the policy instruments and the exogenous variables.

- In the **programming** or **policy mode**, Δy, ΔR, and ΔP_D are policy targets (denoted $\Delta \tilde{y}$, $\Delta \tilde{R}$, and $\Delta \tilde{P}_D$) and the instruments are T or G, ΔE, and ΔL^g. All four possible instruments appear directly in all three equations—T and G, for instance, through κ, as shown in Equation (49), and thus χ_{10}. The system is thus *fully simultaneous*: solution values of the three policy instruments (ΔE, ΔL^g and, say, G) must be calculated at the same time from Equations (53)-(55), for given targets $\Delta \tilde{y}$, $\Delta \tilde{R}$, and $\Delta \tilde{P}_D$ and given values of X, ΔF, T, and the predetermined variables.

Given the solution values for the instruments G and ΔL^g and for given values of T and ΔF^g, Equation (46) is always satisfied. The target values for changes in real output and the domestic price level—and thus, from Equation (38), the target value for the *overall* price level—generate from Equation (37) a programmed value for nominal output and thus private sector credit, ΔL^p, through Equation (40).

The solution of the merged model is illustrated in Figure 9.4. In the panel on the right-hand side, two curves are shown in the Δy-ΔR space. Curve MM is derived from Equation (54) and its slope is given by

$$\frac{\Delta y}{\Delta R}\bigg|_{MM} = -\chi_{21}^{-1} < 0.$$

The second curve is denoted BB and depicts the combinations of Δy and ΔR that satisfy Equation (55); its slope is assumed to be less than that of MM and is given by

$$\frac{\Delta y}{\Delta R}\bigg|_{BB} = -\chi_{31}^{-1} < 0, \quad |\chi_{31}| > |\chi_{21}|.$$

In the panel on the left-hand side, the curve YY depicts the combinations of Δy and ΔP_D that satisfy Equation (53). Its slope is given by

$$\frac{\Delta y}{\Delta P_D}\bigg|_{YY} = \chi_{11}^{-1} > 0.$$

In the **positive mode** (that is, for given values of the exogenous variables and the policy instruments), the intersection of MM and BB (at point E) yields the solution values for Δy and ΔR; the corresponding equilibrium value for ΔP_D is found at the intersection of the horizontal line originating from E and curve YY.

Suppose, for instance, that the policymaker has three objectives, to increase output, lower inflation, and increase official reserves by moving from the initial position at E to a point such as E' in the panel on the right-hand side of

Figure 9.4 and point A' in the panel on the left-hand side. This outcome can be achieved through a combination of three policy actions: a *reduction* in domestic credit to the government, ΔL^g; a *depreciation* of the nominal exchange rate, ΔE; and a *reduction* in government spending, G. In general, as can be inferred from Equations (53)-(55), a change in any of these instruments shifts all three curves, MM, BB, and YY; but as shown in Figure 9.4, all three curves must eventually shift to the right for all three objectives to be satisfied, and this can only be achieved by using all three policy instruments *simultaneously*. This result illustrates once again the **Meade-Tinbergen principle**.

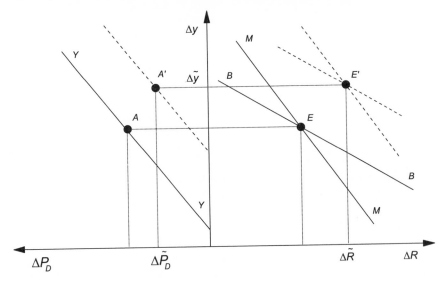

Figure 9.4. The merged IMF-World Bank model.

9.4.2   The RMSM-X Framework

As noted earlier, the RMSM-X model is the expanded version of the RMSM model previously used by the World Bank for its growth and balance-of-payments projections (see World Bank (1997b)). The conceptual basis of RMSM-X is the merged IMF-World Bank model described in the previous subsection, which essentially adds to RMSM a price sector, a monetary sector, and government accounts, along the lines of the IMF's financial programming approach.

In practice, RMSM-X models can be fairly detailed. They typically consist of four economic sectors: the public sector, the private sector, the consolidated banking system, and the external sector, although some models disaggregate further the public sector (into government and public enterprises) and the banking system (into commercial banks and the central bank).

A budget constraint is associated with each sector. These constraints are represented within the framework of a **consistency accounting matrix**, similar to the one developed in Chapter 1. National accounts are derived via aggregation of the sectoral budget constraints and serve to close the model.

On the financial side, standard versions of the model include as before two types of assets, money and foreign assets, but some versions (particularly for middle-income countries) also include domestic bonds—requiring therefore explicit assumptions regarding interest rate formation and substitution patterns between assets.

The specification of money demand in most cases follows the Polak model, in which the (nominal) demand for money is linked to (nominal) income via the assumption of constant velocity. In models where the structure of the banking system is disaggregated, the money supply (which represents the liabilities of the entire banking system) is not simply the sum of central bank credit and official reserves (that is, the monetary base), but is obtained instead as the product of the monetary base (which represents the total liabilities of the central bank) and a (constant or time-varying) money multiplier.

In most RMSM-X models, the fixed relationship between investment and the growth rate of output (through an ICOR that may or may not vary over time) plays a central role, just like in RMSM models.

Relative prices can be introduced by assuming that domestic and foreign goods are imperfect substitutes, so that substitution effects can be analyzed (often on the import side only, as described earlier). Imports are often divided into several categories (for instance, food, other final consumption goods, intermediate goods, and capital goods) and the demand for each category of imports is specified as a function of the real exchange rate and either real GDP or, in the case of imports of capital goods, gross domestic investment. Imports of food are also sometimes made a direct function of private consumption. As was also the case in the RMSM approach, consumption is generally assumed to depend only on disposable income—thereby excluding the type of consumption-smoothing effects discussed in Chapter 2.

Within the RMSM-X framework, several **model closures** can be specified, with each yielding an alternative solution.

- In the **public sector closure**, values for all variables except public sector expenditure and domestic borrowing are specified; the latter two variables are then determined by the model.

- In the **private sector closure**, values for government expenditure and revenue are specified, and the model estimates private sector variables.

In both of these approaches, likely disbursements from external donors provide an estimate of external financing. The *required* amount of external borrowing is determined separately, through the balance-of-payments identity. If there is a gap between what is expected to be available and what is required to equilibrate external accounts, a marginal economic agent is assumed to undertake the necessary borrowing.

Under a public sector closure, for instance, the marginal borrower is the central government. The marginal foreign creditor in both the private and the public sector closures can also be chosen, although in general it is assumed to be foreign commercial banks.

- In the **policy closure**, the values of macroeconomic policy variables as well as the expected behavior of private sector agents are specified so that the model can generate time paths for GDP and other key macroeconomic variables, such as inflation. All external financing is identified in advance and imports are adjusted (positively or negatively) in order to equilibrate the balance of payments. Hence, this type of closure is also called the *availability mode.*

The RMSM-X model is most often operated in the **programming mode**; given a set of macroeconomic objectives, it can be solved for a mix of fiscal, monetary, and exchange rate policies that are consistent with the targeted values. The solution sequence is as follows:

- Step 1. Set targets for the inflation rate, potential GDP growth rate (evaluated at full employment), real exchange rate, real interest rate, and international reserves (specified in months of imports).

- Step 2. Calculate investment requirements, given estimates of ICOR and the actual growth rate of output, the latter being determined by adjusting the potential growth rate on the basis of the projected rate of capacity utilization;

- Step 3. Calculate the demand-side relationships based on the projections of the exogenous variables.

- Step 4. Estimate the initial supply of foreign borrowing on the basis of likely disbursements of external agencies. Calculate the foreign reserve requirements of the central bank for an exogenously given target of imports. Given the demand for foreign borrowing as well as the initial supply, determine the amount of additional foreign borrowing needed.

- Step 5. Determine the growth rates of the monetary base and the broad money supply, given the policy targets for inflation and the output growth rate, and estimates of velocity and the money multiplier. Estimate residually the amount of domestic credit to be supplied by the central bank or the banking system, given the reserve accumulation target.

- Step 6. Close the model by determining the following residuals in the relevant markets: consumption of goods and services, that is, public (private) consumption in the public (private) sector closure; borrowing from the foreign external sector; and credit allocated by the banking system (or, in more specific cases, central bank credit to the nonfinancial public enterprises).

Although the RMSM-X framework is a significant step toward an integrated framework for analyzing the feasibility and sustainability of stabilization and growth-oriented policies, it retains the limitations of the two models that underlie it. The financial programming framework of the IMF, even in the extended versions that are now available, remains rudimentary; its static nature makes it particularly problematic for short-term projections, given the importance of lags (see the discussion below).[16] It does not incorporate many important features of the economic landscape of modern-day developing countries, particularly on the financial side: bond financing of fiscal deficits and its effects on domestic interest rates are often ignored, and so is the endogeneity of private capital flows.

Moreover, all of these models typically assume that the economy produces only one domestic good, which is used for both domestic consumption and exports. A more appropriate framework for developing economies would distinguish between exportables, nontradables, and importables, as discussed in Chapter 7. The short-run link between production and bank credit (a key feature of many developing countries, as emphasized in Chapter 7) is often not taken into account—thereby obviating a critical channel through which monetary policy can affect the real economy.

The supply side of the RMSM-X also reflects the limitations of the basic RMSM model. It does not account for the complementarity between public investment (in infrastructure, most notably) and private investment, as discussed in Chapter 2. Most importantly, the fixed-coefficient production function (the ICOR relationship) remains subject to a number of analytical and practical difficulties. In a study of 146 countries over the period 1950-92, Easterly (1999) found that the assumed linear relationship between growth and investment is significantly rejected by the data. In addition, the ICOR specification rules out substitutability between capital and labor and therefore is unable to account for observed fluctuations in real wages.[17]

Relative prices (and the real exchange rate) influence the allocation of resources only through the demand side, not the supply side. Finally, the model provides no role to expectations (and thus to the degree of policy credibility, as discussed in Chapter 6) and no explicit role for the labor market. It is thus incapable of explaining fluctuations in unemployment.

9.5   Three-Gap Models

The two-gap approach discussed earlier in the context of the RMSM model was extended to a three-gap framework by Bacha (1990) to account for the possibility of a third constraint, the **fiscal gap**.[18] In contrast to the *financing needs*

---

[16]There is an extensive literature analyzing the outcomes (as opposed to the analytical foundations) of IMF stabilization programs. See Conway (1994), Doroodian (1993), Killick (1995), Bird (2002), Przeworski and Vreeland (2000), and Evrensel (2002).

[17]With factor substitution, and constant returns to scale in production and exogenously determined returns to factor inputs, the ICOR would be a function of the ratio of the wage rate to the rate of return to capital. To assume a constant ICOR would thus be equivalent to assuming a constant ratio of factor rewards.

[18]A useful survey of gap models is provided by Taylor (1994). For applications of three-gap models to developing countries, see Sepehri, Moshiri, and Doudongee (2000) to Iran, Iqbal, James, and Pyatt (2000) to Pakistan, and Thanoon and Baharumshah (2003) to Malaysia.

approach described earlier, Bacha's model links foreign exchange availability directly to the rate of growth of productive capacity and only indirectly to the actual level of real output.

The first equation of the model is an ICOR relationship similar to Equation (22), which is repeated here for convenience:

$$I = \Delta y/\sigma, \quad \sigma > 0. \tag{56}$$

In addition, total investment is now assumed to require *imported capital goods*, in quantity J_K:

$$J_K = \delta I, \quad 0 < \delta < 1. \tag{57}$$

Let X be total exports of goods and nonfactor services, J total imports of goods and nonfactor services, and let X_N be the level of exports net of other (noncapital) imports, that is,

$$X_N = X - (J - J_K).$$

Define ΔF_N as net capital inflows, ΔF, minus changes in foreign exchange reserves (previously denoted ΔR), and let O_S be net factor services to the rest of the world (namely, external debt service and other transfers). The standard balance-of-payments identity, given by

$$\Delta R = (X - J) - O_S + \Delta F, \tag{58}$$

can thus be written as

$$\Delta F_N - O_S + (X_N - J_K) = 0.$$

This equation yields, together with Equation (57):

$$I = (X_N + H)/\delta, \tag{59}$$

where $H = \Delta F_N - O_S$.

Suppose that other (noncapital) imports are invariant to the level of domestic income, and that X_N is subject to an upper bound $\tilde{X}_N$, determined by external demand. Equation (59) implies therefore a *foreign exchange constraint* on investment, given by

$$I \leq (\tilde{X}_N + H)/\delta. \tag{60}$$

Equations (56) and (60) imply therefore a constraint on growth as well.

To derive the second gap, consider now the basic saving-investment balance, as derived in Chapter 1:

$$I = (y - C^p) + (T - G) + (J - X),$$

where C^p denotes private expenditure, T government tax revenue, and G public expenditure. Using Equation (58), this equation can be rewritten as

$$I = (y - C^p) + (T - G) + H. \tag{61}$$

Defining private saving as $S^p = y - C^p$, Equation (61) becomes

$$I = S^p + (T - G) + H,$$

which simply decomposes the financing of investment into domestic private and public sector saving, and foreign saving (see Chapter 1).

Suppose, for simplicity, that private consumption is exogenous.[19] Because, as noted earlier, the constraint on investment (60) implies an upper-bound constraint on output, $\tilde{y}$, S^p (being an increasing function of output) is also bounded from above by $\tilde{S}^p = \tilde{y} - C^p$. Thus, investment may also be subject to a **saving constraint**, given by

$$I \le \tilde{S}^p + (T - G) + H. \tag{62}$$

Suppose now that money is the only asset available as a store of value to private agents; all foreign capital inflows serve to finance the government's budget deficit. The private sector's budget constraint can thus be written as

$$S^p - I^p = \Delta M / P, \tag{63}$$

where I^p denotes private investment, M the nominal stock of base money, and P the price level. Assuming constant real money balances, $\Delta M / P$ measures both seigniorage and the inflation tax (see Chapter 3). Revenue from this tax is written as a function of the inflation rate, $\pi \equiv \Delta P / P$, and the **propensity to hoard**, θ, which can be defined as the proportion of any increase in income allocated to the accumulation of cash balances:

$$\Delta M / P = h(\pi, \theta), \quad \theta > 0, \ h_\theta > 0. \tag{64}$$

Because, as noted earlier, all foreign capital flows accrue to the government, the budget constraint of the consolidated public sector can be written as

$$I^g = h(\pi, \theta) + (T - G) + H, \tag{65}$$

where I^g is public investment. Total investment is thus

$$I = I^p + I^g. \tag{66}$$

Suppose that private and public investment are *complements*, so that private investment is bounded from above by the level of public investment:

$$I^p \le \phi I^g, \tag{67}$$

where ϕ is the ratio of private to public capital in the composite capital stock. As discussed in Chapter 2, this assumption is particularly relevant empirically in cases where public investment is directly at increasing public capital in infrastructure.

---

[19] It is straightforward to extend the analysis to consider the case where, as in the Keynesian specification discussed in Chapter 2, consumption is a linear function of disposable income.

From Equations (65) to (67), the **fiscal constraint** on total investment is thus given by

$$I \leq (1 + \phi)[h(\pi, \theta) + (T - G) + H]. \tag{68}$$

Equations (60), (62), and (68) are the three constraints that may determine investment. To illustrate the mechanisms at play, a useful first step is to analyze the effects of a change in the level of foreign financing, H, in the presence of the foreign exchange and saving constraints only.

Figure 9.5 plots aggregate investment, I, against H. The foreign exchange and saving constraints, Equations (60) and (62), are plotted as curves FF and SS, respectively. The slope of SS is unity, whereas the slope of FF is $1/\delta$. The latter is greater than unity, because δ is a fraction.[20] The hatched areas beneath the curves represent the feasible regions for I, that is, the values of I that satisfy the inequalities in (60) and (62). Three cases can be considered.

- If net foreign inflows H are equal to H^*, both constraints are binding and investment is equal to I^*.

- If H is less than H^*, only the foreign exchange constraint binds. Investment (and therefore the change in output) is determined by foreign exchange availability. Because investment will therefore be less than the level that would satisfy Equation (62) as an equality, and because the other components of aggregate demand are fixed, the economy will suffer from *excess capacity* and actual output will be given by

$$y = C^p + G + (1 - \delta)I^c + \tilde{X}_N, \tag{69}$$

  where I^c is the actual, constrained level of investment.

- If H exceeds H^*, the economy will be constrained by domestic saving. Investment will now be determined along SS, and output will be at full capacity, $\tilde{y}$. The actual value of adjusted exports, X_N, will thus be less than their maximum value $\tilde{X}_N$, given by foreign demand; domestic demand, in a sense, "squeezes" exports to

$$X_N = \tilde{y} - C^p - G + (1 - \delta)I^c, \tag{70}$$

  where I^c denotes now the saving-constrained level of investment.

---

[20] The relative position of the two curves in the figure assumes that $\tilde{X}_N/\delta < \tilde{S}^p + (T - G)$.

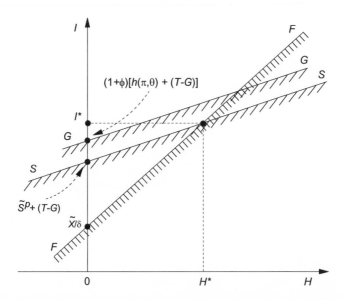

Figure 9.5. The three-gap model. Source: Adapted from Bacha (1990, p. 291).

The foregoing discussion is essentially similar to the previous discussion of the two-gap mode of the RMSM model. Graphically, adding the fiscal gap leads to the following modifications to Figure 9.5.

- Inequality (68) is represented by an area bounded from above by a curve called GG, with slope $1+\phi$ and vertical intercept $(1+\phi)[h(\pi, \theta)+(T-G)]$. The quantity $1+\phi$ may be greater or less than $1/\delta$, so GG may be steeper or flatter than FF; the case illustrated in the figure assumes that $1/\delta > 1+\phi$ and FF is steeper than GG.

- Curves GG and SS have the same slope. However, their relative heights depend on the values of π and ϕ. As long as I^p is positive, the private sector budget constraint, Equation (63), implies that

$$\tilde{S}^p > h(\pi, \theta).$$

- However, the difference between $\tilde{S}^p$ and $h(\pi, \theta)$ decreases with π. Thus, a larger value of π raises the height of GG relative to SS. A larger value of ϕ has a similar effect.

The fiscal constraint can be incorporated in the foregoing analysis in a variety of ways. Two possibilities are the following:

- Treat inflation as an *endogenous* variable, whose role is to ensure that Equation (68) holds as an equality. In this simple case, the fiscal constraint serves only to determine the rate of inflation. Given the value of I,

Equations (66) and (67)—the latter holding as an equality—would determine the levels of I^p and I^g, and, given the latter, Equation (68) holding as an equality would determine π.[21]

- Treat inflation as an *exogenous* policy variable, so that GG serves as an independent constraint.

In this mode, two cases must be considered. If the fiscal constraint does not bind, then ϕ becomes the slack variable. Given I and I^g, private investment I^p is then determined residually, and the constrained value of ϕ implied by I^p and I^g, ϕ_c, may be smaller than the initial value of ϕ. If the fiscal constraint *does* bind, then a rise in H will increase capacity growth, because increased foreign financing will result in higher public investment, which, in turn, will induce more private investment outlays. The actual level of output will rise, through a positive demand effect stemming from higher levels of both private and public investment—bringing the economy closer to full capacity utilization, at a lower level of net exports.

An important lesson of the three-gap model is that a country may face a fiscal constraint independently of its overall saving constraint. However, the model remains subject to a number of limitations. Some of the main variables are only partially endogenized; inflation, for instance, depends on a host of factors in addition to public finance considerations (see Chapter 6). The government budget constraint does not account for the possibility of bond financing—an option, again, that has become available to a number of governments in middle-income developing countries. It also does not account for movements in relative prices.

9.6   The 1-2-3 Model

The 1-2-3 model, developed at the World Bank by Devarajan et al. (1997), captures some of the main features of more complex, highly disaggregated **computable general equilibrium (CGE) models**. CGE models are typically highly disaggregated models (on both the demand and the supply side) designed to study issues such as the allocational and distributional effects of domestic and external shocks (see Bandara, 1991). On the demand side, for instance, they typically consider several types of households, depending on their ownership of production factors. Relative price movements play a central role in CGE models, although price adjustment is not always Walrasian in nature; that is, prices do not always adjust to clear markets instantaneously. Price rigidities, as well as binding wage constraints (in the form of minimum wage rules, for instance) are, in fact, common in CGE models.

---

[21] Graphically, the introduction of the fiscal constraint would entail a shift in the GG curve (brought about by changes in π) to intersect whichever of the two other curves happens to be binding at a point directly above the actual value of $(\Delta F - H)$. An increase in $(\Delta F - H)$ would in this case not only serve to increase the change in capacity output by raising I (as in the two-gap approach), but would also reduce inflation by allowing external financing of the fiscal deficit and reducing reliance on seigniorage.

Although mostly microeconomic in nature, real CGE models (that is, models in which the financial side is suppressed) also have a macroeconomic dimension due to the identity that relates aggregate saving and investment (see Chapter 1). The mechanism that ensures that this identity holds *ex post* is defined as a **closure rule**. As discussed by Dewatripont and Michel (1987), three types of closure rules are commonly used in the CGE literature:

- The *classical rule*, whereby investment is endogenous and determined by aggregate saving.

- The *Keynesian rule*, whereby investment is exogenous and real wages are taken to adjust to changes in aggregate income—thereby permitting saving to equal investment. The labor market, however, may not clear and unemployment can emerge.

- The *Johansen rule*, whereby endogenous public or private consumption adjusts to ensure that total saving equals investment (which can be either exogenous or determined by a specific functional form).

In practice, the sensitivity of numerical results to the particular closure rule chosen is not always clear and may vary depending on the issue under consideration.

The first part of this section presents the simplest version of the 1-2-3 model (with no saving and no investment), and the second uses it to analyze the effects of a terms-of-trade shock. The last part extends the model to account for government activities and investment.

9.6.1 The Minimal Setup

Consider a small open economy in which two representative agents operate: a producer (or firm) and a household. The economy produces two goods: a **home good**, which is used only for final domestic consumption, and an **exportable good**, the price of which is fixed on world markets. In addition, the household consumes an **imported good** which is not produced domestically.[22] The capital stock is fixed within the time frame of the analysis. Given that the economy is assumed small, the demand for domestically produced exportables is perfectly elastic at an exogenous foreign currency price, so that the output of these goods is supply determined. For simplicity, it will be assumed that the output of exportable goods is entirely sold abroad. For the moment, it is also assumed that the economy has no access to capital markets; external equilibrium requires therefore equality between exports and imports, or a zero trade balance.

The domestic **production possibility frontier** (PPF), which defines the maximum achievable combinations of exportables and nontradables that the

---

[22] As noted in Chapter 7, a three-good structure (rather than a dependent-economy framework) is necessary to analyze the effects of shocks such as changes in the terms of trade and changes in tariffs on imports. Adding domestic production of importables is straightforward.

economy can supply, is given by

$$Y = F(Y_X, Y_N^s; \theta), \tag{71}$$

where Y denotes aggregate production, Y_X output of exportables, Y_N output of home goods, and θ a technological parameter. The quantity Y (which is the economy's net output, because no intermediate inputs are used in the production process) will be assumed to be fixed—an assumption that is tantamount to assuming full employment of all production factors. In practical implementations of the 1-2-3 model—as in many CGE models—the functional form $F(\cdot)$ is taken to be of the **constant elasticity of transformation** (CET) type:

$$Y = [\delta Y_X^\mu + (1 - \delta) Y_N^\mu]^{1/\mu}, \quad 0 < \delta < 1, \ 1 < \mu < +\infty,$$

with the parameter θ measuring the **elasticity of transformation**, given by

$$\theta = \frac{1}{\mu - 1}.$$

The *efficient ratio* of output of exportables to nontradables can then be written as a function of their relative prices:

$$Y_X / Y_N^s = h^1(P_X, P_N), \tag{72}$$

where P_N is the (domestic) price of the home good and P_X the domestic price of exportables, given by the product of the nominal exchange rate, E, and the world (foreign-currency) price of the exportable good, P_X^*:

$$P_X = E \cdot P_X^*. \tag{73}$$

The *price of aggregate output*, P_Y, is defined as a function of both P_X and P_N:[23]

$$P_Y = g^1(P_X, P_N). \tag{74}$$

The identity relating aggregate domestic output in nominal terms to output of exportables and nontradables is thus

$$P_Y Y \equiv P_X Y_X^s + P_N Y_N^s. \tag{75}$$

The household consumes both domestic and imported goods. These goods are imperfect substitutes; their combination describes a **composite good**, Q, defined by

$$Q^s = q(Y_N^d, J; \sigma), \tag{76}$$

where σ is a technological parameter.

The motivation for the product differentiation assumption implicit in (76) is the specialization problem in small open economies facing exogenous world

---

[23] Technically, the price function g^1 in Equation (74) is the cost function dual to the firm's first-order condition for profit maximization, from which Equation (72) is derived. See, for instance, Varian (1992, chaps. 5 and 6).

prices (de Melo and Robinson (1989)). By differentiating home and foreign goods, the transmission of changes in world prices on the domestic economy is dampened and drastic swings in the sectoral composition of output are avoided. This also opens the possibility of intra-industry trade, a commonly observed phenomenon. The specification adopted here is the so-called **Armington approach**, in which goods are *exogenously* differentiated by origin (see Armington, 1969). This seems most appropriate for those goods for which the scope for production is limited by a variety of factors (for instance, fruits and vegetables, constrained by climatic considerations). The market share rigidity provided by the Armington specification also serves as a proxy for nonprice considerations, which may play an important role for some goods. This specification may also be modified so that the law of one price applies in the long run (Gielen and van Leeuwen, 1998). However, the Armington approach may not be relevant for sectors where consumers do not pay attention to the origin of the products that they consume.

In numerical applications of the 1-2-3 model (again, as in many CGE models) the functional form $q(\cdot)$ is taken to be of the **constant elasticity of substitution** (CES) variety:

$$Q^s = [\phi Y_N^\rho + (1-\phi)J^\rho]^{1/\rho}, \quad 0 < \phi < 1, \ -\infty < \rho < 1,$$

with the parameter σ measuring the elasticity of substitution, given by

$$\sigma = \frac{1}{1-\rho}.$$

Assuming that utility is linear in Q, and that the household maximizes its utility yields the *desired ratio* of home goods and imported goods as a function of relative prices:

$$J/Y_N^d = h^2(P_J, P_N), \tag{77}$$

where P_J is the domestic price of imported goods, given by the product of the nominal exchange rate, E, and the world (foreign-currency) price of these goods, P_J^*:

$$P_J = E \cdot P_J^*. \tag{78}$$

The price of the composite good is given by[24]

$$P_Q = g^2(P_J, P_N). \tag{79}$$

The identity relating aggregate supply of the composite good to imports and demand for nontradables is thus

$$P_Q Q^s \equiv P_J J + P_N Y_N^d. \tag{80}$$

The household's total income in nominal terms, V, is given by

$$V = P_Y Y. \tag{81}$$

---

[24] Again, the price index defined by Equation (79) can be interpreted as the cost function dual to the first-order condition for utility maximization, from which Equation (77) is derived.

Assuming that all income is spent on the composite good yields the household's demand for this good as

$$Q^d = V/P_Q = P_Y Y/P_Q. \tag{82}$$

This equation can be written in the form of an identity:

$$V \equiv P_Q Q^d, \tag{83}$$

which simply indicates that total purchases of composite goods by the household must be equal (in fact, identical) to the value of expenditure on these goods.

In the above system, Equations (71) and (76) are **linearly homogeneous** (that is, homogeneous of degree one): doubling, for instance, the quantities of exportables and nontradables produced would double aggregate output. The price equations (74) and (79) are also linearly homogeneous. By contrast, Equations (72), (77), and (82) are **homogeneous of degree zero** in all prices (including the exchange rate). Thus only *relative prices* affect the demand for composite goods, the exportables-to-nontradables output ratio, and the home goods-and-imports expenditure ratio.

To close the model requires specifying the *equilibrium conditions* between supply and demand.

- The first condition is the equality between *demand and supply of nontradables*:

$$Y_N^s = Y_N^d. \tag{84}$$

- The second condition requires equality between *demand and supply of composite goods*:

$$Q^s = Q^d. \tag{85}$$

- Finally, because the economy cannot borrow on world capital markets, the third condition requires that *trade be balanced*, that is,

$$P_J^* J - P_X^* Y_X = 0. \tag{86}$$

These three constraints, however, are not independent, as implied by **Walras' law**. The reason is that the model must satisfy three identities: Equations (75), (80), and (83). Multiplying both sides of Equation (84) by P_N, both sides of (85) by P_Q, and both sides of (86) by E yields, adding all three equilibrium conditions,

$$P_N(Y_N^s - Y_N^d) + P_Q(Q^s - Q^d) + P_J J - P_X Y_X = 0,$$

which shows that, as long as, say, the equilibrium conditions (84) and (85) for instance are satisfied, condition (86) will also be satisfied.

The model is summarized in Table 9.5. As indicated earlier, only relative prices affect demand for composite goods and the ratios Y_X/Y_N^s and J/Y_N^d. A **numéraire price** (that is, a *unit of account*) must thus be defined. A conventional choice is to assume that it is the price of foreign exchange, $E = 1$. It is also convenient to normalize world prices to unity, so that $P_X^* = P_J^* = 1$.

Table 9.5. The Minimal 1-2-3 Model

Equation	Definition
	Flows
$Y = F(Y_X, Y_N^s; \theta)$	Production possibility frontier
$Y_X/Y_N^s = h^1(P_X, P_N)$	Allocation of production resources
$Q^s = q(Y_N^d, J; \sigma)$	Composite good
$J/Y_N^d = h^2(P_J, P_N)$	Allocation of demand
	between home and imported goods
	Prices
$P_X = EP_X^*$	Domestic price of exports
$P_Y = g^1(P_X, P_N)$	Output deflator
$P_J = EP_J^*$	Domestic price of imports
$P_Q = g^2(P_J, P_N)$	Cost-of-living index
	Equilibrium conditions
$Y_N^s = Y_N^d$	Market for home goods
$Q^s = Q^d$	Supply and demand of composite good
$P_J^* J - P_X^* X = 0$	Balanced trade
	Identities
$P_Y Y \equiv P_X X + P_N Y_N^s$	Value of output of domestic goods
$P_Q Q^s \equiv P_Z Z + P_N Y_N^d$	Value of composite goods
$V \equiv P_Q Q^d$	Sales and purchases of composite goods

Source: Adapted from Devarajan et al. (1997, p. 159).

The equilibrium of the model is illustrated in Figure 9.6. The PPF, as given by Equation (71), is shown in the Southeast quadrant.

For any given price ratio P_N/P_X, the point of tangency between that ratio and the transformation frontier determines the allocation of total resources between production of exportables and production of nontradables (point A). The balance of trade constraint, which requires equality between exports and imports $(J - Y_X = 0)$ is shown as the 45-degree line in the Northeast quadrant.

Given the level of output of exportables determined at point A, the level of imports is determined at point B. The **consumption possibility frontier** (CPF), which shows the combinations of the domestic and imported goods that the household can purchase (given the production technology, as reflected in the PPF and the foreign exchange constraint), is depicted in the Northwest quadrant. Because foreign trade is balanced, the CPF is simply the mirror image of the PPF. The composite quantity Q defined by Equation (76) can be referred to as **domestic absorption**. For varying values of imports and demand for nontradables, it is depicted in the Northwest quadrant as an **isoabsorption curve**, which is similar to a conventional, convex utility curve in a two-good space. Maximizing the level of absorption requires tangency between an isoabsorption curve and the CPF; the tangency point, C, determines the optimal allocation of imports and nontradables demanded by the household, given the price ratio P_N/P_J.

The case illustrated in Figure 9.6 assumes that the elasticity of substitution between imports and home goods in the composite good aggregation function,

σ, is positive and less than infinite $(0 < \sigma < \infty)$. With $\sigma \to 0$, the indifference curves in the Northwest quadrant would be L-shaped; by contrast, with $\sigma \to \infty$, the indifference curves would be almost flat. Distinguishing the three cases is important in assessing the general equilibrium effects of policy and exogenous shocks.

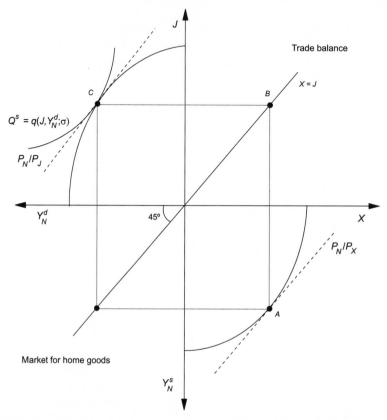

Figure 9.6. Equilibrium in the 1-2-3 model. Source: Adapted from Devarajan et al. (1997, p. 164).

9.6.2 An Adverse Terms-of-Trade Shock

To illustrate the functioning of the simple version of the 1-2-3 model, suppose that there is an adverse terms-of-trade shock, captured by an increase in the world price of the imported good, P_J^*. The results are illustrated in Figure 9.7, in the general case in which $0 < \sigma < \infty$. At the initial level of P_N/P_X, output of exportables does not change; however, the increase in P_J^* implies that the country must reduce the quantity of goods imported, because they are now more expensive. Graphically, the line capturing the balanced trade constraint in the Northeast panel rotates clockwise, that is, its slope becomes less steep. Balanced trade now occurs at B'. At the same time, the fall in the relative price of home goods, P_N/P_J, leads to an inward rotation of the CPF, as shown in the Northwest quadrant. The new equilibrium consumption point, C', is obtained at a lower level of utility. Consumption of both home and imported goods falls. The equality between demand and supply of home goods (as shown in the Southwest quadrant) implies that the equilibrium allocation of resources on the supply side is now at A'. Because the value of imports rises (the increase in import prices is proportionally higher than the fall in the volume of imports), exports must increase to maintain trade balance equilibrium. The increase in output of exportables is brought about through an increase in the relative price of these goods, which shifts incentives away from the production of nontradables. Thus, the *real exchange rate* (defined either as P_X/P_N or as a weighted average of P_X and P_J over P_N) must *depreciate* in the case illustrated in Figure 9.7.

In general, however, whether the real exchange rate depreciates or not in response to an adverse shock in the terms of trade depends crucially on the value of the elasticity of substitution between imports and home goods, σ.[25]

- If $\sigma \to 0$, so that (as indicated earlier) the isoabsorption curves are L-shaped, both production and consumption of home goods will fall, and the real exchange rate will *depreciate*, as in Figure 9.7.

- If $\sigma \to \infty$, the isoabsorption curves are flat; the tangency point between one of these curves and the new CPF will necessarily occur to the left of the initial equilibrium consumption point, C. This is because, as shown in Figure 9.7, the rotation flattens the CPF curve. The demand for home goods therefore increases; output of home goods rises and the real exchange rate *appreciates*.

The effect of the shock on the real exchange rate depends also on whether σ is less than, greater than, or equal to 1. The reason is that the increase in the price of imports generates two types of effects, as standard microeconomic analysis would predict (see Varian, 1992): an **income effect**, which captures the reduction in the household's real income, and a **substitution effect**, which results from the fact that domestically produced goods have now become relatively cheaper. The resulting equilibrium will depend on which effect dominates.

- If $\sigma < 1$ (that is, there is relatively low substitutability between imports and home goods) the income effect dominates. The equilibrium response is a reduction in output of nontradables and an increase in output of exportables, which is brought about by a real depreciation.

- If $\sigma > 1$, substitutability between imports and home goods is relatively high; the substitution effect dominates. The equilibrium response is to reduce output of exportables (and therefore also imports) and increase output of nontradables. In that case, the real exchange rate appreciates.

---

[25] A formal algebraic analysis of the relationship between the response of the economy to a terms-of-trade shock and the elasticity of substitution in the 1-2-3 model is provided by Devarajan, Lewis, and Robinson (1993).

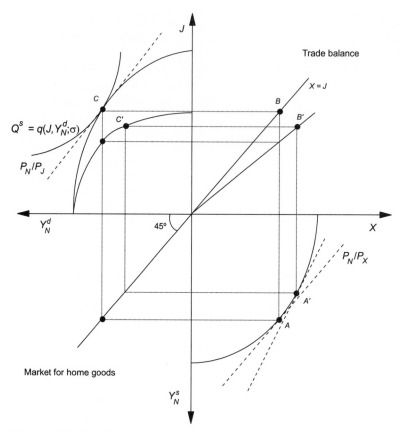

Figure 9.7. An adverse terms-of-trade shock in the 1-2-3 model. Source: Adapted from Devarajan et al. (1997, p. 167).

- If $\sigma = 1$, there is no change in either the real exchange rate or the allocation of productive resources in the economy.

9.6.3 Investment, Saving, and the Government

The minimal version of the 1-2-3 model described earlier can be extended in various directions. Two of these extensions are now considered: the introduction of a government sector (with both taxes and expenditure) and investment.[26] The first extension is important to analyze the effect of fiscal policy measures on relative prices and resource allocation, whereas the second is important to integrate the saving-investment balance.

The PPF remains as defined earlier in Equation (71), with the allocation of resources given as in (72). The domestic price of exports and the output

---

[26] Other extensions to the static 1-2-3 framework are discussed by Devarajan, Lewis, and Robinson (1990). A dynamic formulation of the model is presented by Devarajan and Go (1998).

deflator are also given by Equations (73) and (74), respectively. The identity relating aggregate domestic output in nominal terms to output of exportables and nontradables is again given by Equation (75).

The composite good is defined as before by Equation (76), with the desired ratio of home goods and imports given as a function of relative prices [Equation (77)]. However, because the government is now assumed to impose a tariff on imported goods at the rate $0 < \iota_J < 1$, the domestic price of imported goods, P_J, is now determined by

$$P_J = (1 + \iota_J)E \cdot P_J^*. \tag{87}$$

Although the price of the composite good remains given by Equation (79), the market price of the good (or the *cost-of-living index*), P_S, is now different from P_Q because the government levies a tax, at the rate $0 < \iota_S < 1$, on domestic sales. Thus

$$P_S = (1 + \iota_S)P_Q. \tag{88}$$

The accounting identity relating domestic sales and purchases of goods is now determined by, instead of Equation (80),

$$P_Q Q^s \equiv P_J J + P_S Y_N^d. \tag{89}$$

The household's total income in nominal terms, V, is now given by

$$V = P_Y Y + P_Q NT_g^h + E \cdot NT_f^h, \tag{90}$$

where NT_g^h are *net transfers* from the government, and NT_f^h net transfers from abroad, measured in foreign-currency terms. It is now assumed that only a fraction of the household's income is spent on the composite good, specifically,

$$P_S Q_h^d = (1 - s_h - \iota_V)V, \tag{91}$$

where s_h is the household's saving rate, and $0 < \iota_V < 1$ the (direct) tax rate on income. Note also that expenditure is now valued at the sales price, P_S. Assuming that the government consumes a quantity G of composite goods, and that investment requires a quantity I of composite goods, total demand for the composite good is now written as

$$Q^d = Q_h^d + I + G. \tag{92}$$

Consider now the government sector. Total government revenue, T, consists of both direct and indirect tax revenue and is given by

$$T = \iota_J E P_J^* J + \iota_S P_Q Q^d + \iota_V V. \tag{93}$$

Government spending consists of purchases of composite goods, $P_Q G$, and transfers to households, $P_Q NT_g^h$. Government saving, S^g, is thus given by the difference between revenue and expenditure:

$$S^g = T - P_Q G - P_Q NT_g^h. \tag{94}$$

Aggregate saving, S, is therefore given by

$$S = s_h V + S^g. \tag{95}$$

To close the model requires again specifying the market-clearing conditions. Equations (84) and (85), with Q^d defined as in Equation (76), remain identical. Because of the existence of private transfers from abroad, the external balance condition, Equation (86), now takes the form

$$P_J^* J - P_X^* X - NT_f^h = 0. \tag{96}$$

There is an additional condition now, which is the equality between aggregate investment and saving:

$$P_S I = S. \tag{97}$$

It can be verified that the four equilibrium conditions, (84), (85), (96), and (97), are not independent, given the identities that the model satisfies— Equations (75), (89), and (92).

The extended model, assuming again that the nominal exchange rate is used as numéraire, is summarized in Table 9.6. The government, in this setup, possesses three tax instruments: the import tariff rate, ι_J, the (indirect) tax rate on domestic sales, ι_S, and the (direct) tax rate on income, ι_V. In the present setting aggregate output is fixed, and foreign saving is fixed. Thus, aggregate saving is given, and *investment adjusts to savings*. The closure rule is thus *classical* in nature, as noted earlier. The model possesses 19 endogenous variables. By **Walras' law**, as previously discussed, one of the equations [for instance the savings-investment identity, Equation (97)] can be dropped from the system, as it is implied by the others.

Despite its simplicity, the 1-2-3 model (in both its minimal and its extended forms) is an informative setup for analyzing a variety of policy issues of crucial importance to policymakers in developing countries. In particular, it is a useful device to understand and quantify the effects of changes in fiscal policy instruments (such as a domestic indirect taxes), trade policy instruments (such as a reduction in tariffs, compensated by an increase in the sales tax to maintain the government's budget balance), as well as external shocks (as illustrated earlier), on relative prices and resource allocation in the medium term. However, the model is static in nature and because changes in *productive capacity* are not accounted for, it cannot adequately address longer-term issues related to growth and capital accumulation. The static structure also makes it inappropriate to understand the transitional dynamics of policy shocks and the potential trade-offs between short- and longer-term effects.

Another limitation of the 1-2-3 model is that it focuses only on the real side of the economy. In recent years, much effort has gone into strengthening the macroeconomic dimension of CGE models. A good example is the **Maquette**, developed by Bourguignon, De Melo, and Suwa (1991), and described as a *micro-macro framework* that attempts to combine the long-run features of CGE models, which are essential for the analysis of the allocational and distributional effects of adjustment policies (such as trade and tax policies), and the short-run features of macroeconomic models—namely a detailed financial side. Specifically, the Maquette attempts to capture the short-run effects through which stabilization policies affect the distribution of income and wealth, and to link them with the effect of structural adjustment measures that alter relative prices. There are a number of methodological issues associated with the introduction of financial variables in CGE models, and some of these are not yet fully resolved.[27] ·A more recent approach to this issue, which emphasizes the role of net worth on the risk premium that firms face on capital markets— along the lines of the **financial accelerator** mechanism discussed in Chapter 4—is developed in Agénor, Izquierdo, and Fofack (2003) in the context of the **Integrated Macroeconomic Model for Poverty Analysis** (IMMPA).

Table 9.6. The 1-2-3 model with a government sector

Equation	Definition
	Flows
$Y = F(Y_X, Y_N^s; \theta)$	Production possibility frontier
$Y_X/Y_N^s = h^1(P_X, P_N)$	Allocation of production resources
$Q^s = q(Y_N^d, J; \sigma)$	Composite good
$J/Y_N^d = h^2(P_J, P_N)$	Allocation of demand
	between home and imported goods
	Prices
$P_X = EP_X^*$	Domestic price of exports
$P_Y = g^1(P_X, P_N)$	Output deflator
$P_J = (1 + \iota_J)EP_J^*$	Domestic price of imports
$P_Q = g^2(P_Z, P_N)$	Price of the composite good
$P_S = (1 + \iota_S)P_Q$	Sales price of the composite good
	Equilibrium conditions
$Y_N^s = Y_N^d$	Market for home goods
$Q^s = Q^d$	Supply and demand of composite goods
$P_J^*J - P_X^*X - NT_f^h = 0$	Balanced trade
$P_S I = S$	Savings-investment balance
	Identities
$P_Y Y \equiv P_X X + P_N Y_N^s$	Value of output of domestic goods
$P_Q Q^s \equiv P_J J + P_S Y_N^d$	Value of composite goods

Source: Adapted from Devarajan et al. (1997, p. 172).

9.7 Lags and the Adjustment Process

As noted earlier, accounting for lags can be critical for establishing short-term projections. From a policy perspective, it is convenient to distinguish between two types of lags:

- **Inside lags**, which refer to the legal and institutional delays involved in implementing a change in policy;

---

[27]See Robinson (1991) and Adam and Bevan (1998) for a discussion of some of these issues.

- **Outside lags**, which relate to the delay involved between implementation of a policy and its effects on the target variables.

Empirical studies suggest that structural policies often involve relatively long lags of both types relative to short-term macroeconomic policies, with outside lags being typically much longer. Among the latter group of policies, there are also significant differences; monetary policy is usually considered to encompass relatively short inside lags and relatively long outside lags (see Chapter 4). A change in *domestic credit*, for instance, may take a substantial amount of time to affect the ultimate target variables—aggregate demand, inflation, and the current account. Changes in the *nominal exchange rate* often have a rather rapid impact on prices (because, for instance, domestic prices are set as a markup over the cost of domestic and imported inputs) but they usually take time (up to 18 months) to affect trade flows and the trade balance. By contrast, *fiscal policies* are often characterized by relatively long inside lags and relatively short outside lags.

Accounting for lags in the adjustment process to policy and exogenous shocks is important in practice, particularly when projections are required at a relatively short horizon—say, on a quarterly basis. Lags can generate complex dynamics; the way they are introduced in the model may thus have a significant effect on the formulation and validity of macroeconomic projections. Unfortunately, such lags are often difficult to estimate with any degree of precision—thereby complicating policy responses and the timing of policy measures. Moreover, lags may be to some extent *endogenous*; they are often affected by private agents' expectations about the sustainability of the various policies. A policy that is perceived to be *highly credible* (that is, with a low probability of reversal) may exert its effect on the target variable relatively quickly, compared with the average historical lag.

Another source of endogeneity in lags is the fact that the behavioral functions themselves may change over time. In particular, behavioral functions are often difficult to estimate in the context of a country undergoing a comprehensive reform program or large shifts in policy. Money demand functions, for instance, are notoriously difficult to estimate in an environment of financial liberalization. In such a context, the use of relatively sophisticated econometric techniques (such as the **error correction framework** described in the appendix to this chapter) may not be enough to detect stable relationships. This instability in behavioral parameters will make the timing of policy effects even more difficult to establish and may make the lag between changes in policy instruments and the economy's response more uncertain.

9.8 Summary

- Analyzing macroeconomic fluctuations is useful to specify applied macroeconomic models, to assess the *type of shocks* that have dominated fluctuations over a particular period of time, and to assess the likely effect (given the pattern of *leads* and *lags*) between changes in policy instruments and domestic output.

- A simple procedure is first to use the **Hodrick-Prescott (HP) filter** to extract the trend component of each series. The two main hypotheses underlying the HP decomposition are that the trend is *stochastic* but moves slowly over time, and that the *secular* and *cyclical components* are *independent*. Other filtering techniques, such as the **band pass filter**, can also be used for checking robustness.

- **Financial programming**, based on the **Polak model** and its extensions, remains at the core of macroeconomic policy exercises conducted by the International Monetary Fund. The extended model endogenizes prices but continues to take real output as given.

- The World Bank's **RMSM** model makes explicit the link between medium-term growth and its financing. It is a real model that takes prices as given and highlights the interplay between the domestic **saving constraint** and the **foreign exchange constraint**.

- The **merged IMF-World Bank** model endogenizes both real output and prices. It forms the analytical basis of the **RMSM-X** model, currently used by the World Bank for its macroeconomic projections. The model remains, however, subject to a number of limitations, related in particular to a rudimentary supply side, an inadequate financial structure, and mechanical behavioral rules.

- **Three-gap models** extend the two-gap approach of the RMSM model to include the **fiscal constraint**. However, they are also subject to limitations due, in particular, to the absence of relative price effects.

- The **1-2-3 model**, also developed at the World Bank, is a simple, static, computable general equilibrium model with two production sectors and three goods. It provides a useful and tractable framework for the analysis of the medium-term effects of external shocks and policies such as tariff and tax reforms on relative prices and the allocation of resources. However, its static nature prevents it from addressing issues related to growth and capital accumulation, as well as the transitional dynamics of policy shocks.

- Macroeconomic policies operate with lags that can be fairly long, although short-run policies are deemed to have a more rapid impact than, say, supply-side measures. Long policy lags may be partly related to private agents' expectations about the perceived sustainability of the policy measures—the higher the probability of policy reversal, the more delayed the response. Accounting for these lags in operational exercises is important.

Appendix to Chapter 9
Money Demand and Cointegration

Behavioral equations derived from economic models are often **long-run equilibrium** relationships. To determine if these relationships hold in practice, economists have in recent years increasingly relied on **cointegration tests**.[28]

The main idea behind cointegration is a specification of models that include beliefs about the movements of variables relative to each other in the long run, such as the money demand function discussed in Chapter 4. Intuitively, cointegration requires that, for a long-run equilibrium relationship between different **nonstationary** variables to exist, these variables should not move too far away from each other.[29] Individually these variables might drift apart in the short run, but in the long run they are constrained. More formally, two or more nonstationary time series are cointegrated if a linear combination of these variables is stationary, that is, converges to an equilibrium over time. Thus, if the money demand function describes a stationary long-run relationship among real money balances, m_t, a transactions variable (real income), y_t, and the opportunity cost of holding money (say, the domestic interest rate), i_t,

$$m_t = m(y_t, i_t), \tag{A1}$$

it can be interpreted to mean that the stochastic trend in real money balances is related to the stochastic trends in real income and interest rates. In other words, if these variables are cointegrated they will be constrained to an equilibrium relationship in the long run. Deviations from the long-run equilibrium may occur in the short run, but they are **mean reverting**.

In practical terms, there are three steps involved in this methodology.

- Show that all the variables appearing in Equation (A1) are nonstationary. A common test is the **Augmented Dickey-Fuller (ADF) test**.

- Show that a linear combination between these (nonstationary) variables is stationary. This can be done by determining whether the residual term of the second-step regression is stationary, using also an ADF test.

- After confirming that Equation (A1) represents a cointegrating (long-run) relationship, study the short-run dynamics of the relationship by specifying an **error-correction (EC) model**, which takes the form:

$$\Delta m_t^d = \alpha_0 + \sum_{h=0}^{n_1} \alpha_{1h} \Delta y_{t-h} + \sum_{h=0}^{n_2} \alpha_{2h} \Delta i_{t-h} + \sum_{h=1}^{n_3} \beta_h \Delta m_{t-h} - \gamma ec_{t-1}.$$

---

[28] See, for instance, Greene (2000) for a detailed treatment of the cointegration methods discussed in this appendix.

[29] A process is stationary if it fluctuates around a constant mean and its variance does not depend on time. More formally, let x_t, for $t = 1, ..., T$, denote a stochastic process; x_t is (weakly) stationary if its mean is independent of t, its variance is constant and independent of t, and its covariance $\text{Cov}(x_t, x_s)$ is a function of $t - s$ but not of t or s. If any of these conditions are violated, x_t is nonstationary.

This specification relates a change in real money balances in period t to current and lagged changes in real income, changes in interest rates, and lagged real money balances, as well as an **error-correction term** ec_{t-1} obtained as the residual from the long-run relationship (A1)—that is, the difference between the actual level of real money balances and its predicted value. This variable approximates deviations from long-run equilibrium values of real money balances and represents the *short-run response* necessary to move money demand toward its long-run equilibrium level. When the coefficient of the error-correction term, γ, is significant and positive, convergence is assured. If γ is less than unity in absolute value, the adjustment process is stable and m^d will adjust toward its long-run value. The closer γ is to unity, the faster the adjustment process will be.

A standard method for testing for the existence of a long-run relationship is the **Johansen technique**. It consists essentially of applying the **maximum likelihood principle** to determine the presence of cointegrating relationships in nonstationary time series (see Greene, 2000). Such relationships are detected and tests of hypotheses regarding elements of the cointegrating relationships can be conducted. Two different tests are provided to determine the number of cointegrating relationships, the *trace test* and the *maximum eigenvalue test*. If a nonzero vector (or vectors) is indicated by these tests, a stationary long-run relationship is implied. As noted in Chapter 4, examples of money demand studies using the Johansen technique are those of Hoffman and Tahiri (1994), Choudhry (1995), Cheong (2003), Ghartey (1998), Price (1994), Thornton (1996), Fielding (1994), and Feliz and Welch (1997).

Chapter 10

Growth, Poverty, and Inequality: Some Basic Facts

No Society can surely be flourishing and happy, of which the far greater part of the members are poor and miserable.

Adam Smith, *The Wealth of Nations*, 1776 (Book 1, Chapter 8).

After a long period of relative neglect in mainstream economics, the study of economic growth has gone through a revival since the early 1980s. A key motivation for this renewed interest is the observation that average annual growth rates (calculated over several decades) vary substantially across countries. The conventional neoclassical theory, which attributes growth to (mostly exogenous) technological progress, has proved incapable of explaining in a satisfactory manner the wide disparities in the rates of per capita output growth across countries.

This chapter and the next three provide a thorough discussion of theories and recent evidence on the determinants of economic growth. The present chapter reviews some basic empirical facts and is organized as follows. Section 10.1 reviews the evidence on economic growth for both industrial and developing countries from 1820 to the early 1990s. Section 10.2 uses simple arithmetic to illustrate the dramatic effects that small differences in growth rates can have, over time, on standards of living. Section 10.3 summarizes some of the basic facts that appear to characterize the process of economic growth in developing countries. It discusses, in particular, the links between growth, poverty, and inequality, as well as the interactions between inflation, financial development, and economic growth.

10.1   A Long-Run Perspective

Tables 10.1 and 10.2 summarize the evidence on long-run growth compiled by Maddison (1995). Table 10.1 shows that per capita growth between 1820 and 1992 was the fastest in countries that were already the most prosperous in the early nineteenth century. GDP per capita recorded a 13-fold increase in European countries such as France and Germany, and a 17-fold increase in North America. By contrast, in Latin America, real per capita income increased by only seven times between 1820 and 1992. Africa (the region with the lowest per capita income in 1820) had an average income in 1992 that was about the same as some European countries achieved in 1820. Income per capita in some of the Asian countries was actually below the average observed in Africa in 1950, but they are now well ahead. Within Asia, per capita income in Japan rose by nearly 28-fold between 1820 and 1992 (by far the largest increase ever recorded) and was in 1992 the third highest in the world.

Table 10.2 shows the average rate of growth per capita for the same group of countries shown in Table 10.1 and for the five **phases of growth** identified by Maddison (1995): 1820-70, 1870-1913, 1913-50, 1950-73, and 1973-92.[1]

- The data suggest that during the first period (1820-70) growth occurred mostly in the now-industrialized countries, at relatively low rates.

- By contrast, in the second phase (1870-1913), growth accelerated in all industrial countries (as well as in some developing regions), in part as a result of a sharp increase in international trade, factor mobility (both capital and labor), and improved communication technologies.

- The period 1913-50 was characterized by a sharp slowdown in rates of economic growth, again in almost all countries and regions—reflecting partly the disruptions of the two world wars, the collapse of world trade, and the Great Depression of the 1930s.

- The years 1950 to 1973, the so-called **golden age of prosperity**, were characterized by unprecedented increases in incomes and growth rates. During that period, world real income per capita grew by about 2.9 percent per annum, more than three times as fast as during the period 1913-50 (Maddison, 1995, p. 73). Although the acceleration in growth rates was recorded in all regions, it was particularly impressive in Asia.[2]

---

[1] These phases do not correspond to stages of development, as identified, for instance, in a classic contribution by Rostow (1960). Nor are they derived from a Kondratieff-type view of long-run fluctuations. See Maddison (1995, pp. 59-86) for a full discussion.

[2] Various factors were at play—including a large increase in physical capital, improved skill levels of the labor force, and a significant expansion of trade among the most advanced economies (which provided a strong impetus to world economic activity). Many of these factors are discussed in the next chapters.

Table 10.1. GDP per capita, in 1990 U.S. dollars

Countries	1820	1870	1900	1913	1950	1973	1992
Industrial							
Canada	893	1,620	2,758	4,213	7,047	13,644	18,159
France	1,218	1,858	2,849	3,452	5,221	12,940	17,959
Germany	1,112	1,913	3,134	3,833	4,281	13,152	19,351
Italy	1,092	1,467	1,746	2,507	3,425	10,409	16,229
Japan	704	741	1,135	1,334	1,873	11,017	19,425
United Kingdom	1,756	3,263	4,593	5,032	6,847	11,992	15,738
United States	1,287	2,457	4,096	5,307	9,573	16,607	21,558
Developing							
Argentina	—	1,311	2,756	3,797	4,987	7,970	7,616
Brazil	670	740	704	839	1,673	3,913	4,637
Chile	—	—	1,949	2,653	3,827	5,028	7,238
Colombia	—	—	973	1,236	2,089	3,539	5,025
Mexico	760	710	1,157	1,467	2,085	4,189	5,112
Peru	—	—	817	1,037	2,263	3,953	2,854
Venezuela	—	—	821	1,104	7,424	10,717	9,163
Bangladesh	531	—	581	617	551	478	720
India	531	558	625	663	597	853	1,348
Indonesia	614	657	745	917	874	1,538	2,749
Pakistan	531	—	687	729	650	981	1,642
Philippines	—	—	1,033	1,418	1,293	1,956	2,213
South Korea	—	—	850	948	876	2,840	10,010
Thailand	—	717	812	846	848	1,750	4,694
Egypt	—	—	509	508	517	947	1,927
Ethiopia	—	—	—	—	277	412	300
Ghana	—	—	462	648	1,193	1,260	1,007
Kenya	—	—	—	—	609	947	1,055
Morocco	—	—	—	—	1,611	1,651	2,327
Nigeria	—	—	—	—	547	1,120	1,152
Tanzania	—	—	—	—	427	655	601

Source: Maddison (1995, pp. 23-24).

- The last period, 1973-92, was characterized by severe disruptions to world economic activity (such as the two oil shocks of 1973 and 1979, and the developing-country debt crisis of the early 1980s) and a sharp reduction in growth rates—except in Asia.[3] In Africa, in particular, with high growth rates of population, average real per capita income fell by about 8 percent between 1973 and 1992 (Maddison, 1995, p. 78). The growth performance

---

[3] See Cline (1995) for a retrospective on the debt crisis of the early 1980s.

of most Latin American countries—several of which were characterized throughout the period by major macroeconomic imbalances, such as high inflation and large fiscal deficits—was also poor. By contrast, in Asia, per capita growth accelerated further relative to the period 1950-73, in part as a result of a reduction in the rate of population growth and large imports of capital goods (see Chapter 13).

Table 10.2. Average annual per capita real GDP growth rates

Countries	1820-70	1870-13	1913-50	1950-73	1973-92
Industrial					
Canada	1.2	2.2	1.4	2.9	1.5
France	0.8	1.5	1.1	4.0	1.7
Germany	1.1	1.6	0.3	5.0	2.1
Italy	0.6	1.3	0.8	5.0	2.4
Japan	0.1	1.4	0.9	8.0	3.0
United Kingdom	1.2	1.0	0.8	2.5	1.4
United States	1.3	1.8	1.6	2.4	1.4
Developing					
Argentina	—	2.5	0.7	2.1	-0.2
Brazil	0.2	0.3	1.9	3.8	0.9
Chile	—	—	1.0	1.2	1.9
Colombia	—	—	1.4	2.3	1.9
Mexico	-0.1	1.7	1.0	3.1	1.1
Peru	—	—	2.1	2.5	-1.7
Venezuela	—	—	5.3	1.6	-0.8
Bangladesh	—	—	-0.3	-0.6	2.2
India	0.1	0.4	-0.3	1.6	2.4
Indonesia	0.1	0.8	-0.1	2.5	3.1
Pakistan	—	—	-0.3	1.8	2.7
Philippines	—	—	-0.2	1.8	0.7
South Korea	—	—	-0.2	5.2	6.9
Thailand	—	0.4	0.0	3.2	5.3
Egypt	—	—	0.0	2.7	3.8
Ethiopia	—	—	—	1.7	-1.7
Ghana	—	—	1.7	0.2	-1.2
Kenya	—	—	—	1.9	0.6
Morocco	—	—	—	0.1	1.8
Nigeria	—	—	—	3.2	0.1
Tanzania	—	—	—	1.9	-0.5

Source: Maddison (1995, pp. 62-63).

The overall pattern suggested by Tables 10.1 and 10.2 is one of *convergence* in income per capita levels over the very long run among the group of the currently most advanced industrial countries, but also *significant divergence between rich and poor countries* over time. According to calculations made by Pritchett (1997) and based in part on Maddison's data, from 1870 to 1990, the ratio of per capita incomes between the richest and the poorest countries increased by a factor of five. The standard deviation of per capita income of rich and poor countries (a measure of dispersion in standards of living) increased from 0.51 in 1870 to 0.88 in 1960 and 1.06 in 1990.

The data also suggest that the *pace* of economic growth as well as patterns of convergence and divergence has changed considerably across periods. Most importantly, there appears to have been a *substantial catch-up* among some groups of countries since 1950. In that year, in particular, the United States had a per capita income that was about 1.7 times the per capita income in France and Germany. By 1992, the gap was substantially narrowed.

In Asia, after a long period of almost 130 years during which growth in per capita income was limited and gaps with respect to the now-industrialized countries rose substantially, a significant narrowing of income differentials occurred between 1950 and 1992. For instance, the difference in levels of income per capita between the United States and South Korea dropped from 11:1 in 1950 to about 2:1 in 1992. For Thailand, the difference (which was roughly the same as the one recorded by South Korea in 1950) dropped to about 5:1 in 1992. Thus, there is evidence within Asia of a significant catch-up—even though large differences remain across countries of the region. The 1997-98 economic and financial crisis in the region (documented in Chapter 8) had a relatively short-lived impact on standards of living.

In contrast to the experience of Asian countries such as South Korea and Thailand, the postwar evidence for African and Latin American countries shows no sign of convergence. Between 1950 and 1992, the per capita income gap vis-à-vis the United States rose for almost all of the African countries and for four out of the seven Latin American countries shown in Table 10.1. In the three cases in which the income gap narrowed, the improvement was relatively small. Thus, until the early 1990s, there were *large disparities* in patterns of growth in the developing world, both across countries and over time. For instance, during the period 1973-92, average growth rates per annum ranged from -1.7 percent in Ethiopia and Peru to 6.9 percent in South Korea.

10.2   The Power of Compounding

10.2.1   Growth and Standards of Living

The data displayed in Tables 10.1 and 10.2 are useful to understand the importance of even small differences in output growth for standards of living over a relatively long period. Consider, for instance, the United States and India. In 1992, measured in 1990 U.S. dollars, income per capita was US$21,558 in the United States, and US$1,348 in India; per capita income in India thus represented only 6.3 percent of income in the United States. Suppose that both countries experience, for the next two centuries, the same annual growth rate that they recorded on average during the period, say, 1913-92—1.8 percent for the United States, and 1.2 percent for India. Under these assumptions, in the United States, per capita income would reach US$21,558·$(1.018)^8$ = US$24,865 in the year 2000, US$60,671 in the year 2050, and US$148,036 in the year 2100. The same numbers for India would be, respectively, US$1,348·$(1.012)^8$ = US$1,483, US$2,693, and US$4,889. Thus, in proportion of U.S. per capita income, India's income per person would fall to 6.0 percent in the year 2000, 4.4 percent in the year 2050, and 3.3 percent in the year 2100.

10.2.2 How Fast Do Economies Catch Up?

Now suppose that, given the average growth rates achieved during the period 1913-92, one wants to calculate the amount of time (in years) that it would take for both countries to double their real per capita income, from the levels observed in 1992. For India, doubling income in N years requires that $y_N = 2 \cdot 1,348 = 1,348 \cdot (1.012)^N$, so that

$$2 = (1.012)^N \Rightarrow N = \ln 2/\ln(1.012) \simeq 58.1$$

For the United States, the same calculations yield $N = \ln 2/\ln(1.018) \simeq 38.9$. Thus, it would take India about 58 years and the United States about 39 years to achieve these results.

By way of comparison, suppose that both South Korea and the United States continue to grow at the average rate observed during the period 1950-92 (6.1 percent and 1.9 percent, respectively). How long would it take South Korea to reach the same level of per capita income as the United States, using 1992 as a base period? This value is obtained by solving for N in the equation

$$21,558 \cdot (1 + 0.019)^N = 10,010 \cdot (1 + 0.061)^N,$$

so that

$$N = \ln(21,558/10,010)/\ln(1.061/1.019) \simeq 18.9,$$

which indicates that it would take Korea only 19 years.

Another interesting question is the following: suppose that India's objective is to attain a per capita income that is equal to 30 percent of the level of per capita income in the United States by the year 2100. By how much should India grow per year? Let y_0^{US} (y_0^{IN}) denote per capita income in the United States (India) in the year 1992, and $g_{US} = 0.018$ and g_{IN} the average growth rate over the period 1913-92 for each country. Because it takes 108 years to reach 2100 beginning in 1992, the value of g_{IN} that is to be calculated is the solution of

$$0.3 \cdot y_0^{US}(1.018)^{108} = y_0^{IN}(1 + g_{IN})^{108},$$

so that

$$(1 + g_{IN})^{108} = C, \quad \text{with } C \equiv 0.3 \cdot y_0^{US}(1.018)^{108}/y_0^{IN},$$

or

$$\ln(1 + g_{IN}) = \ln C/108 \Rightarrow 1 + g_{IN} = e^{\ln C/108},$$

and finally $g_{IN} = e^{\ln C/108} - 1 \simeq 0.0329$.

Put differently, the target growth rate of output must be about 3.3 percent per annum—almost three times the level observed during the period 1913-92. If, instead of 3.3 percent, India grows by a slightly lower number of 3.0 percent per annum, in the year 2100 its per capita income would be only about 22 percent of the U.S. level. Thus, when compounded over fairly long periods of time, even small differences in growth rates can have dramatic effects on standards of living.

10.3   Some Basic Facts

Studies of the growth patterns of industrial and developing economies suggest a set of propositions (or *basic facts*) that can be viewed as broadly consistent with long-run trends. This section summarizes some of these facts as they relate to the growth experience of developing countries.

10.3.1   Output Growth, Population, and Fertility

The evidence on the growth rates of output, production inputs, and population across countries suggests the following basic facts.

> Fact 1. Output per worker (or average labor productivity) and income per capita tend to grow at widely different rates across countries.

> Fact 2. The rate of growth of factor inputs (capital and labor) does not fully account for the rate of growth of output.

> Fact 3. The mean growth rate of output is unrelated to the initial level of per capita income across countries.

> Fact 4. Population growth rates, and fertility rates, are negatively correlated with both the level and the rate of growth of income per capita across countries.

The first fact is directly corroborated by the evidence reviewed in the first part of this chapter and is discussed for instance by Durlauf and Quah (1999). The second empirical observation, which has been emphasized notably by Easterly and Levine (2001), will be discussed at length in Chapter 13. It has important analytical implications, because it suggests that even after appropriate adjustments are made to measure factor inputs (such as the degree of utilization of the capital stock, or quality adjustments for labor categories), other factors need to be introduced to fully explain the growth rate of output.

Fact 3 is illustrated in Figure 10.1. The horizontal axis in the figure measures the ratio of per capita income in a given country relative to that in the United States in 1970, with incomes in both countries measured in 1995 U.S. dollars.

The vertical axis measures the growth rate of per capita income during the period 1980-2001. The data cover 99 industrial and developing countries.

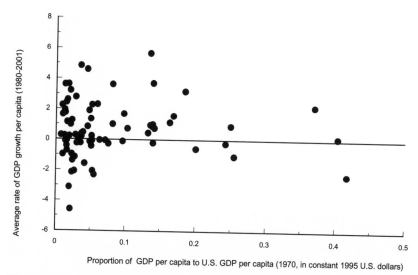

Figure 10.1. Average rate of growth per capita and proportion of GDP per capita to U.S. GDP per capita (1980-2001). Source: World Bank.

The figure suggests, indeed, that the growth rate of output appears to bear no systematic correlation with the initial level of income. Similar results are obtained when the sample period is extended to cover the 1960s (Barro and Sala-i-Martin, 1995). This is seemingly in contrast to the main prediction of the standard neoclassical model, which suggests (as discussed in the next chapter) that low-income countries should grow *faster* (at least during a transitory period of time) than rich countries.

Fact 4 is illustrated in Figures 10.2 and 10.3 for a group of industrial and developing countries. As discussed in the next chapter, the standard neoclassical model does predict a relationship between the population growth rate and the *level* of income per capita, but no relationship between the former variable and the *growth rate* of income per capita.

10.3.2   Saving, Investment, and Growth

The evidence on saving, investment, and output growth rates across countries suggests the following basic facts.

Fact 5. Saving rates are positively related to both the level and the growth rate of income per capita.

Fact 6. Both the rate of growth of investment and the share of investment in output are positively related to the rate of growth of income per capita.

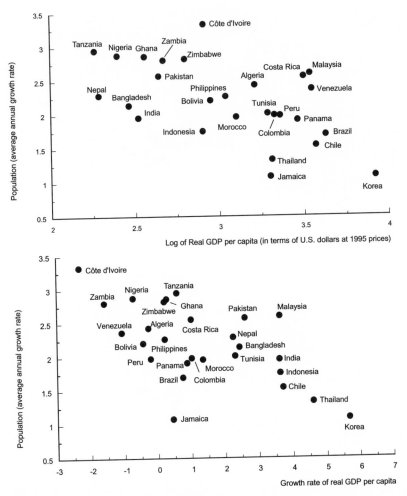

Figure 10.2. Population growth and real income per capita (averages over 1980-2001). Real GDP per capita in terms of U.S. dollars at 1995 prices. Source: World Bank.

Fact 5 captures the widely held view that saving is crucial to economic growth. Countries that have achieved high saving rates have also tended to enjoy high levels and growth rates of per capita income—although the direction of *causality* between savings and growth remains a matter of controversy (see Chapter 13).

Figure 10.4 shows cross-sectional scatter plots of domestic saving rates—measured as gross domestic savings as a fraction of GDP—against both the *level* and the *rate of growth* of per capita real income over the period 1980-2001 in a group of developing countries. The data suggest a positive association between these variables. This evidence is corroborated by a large number of studies, as discussed for instance by Schmidt-Hebbel, Servén, and Solimano (1996).

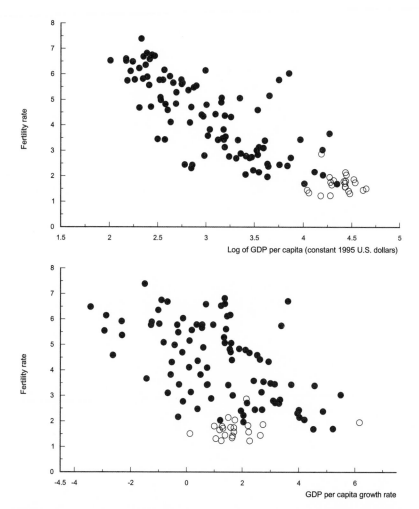

Figure 10.3. Fertility rate and income per capita (annual averages, 1990-99). Total fertility rate represents the number of children that would be born to a woman if she were to live to the end of her childbearing years and bear children in accordance with prevailing age-specific fertility rates. Source: World Bank.

The role of savings in the processs of growth and development was emphasized early on by Rostow (1960), who argued that growth tends to evolve in three stages:

- an initial period of **low savings** (5 percent of GDP or less) and slow economic growth;

- a **takeoff** period, during which the saving rate increases dramatically to more than, say, 10 percent of GDP, and perhaps to as much as 20 or 30 percent;

- a **mature** phase, marked by declining saving and growth rates.

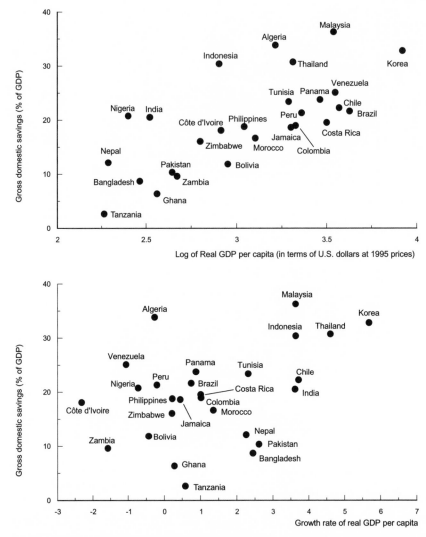

Figure 10.4. Saving rate and per capita income (averages over 1980-2001). Real GDP per capita in terms of U.S. dollars at 1995 prices. Source: World Bank.

He also emphasized that breaking out of the initial phase may be the most important step toward economic development. However, reaching the take-off point can be difficult, as a result of a **savings trap**, which was described by Ragnar Nurkse (1953, p. 5) in the early 1950s:[4]

---

[4]Various models of the savings trap have been developed in recent years. Some models emphasize the role that cultural and institutional factors may have on saving rates. Others have emphasized the idea that a low savings equilibrium may result from a lack of coordination among agents and that, in the absence of policy interventions or other exogenous shocks, such an outcome may persist over time (see Agénor, 2004d).

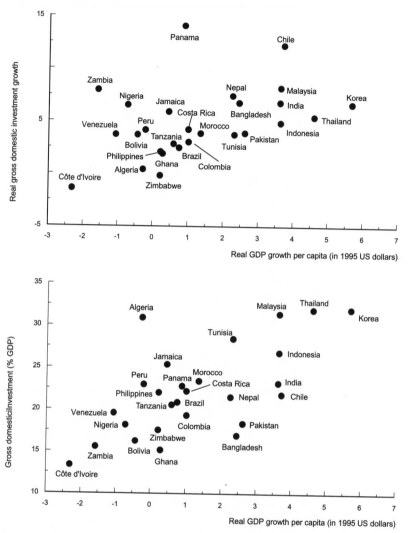

Figure 10.5. Investment growth, investment share, and growth (averages over 1980-2001). Source: World Bank.

On the supply side, there is a small capacity to save, resulting from the low level of income. The low real income is a reflection of low productivity, which in its turn is due largely to the lack of capital. A lack of capital is the result of the small capacity to save, and so the circle is complete.

Figure 10.5 displays the positive relation between the rate of growth of investment, the share of investment in output, and the rate of growth of income per capita for a group of developing countries, as summarized by Fact 6.

It is important to note that the data shown in the figure refer to the accumulation of *physical* capital; as discussed in Chapters 12 and 13, new theories of growth have suggested that the accumulation of *human* capital plays a critical role in the growth process.

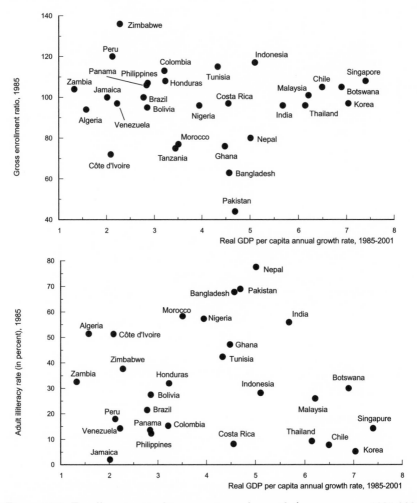

Figure 10.6. Enrollment ratio, literacy rate, and growth (averages over 1985-2001). The gross enrollment ratio is the ratio of total enrollment, regardless of age, to the population of the age group that officially corresponds to the level of education shown. The adult illiteracy rate is the proportion of adults aged 15 and above who cannot, with understanding, read and write a short, simple statement on their everyday life. Source: World Bank.

Figure 10.6 shows scatter diagrams relating the rate of growth of real income per capita and two proxies for human capital accumulation: the **gross enrollment ratio** and the **adult literacy rate**. The data do not suggest a close correlation. However, in part because of the limitations of the measures used, firm conclusions cannot be established on the basis of these figures alone.

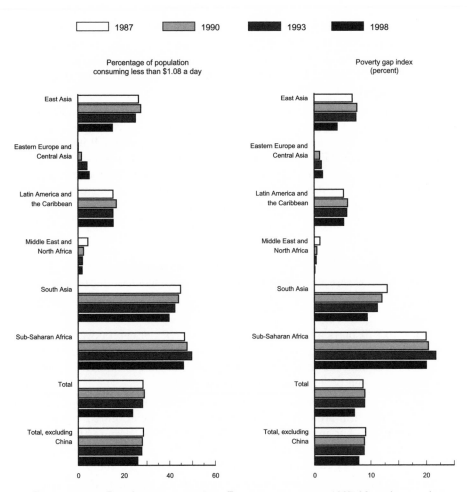

Figure 10.7. Developing countries: Poverty measures, 1987-98, using an international poverty line of $1.08 per person per day at 1993 purchasing power parity exchange rates. Source: World Bank.

10.3.3 Growth and Poverty

Economists typically use two indicators to measure poverty:[5]

- the **poverty headcount index**, which measures the proportion of individuals or households earning less than a given absolute level of income;

- the **poverty gap index**, which is the average shortfall of the income of the poor with respect to the poverty line, multiplied by the headcount index.

---

[5] See Ravallion (1994) and Lipton and Ravallion (1995) for a discussion of the limitations of these indicators.

Both types of indicators are shown in Figure 10.7, using a uniform, 1993 PPP-adjusted, US$1.08 a day line to measure poverty across countries.[6] The data suggest that the *incidence* of poverty in developing countries, as measured by the headcount index, fell significantly between 1987 and 1998 only when China is included in the sample.

Similarly, the *depth* of poverty, as measured by the average distance below the poverty line, fell only marginally when China is excluded. More generally, there were sharp differences across regions; poverty incidence fell in East Asia, South Asia, and the Middle East and North Africa, and rose in Eastern and Central Europe, Latin America, and sub-Saharan Africa. Moreover, in many countries, although poverty is becoming increasingly an urban problem, the rural poor are still poorer than the urban poor.

The evidence linking poverty and growth leads to the following observation.

> Fact 7. Maintaining sustained rates of economic growth is necessary, although not always sufficient, to ensure durable reductions in poverty.

Figure 10.8 displays average growth rates of GNP per capita over the period 1981-93 and the proportion of poor (those earning less than US$1.08 a day in both the rural and the urban sectors). The data indeed suggest a negative correlation between poverty and economic growth.[7]

It is also worth emphasizing that growth seems to have an *asymmetric effect* on poverty: in Latin America, for instance, poverty deteriorated significantly during the 1980s, but improved only little in the 1990s, despite the economic recovery and an increase in GDP per capita in the region of almost 6 percent in real terms between 1990 and 1995 (Londoño and Székely, 2000).

As shown in various empirical studies, several other factors affect poverty in addition to the rate of growth. The cross-country econometric results presented by Agénor (2002b) suggested that inflation and macroeconomic instability have a significant adverse effect on the poor. Londoño and Székely (2000) suggested that, at least in Latin America, poverty is strongly associated with a high degree of income inequality. Other important variables are access to education, health services, and employment opportunities (Lipton and Ravallion, 1995).

---

[6] Some researchers have argued that a *country-specific* poverty line should be used for cross-country comparisons, because there are significant differences in consumption patterns across countries and over time—differences that make it difficult to establish a common criterion. However, it has been shown that the elasticity of the poverty line with respect to average income appears to be very low in practice, implying that it is unlikely that changes in consumption patterns over time will significantly alter the value of country-specific poverty lines.

[7] More generally, the empirical evidence suggests that the depth of poverty, as reflected in the poverty gap index, is more responsive to growth than is the incidence of poverty (Lipton and Ravallion, 1995).

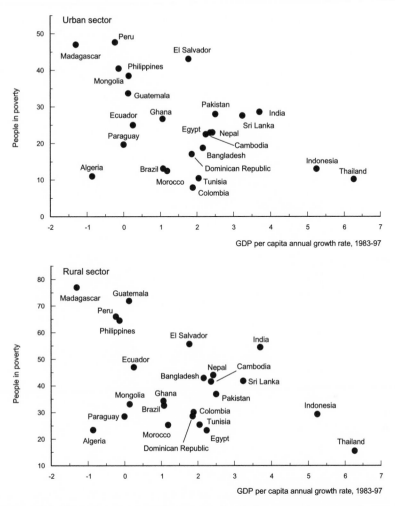

Figure 10.8. Growth and people in poverty (period average, in percent). People in poverty = proportion of the population earning US$1.08 or less, in 1993 PPP-adjusted U.S. dollars, various survey years. Source: World Bank.

10.3.4   Inequality, Growth, and Development

To measure income inequality and capture some of the most important characteristics of income distribution in a given country, economists often use three types of indicators:

- the share of the top to the bottom income deciles or quintiles, which only attaches weight to the two tails of the income distribution;

- the **Gini coefficient**; and

- the **Theil inequality index**, which can be decomposed into two terms: one that captures inequality due to differences *between groups*, and another that captures inequality *within groups*.

In practice, the Gini coefficient remains the most widely used indicator. Like the first indicator, it is derived from the **Lorenz curve**, which shows the cumulative share of total income received by cumulative shares of the population, starting from the poorest income-receiving groups. The graph of the Lorenz curve contains a reference line representing *perfect equality*, which indicates what the distribution would be if every individual received an identical income. The Gini coefficient measures the area between the actual curve for a population and the line of perfect equality; it varies between 0 (maximum equality) and unity (maximum inequality).[8]

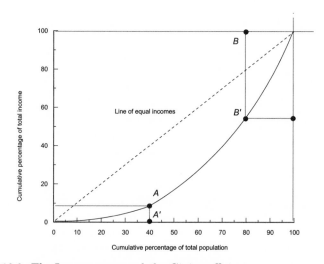

Figure 10.9. The Lorenz curve and the Gini coefficient.

Figure 10.9 shows the Lorenz curve and the Gini coefficient for a hypothetical country. The horizontal axis shows the cumulative proportion of the population (in terms of quintiles and deciles), and the vertical axis represents the proportion of total income accruing to the corresponding proportion of the population. The distance AA' in the figure measures the income share of the poorest 40 percent of the population, whereas the distance BB' measures the income share of the richest 20 percent. The more unequal the distribution of income, the greater the distance of the Lorenz curve from the diagonal, and the greater the Gini coefficient. It should be noted, however, that the Gini index may not always fully capture changes in inequality. A complementary measure, discussed in the appendix to this chapter, is the **polarization index**.

---

[8] In practice, many researchers (see, for instance, Londoño and Székely, 2000) use an approximation to obtain the arc of the Lorenz curve even when information is only available by quintiles (see Lipton and Ravallion, 1995). A popular method is the Villaseñor-Arnold procedure, which uses a quadratic equation for estimation.

The evidence on income shares for industrial countries suggests that the share of income accruing to capital (and thus labor) is approximately constant, although in some cases there appears to be a slight reduction (increase) over long periods of time (Romer, 1989). In a broader study focusing on a group of 49 industrial and developing countries over the period 1947-94, Li, Squire, and Zou (1998) found that although there is considerable variation in the degree of income inequality (as measured by the Gini coefficient) *across* countries, there is considerable stability over time *within* countries.

The Kuznets Curve

The link between growth and inequality appears to be more tenuous. Figure 10.10 shows the correlation for a group of about 30 countries between the rate of growth of income per capita and two measures of income inequality, both derived (as indicated earlier) from the Lorenz curve: the ratio of the share of the richest 20 percent to the share of the poorest 20 percent, and the Gini coefficient. The data do not suggest any clear pattern.

However, it should be recognized that Figure 10.10 focuses on a relatively short period (about 15-16 years); there are good theoretical reasons, related in particular to political economy considerations, to argue that the link between growth and inequality may be ambiguous at relatively short horizons (Bénabou, 1997). By contrast, in a longer-run perspective, there are several arguments to support the existence of a significant link between inequality, the pattern of growth, and development.

In particular, a long-held view in development economics is that income distribution changes in a predictable manner during the process of economic development. According to the **Kuznets hypothesis** (see Kuznets, 1955), income inequality should increase in the early stages of growth and development, and then decrease. This **inverted-U shape** pattern reflects the view that the process of economic development involves a transition from a *low-productivity, agrarian economy* to a *high-productivity, industrial economy*.

More specifically, during the process of industrialization, income inequality tends to rise not only on account of earnings differentials between agriculture and industry, but also because of the increased importance of industrial incomes, which are distributed less equally than agricultural incomes. However, as industry takes over and average incomes rise, earnings differentials associated with productivity differences tend to fall. Consequently, a *turning point* is eventually reached; beyond that point, income distribution begins to improve as the level of income rises. In this perspective, therefore, growth and development tend to raise inequality at first, before reducing it.[9]

---

[9] Anand and Kanbur (1993) provided a formal derivation of the conditions under which the development-inequality relationship has the form hypothesized by Kuznets, for six commonly used indices of inequality.

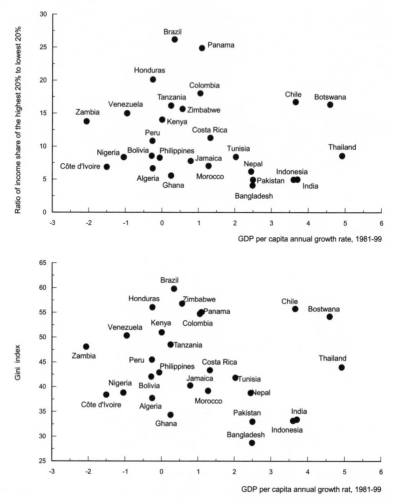

Figure 10.10. Growth and income distribution (average over 1981-99). Source: World Bank.

Galor and Tsiddon (1996) provided an alternative interpretation of the inverted-U shape relationship between development and inequality. They focused on the role of human capital and technological progress. In their analysis, the "backward" sector uses an "old" technology, whereas the "advanced" sector uses more recent production techniques. Mobility from the "backward" to the "advanced" sector requires a process of adaptation and skills acquisition.

In this context, technological innovations (such as electric power or computers) tend initially to raise inequality, because initially few individuals get to share in the relatively high incomes of the technologically advanced sector. But subsequently, as more people acquire skills and take advantage of the superior techniques, inequality begins to fall. This equalization occurs because eventually relatively few people remain behind, and because newcomers to the more advanced sector tend to catch up with those who started ahead. The relative wage of those staying in the backward sector may also rise as the supply of factors in that sector falls.

Another explanation of the U-shape pattern between development and inequality was proposed by Aghion and Bolton (1997) and discussed by Aghion, Caroli, and Garcia-Penalosa (1999). In that view, capital market imperfections induce different investment behavior among the rich and the poor in the early stages of growth; these differences lead the rich to get richer while the poor remain poor. Economic growth is driven by the investment of the rich; as the economy grows and accumulates physical capital, the rate of interest declines, leading to an improvement in the requirements for risky loans. At some point requirements are improved sufficiently to allow the poor to obtain credit and to take advantage of profitable opportunities. Thus, their wealth eventually converges to that of the rich and inequality falls.[10]

Early evidence based on cross-country analysis of the relationship between per capita income and inequality broadly confirmed the existence of the inverted-U pattern in which inequality is lowest in low-income and high-income countries and highest in middle-income countries. Similar results were obtained more recently by Barro (2000b) and Bulir (2001). Barro (2000b), however, found that the Kuznets curve explains only a fraction of the variations in inequality across countries or over time. Other studies have also failed to provide much support, as indicated in two comprehensive surveys by Bruno, Ravallion, and Squire (1998) and Fishlow (1995). This evidence can be summarized in the following fact.

Fact 8. The link between income inequality and income per capita (or possibly growth itself) appears to be nonlinear, but there remains some controversy about the causal nature and degree of robustness of this relationship.

Education and Income Distribution

In addition to growth, there appears to be significant evidence of an adverse effect of **education inequality** on the distribution of income, as is the case for poverty. Psacharopoulos et al. (1995), for instance, suggested that educational attainment has the greatest correlation with both income inequality and the probability of being poor. Londoño and Székely (2000) suggested also that changes in income inequality in Latin America during the past two decades have largely reflected growing inequalities in educational opportunities. Moreover, the evidence reviewed by Lipton and Ravallion (1995) suggests that the relationship between education levels and inequality is typically *nonlinear*. The first phases of growth in education are associated with *increased inequality*; for example, an increase from 1 to 2 years of education in the labor force is typically associated with a 3-point increase in the Gini coefficient. An increase from 4

---

[10]Note that the Aghion-Bolton model focuses on the relationship between wealth inequality and development, as opposed to income inequality and development.

to 5 years is associated with a 1 point increase. The turning point arises when the workforce attains between 5 and 6 years of education. From that point on, inequality decreases; on going from 6 to 7 years, inequality *falls* by half a point. On passing from 9 to 10 years, it falls by 2 points. The link between education and income distribution has, of course, important implications for *public policy*. Improving access to education and the quality of education may lead over time to a reduction in income differentials associated with disparities in average levels of schooling, and should contribute significantly to reductions in income inequality and foster growth (see Chapter 12).

In addition to growth and education, studies have shown that various other factors may affect the pattern of income distribution. Cardoso et al. (1995), for instance, identified inflation and unemployment as determinants of income inequality in Brazil during the 1980s. In a cross-section study of 75 countries, Bulir (2001) found that inflation and income inequality (as measured by the Gini coefficient) are positively related. This relationship appears to be *nonlinear*: a reduction in inflation from very high levels significantly lowers inequality, whereas further reductions toward very low levels (below, say, 5 percent a year) bring about only negligible improvements in income distribution.[11] Finally, several studies suggested that inequality in developing countries is often closely associated with a high degree of concentration of *material wealth*. Inequality in the ownership and distribution of assets (most importantly, land) tend to interact with the other variables listed above, such as education, and often compound their effects.

10.3.5   Trade, Inflation, and Financial Deepening

Fact 9. Growth in the volume of both exports and imports is positively related to the rate of growth of output. The relationship between the degree of openness and growth, however, may involve some nonlinearities.

Figure 10.11 shows that growth in both export and import volumes appears to be positively related to output growth per capita in developing countries. The first result provides support for advocates of *export-led growth* strategies. The second result may stem from the importance of imports of capital goods and intermediate products in total imports of most developing countries (as noted in Chapter 2).

Figure 10.12, which displays the correlation between the rate of growth of income per capita and the **degree of openness**, measured as either the sum of exports plus imports of goods and services divided by GDP, or one over the average tariff rate, does not suggest that outward orientation is strongly associated with high standards of living, although other measures of openness, such as the index devised by Sachs and Warner (1997a), indicate a stronger correlation.[12]

---

[11]Sarel (1997), however, found no significant effect of inflation (in either level or in terms of variability) on income distribution.

[12]See Edwards (1998b), Harrison (1996), and Harrison and Hanson (1999) for further discussion of measures of openness and their relation with the rate of economic growth. Harrison

As discussed by Agénor (2004*a*), Greenaway, Morgan, and Wright (2002), and Winters (2004), possible *nonlinearities* may be involved in the growth-openness relationship.

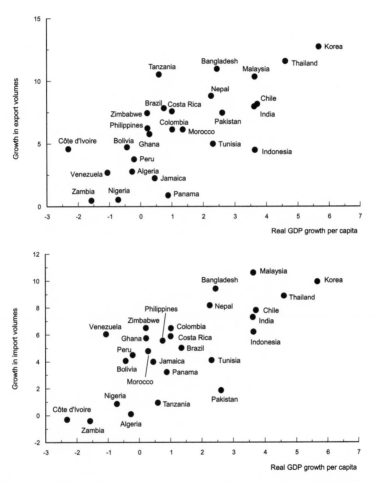

Figure 10.11. Exports, Imports, and Growth (averages over 1980-2001). Source: World Bank.

Fact 10. The association between inflation and growth tends to be negative and nonlinear.

The negative correlation between inflation and growth (possibly resulting from the effect of the former variable on the incentives to invest, as discussed in Chapter 2) is shown in Figure 10.13. This link is often viewed as a key argument for advocating **macroeconomic stability**.

and Hanson, in particular, argue that the Sachs-Warner index is not a robust measure of trade openness.

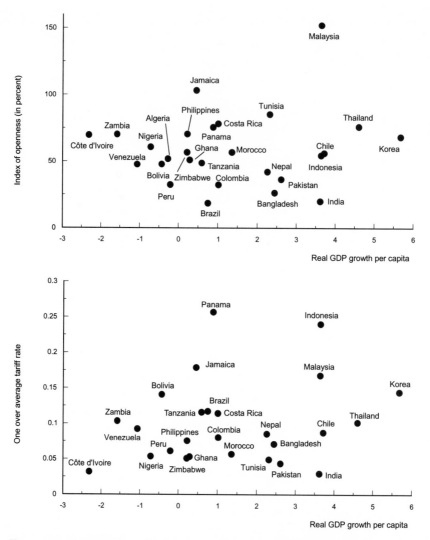

Figure 10.12. Openness and growth (averages over 1980-2001). Openness is measured by the ratio of the sum of exports of goods and services and imports of goods and services (both at current prices), relative to GDP at current prices. The tariff rate is defined as import duties in percent of imports. Source: World Bank.

Much of the recent literature, however, suggests that the inflation-growth link is nonlinear: at low levels of inflation, changes in inflation have only a negligible impact on growth rates; at higher levels (above, say, 30-40 percent per annum), inflation stabilization is conducive to higher growth rates. These issues are discussed further in Chapters 12 and 13.

Fact 11. The degree of development of the financial system is positively related to the rate of growth of output.

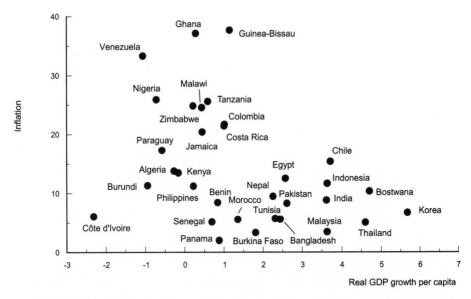

Figure 10.13. Inflation and growth (average annual percentage change, 1980-2001). Source: World Bank.

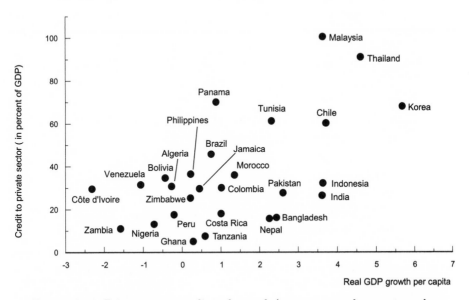

Figure 10.14. Private sector credit and growth (average annual percentage change, 1980-2001). Source: World Bank.

The link between financial deepening and economic growth is documented by Levine (1997) and corroborated by the study of Levine, Loayza, and Beck (2000), although some dissenting views persist (see Driffill, 2003, and the discussion in Chapter 13). Various indicators have been used to measure the degree of financial development in empirical work.

Figure 10.14 relates one of those indicators, the ratio of private sector credit to GDP, to real growth in per capita terms. The figure suggests indeed a positive correlation between these two variables. Other indicators, such as the proportion of quasi-money in the broad money stock, yield similar results. However, although the link between finance and growth is a well-documented fact, the direction of *causality* remains a matter of controversy, as discussed in subsequent chapters.

10.4   Summary

- The evidence on growth since the end of the nineteenth century suggests a pattern of *convergence* in income per capita levels among the group of the currently most advanced industrial countries, but also significant *divergence* between rich and poor countries.

- Simple arithmetic reveals that even small differences in growth rates, once compounded, can add up over time to very large differences in levels of income and standards of living.

- Empirical evidence on the patterns of growth in industrial and developing countries suggest the following basic facts, which theories of growth must explain.

  - 1. Output per worker grows at widely different rates across countries.

  - 2. Growth of capital and labor does not fully account for the rate of growth of output.

  - 3. Output growth rates across countries appear to be unrelated to initial levels of per capita income.

  - 4. Population growth rates, as well as fertility rates, are negatively correlated with both the level of income per capita and the rate of growth of income per capita across countries.

  - 5. Countries with low (high) saving rates tend to have low (high) income levels and growth rates per capita.

  - 6. Both the rate of growth of investment and the share of investment in output are positively related to the rate of growth of income per capita.

  - 7. Poverty rates appear to be negatively related with growth. But although maintaining sustained rates of economic growth is necessary to ensure durable reductions in poverty, it is not always sufficient.

  - 8. The link between income inequality and income per capita (or possibly growth itself) appears to be nonlinear.

- 9. Growth in the volume of exports and imports is positively correlated with growth. The relationship between the degree of openness and growth may involve some nonlinearities.

- 10. The association between inflation and growth is negative and nonlinear.

- 11. The degree of development of the financial system is positively related to the rate of growth of output.

- A reduction in poverty is not necessarily accompanied by reduced inequality as conventionally measured. A policy, for instance, that leads to income being redistributed toward the *extreme groups* of the distribution, accompanied at the same by a fall in the percentage received by the middle groups, may lead to an increase in **polarization** even though it reduces inequality at the same time.

Appendix to Chapter 10
Common Measures of Poverty and Inequality

While there is a broad consensus that poverty alleviation should be a main concern in policy design, the measurement of poverty is itself the subject of intense debate. The basic requirement for the measurement of poverty is the definition of a poverty line that delineates the poor from the nonpoor. Disputes over the choice of a poverty line arise because the standard of living is a multidimensional concept, and there is no objective standard for what constitutes basic requirements. For that reason, some policy analysts prefer to use physical measures related to a specific requirement on which there may be greater consensus, such as nutrition or health, as the basis for defining poverty. Dwelling on this, the definition of a poverty line in terms of income is often done by first calculating the expenditure required to achieve a minimum nutritional intake and then inflating this expenditure by an appropriate ratio to take into account nonfood requirements.

Assuming that one has defined such a poverty line x^*, several measures of the extent of poverty exist. The most commonly used index is the **headcount index** or **ratio**,

$$P_H = n/N,$$

that is, the share of households which are below the poverty line, n, in total population, N. This index, however, does not give a measure of the *extent* of poverty (or how poor the poor really are). One indicator that overcomes this shortcoming is the **poverty gap**, P_G, defined as

$$P_G = \frac{1}{nx^*} \sum_{i \in L} (x^* - x_i),$$

where $x^* - x_i$ measures, for individual i in poverty, the gap between income x_i and the poverty line x^*, L is the set of all poor, and n is the total number of poor.

Because the poverty gap does not take into account the number of poor, researchers sometimes use the product of the two previous measures, denoted P_{HG}:

$$P_{HG} = P_H \cdot P_G = \frac{1}{Nx^*} \sum_{i \in L} (x^* - x_i).$$

P_{HG} measures the level of income transfer needed to bring all poor to the poverty line, normalized by Nx^*. The shortcoming of this index is that it does not capture inequality among the poor, because a dollar of income gap for the extreme poor has the same weight as a dollar of income gap for those who are just under the poverty line.

The **Sen poverty index** combines the two basic poverty measures P_H and P_G with a measure of inequality within the poverty group; it is defined as

$$P_S = P_H[P_G + (1 - P_G)\gamma],$$

where γ is the Gini coefficient of inequality among the poor, derived from the Lorenz curve of income distribution. If the Lorenz curve is constructed with individual income data, γ is given by (see Pyatt, Chen, and Fei, 1980):

$$\gamma = \frac{2}{N\bar{y}}\left(-\frac{Y(1+N)}{2} + \sum_j r_j y_j\right) = \frac{2}{N\bar{y}}\mathrm{Cov}(y,r),$$

where y_i is income of individual i, $Y = \sum_i y_i$ total income, $\bar{y} = Y/N$ mean income, r_i the rank of individual i when the population is ordered by increasing income and $\mathrm{Cov}(y,r)$ the covariance between the income and rank series.

Alternatively, and to better capture the importance of extreme poverty, Foster, Greer, and Thorbecke (1984) have suggested the following index, called the **FGT index**:

$$P_{FGT} = \frac{1}{Nx^{*2}}\sum_{i \in L}(x^* - x_i)^2.$$

One property of this index, which proves to be convenient in policy analysis, is that it is *decomposable across subgroups*. Hence, the aggregate poverty index P_{FGT} of a population is a weighted average of the indices $P_{FGT}(k)$ calculated for groups $k = 1, ...,$ each of size N_k:

$$P_{FGT} = \frac{1}{N}\sum_k N_k P_{FGT}(k).$$

Conventional measures of income distribution, such as the Gini index defined in the text, may not fully capture changes in inequality. An alternative (or, rather, complementary) measure that economists often use is the **polarization index**. Generally speaking, income distribution in country 1 is said to be more polarized than in country 2 if incomes in country 1 tend to be *more bimodal*, in that there are more poor and rich, but fewer people in the middle (Wolfson, 1994). In concrete terms, following Ravallion and Chen (1997), consider an economy composed of four individuals (A, B, C, and D), with incomes of $100, $200, $300, and $400 respectively. Suppose that $50 is taken by a benevolent government from individual B, with an income of $200, and given to individual A, with an income of $100. Suppose also that the same amount is taken from individual D, with an income of $400, and given to individual C, with an income of $300. The new distribution is thus $150, $150, $350, and $350. Inequality, as measured by the Gini index, has fallen because the gainers (individuals A and C) were poorer than the losers (individuals B and D); but *polarization has increased* because the new distribution is more sharply divided between "poor" individuals (A and B) and "rich" individuals (C and D).

A commonly used index of polarization is the **Wolfson index**, W, which is defined as

$$W = 2(\mu^* - \mu_L)/m,$$

where μ^* is the distribution-corrected mean income (given by the actual mean times 1 minus the Gini index), μ_L is the mean income of the poorest half of the population, and m is median income.

Although in practice common measures of inequality and polarization are often closely associated, there may be situations in which measuring inequality through conventional indicators may miss relevant aspects of how distribution has changed. This may be particularly important from a political economy point of view; a more polarized distribution may exacerbate social tensions and lead (as discussed in Chapter 17) to the collapse of a reform program.

Chapter 11

Growth and Technological Progress: The Solow-Swan Model

The starting point of many of the attempts aimed at explaining analytically the facts described in the previous chapter is the so-called neoclassical growth model, developed in the 1950s by Solow (1956) and Swan (1956). Whether one is for or against it, the Solow-Swan model continues to be at the center of the debate between "old" and "new" theories of economic growth. It is therefore important to understand its properties and predictions, regarding notably the effects of the allocation of output between consumption and investment on capital accumulation, and the critical role played by technological progress.

Section 11.1 presents the basic structure and the main assumptions of the Solow-Swan model. Section 11.2 derives the dynamic path of output and the capital stock, under the assumptions that labor and knowledge grow exogenously. Section 11.3 considers briefly the case in which the rate of growth of the population is nonlinearly related to the capital-effective labor ratio. Section 11.4 analyzes the effects of changes in the rate of growth of the labor force and the saving rate on the rate of growth of output per capita in the short and long run. Factors affecting the speed at which adjustment to the long-run equilibrium proceeds are analyzed in section 11.5. Section 11.6 assesses the model's ability to explain the basic facts discussed in the previous chapter.

11.1 Basic Structure and Assumptions

The basic version of the Solow-Swan model considers a closed economy producing one single (composite) good using both *labor* and *capital*. It takes **technological progress** as given and the *saving rate* as exogenous.[1] There is no

---

[1] More precisely, the model takes the saving *function* as given.

government; there is a fixed number of firms in the economy, each with the same production technology. Normalizing the number of firms to unity for simplicity, aggregate output can thus be characterized by an *aggregate production function*. The price of output is constant and factor prices (including wages) adjust to ensure full utilization of all available inputs.

Formally, the model focuses on four variables:

- the flow of output, Y;

- the stock of capital, K;

- the number of workers, L;

- *knowledge* or the **effectiveness of labor**, A.

The economy combines capital, labor, and knowledge to produce output. The aggregate production function is[2]

$$Y = F(K, AL), \tag{1}$$

where capital and effective labor are assumed to be **gross (Edgeworth) complements** $(F_{KL} > 0)$.

Three features of the production function (1) must be noted at the outset.

- Because K and L are *stock* variables, strictly speaking it is the *flow rates of services* of these factors—for instance, the stock of capital times the rate of utilization of capital services—that should enter the production function. For simplicity, the utilization rates of both factors are assumed constant and normalized to unity.

- *Time* does not enter directly but only through K, L, and A. That is, output changes over time only if the production inputs change.

- A and L enter multiplicatively. AL is referred to as **effective labor**, and technological progress that enters in this fashion is known as **labor augmenting** or **Harrod neutral**.

If knowledge enters in the form $Y = F(AK, L)$, technological progress is deemed **capital augmenting** or **Solow neutral**. If it enters in the form $Y = AF(K, L)$, technological progress is **Hicks neutral**. The assumption that technological progress is Harrod neutral implies, as shown below (and given the other assumptions on which the model relies), that the relative shares of capital and labor in output remain constant along paths for which the capital-output ratio itself remains constant. Although there exists limited evidence on the relevance of these facts for developing countries, they appear to hold over the long run for industrial countries (see Romer, 1989).

Several additional assumptions characterize the model:

---

[2]In practice, there are serious aggregation problems involved in the measurement of aggregate stocks of inputs—particularly stocks of physical capital—as specified in Equation (1). However, such issues do not arise here, because of the assumption that the economy produces only one good.

- The **marginal product** of each factor is positive ($F_h > 0$, where $h = K$, AL) and there are **diminishing returns** to each input ($F_{hh} < 0$).

- The production function exhibits **constant returns to scale** (CRS) in capital and effective labor; that is, doubling the quantities of K and AL doubles the amount of output produced. More formally, the CRS assumption implies that, multiplying K and AL by any nonnegative constant m changes output by the same factor:[3]

$$F(mK, mAL) = mF(K, AL), \quad m \geq 0.$$

- Inputs other than capital, labor, and knowledge are relatively unimportant. In particular, the model neglects *land* and other *natural resources*. If natural resources are a constraining factor—as one would expect to be the case in, say, island economies—doubling capital and effective labor could less than double output. The assumption of constant returns to capital and effective labor alone may therefore be inappropriate. Nevertheless, it will be assumed to hold.[4]

Under the CRS assumption, the production function can be written in terms of the *ratio* of production factors. Setting $m = 1/AL$ in Equation (1) results in

$$F(\frac{K}{AL}, 1) = \frac{1}{AL} F(K, AL) = \frac{Y}{AL}, \tag{2}$$

where K/AL is the amount of physical capital per unit of effective labor, and Y/AL is output per unit of effective labor.

Let $k = K/AL$, $y = Y/AL$, and $f(k) = F(k, 1)$. Equation (2) can be rewritten as

$$y = f(k), \quad f(0) = 0. \tag{3}$$

Equation (3) relates output per unit of effective labor to capital per unit of effective labor. The function $f(k)$ is the *intensive-form* production function. Positive output is assumed to require a positive level of capital; put differently, capital is an indispensable factor of production.

Given the earlier assumptions regarding the signs of F_K and F_{KK}, the intensive-form production function must satisfy the following conditions:

$$f'(k) > 0; \quad f''(k) < 0.$$

The quantity $f'(k)$ is the marginal product of capital, F_K, because

$$Y = F(K, AL) = ALf(\frac{K}{AL}) \Rightarrow F_K = \frac{\partial F(K, AL)}{\partial K} = ALf'(\frac{K}{AL}) \cdot \frac{1}{AL} = f'(k),$$

---

[3] The CRS condition is an important assumption of the Solow-Swan model and will be further discussed later.

[4] Romer (1995) discusses an extension of the Solow-Swan model in which the presence of natural resources implies the existence of diminishing returns to capital and labor. The next chapter will examine the implications of increasing returns.

and is thus positive. Similarly, $f''(k) < 0$ because

$$F_{KK} = \frac{\partial^2 F(K, AL)}{\partial K^2} = \frac{\partial}{\partial K}\left\{ALf'(\frac{K}{AL}) \cdot \frac{1}{AL}\right\} = \frac{\partial}{\partial K}\left\{f'(\frac{K}{AL})\right\} = \frac{f''(k)}{AL}.$$

Thus, the above assumptions imply that

- the marginal product of capital is *positive*;

- the marginal product of capital *decreases* as capital (per unit of effective labor) rises.

In addition, the intensive-form production function is assumed to satisfy the **Inada conditions**:

$$\lim_{k \to 0} f'(k) = \infty, \quad \lim_{k \to \infty} f'(k) = 0.$$

These conditions state that the marginal product of capital is very large when the capital stock is sufficiently small, and that it becomes very small as the capital stock becomes very large; their role is to ensure that the path of the economy does not diverge, as discussed below.[5]
A specific production function satisfying all the above conditions is the **Cobb-Douglas function**:

$$Y = F(K, AL) = K^\alpha(AL)^{1-\alpha}, \quad 0 < \alpha < 1. \tag{4}$$

This production function is easy to use, and it appears to be a reasonable first approximation to actual production technologies. To show that the Cobb-Douglas function has constant returns to scale, multiply both inputs by m to obtain

$$(mK)^\alpha(mAL)^{1-\alpha} = m^\alpha m^{1-\alpha}K^\alpha(AL)^{1-\alpha} = mY.$$

The intensive-form Cobb-Douglas function is obtained by dividing both inputs in Equation (4) by AL, so that

$$y = f(k) = (\frac{K}{AL})^\alpha = k^\alpha. \tag{5}$$

Equation (5) implies that

$$f'(k) = \alpha k^{\alpha-1} > 0, \quad f''(k) = -(1-\alpha)\alpha k^{\alpha-2} < 0.$$

It can also be verified that the Inada conditions are satisfied:

$$\lim_{k \to 0} \alpha k^{\alpha-1} = \infty, \quad \lim_{k \to \infty} \alpha k^{\alpha-1} = 0. \tag{6}$$

---

[5] These conditions are, in fact, stronger than is needed for the model's central results. See Burmeister and Dobell (1970, pp. 25-26).

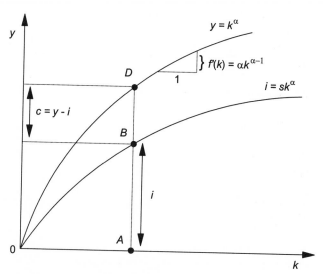

Figure 11.1. The production function in the Solow-Swan model.

The function k^α is illustrated in Figure 11.1. The slope of the function is the marginal product of capital, $\alpha k^{\alpha-1}$. It becomes flatter as k increases, as implied by the assumption of diminishing marginal product of capital.

It can also be verified that, with the Cobb-Douglas production function, labor-augmenting, capital-augmenting, and Hicks-neutral technological progress (as defined earlier) are all basically the same. This is because all factors of production enter multiplicatively. Because of its tractability, the Cobb-Douglas specification will be used systematically in this chapter and next.

To complete the description of the model requires specifying the allocation of resources between consumption, saving, and investment, and the evolution over time of the stocks of capital, labor, and knowledge. Both labor and knowledge are assumed to grow at exogenous, constant rates:

$$\dot{L}/L = n, \quad \dot{A}/A = \gamma, \tag{7}$$

where γ can be interpreted as the rate at which knowledge, other than technological know-how embodied in equipment, improves—for instance, efficiency gains in organizational structures and management procedures.

The expressions in (7) imply that, denoting by L_0 and A_0 the initial values of L and A:[6]

$$L = L_0 e^{nt}, \quad A = A_0 e^{\gamma t}. \tag{8}$$

Output is divided between consumption, C, and investment, I:

$$Y = C + I. \tag{9}$$

---

[6] To verify this, note, for instance, that $L = L_0 e^{nt}$ implies that $\dot{L} = nL_0 e^{nt} = nL$ and that the initial value of L is $L_0 e^0 = L_0$.

Savings, S, defined as $Y - C$, is assumed to be a constant fraction, s, of output:

$$S \equiv Y - C = sY, \quad 0 < s < 1. \tag{10}$$

All savings are assumed absorbed by firms for capital accumulation. Combining Equations (9) and (10) the saving-investment equality can therefore be written as:

$$S = I = sY, \tag{11}$$

which shows that the saving rate is also the fraction of output allocated to investment.[7]

Finally, assuming that one unit of output allocated to investment yields one unit of new capital, that the existing capital stock depreciates at the constant rate $\delta > 0$, and using Equation (11), changes in the capital stock (or net investment) can be written as

$$\dot{K} = sY - \delta K. \tag{12}$$

Let $c = C/AL$ and $i = I/AL$ denote consumption and investment per effective units of labor, respectively. Using Equation (4) yields:

$$c = (1 - s)k^{\alpha}, \quad i = sk^{\alpha}. \tag{13}$$

Figure 11.1 shows graphically how output (per effective units of labor) is allocated between consumption, saving, and investment.

11.2   The Dynamics of Capital and Output

To determine the behavior of the economy over time under the preceding set of assumptions requires only examining the behavior of the capital stock, because labor and knowledge grow exogenously. To do so, it is convenient to focus on the capital stock per units of effective labor, k, rather than the capital stock itself. Differentiating the expression $k = K/AL$ with respect to time implies that

$$\dot{k} = (\frac{1}{AL})\dot{K} - (\frac{K}{A})\frac{\dot{L}}{L^2} - (\frac{K}{L})\frac{\dot{A}}{A^2},$$

or equivalently

$$\dot{k} = \frac{\dot{K}}{AL} - (\frac{K}{AL})\frac{\dot{L}}{L} - (\frac{K}{AL})\frac{\dot{A}}{A} = \frac{\dot{K}}{AL} - (\frac{\dot{L}}{L} + \frac{\dot{A}}{A})k. \tag{14}$$

From Equation (8), $\dot{L}/L = n$ and $\dot{A}/A = \gamma$; and $\dot{K}$ is given by Equation (12). Substituting these expressions into the right-hand side of Equation (14) results in

$$\dot{k} = \frac{sY - \delta K}{AL} - (n + \gamma)k,$$

---

[7] For simplicity, the assumption that savings are a constant fraction of income will be maintained in this chapter and the next. Models with a variable saving rate can be derived from full-blown optimization problems by households but are mathematically more demanding. For a discussion, see Barro and Sala-i-Martin (1995).

or

$$\dot{k} = \frac{sY}{AL} - \delta k - (n + \gamma)k,$$

and finally, using the fact that, from Equation (4), $Y/AL = k^\alpha$:

$$\dot{k} = sk^\alpha - (n + \gamma + \delta)k, \quad n + \gamma + \delta > 0, \tag{15}$$

with initial condition $k_0 = K_0/A_0 L_0$.

Equation (15) is a *nonlinear, first-order differential equation*; it represents the key equation of the Solow-Swan model. It states that the rate of change of the capital stock per units of effective labor is the difference between two terms:

- sk^α, which measures *actual investment* per unit of effective labor. Output per units of effective labor is k^α, and the fraction of that output that is invested is s.

- $(n + \gamma + \delta)k$, which measures *required investment*, that is, the amount of investment that must be undertaken in order to keep k at its existing level.

There are two reasons why some investment is needed to prevent k from falling.

- The existing capital stock is depreciating; this capital must be replaced to prevent the capital stock from falling. This is measured by the term δk in Equation (15).

- The quantity of effective labor is growing. Thus, investing just enough to keep the capital stock, K, constant is not sufficient to maintain capital per unit of effective labor, k, constant. Instead, because the quantity of effective labor is growing at the rate $n + \gamma$, the capital stock must grow at the rate $n + \gamma$ to keep k constant. This is the $(n + \gamma)k$ term in Equation (15).

Equation (15) indicates, therefore, that the capital-effective labor ratio rises at a rate proportional to the difference between actual and required investment:

- When actual investment exceeds required investment, so that $sk^\alpha > (n + \gamma + \delta)k$, k is rising.

- When actual investment falls short of required investment, k is falling.

- When the two terms are equal, k is constant.

Figure 11.2 extends Figure 11.1 to represent both terms of the expression for $\dot{k}$ as functions of k. Required investment, $(n + \gamma + \delta)k$, is proportional to k and is represented as a *straight line* with a positive slope. Actual investment is a *concave curve* (like the production function itself) because it is a fraction of output per units of effective labor and, as shown earlier, $\alpha k^{\alpha-1} > 0$, $-(1 - \alpha)\alpha k^{\alpha-2} < 0$.

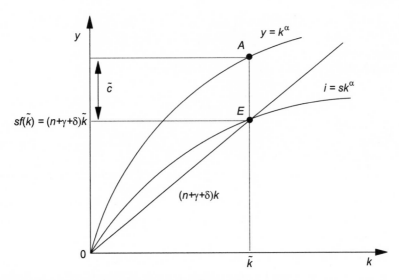

Figure 11.2. The equilibrium capital-effective labor ratio.

At $k = 0$, $y = 0$ and actual investment and required investment are equal. To show that this equality does occur only once for $k > 0$ proceeds in three steps.

- The first Inada condition in (6) implies that for k slightly greater than 0, the marginal productivity of capital $\alpha k^{\alpha-1}$ is large, and thus that the sk^α curve is steeper than the $(n + \gamma + \delta)k$ line. Thus, for positive but small values of k, actual investment is larger than required investment.

- The second Inada condition in (6) implies that $\alpha k^{\alpha-1}$ drops toward zero as k becomes large. At some point, the slope of the actual investment line falls below the slope of the required investment line. With the sk^α curve flatter than the $(n + \gamma + \delta)k$ line, the two must eventually cross.[8]

- The fact that $-(1-\alpha)\alpha k^{\alpha-2} < 0$ implies that the two curves will intersect *only once* for $k > 0$—at the unique value of k for which actual investment equals required investment.

Let $\tilde{k}$ denote this unique value, which is the *equilibrium point* of the system; it is determined by setting $\dot{k} = 0$ in Equation (15), so that

$$s\tilde{k}^\alpha - (n + \gamma + \delta)\tilde{k} = 0. \tag{16}$$

Solving this equation yields

$$\tilde{k} = \left\{ \frac{s}{n + \gamma + \delta} \right\}^{1/(1-\alpha)}. \tag{17}$$

---

[8] Clearly, if there is no range of values of k for which the sk^α curve is above the $(n+\gamma+\delta)k$ line, the two curves cannot intersect and there is no equilibrium.

Equation (17) implies that, in particular, $\partial \tilde{k}/\partial s > 0$. An increase in the saving rate raises the equilibrium capital-effective labor ratio—and thus per capita income, given by $A\tilde{k}^{\alpha}$.

Figure 11.3 shows the **phase diagram** relating $\dot{k}$ to k.

- If initially $k < \tilde{k}$, actual investment exceeds required investment and so $\dot{k}$ is positive, that is, k is rising.

- If initially $k > \tilde{k}$, $\dot{k}$ is negative and k is falling.

- If initially $k = \tilde{k}$, $\dot{k}$ is zero.

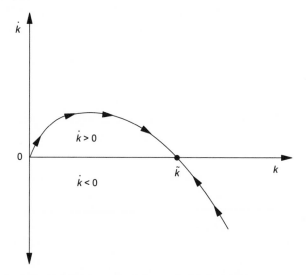

Figure 11.3. Adjustment process of the capital-labor ratio.

Thus, regardless of where the economy's initial stock of capital is (as long as it is positive), it converges to $\tilde{k}$—the point at which the phase line crosses the horizontal axis.[9] The dynamic process described by Equation (15) is thus **globally stable**. The explicit dynamic path of k is derived in the appendix to this chapter.

In the steady-state equilibrium, with k constant at $\tilde{k}$, the capital stock, which by definition is equal to ALk, is growing at the rate

$$\tilde{g}_K = \left.\frac{\dot{K}}{K}\right|_{k=\tilde{k}} = \frac{\dot{A}}{A} + \frac{\dot{L}}{L} = n + \gamma, \tag{18}$$

which is also the growth rate of the effective labor force, AL.

Output is given by ALy. Its steady-state growth rate, $\tilde{g}_Y$, is thus

$$\tilde{g}_Y = \frac{\dot{A}}{A} + \frac{\dot{L}}{L} = n + \gamma, \tag{19}$$

[9] If k is initially zero, it remains there. This possibility is ignored in what follows.

because y is constant at $\tilde{k}^\alpha$, so that $\dot{y}/y|_{k=\tilde{k}} = 0$. Thus, output is also growing at the same rate as capital and effective labor.

From the above results, the rates of growth of capital per worker, and output per worker (that is, labor productivity), are given by

$$\tilde{\mathbf{g}}_{K/L} = \tilde{\mathbf{g}}_K - \frac{\dot{L}}{L} = \gamma, \quad \tilde{\mathbf{g}}_{Y/L} = \tilde{\mathbf{g}}_Y - \frac{\dot{L}}{L} = \gamma. \tag{20}$$

Thus, the Solow-Swan model implies that, regardless of its starting point, the economy converges to a **balanced growth path**—a situation where each variable of the model is growing at a constant rate. On the balanced growth path, the growth rate of output per worker is determined solely by the rate of growth of technological progress. It depends, in particular, neither on the saving rate nor on the specific form of the production function.

By definition, if markets are competitive, the **rate of return to capital**, r, must equal the *net* marginal product of capital, that is, $\alpha k^{\alpha-1}$ minus the depreciation rate, δ:

$$r = \alpha k^{\alpha-1} - \delta,$$

whereas the **wage rate**, w, is equal to the marginal product of labor

$$w = \frac{\partial}{\partial L}(ALk^\alpha) = (1-\alpha)Ak^\alpha.$$

On the balanced growth path, therefore, the rate of return to capital (or the net real interest rate) is constant, whereas wages are rising at the rate γ. Using the above results, the *relative shares of capital and labor*, as given by

$$\frac{(r+\delta)K}{Y} = \frac{(r+\delta)k}{y} = \frac{\alpha k^{\alpha-1}k}{k^\alpha} = \alpha,$$

$$\frac{wL}{Y} = \frac{w}{Y/L} = \frac{w}{Ay} = \frac{(1-\alpha)Ak^\alpha}{Ak^\alpha} = 1-\alpha,$$

are also constant along the balanced growth path.

11.3 A Digression on Low-Income Traps

The foregoing discussion assumed that the population growth rate, n, is exogenous [Equation (7)]. Suppose for a moment that the rate of population growth is *endogenous* and *nonlinearly* related to the capital-effective labor ratio. As shown in early contributions by Buttrick (1958) and Nelson (1956), in such conditions the Solow-Swan model can lead to a **dynamically stable**, low-steady-state level of per capita income.[10]

---

[10] Becker, Murphy, and Tamura (1990) provide an alternative treatment based on an endogenous fertility rate.

Formally, suppose that $n = n(k)$; the basic dynamic equation of the Solow-Swan model, Equation (15), becomes

$$\dot{k} = sk^\alpha - [n(k) + \gamma + \delta]k.$$

Suppose, specifically, that the function $n(k)$ is such that the population growth rate is

- *negative* at low levels of the capital-effective labor ratios, because the population is unable to satisfy its basic needs;

- *positive* at intermediate values of k (and thus of the wage rate);

- again *negative* at higher values of k.

Such a scenario may be a plausible one for developing countries. A function $n(k)$ that satisfies these conditions is illustrated in the upper panel of Figure 11.4, which is taken from Burmeister and Dobell (1970). As shown in the lower panel of the figure, the nonlinearity of $n(k)$ implies that **multiple equilibria** (some of them unstable) may emerge.[11]

In particular, the figure illustrates the possibility of a **low-level trap** (point E) at which, for small changes in k, population effects prevent any increase in the capital-effective labor ratio and force a return to the stable equilibrium, $\tilde{k}_S$. A **big push**, however, taking the form of an exogenous increase in the saving rate for instance, would increase the capital-effective labor ratio beyond the high, unstable equilibrium point $\tilde{k}_U$, and would set the economy on a path of rising capital and income per capita. This possibility was pointed out by Rosenstein-Rodan (1961); a modern restatement of this view is offered by Murphy, Shleifer, and Vishny (1989).

11.4 Population, Savings, and Output

Return now to the case in which the rate of growth of the labor force is indeed exogenous, and consider the effects of a change in n and a change in the saving rate, s.

Suppose that the economy's initial position is on the balanced growth path and assume first that the rate of population growth falls, at $t = 0$, from n_H to n_L. Figure 11.5 illustrates the effects of this change.

---

[11]Burmeister and Dobell (1970, pp. 36-38) discuss endogenous labor growth in the basic Solow-Swan model by relating participation rates to the wage rate. As discussed later, this extension does not affect the qualitative properties of the model, only the *speed of convergence* to the balanced growth path.

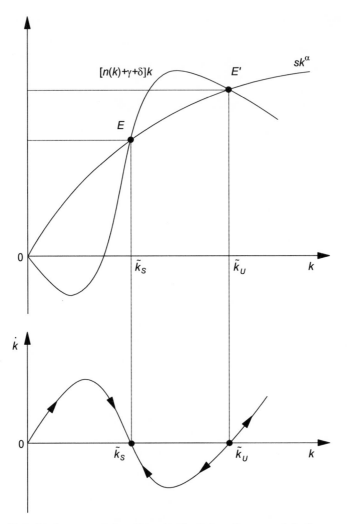

Figure 11.4. Endogenous labor force in the Solow-Swan model. Source: Adapted from Burmeister and Dobell (1970, p. 37).

The break-even investment line shifts downward; on impact, with k given at $k_0 = \tilde{k}_H$, the fall in required investment relative to actual investment (by the quantity EA) implies that $\dot{k}_0 > 0$. Thus k begins to rise and continues to do so until reaching the new steady state, which is characterized by a higher capital stock per worker ($\tilde{k}_L > \tilde{k}_H$). Output per worker, which is equal to $A\tilde{k}^\alpha$, is thus also higher in the new steady state. This positive long-run effect can be directly verified from (17). However, no rate of growth of any variable measured in per capita terms is affected in the long run; although the reduction in n is *permanent*, the increase in the growth rate of output per worker is only *transitory*. In the long run, Y/L grows at the same rate γ.

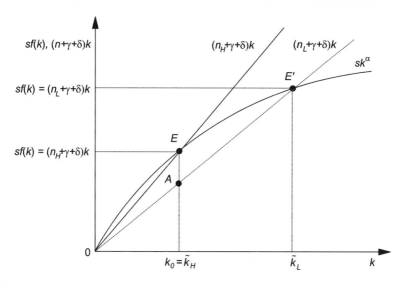

Figure 11.5. Reduction in the population growth rate in the Solow-Swan model.

Suppose now that the saving rate, s, increases—as a result, say, of a sudden appetite for thrift. The increase in s (from s_L to s_H) shifts the actual investment curve, sk^α, as illustrated in Figure 11.6. The steady-state capital stock therefore increases from $\tilde{k}_L$ to $\tilde{k}_H$. At the initial level of k, actual investment exceeds required investment (by the quantity EA) and so $\dot{k}_0 > 0$; k begins to rise and continues to do so until the new steady-state level $\tilde{k}_H$ is reached. Thus, an increase in the saving rate raises the capital-effective labor ratio in the long run as can be seen, again, directly from Equation (17).

Output per worker, Y/L, is equal to Ak^α. When k is constant, Y/L grows at rate γ, as shown earlier. During the transition from $\tilde{k}_L$ to $\tilde{k}_H$, with k increasing, the rate of growth of Y/L will exceed γ. A *permanent* increase in the saving rate therefore leads only to a *transitory* increase in the growth rate of output per worker. Moreover, the increase in the saving rate has *no long-run effect* on the rate of growth of output and the capital stock.

As shown in Equation (13), consumption per unit of effective labor, c, is initially given by

$$c = (1 - s_L)k^\alpha. \tag{21}$$

By definition, k cannot change in discrete fashion. Thus, the step increase in s from s_L to s_H implies that consumption jumps downward. After falling initially, consumption rises gradually as k rises and s remains at s_H.

To establish whether consumption per unit of effective labor rises or falls in the long run relative to its initial level, note that on the balanced growth path, $\tilde{c}$ is given by the difference between output and actual investment:

$$\tilde{c} = \tilde{k}^\alpha - s\tilde{k}^\alpha, \tag{22}$$

which is given in Figure 11.2 by the distance EA. As shown by Equation (16), on the balanced growth path, actual investment, $s\tilde{k}^\alpha$, is also equal to required investment.

Substituting Equation (16) in (22) results in

$$\tilde{c} = \tilde{k}^\alpha - (n + \delta + \gamma)\tilde{k},$$

which implies that

$$\frac{\partial \tilde{c}}{\partial s} = [\alpha \tilde{k}^{\alpha-1} - (n + \gamma + \delta)]\frac{\partial \tilde{k}}{\partial s} \gtrless 0.$$

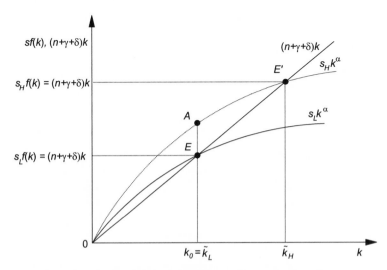

Figure 11.6. Increase in the saving rate in the Solow-Swan model.

Because $\partial \tilde{k}/\partial s > 0$, the sign of $\partial \tilde{c}/\partial s$ depends on whether the marginal product of capital, $\alpha \tilde{k}^{\alpha-1}$, is greater or lower than $n + \gamma + \delta$.

- If $\alpha \tilde{k}^{\alpha-1}$ is *less* than $n + \gamma + \delta$, then the additional output from the increased capital is not enough to maintain the capital stock at its higher level. In this case, consumption must fall to maintain the higher capital stock.

- If $\alpha \tilde{k}^{\alpha-1}$ is *greater* than $n + \gamma + \delta$, there is more than enough additional output to maintain k at its higher level, and so consumption rises.[12]

Establishing the effect of the increase in the saving rate on the long-run value of output per unit of effective labor is a bit more involved. As derived in the appendix to this chapter, the long-run elasticity of y with respect to s, η, is given by

$$\eta = \frac{\alpha}{1 - \alpha}. \tag{23}$$

[12] The value of $\tilde{k}$ for which an increase in the saving rate has no effect on consumption ($\partial \tilde{c}/\partial s = 0$) is known as the *golden-rule* level of the capital stock. Consumption is at its maximum possible level among balanced growth paths. See Barro and Sala-i-Martin (1995).

Suppose that α, the share of income paid to capital, is about 0.3—a value that appears to be consistent with the evidence for developing countries. Substituting this value in the above expression yields

$$\eta = \frac{0.3}{1 - 0.3} \simeq 0.43.$$

This result implies that, for instance, a 10 percent increase in the saving rate (from, say, 10 percent of output to 11 percent) raises output per unit of effective labor by only 4.3 percent in the long run relative to its initial path. Even a 50 percent increase in s (from, say, 10 percent to 15 percent) would raise $\tilde{y}$ by only about 21 percent. Thus, large changes in saving rates have only *moderate effects* on the level of output on the balanced growth path.

Intuitively, a small value of α makes the impact of saving on output low for two reasons (Romer, 1995, p. 21):

- a low value of α means that the impact of a change in $\tilde{k}$ on $\tilde{y}$ is small;

- it implies that the actual investment curve, sk^α, bends fairly sharply; as a result, an upward shift of the curve moves its intersection with the required investment line relatively little. As a result, the impact of a change in s on $\tilde{k}$ is small.

11.5   The Speed of Adjustment

The foregoing discussion has focused on the *long-run* effects of changes in the population growth rate and the saving rate; in practice, it is also important to assess the *speed* at which adjustment to the new equilibrium proceeds, that is, how fast is k approaching $\tilde{k}$.

Consider first the behavior of the capital stock per unit of effective labor. As shown in the appendix to this chapter, changes in k in the vicinity of the balanced growth path can be approximated by

$$\dot{k} \simeq \Lambda(k - \tilde{k}), \tag{24}$$

where

$$\Lambda = -(1 - \alpha)(n + \gamma + \delta) < 0.$$

Equation (24) indicates that (in the neighborhood of the balanced growth path), capital per unit of effective labor evolves toward its steady-state level at a speed *proportional to its distance* from $\tilde{k}$, with a coefficient of proportionality Λ.

Equation (24) is a *first-order, nonhomogeneous differential equation*, whose solution, as derived for instance in Chiang (1984, pp. 472-74), is given by

$$k - \tilde{k} \simeq e^{\Lambda t}(k_0 - \tilde{k}),$$

where k_0 denotes the initial value of k. As shown in the appendix, y approaches $\tilde{y}$ at the same rate that k approaches $\tilde{k}$:

$$y - \tilde{y} \simeq e^{\Lambda t}(y_0 - \tilde{y}). \tag{25}$$

Equation (25) can be used to assess the speed at which a Solow-Swan economy approaches its balanced growth path. Specifically, $|\Lambda|$ in the above equation measures the **speed of adjustment** of output per worker, that is, the rate at which the economy catches up to its steady-state level of y, given some initial position y_0. Put differently, Equation (25) indicates that $|\Lambda| \cdot 100$ percent of the initial gap between the actual level of output per worker and its steady-state level is closed every year. In particular, the speed of adjustment is a decreasing function of the capital share, α.

Suppose, for instance, that the annual rate of growth of the labor force, n, is 2 percent, technological progress γ grows at the yearly rate of 2 percent, and that the annual rate of depreciation of the capital stock, δ, is 4 percent (which implies that capital lasts an average of 25 years). Suppose, again, that capital's share in output is about 0.3. Then,

$$\Lambda = -(1 - 0.3)(0.02 + 0.02 + 0.04) \simeq -0.056,$$

that is, output per worker (as well as the capital-effective labor ratio) moves about 6 percent of the remaining distance toward its long-run equilibrium value $\tilde{y}$ each year. Let the **adjustment ratio**, μ, be defined as the fraction of the change from y_0 to $\tilde{y}$ completed after t years:

$$\mu = \frac{y - y_0}{\tilde{y} - y_0}.$$

Using (25), this equation can be rewritten as

$$\mu = \frac{(y - \tilde{y}) + (\tilde{y} - y_0)}{\tilde{y} - y_0} = 1 - e^{\Lambda t},$$

or equivalently

$$e^{\Lambda t} = 1 - \mu. \tag{26}$$

The time taken to achieve a given fraction μ of the adjustment from y_0 to $\tilde{y}$ is thus given by[13]

$$t^* = \ln(1 - \mu)/\Lambda \simeq -\mu/\Lambda, \tag{27}$$

where the last result is obtained by using the approximation $\ln(1 + x) \simeq x$, for x small enough. For instance, calculating the **half-life** of the process—the time needed to eliminate one-half of the initial deviation of y from its steady-state value—requires setting $\mu = 0.5$. Given the value of Λ calculated earlier, Equation (27) yields

---

[13] Equation (26) can also be used to calculate the percentage μ^* of the steady-state value achieved for a given convergence rate after t years as $1 - e^{-\Lambda t} \simeq -\Lambda t$.

$$t^* = -0.69/(-0.056) \simeq 12.4,$$

that is, it takes approximately 12 years to get half way to the steady state $\tilde{y}$. Table 11.1 provides a more complete set of numerical results for $\delta = 0.04$. In particular, for $\alpha = 0.3$, $n = 0.01$, and $\gamma = 0.02$, the speed of adjustment is 4.9 percent and it takes 32.8 years to achieve 80 percent of the adjustment from y_0 to $\tilde{y}$. Thus, as emphasized very early on by Sato (1963) in an important contribution, reaching the steady-state equilibrium in the Solow-Swan model can be a fairly long process.

Table 11.1. Solow-Swan model: Years to adjustment ($\delta = 0.04$)

γ	μ	$\alpha = 0.3$		$\alpha = 0.4$	
		$n = 1\%$	$n = 2\%$	$n = 1\%$	$n = 2\%$
		$|\Lambda| = 4.2\%$	$|\Lambda| = 4.9\%$	$|\Lambda| = 3.6\%$	$|\Lambda| = 4.2\%$
	0.2	05.3	04.6	06.2	05.3
0.01	0.5	16.5	14.1	19.3	16.5
	0.8	38.3	32.8	44.7	38.3
		$|\Lambda| = 4.9\%$	$|\Lambda| = 5.6\%$	$|\Lambda| = 4.2\%$	$|\Lambda| = 4.8\%$
	0.2	04.6	04.0	05.3	04.6
0.02	0.5	14.1	12.4	16.5	14.4
	0.8	32.8	28.7	38.3	33.5
		$|\Lambda| = 5.6\%$	$|\Lambda| = 6.3\%$	$|\Lambda| = 4.8\%$	$|\Lambda| = 5.4\%$
	0.2	04.0	03.5	04.6	04.1
0.03	0.5	12.4	11.0	14.4	12.8
	0.8	28.7	25.5	33.5	29.8

Source: Author's calculations.

The implication of these results is also that policy changes in the model may be associated with long periods of adjustment. Suppose indeed that $|\Lambda| = 0.056$. In the previous example of a 10 percent increase in the saving rate, output per worker is $0.056(5\%) = 0.28$ percent above its previous path after 1 year; $0.5(5\%) = 2.5$ percent above after about 12 years; and asymptotically approaches 5 percent above the initial path. Put differently, not only is the overall impact of a substantial change in the saving rate modest, it does not occur very quickly.

A procedure similar to the one outlined above can be used to study the speed of adjustment of the *growth rate* of output, as opposed to its *level*, to its steady-state value. To do so, note first that the solution to Equation (24) can be written as

$$k = \tilde{k} + \eta e^{\Lambda t},$$

where η is a **constant of integration**. Substituting this result back in Equation

(24) then yields

$$\dot{k}/k = \Lambda \left\{ 1 - \frac{\tilde{k}}{\tilde{k} + \eta e^{\Lambda t}} \right\}. \tag{28}$$

Because output is equal to $Y = ALk^{\alpha}$, the actual growth rate of output is equal to

$$\mathbf{g}_Y \equiv \dot{Y}/Y = \alpha \dot{k}/k + n + \gamma = \alpha \dot{k}/k + \tilde{\mathbf{g}}_Y, \tag{29}$$

where, as shown earlier [Equation (19)], $\tilde{\mathbf{g}}_Y = n + \gamma$.

Substituting Equation (28) in (29) yields

$$\mathbf{g}_Y = \alpha \Lambda \left\{ 1 - \frac{\tilde{k}}{\tilde{k} + \eta e^{\Lambda t}} \right\} + \tilde{\mathbf{g}}_Y. \tag{30}$$

Setting $t = 0$ in this equation implies that

$$\alpha \Lambda \left\{ 1 - \frac{\tilde{k}}{\tilde{k} + \eta} \right\} = \mathbf{g}_Y^0 - \tilde{\mathbf{g}}_Y,$$

where $\mathbf{g}_Y^0$ is given by the initial condition. Solving this equation for the constant term η yields

$$\eta = \frac{(\mathbf{g}_Y^0 - \tilde{\mathbf{g}}_Y)\tilde{k}}{\tilde{\mathbf{g}}_Y - \mathbf{g}_Y^0 + \alpha \Lambda},$$

which can be substituted back into Equation (30) to give

$$\mathbf{g}_Y = \alpha \Lambda \left\{ 1 - \tilde{k} \left[\tilde{k} + \frac{(\mathbf{g}_Y^0 - \tilde{\mathbf{g}}_Y)\tilde{k}e^{\Lambda t}}{\tilde{\mathbf{g}}_Y - \mathbf{g}_Y^0 + \alpha \Lambda} \right]^{-1} \right\} + \tilde{\mathbf{g}}_Y. \tag{31}$$

The **adjustment ratio** can now be defined as

$$\mu = \frac{\mathbf{g}_Y - \mathbf{g}_Y^0}{\tilde{\mathbf{g}}_Y - \mathbf{g}_Y^0}. \tag{32}$$

Substituting Equation (31) in (32) and solving for the time t^* (in years) required to get a fraction λ of the way from $\mathbf{g}_Y^0$ to $\tilde{\mathbf{g}}_Y$ yields

$$t^* = \Lambda^{-1} \ln \left\{ \frac{(1 - \mu)(\tilde{\mathbf{g}}_Y - \mathbf{g}_Y^0 + \alpha \Lambda)}{(1 - \mu)(\tilde{\mathbf{g}}_Y - \mathbf{g}_Y^0) + \alpha \Lambda} \right\}.$$

11.6   Model Predictions and Empirical Facts

The following are the predictions of the Solow-Swan model regarding the long-run behavior of output, consumption, and investment and the response of these variables to changes in the population growth rate and the saving rate.

- The capital-effective labor ratio, the marginal product of capital, and output per units of effective labor are constant on the balanced growth path.

- The steady-state growth rate of capital per worker K/L and output per worker Y/L are determined solely by the rate of technological progress. In particular, neither variable depends on the saving rate or on the specific form of the production function.

- Output, the capital stock, and effective labor all grow at the same rate, given by the sum of the growth rate of the labor force and the growth rate of technological progress.

- A reduction in the population growth rate raises the steady-state levels of the capital-effective labor ratio and output in efficiency units and lowers the rate of growth of output, the capital stock, and effective labor.

- A rise in the saving rate also increases the capital-effective labor ratio and output in efficiency units in the long run, but has no effect on the steady-state growth rates of output, the capital stock, and effective labor.

How do these predictions compare with the empirical evidence on growth and the basic facts described in the previous chapter? First, the evidence for industrial countries suggests that it is a reasonable first approximation to argue that the growth rates of labor, capital, and output are each roughly constant in the long term (Romer, 1989). The growth rates of output and capital are about equal (so that the capital-output ratio is approximately constant) and are larger than the growth rate of labor; as a result, output per worker and capital per worker are rising over time. The limited evidence available for developing countries, however, does not allow any generalization.

Second, the model's predictions regarding the effects of changes in the population growth rate and the saving rate on the *level* of income (or standard of living) are also consistent with the evidence. The upper panel of Figure 10.2 showed that, indeed, as predicted by the model, lower population growth rates tend to be associated with higher levels of income per capita; a similar result is illustrated in the upper panel of Figure 10.3, in which the fertility rate (which corrects for the age structure of the population, and subtract out the effects of mortality and migration) is used. Similarly, the upper panel in Figure 10.4 showed that the saving rate is positively associated with the level of income per capita.

However, there are several stylized facts that the model is unable to explain. First, as discussed in the previous chapter, and as shown in the lower panels in Figures 10.4 and 10.5, both the saving rate and the share of investment in output are positively correlated (over a sufficiently long period of time) with the *growth rate* of income per capita (as an approximation for output per worker). More formal evidence (reviewed in Chapter 13) indicates also that variations in the accumulation of physical capital account for a significant part of cross-country income differences in economic growth. By contrast, the Solow-Swan model predicts *no association* between these variables in the steady state.

Second, differences in *physical capital per worker* cannot account for the observed differences in output per worker (or income per capita)—at least if capital's contribution to output is roughly reflected by its private returns. Specifically, two difficulties arise:

- The required differences in capital are *far too large*. For instance, output per worker in the United States today is on the order of *ten times* larger than it is in, say, India today. With the Cobb-Douglas production technology used earlier, the share of capital in output, α, is also the elasticity of output with respect to the capital stock. Accounting for a tenfold difference in output per worker on the basis of differences in capital requires a difference of a factor of $10^{1/\alpha}$ in capital per worker. For $\alpha = 0.3$, this is a factor of one thousand. Even if $\alpha = 0.5$, a value that exceeds most estimates available, one still needs a difference of a factor of one hundred. However, capital per worker in the United States is no more than twenty to thirty times larger than in India.[14]

- Attributing differences in output to differences in capital without differences in the effectiveness of labor implies large variations in the rate of return on capital (Lucas, 1990).

As noted earlier, the net rate of return to capital, r, equals its marginal product, $\alpha k^{\alpha-1}$, minus depreciation, δ. Because the production function can be written as $k = y^{1/\alpha}$, the marginal product of capital is $\alpha y^{-(1-\alpha)/\alpha}$; this implies that the elasticity of the marginal product of capital with respect to output is $-(1-\alpha)/\alpha$. If $\alpha = 0.3$, a *tenfold difference* in output per worker arising from differences in capital per worker thus implies a *hundredfold difference* in the marginal product of (and the rate of return to) capital. Again, there is no evidence of such huge differences in rates of return across countries; they would lead to massive and sustained flows of capital from rich to poor countries—something that has not happened.

Third, and most importantly, the only source of variation in the growth rate of output per worker (or income per capita) in the Solow-Swan model in the long run is the rate of growth of labor effectiveness, γ. But the model is *incomplete* because the driving force of long-run growth, the rate of increase in the effectiveness of labor, is *exogenous*.[15] The effectiveness of labor is no more than a catchall for factors other than labor and physical capital that affect

---

[14] The same argument can be presented in terms of the rates of saving, population growth, and so on that determine capital per worker. For instance, the elasticity of $\tilde{y}$ with respect to s is $\alpha/(1-\alpha)$; see Equation (23). Thus, accounting for a difference of a factor of ten in output per worker on the basis of differences in s would require a difference of a factor of one hundred in s if $\alpha = 0.3$ and a difference of a factor of ten if $\alpha = 0.5$. Variations in actual saving rates across countries are much smaller than this.

[15] It should be noted that, away from the steady state, fluctuations (over time as well as across countries) in the rate of growth of output per worker can result not only from differences in the rate of growth of the effectiveness of labor, A, but also from differences in the growth rate of capital per worker, K/L. As discussed earlier, however, in most reasonable cases the impact of changes in capital per worker on output growth rates is likely to be modest.

output. Much of the recent research in this area has focused on defining what the effectiveness of labor is, and what causes it to vary over time, in order to understand cross-country differences in the growth rates of real income. The next chapter will consider in detail several alternative interpretations.

11.7 Summary

The Solow-Swan growth model makes the following predictions.

- The capital-effective labor ratio, the marginal product of capital, and output per units of effective labor are *constant* on the **balanced growth path**.

- The steady-state growth rates of capital per worker are determined only by the rate of technological progress.

- Output, the capital stock, and effective labor grow at the *same rate*, given by the sum of the growth rate of the labor force and the growth rate of technological progress.

- Changes in the *population growth rate* and the *saving rate* affect the steady-state *levels* of the capital-effective labor ratio and output per worker but have *no effect* on the *steady-state growth rate* of income per capita.

- If the rate of growth of the population is *nonlinearly* related to the capital-effective labor ratio (or income), the Solow-Swan model may lead to a *dynamically stable, low-steady-state level of per capita income.*

Several of these predictions are consistent with the empirical evidence on long-run growth in industrial and developing countries. The basic model remains, however, subject to a number of limitations.

- It does not account for the positive correlation between *saving* and *investment rates* and *growth* in income per capita across countries, as documented in the previous chapter.

- Differences in long-run per capita income levels across countries can result in the model only from differences in capital-effective labor ratios—which in turn may differ across countries only as a result of differences in population growth rates, rates of technological progress, and saving rates. However, observed differences in capital per worker are *far smaller* than those needed to account for the differences in output per worker (or income per capita) shown in the data.

- It provides an *incomplete* description of the growth process, because the driving force of long-run growth, the rate of increase in the effectiveness of labor, is *exogenous.*

Appendix to Chapter 11
Dynamics of k, the Output Effect of s,
and the Speed of Adjustment

To find the explicit dynamic path of k, note that Equation (15) can be written as

$$\dot{k} + (n + \gamma + \delta)k = sk^{\alpha},$$

whose particular form is known as a **Bernoulli equation** (see Chiang, 1984, p. 500). Let $z = k^{1-\alpha}$, so that $\dot{z} = (1 - \alpha)k^{-\alpha}\dot{k}$; from these two results,

$$k = zk^{\alpha}, \quad \dot{k} = \frac{\dot{z}k^{\alpha}}{1 - \alpha},$$

so that the above equation can be written as

$$\dot{z} + (1 - \alpha)(n + \gamma + \delta)z = (1 - \alpha)s,$$

which is a standard linear nonhomogeneous differential equation in z, whose solution is therefore

$$z = \left\{ z_0 - \frac{s}{n + \gamma + \delta} \right\} e^{-(1-\alpha)(n+\gamma+\delta)t} + \frac{s}{n + \gamma + \delta}.$$

Substituting for z yields

$$k^{1-\alpha} = \left\{ k_0^{1-\alpha} - \frac{s}{n + \gamma + \delta} \right\} e^{-(1-\alpha)(n+\gamma+\delta)t} + \frac{s}{n + \gamma + \delta},$$

which shows that, because $(1-\alpha)(n+\gamma+\delta) > 0$, $k^{1-\alpha}$ tends to $s/(n+\gamma+\delta)$—or the solution $\tilde{k}$ given in Equation (17).

To establish the effect of the increase in the saving rate on output per unit of effective labor on the balanced growth path, note that because $\tilde{y} = \tilde{k}^{\alpha}$ it must be that

$$\frac{\partial \tilde{y}}{\partial s} = \alpha \tilde{k}^{\alpha-1}\left(\frac{\partial \tilde{k}}{\partial s}\right). \tag{A1}$$

As shown above, $\tilde{k}$ is determined by the equality between actual and required investment [Equation (16)], that is,

$$s\tilde{k}^{\alpha} - (n + \gamma + \delta)\tilde{k} = 0. \tag{A2}$$

Implicit differentiation of this expression with respect to s yields

$$s\alpha\tilde{k}^{\alpha-1}\left(\frac{\partial \tilde{k}}{\partial s}\right) + \tilde{k}^{\alpha} - (n + \gamma + \delta)\frac{\partial \tilde{k}}{\partial s} = 0,$$

which can be rearranged as

$$\frac{\partial \tilde{k}}{\partial s} = \frac{\tilde{k}^{\alpha}}{(n + \gamma + \delta) - s\alpha\tilde{k}^{\alpha-1}}.$$

Substituting this expression for $\partial \tilde{k}/\partial s$ in (A1) results in

$$\frac{\partial \tilde{y}}{\partial s} = \frac{\alpha \tilde{k}^{\alpha-1} \tilde{k}^{\alpha}}{(n+\gamma+\delta) - s\alpha \tilde{k}^{\alpha-1}}.$$

To interpret this expression, it is convenient to use Equation (16) to substitute for s and convert it into an elasticity by multiplying both sides by $s/\tilde{y}$. The result is

$$\eta \equiv \frac{\partial \tilde{y}/\tilde{y}}{\partial s/s} = (\frac{s}{\tilde{k}^{\alpha}}) \frac{\alpha \tilde{k}^{\alpha-1} \tilde{k}^{\alpha}}{(n+\gamma+\delta) - s\alpha \tilde{k}^{\alpha-1}},$$

or, noting from (A2) that $s\tilde{k}^{\alpha-1} = (n+\gamma+\delta)$:

$$\eta = \frac{\alpha(n+\gamma+\delta)\tilde{k}^{\alpha}}{[(n+\gamma+\delta) - \alpha(n+\gamma+\delta)]\tilde{k}^{\alpha}},$$

which can be simplified to give Equation (23) in the text.

To derive Equation (24), note first that from Equation (15), $\dot{k}$ is a function of k; this relationship can be written as

$$\dot{k} = \Phi(k). \tag{A3}$$

When $k = \tilde{k}$, $\dot{k}$ is zero. Around the long-run equilibrium ($k = \tilde{k}$), therefore, a **first-order Taylor-series approximation** of the function $\Phi(k)$ yields (see Chiang, 1984, pp. 256-58):[16]

$$\dot{k} \simeq \Phi(\tilde{k}) + \Phi'|_{k=\tilde{k}} (k - \tilde{k}),$$

or, because $\Phi(\tilde{k}) = 0$ when $\dot{k}$ is zero (in the neighborhood of the long-run equilibrium):

$$\dot{k} \simeq \Phi'|_{k=\tilde{k}} (k - \tilde{k}), \tag{A4}$$

where $\Phi'|_{k=\tilde{k}}$ is the first-order derivative of $\dot{k}$ evaluated at $k = \tilde{k}$.

Differentiating Equation (15) with respect to k and evaluating the resulting expression at $k = \tilde{k}$ yields

$$\Phi'|_{k=\tilde{k}} = s\alpha \tilde{k}^{\alpha-1} - (\gamma+n+\delta),$$

or, using Equation (16) to substitute for s:

$$\Phi'|_{k=\tilde{k}} = \Lambda = -(1-\alpha)(n+\gamma+\delta) < 0,$$

---

[16] The speed of adjustment derived from this procedure provides, strictly speaking, a reliable estimate only in an arbitrarily small neighborhood around the balanced growth path. For the Solow-Swan model with conventional production functions, and for moderate changes in parameter values (such as the change in s considered earlier), the Taylor-series approximation is reliable. In general, however, Taylor-series approximations do not provide reliable estimates for *finite changes*. See Mulligan and Sala-i-Martin (1993) for a discussion.

which can be substituted in (A4) to yield Equation (24).

To show that y approaches $\tilde{y}$ at the same rate that k approaches $\tilde{k}$, note first that, from Equation (5), $\dot{y} = \alpha k^{\alpha-1}\dot{k}$; using (A3) and the fact that $k = y^{1/\alpha}$ yields

$$\dot{y} = \alpha k^{\alpha-1}\Phi(k) = \alpha y^{(\alpha-1)/\alpha}\Phi(y^{1/\alpha}) = \Gamma(y).$$

A *linear approximation* in the vicinity of $y = \tilde{y}$ now yields, because $\Gamma(\tilde{y}) = 0$,

$$\dot{y} = \Gamma'|_{y=\tilde{y}}\,(y - \tilde{y}),$$

where, because $\Phi(\tilde{y}^{1/\alpha}) = 0$,

$$\Gamma'|_{y=\tilde{y}} = \alpha y^{(\alpha-1)/\alpha}\,\Phi'|_{y=\tilde{y}} = \alpha\tilde{y}^{(\alpha-1)/\alpha}[sy - (\gamma + n + \delta)y^{1/\alpha}]'_{y=\tilde{y}},$$

that is,

$$\Gamma'|_{y=\tilde{y}} = \alpha s\tilde{y}^{(\alpha-1)/\alpha} - (\gamma + n + \delta).$$

Using Equation (16) yields $s = (\gamma + n + \delta)\tilde{y}^{1/\alpha}/\tilde{y}$, which can be substituted in the above expression to give $\Gamma'|_{y=\tilde{y}} = \Lambda$.

Chapter 12

Knowledge, Human Capital, and Endogenous Growth

As discussed in the previous chapter, the only determinant of per capita income growth in the long run in the Solow-Swan model is the effectiveness of labor, A, whose exact meaning is not specified and whose behavior is taken as exogenous. Moreover, assuming that the rate of return on capital reflects its contribution to output and that its share in total income is set at plausible levels, differences in capital intensity cannot account for cross-country income differences. In part because of these limitations, much thinking has been devoted in the past few years to understanding the sources of growth and the divergent patterns of income observed across countries. This research has highlighted the existence of a variety of *endogenous mechanisms* that foster economic growth, and has suggested new roles for public policy. This revival of interest has largely been the result of influential contributions by Lucas (1988), Grossman and Helpman (1991), and Romer (1986). This chapter considers several of these new perspectives on growth.[1]

Section 12.1 focuses on the view that the driving force of growth is the *accumulation of knowledge*. It examines various mechanisms through which knowledge is produced and resources are allocated to knowledge production. The second perspective, examined in section 12.2, takes a broader view of capital to include *human* capital. These models (which in some regards can be seen as extensions of the Solow-Swan model) imply that the income share of *physical* capital alone may not be an accurate measure of the overall importance of capital. A broad measure of capital raises the possibility that differences in capital intensity may be able to account, after all, for cross-country differences

---

[1] For comprehensive overviews, see Aghion and Howitt (1998), and Barro and Sala-i-Martin (1995). Jones and Manuelli (1997) provide a more technical survey of some important classes of endogenous growth models.

in incomes per capita. Section 12.3 discusses the links between human capital accumulation, public policy toward education, and growth. Section 12.4 considers various other determinants of growth emphasized in the recent growth literature—including fiscal policy (changes in government spending, taxation, and fiscal deficits), inflation and macroeconomic stability, trade liberalization, the degree of financial development, political factors and income inequality, and the role of institutions.

12.1   The Accumulation of Knowledge

There are two main mechanisms through which the creation of knowledge is captured in endogenous growth models: as a by-product of economic activity or as a production activity in its own right. Of course, these approaches are rather mechanical; in reference to the latter, Solow (1994, pp. 51-52), for instance, wrote

> There is probably an irreducibly exogenous element in the research and development process, at least exogenous to the economy. Fields of research open up and close down unpredictably, in economics as well as in science and technology. This is reflected, for instance, in the frequency with which research projects end up by finding something that was not even contemplated when the initial decisions were made. There is an internal logic—or sometimes non-logic— to the advance of knowledge that may be orthogonal to the economic logic. This is not at all to deny the partially endogenous character of innovation but only to suggest that the "production" of new technology may not be a simple matter of inputs and outputs.

Nevertheless, it is worth presenting illustrative models of both mechanisms because they have very different implications regarding the determinants of an economy's steady-state growth rate.

12.1.1   Knowledge as a By-Product: Learning by Doing

A key source of technological progress, as emphasized by Arrow (1962), results from **learning by doing**. In such a framework, experience, measured in various ways (in terms, for instance, of cumulative past investment or output) plays a critical role in raising labor productivity over time.

A simple way to illustrate Arrow's learning-by-doing approach is to assume that the level of productivity, A, is related to the absolute size of the capital stock and to an autonomous factor, Z, so that

$$A = ZK^{\theta}, \tag{1}$$

where θ is a positive coefficient. Differentiating this expression with respect to time yields

$$\frac{\dot{A}}{A} = \theta(\frac{\dot{K}}{K}) + \gamma, \quad 0 < \theta < 1, \tag{2}$$

where $\gamma \ (\equiv \dot{Z}/Z)$ can be viewed, as before, as the exogenous rate of labor-augmenting technical change. The parameter θ is often described as the *learning coefficient*, which may depend, in particular, on government spending on education (as discussed later). Thus, technological change is partly exogenous and partly endogenous. The Solow-Swan model corresponds to the case in which $\theta = 0$.[2]

To examine the implications of this specification, consider again the case in which the production technology is Cobb-Douglas, which in intensive form is given by

$$y = k^{\alpha}, \tag{3}$$

where $k = K/AL$. Capital accumulation and the labor force growth rate are again given by

$$\dot{K} = sY - \delta K, \quad \dot{L}/L = n. \tag{4}$$

From Equations (3) and (4), the growth rate of the capital stock is given by

$$\frac{\dot{K}}{K} = s(\frac{Y}{AL})(\frac{AL}{K}) - \delta = \frac{sk^{\alpha}}{k} - \delta, \tag{5}$$

whereas the growth rate of labor in efficiency units is given by, using Equation (2):

$$\frac{\dot{A}}{A} + \frac{\dot{L}}{L} = \theta(\frac{\dot{K}}{K}) + \gamma + n. \tag{6}$$

Differentiating the expression $k = K/AL$ with respect to time yields

$$\frac{\dot{k}}{k} = \frac{\dot{K}}{K} - (\frac{\dot{A}}{A} + \frac{\dot{L}}{L}), \tag{7}$$

so that, using Equations (5) and (6):

$$\dot{k} = s(1 - \theta)k^{\alpha} - [\gamma + n + \delta(1 - \theta)]k, \tag{8}$$

which is a nonlinear, first-order differential equation in k similar to the one derived in the previous chapter for the Solow-Swan model. The equilibrium capital-effective labor ratio is thus given by

$$\tilde{k} = \left\{ \frac{s(1 - \theta)}{n + \gamma + \delta(1 - \theta)} \right\}^{1/(1-\alpha)},$$

from which it can readily be established that an increase in the learning coefficient θ, by raising the level of effective labor, reduces the steady-state value of the capital-effective labor ratio.

Setting $\dot{k} = 0$ in Equation (7), the steady-state growth rate of the capital stock is thus given by, using Equation (6),

$$\tilde{g}_K \equiv \left. \frac{\dot{K}}{K} \right|_{k=\tilde{k}} = \theta\tilde{g}_K + \gamma + n,$$

---

[2] Assuming that knowledge accumulation occurs as a side effect of goods production, rather than capital accumulation, leads to qualitatively similar conclusions to those derived here.

so that

$$\tilde{\mathbf{g}}_K = \frac{\gamma + n}{1 - \theta}.$$

The steady-state growth rate of output, ALk^α, is thus equal to

$$\tilde{\mathbf{g}}_Y = \theta\tilde{\mathbf{g}}_K + \gamma + n = \frac{\gamma + n}{1 - \theta},$$

so that income per worker, Y/L, grows on the balanced growth path at the rate

$$\tilde{\mathbf{g}}_{Y/L} = \tilde{\mathbf{g}}_Y - n = \frac{\gamma + \theta n}{1 - \theta}. \tag{9}$$

Thus, in Arrow's model, although the learning coefficient has a positive effect on the steady-state growth rate of output, the latter remains *independent of the saving rate*. In addition, this model predicts that an increase in the population growth rate, n, *raises* the steady-state growth rate of output per worker—in contrast to the Solow-Swan model, where an increase in n has no effect on Y/L. The evidence reviewed in Chapter 10, however, suggests that the population growth rate and the growth rate of income per capita (or output per worker) are *negatively* correlated.

Thus, although Arrow's formulation of learning by doing is capable of explaining differences in growth rates in per capita incomes by differences in the ability to learn from experience (going in this sense beyond the Solow-Swan model, which relies only on differences in the rate of technological progress), it still gives no role to saving and investment rates. An extension of Arrow's learning-by-doing model presented by Villanueva (1994) addresses this issue. The introduction of learning through experience in Villanueva's model has three attractive consequences.

- The equilibrium growth rate becomes *endogenous* and may be influenced by government policies.

- The *speed of adjustment* to the equilibrium growth path is faster than in the Solow-Swan model, and enhanced learning reduces adjustment time.[3]

- The equilibrium rate of output growth exceeds the sum of the exogenous rates of technical change and population growth.

The key relationship of Villanueva's modified Arrow model is the equation driving the efficiency of labor, which is given by, instead of Equation (2),

$$\dot{A} = \theta(\frac{K}{L}) + \gamma A, \quad \theta > 0. \tag{10}$$

Equation (10) indicates that technical change is positively related to the capital stock per worker, K/L.[4] Put differently, the productivity of workers

---

[3] For a general comparison of the speed of convergence in the Solow-Swan model and endogenous growth models with human capital accumulation, see Ortigueira and Santos (1997).

[4] This specification is reminiscent of an early contribution by Conlisk (1967), who related the rate of growth of the labor force not only to an exogenous component, n, but also to output per worker, Y/L.

increases when the relative availability of capital goods (for instance, the stock of high-performance computers) rises.

Suppose again that the production technology is Cobb-Douglas [as assumed in Equation (3)] and that capital accumulation and the labor force growth rate are given by Equation (4). The growth rate of the capital stock is thus again given by Equation (5). Using Equation (10), the growth rate of labor in efficiency units is now given by

$$\frac{\dot{A}}{A} + \frac{\dot{L}}{L} = \theta k + \gamma + n. \tag{11}$$

Differentiating the expression $k = K/AL$ with respect to time and substituting Equation (11) now yields

$$\dot{k}/k = sk^{\alpha-1} - \theta k - (\gamma + n + \delta), \tag{12}$$

an equation for which no explicit solution can be derived—in contrast to the case studied in the appendix to Chapter 11, which corresponds to $\theta = 0$. The equilibrium capital-effective labor ratio can nevertheless by obtained from Equation (12) by setting $\dot{k} = 0$, so that

$$s\tilde{k}^{\alpha-1} - \theta\tilde{k} - (\gamma + n + \delta) = 0.$$

Using the **implicit function theorem**, it can be established from the above expression that $\partial\tilde{k}/\partial\theta < 0$.[5] Thus, as in Arrow's model, an increase in the speed of learning lowers the equilibrium capital-effective labor ratio.

The steady-state growth rates of the capital stock and output are now equal to

$$\tilde{g}_Y = \tilde{g}_K = \theta\tilde{k} + \gamma + n,$$

whereas income per worker, $Y/L = Ak^\alpha$, which grows away from the steady state at the rate

$$\frac{\dot{Y}}{Y} - n = \alpha(\frac{\dot{k}}{k}) + \theta k + \gamma, \tag{13}$$

has an equilibrium growth rate given by

$$\tilde{g}_{Y/L} = \theta\tilde{k} + \gamma.$$

In contrast to Arrow's model [Equation (9)], $\tilde{g}_{Y/L}$ now depends on the steady-state value of the capital-effective labor ratio—as long as θ is different from zero.

The determination of the equilibrium growth rate in the modified Arrow model is depicted in Figure 12.1.

---

[5] The implicit function theorem states that for a given equation in the form $H(y, x_1, ..., x_n) = 0$, to define an implicit function $y = h(x_1, ..., x_n)$ it is sufficient that (a) the function H has continuous partial derivatives; and (b) at a point $(y^0, x_1^0, ..., x_n^0)$ satisfying the equation $H(\cdot) = 0$, H_y is not zero; then $\partial y/\partial x_i = -H_{x_i}/H_y$. In this case, $H(\cdot)$ is defined as $H(\tilde{k}, s, n, \theta)$, with $y = \tilde{k}$, so that $\partial\tilde{k}/\partial\theta = -H_\theta/H_{\tilde{k}} = \tilde{k}/[s(\alpha-1)\tilde{k}^{\alpha-2} - \theta] < 0$. See Chiang (1984, pp. 206-8) for more details.

- Curve KK corresponds to Equation (5), and shows the growth rate of the capital stock, $\dot{K}/K$, as a function of the capital-effective labor ratio, k. It is *downward sloping* as a result of diminishing marginal returns to capital ($\alpha < 1$).

- The line NN corresponds to the growth rate of effective labor in the modified Arrow model, as given by Equation (11); it is *upward sloping* because $\theta > 0$.

- The line SS corresponds to the growth rate of effective labor in the Solow-Swan model, which is constant and equal to $n + \gamma$ [that is, Equation (11) with $\theta = 0$].

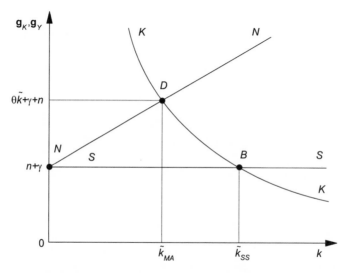

Figure 12.1. The steady-state growth rate in the Solow-Swan and modified Arrow models. Source: Adapted from Villanueva (1994, p. 8).

The balanced growth path of the Solow-Swan model is obtained at point B, which corresponds to the intersection of KK and SS. The balanced growth path of the modified Arrow model, by contrast, is obtained at the intersection of KK and NN (point D). The growth rate of output, g_Y, is thus *higher* in the modified Arrow model by the magnitude $\theta\tilde{k}$, which reflects induced learning by doing. The capital-effective labor ratio, however, is lower in the modified Arrow model ($\tilde{k}_{MA} < \tilde{k}_{SS}$), because of a higher level of effective labor.

To illustrate the properties of this model, it is worth examining the effects of an *increase in the saving rate*, s, as was done in the previous chapter in the context of the Solow-Swan model. Such effects are illustrated in the upper panel of Figure 12.2, in which the initial positions of the Solow-Swan and modified Arrow models are indicated by Points B and D, respectively. An increase in the saving rate shifts the KK curve to the right in both models. The new equilibrium positions are given respectively by point B' in the Solow-Swan model and point D' in the modified Arrow model. In both models, the capital-effective labor ratio rises, although the new ratio remains lower in the modified Arrow model (as a result of learning by doing) relative to the Solow-Swan model. But the new steady-state growth rate *rises* in the former, whereas it does not change in the latter.

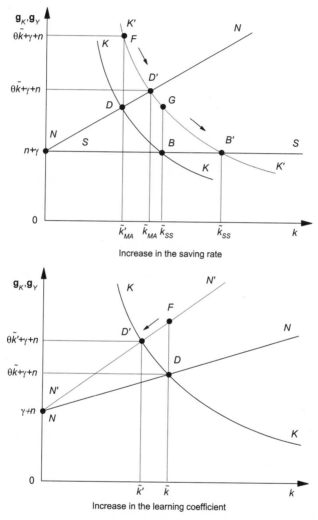

Figure 12.2. Properties of the modified Arrow model. Source: Adapted from Villanueva (1994, pp. 11, 13).

During the transition between equilibrium points B and B', the rate of output growth in the Solow-Swan model is temporarily higher—as measured by the distance BG—than the natural rate $n + \gamma$ because the growth of capital increases as a result of the rise in the saving rate. Formally, from Equation (13) with $\theta = 0$, because $\dot{k}/k$ is positive anywhere between $\tilde{k}_{SS}$ and $\tilde{k}'_{SS}$, $\dot{Y}/Y$ must be greater than $n + \gamma$ throughout the transition from B to B'. Nevertheless, the growth rate of output falls over time (the vertical distance between the horizontal curve SS and $K'K'$ diminishes continuously between $\tilde{k}_{SS}$ and $\tilde{k}'_{SS}$) as a result of diminishing marginal returns. In the new steady state (point B'), because $\dot{k} = 0$, $\dot{Y}/Y$ is again equal to $n + \gamma$. Thus, as shown in the previous chapter, the long-run effect of a rise in the saving rate is an increase in the capital-effective labor ratio, with no change in the economy's steady-state rate of output growth.

In the modified Arrow model, by contrast, the increase in the saving rate shifts the long-run equilibrium position (the point of intersection of $K'K'$ and NN) to D'. At the initial level of the capital-effective labor ratio $\tilde{k}_{MA}$, the growth rate of the capital stock jumps from point D to point F (implying that the growth rate of output jumps also), and the capital-effective labor ratio begins to increase along $K'K'$. This increase tends to reduce over time the marginal (and average) product of capital, thereby lowering the level of saving per unit of capital and reducing the growth rate of the capital stock—from point F to point D'. At the same time, because the increase in the capital-effective labor ratio tends to raise the rate of labor-augmenting technical change, the rate of growth of effective labor begins to increase also—rising from point D to point D' along NN. This process continues until a new long-run equilibrium is achieved, in which the growth rates of the capital stock and effective labor are equal (point D').

Another important feature of the modified Arrow model is the dynamic adjustment process associated with an *increase in the learning coefficient, θ.* As illustrated in the lower panel of Figure 12.2, an increase in θ shifts the NN curve to the left, and its slope becomes steeper. The adjustment dynamics are as follows. Following the increase in θ, and at the initial equilibrium point $\tilde{k}_{MA}$, the rate of change of effective labor rises above $\gamma + n$ [as implied by Equation (11)], jumping from point D to point F, whereas the rate of change of the capital-effective labor ratio, $\dot{k}/k$, turns negative [as implied by Equation (12)]. From Equation (7), this last result implies that the rate of growth of effective labor is higher than the growth rate of the capital stock, and the capital-effective labor ratio begins to fall toward $\tilde{k}'_{MA}$. As k falls, income per unit of capital [Y/K, which is equal to $1/k^{1-\alpha}$ from Equation (5)] increases, stimulating saving and investment, and the growth rate of the capital stock begins rising. At the same time, the fall in the capital-effective labor ratio reduces over time the rate at which technological progress is occurring [$\dot{A}/A = \theta k + \gamma$, from Equation (10)]. The growth rate of effective labor, $\dot{A}/A + n$, therefore falls also over time [Equation (11)]. This process continues until the growth rates of the capital stock and effective labor are equal (point D'). The new long-run equilibrium is characterized by a lower level of the capital-effective labor ratio and a higher growth rate of per capita output and income.

The model also has interesting implications—as does the original Arrow model of learning by doing presented earlier—for the *speed of adjustment* to the steady state. From Equation (12), it can be shown that[6]

$$\dot{k} = \Lambda(k - \tilde{k}), \quad \Lambda < 0. \tag{14}$$

As in the previous chapter, the speed of adjustment of the actual growth rate of output to its steady-state value, $\tilde{\mathbf{g}}_Y = \theta \tilde{k} + \gamma + n$, can be easily calculated. The **adjustment ratio** can again be defined as

$$\mu = \frac{\mathbf{g}_Y - \mathbf{g}_Y^0}{\tilde{\mathbf{g}}_Y - \mathbf{g}_Y^0}.$$

Solving for $\mathbf{g}_Y$ and substituting the result in this equation implies that the time t^* (in years) required to get a fraction μ of the way from $\mathbf{g}_Y^0$ to $\tilde{\mathbf{g}}_Y$ is given by

$$t^* = \Lambda^{-1} \ln \left\{ \frac{(1-\mu)(\tilde{\mathbf{g}}_Y - \mathbf{g}_Y^0 + \alpha\Lambda)}{(1-\mu)(\tilde{\mathbf{g}}_Y - \mathbf{g}_Y^0) + \alpha\Lambda} \right\}.$$

Simulation results performed by Villanueva (1994) showed that the adjustment time in this model is about a quarter to a third of what the Solow-Swan model predicts, depending on the value of the learning coefficient θ (which affects Λ). Thus, the presence of learning by doing implies that convergence to the balanced growth path occurs *more quickly*. Of course, the generality or empirical relevance of Villanueva's specification remain open to question. At the conceptual level, nevertheless, it provides a useful illustration (consistent with various other models) of the importance of learning for the growth process. More generally, Villanueva's variant of Arrow's specification of endogenous technical change is potentially capable of explaining the diversity in per capita growth rates across countries indicated by the data. Such diversity can be explained not only in terms of differences in population growth rates, but also in terms of differences in saving rates and parameters that influence the learning process—such as government spending on education (as discussed later).

12.1.2 The Production of Knowledge

The foregoing discussion assumed that the accumulation of knowledge occurs as a natural *by-product* of economic activity. This section discusses the case where, on the contrary, knowledge must be produced, like any other good.

Following Romer (1990), consider an economy with two production sectors:

---

[6] Following the procedure outlined in the appendix to Chapter 11, Equation (12) can be written as

$$\dot{k} = sk^\alpha - \theta k^2 - (\gamma + n + \delta)k = \Phi(k).$$

Taking a linear approximation in the neighborhood of $\tilde{k}$ yields

$$\dot{k} \simeq \Phi(\tilde{k}) + \Phi'|_{k=\tilde{k}} (k - \tilde{k}),$$

which, because $\Phi(\tilde{k}) = 0$, corresponds to Equation (14) with

$$\Phi'|_{k=\tilde{k}} = \Lambda \equiv s\alpha\tilde{k}^{\alpha-1} - 2\theta\tilde{k} - (\gamma + n + \delta).$$

Note that Λ is, in general, ambiguous; ensuring stability requires assuming that $\Lambda < 0$.

- a *goods-producing sector*, which uses physical capital, knowledge, and labor in the production process; and

- a *knowledge-producing sector*, where additions to the stock of knowledge are made using the same inputs.

A fraction ϕ_L of the labor force is used in the knowledge-producing sector, and a fraction $1 - \phi_L$ in the goods-producing sector. Similarly, a fraction ϕ_K of the capital stock is used in the knowledge-producing sector, and a fraction $1 - \phi_K$ in the goods-producing sector.

Both sectors use the *full stock of knowledge*, A. The rationale here is **non-rivalry**: the use of an element or component of knowledge in one sector does not preclude its use in the other sector.

Output in the goods-producing sector is given by a conventional Cobb-Douglas function

$$Y = [(1 - \phi_K)K]^\alpha [A(1 - \phi_L)L]^{1-\alpha}, \quad 0 < \alpha < 1, \tag{15}$$

which implies constant returns to *both* capital and (effective) labor. By contrast, the production of knowledge is determined by the **generalized Cobb-Douglas** form

$$\dot{A} = \gamma(\phi_K K)^\beta (\phi_L L)^\eta A^\kappa, \quad \beta, \eta, \gamma \geq 0. \tag{16}$$

If $\kappa = 1$, $\dot{A}$ is proportional to A; the effect is stronger if $\kappa > 1$, and weaker if $\kappa < 1$. The production function for knowledge is not assumed to have constant returns to scale to capital and labor, that is, $\beta + \eta$ may exceed unity.[7] Setting $\beta = \eta = \phi_K = \phi_L = 0$, and $\kappa = 1$, the production function for knowledge accumulation becomes $\dot{A}/A = \gamma$, which implies that A grows at a constant rate, as in the Solow-Swan model.

Unlike the previous models of learning by doing, the dynamics of the above model cannot be characterized by a single differential equation in the capital-effective labor ratio; they now involve two endogenous stock variables, K and A, making the model more complicated to analyze.[8]

As shown by Romer (1990), under the same assumptions as above regarding capital accumulation and the labor force growth [Equation (4)], the steady-state growth rates of knowledge and capital are given by

$$\tilde{g}_A = \frac{\beta + \eta}{1 - (\kappa + \beta)} n, \quad \tilde{g}_K = \tilde{g}_Y = \tilde{g}_A + n,$$

and the growth rate of output per worker by

$$\tilde{g}_{Y/L} = \tilde{g}_K - n = \tilde{g}_A.$$

---

[7] The fact that the function does not necessarily have constant returns to scale is the reason for referring to it as a generalized Cobb-Douglas function.

[8] Arnold (2000) provided a complete characterization of the dynamics of Romer's (1990) model in the neighborhood of its steady state (that is, the balanced growth path). He showed that the growth path converging to this steady state is unique and monotonic.

Thus, the economy's growth rate is an increasing function of population growth and is zero if population growth is zero—because in that case $\tilde{\mathbf{g}}_A = 0$. The fractions of the labor force and the capital stock used in the knowledge-producing sector, ϕ_L and ϕ_K, have no effect on the growth rate, nor does the saving rate, s.

Thus, the specific mechanism by which a knowledge-producing sector was introduced does not alter significantly the predictions of the Solow-Swan model. Consequently, the model suffers from the same limitations regarding its ability to explain some of the basic empirical facts that appear to characterize the growth process.

12.2 Human Capital and Returns to Scale

Another strand of the recent literature on growth focuses on the accumulation of human capital—as distinct from the accumulation of knowledge. Human capital is viewed as consisting of the abilities, skills, and knowledge of individual workers. In that perspective, it has been emphasized that human capital, very much like conventional economic goods, is *rival* (use of a particular good by one individual precludes its use by another individual at the same time) and *excludable* (an individual can prevent others from using the good that he or she is using).

By contrast, as indicated earlier, aggregate knowledge is typically nonrival. This section presents two models of growth with both physical and human capital accumulation: the model of Mankiw, Romer, and Weil (1992), and the so-called AK model of Rebelo (1991).[9]

12.2.1 The Mankiw-Romer-Weil Model

Aside from the inclusion of human capital, the model developed by Mankiw, Romer, and Weil (1992) is similar to the Solow-Swan model in the sense that it assumes constant returns to scale. However, it differs in an important way from that model because relatively small changes in the resources devoted to physical and human capital accumulation may lead to large changes in output per worker. As a result, it is more capable to account for large differences in real incomes across countries.

There is only one production sector, with output given by

$$Y = K^\alpha H^\beta (AL)^{1-\alpha-\beta}, \quad \alpha, \beta > 0, \ \alpha + \beta < 1, \tag{17}$$

where H is the stock of human capital, and L the number of workers, as before. Thus, there are *decreasing returns* to K and H, but *constant returns* to K, L

---

[9] For other models of human capital accumulation and growth, see Lucas (1988) and Azariadis and Drazen (1990).

and H.[10] As before, it is assumed that

$$\dot{K} = s_K Y - \delta K, \quad \dot{L}/L = n, \tag{18}$$

where now s_K denotes the fraction of output devoted to investment.

As in the Solow-Swan model, technological progress is taken to be exogenous:

$$\dot{A}/A = \gamma. \tag{19}$$

Investment in human capital is also assumed to represent a fixed fraction of output:[11]

$$\dot{H} = s_H Y - \delta H, \tag{20}$$

where for simplicity the rate of depreciation of human capital is assumed to be the same as for physical capital.

Let $h = H/AL$ be the **human capital-effective labor ratio**. The production function (17) can be written in intensive form as

$$y = k^\alpha h^\beta, \tag{21}$$

where, as before, $k = K/AL$ and $y = Y/AL$.

To determine the dynamics of k, note that from the definition of k, as shown in the previous chapter,

$$\dot{k} = \frac{\dot{K}}{AL} - \left(\frac{K}{AL}\right)\frac{\dot{L}}{L} - \left(\frac{K}{AL}\right)\frac{\dot{A}}{A},$$

which can be written as, using Equations (18) and (19):

$$\dot{k} = s_K y - \varphi k,$$

where $\varphi = n + \gamma + \delta$. Equivalently, using Equation (21), this equation can be rewritten as:

$$\dot{k} = s_K k^\alpha h^\beta - \varphi k. \tag{22}$$

Similarly, from the definition of h,

$$\dot{h} = \frac{\dot{H}}{AL} - \left(\frac{H}{AL}\right)\left\{\frac{\dot{L}}{L} + \frac{\dot{A}}{A}\right\},$$

which can be written as, using Equations (19), (20), and (21):

$$\dot{h} = s_H k^\alpha h^\beta - \varphi h. \tag{23}$$

---

[10] Temple (1998) introduced the distinction between equipment and structures (buildings) as two components of capital in the Mankiw-Romer-Weil framework. His production function generalizes (17) to give $Y = K_S^{\alpha_S} K_E^{\alpha_E} H^\beta (AL)^{1-\alpha_S-\alpha_E-\beta}$, where K_S is the stock of structures, K_E the stock of equipment goods, $0 < \alpha_S, \alpha_E, \beta < 1$, and H and L are defined as before. There are now constant returns to K_S, K_E, L, and H.

[11] See Cohen (1996b) for a more general specification of the law of motion of human capital. Cohen's specification assumes that knowledge and output are not proportional, and that human capital plays a larger role in the production of knowledge than in the production of goods.

Equations (22) and (23) form a first-order differential equation system in k and h, which can be linearized around the steady state to give

$$\begin{bmatrix} \dot{k} \\ \dot{h} \end{bmatrix} = \begin{bmatrix} a_{11} & a_{12} \\ a_{21} & a_{22} \end{bmatrix} \begin{bmatrix} k - \tilde{k} \\ h - \tilde{h} \end{bmatrix}, \tag{24}$$

where

$$a_{11} = \alpha s_K \tilde{k}^{\alpha-1} \tilde{h}^\beta - \varphi, \quad a_{12} = \beta s_K \tilde{k}^\alpha \tilde{h}^{\beta-1} > 0,$$

$$a_{21} = \alpha s_H \tilde{k}^{\alpha-1} \tilde{h}^\beta > 0, \quad a_{22} = \beta s_H \tilde{k}^\alpha \tilde{h}^{\beta-1} - \varphi,$$

and $\tilde{k}$ and $\tilde{h}$ are the steady-state values obtained by setting $\dot{k} = 0$ and $\dot{h} = 0$ in Equations (22) and (23):

$$s_K \tilde{k}^\alpha \tilde{h}^\beta = \varphi \tilde{k}, \quad s_H \tilde{k}^\alpha \tilde{h}^\beta = \varphi \tilde{h}. \tag{25}$$

Because $0 < \alpha < 1$ and $0 < \beta < 1$, these two equations imply that $a_{11} < 0$ and $a_{22} < 0$. They also yield two relationships between k and h,

$$\tilde{k} = \left\{ \left(\frac{s_K}{\varphi}\right) \tilde{h}^\beta \right\}^{1/(1-\alpha)}, \quad \tilde{k} = \left\{ \left(\frac{\varphi}{s_H}\right) \tilde{h}^{1-\beta} \right\}^{1/\alpha}, \tag{26}$$

which can be solved for $\tilde{k}$ and $\tilde{h}$.

The first equation of (26) is shown in Figure 12.3 as curve KK in the k-h space.[12] The slope of this curve is positive and given by

$$\left.\frac{dh}{dk}\right|_{KK} = -\frac{a_{11}}{a_{12}} > 0. \tag{27}$$

In addition, Equation (22) implies that $\dot{k}$ is increasing in h. Thus, $\dot{k}$ is positive (negative) to the right (left) of the KK curve, as illustrated by the horizontal arrows. Similarly, the second Equation in (26) is illustrated in Figure 12.3 as curve HH. The slope of HH is also positive and given by

$$\left.\frac{dh}{dk}\right|_{HH} = -\frac{a_{21}}{a_{22}} > 0. \tag{28}$$

Again, Equation (23) implies that $\dot{h}$ is positive (negative) above (below) HH as shown by the vertical arrows.

---

[12] See Chiang (1984, pp. 628-634) for a discussion of two-variable phase diagrams.

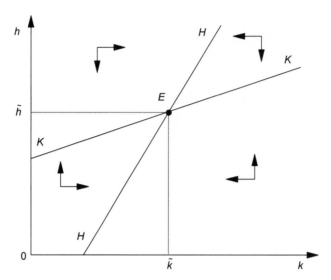

Figure 12.3. Dynamics of human and physical capital per unit of effective labor in the Mankiw-Romer-Weil model.

Local stability of the linearized system (26) requires the following conditions:

- The determinant of the matrix of coefficients, $\mathbf{A}$, must be positive, to guarantee that the two roots of the system have the same sign:

$$\det \mathbf{A} = a_{11}a_{22} - a_{12}a_{21} > 0;$$

- The trace of matrix $\mathbf{A}$ must be negative, to ensure at least one negative root:

$$\det \mathbf{A} = a_{11} + a_{22} < 0.$$

It can readily be seen that the second condition is always satisfied. The first is also always satisfied, as can be verified by substituting (25) in the definition of the a_{ij} coefficients. This yields

$$\det \mathbf{A} = (1 - \alpha)(1 - \beta)\varphi^2 - \alpha\beta\varphi^2 = \varphi^2(1 - \alpha - \beta),$$

which is always positive, given the assumption $\alpha + \beta < 1$. In fact, the model is **globally stable**: whatever the initial values of k and h, the economy *always converges* to the balanced growth path. This is shown in Figure 12.3, where HH cuts KK from below (because $-a_{11}/a_{12} < -a_{21}/a_{22}$). The long-run equilibrium values of physical and human capital, $\tilde{k}$ and $\tilde{h}$ (corresponding to point E in the figure), can be solved from Equations (26):

$$\tilde{k} = \left\{ \frac{s_K^{1-\beta} s_H^{\beta}}{\varphi} \right\}^{1/(1-\alpha-\beta)} , \quad \tilde{h} = \left\{ \frac{s_K^{\alpha} s_H^{1-\alpha}}{\varphi} \right\}^{1/(1-\alpha-\beta)} ,$$

which yields

$$\frac{\tilde{k}}{\tilde{h}} = \frac{s_K}{s_H}. \qquad (29)$$

Total physical capital, human capital, and output (K, H, and Y) are growing at rate $n + \gamma$; and physical capital per worker, human capital per worker, and output per worker (K/L, H/L, and Y/L) are growing at rate γ. Thus, as in the Solow-Swan model, the long-run growth rate of output per worker is determined by the exogenous rate of technological progress.

Consider again an increase in the *saving rate* s_K, under the assumption that the economy is initially on a balanced growth path. The economy's path is illustrated in Figure 12.4. Because, as shown in Equation (26), the dynamics of h do not depend on s_K, the curve HH is not affected; its slope, as given by (28), remains the same. The slope of the KK curve, by contrast, becomes steeper, as can be inferred from (27). The new balanced growth path is now at E', located on the North-East of E. Initially (at $t = 0$) k increases ($\dot{k}_0 > 0$). The economy's position therefore moves above HH, implying that the stock of human capital-effective labor ratio, h, begins to rise also. During the transition, both k and h increase until the new balanced growth path is reached at point E'.

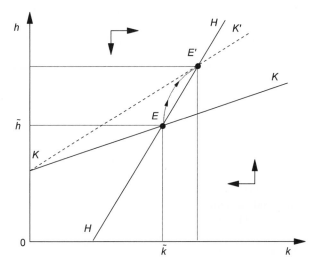

Figure 12.4. An increase in the saving rate in the Mankiw-Romer-Weil model.

From Equation (21), output per worker is equal to

$$Y/L = Ak^\alpha h^\beta.$$

During the transition between the two balanced growth paths, output per worker is rising both because A is rising and because k and h are rising. Thus, output per worker is growing at a rate greater than γ. When the economy reaches the new balanced growth path, k and h are again constant [with a ratio given by (29)], and the rate of growth of output per worker returns to γ. Thus, as in the Solow-Swan model, a permanent increase in the saving rate leads to only a *temporary increase* in the economy's growth rate.

However, the implication of the model regarding the *magnitude* of the effects of changes in the saving rate and the population growth rate differ considerably from the Solow-Swan model. To see this, calculate first the level of y on the balanced growth path, $\tilde{y}$. From Equations (22) and (26), with $\dot{k} = \dot{h} = 0$ on the balanced growth path,

$$s_K \tilde{k}^\alpha \tilde{h}^\beta = \varphi \tilde{k}, \quad s_H \tilde{k}^\alpha \tilde{h}^\beta = \varphi \tilde{h},$$

which can be rewritten, taking logs, as

$$\alpha \ln \tilde{k} + \beta \ln \tilde{h} = \ln \varphi + \ln \tilde{k} - \ln s_K,$$

$$\alpha \ln \tilde{k} + \beta \ln \tilde{h} = \ln \varphi + \ln \tilde{h} - \ln s_H.$$

These two equations are linear in $\ln \tilde{k}$ and $\ln \tilde{h}$. The solution is

$$\ln \tilde{k} = \frac{1}{1 - \alpha - \beta} \left\{ (1 - \beta) \ln s_K + \beta \ln s_H - \ln \varphi \right\},$$

$$\ln \tilde{h} = \frac{1}{1 - \alpha - \beta} \left\{ \alpha \ln s_K + (1 - \alpha) \ln s_H - \ln \varphi \right\}.$$

From the production function (21),

$$\ln \tilde{y} = \alpha \ln \tilde{k} + \beta \ln \tilde{h}.$$

Substituting in this expression the solutions for $\ln \tilde{k}$ and $\ln \tilde{h}$ derived above yields

$$\ln \tilde{y} = \frac{\alpha}{1 - \alpha - \beta} \ln s_K + \frac{\beta}{1 - \alpha - \beta} \ln s_H - \frac{\alpha + \beta}{1 - \alpha - \beta} \ln \varphi. \tag{30}$$

The analogous expression for the Solow-Swan model is identical to Equation (30) with $\beta = 0$, and is thus given by

$$\ln \tilde{y} = \frac{\alpha}{1 - \alpha} \ln s_K - \frac{\alpha}{1 - \alpha} \ln \varphi. \tag{31}$$

Suppose, for instance, that β, human capital's share in output, is equal to 0.4, and that $\alpha = 0.35$. Equation (30) implies that with these parameter values output has elasticities of 1.4 with respect to s_K, 1.6 with respect to s_H, and -3 with respect to φ. In the model without human capital, by contrast, a value for α of 0.35 implies that the elasticity of output with respect to s_K is 0.54 and its elasticity with respect to φ is -0.54. Thus, unlike the Solow-Swan model, the Mankiw-Romer-Weil model can, because of the large elasticities of output with respect to its underlying determinants, potentially account for the observed large income differences across countries (empirical tests of the Mankiw-Romer-Weil model are discussed in the next chapter). However, because the model assumes diminishing marginal products of physical and human capital, it also implies that rates of return are lower in rich than in poor countries. Thus the model does not answer the question of why capital does not flow to poor countries—at least not in the massive and sustained amounts that the theory predicts.[13]

12.2.2 The AK Model

The foregoing analysis focused on the case of diminishing returns to physical and human capital taken together. But it is possible for returns to both types of capital to be **constant** or **increasing**. There are at least three reasons for this to happen.

- Production methods can lead to **internal economies of scale**, once output reaches a sufficiently high level.

- Knowledge can occur as a by-product of capital accumulation (as in the learning-by-doing models discussed earlier), which then creates **positive externalities**.

- The production technology may generate **external economies of scale**. For instance, a doubling of inputs by a single firm may only double its own output, but a doubling of inputs by all firms *together* may more than double their total output.[14]

A simple growth model that views production as exhibiting constant returns to scale to physical and human capital together is the so-called *AK* model proposed by Rebelo (1991). All production inputs in the model are viewed as *reproducible capital*, including not only physical capital (as emphasized in the basic neoclassical framework), but also human capital. Specifically, denoting by K^T this composite measure of capital, the production function is assumed given by the linear form

$$Y = AK^T, \tag{32}$$

where A is again a parameter that captures factors affecting the level of technology.[15]

Using (4) and (32) implies that $\dot{K}^T = sY - \delta K^T = (sA - \delta)K^T$, so that $\mathbf{g}_{K^T} = sA - \delta$. The steady-state growth rate of the capital stock per worker is thus equal to

$$\tilde{\mathbf{g}}_{K^T/L} = sA - (n + \delta),$$

---

[13] Tax policies, expropriation risk, and various forms of capital-market imperfections could cause capital not to flow to poorer countries in the face of rate-of-return differentials—even if these differentials are large.

[14] For instance, the presence of a large number of firms producing similar products can foster the development of specialized support firms, thereby making the production process at any given firm more efficient.

[15] Another route to obtaining an equation like Equation (32) is to postulate that an increasing variety or quality of machinery or intermediate inputs offsets the propensity to diminishing returns. In this interpretation, K^T now represents the variety or quality inputs. Research and development are necessary to obtain this variety, and firms devote skilled labor to this activity. To ensure that outlays for research and development that generate these inputs are recuperated (in the form of rents) by firms that engage in such activities, imperfect competition must prevail in some form. See Grossman and Helpman (1991) and Romer (1990).

whereas the steady-state growth rate of output per worker is given by

$$\tilde{g}_{Y/L} = sA - (n + \delta). \tag{33}$$

This equation implies that income per capita grows at a positive and constant rate as long as $sA > n + \delta$. An important implication of the AK model is thus that, in contrast to the Solow-Swan and Mankiw-Romer-Weil models discussed earlier, an increase in the saving rate *permanently* raises the growth rate of output per capita. In addition, and again in contrast with the neoclassical growth model, which predicts that poor countries should grow faster than rich countries during the transition to the steady state, the AK model implies that poor countries whose production process is characterized by the same degree of technological sophistication as richer countries should always grow at the same rate as these countries, *regardless* of the initial level of income. Thus, the AK model does not predict convergence in per capita income even if countries share the same technology and are characterized by the same pattern of saving— a prediction that seems to accord well with some of the empirical evidence. However, recent time-series tests do not appear to support the basic assumptions of the AK model (Jones, 1995).

12.3 Human Capital and Public Policy

Educational attainment is a crucial determinant of an individual's earnings capacity and of a country's stock of human capital. Poor families are often caught in a **low-education**, **low-skill**, and **low-income trap**: they cannot afford to save a significant fraction of current income and invest it in education.[16] The higher the initial degree of inequality in income and asset distribution, the more difficult it is for some individuals to invest in the acquisition of skills, and the more likely it is that the trap will operate. Poverty therefore becomes a self-perpetuating process.

In an important contribution, Azariadis and Drazen (1990) developed a model in which sufficient human capital must be acquired before the economy can take off. Specifically, they showed that in an extended Solow-Swan setting in which the *private* rate of return on human capital depends positively on the existing *average* quality of the stock of human capital (that is, when the technology that drives human capital accumulation is characterized by *positive externalities*), small differences in initial conditions may lead to very different equilibrium growth paths. In particular, if the private return to training is too low to induce agents to acquire training and accumulate skills—a possibility that arises when the average initial stock of human capital is relatively low— the economy will converge to a no-training, low-income equilibrium path. This occurs even if the *social return* to higher average human capital is high.

---

[16] Skill acquisition through on-the-job training and apprenticeship may make it possible to escape from the poverty trap, but this may be the case only for jobs requiring moderate levels of education.

Various models of endogenous growth have emphasized that in the presence of collateral requirements and other forms of credit market imperfections, (poor) individuals may find it impossible to borrow on capital markets and finance human capital accumulation (see, for instance, De Gregorio, 1996). Restrictions on the ability to borrow may act therefore as a constraint on the rate of economic growth in the long run. Some economists have also argued that, in such conditions, the provision of *free basic education* (at the primary and secondary levels) or the creation of *public credit schemes* to cover the costs of skill acquisition may be welfare enhancing (Stern, 1989). The social value of this investment is clear: it creates **positive externalities** (because they benefit society as a whole) and raises the steady-state rate of economic growth, in addition to reducing income disparities.

However, while intuitively appealing, these conclusions must be treated with caution, as suggested in two studies.

- Zhang (1996) argued that although government subsidies to private education unambiguously stimulate growth, the *direct provision of education* by the public sector may actually *reduce* growth—despite reducing income inequality. This may occur if public education is financed through a **distortionary tax**. The positive externalities generated by higher education levels must be sufficiently high for government intervention to be welfare improving.

- Upadhyay (1994) showed that government subsidies can produce *too much education*. This is because a subsidy may increase the demand for higher education at the cost of investment in physical capital, thereby leading to *inefficient substitution* between skilled and unskilled labor in the long run. Paradoxically, in the long run, output can be constrained by a lack of unskilled labor, while at the same time skilled workers may be unemployed.

12.4 Other Determinants of Growth

In addition to the endogenous channels of growth highlighted in the foregoing discussion, the recent literature has identified a number of other mechanisms through which government intervention can affect, directly or indirectly, the rate of growth in the long run. This section offers a review of some of these mechanisms. It focuses, in particular, on the role of fiscal policy, inflation and macroeconomic stability, openness to trade and capital flows, financial development, and the role of political and institutional factors.

12.4.1 Fiscal Policy

Recent models of endogenous growth have shown that there are a variety of channels through which fiscal policy can have long-run effects on growth. In particular, different types of government expenditure and different forms of taxation may have very conflicting effects on growth, through their impact on private investment and the productivity of private factors of production.

Government Spending

As discussed by Tanzi and Zee (1997) and Zagler and Durnecker (2003), government expenditure may affect the rate of economic growth in at least two ways:

- directly by increasing the economy's capital stock through, for instance, public investment in *infrastructure*, which, as noted in Chapter 2, can be complementary to private investment;

- indirectly by raising the marginal productivity of privately supplied factors of production—through spending on education, health, and other services that contribute to the accumulation of human capital.

Regarding the first channel, however, it should be noted that public capital, like any other production factor, is subject to diminishing marginal returns. This raises the possibility that excessive government spending on infrastructure (relative to private investment) may be *inefficient.* A key policy issue is thus to determine the optimal ratio of government to private capital formation (see Glomm and Ravikumar, 1994, 1997, and Agénor, 2004c). Another issue, of course, is that the effect of public investment also depends on the way these outlays are financed. Cashin (1995), in particular, analyzed how the effect of public investment on private investment and growth may depend on the form of taxation used to finance it. If public capital expenditure is financed by an increase in *direct taxes* and a reduction in private saving, the net effect on growth may be *negative* despite a positive effect on the marginal productivity of capital. As discussed next, there may be therefore a trade-off if the only financing instrument available is distortionary taxation.

The Dual Effects of Taxation

In assessing the effects of taxes on economic growth, the distinction made in Chapter 3 between **lump-sum taxes** and **distortionary taxes** is essential. In practice, most taxes are distortionary; they tend therefore to distort the allocation of resources through their impact on saving and investment.[17] However, whether or not they have a detrimental effect on growth *in net terms* depends on the growth benefits of the expenditures that they serve to finance. Distortionary taxes may also have a net positive effect on long-run economic growth if they are used to correct for **negative externalities** or other related distortions.

Barro (1990) developed a model that illustrates well the *dual effects* of taxation on growth. The key idea of Barro's model is that the flow of government

---

[17]The impact of taxation on the level of investment operates through the cost of capital. As discussed in Chapter 2, the evidence on this effect is limited for developing countries. Taxation may, nevertheless, affect the *composition* of investment through a differentiated structure of tax rates on profits.

spending, G, has a positive effect on private production. Specifically, Barro considered the following production function for firm h, with $h = 1, ..., n$:

$$Y_h = AG^{1-\alpha}L_h^{1-\alpha}K_h^\alpha, \quad 0 < \alpha < 1, \tag{34}$$

where K_h is the capital stock held by h and L_h the amount of labor used by h.[18] This specification implies that for each firm h, the production function exhibits constant returns to G and K_h.

Suppose that the government runs a *balanced budget* financed by a proportional tax on output, τ, so that

$$G = \tau Y, \quad 0 < \tau < 1, \tag{35}$$

where Y is aggregate output. Given that G rises along with the aggregate private capital stock and that the individual firm's production function exhibits constant returns to G and K_h, the model produces endogenous steady-state growth. Barro shows that in fact the economy's growth rate of output per capita is given by

$$\tilde{g}_{Y/L} = \alpha A^{1/\alpha}\tau^{(1-\alpha)/\alpha}(1-\tau) - (\rho + \delta), \tag{36}$$

where ρ is the subjective **rate of time preference** (as discussed in Chapter 2) and δ the rate of depreciation of capital.[19] Equation (36) shows that the effect of government spending on growth operates through two channels:[20]

- the term $1 - \tau$, which represents the *negative* effect of taxation on the after-tax marginal product of capital; and

- the term $\tau^{(1-\alpha)/\alpha}$, which represents the *positive* effect of the provision of public services on the after-tax marginal product of capital.

Expression (36) implies therefore that the growth rate rises at first with increases in the tax rate (with the positive effect dominating the negative effect), reaches a maximum at τ^*, and then begins to decrease with further rises in the tax rate, as illustrated in Figure 12.5. Thus for $\tau > \tau^*$, taxation and government expenditure are inefficient, as argued earlier.

---

[18] The derivations that follow are actually based on Barro and Sala-i-Martin (1992, pp. 153-55). Futagami, Morita, and Shibata (1993) extended Barro's analysis to include the *stock* of public capital, rather than the flow of government spending, in the production function. Bajo-Rubio (2000) followed a similar approach in the context of the Solow-Swan framework.

[19] The derivation of the growth rate involves solving a representative household's optimization problem and is omitted here. The expression given in Equation (36) assumes that the degree of intertemporal substitution (as defined in Chapter 2) is unity.

[20] Empirical evidence on these two effects is provided by Cashin (1995).

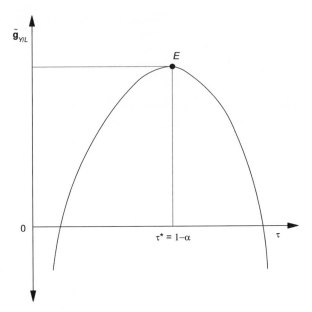

Figure 12.5. Growth and the tax rate in Barro's model.

The optimal tax rate is such that it maximizes the growth rate given in Equation (36), that is, $d\tilde{g}_{Y/L}/d\tau = 0$. The condition that determined τ^* is thus

$$\frac{d\tilde{g}_{Y/L}}{d\tau} = \alpha A^{1/\alpha}\tau^{(1-\alpha)/\alpha}\left[\frac{(1-\tau)(1-\alpha)}{\alpha\tau} - 1\right] = 0,$$

which yields

$$\tau^* = 1 - \alpha.$$

In a related contribution that bears particular relevance for developing countries, Loayza (1996) proposed a model that captures the idea that the imposition of high tax rates in the **formal sector** by governments that lack the capability to enforce compliance leads to a growing **informal sector**, where taxes are evaded. High tax rates therefore lower the capacity of the government to generate revenue and exert an adverse effect on growth.

Loayza's analysis dwells on a model of an economy producing one good, which can be either consumed or invested. Agents are endowed with a broad measure of human and physical capital, and production takes place using a technology that exhibits constant returns to capital, as in the AK model of Rebelo (1991) discussed earlier. Thus, raw labor does not have any direct role in the production process. As in Barro (1990), production depends also on the *flow* of public services, G, but this time it is the ratio of G to aggregate output that matters:

$$Y_h = A(\frac{G}{Y})^\alpha K_h, \quad 0 < \alpha < 1, \tag{37}$$

where Y_h is production of firm h, K_h the stock of capital owned by h, A an exogenous productivity parameter, and Y the economy's aggregate output. The coefficient α measures the elasticity of output with respect to G/Y.

At any point in time, each firm can choose to belong either to the formal economy or to the informal sector.

- Firms operating in the formal economy are subject to a proportional tax on income, τ, the proceeds of which are used to finance government expenditure, which consists not only of the flow of services that are used in the production process but also of the spending required to enforce the rule of law.

- Firms operating in the informal sector are able to evade the tax on profits paid by firms in the formal sector, but they lose a fraction of their income, $\phi < \tau$, to maintain their informal sector status (through the payment of, say, bribes to government officials). At the same time, because of their illegal status, informal firms have access only to a fraction of public services that are available to society at large.

Thus, if firm h belongs to the formal sector, its net-of-tax income is given by

$$Y_h^F = (1 - \tau)A(\frac{G}{Y})^\alpha K_h, \quad 0 < \tau < 1, \tag{38}$$

whereas if it belongs to the informal sector, its income is

$$Y_h^I = (1 - \phi)A(\frac{\theta G}{Y})^\alpha K_h, \quad 0 < \phi, \theta < 1, \tag{39}$$

where θ is the fraction of public services to which firms operating in the informal sector have access to.

The flow of public services that are used in the production process are financed by a fraction η of the taxes levied on formal-sector output, such that

$$G = \eta(\overset{+}{q}, \overset{-}{\lambda})\tau Y^F, \quad 0 < \eta \leq 1. \tag{40}$$

The coefficient $1 - \eta$ represents the fraction of government revenue that is either used unproductively (to finance enforcement costs) or misused, and thus wasted. η is assumed to be related positively to the *quality* (or *efficiency*) of government institutions, measured by the parameter q, and negatively to the government's capacity to enforce the rule of law, measured by the parameter λ. In addition, Loayza posits that $\eta_{q\lambda} > 0$, an assumption that captures the view that the amount of resources it takes to raise enforcement strength decreases with the quality of government institutions.

Let Ω denote the relative size of the informal sector, defined as

$$\Omega = Y_I/Y, \tag{41}$$

where Y is total output. Using Equations (40) and (41), the ratio of public services to output can be written as

$$\frac{G}{Y} = \eta(q, \lambda)\tau(1 - \Omega). \tag{42}$$

Finally, the fraction of income spent by informal-sector firms to maintain their illegal status, ϕ, is assumed to depend positively on the size of the informal sector. Specifically, ϕ is assumed given by

$$\phi = \kappa\Omega, \quad \kappa > 0. \tag{43}$$

In equilibrium, and in the absence of restrictions on mobility between the formal and informal sectors, rates of return in both sectors must be equalized. This equality determines the relative size of the informal economy. To see this, note that from Equations (38), (39), and (43):

$$(1 - \kappa\Omega)\theta^\alpha = 1 - \tau,$$

so that[21]

$$\Omega = \frac{\theta^\alpha - (1 - \tau)}{\kappa\theta^\alpha} = \Omega(\bar{\kappa}, \overset{+}{\tau}, \overset{+}{\theta}, \bar{\alpha}). \tag{44}$$

Equation (44) shows, in particular, that the relative size of the informal sector *increases* with the tax rate in the formal economy and the fraction of public services to which firms operating in the informal sector have access.

The equilibrium **after-tax rate of return on capital**, r, is given by

$$r = A(1 - \tau)\tau^\alpha[\eta(q, \lambda)(1 - \Omega)]^\alpha. \tag{45}$$

The term $A(1-\tau)\tau^\alpha$ represents the economy's after-tax rate of return in the absence of waste ($\eta = 1$) and with no informal economy ($\Omega = 0$). In the presence of an informal sector, this term is multiplied by the quantity $[\eta(1-\Omega)]^\alpha$—which is less than unity, because both η and Ω are less than unity. Thus, the economy's after-tax rate of return is *lower* than it would be otherwise. Equation (45) shows also that, as in Barro's model, with no informal activities ($\Omega = 0$), an increase in the tax rate has at first a positive and then a negative effect on the after-tax rate of return. In the presence of an informal sector ($\Omega > 0$), there is an additional, *negative* effect of the tax rate on the rate of return on capital, resulting from the positive effect of τ on the size of the informal sector.

As shown by Loayza, the model has no transitional dynamics: capital and formal- and informal-sector output (and thus aggregate output) all grow at the constant rate of growth of per capital income, $\tilde{g}_{Y/L}$, given by[22]

$$\tilde{g}_{Y/L} = A(1 - \tau)\tau^\alpha[\eta(1 - \Omega)]^\alpha - (\rho + \delta). \tag{46}$$

It can be seen from Equation (46) that an increase in the tax rate can have either a positive or negative effect on the steady-state growth rate—as shown earlier in the analysis of Equation (45)—depending on the initial level of taxation. At low levels of taxes, an increase in the tax rate leads to a rise in

---

[21] For Equation (44) to provide an interior solution for Ω (that is, $0 < \Omega < 1$) requires imposing the parameter restrictions $\theta^\alpha > 1 - \tau$ and $(1 - \kappa)\theta^\alpha < 1 - \tau$.

[22] The derivation of the growth rate is relatively involved and is omitted here. Again, the expression given in Equation (46) assumes that the degree of intertemporal substitution is unity.

the amount of public services that is large enough to offset the adverse effect of public-service congestion due to increased informality, and its negative impact on the net rate of return on private capital.

The optimal tax rate is determined, as in Barro's model, as the rate τ^* that maximizes the growth rate, Equation (46). In Loayza's model, however, in the general case, there is no explicit solution for τ^*.[23] Nevertheless, by again applying the implicit function theorem it can be shown that[24]

$$\tau^* = \tau(\overset{+}{\alpha}, \overset{+}{\kappa}, \overset{-}{\delta}). \tag{47}$$

Equation (47) indicates, in particular, that an increase in the cost of remaining informal (a rise in κ) raises the optimal tax rate. The reason is that a higher κ makes informality less attractive, so that a sufficiently small increase in the tax rate does not lead to more public-service congestion due to informality.

There are a number of important aspects of the links between informal sector activities and growth that Loayza's model does not account for, such as labor market regulations and segmentation, the size of production units, and differences in factor intensity, which may be important for understanding the size of the informal sector.[25] Nevertheless, a key implication of the model is that in countries where tax rates are high (or larger than optimal) and the enforcement system is weak, the relative size of the informal sector will be *negatively* correlated with the rate of economic growth. Thus, measures aimed at reducing the tax burden and improving the quality of government institutions, for instance, would not only help to reduce the relative size of the informal economy but would also promote economic growth and increases in standards of living.

Other models have identified various additional channels through which the level and nature of government taxes affect economic growth, particularly through their impact on the supply and demand for capital and labor. For instance, Milesi-Ferretti and Roubini (1998) examined the effects of *consumption* and *income taxes* on growth. Their analysis emphasized, in particular, the adverse role that taxation of human capital accumulation may have on the expansion of the *education sector*. Labor income taxation reduces individuals' incentive for human capital accumulation and may thus affect the rate of economic growth when tax revenues are spent unproductively by the government. As discussed below, *trade taxes* may also have steady-state effects on growth: *tariffs*, for instance, can raise the relative price of *intermediate goods*, and thus reduce the steady-state marginal rate of return of these inputs.

Finally, it should be noted that the effect of taxes on growth can operate through their effect on macroeconomic stability (as discussed later) and may, as

---

[23] In the particular case where $\kappa = 1$ (that is, the cost of bribery is so high that no firm would choose to operate in the informal sector), the optimal tax rate is $\tau^* = \alpha/(1 + 2\alpha)$.

[24] If $1 - \theta^\alpha < \alpha\lambda/(\alpha + \kappa + \alpha\kappa)$, the growth-maximizing tax rate would imply some informality. If this inequality is reversed, the optimal tax rate would bring about a fully formal economy. The first inequality is assumed to hold.

[25] Another limitation of the model is that it does not capture the effect of taxes on labor supply, that is, the effect on agents' labor-leisure trade-off. A reduction in taxes, for instance, by increasing income, may lead agents to opt for more leisure, which would lower the steady-state rate of economic growth. The same issue arises in the context of Barro's model.

a result, be *nonlinear*. For small tax rates, the effect might be positive because of the contribution of taxes to macroeconomic stability (the **automatic stabilizer** effect); for higher tax rates, however, the relationship could become *negative*, as the distortionary effects (on, say, production incentives and the supply of labor) start to dominate.

Budget Deficits and Growth

In addition to spending and taxes, the government's *overall* budgetary position may also affect growth, through three channels:

- By lowering *aggregate saving*, in the realistic case in which Ricardian equivalence does not strictly hold (see Chapter 2).

- By contributing to higher *inflation* (as discussed later), when deficits are monetized. Inflation may in turn distort relative price signals and increase **macroeconomic instability**, thereby contributing to inefficiencies in the allocation of resources.

- By leading to a buildup of *domestic debt* when deficits are financed by issuance of liabilities; this type of financing may **crowd out** private investment through pressures on interest rates or the availability of domestic credit.[26] It may also raise the risk of *future taxation* and thus adversely affect private saving and investment decisions.

Weak fiscal discipline may also have an indirect, adverse effect on long-run growth if it leads to balance-of-payments pressures and stop-and-go corrective policies. Both factors may increase macroeconomic uncertainty (the former by raising the prospects of a nominal devaluation, the second by affecting the *credibility* of the policy process) and thus reduce private investment.

12.4.2   Inflation and Macroeconomic Stability

Endogenous growth models identify various channels, both direct and indirect, through which inflation can affect steady-state growth. De Gregorio (1993), for instance, suggested that inflation may have a negative effect on the economy's balanced growth path because it reduces the *rate* of investment and lowers the *efficiency* of investment. At the heart of De Gregorio's model is the assumption that firms (as well as households) use money because it reduces transactions costs. Inflation lowers the optimal level of real money balances and raises the cost of investing; it thus lowers the rate of capital accumulation and the productivity of capital, thereby adversely affecting the rate of growth in the long run. In a related analysis, Palokangas (1997) argued that inflation negatively affects the steady-state growth rate because higher inflation raises nominal interest

---

[26]The latter possibility is particularly relevant under a regime of financial repression (as defined in Chapter 4), in which the structure and regulation of the financial system are deeply dependent on the financing needs of the government.

rates and reduces the demand for real money balances—thereby subjecting private agents to larger transactions costs. This, in turn, lowers the rate of return on physical and human capital and reduces investment and long-run growth rates.[27]

What causes inflation is important, not only to assess its ultimate effects on growth but also to understand the type of policies that may be needed to limit these effects. As indicated in Chapter 6, inflation in developing countries is often caused by large fiscal deficits and a high degree of monetization. In such conditions, reductions in government spending may be necessary. Roubini and Sala-i-Martin (1995), for instance, argued that to the extent that inflation can be viewed as a proxy for financial repression, the negative effect of inflation on investment and growth may reflect government-imposed restrictions on financial markets. An alternative interpretation is to view inflation directly as a tax, which is determined (as discussed in Chapter 3) by the government to maximize seigniorage revenue (given an expenditure or deficit target) subject to the constraint that *conventional* taxes are subject to *rising marginal collection costs*. In that perspective, then, what causes inflation (and thus low growth) is an *inefficient tax system*, as emphasized most notably by De Gregorio (1993).

The data reviewed in Chapter 10 suggested a negative correlation between inflation and growth. As discussed in the next chapter, this result is largely corroborated by formal econometric studies. In addition, several of these studies have shown that the effect of inflation on growth is *nonlinear*, being small at low levels of inflation but significantly negative at high levels. Thus, in countries where inflation is high to begin with, achieving and maintaining inflation in the single-digit range may be very beneficial for increasing output growth.

High inflation and large fiscal deficits are often viewed as key symptoms of **macroeconomic instability**. Such instability is, in general, more pronounced in developing countries relative to industrial countries because the former group of countries tends to be *less diversified* and less able to absorb external shocks. In addition, however, macroeconomic instability often reflects weaknesses in macroeconomic management. By increasing overall uncertainty and distorting information on underlying economic fundamentals, macroeconomic instability hampers private investment and saving decisions, thereby leading to an inefficient allocation of resources. Macroeconomic instability also has an adverse effect on confidence, which can discourage domestic investment and lead to capital flight—with potentially adverse effects on long-run growth.

The effect of macroeconomic policy uncertainty on growth is well illustrated in the model developed by Aizenman and Marion (1993).[28] Endogenous growth emerges in their model because knowledge is one input in the production process

---

[27] It is worth noting that this result appears to be in contrast with the prediction of early monetary growth models, which argued that higher inflation would lead to increased output through a shift away from money balances (as real interest rates fall) and toward real capital accumulation, as predicted by the Tobin-Mundell effect (mentioned in Chapter 2). See Burmeister and Dobell (1970) for a formal treatment.

[28] Hopenhayn and Muniagurria (1996) developed an alternative model in which policy variability lowers the economy's steady-state growth rate.

and investment in human capital and physical capital are linked. Policy uncertainty arises because the *future tax rate on capital* is unknown at the moment investment decisions are made. The key result of the model stems from the interaction between **irreversibility effects** in investment decisions and **policy persistence**. As noted in Chapter 2, when investment is subject to sunk costs, uncertainty generates an **option value of waiting**. Put differently, irreversibilities in the investment process generate *delays*, as entrepreneurs may opt to wait for the resolution of uncertainty. Firms are cautious in their decisions to expand capacity under uncertainty, because investment today can lead to excessive capacity tomorrow if circumstances change. Aizenman and Marion showed, however, that macroeconomic policy uncertainty generates an option value of waiting only if policy is characterized by persistence. With persistence, higher macroeconomic uncertainty alters the expected net present value of the marginal product of capital and hence the pattern of investment. Moreover, with investment in physical capital linked to investment in human capital, the interaction of macroeconomic uncertainty and persistence influences the steady-state growth rate of output.[29]

12.4.3 Trade and International Financial Openness

Conventional trade theory, as discussed in Chapter 14, suggests that openness generates **static economic gains**—under free trade, productive resources tend to be reallocated toward activities where they are used with comparatively greater efficiency and away from less efficient activities. However, these gains (which tend to be relatively small in practice) generally take the form of a *level* effect on output, not a *growth* effect.[30] Recent research in growth theory provides various mechanisms through which trade and openness may generate **dynamic gains** and thereby affect the economy's growth rate in the long run. In particular, it has been shown that trade openness may have the following effects.

- It may lead to improved allocation of resources among sectors by eliminating distortions—including lower incentives to engage in **rent-seeking activities**.[31]

- It may facilitate the acquisition of new inputs, intermediate goods, and improved technologies, which enhance the *overall productivity* of the econ-

---

[29] In the Aizenman-Marion model, policy uncertainty affects growth only through the supply side. This is because the household utility function that they specify prevents any effect of uncertainty on consumption and saving decisions. In general, of course, the effects of policy uncertainty on growth may also result from the demand side.

[30] In practice, of course, a level effect can appear as a growth effect for a given period of time, because the adjustment process to any given shock in real economies can be very slow.

[31] The concept of rent seeking is attributed to Krueger (1974). The argument, essentially, is that public policy—especially in the domain of import duties, tariffs, quotas, and licensing systems—has the potential of increasing the incomes of certain individuals and groups. These incomes accrue in the form of rents. Pressure groups, acting rationally, seek rents by spending money and lobbying in order to get government authorities to allocate to them import licences, foreign exchange, and so on.

omy. In particular, imported equipment may lead to permanently higher growth rates, if it costs less than domestic equipment (Mazumdar, 2001). Imported capital goods may also have a persistent effect on growth through **learning-by-doing effects**, as discussed earlier (Goh and Olivier, 2002).

- It may reduce the **risk premium** on world capital markets (see Chapter 16), thereby improving the terms under which a country can borrow to finance domestic capital formation. If the marginal productivity of domestic investment is *higher* than the world interest rate, trade openness will also increase the supply of foreign capital and may improve domestic welfare.

The second channel, the international diffusion and adoption of new technologies or new goods, has been a major focus of attention in the recent literature. Grossman and Helpman (1991) and Rivera-Batiz and Romer (1991), for instance, developed models in which technology is produced by profit-maximizing firms. They showed that openness to international markets can increase the growth rate of technology by increasing the *size of the market* available to technology producers and allowing those countries with a comparative advantage in technology production to specialize in that activity. International trade may also improve domestic productivity and economic growth by increasing **knowledge spillovers** from more advanced trading partners, as in some of the "North-South" models reviewed by Chui, Levine, Murshed, and Pearlman (2002). The empirical evidence provided by Coe, Helpman, and Hoffmaister (1997) suggests indeed that trade flows provide a conduit through which advanced production techniques and technological knowledge are transmitted across countries.[32] The empirical evidence also suggests that the learning-by-doing and growth effects of these spillovers are largest in countries with *higher levels of education*. As discussed in the next chapter, this appears to have played an important role in the rapid growth of some East Asian countries since the end of World War II.

Another important idea that has been explored in some recent models of growth is that trade liberalization increases the *variety of goods* available to domestic agents and raises productivity by providing *less expensive* or *higher-quality intermediate goods*. Romer (1994), for instance, emphasized both the productivity of specialized resources and the limitations imposed by the size of the market. In an economy subject to trade restrictions, only a narrow range of specialized intermediate goods or capital goods can be profitably produced and therefore the full range of technological possibilities, which rely on a potentially broader range of inputs, cannot be exploited effectively. In this model a *greater variety of inputs* does more for production than a *greater quantity of a narrow range of inputs*. Thus, access to a variety of foreign inputs at a lower cost shifts the economy-wide **production possibility frontier** outward, thereby raising productivity.

---

[32] As discussed later, foreign direct investment provides another route through which technology and advanced managerial and production techniques can flow from industrial to developing countries, thereby raising growth rates.

In contrast to the early literature on trade and growth, which emphasized solely the role of exports as an engine to growth, the new literature provides important new insights. A number of caveats, however, are worth highlighting.

- The effects of scale economies and learning by doing emphasized in the new theories of trade and growth take place mostly in the production of advanced manufactured products, such as *high-technology goods*. Exports of many developing countries continue, however, to consist of *raw materials* (including energy and agricultural products) and relatively *low-technology* manufactured goods (such as textiles). It may be argued, nevertheless, that openness to trade (and capital flows) may help these countries to assimilate technologies and production techniques over time, thereby enabling them to shift gradually toward the production of goods and services that are characterized by dynamic gains.

- Some models suggest that, under some conditions, opening an economy to trade may discourage *domestic* research and development activities, for instance by inducing the poorer countries to allocate too much of their limited supply of skilled labor to the production of manufactured goods. In such conditions, paradoxically, restrictions on trade may *accelerate* growth.

- In several models, the mechanism through which increased productivity and growth rates occur as economies become open to international trade focuses on the adoption of more specialized intermediate inputs and machinery available from trading partners. However, there are many types of useful knowledge that are not embodied in material inputs, such as production engineering and information about changing product patterns, which can also be transferred as a result of trade with more advanced countries. As argued by Romer (1992), in practice, the transmission of *ideas* may be as important, if not more important, than the transmission of new inputs.

Some recent papers in the endogenous growth literature have also argued that international *financial* openness (or capital account liberalization) may provide significant long-run benefits, in addition to other "conventional" ones—such as consumption smoothing.[33] Indeed, the ability to draw upon the international pool of resources that financial openness gives access to may have a strong effect on domestic investment and growth. Openness to capital flows may increase opportunities for portfolio risk diversification; and producers who are able to diversify risks on world capital markets may invest in riskier (and higher-yield) projects, thereby raising the country's rate of economic growth (Obstfeld, 1994). More generally, in countries where the capacity to save is constrained by

---

[33] The smoothing argument is that access to world capital markets may allow a country to borrow in "bad" times (say, following a sharp deterioration in the country's terms of trade) and lend in "good" times. By enabling domestic households to smooth out their consumption over time, capital flows can therefore increase welfare. This countercyclical role of world capital markets is particularly important if shocks are temporary in nature.

a low level of income and the marginal return from investment is at least equal to the cost of capital, net foreign resource inflows can supplement domestic saving, increase levels of physical capital per worker, and help the recipient country raise its rate of economic growth and improve living standards. These potential benefits can be particularly large for some types of capital inflows, most notably foreign direct investment (see Chapter 7).

In addition to this direct effect on growth, foreign direct investment may also have significant indirect long-run effects. As emphasized by Borensztein, De Gregorio, and Lee (1998), and Grossman and Helpman (1991), FDI may facilitate the transfer or diffusion of managerial and technological know-how—particularly in the form of new varieties of capital inputs—and improve the skills composition of the labor force as a result of learning-by-doing effects, investment in formal education, and on-the-job training. In addition, as suggested by Markusen and Venables (1999), although the increased degree of competition in the product and factor markets induced by foreign direct investment may tend to reduce profits of local firms, spillover effects through linkages to supplier industries may reduce input costs, raise profits, and stimulate domestic investment.

To highlight the complementarity (through productivity effects) between foreign direct investment and skilled human capital in the growth process consider, following Borensztein, De Gregorio, and Lee (1998), an economy in which the source of technological progress is an increase in the number of varieties of capital goods available to producers, which consist of local and foreign firms. Suppose also that the economy produces a single final consumption good using the following technology:

$$Y = S^\alpha K^{1-\alpha}, \tag{48}$$

where $0 < \alpha < 1$ and S is the economy's fixed endowment of skilled labor and K is the stock of physical capital, which is itself a composite of a continuum of different varieties of capital goods, each one denoted by x_j:

$$K = \int_0^N [x_j^{1-\alpha} dj]^{1/(1-\alpha)}, \tag{49}$$

with N denoting the total number of varieties. Physical capital accumulation therefore takes place through an increase in the number of varieties of capital goods produced domestically. (48) and (49) imply that there are diminishing returns with respect to each variety of capital goods, but that there are constant returns with respect to all of them taken together.

Suppose that there are two types of firms producing capital goods: foreign firms, which produce $n^* < N$ varieties, and domestic firms, which produce the other $N - n^*$ varieties. Specialized firms produce each variety j of capital goods and rent it out to producers of final goods at a rate m_j. The optimal demand for each variety j is thus determined by equating the rental rate and the marginal productivity of j in the production of the final good:

$$m_j = (1 - \alpha)S^\alpha x_j^{-\alpha}. \tag{50}$$

An increase in the number of varieties of capital goods available to producers is assumed to require the adaptation of technology available in more advanced countries. This adaptation to local needs is assumed to require a fixed setup cost, F, which is assumed to depend negatively on the ratio of foreign firms operating domestically to the total number of firms, n^*/N. Thus, $F = F(n^*/N)$, with $F' < 0$.[34] This assumption captures the idea that foreign firms make it easier to adopt the more advanced technology required to produce new varieties of capital, by bringing in the knowledge already available elsewhere.

In addition to this fixed cost, once a capital good is introduced, its owner must spend a constant maintenance cost per period of time. This is equivalent to assuming that production of x_j involves a constant marginal cost equal to unity and that capital goods depreciate fully.[35] Assuming that the interest rate r that firms face is constant, profits for the producer of a variety j, denoted Π_j, are given by

$$\Pi_j = -F + \int_0^\infty (m_j x_j - x_j)e^{-rs}ds. \tag{51}$$

Maximization of (51) subject to (50) yields the equilibrium level of production of each capital good:

$$x_j = S(1 - \alpha)^{2/\alpha},$$

which shows that, given the assumption of symmetry among producers, the level of production of the different varieties of capital is the same. Assuming free entry, it can be shown that the zero-profit condition implies that

$$r = \phi S/F, \tag{52}$$

where $\phi \equiv \alpha(1 - \alpha)^{(2-\alpha)/\alpha} > 0$.

To close the model requires specifying savings decisions, which determine the process of capital accumulation. Suppose that households face a rate of return also equal to r and that they maximize a standard intertemporal utility function given by the discounted present value of consumption. Assuming that the intertemporal elasticity of substitution is equal to unity, it can be shown that the optimal solution is such that the rate of growth of consumption, g_c, is driven by:

$$\mathbf{g}_c = r - \rho, \tag{53}$$

where ρ is the rate of time preference. In a stationary state, the rate of growth of consumption must be equal to the rate of growth of output, $\tilde{\mathbf{g}}$, that is, $\tilde{\mathbf{g}} = \tilde{\mathbf{g}}_c$. Substituting (52) in (53) therefore yields the economy's growth rate:

$$\tilde{\mathbf{g}} = \phi S/F(n^*/N) - \rho. \tag{54}$$

---

[34] Borensztein, De Gregorio, and Lee (1998) also discuss a second possible influence on F, namely, the possibility of a "catch-up" effect in technological progress, reflecting the fact that it may be cheaper to imitate products already in existence than to create new ones at the cutting edge of innovation. This notion is implemented in their model by assuming that setup costs depend positively on the number of capital varieties produced domestically, compared with those produced in more advanced countries.

[35] Substituting the optimal level of production into Equation (50) yields the constant equilibrium rental rate, $m_j = 1/(1 - \alpha)$, as a markup over maintenance costs.

Equation (54) shows that foreign direct investment, as measured by the fraction of capital goods produced locally by foreign firms in the total number of these goods, n^*/N, has a positive effect on the economy's long-term growth rate. The reason is that foreign direct investment reduces the cost of introducing new varieties of capital, thereby increasing the rate at which these goods are introduced.[36] Moreover, the effect of foreign direct investment on the economy's growth rate is positively related to the existing stock of skilled labor employed in production—this is the complementarity effect mentioned earlier. Put differently, absorbing the more advanced technologies that foreign direct investment provides requires the presence of a sufficiently high level of human capital. There is therefore a nonlinearity associated with the level of education.

But financial openness may also have adverse effects on growth. Exposure to volatile international financial markets may increase domestic instability and hamper growth. In particular, Devereux and Smith (1994) studied the effects of international risk sharing (the ability to diversify portfolios of risky assets) in a multicountry world in which growth is based upon the spillover effects of human capital accumulation, and agents have preferences characterized by **constant relative risk aversion** (or CRRA, see Chapter 2). They showed that when countries share endowment risk via international capital markets, the saving and growth rates can be lower than in autarky. The reason is that by eliminating country-specific income risk, financial market integration eliminates the impact of this risk on savings, and therefore on economic growth. Put differently, the average growth rate is lower under openness, because the elimination of income risk reduces world savings and growth rates in all countries are lower under financial openness. The reason is that, as discussed in Chapter 2, with CRRA preferences riskier income leads to greater saving as a result of a precautionary motive. With full risk sharing, income risk is diversified away, reducing the equilibrium saving rate in each country. Lower saving in turn tends to lower the growth rate in each country.

The results of Devereux and Smith are sensitive to the assumption that there is only one investment technology available. As can be inferred from the results of Greenwood and Jovanovich (1990) and Obstfeld (1994), if there are many (risky) technologies available, financial openness may increase the equilibrium growth rate—even if it reduces saving rates, as a result of the "reverse" precautionary effect alluded to earlier—by leading to a reallocation of savings to projects with high risk and return. In addition, it should be noted that the Devereux-Smith model takes the depth of the financial system as given when assessing the impact of financial integration; but it is possible that the two may be positively related. In Agénor and Aizenman (1999), for instance, financial openness translates into lower markups over funding costs and more efficient

---

[36] In addition to reducing costs associated with innovation activity, foreign direct investment can also have a more direct effect on growth—if, for instance local firms involved in research activities are able to use at least in part the advanced knowledge that foreign firms possess. In such conditions, as discussed by Berthélemy and Démurger (2000), it would be the number of varieties of capital goods, and not the rate of change of the capital stock, that would affect long-run growth.

intermediation by domestic banks. In that case, international financial openness may bring additional benefits, which could mitigate the adverse impact of a greater opportunity for risk diversification on savings and growth.

12.4.4   Financial Development

As noted in Chapter 4, government restrictions imposed on financial institutions (such as interest rate ceilings, high reserve requirements, and directed credit programs) tend to restrain the process of financial intermediation and, consequently, impede economic growth. Several contributions to the endogenous growth literature have examined the potential linkages between economic growth and financial markets (see Pagano, 1993, for a brief overview). They have highlighted the fact that financial institutions play a key role in evaluating prospective entrepreneurs and financing those that carry the best promise of future innovation—with the resulting increase in productivity leading to higher growth. More specifically, financial institutions emerge to mitigate problems such as economies of scale in information gathering and the allocation of risk under **asymmetric information** (as defined in Chapter 4). Greenwood and Jovanovich (1990), for instance, stressed the role of financial intermediaries in *pooling funds* and *acquiring information* that enables them to allocate capital to its highest valued use, thereby raising the average return to capital. Specifically, they considered a situation in which capital can be invested in safe, low-yielding investments or risky, high-yielding investments. Risk results from both aggregate and project-specific shocks. Potential entrepreneurs cannot differentiate between the two types of shocks. With large portfolio holdings, however, financial intermediaries can experiment with a small sample of high-yielding projects to determine the state of the world. By spending on the collection and analysis of information, financial intermediaries determine their investment strategies knowing the realization of the current-period aggregate shock. Provided the cost of information collection and analysis is sufficiently small, the ability to choose the appropriate set of projects knowing the realization of the aggregate shock raises the expected return on the intermediaries' portfolios above that of individuals who must choose one or the other technology without any information about the aggregate shock. Thus, financial intermediation improves the allocation of resources and raises the long-run rate of economic growth.

Another approach is followed by Bencivenga and Smith (1991, 1992) and Greenwood and Smith (1997). Their analysis emphasized the fact that, with the introduction of banks, individuals can hold deposits that financial intermediaries (essentially banks) then invest in currency and capital. At the same time, banks can exploit the **law of large numbers** to estimate deposit withdrawals (which are unpredictable at the individual level but predictable for the economy as a whole) and thus ensure that they never have to liquidate capital prematurely.[37]   Hence, banks avoid the uncertainty that leads individuals

---

[37]Consider a set of n independent random variables that follow the same distribution function with mean μ. Then the mean of these variables, $\bar{x}_n$, also has mean μ, whatever the value of n. The (weak) law of large numbers states that, in effect, $\bar{x}_n$ becomes more and more

to misallocate resources. By engaging in **maturity intermediation** (one of the key functions of banks, as noted in Chapter 4) financial institutions offer liquidity to savers and, at the same time, long-term funding to entrepreneurs. In so doing, they stimulate productive investment by inducing savers to switch from unproductive investment (in physical assets such as land or foreign exchange) to productive investment in firms. As a result, financial intermediation leads to higher capital-labor ratios and higher steady-state rates of economic growth. Finally, yet another approach is developed by Boyd and Smith (1996) and Blackburn and Hung (1998). Both studies emphasize the role of *monitoring costs*, in a context where the returns associated with the various technologies available are not costlessly observable *ex post* (see Chapter 4). Whereas Boyd and Smith focus on the interactions between monitoring costs, growth, and the evolution of debt and equity markets, Blackburn and Hung focus on the interactions between financial liberalization, trade openness, financial intermediation and growth.

As noted in Chapter 2, financial development may lead to higher saving rates, and thus higher rates of increase in output per capita in many endogenous growth models. Whether a similar effect may operate through *borrowing constraints* has been subject to debate. Jappelli and Pagano (1994) have pointed out that these constraints may increase saving and lead to a permanently higher growth rate in an endogenous growth setting, by raising the rate of capital accumulation. The issue therefore is on the implications of credit rationing for the behavior of *households*, as opposed to firms. To illustrate the argument more formally, consider a world in which individuals live for three periods. They earn (labor) income in the second period of their life only. Individuals borrow when young (first period) to finance current consumption, whereas when they are middle-aged (second period) they repay the loan and save for retirement (which occurs in the third period). When retired, they consume all the savings accumulated in the second period and leave no bequests upon death. If capital markets are perfect, the young can borrow whatever amount they desire in the first period. But if liquidity constraints are binding, they can borrow at most a proportion ϕ of the present value of their lifetime income. Population is stationary, and the size of each generation is normalized to unity.

Preferences are given by

$$u(c_{t,t}, c_{t,t+1}, c_{t,t+2}) = \ln c_{t,t} + \beta \ln c_{t,t+1} + \beta^2 \ln c_{t,t+2}, \tag{55}$$

where c is consumption (with the first subscript indicating the generation, and the second the timing of consumption) and $\beta > 0$ the discount factor.

Individuals in each generation t maximize utility subject to

$$c_{t,t} + \frac{c_{t,t+1}}{R_{t+1}} + \frac{c_{t,t+2}}{R_{t+1}R_{t+2}} \leq \frac{e_{t+1}}{R_{t+1}}, \tag{56}$$

$$c_{t,t} \leq \phi \frac{e_{t+1}}{R_{t+1}}, \tag{57}$$

narrowly dispersed about μ as n increases. This theorem remains valid even if the variance of the underlying random variables does not exist.

where e_{t+1} is real labor earnings at $t+1$, and R_{t+1} is the gross interest rate between t and $t+1$. Equation (56) is the individual's intertemporal budget constraint; as noted earlier, labor income in the first period of life and in retirement is zero. Equation (57) captures the liquidity constraint that prevails with imperfect capital markets; the young can borrow at most a fraction ϕ of their discounted lifetime income. If the liquidity constraint (57) is not binding, maximization of (55) consists of

$$\max_{c_{t,t},c_{t,t+1},c_{t,t+2}} u(c_{t,t}, c_{t,t+1}, c_{t,t+2}),$$

subject to (56), holding with equality. Let λ denote the Lagrange multiplier associated with this problem; the first-order conditions are

$$1/c_{t,t} = \lambda, \quad \beta/c_{t,t+1} = \lambda/R_{t+1}, \quad \beta^2/c_{t,t+2} = \lambda/R_{t+1}R_{t+2},$$

which imply that

$$c_{t,t} = c_{t,t+1}/\beta R_{t+1} = c_{t,t+2}/\beta^2 R_{t+1}R_{t+2}.$$

Substituting these results in the budget constraint (56) give

$$c_{t,t} + \frac{\beta R_{t+1}c_{t,t}}{R_{t+1}} + \frac{\beta^2 R_{t+1}R_{t+2}c_{t,t}}{R_{t+1}R_{t+2}} = \frac{e_{t+1}}{R_{t+1}},$$

implying that the consumption of the young is

$$c_{t,t} = \chi \frac{e_{t+1}}{R_{t+1}}, \qquad \chi \equiv \frac{1}{1 + \beta + \beta^2}.$$

As long as $\phi < \chi$, the borrowing constraint is binding and first-period consumption is equal to the borrowing limit, as given by the right-hand side of (57). Aggregate net wealth, W_t, is given by the sum of the wealth of the middle-aged, minus the debt of the young:

$$W_t = \frac{\beta(1 - \phi)}{1 + \beta} e_t L - \phi \frac{e_{t+1}}{R_{t+1}} L, \tag{58}$$

where L is the population size and $\phi = \chi$ when liquidity constraints are not binding. The lower the value of ϕ, the more severe the liquidity constraints are, and the greater the value of wealth.

The aggregate production function is of the Cobb-Douglas form,

$$Y_t = A_t K_t^\alpha L^{1-\alpha}, \tag{59}$$

where Y_t is aggregate output, A_t technological progress, K_t capital, and L the constant labor force (set to unity in what follows). Capital is assumed to depreciate fully within one period. The capital market equilibrium condition is thus

$$W_t = K_{t+1}. \tag{60}$$

As in the previous chapter, consider first the Solow-Swan case where A_t is a function only of time:

$$A_t = Z(1+\gamma)^t, \tag{61}$$

where Z is a constant term and $\gamma > 0$. The first-order conditions for profit maximization are given by, with $L = 1$:

$$e_t = (1-\alpha)A_t K_t^\alpha, \qquad R_t = \alpha A_t K_t^{\alpha-1},$$

which can be substituted in the expression for wealth (58) to give

$$W_t = \frac{\beta(1-\phi)(1-\alpha)}{1+\beta}A_t K_t^\alpha - \phi\frac{(1-\alpha)K_{t+1}}{\alpha}.$$

Substituting this result into the capital market equilibrium condition (60) yields

$$\left\{1 + \phi\frac{(1-\alpha)}{\alpha}\right\}K_{t+1} = \frac{\beta(1-\phi)(1-\alpha)}{1+\beta}A_t K_t^\alpha,$$

which implies, using (61), that the law of motion of capital is

$$(1+\beta)[\alpha + \phi(1-\alpha)]K_{t+1} = \beta(1-\phi)\alpha(1-\alpha)Z(1+\gamma)^t K_t^\alpha. \tag{62}$$

Re-arranging (62) and taking logs yields

$$\ln K_{t+1} = \ln \Lambda + t\ln(1+\gamma) + \alpha \ln K_t,$$

where

$$\Lambda = \frac{\beta(1-\phi)\alpha(1-\alpha)Z}{(1+\beta)[\alpha + \phi(1-\alpha)]}.$$

The solution to this difference equation is

$$\ln K_t = \left\{\ln K_0 - \frac{\ln \Lambda}{1-\alpha} + \frac{\ln(1+\gamma)}{(1-\alpha)^2}\right\}\alpha^t + \frac{\ln \Lambda}{1-\alpha}$$

$$- \frac{\ln(1+\gamma)}{(1-\alpha)^2} + \frac{\ln(1+\gamma)}{1-\alpha}t.$$

Along a steady-state growth path, the initial capital stock K_0 is given by

$$\ln K_0 = \frac{\ln \Lambda}{1-\alpha} - \frac{\ln(1+\gamma)}{(1-\alpha)^2}.$$

Substituting this expression into the preceding one yields the law of motion of the capital stock along the steady-state growth path:

$$\ln K_t = \frac{\ln \Lambda}{1-\alpha} - \frac{\ln(1+\gamma)}{(1-\alpha)^2} + \frac{\ln(1+\gamma)}{1-\alpha}t.$$

Taking the antilog of this expression and substituting for Λ implies that in the steady state the capital stock grows according to

$$K_t = K_0(1+\gamma)^{t/(1-\alpha)}, \tag{63}$$

where

$$K_0 = \left\{ \frac{\beta(1-\phi)\alpha(1-\alpha)Z(1+\gamma)^{-1/(1-\alpha)}}{(1+\beta)[\alpha+\phi(1-\alpha)]} \right\}^{1/(1-\alpha)}.$$

In the steady state, capital and output grow at the same rate:

$$\frac{K_{t+1} - K_t}{K_t} = \frac{Y_{t+1} - Y_t}{Y_t} = (1+\gamma)^{1/(1-\alpha)} - 1. \tag{64}$$

The steady-state net saving rate, $S_t/Y_t = (K_{t+1} - K_t)/Y_t$, is thus equal to the growth rate of capital multiplied by the constant capital-output ratio, that is

$$\frac{S_t}{Y_t} = \left(\frac{K_{t+1} - K_t}{K_t}\right)\left(\frac{K_t}{Y_t}\right) = [(1+\gamma)^{1/(1-\alpha)} - 1]\frac{K_0}{Y_0},$$

that is, using (63), and noting that from (59) with $L = 1$ and (61) with $t = 0$, $Y_0 = ZK_0$,

$$\frac{S_t}{Y_t} = [(1+\gamma)^{1/(1-\alpha)} - 1]\left\{ \frac{\beta(1-\phi)\alpha(1-\alpha)(1+\gamma)^{-1/(1-\alpha)}}{(1+\beta)[\alpha+\phi(1-\alpha)]} \right\}. \tag{65}$$

This expression implies that a rise in the steady-state growth rate increases the saving rate, that is

$$\frac{\partial(S_t/Y_t)}{\partial(K_{t+1}/K_t)} = (1+\gamma)^{-1/(1-\alpha)}\frac{K_0}{Y_0} > 0.$$

As can be seen from (64), the steady-state growth rate is independent of ϕ and thus does not depend on the existence of borrowing constraints on household consumption. However, as shown by (65), the saving rate in an economy with liquidity constraints ($\phi < \theta$) is higher than in an economy with perfect markets ($\phi \geq \chi$); and if in the former case borrowing constraints become less binding (so that ϕ increases), the saving rate falls. Moreover, the larger the intensity of liquidity constraints, the stronger the effect of growth on saving; that is, $\partial(S_t/Y_t)/\partial(K_{t+1}/K_t)$ varies inversely with the magnitude of ϕ.[38]

Suppose now that productivity is a function of the capital stock, as in Equation (1) above:

$$A_t = ZK_t^\theta, \tag{66}$$

where $\theta \geq 0$. Substituting (66) in (59) yields the production function

$$Y_t = ZK_t^{\alpha+\theta}.$$

Using this expression together with (58) and (60), the law of motion of capital can be written as, instead of (62),

$$(1+\beta)[\alpha+\phi(1-\alpha)]K_{t+1} = \beta(1-\phi)\alpha(1-\alpha)ZK_t^{\alpha+\theta}. \tag{67}$$

[38] Note that liquidity constraints affect saving only by interacting with growth; in the absence of growth ($\gamma = 0$), saving would be zero, independently of whether liquidity constraints are binding or not. In addition, as shown by Jappelli and Pagano (1994), in an open economy (where the marginal productivity of capital is exogenous) growth would have an ambiguous effect on saving.

Taking logs, Equation (67) becomes

$$\ln K_{t+1} - \ln K_t \simeq \frac{K_{t+1} - K_t}{K_{t+1}} = \ln \Lambda - (1 - \alpha - \theta) \ln K_t, \qquad (68)$$

where

$$\Lambda = \frac{\beta(1 - \phi)\alpha(1 - \alpha)Z}{(1 + \beta)[\alpha + \phi(1 - \alpha)]}.$$

If $\alpha + \theta < 1$, the solution of this equation is

$$\ln K_t = \left\{ \ln K_0 - \frac{\ln \Lambda}{1 - \alpha - \theta} \right\} (\alpha + \theta)^t + \frac{\ln \Lambda}{1 - \alpha - \theta},$$

so that the growth rate of the capital stock is

$$(\Lambda/K_0^{1-\alpha-\theta})^{(\alpha+\theta)^{t-1}} - 1,$$

which is positive only if the economy starts with a capital stock below the steady-state level, $\Lambda^{1/(1-\alpha-\theta)}$, whereas in the steady state the growth rate of capital is zero (when $\theta = 0$, the model reduces to the previous case with $\gamma = 0$). If instead $\alpha + \theta = 1$, the solution is

$$\ln K_t = \ln K_0 + t \ln \Lambda,$$

and the growth rate of capital is $\Lambda - 1$.[39]

An economy with liquidity constraints therefore grows faster because the constant term Λ in Equation (68) is inversely related to ϕ. In particular, if $\alpha + \theta = 1$, the growth rate in the presence of binding liquidity constraints would be *permanently higher* than that of an economy with perfect capital markets. The same applies to the saving rate, which in this case is simply equal to $(\Lambda - 1)/Z$.

The empirical evidence provided by Jappelli and Pagano (1994) suggests that liquidity constraints are indeed positively correlated to growth. However, it is also important to note, as emphasized by De Gregorio (1996), that although liquidity constraints may raise saving and therefore stimulate growth, they may end up lowering growth, in net terms, because they lower the rate of **human capital accumulation**. This effect is absent in the Jappelli-Pagano model, but it may be quite relevant in practice for developing countries. Moreover, the model also ignores efficiency losses in financial intermediation associated with changes in ϕ. Thus, the policy implication of the foregoing discussion is *not* that growth-minded governments should encourage banks to impose tighter borrowing constraints; this may end up being more costly than alternative policies.

12.4.5 Political Factors and Income Inequality

Although there exists a large literature, by both economists and political scientists, focusing on the linkages between economic performance in general and

---

[39] The economy exhibits explosive growth if $\alpha + \theta > 1$.

political factors (see Chapter 17), the analytical literature focusing on the interactions between these factors and growth in an endogenous growth setting is more limited. Moreover, much of this literature, as reviewed by Alesina and Perotti (1994), remains inconclusive. In particular, much of the evidence (as discussed in the next chapter) is ambiguous on whether democracy is good or bad for growth—most *developed* countries today are indeed democracies, but democratic regimes have failed to foster economic growth in many developing countries. Nevertheless, some economists have argued that democracy can have an indirect, positive effect by influencing the *quality of governance* (Rivera-Batiz, 2002). Better governance institutions can improve the incentives of individuals to engage in innovative activities, by making them more profitable.

There is some evidence suggesting that fertility is lower in countries where citizens enjoy more civil and political liberties (Dasgupta, 1995). There is also some empirical support, as discussed in the next chapter, for the view that political instability may have an adverse effect on long-run growth. One possible explanation for this negative effect is that the political environment has an influence on the *choice of public policy*, which in turn affects growth. Different political environments may set different constraints on the available public policy instruments. For instance, the quantity and quality of public investment, the role of the government in production activities, the extent of regulation, and many other factors may be determined by the characteristics of the political system.

Another possibility is that political instability affects the growth rate in the long run through its effect on investment. Alesina and Tabellini (1989), for instance, examined the implications of political uncertainty in a model in which two governments with *conflicting distributional objectives* randomly alternate in office. Each government represents a different interest group; as a result, the incumbent government makes transfers only to its constituent interest group. These transfers are financed by taxing the other group and by borrowing. However, the incumbent government recognizes the possibility of a different type of government coming to power in the future and having to service the debt. To the extent that the future cost of debt servicing is not fully internalized in the borrowing decision, the result will be a level of borrowing above what is optimal.[40] Private agents realize that the future costs of debt servicing will fall disproportionately on one group, depending on which government is in power. They accumulate foreign assets as insurance against the risk of taxation. Political uncertainty thus generates overborrowing, capital flight, and low domestic investment—with potentially adverse effects on the rate of economic growth.[41]

The link between income inequality and growth has also been the subject of much investigation in recent years. The recent literature goes beyond the **Kuznets curve**, which (as noted in Chapter 10) relates income distribution

---

[40]More precisely, the level of debt will be higher than that consistent with economic efficiency. Of course, it will still be constrained by the limit imposed by lenders.

[41]Overborrowing may also occur when, in addition to political uncertainty, polarization—defined as the extent of disagreement over the composition of public goods—prevails, leading to a stronger preference for present government consumption (Ozler and Tabellini, 1991).

and the *level* of income. It has also emphasized the role of the political system in affecting this link, because of the key role played by the political process in aggregating conflicting interests into public policy decisions (Persson and Tabellini, 1994). From that perspective, inequality and growth are *both* endogenous outcomes of the politico-economic process, as illustrated formally by Chang (1998) in a two-class, bargaining framework that accounts simultaneously for the growth-enhancing and distributional aspects of taxation.

A common argument is that income inequality is necessary for rapid capital accumulation because the rich have a higher propensity to save and invest than the poor. Recent research has shown, however, that there are at least two channels through which inequality in income distribution can *lower* the rates of capital accumulation and economic growth.[42]

- Inequality can trigger *political and social pressures* that contribute to social and political instability and may eventually undermine incentives to save and invest. The adverse effect on growth may further increase inequality, leading to a **vicious circle** of increasing inequality and low growth.

- Inequality can reduce the average *skill level* of the labor force by making it more difficult for the poor to finance their education and that of their children. This effect may be particularly large if, as discussed earlier, low-income families have only limited access to capital markets.

Galor and Zeira (1993), in particular, showed that in the presence of credit market imperfections and indivisibilities in investment in human capital, the initial distribution of wealth affects aggregate output and investment both in the short run and in the long run. Alesina and Rodrik (1994) presented a theoretical model that suggested that income inequality affects growth negatively:

- income (and wealth) inequality causes the tax rate to rise above its optimal level, because the median voter gains from the redistributive effects of a higher tax rate if the degree of inequality is large;

- a higher than optimal tax rate reduces the propensity to invest.

12.4.6 Institutions and the Allocation of Talent

Various economists have argued in recent years that one reason why growth rates differ across countries is that the *economic environment* in which individuals operate also differs. This environment comprises the country's laws, institutions, and government rules, policies, and regulations. An environment that provides adequate protection for *property rights* and gives agents the incentive to produce, invest, and accumulate skills is a *growth-enhancing* environment.[43] In

---

[42] See Alesina and Rodrik (1994), Alesina and Perotti (1996), Bruno, Ravallion, and Squire (1998), and Persson and Tabellini (1994). Alesina and Perotti (1994) and Bénabou (1997) provide surveys of this literature.

[43] Evidence on the link between property rights and private investment is provided by Svensson (1998).

particular, legal reforms that strengthen creditor rights, contract enforcement, and accounting practices can stimulate financial development (Levine, Loayza, and Beck, 2000). By contrast, a *growth-deterring* environment discourages production and effort and has an adverse effect on economic performance. A highly corrupt bureaucracy, for instance, operates as a *tax* on production activities.[44] Entrepreneurs must allocate some of their time and resources to bribing government officials to obtain the necessary authorizations (such as permits and licenses) for operating. As Shleifer and Vishny (1993) argued, if the structure of government is such that different groups of bureaucrats have *hold-up power* over an investment project, the result may be a level of capital formation that is dramatically lower than would be achievable in different circumstances: because the bureaucrats may be unable to collude or coordinate, the total sum of bribes required to have the project approved may exceed the private gains from investing in the first place.

The opportunity to divert resources in this way through government can have important dynamic consequences for the **allocation of talent**, as emphasized by Baumol (1990) and Murphy, Shleifer, and Vishny (1991). Individuals who might have chosen to become entrepreneurs may instead devote their energies to **rent seeking** or other forms of diversion in the public sector. Individuals may be tempted to accumulate not the type of skills that would increase the productive capacity of the economy but rather those that maximize their own chance of securing a *strategic position* in the government bureaucracy. Douglass North's description of pirates investing in technologies and skills to make piracy more effective is a classic example of this diversion of talent (see North, 1990, pp. 77-78):

> To be a successful pirate one needs to know a great deal about naval warfare; the trade routes of commercial shipping; the armament, rigging, and crew size of potential victims; and the market for booty. Successful pirates will acquire the requisite knowledge and skills. Such activities may well give rise to a thriving demand for improved naval warfare technology by both the pirates and the victims . . . If the basic institutional framework makes income redistribution (piracy) the preferred (and most profitable) economic opportunity, we can expect a very different development of knowledge and skills than a productivity-increasing . . . . economic opportunity would entail . . . The incentives that are built into the institutional framework play the decisive role in shaping the kinds of skills and knowledge that pay off.

A key implication of this analysis is that effective government institutions are essential to avoid biasing individual choices in favor of rent seeking (or corruption, as discussed in the appendix to this chapter) instead of production. Such institutions include a *strong judiciary* and *secure property rights*.[45]

---

[44] See the appendix to Chapter 17 for a discussion of corruption and its economic costs.

[45] In an environment characterized by a strong judicial system, limited resources may actually be needed to enforce the laws, because of the deterrent effect of a credible threat of enforcement.

Related arguments were made by Tornell and Velasco (1992), Hall and Jones (1999), and Olson (1996). Tornell and Velasco developed a model in which poorly defined property rights lead investors to prefer external investment, even if domestic investments have a higher social (but a lower private) expected rate of return. As a result, growth in per capita income is lower than it would be otherwise. Hall and Jones found that differences in *social infrastructure* (which they define as institutions and government policies that determine the environment within which economic agents operate) are key factors in explaining cross-country differences in capital accumulation, educational attainment, productivity, and thus income per capita. Olson argued that a key factor that explains the low-growth performance of poor countries is that they tend to *waste more resources* (both capital and knowledge) than richer countries. The problem, then, may not be to accumulate more resources (by investing in physical and human capital, for instance) but to waste less of the resources that *already exist*. This, in turn, calls for the adoption of policies and institutions that can raise the ability to use existing resources more efficiently.

12.5   Summary

- Recent developments in the theory of economic growth have emphasized the potential growth-enhancing roles of knowledge, **human capital**, and **research and development**, as well as the possibility of **increasing returns** to scale at the aggregate level.

- This literature contrasts with the traditional, neoclassical model, in which capital accumulation raises the *level* of output, or the rate of output growth during the *transition* to a new steady state, but not its *long-term growth rate*. In the Solow-Swan model, because of the assumption of **constant returns to scale** in all inputs (and hence diminishing returns to capital), policies that stimulate saving and investment raise output growth only *temporarily* because each addition to the capital stock is assumed to generate diminishing amounts of additional output.

- By contrast, the new endogenous growth theories assume either that investment does not have such diminishing returns, or that some of the additional output is used in activities that directly increase the rate of technological change and economic growth.

- The production of knowledge may occur either as a *by-product* of economic activity (as in **learning-by-doing** models) or through a production activity. In most of these models, an increase in the *saving rate* may raise the steady-state growth rate of income per capita.

- The Mankiw-Romer-Weil model extends the Solow-Swan model to include human capital. It retains the assumption of constant returns to scale in all inputs (and thus diminishing returns to physical and human capital taken together). However, it implies that relatively small changes in the resources devoted to physical and human capital accumulation may lead to large changes in output per worker. As a result, it is better equipped to account for large differences in *levels* of real income across countries.

- The *AK* model assumes that there are *constant returns* to capital, defined broadly to include both physical and human capital. In the *AK* model, an increase in the saving rate *permanently* raises the growth rate of output per capita. Whereas the Solow-Swan model predicts that poor countries should grow faster than rich countries, the *AK* model implies that poor countries with the *same level of technology* and the same structural parameters as richer countries should grow at the same rate as these countries, *regardless* of the initial level of income. Thus, the *AK* model *does not predict* (absolute) *convergence*.

New growth theories have identified various other factors, both structural and policy related, that may alter the long-run growth process.

- *Fiscal policy* affects steady-state growth through *direct effects* stemming from expenditures and taxes, and *indirect effects* through macroeconomic stability.

- Public investment in *infrastructure* (which is generally complementary to private investment) has a direct effect on growth by increasing the economy's capital stock. Government spending may also alter growth indirectly by raising the *marginal productivity* of privately supplied factors of production—through spending on *education, health,* and other services that contribute to the accumulation of human capital.

- An increase in the tax rate lowers the after-tax marginal product of capital (and thus investment and growth) because of its direct impact on rates of return; it also raises it, however, because of its impact on the provision of public services. Taxes and growth are thus *nonlinearly* related. High rates of taxation, in addition, may contribute to the growth of the **informal economy**.

- *Inflation* has a negative effect on steady-state growth through various channels. In particular, it may reduce both the *rate* and the *efficiency* of investment. If firms use money because it reduces *transactions costs*, inflation will lower the optimal level of real money balances and raise the cost of investing. By lowering the rate of capital accumulation and the productivity of capital, inflation adversely affects the rate of growth in the long run.

- High inflation and large fiscal deficits are key symptoms of *macroeconomic instability*. Such instability is pervasive in countries that are *poorly diversified* (and thus less able to absorb domestic and external shocks) and where macroeconomic management is weak. By increasing *overall uncertainty* and *distorting information* on underlying economic fundamentals, macroeconomic instability hampers private investment and saving decisions, and thus long-run growth.

- Greater openness to trade may generate **dynamic gains** and thereby affect the economy's rate of growth in the long run. The specialization in production that results from free trade, for instance, not only leads to a higher level of *efficiency* in production but can also raise the long-run growth rate. Integration with the world economy effectively expands the markets open to firms and allows more efficient use of existing productive capacity. The increased scale of production in industries where a country has comparative advantage provides larger benefits through **learning by doing** and increases the incentives for human capital accumulation and for fixed investment aimed at improving technology. All these effects have the potential to raise growth rates.

- However, the effects of scale economies and learning by doing emphasized in the new theories of trade and growth take place mostly in the production of advanced manufactured products. In countries where the level of skills is relatively low, and exports consist mainly of *raw materials* or *low-technology* manufactured goods, the rate at which technologies and production techniques are assimilated may be too slow to foster a rapid shift toward the production of goods and services that are characterized by dynamic gains. The effect on long-run growth rates would therefore be limited.

- Financial openness may provide significant long-run benefits. Producers who are able to diversify risks on world capital markets may invest in riskier (and higher-yield) projects, thereby raising the country's rate of economic growth. In countries where the capacity to save is constrained by a low level of income, the ability to draw upon foreign resources may lead to higher domestic investment and growth. This effect can be particularly large for *foreign direct investment.* In addition, foreign direct investment may facilitate the transfer or diffusion of managerial and technological know-how, and improve the skills composition of the labor force as a result of learning-by-doing effects, investment in formal education, and on-the-job training.

- But financial openness may also have adverse effects on growth. Exposure to greater volatility of capital flows on international financial markets may increase domestic instability and reduce private investment, thereby hampering growth.

- *Financial development* affects long-run growth through a variety of channels. Financial institutions play a key role in screening among potential entrepreneurs and financing the best prospects. The resulting increase in productivity may lead to higher growth.

- Financial development also leads to higher saving rates, and thus higher rates of economic growth. Financial institutions possess *economies of scale* in gathering and processing information, monitoring performance, and enforcing contracts, and therefore help reduce the cost of transforming savings into productive investment.

- By pooling together the assets of a multitude of individual savers, such institutions can also finance projects that would not be undertaken otherwise because of their *size*, their *riskiness*, or their long *gestation period*. Moreover, combining assets allows financial institutions to reduce any single individual's exposure to the risks of liquidity and failure inherent in any project compared with a situation in which financing is provided directly.

- In general, whether democracy is good or bad for growth remains an open issue. However, *political instability* may have a significant adverse effect on long-run growth. A possible reason is that the political environment has an influence on the *choice of public policy*, which in turn affects growth.

- The *economic environment* in which individuals operate (a country's laws, institutions, and policies) may have a strong impact on its growth performance. An environment that provides agents with the incentive to produce, invest, and accumulate skills fosters economic growth. By contrast, an environment that discourages production and effort will have an adverse effect on economic performance. A highly corrupt bureaucracy, for instance, operates as a *tax* on production activities. The opportunity to divert resources can have important dynamic consequences for the **allocation of talent**. Individuals who might have chosen to become entrepreneurs may instead devote their energies to **rent-seeking** activities in the public sector.

Appendix to Chapter 12
Determinants and Costs of Corruption

Corruption is generally defined as the abuse of public office for private gain (see Klitgaard, 1988, and Jain, 2001). Although corruption is a widespread phenomenon, its incidence is particularly pervasive where, as is the case in many developing countries, large and inefficient bureaucracies exist, regulations lack transparency, property rights are not well defined, and judicial systems are deficient. More specifically, the incidence of corruption is closely related to **rent-seeking behavior**, as defined earlier. Such behavior may be exacerbated by the presence of government-induced sources of rents—quantitative restrictions on trade (such as quotas on imports), subsidies (for instance to public enterprises), price controls, foreign exchange allocation schemes, and low wages in the public sector—or the existence of large resource endowments (Bardhan, 1997).

As discussed by Aidt (2003), most of the economic literature on corruption uses the **principal-agent framework** to analyze the relationship between the government (the principal) and the bureaucrats (the agents).[46] Corruption is seen as the result of **imperfect monitoring** by the government. Bureaucrats take bribes in the process of buying and selling goods from the private sector on behalf of the government. Such a framework is used to examine the extent to which bribery is affected by alternative sanctions or incentives, monitoring technologies, and the degree of competition among agents and private individuals in providing government goods to the private sector and in selling privately produced goods to the government.

A good example of this type of model is the one developed by Shleifer and Vishny (1993). In the Shleifer-Vishny framework, bureaucrats take bribes from private individuals demanding government-produced goods. Taking this relationship as given, the model attempts to explain both the *incidence* of corruption and its *costs*. To explain the incidence of corruption requires assessing the degree of competition among bureaucrats and consumers. The model assumes that the private sector needs various complementary government goods as inputs (that is, licenses, permits, and so on) provided through various public agencies—each run by a bureaucrat. With multiple government goods, the market structure, in the provisions of these goods, helps to explain the incidence of corruption. Shleifer and Vishny analyzed three types of market structure:

- the different bureaucratic agencies, each supplying one (and only one) of the complementary government goods, collude in *one monopoly*;

---

[46] The use of economic analysis to study corruption (or, rather, crime and law enforcement in general) was pioneered by Becker (1968). Becker showed that the amount of resources (spent on police, courts, and so on) and the punishment that should be used to enforce the rule of law are determined by minimizing a social loss function—which captures the net cost of crime to society, the cost of apprehension and conviction, and the cost of punishing offenders. He concluded that the probability of apprehension and conviction (which depends on the level of resources spent) and the potential punishment deter offenders at the margin; thus crime not paying off (at the margin) is an optimality condition and not a statement about the efficiency of police activities and the judicial system.

- the agencies, each supplying one (and only one) of the complementary government goods, act as *independent monopolists*;

- the agencies, each supplying more than one of the government-produced goods, *compete* in the provision of these goods.

The authors concluded that the third case (competition) yields the lowest level of bribes, the second (independent monopolists) the highest, and the first (collusion) in between. The total bribe revenue collection, however, is the highest in the first case, where the agencies collude, precisely to maximize the total value of bribes.

The consequences of corruption are pervasive. Because bribes to corrupt officials act as an implicit tax, they reduce the incentive to invest—and thus, ultimately, hinder economic growth. Corruption also has an adverse effect on the allocation of talent and skills, as emphasized by Murphy, Shleifer, and Vishny (1991): in an environment where the return to corruption is high, the more talented and highly educated will be more likely to engage in rent-seeking activities than in productive ones—again, with potentially adverse effects on long-run growth. It also implies a loss of tax revenue (as a result, for instance, of illegal use of tax exemptions), higher public expenditure (through higher subsidies, for instance), and lower quality of public services. Finally, corruption may also reduce the effectiveness of foreign aid (discussed in Chapter 16), by channeling funds to unproductive government expenditures.

Because of its very nature, corruption is difficult to measure. Various attempts have been made, in recent years, to construct (subjective) indices of the degree of corruption across countries. These indices are subject to a number of limitations; in particular, they typically do not distinguish between *high-level* corruption (involving, say, senior government officials) and *low-level* corruption (involving bureaucrats at the low end of public administrations); these two types of activities are likely to be substantially different in their economic effects. Nevertheless, several studies (based on cross-section regressions) have provided evidence suggesting that corruption may have a large, adverse effect on investment and growth. Mauro (1997), in particular, estimates that to a large extent the effects of corruption on growth operate through investment.

Chapter 13

The Determinants of Economic Growth: An Empirical Overview

The past few years have witnessed a flurry of empirical studies on the determinants of economic growth, in parallel with the development of the various analytical approaches reviewed in the previous chapter. Two main techniques have been used: country-specific growth accounting, which evolved mostly from the Solow-Swan growth model presented in Chapter 11, and cross-country regressions, which rely on econometric techniques and large data sets. This chapter reviews the recent evidence on the determinants of growth based on both approaches and highlights some of the methodological issues confronting many of the existing studies. Section 13.1 presents the growth accounting methodology and section 13.2 illustrates its usefulness (and limitations) by analyzing the controversy over the sources of growth in East Asia since the early 1950s. Section 13.3 discusses the econometric issues that arise in using cross-country growth regressions. Section 13.4 provides a selective summary of the recent literature in this area. The last part concludes by assessing whether the evidence supports any firm conclusion regarding the speed of convergence in income per capita across countries.

13.1 Growth Accounting

A widely used methodology to explain differences in growth rates across countries is **growth accounting**, which consists essentially in adding the different contributions of the growth of basic factor inputs (labor and capital) and an unexplained element or residual that is often viewed as capturing *improvements in technology,* or more generally overall gains in economic efficiency.

To derive the basic growth accounting equation, suppose that aggregate output in the economy can be described by the production function

$$Y = AF(K, L), \tag{1}$$

where K is the stock of capital, L the number of workers, and A measures the efficiency of the production process or the level of technological progress. This specification implies that technological progress raises the level of output that can be produced with a given combination of inputs, without affecting their marginal products. In the terminology described in Chapter 11, technological progress is assumed to be **Hicks neutral**.

Differentiating Equation (1) with respect to time yields

$$\dot{Y} = \dot{A}F + AF_K\dot{K} + AF_L\dot{L},$$

which can be rewritten as

$$\frac{\dot{Y}}{Y} = \frac{\dot{A}}{A} + F_K(\frac{AK}{Y})\frac{\dot{K}}{K} + F_L(\frac{AL}{Y})\frac{\dot{L}}{L} = \frac{\dot{A}}{A} + (\frac{KF_K}{F})\frac{\dot{K}}{K} + (\frac{LF_L}{F})\frac{\dot{L}}{L}.$$

Equivalently, letting $\mathbf{g}_x = \dot{x}/x$ and denoting by $\eta_K = F_K K/F$ and $\eta_L = F_L L/F$ the elasticities of output with respect to capital and labor, respectively, the above expression yields

$$\mathbf{g}_Y = \mathbf{g}_A + \eta_K\mathbf{g}_K + \eta_L\mathbf{g}_L.$$

Let w and r denote, respectively, the wage rate and the rental rate of capital. Under conditions of perfectly competitive factor pricing, factors are paid their marginal product, so that $w = F_L$ and $r = F_K - \delta$, where δ is the rate of depreciation of capital. Thus, with $\delta = 0$ for simplicity, $\eta_L = wL/Y$ and $\eta_K = rK/Y$; η_L and η_K are simply equal to the share of, respectively, labor and capital income in total output. **Euler's theorem** on homogeneous functions— see for instance Chiang (1984, pp. 411-414)—guarantees that for a CRS function $F(K, L)$,

$$KF_K + LF_L = F \quad \Rightarrow \quad \frac{KF_K}{F} + \frac{LF_L}{F} = 1,$$

or equivalently that the sum of the share coefficients η_K and η_L is equal to unity ($\eta_K + \eta_L = 1$). The equation for $\mathbf{g}_Y$ can thus be rewritten as

$$\mathbf{g}_Y - \mathbf{g}_L = \mathbf{g}_A + \eta_K(\mathbf{g}_K - \mathbf{g}_L),$$

or equivalently

$$\mathbf{g}_{Y/L} = \mathbf{g}_A + \eta_K\mathbf{g}_{K/L}, \tag{2}$$

which relates the growth of output per worker to the rate of technological progress (often referred to as the **Solow residual** or the rate of growth of **total factor productivity**, TFP) and the rate of growth of capital per worker, weighted by the share of total income going to capital (or, more accurately, capital owners).

In practice, researchers often use a **Cobb-Douglas** specification, that is,

$$Y = AK^\alpha L^{1-\alpha}.$$

This function, as discussed in Chapter 11, is characterized by *constant returns to scale* and *constant factor income shares*, with a capital share of α ($= \eta_K$) and a labor share of $1 - \alpha$.

Once estimates of the growth rates of output, capital, and the labor force are obtained, and an estimate of η_K (or α) is derived, Equation (2) can be solved for the rate of technological progress:

$$\mathbf{g}_A = \mathbf{g}_{Y/L} - \eta_K \mathbf{g}_{K/L} = \eta_K \mathbf{g}_{K/Y} + (1 - \eta_K)\mathbf{g}_{Y/L}, \tag{3}$$

where the last expression defines TFP growth as the weighted average of the growth rates of the capital-output ratio and output per unit of labor.

In practical applications, income is generally measured in per capita terms rather than per worker; Equation (2) in this case is written as

$$\mathbf{g}_{Y/N} = \mathbf{g}_Y - \mathbf{g}_N = \mathbf{g}_A + \eta_K \mathbf{g}_{K/N} + (1 - \eta_K)\mathbf{g}_{L/N},$$

where $\mathbf{g}_N$ is the rate of growth of the population as a whole. The Solow residual is thus given by

$$\mathbf{g}_A = \mathbf{g}_{Y/N} - \eta_K \mathbf{g}_{K/N} + (1 - \eta_K)\mathbf{g}_{L/N}, \tag{4}$$

which is simply (2) if $\mathbf{g}_L = \mathbf{g}_N$.

The basic growth accounting framework has been extended in various ways to include not only investment in physical and human capital but also a large number of additional variables, including, as noted by Maddison (1995, pp. 40-49) and Hulten (2001), changes in the *composition* and *quality* of factor inputs, changes in levels of research and development, foreign trade, economies of scale in domestic markets, government regulations, labor hoarding, and changes in rates of capacity use.

Nevertheless, growth accounting exercises remain fraught with difficulties. The inclusion of the variables mentioned earlier has often proceeded in an *ad hoc* manner, without always being based on well-accepted theoretical considerations. The role of land as a separate factor of production is generally ignored—partly because of inadequate data. The share of capital in the production function is, as a result, overstated, and the rate of TFP growth underestimated. No standard measurement method exists for estimating the growth rates of capital and labor. Capital stock series are typically constructed by using the **perpetual inventory method**, which essentially consists in cumulating data on investment flows at constant prices, obtained either from national sources or international databases, such as the *Penn World Tables*, assuming a constant depreciation rate (generally in the 4-6 percent range). The choice of the starting year for the sample, however, is often arbitrary and may lead to large estimation errors, particularly in the early periods. Several authors have attempted to use a quality-adjusted measure of capital. Roldós (1997b), for instance, estimated an index of the quality of capital in Chile as a weighted average of investment in machinery and equipment, on the one hand, and investment in buildings and structures, on the other, with weights given by relative rental rates. However, quality adjustments (which may have drastic implications for measured TFP growth rates) are often viewed as having an *ad hoc* nature.

Labor is often measured from data on participation rates and working hours. Differences among types of workers and data reliability across countries create serious problems for comparative analysis. To answer the first problem, several researchers (for instance, Young, 1995) have used measures of quality-adjusted labor as a production input. These measures are often constructed as a weighted average of labor with different levels of education, with weights given by relative wages. However, such adjustments may lead to an underestimation of the true rate of TFP growth by attributing a larger part of the increase in output to a better or more educated labor force (Sarel, 1997).[1]

Estimation of factor shares—the parameter η_K or α given above, which may significantly affect estimates of TFP growth—can also be problematic. The most commonly used method to estimate these shares is to use national accounts data to calculate (generally period by period) the share of income that is distributed to each factor of production.[2] As noted earlier, this approach requires that markets of capital and labor be perfectly competitive and that the income of each factor be equal to the value of its marginal product. In practice, of course, market imperfections abound. Noncompetitive wage determination and monopolistic product markets may significantly distort the relationship between income shares and marginal products. The absence of perfect competition, in the context of a constant returns to scale production function, can lead to large errors in estimating the elasticity of output with respect to each input, because factor shares need no longer reflect output elasticities. In particular, to the extent that monopoly profits are reflected in capital income, capital's share of income will tend to overstate the elasticity of output with respect to capital. Researchers often attempt to adjust for such biases, but the practice has an *ad hoc* nature, with potentially large effects on estimated TFP growth rates.

The method also ignores government policies and regulations, most notably tax policy, which may have a significant impact on the rate of return to capital. Subsidies to capital-intensive industries, for instance, may raise the rate of return to capital above its physical marginal product; estimating factor shares by using income shares would thus lead to an overestimation of the share of capital in the production process. There are also problems involved in using national accounts data, related notably to the classification of workers (see Sarel, 1997, pp. 386-87). Moreover, the very use of a Cobb-Douglas production function has come under scrutiny. The presence of **positive externalities** implies

---

[1] This argument loses some strength if TFP growth is viewed merely as a measure of ignorance, a true residual.

[2] The second approach used to estimate factor shares is the regression approach, which suffers in particular from the assumption that the estimated weights are constant over the estimation period. In practice, the relative importance of production inputs is likely to change over time, especially when an economy undergoes rapid transformation and structural change.

that standard growth accounting techniques can provide misleading estimates of total factor productivity growth. In particular, if the aggregate production function is indeed characterized by **increasing returns to scale**—as a result, for instance, of externalities generated by the economy-wide capital stock, as discussed by Romer (1986)—then the standard approach based on the assumption of constant returns to scale will underestimate the contribution of capital and the residual obtained will overestimate TFP growth. A simple illustration of this result, due to Barro (2000a), is presented in the appendix to this chapter.[3]

A **dual approach to growth accounting**, based on the identity relating national income to factor incomes (and thus factor prices), could alleviate some of the data problems that the conventional methodology faces and can therefore be viewed as a useful complement (see Hsieh, 1999). For instance, if growth is indeed driven by physical capital accumulation rather than by exogenous technological progress, the return to capital should fall over time in the presence of diminishing returns.

13.2   The East Asian "Miracle"

An interesting application of the growth accounting framework has been to the issue of growth in East Asian countries between the early 1950s and the mid-1990s (for an overview, see Krueger, 1995). Growth in some of these countries averaged 6 percent between 1950 and 1992. Output per worker increased by more than 5 percent during the period 1960-94 in Korea, Singapore, Thailand, and Taiwan. Just during the period 1980-95, Indonesia, Malaysia, Singapore, and Thailand more than doubled their real income per capita, compared with an increase of only 20 percent in the United States (Sarel, 1997, p. 369). In all of these countries, investment in *physical capital* appears to have played an important role. In Singapore for instance, the rate of growth during the period 1960-91 averaged 6.3 percent a year in per capita terms. The scale of investment (mostly by the private sector) since the early 1960s has been impressive: the ratio of gross fixed investment to GDP has exceeded, on average, 35 percent since the early 1970s. On the basis of cumulative net investment data, Singapore's capital stock has increased 33-fold between 1960 and 1992, doubling on average once every six years. This rapid pace of physical investment resulted in a tenfold increase in the capital-labor ratio between 1960 and 1992. However, whether investment in physical capital alone accounts for the high growth rates observed in East Asia remains a hotly debated issue among economists.

In a well-publicized study, Young (1995) argued, using the framework described above, that the very high growth rates experienced by Hong Kong, Singapore, South Korea, and Taiwan over the past three decades are almost entirely due to rising investment, increasing labor force participation, and improving labor quality (as reflected in an increase in the proportion of skilled workers), and not to rapid technological progress and other forces affecting the Solow residual. More specifically, Young estimated the growth rate of TFP in

---

[3] For some evidence on increasing returns, see Ades and Glaeser (1999).

these countries to be very low in comparison with industrial countries. Thus, in Young's view, there is nothing *miraculous*—in the sense of something that can be explained only by referring to divine intervention—about growth in East Asian countries. These conclusions found some support in a subsequent study by Collins and Bosworth (1996). For the period 1960-94, they estimated that of an average growth of output per worker equal to 4.2 percent for East Asia, 1.1 percentage points can be attributed to TFP growth; most of the increase (2.5 percentage points) resulted from the high rate of accumulation of physical capital per worker. Results for individual countries (most notably Korea and Singapore) suggested a similar pattern. In a more recent study, Collins and Bosworth (2003) expanded their initial analysis to the period 1960-2000 and found similar results. Output per worker grew at an average yearly rate of 3.9 percent in East Asia, with much of it resulting again from accumulation of physical capital (2.3 percentage points) and the quality of human capital (0.5 percentage points), as opposed to TFP growth (1 percentage point).

Several authors, including Pack and Page (1994) and Sarel (1997) questioned the validity of Young's calculations and argued that TFP growth in East Asia was *much higher* than Young's results suggested. Sarel's analysis focused on five East Asian countries: Indonesia, Malaysia, the Philippines, Singapore, and Thailand (with the United States as a comparator country) for the period 1978-96. Sarel's approach differed from the standard growth accounting framework used by Young in that he estimated technological factor shares not by using *income shares* (as described earlier) but by a method that attempted to capture differences in the structure of production across countries and differences in the level of development.[4] The estimated capital share, α, varied from 0.28 for Thailand to 0.34 for Singapore. Young (1995), in contrast, obtained a capital share of 0.5 for Singapore. Sarel's results indicate that the rates of TFP growth were very strong in Singapore (2.2 percent), Malaysia and Thailand (2 percent), and much less so in Indonesia (1.2 percent). These rates are well above the rate observed in the United States for the sample period (0.3 percent) and those obtained by Collins and Bosworth (1996). In all four Asian countries, TFP growth rates accounted for a significant proportion of the growth rate of output per capita during the period.

Thus, Sarel's results differ significantly from Young's calculations. Several methodological factors may account for these differences. In the case of Singapore, in particular, the difference between the two studies appears to result essentially from the use of different estimates of the capital share. But for the other countries, various other factors may also be important. The studies cover different periods; and the methods used for the measurement of the capital stock

---

[4]Specifically, Sarel calculated the aggregate capital share in each country, for every year during the sample period, as the weighted average of the capital shares in each major economic activity (as defined in the United Nations' *National Accounts Statistics*), using as weights the relative shares of these activities in output at factor cost. Implicit in this approach, however, is the assumption that no systematic differences in factor shares would exist once cross-country differences are controlled for in the structure of production and the level of development. As can be inferred from the previous section, this is far from being an innocuous hypothesis.

and the stock of labor differed substantially. In particular, Sarel did not adjust his measure of labor input for education levels, in contrast to Young and many other authors.

The conclusion of this brief overview of growth accounting studies is that no consensus has yet emerged regarding the relative importance of productivity growth versus growth in factor inputs in accounting for the high growth rates observed in East Asia from the early 1960s to the mid-1990s. Various aspects of the methodology, as indicated earlier, remain sources of controversy. The experience of industrial countries does suggest that the accumulation of physical capital is an important source of growth in the early stages of development; once a relatively high level of capital intensity (as measured by the capital-to-labor ratio) is reached, technological progress tends to become the principal driving force. At the same time, as argued by Nelson and Pack (1999), what appears to have been an important factor underlying the East Asian miracle is the ability of the local populations to *assimilate* new technologies (through greater entrepreneurship, innovation, and learning), and thereby enhance the growth effect of physical capital accumulation. Thus, both physical and human capital accumulation matter in the growth process, along with TFP growth. Moreover, policies aimed at increasing TFP growth may also raise the rate of physical capital accumulation, and policies aimed at promoting education (the rate of accumulation of human capital) may improve efficiency and raise TFP growth. Finally, it is worth emphasizing that it is not only the *quantity* of investment that matters, but also its *quality*. As noted in Chapter 8, this may have been one of the lessons of the recent crisis in East Asia.

13.3   Growth Regressions and Convergence

13.3.1   Diminishing Returns and Convergence

An issue that has attracted considerable attention in the recent empirical literature on growth is whether poor countries tend to grow faster than rich countries; that is, whether a process of *convergence* in growth rates occurs over time. As discussed in Chapter 11, the Solow-Swan model predicts that countries with different production technologies, saving rates, and population growth rates, but with the same rate of technological progress, γ, will all converge to a balanced growth path with a *growth rate* of income per capita equal to γ. Moreover, if production technologies, saving rates, and population growth rates are the same across countries, they will all converge to the same *level* of income per capita as well.

But to the extent that countries are at different points in their transition to the balanced growth path, differences in growth rates of output per worker will arise; one would then expect the poorer countries to grow faster than the richer countries—even with identical technology, saving rates, and population growth rates. The reason is that *diminishing returns to capital* imply that each addition to the capital stock generates large additions to output when the capital stock is small to begin with (see Chapter 11). The opposite is true when the capital stock is large initially. This observation has important implications for econometric testing.

13.3.2 Convergence and Cross-Section Regressions

From an empirical point of view, various concepts of convergence have been used in the literature(see Islam, 2003, for a detailed discussion). The two concepts emphasized by Barro and Sala-i-Martin (1995) and Mankiw, Romer, and Weil (1992) are β-convergence (absolute and conditional) and σ-convergence, which are commonly analyzed through cross-country regression techniques.[5]

- **Absolute β-convergence**, or **mean reversion**, occurs in a cross section of countries (that is, a sample of country observations all drawn at the same moment in time) if a negative relationship can be found between the growth rate of real income per capita and the *initial level* of real income per capita. Put differently, absolute β-convergence occurs if poor economies tend to grow faster than richer ones, as indicated earlier.

- **σ-convergence** occurs across a group of countries when the *dispersion* of real per capita income tends to fall over time. In other words, σ-convergence requires that the distribution of world income become *more equitable* over time.

To see how these two concepts of convergence are related, consider a group of N countries, with real per capita income for country h given by y_h, $h = 1, ...,$ N. Consider also the following regression model, in discrete time, of $\ln y_h$ over a constant term, a_0, and its lagged value:

$$\ln y_{ht} = a_0 + (1 - \beta) \ln y_{ht-1} + u_{ht}, \quad h = 1, ..., N, \tag{5}$$

where β is a parameter to be estimated and u_{ht} is a disturbance term with mean zero and constant variance σ_u^2, which captures temporary shocks to the production technology, the propensity to save, and so on. This term is also assumed to be *independent* over time and across countries. Equation (5) can also be written as

$$\ln(y_{ht}/y_{ht-1}) = a_0 - \beta \ln y_{ht-1} + u_{ht}, \quad h = 1, ..., N. \tag{6}$$

Equation (6) shows that for β-convergence to hold, the condition $\beta > 0$ must be satisfied; indeed, $\beta > 0$ implies *mean reversion* because the annual growth rate of per capita income, $\ln(y_{ht}/y_{ht-1})$, is inversely related to $\ln y_{ht-1}$.[6] The

---

[5] See Greene (2000) for a discussion of these techniques. An alternative statistical approach to testing for β-convergence, based on changes in the ranking of income levels over time, is discussed by Boyle and McCarthy (1997).

[6] The condition $\beta < 1$ is also generally required to exclude the possibility that real income per capita in poor countries exceeds income per capita in richer ones at some point in the future.

higher β is, the greater the tendency to converge. As shown by Bernard and Durlauf (1996), with ordinary least squares (OLS) estimation, β can be written as a weighted average of the ratio of differences of growth rates from the sample mean to differences of initial incomes from the sample mean. The requirement that $\beta > 0$ in a cross-section regression may therefore be expressed as requiring that a weighted average of countries with above-average initial incomes grows at a slower rate than the mean growth for the cross section.

In the long run, with $y_{ht-1} = y_{ht}$, *expected* real income per capita is

$$\mathbf{E} \ln y_h = a_0/\beta,$$

where $\mathbf{E}$ is the mathematical expectations operator.

To define σ-convergence, consider as a measure of the dispersion of income across countries the **sample variance** of $\ln y_{ht}$:

$$\sigma_t^2 = \frac{1}{N-1} \sum_{h=1}^{N} (\ln y_{ht} - \mu_t)^2, \tag{7}$$

where μ_t is the sample mean of $\ln y_{ht}$. If N is sufficiently large, then the sample variance can be viewed as a relatively accurate measure of the **population variance**. Equation (5) can then be used to calculate the process driving σ_t^2 over time:

$$\sigma_t^2 \simeq (1-\beta)^2 \sigma_{t-1}^2 + \sigma_u^2. \tag{8}$$

Equation (8) is a **first-order difference equation** in σ_t^2, which, as long as $0 < \beta < 1$, provides a stable steady-state solution, $\tilde{\sigma}^2$, given by (see Chiang, 1984, pp. 554-56):

$$\tilde{\sigma}^2 = \frac{\sigma_u^2}{1-(1-\beta)^2}. \tag{9}$$

Equation (9) shows that the long-run value of the variance of per capita income across countries is increasing in the variance of the disturbance term σ_u^2, and decreasing in β.

Equation (8) also reveals that if absolute β-convergence does not hold in the sample, that is if $\beta < 0$, $(1-\beta)^2$ will be greater than unity and the process driving σ_t^2 will be **unstable**: the cross-sectional variance of income will tend to increase over time without bound. Thus, absolute β-convergence is *necessary* for σ-convergence to occur.

The solution of Equation (8) can be written as

$$\sigma_t^2 - \tilde{\sigma}^2 = (1-\beta)^2 (\sigma_{t-1}^2 - \tilde{\sigma}^2), \tag{10}$$

which shows that if absolute β-convergence holds ($\beta > 0$), then σ_t^2 will approach its long-run value $\tilde{\sigma}^2$ monotonically. Equation (10) also shows that whether σ_t^2 is rising or falling toward $\tilde{\sigma}^2$ depends on whether its initial value is greater, or lower, than the long-run value. In particular, σ_t^2 may be increasing during the transition even if $\beta > 0$. Thus, although absolute β-convergence is *necessary* for σ-convergence (as shown earlier), it is *not sufficient*.[7]

The third concept of convergence emphasized in the literature is the concept of **conditional β-convergence**, which is taken to occur in a group of countries if the *partial correlation* between the rate of growth of, and the initial level of, per capita real income is *negative*. To illustrate this concept, consider a cross-section regression of per capita income growth rates on initial per capita income and various other *control variables* summarized in the vector Z_t, which captures other determinants of income—such as inflation, the degree of openness, or financial factors (as discussed below):

$$\ln y_{ht} = a_0 + a_1 Z_t + (1 - \beta) \ln y_{ht-1} + u_{ht}. \tag{11}$$

It can be shown that, as long as the process driving the variables contained in Z_t is stable, conditional β-convergence once again requires $\beta > 0$. Similarly, σ-convergence can also be defined in the context of Equation (11); and once again, conditional β-convergence is *necessary* for σ-convergence to occur. There are, however, two differences:

- Even if $0 < \beta < 1$, σ_t^2 does not approach its steady-state value *monotonically*: there may be, during the transition process, periods during which σ_t^2 increases and then falls, depending on the process driving the variables contained in Z_t, as well as their initial and long-run values.

- The dispersion of income per capita in the long run depends not only [as in Equation (9)] on the variance of the shocks, σ_u^2, but also on the dispersion of *country-specific characteristics*, as summarized by σ_Z^2.

13.3.3 Testing the Mankiw-Romer-Weil Model

A key implication of the growth model with physical and human capital accumulation developed by Mankiw, Romer, and Weil (1992), as indicated in the previous chapter, is that differences in population growth and capital accumulation can potentially account for the observed large variations in incomes across countries. The income per capita equation of their model, as derived in the previous chapter, is

$$\ln \tilde{y} = \frac{\alpha}{\Omega} \ln s_K + \frac{\beta}{\Omega} \ln s_H - \frac{\alpha + \beta}{\Omega} \ln(n + \gamma + \delta),$$

where $\Omega = 1/(1 - \alpha - \beta)$. To test this equation, Mankiw, Romer, and Weil use the following measures:

- y: the logarithm of output per person in the population of working age (15 to 64);

---

[7] Quah (1996*a,b*) explains the difference between β- and σ-convergence by means of *Galton's fallacy*: the convergence to the intergenerational mean in the height of the members of a family (β-convergence) does not imply that the dispersion of heights within the population diminishes throughout time (σ-convergence).

- n: average rate of growth of the working-age population;

- s_K: average share of total investment in GDP;

- s_H: the average fraction of the population of working age that is enrolled in secondary school over the period 1960-85;[8]

- $\gamma + \delta$: set to 0.05 for all countries.

The cross-section regression results show that the model appears to fit the data fairly well; the regression accounts for almost 80 percent of the cross-country variation in output per worker. In addition, the estimates of α and β (0.31 and 0.28, respectively, for the sample of nonoil-exporting countries) are reasonable and indeed imply decreasing returns to total capital. However, the estimation method used by Mankiw, Romer, and Weil (OLS) exposes them to both **specification** and **endogeneity biases**, as discussed below.

In the Mankiw-Romer-Weil model, as in the standard Solow-Swan model, countries with different levels of s_K, s_H, and n have different levels of output per worker on their balanced-growth paths; thus, there is a component of cross-country income differences that persists over time. But differences that arise because countries are initially at different points on their balanced-growth paths gradually disappear as convergence to those paths occurs. The model therefore also predicts convergence once the determinants of income on the balanced-growth path are properly controlled for, that is, **conditional convergence**, as defined earlier.

Specifically, the model implies that, in the vicinity of the balanced growth path, y converges to $\tilde{y}$ at the rate

$$|\Lambda| = (1 - \alpha - \beta)(n + \gamma + \delta),$$

which differs from the speed of adjustment derived for the Solow-Swan model (see Chapter 11) by the term in β. By definition, therefore, changes in real income over time can be approximated by

$$\frac{d\ln y}{dt} \simeq -|\Lambda|(\ln y - \ln \tilde{y}).$$

This equation implies that $\ln y$ approaches $\ln \tilde{y}$ exponentially:

$$\ln y - \ln \tilde{y} \simeq e^{-|\Lambda|t}(\ln y_0 - \ln \tilde{y}), \tag{12}$$

where y_0 is some initial value. For instance, if α and β are each 0.3 and $n+\gamma+\delta$ is 6 percent, $|\Lambda|$ is 2.4 percent; this implies that a country moves half way to its balanced growth path in $\ln(0.5)/\Lambda \simeq 29$ years.

---

[8] This variable may be subject to large measurement errors. In general, proxies for human capital, such as the average number of years of schooling of the labor force, the proportion of the labor force with higher education, and so on, not only are largely arbitrary measures but also fail to reflect fully the large differences across countries in the quality of education. See Barro and Lee (2001) for a comprehensive database on human capital.

Adding $\ln \tilde{y} - \ln y_0$ to both sides of Equation (12) yields an expression for the growth of income:

$$\ln y - \ln y_0 \simeq -(1 - e^{-|\Lambda|t})(\ln y_0 - \ln \tilde{y}). \tag{13}$$

Equation (13) implies **conditional convergence**: countries with initial incomes that are low relative to their balanced growth paths have higher growth. Finally, using the solution for $\ln \tilde{y}$ derived in the previous chapter [Equation (30)] yields

$$\frac{\ln y - \ln y_0}{1 - e^{-|\Lambda|t}} \simeq \frac{\alpha}{\Omega}[\ln s_K - \ln(n + \gamma)] + \frac{\beta}{\Omega}[\ln s_H - \Delta \ln(n + \gamma)] - \ln y_0.$$

The parameter estimates obtained by Mankiw, Romer, and Weil are, for their sample of nonoil-exporting countries, $\alpha = 0.48$, $\beta = 0.23$, and $|\Lambda| = 0.014$. These estimates are broadly in line with the predictions of the model: countries converge toward their balanced-growth paths at about the rate that the model predicts, and the estimated capital shares are plausible. Overall, the results obtained by Mankiw, Romer, and Weil suggest that a model that maintains the assumption of diminishing returns to capital but that adopts a *broader definition of capital* than traditional physical capital, and therefore implies a total capital share close to $\alpha + \beta = 0.7$, appears to provide a good approximation to the cross-country data.

Results qualitatively similar to those obtained by Mankiw, Romer, and Weil were obtained by Gundlach (1995) and Bernanke and Gurkaynak (2001), with the latter study essentially replicating the earlier results with a longer sample period (1960-95, instead of 1960-85). De la Fuente (1997), however, reestimated the Mankiw-Romer-Weil model over two subperiods (1960-75 and 1975-85) and found that it does not explain well the growth slowdown that characterized the 1975-85 period—suggesting some important *omitted variables* in the model. Grossman and Helpman (1994) criticized the assumption of an identical rate of technological progress for all the countries in the sample considered by Mankiw, Romer, and Weil. Specifically, Grossman and Helpman (1994, p. 29) argued that

> If technological progress varies by country, and [these variations are] treated as part of the unobserved error term, then ordinary least squares estimates of the . . . equation will be biased when investment-GDP ratios are correlated with country-specific productivity growth. In particular, if investment rates are high when productivity grows fast, the coefficient on the investment [or saving] variable will pick up . . . part of the variation due to their different experiences with technological progress . . . [In addition, one] would certainly expect investment to be highest where capital productivity is growing the fastest.

Thus, the estimate of the effect of the saving-investment variable derived by Mankiw, Romer, and Weil may be overstated and the slope-coefficient test may consequently be biased. How large this bias is has not been precisely evaluated.

But in any case, it relates only to the ability of the model to explain cross-section differences in income levels, not in growth rates.[9]

At a more conceptual level, another criticism of the Mankiw-Romer-Weil approach is offered by Barro, Mankiw, and Sala-i-Martin (1995), who introduced not only human capital but also **partial capital mobility** in a Solow-Swan framework by assuming that only a fraction of the capital stock can be used as *collateral* against borrowing on world capital markets. Specifically, in the model physical capital is assumed to be mobile across countries, but human capital is not. Moreover, physical capital can be used (at least in part) as collateral for international borrowing, but human capital cannot.

In this setting, adjustment to the steady-state level of physical capital is fast due to the possibility of international borrowing, but adjustment to the steady-state level of human capital is relatively slow. The relative size of the accumulated stocks of physical and human capital determines the fraction of the capital stock that can be used as collateral. These assumptions have no effect on the predicted steady state itself, but affect the rate of convergence. Specifically, the convergence rate derived by Barro, Mankiw, and Sala-i-Martin (1995), based on a production function similar to the one used by Mankiw, Romer, and Weil, is

$$|\Lambda| = (1 - \frac{\beta}{1 - \alpha})(n + \gamma + \delta).$$

For instance, assuming again that α and β are each 0.3 and that $n + \gamma + \delta$ is 6 percent, $|\Lambda|$ is now 3.4 percent (instead of 2.4 percent); a country would move halfway to its balanced growth path now in only $\ln(0.5)/\Lambda \simeq 20$ years.

The main implication of the analysis is that the speed of convergence predicted for a *closed* economy (with no capital mobility) is very similar to the speed predicted for an *open* economy when the share of mobile capital that can be used as collateral—physical capital only—does not exceed one-half. For all practical purposes, therefore, the assumption of a closed economy is not completely misleading, as long as *capital mobility is imperfect*—a view that is supported by much of the evidence for developing countries (see Chapter 7). Thus, the neoclassical model with partial capital mobility appears to be consistent with the empirical evidence on convergence in levels of per capita income.

13.4   The Empirics of Growth

Much of the empirical literature on growth, following an early study by Barro (1991), has focused on estimating cross-country regressions in search of a set of stable relations among the various variables suggested by the old and new theories. This literature has been plagued, however, by severe methodological

---

[9]Islam's (1995) approach to conditional convergence allowed some production function parameters to differ across countries. He retained, however, the assumption that the rate of technological progress is the same for all countries.

problems.[10] From an econometric standpoint, many studies suffer from an inappropriate treatment of **measurement** and **specification errors**, and a lack of appreciation of the potential for **simultaneity bias**.

A first difficulty is that the data necessary to adequately test the predictions of the new models of growth do not exist or are difficult to construct. In many cases, the quality of the data is also inadequate. As a result, some of the explanatory variables introduced in cross-sectional growth regressions suffer from **measurement errors**. Bosworth and Collins (2003) argued that basic measurement problems (such as the reliance on investment shares to proxy changes in the capital stock, and the valuation of investment at domestic or international prices) may be a source of divergence across empirical studies. In addition, Arcand and Dagenais (1999) found that results derived from Barro-type regressions, as well as those of Mankiw, Romer, and Weil (1992) reviewed earlier, are fragile when such errors are properly accounted for in the econometric procedure. A few authors—such as Persson and Tabellini (1994)—have attempted to gauge the sensitivity to measurement errors of the parameter estimates obtained in their cross-section studies by using more appropriate econometric techniques, but the practice is far from being systematic.

Even with adequately measured variables, the basic approach that characterizes many cross-country empirical studies of growth (consisting of regressing the *time-averaged* growth rate for a group of countries on a set of ad hoc explanatory variables) faces a number of other difficulties.

- Heterogeneity between developing countries regarding growth patterns may be such that it is simply inappropriate to perform cross-country regressions. The practice of using **regional or continent dummies** in pooled cross-section, time-series analyses is based on the presumption that geographical factors may yield a homogeneous sample.[11] In practice, however, appropriate **statistical tests for pooling** are seldom applied. Yet various techniques exist for doing so (see Maddala and Wu, 2000).

- There are considerable variations in *data definitions* across countries; classifications of government expenditures, for instance, vary depending on the institutional coverage (for example, central government or general government), and on arbitrary conceptual definitions. Such differences are seldom taken into account.

---

[10]Levine and Renelt (1992) provided a comprehensive methodological and conceptual review of early cross-country growth equations. They made general recommendations aimed at improving the econometric techniques used to estimate these equations and improve the data used. They also provided a more detailed discussion of the general statistical problems (sampling, aggregation, causality, data selection, measurement errors, etc.) that cross-country econometric analysis faces. Temple (1999) provided an updated presentation (and criticism) of the new econometric procedures used in the current literature. See also Brock and Durlauf (2001).

[11]Alternatives followed by some authors are to focus only on one specific region (for instance, Rodrik, 1998a or Hoeffler, 2000) or to exclude a subset of countries—such as major oil-exporting countries.

- The behavior of the actual growth rate of output reflects both a *trend* (or long-term) component and a *cyclical* component—that is, **transitional movements** around the steady state (see Chapter 9). Attempts to measure the trend component often take the form of *averaging* both output growth rates and explanatory variables over a relatively long period (five years, ten years, and sometimes up to thirty years), to create a cross-section of observations. However, the *length of the period* used to average the data is in practice *largely arbitrary*, because the frequency of cycles is not generally known (making it difficult to separate the trend component from the cyclical component), and because cycles have different frequencies across countries and across variables. Using a *uniform* averaging period is thus likely to distort the long-run relationships between variables.

- In addition, as emphasized by Pesaran and Smith (1995), whereas the dependent variable is a time average of growth rates, explanatory variables are often a combination of time averages of *flows* (such as fixed investment) and beginning-of-period *stock* variables (such as an index of schooling). Such variables, however, have different time-series properties; mixing **stationary** and **nonstationary** variables in estimation can lead to spurious results—a point well emphasized in modern time-series econometrics (see Greene, 2000).

- Averaging implies that cross-country regressions do not represent *typical behavioral equations*. Parameter estimates represent cross-country averages which may not be representative of any individual country.

Other criticisms focus on the econometric techniques used by some researchers in estimating cross-country regressions. Particularly in the early literature, *linear* models and OLS were used most of the time. Caselli, Esquivel, and Lefort (1996) and Pesaran and Smith (1995), for instance, argued that such techniques give unreliable results because they are subject to the following problems:

- An **omitted variable** (or **specification**) **bias**, resulting from the incorrect treatment of country-specific effects—associated notably with differences in technology and tastes. OLS estimates in a cross-section regression are consistent only to the extent that the individual effects are *uncorrelated* with other explanatory variables. This condition is unlikely to hold in practice.[12]

- An **endogeneity** (or **simultaneity) bias**, resulting from the failure to account for the endogenous nature of some of the explanatory variables.[13]

---

[12]Pesaran and Smith (1995) also argued that the assumption that the error term is uncorrelated with the explanatory variables is likely to be violated due to the inherently dynamic nature of growth regressions.

[13]Hoeffler (2000) estimated the augmented Solow-Swan model for sub-Saharan Africa using an instrumental variable technique. Temple (1998) also used instrumental variables in estimating a variant of the Mankiw-Romer-Weil model with equipment investment.

The specification bias may also result from the fact that the growth regression takes the relationship between the explanatory variables and growth to be *linear*, whereas in fact it is *nonlinear*—as discussed for instance in Chapter 12 in the case of taxation, or as discussed later in the context of the link between inflation and growth. This makes it difficult to detect a significant correlation with a linear estimation procedure. Finally, as noted by Evans (1997), unless the control variables that are typically incorporated in growth regressions (the vector Z_t defined above) account for all cross-country heterogeneity, estimates of convergence rates will be inconsistent. The reason is that any remaining heterogeneity affects both the initial level of output per capita and the error term in the same direction, biasing estimated convergence rates toward zero.

Some studies have attempted to correct for one or some of these problems; others have tried to do so simultaneously. The estimation method used by Knight, Loayza, and Villanueva (1993), for instance, provided a proper treatment of country-specific effects but failed to address the endogeneity issue. Aizenman and Marion (1993) used instrumental variables estimation to account for simultaneity bias but did not test for specification bias. By contrast, several studies have used **dynamic panel data techniques** to address both the omitted variable and endogeneity issues (see Greene, 2000, chap. 14). Panel data sets contain observations at several points in time (for instance, annual time series on income per capita, investment, and so on), and can be either balanced (if they cover the same period for all countries) or unbalanced (covering different periods for different countries). A common approach in this context is the use the **Arellano-Bond estimator**, which can be briefly described as follows. Consider the following regression equation,

$$\ln(y_{it}/y_{it-1}) = (\alpha - 1) \ln y_{it-1} + \beta' Z_{it} + \eta_i + \varepsilon_{it},$$

where y is income per capita, α a scalar coefficient, β a vector of parameters, Z the set of explanatory variables (other than the lagged saving rate), η_i an unobserved country-specific effect, ε_{it} the error term, and the subscripts i and t represent country and time periods, respectively. This equation can be rewritten as

$$\ln y_{it} = \alpha \ln y_{it-1} + \beta' Z_{it} + \eta_i + \varepsilon_{it},$$

and we can take first differences to eliminate the country-specific effect:

$$\ln(y_{it}/y_{it-1}) = \alpha \ln(y_{it-1}/y_{it-2}) + \beta' (Z_{it} - Z_{it-1}) + \varepsilon_{it} - \varepsilon_{it-1}.$$

The use of instruments is required to deal with both the endogeneity of the explanatory variables and the fact that, by construction, the new error term, $\varepsilon_{it} - \varepsilon_{it-1}$, is correlated with the lagged dependent variable, $\ln y_{it-1} - \ln y_{it-2}$. Under the assumptions that (a) the error term is not serially correlated, and (b) the explanatory variables are weakly exogenous (that is, the explanatory variables are uncorrelated with future realizations of the error term), the Arellano-Bond estimator uses the following moment conditions:

$$\mathbf{E}[\ln y_{it-h}(\varepsilon_{it} - \varepsilon_{it-1})] = 0, \quad \text{for } h \geq 2, \text{ and } t = 3, ..., T,$$

$$\mathbf{E}[Z_{it-h}(\varepsilon_{it} - \varepsilon_{it-1})] = 0, \quad \text{for } h \geq 2, \text{ and } t = 3, ..., T,$$

which must be satisfied by the instrumental variables. Studies using dynamic panel data techniques include Islam (1995), Caselli, Esquivel, and Lefort (1996), Easterly, Loayza, and Montiel (1997), Temple (1998), Hoeffler (2001, 2002), and Easterly and Levine (2001). Hoeffler (2002) for instance estimated both the Solow-Swan and the Mankiw-Romer-Weil models for sub-Saharan Africa, whereas Temple (1998) estimated a variant of the second model with equipment investment.

Another issue with the early literature is that it was characterized by considerable diversity in the country coverage, the periods examined, and the set of explanatory variables; this made it difficult to generalize or to consider any particular study as reliable. Moreover, the *lack of clear theoretical underpinnings* for many empirical studies made it difficult to attach any analytical interpretation to some of these results. In a comprehensive study of the early literature on cross-country empirical studies of economic growth, Levine and Renelt (1992) found that almost all of the cross-country regression results that they reviewed were fragile: minor alterations in the list of explanatory variables often destroyed the properties of the growth equation. Subsequently, however, the Levine-Renelt methodology for testing for robustness was criticized by some researchers as being too stringent. Doppelhofer, Miller, and Sala-i-Martin (2000) proposed an alternative methodology based on a **Bayesian approach**. They found that four variables appear to be strongly correlated with growth: the initial level of per capita income, the share of mining in GDP, a measure of trade openness, and the fraction of Confucians in the population (which can be interpreted as a dummy variable for Hong Kong and some East Asian countries). A second group of seven variables (initial life expectancy, initial primary schooling enrollment rate, dummies for sub-Saharan Africa and Latin America, the fraction of Protestants in the population, the fraction of primary exports in total exports, and a measure of real exchange rate distortions) appears to have weaker explanatory power, but nevertheless coefficients are still quite precisely estimated.

Several alternative approaches to the standard cross-country regression framework discussed above have been developed in recent years. Quah (1996*a,b*, 1997) argued that focusing on cross-section averages over long periods of time may be misleading, and proposed to analyze the evolution of the entire distribution. Other researchers, such as Bernard and Durlauf (1996) and Arestis and Demetriades (1997), suggested that **time-series regression** for *individual* countries may be more appropriate to assess the effects of various variables on growth. As indicated earlier, cross-country regressions typically involve averaging out variables over relatively long periods of time—a procedure that makes cross-country variations in results difficult to interpret. In addition, the question of *causality* is difficult to address in a cross-section framework; causal inferences as conventionally drawn in the empirical literature require statistical assumptions that are often implausible (see Brock and Durlauf, 2001, and Durlauf and Quah, 1999). The time-series approach allows the investigator not only to analyze the possibility of **bidirectional causality** but also to account for differences in the *institutional framework* and the *policy regimes*, which may affect (as noted in the previous chapter) in a crucial manner the effect of various variables on growth.[14]

Arestis and Demetriades (1997), in particular, use a **cointegration approach** (as briefly discussed in the appendix to Chapter 9) to analyze the determinants of growth in an individual-country context. This alternative approach, of course, also has its limitations. One is the limited number of observations available in a time-series context for many developing countries. Another is the fact that cointegration analysis does not allow the investigator to capture changes in the *steady state itself*, which may result from structural change. Recent developments in *panel data econometrics* and their application to growth issues (as discussed by Temple, 1999) provide a promising framework for integrating the cross-country and time-series approaches. One example of **panel cointegration analysis** is by Christopoulos and Tsionas (2004), which is discussed later.

13.5   The Econometric Evidence: Overview

This section provides a selective overview of the recent literature on cross-country growth regressions, broadly along the lines of the discussion on the determinants of growth provided in Chapters 11 and 12. The focus on recent studies is motivated by the results of the extensive review by Levine and Renelt (1992), which, as indicated earlier, argued that many of the cross-country regression results that they reviewed lack robustness. Although some of the recent studies continue to suffer from some of the problems identified by Levine and Renelt, many of them have used improved econometric methods (such as dynamic panel data techniques) and can therefore be viewed, at least to some extent, as more reliable. The evidence on the role played by saving and capital accumulation (physical and human), fiscal variables, inflation and macroeconomic stability, financial factors, the degree of trade and financial openness, and political variables and income inequality, are examined in turn.

13.5.1   Saving and Physical and Human Capital

Levine and Renelt (1992), in their review of the early evidence on the determinants of growth, suggested that both *saving* and *physical investment* rates were positively and significantly correlated with average growth rates across a wide variety of samples and specifications. These results have been corroborated in a variety of more recent studies, including Easterly, Loayza, and Montiel (1997) and Hoeffler (2002). However, few researchers have attempted to account for the *quality* of investment in their growth regressions; as the Asia crisis discussed

---

[14]Durlauf and Quah (1999) derive a general framework that nests a variety of alternative growth models.

in Chapter 8 amply demonstrated, high rates of investment are not necessarily conducive to sustained growth.

As indicated in the previous chapters, investment in education and human capital leads to the acquisition of skills that increase efficiency, raise the intensity with which existing technologies are used, and promote technological advances. Econometric evidence provided by Barro (1991, 1997, 2001), Benhabib and Spiegel (1994), and various other researchers suggests that the *initial level of education* (a proxy for human capital), especially at the primary level, is an important determinant of subsequent growth. Public spending on education as a share of GDP has also been found to have a positive impact on growth. This is in contrast to the early review by Levine and Renelt (1992), which suggested that the significance of human capital indicators in growth regressions was not always robust to the inclusion of other variables.

Some of the recent evidence, however, is not entirely conclusive for at least two reasons:

- As noted by Pack and Page (1994), most cross-section regressions do not take into account changes in the *sectoral composition* of output, although such shifts in the production structure may explain part of aggregate growth. These authors argued that some of the growth effects attributed to investment and education may reflect the fact that they facilitate a change in the *sectoral structure* of production.

- Bils and Klenow (1998) emphasized that the positive correlation between initial schooling enrollment and subsequent movements in growth rates found in several empirical studies may be consistent with causality running from *expected* growth to schooling (through its effect on expected earnings, for instance), rather than the other way around. They noted, in particular, that for the group of 93 countries in their sample, schooling attainment implied by enrollment rates increased by one-third between 1960 and 1975; yet the average growth rate of per capita income in the same group fell from 2.9 percent per year during 1960-75 to 11.1 percent during 1975-90.[15]

The issue of potential causality was addressed in studies by Easterly and Levine (2001), Barro (2001), and De la Fuente and Doménech (2000). Easterly and Levine found that greater human capital, as measured by average years of schooling of the working-age population, has a significant effect on growth. Barro (2001) found a similar result, using the adult male secondary and higher schooling ratio (as described in Barro and Lee, 2001), and so did De la Fuente and Doménech (2000), using a different measure of educational attainment for industrial countries. In addition, Barro found, as did Hanushek and Kimko (2000) and Bosworth and Collins (2003), that the *quality* of education— measured by using data on students' scores on internationally comparable examinations in science, mathematics, and reading—mattered. In fact, he found that

---

[15] The drop in the growth rate of per capita income between the two periods was actually larger in countries where growth in schooling exceeded the average rate.

the impact of school quality was more important than the quantity of schooling, with scores on science tests having a particularly strong effect on growth.

13.5.2   Fiscal Variables

A large part of the recent empirical growth literature has examined the impact on growth of the levels of government current and investment expenditure, and the composition of such expenditure. Overall, the evidence on the nature of this relationship is mixed. Devarajan, Swaroop, and Zou (1996), for instance, found no significant relationship between growth and the *level* of expenditures (as measured by their share in GDP). The empirical literature on the effects of the *composition* of expenditures has also produced mixed results. Barro (1997) found that government consumption expenditures—calculated by deducting defense and education expenditures from general consumption spending—measured in proportion of GDP was negatively correlated with growth. Devarajan, Swaroop, and Zou (1996), in contrast, found a positive relationship between public consumption expenditures (as measured by current outlays as a share of total expenditures) and economic growth. Caselli, Esquivel, and Lefort (1996) also found a positive effect on growth of government expenditure (net of military and educational spending) as a share of output. Easterly, Loayza, and Montiel (1997) found no significant effect of the share of government consumption in GDP on growth in Latin America.

Recent analytical studies have emphasized the differential role of public and private investment in the growth process. As discussed in Chapters 2 and 12, public investment in infrastructure can increase the marginal product of private production inputs and raise private investment through a *complementary* effect—thereby raising the economy's growth rate. This is a particularly important link in developing countries. In contrast, if public production activities compete with private initiative, there may be **substitution** or **crowding-out effects** that may lead to adverse effects on growth. However, the evidence on the relationship between public investment and growth remains inconclusive. Knight, Loayza, and Villanueva (1993) and Nelson and Singh (1994) found that the level of public investment in infrastructure had a significant effect on growth, particularly during the 1980s. But Khan and Kumar (1997), using a sample of 95 developing countries over the period 1970-90, found that the effects of private and public investment on growth differed significantly, with private investment being consistently more productive than public investment. Easterly and Rebelo (1993), using a cross-section study of 119 countries, estimated that public investment in *transportation* and *communications* was positively related to growth. In contrast, public investment in *state-owned enterprises* had no effect on growth, whereas public investment in *agriculture* had a negative effect. Milbourne, Otto, and Voss (2003) estimated the Mankiw-Romer-Weil model found evidence of a positive correlation between public investment and economic growth in a sample of 74 industrial and developing countries only when using OLS, not when using instrumental variables methods.

Several empirical studies have found evidence of an inverse relationship between *taxes* and economic growth, but overall the results are not very robust. Nelson and Singh (1994) found no significant effect of **fiscal deficits** on growth in developing countries during the 1970s and 1980s. Rodrik (1998*a*), in contrast, provided evidence suggesting that long-term growth in sub-Saharan Africa during 1965-90 was significantly affected by fiscal policy (in addition to human resources, demography, and a catch-up variable). Low central government surpluses tended to slow the rate of growth in income per capita in the region.

The lack of robustness of the evidence on fiscal policy and growth may be related in part to the *nonlinear* nature of the relationship between these variables. As discussed in the previous chapter, in Barro's (1990) model, growth increases with taxation and expenditures at low levels and then decreases as the distortionary effects of taxation exceed the beneficial effects of public goods. Government expenditures and growth are positively correlated when government expenditures are below the optimum amount, negatively related when they are above, and are uncorrelated when governments are providing the optimal amount of services. Cross-country empirical studies have, in general, failed to account for this nonlinearity and may therefore be unable to detect it in the data. Despite the inconclusive nature of the empirical literature, however, the consensus view seems to be that changes in the composition of government spending toward higher outlays on health, education, and basic infrastructure tend to have a positive impact on growth.

13.5.3   Inflation and Macroeconomic Stability

The effect of inflation and macroeconomic stability on long-run growth has been a key area of investigation, at both the analytical and the empirical level. In one of the early contributions to this literature, Fischer (1993) found empirical evidence for a large group of countries of a positive link between growth and macroeconomic stability—defined in terms of the level of inflation and its volatility, the *parallel market premium* (the ratio of the parallel exchange rate to the official rate, see Agénor, 1992), the ratio of the budget deficit to GDP, and changes in the terms of trade. The negative correlation between the overall budget deficit and growth appeared particularly robust. De Gregorio (1992, 1993) also found evidence of a negative relationship between the level of inflation (an indicator of tax system inefficiency rather than financial repression, as argued earlier), the variability of inflation, and growth in Latin America, using a cross section of 12 Latin American countries over the period 1950-85.

In another contribution, Sarel (1996) found that the effects of inflation on economic growth are *nonlinear*. When inflation is low, it has no significant effect on growth. But when inflation is high (above 8 percent per annum), it has a negative and statistically significant effect on growth. A doubling in the rate of inflation (from, say, 20 to 40 percent) reduces the economy's growth rate by 1.7 percentage points. This is much higher than the estimate derived in several other studies. Barro (1997) also found that inflation has a negative effect on output growth rates per capita (and the share of investment in output) in a cross-country regression over the period 1960-90. This effect, however, is not large; an increase in average inflation by 10 percentage points per year lowers the growth rate of real per capita GDP on impact by 0.2 to 0.3 percentage point per year.[16] In addition, the effect exists only when the high-inflation observations, that is, countries in which inflation exceeded 40 percent a year (a sample that included a large proportion of Latin American countries), are included in the sample. Along the same lines, Bruno and Easterly (1998) found no robust evidence of a long-run relationship between inflation and growth at annual inflation rates less than 40 percent. They argued that the significant effect reported in some early cross-country studies was an artifact that resulted from both the sample period used and the inclusion of some high-inflation outliers.

Various other studies have used a series of indicators, in addition to inflation variability, to assess the degree of uncertainty associated with macroeconomic policies. A simple (albeit crude) composite measure of macroeconomic instability is the unweighted sum of the mean inflation rate, the standard deviation of inflation, mean budget and external current account deficits as a percentage of GDP, and mean terms-of-trade changes. A more precise measure of *policy variability* was proposed by Aizenman and Marion (1993); they used the standard deviation of the real exchange rate, the standard deviation of inflation, and domestic credit growth, as well as composite indicators including all of the foregoing variables. The evidence that they provided generally supports the existence of a negative relationship between policy variability and growth, although the relationship was not robust for some indicators. Bleaney (1996), in a cross-section study covering the period 1980-90, found that macroeconomic instability (measured by the fiscal balance and the degree of volatility of the real exchange rate) had a significant negative effect on the rate of economic growth and possibly also a negative effect on investment. Finally, Brunetti (1998) found that policy volatility, as measured by the standard deviation, the coefficient of variation, or the standard errors of various fiscal and monetary variables, are significantly related to cross-country differences in the rate of economic growth. The results, however, were also found to be sensitive to variations in country samples and to variations in the specification of the growth regression.

13.5.4 Financial Factors

The recent evidence on the role of financial variables on growth, as reviewed by Levine (1997, 2003), appears to be highly supportive of a positive link between these variables. In an early contribution, King and Levine (1993), for instance, found a robust correlation between the degree of financial development and growth, investment, and the efficiency of capital. The financial indicators that they used included the size of the formal financial sector (as measured by the liquid liabilities to the financial system) relative to output, the importance of banks relative to the central bank, the ratio of credit allocated to firms relative to output, and the share of total credit allocated to firms.

---

[16] As noted in Chapter 10, however, even small reductions in the rate of growth of output may translate over a sufficiently long period of time (say, 20 or 30 years) into large effects on standards of living.

The problem with most of the early literature, however, is that (as noted earlier) it does not address the issue of *causality*.[17] A more recent study by Levine, Loayza, and Beck (2000), using instrumental variables and dynamic panel techniques, found a significant causal relationship between financial development and growth. Easterly and Levine (2001) also found a significant and positive effect of private sector credit (as a share of output) on growth. By contrast, Demetriades and Hussein (1996), using time-series data and co-integration techniques for 16 countries, suggested that the causality between financial depth—as measured by the ratios of bank deposits to GDP and bank claims on the private sector to GDP—and growth varies across countries. In only two cases (Honduras and Sri Lanka) did financial development appear to cause economic growth. In seven of the countries in their sample (Guatemala, Honduras, India, Korea, Mauritius, Thailand, and Venezuela) they detected a **feedback relationship** between finance and growth; and in four others (El Saldavor, Pakistan, South Africa, and Turkey) the causality relationship was instead from growth to finance—which may occur as a result, for instance, of an increased demand (induced by higher income) for financial services. Using pooled data on 109 developing and industrial countries from 1960 to 1994, Calderón and Liu (2003) also found evidence of **bidirectional causality** between financial development and economic growth.

Because time-series studies may yield unreliable results due to the short time spans of typical data sets, Christopoulos and Tsionas (2004) used panel unit root tests and **panel cointegration analysis** to examine the relationship between financial development and growth in developing countries. By using time-series tests of causality in a panel context, they were able to increase significantly sample size. In contrast to the previous studies, they found strong evidence in favor of long-run causality running from financial development to growth, and no evidence of bi-directional causality. Furthermore, they find a unique cointegrating vector between financial development and growth in most cases.

There is also some evidence showing that **financial repression** has an adverse effect on economic performance. Roubini and Sala-i-Martin (1995), for instance, found a negative effect of the *bank reserve ratio* on growth. However, this evidence is not entirely conclusive because reserve ratios can be a poor proxy for the degree of financial repression. As an alternative approach, Arestis and Demetriades (1997) used as proxy a weighted index of the principal components of five types of controls on the banking sector—the ceiling on deposit rates, the ceiling on lending rates, the proportion of total credit covered by the directed credit program, and the minimum reserve requirement rate on demand and time deposits. Their econometric results suggested a mildly positive effect of financial repression on economic growth in Korea.

---

[17]Another problem with some of the empirical literature is that the apparently significant effect of financial variables on growth may be capturing regional differences. See Driffill (2003) for a discussion.

13.5.5   External Trade and Financial Openness

As noted in the previous chapter, endogenous growth models emphasizing the role of international trade suggest that trade openness allows poorer countries to benefit from **technology spillovers**, such as through the stock of knowledge embedded in capital goods. In turn, increases in the stock of knowledge may raise total factor productivity and the economy's growth rate (Winters, 2004). Openness to international trade may also increase the number of specialized inputs, thereby increasing growth rates in the long run.[18] Studies that highlighted the importance of the degree of openness and, more generally, an outward orientation for growth are those of Dollar (1992), Edwards (1998), Khan and Kumar (1997), Knight, Loayza, and Villanueva (1993), and Sachs and Warner (1997a,b). Trade distortions, in all of these studies, have a negative effect on growth.[19]

Sachs and Warner (1997a) in particular focused on a sample of 117 countries classified into two groups: those who protected *property rights* and kept trade open during the 1970-89 period, and those who did not. The *index of openness* that the authors constructed was based on five criteria—nontariff barriers, average tariff levels, the parallel market exchange rate, whether state monopolies existed for major exports, and whether the economy was socialist or not. They found that, on average, the more open countries grew by 2 to 2.5 percentage points more than others. As noted in Chapter 10, however, the robustness of the Sachs-Warner index of trade openness was questioned by Harrison and Hanson (1999) and the econometric results were qualified by Hoeffler (2001). Rodriguez and Rodrik (1999) also criticized the Sachs-Warner approach, as well as the methodology and results in Dollar (1992) and Edwards (1998).

Another study by Greenaway, Morgan, and Wright (2002) used a cross-country data set of up to 73 countries. The regression model that they specified includes not only a measure of openness but also various other control variables—initial income per capita, the ratio of domestic investment to output, and an index of the terms of trade. They also used several alternative indicators of openness, among which was the Sachs-Warner index described earlier, as well as an index based on average nominal tariffs, a measure of quantitative restrictions on imports, and average parallel market premia. In contrast to many earlier studies, Greenaway, Morgan, and Wright used a *dynamic* regression framework to investigate potential lagged effects. They found that trade openness appeared to have an identifiable impact on growth; this effect was

---

[18]Note that if the degree of openness to international trade and the resulting transfer of knowledge and inputs affects the rate of productivity growth, then the standard growth accounting framework described earlier (which is based on a pure production function approach) may be inadequate, because the level of technology will change with the allocation of output between domestic sales and exports—partly offsetting the effect of diminishing returns to capital.

[19]The parallel market premium is used in a number of studies as an indicator of structural distortions, particularly in the trade and financial areas; see, for instance, Easterly (1992). Results were often highly significant but, as noted by Levine and Renelt (1992), the precise channels through which the premium may affect growth is usually not specified.

robust relative to the indicator used. At the same time, however, the growth effect had a **J-curve** feature: the impact of trade openness on output growth rates was found to be small or negative initially; only over time did it become positive. This result has implications for the *sustainability* of trade reforms, as discussed in the next chapter.

There is also evidence of a direct link between imports of capital goods and growth. Lee (1993, 1995), for instance, found a close relationship between these two variables in a large group of developing countries, and Temple (1998) found that equipment investment (much of it coming from abroad, in developing countries) is strongly correlated with growth.[20] Along the same lines, Roldós (1997) found that in Chile over the period 1971-95, TFP growth appeared to be correlated with the ratio of imported capital to total physical capital—perhaps reflecting the process of technology diffusion and adoption alluded to earlier. By contrast, Mazumdar (2001) found that only investment in *imported* equipment tends to increase the growth rate, whereas equipment investment in domestically produced goods tends to reduce it. Finally, there is some firm-level empirical evidence of the importance of transfers of knowledge, rather than machinery, for several Asian countries (including Korea and Taiwan), as pointed out by Pack and Page (1994). Also using firm-level data, Krishna and Mitra (1998) found significant evidence of productivity growth in the Indian manufacturing industry, following the trade reform of 1991.

As noted in the previous chapter, the growth in productivity stemming from increasing international trade may be facilitated by improved domestic absorptive capacity made possible by higher levels of *human capital*; education, in particular, increases the ability of individuals to deal with rapid changes in knowledge. What this suggests is that the effect of the degree of openness on growth may be *nonlinear*: low in countries with low levels of education, and high in countries with a highly skilled workforce. A review of the East Asia growth experience by the World Bank (1993) suggested indeed that Asian countries during the "miracle" years benefited from the interaction of rapid transfers of technology and a highly skilled labor force to adapt the technology to local needs. More formal econometric results were provided by Dinopoulos and Thompson (2000), who found that the degree of trade openness increases the effectiveness with which human capital generates new knowledge.

Nevertheless, it should be emphasized that the empirical evidence has not yet clearly established the direction of causality between trade openness and growth. There are several mechanisms that could imply a positive effect of growth on openness, or channels through which other factors may affect *both* openness and growth in the same direction. For instance, as income grows, the demand for luxury imported goods may rise fast enough to lead to an increase in the degree of openness, as conventionally measured. In such conditions, the case for advocating outward orientation as a growth-enhancing strategy would

---

[20] Temple also argued on the basis of his results that the Mankiw-Romer-Weil model is not adequate for describing the growth process in developing countries. He suggested that a framework allowing for externalities to equipment investment—as in Hendricks (2000), for instance—might be necessary.

be significantly weakened. Two studies, however, by Frankel and Romer (1999) and Irwin and Tervio (2002), have used instrumental variables techniques to control for the endogeneity of trade openness; their conclusion is that trade openness has indeed a quantitatively large and robust positive effect on the level and growth rate of income per capita. In their overview of the recent empirical literature, Lewer and Van den Berg (2003) estimated that a one percentage point increase in the growth rate of exports per annum is associated with a one-fifth percentage point increase in the rate of economic growth per year. As a result of compounding, trade can therefore have a large impact on standards of living.

Finally, it is worth emphasizing that the exact method of measuring trade openness remains a matter of controversy. Yanikkaya (2003), for instance, compared the performance of two sets of indicators: those based on trade volumes, and those based on trade restrictions. While regression results based on the first set suggest indeed a positive effect of trade openness on growth, those based on the second set go the opposite way. However, given the notorious difficulty of measuring trade restrictions (particularly nontariff barriers), it appears unwise to infer from these results that countries can actually benefit from trade restrictions. The experience of many developing countries with import-substituting policies would suggest quite the contrary (see Chapter 14).

Regarding financial openness, studies examining the impact of international financial integration on domestic investment and growth can be classified in two groups:

- The first group attempts to measure directly the impact of capital account liberalization by exploiting qualitative information on restrictions on capital movements;

- the second group uses the level of capital flows as a proxy measure for the degree of financial openness.

Two studies focusing directly on the impact of capital account liberalization on growth are those of Arteta, Eichengreen, and Wyplosz (2001) and Edison, Levine, Ricci, and Slok (2002). In the first study the degree of capital account liberalization is measured by an index of capital account restrictions. The authors found some evidence of a positive link between the index of capital account openness and growth, but only when countries are already sufficiently open commercially and face limited macroeconomic imbalances. This is an important result, because it brings to the fore the issue of *sequencing* of reforms (see Chapter 17). The second study, using a variety of measures of financial openness and advanced econometric techniques, found that international financial integration has no discernible effect on growth in a group of 57 countries. However, to the extent that capital account liberalization reduces inflation (as found by Gruben and McLeod, 2002), it may have an indirect, positive effect on growth.

The second group of studies is based on the view that actual levels of capital movements provide a good proxy for the effective degree of financial openness.

It includes those of Bosworth and Collins (2000), Borensztein, De Gregorio, and Lee (1998), and Choe (2003). Bosworth and Collins (1999) used panel regression techniques to evaluate the impact of capital inflows on investment on a group of 58 developing countries for the period 1978-95. They found that foreign direct investment flows have a positive (and almost one for one) impact on investment, whereas portfolio flows have no discernible effect. Borensztein, De Gregorio, and Lee (1998), using foreign direct investment flows from industrial countries to 69 developing countries during the period 1970-89, found that the link between foreign direct investment and growth was positive and significant. Moreover, they also found that there is complementarity between foreign direct investment and human capital (proxied by a measure of educational attainment) in affecting growth, as hypothesized in the growth model highlighted in the previous chapter, and that foreign direct investment has a positive (although not very robust) impact on aggregate domestic investment. In a study covering 80 countries over the period 1971-95, Choe (2003) also found evidence of a positive effect of foreign direct investment on growth, although the causality seems to be going in both directions.

Thus, to the extent that the size of capital flows can be seen as an adequate proxy for the degree of financial openness, it would appear that financial integration has a positive effect on domestic investment and growth, with possibly significant feedback effects as well.[21] The foregoing discussion relied on the assumption that greater financial openness translates into larger capital inflows. There is indeed evidence supporting this contention, at least on average and over a sufficient period of time. As a result, using the size of capital inflows as a proxy for the degree of financial integration is a sensible approach when the focus is on longer-term movements in investment and growth, given also the practical difficulties involved in constructing a quantitative index of financial openness. However, the relation between the degree of capital account openness and capital inflows is not always very close, particularly in the short term; a country can experience periods of low inflows (as a result, say, of a change in market sentiment), regardless of how open its capital account is.

In addition, none of the econometric studies referred to above tests for the existence of an adverse effect of the *volatility* of capital flows (as opposed to their level) on investment and growth. As emphasized in the literature on uncertainty and irreversibility in investment decisions (see Chapter 2), uncertainty about the availability of external finance in the future may deter investment, particularly in projects that have a long gestation periods, thereby negatively affecting per capita growth rates. In addition, the volatility of capital flows is itself endogenous, because it may arise not only from external factors but also from domestic causes. In such conditions, modeling the sources of volatility is essential. For all these reasons, one should therefore be cautious in judging the robustness of the available empirical evidence.

---

[21]It should be noted, however, that some studies are not consistent with this view. For instance, in a study based on data for 72 countries over the period 1985-96, Soto (2003) found that bank flows are the sole source of foreign financing that displays a positive and robust correlation with growth.

Finally, it should also be noted that there is some *microeconomic* evidence suggesting that private capital flows may enhance productivity (and therefore the rate of output growth), particularly in countries with a relatively skilled labor force and a well-developed physical infrastructure. Haddad and Harrison (1993), for instance, in a study of the impact of foreign investment on firms in Morocco's manufacturing sector during the period 1985-89, found that although domestic firms exhibit lower levels of total factor productivity, their rate of productivity growth is higher than that for foreign firms. Moreover, domestic firms exhibit higher levels of productivity in sectors with a larger foreign presence. At the same time, however, there is some evidence suggesting that domestic firms may not be able to capitalize on the transfer of knowledge associated with foreign direct investment because the entry of foreign firms may lead to losses in market share and reduced productivity, as a result of a contraction in output (Aitken and Harrison, 1999). More generally, microeconomic evidence is important in judging the impact of capital flows on the quality of domestic investment and growth. Indeed, one lesson from the Asia crisis is that high, aggregate ratios of capital formation to GDP can mask a sharp decline in the productivity of these investments.

13.5.6   Political Variables and Income Inequality

As noted in the previous chapter, it is now well recognized that political and civil liberties are not only desirable in themselves; by providing a foundation for imposing the rule of law, and thereby ensuring the security of property and the enforcement of contracts, they may also play an important economic role. Indeed, recent evidence suggests that these liberties are positively and significantly correlated with improvements in income per capita, life expectancy at birth, and the infant survival rate (Dasgupta, 1995).

Specifically, the *growth effects* of political factors have been the subject of a variety of cross-country empirical studies. Brunetti (1997) classified the political variables used in these studies in four groups:

- Measures of democracy, which include indicators such as the **Gastil index**—an annual rating of political rights and civil liberties in individual countries based on a seven-point scale.

- Measures of government (or institutional) instability, namely the number of, or the probability of, changes in government. These measures sometime include not only the number of regular executive transfers (through conventional legal procedures) but also the number of irregular transfers of power (or successful coups).

- Indicators of political violence, including measures of political strikes, protest demonstrations, riots, armed attacks, political assassinations, and executions.

- Subjective political indicators, as measured by surveys of the perceptions of local or international experts of the political situation in various countries. The empirical growth literature has often relied on indicators provided by three well-established country-risk evaluation firms: Business International, the International Country Risk Guide (ICRG), and Business Environmental Risk Intelligence (BERI).

The results summarized by Brunetti (1997) suggested that democracy indicators, measures of government stability, and indicators of political violence were not robustly correlated with growth. The same conclusion was reached by Levine and Renelt (1992) in their sensitivity analysis of the early literature, including studies such as Barro's (1991), which found that social indicators of war, revolution, and civil liberties were negatively related to growth. More recent work, however, by Tavares and Wacziarg (2001), suggests that democracy has both positive and negative effects on growth. On the one hand, it leads to greater accumulation of human capital and somewhat greater income equality; on the other, it tends to lower the rate of physical capital accumulation and to increase the share of government consumption in output. The net, overall effect of democracy on growth is moderately negative. Survey-based measures of political risk appear, in contrast, to be more closely correlated with growth, as suggested, for instance, by Mauro (1997).

The available evidence also suggests no clear correlation between the degree of income inequality and the rate of economic growth. In most empirical studies, inequality and growth were found either to be unrelated or the relationship lost its significance when other variables were included (see Alesina and Perotti, 1994, and Fishlow, 1995). Even where an inverse relationship was found, the impact of inequality on growth was fairly small (Clarke, 1995). Studies have also found no systematic relationship and no clear causal link between income inequality and political instability. However, most of the existing studies do not test for the existence of a *nonlinear* relationship between inequality and growth. One should therefore refrain, at this stage, from arguing that the degree of inequality does not matter for long-run growth.

13.6   Catching Up or Falling Behind?

As discussed earlier, the Solow-Swan model implies convergence across countries in both growth rates and income levels if all structural parameters (notably the production technology, the rate of population growth, and the saving rate), as well as the rate of technological progress, are the same. Poor countries will initially exhibit lower capital-labor ratios than richer ones, implying a higher marginal product of capital. Given equal rates of technological progress, labor force growth, and domestic saving rates, poor nations' capital stock growth will exceed that in richer countries during a transitional period, but they should ultimately converge to the capital-labor and capital-output ratios (and income levels) of richer countries. Of course, convergence will not occur if countries differ in their production technology, population growth rates, saving rates, or their rate of technological progress. For instance, if trade barriers are such that poor countries have limited possibilities to acquire the more advanced technologies available in the richer countries, the rate of income growth per capita in the poor countries may well be permanently lower than in rich countries, implying sustained and growing differences in standards of living.

Many endogenous growth models (such as the *AK* model) indeed imply the possibility of sustained differences in both levels and rates of growth of income. Because of the externalities or the productivity gains obtained from the availability of specialized inputs made possible by research and development activities, diminishing returns to human and physical capital do not occur, and the main force behind convergence disappears. Thus, the fact that the Solow-Swan model (with uniform parameters) predicts convergence and endogenous growth models do not, explains in part why the convergence hypothesis has received so much attention in the empirical literature of the last few years: it has been viewed as one way to discriminate between the two models. However, as pointed out in particular by Romer (1989), the convergence hypothesis is strictly speaking a test of the absence of diminishing returns, not a test of endogenous growth; the two issues should not be confused. For instance, suppose that the production process in the Solow-Swan model is characterized by a *CES technology*, as defined in Chapter 9. It can then be shown that, for a sufficiently high elasticity of substitution, the model can generate an endogenous steady-state growth and at the same time guarantee convergence (see Jones and Manuelli, 1997). The reason is that the key condition for endogenous growth is the violation of the **Inada conditions** (given in Chapter 11), whereas the key for ensuring convergence is the existence of diminishing returns to capital. The CES production function displays diminishing returns to capital, and therefore predicts convergence, but it does not satisfy the Inada conditions—thereby making it possible for the model to generate endogenous growth.[22]

The informal evidence discussed in Chapter 10 suggested that poor countries do not grow faster than richer countries; *absolute* or *unconditional* β-convergence (in the sense defined above) did not appear to hold. There is also evidence of σ-convergence, as documented by Islam (2003), and as found for instance by Dobson and Ramlogan (2002) for Latin America. However, several of the cross-country studies described earlier have confirmed the existence of *conditional* convergence: the level of GDP per capita at the start of the period is generally found to have a negative sign, once other factors are controlled for. Put differently, relative income levels eventually stabilize; but the long-run equilibrium position *itself* varies across countries, reflecting underlying differences in economic fundamentals—the level of education (a proxy for human capital), the rate of investment, the degree of openness, and so on. Thus, divergence in income levels across countries may persist over time. Early empirical estimates based on the econometric approach described earlier suggested that the rate of convergence varies between 1 and 2 percent—although estimates tended to be

---

[22]See also the production functions proposed by Jones and Manuelli (1990).

quite sensitive to sample size and the list or control variables. Ghura and Had-jimichael (1996), for instance, in a study focusing on 29 sub-Saharan countries during the period 1981-92, found the speed of convergence to be about 2 percent when correcting for simultaneity bias.

Caselli, Esquivel, and Lefort (1996), however, using an estimator that relies on first differencing and instrumental variable and a general growth regression framework, found that the speed of convergence is very large compared with the early estimates—in the range of 6 to 10 percent per annum. Easterly, Loayza, and Montiel (1997) also found, for Latin America, a rate of 5.4 percent per year, which implies a half-life of 12.8 years. Similarly, using an estimating technique that controls for cross-country heterogeneity, Evans (1997) found a β-convergence rate of 5.9 percent per annum for a group of 48 industrial and developing countries over the period 1950-90, whereas Lee, Pesaran, and Smith (1997) found even higher estimates of convergence rates using a panel of data for 102 countries covering the period 1960-89. The key implication of these results is that observed differences in income per capita may reflect to a significant extent differences in *steady-state levels* of per capita income, rather than differences in countries' *relative positions* along similar transitional paths leading to the same steady state.

The evidence also suggests that since the end of World War II the *dispersion* of levels of income per capita across industrial countries has fallen significantly— an indication of σ-convergence (De la Fuente, 1997). At the same time, how-ever, the dispersion of income levels between industrial and developing countries has increased substantially. Poor countries, particularly those in sub-Saharan Africa, appear to be more and more concentrated in the tails of the distrib-ution of income. A similar tendency for divergence of cross-country incomes is obtained in a series of studies by Quah (1996 a,b, 1997). His analysis sug-gested that in the postwar era, rich countries have tended to become richer and poor countries poorer—leading to the emergence of **convergence clubs**. Although these results have been challenged by some—Kremer, Onatski, and Stock (2001) have argued that Quah's results are fairly sensitive to sample se-lection and testing procedures—other studies have corroborated them. For in-stance, Li (1999) and Mayer-Foulkes (2002), using methodologies different from Quah's, have found convergence among the goup of high-income countries and divergence among that group and various clusters of developing countries. Go-ing further, McCoskey (2002), using panel cointegration techniques, found little support for convergence within sub-Saharan Africa in general, although smaller convergence clubs appear to exist.

13.7   Summary

- **Growth accounting** aims to quantify the immediate sources of growth by measuring the rates of accumulation of various productive factors and weighting them according to their observed shares in national income.

- The methodology is subject to important limitations. The main difficulty with the concept of **total factor productivity** (or **Solow residual**) is that it encompasses the effects of a wide variety of factors, including technology, efficiency in resource allocation, managerial skills and administrative efficiency, and **economies of scale**. It may also reflect changes in the quality of factors of production; such changes can be very difficult to measure.

- Growth accounting techniques have been used to assess the sources of economic growth in East Asia between the 1950s and the early 1990s. Some economists have argued that the growth performance in the region was essentially the result of a high rate of physical capital accumulation; others have argued that it stemmed mostly from a high rate of growth of total factor productivity. The debate is difficult to settle because of a number of methodological and econometric issues.

- The assumption of *diminishing returns to capital* implies that in the Solow-Swan model countries with different production technologies, saving rates, and population growth rates but with the same rate of technological progress, γ, will all converge to a balanced growth path in which the *growth rate* of income per capita is equal to γ. If production technologies, saving rates, and population growth rates are the same across countries, they will all converge to the same *level* of income per capita as well.

- This prediction has been tested in both its absolute form and relative form (given differences among structural parameters and characteristics across countries) using cross-country regression techniques. Conditional β-**convergence** of per capita income is defined as the tendency for poor economies to grow faster than rich economies, once the determinants of their steady state are held constant.

- Another concept of convergence is that of σ-**convergence**, which is deemed to occur across a group of countries when the *dispersion* of real per capita income tends to fall over time. β-convergence is necessary, but not sufficient, for σ-convergence.

- Cross-country estimates of the model of Mankiw, Romer, and Weil (1992) suggest that maintaining the assumption of diminishing returns to capital but accounting for both physical and human capital yields empirical predictions that appear to be consistent with the observed cross-country differences in *levels* of income. However, robustness tests provided mixed support for the model.

- Much of the empirical literature on growth has focused on estimating cross-country regressions in search of a set of stable relations among the variables suggested by the old and new theories. This literature has been plagued, however, by severe methodological problems. The data necessary to test adequately the predictions of the new models of growth do not exist or are difficult to construct. The quality of the data may also be inadequate. From an econometric standpoint, many studies suffer from an inappropriate treatment of **measurement** and **specification errors** (for instance, **omitted variable bias** due to incorrect treatment of individual country-specific effects), **simultaneity bias**, and lack of appreciation of the potential for **bidirectional causality**. As a result, the bulk of the early evidence lacks robustness.

- More recent cross-country studies, based on **dynamic panel data techniques**, have been able to correct some of these problems. An alternative approach that is gaining popularity in the analysis of the determinants of growth is the **time-series approach**, which is more suited to assess, for instance, the issue of *causality* among variables. Detailed case studies may also be able to capture more accurately salient differences in policy regimes than many broad cross-country studies. **Panel cointegration analysis** is a promising approach to testing for causality among growth and other variables.

A selective review of the more recent cross-country evidence suggests the following regularities.

- *Saving* and *physical investment* are positively and significantly correlated with average growth rates across countries in a wide variety of samples and specifications. The evidence on the role of *human capital* is less conclusive.

- Most of the evidence on the effects of *taxes* and *government expenditure* (current and capital) on growth is inconclusive, although it would appear that public investment in infrastructure, which tends to raise the productivity of private inputs and to be *complementary* to private investment, has a positive effect on growth. *Nonlinearities* may explain this apparent lack of robustness. Evidence for sub-Saharan Africa suggests that *fiscal deficits* have had an adverse effect on growth.

- *Inflation* has an adverse, and possibly *nonlinear*, effect on growth. *Macroeconomic instability* (as measured by the variability of inflation or the standard deviation of the real exchange rate) also tends to be negatively correlated with growth.

- Indicators of *financial depth* (such as the ratio of liquid liabilities to the financial system to GDP, the percentage of credit allocated by commercial banks, the percentage of domestic credit received by the private sector, and the ratio of credit to the private sector in proportion of GDP) have a positive and statistically significant correlation with long-term economic growth, the investment ratio, and total factor productivity. However, time-series evidence suggests that the *causality* may run from growth to finance, or may operate in *both directions*.

- *Trade openness* tends to be positively associated with growth, but again, the direction of causality is not well established. Recent evidence also suggests a *nonlinear* (**J-curve**) pattern: the initial effect on output growth tends to be small or negative; it is only over time that the effect becomes positive.

- *Political variables* (including measures of democracy, measures of government instability, indicators of political violence, and subjective indicators) are not robustly correlated with growth.

- **Absolute** β-convergence does not appear to hold, but **conditional** β-convergence does. Put differently, relative levels of income per capita eventually stabilize; but the long-run equilibrium position *itself* varies across countries, reflecting underlying differences in economic fundamentals, such as the level of education (a proxy for human capital), the rate of investment, and the degree of openness.

- Thus, divergence in income levels across countries may persist over time. Some early empirical studies suggested that the *rate of convergence* was around 2 percent, but a much higher number was found in some of the more recent studies. These estimates, however, remain quite sensitive to sample size and the list or control variables.

- Convergence appears to occurs in clusters.

Appendix to Chapter 13
Growth Accounting with Increasing Returns

This appendix, which is based on Barro (2000a), shows that if the production technology is characterized by **increasing returns to scale**, then standard growth accounting techniques based on the assumption of constant returns to scale will underestimate the contribution of capital and overestimate total productivity growth.

Following Romer (1986), suppose that output Y_h of each firm h in the economy depends not only on the stock of physical capital and the quantity of labor used by the firm, K_h and L_h, but also on the economy-wide capital stock, K. The scale of production at each individual firm is thus a function of the aggregate stock of knowledge, embodied in the capital stock (see Chapter 12). Assuming identical firms and a generalized Cobb-Douglas production function yields

$$Y_h = AK_h^\alpha L_h^{1-\alpha} K^\beta, \quad 0 < \alpha < 1, \ \beta \geq 0, \tag{A1}$$

where A measures the efficiency of the production process or technological progress. Thus, production exhibits constant returns to scale only in the firm's specific inputs, K_h and L_h. The coefficient β measures the strength of the spillover effects associated with the diffusion of knowledge across firms.

Let w and r denote again the economy-wide wage rate and the rental rate of capital. Under perfect competition, each firm equates factor prices (taken as given) to the marginal product of each production factor. Assuming, in addition, that the aggregate stock of capital is also taken as given yields, from Equation (A1),

$$r = \frac{\alpha Y_h}{K_h} - \delta, \quad w = \frac{(1-\alpha)Y_h}{K_h},$$

where δ is the rate of depreciation. Factor income shares are thus simply $\eta_K = \alpha$ and $\eta_L = 1 - \alpha$.

Let $k = K/L$, where L is the aggregate supply of labor. k is therefore the economy-wide capital-labor ratio. The production function (A1) can be written as

$$Y_h = Ak_h^\alpha L_h K^\beta = Ak_h^\alpha L_h L^\beta k_h^\beta. \tag{A2}$$

In equilibrium, each firm must adopt the same capital-labor ratio. Setting $k_h = k$ in Equation (A2) yields

$$Y_h = Ak^{\alpha+\beta} L_h L^\beta.$$

Linear aggregation across all firms implies

$$Y = Ak^{\alpha+\beta} L^{1+\beta} = AK^{\alpha+\beta} L^{1-\alpha}, \tag{A3}$$

given the definition of k. Equation (A3) shows that, as long as $\beta > 0$, then aggregate production will exhibit increasing returns to scale. A doubling of K

and L, in particular, will raise aggregate output by $1 + \beta$. Taking growth rates, Equation (A3) also implies that

$$\mathbf{g}_A = \mathbf{g}_Y - (\alpha + \beta)\mathbf{g}_K - (1 - \alpha)\mathbf{g}_L,$$

which can be rewritten as

$$\mathbf{g}_A = \mathbf{g}_{Y/L} - \alpha\mathbf{g}_{K/L} - \beta\mathbf{g}_K. \tag{A4}$$

Comparing Equations (3) and (A4) shows that using the conventional growth accounting framework, based on constant returns to scale ($\beta = 0$), will underestimate by β the contribution of the growth rate of capital when in fact production is characterized by increasing returns. It will thus lead to overestimation of the true rate of TFP growth. The larger the difference between the social marginal product of capital, $(\alpha + \beta)Y/K$, and the private marginal product, $r = \alpha Y/K$ (that is, the larger β is), the larger the bias. How to estimate in practice the size of the coefficient β remains, however, a matter of debate.

Chapter 14

Trade and Labor Market Reforms

> If to do were as easy as to know what were good to do, chapels had been churches, and poor men's cottages princes' palaces . . . . I can easier teach twenty what were good to be done, than be one of the twenty to follow mine own teaching.
>
> Portia, in William Shakespeare, *The Merchant of Venice*, 1600, Scene 2.

Structural reforms are generally defined as policy measures that lead to a rise in the productive capacity, or the degree of flexibility, of the economy. They are also often referred to as *microeconomic policies*, because their ultimate objective is to improve efficiency in resource allocation by reducing the various distortions (government-induced or otherwise) that may hinder the functioning of specific markets. In addition to their microeconomic or sectoral effects, however, structural reforms often have a significant impact on the behavior of aggregate variables, such as interest rates, prices, fiscal deficits, and the current account. For instance, as noted in Chapter 4, and as further discussed in the next chapter, ceilings on interest rates that lead to negative real rates of return often have an adverse effect on aggregate savings, investment, and thus on the rate of economic growth. Conversely, structural policies that make markets *more flexible* may enhance the economy's ability to absorb domestic macroeconomic shocks and external disturbances—thereby limiting their effects on inflation and the balance of payments. Recognizing that microeconomic rigidities may have a large impact on macroeconomic imbalances is essential for the sequencing of reforms and the overall design of adjustment programs, as further discussed in the last chapter of this book.

This chapter focuses on the conceptual and empirical aspects of structural adjustment policies that directly affect the *real side* of the economy.[1] Section

---

[1] Measuring the effects of structural reforms is in general difficult; there is no straightforward

547

14.1 assesses the benefits, costs, and evidence on trade liberalization, including their effects on wage inequality—an issue that has attracted much attention in recent years. The trend toward regional trade integration and preferential trade arrangements is discussed in section 14.2. Section 14.3 focuses on the role of the labor market in economic adjustment. It begins with a review of the main features of labor markets in developing countries, including wage formation mechanisms and the sources of labor market segmentation. It then discusses the impact of minimum wages on employment and the role of trade unions in the wage bargaining process. It concludes with an assessment of measures aimed at increasing labor market flexibility, particularly those aimed at reducing job security provisions. The appendix discusses briefly the role of of price reform in stimulating agricultural output in low-income countries.

14.1 Trade Liberalization

Growing recognition of the severe allocative distortions associated with **import substitution strategies** has led an increasing number of countries in the developing world to adopt more liberal external trade regimes.[2] Traditional economic arguments suggest that a reduction in trade barriers (such as *tariffs* and *import quotas*) fosters an adjustment in relative prices that leads to a reallocation of resources toward the exportable sector. In the long run, trade reform leads to an expansion of output of exportables and a contraction of activity in import-competing industries, as well as to an overall transfer of resources from sectors producing nontradables toward those producing tradables. The improvement in the allocation of resources does not only lead to a static output gain; as noted in Chapter 12, there are also *dynamic gains* from free trade. In particular, the removal of barriers to trade may lead to a permanent increase in the economy's growth rate as a result of **technological spillovers** from rich to poor countries.

This section begins by showing, using both partial and general equilibrium settings, the efficiency loss associated with tariffs—and thus the gain from removing them. It then discusses recent experiences with trade reform, and reviews the impact of such reforms on employment and wage inequality. It concludes by examining various obstacles to trade reform, such as political resistance and adverse effects on fiscal deficits.

14.1.1 The Gains from Trade

Understanding the gains from trade reform requires understanding the efficiency loss associated with the imposition of a tariff in the first place. A simple analysis of the impact of tariffs is illustrated in the two panels of Figure 14.1, which

---

way of assessing, for instance, the increase in the degree of flexibility in response to shocks that structural reforms may bring. The appendix to Chapter 15 discusses an index-based approach that has been used in a study on Latin America.

[2] See Bruton (1989) for a critical discussion of arguments for and against import substitution policies.

are constructed using the assumptions underlying the standard *Hekscher-Ohlin-Samuelson model*—perfectly competitive and efficient markets, incomplete specialization in accordance with relative factor endowments, international immobility of factors, and exogenous terms of trade for the domestic economy (see, for instance, Mikić, 1998).

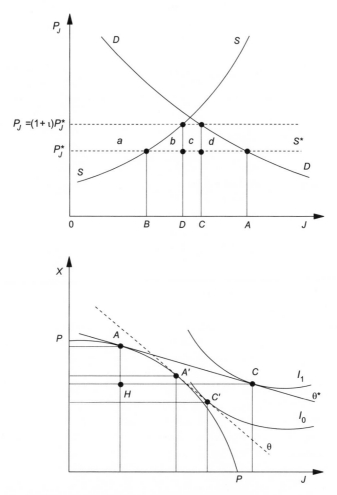

Figure 14.1. Effects of a tariff in a small open economy.

The upper panel in Figure 14.1 describes the case of a small open economy producing one importable good in a *partial equilibrium* setting. D, S, and S^* denote domestic demand, domestic supply, and foreign supply, respectively, of the import substitute. At the world price of P_J^*, OA is consumed, with OB supplied by domestic producers and BA by foreign producers. If an *ad valorem* tariff of ι is levied on imported goods, the domestic price, P_J, becomes

$$P_J = (1 + \iota)P_J^*.$$

At this price demand falls by the quantity AC to OC, domestic supply increases by BD to OD, and imports drop to DC. The welfare effects of the imposition of the tariff are

- a reduction in the **consumers' surplus** by the area $a + b + c + d$;

- an increase in the **producers' surplus** by a;

- an increase in **government revenue** by c (from an initial value of zero).

The **deadweight loss** (or net welfare loss) associated with tariff protection is thus equal to $b + d$. The area b represents the excess cost of producing domestically goods that could otherwise be imported; the area d represents the loss resulting from the fact that, at the margin, some consumers are "squeezed out" as a result of the higher cost of importables. The area of triangle b is measured by $\iota(OD - OB)/2$ and the area of d by $\iota(OA - OC)/2$. The welfare loss due to the tariff, ΔW, is thus approximately

$$\Delta W \simeq \iota[(OD - OB) + (OA - OC)]/2 = \iota \Delta J/2,$$

where ΔJ is the change in imports, $(OA - OB) - (OC - OD) = AC + BD$. If the domestic good is measured in units such that its free-trade price, P_J^*, is normalized to unity, the change in imports can be written as

$$\Delta J = \iota J \eta_J,$$

where η_J is the price elasticity of the demand for imports, and ι, the tariff rate, represents the proportionate price change between the two regimes (that is, $\Delta P_J/P_J^*$). Using this result, the welfare loss can be approximated by the **Meade formula** given by[3]

$$\Delta W = \iota^2 J \eta_J/2.$$

The lower panel in Figure 14.1 illustrates the same result in a *general equilibrium* setting. Let X denote the exportable good (whose price is P_X) and J the importable good (whose price, before the imposition of tariffs, is P_J^*). PP is the **production possibilities frontier** (PPF), which shows the maximum physical production of X and J that can be produced, given the economy's productive resources and the state of technology. It is concave to the origin, as noted in Chapter 9. Its slope, the **marginal rate of transformation** of X into J, reflects the assumption of diminishing marginal productivity of factors of production. The convex curves I_0 and I_1 are **social indifference curves**, which show the various combinations of X and J between which society is indifferent in choosing. The slope of these curves measures the **marginal rate of substitution** of X into J. Finally, θ is the relative price of importables in

---

[3] Note that this formula provides a good approximation only in the case of a small market, with (approximately) linear demand and supply schedules.

terms of exportables, and is taken as exogenous. The slope of θ measures the rate at which goods can be transformed through trade.

Free trade production is located at point A on the PPF, and consumption at C on the social indifference curve I_1. Trade is shown by triangle AHC; the country exports AH of good X and imports HC of good J.

Suppose now that an *ad valorem* tariff is levied on imports of J. The tariff distorts the domestic relative price ratio from θ^* to

$$\theta = (1 + \iota)P_J^*/P_X.$$

At this price ratio, production shifts from A to A' as the exportable sector contracts and the importable sector expands. Consumption shifts from point C to C', with the restriction of consumption possibilities taking the economy from I_1 to I_0. The tariff equilibrium is thus *suboptimal*.

- On the producers' side, the shift from A to A' entails a loss in the value of domestic output at world prices.[4]

- On the consumers' side, there is a loss in utility because I_0 is not the highest social indifference curve that can be attained, even at a relative price θ. This is the analog to the deadweight loss identified in the upper panel of the figure.

The overall conclusion, therefore, is that (in the absence of initial distortions) an import tariff results in net welfare losses in a small open economy.[5] But can an import tariff be nevertheless optimal? It has been argued, for instance, that if collection costs of alternative means of generating revenue—including income and consumption taxes—are relatively high, reliance on tariffs as a revenue-raising device may indeed be optimal. For instance, Aizenman (1987) showed that, in the absence of collection costs associated with tariffs, and with an inelastic supply of labor, the optimal tariff rate is given by

$$\iota = \frac{\phi}{\eta - \phi},$$

where ϕ is the cost (in percent) of collecting alternative, domestic taxes and η the price elasticity of the demand for imports. However, the argument that trade taxes are necessary to raise revenue in developing countries (because of their lower administrative costs) was criticized by Dixit (1985), who showed that it is possible to derive a combination of domestic taxes levied neutrally on domestic and foreign goods that yields the same revenue as an import tax, for instance, but with a lower efficiency loss. Moreover, there are many cases where even if *collection* costs associated with tariffs are low (as assumed by Aizenman), *enforcement* costs may be high (because tariffs create incentives to

---

[4] World prices measure the true value of domestic goods, because both goods can be converted at that rate through trade.

[5] This result, however, does not hold for a large open economy; see, for instance, Greenaway and Milner (1994, pp. 14-15).

smuggle); thus the net effect may well be a reduction in welfare, as indicated earlier.

The foregoing discussion focused on the *static* gains from trade. As discussed in Chapter 12, the recent growth literature has emphasized that the benefits of trade openness may be largely *dynamic* in nature. As noted by Rivera-Batiz and Romer (1991), lowering barriers to trade could affect economic growth through at least three mechanisms:

- Trade integration with the industrial world increases the *transmission of technology* to developing countries (most importantly through imports of capital goods), thereby reducing the duplication of research and development activities. To the extent that knowledge is a *public good*, its accumulation may increase the rate of productivity growth in the economy.

- The international integration of sectors characterized by *increasing returns to scale* raises output without requiring more inputs.

- Trade liberalization reduces *price distortions*, reallocating resources across sectors and increasing economic efficiency.

The first two effects unambiguously raise the rate of economic growth; the third may raise growth rates (at least during a transitional period) to the extent that greater efficiency leads to more resources being invested in research and development—but it could also lower growth if the change in relative prices causes resources to shift out of research and development activities.[6]

In recent years a new approach to the analysis of the benefits of free trade has led to the development of **strategic trade theory** (Helpman and Krugman, 1985). At the heart of the new approach is the consideration of **scale economies** and **externalities**. Because both factors tend to lower *average costs*, large producers have an advantage over small ones. An important feature of the theory is its emphasis on the role of *alternative market structures* in assessing the impact of trade liberalization.[7] The case considered by Rodrik (1988), for instance, is that of a country where tariffs are high and imperfect competition prevails. In such a setting, trade reform (a reduction in tariffs) affects welfare through a variety of channels, some traditional (such as the *volume of trade* effect, which results from the fact that imports should expand in those sectors where the domestic price rises) and some that depend on assumptions about market structure. Whether the net effect of a reduction in tariffs is beneficial or not is a priori ambiguous, because these effects operate in conflicting directions. Nevertheless, it is possible for trade intervention to be efficient. But as argued in particular by Baldwin (1992), the results of strategic trade theory are not easily generalizable; the policy recommendations that it leads to are

---

[6] How to identify and measure the dynamic gains from trade, and thus the net effect of the channels identified here, remains a difficult task, as noted in Chapter 13.

[7] Vousden (1990) contains a thorough treatment of trade policy with various market structures.

very sensitive to assumptions about market structure, entry and exit restrictions, and intersectoral linkages—information that is in practice very difficult to obtain.

14.1.2   Recent Evidence on Trade Reforms

Trade liberalization (elimination of nontariff barriers and reductions in tariffs) gained momentum in developing countries in the mid-1980s, particularly in Latin America. A simple policy indicator of the change in the level of trade intervention is some average measure of nominal tariffs. However, there are at least four reasons to be careful in interpreting data on nominal tariff rates (Greenaway and Milner, 1994):

- There may be *instrument substitution* taking place; nominal tariffs may indeed be lowered, but at the same time they may be replaced by other restrictions—such as *antidumping measures.*

- *Nominal* tariffs may decline, but *effective* tariffs may be increasing. This is the case if, at the same time, exemptions are being eliminated.

- There may have been a degree of *tariff redundancy* prior to reform. If so, the overall structure of tariffs may become more, rather than less, protective.

- Trade liberalization, in practice, includes not only tariff cuts but also reductions in *anti-export-biased policies* (such as distorted exchange rate regimes), and the substitution of more efficient for less efficient forms of interventions—such as the replacement of tariffs for *quotas.*

The bias of a trade regime is better assessed by looking not at nominal protection rates (that is, the nominal tariffs themselves, if they are ad valorem), but at **effective protection rates**, which are defined as the amount by which the value added in a given sector at domestic prices exceeds the value added in that sector at international prices, expressed as a percentage of the latter (see, for instance, Anderson, 1994). These rates depend therefore not only on the tariff on the (final) good produced in the sector, but also on the *input coefficients* and the *tariffs on inputs*. As a result, calculations of effective rates of protection usually require detailed *input-output tables* and a variety of other microeconomic data for a large number of sectors if they are to be accurate and useful.[8] Thus, despite their limitations, nominal tariff rates are often used as indicators of changes in the trade regime.

Figure 14.2 shows movements in nominal tariffs for a group of developing countries in 1980 and 2000. It highlights the fact that average tariff rates fell substantially in several developing countries. In India, for instance, the maximum tariff on imports fell from 400 percent in 1990 to 50 percent in 1995, and

---

[8]Note also that effective rates of protection are relevant only for analyzing the production (or supply side) effects of protection, not consumption (or demand side) effects, which should still be analyzed in terms of nominal tariff rates on goods.

average tariff rates dropped from well above 80 percent to under 30 percent over the same period. In Latin America tariffs were cut from 41.6 percent in 1985 to 13.7 percent in 1995 (Lora and Olivera, 1998, p. 13). In South Asia, unweighted tariff averages on *manufactured goods* fell in the early 1990s to 11 percent in Korea, 15 percent in Malaysia, and 11 percent in Taiwan; at the same time, however, they remained at 42 percent in Thailand, 56 percent in India, 64 percent in Pakistan, and 85 percent in Bangladesh (Bandara and McGillivray, 1998). Figure 14.3 suggests that the reduction in mean tariffs was also associated with a reduction in the *dispersion* of tariff rates.

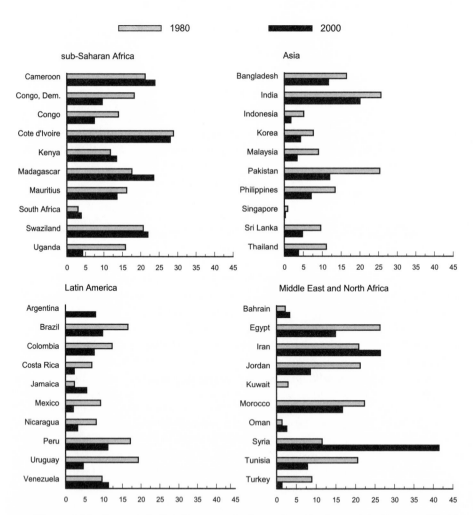

Figure 14.2. Import duties (in percent of merchandise imports). Source: World Bank.

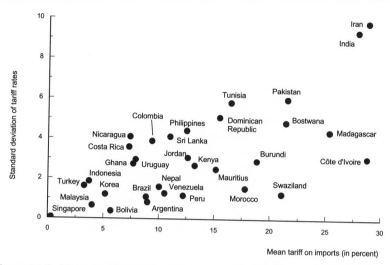

Figure 14.3. Mean tariffs and tariff dispersion (averages over 1990-2000). Source: World Bank.

Finally, it is worth noting that the region where the least progress has been achieved in trade liberalization is sub-Saharan Africa. In fact, the region's importance in global trade has declined significantly over the past 30 to 40 years. Exports from sub-Saharan Africa accounted for about 3 percent of world exports in 1955; by 1990 its share had fallen to barely above 1 percent. Part of this outcome reflects declining global demand for key export products of the region, but part is due to a substantial erosion of its market shares. World Bank estimates suggest that if sub-Saharan Africa had maintained its 1962-64 export shares for major products, the region's exports would now be more than double their current value. In turn, the evidence suggests that the loss of market share and marginalization of the region in world trade appears to be the *antiexport bias* that still characterizes the trade regime in many of the countries of sub-Saharan Africa today (Ng and Yeats, 1997). Trade policy reform may thus be an essential component of an adjustment program aimed at reversing the marginalization process that the region has experienced since the early 1960s.

14.1.3   Trade Reform, Employment, and Wage Inequality

While there appears to be broad agreement on the allocative effects of trade liberalization in the long run, the short- and intermediate-run impact of trade reform on wages and employment remains imperfectly understood. The evidence gathered in the comprehensive study of trade reform episodes in developing countries conducted in the early 1980s at the World Bank and summarized by Papageorgiou, Choksi, and Michaely (1990) appeared to be largely inconclusive in that regard. Although most individual-country studies suggested that total employment in the manufacturing sector either fell or remained stable in the aftermath of the liberalization program, they often did not distinguish between traded and nontraded manufacturing goods and were therefore unable to characterize changes in the *distribution* of employment. In addition, almost no evidence was provided either on changes in employment in production activities other than manufacturing or on changes in the aggregate unemployment rate. These limitations (which in several cases resulted from the paucity of relevant data) are compounded by the methodological shortcomings that affect many of the specific country studies. For instance, although in several cases trade reforms were implemented simultaneously with macroeconomic stabilization programs—and in an environment characterized by severe external shocks—few authors attempted to disentangle rigorously the employment effects associated with each set of measures (Edwards, 1993). Despite this important caveat, Papageorgiou, Choksi, and Michaely (1990) attributed the fall in manufacturing sector employment observed in a few cases in the aftermath of reform mostly to restrictive macroeconomic policies.

Other studies have attempted to study directly the effects of tariff reform on the labor market.

- Rama (1994) examined the relationship between tariffs, employment, and wages in the manufacturing sector in *Uruguay*. He found no impact of the reform on wages, but a negative effect on employment. Rama's estimates indicated that a reduction in the tariff-inclusive price of imports by 1 percentage point led to an employment drop in manufacturing of between 0.4 and 0.5 percentage points.

- In a study of the trade liberalization program implemented in Mexico between 1985 and 1988, Revenga (1997) estimated that the reduction in tariffs during the period (of about 10 percentage points) led to a much smaller reduction in aggregate employment in the manufacturing sector (by 2 to 3 percentage points) and an increase in average wages. However, her study also suggested that, despite relatively limited aggregate effects, significant changes occurred in the *composition* of employment at the industry level.

- Currie and Harrison (1997) found that the comprehensive trade reform that was implemented in Morocco between 1984 and 1990—which led to a reduction in the coverage of import licenses from 41 percent of imports in 1984 to 11 percent in 1990 and a reduction in the maximum tariff rate from 165 percent to 45 percent—also had a small, albeit significant, impact on aggregate wages and employment in the formal manufacturing sector. As in the case of Mexico, pronounced sectoral shifts in employment appeared to have taken place, particularly in the manufacturing industries that were subject to large tariff reductions.

- Márquez and Carmen Pagés-Serra (1998) estimated the effect of changes in trade openness and real exchange rates on the demand for labor in the manufacturing sector in a group of 18 countries in Latin America and the Caribbean. They found that trade reforms had a negative but small effect on employment growth, and that this effect was reinforced by real exchange rate appreciation. Changes in domestic protection did not have a significant effect on unemployment, suggesting that movements in and out of the labor force dominated over flows into unemployment.

The impact of trade liberalization on *income distribution* has also been the subject of much research in recent years. In a number of countries (particularly in Latin America), openness to trade since the early or mid-1980s has coincided with an increase in the demand of, and the return to, *skilled labor* relative to *unskilled labor*, and a worsening of income distribution.[9] Revenga (1997) noted that the increase in average manufacturing wages in Mexico in the aftermath of trade reform may have reflected a change in the *composition* of the labor force— a shift toward high-skill, high-wage workers. A similar shift in the composition of the workforce was noted by Currie and Harrison (1997) in their analysis of trade reform in Morocco. Increases in relative wages of skilled workers have been noted in several other countries implementing trade reforms; in Chile, wages of university graduates rose by 56 percent relative to those of high school graduates between 1980 and 1990 (Beyer, Rojas, and Vergara, 1999). Similar evidence is also available for Argentina, Colombia, Costa Rica, and Uruguay (Robbins, 1996), as well as Brazil (Arbache, Dickerson, and Green, 2004)—although the evidence provided by Behrman, Birdsall, and Székely (2000) is less supportive.

The theory often referred to in interpreting these links is the standard *Hecksher-Ohlin-Samuelson* (HOS) *model* of international trade (see, for instance, Bhagwati, Panagariya, and Srinivasan, 1998). The model relies on the **principle of comparative advantage** and predicts the pattern of trade across countries by reference to the relative abundance of factors of production among them. Specifically, the HOS model predicts that between two countries A and B that share the same production technology, country A will export commodities that are produced with relatively more of the factor of production that is relatively abundant in country A and will import commodities produced with relatively more of the factor of production that is relatively abundant in country B.[10]

Two theorems derived from the HOS model deal explicitly with the effect of trade on wages and other factor prices: the **factor price equalization** (FPE) **theorem** and the **Stolper-Samuelson** (S-S) **theorem**.

- The FPE theorem asserts that under the assumptions of the HOS model and a regime of unrestricted free trade, prices of *production factors* will be *equalized* among trading partners.[11] Free trade between the United

---

[9] The link between trade and wage inequality has also been a key policy issue in industrial countries in recent years.

[10] The HOS model is subject to a number of limitations. In particular, the validity of the assumption of constant returns to scale, which is central for some of the model's predictions, is debatable.

[11] The original proof of the FPE theorem (attributed to Paul Samuelson) was based on a model in which two inputs were used to produce two goods. It was subsequently shown that the result remains valid under appropriate assumptions for additional goods and factors, as long as the number of goods exceeds the number of factors of production.

States and Mexico, for instance, should lead to an equalization of U.S. and Mexican wages for the same category of labor. It will also equalize the price of *land* across these countries—even if land cannot be moved across borders.

- The S-S theorem asserts that an increase in the domestic price of a good, brought about by a higher tariff or increased nontariff protection (such as quotas), will raise the real price of the factor of production that is used relatively intensively in producing that good. If computers, for instance, are produced using labor intensively and land sparingly, whereas wheat is produced using land intensively and labor sparingly, then an increase in tariffs on computers will raise the real wage received by workers involved in the production of that category of goods.

By implication, the S-S theorem predicts that a reduction in tariff protection on manufacturing goods (such as apparel and footwear) that are relatively *intensive in unskilled labor* will tend to reduce the real wage received by that category of workers, relative to wages earned by skilled workers. Thus trade liberalization may lead to an *increase in wage inequality*.

The S-S theorem is illustrated in Figure 14.4 for the case of an economy producing an exportable good that is more capital intensive than the importable good.[12] The wage rate and rental rate of capital are denoted by w and r, respectively. Curves $P_X P_X$ and $P_J P_J$ are the **iso-price curves** for the exportable and importable goods, respectively, produced by the domestic economy. These curves show the combinations of factor prices consistent with zero profits in producing exportables and importables at a given price. They are convex to the origin because the capital-labor ratio in each sector is an increasing function of the ratio of the wage rate and the rental rate of capital.[13] The intersection of the two curves, at point E, determines the economy's equilibrium wage and rental rates consistent with *zero profits* in both industries. At point E, the country produces both goods.

Suppose now that the country's price of exportables increases, and that it begins trading with the rest of the world at the new prices. The curve $P_X P_X$ shifts outward by the same proportion as the price increase. Measured along the ray from the origin to point E, the price increase is given by EE'/OE. But, because the price of importables does not change, curve $P_J P_J$ does not change either. The intersection of the iso-price curves now occurs at point E'', which corresponds to the new competitive equilibrium. At E'', factor prices have changed: the price of capital has increased while the price of labor has fallen. Moreover, the increase in the rental rate of capital is relatively *larger* than the increase in the price of exportables, because $r_E r_{E''} > EE'/OE$. Put differently, there is a *magnification effect*—the price of a factor changes more than proportionately in response to a change in the price of a good intensive in

---

[12] For an algebraic proof, see, for instance, Mikić (1998, pp. 91-92).

[13] For a derivation see, again, Mikić (1998, pp. 131-32). Note also that, as drawn, the curves intersect only once; this is due to the exclusion of *factor intensity reversals*.

that factor. Relative to both commodity prices, the rental rate has increased whereas the wage rate has fallen, as predicted by the S-S theorem.

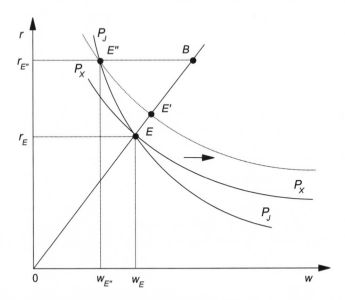

Figure 14.4. The Stolper-Samuelson Theorem.

The implication of the theorem is that changes in *factor prices* can be inferred from changes in *relative goods prices*. Assuming continuous full employment of both factors, an increase in the relative price of a good will unambiguously increase the real return to the factor of production used relatively intensively in the production of that good, while the real return to the other factor of production will be reduced in terms of both goods.

In the particular case that is being considered here, a reduction in the relative price of unskilled labor-intensive goods (brought about by a reduction in tariffs) will unambiguously reduce the real return to the factor of production used relatively intensively in the production of that good—unskilled labor. Tests of this proposition, however, have been inconclusive, as noted by Robbins (1996) in a study covering seven countries in Latin America and East Asia.

An alternative explanation is that trade liberalization was associated with the introduction of higher-level technology, the use of which required highly skilled labor. The reason is that the *cost of capital* depends not only on the relative price of capital goods (as noted in Chapter 2), but also on *financial costs*, *tariffs*, and *taxes* that must be incurred in order to be able to purchase and use an additional unit of capital goods. To the extent that a fall in tariffs translates into a fall in the cost of capital, a high degree of complementarity between skilled labor and capital, and a high degree of substitutability between unskilled labor and capital, will entail an increase in the demand for skilled workers—thereby leading to a widening of the wage gap between skilled and unskilled labor. There is indeed evidence for some countries (such as Colombia) that the price of capital fell significantly following the beginning of trade reform. A problem with the argument, however, is that it suggests that one should observe a significant increase in *imports of capital goods*, and a concomitant expansion in *exports of skill-intensive goods*. Yet the evidence, at least for Latin America, does not suggest anything of this sort. In 1992, for the seven major Latin American countries taken together, investment in machinery and equipment (most of it imported) was *lower* than in the early 1980s. There has also been no dramatic increase in the relative share of skill-intensive goods in the region's total exports.

Spilimbergo, Londoño, and Székely (1999) emphasized the role of *relative factor endowments* in analyzing the relationship between trade liberalization, increases in wage differentials, and income inequality. In an analysis covering postwar data and focusing on 88 countries, they found that the relationship between trade liberalization and total income distribution depended essentially on factor endowments (natural resources, skilled and unskilled labor, and capital) relative to world patterns. In turn, world endowment patterns appeared to have changed with trade: growing participation by Asian countries (most notably China) with abundant unskilled labor resources altered the traditional comparative advantage patterns of Latin America. They also found that changes in rates of return on natural resources and physical capital that often accompany trade liberalization tended to have a smaller effect in bridging the income gap in those countries in which assets were more concentrated in a few hands, as was (and continues to be) the case for Latin America.

14.1.4 Obstacles to Trade Reform

Although many developing countries have implemented far-reaching programs of trade liberalization in recent years, progress has remained relatively slow in others—particularly in sub-Saharan Africa, as indicated earlier. In a detailed review of the empirical evidence, Matusz and Tarr (1999) argued that adjustment costs associated with trade liberalization (notably in terms of employment losses in manufacturing and increases in fiscal deficits and inflation) are typically very small compared with the benefits of reform. Why, then, is trade reform so unpopular at times? The reason is often that trade policies are heavily influenced by the interests of *powerful groups* and *political considerations* rather than by an assessment of costs and benefits. **Rent-seeking activities** (aimed at maintaining and extending existing tariff protection, or at influencing the allocation of import quotas) for instance, tend to magnify the distortions and inefficiencies in resource allocation. Two main obstacles to trade reform have been identified in the literature (Rodrik, 1995c):

- the **status quo bias**, associated with individual uncertainty regarding the benefits of reform;

- the high political cost compared with relatively small efficiency gains associated with trade reform.

Regarding the first obstacle, Fernández and Rodrik (1991) argued that *idiosyncratic uncertainty* associated with the effect of reforms (the fact that individual gainers and losers cannot always be clearly identified before implementation) may generate *ex ante* opposition to them, even if, *ex post*, everyone should support them. To illustrate this result in a simple manner, consider the case of an economy populated by 100 workers, employed in two sectors, identified by W and L. Initially, 40 workers operate in sector W and 60 in L:

$$L \qquad\qquad\qquad W$$

| 60 workers | 20 workers | 40 workers |
| -0.2 each | $\Longrightarrow$ | +0.2 each |

Consider now a reform whose outcome is such that each worker in sector W gains 0.2, whereas workers in sector L each lose 0.2. The reform is anticipated to induce 20 workers to move from L to W. If there is *full information* regarding the identity of the workers moving from L to W, the majority of voters will approve the reform, because 60 will benefit (the original 40 in W plus the 20 that will be relocated in W).

However, suppose that there is *individual uncertainty* regarding the identity of the workers moving from L to W. Specifically, suppose that the *probability of relocation* in W is the same for all workers in sector L; this probability can thus be approximated by 20/60, whereas the probability of remaining in L is simply 40/60. In the first case, as indicated earlier, each worker gains 0.2, whereas in the second he or she loses 0.2; the *expected gain from the reform* is thus the weighted average given by

$$0.2 * (1/3) - 0.2(2/3) < 0,$$

which implies that each worker expects to *lose* from the reform—implying that the majority of workers in the L sector will rationally *vote against it*. The paradox is that if a "benevolent" dictator (assuming of course that such dictators exist) were to implement the reform discretionarily, the majority of workers would *ex post* support it, because *ex post* individual uncertainty disappears.

As this example illustrates, status quo bias reduces welfare. Overcoming it (in a democratic setting) requires policies that mitigate personal uncertainty, such as the design of appropriate *transfer schemes* or more generally the operation of an *insurance market*, which would allow individuals to protect themselves from uncertain outcomes. In practice, of course, such markets are difficult to create because of asymmetric information problems.

Another source of resistance to trade reform stems from the existence of relatively high political costs. Empirical evidence suggests that the welfare cost of trade distortions (such as tariffs and quotas), as measured by **Harberger triangles** (the loss in social welfare resulting from the misallocation of resources due to market imperfections), are frequently relatively small—often on the order of 2 percent of GDP or less.[14] Although trade liberalization will typically

---

[14] See Chapter 15 for a discussion of Harberger triangles in the context of financial repression. Note, however, that the use of these triangles to assess welfare losses has been criticized,

improve welfare by eliminating these distortions, they involve at the same time potentially *large reallocations of income*; these movements may be associated with high political costs and may generate resistance to reform (Rodrik, 1992).

Consider, for instance, a small open economy facing a given world relative price of importables to exportables, denoted θ^*. Initial tariffs are such that the relative price faced by domestic agents is $\theta > \theta^*$. A reduction in tariffs leads to a fall from θ to θ^*—or, using Figure 14.1 to illustrate, a reduction from P_J to P_J^*—and implies that consumers gain area $a+b+c+d$, whereas the government loses area a (foregone tariff revenue), and producers lose area c. In other words, there is a redistribution of income from producers and the government to consumers (area $a+c$, respectively) and an increase in efficiency given by area $b+d$. Rodrik defines the ratio of the income redistributed to the efficiency triangles, that is, area $(a + c)/(b + d)$, as a measure of the political resistance to reform. He points out that this ratio is typically high in practice—possibly reaching values exceeding 10.

In another study, Rodrik (1998) argued that the large distributional effects associated with trade liberalization (and its potential for exacerbating social conflict) explains the erratic pattern and low credibility of trade reform in many sub-Saharan African countries during the past two decades. What may compound the problem (as argued by Tommasi and Velasco, 1996) is the fact that opposition to trade reform is often more localized, more organized, and more effective than political opposition to macroeconomic stabilization—which may be more diffuse, less organized, and relatively ineffective.

Another possible obstacle to reform may be the **lack of credibility** of the reform process. As emphasized by Calvo (1989), a low degree of credibility acts fundamentally as a *distortion* or a *production tax* because it impairs the beneficial effects of an otherwise desirable policy. The example considered by Calvo is a situation where the authorities announce that all tariffs will be permanently abolished, but the private sector expects that such a policy will be modified in the future and that a new set of tariffs will be put in place. If there is no substitution in production and consumption, but consumption goods can be stored at a low cost, the lack of credibility of the tariff reform will trigger speculative accumulations of inventories. Although this activity may be profitable from the point of view of the private sector, it will not be necessarily desirable for the society as a whole because the accumulation of inventories may crowd out the acquisition of other types of assets—such as physical capital formation—with a higher social rate of return. In this setting, the *social cost* of this misallocation is a function of the structure of capital markets: in a regime of perfect capital mobility, unlimited funds could be obtained from abroad for speculation in inventories; with binding controls on capital flows, a lesser amount of capital could be tied up in this form.[15]

---

because they do not take into account the potential benefits of all production activities that are, in a sense, missing because of high levels of tariffs. See Romer (1993) for a simple example.

[15] This does not necessarily imply that capital controls should be retained or reintroduced, but rather that reform efforts in other areas should be accelerated.

Finally, concerns about possible *adverse revenue effects* may also explain the slow pace of trade liberalization (see Ebrill, Stotsky, and Gropp, 1999). In countries where the share of trade taxes in total revenues is large, trade barriers have often been gradually dismantled due to fiscal constraints. The extent to which total tax revenue fall depends, of course, on what alternative tax bases the government can rely on following a cut in tariffs, as illustrated by Konan and Maskus (2000) in the case of Egypt. More generally, although trade liberalization may lead to a fall in revenue in the short term (sometimes forcing governments to implement concomitant cuts in expenditure) some trade liberalization measures (such as the replacement of quotas by tariffs) can be implemented without significant declines in revenue. Lifting *quantitative restrictions* may even lead to an increase in revenue if the newly liberalized categories of imports increase and are subject to tariffs. Moreover, in countries where the foreign exchange market is being liberalized at the same time, and the official exchange rate depreciates significantly as a result, the increase in the *domestic-currency price* of imports may be large enough to lead to higher revenue, even with falling tariff rates (see Agénor, 1992).

14.2 Trade and Regional Integration

Since the early 1970s key changes have taken place in the composition of exports of developing countries. In Asia, the share of manufacturing exports relative to that of primary commodities has increased substantially, from 42 percent of total exports of goods in 1970 to 48 percent in 1980 and 74 percent in 1990. The share of manufactures in total merchandise exports in Latin America has also increased, from about 12 percent in 1970 to 18 percent in 1980 and 34 percent in 1990. By contrast, in Africa, the export share of manufactured goods fell from 27 percent in 1980 (after increasing from 15 percent in 1970) to 22 percent in 1990. These changes in export composition were in part the result of the removal of distortions in domestic markets and reductions in trade barriers. Most importantly, they reflect an underlying shift in the comparative advantage of many developing countries toward manufacturing activities. Relatively low wage costs coupled with increased investment have made some developing countries highly competitive in the production of many manufactured goods. This is particularly so in some of the Asian countries, where high domestic saving and investment rates have been reflected in increases in the stock of capital. The composition of manufactured exports in a number of Asian countries now includes a significant proportion of advanced, high-technology manufactured goods.[16]

At the same time, there has been an increase in the degree of diversification of export markets of developing countries and a marked rise in *intraregional trade*. Between the late 1980s and mid-1990s, the growth in intraregional trade was particularly marked during the period in Asia, where almost 40 percent of the

---

[16] At the same time, the comparative advantage of many industrial countries has shifted toward *services*, many of which are now tradable owing to changes in technology, especially improvements in communications and information technologies.

region's exports are now going to other Asian countries. The expansion of markets in Asia has benefited other regions—all industrial and developing-country regions have increased the share of their exports going to Asia. Intraregional trade has also risen markedly among Latin American countries, although export diversification has been more limited—with almost 50 percent of the region's exports being shipped to North America.

By contrast, export markets among African countries have remained relatively undiversified, with almost 50 percent of the region's exports going to Europe, and the level of intraregional trade remaining modest. A key problem in sub-Saharan Africa is that nonoil exports are highly concentrated in a few products, none of which are important in regional imports; this "noncomplementarity" raises doubts about the potential for greater trade within the region (Yeats, 1998). The level of intraregional trade among the countries of the Middle East and Eastern Europe is also relatively small, and in contrast to the other developing-country regions, the importance of intraregional trade actually diminished between 1984 and 1994.

The increase in intraregional trade in some regions has coincided with the development of **preferential trade agreements** (PTAs). An example of such arrangements is the *Mercosur agreement* between Brazil, Argentina, Paraguay, and Uruguay that took effect on January 1, 1995. Regional trade integration can allow firms to spread the costs of research and development over a larger market, thus reducing unit costs and encouraging greater innovation and technical progress. This can, in turn, generate positive spillovers as successful innovations are applied more broadly. Integration can also boost productivity growth by allowing increased specialization; there are also efficiency gains from increased competition, which can be reinforced by foreign direct investment.[17] Estimating the actual gains from growing regional trade integration is very difficult, because it occurs in different ways and with a variety of different effects.

PTAs raise some fundamental policy issues, which have been reviewed by DeRosa (1998) and Bhagwati and Panagariya (1996). Both studies concluded that some of the common arguments in favor of such agreements are not valid and that they may conflict with *multilateral, nonpreferential trade liberalization*, as pursued through international institutions like the World Trade Organization (WTO). Indeed, it has been argued that PTAs can be viewed as a threat to a multilateral trading system, defined as a cooperative arrangement among governments that is designed to eliminate inefficient trade restrictions (Bagwell and Staiger, 1998). Two issues are particularly important:

- PTAs may lead to **trade creation**, by replacing relatively high-cost domestic production with lower-cost imports from partner countries. However, there is also scope for **trade diversion**, which occurs when imports are switched from efficient nonmember suppliers to less efficient member

---

[17]As argued by Eichengreen (1998) in the context of Mercosur, realizing the full benefits of trade integration may require, in addition to a customs union, complete monetary integration to prevent potentially disruptive effects of exchange rate changes on trade flows.

countries benefiting from tariff preferences.[18]

- Higher trade volumes between member countries that result from the agreement may lead to *greater*, not *smaller*, losses to an individual member Z who joins the agreement from a higher initial set of tariffs, because joining the agreement at a common lower tariff leads to a redistribution of tariff revenues from Z to other member countries with initially lower tariffs.[19]

The concepts of trade diversion and trade creation, attributed to Viner (1950), can be illustrated in a partial equilibrium setting. Consider two countries, A and B, producing the same good and suppose that these countries are considering forming a PTA whose main element is a customs union. Both countries are small relative to the rest of the world; they therefore face a constant world price, P^*, for their imports and exports. Suppose also that country A imports the good before the customs union is created, and that B is a net exporter, but with a volume of exports that does not completely satisfy the demand for imports by A. Country A is thus also importing from the rest of the world. Before the customs union is formed, A imposes a nondiscriminatory tariff of ι on all imports; the same tariff rate is used as the common external tariff by the union (B initially has no tariff). Finally, prior to the creation of the union B exports only to A, and once the union is in place the two countries are self-sufficient at a price P_U which is above the world price P^* but below the tariff-inclusive price $(1+\iota)P^*$. As shown in Figure 14.5, before the union is formed the domestic price of the good in country A is $(1+\iota)P^*$, domestic production is Q_E^A, and consumption is $Q_C^A > Q_E^A$. Country A is thus importing $J^A = Q_C^A - Q_E^A$; the quantity $Q_J^A - Q_E^A$ is from country B, whereas the remainder, $Q_C^A - Q_J^A$, is provided by the rest of the world. Country B produces Q_E^B and faces a pre-union domestic price equal to P^*. It consumes Q_C^B and exports a quantity $X^B = Q_E^B - Q_C^B$ (equal to $Q_J^A - Q_E^A$) to country A.

Once the customs union is in place, country B channels all its exports to country A, and trade with the rest of the world ceases.[20] Demand by member countries for the good is met entirely by union production, at the price $P_U < (1+\iota)P^*$. Thus, the formation of the customs union has three types of effects in country A:

- A *trade creation* effect, which results from the replacement of an amount $Q_E^A - Q_{E'}^A$ of domestic output by cheaper imports from country B. This is measured by area b in Figure 14.5.

---

[18] Yeats (1997) for instance argued that the Mercosur agreement has led to the replacement of efficiently produced goods from outside the arrangement by inefficiently produced goods from inside. However, his methodology (based on comparing shifts in intraregional exports with a measure of relative efficiency in production) has been questioned by various researchers.

[19] Bhagwati and Panagariya (1996) also stressed that PTAs are worth pursuing only for countries whose ultimate goal is complete dismantling of barriers to labor and capital mobility, and complete integration of political structures.

[20] Producers in country B have the incentive to sell to consumers in country A only because P_U, by assumption, is above the world price, P^*.

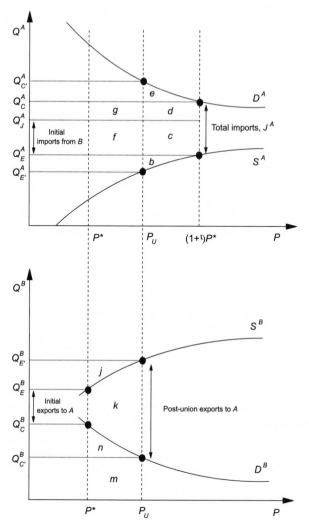

Figure 14.5. Customs union: Trade diversion and trade creation.

- A *trade diversion* effect, as the lower-cost imports from the rest of the world, $Q_C^A - Q_J^A$, are replaced by more expensive imports from the union's other member, B. This is measured by area g in Figure 14.5.

- A *consumption* effect, $Q_{C'}^A - Q_C^A$, which results from the fall in the (tariff-inclusive) domestic price of the good from $(1 + \iota)P^*$ to P_U. This is measured by area e in Figure 14.5.

In country B, production expands by $Q_{E'}^B - Q_E^B$, consumption falls by $Q_C^B - Q_{C'}^B$ and exports increase from $Q_E^B - Q_C^B$ to $Q_{E'}^B - Q_{C'}^B$. The producers' surplus gain in that country is given by the area $k + m + n$, whereas the consumers' loss is given by the area $m + n$. Country B therefore realizes a net welfare gain, equal to k, from the union. Essentially, this gain reflects the increase in exports to country A at a price P_U that exceeds the pre-union price, P^*. For country A, however, the impact of the union on net welfare is in general ambiguous and depends on the relative strength of the three different effects identified earlier. As shown in the figure, the producers' surplus falls by a, the consumers' surplus gain is equal to $a+b+c+d+e$, and tariff revenue falls by the area $c+d+f+g$. The net effect is thus equal to

$$(b+e) - (f+g).$$

Areas b, g, and e, as defined earlier, measure the trade creation, trade diversion, and consumption expansion effects; area f measures the *terms-of-trade loss* with country B. Thus, country A will incur a net welfare improvement only if the gains associated with the trade creation and consumption expansion effects (area $b+e$) exceed the losses resulting from the trade diversion and terms-of-trade loss (area $f+g$).

If country A gains, the union as a whole is also gaining. But in general, whether the union is welfare improving or welfare reducing is ambiguous. In particular, the larger the difference between the union price and the world price, the larger the volume of imports by country A prior to the union; and the lower the price elasticity of domestic supply and demand, the more likely it is that country A will lose. Country A's loss may be large enough to outweigh country B's gain, implying that the union is welfare reducing. As long as the union leads primarily to trade creation (diversion), it will tend to increase (reduce) aggregate welfare.

A number of additional results can be established from the foregoing analysis and other research on customs unions.

- The more competitive and the more complementary are the production structures of the union partners, the more likely it is that the customs union will lead to an increase in welfare. The reason is that there is more scope for trade creation among countries whose production structures are similar, because less efficient domestic production tends to be replaced by imports from partner countries.

- The larger the cost differentials between the countries of the union in the goods that they both produce, the larger will be the scope for gains from trade creation effects. The reason is that a large cost difference will increase the possibilities for resource reallocation and trade-creation effects.

- The higher the initial tariffs between the union partners, the greater is the scope for trade creation and an increase in welfare. This is because the lower the tariffs imposed on goods imported from the rest of the world, the smaller the losses resulting from trade diversion.

- The larger the part of trade originally covered by trade between the union partners (that is, the smaller the share of goods imported from nonmember countries in total consumption prior to the union), the greater the likelihood that the union will be beneficial for all members.

In addition, recent research on customs unions and preferential trade arrangements suggests that assessing the net welfare effects of these arrangements requires examining their *dynamic effects*, associated with greater scope for economies of scale, increased competition, and larger investment and technology flows across member countries (see Baldwin and Venables, 1995). However, evaluating the practical importance of these effects may require the use of relatively complex models, whose sensitivity to certain behavioral parameters may be quite high—as is typically the case in applied general equilibrium models.

14.3 Reforming Labor Markets

A large literature in development economics has emphasized the role of *labor market flexibility* in the process of economic growth. For instance, it has been argued by a number of observers that one of the key features of the East Asian growth miracle of the second half of the past century was the limited impact of trade unions and other distortions on the labor market (Fields and Wan, 1989) and the unusually high levels of employment growth without excessive wage pressures. In turn, this was viewed as the result of large investments in primary and secondary education, which ensured an ample supply of skilled workers and helped to prevent large changes in relative incomes (Fields, 1994).

Advocates of labor market reform have argued that circumventing the scope of hiring and firing regulations, reducing nonwage labor costs, eliminating (or restricting the scope of) minimum wage laws, limiting unemployment benefits, and curtailing the role of trade unions in the wage bargaining process would enhance flexibility and have a positive effect on growth.

This section attempts to provide a balanced view of the effects of such reforms. It begins by reviewing some of the known facts about the structure of labor markets in developing countries—including the composition of employment, the role of minimum wages, and the role of trade unions in wage negotiations. It then considers various types of labor market reforms aimed at increasing economic flexibility. It concludes by examining the link between labor market regulations and growth—an issue that has received insufficient attention in the recent literature on structural adjustment.

14.3.1 Labor Markets in Developing Countries

Labor markets play an important role in the transmission process of macroeconomic policy shocks and structural adjustment policies. The degree of wage flexibility, in particular, plays an important role in the adjustment process to policy and exogenous shocks.[21]

---

[21] For instance, as discussed in Chapter 5, the degree of wage inertia plays an important role in determining whether or not a nominal devaluation is contractionary.

Basic Structure

The labor market in developing countries typically consists of three sectors:

- The **rural sector**, which continues to employ a sizable proportion of the labor force in some countries, particularly in sub-Saharan Africa.

- The **informal urban sector**, which is characterized mostly by *self-employment* and a limited proportion of hired labor. Wage flexibility, both nominal and real, is high and employment security low.[22] *Labor regulations* (including minimum wage laws) do not apply or are not enforced.

- The **formal urban sector**, where workers are hired on the basis of *explicit contracts* and the degree of compliance with labor market legislation, is relatively high. Wage determination often departs from *market-clearing mechanisms* as a result of legal restrictions, the existence of labor unions, and considerations internal to firms.

Employment Distribution and Unemployment

Although existing data on employment and unemployment in developing countries are not very reliable, they indicate that the proportion of *wage earners* in total employment is relatively high in Asia and Latin America, and very low in sub-Saharan Africa (sometimes less than 10 percent). In some countries, the public sector absorbs a large share of formal wage employment. The share of informal sector employment in total urban employment is sizable in many developing countries—exceeding, for instance, 60 percent in a countries like India and Kenya. In many countries in Latin America, the informal sector grew in importance during the 1980s and early 1990s, accounting for more than 50 percent of total employment in 1992 (see Agénor, 1996). It remains at these levels in many countries today, as documented, for instance, by Saavedra (2003) for Latin America.

Published measures of *unemployment* mostly include unemployed workers looking for jobs in the formal sector, but not *underemployed* workers in the informal and rural sectors—**disguised unemployment**. The available evidence suggests, nevertheless, that underemployment is far more pervasive than open unemployment. Open and disguised unemployment amounts to anywhere between 25 and 60 percent of the labor force in some countries.

Unemployment insurance or **compensation schemes** are not well developed in developing countries. Whether they should be is an open question. It has been argued that such schemes act, to some extent, as a *disincentive to search* for (or to accept) employment, and that they may act as an incentive to enter the labor force in order to collect unemployment benefits. However, unemployment insurance may also have positive effects in encouraging labor force

---

[22]Nominal wage flexibility refers to the elasticity of the nominal wage with respect to aggregate prices; real wage flexibility refers to the responsiveness of the real wage to unemployment.

participation and favoring regular, as opposed to marginal, employment (Atkinson and Micklewright, 1991). Because of limited data on variables such as the duration of unemployment benefits in the developing countries where they are available, it has proved difficult to test alternative views on these issues. The elasticity of unemployment with respect to *replacement rates* (benefits before taxes as a percentage of previous earnings) may be relatively low; but whether high unemployment benefits tend to increase open unemployment remains an open issue.

Wage Formation and Labor Market Segmentation

The labor market in many developing countries is characterized by **segmentation**, that is, a situation where observationally identical workers (that is, workers with similar qualifications) receive different wages depending on their sector of employment. Labor market segmentation may be induced by various factors:

- government intervention in the form of **minimum wages** (discussed below);

- **trade unions**, which may prevent wages from being equalized across sectors by imposing a premium for their members (also discussed below);

- **efficiency wages**, resulting from nutritional factors (Bliss and Stern, 1978), large turnover costs (Stiglitz, 1974) or productivity considerations (Stiglitz, 1982).

The basic idea of efficiency wages is that firms set wages so as to minimize labor costs *per efficiency unit*, rather than labor costs *per worker*. For instance, workers' level of effort may depend positively on the wage paid in the current sector of employment (say, the urban formal sector), relative to the wage paid in other production sectors (say the informal economy). The outcome of the firms' wage-setting decisions may be a **markup** of formal-sector wages over informal-sector wages. Because the efficiency wage may exceed the market-clearing wage, such models also help to explain the existence of **involuntary unemployment**. Agénor and Aizenman (1997) present a two-sector model of the labor market (with a primary, or formal, sector, and a secondary, or informal, sector) in which efficiency considerations lead to market segmentation and equilibrium unemployment of both skilled and unskilled workers. The model dwells on the **shirking model** developed by Shapiro and Stiglitz (1984). In this type of model, unemployment is both involuntary (for the reason mentioned earlier) and *voluntary*, because workers could work if they choose to in the secondary, or informal, sector at the going wage.

Minimum Wages

Development economists have long debated the role of minimum wage legislation in labor market adjustment. Advocates have often viewed minimum wages as having positive nutritional effects, as being an instrument of income redistribution and social justice, or as fostering higher productivity. By contrast, opponents argue that minimum wage legislation, by preventing wages from adjusting downward to excess supply of labor, imposes an *implicit tax* on employers in the formal economy, leads to *misallocation of labor* (by preventing wages from adjusting downward to clear the labor market), creates unemployment (particularly for young, unskilled workers, and women), induces labor market segmentation, and depresses wages in the informal urban sector. The last two categories of effects may have an adverse impact on urban poverty. A high minimum wage increases the relative cost of employing unskilled workers, thereby accelerating the substitution of capital for unskilled labor and reducing profits—and thus firms' capacity to invest. As a result of both factors, high minimum wages restrain the expansion of labor demand over time.

The empirical evidence on the effects of minimum wages on relative earnings and employment in developing countries is mixed and often inconclusive. In part, this is because assessing these effects is inherently difficult in this type of environment. *Lack of compliance* with the law makes studies based on the formal sector highly imprecise. For instance, a significant share of workers in one formal sector industry may be paid below-minimum wages whereas the other share may earn wages in excess of the minimum wage. Controlling for these differences is not always easy, because they are not necessarily related to observable workers' (or firms') characteristics. The lack of consensus is evident in some recent studies. Bell (1997), for instance, found that although changes in the minimum wage seemed to affect the *distribution* of wages in Colombia and Mexico, they appeared to have a limited impact on employment. Maloney and Mundez (2003) also found a large impact of changes in the minimum wage on the distribution of wages in Latin America—including the informal sector in countries like Argentina, Brazil, Mexico, and Uruguay—but detected large employment effects only in Colombia. Large adverse effects on employment rates of the youth and the unskilled were also detected in Chile by Montenegro and Pagés (2003). Nevertheless, most researchers agree that changes in the minimum wage are likely to have important distributional effects among workers, for instance, between those employed in the formal sector and those in the informal sector. As noted in Chapter 12, changes in distribution may have an indirect effect on growth. Explicit consideration of the informal economy, and wage differentials across sectors, may thus be important in analyzing the aggregate effects of changes in the minimum wage.

Trade Unions and the Bargaining Process

In assessing the role of trade unions in the bargaining process and wage formation in developing countries, two considerations are important (Nelson, 1994).

- Trade union movements in developing countries are typically not very centralized, making it difficult to organize collective labor action.

- The **degree of unionization** is a highly imperfect measure of the influence of trade unions on wage formation and the labor market. Trade unions in certain strategic sectors or industries may exert considerable influence on wage formation and working conditions at the national level, even if overall union membership is low in proportion to the workforce. Within individual firms, for instance, collective bargaining agreements may be extended to the nonunionized workers.

Whether a low degree of centralization has beneficial effects on wage formation remains a matter of debate. It has been argued, most notably by Calmfors (1993), that the relationship between the degree of centralization in wage bargaining—defined as the extent to which unions and employers cooperate in wage negotiations—and wage pressures is not monotonic but rather has an **inverted U-shape**. Wage push is limited when bargaining is *highly centralized* (that is, conducted at the national level) and when *highly decentralized* (when it takes place at the level of individual firms). The highest degree of influence on wage formation would thus tend to occur in countries where centralization is in the intermediate range, that is, at the industry level.

Various types of **externalities** have been used to explain why centralized bargaining is likely to produce lower aggregate real wages and higher employment (see Calmfors, 1993):

- A high degree of cooperation between unions and employers (as is the case under centralized bargaining) implies that the effects on others of a wage increase in one part of the economy will be *internalized*, thereby lowering the marginal benefit of an increase in wages. In particular, if unions are averse to inflation, they will tend to moderate their wage demands in order to induce the central bank to inflate at a lower rate.

- Decentralized bargaining systems produce real wage moderation because of the restraint imposed by *competitive forces*—although moderation may occur at the cost of increased wage dispersion.

- With intermediate centralization, neither internalization effects nor competitive forces are sufficiently strong to restrain unions' incentives to demand higher wages.

However, a higher degree of centralization may not always reduce wage pressures. Cukierman and Lippi (1999), in particular, argued that an increase in the degree of centralization of wage bargaining (as measured by a fall in the number of trade unions in the economy) triggers two opposite effects on real wages:

- The reduction in the number of unions tends to reduce the degree of effective competition among unions; this *competition effect* tends to raise real wages.

- The fall in the number of unions strengthens the moderating influence of inflationary fears on the real wage demands of each union. This *strategic effect* tends to lower wages.

The net effect is thus ambiguous. In addition, it is not always easy in practice to classify wage bargaining systems into completely centralized or decentralized systems. In Argentina in recent years, the government has sought to decentralize collective bargaining agreements from the sectoral to the firm level. In 1995, Mexico also moved toward terminating centralized wage agreements in favor of decentralized bargaining arrangements. In Brazil, by contrast, the evidence seems to suggest that wage negotiations became more centralized in a number of industries during the 1980s (Amadeo, 1994). Whether any of these countries can be rigidly categorized under a particular wage bargaining system is unclear.

Nevertheless, the influence of trade unions in the wage bargaining process can be evaluating by assessing directly their impact on wages, using econometric techniques.[23] Unfortunately, the literature in that area is somewhat limited. Nelson (1994) noted that in Latin America, unions seem to cause wages to rise above the opportunity cost of labor through a combination of union pressure, minimum wage legislation, and wage policies in the public sector. In Taiwan and Korea, the evidence also suggests that unions have limited power in bargaining over wages (Fields, 1994). Other studies have attempted to estimate econometrically the bargaining strength of organized labor, as reflected in the union-nonunion wage differential. Park (1991), for instance, estimated that blue-collar workers in the unionized manufacturing sector in Korea are paid on average only 4 percent more than their counterparts in the nonunionized sector. Panagides and Patrinos (1994) estimated that the union-nonunion wage differential in Mexico was about 10 percent in the late 1980s, which would appear to indicate the existence of some bargaining strength. In interpreting these wage premia, however, some caution is required. If union workers are more productive than their nonunion counterparts (as a result of reduced shirking induced by greater job security, for instance) the productivity differential between the two categories of labor may be large enough to offset the union-nonunion wage differential. In that case, the "union premium" would be economically justified.

14.3.2 Labor Market Reforms and Flexibility

Various economists have argued that **job security provisions**, despite being commendable in principle (to the extent that their objective is the protection of workers against unsafe work practices and unjustified dismissals), have had in practice a variety of adverse consequences.

---

[23] An alternative approach to examining the impact of trade unions on wage differentials, employment, and growth is to use a general equilibrium model and simulation techniques. See Agénor, Nabli, Yousef, and Jensen (2003), who examine the impact of a reduction in union bargaining strength in the "real" version of the IMMPA framework developed by Agénor (2003) and Agénor, Izquierdo, and Fofack (2003).

- Job security provisions have led in some cases to a general loss of profitability, reduced flexibility at the firm level to relative price shocks and shifts in aggregate demand, and distortions in favor of more capital-intensive production techniques.

- Firms tend to become reluctant to take on new employees when faced with high **hiring** and **firing costs**. In addition, employers may become cautious about hiring new workers with contracts of indefinite duration, opting instead to rely on casual labor, subcontracting, or fixed-term contractual relationships. In situations where demand conditions tend to fluctuate, the average level of employment in the affected industries or occupations could thus become lower than optimal.[24]

- High **mandatory severance payments** have effects that are fundamentally similar to a *contingent tax* on labor use; they tend to impede the speed of adjustment in employment in response to adverse sectoral and aggregate shocks.

Tokman (1992), for instance, estimated that during the 1980s labor regulations contributed to an increase in labor costs of about 20 percent on average in a group of Latin American countries. This increase was about equally divided between fringe benefits (such as health insurance and sick leave) and social security contributions. Montenegro and Pagés (2003), in a study of the labor market in Chile during the period 1960-98, found that employment security provisions had an adverse effect on the employment rates of the youth and the unskilled. Heckman and Pagés (2003), who provide a detailed review of existing job ssecurity regulations in Latin America, found similar results for a larger group of countries in that region.

Thus, by inhibiting the reallocation of labor and wage flexibility, labor regulations may lead to higher, and more persistent, unemployment. At the same time, by increasing the incidence of long-term unemployment through reduced labor turnover, regulations may compound the loss of skills among the unemployed and reduce the downward pressure exerted by the unemployed on wages. Moreover, employment security provisions often lead to increased reliance on *temporary labor* and may limit (most notably by raising the cost of dismissing redundant workers) labor mobility across sectors. In effect, as noted by Fallon and Riveros (1989), labor may become a *quasi-fixed factor* of production—thereby raising the short-term costs of adjustment policies. Finally, employment regulations may negatively *reinforce* each other, aggravating their direct effects on the labor market. For instance, it has been argued that high minimum wages and job protection legislation may combine to reduce employment prospects of unskilled workers by pricing them out of jobs and reducing incentives to search and invest in acquisition of new skills. Removing (or reducing the scope of) these

---

[24]The use of repeated temporary contracts to circumvent regulations on hiring and firing may also increase with competitive pressures, as for instance in the aftermath of trade liberalization (Currie and Harrison, 1997).

regulations would reduce nonwage labor costs and eliminate rigidities that impede labor mobility and the efficient allocation of resources. Thus, as argued by Coe and Snower (1997), there are important **policy complementarities** to exploit, and substantial benefits in terms of growth and employment to obtain, by following a comprehensive approach to labor market reforms. In that perspective, labor market reforms must be sufficiently broad (in the sense of covering a wide range of complementary policies) and deep (of substantial magnitude) to have much of an effect.

However, this view has become the subject of renewed controversy in recent years, in both industrial and developing countries. For industrial countries (particularly Europe), there appears to be limited empirical evidence supporting the view that employment protection measures (such as hiring and dismissal procedures) are sources of unemployment persistence. An examination of employment protection measures in Germany, France, and Belgium in the mid-1980s by Abraham and Houseman (1994) found no evidence that changes in such provisions affected the speed of labor market adjustment.[25] In fact, they have argued that the standardization of contractual rules across firms may reduce **information** and **transaction costs**, thereby making the labor market more efficient than it would be otherwise.

In the context of developing countries, high hiring and firing costs may have more limited practical effects than is often thought where (at least segments of) labor markets are highly flexible—precisely in part due to *poor compliance* with existing regulations (Freeman, 1993). Job security provisions may not have any *direct* effects on employment and unemployment, if wages are *de facto* flexible.[26] More generally, as argued by Standing (1991), there may be several benefits associated with employment security regulations:

- They can improve workers' commitment to the enterprise and thus raise *work motivation* and *productivity.*

- They may reduce transaction costs associated with employment by reducing *labor turnover*—a consideration that carries particular importance when productivity rises with on-the-job learning.

- They may improve job and work flexibility, that is, improve the willingness of workers to accept (or initiate) occupational and work environment changes.

- They may induce workers to accept lower wage rises.

---

[25] It should be noted, however, that employment protection measures may only have a second-order impact on labor market flexibility in the presence of other (more important) distortions, such as high minimum wages (as in France) or generous long-term unemployment benefits schemes.

[26] However, if employment protection legislation is not applied uniformly to all firms in all production sectors (or if the degree of enforcement varies according to firm size), it will distort labor allocation and firm size, and foster expansion of the informal economy, as producers strive to avoid taxation.

- They may reduce the probability of *frictional unemployment*, by enabling workers that have been made redundant to get adequate notice and begin searching for alternative opportunities, thereby reducing both individual and social costs of mobility.

In developing countries (where, again, one would expect some types of labor regulations to have limited employment effects, due to extensive noncompliance) it appears that the recent literature has focused almost exclusively on the alleged costs of job security provisions. A more balanced evaluation, based on detailed case studies, appears warranted. In the absence of such studies, it appears difficult to conclude (as many observers have done) that easing employment protection regulations (such as minimum wage laws) would help increase labor mobility. For instance, high minimum wages may lead formal-sector firms to adopt more efficient managerial practices and to invest in labor-saving technology rather than rely on low wages as the main source of profitability. The overall effect in the longer run may be an increase in productivity and competitiveness, which could outweigh adverse short-term effects on employment. Rama (1995), in a study based on cross-section data for 31 countries in Latin America and the Caribbean covering the period 1980-92, found that labor market regulations such as social security contributions, minimum wages, and severance pay requirements did not appear to affect significantly the rate of economic growth.[27] Higher minimum wages appeared, in fact, to be positively correlated with employment growth. In a related study covering a broader sample of almost 120 countries, Forteza and Rama (2001) found that labor market rigidities taking the form of minimum wages and mandatory benefits were not detrimental to growth. These results do cast doubt on the simplistic view that policies aimed at eliminating labor market distortions would necessarily enhance economic performance.[28] Determining the *net cost* of employment security regulations requires taking into account all of their potential benefits.

14.4   Summary

- **Structural policies** operate primarily through the supply side of the economy, by influencing the level of potential output and by affecting the flexibility with which the economy responds to economic shocks.

- The trend toward **trade liberalization** in developing countries (except for sub-Saharan Africa) was fostered by the large body of evidence on the high costs of import-substitution policies (despite high rates of **effective**

---

[27] Rama's results also suggest a negative relationship between the relative size of government employment, the unionization rate, and the rate of growth.

[28] In addition, the distortionary effects of employment protection regulations are often judged by comparison to a situation of perfect competition—a probably inappropriate benchmark. As argued by Blank and Freeman (1994), in a setting where government-induced restrictions tend to overlap, some employment security regulations may offset the inefficiencies and distortions caused by other regulations.

protection) and resource losses associated with **rent-seeking activities**. In addition to the traditional *static* gains from trade, it has been increasingly recognized that there are also *dynamic* gains from free trade (resulting, in particular, from **technological spillovers**), which may lead to a *permanent* increase in the economy's growth rate.

- Although the recent literature on **strategic trade theory** does consider cases in which trade intervention can be an efficient form of intervention, its results are not easily generalizable. Its practical implications have been rather limited.

- Recent evidence on the effects of trade reform on employment suggests that the *level* effect has been limited but that changes in the *composition* of employment (namely, a relative increase in the demand for skilled labor) have been quite pronounced in some cases. Shifts in the structure of employment have been associated with a *worsening of income differentials* between skilled and unskilled workers in many countries.

- One explanation of the movements in relative wages is based on the **Stolper-Samuelson theorem**, which asserts that under the assumptions of the Hecksher-Ohlin-Samuelson model and a regime of unrestricted free trade, a reduction in the domestic price of a good, brought about by a lower tariff or reduced nontariff protection (such as quotas), will lower the real price of the factor of production that is used *relatively intensively* in producing that good. Thus, a reduction in tariff protection on manufacturing goods that are relatively *intensive in unskilled labor* will tend to reduce the real wage received by that category of workers and increase wage inequality. The evidence, however, remains mixed. A high degree of *complementarity* between (imported) capital goods and skilled labor provides an alternative explanation of the increase in wage differentials.

- Obstacles to trade liberalization may result from **status quo bias** associated with *individual uncertainty* regarding the benefits of reform, the high political cost compared with the relatively small efficiency gains associated with trade reform, and the lack of credibility of the reform process, which may create expectations of a future *policy reversal*.

- Another obstacle to trade reform is the fact that it may have an adverse effect on the *fiscal deficit*, as a result of the negative impact of a reduction in import duties on revenue. However, if **exchange market unification** occurs at the same time that tariff rates are reduced, the higher domestic-currency price of imports at the liberalized market exchange rate may have an offsetting effect.

- **Intraregional trade** in developing countries (particularly in Asia and Latin America) has increased significantly during the past two decades. **Preferential trade agreements** have also become more common. Such arrangements can provide significant benefits, because they may generate *positive spillovers* through a broader application of successful innovations. They can also lead to higher *productivity growth* rates by allowing increased specialization.

- At the same time, however, they may conflict with *multilateral, nonpreferential trade liberalization* and can lead to **trade diversion** (a shift in imports from low-cost nonmember countries to higher-cost members) instead of **trade creation** (a shift from high-cost domestic producers to lower-cost producers from other union members).

- The *labor market* plays an important role in the transmission process of macroeconomic policy shocks and structural adjustment policies. It typically consists of three sectors: the **rural sector**, the **informal urban sector** (characterized by self-employment and flexible wages), and the **formal urban sector**. **Disguised unemployment** and **labor market segmentation** (induced either by government-imposed regulations, such as minimum wages, the existence of trade unions, or efficiency considerations by wage-setting firms) prevail in most countries.

- Labor market regulations have a variety of adverse consequences, including loss of profitability, reduced flexibility at the firm level to relative price shocks and shifts in aggregate demand, and distortions in favor of more capital-intensive production techniques. Firms may rely more on temporary employment when faced with high **hiring** and **firing costs**. Such costs also limit labor mobility across sectors.

- At the same time, there are several benefits of employment regulations, including an increase in workers' commitment to the firm that employs them (raising work motivation and productivity), reduced labor turnover costs, improved job flexibility, mitigation of wage pressures, and reduced **frictional unemployment**.

- Assessing the desirability of labor market reforms aimed at enhancing economic flexibility requires a *broad measure* of the benefits and costs of labor market regulations. Available studies have not gone far enough in assessing potential benefits. The limited cross-country evidence that exists does not suggest an adverse effect of labor market regulations on growth, but here again the literature remains scant.

- The agricultural sector in many developing countries plays an important role in providing employment opportunities and a source of revenue for government operations. Tax and pricing policies with regard to agriculture can, therefore, have a profound effect on the labor market and government revenue.

- *Food subsidies* to households are not an efficient means of redistributing income, compared with direct and well-targeted transfers. By artificially lowering prices for food products, subsidies tend to reduce domestic production. Taxation of agricultural exports (often through *marketing boards*), by lowering the profitability of agricultural activities, has also contributed to the creation of distortions and disincentives to produce. In countries where much of the labor force is concentrated in rural areas, the *distribution of income* is greatly influenced by agricultural policies.

- Reforms of agricultural pricing and tax policies have aimed at increasing the profitability of agricultural production, through either the elimination of export duties or a reduction in the gap between world and domestic producer prices of agricultural commodities. However, evidence on the impact of these reforms on rural incomes and income distribution remains mixed.

Appendix to Chapter 14
Reforming Price Incentives in Agriculture

A common argument made in much of the development literature is that agriculture has borne a high *implicit tax* burden, through government food price policy, often to the benefit of urban citizens.[29] In several developing countries, food products (often basic staple commodities) continue to be directly subsidized, and government-controlled marketing boards continue to pay domestic producers significantly less than the world market prices for their output. Such policies are frequently undertaken as a direct attempt to alter the *distribution of income* in the economy, particularly to increase the per capita consumption of low-income groups. There are at least two problems, however, associated with food subsidies:

- They are not an *efficient means* of redistributing income compared with direct and well-targeted transfers.

- By artificially lowering prices for food products, they tend to *reduce domestic production* (thereby increasing imports) and employment in the rural sector, thereby raising migration flows to urban areas and increasing urban unemployment.

The consequence is that subsidization of food products may not only impose a direct drain on the budget but also exacerbate balance-of-payments difficulties and unemployment.

Taxation, by lowering the profitability of agricultural activities, may lead to similar effects. Although export taxes (as documented in Chapter 3) have now lost most of their importance in developing countries, for a long time they represented the main mechanism through which agriculture was taxed.[30] In some countries, agricultural producer prices were kept at artificially low levels; this had an effect on production equivalent to that of a tax on output, and an effect on consumption equivalent to that of a subsidy. Pricing policy can raise significant revenue; for instance, Benjamin and Deaton (1993) concluded that coffee and cocoa pricing policies in Côte d'Ivoire raised as much as 40 percent of total government revenue in the early 1980s.

The experience of sub-Saharan Africa illustrates the dire consequences of excessive agricultural taxation. The tax burden imposed on major export crops through marketing boards has long been considered to be one of the major sources of the region's economic difficulties—stagnation of output per capita and a high incidence of poverty, as discussed in Chapter 10—not only because it created distortions and disincentives in agriculture, but also because it shifted income distribution against the rural sector, where most of the poor are located. As argued by Schiff and Valdés (2001), for instance, inadequate agricultural

---

[29] See Sah and Stiglitz (1992) and Schiff and Valdés (1998) for an extensive discussion.

[30] For a review of explicit and implicit instruments of agricultural taxation in developing countries, see United Nations (1993).

pricing policy, together with currency overvaluations, has led to an **urban bias** in many of these countries.

Partly in response to a better understanding of the cost of these distortions and disincentives, a number of sub-Saharan African countries have in recent years implemented reforms of agricultural pricing and tax policies. These reforms have aimed at increasing the profitability of agricultural production, through either the elimination of export duties or a reduction in the gap between world and domestic producer prices of agricultural commodities. In sub-Saharan Africa, in particular, major areas of reform have been the deregulation of agricultural prices and the dismantling of marketing boards. Price controls have been eliminated, subsidies reduced or eliminated, and prices set by the remaining marketing boards more closely linked with world prices.

However, the available evidence suggests that the impact of these reforms on farm income and income distribution in the region has been so far limited. Estimates by the World Bank (1994, tables A9 and A18) for a group of 27 sub-Saharan African countries indicated that the average *domestic terms of trade* for export crops (as measured by producer prices relative to overall price movements) improved during the periods 1981-83 and 1989-91 in only ten countries. Of course, these results may point toward the possible role of *market imperfections* (such as the fact that markets for export crops are often dominated by a few traders) and shortcomings in the institutional aspects of the implementation of reforms. Nevertheless, a legitimate question is whether policies designed to remove price distortions in agriculture are sufficient to strengthen incentives for production and promote greater income equality. In many cases, reform of agricultural taxation may need to be complemented with land reform, increased provision of infrastructure, development of rural credit markets, and the encouragement of small-scale production methods in order to achieve these objectives.

Reforms in agricultural tax and pricing policies may also have benefits for other sectors as well. To the extent that they lead to a rise in net agricultural and rural incomes, they may reduce incentives to migrate out of agriculture.[31] To the extent that it affects the supply of labor, reduced rural-urban migration has important effects on the determination of urban unemployment, as well as on wages and employment in the urban informal sector. But although these reforms may reduce fiscal imbalances (as is the case with the elimination of subsidies, for instance), they may also have adverse budgetary effects in the short run. The elimination of taxes on agricultural exports, for instance, creates a loss in revenue that may need to be offset by an increase in domestic taxes. In general, therefore, tax reform in agriculture cannot be dissociated from the overall reform of the tax system.

---

[31] The World Bank (1993) noted that the gap between urban and rural incomes is generally much smaller in the high-performing Asian developing economies than that in other developing economies; the level of agricultural taxation has typically also been lower in the former than in the latter.

Chapter 15

Fiscal Adjustment and Financial Sector Reforms

As noted in Chapter 3, many developing countries continue to have a tax structure that is overly complex (in some cases several hundred taxes yielding little revenue) and difficult to administer. High rates of taxation levied on a narrow base have contributed to the expansion of the informal economy, exacerbating fiscal constraints. Unproductive expenditure, often resulting from rent-seeking activities, and an excessive wage bill, resulting from overstaffed public administrations, are widespread. Large **quasi-fiscal operations**, as also discussed in Chapter 3, have contributed in many countries to distortions in fiscal accounts. At the same time, **financial repression**, often resulting from the inability to extract sufficient resources through conventional taxation, continues to generate distortions in the allocation of resources—with adverse effects on rates of economic growth and standards of living.

Growing recognition of the cost associated with these distortions has led many developing countries to implement adjustment programs in which fiscal and financial sector reforms have figured prominently. Issues associated with the design and effects of such reforms are examined in this chapter.[1] Section 15.1 focuses on fiscal adjustment. It begins by reviewing the efficiency loss of taxation and practical guidelines for tax reform. It then considers issues associated with public expenditure control and management, and civil service reform. The role of fiscal decentralization is also assessed. Section 15.2 discusses pension reform, which also affects the public sector. Section 15.3 focuses on one aspect of financial reform, interest rate liberalization.[2] Following a formal presentation of the effects of these reforms on the credit market, saving, and investment, po-

---

[1] For lack of space, privatization of state-owned enterprises is not addressed here. For a discussion of the analytical issues involved, see International Finance Corporation (1995) and Gylfason (1998a). Campbell, White, and Bhatia (1998) review the experience of sub-Saharan Africa with privatization during the early to mid-1990s.

[2] Another aspect of financial reform that is not discussed here involves exchange market unification; see Agénor (1992) and Agénor and Ucer (1999) for a thorough discussion.

tential pitfalls are highlighted. Sections 15.4 and 15.5 discuss sources of financial fragility in general, and identify ways through which countries can strengthen their financial systems.

15.1   Fiscal Adjustment

Fiscal adjustment consists of a variety of policies aimed at improving the efficiency and transparency of public finances. This section focuses on the following aspects of fiscal adjustment: tax reform, expenditure control and management, public sector retrenchment, and fiscal decentralization.

15.1.1   Reforming Tax Systems

Tax reform has been at the heart of adjustment programs in many developing countries. As noted in Chapter 3, the inability to levy sufficient revenue through conventional instruments of taxation has often led to excessive reliance on the inflation tax—a highly distortionary source of revenue. However, conventional taxation may also entail efficiency and welfare costs.

The Excess Burden of Taxation

There are essentially two types of taxes: lump-sum taxes and *ad valorem* taxes. A lump-sum tax, by definition, does not alter relative prices; it therefore generates no efficiency losses. By contrast, an ad valorem tax on any given good does distort the relative price of the good and reduces the welfare of consumers through two channels:

- a direct transfer of income to the government;

- an indirect effect resulting from the rise in the (tax-inclusive) price of the good relative to other goods that are not subject to taxation. This effect can be decomposed into an (indirect) **income effect** and a **substitution effect**—as in the standard microeconomic analysis of a change in a relative price (see, for instance, Varian, 1992).

The *efficiency loss* of a (distortionary) tax, also called the **deadweight loss** or **excess burden** of the tax, can thus be defined as the excess of the reduction in the consumers' welfare above and beyond the welfare loss that can be accounted for by the fall in income resulting from the payment of the tax (see Zee, 1995).[3]

In practice, as is the case with tariffs discussed in the previous chapter, the efficiency loss is measured by the loss in the **consumers' surplus** associated with the tax. To illustrate, consider the case of an economy producing a single

---

[3]More generally, a (distortionary) tax causes an excess burden vis-à-vis a lump-sum tax if it reduces utility in excess of what would have occurred had the tax been collected as a lump-sum payment.

good. In Figure 15.1, the market demand curve is shown as DD, with Q_A the quantity demanded at the initial, pretax price P_A. The consumers' surplus is then the area below DD and above the price line, that is, the triangle BP_AA. Suppose now that the government imposes an *ad valorem* tax at the rate ι, which brings the market price to $P_T = (1+\iota)P_A$. The quantity demanded for the good drops from Q_A to Q_T, and the consumers' surplus falls to BP_TA', or equivalently a reduction of $P_TA'AP_A$ relative to the initial situation. The rectangular area $P_TA'CP_A$, however, measures the total amount of taxes paid, $(P_T - P_A)Q_T$, which is ιP_AQ_T. Hence, the **excess burden** of the tax is the triangle $A'AC$, which measures (as defined earlier) the reduction in the consumers' surplus above and beyond that associated with the payment of the tax. The area $A'AC$ is also known as the **Harberger triangle**.

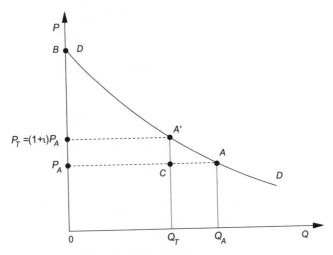

Figure 15.1. The efficiency cost of taxation.

To calculate the area $A'AC$, note that $AC = -(Q_T - Q_A) = -\Delta Q$, and that $A'C = P_T - P_A = \Delta P$. Thus, approximately,

$$\text{area } A'AC \simeq -\Delta Q \Delta P/2.$$

By definition, the absolute value of the price elasticity of the demand for the good before the imposition of the tax is $\eta = -(\Delta Q/Q_A)/(\Delta P/P_A)$. As a result,

$$-\Delta Q = \eta \Delta P(Q_A/P_A).$$

Combining the last two equations, and noting that $\Delta P = \iota P_A$, yields the **Meade formula** already used in Chapter 14:

$$\text{area } A'AC \simeq \eta \iota^2(P_AQ_A)/2, \tag{1}$$

which indicates that the excess burden of the tax varies, in particular, with the squared value of the tax rate.[4]

How, then, should taxes be set if the objective is to minimize efficiency losses? The theory of *optimal taxation* suggests that for efficiency reasons tax rates on consumption goods should be inversely related to the elasticity of demand for each commodity (the so-called **Ramsey rule**) and taxation of production should fall on final goods rather than on intermediate goods (see, for instance, Myles, 1995). As discussed below, value-added taxes attempt precisely to avoid taxing intermediate inputs and instead focus on final consumption.

In practice, however, taxation of goods and services in many developing countries is far from efficient:

- Tax collection is difficult to administer, leading to revenue losses.

- Tax systems continue to be characterized by the imposition of multiple tax rates on both consumption and production activities.

- Inefficiencies often arise because of a *cascading effect*, resulting from the fact that taxes fall not only on production at a given stage but also on taxes paid in earlier stages.

- Taxes often have an adverse effect on international competitiveness because they are often levied at the *manufacturing* stage rather than the *retail* stage, implying that exporters are also subject to them.

In the area of income taxation as well, tax systems in developing countries suffer from severe inefficiencies. Legislation often incorporates multiple exemptions and high rates, as for instance in Cameroon (see Gauthier and Gersovitz, 1997), and it often does not integrate taxation of personal and corporate incomes. Income brackets are usually not indexed on inflation. The implications have been low revenue productivity (as tax evasion became pervasive), inequities reflecting narrow tax bases, and inefficiencies in resource allocation.

Fighting Tax Evasion

Limited capability to administrate the tax system is only one of the reasons why tax evasion is a widespread phenomenon in developing countries. The theoretical literature on tax evasion emphasizes that the level of taxes itself and the shape of the tax schedule are major factors affecting the decision to evade.[5] It follows two main approaches: the **expected utility maximization** (EUM) approach, developed by Allingham and Sandmo (1972), and the **expected income maximization** (EIM) approach proposed by Srinivasan (1973).[6]

---

[4] Formula (1) is not without problems; in particular, as discussed by Zee (1995), it provides a correct approximation only in the case where the market demand curve is approximately linear, as drawn in Figure 15.1. It remains, however, widely used in practice.

[5] It is common to distinguish tax avoidance from tax evasion; the former is legal, whereas the latter is not. From an economic point of view, however, the distinction is less meaningful, because both types of activities tend to have similar fiscal effects.

[6] See Andreoni, Erard, and Feinstein (1998) for a detailed review of these models.

The EUM approach assumes that the taxpayer has two options:

- to declare his or her *total* actual income, and thus pay the full amount of the taxes due;

- to declare *less* than total actual income—which implies facing a nonzero probability, π, of being detected and penalized.

Given these two options, the taxpayer maximizes his (or her) expected utility, $E(U)$. Let Y denote the taxpayer's actual income (assumed exogenous), $0 < \iota < 1$ the statutory tax rate on income (assumed constant), X the income reported to the tax administration, and $0 < \eta \leq 1$ the penalty rate that the taxpayer must face on unreported income, $Y - X$, if detected; expected utility can thus be written as

$$E(U) = (1 - \pi)U(Y - \iota X) + \pi U[Y - \iota X - \eta(Y - X)]. \tag{2}$$

The taxpayer chooses reported income, X, to maximize expected utility, Equation (2). Assuming **decreasing absolute risk aversion** (see the appendix to Chapter 2), Allingham and Sandmo showed that the optimum level of reported income, X^*, responds as follows to changes in ι, η, and π:

$$dX^*/d\iota \gtrless 0, \quad dX^*/d\eta > 0, \quad dX^*/d\pi > 0.$$

The first result implies that a rise in the statutory tax rate on income has an ambiguous effect on the reported value of income. The reason is the interaction between **substitution** and **income effects** associated with a change in the tax rate:

- The substitution effect is *negative* because an increase in ι makes it more profitable (at the margin) to evade taxes. Reported income therefore tends to fall.

- The income effect, by contrast, is *positive* because a higher ι lowers (disposable) income; under decreasing absolute risk aversion, this tends to reduce tax evasion and to increase reported income.

If the degree of absolute risk aversion is assumed constant, rather than increasing, the income effect would disappear, and a rise in the statutory tax rate would unambiguously reduce reported income.

The second and third results imply that a rise in the penalty rate, η, or the probability of detection, π, has an unambiguously positive effect on optimum level of reported income and thus a negative effect on tax evasion, as measured by $Y - X^*$. These effects hold regardless of whether the degree of absolute risk aversion is constant, decreasing, or increasing.

The EIM approach assumes that the objective of the taxpayer is to maximize the expected value of his income, $E(Y)$, after taxes and (possible) penalties. The taxpayer is thus, in contrast to the EUM approach, assumed to be **risk neutral**.

Following Srinivasan (1973), let $0 < x < 1$ be the proportion by which income is unreported, $\tau(\cdot)$ the *tax function* based on the reported value of income—Y if total income is reported, or $(1-x)Y$ if evasion occurs—and $h(x)$ the *penalty function* on tax offenders, which depends on the proportion of income that goes undeclared. Thus, the quantity $h(x)xY$ is the income penalty assessed on the taxpayer if he is caught evading. Formally, the taxpayer chooses the level of reported income so as to maximize

$$E(Y) = (1-\pi)[Y - \tau[(1-x)Y]] + \pi[Y - \tau(Y) - h(x)xY].$$

Suppose that the tax function $\tau(\cdot)$ is a positive, increasing, and convex function of declared income, that is, $\tau > 0$, $0 < \tau' < 1$, and $\tau'' \geq 0$. The tax system is therefore **progressive**. Suppose also that the penalty function $h(x)$ is a positive, increasing, and convex function of the proportion by which income is unreported; thus, $h > 0$, $h' > 0$, and $h'' \geq 0$.[7] Under these assumptions, Srinivasan showed that the optimum proportion of unreported income, x^*, responds as follows to changes in π and Y:

$$dx^*/d\pi < 0, \quad \left.\frac{dx^*}{dY}\right|_{\pi \text{ given}} > 0.$$

The first result indicates that an increase in the probability of detection lowers the proportion of undeclared income. The second result indicates that, given a progressive tax function $(\tau'' > 0)$, and for π given, the larger the level of income, the larger the optimal proportion of income that is undeclared. This result, however, holds only when the probability of detection is given; Srinivasan showed that if π is an increasing function of income and the tax rate is proportional (so that $\tau'' = 0$), the proportion of understated income will *fall* as total income rises.[8] More generally, the source of differences in the qualitative predictions of the EUM and EIM models lies in their treatment of the taxpayer's objective function—not in differences in the treatment of taxation and penalties (proportional in one case, progressive in the other). The Allingham-Sandmo model, which explicitly accounts for attitude toward risk (and therefore excludes a monotonic relation between expected income and utility), can be viewed as a more general approach.

The EUM and EIM approaches have been extended in a number of directions (see Cowell, 1990; Pyle, 1991; and Andreoni, Erard, and Feinstein, 1998). There is general consensus that *penalties*, if properly enforced, can deter tax evasion.[9] This is an important consideration when designing sanctions and penalty systems in the context of tax reforms, as discussed later. There is also agreement that a sufficiently high *probability of detection* tends to reduce the propensity

---

[7] Imposing $\tau'' \geq 0$ and $h'' \geq 0$ are necessary in Srinivasan's model to ensure the existence of an optimum solution.

[8] Srinivasan's analysis also implies that an increase in the penalty rate lowers tax evasion and increases reported income, as in the EUM approach.

[9] Besley and McLaren (1993) discuss the role of wage incentives for tax inspectors in reducing tax evasion, whereas Garoupa (1997) offers a general discussion of the theory of optimal law enforcement.

to evade. However, several theoretical contributions have shown that the relationship between an increase in *statutory tax rates* and tax evasion can be either positive or negative; the outcome depends, in particular, on the manner in which penalties are assessed and the shape of the tax schedule. Yitzhaki (1974), for instance, showed that if the penalty imposed on evaders is levied on the evaded tax liabilities (rather than on the amount of unreported income, as assumed by Allingham and Sandmo), an increase in the tax rate will unambiguously reduce evasion. The reason is that in this alternative case the penalty rate will increase *proportionally* with the statutory tax rate, ι. A rise in ι has therefore no substitution effect (as discussed earlier), only a pure income effect. Also using the EUM approach, Koskela (1983) found that a compensated increase in the tax rate raises tax evasion if penalties are imposed on the amount of income evaded, whereas it reduces tax evasion if penalties are imposed on the amount of tax evaded.[10] When penalties are imposed on undeclared income, the negative income effect associated with an increase in the statutory tax rate is offset by a lump-sum transfer from the government, leaving only the positive substitution effect. On the contrary, when penalties are levied on evaded tax liabilities, the amount of penalty will increase proportionally with the tax, as argued by Yitzhaki (1974); an increase in the statutory tax rate has therefore no substitution effect, only a negative income effect.

Guidelines for Reform

During the 1980s several developing countries implemented far-reaching reforms of their tax systems. Simplifying the tax structure and improving the efficiency, equity, and neutrality of these systems have been key objectives of reform in these countries.

Thirsk (1997) summarized the experience of a group of eight countries (Bolivia, Colombia, Indonesia, Jamaica, South Korea, Mexico, Morocco, and Turkey) with tax reform during the 1980s and early 1990s. Although these countries faced very different initial conditions (in terms of both macroeconomic and structural indicators) prior to reform, they all aimed at the same broad objectives:

- reduce the allocative distortions of the tax system, notably by reducing incentives for rent seeking and tax evasion, and broaden its application;

- improve compliance, in order to not only reduce (marginal) tax rates but also generate higher tax revenue over time;

- simplify the tax structure in order to reduce administrative requirements and enforcement costs.

---

[10] In Koskela's analysis, a compensated increase in the tax rate is a rise in ι that is accompanied by a lump-sum transfer that is such that the amount of tax revenue expected by the tax authority remains unchanged.

In all countries, tax rates on both corporate and personal incomes were reduced significantly. Income tax bases were broadened in a variety of ways— including reduced reliance on tax incentives, elimination of exemptions, and greater use of presumptive methods of taxation. A broad-based sales tax (typically a value-added tax, with exemptions for either basic necessities or sectors that are hard to tax) has become a key source of revenue. A good example is Colombia, whose tax reform program during the period 1980-92 led to an increase of 4 percentage points of GDP in the revenue collected by the central administration.[11] The first major step in the reform program occurred in 1983, and was aimed at reducing double taxation (of both enterprises and individuals) and increasing tax incentives for saving and investment.

An important lesson of these experiences, as emphasized by Thirsk (1997, p. 30), is that in developing countries *broad-based indirect taxes* may often be easier to design and implement than broad-based income taxes as a result of a variety of constraints—including a large informal sector (which makes it difficult to assess levels of production and income) and powerful interests that tend to reduce the base of the personal income tax. A somewhat similar conclusion was reached by Burgess and Stern (1993) in their review of the experience of some of the same countries as well as a few others (Colombia, Indonesia, Jamaica, Korea, Mexico, Sri Lanka, and Turkey) with tax reform during the 1980s: the reform of indirect taxation was in general more successful than that of direct taxation, in part because indirect taxes, being less visible, tend to encounter less political resistance than direct taxes.

There is indeed considerable scope in many developing countries to enhance revenues without worsening distortions and reducing efficiency, by broadening the tax base and improving tax collection and tax administration. To encourage taxpayers to voluntarily comply with their tax obligations, there is general consensus that penalties are more effective than a high probability of detection to deter tax evasion. Theory and empirical evidence also support the intuitive view that lower penalties applied consistently are more effective in deterring tax evasion than high penalties applied fairly infrequently (see Pyle, 1991).

Another aspect of reform of the tax structure involves a significant reduction in personal and corporate income tax rates and the imposition of strict limitations on ad hoc exemptions that tend to narrow the tax base and reduce efficiency. Lower personal income tax rates, in particular, help to

- promote a more equitable tax system in countries where, because of inadequate tax administration, high marginal tax rates are applied in an ad hoc and discriminatory fashion;

- reduce the size of the informal economy (by reducing incentives to evade taxes) and improve allocative efficiency.

In sum, the "ideal" tax system for a typical low- or middle-income developing country would have the following characteristics (see Stotsky, 1995):

---

[11] Other countries also recorded significant increases in their tax revenue-GDP ratios in the aftermath of reform.

- Heavy reliance on a broadly based sales tax, such as the **value-added tax**, with one or two rates and minimal exemptions, and excise taxes on petroleum products, alcohol, tobacco, and perhaps a few luxury items. Small production units should be excluded from coverage to lower collection costs and a system of *presumptive assessment* should be used instead (Cnossen, 1991).

- No reliance on export duties, except as a transitory alternative to income taxation.

- Reliance on import taxation for protective purposes only—because the domestic sales tax is assigned the revenue-raising function—with a low average rate and a limited dispersion of rates to minimize effective rates of protection and reduce incentives for smuggling.

- An administratively simple form of the personal income tax, with exemptions limited to allowances for dependents, a relatively low top marginal rate, an exemption limit large enough to exclude individuals or households with modest resources, and a substantial reliance on withholding.

- A corporate income tax levied at only one moderate-to-low rate, with depreciation and other noncash expenditure provisions uniform across sectors and minimal recourse to incentive schemes for new ventures.

It is important to realize that the type of reforms that would bring about this tax system may have significant *distributional implications*:

- A simplified tax system reduces opportunities for tax evasion. Together with the elimination of special treatments, they tend to reduce the benefits enjoyed by the more influential and higher-income groups.

- Broadening the base of consumption or income taxes may lead to lower tax pressure on middle-income groups that are taxed more heavily to begin with, because they are easy to monitor, for instance public sector employees in the formal sector. This should improve income distribution.

- A more neutral tax system, to the extent that it encourages investment, may lead to the creation of new job opportunities that may benefit the poor.

In addition, it must be recognized that there can also be *regressive* effects associated with tax reforms:

- Reducing marginal income tax rates benefits higher-income individuals and corporations.

- Value-added taxes are taxes on consumption; they tax less those who save more, that is, higher-income individuals.

- The elimination of tax exemptions for basic goods and reductions in tax rates on luxury consumption goods hurt the poor and benefit richer households.

- The elimination of special tax exemptions for labor-intensive firms in particular production sectors may have an adverse effect on job creation and raise poverty.

Finally, it should be noted that tax reform may affect *short-* and *longer-term* economic prospects in *opposite directions*. The elimination of an export tax on a commodity such as *cocoa*, for instance, would in the short run tend to reduce public sector revenue and to raise the fiscal deficit—with possibly inflationary consequences. At the same time, however, the removal of the tax tends to increase the domestic price of cocoa, which would not only reduce domestic consumption but also encourage cocoa producers to expand output. This, in turn, may raise exports and lead to an improvement in the trade balance. Thus the microeconomic aspects of fiscal policy (and the possible *trade-offs* that are involved) must be taken into account in the design of stabilization programs.

15.1.2 Expenditure Control and Management

As noted in Chapter 6, fiscal adjustment is often characterized by excessive and disproportionate cuts in public investment and expenditure on materials, supplies, and maintenance relative to other types of expenditure. Such cuts may have adverse effects on growth, as discussed in Chapter 12.[12] The source of fiscal imbalances, however, is often elsewhere, most notably in large increases in the public sector wage bill. More generally, fiscal deficits and inefficiencies in the management of public sector resources often result from the lack of control over all four major categories of spending—government consumption (including wages and salaries), public investment, transfers and subsidies, and interest payments on the public debt. Thus, the issue that often arises in the conduct of fiscal policy is not only to maintain the *level* of expenditure on key infrastructure projects and high-priority spending on health and education, but also to ensure the overall *quality* of budget outlays. In turn, improving budgeting and expenditure control systems may play an important role in this process.

Public finance experts regard an efficient public expenditure management system as containing the following elements (see Premchand, 1993):

- A *transparent budget* that integrates current and capital expenditure plans and relies on efficient appraisal techniques to decide among alternative expenditure options;

---

[12]Nonlinearities are quite important in this context. As also noted in Chapter 12, at high levels of taxation, a further increase in taxes is not necessarily conducive to higher growth rates—even when the resources taken away from the private sector are invested productively by the government.

- Aggregate *expenditure ceilings*, with effective control over expenditure during the year, coordination of domestic- and foreign-financed expenditure, and effective management of cash and public debt;

- A *reporting system* that compiles clear, reliable, comprehensive, and timely data on budget execution.

The public expenditure management system also needs to embed the budgetary process in an appropriate *medium-term macroeconomic framework*, comprising a medium-term, fiscal-policy forecasting component capable of addressing issues such as the sustainability of public debt (see Chapter 3). In practice, however, very few developing countries have been able to implement a system along these lines, mainly because of administrative and human capital constraints.

15.1.3   Civil Service Reform

In many developing countries government wage and employment decisions are determined more by political considerations than by conventional economic factors (namely, the marginal productivity of workers). As noted earlier, when faced with budgetary pressures, it is often easier politically for governments to cut investment outlays or maintenance expenditures than to fire public sector workers. An unstable political climate may lead to increases in employment or higher wages to attract followers (prior to elections, in participatory democracies) or to retain them (by rewarding key followers). Public sector employment has also been used to offset the effect of adverse shocks on the labor market, in part to avoid growing political dissent.

In part because of large and unsustainable fiscal deficits, downsizing of the public sector workforce has become in recent years a key policy issue in the developing world. Lienert and Modi (1997) for instance examined the process of civil service restructuring in sub-Saharan Africa between the mid-1980s and the mid-1990s. Their analysis suggested that during that period nominal wage bills declined on average—particularly so in CFA franc countries, after the devaluation of 1994. To a large extent, however, this decline resulted from a substantial and almost continuous fall in real wages (since 1991 in non-CFA franc countries and since 1994 for CFA franc countries). The number of civil servants did not change much on average, although some progress was made in CFA franc countries after 1994. In many cases, *voluntary retirement* was encouraged and attractive *severance packages* (based on length of service and, in some cases, the retiree's age) were offered. One problem confronted by many countries was that eligibility for severance packages was not conditional on performance, and many highly skilled workers ended up leaving the civil service.

How to alter or design severance packages in a way that induces only poor performers to leave remains a challenge in many countries. A recent analytical overview of some of the issues involved was provided by Rama (1997*b*). The point of departure of his analysis is the observation that *individual productivity* is often difficult to observe in government administration. Thus, identifying the truly redundant workers is also complicated. In such conditions, severance pay may be a potentially *perverse selection mechanism*—in the sense that it may lead to a "wrong" composition between those who stay and those who leave.

To show this, consider the following example provided by Rama (1997*b*). Suppose that there are two sectors in the economy, the public and the private sectors. The number of workers is also given; they are all identical, except in their degree of *aversion to effort*. Suppose also, for simplicity, that there are only two levels of effort aversion, so that workers are either *productive* or *unproductive*.[13] Suppose that any worker who leaves (voluntarily or involuntarily) his or her job in one sector is immediately rehired in the other sector. Thus, there is no (transitory) unemployment. Assume also that private sector firms are effective at monitoring effort; all workers employed there are therefore productive. In contrast, the public sector cannot effectively monitor the level of effort; workers can, if they so choose, be unproductive. The problem is how to identify these unproductive workers.

The first step in the analysis consists in comparing the welfare loss of both types of workers in case of separation. In the above example, both types of workers would earn the same income in the public sector. Because the level of effort is difficult to measure, public sector pay tends to be based on *observable characteristics*, such as education and years on the job, and both types of workers are identical in that respect. Moreover, both types of workers would earn the same income out of the public sector as well, because private sector pay depends on productivity, and monitoring ensures a uniform level of productivity across workers. The change in *income* is therefore the same for both types of employees. But the change in *effort* is not. The effort level remains unchanged for the productive workers, whereas it increases for unproductive ones. The total welfare loss is therefore larger for the latter. In such conditions, if severance pay is used to induce voluntary separations, productive workers would be the first ones to leave, whereas unproductive workers would be the last ones. There is therefore a **perverse selection** effect.

The extent and composition of downsizing depends on the amount of severance offered to induce voluntary departures. In the example considered, there are three possible outcomes.

- The package offered can be less than the loss in income of the productive workers. None of these workers would then leave. However, none of the unproductive workers would leave either, because their welfare loss (in terms of income and effort) is even larger.

- The package could be generous enough to offset completely the welfare loss to unproductive workers. Because the loss to the productive workers is smaller, all workers would then accept the offer and leave.

---

[13]The argument could be easily generalized to the case in which there is a continuum of effort levels.

- In between these two possibilities, the package could be higher than the welfare loss to productive workers, but lower than that of unproductive workers. In this case, only the latter would stay.

The *net social benefit* from public sector downsizing differs in each of these three alternatives, but no ranking is valid under all circumstances. In the second and third possibilities, private sector output increases whereas public sector output decreases. Both the increase in private sector output and the decline in public sector output are larger in the second case, because more people are reallocated across sectors. The decline in public sector output could be similar in the second and third cases if the level of effort of unproductive workers was very low to begin with. In turn, this implies that the net social benefit in the second case could be higher than in the third case. It could also be negative in both cases, which implies that offering severance across the board (that is, indiscrimately to all workers) may reduce efficiency.

Various mechanisms have been proposed to mitigate the adverse selection problem that arises when individual productivity is unobservable. In essence, these mechanisms try to find ways, through **self-selection**, to separate productive workers from unproductive ones. In practice, however, they remain difficult to implement, as noted by Rama (1997*b*).

15.1.4 Fiscal Decentralization

In recent years, a number of developing countries have begun to decentralize spending and revenue-raising responsibilities from national or central levels of government to subnational levels.[14] This shift can be viewed as reflecting two main factors (Ter-Miniassan, 1997):

- the general tendency of political processes to move toward more democratic and participatory forms of government, which attempt to make political leaders more accountable to their constituencies for their actions and decisions;

- the attempt to ensure a closer correspondence between the level, composition, and quality of goods and services provided by governments and the preferences of beneficiaries or constituents.

From the point of view of macroeconomic management, the process of decentralization may provide some potential benefits. Decentralizing spending responsibilities to the level of government that is most closely associated with potential beneficiaries, for instance, may increase the efficiency with which public sector resources are allocated and used—assuming, of course, that these sublevel government institutions are themselves sufficiently competent.

Decentralization may also, however, complicate significantly the conduct of macroeconomic policy (Ter-Miniassan, 1997):

---

[14]In most cases, the central government has retained direct administrative control over foreign borrowing by subnational governments.

- Giving subnational governments too much latitude to tax may excessively reduce the number of tax instruments available for macroeconomic management by the central government.

- Even if subnational governments are limited in their ability to tax and borrow, changes in the *composition* of their expenditures—toward, for instance, higher transfers to consumers or unemployment benefits—can affect aggregate demand and the balance of payments in ways that may conflict with the macroeconomic policy targets set by the central government.

The solution to the latter problem is that expenditures that have a large impact on demand should remain under the control of central governments. The solution to the first is more complicated. Clearly, arrangements that assign all taxing powers to the central government are undesirable, because they imply no connection between the ability to spend and revenue-raising responsibilities. The solution, in practice, is a *revenue-sharing arrangement*, which assigns to each level of government its own source(s) of revenue and provides for various types of intergovernmental transfers to bridge any deficit between revenue and expenditure assignments.

The viability of such arrangements requires, however, a high degree of *policy coordination* among the various levels of government. In addition, because most major taxes are typically assigned to the central government, whereas substantial and growing expenditure responsibilities are devolved to regional and local governments, sizable **vertical imbalances** (pretransfer fiscal deficits) frequently emerge at the level of subnational governments. There are also **horizontal imbalances**, which result notably from the fact that the revenue-raising capacity of subnational governments varies across regions. Designing a robust system of *intergovernmental transfers* is crucial not only to redistribute resources within a country but also to ensure that limits on borrowing by subnational governments can be set and properly enforced.

Decentralization can also lead to *bigger*, and thus *less efficient*, governments. Stein (1997), in particular, found in a study focusing on Latin America that the political distortions associated with decentralization may lead to soft budget constraints. Imposing hard budget constraints on subnational governments requires ensuring that proper limits are in place on vertical fiscal imbalances—as measured by the ratio of intergovernmental transfers from the central government, including tax sharing, over total revenues (own plus transferred) of the subnational level—by proper assignment of revenue bases (on the basis of the degree of efficiency in collection) and by limiting the degree of autonomy in borrowing by lower-level jurisdictions.

15.2   Pension Reform

Reforming pension systems has been high on the policy agenda of a growing number of developing countries since Chile's pioneering privatization program in the early 1980s. The first part of this section examines the basic features of pension plans. The second develops a simple analytical framework for understanding how the design of pension regimes (together with the structure of household preferences) affects saving, whereas the third examines some of the recent evidence on pension reform in developing countries.

15.2.1 Basic Features of Pension Systems

Pension systems differ in the way they finance and provide pensions, whether they fix *benefits* or *contributions*, and in whether they are run by the state or by the private sector. Until recently, pension systems were mostly state run in developing countries and offered benefits that were determined by law rather than lifetime contributions.

Pension plans may be either unfunded "pay as you go" (PAYG), partially funded, or fully funded. Most public plans in the developing world remain either PAYG or partially funded; Chile's plan (which is discussed below), was a notable first exception.

In a funded system, each working generation accumulates savings to provide for its own retirement. Unfunded, defined-benefits systems operate on a **pay-as-you-go basis** and transfer resources from the current contributors to the beneficiaries. Resources are often collected through *payroll taxes* on employers or direct contributions by workers. Payroll tax rates are in principle adjusted when needed to ensure adequate balance between *current revenue* and current payment obligations. Reserves are maintained only to finance temporary shortfalls in revenue. By contrast, with a funded system, the tax rate is set so as to ensure equality between the expected present value of benefits and the *expected present value of contributions* over an essentially indefinite future.

A further distinction is between defined-benefits and defined-contributions plans. A **defined-benefits plan** typically defines plan participants' benefits as a function of salary and work history. Let B be the value of the pension, N the number of years of coverage, and Y pensionable income; a standard formulation for an earnings-related pension is

$$B = bYN,$$

where b is the **replacement ratio**, that is, the ratio of the pension benefit, B, to the measure of income earned during the contribution period, YN. In practice, N is typically subject to a maximum of 30-35 years, whereas Y is usually an average of income over some subperiod within the contribution period, generally near the end of working life. If the replacement ratio varies inversely with the level of income, the pension plan will have redistributive effects. Most earnings-related pension plans do have a redistributive component because most have some combination of minimum and maximum pensions and contribution levels.

A **defined-contributions plan** does not define the benefit; plan participants, upon retirement, get back their contributions plus their accumulated return, with the pension benefit taking the form of one lump-sum payment or a series of lump-sum payments, or an annuity (generally indexed on the consumer price index). Most public pension plans are defined-benefits plans rather than defined-contributions plans; Chile, again, is an exception. A defined-contributions plan is fully funded by definition; if its investment experience is poor, the average pension benefit will be reduced. A defined-benefits plan may be either funded to some degree or unfunded. Its "fundedness" is never perfect, in that any calculation of the actuarial soundness of a plan is based on uncertain assumptions, especially as to the rate of return to plan assets. Whereas the replacement ratio is, in principle, known in a defined-benefits plan, a defined-contributions plan, by definition, cannot guarantee any particular ratio.

Let B denote the average pension, ι_p the payroll tax rate (assumed to be the only source of funding for the pension plan), L the number of contributors, w the contributions base (the average wage), and P the number of pensioners. **Cash-flow equilibrium** of a PAYG plan requires the following:

$$B \cdot P = \iota_p(w \cdot L), \quad \text{or} \quad \iota_p = (P/L)(B/w).$$

Thus, the required contribution rate varies directly with the **dependency ratio**, P/L, and the **average replacement ratio**, B/w. As the dependency ratio rises, working generations may face large increases in payroll taxes in a PAYG system. Such increases may not only be unpopular, they may also have an adverse effect on employment, private investment, and growth—thereby mitigating their overall effect on fiscal revenue. Alternatively, the impact of a higher dependency ratio can be mitigated by an increase in the retirement age in line with life expectancy, a reduction in the average replacement ratio (that is, the ratio of pensions to wages), or by switching toward less generous *pension indexation formulas* (which would imply a lower weight attached to wages, as opposed to inflation). A more drastic option is to replace the PAYG system with a funded system—but this may entail significant transition costs. The generation under which the reform is implemented needs to pay not only for the current generation of pensioners, but must also save enough for its own retirement.

15.2.2 Pension Regimes and Saving: A Framework

The life-cycle model described in Chapter 2 provides a convenient starting point for studying the impact of pension regimes on private saving. Recall that in its simplest form the model implies that consumption is a function only of the interest rate (with typically a very low elasticity in practice) and lifetime wealth—defined broadly to include not only real and financial assets but also the expected value of future income from human capital (labor). Changes in the pattern of disposable income over time *per se* have no effect on consumption and saving; as a result, the propensity to save out of current income will vary over an individual's life, being high in middle age (when earnings are high) and low or negative in retirement. The implication of the life-cycle model for the design of pension systems is straightforward: in order to affect private savings, such systems must affect the wealth of those participating in it—either by affecting the average wealth of contributors, by redistributing wealth *across* age groups with different propensities to save, or by redistributing wealth *within* members of the same age group with different propensities to save. Unless that happens, pension regimes will end up affecting the *distribution* of national saving between the public and the private sectors, but not its total amount. For instance, the increase in public saving resulting from an across-the-board increase in the contribution rate to a funded public pension plan, in the absence of the distributional effects identified above, may well be exactly offset by a reduction in private saving.

As discussed in Chapter 2, however, there are a number of reasons why the life-cycle model, in its simple form, may not be applicable in a developing-country context. Binding borrowing constraints, for instance, may result in a close correlation between changes in current income and consumption, resulting in lower saving. Uncertainty about future income, and the inability to rely on an extended family when old, may lead to precautionary saving. Accordingly, to illustrate the impact of pension regimes and pension reform on savings, this section presents an overlapping-generations model, along the lines of Blanchard and Fischer (1989, chap. 3), that accounts for imperfect capital markets and imperfect information about the future.[15]

Formally, consider an economy in which individuals live for two periods and have a lifetime utility, U, given by

$$U = u(c_t) + \frac{u(c_{t+1})}{1 + \beta}, \tag{3}$$

where $\beta > 0$, c is consumption, and $u(\cdot)$ is the instantaneous utility function, characterized by $u' > 0$, $u'' < 0$. Individuals work only in the first period of their lives, supplying labor inelastically and earning a wage w_t. They consume part of their labor income and save the rest, investing their savings to finance their second-period consumption.

The saving of the young in period t, s_t, generates the capital stock that is used in $t + 1$ in combination with the labor supplied by the young generation in that period. The number of individuals born at time t and working in that period is N_t. Population growth is given exogenously at rate n.

Firms behave competitively and produce output using a production function with the constant returns to scale, $Y_t = F(K_t, N_t) = K_t^\alpha N_t^{1-\alpha}$, where $0 < \alpha < 1$. Output per worker is therefore given by $y_t = f(k_t) = k_t^\alpha$, where k is the capital-labor ratio. The production function satisfies the Inada conditions (see Chapter 11) and firms take the wage rate, w_t, and the rental price of capital, r_t, as given when maximizing profits.

Each individual maximizes (3) subject to

$$c_t + s_t = w_t,$$

---

[15]Lindbeck and Persson (2003) develop a more general framework to analyze the impact of pension regimes and pension reforms on labor supply and savings.

$$c_{t+1} = (1 + r_{t+1})s_t.$$

The first condition shows the allocation of wage income to consumption and savings. The second condition indicates that individuals (who do not work in the second period of their life) consume all their savings (principal and interest) in retirement.

The first-order condition for optimization is

$$u'(w_t - s_t) - \frac{(1 + r_{t+1})u'[(1 + r_{t+1})s_t]}{1 + \beta} = 0, \tag{4}$$

which yields a saving function of the form

$$s_t = s(\overset{+}{w_t}, \overset{?}{r_{t+1}}), \tag{5}$$

where $0 < s_w < 1$ and the sign of s_r is ambiguous, as a result of offsetting **income** and **substitution effects** (see Chapter 2).

Assuming that capital does not depreciate, the first-order conditions for profit maximization by firms take the familiar form (see Chapter 11):

$$(1 - \alpha)k_t^\alpha = w_t, \quad \alpha k_t^{\alpha-1} = r_t. \tag{6}$$

The equilibrium condition of the goods market can be expressed equivalently as the equality between saving and investment, that is, the stock of capital at $t + 1$ must be equal to the savings of the young generation at t:

$$K_{t+1} = N_t s_t,$$

that is, noting that $N_{t+1} = (1 + n)N_t$ and using (5):

$$(1 + n)k_{t+1} = s(w_t, r_{t+1}). \tag{7}$$

From these equations, one can derive a dynamic relation between k_{t+1} and k_t. As shown by Blanchard and Fischer (1989, p. 112), stability requires that

$$\left| \frac{dk_{t+1}}{dk_t} \right| = \left| \frac{s_w \alpha (1 - \alpha) \tilde{k}^{\alpha-1}}{1 + n + s_r \alpha (1 - \alpha) \tilde{k}^{\alpha-2}} \right| < 1,$$

a condition that requires, in particular, the marginal propensity to save out of wage income, s_w, to be sufficiently small.

Three types of pension reform are analyzed: the introduction of funded and unfunded social security systems, and the replacement of an unfunded system with a funded one (that is, a defined-contributions plan). Consider first the case of the introduction of a *fully funded* system. In such a regime, the pension fund (or, more generally, the government) collects in period t contributions of d_t from the young and acquires physical capital with the proceeds. It also pays benefits to the old (whose contributions were invested in period $t - 1$) in an amount $b_t = (1 + r_t)d_{t-1}$. Equations (4) and (7) thus become

$$u'[w_t - (s_t + d_t)] - \frac{(1 + r_{t+1})u'[(1 + r_{t+1})(s_t + d_t)]}{1 + \beta} = 0, \tag{8}$$

and

$$(1+n)k_{t+1} = s_t + d_t. \tag{9}$$

Comparing Equations (4) and (7) with (8) and (9) reveals that if k_t solves the former set of equations, it will also solve the latter, as long as $d_t < (1+n)k_{t+1}$. That is, as long as the required contribution under the fully funded scheme does not exceed the level of voluntary saving that would exist without the pension scheme, the introduction of a fully funded scheme does not affect the level of private saving. Individuals earn the same return on pension savings as on any other form of savings and are therefore indifferent between the allocation of s and d. They simply adjust their voluntary saving s to take into account any mandatory savings d.

Consider now the introduction of an *unfunded* system. In that case, the young individual's first-period income again falls by d_t, but now the benefits paid in period t (to the old) are equal to the contributions collected during the same period; that is, $b_t = (1+n)d_t$. Put differently, if each individual's contribution to the pension fund is constant over time (as is the case in the steady state), the gross rate of return on pension contributions is only $1+n$ rather than $1+r$. Equations (4) and (7) thus become

$$u'[w_t - (s_t + d_t)] - \frac{(1+r_{t+1})u'[(1+r_{t+1})s_t + (1+n)d_t]}{1+\beta} = 0, \tag{10}$$

and

$$(1+n)k_{t+1} = s_t. \tag{11}$$

Differentiating Equation (10) with respect to the contribution rate (and assuming that $d_{t+1} = d_t$) yields

$$\frac{\partial s_t}{\partial d_t} = -\left[\frac{u''(x_t)(1+r_{t+1})^2 u''[\cdot]}{1+\beta}\right]^{-1}\left[u''(x_t) + \frac{(1+r_{t+1})(1+n)u''[\cdot]}{1+\beta}\right] < 0,$$

where $x_t = w_t - (s_t + d_t)$, and $[\cdot]$ refers to the argument of u' in the second term on the left-hand side of (10). Differentiating Equation (11), using the **implicit function theorem**, yields

$$\frac{\partial k_{t+1}}{\partial d_t} = -\frac{\partial s_t/\partial d_t}{1+n+s_r\alpha(1-\alpha)\tilde{k}^{\alpha-2}} < 0.$$

The above results indicate that both the private saving rate and the per capita stock of capital fall in response to the introduction of an unfunded pension scheme.

Suppose now that an existing, unfunded PAYG system is replaced by a fully funded regime. The pension fund must borrow from the young generation (at the market interest rate) in order to finance the payment of benefits to the current old generation. But because the value of these benefits is not affected by the regime change, the amount the fund borrows per individual in the new system, z_t, must be the same as the amount it would have collected from the young under the previous regime, d_t. Thus, Equations (4) and (7) become

$$u'[w_t - (s_t + z_t)] - \frac{(1 + r_{t+1})u'[(1 + r_{t+1})(s_t + z_t)]}{1 + \beta} = 0, \quad (12)$$

and

$$(1 + n)k_{t+1} = s_t. \quad (13)$$

Suppose that, as before, $d_{t+1} = d_t$; then Equations (12) and (13) are identical to (10) and (11), except that the portion of savings going to finance the retirement consumption of the currently old generation earns a return of r_{t+1} instead of n. This increase in the inframarginal rate of return will generate a pure income effect that will tend to discourage current-period saving. Thus, the switch from a PAYG system to a fully funded regime generates an immediate income effect that lowers private saving.

Assuming that no fiscal consolidation accompanies the pension reform, the government will have to continue to borrow to repay its debt. Thus, to repay in period $t + 1$ the funds it borrowed in period t, the government will need to borrow $z_{t+1} = (1 + r_{t+1})z_t/(1 + n)$ from each young individual in period $t+1$. The first-order optimality conditions for a young individual in period $t+1$ become

$$u'[w_{t+1} - (s_{t+1} + z_{t+1})] - \frac{(1 + r_{t+2})u'[(1 + r_{t+2})(s_{t+1} + z_{t+1})]}{1 + \beta} = 0, \quad (14)$$

and

$$(1 + n)k_{t+2} = s_{t+1}. \quad (15)$$

If the interest rate is greater than n (the most common case), the stock of debt per worker increases in each period, leading (in partial equilibrium) to a decrease in savings, and thus a lower capital stock. From Equation (14), increases in z are fully offset by decreases in s (given that individuals are indifferent between buying government debt and investing in capital) until voluntary savings are exhausted. However, this is a partial equilibrium result in that it treats the interest rate as given. As the stock of capital falls, the rate of interest will rise and labor income will fall, both of which will influence the level of saving, as shown for instance in (4). To assess the general equilibrium effects of an increase in public borrowing, one can differentiate equation (15) with respect to z_{t+1} to give

$$\frac{dk_{t+2}}{dz_{t+1}} = \frac{\partial s_{t+1}/\partial d_{t+1}}{1 + n + s_r\alpha(1 - \alpha)\tilde{k}^{\alpha-2}}.$$

This result implies that, as long as s_r is nonnegative, the effect of an increase in government borrowing per worker is an unambiguous reduction in the stock of capital.[16]

In this scenario, public borrowing grows at the rate $(1 + r_t)/(1 + n)$; this is unsustainable as long as $r_t > n$ (see the discussion in Chapter 3). Financing

---

[16] The condition on s_r is of course sufficient, not necessary, to obtain $dk_{t+2}/dz_{t+1} < 0$.

the transition with debt leads to spiraling government deficits, even though the underlying primary fiscal balance is constant. Although the decline in the capital stock will lead to an increase in the interest rate and generate additional savings, the explosive path of z_t will eventually exhaust output. Accordingly, an increase in the primary fiscal surplus will be required to ensure stability. A switch from a PAYG to a fully funded scheme may thus encourage saving in this indirect sense.

In summary, the above analysis has shown that

- the introduction of a fully funded pension scheme should have no impact on the level of private savings unless the mandatory contribution rate is very high;

- the introduction of an unfunded PAYG system will tend to decrease private saving;

- the replacement of an existing PAYG system with a fully funded regime will not typically increase saving, unless it is accompanied by a fiscal consolidation.

15.2.3   Recent Evidence on Pension Reform

Public pension systems in many countries continue to offer generous coverage, as measured by high replacement ratios, and extensive protection to retirees. However, there has been growing recognition that such systems suffer from serious deficiencies. In particular, the lack of a direct relationship between benefits and contributions has imposed serious strains on government budgets in some countries—in part exacerbated by the relative increase in the number of retirees due to population aging. In others, the use of payroll taxes to generate revenue has distorted labor markets and encouraged tax evasion.

Partly as a result, several developing countries (particularly in Latin America) have moved toward **fully funded pension schemes**, both public and private. The country that pioneered many of these reforms is Chile. As a result of the funding problems developed by the country's pay-as-you-go government pension scheme in the late 1970s, pension reform began in 1981, at a time when the fiscal surplus was sufficiently large to finance the transition to a fully funded system, and after the retirement age was increased to 65 for men and 60 for women. A privatized savings plan requiring workers to place 10 percent of their earnings in one of a number of highly regulated intermediaries was also introduced. Participants pay a contribution that is a fixed percentage of their gross salary to an account registered in their name with the pension fund of their choice, as well as a management fee with a fixed percentage and a flat component. Upon retirement, contributors may choose among several combinations of lump-sum payments (or phased withdrawals) or an indexed annuity.[17]

---

[17]However, in contrast to a defined benefit system, uncertainties regarding the length of the working life, the duration of retirement, and the return on invested contributions has made pension benefits somewhat unpredictable.

Following Chile, six countries in Latin America reformed their pension systems in the 1990s. But reforms in some of these countries have moved away from exclusive reliance on an individual capitalization system. Peru (1993) and Colombia (1994) opted for a dual pay-as-you-go, fully funded scheme in which the government system and the new private pension funds have to compete with each other. Argentina (1994) and Uruguay (1996) adopted a system in which the two are complementary; and Mexico (1997) is maintaining the public system solely as a guarantor of benefits for those currently enrolled. In all cases, reforms have entailed major corrections of the financial weaknesses and imbalances between contributions and benefits provided by the government pension system.

Countries in East Asia have used fully funded schemes for a number of years. Some have used variants of the defined contribution system, in part as a tool of development policy. The pension systems in Malaysia and Singapore, for instance, rely primarily on fully funded, defined-contribution schemes, where compulsory contributions are maintained in a central fund with separate accounts for individual contributors. Upon retirement, benefits consist of accumulated contributions plus interest and take the form of a lump-sum payment. Compulsory coverage is generally restricted to wage earners in the formal sector, and those with low wages or with short employment records receive limited coverage.

The experience of developing countries that have reformed their pension system suggests that the combination of a *mandatory, fully funded scheme* with a *supplementary, defined-benefit arrangement* may provide the best strategy to reduce pressures on the government budget while at the same time providing adequate protection for retirees. The mandatory, fully funded component of the system may lead to higher saving by making households more aware of the need to save for the future, and through forced saving (see Chapter 2) the investment needs of pension funds are also likely to foster the development of domestic capital markets. To the extent that pension reform leads to higher saving, it is likely to have a direct, positive effect on growth (see Chapter 12). The development of domestic capital markets that results from the reform may also lead to higher investment and thus indirectly to higher output growth and income per capita—which in turn may lead to higher saving rates.

What is the evidence on these effects? At an informal level, although it is possible that voluntary private saving may be reduced as compulsory saving increases, the experience of Malaysia and Singapore suggests that pension systems have contributed to high national saving rates. In the case of Chile, a comprehensive empirical analysis by Corbo and Schmidt-Hebbel (2003) showed that pension reform contributed substantially to growth during the period 1981-2001, through higher saving and investment, fiscal adjustment, and factor productivity gains—the latter by fostering the development of domestic financial markets and improving labor market performance. The theoretical predictions, therefore, appear to be largely corroborated by the facts: the shift from an unfunded to a funded pension scheme, supported by an adequate fiscal policy, is likely to lead to higher saving rates and positive externalities (through labor and financial markets) that may accelerate improvements in standards of living.

15.3   Interest Rate Liberalization

Broadly defined, financial liberalization entails, on the one hand, the abolition of explicit controls on domestic interest rates and restrictions on the allocation of credit by commercial banks, and, on the other, the elimination of restrictions on capital movements. The present section begins by using a simple graphical framework to discuss issues associated with interest rate liberalization and the elimination of credit restrictions. It then examines the potential pitfalls associated with interest rate liberalization.

15.3.1   A Simple Framework

The traditional analysis of interest rate repression and liberalization is illustrated in Figures 15.2 to 15.4 (see Caprio, Hanson, and Honohan, 2001). Figure 15.2 illustrates how financial repression reduces loanable funds, loans, and efficiency of credit use; Figure 15.3 the effects of a cross subsidy under financial repression; and Figure 15.4 the impact of liberalization.

In Figure 15.2, the supply of loanable funds, SS, is shown as being positively related to the deposit interest rate, R. With no restrictions on credit allocation and interest rate setting, and with full information, banks would allocate credit to borrowers who are ranked according to the demand curve LL. The equilibrium occurs at point E, which corresponds to an interest rate R^*, for the "last" borrower, that is, the one not showing any interest rate premium for risk. The use of a single interest rate is of course a gross simplification—in the real world different borrowers are charged different rates. The figure also neglects the issues of moral hazard, adverse selection, and bankruptcy problems that can lead to credit rationing, as discussed in Chapter 4. Under credit rationing, borrowers would not receive all the credit they want, and the interest rate charged might be substantially below what borrowers are willing to pay.

Imposing a ceiling on the interest rate on deposits, say at r', reduces the amount of loanable funds available, to an extent that depends on the elasticity of supply. A mechanism also must be chosen to allocate the reduced supply of loanable funds, which is now Q_2. One possibility is to let the lending rate increase to R' (corresponding to point B on the demand curve). A spread would then emerge between the lending and deposit rates, equal to $R' - r'$. The resulting "rent," measured by the rectangular area $ABR'r'$, can be divided up between the banks and the government (through taxes, bank license fees, and so on). There is also a loss in efficiency in the full information model, which is measured by the **Harberger triangle** ABE. The efficiency loss will be lower the smaller the degree of interest rate repression is, and the more inelastic the supply of deposits is. Another mechanism is to assume that at the deposit rate r', the government provides a direct allocation of credit. The recipients of credit end up therefore "capturing" some of the rents associated with financial repression.

Alternatively, if financial repression consists in the imposition of a low ceiling on *lending* rates, rather than deposit rates as described above, political pressures may develop to access these cheap funds. Financial repression is thus likely to lead also to directed credit allocation, which may end up reducing efficiency beyond the conventional loss measured by Hargerger triangles. This is because directed credit allocation is likely to exclude some of the borrowers who would receive credit under a market allocation, and replaces them with others who can generate political support but whose use of credit is less productive. The lower productivity may manifest itself in lower returns, which may nonetheless be sufficient to cover the lower lending rate, or higher nonperforming assets.

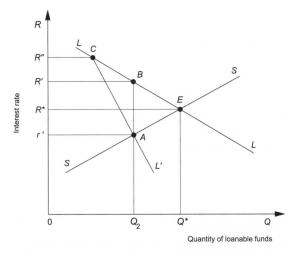

Figure 15.2. Financial repression and the supply of loanable funds.

These issues are illustrated in Figure 15.2 by assuming that a ceiling on the lending rate is set at r', and a credit allocation process is put in place. For instance, the government may require a higher percentage of credit to go to some sectors than would be the case with a market allocation, with the remainder of the credit to be freely allocated by the banks. In Figure 15.2, the actual recipients of credit are described by a *pseudo demand curve for credit*, LCL', which ranks the actual recipients of credit under the nonmarket allocation by what they would have been willing to pay.[18] The lower productivity of credit under the nonmarket allocation process, because some borrowers who would be willing to pay high rates are "crowded out" by the forced allocation of funds to other borrowers, is shown graphically by the portion of the pseudo demand curve CL', which lies below the unconstrained demand curve, CL. The kink in the curve (at point C) reflects the assumption that all borrowers who can pay more than R'' receive credit.

The triangle ABC is the additional loss in efficiency, compared to the market allocation of loanable funds under a ceiling deposit rate (which entails, as noted earlier, a loss equivalent to ABE), bringing the total loss to ACE. Note that this efficiency loss occurs even if the supply curve of loanable funds is ver-

---

[18] For simplicity the process is assumed to equilibrate the rate to the "last" borrower with the (cost-adjusted) deposit rate.

tical. As usually occurs with the ceiling rate or nonmarket credit allocation, Figure 15.2 also shows the elimination of the potential spread between what the most productive borrowers would be willing to pay, R', and the ceiling rate on deposits. Of course, the deposit ceiling rate itself may have to be adjusted downward as part of the process of limiting any reduction in the profitability of banks, because of poor performance by the borrowers who receive credit under the nonmarket allocation process.

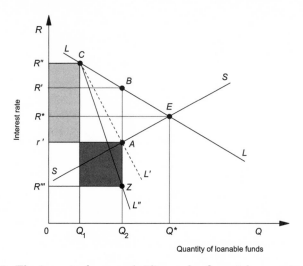

Figure 15.3. The impact of cross subsidies under financial repression.

Typically, all credit is not allocated by directed credit processes at a single, ceiling loan rate, as assumed for simplicity in Figure 15.2; usually, some borrowers receive a cross-subsidy from other borrowers. This means that the credit allocation process generates a *redistribution of income* from those who pay a high rate to those who pay a low rate. The allocation process is also likely to generate a further loss of efficiency, because additional, low productivity activities typically will receive credit.

Figures 15.3 illustrates this process. Half the available credit is assumed to be allocated by a market determined process and interest rate, the other half is allocated to a directed credit pool, where borrowers pay a fixed, below-market rate. For simplicity, the allocation process is assumed to be capable of forcing anyone who can pay the market determined rate, R'', to pay it, and to offer the remaining credit to the favored borrowers at rate R'''. However, the allocation mechanism does not permit banks to fully discriminate between the highest productivity investments and those that can simply pay the directed credit rate R''', as is usually the case. Those receiving directed credit get a subsidy equal to the spread $r'R'''$, multiplied by the volume of directed credit, Q_1Q_2; those without access pay the spread $r'R''$ multiplied by OQ_1, which covers the subsidy. The amounts received and paid (the two shaded areas) are equal because of the need to cover the intermediaries' average cost of funds,

r'. Also, note that the banks' inability to exclude some additional borrowers results in additional inefficiency. That is, the pseudo demand for funds under the cross-subsidy allocation process falls from CL' to CL''. Hence, the cross subsidy process results in an additional loss of efficiency, compared to the single-ceiling loan rate, equal to the triangle CAZ.

Note that the cross-subsidized, directed credit lending rate need not be below the deposit rate, because the supply curve/cost of funds includes the reserve requirement and intermediation costs as well as the deposit rate.[19] However, in practice, some directed credit rates have sometimes been set below deposit rates. In such conditions, the demand for loanable funds effectively becomes infinite—the borrower can simply take the loan to the "deposit window" and get a positive return. In this case, the distributional effects of directed credit become dominant. It becomes almost impossible to ensure that the directed credit is used for its stated purpose, such as providing investment and working capital funds for agriculture or small-scale entrepreneurs.

Consider now the impact of financial liberalization (the easing of directed credit restrictions and interest rate ceilings) on the credit market. Traditional analysis of this policy suggests that it permits a better allocation of credit and a possible rise in loanable funds. This is shown in Figure 15.4, which reproduces Figure 15.2 and ignores cross subsidies.

Raising the deposit rate from r' to, say, r'' increases the amount of funds available, from Q_2 to Q_1. Moreover, allowing financial institutions more choice in allocation credit rations out some of the low-productivity borrowing, replacing it by higher productivity borrowing. For instance, if directed credit were eliminated and allocation was made solely by the financial institutions, then the nonmarket directed credit allocation process, represented by the portion CL', would be eliminated and borrowers would pay R'''. The misallocation of resources is reduced to the triangle $A'B'E$, from ACE. Quite importantly, this analysis suggests that, although interest rate liberalization can raise deposit and average lending rates, it can also generate an increase in the volume of credit and the productivity of its use.

There are other positive effects of interest rate liberalization, to the extent that it translates into positive real interest rates (Fry, 1997, p. 755):

- Positive real rates attract savings that were previously held outside the formal financial sector (gold held under the mattress, for instance), which increases the resources available to the financial system, raising the level of investment and stimulating growth.

- Positive real rates tend to deter entrepreneurs from investing in low-yielding projects that are no longer profitable at the higher cost of loanable funds; hence, the average return to, or efficiency of, aggregate investment tends to increase.

---

[19] Graphically, R''' lying below r' does not mean that R''' is necessarily below the average deposit rate, because SS includes the costs of intermediation and reserve requirements.

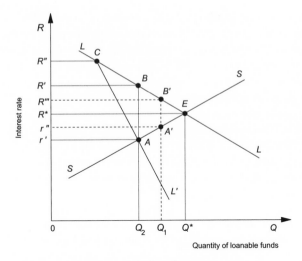

Figure 15.4. The impact of financial liberalization.

The increase in both the quantity and the quality of investment have positive effects on the growth rate of output. Interest rate liberalization is also an important step toward the development of an interbank market and a secondary market for government securities, which are necessary, as noted in Chapter 4, for controlling the supply of money through indirect monetary policy instruments, such as open-market operations.[20]

15.3.2 Potential Pitfalls

The liberalization of domestic interest rates has been at the core of programs of financial reform in many developing countries—in large part as a result of the growing evidence on the adverse effects associated with financial repression. Demetriades and Luintel (1997), for instance, found that financial repression—as measured by a composite index based on various types of interest rate controls, reserve and liquidity requirements, and directed credit—had an adverse effect on financial development (as measured by the ratio of bank deposits over GDP) in India during the period 1960-91. Using firm-level panel data for 12 developing countries (Argentina, Brazil, Chile, India, Indonesia, Korea, Malaysia, Mexico, Pakistan, Philippines, Taiwan, and Thailand), Galindo, Schiantarelli, and Weiss (2001) found that financial liberalization (as measured by various indicators of financial depth) led in the majority of cases to an increase in the efficiency of allocation of investment funds (as measured by the share of investment going to firms with a higher marginal return to capital).

There are, however, a number of potential dangers associated with interest rate liberalization.

---

[20] Although seldom discussed, the order in which interest rates must be freed—taking into account the overall fragility of the financial system—may also be an important consideration. In practice, countries have often started by liberalizing interbank market rates first, then lending rates, and last deposit rates.

- As indicated in Chapter 2, some empirical studies (notably by Ogaki, Ostry, and Reinhart, 1996) concluded that the real interest elasticity of total savings is not significantly different from zero for *low-income* countries. Moreover, even in *higher-income* countries, these studies found that the effect of interest rate changes on saving, although significant, remains small. Interest rate liberalization may thus have only a limited impact on aggregate savings. In a review of financial liberalization episodes in the mid-1970s in Chile and Malaysia, and in the early 1980s in Indonesia, Korea, Malaysia, and Turkey, Atiyas, Caprio, and Hanson (1994) indeed found that higher real interest rates had a small effect on saving rates, except in cases where the change in interest rates was from a severely negative level to a positive one.[21]

- Interest rate liberalization may have an adverse effect on the *fiscal deficit*; a rise in interest rates may increase the cost of borrowing and the interest payments on the domestic public debt. In the presence of fiscal rigidities (namely, the inability to reduce expenditure and increase conventional tax revenue), the government may be induced to rely more heavily on the **inflation tax** (see Chapter 6).

- Once interest rates are liberalized, endogenous constraints in the credit market, such as those resulting from **imperfect information**, can remain significant barriers to efficient credit allocation (Gibson and Tsakalotos, 1994). Specifically, the Stiglitz-Weiss model discussed in Chapter 4 suggests that even under a regime of free interest rates, banks may not provide loans to potential borrowers that are perceived to be too risky. The persistence of credit rationing may hamper the expansion of private investment.

- The high real interest rates that are sometimes associated with financial liberalization (as a result for instance of greater bank competition for deposits) may make the financial system more vulnerable to crises by worsening the problems of **adverse selection** and **moral hazard**, and by raising the **incidence of default** on loan commitments.

- To the extent that interest rate liberalization is accompanied by an easing of *liquidity constraints* (through easier access to consumer credit, for instance), it can lead to a temporary expansion of consumption and a *reduction*, rather than an increase, in saving rates. In turn, the credit boom may lead to asset price bubbles, a weakening of bank balance sheets (because of inflated values of collateral), and greater vulnerability of the financial system to adverse shocks, as discussed next.

---

[21]However, they also noted that other aspects of financial reform (such as an increase in bank branches, or a greater menu of financial products) may have a positive effect on savings rates.

15.4   Sources of Financial Fragility

The experience of the 1980s and 1990s has made it abundantly clear that financial liberalization (above and beyond interest rate liberalization), though potentially beneficial, can be risky if undertaken in a fragile financial environment. This section reviews the main sources of financial fragility in developing countries, whereas the next section considers various measures aimed at strengthening the financial system and limiting the risks of financial instability associated with liberalization. The analysis, overall, emphasizes two major preconditions for successful financial sector reform: a stable macroeconomic environment and a proper system of bank prudential regulation and supervision.

15.4.1   The Nature of Banks' Balance Sheets

As noted in Chapter 4, banks remain at the center of the financial system in most developing countries. Any analysis of the sources of financial fragility must therefore pay particular attention to the conditions under which banks operate.

In general, banks are perceived to be more fragile than nonfinancial firms primarily because they tend to have low capital-to-assets ratios (that is, they are *highly leveraged*), a low cash-to-assets ratio (as a result of *fractional reserve banking*), and high ratios of short-term demand deposits to total liabilities—which create a high potential for a bank run. As discussed later, prudential supervision in many countries has failed to ensure that these **fragility ratios** remain at reasonable levels.

The severity of banking sector problems can be measured in terms of the ratio of *nonperforming loans* to total loans, the volume of *restructured loans*, and the extent of direct and indirect *government support* for the banking system.[22] The evidence reviewed by Lindgren, Garcia, and Saal (1996), for instance, suggests that (as noted in Chapter 8) a significant number of developing countries experienced severe banking sector problems or full-fledged banking crises during the past two decades. The macroeconomic costs imposed by these problems have been large in terms of efficiency losses in financial intermediation, adverse effects on output, and pressures on public finances, because the resolution costs have been born mostly by the public sector. For instance, the cumulative fiscal and quasi-fiscal costs associated with bank restructuring were in the range of 12 to 15 percent of GDP in Mexico for the period 1994-95, 0 to 17 percent in Venezuela for 1994-96, and 19 to 41 percent in Chile for 1981-85.

A growing body of evidence suggests that key sources of financial fragility and banking sector weaknesses are *microeconomic* and *institutional failings*. These failings include poor management and weaknesses in the legal framework, inadequate supervision, and perverse incentives and moral hazard created by implicit or explicit government guarantees. In addition, *macroeconomic instability* and *premature liberalization* may also have played an important role.

---

[22]However, the ratio of nonperforming loans is not necessarily a good indicator of bank soundness. Banks could be rolling over problem loans, thereby making them look as if they are "performing," while in fact they are not. This is the so-called evergreening problem.

15.4.2   Microeconomic and Institutional Failings

Poor management within financial institutions is often the first source of fragility. Inadequate internal control procedures, concerted lending, insider dealing, and outright fraud have in many cases led to *excessive risk concentration*—a large proportion of loans allocated to a single borrower (related companies or the banks' own managers), a specific region, or a specific industry. The consequence is often a *poor quality* of loan portfolios and a high ratio of nonperforming loans.[23]

Weaknesses in the *legal framework* have compounded the problems of inadequate management and weak corporate governance, in particular by making it difficult for banks to seize, in case of default, the *collateral* pledged by borrowers on their loans. In general, lack of pledgeable collateral (in the form, for instance, of physical assets) acts as a constraint on the ability of firms to take advantage of the greater access to credit markets that financial liberalization is assumed to promote. For instance, using firm-level data for Ecuador, Jaramillo, Schiantarelli, and Weiss (1996) found that financial liberalization did not help to relax financial constraints for small firms—a result that may be related to the inability of these firms to offer sufficient collateral to secure loans. By contrast, Gelos and Werner (2002), using data for the manufacturing sector for Mexico during 1984-94, found that collateral-based lending increased significantly as a result of financial liberalization. As discussed in Chapter 4, the importance of collateral may be the consequence of high monitoring and enforcement costs associated with loan contracts, themselves resulting from a poor legal environment and uncertain property rights.

The absence of effective market discipline (in part resulting from the lack of relevant information about the operations of financial institutions), inadequate prudential regulations, and *supervisory forbearance* have also tended to compound the problem. In many cases supervisors either failed to identify potential weaknesses in banks' balance sheets or did not take appropriate action to force banks to address these weaknesses in a comprehensive and timely fashion. In turn, the *persistence* of these large weaknesses—and inadequate information on the *magnitude* of potential loan losses—affected the effective and uniform enforcement of prudential norms, further delaying the process of strengthening banking supervision and compounding the problems posed by loan losses. As a result, the quality of banks' asset portfolios deteriorated significantly, increasing the vulnerability of the financial system to macroeconomic shocks.

15.4.3   Moral Hazard and Perverse Incentives

The lack of adequate prudential regulation and supervision often leaves too much room for weak financial institutions to take excessive risks (as noted above), leading to inefficient intermediation and creating the preconditions for a potential financial crisis. The temptation for banks to increase the riskiness of their

---

[23]Mismatches between assets and liabilities in terms of either currencies or maturities (as discussed later) can also be viewed as a form of mismanagement.

loan portfolios is in part fostered by the existence of implicit or explicit **government bailout guarantees**, such as **deposit insurance schemes**. Such guarantees create moral hazard problems, that is, weak incentives for banks and borrowers to internalize the consequences of their actions, and may increase the likelihood of a banking crisis ((Demirgüç-Kunt and Detragiache, 2002). These problems tend to be particularly acute when banks and borrowers have low net worth and may be tempted to "gamble" by engaging in high-return but risky projects.[24]

The adverse incentive effects of implicit government insurance were described for instance by Díaz-Alejandro (1985, p. 18) in a classic review of the financial crises of the early 1980s in Argentina, Chile, and Uruguay that followed financial liberalization:

> "Public opinion," including generals and their aunts, simply [did] not believe that the state would (nor could) allow most depositors to be wiped out by the failure of banks and financial intermediaries. It may be that private financial agents, domestic and foreign lenders, borrowers and intermediaries, whether or not related to generals, (knew) that the domestic political and judicial systems (were) not compatible with [the] laissez-faire commitments [that] a misguided Minister of Finance or Central Bank President may occasionally utter in a moment of dogmatic exaltation. When a crisis hits, agents will reason, bankruptcy courts will break down; when . . . everyone (who counts) is bankrupt, nobody is!

The increased riskiness of bank portfolios may turn into actual losses when a price bubble bursts or economic activity slows down sharply—as a result either of a tightening of macroeconomic policies or adverse external shocks. In such conditions, even loans that are fully collateralized can become nonperforming, because the same shock that reduces the borrower's ability to repay may simultaneously reduce the value of the collateral pledged to obtain the loan. For instance, a developer who borrows to invest in real estate and pledges land for collateral would put the lender doubly at risk if property prices experience a sudden collapse. Because banks' own capital generally does not offer sufficient protection against these risks and losses, actual losses often end up being absorbed by the public sector—often at substantial costs, as noted earlier.

The role of **lender of last resort** of the central bank is also a source of moral hazard problems. The rationale for this role is that the central bank should provide liquidity support only to *solvent* but *illiquid banks*, and let insolvent banks fail.[25] The reason is that liquidity support to insolvent banks provides perverse incentives and fails to address underlying problems. Abstracting from the issue

---

[24]Bhattacharya, Boot, and Thakor (1998) provide a detailed overview of the analytical issues that arise in the context of bank regulation, including measures aimed at reducing moral hazard problems induced by the existence of deposit insurance schemes.

[25]A bank is solvent if the value of its assets is greater than the value of its liabilities to depositors and other creditors. A bank is liquid as long as it can meet day-to-day operating expenses and withdrawals. A highly leveraged bank can remain liquid even if it is insolvent.

of whether insolvency problems can be easily distinguished from illiquidity problems in practice, the major problem is that the regulatory authorities cannot credibly commit to such an intervention rule. The reason is the **too-big-to-fail problem**: to avoid a financial crisis, central banks may deviate from their policy and provide liquidity to support large banks, even if they are insolvent. Large banks therefore face perverse incentives.

15.4.4   Macroeconomic Instability

As noted in previous chapters, macroeconomic instability tends to be high in developing countries. This instability is induced by either inadequate economic management by the government (such as **stop-and-go** macroeconomic policies) or a high degree of vulnerability to exogenous (domestic and external) shocks. Such instability has been associated with serious problems in the financial system, primarily in the banking sector.

The effects of macroeconomic instability on banks operate through both the asset side and the liability side of their balance sheets. Macroeconomic volatility (as measured, for instance, by a highly variable rate of inflation) may considerably distort the accuracy of the rates of return calculated by firms, thereby creating cash-flow problems and repayment difficulties.

More generally, banks' *stock* problems (a large share of nonperforming loans in their portfolios) as well as *flow* problems (operational inefficiencies) tend to be exacerbated by economic downturns. In a highly open economy, as noted in Chapter 8, inconsistent macroeconomic policies tend to exacerbate the volatility of short-term capital flows. To the extent that these flows are intermediated through the banking system, an abrupt reversal can cause a **liquidity crisis** and force banks to default on their obligation to convert deposits into cash at par—a decision that may in turn exacerbate macroeconomic instability. The reasons may be a **maturity mismatch** (the deposit base is short term, whereas loans are often for a longer term) or a **currency mismatch** (deposits may be in a foreign currency, whereas loans are denominated in the domestic currency). Again, as noted in Chapter 8, greater financial openness and the possibility of abrupt shifts in market sentiment have led to renewed emphasis on maintaining a stable macroeconomic environment. Weak and inefficient banking systems are less able to cope with volatile capital flows and exchange market pressures, and more likely to propagate and magnify the effects of financial crises occurring elsewhere (as a result of **contagion effects**). The implication, again, is the need to strengthen standards for banking supervision, as discussed in the next section.

15.4.5   Premature Financial Liberalization

There is also evidence that financial liberalization has exacerbated the financial weaknesses present in developing countries. The data compiled by Williamson and Mahar (1998) for more than 30 industrial and developing countries during the 1980s and early 1990s indicated that in more than half of them financial liberalization was followed by a financial crisis. At a more formal level, Demirgüç-Kunt and Detragiache (2001) constructed an index of financial liberalization (reflecting mostly the deregulation of bank interest rates) for a group of more than 50 developed and developing countries for the period 1980-95 and found that, everything else equal, banking crises were more likely to occur in liberalized financial systems. This relationship was stronger in countries where the institutional environment was weak, particularly in the area of prudential regulation and supervision of financial intermediaries and contract enforcement mechanisms.

Various channels may account for the link between financial liberalization and financial crises. An important element is the fact that prior to financial liberalization, banks and other financial institutions in a number of countries often enjoy substantial *rents*. Financial liberalization leads to *increased competition* (as noted earlier) for resources and thus a higher marginal cost of funds, as measured by interest rates on bank deposits. In turn, higher funding costs lead to higher lending rates. To compensate for the adverse effect of higher lending rates on the demand for credit, banks often respond by *increasing the riskiness* of their loan portfolios—a strategy that may be exacerbated by the existence of implicit or explicit government bailout guarantees, as also noted earlier. The rapid expansion of loans on banks' balance sheets often tends to be associated with a growing concentration of risk exposure to particular sectors (such as real estate) and groups. Again, realized and expected losses impose significant burdens on fiscal and, in some cases, monetary policy as policymakers attempt to preserve financial stability. More generally, if banks are, to begin with, *insolvent*, interest rate liberalization may exacerbate **adverse selection** and **moral hazard effects**, because these banks may be willing to borrow at a very high cost to avoid illiquidity.[26]

The experience of sub-Saharan Africa provides a useful illustration of the potentially adverse effects of premature financial liberalization. As noted by Pill and Pradhan (1997), banks in many sub-Saharan African countries continue to be publicly owned and therefore remain susceptible to government interference—even after controls on credit pricing and allocation have been formally abolished. Moreover, because of the stock of nonperforming loans inherited from the administratively directed lending programs of the prereform period, the solvency of many privatized banks has remained dependent on *subsidized credit* from the central bank, even after liberalization. Because banks have remained dependent on the government, and their lending decisions continue to be subject to its discretion, liberalization has done little to improve credit allocation or deepen financial markets in the region.

Another point emphasized by Pill and Pradhan (1997) is that if *competition* among banks in the newly deregulated financial sector is weak, financial liberalization may result in *lower* real deposit rates rather than higher, positive

---

[26] In countries where financial liberalization was accompanied by a reduction or removal of restrictions on international capital movements, financial intermediaries took an additional risk (*currency risk*) by increasing their foreign exchange exposure and lending in domestic currency to local borrowers.

levels. *Monopolistic banks* can exploit the opportunity offered by the abolition of interest rate controls to widen the margins between their deposit and lending rates to increase profits. Pill and Pradhan argued that the lack of competition explains why in countries like Kenya, Madagascar, and Malawi financial liberalization has in fact led to a *reduction* in the attractiveness of bank deposits to domestic savers, and has so far resulted in little financial deepening in these countries.

These results, of course, do not imply that financial liberalization *per se* should be avoided; rather, what they suggest is that because of its potentially high costs in terms of increased financial fragility, strengthening the financial system is an *important prerequisite* for liberalization to be successful. In cases where administrative constraints are severe (as is the case in many developing countries), a *gradual* process of liberalization may be optimal.

15.5   Strengthening Financial Systems

The foregoing discussion suggests that reforming banking systems in developing countries requires a comprehensive approach addressing not only the immediate stock and flow problems of weak and insolvent banks but also correcting shortcomings in the accounting, legal, regulatory, and supervisory framework.

Bank supervision, in particular, needs to be restructured before financial liberalization in order to cope with the risks that liberalization entails. The globalization of financial markets and the associated increase in the volatility of capital flows has also underscored the importance of strengthening prudential supervision and related information systems in order to deal effectively with interest rate and exchange rate risks, as well as other banking risks, particularly in the context of capital account liberalization.

Strengthening prudential supervision entails a variety of institutional reforms, including establishing an exposure limit on lending to connected parties (most importantly owners and affiliated companies), preventing concentration of credit to single borrowers, and raising *bank capital* to levels commensurate with the volatile macroeconomic environment in many developing countries. **Capital adequacy standards** are particularly needed to compensate for the effect of deposit insurance in weakening market discipline of financial institutions and may be important in mitigating the incentives to take on excessive risk.[27]

In addition to prudential supervision, reforming banking systems in developing countries includes a number of other aspects, such as encouraging better public disclosure of banks' financial condition, adopting strict international accounting standards, upgrading banks' internal controls, and legislation to ensure arm's length (anonymous) credit allocation decisions. It is also important to bring greater transparency to excessive government involvement or ownership in banking systems (as the example of sub-Saharan Africa illustrates) and redesign official safety nets to include safeguards against strong political pressures

---

[27]However, Rochet (1992) argued that such requirements may distort a bank's investment behavior to such an extent that they may make insolvency more, rather than less, likely.

for regulatory forbearance.[28] An important question in this context is how to ensure that regulators have the *proper incentives* to intervene. If regulatory action can be interpreted as a signal that the regulatory agency did not perform properly in the past, the agency has an incentive to *cover up* and be inactive when action is required (Boot and Thakor, 1993).

All these reforms are likely to take time and require adequate administrative capacity. In such conditions, then, there is a strong case for liberalizing the domestic financial system and opening the capital account only gradually, while an adequate system of prudential regulation and effective supervision is being put in place. There is thus a *second-best argument* for maintaining some degree of financial repression and limits on capital inflows through various types of controls during a transitional phase.

15.6 Summary

- *Fiscal reform* is necessary in many developing countries to improve the structure of taxation and the efficiency of tax administration. An important aspect of reform consists of rationalizing and consolidating tax structures to reduce distortionary effects and move toward broad-based consumption taxes. Strengthening public expenditure management is also important.

- *Public sector downsizing* is often a priority in countries facing budgetary pressures. *Severance pay* is a potentially **perverse selection mechanism**. Because workers differ in unobservable ways, offering severance pay across the board creates an incentive for the most productive workers to leave the public sector and for the less productive ones to stay. Severance pay should be offered only to those workers who are targeted to leave, but identifying them can be difficult in practice.

- *Fiscal decentralization* can help to improve resource allocation by bringing taxation and spending decisions closer to voter preferences. It can also help to make governments more accountable. However, it can give rise to coordination problems, which may translate into **soft budget constraints** at the subnational level and large aggregate fiscal imbalances.

- In many developing countries, public pension plans are defined-benefit plans financed on a **pay-as-you go** basis. Saving may increase after the establishment of a pay-as-you-go pension system if it induces workers to begin planning for an earlier retirement. The evidence suggests that the reform implemented in Chile in 1981 contributed significantly to the subsequent increase in private saving, financial deepening, and the higher output and productivity growth rates.

---

[28] As discussed in Chapter 8, regulations affecting the asset and liability positions of domestic financial institutions are prudential measures that limit the exchange rate, interest rate, and maturity risk assumed by these institutions, as well as their exposure to sudden changes in capital flows. They can also be viewed as restrictions on capital movements.

- Advocates of *interest rate liberalization* and abolition of credit ceilings argue that they should lead to an increase in both the quantity of, and the quality of, financial intermediation by the banking system and thereby raise the rates of output and productivity growth. They provide an incentive for borrowers to invest in more productive activities, thereby improving productivity. However, by easing **liquidity constraints**, these measures can lead to a temporary stimulus to consumption and a *reduction*, rather than an increase, in saving.

- Moreover, the real interest elasticity of total savings is not significantly different from zero for *low-income* countries and remains small in *higher-income* countries; interest rate liberalization may thus have only a limited impact on aggregate savings.

- Finally, interest rate liberalization may increase the cost of borrowing and interest payments on the domestic public debt and lead to a higher *fiscal deficit*—with consequent inflationary pressures.

- The perverse nature of the incentive system and regulatory environment is often at the root of banking sector problems in developing countries. The presence of implicit or explicit **government bailout guarantees** (such as **deposit insurance schemes**) creates **moral hazard problems**, that is, weak incentives for banks and borrowers to internalize the consequences of their decisions. Banks, as a result, are often saddled with overly risky loan portfolios.

- *Financial instability* in developing countries can be attributed to a wide range of microeconomic and institutional failings, including poor management, an inadequate legal framework, implicit or explicit government guarantees that lead to excessive risk taking (and often translate into large fiscal and quasi-fiscal costs) and macroeconomic instability.

- *Premature financial liberalization* has also played a role in many countries. Perverse incentives and increased risk taking by financial intermediaries in the aftermath of financial liberalization (which translated into a sharp expansion in bank lending and, in some cases, a growing concentration of loans to particular sectors) have been important sources of financial fragility.

- The speed at which financial liberalization should proceed, the prerequisites for a successful liberalization, and the way financial reforms should be sequenced within an overall reform program are key policy issues. In the absence of improvements in prudential regulation and supervision of the banking system, financial liberalization can be costly and counterproductive. The need for effective prudential supervision may be even greater in a deregulated financial environment than in a regime of financial repression.

- In addition to an adequate regulatory framework, financial liberalization must also be implemented in a stable macroeconomic environment. In particular, to be successful, it may need to be accompanied by *fiscal adjustment* to reduce the need for alternative sources of implicit revenue.

- Other ways to strengthen financial systems include various safeguards that may encourage prudent behavior by banks—including minimum capital standards, criteria for provisioning for nonperforming loans, limits on loan concentration, collateral requirements, and enforcement mechanisms. Financial reporting and disclosure standards are also needed to improve transparency, so that the market and the central bank can play their roles in ensuring financial discipline.

Appendix to Chapter 15
Structural Policy Indices

To assess the effect of structural reforms on economic variables such as growth, employment, investment, and financial depth, some studies have attempted to build a *structural policy index*. A good example is the index devised by Lora (1997) for various countries in Latin America. The index attempts to measure the extent to which structural reforms lead to greater efficiency in resource allocation, essentially by reducing distortions caused by policies that prevent the smooth functioning of markets or that impose large costs on transactions and the production process.

Specifically, Lora's index focuses on five areas, each with a set of indicators taking generally a value between 0 and 1, based on the worst and best observations in the sample:

- *Trade policy*, with indicators consisting of average tariffs (including surcharges) and tariff spreads. Trade restrictions associated with quotas, while often important in practice, are not accounted for, because of lack of information.

- *Tax policy*, with indicators consisting of the maximum *marginal* income tax rates on corporations and individuals,[29] the basic value-added tax rate, and the productivity of the value-added tax (defined as the ratio of the basic rate times actual revenue collected over GDP).

- *Financial policy*, with indicators consisting of whether interest rates on deposits and loans are free to vary, the real level of reserves on bank deposits, and the quality of banking and financial supervision. The latter indicator is based on a discrete and subjective scale, with three possible levels.

- *Privatization*, measured as the cumulative sums resulting from sales and other property transfers since a benchmark period (1988 in Lora's study), as a proportion of average public investment over a previous period (1985-87 in Lora's analysis).[30]

- *Labor legislation*, with indicators of flexibility consisting of criteria assessed on a discrete scale: hiring costs, costs of dismissal after one year of work and ten years of work, overtime pay, and social security contributions.

Indices in these five areas are first calculated as simple averages of the indices for the policy variables considered in each case. The *total structural policy index* is then derived as the simple average of the five indices.

---

[29] An alternative would be to use *average* marginal tax rates, although Lora's measure is more appropriate to assess the effect of taxation on investment and labor supply decisions.

[30] An alternative and perhaps more appropriate measure would be to calculate the percentage of a country's total stock of physical assets held and operated by the private sector. There are, however, considerable practical difficulties in constructing such a measure.

Using this index, Lora (1997) showed that structural reforms have made significant progress in Latin America between the mid-1980s and the mid-1990s—although the timing and pace of reform has varied considerably across countries. Without reforms, Lora estimates that on average the rate of economic growth would have been 1.9 percentage points lower, and income per capita 12 percent lower, than it is at the moment in Latin America. At the same time, however, there appears to remain considerable scope for improvement (particularly in the areas of labor legislation, tax reform, and the regulation and supervision of financial systems), with potentially large effects on investment, growth, and standards of living in the region.

An important limitation of the above index is that it does not attempt to measure in a comprehensive manner the *qualitative* aspects of economic reforms. For instance, it does not capture the fact that although changes in labor legislation may increase the flexibility of firms to hire and fire workers in response to changes in demand, they may reduce at the same time workers' protection and employment stability (as discussed in Chapter 14). In turn, this may affect the supply of labor, saving, and consumption decisions, with feedback effects on growth and employment.

Chapter 16

Aid, External Debt, and Growth

The debt crisis of the early 1980s had a severe impact on the economic performance of many developing countries. In some cases, the lack of access to world capital markets led to a surge in inflationary finance of fiscal deficits, a slowdown in investment, and reduced rates of economic growth.

But although many of the most severely affected middle-income economies were subsequently able to regain access to world capital markets—in part as a result of international initiatives such as the *Brady Plan*—servicing external debt continues to be a key concern for policymakers in low-income countries.[1] The inability of the poorest of these countries (many of them in sub-Saharan Africa) to meet their debt-service obligations has led in recent years to a variety of new proposals aimed at ensuring that the debt burden does not hamper capital formation and economic growth.

This chapter examines various policy issues associated with foreign borrowing, growth, and the process of adjustment in highly-indebted low-income countries. It begins in section 16.1 by examining the effects of foreign aid on the government budget, domestic investment, and growth. Section 16.2 then presents a simple endogenous growth model that captures the links between external debt and capital accumulation in a world of imperfect capital markets, and analyzes the short- and long-run response of the economy to fiscal adjustment.

Section 16.3 discusses the notions of debt overhang and debt Laffer curve, which have proved useful to understand the adverse effect of a high burden of debt on investment and production incentives and to justify debt relief. Section 16.4 reviews various practical measures of a country's debt burden and discusses a more formal approach to assessing that burden, namely, external solvency, which dwells on an open-economy intertemporal budget constraint. Section 16.5 reviews the mechanics of debt reschedulings as well as recent international

---

[1] For a retrospective on the debt crisis of the early 1980s and the performance of the Brady Plan since its inception, see Cline (1995), Bowe and Dean (1997), and Miles (1999).

initiatives aimed at alleviating the debt burden of the poorest countries in the developing world.

16.1   The Effects of Foreign Aid

The effects of foreign aid on the recipient country have been the subject of a vast literature, some of it aptly reviewed by White (1992). These effects include the impact of aid on savings, the government budget and fiscal policy, the real exchange rate and the level of investment, the rate of economic growth, and more recently poverty and the incentives for reform. For instance, it has been argued that aid may lead to a decline in public savings through lower tax revenues, as governments reduce either levels of taxation or collection effort. Various types of **fiscal response models** have indeed been used to estimate the impact of aid on taxes and government expenditure, that is, the *degree of fungibility* of aid (see Franco-Rodriguez, 2000). van Wijnbergen (1986) emphasized that foreign aid can have **Dutch disease effects** (see Corden, 1984). To the extent that aid is partially spent on nontradable goods, it puts upward pressure on domestic prices and may lead to a real exchange rate appreciation. In turn, the real appreciation leads to a reallocation of labor toward the nontradable goods sector, thereby raising real wages in terms of the price of tradable goods. The resulting deterioration in competitiveness may lead to a decline in export performance and an adverse effect on growth.[2]

It has also been argued that shortfalls in aid tend to translate into shortfalls in domestic revenue (Bulir and Hamann, 2003), although the magnitude of this effect may depend on the composition of aid (Gupta (2003)). Others have emphasized that foreign aid may lead to higher growth rates through two channels: by leading to a direct increase in public investment and raising the level of the capital stock or the efficiency with which the existing stock is utilized; and by inducing policy changes that lead to reduced distortions, and thus indirectly stimulate private investment. This latter channel, however, is more debatable, because the donor-recipient relationship may be *noncooperative*. In such conditions, as noted by Svensson (2000), moral hazard problems can lead to aid having little impact on the problems it is intended to alleviate. In particular, aid may simply lead to a relaxation of the budget constraint of the recipient government, without having much impact on the amount of that budget that is used for investment. In countries where the government's incentives to undertake structural reform are indeed subject to a moral hazard problem, conditionality (or outright delegation of part of the aid budget to an external agency) may help to strengthen the impact of aid on growth and poverty reduction. Azam and Laffont (2003) also showed that, under certain conditions, conditionality

---

[2]See Yano and Nugent (1999) for a more detailed discussion of the impact of foreign aid on the priced of nontraded goods. Note also that if there is learning by doing (endogenous productivity) and learning spillovers between sectors, or if aid has a direct effect on public investment in infrastructure, then the longer-run effect on the real exchange rate may be ambiguous. See Torvik (2001) and Adam and Bevan (2003).

may increase the impact of aid on the consumption of the poor.[3]

This section offers a brief review of some of these issues, examining first aid effectiveness and the fungibility problem, the impact of foreign aid on investment and growth, and the cross-country empirical evidence on the impact of aid and growth.

16.1.1   Aid Effectiveness and the Fungibility Problem

One of the main issues that arises in assessing aid effectiveness relates to the so-called **fungibility problem**. The conventional approach to this issue focuses on whether a recipient has the ability to treat aid as resources that can be spent as it wishes. If aid provided by donors to finance a specific activity can be as freely spent as aid provided as general budgetary support, then aid is fully fungible; otherwise it is partially fungible. According to a comprehensive report on aid by the World Bank (1998), while aid generally causes government spending to increase, it is not generally true that each additional dollar of aid results in a one dollar increase in this spending, and this supports the view that aid is (at least partially) fungible. Similar conclusions are drawn with respect to development expenditure. Specifically, the study concluded that although aid causes public investment to increase, only 29 cents of each additional dollar of aid typically goes to this sort of expenditure, with most of the balance being allocated to consumption.

There are two problems with these results. First, they are not reliable. A number of other studies (cited by McGillivray and Morrissey, 2000) found that aid leads to larger increases in investment than in consumption. Second, they focus exclusively on the impact of aid on expenditure. To understand why this could be misleading, consider the following simple example, due to McGillivray and Morrissey (2000). Suppose that the recipient allocates funds to two expenditure items, roads and schools, and that the donor provides aid to a recipient with the understanding that it will be allocated fully to roads. There is *full fungibility* if the recipient allocates the entire amount of aid to schools in the absence of effective restrictions on the use of aid. If the donor attempts to restrict aid to a specific project, there is *partial fungibility*. This may prevent the recipient from allocating aid as it wishes, but the recipient would still be better off compared with the case where no aid is received.

However, this conventional view overlooks two possible channels: aid-financed reductions in tax revenue and income feedback effects. Assuming that the tax revenues allocated to roads fall, expenditure on roads would not increase by the full extent of the aid flow. The conventional approach overlooks this possibility because it concentrates on expenditures rather than on both sides of the budget. There are indeed several empirical studies showing an often strongly negative incremental impact of aid on tax revenue, although calculating the net impact of aid on public finances would require a focus on fiscal deficits. In addition,

---

[3]In practice, however, conditionality is hard to enforce. In a study of net resource transfers to sub-Saharan Africa during the period 1978-98, Birdsall, Claessens, and Diwan (2003) found that aid largely went to countries pursuing inadequate growth policies.

the conventional approach assumes that aid has a zero income multiplier. But aid must have some impact on aggregate income. Suppose that aid results in increased expenditure with respect to both roads and schools, thereby leading to a higher level of national income and higher tax and nontax revenue. Further, suppose also that some portion of these revenues are allocated back to roads and schools, raising spending on both items. Thus, if multiplier effects are sufficiently large and positive, fungibility may not be much of an issue. To estimate the impact of aid on tax revenue (as well as government borrowing) and account for income multiplier effects, various types of **fiscal response models** have been proposed by researchers (see, again, Franco-Rodriguez, 2000). A limitation of this literature, however, is that it presumes the existence of well-defined targets for government expenditure and revenue, and those targets can be difficult to estimate.

More fundamentally, fungibility only indicates that donors and recipients have different views on how expenditures should be allocated. To the extent that aid is treated as general revenue, and assuming constant preferences over time, the initial allocation is a good indicator of the proportions in which aid will be allocated to different areas. If donors approve of the initial and planned allocation, they can grant aid without restrictions. If donors do not approve of the initial and planned allocations, they have two options: they may try to alter the allocation so that fungibility is not a concern, or alternatively they can attempt to constrain the use of aid—a policy that is often difficult to enforce in practice.

16.1.2 Aid, Investment, and Growth

The impact of foreign aid on domestic investment (both public and private) and growth has been the subject of an extensive analytical and empirical literature. A useful framework for analyzing the effects of foreign aid on domestic investment is that of Pedersen (1996), who investigates the way a donor organization should behave if it wants to contribute as efficiently as possible to investment and growth given the preferences and the administrative capacity of the recipient government and other domestic factors. Specifically, using a two-period game-theoretic framework (with the donor giving aid in period 1 to boost domestic capital formation), Pedersen showed that the effect of aid on investment depends critically on how donors choose to intervene in the recipient country's decision-making process. His model is presented below, beginning first with the case without aid.

The Situation without Aid

Consider a two-period economy is which C_1 and C_2 represent average consumption in periods 1 and 2, respectively. The intertemporal distribution of consumption is determined by the government through maximizing the following welfare function:

$$U = \ln C_1 + \rho \ln C_2, \tag{1}$$

where $0 \leq \rho \leq 1$ is a discount factor.

Y_1 and Y_2 denote output in periods 1 and 2, respectively, and are assumed exogenous. Domestic investment in period 1, I, is

$$I = S + R, \tag{2}$$

where S is domestic saving and R the inflow of international credit.

Investment is assumed to be non-negative, which implies that $S \geq -R$. Let $f(I)$ be the return in period 2 to investment in period 1. R is assumed exogenous and $\partial f / \partial I > 1 + r$, where r is the interest rate paid on international loans. For simplicity, it is also assumed that the marginal benefit of investment is constant, $\partial f / \partial I \equiv \eta$. Thus, consumption in periods 1 and 2 is

$$
\begin{aligned}
C_1 &= Y_1 - S, \\
C_2 &= Y_2 + \eta I - (1+r)R.
\end{aligned} \tag{3}
$$

The optimal level of saving, S^*, is obtained by maximizing (1) with respect to S, subject to (2) and (3), that is, by solving:

$$\max_S \ln(Y_1 - S) + \rho \ln[Y_2 + \eta(S + R) - R(1+r)].$$

Solution of this problem yields

$$S^* = \frac{1}{1+\rho} \left[\rho Y_1 - \frac{\bar{Y}}{\eta} \right], \tag{4}$$

where $\bar{Y} = Y_2 + [\eta - (1+r)]R$. From Equation (2), the optimal level of investment is

$$I^* = \frac{1}{1+\rho} \left[\rho Y_1 - \frac{\bar{Y}}{\eta} \right] + R. \tag{5}$$

Substituting (4) and (5) into (3) yields consumption levels in both periods:

$$C_1^* = \frac{1}{1+\rho} \left[Y_1 + \frac{\bar{Y}}{\eta} \right], \qquad C_2^* = \frac{\eta \rho}{1+\rho} \left[Y_1 + \frac{\bar{Y}}{\eta} \right]. \tag{6}$$

Equations (6) indicate that the intertemporal distribution of consumption is determined by the marginal benefit of investment and the discount factor:

$$C_2^* / C_1^* = \eta \rho.$$

The higher ρ and the higher η, the higher the growth of consumption between periods 1 and 2. The optimal solution is illustrated in Figure 16.1 at point Z, which corresponds to the point where the welfare curve U^*, whose slope is $dC_1 / dC_2 = -\rho C_1 / C_2$, is tangent to the intertemporal budget line, whose slope is $dC_1 / dC_2 = -1/\eta$.

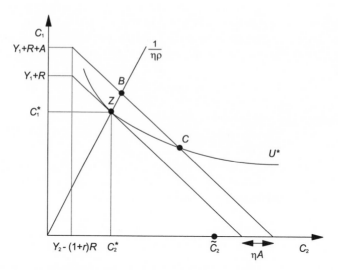

Figure 16.1. Consumption allocation without aid and with active donor behavior. Source: Adapted from Pedersen (1996, p. 428).

The Effects of Aid on Investment

Suppose now that an aid organization decides to help the recipient government in period 1 to increase investment, in order to contribute to growth and consumption in period 2. The inflow of aid is taken to be exogenous and equal to A. The country qualifies for aid if expected period 2 consumption without aid is below a certain level, $\widetilde{C}_2$, or equivalently, investment without aid is below a certain level, $\widetilde{I}$. The consequences of the donor's activities for the country will depend on what "type" the aid organization is, either a **passive Stackelberg leader**, an **active Stackelberg leader**, or a **Stackelberg follower**:

- A passive Stackelberg leader is passive in the sense that it does not intervene in the recipient country's decision-making process.

- An active Stackelberg leader is active in the sense that it intervenes in the recipient country's decision-making process (regarding, namely, the allocation of aid), and a Stackelberg leader in the sense that its decisions are not subject to manipulation by the recipient.

- When the organization is a Stackelberg follower, the aid inflow can be manipulated by the recipient country.

The Passive Stackelberg Leader This type of organization gives aid without conditions and let the government of the recipient country use it in accordance with its own preferences, assumed to be reflected in the welfare function (1). The government takes aid as given and does not adjust its behavior or decisions in order to qualify for aid. Equation (2) becomes therefore

$$I = S + R + A.$$

The non-negativity of investment implies now that $S \geq -(R + A)$. Given that A is exogenous, the levels of saving and investment can be obtained in a manner similar to the case without aid, by maximizing the following equation:

$$\max_{S} \ln(Y_1 - S) + \rho \ln[Y_2 + \eta(S + R + A) - R(1 + r)].$$

The solutions are, for saving and investment:

$$S = \frac{1}{1+\rho}\left[\rho Y_1 - (A + \frac{\bar{Y}}{\eta})\right], \quad I = R + \frac{1}{1+\rho}\left[\rho Y_1 - (A + \frac{\bar{Y}}{\eta})\right] + A, \quad (7)$$

and for consumption in both periods:

$$C_1 = \frac{1}{1+\rho}\left[Y_1 + \frac{\bar{Y}}{\eta} + A\right], \quad C_2 = \frac{\eta\rho}{1+\rho}\left[Y_1 + \frac{\bar{Y}}{\eta} + A\right]. \quad (8)$$

Equations (8) imply that the intertemporal distribution of consumption is the same as in the case without aid, that is, $C_2^*/C_1^* = \eta\rho$. The optimal solution is shown in Figures 16.1 and 16.2 at point B. As long as ρ is less than infinity, A crowds out domestic savings to some extent. Specifically, $\partial S/\partial A = -1/(1+\rho)$ tends to be -0.5 when ρ gets close to 1, and to be -1 when ρ gets close to 0.

Figure 16.2 shows the relationship between A and I as $A(I)|_{pl}$, where the subscript pl stands for "passive leader." From the second equation in (7), this relationship is given by

$$A = \frac{1+\rho}{\rho}\left[I - R - \frac{\rho Y_1}{1+\rho} + \frac{\bar{Y}}{\eta(1+\rho)}\right].$$

The slope of $A(I)|_{pl}$ is thus

$$\left.\frac{dA}{dI}\right|_{pl} = \frac{1+\rho}{\rho}. \quad (9)$$

The second equation in (8) yields a relationship between A and C_2, denoted $A(C_2)|_{pl}$, given by

$$A = \frac{(1+\rho)}{\eta\rho}C_2 - Y_1 - \frac{\bar{Y}}{\eta},$$

whose slope is

$$\left.\frac{dA}{dC_2}\right|_{pl} = \frac{1+\rho}{\eta\rho}. \quad (10)$$

Equation (9) shows that the cost of a one-unit increase in I gets close to 2 when ρ tends to 1, and tends to infinity when ρ tends to 0. Equation (10) indicates that the unit cost of C_2 will be affected not only by the discount factor but also by the marginal benefit of capital. The higher η is, the cheaper (in terms of additional aid) it is to increase C_2 for a given ρ.

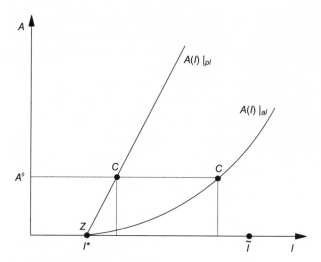

Figure 16.2. Aid and investment with active donor behavior. Source: Adapted from Pedersen (1996, p. 428).

The Active Stackelberg Leader Suppose that now the donor intervenes in the domestic decision-making process, in an attempt to generate more investment than the passive leader. In this case a contract is used to specify the required level of domestic saving, investment and consumption in period 2. For the recipient to accept the contract, the welfare level should obviously be higher than the one without aid. This means that the following constraint has to be satisfied:

$$\ln C_1 + \rho \ln C_2 - U^* \geq 0, \tag{11}$$

where $U^* = \ln C_1^* + \ln C_2^*$. C_1 and C_2 will of course be a function of the terms of contract.

- If A and I enter the contract, $C_1 = Y_1 + R + A - I$ and $C_2 = Y_2 - R(1+r) + \eta I$ from equations (3) and (6).

- If A and C_2 enter the contract, $C_1 = Y_1 - (1/\eta)(C_2 - \bar{Y}) + A$.

Equation (11) is binding because the donor is not willing to give more aid than required to obtain a specific I or C_2. Differentiating (11) with respect to A and I, or A and C_2, yields the amount of aid necessary to motivate the government to increase I or C_2 by one unit:

$$\left.\frac{dA}{dI}\right|_{al} = 1 - \rho\eta\frac{C_1}{C_2} \quad \text{and} \quad \left.\frac{dA}{dC_2}\right|_{al} = \frac{1}{\eta}\left(1 - \rho\eta\frac{C_1}{C_2}\right),$$

where the subscript al stands for "active leader."

The above equations are the slopes of the functions relating A and I, $A(I)|_{al}$, shown in Figure 16.2, and the relationship between A and C_2, $A(C_2)|_{al}$. As long as $\rho > 0$, the cost of both increased investment and consumption goes to zero when A tends to zero, because C_1/C_2 tends to $C_1^*/C_2^* = 1/\eta\rho$. When A increases, C_1/C_2 rises above $\rho\eta$ and the cost will be positive. The increase in I will be higher than the extra inflow of A. The government may reduce C_1 in return for extra A. The higher the amount of aid given, the larger the amount of extra aid required in order to motivate the government to increase I or C_2 by one unit. For a given inflow of A, the optimal solution is shown at point C in Figures 16.1 and 16.2.

When ρ gets close to zero, the government will insist on getting the donor to finance investment entirely. In this case $dA/dI|_{al}$ gets close to 1 and $dA/dC_2|_{al}$ tends to $1/\eta$. Thus, having an aid organization playing the role of an active leader is more efficient than the passive leader, in the sense that the recipient country is able to generate higher levels of I and C_2.

The Stackelberg Follower   Consider now the case of the Stackelberg follower, in which a recipient qualifies as long as I^* is lower than maximum investment with aid, $\widetilde{I}$, and C_2^* is lower than $\widetilde{C}_2$, where $\widetilde{C}_2 = Y_2 + \eta\widetilde{I} - R(1+r)$. As long as these criteria hold, the activities of a Stackelberg follower will have the same consequences as the activities of the passive Stackelberg leader. The reason is that the government has no incentive to manipulate the contract to its own advantage.

The problem that arises in the case of a follower organization relates to a situation where I^* is higher than $\widetilde{I}$ and C_2^* is higher than $\widetilde{C}_2$. In this case, the government may find it advantageous to adjust in order to qualify for aid because it knows the aid allocation criterion. If $\widetilde{I}$ refers indeed to investment *before* the aid has been received, the government must make sure that $R+S \leq \widetilde{I}$ in order to qualify for aid. This means that S should not exceed $\widetilde{I} - R$. Because adjustment is costly to the government, the constraint on S will bind. As a result of this, saving, $\widehat{S}$, investment, $\widehat{I}$, and consumption in period 2, $\widehat{C}_2$, will be determined by the criterion set by the donor. Given the amount of aid, A^0:

$$\widehat{Z} = \widetilde{I} - R, \quad \widehat{I} = \widetilde{I} + A^0, \quad \widehat{C}_2 = Y_2 + \eta(\widetilde{I} + A^0) - (1+r)R.$$

Figure 16.3 illustrates the adjustment of the government as a movement from point Z to E along the intertemporal budget line. This is a distortion favoring the present against the future. After the adjustment has been made, any aid obtained is invested and this affects consumption in period 2. This is represented as a movement to the right from point E. Figure 16.4 shows the relationship between the inflow of aid and investment, $A(I)|_f^1$, where f stands for "follower." A^0 is high enough to make it worthwhile for the government to make the required adjustment in order to qualify for aid. The solution, that is, the triplet $\widehat{C}_1$, $\widehat{C}_2$, and $\widehat{I}$, is shown as point F in Figures 16.3 and 16.4.[4]

---

[4] Point Z in Figures 16.2 and 16.4 corresponds to the optimal level of investment without aid, as given by Equation (5), and the consumption allocation shown at the same point in Figures 16.1 and 16.3.

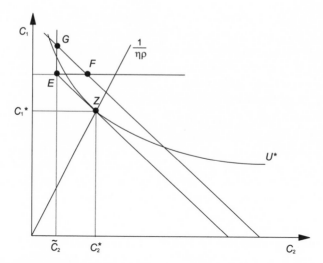

Figure 16.3. Consumption allocation with passive donor behavior. Source: Adapted from Pedersen (1996, p. 431).

The results change if the criterion is related to investment *after* the aid has been received. In this case investment, which is equal to $R + S + A^0$, must be lower than $\widetilde{I}$ if the country is to qualify for aid, so that S should not exceed $\widetilde{I} - (R + A^0)$. In this case aid totally crowds out S even after the adjustment has been made. The optimal values of the variables are

$$\widehat{I} = \widetilde{I}, \quad \widehat{S} = \widetilde{I} - (R + A^0),$$

$$\widehat{C}_2 = Y_2 + \eta\widetilde{I} - (1 + r)R, \quad \widehat{C}_1 = Y_1 + R + A^0 - \widetilde{I}.$$

Once the adjustment has taken place, any aid will lead to an upward movement from point E to G in Figures 16.3 and 16.4, where the relationship between aid and investment is shown as $A(I)|_f^2$.

Several other recent contributions, most notably by Boone (1996), Obstfeld (1999), and Lensink and White (2001), have focused on other aspects of the relationships between aid, investment, and economic growth. Boone (1996) analyzed the effect of aid on growth in the context of the Solow-Swan framework, modified to account for productive public expenditure as in Barro (1990). He argued that in countries where politicians maximize the welfare of a wealthy elite, (unconditional) foreign aid will have a limited effect on standards of living—because it is usually not optimal for politicians to adjust distortionary policies as a result of an increase in aid flows. His empirical results showed indeed that aid has no effect in the long run because it is consumed rather than invested. However, these results were qualified by Obstfeld (1999), who showed that within the class of growth models considered by Boone, an increase in aid raises both consumption and investment as well as the growth rate—provided that the economy is initially below its steady-state equilibrium.

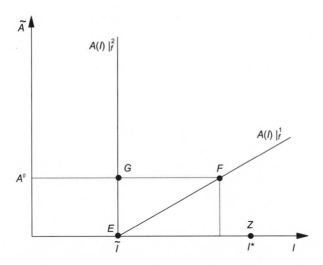

Figure 16.4. Aid and investment with passive donor behavior. Source: Adapted from Pedersen (1996, p. 431).

Lensink and White (2001) also used Barro's assumption of productive government expenditure to analyze the link between aid and growth, but this time in an endogenous growth framework. They showed that aid, by increasing government purchases of goods, and hence the production of public services, has a positive effect on steady-state growth. However, this effect operates only at low levels of aid; beyond a certain threshold, aid has a negative impact on growth. The reason is that aid-financed government expenditure exerts diminishing returns on private production. An alternative explanation is related to the existence of a gradual tightening of constraints on absorptive capacity.

16.1.3   Aid and Growth: Cross-Country Evidence

The empirical relationship between aid and growth has received much attention in recent years. Burnside and Dollar (2000) argued that aid "works" (in the sense of being effectively beneficial to growth) only in an enabling policy environment. They assumed that aid can affect output only through capital accumulation, and measure its impact on growth by the product of the marginal productivity of capital and the marginal propensity to invest aid.[5] Using cross-country regressions for 56 developing countries and six four-year periods over 1970-93, they found that aid has no impact on growth in countries with poor macroeconomic policies, as measured by high inflation, high fiscal deficits, and a low degree of openness. They also found no evidence that aid has had any systematic effect on economic policies, or that aid (particularly on a bilateral basis) had a strong positive impact on government consumption, which in turn has no positive effect on growth. These results led the World Bank (1998) to

---

[5] In contrast to previous studies in the literature, Burnside and Dollar provided a more accurate estimate of foreign aid by adding to outright grants the grant components of concessional loans.

advocate a selective approach, whereby donors should direct foreign aid only to countries with "good" economic policies. This conclusion is somewhat at odds with another study by Dollar and Svensson (2000), in which the authors argue that policy-based aid may increase the probability of reform and the success of an adjustment program—thereby affecting growth indirectly. Put differently, aid and "good" policies are not independent.

More importantly, a number of subsequent studies have questioned the empirical robustness of the alleged dependence of the aid-growth link on the policy regime. Dalgaard and Hansen (2001) found that the Burnside-Dollar results are very fragile. Five observations, which are excluded in Burnside and Dollar's "preferred" regressions, have a critical influence on the parameter of interest. Dalgaard and Hansen argued that, in fact, aid spurs growth *unconditionally* (that is, regardless of whether policies are "good" or "bad") but with decreasing marginal returns—perhaps as a result of gradually binding constraints on absorptive capacity, as noted earlier. Lensink and White (2001) and Hansen and Tarp (2001) found similar results; the latter study used an estimation technique based on instrumental variables to account for the endogeneity of aid alluded to earlier. Moreover, Hansen and Tarp found that when physical investment and human capital are controlled for, aid has no direct effect on growth but only an indirect one, through its impact on capital formation. Finally, Easterly, Levine, and Roodman (2003), using a specification similar to Burnside and Dollar but with an extended sample, found that the interaction term between aid and policies was insignificant. In addition, Easterly (2003) found that even in the same sample as Burnside and Dollar, the result was not robust to alternative (and equally plausible) definitions of aid, policies, and long-run growth.

16.2   Growth, Debt, and Fiscal Adjustment

As discussed in Chapter 2, a high level of foreign debt can have adverse effects on savings and investment. In turn, the positive correlation between savings, capital accumulation, and growth documented in Chapter 10 suggests that a high burden of debt can severely constrain growth rates and limit improvements in standards of living. To illustrate the joint dynamics of foreign debt, capital accumulation, and growth, this section uses an extension of the learning-by-doing model of endogenous growth developed by Villanueva (1994) and discussed in Chapter 11.[6] The relative simplicity of the model makes it a convenient framework for analyzing the links between domestic adjustment policies, foreign borrowing, and growth.

As in Chapter 11, consider the Cobb-Douglas production function

$$Y = K^{\alpha}(AL)^{1-\alpha}, \quad 0 < \alpha < 1, \tag{12}$$

---

[6]See Cohen (1994) for a model of growth and debt based on the AK framework also discussed in Chapter 11. The appendix to this chapter reviews briefly the alternative perspective on debt issues developed in the literature on stages in the balance of payments, which takes foreign saving as an outcome rather than a constraint.

where Y is the flow of output, K the stock of capital, L the number of workers, and A the effectiveness of labor. In intensive form, Equation (12) can be written as

$$y = k^\alpha, \tag{13}$$

where $y = Y/AL$ and $k = K/AL$ is the capital-effective labor ratio.

Let D^* denote the country's net stock of external debt. National income, Q, is given by

$$Q = Y - r^* D^*,$$

where r^* is the *cost of borrowing* that the country faces on world capital markets. National income per unit of effective labor, q, can thus be written as

$$q = k^\alpha - r^* d^*, \tag{14}$$

where $d^* = D^*/AL$ is foreign debt per unit of effective labor. Changes in net external debt are equal to foreign saving, S^*:

$$\dot{D}^* = S^*. \tag{15}$$

Domestic saving, S, is the sum of private saving, S^p, and government saving, S^g, which are defined as follows. Private saving is a constant fraction, s, of disposable income, given by $1 - \iota$, where $0 < \iota < 1$ is the tax rate, multiplied by national income. Thus

$$S^p = s(1 - \iota)Q. \tag{16}$$

Government saving is the difference between tax revenue (a fraction, ι, of national income) and government spending, G. Thus

$$S^g = \iota Y - G. \tag{17}$$

Changes in the capital stock, assuming a depreciation rate of δ, are given by

$$\dot{K} = I - \delta K. \tag{18}$$

In equilibrium, domestic investment must be financed by domestic and foreign saving:

$$I = S = (S^p + S^g) + S^*. \tag{19}$$

Using Equations (15) and (18), this condition becomes

$$\dot{K} + \delta K - \dot{D}^* = S. \tag{20}$$

Labor is assumed to grow at an exogenous rate:

$$\dot{L}/L = n, \tag{21}$$

whereas, following Villanueva's (1994) **learning-by-doing** specification (see Chapter 12), the efficiency of labor changes according to

$$\dot{A} = \theta(\frac{K}{L}) + \gamma A, \quad \theta > 0.$$

This equation, together with Equation (21), implies that the growth rate of labor in efficient units is given by

$$\frac{\dot{A}}{A} + \frac{\dot{L}}{L} = \theta k + n + \gamma. \tag{22}$$

The rate of change of foreign debt is assumed to depend on the difference between the marginal productivity of capital, $\alpha k^{\alpha-1}$, net of depreciation, δ, and the marginal cost of funds on world capital markets, r^*:

$$\dot{D}^*/D^* = \beta(\alpha k^{\alpha-1} - \delta - r^*), \quad \beta > 0, \tag{23}$$

where β measures the speed of adjustment.

In turn, the marginal cost of funds on world capital markets is assumed to consist of a *risk-free rate*, r_f^*, and a *risk premium*, ρ, which depends on the economy's stock of debt in effective units of labor, d^*:

$$r^* = r_f^* + \rho(d^*, \lambda), \quad \rho_{d^*}, \rho_\lambda > 0, \tag{24}$$

where λ represents a shift factor capturing exogenous changes in market perceptions of country risk. This specification captures the idea that the higher the level of foreign debt, the higher the *probability of default*, and thus the higher the cost of borrowing for the domestic country.[7] It is also plausible to assume that the premium rises at an increasing rate (so that $\rho_{d^*d^*} > 0$) and that the domestic economy may lose complete access to world capital markets for a level of debt that is sufficiently high. For the moment, however, it will be assumed that the economy operates in a region in which complete rationing does not occur.

As shown in Chapter 11, changes in the capital-effective labor ratio can be written as

$$\dot{k} = \frac{\dot{K}}{AL} - (\frac{\dot{A}}{A} + \frac{\dot{L}}{L})k,$$

that is, using Equation (22):

$$\dot{k} = \frac{\dot{K}}{AL} - [\theta k + (n + \gamma)]k,$$

or, using Equation (20):

$$\dot{k} = -[\theta k + (n + \gamma)]k + \frac{(S^p + S^g) - \delta K + \dot{D}^*}{AL}.$$

This equation becomes, using Equations (16) and (17):

$$\dot{k} = [\iota + s(1 - \iota)]q + (\frac{\dot{D}^* - G}{AL}) - [\theta k + (n + \gamma + \delta)]k. \tag{25}$$

---

[7] The analysis could be extended to the case where the risk premium depends on the ratio of the country's debt to its national income, D^*/Q.

Using Equation (23), the term $\dot{D}^*/AL$ in the above expression can be written as

$$\frac{\dot{D}^*}{AL} = (\frac{\dot{D}^*}{D^*})(\frac{D^*}{AL}) = \beta(\alpha k^{\alpha-1} - \delta - r^*)d^*.$$

Using this result, setting $\phi = \iota + s(1 - \iota)$ and $g = G/AL$ in Equation (25), yields

$$\dot{k} = \phi q + \beta(\alpha k^{\alpha-1} - \delta - r^*)d^* - g - [\theta k + (n + \gamma + \delta)]k.$$

Using Equation (14) to substitute out for q yields

$$\dot{k} = \phi k^\alpha + \left\{\beta(\alpha k^{\alpha-1} - \delta) - (\phi + \beta)r^*\right\}d^* - g - [\theta k + (n + \gamma + \delta)]k, \quad (26)$$

with r^* given by Equation (24) and g assumed to be constant.

Finally, it can be noted that

$$\frac{\dot{d}^*}{d^*} = \frac{\dot{D}^*}{D^*} - (\frac{\dot{A}}{A} + \frac{\dot{L}}{L}) = \beta(\alpha k^{\alpha-1} - \delta - r^*) - \theta k - (n + \gamma). \quad (27)$$

Equations (26) and (27) consist of a system of two differential equations in the capital-effective labor ratio, k, and the external debt-effective labor ratio, d^*, which can be linearized around the steady state to give

$$\begin{bmatrix} \dot{d}^* \\ \dot{k} \end{bmatrix} = \begin{bmatrix} a_{11} & a_{12} \\ a_{21} & a_{22} \end{bmatrix} \begin{bmatrix} d^* - \tilde{d}^* \\ k - \tilde{k} \end{bmatrix}, \quad (28)$$

where

$$a_{11} = -\tilde{d}^* \beta \rho_d < 0,$$

$$a_{12} = \tilde{d}^*[\beta\alpha(\alpha - 1)\tilde{k}^{\alpha-2} - \theta\tilde{k}] < 0,$$

$$a_{21} = -\tilde{d}^*(\phi + \beta)\rho_d - \phi r^* < 0,$$

and

$$a_{22} = \phi\alpha\tilde{k}^{\alpha-1} + \tilde{d}^*\beta\alpha(\alpha - 1)\tilde{k}^{\alpha-2} - 2\theta\tilde{k} - (n + \gamma).$$

The sign of coefficient a_{22} is in general ambiguous. It will be assumed in what follows that $a_{22} < 0$; a sufficient (although not necessary) condition for this restriction to hold is for the speed of adjustment of external debt, β, to be sufficiently high:

$$\beta > (\frac{\phi}{1-\alpha})\frac{\tilde{d}^*}{\tilde{k}},$$

or, equivalently, the initial debt-to-capital ratio must not be too large ($\tilde{d}^*/\tilde{k} < \beta(1-\alpha)/\phi$).

A graphical illustration of the economy's equilibrium path is provided in Figure 16.5. Curve DD denotes the combinations of d^* and k for which the stock of debt in effective units of labor is constant over time ($\dot{d}^* = 0$), whereas curve KK depicts the combinations of d^* and k for which the capital-effective labor ratio remains constant over time ($\dot{k} = 0$). The steady-state equilibrium position of the economy is obtained at point E.

Dynamic stability requires DD to be steeper than KK. To see this, note that stability requires that the trace of the matrix of coefficients in Equation (28), which is equal to the sum of the roots, be negative ($a_{11} + a_{22} < 0$), and that the determinant of that matrix be positive, that is, $a_{11}a_{22} - a_{12}a_{21} > 0$. The first condition is always satisfied, given the assumption that $a_{22} < 0$. The second can be rewritten as $a_{11}/a_{12} > a_{21}/a_{22}$, which is indeed the condition that slope of DD be steeper than that of KK.

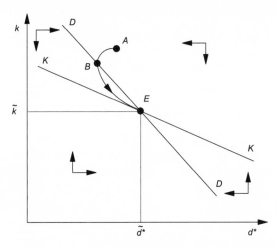

Figure 16.5. Foreign debt and the capital-effective labor ratio: Long-run equilibrium.

To illustrate the functioning of the above model, consider an adjustment strategy that calls for a permanent reduction in the ratio of government spending to effective labor, g.[8] As illustrated in Figure 16.6, this shock leads to an upward shift in the KK curve. In the long run, the reduction in government spending increases government saving and reduces the level of foreign borrowing required at the initial levels of domestic saving and investment.

The reduction in debt also reduces debt service payments—both directly and indirectly, the latter as a result of the fall in the risk premium—thereby raising national disposable income and thus private saving. The net effect is higher investment and a higher capital stock (measured in effective units of labor) in the long run.

During the transition to the new steady-state equilibrium (located at point E' in Figure 16.6), foreign borrowing falls continuously, whereas the capital-effective labor ratio increases monotonically. The higher capital-effective labor ratio is also associated with a higher growth rate of output per capita in the

---

[8] Other interesting experiments with the model include an increase in the risk-free interest rate, r_f^*, or in the autonomous component of the risk premium, λ. As discussed by Eaton (1993), the presumption in many endogenous growth models with foreign debt is that a permanent increase in the world interest rate would lower the steady-state rate of economic growth. It can be verified that this is indeed verified in the present case.

steady state, which, as shown in Chapter 12, is given by

$$\tilde{g}_{Y/L} = \theta\tilde{k} + \gamma.$$

Thus, fiscal adjustment does not only reduce the foreign debt burden; by raising the capital-effective labor ratio, it also has permanent (and positive) growth effects.

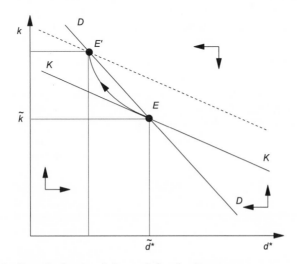

Figure 16.6. Growth, foreign debt, and fiscal adjustment.

An important limitation of the above analysis is that it does not account for the *supply-side effects* of government spending. For instance, if as in Barro's (1990) model flow government expenditure has a positive impact on private production (at least at low levels of taxation, as discussed in Chapter 12), a cut in the ratio of government spending to effective labor, g, would exert an adverse effect on output in both the short and the long run. This effect would tend to offset the positive impact of induced by higher national income (itself resulting from the lower risk premium).

More generally, it is not only the level of government spending that affects growth, but also its composition, that is, the allocation of expenditure between transfers and spending on goods and services, and the allocation of investment between spending on education, health, and infrastructure. What determines the optimal composition of government spending, given a growth target, tax collection constraints, congestion effects associated with the use of public services, and possibly constraints on the allocation of foreign aid, is an important area for further research.

16.3 The Debt Overhang and the Debt Laffer Curve

A key channel through which a large level of foreign debt affects economic performance in the model of the previous section is the risk premium charged by foreign lenders in their attempt to internalize the risk of default. Several economists have pointed out, however, that the medium-term uncertainty associated with a high burden of debt may have an adverse effect on *investment incentives* domestically—a phenomenon that the model did not capture. Helpman (1989), Krugman (1988), and Sachs (1989) argued that, beyond a certain point, a high level of external debt acts as a marginal tax on investment because a fraction of the gains in output resulting from increased capital formation accrues to creditors in the form of debt repayment. To the extent that individual investors internalize the tax effect of the debt—an assumption that is not as innocuous as it seems—the fear of appropriation will reduce the expected after-tax rate of return on capital. High indebtedness can therefore lead to low investment, low growth, and ultimately to low repayment. Highly indebted countries would suffer, in this case, from a **debt overhang**.

More formally, a debt overhang refers to a situation in which the *expected repayment* on foreign debt falls short of its *contractual value*. To illustrate, consider the case of a country whose current level of foreign debt, D^*, must be repaid in full in the next period. Lenders (through trade sanctions, for instance) can enforce repayment but only up to a certain extent; the debtor country can always keep a minimum amount, C_{min}, of domestic output, Y, for consumption. Repayment, R, is thus given by

$$R = \min(D^*, Y - C_{min}).$$

Suppose that the production function is given by

$$Y_s = u_s I^\alpha, \quad 0 < \alpha < 1,$$

where s denotes the *state of nature*, I investment output, and u_s a productivity shock that can take two values: a high value $u_s = u_H$ in good states of nature, and a low value $u_s = u_L < u_H$ in bad states of nature. Suppose that there is a physical upper limit to the amount of investment that the country can achieve, I_{max}, and that the two states are so different that there is no overlap of output, that is,

$$Y_L = u_L I_{max}^\alpha < u_H I^\alpha.$$

In this setting, a debt overhang exists if

$$D^* > Y_L - C_{min},$$

because in this case the debt cannot be fully serviced in the bad state of nature.

To see how the debt overhang reduces the incentive to invest, suppose that

$$Y_L - C_{min} < D^* < Y_H - C_{min}.$$

In the good state of nature the debt is fully repaid, whereas in the bad state of nature repayment is equal to realized output minus the minimum consumption level. Let π denote the probability of the good state; for simplicity, this probability is taken to be constant. Because $D^* > Y_L - C_{min}$, the expected marginal return to an additional unit of investment is thus

$$\pi u_H \alpha I^{\alpha-1} + (1 - \pi) \cdot 0,$$

whereas, in the absence of a debt overhang, the expected marginal return to an additional unit of investment is

$$\pi u_H \alpha I^{\alpha-1} + (1 - \pi) u_L \alpha I^{\alpha-1} > \pi u_H \alpha I^{\alpha-1},$$

which implies that investment will never take place. In addition, in the case where $D^* > Y_H - C_{min}$, the expected marginal return to an additional unit of investment is actually zero and the incentive to invest disappears completely. However, Aizenman and Borensztein (1993) showed that, in a strategic investment framework, the effect of the overhang on the incentive to invest can be ambiguous. In particular, there are conditions under which the overhang acts as a *subsidy* to (that is, increases the incentives for) investment. In their model, if a debtor is unable to meet its repayment obligations, the level of repayment is determined by a bargaining game. If domestic capital is a good substitute for imported inputs, the threat of trade sanctions (or autarky) loses its effectiveness. Thus, it is possible that an increase in investment (which raises the stock of domestic capital) strengthens the country's bargaining position and therefore reduces its level of repayment. In such a case high indebtedness may raise the incentive for investment.

An alternative way of presenting the concept of a debt overhang is through the derivation of the **debt Laffer curve**, which relates a country's nominal debt obligations to the *market's expectation* of the repayments that these loans will generate. Let D^* denote once again the contractual value of debt, and V the expected resource transfer that the country is expected to make to service it. The relationship between D^* and V, the debt Laffer curve, is illustrated in Figure 16.7. At low levels of D^*, expected repayments increase one for one with the contractual value of debt. The first segment of the debt Laffer curve, OA, is thus along the 45-degree line. As D^* increases, however, the risk of default rises as well, and the probability of repayment, θ, falls below unity. Beyond point E (corresponding to $\tilde{D}^*$) contractual levels of debt and the risk of default are so high that V begins to decline. Additional amounts of debt actually *lower* expected repayments. Thus, beyond $\tilde{D}^*$, a country is said to be on the *wrong side* of the debt Laffer curve; the disincentive effects on potential investors are so strong that a reduction in the stock of debt would result in an increase in its market value.[9] In such conditions, a reduction in the **debt tax rate**—that is,

---

[9]Husain (1997) argued that the disincentive to investment generated by a large level of debt can place a country on the wrong side of the debt Laffer curve only in the presence of significant distortions in the domestic tax system.

the proportion of output that is allocated to servicing the debt—would translate into an increase in actual debt payments (Sachs, 1989).

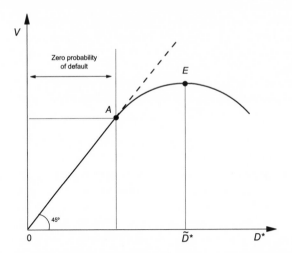

Figure 16.7. The debt Laffer curve. Source: Adapted from Krugman (1989*b*).

Froot and Krugman (1989) attempted to estimate the position on the debt Laffer curve of various countries in a group of 35 heavily indebted countries (12 of which were low-income countries), by examining the relationship between the *secondary market price* of debt and the face value of debt claims. Multiplying the existing stock of debt by the secondary market price provides an estimate of market expectations of repayments. A debt overhang exists when further increases in obligations are discounted at such a high rate (as implied by a sufficiently large fall in the secondary price) that they are associated with a *decline* in the market value of the debt stock. They found that for 5 of the 12 low-income countries (Bolivia, Madagascar, Nicaragua, Sudan, and Zambia) debt-to-export ratios were sufficiently high to place them on the wrong side of their debt Laffer curves.[10] However, there are two problems with these results:

- The Froot-Krugman technique cannot be applied to low-income countries for which there is no secondary debt market. This is often because of the relatively small proportion of debt owed to commercial creditors by these countries.

- Claessens (1990), using data for 29 countries for the period 1986-88, found that although the present value of repayment, measured by the secondary market price, is concave with respect to the face value of outstanding debt, there are very few cases (actually, 6 countries) for which it actually begins to slope downward.

---

[10] The other low-income countries included in the Froot-Krugman sample were Côte d'Ivoire, Honduras, Liberia, Nigeria, Senegal, Togo, and the former Zaire.

Other studies have attempted to estimate directly the effect of a large burden of debt on domestic capital formation. Deshpande (1997), for instance, examined the behavior of domestic fixed investment in 13 highly indebted countries (including Algeria, Argentina, and Côte d'Ivoire) during the period 1971-92. He argued that a debt overhang has an adverse effect on investment through two channels:

- a direct disincentive effect, which results from the *fear of appropriation* of funds invested (or the returns from the investment) for the purpose of debt servicing, as described earlier;

- an indirect effect through the *adjustment measures* undertaken to face (or avoid) debt-servicing difficulties—such as cuts in imports (including reductions in imported capital goods) and reductions in public sector investment required to reduce fiscal deficits.[11]

The second argument suggests that to the extent that public and private capital outlays are *complementary* (as discussed in Chapter 2), a fiscal adjustment program that brings about a fall in public capital outlays would also tend to reduce private investment.[12] Deshpande found that there is a significantly negative relationship between the level of external debt and investment. Similar results were obtained by Elbadawi, Ndulu, and Ndung'u (1997) and Pattillo, Poirson, and Ricci (2002) in studies focusing on *private* capital formation in sub-Saharan Africa.

The foregoing discussion therefore suggests that eliminating the debt overhang in a highly indebted country may create renewed incentives for capital formation, which can benefit *both* the country itself and its creditors. In general, for debt relief to benefit creditors—that is, for expected repayment V to increase despite the decline in the contractual value of foreign debt from D^* to $D^* - x$—the increase in the secondary market price of debt (as measured by the ratio of V over the contractual value of debt) must be large enough to outweigh the potential loss to creditors that would occur *ex post* if the state of nature turns out to be so favorable that full repayment would have occurred anyway in the absence of debt relief. Formally, assuming as before that the relation between output and investment is of the form $Y = I^\alpha$, this condition can be written as (Krugman, 1989b):

$$\frac{dV}{dx} = -\theta + (1 - \theta)\frac{dI}{dx}\alpha I^{\alpha-1} > 0,$$

where dI/dx measures the increase in investment induced by debt relief, and $\alpha I^{\alpha-1}$ the marginal product of investment in terms of increased debt payment

[11] As pointed out by Krugman (1988), there is also an illiquidity effect, which results from the fact that a debt overhang may shut countries out of world capital markets—preventing additional borrowing to finance high-yielding investments.

[12] At the same time, however, if fiscal consolidation is accompanied by a reduction in (unproductive) government spending, it may lead to an expansion in private investment—by reducing, for instance, the demand for credit by the public sector.

capacity. The first term, θ, represents the loss incurred by creditors in good states of nature, whereas the second measures the expected payoff resulting from debt relief and higher investment. In Figure 16.7, $dV/dD^* < 0$ beyond point A, and $dV/dx > 0$. In the particular case where $dI/dx = 0$,

$$\frac{dV}{dx} = -\theta < 0.$$

Thus, without any induced effect on investment, debt relief would never be optimal from the point of view of creditors.[13]

It is important to stress, however, that the argument for reducing the debt burden of highly indebted countries does not depend only on the existence of a debt overhang. The problem of providing incentives to repay is relevant only insofar as a country has the **ability to repay**, as discussed later. Low growth rates in heavily indebted countries may make full repayment of their outstanding level of debt impossible despite any incentives.[14] To the extent, for instance, that debt relief lowers the risk premium charged to borrowers on world capital markets, it may have a direct effect on growth (as indicated in the previous section) and expected repayment.

16.4   Measuring the Debt Burden

A common practice to evaluate the debt burden and the sustainability of the external position of a country is to examine the evolution of the ratios of debt and debt service to various indicators of economic performance. When these ratios are so high as to make a country unable to meet its contractual debt-service payments without debt reschedulings, and the ratios are expected to remain at high levels, the external position is deemed unsustainable. An alternative approach is based on external solvency.

16.4.1   Conventional and Present Value Indicators

Conventional measures of the debt burden include

- The ratio of the *stock of debt to output* (or exports of goods and services). This indicator can be misleading to the extent that it fails to capture the effects of new financing and of debt relief on more concessional terms, that is, lower interest rates and longer repayment periods.

- The ratio of *actual debt service to exports*, which captures the impact of debt-service obligations on foreign exchange cash flow. This measure,

---

[13] As noted by Bowe and Dean (1997, p. 34) these formulas do not account for some of the indirect benefits associated with debt relief, such as the reduction in the costs of default, negotiations with creditors, and enforcement of penalties.

[14] Warner (1993) argued that it is the slow growth experienced by highly indebted middle-income developing countries that led to debt difficulties during the 1980s, rather than the reverse.

which is also viewed as a measure of a country's *foreign exchange constraint*, takes into account debt relief provided by debt-service reschedulings (as well as debt cancellations, as discussed later) and arrears on payments. A limitation of this indicator is that, given the uncertain nature of debt relief, a low value may reflect an **unwillingness to pay**.

- The ratio of *scheduled interest payments to exports*, which measures the ongoing cost of the accumulated stock of debt.

The second and third measures tend to diverge as a result of *increased concessionality* in new lending and rescheduling agreements, which often lead to changes in the concessionality of interest rates and changes in grace and repayment periods.

Two conventional measures aim at capturing the *fiscal impact* of the external debt burden:

- The ratio of *scheduled interest payments* to *government revenue*, which measures the country's capacity to repay as scheduled.[15] This ratio is often considered low if it is less than 0.2, moderate if it is between 0.2 and 0.5, and high if it is above 0.5. However, a high value may simply reflect the country's inability to collect revenue through explicit taxation (see Chapter 3).

- The ratio of *scheduled interest payments* to *government expenditure*, which measures the constraint imposed by debt servicing on the country's ability to expand other (current and capital) expenditures.

An alternative to the conventional measures defined above is to compare the discounted present value of *future debt-service obligations* with the discounted present value of *future export receipts*. The discounted present value of debt is obtained by taking all future debt service obligations (including interest payments at the original rate of the loan and amortization payments) until full repayment of the debt, and dividing them by a factor based on a given *discount rate*. If the discount rate is equal to the original interest rate of the loan, the present value will be equal to the face value of the debt. If the discount rate used is higher than the original interest rate of the loan, future repayments will matter less and the present value will be lower. The present value of future export receipts is obtained in a similar fashion and requires estimates of the growth rate of exports until the horizon of the debt. A variant of this measure is the ratio of the present value of *future debt-service payments* to *current exports*. To the extent that the expected future growth rate of exports is higher than the discount rate, this variant would lead to a higher ratio than the present value debt-to-export ratio. Practitioners often consider that, for this ratio to be consistent with debt sustainability (and thus avoid default or reschedulings, as discussed below), it should not exceed 200 percent.

---

[15] Government revenue in this definition is typically taken to refer only to permanent resources, and therefore excludes foreign grants and privatization proceeds.

An attractive feature of these two alternative indicators is that they take into account the *concessionality* or *grant element* of debt obligations—that is, the fact that loans may be contracted at a rate of interest that is substantially below the prevailing market rate. The present value approach, in particular, can be used to measure the grant element of a concessional loan. In that case, the debt service flow is calculated at the concessional rate but is discounted at the higher market rate. The face value of the debt is higher than its present value, and the difference measures the grant element.

However, these indicators are subject to three major weaknesses:

- Data requirements can be quite complex. Estimates of future export receipts needed to construct the ratio of scheduled interest payments to exports, for instance, may be subject to considerable uncertainty over volume flows and world prices.

- The results can be highly sensitive to the discount rate assumed to calculate present values. Applying a discount rate that is higher than the original interest rate (concessional or not) on a loan would give a present value that is lower than the face value of the loan, thus understating the actual burden of debt for debtor countries.

- The calculated ratio does not provide information about the *debt-service profile*—which may be of paramount importance for a country contemplating a rescheduling agreement and requiring an assessment of the immediate cash-flow requirements of debt-service obligations associated with alternative options.

16.4.2   Sustainability and External Solvency

An alternative approach to assessing the debt burden and its sustainability is to focus on **external solvency** in a way that is analogous to the assessment of fiscal solvency (see Chapter 3). As derived in Chapter 1, the basic identity defining the current account deficit CA is, after normalizing the exchange rate to unity,

$$CA \equiv D^* - D^*_{-1} = -(Y - A) - NT + i^* D^*_{-1}, \qquad (29)$$

where Y is nominal GDP, D^* net external debt (that is, gross debt minus gross private assets and official reserves), A domestic absorption (the sum of private and public expenditure on goods and services), NT net transfer receipts from the rest of the world, and i^* the interest rate on foreign liabilities. This identity relates the current account deficit (which is algebraically equal to the flow increase in the economy's *total* external liabilities) to the difference between total expenditure (absorption and interest payments on foreign debt) to the economy's aggregate income at the end of period t, which consists of domestic income plus net transfers from abroad.

As also shown in Chapter 1, the trade balance surplus, TB, which is equal to the difference between exports and imports of goods and services, is equal to GDP minus domestic absorption:

$$TB = Y - A.$$

Combining this result with Equation (29) yields

$$D^* - D^*_{-1} = -(TB + NT) + i^* D^*_{-1},$$

which can be rewritten as

$$D^* = (1 + i^*)D^*_{-1} - Z, \tag{30}$$

where Z is the *net external surplus*, defined as

$$Z = TB + NT.$$

Suppose that the world interest rate i^* is constant and that output grows at the constant rate θ, so that $Y = (1 + \theta)Y_{-1}$. Setting $d^* = D^*/Y$ and $z = Z/Y$, Equation (30) becomes

$$d^* = \frac{(1 + i^*)}{(1 + \theta)} d^*_{-1} - z. \tag{31}$$

Solving Equation (31) recursively forward yields[16]

$$d^*_0 = \sum_{h=1}^{\infty} \left(\frac{1 + \theta}{1 + i^*}\right)^h z_h + \lim_{N \to \infty} \left(\frac{1 + \theta}{1 + i^*}\right)^{N+1} d^*_{N+1}. \tag{32}$$

As in Chapter 3, external solvency requires that the **no-Ponzi game condition** hold, so that

$$\lim_{N \to \infty} \left(\frac{1 + \theta}{1 + i^*}\right)^{N+1} d^*_{N+1} \leq 0. \tag{33}$$

This condition simply states that a country cannot roll over its external liabilities forever. Thus, from Equation (32):[17]

$$d^*_0 \leq \sum_{h=1}^{\infty} \left(\frac{1 + \mathbf{g}}{1 + i^*}\right)^h z_h. \tag{34}$$

---

[16]The forward solution of Equation (31) with variable output and world interest rates is given by

$$d^*_0 = \sum_{h=1}^{\infty} \Pi^h_{j=1}\left(\frac{1 + \theta_j}{1 + i^*_j}\right) z_h + \lim_{N \to \infty} \Pi^{N+1}_{j=1}\left(\frac{1 + \theta_j}{1 + i^*_j}\right) d^*_{N+1}.$$

[17]With variable output growth and world interest rates, the no-Ponzi game condition for external solvency is $\lim_{N \to \infty} \Pi^{N+1}_{j=1}[(1 + \theta_j)/1 + i^*_j)]d^*_{N+1} \leq 0$, so that Equation (34) becomes $d^*_0 \leq \sum_{h=1}^{\infty} \Pi^h_{j=1}[(1 + \theta_j)/1 + i^*_j)]z_h$.

Thus external solvency requires that the current ratio of net foreign liabilities to output be less than or equal to the maximum level of debt that can be sustained by prospective net external surpluses (measured as a fraction of output). The current policy stance is sustainable as long as it does not lead to a violation of condition (34).[18] As shown in the context of fiscal solvency, the no-Ponzi game condition matters only if the interest rate on external debt exceeds the growth rate of output; otherwise, the foreign debt-output ratio will tend to zero anyway if the horizon N is sufficiently long.

From an analytical standpoint, the concept of external solvency suffers from the same limitations as those faced by the notion of fiscal solvency discussed in Chapter 3; in particular, the solvency constraint imposes only *weak restrictions* on the size and behavior of the current account deficits that lead to the accumulation of foreign liabilities over time. Practical applications are also hampered by difficulties associated with the projection of trade flows (which depend on the real exchange rate and foreign demand for domestic goods) and the choice of an appropriate interest rate. Nevertheless, a number of recent empirical studies have attempted to estimate operational models of external solvency in developing countries. Sawada (1994), for instance, used various econometric tests to assess the sustainability of current account deficits in a group of heavily indebted developing countries in the early 1980s, and so did Baharumshah, Lau, and Fountas (2003) for a group of four Asian countries (Indonesia, Malaysia, the Philippines, and Thailand). Most of these tests, however, are based on **unit root tests** and **cointegration techniques** (see Greene, 2000) that lack power in small samples.

16.5 Debt Rescheduling and Debt Relief

The theoretical literature on sovereign debt distinguishes two approaches to debt repayment (see Kletzer, 1988):

- the **ability-to-pay** approach, which refers to a situation in which a country is unable to meet its current debt servicing requirements, directly or through further borrowing;

- the **willingness-to-pay** approach, which focuses on the case where the borrower has the resources for repayment but finds it optimal not to repay.

The high levels of foreign debt and debt service faced by the low-income developing countries and the severe difficulties they have encountered in ensuring payments has led to increased recognition that many of these countries face an ability-to-pay problem: required debt service exceeds their debt-servicing capacity.[19] Moreover, this ability-to-pay problem is in general a reflection of

---

[18] See Milesi-Ferreti and Razin (1996) for a detailed discussion of the concepts of external solvency and sustainability.

[19] See Kraay and Nehru (2003) for an empirical analysis of the factors that often lead countries to run into debt difficulties, most notably the initial debt level and the quality of policies and institutions.

not a **liquidity problem** but rather a **solvency problem**—that is, a situation in which the present value of a country's current and future income (taken over the whole future) is less than its debt obligations.[20]

Debt relief to poor countries has often taken the form of debt reschedulings at highly concessional terms by official bilateral creditors, organized into an informal group called the **Paris Club** (see http://www.clubdeparis.org/). In general, there are two main types of debt rescheduling operations:

- **flow reschedulings**, which provide for the rescheduling of debt service on eligible medium- and long-term debt falling due during the so-called *consolidation period*;

- **stock-of-debt operations**, under which the entire stock of eligible debt, before a so-called *precutoff date*, is rescheduled at concessionary terms.[21]

The conditions guiding rescheduling agreements have improved gradually over time, from the **Toronto terms** (October 1988-June 1991), to the **London terms** (December 1991-December 1994), the **Naples terms** (January 1995-1999), the **Cologne terms** (1999-September 2003), to the **Evian terms** (since October 2003). Despite these improvements (which include a greater percentage of debt reduction), it was recognized that debt reschedulings would not prove to be an effective and durable solution for many low-income countries, the so-called group of about 40 countries or so currently classified as **heavily indebted poor countries** (HIPCs) by the Bretton-Woods institutions (see http://www.worldbank.org/hipc/). Part of the reason is that, for the HIPCs, *multilateral debt* represents a large fraction of total external debt—about 31 percent at the end of 1996, compared with 42 percent for bilateral official creditors.

In September 1996 a joint IMF-World Bank proposal, the **HIPC Debt Initiative**, was put forward to tackle the issue of debt owed to multilateral official creditors (see Boote and Thugge, 1999). The initiative was enhanced in 1999 in order to provide faster, broader, and deeper debt relief. The HIPC Initiative requires countries to show a track record of *good policy performance* as monitored by the IMF and the Bank. A **debt sustainability analysis** determines the eligibility of debtor countries, and eventually the amount of debt relief necessary for the country to achieve a sustainable level of debt. Once a country reaches the **completion point**, provided that the country has met the performance criteria under the Initiative, Paris Club creditors provide a reduction in the stock of debt of up to *90* percent in net present value terms (or more if necessary to achieve sustainability), with at least comparable treatment

---

[20] A country is illiquid if it is solvent but cannot borrow to meet its current debt servicing requirements. It should be noted that if a country is solvent, lenders should always be willing to lend to it the resources needed to make current repayments—unless they expect the country to repudiate the debt at some point in the future.

[21] These operations typically require countries to maintain what is deemed to be a "satisfactory track record" for several years with respect to both payments under rescheduling agreements and performance under a credit arrangement with multilateral institutions.

provided by other bilateral and commercial creditors. Multilateral institutions must provide a reduction in net present value terms of their claims necessary for the total debt to reach a sustainable level.

By September 2002, twenty-six countries had benefited from the HIPC Initiative. However, how effective this approach is remains a matter of debate (see, for instance, Sachs, 2002). It has been argued that debt reduction for highly indebted poor countries should be based not on some arbitrary set of criteria (such as a debt-to-exports ratio of 150 percent) but rather in terms of a thorough assessment of a country's needs for debt relief and increased foreign assistance, given a set of of explicit development objectives—such as poverty reduction and reduced manutrition. Since 1999, HIPC countries have been required to prepare a Poverty Reduction Strategy Paper (PRSP), which aims to improve low-income countries' public actions for poverty reduction and to increase the effectiveness of both domestic resources (including savings associated with debt relief) and development assistance. The approach is, in principle, country-driven. But as discussed by Booth (2003), the evidence on whether the PRSP approach can promote changes leading to more effective poverty reduction strategies is rather mixed. Moreover, the HIPC initiative is not meant to benefit all low-income countries; and even if it succeeds in "undoing" the mistakes of the past, it provides no guarantee that the very same mistakes will not be repeated in the future.

16.6 Summary

- Assessing the effects of **foreign aid** on the recipient country has been the subject of a vast literature, focusing on the impact of aid on the government budget, the real exchange rate and the current account, investment, growth, and more recently poverty.

- The conventional view of the **fungibility problem** focuses on the impact of aid on government spending. If aid provided by donors to finance a specific activity can be as freely spent as aid provided as general budgetary support, then aid is fully fungible. Otherwise, it is partially fungible.

- This conventional approach overlooks the fact that aid may have an adverse impact on tax revenue, both directly and indirectly (through a multiplier effect on aggregate income).

- Burnside and Dollar (2000) found that aid has a positive impact on growth only in good policy environments. However, Hansen and Tarp (2001) and Dalgaard and Hansen (2001) found this result to be statistically fragile. Aid has an unconditional positive impact on growth, although it appears to be subject to diminishing returns.

- In a world of imperfect world capital markets, fiscal adjustment in low-income countries may lead to a lower burden of foreign debt both by reducing the level of indebtedness and by lowering the **external risk premium** that domestic agents face on foreign borrowing. In an endogenous growth setting with learning by doing, the resulting higher capital-effective labor ratio may also lead to a *permanent* increase in the economy's growth rate.

- A **debt overhang** arises when a debtor country benefits very little from the return to any additional investment, because of high debt service obligations. It can be measured as the difference between the present value of a country's contractual debt obligations and the expected resource transfers that are needed to service it.

- When foreign obligations cannot be met fully with existing resources and actual debt payments are determined by some negotiation process between the debtor country and its creditors, the amount of payments can become linked to the economic performance of the debtor country, with the consequence that at least part of the return to any increase in production would in fact be devoted to debt servicing. This creates a *disincentive to invest*.

- A country is on the wrong side of its **debt Laffer curve** when a reduction in the **debt tax rate** (that is, the proportion of output that is allocated to servicing the debt) would translate into an *increase* in actual debt payments. Reducing the debt overhang would benefit both the debtor country and its creditors.

- Conventional measures of the debt burden include the ratio of the stock of debt to output or exports, the ratio of actual debt service to exports (which is also a measure of the foreign exchange constraint), and the ratio of scheduled debt service to exports. Alternative measures include the ratio of the discounted present value of future debt-service obligations relative to either the discounted present value of future export receipts or the current value of exports.

- When loans are contracted (or rescheduled) at concessional interest rates, indicators based on the net present value of foreign liabilities are more meaningful measures of the actual burden of debt than those based on the face value of these liabilities. The lower the concessional rate, the lower the net present value of future debt service obligations discounted at the market rate. The difference between the face value of debt and its present value measures the *grant element*.

- External debt sustainability can be assessed by evaluating **external solvency**, in a manner analogous to the assessment of domestic public debt solvency (see Chapter 3). The **no-Ponzi game condition** prevents a country from rolling over its external obligations indefinitely. Under this condition, external solvency requires the present discounted value of trade surpluses to be sufficiently large to repay the country's existing net stock of foreign liabilities. However, external solvency analysis is subject to some of the same conceptual and empirical limitations that fiscal solvency analysis faces.

- The debt problem of many low-income countries reflects an **ability-to-pay** problem, rather than a **willingness-to-pay** problem; debt service payments exceed in many cases the country's debt-servicing capacity. Since the mid-1980s many low-income countries have been engaged in rescheduling operations at concessional terms.

- The **HIPC Initiative**, launched in September 1996 and modified in 1999, is an attempt to recognize the fact that a significant portion of the foreign debt of low-income countries is owed to multilateral institutions. A two-stage process eventually leads to a *completion point* where debt relief through *stock-of-debt operations* is implemented. HIPC countries are now required to prepare a **Poverty Reduction Strategy Paper** to increase the impact of development assistance and allocate the savings associated with debt relief. The process, however, has remained slow and its effectiveness is a matter of debate.

Appendix to Chapter 16
The Theory of Stages in the Balance of Payments

The literature on **stages in the balance of payments** analyzes the pattern of foreign borrowing and lending that an initially capital-poor economy goes through during the process of development. This literature links the behavior of external accounts over time to *growth paths* in which investment first exceeds saving, then saving overtakes investment. Specifically, five phases are typically distinguished in this literature:

- a *young debtor-borrower stage*, in which both the trade balance and the current account are in deficit and the country is a net debtor;

- a *mature debtor-borrower stage*, in which the trade balance has turned to surplus but the current account is still in deficit due to debt-service obligations;

- a *debtor-repayer stage*, in which the country is still a net debtor but the current account is in surplus;

- a *young creditor-lender stage*, with both the current account and trade balance in surplus, and the country has become a net creditor;

- a *mature creditor-lender stage*, in which the trade balance has turned to deficit but the current account is still in surplus due to interest income from abroad.

Thus, in the early stages of growth when investment opportunities exceed saving, countries tend to borrow abroad. As income and saving rise above investment requirements, and as the marginal productivity of capital falls toward the world rate of interest (thereby reducing the investment motive for borrowing), countries pay back their debt and accumulate foreign assets. In the steady state, characterized by a zero current account deficit, a country that has passed through the last two stages will be a net creditor running a trade deficit exactly offsetting its earnings on foreign assets.

The analytical literature suggests that various conditions must be satisfied for stages in the balance of payments to emerge. In the growth model developed by Fischer and Frenkel (1972, 1974), for instance, for a country starting with a low level of capital and low per-capita wealth, a transition from debtor to creditor requires the *assumption* that the steady-state position is one in which the country becomes a net creditor. The model, however, does not necessarily generate nonmonotonic dynamics of foreign debt (asset) accumulation; it is also consistent with patterns of foreign borrowing in which debt may increase or decrease continuously over time—raising possibly solvency issues (see the earlier discussion).

In general, both consumption dynamics and capital accumulation are important in reproducing in analytical models stages in the balance of payments. More importantly perhaps, as pointed out by Manzocchi (1990), is that the whole literature is subject to an important limitation: because of the assumption of perfect international capital markets (which implies a perfectly elastic supply of funds), the balance of payments is viewed as an *outcome* of the process of economic growth, not a *constraint*—a treatment that would appear to be more realistic for many developing countries. The model discussed in the first part of this chapter illustrates some of the implications of capital market imperfections for the dynamics of growth and external debt.

Chapter 17

Sequencing, Gradualism, and the Political Economy of Adjustment

> There is nothing more difficult to carry out, nor more doubtful of success, nor more dangerous to handle, than to initiate a new order of things. For the reformer has enemies in all those who profit by the old order, and only lukewarm defenders in all those who would profit by the new order . . . Thus it arises that on every opportunity for attacking the reformer, his opponents do so with the zeal of partisans, the others defend him half-heartedly, so that between them he runs great danger.
>
> Machiavelli, *The Prince*, 1513 (Chapter 6).

In designing reform programs in an environment where various distortions exist, a key issue for policymakers is the choice of an appropriate sequence of policy measures. A related issue is the speed at which economic reforms should be implemented. The answer to both questions depends not only on economic considerations (such as the type of adjustment costs that alternative policy sequences entail) but also on the political constraints that policymakers face.

The political dimension of adjustment has been one of the main areas of interest of the *new political economy*, which studies, using modern analytical tools, the interactions between the political system, institutional structures, policy formulation, and policy outcomes.[1] Economic policy decisions are viewed in this

---

[1] The impact of political factors on reform outcomes is well illustrated in the study by Dollar and Svensson (2000). In an analysis of more than 200 reform programs implemented in developing countries during 1980-95 with the support of adjustment loans from the World Bank, they found that political economy factors—such as the length of tenure of the government (measured by the length of time the incumbent has been in power prior to the reform), the degree of political instability (measured by the average number of government crises during the reform period), and whether leaders are democratically elected or not—all strongly influence the success or failure of these programs.

perspective as the *endogenous* outcome of these interactions. This approach seeks to provide a better empirical explanation of economic policy formation than conventional models in which policy is chosen either *exogenously* or by a benevolent social planner, often with no interaction between public and private agents. More specifically, the recent literature on the political economy of reform in developing economies has focused on three issues (Williamson and Haggard, 1994):

- The **timing** of reforms, that is, understanding the conditions or circumstances that determine *why* and *when* reforms are implemented.

- The **sequencing** of reforms, that is, the analysis of the reasons why some reforms are implemented *earlier* than others, and why reforms are implemented sometimes in a piecemeal fashion and sometimes in the context of a comprehensive program.

- The **speed** of reforms, that is, the factors explaining why reform programs, once they are selected, are sometimes implemented *overnight* and sometimes *gradually*.

This chapter reviews various recent contributions to these issues. Section 17.1 examines *complementarities* and *trade-offs* that arise in the use of policy instruments for stabilization and adjustment purposes. Section 17.2 focuses on the order of liberalization and considers issues associated with both the liberalization of external accounts and the sequencing of domestic and external financial reforms. The links between political constraints and the design of economic reforms are discussed in Section 17.3. It begins by considering alternative approaches to modeling political conflict among agents. It then examines the extent to which economic crises may be conducive to reform, and the relation between income distribution, the political acceptability of reform, and the sustainability of the reform process. Part 4 studies how the pace of reform is affected by factors such as preexisting distortions, imperfect credibility of policies, congestion externalities, financial sector weaknesses, and distributional considerations.

17.1 Stabilization and Structural Adjustment

Most policy decisions have both short-term and structural effects, which may or may not operate in the same direction. A cut in government spending aimed, for instance, at improving macroeconomic performance (by reducing government borrowing needs, money supply growth, and inflation) may have an effect on the **incentives structure** as well as on the efficiency of resource utilization—by leading to a reduction in taxation, and thus reducing the propensity to evade taxes (see Chapter 12). Moreover, although macroeconomic policy measures operate primarily through the demand side of an economy, and structural policies primarily through the supply side, the ultimate objectives of both sets of policies are often the same: output growth, low unemployment, price stability, and a viable current account. As a result, it has often been argued that stabilization and structural adjustment should proceed in parallel because they may reinforce each other. The existence of **policy complementarities** is one of the main arguments in favor of shock therapy, as discussed later.

However, macroeconomic and structural policies may also have *conflicting effects*, particularly in the short run. Eliminating a distortionary agricultural subsidy, for instance, may help to improve the government budget in the short run (thereby lowering inflationary pressures) and may raise the welfare of consumers of nonagricultural goods in the longer run by improving resource allocation. However, it will also lower farm income and raise food prices in the short run. Agricultural households may suffer, and consumers may pay higher food prices. Similarly, the elimination of a tax on agricultural exports may increase output of these goods and income in the rural sector in the medium and long run, but it may also increase the budget deficit in the short run.

Moreover, structural policies have a longer time frame than short-run macroeconomic policies, because *potential output* responds more slowly and with highly variable lags to structural policies than does actual output to, say, monetary and fiscal policies. The slow (and uncertain) adjustment of the economy to structural measures and the possible adverse macroeconomic effects of these measures in the short run have led some economists to argue that structural adjustment policies must be introduced gradually, to avoid derailing stabilization objectives and eroding political support to a point where the sustainability of the overall reform process is called into question (see below).

An important economic argument in favor of ensuring that the stabilization objective is achieved first is that in an environment in which inflation is high and relative prices are distorted, the ability of agents to understand and interpret correctly *price signals* (that is, changes in relative prices) may be seriously hampered (Rodrik, 1995a). In such conditions, structural adjustment policies, which operate to a great extent through their effects on the structure of incentives faced by agents, may not be successful because markets cannot play their role in allocating resources.

17.2   The Order of Liberalization

Much of the discussion in Chapters 14 and 15 focused on various types of economic reforms aimed at removing or alleviating government-induced distortions. In practice, of course, many of these distortions are present simultaneously, and the issue of what to do in such conditions arises. In principle, the *optimal* or *first-best solution* would be to remove all market distortions at once; such a strategy is unambiguously welfare improving. In practice, however, this is almost never a realistic option because of various administrative, political, and other constraints. The issue of sequencing arises therefore naturally in such conditions. The reason is that, in a *second-best environment*, the impact of a particular measure in a given sector depends on prevailing circumstances in

other sectors of the economy. When distortions exist in various sectors of the
economy, the removal of a distortion in one sector does not necessarily lead to
an improvement in social welfare—despite its direct potential benefits. Consequently, an analysis of the aggregate welfare effects of reform that limits itself
to the sector where the policy change is occurring may be misleading. The general implication of the theory of second best is that economic reforms should
be broad in scope in order to ensure a first-best solution in the long run. However, as noted earlier, in a world in which policy measures entail short-term adjustment costs—resulting from the fact that productive resources cannot move
instantaneously among alternative uses, or product and factor prices cannot adjust immediately to clear all markets—economic and political impediments can
make an immediate and comprehensive reform of all markets neither feasible
nor desirable. Again, in such conditions, the question of what should be the
appropriate sequence of economic reforms arises.

More specifically, the sequencing of reforms refers to the order in which individual markets should be liberalized in the transition from a distorted economy
toward a market-oriented economy.[2] As noted by Falvey and Kim (1992, p.
909), getting the timing and sequencing of economic reforms right is important
because inappropriate timing and sequencing may foster doubts about the *sustainability* of the reform program and deter private agents from undertaking
appropriate adjustments in their supply and demand decisions.[3]

The literature on sequencing has focused on two main dimensions of the
debate (see McKinnon, 1993): the order of liberalization of the trade and capital accounts, and whether domestic financial liberalization should precede or
follow the opening of the capital account. More recently, there has also been
some thinking on the role of labor market reforms in the overall sequence of
liberalization measures.

17.2.1   Liberalization of External Accounts

The experience of the Southern Cone countries of Latin America (Argentina,
Chile, and Uruguay), Indonesia, and Korea with structural reform in the late
1960s and 1970s was the main source of the initial debate on the order of liberalization. Several economists concluded that the trade account should be opened
before the capital account, in order to avoid destabilizing effects associated with
capital flows. Opening the capital account while trade liberalization is still in
its initial stages could jeopardize the success of trade reform; this is because
the successful liberalization of the trade account requires a *real depreciation*

---

[2]There are also issues associated with the sequencing of a given set of policy instruments.
For instance, there is a sequencing issue in the context of fiscal adjustment, to the extent that
inadequate tax administration may force the government to reduce its fiscal deficit by cutting
expenditure (often current outlays on nonwage goods and services and on capital projects,
with little reduction in wages and salaries) rather than by increasing revenue. As noted in
Chapters 6 and 13, such cuts may have an adverse effect on a country's growth prospects.

[3]In practice, a politically sustainable reform program requires not only a large degree of
social acceptability but also a sufficient degree of parliamentary support for reforms (Tommasi
and Velasco, 1996).

(in order to generate a reallocation of resources from the nontradables sector to the tradables sector, as noted in Chapter 14), whereas opening the capital account may be associated with a *real appreciation* (as documented in Chapter 7), induced by large capital inflows.

A more formal analysis of this issue was provided by Edwards and van Wijnbergen (1986). They assessed the desirability of alternative sequences by evaluating their welfare effects in the context of a multi-period model. The first conclusion of their analysis was that liberalization can have an ambiguous impact on welfare because of three types of (possibly conflicting) effects:

- **direct effects**, which occur in the market in which the reform has taken place and within the *same time period*;

- **intratemporal indirect effects**, which occur within the period in which the reform occurs, because of the interaction between two or more distortions in different markets;

- **intertemporal indirect effects**, which result from the inherently dynamic nature of liberalization policies. They imply that a reform in one period may alter the equilibrium in distorted markets in the *next period*.

The second conclusion reached by Edwards and van Wijnbergen was that the current account should be opened first, because the negative indirect welfare effect of opening the capital account in the presence of trade distortions will be greater than the indirect effects resulting from the opposite ordering. Extension of the Edwards-van Wijnbergen analysis by Kahkonen (1987) to include **financial repression** (as defined in Chapter 4) broadly supports this policy prescription, as discussed more formally below.

The implication of uncertainty for the sequencing of trade and capital account measures was discussed by Conley and Maloney (1995). They considered a two-period model in which the benefits of economic liberalization are uncertain. Specifically, they considered a two-part liberalization program, consisting of

- a liberalization of the current account—say, a reduction in tariffs—in the first period, which is assumed to translate into an increase in the marginal productivity of capital in the second period. The magnitude of this increase, however, is assumed to fluctuate randomly;

- a complete opening of the capital account, which allows agents to borrow and lend freely on world capital markets—and thus to engage in **intertemporal smoothing** of consumption (see Chapter 2).

Because the benefits of current account liberalization are uncertain, private agents base their consumption path (for both the first and the second periods) on their *expectations* of the value of the marginal productivity of capital in the second period. Conley and Maloney showed that in such conditions, if agents are at the same time free to borrow and lend on world capital markets, economic liberalization will lead to a surge in consumption, a current account deficit, and an increase in private foreign borrowing. However, *ex post*, private sector expectations may turn out to be incorrect; indeed, if private agents borrow in the first period, and the marginal productivity of capital turns out to be significantly *less* than expected, consumption in the second period may have to fall by a large amount to ensure repayment of the first-period debt. Policymakers may be averse to such **boom-bust cycles**; and if the probability of a low realization of the marginal productivity of capital is sufficiently high, they may choose to delay the opening of the capital account. Such an outcome depends importantly on the distribution function characterizing the marginal productivity of capital and government preferences.[4] It may occur even if the liberalization program is internally consistent.

17.2.2   Financial Reform and the Capital Account

The experience of developing countries suggests that opening the capital account has often resulted, at least in the short run, in large destabilizing capital flows.[5] If the capital account is opened at a moment when domestic capital markets are still subject to financial repression, with interest rates in particular fixed at artificially low levels, massive capital outflows are likely to take place—thereby threatening the viability of pegged exchange rate regimes and possibly increasing the fragility of the domestic banking system (see Chapter 15). Such flows may be particularly large in countries where the credibility (and thus the sustainability) of the structural reform program within which capital account liberalization is embedded is not fully established. For these reasons, many economists agree that the capital account should only be opened *after* the domestic financial market has been liberalized and interest rates have been raised (see, for instance, Hanson, 1995).

In addition, the experience of the 1980s and 1990s has highlighted the importance of strengthening **prudential supervision** and **regulation** of the banking system at the same time that domestic interest rates are liberalized, before opening the capital account (see Chapter 15). Large capital inflows intermediated by the banking system may lead, as noted in Chapter 7, to excessive risk taking and greater financial fragility if proper regulatory structures are not in place.

17.2.3   A Formal Framework

An analytical framework that is useful to understand some of the issues associated with the sequencing of reforms is provided by Kahkonen (1987). Consider a two-period, small open economy that produces two traded goods (an exportable,

---

[4]In the Conley-Maloney model, it is crucial that the government's welfare function depends not only on the expected utility of the representative household but that it also cares about increases in standards of living—defined in their model as a situation in which second-period consumption is greater than first-period consumption.

[5]See for instance Valdés-Prieto (1994) for a discussion of Chile's experience in the late 1970s and early 1980s.

denoted by x, and an importable, y) using capital and two other factors of production (land and labor) as inputs. Physical capital is invested in the first period, and investment becomes productive in the second period. Land and labor are supplied inelastically in both periods. The home country is taken to be initially a net debtor with respect to the rest of the world. There are four types of agents: households, firms, banks, and the government. Households are identical, live for two periods, and consume both goods. The importable, y, is taxed in both periods. Bank deposits are the only form of saving available to households.

There are three policy-induced distortions in the economy:

- the domestic deposit rate, r_D, is kept below the world market interest rate, r^*;

- the domestic (marginal) loan rate, r_L, is above r^* as a result of capital controls. This is because the government "owns" the banking sector and is assumed to control capital movements by imposing a tax (given by $r_L - r^*$) on transactions conducted on world capital markets;

- there is a tariff, ι, on imports of y in the first period. In the second period, trade is fully liberalized, so that $\iota = 0$.

The lifetime budget constraint of the representative household is

$$c_x^1 + p_1 c_y^1 + \delta_D c_x^2 + \delta_D p_2 c_y^2 = y^1 + \delta_D y^2 \equiv y, \tag{1}$$

where c_j^i is consumption of good j in period i, with $i = 1, 2$ and $j = x, y$; p_i is the relative price of good y in period i ($p_1 = p_1^* + \iota$, where p_1^* is the world market relative price of y, and ι is the tariff rate); $\delta_D = 1/(1 + r_D)$ is the household's discount factor; y^i is the household's income in period i; and y is the present value of lifetime income. The relative price of the exportable good in both periods is set to unity.

First-period saving is given as

$$s = y^1 - c_x^1 - p_1 c_y^1.$$

Households' behavior is characterized by an expenditure function, defined as the minimum expenditure needed to achieve utility level u, given prices (see Varian, 1992). Assuming that the utility function is weakly separable and that the subutility functions z^1 and z^2 are homothetic yields

$$u(c_x^1, c_y^1, c_x^2, c_y^2) = \tilde{u}[z^1(c_x^1, c_y^1), z^2(c_x^2, c_y^2)].$$

The expenditure function can be derived in two steps. In the first step, first-period spending, which is minimized for z^1, is defined as

$$\pi^1(1, p_1) z^1 = \min(c_x^1 + p_1 c_y^1), \quad \text{such that} \quad z^1(c_x^1, c_y^1) \geq z^1,$$

where π^1 is the exact price index for period 1. Because the subutility functions are homothetic, the first-period expenditure function can be written as multiplicatively separable in z^1. The second-period expenditure function is

$$\pi^2(1, p_2)z^2 = \min(c_x^2 + p_2 c_y^2), \quad \text{such that} \quad z^2(c_x^2, c_y^2) \geq z^2,$$

where π^2 is the exact price index for period 2.

In the second step, the overall expenditure function can be written as

$$e = \min(c_x^1 + p_1 c_y^1 + \delta_D c_x^2 + \delta_D c_y^2) \quad \text{such that} \quad u(c_x^1, c_y^1, c_x^2, c_y^2) \geq u,$$

that is, using the above results,

$$e = \min[\pi^1(1, p_1) + \delta_D \pi^2(1, p_2)] \quad \text{such that} \quad \tilde{u}(z^1, z^2) \geq u,$$

and finally

$$e = e[\pi^1(1, p_1), \delta_D \pi^2(1, p_2), u]. \tag{2}$$

The properties of the expenditure function are that it is increasing in all of its arguments, it is concave, and it is homogeneous of degree one in prices. In addition, the function's partial derivatives with respect to prices yield the Hicksian (compensated) demand functions:

$$c_x^1[\pi^1(1, p_1), \delta_D \pi^2(1, p_2), u] = e_{11}, \tag{3}$$

$$c_y^1[\pi^1(1, p_1), \delta_D \pi^2(1, p_2), u] = e_{p_1}, \tag{4}$$

and

$$\delta_D c_x^2[\pi^1(1, p_1), \delta_D \pi^2(1, p_2), u] = e_{21},$$

$$\delta_D c_y^2[\pi^1(1, p_1), \delta_D \pi^2(1, p_2), u] = e_{p_2},$$

where $e_{11} \equiv (\partial e / \partial \pi^1) \pi_1^1$, $e_{p_1} \equiv (\partial e / \partial \pi^1)(\partial \pi^1 / \partial p_1)$, $e_{21} \equiv (\partial e / \partial \pi^2) \pi_1^2$, and $e_{p_2} \equiv (\partial e / \partial \pi^2)(\partial \pi^2 / \partial p_2)$.

Firms produce the two traded goods in both periods and invest in the first period. Only x is used in investment. Investment is financed entirely by loans at the interest rate $r_L > r^*$. Thus, the representative firm's discount factor is

$$\delta_L = 1/(1 + r_L),$$

which is lower than the world discount rate, $\delta^* = 1/(1 + r^*)$.

The revenue functions for each period are defined as the maximum revenue obtainable from the production of the two goods, given prices and factor supplies:

$$R^1(1, p_1) \text{ and } R^2(1, p_2, \bar{k} + I),$$

where $\bar{k}$ is the initial capital stock, I is investment, and the exogenous supplies of land and labor are omitted. The revenue functions are convex and homogeneous of degree one in prices and concave in factor supplies. The supply functions of the goods are given by the partial derivatives of $R^1(\cdot)$ and $R^2(\cdot)$ with respect to prices. R_1^1 and R_1^2 are the supply of the exportable good in the first and second periods, respectively; and R_2^1 and R_2^2 are the supply of the importable good in the first and second periods, respectively.

The profit function is defined as:

$$\max_I R^1(1, p_1) + \delta_L R^2(1, p_2, \bar{k} + I) - I.$$

Profit maximization with respect to I yields the first-order condition

$$\delta_L R_3^2(1, p_2, \bar{k} + I) = 1, \tag{5}$$

where R_3^2 is the partial derivative of R^2 with respect to I. This condition defines I implicitly as

$$I = I(\delta_L), \qquad I' < 0. \tag{6}$$

The banking system, which (as noted earlier) is owned by the government, receives deposits (or savings, s) from households at the interest rate r_D, borrows abroad at the rate r_L (with a tax equal therefore to $r_L - r^*$), and uses its funds to finance firms' investments at the rate r_L. Banks' profits, PR^B, are thus

$$PR^B = r_L I - r_D s - r_L (I - s) = (r_L - r_D)s = (\frac{1}{\delta_L} - \frac{1}{\delta_D})s, \tag{7}$$

where $I - s$ represents the amount borrowed abroad.

The government receives all profits from banks and collects revenues from tariffs, in an amount $\iota(e_{p_1} - R_2^1)$—where $(e_{p_1} - R_2^1)$ is the difference between demand for, and supply of, importable goods (that is, the quantity of imports)— and capital controls, in an amount

$$(r_L - r^*)(I - s) = (\frac{1}{\delta_L} - \frac{1}{\delta^*})(I - s). \tag{8}$$

where $r_L - r^*$ is the effective tax on foreign borrowing $I - s$ at the rate r_L. Revenues (tariffs in period 1, the others in period 2) are rebated to households in the same period in which they are collected. All categories of revenues are handed back in lump-sum fashion.

In general equilibrium, expenditure equals income:

$$e[\pi^1(1, p_1), \delta_D \pi^2(1, p_2), u] = y^1 + \delta_D y^2. \tag{9}$$

Total income in period 1, y^1, consists of income from production in the first period, R^1, and of tariff revenue:

$$y^1 = R^1 + \iota(e_{p_1} - R_2^1). \tag{10}$$

Total income in period 2, y^2, consists of revenue from production in the second period, $R^2 - I/\delta_L$, and lump-sum transfers from the government (banks' profits and revenue from capital controls), that is, using (7) and (8):

$$y^2 = R^2 - I/\delta_L + (\frac{1}{\delta_L} - \frac{1}{\delta_D})s + (\frac{1}{\delta_L} - \frac{1}{\delta^*})(I - s). \tag{11}$$

Households' first-period saving is given by

$$s = y^1 - c_x^1 - p_1 c_y^1,$$

that is, using (3), (4), and (10),

$$s = R^1 + \iota(e_{p_1} - R_2^1) - e_{11} - p_1 e_{p_1}. \tag{12}$$

Combining Equations (11) and (12), households' discounted lifetime income,

$$y = y^1 + \delta_D y^2,$$

is equal to

$$y = R^1 + \iota(e_{p_1} - R_2^1) + \delta_D R^2 - (\frac{\delta_D}{\delta^*})I + (\frac{\delta_D}{\delta^*} - 1)s,$$

that is

$$y = \frac{\delta_D}{\delta^*}[R^1 - I + \iota(e_{p_1} - R_2^1)] + \delta_D R^2 - (\frac{\delta_D}{\delta^*} - 1)(e_{11} + p_1 e_{p_1}). \tag{13}$$

In a world without distortions ($\delta_D = \delta_L = \delta^*$, $\iota = 0$), lifetime income would be

$$y = R^1 - I + \delta^* R^2.$$

Substituting Equation (13) into Equation (9) and assuming that the prices of the traded goods are exogenous to a small economy (that is, $p_1 = p_1^* + \iota$ and $p_2 = p_2^*$, where an asterisk indicates the given world market level of the variable) produces the equilibrium condition:

$$\begin{aligned}
& e[\pi^1(1, p_1), \delta_D \pi^2(1, p_2), u] \\
= \; & \frac{\delta_D}{\delta^*}\{R^1(1, p_1^* + \iota) - I(\delta_L) + \iota[e_{p_1}(\cdot) - R_2^1(1, p_1^* + \iota)]\} \\
& + \delta_D R^2[1, p_2^*, \bar{k} + I(\delta_L)] \\
& - (\frac{\delta_D}{\delta^*} - 1)[e_{11}(\cdot) + (p_1^* + \iota)e_{p_1}(\cdot)].
\end{aligned} \tag{14}$$

In what follows, this equilibrium condition is used to analyze the effects of liberalization policies on welfare.

Analysis of Liberalization Policies

Welfare effects can be analyzed by looking at changes in u, in response to changes in the exogenous variables δ_D, δ_L, and ι. Financial deregulation is measured by $d\delta_D < 0$ (an increase in the domestic deposit rate); relaxation of capital controls is measured by $d\delta_L > 0$ (a reduction in the loan rate); and trade liberalization is measured as $d\iota < 0$ (a cut in the tariff rate).

The effects of liberalization policies are obtained by totally differentiating Equation (14), which yields

$$a \, du = b_1 d\delta_D + b_2 d\delta_L + b_3 d\iota, \tag{15}$$

where $a, b_2 > 0$, and b_1 and b_3 are ambiguous in sign. The derivation of all four coefficients is discussed in the appendix of this chapter.

Financial Deregulation

An increase in the domestic deposit rate (that is, $dr_D > 0$) is equivalent to a reduction in the discount rate ($d\delta_D < 0$). From Equation (15), the welfare effect is thus

$$\frac{\partial u}{\partial \delta_D} = \frac{b_1}{a} \gtrless 0, \tag{16}$$

because $a > 0$ and b_1 is ambiguous in sign. Intuitively, this effect can be explained as follows. In the initial situation, saving is distorted for two reasons: on the one hand, the low deposit rate discourages saving; on the other, the existence of a tariff in the first period forces households to postpone consumption and increase saving. If the tariffs are too high, there can initially be too much saving. In that case, a rise in the deposit rate, which increases saving, worsens intertemporal allocation by causing excessive saving. Thus, in a high-tariff economy (and regardless of whether capital controls are in place or not), attempts to end financial repression by raising the artificially low deposit rate may lead to a lower level of welfare. By contrast, if the tariff is sufficiently low, financial deregulation will increase welfare unambiguously.

The second-best optimal deposit rate is obtained by setting $\partial u / \partial \delta_D = 0$ and solving for δ_D^{**}, the second-best optimal households' discount rate. The result is

$$\delta^{**} = [1 + \iota e_{p_1,2}^+ / (e_{11,2} + p_1^* e_{p_1,2}^+)] \delta^*. \tag{17}$$

This expression shows that, because in the first period $\iota > 0$, $\delta^{**} > \delta^*$. The optimal deposit rate is thus lower than the world market interest rate. The reason is that a first-period tariff makes saving higher than it would be under free trade. Hence, to prevent saving from rising above the optimal level, the interest rate on deposits has to be kept below the world market rate. An important implication of Equation (17) is that, in the presence of tariffs, gradual liberalization of domestic financial markets is the optimal strategy.

Relaxation of Capital Controls

Relaxing capital controls (that is, $d\delta_L > 0$) increases welfare unambiguously, because

$$\frac{\partial u}{\partial \delta_L} = \frac{b_2}{a} > 0, \tag{18}$$

and both a and $b_2 > 0$. The reason for this result is as follows. The initial distortion in investment is the high loan rate, which discourages the accumulation of physical capital. Lowering the loan rate therefore increases investment and thereby improves welfare.

Setting $\partial u / \partial \delta_L = 0$, the (second-best) optimal domestic loan rate is

$$\delta_L^{**} = \delta^*,$$

which indeed indicates that the optimal lending rate is simply equal to the world market interest rate.

Trade Liberalization

A cut in the tariff rate in the first period ($d\iota < 0$) yields

$$\frac{\partial u}{\partial \iota} = \frac{b_3}{a} = [(\frac{\delta_D}{\delta^*})(e_{p_1 p_1} \overset{-}{-} R^1_{22})\iota - (\frac{\delta_D}{\delta^*} \overset{+}{-} 1)(e_{11,p_1} \overset{-}{+} p_1 e_{p_1 p_1})]/\overset{+}{a} \gtrless 0. \quad (19)$$

The reason for this ambiguity is that tariffs cause two types of welfare loss in this economy. First, there is the standard static welfare loss resulting from overproduction and underconsumption of the protected good, y. Second, the presence of a first-period tariff shifts consumption to the second period, with the shift leading to excess saving (as discussed above). In the absence of other distortions, trade liberalization would reduce both types of welfare losses. But the presence of financial repression complicates the situation. A low deposit rate leads to low saving so that, with a sufficiently small tariff, the combined effect of a tariff and financial repression is suboptimal saving. In such conditions, trade liberalization worsens the intertemporal allocation of consumption by reducing saving further, and this intertemporal welfare loss may outweigh the static welfare gain. By contrast, if the initial tariff rate is sufficiently high, there would be excess saving to begin with, and trade liberalization would improve both intertemporal and static resource allocation, thereby unambiguously raising welfare.

Setting $\partial u/\partial \iota = 0$, we obtain the (second-best) optimal first-period tariff rate:

$$\iota^{**} = (1 - \frac{\delta^*}{\delta_D})(e_{11,p_1} + p_1 e_{p_1 p_1})/(e_{p_1 p_1} - R^1_{22}). \quad (20)$$

Trade liberalization would reduce (increase) welfare if the initial tariff is below (above) ι^{**}. Because ι^{**} is positive as long as $\delta_D > \delta^*$, gradual liberalization (keeping the tariff positive in the first period) is superior to "big bang" liberalization (removing the tariff in the first period) as long as the deposit rate differs from the world market interest rate.

Finally, note that the above model does not yield the conclusion that the current account should be liberalized before the capital account is opened. On the contrary, the analysis suggests that the welfare effects of these two types of reform are largely independent of each other. In fact, independently of whether capital movements are regulated or not, a simultaneous liberalization of trade and *domestic* financial markets would appear to be the best option—tariff reductions increase welfare unambiguously only if the domestic financial market is unregulated, and raising the deposit rate unambiguously raises welfare only under free trade.[6] Partial reforms that are beneficial in the long run may result in welfare losses in the short run. This may affect the political feasibility of a reform program, as discussed later.

---

[6] A similar conclusion is reached by Battle (1997), in an extension of Kahkonen's model to account for nominal wage rigidity.

17.3   Sequencing and Labor Market Reforms

As noted in Chapter 14, labor market regulations continue to play a pervasive role in developing countries. Although the extent to which some of these regulations translate into actual distortions is not entirely clear, assessing the role of labor market reform in the overall sequencing of reforms is an important (and as yet unresolved) issue. Edwards (1989) was one of the first to emphasize that labor market reform may need to precede trade reform in order to increase the speed of labor mobility and facilitate the reallocation of resources across sectors. The issue, however, arises in the context of other policies as well. In particular, reforms aimed at altering the process of wage formation in the formal economy (such as changes aimed at indexing nominal wages on future, rather than past, inflation) may be critical in reducing inflation. It may therefore be argued that labor market reforms should precede (or at least accompany) macroeconomic adjustment measures.

Experience suggests, however, that labor market reforms are often difficult to introduce (see Agénor, 1996, and World Bank, 2003). They often are relegated, for various political reasons, to the end of the reform sequence—thereby giving powerful groups the opportunity to block the overall reform process. Moreover, the fear of unemployment often retards critical reforms in other areas, such as privatization or restructuring loss-making public enterprises. Both factors suggest that there may be a strong case for placing labor market reforms early in the overall sequence of economic reform.

17.4   Political Constraints and Reforms

As noted earlier, the new political economy analyzes economic policy formation from both a *normative* and a *positive* perspective.

- The normative perspective focuses, in particular, on issues related to the effect of institutions on policy formation.

- The positive perspective focuses on the type of policies that are more likely to emerge from specific political and institutional settings, and thus the specification of politically sustainable policies.

Using both the normative and the positive perspectives, this section examines three issues that have figured prominently in recent research on the new political economy: the modeling of political conflict among interest groups, the role of economic crises in inducing the adoption of reform programs, and the impact of distributional factors on the political acceptability and sustainability of these programs.

17.4.1   Modeling Political Conflict

A key step in understanding the timing of economic reforms (such as trade liberalization, as discussed in Chapter 14) is to recognize that they typically generate gains for some sectors and losses for others—even if they lead to a net welfare gain for the economy as a whole. If the losing sectors are politically powerful, they may block efforts to adopt adjustment measures that would hurt their interests. Moreover, because *short-run* winners and losers may differ from *long-run* winners and losers, **backtracking** (or policy reversals) may occur in the absence of appropriate compensation schemes, as discussed below.

Analytically, the possibility of conflict (or divergence of interest) between winners and losers suggests that assuming the existence of a welfare-maximizing, **benevolent social planner** that chooses and implements reforms does not accurately describe the way policy decisions are actually made. Instead, as emphasized by Drazen (1996), it must be explicitly recognized that policy choices in reform programs reflect the resolution of *conflicts of interest* between groups with *different goals*. The question then is to identify the reasons why such conflicts, and the mechanisms by which they are resolved, may lead to delays in the adoption of beneficial reforms. Two basic approaches have been proposed in recent years; each emphasizes heterogeneity of interests and some sort of uncertainty about the net benefits of reform, although they do so in quite different ways:[7]

- The **distributional conflict** approach, due to Alesina and Drazen (1991) and Drazen and Grilli (1993), dwells on the basic idea that there is a conflict over how the *known* cost of policy change will be divided among interest groups, so that what matters is *ex post heterogeneity*, that is, heterogeneity caused by the change in policy. Although each interest group knows the net benefit it would receive from the change under a proposed allocation of costs, each group is *uncertain* about the net benefits other groups will enjoy and hence about their willingness to pay for the reform.

- The **uncertain-benefits** approach dwells on the key idea that some groups may be uncertain about the net benefits they themselves would receive if a reform is adopted. Thus, reforms that could end up benefitting a majority of the population are not adopted and there is **status quo bias**. An example of this type of model is provided by Fernández and Rodrik (1991), reviewed in Chapter 14, which focuses on the nonadoption of beneficial reforms in a *static* context rather than *delay over time*. But models along the lines of the Fernández-Rodrik formulation have also been developed to explain delay in a *dynamic* context.

The distributional conflict approach of Alesina and Drazen (1991) and Drazen and Grilli (1993) is based on models of **wars of attrition**. A war of attrition takes place when two (or more) groups disagree over the *burden sharing* that needed policy measures (such as government spending cuts) entail. *Uncertainty* is crucial in this setting—if a group knew it would eventually have to concede, it would be in its interest to do so early on (at the beginning of the reform

---

[7]Drazen (1996) provides an analytical framework that synthesizes the main features of these approaches.

program), thereby avoiding a costly delay. As time goes by, each group learns about the strength of rival groups (namely, how costly it is for *them* to concede) or the costs of the *status quo*. The war ends when one or both groups find the continuation of the status quo more costly than conceding or compromising.

Specifically, Alesina and Drazen describe an economy where government deficits are financed by distortionary taxes (a proxy for inflation), which impose welfare losses on consumers. These welfare losses, which differ across consumers' types, are private information and could be avoided if consumers agreed to "stabilize" the economy—that is, if agreement is achieved on higher (but not distortionary) taxes or lower government transfers. The authors assume that the costs of stabilization are borne unevenly, with the group conceding first incurring the largest share. In equilibrium, each faction hesitates to concede, hoping to outlast its rivals. Although a fully informed social planner would stabilize immediately, delay is individually rational.

The model can be summarized as follows. Prior to stabilization, government expenditure is financed by distortionary taxes, τ, and for simplicity, government expenditure per period, g, is constant over time.[8] Therefore, at time t:

$$\tau_t = g.$$

There are two consumers, both earning the same constant income y and paying an equal share of taxes in each period. Besides reducing consumers' disposable incomes, taxes cause distortions that result in utility losses. These losses are assumed to be proportional to the amount of taxes but different across consumers; they are captured by a parameter θ_i, which is private information.

In equilibrium, each player consumes his disposable income. Ignoring the constant income term, the two players' flow utilities in each period (before stabilization) are, with $i = 1, 2$:

$$u_i = -(\theta_i + 0.5)\tau_t = -(\theta_i + 0.5)g.$$

The parameter θ_i lies between known extremes, θ_L and θ_H. Both players estimate the opponent's cost θ according to the density function $f(\theta)$ and cumulative probability distribution function $F(\theta)$.

At the date of stabilization T, nondistortionary taxes become available and are raised so as to cover all fiscal expenditure. These taxes are divided unequally between players, with the player conceding first (the "loser") shouldering a larger tax burden forever. The tax shares of the "loser" and the "winner" are α (greater than 0.5) and $(1 - \alpha)$, respectively.

---

[8] In Alesina and Drazen's model, government spending before stabilization is financed either by distortionary taxation or by new bond issues, in fixed proportions. Total government spending is then the sum of primary government expenditure and interest costs. Although primary expenditure is assumed to be constant, the rising stock of bonds outstanding causes an increase over time in interest costs and thus in total spending. Allowing for bond financing has no important effect on the game and may create the misleading impression that an increasing debt burden is required to induce stabilization. To make clear that this is not so, and to present the model in its simplest form, all government expenditure here is taken to be financed by taxation.

Because taxes are nondistortionary, the only utility loss following stabilization is associated with the reduction in disposable income. Flow utilities at all times after stabilization are

$$U_L = -\alpha g, \quad U_W = -(1 - \alpha)g,$$

where L denotes the loser and W the winner. Discounted lifetime utilities evaluated at the date of stabilization are

$$V_L = -\alpha g / r, \quad V_W = -(1 - \alpha)g / r,$$

where r is the constant interest rate.

In each period, each player can concede and bring about stabilization by agreeing to pay higher taxes forever. Alternatively, he can wait, hoping that his opponent will concede but enduring distortionary taxes in the interim. The solution of the game is a function $T(\theta_i)$, mapping the idiosyncratic cost of living in the destabilized economy, θ_i, into an optimal time of concession, T. In equilibrium, T is such that the marginal benefit of conceding at T instead of at $T + dt$ equals the marginal benefit of waiting:

$$-u_i + U_L - \frac{dV_L}{dT} = \Omega(T, \theta_j)(V_W - V_L), \tag{21}$$

where $\Omega(T, \theta_j)$ is the probability that the opponent concedes between T and $T + dt$, given that he has not yet conceded, and is given by:[9]

$$\Omega(T, \theta_j) = -\frac{f(\theta_j)}{F(\theta_j)} \cdot \frac{1}{T'(\theta_j)}. \tag{22}$$

Substituting the functional forms assumed above and concentrating on the symmetric equilibrium, Equation (21) can be written as

$$T'(\theta) = -\frac{f(\theta)}{F(\theta)} \cdot \frac{(2\alpha - 1)}{r(\theta + 0.5 - \alpha)}. \tag{23}$$

The additional assumption $\theta_L > \alpha - 0.5$ guarantees that all types $\theta > \theta_L$ concede in finite time. As shown by (23), the optimal concession time T depends negatively on θ: the higher is the idiosyncratic cost from distortionary taxation, the earlier a player concedes.

Moreover, the player with the highest possible cost, θ_H, concedes immediately, because he knows that any other type will wait. Thus,

---

[9]To derive this expression, let $G[T(\theta)]$ be the cumulative distribution function of the time of concession T, and $g[T(\theta)]$ the corresponding density function. Then, it can be shown that the probability Ω is given by

$$\Omega(T, \theta) = \frac{g[T(\theta)]}{1 - G[T(\theta)]}.$$

But $1 - G[T(\theta)] = F(\theta)$, and differentiating this expression yields $-g[T(\theta)]T'(\theta) = f(\theta)$. Substituting these two expressions in the equation above yields Equation (22). Note also that in (21), $dV_L/dT = 0$.

$$T(\theta_H) = 0. \tag{24}$$

The differential equation (23) together with boundary condition (24) completely characterize the symmetric equilibrium. If, for instance, the distribution of θ is uniform between θ_L and θ_H, that is, $f(\theta) = 1/(\theta_H - \theta_H)$, Equations (23) and (24) imply

$$T(\theta) = \frac{(2\alpha - 1)}{r(\theta + 0.5 - \alpha)} \left\{ \ln \left[\frac{\theta + 0.5 - \alpha}{\theta_H + 0.5 - \alpha} \right] - \ln \left[\frac{\theta - \theta_L}{\theta_H - \theta_L} \right] \right\},$$

which is illustrated in Figure 17.1.

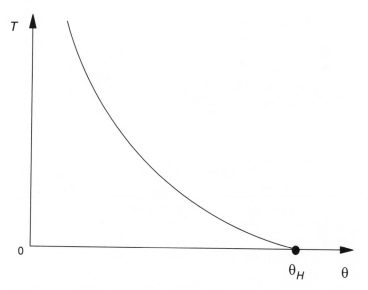

Figure 17.1. The optimal concession time in the Alesina-Drazen war of attrition model.

A key factor affecting the length of the period of inaction is an *unequal distribution* of the burden of adjustment—which delays reform because losing is more costly for at least one group. The war of attrition specification may explain why (without resorting to, say, irrationality of economic agents) governments may at first face little difficulty in implementing a reform package, but then become unable to proceed with further reforms. The crucial issue then becomes the identification of a mechanism that can break the deadlock and restart the reform process. Casella and Eichengreen (1996) argued that *foreign assistance* may play such a role.

In the Alesina-Drazen framework, the delay in implementing fiscal stabilization is endogenous, but the initial fiscal deficit is not. Velasco (1997b), and Mondino, Sturzenegger, and Tommasi (1996) developed dynamic models that endogenize the deficit (as well as inflation). Velasco (1997b) modeled fiscal policy as the outcome of a political process in which spending power is in the hands of several agents (controllers) who represent different interest groups and who behave *noncooperatively*. A key feature of the model is that the benefits of spending are *group specific*, whereas the costs (debt service, in particular) are borne by all groups *jointly*. In this setting, the benefit from public saving, as perceived by each group, is not the rate of interest (that is, the rate of return on saving) but the rate of interest adjusted to account for what other groups spend. As a result, incentives are distorted, each group overspends, and debt accumulates over time. As noted in Chapter 3, this **tragedy of the commons** may explain the **deficit bias** that characterizes fiscal policy in some countries.

17.4.2   The Benefits of Crises

A second issue that has attracted much attention in the new political economy literature is the role of economic and political crises in generating incentives to reform. Krueger (1993, pp. 124-25) argued that economic crises may weaken the political influence of those groups that had earlier resisted policy changes and contributed to a political impasse, thereby providing renewed impetus for reform. At a more formal level, Drazen and Grilli (1993) developed a model in which the cost of inflation increases exogenously. They showed that by making delay more costly, a sudden upward shock to inflation (a "crisis") can accelerate the implementation of a stabilization program. Crises can even make everyone better off and increase welfare if the indirect, beneficial effect of a "bad" shock (a reduction in delay) outweighs the direct (adverse) effect of the crisis.

The notion that economic crises may facilitate the implementation of economic reforms is appealing and somewhat intuitive. As noted in Chapter 6, the historical record seems to indicate that episodes of **hyperinflation** (which are typically periods of severe economic disruptions) have often been easier to terminate than episodes of chronic inflation. An important reason is that periods of very high price instability may allow governments to gather political support more rapidly and to implement drastic stabilization measures. However, the argument also faces some difficulties. At the analytical level, as noted by Tommasi and Velasco (1996, pp. 198-199), the definition of crisis used in the Drazen-Grilli framework is somewhat unconventional: a "crisis" in the model consists of an increase in the costs of lax policies that are in place prior to reform, rather than a sharp and unexpected increase in such costs (as would happen, for instance, with a sudden hyperinflation) shortly before a reform program is implemented. In addition, as also noted by Tommasi and Velasco, the Drazen-Grilli analysis relies on dynamic game models which yield equilibria whose features are not robust to relatively minor changes in model specification. The positive link between crisis and reform may thus depend on which specification (or which equilibrium) is being considered by the analyst.

More generally, Rodrik (1996) argued that the view that crises can be beneficial for reform suffers from two problems. First, it contains an element of tautology (Rodrik, 1996, p. 27): "Reform naturally becomes an issue only when policies are perceived to be not working. A crisis is just an extreme case of policy failure. That reform should follow crisis, then, is no more surprising than smoke following fire." Second, it is difficult to refute, because "if an economy in crisis has not yet reformed, the frequently preferred explanation is that the crisis has not yet become 'severe enough.'"

17.4.3 Political Acceptability and Sustainability

Uncertainty about the distributional consequences of economic reforms also has important implications for the *acceptability* of an adjustment program—particularly, as argued by Wyplosz (1993), in a setting where reforms raise productivity and lead to full employment in the long run but cause unemployment in the short run. Along the lines of the Alesina-Drazen approach, Wyplosz also emphasized that in the presence of uncertainty about the distributional consequences of reforms, it is harder politically to *sustain* them over time (that is, to carry out the reform program to its completion) than it is to *start* them.

Formally, Wyplosz's analysis can be illustrated as follows. Consider an economy in which there are N identical workers. The initial situation, at $t = 0$, is such that each worker's marginal (and average) productivity is θ_L and all workers are employed by the government or public enterprises.[10] National income is thus $Y_0 = N\theta_L$.

In period $t = 1$, an adjustment program, calling for a cut in the public sector labor force, is put in place. Specifically, public enterprises fire a fraction α of their workforce. Employment therefore falls to $(1-\alpha)N < N$ and national income drops to $Y_1 = (1-\alpha)N\theta_L$ (assuming that productivity remains the same as in period 0) and the unemployment rate jumps to α. Because all workers are identical, firing occurs in a *random* fashion. Although the total number of jobs to be cut is known *ex ante*, individual workers do not know for sure whom will be affected.

In period $t = 2$, reform leads to an increase in productivity from θ_L to $\theta_H > \theta_L$. All workers who lost their job in period 1 regain employment in period 2. National income therefore rises to $Y_2 = N\theta_H$.

Let r denote the constant rate at which agents can borrow and lend—for simplicity, the world interest rate. The reform program is *efficient* if the **present value** of national income rises relative to no reform, that is,

$$Y_1 + \frac{Y_2}{1+r} > Y_0 + \frac{Y_0}{1+r},$$

or equivalently, setting $\beta = 1/(1+r)$:

$$Y_1 + \beta Y_2 > (1+\beta)Y_0. \tag{25}$$

Consider a worker who loses his (or her) job when the reform is implemented in period 1 and receives no compensation of any sort. His income is thus 0 in period 1 and θ_H in period 2, because full employment is restored. If the reform

---

[10] Wyplosz's argument was developed in the context of transition economies, but it applies with equal force to developing countries engaged in public sector downsizing (see Chapter 15).

is not implemented, his income is θ_L in both periods. In present value terms, the worker would therefore lose from the reform if

$$\theta_L + \frac{\theta_L}{1+r} > 0 + \frac{\theta_H}{1+r},$$

that is,

$$(1+\beta)\theta_L > \beta\theta_H. \tag{26}$$

Given the definitions of Y_0, Y_1 and Y_2, Equation (25) can be rewritten as

$$(1-\alpha)N\theta_L + \beta N\theta_H > (1+\beta)N\theta_L,$$

that is,

$$(1-\alpha) + \beta\frac{\theta_H}{\theta_L} > (1+\beta).$$

This inequality can be rewritten as

$$\frac{\theta_H}{\theta_L} > \frac{1+\beta}{\beta} - \frac{1-\alpha}{\beta} = \frac{\alpha+\beta}{\beta}. \tag{27}$$

From Equation (26), $\theta_H/\theta_L < (1+\beta)/\beta$. Combining this result with Equation (27) implies that the economic reform program must guarantee the **efficiency condition**

$$\frac{\alpha+\beta}{\beta} < \frac{\theta_H}{\theta_L} < \frac{1+\beta}{\beta}, \tag{28}$$

which ensures that from the point of view of society as a whole *and* from the point of view of the individual worker who runs the risk of being fired, the program is worth implementing. Condition (28) will be assumed to hold in what follows. However, it does not ensure that the program is *welfare enhancing*. Let $v(c_h)$, where c_h is consumption at period h, denote the utility function of each identical worker; $v(\cdot)$ is taken to satisfy the usual conditions for positive and decreasing marginal utility, $v' > 0$ and $v'' < 0$ (see Chapter 2). For a reform to be *ex ante* **politically acceptable**, it must be that workers expect their own situation to improve, that is,

$$\mathbf{E}[v(c_1) + \rho v(c_2)] \geq (1+\rho)v(\tilde{c}), \tag{29}$$

where $\mathbf{E}$ is the mathematical expectations operator (conditional on information available at the beginning of period 1), ρ is the time-preference factor, which need not be equal to the discount factor β, and $\tilde{c}$ the (constant) level of consumption if no reform is implemented.

Condition (29) is the *ex ante* **political acceptability condition**: when it is not satisfied, all workers will rationally choose to reject an adjustment program that is economically efficient. The reason is that if condition (29) is not satisfied, the program will immediately face political opposition upon implementation because, *ex post*, workers are *not* all identical: some become unemployed whereas others end up keeping their jobs. Consequently, the condition for *ex* *post* political acceptability differs from condition (29) and may not be satisfied even when condition (29) is, because some workers are worse off.

The question, then, is under what conditions will the government generate sufficient support (or a sufficient degree of consensus) to implement the program anyway? In the present case, suppose that the government cares about income distribution between those workers who retain their jobs and those who become unemployed during the transition period. This concern about income distribution can be captured by the way the government manipulates unemployment benefits in period 1, b.

To begin with, suppose that neither the government nor individuals are able to borrow against future income, either at home or abroad. Workers consume current income ($c_1 = \theta_L$ or 0 in period 1, $c_2 = \theta_H$ in period 2) and the government must finance unemployment benefits out of taxes, τ, levied in period 1 on employed workers who continue to earn prereform income, θ_L. As a result, *all* citizens are worse off in period 1 compared with their pre-reform situation. The *ex ante* political acceptability condition (29) requires that utility increase by a sufficient amount:

$$\mathbf{E}[v(c_1) + \rho v(\theta_H)] \geq (1+\rho)v(\theta_L),$$

where $\tilde{c} = \theta_L$. In the presence of an unemployment benefit b, given that c_1 depends on the state of nature and that firing occurs randomly (and thus with probability α), this condition can be rewritten as

$$[(1-\alpha)v(\theta_L - \tau) + \alpha v(b)] + \rho v(\theta_H) \geq (1+\rho)v(\theta_L). \tag{30}$$

The government budget constraint is given by

$$\alpha N b = \tau(1-\alpha)N,$$

so that

$$\tau = \frac{\alpha b}{1-\alpha}. \tag{31}$$

Substituting this result in (30) yields

$$(1-\alpha)v\left\{\theta_L - \frac{\alpha b}{1-\alpha}\right\} + \alpha v(b) \geq (1+\rho)v(\theta_L) - \rho v(\theta_H). \tag{32}$$

Ex post, once job losses have actually occurred, workers are not all alike anymore. There are now *two* conditions for *ex post* political acceptability: one for the losers,

$$v(b) \geq (1+\rho)v(\theta_L) - \rho v(\theta_H), \tag{33}$$

and one for the winners,

$$v\left\{\theta_L - \frac{\alpha b}{1-\alpha}\right\} \geq (1+\rho)v(\theta_L) - \rho v(\theta_H). \tag{34}$$

The *ex ante* condition (32) is thus a weighted average of the two *ex post* conditions: if (33) and (34) are both satisfied, (32) will also be satisfied, but the reverse is not true. The range of acceptable income distributions is wider *ex ante* than *ex post*, as seen in Figure 17.2, which displays the left-hand side of the three conditions. This result is important, because it may explain why the transition phase of an adjustment program may be problematic. Because the set of politically acceptable distributions tends to narrow, majority support tends to erode during the transition—possibly leading to an abandonment of the adjustment program. For instance, if the initial position is at point A, a shift to a point such as B in the course of the program may lead to a collapse of the adjustment effort.

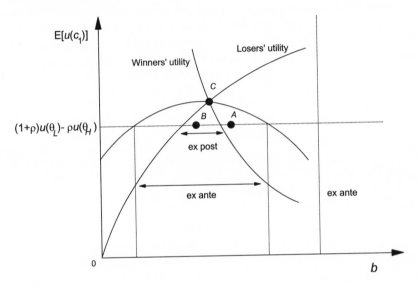

Figure 17.2. Income distribution and political acceptability regions. Source: Wyplosz (1993, p. 383).

Maximizing *ex ante* the likelihood that the program will not be abandoned requires the government to choose an income distribution scheme (that is, an unemployment benefit level, b) that maximizes the left-hand side of (32). The first-order condition is

$$-\alpha v' \left\{ \theta_L - \frac{\alpha b}{1 - \alpha} \right\} + \alpha v'(b) = 0,$$

or equivalently

$$b = \theta_L - \frac{\alpha b}{1 - \alpha},$$

that is

$$b = (1 - \alpha)\theta_L.$$

This solution is represented as point C in Figure 17.2. It implies full *ex post* income equality among *ex ante* identical citizens. If this solution is such that condition (32) is satisfied, then both (33) and (34) will also be satisfied: a reform that is welfare increasing for the country as a whole must also be welfare increasing for each citizen if all receive equal treatment.

To summarize the foregoing discussion, therefore, if all workers face the same probability of becoming unemployed and if economic prospects are expected to improve sufficiently, a redistributional scheme that ensures sufficient support for the implementation of reforms can be readily devised. However, once reforms are implemented and unemployment emerges, even an *ex ante* well-designed redistributional scheme may not prevent individuals that are harmed by the reforms from opposing the continuation of the adjustment program and militating for a policy reversal.

The foregoing discussion assumed that the government was unable to borrow abroad; consequently, the compensation scheme had to be financed through taxes on those workers remaining employed in period 1. Suppose now that the government is able to borrow abroad to finance the benefits paid out during the transition. Taxes, τ_1 and τ_2, are levied in both periods to repay the debt. The *ex ante* political acceptability condition (32) is now

$$(1 - \alpha)v(\theta_L - \tau_1) + \alpha v(b) \geq (1 + \rho)v(\theta_L) - \rho v(\theta_H - \tau_2), \qquad (35)$$

with *ex post* conditions similar to (33) and (34). The intertemporal government budget constraint is now

$$b = \frac{(1 - \alpha)}{\alpha}\tau_1 + \frac{\beta}{\alpha}\tau_2. \qquad (36)$$

Although condition (35) is less stringent than (32), most of the qualitative results derived earlier continue to apply. In particular, the economic efficiency condition (25) still does not necessarily imply *ex ante* support, nor does *ex ante* support provide complete guarantee of *ex post* acceptability of the reform program.

Again, maximizing *ex ante* political support requires the government to maximize Equation (35), subject to (36), with respect to b, τ_1, and τ_2. Let μ be the Lagrange multiplier associated with (36); the first-order conditions are

$$\alpha v'(b) = \mu,$$

$$-(1 - \alpha)v'(\theta_L - \tau_1) = -\frac{(1 - \alpha)\mu}{\alpha},$$

$$-\rho v'(\theta_H - \tau_2) = -\frac{\mu\beta}{\alpha}.$$

These equations can be combined to give

$$\frac{v'(b)}{v'(\theta_L - \tau_1)} = 1, \quad \frac{v'(b)}{v'(\theta_H - \tau_2)} = \frac{\rho}{\beta},$$

or equivalently,

$$v'(b) = v'(\theta_L - \tau_1) = (\frac{\rho}{\beta})v'(\theta_H - \tau_2). \qquad (37)$$

With a **logarithmic** utility function,[11]

$$v(c) = \ln c, \tag{38}$$

Equation (37) becomes

$$b = \theta_L - \tau_1 = (\frac{\beta}{\rho})(\theta_H - \tau_2). \tag{39}$$

Using Equations (38) and (39), Equation (35) can be rewritten as, after some manipulations,

$$\frac{\theta_H}{\theta_L} \geq \frac{\alpha + \rho}{\beta}. \tag{40}$$

Given condition (28), a *sufficient* condition for political acceptability is thus

$$\beta \geq \rho, \tag{41}$$

that is, the government must be able to borrow at an interest rate that is lower than the rate of time preference. In that case, *ex post* acceptability is guaranteed. On the contrary, a sufficient (though not necessary) condition for (40) to be *rejected*, using condition (28), is:

$$1 + \beta \leq \alpha + \rho. \tag{42}$$

Thus, the higher the rate of unemployment in period 1, α, or the lower the discount factor, β (or equivalently the higher the interest rate), the more likely condition (40) will be rejected. Hence, only in cases where the cost of borrowing is not too high will access to international capital markets and foreign loans (by private agents or the government itself) be able to help alleviate the costs of transition and hence facilitate political sustainability.

The foregoing analysis suggests therefore that assessing the political consequences of its actions is a crucial step for a reform-minded government; these consequences determine, at least in part, the sustainability of the initial decisions and whether or not delays (or partial reversals) occur in the implementation of the reform program. In that perspective, it has been increasingly recognized that adjustment programs must include a **social safety net**, that is, a combination of measures aimed at mitigating the short-term adverse effects of economic reform on *losers*—often the poorest segments of the population. Such measures, advocates claim, may help to enhance the political sustainability of the program. Typical reforms with potentially adverse consequences for the most vulnerable include reduction of generalized price subsidies on basic necessities, restructuring of state enterprises, and civil service downsizing (see Chapter 14). Safety nets often include the following components:

- *Targeted subsidies* and *cash compensation.* These schemes have sought to protect the consumption of basic food items by the poor in the face of rising prices, while reducing budgetary expenditure.

---

[11]Wyplosz considers a more general utility function, which generalizes conditions (41) and (42).

- *Unemployment benefits, severance pay,* and *public works schemes.* Because reforms usually involve a temporary increase in unemployment, an important aspect of social safety nets has been enhanced unemployment benefit schemes, the provision of severance pay, and low-wage public jobs in construction, transportation, and so on.

In practice, however, even a well-designed social safety net may not be politically effective, in the sense of enhancing the political acceptability and sustainability of the reform process. The reason is that losers of economic reform are not necessarily the poor; for instance, a sharp reduction in tariff protection will hurt *producers* (and not only workers) in import-substitution industries. As a group, these producers (who presumably do not benefit from the safety net) may be quite effective in blocking further reform or forcing the government to reverse the process of trade liberalization.

17.5   Shock Treatment or Gradual Approach?

As indicated earlier, various economists have argued that shock therapy is preferable in implementing reform programs, because of complementarities between policy instruments. Also as noted earlier, however, trade-offs may arise in the use of policy instruments, making gradualism a less risky approach. In general, the *economic* arguments in favor of gradualism are the following:

- **Preexisting distortions**, which cannot be removed at the time the reform program is announced. Such distortions include labor market rigidities, which are often pervasive in developing countries (as noted earlier), capital market imperfections, and a propensity by private agents to overborrow (Edwards and van Wijnbergen, 1986). Imperfect intersectoral labor mobility, for instance, can be an argument for gradual trade liberalization (Furusawa and Lai, 1999).[12]

- **Imperfect credibility**, which, as stressed by Calvo (1989), is tantamount to a distortion in the intertemporal price of tradable goods. As noted in Chapter 14, if the public wrongly believes that trade liberalization will be reversed in the future, maintaining (or reinforcing) quantitative controls on the capital account may be called for.[13]

- **Congestion externalities**, which may create too much transitional unemployment (relative to the market optimum) after a shock treatment (Gavin, 1996).

---

[12]However, Auernheimer and George (1997) provide an example in which a gradual reform (a reduction in tariffs) itself causes transitory intertemporal distortions (through consumption arbitrage over time), which may outweigh intratemporal gains.

[13]Rodrik (1989), among others, claimed that if imperfect credibility arises because the public is unsure about the true preferences of the government, shock therapy may be preferable to a gradual approach because overshooting can act as a signaling device. However, as noted in Chapter 5, if drastic policies are not perceived to be sustainable, they may be counterproductive.

- **Weak financial system**. Experience with capital account liberalization in recent years supports the view that, although desirable, financial openness may need to proceed gradually over time. As discussed in Chapter 15, premature liberalization can be risky in the absence of adequate prudential regulation and supervision of the banking system.

In addition, there are a number of *political economy* arguments for and against gradualism. The fundamental reason why the pace of reform can be heavily influenced by political constraints is because all structural reforms involve (as emphasized in the previous section) some **distributional changes** in favor of some groups and against others, and there are limits to how much such changes can be tolerated. Along these lines, proponents of shock therapy have argued that such an approach does not allow time for opposition to build up and for interest groups to get together to increase their lobbying activities against the reforms. In particular, for a new, reformist government, maintaining the momentum for reform may be difficult beyond a **honeymoon period**; a gradual approach would give the political opposition time to organize itself and gather strength.

There are also, however, political arguments in favor of a gradualist approach to structural reforms. The general idea is that it may help to minimize adjustment costs and limit the distributional burdens on particular groups in the initial phases of reform. Dewatripont and Roland (1992a, 1992b) provided a good example of this type of argument.

Following the logic of their analysis, consider a reform-minded government facing an inefficient public sector with workers who are heterogeneous in terms of the employment opportunities that they face in the private sector. Improving allocative efficiency requires a shift to higher-productivity activities and layoffs in the public sector, as in Wyplosz's model discussed earlier. In order to make shock therapy *politically acceptable*, all workers in the public sector (who are indistinguishable to the government) must be paid the same compensation, which is determined by the income loss of the less productive worker and therefore ends up being very costly for the state budget. A trade-off therefore appears between allocative efficiency and the fiscal cost of reform. If raising revenue is *distortionary*, a gradual reform, which involves laying off only those workers with the highest relative outside opportunities, generates less of a budgetary burden than shock therapy and may be preferable on welfare grounds—even though it is inferior in terms of allocative efficiency. However, the argument loses weight if governments can indeed finance compensation costs, for instance through *foreign assistance* or by providing a well-targeted *social safety net* (as discussed earlier). In such conditions, shock therapy may remain preferable.[14]

Mehlun (2001) also considered the case of a reform program taking the form of lay-offs in the public sector. In his model, big bang reform leads to a sharp drop in real wages whereas gradual reform leads to a more modest decline. In both cases, output and employment rise over time as capital accumulation

---

[14] At the same time, as noted earlier, even a well-designed safety net may not have much effect on the political sustainability of reform programs.

sustains growth. But if there is resistance to large wage cuts (as a result, for instance, of a subsistence constraint), gradual reform may be preferable not only because it implies a lower cut in wages (thereby ensuring that the reform is both feasible and sustainable), but also because it avoids **multiple equilibria**, which depend on the speed of reform: the initial drop in wages is larger if agents expect the reform to be abandoned in the future, and abandonment is itself dependent on the severity of the initial fall in wages.

Yet another argument in favor of gradualism was proposed by Dewatripont and Roland (1995), who argued that if partial reforms are *unstable*—in the sense that they cannot yield full results unless they are complemented by other reforms—at each stage of the reform process the issue is between accepting the next set of reforms or reversing the previous one. If the previous reforms are deemed successful, people are more willing to accept further (possibly less popular) reforms so as not to lose the gains achieved as a result of the previous set of reforms and to avoid a costly policy reversal.

A related argument was presented by Wei (1998), who argued that a gradual approach to reform may allow a reform-minded government to build constituencies to support the reform process.[15] A package of reforms that would have been rejected by majority voting may gain approval if submitted *piecemeal*, thus allowing information about costs to flow and alliances to form. This argument is diametrically opposite to the one conventionally made about shock therapy— the ability to prevent vested interests from getting organized and blocking the reform process.

Martinelli and Tommasi (1998), however, criticized Wei's argument on the ground that, in societies with powerful interest groups and characterized by a myriad of redistributive and distortionary policies, unbundling a reform program may be **time inconsistent**. Winners of early reforms who are hurt by later reforms have an incentive to *stop* a gradual reform process in its later stages. Knowing that, losers from early reforms will oppose the earlier measures. In such conditions, there may be no alternative to shock therapy.

The implication of the foregoing discussion is that there is no general rule for determining the optimal pace of economic reforms. Initial economic and political conditions facing the reforming economy, and possibly the amount of foreign assistance available, determine the optimal pace of reform. On the one hand, a faster pace of reform may enhance credibility in the reform process if the results achieved in the short run are sufficiently favorable to vindicate the reforms and those who implement them, and thereby ensure against reversibility. On the other, shock therapy may impose *high transitional costs* and hence weaken political support for reform. A gradualist approach can generate greater credibility if it avoids unnecessary disruptions in the short run and allows time for those who benefit from the reforms to gather strength and develop a vested interest in their continuation.

---

[15] Wei's analytical framework is based on the model developed by Fernández and Rodrik (1991), which emphasizes individual-specific uncertainty (see Chapter 14).

17.6 Summary

- Stabilization and adjustment policies have effects that often operate in the same direction; these **policy complementarities** provide arguments for a comprehensive approach to reform and, to some extent, for **shock therapy**. However, macroeconomic and structural policies may also have conflicting effects, particularly in the short run. In such conditions, it may be optimal to adopt a less comprehensive and more gradual program.

- If productive resources could move instantaneously and without cost among alternative uses, and if product and factor prices could adjust immediately to clear all markets, the optimal reform program would entail removing all distortions immediately and simultaneously.

- In practice, however, productive resources cannot be moved instantaneously and costlessly among contracting and expanding sectors of the economy, and the various markets concerned adjust with different speeds toward their long-run equilibrium in response to various reforms.

- The opening of the *capital account* should occur in general after trade account liberalization and domestic financial reforms. Because large capital flows tend to increase the vulnerability of weak financial systems, an adequate prudential, regulatory, and supervision infrastructure must be put in place before the capital account is liberalized.

- Beyond that, however, there are few general principles on the proper sequencing of reforms. The analytical basis for comparing different sequences for removing structural distortions (including those on labor markets) in a **second-best world** is limited. In practice, therefore, the appropriate sequence will depend on characteristics that are specific to each country.

- Changes associated with the beginning of a process of economic reform almost inevitably give rise to **distributional conflicts**. Such conflicts are particularly likely to emerge in cases where the winners and losers from reform are difficult to identify *ex ante*.

- If the political system is fragmented or a large degree of consensus is needed for the continuation of reforms, these conflicts will make it more difficult to sustain politically the reform process. Indeed, they may engender a situation where the reform process stalls because no sufficient consensus can be gathered for a continuation or reversal of policies—a **status quo bias**.

- There is no general rule for choosing between **shock treatment** and a **gradualist approach** in economic reforms. Initial economic and political conditions, and possibly the level of foreign aid, determine the optimal pace of reform. On the one hand, a faster pace of reform may enhance *credibility* in the adjustment process and reduce the risk of policy reversals if the short-run outcomes are favorable enough to vindicate the initial decisions. On the other, shock therapy may impose *high transitional costs* and hence weaken political support for reform.

Appendix to Chapter 17
Calculating the Welfare Effects of Reform

Coefficients a, b_1, b_2, and b_3 in Equation (15) are obtained as follows. First, total differentiation of the equilibrium condition (14) yields the following expression for a:

$$a = e_u - \frac{\delta_D}{\delta^*} \iota e_{p_1,u} + (\frac{\delta_D}{\delta^*} - 1)[e_{11,u} + (p_1^* + \iota)e_{p_1,u}]. \tag{A1}$$

In order to simplify Equation (A1), define the marginal propensities to spend lifetime income y on the two goods in the first period as

$$MPC_x^1 = \partial d_x^1 / \partial y, \qquad MPC_y^1 = p_1 \partial d_y^1 / \partial y,$$

where $d_x^1[\pi^1(\cdot), \delta_D \pi^2(\cdot), y]$ and $d_y^1[\pi^1(\cdot), \delta_D \pi^2(\cdot), y]$ are the Marshallian (uncompensated) demand functions. Let $V[\pi^1(\cdot), \delta_D \pi^2(\cdot), y]$ be the **indirect utility function**, obtained by substituting the Marshallian demand functions into the utility function (see Varian, 1992). Then the following identities must hold:

$$e_{11}[\pi^1, \delta_D \pi^2, V(\pi^1, \delta_D \pi^2, y)] = d_x^1(\pi^1, \delta_D \pi^2, y), \tag{A2}$$

$$e_{p_1}[\pi^1, \delta_D \pi^2, V(\pi^1, \delta_D \pi^2, y)] = d_y^1(\pi^1, \delta_D \pi^2, y), \tag{A3}$$

$$e[\pi^1, \delta_D \pi^2, V(\pi^1, \delta_D \pi^2, y)] = y. \tag{A4}$$

Differentiating Equations (A2) and (A3) with respect to y yields $\partial d_x^1 / \partial y = e_{11,u} V_y$ and $\partial d_y^1 / \partial y = e_{p_1,u} V_y$, whereas differentiating (A4) yields $e_u V_y = 1$. Then $MPC_x^1 = e_{11,u} V_y = e_{11,u}/e_u$ and $MPC_y^1 = p_1 e_{p_1,u} V_y = p_1 e_{p_1,u}/e_u$. Substituting these marginal propensities into Equation (A1) yields:

$$a = e_u - \frac{\delta_D}{\delta^*}(\iota/p_1)MPC_y^1 e_u + (\frac{\delta_D}{\delta^*} - 1)(MPC_x^1 e_u + MPC_y^1 e_u),$$

that is,

$$a = e_u - [\frac{\delta_D}{\delta^*}(\iota/p_1) - (\frac{\delta_D}{\delta^*} - 1)]MPC_y^1 e_u + (\frac{\delta_D}{\delta^*} - 1)MPC_x^1 e_u,$$

or finally

$$a = \overset{+}{e_u}\{1 + [\frac{\delta_D}{\delta^*}(1 - \iota/p_1) - 1]\overset{+}{MPC_y^1} + (\frac{\overset{+}{\delta_D}}{\delta^*} - 1)\overset{+}{MPC_x^1}\} > 0,$$

where in indicating the signs of the expressions it has been assumed that all goods are normal, so that both of the marginal propensities, MPC_x^1 and MPC_y^1, are between zero and unity.

Differentiating the equilibrium condition (14) with respect to $\Delta \delta_D$ yields the following expression for b_1 in Equation (15):

$$b_1 = \pi^2 e_{\pi^2} - (\frac{1}{\delta^*})[R^1 - I + \iota(e_{p_1} - R_2^1)] - (\frac{\delta_D}{\delta^*})(\iota e_{p_1,2} \pi^2) - R^2$$

$$+ (\frac{1}{\delta^*})(e_{11} + (p_1^* + \iota)e_{p_1} + (\frac{\delta_D}{\delta^*} - 1)[e_{11,2}\pi^2 + (p_1^* + \iota)e_{p_1,2}],$$

that is

$$b_1 = -(\frac{1}{\delta^*})[e_{11} + p_1 e_{p_1} + \delta^* \pi^2 e_{\pi^2} + I - R^1 - \iota(e_{p_1} - R_2^1) - \delta^* R^2] \;\text{(A5)}$$

$$+ [\iota e_{p_1,2} - (\frac{\delta_D}{\delta^*} - 1)(e_{11,2} + p_1^* e_{p_1,2})]\pi^2.$$

This equation can be simplified in the following way. Because the expenditure function is homogeneous of degree one in prices,

$$e(\pi^1, \delta_D \pi^2, u) = e_{11} + p_1 e_{p_1} + \delta_D \pi^2 e_{\pi^2}.$$

Rearranging this equation yields

$$e + (\frac{\delta_D}{\delta^*} - 1)(e_{11} + p_1 e_{p_1}) = (\frac{\delta_D}{\delta^*})(e_{11} + p_1 e_{p_1} + \delta^* \pi^2 e_{\pi^2}),$$

so that

$$e_{11} + p_1 e_{p_1} + \delta^* \pi^2 e_{\pi^2} = (\frac{\delta^*}{\delta_D})[e + (\frac{\delta_D}{\delta^*} - 1)(e_{11} + p_1 e_{p_1})]. \qquad \text{(A6)}$$

Plugging Equation (14) into (A6) yields

$$e_{11} + p_1 e_{p_1} + \delta^* \pi^2 e_{\pi^2} = (\frac{\delta^*}{\delta_D})\{(\frac{\delta_D}{\delta^*})[R^1 - I + \iota(e_{p_1} - R_2^1)]$$

$$+ \delta_D R^2 - (\frac{\delta_D}{\delta^*} - 1)(e_{11} + p_1 e_{p_1}) + (\frac{\delta_D}{\delta^*} - 1)(e_{11} + p_1 e_{p_1})\},$$

that is

$$e_{11} + p_1 e_{p_1} + \delta^* \pi^2 e_{\pi^2} = (\frac{\delta^*}{\delta_D})\{(\frac{\delta_D}{\delta^*})[R^1 - I + \iota(e_{p_1} - R_2^1)] + \delta_D R^2\},$$

$$= R^1 - I + \iota(e_{p_1} - R_2^1) + \delta^* R^2.$$

This equality implies that

$$e_{11} + p_1 e_{p_1} + \delta^* \pi^2 e_{\pi^2} - R^1 + I - \iota(e_{p_1} - R_2^1) - \delta^* R^2 = 0. \qquad \text{(A7)}$$

By plugging Equation (A7) into (A5), b_1 can be written as

$$b_1 = [\iota \overset{+}{e_{p_1,2}} - (\frac{\delta_D}{\delta^*} - 1)(\overset{+}{e_{11,2}} + p_1^* \overset{+}{e_{p_1,2}})]\pi^2 \gtrless 0,$$

where in indicating the signs of the expression it has been assumed that all goods are *gross substitutes*, so that

$$e_{11,2}, e_{p_1,2} > 0, \quad \text{and} \quad e_{11,p_1} + p_1 e_{p_1 p_1} < 0. \qquad \text{(A8)}$$

Differentiating the equilibrium condition (14) with respect to $\Delta\delta_L$ yields the following expression for b_2:

$$b_2 = -(\frac{\delta_D}{\delta^*})I' + \delta_D R_3^2 I'. \tag{A9}$$

Using Equations (5) and (A9), this expression can be rearranged as

$$b_2 = \delta_D(\frac{1}{\delta_L} - \frac{1}{\delta^*})\overset{-}{I'} > 0.$$

Finally, differentiating (14) with respect to $\Delta\iota$ yields the following expression for b_3:

$$b_3 = (\frac{\delta_D}{\delta^*})(e_{p_1 p_1} - R_{22}^1)\iota - (\overset{+}{\frac{\delta_D}{\delta^*}} - 1)(e_{11,p_1} + \overset{-}{p_1 e_{p_1 p_1}}) \gtrless 0,$$

where $e_{p_1 p_1} < 0$, R_{22}^1, and e_{11,p_1} represent the derivatives of e_{p_1}, R_2^1, and e_{11} with respect to p_1. In indicating signs in the above expression, all goods are again assumed to be gross substitutes, as indicated in (A8).

References

Abel, Andrew B., "Optimal Investment under Uncertainty," *American Economic Review*, 73 (March 1983), 228-33.

Abel, Andrew B., and Janice C. Eberly, "The Effects of Irreversibility and Uncertainty on Capital Accumulation," *Journal of Monetary Economics*, 44 (December 1999), 339-77.

Abraham, Katharine, and Susan Houseman, "Does Employment Protection Inhibit Labor Market Flexibility? Lessons from Germany, France, and Belgium," in *Social Protection versus Economic Flexibility: Is There a Trade-off?* ed. by Rebecca M. Blank, University of Chicago Press (Chicago, Il.: 1994).

Adam, Christopher, "Fiscal Adjustment, Financial Liberalization, and the Dynamics of Inflation: Some Evidence from Zambia," *World Development*, 23 (May 1995), 735-50.

Adam, Christopher, and David Bevan, "Costs and Benefits of Incorporating Asset Markets into CGE Models—Evidence and Design Issues," Working Paper No. 202, Institute of Economics and Statistics, University of Oxford (October 1998).

——, "Aid, Public Expenditure and Dutch Disease," Working Paper No. 2003-02, Centre for the Study of African Economies, Oxford University (February 2003).

Ades, Alberro, and Edward Glaeser, "Evidence on Growth, Increasing Returns, and the Size of the Market," *Quarterly Journal of Economics*, 14 (August 1999), 1025-46.

Agell, Jonas, Lars Calmfors, and Gunnar Jonsson, "Fiscal Policy When Monetary Policy Is Tied to the Mast," *European Economic Review*, 40 (August 1996), 1413-40.

Agénor, Pierre-Richard, *Parallel Currency Markets in Developing Countries: Theory, Evidence, and Policy Implications*, Princeton Essays in International Finance, No. 188 (November 1992).

——, "Credibility and Exchange Rate Management in Developing Countries," *Journal of Development Economics*, 45 (August 1994), 1-16.

——, "Credibility Effects of Price Controls in Disinflation Programs," *Journal of Macroeconomics*, 17 (Winter 1995), 161-71.

——, "The Labor Market and Economic Adjustment," *IMF Staff Papers*, 43 (June 1996), 261-335.

——, "Monetary Policy under Flexible Exchange Rates: An Introduction to Inflation Targeting," in *Inflation Targeting: Design, Performance, Challenges*, ed. by Norman Loayza and Raimundo Soto, Central Bank of Chile (Santiago: 2002a).

——, "Macroeconomic Adjustment and the Poor: Analytical Issues and Cross-Country Evidence," PRE Working Paper No. 2788, World Bank (January 2002b). Forthcoming, *Journal of Economic Surveys.*

——, "Credit Market Imperfections and the Monetary Transmission Mechanism in an Open Economy," unpublished, World Bank (December 2002c).

——, "Mini-IMMPA: A Framework for Assessing the Unemployment and Poverty Effects of Fiscal and Labor Market Reforms," Policy Research Working Paper No. 3067, World Bank (May 2003).

——, "Does Globalization Hurt the Poor?," *Journal of International Economics and Economic Policy*, 1 (January 2004a), 1-31.

——, "Orderly Exits from Adjustable Pegs and Exchange Rate Bands: Policy Issues and the Role of Capital Flows," unpublished, World Bank (February 2004b). Forthcoming, *Journal of Policy Reform.*

——, "Infrastructure, Public Education and Growth with Congestion Costs," unpublished, World Bank (April 2004c).

——, "Escaping from Poverty Traps," unpublished, World Bank (April 2004d).

Agénor, Pierre-Richard, and Joshua Aizenman, "Technological Change, Relative Wages, and Unemployment," *European Economic Review*, 41 (February 1997), 187-205.

——, "Contagion and Volatility with Imperfect Credit Markets," *IMF Staff Papers*, 45 (June 1998), 207-35.

——, "Volatility and the Welfare Costs of Financial Market Integration," in *The Asian Financial Crisis: Causes, Contagion and Consequences*, ed. by Pierre-Richard Agénor, Marcus Miller, David Vines, and Axel Weber (Cambridge University Press: 1999).

——, "Savings and the Terms of Trade under Borrowing Constraints," unpublished, World Bank (November 2002). Forthcoming, *Journal of International Economics.*

Agénor, Pierre-Richard, and Robert P. Flood, "Macroeconomic Policy, Speculative Attacks and Balance of Payments Crises," in *The Handbook of International Macroeconomics*, ed. by Frederick Van der Ploeg, Basil Blackwell (Oxford: 1994).

Agénor, Pierre-Richard, and Nadeem Ul Haque, "Macroeconomic Management with Informal Financial Markets," *International Journal of Finance and Economics*, 1 (April 1996), 87-102.

Agénor, Pierre-Richard, Alejandro Izquierdo, and H. Fofack, "IMMPA: An Integrated Macroeconomic Framework for the Analysis of Poverty Reduction Strategies," Policy Research Working Paper No. 3092, World Bank (June 2003).

Agénor, Pierre-Richard, and Paul R. Masson, "Credibility, Reputation, and the Mexican Peso Crisis," *Journal of Money, Credit, and Banking*, 31 (February 1999), 70-84.

Agénor, Pierre-Richard, C. John McDermott, and Eswar Prasad, "Macroeconomic Fluctuations in Developing Countries: Some Stylized Facts," *World Bank Economic Review*, 14 (May 2000), 251-86.

Agénor, Pierre-Richard, C. John McDermott, and E. Murat Ucer, "Fiscal Imbalances, Capital Inflows, and the Real Exchange Rate: Evidence for Turkey," *European Economic Review*, 41 (April 1997), 819-25.

Agénor, Pierre-Richard, and Peter J. Montiel, *Development Macroeconomics*, Princeton University Press, 2nd ed. (Princeton, New Jersey: 1999).

Agénor, Pierre-Richard, Mustapha K. Nabli, Tarik Yousef, and Henning T. Jensen, "Labor Market Reforms, Growth, and Unemployment in Labor-Exporting MENA Countries," unpublished, World Bank (June 2003).

Agénor, Pierre-Richard, and E. Murat Ucer, "Exchange Market Reform, Inflation and Fiscal Deficits," *Journal of Policy Reform*, 3 (March 1999), 81-96.

Agénor, Pierre-Richard, and Mark P. Taylor, "Testing for Credibility Effects," *IMF Staff Papers*, 39 (September 1992), 545-71.

Aghion, Philippe, Philippe Bacchetta, and Abhijit Banerjee, "Currency Crises and Monetary Policy in an Economy with Credit Constraints," *European Economic Review*, 45 (June 2001), 1121-50.

Aghion, Philippe, Abhijit Banerjee, and Thomas Piketty, "Dualism and Macroeconomic Volatility," *Quarterly Journal of Economics*, 114 (November 1999), 1359-97.

Aghion, Philippe, and Patrick Bolton, "A Theory of Trickle-Down Growth and Development," *Review of Economic Studies*, 64 (April 1997), 151-72.

Aghion, Philippe, Eve Caroli, and Cecilia Garcia-Penalosa, "Inequality and Growth: The Perspective of New Growth Theories," *Journal of Economic Literature*, 27 (December 1999), 1615-60.

Aghion, Philippe, and Peter Howitt, *Endogenous Growth Theory*, the MIT Press (Cambridge, Mass.: 1998).

Ahmed, Shaghil, "Sources of Economic Fluctuations in Latin America and Implications for the Choice of Exchange Rate Regimes," *Journal of Development Economics*, 72 (October 2003), 181-202.

Aidt, Toke S., "Economic Analysis of Corruption: A Survey," *Economic Journal*, 113 (November 2003), 632-52.

Aitken, Brian J., and Ann E. Harrison, "Do Domestic Firms Benefit from Direct Foreign Investment? Evidence from Venezuela," *American Economic Review*, 89 (June 1999), 605-18.

Aizenman, Joshua, "Inflation, Tariffs and Tax Enforcement Costs," *Journal of International Economic Integration*, 2 (September 1987), 12-28.

Aizenman, Joshua, and Eduardo Borensztein, "Strategic Investment in a Debt Bargaining Framework," *Journal of International Trade and Economic Development* (June 1993), 2:43-63.

Aizenman, Joshua, and Nancy P. Marion, "Policy Uncertainty, Persistence and Growth," *Review of International Economics*, 1 (June 1993), 145-63.

——, "Volatility and Investment: Interpreting Evidence from Developing Countries," *Economica*, 66 (May 1999), 157-79.

——, "The High Demand for International Reserves in the Far East: What Is Going On?," *Journal of the Japanese and International Economies*, 17 (September 2003), 370-400.

Alba, Joseph D., and David H. Papell, "Exchange Rate Determination and Inflation in Southeast Asian Countries," *Journal of Development Economics* (April 1998), 421-37.

Alba, Pedro, Amar Bhattacharya, Stijn Claessens, Swati Ghosh, and Leonardo Hernandez, "The Role of Macroeconomic and Financial Sector Linkages in East Asia's Financial Crisis," in *Financial Crises: Contagion and Market Volatility,* ed. by Pierre-Richard Agénor, Marcus Miller, David Vines, and Axel Weber (Cambridge University Press: 1999).

Alesina, Alberto, and Allan Drazen, "Why Are Stabilizations Delayed?," *American Economic Review,* 81 (December 1991), 1170-88.

Alesina, Alberto, Vittorio Grilli, and Gian Maria Milesi-Ferretti, "The Political Economy of Capital Controls," in *Capital Mobility: The Impact on Consumption, Investment, and Growth,* ed. by Leonardo Leiderman and Assaf Razin, Cambridge University Press (Cambridge: 1994).

Alesina, Alberto, and Roberto Perotti, "The Political Economy of Growth: A Critical Survey of the Recent Literature," *World Bank Economic Review,* 8 (September 1994), 351-71.

——, "Income Distribution, Political Instability, and Investment," *European Economic Review,* 40 (June 1996), 1203-28.

Alesina, Alberto, and Dani Rodrik, "Redistributive Politics and Economic Growth," *Quarterly Journal of Economics,* 109 (May 1994), 465-90.

Alesina, Alberto, and Guido Tabellini, "External Debt, Capital Flight, and Political Risk," *Journal of International Economics,* 27 (November 1989), 199-20.

——, "Positive Theory of Fiscal Deficits and Government Debt," *Review of Economic Studies,* 57 (July 1990), 403–14.

Alexander, William E., Tomás J. Baliño, and Charles Enoch, *The Adoption of Indirect Instruments of Monetary Policy,* Occasional Paper No. 126, International Monetary Fund (Washington DC: 1995).

Alexander, William E., and Francesco Carramazza, "Money versus Credit: The Role of Banks in the Monetary Transmission Process," in *Frameworks for Monetary Stability,* ed. by Tomás J. Baliño, International Monetary Fund (Washington DC: 1995).

Allingham, Michael G., and Agnar Sandmo, "Income Tax Evasion: A Theoretical Analysis," *Journal of Public Economics,* 1 (November 1972), 323-38.

Alston, Julian M., Colin A. Carter, Richard Green, and Daniel Pick, "Whither Armington Trade Models?," *American Journal of Agricultural Economics,* 72 (May 1990), 455-67.

Amadeo, Edward J., "Bargaining Power, Mark-up Power, and Wage Differentials in Brazil," *Cambridge Journal of Economics,* 18 (June 1994), 313-22.

Anand, Ritu, and Sweder van Wijnbergen, "Inflation and the Financing of Government Expenditure: An Introductory Analysis with an Application to Turkey," *World Bank Economic Review,* 3 (March 1989), 17-38.

Anand, Sudhir, and Ravi Kanbur, "Inequality and Development: A Critique," *Journal of Development Economics,* 41 (June 1993), 19-43.

Anderson, J. E., "The Theory of Protection," in *Surveys of International Trade,* ed. by David Greenaway and L. Alan Winters, Basil Blackwell (Oxford: 1994).

Ando, Albert, and Franco Modigliani, "The Life-Cycle Hypothesis of Saving: Aggregate Implications and Tests," *American Economic Review*, 53 (March 1963), 55–84.

Andreoni, James, Brian Erard, and Jonathan Feinstein, "Tax Compliance," *Journal of Economic Literature*, 36 (June 1998), 818-60.

Arbache, Jorge S., Andy Dickerson, and Francis Green, "Trade Liberalisation and Wages in Developing Countries," *Economic Journal*, 114 (February 2004), 73-96.

Arcand, Jean-Louis, and Marcel G. Dagenais, "Measurement Error and the Empirics of Economic Growth," unpublished, University of Montréal (October 1999). Forthcoming, *Oxford Bulletin of Economics and Statistics*.

Arestis, Philip, and Panicos Demetriades, "Financial Development and Economic Growth: Assessing the Evidence," *Economic Journal*, 107 (May 1997), 783-99.

Argy, Victor, "Choice of Exchange Rate Regime for a Smaller Economy: A Survey of Some Key Issues," in *Choosing an Exchange Rate Regime: The Challenge for Smaller Industrial Countries*, ed. by Victor Argy and Paul De Grauwe, International Monetary Fund (Washington DC: 1990).

Ariyoshi, Akira, and others, *Capital Controls: Country Experiences with their Use and Liberalization*, Occasional Paper No. 190, International Monetary Fund (Washington DC: 2000).

Armington, P. S., "A Theory of Demand for Products Distinguished by Place of Production," *IMF Staff Papers*, 16 (March 1969), 159-76.

Arnold, Lutz G., "Stability of the Market Equilibrium in Romer's Model of Endogenous Technological Change: A Complete Characterization," *Journal of Macroeconomics*, 22 (January 2000), 69-84.

Arrow, Kenneth, "The Economic Implications of Learning by Doing," *Review of Economic Studies*, 29 (June 1962), 155-73.

Arteta, Carlos, Barry Eichengreen, and Charles Wyplosz, "When Does Capital Account Liberalization Help More than It Hurts?," Working Paper No. 8414, National Bureau of Economic Research (August 2001).

Ashworth, John, and Lynne Evans, "Seigniorage and Tax Smoothing in Developing Countries," *Journal of Economic Studies*, 25 (December 1998), 486-95.

Aspe, Pedro, *Economic Transformation: The Mexican Way*, Cambridge University Press (Cambridge, Mass.: 1993).

Atkinson, Anthony B., and John Mickelwright, "Unemployment Compensation and Labor Market Transitions: A Critical Review," *Journal of Economic Literature*, 29 (December 1991), 1679-727.

Atiyas, Izak, Caprio, Gerard Jr., and James A. Hanson, "An Overview of Financial Reform Episodes," in *Financial Reform: Theory and Experience*, ed. by Gerard Caprio, Jr., Izak Atiyas, and James A. Hanson, Cambridge University Press (Cambridge: 1994).

Attanasio, Orazio P., "Consumption," in *Handbook of Macroeconomics*, ed. by John B. Taylor and Michael Woodford, Vol. IA, North Holland (Amsterdam: 1999).

Auerbach, Alan, "The Cost of Capital and Investment in Developing Countries," in *Fiscal Incentives for Investment and Innovation*, ed. by Anwar Shah, Oxford University Press (Oxford: 1995).

Auernheimer, Leonardo, and Susan M. George, "Shock versus Gradualism in Models of Rational Expectations: The Case of Trade Liberalization," *Journal of*

Development Economics, 54 (December 1997), 307-22.

Azam, Jean-Paul, and Jean-Jacques Laffont, "Contracting for Aid," *Journal of Development Economics*, 70 (February 2003), 25-58.

Azariadis, Costas, and Allan H. Drazen, "Thresholds in Economic Development," *Quarterly Journal of Economics*, 105 (May 1990), 501-25.

Bacha, Edmar L., "A Three-Gap Model of Foreign Transfers and the GDP Growth Rate in Developing Countries," *Journal of Development Economics*, 32 (April 1990), 279-96.

Baffoe-Bonnie, John, and Mohammed Khayoum, "Economic Development, Life-Cycle Consumption, and Planning Horizon," *International Economic Journal*, 1 (December 1997), 17-37.

Bagwell, Kyle, and Robert W. Staiger, "Will Preferential Agreements Undermine the Multilateral Trading System?," *Economic Journal*, 108 (July 1998), 1162-82.

Baharumshah, Ahmad Z., Evan Lau, and Stilianos Fountas, "On the Sustainability of Current Account Deficits: Evidence from Four ASEAN Countries," *Journal of Asian Economics*, 14 (June 2003), 465-87.

Bahmani-Oskooee, Mohsen, "Real and Nominal Effective Exchange Rates for 22 LDCs: 1971:1-1990:4," *Applied Economics*, 27 (July 1995), 591-604.

Bailey, Martin J., "The Welfare Cost of Inflationary Finance," *Journal of Political Economy*, 64 (April 1956), 93-110.

Bajo-Rubio, Oscar, "A Further Generalization of the Solow Growth Model: The Role of the Public Sector," *Economics Letters*, 68 (July 2000), 79-84.

Baldwin, Richard, and Paul R. Krugman, "Persistent Trade Effects of Large Exchange Rate Shocks," *Quarterly Journal of Economics*, 104 (November 1989), 635-54.

Baldwin, Richard, and Anthony Venables, "Regional Economic Integration," in *Handbook of International Economics*, Vol. 3, ed. by Gene M. Grossman and Kenneth Rogoff, North Holland (Amsterdam: 1995).

Baldwin, Robert E., "Are Economists' Traditional Trade Policy Views Still Valid?," *Journal of Economic Literature*, 30 (June 1992), 804-29.

Baliño, Tomás J., amd Charles Enoch, *Currency Board Arrangements: Issues and Experiences*, Occasional Paper No. 151, International Monetary Fund (Washington DC: 1997).

Bandara, Jayatilleke S., "Computable General Equilibrium Models for Development Policy Analysis in LDCs," *Journal of Economic Surveys*, 5 (January 1991), 3-69.

Bandara, Jayatilleke S., and Mark McGillivray, "Trade Policy Reforms in South Asia," *The World Economy*, 21 (September 1998), 881-96.

Bandiera, Oriana, Gerard Caprio, Jr., Patrick Honohan, and Fabio Schiantarelli, "Does Financial Reform Increase or Reduce Savings?," *Review of Economics and Statistics*, 82 (May 2000), 239-263.

Bardhan, Pranab, "Corruption and Development: A Review of Issues," *Journal of Economic Literature*, 35 (September 1997), 1320-46.

Bar-Ilan, Avner, and William C. Strange, "Investment Lags," *American Economic Review*, 86 (June 1996), 610-22.

Barro, Robert J., "Are Government Bonds Net Wealth?," *Journal of Political Economy*, 82 (November 1974), 1095-117.

——, "Inflationary Finance under Discretion and Rules," *Canadian Journal of Economics,* 16 (February 1983), 1-16.

——, "The Ricardian Approach to Budget Deficits," *Journal of Economic Perspectives,* 3 (March 1989), 37-54.

——, "Government Spending in a Simple Model of Endogenous Growth," *Journal of Political Economy,* 98 (October 1990), s103-s125.

——, "Economic Growth in a Cross Section of Countries," *Quarterly Journal of Economics,* 106 (May 1991), 407-43.

——, *Determinants of Economic Growth,* MIT Press (Cambridge, Mass.: 1997).

——, "Notes on Growth Accounting," *Journal of Economic Growth,* 4 (June 2000*a*), 119-37.

——, "Inequality and Growth in a Panel of Countries," *Journal of Economic Growth,* 5 (March 2000*b*), 5-30.

——, "Human Capital and Growth," *American Economic Review,* 91 (May 2001), 12-17.

Barro, Robert J., and David B. Gordon, "A Positive Theory of Monetary Policy in a Natural Rate Model," *Journal of Political Economy,* 91 (August 1983), 589-610.

Barro, Robert J., and Jong-Wha Lee, "International Data on Educational Attainment: Updates and Implications," *Oxford Economic Papers,* 53 (July 2001), 541-63.

Barro, Robert J., N. Gregory Mankiw, and Xavier Sala-i-Martin, "Capital Mobility in Neoclassical Models of Growth," *American Economic Review,* 85 (March 1995), 103-15.

Barro, Robert J., and Xavier Sala-i-Martin, "Public Finance in Models of Economic Growth," *Review of Economic Studies,* 59 (October 1992), 645-61.

——, *Economic Growth,* McGraw-Hill (New York: 1995).

Barry, Frank, and Michael B. Devereux, "The 'Expansionary Fiscal Contraction' Hypothesis: A Neo-Keynesian Analysis," *Oxford Economic Papers,* 47 (April 1995), 249-64.

——, "Expansionary Fiscal Contraction: A Theoretical Exploration," *Journal of Macroeconomics,* 25 (March 2003), 1-23.

Basu, Kaushik, *Analytical Development Economics,* 2nd ed., MIT Press (Cambridge, Mass.: 1997).

Battle, Ann Marie, "Welfare Effects of Liberalization Reforms with Distortions in Financial and Labor Markets," *Journal of Development Economics,* 52 (April 1997), 279-94.

Baumol, William J., "Entrepreneurship: Productive, Unproductive, and Destructive," *Journal of Political Economy,* 98 (October 1990), 893-921.

Beaugrand, Philippe, "Zaïre's Hyperinflation, 1990-96," Working Paper No. 97/50, International Monetary Fund (April 1997).

Becker, Gary, "Crime and Punishment: An Economic Approach," *Journal of Political Economy,* 76 (March/April 1968), 169-217.

Becker, Gary, Kevin Murphy, and Robert Tamura, "Human Capital, Fertility, and Economic Growth," *Journal of Political Economy,* 98 (October 1990), 12-37.

Behrman, Jere, Nancy Birdsall, and Miguel Székely, "Economic Reforms and Wage Differentials in Latin America," unpublished, Inter-American Development Bank

(September 2000).

Bell, Linda A., "The Impact of Minimum Wages in Mexico and Colombia," *Journal of Labor Economics*, 15 (July 1997), s102-s135.

Bénabou, Roland, "Inequality and Growth," in *NBER Macroeconomics Annual 1996*, ed. by Ben S. Bernanke and Julio J. Rotemberg, MIT Press (Cambridge, Mass.: 1997).

Bencivenga, Valerie R., and Bruce D. Smith, "Financial Intermediation and Endogenous Growth," *Review of Economic Studies*, 58 (April 1991), 195-209.

——, "Deficits, Inflation, and the Banking System in Developing Countries: The Optimal Degree of Financial Repression," *Oxford Economic Papers*, 44 (October 1992), 767-90.

Benhabib, Jess, and Mark M. Spiegel, "The Role of Human Capital in Economic Development: Evidence from Aggregate Cross-Country Data," *Journal of Monetary Economics*, 34 (October 1994), 143-73.

Benjamin, Dwayne, and Angus Deaton, "Household Welfare and the Pricing of Cocoa and Coffee in Côte d'Ivoire: Lessons from the Living Standards Surveys," *World Bank Economic Review*, 7 (September 1993), 293-318.

Bennett, Herman, Norman Loayza, and Klaus Schmidt-Hebbel, "A Study of Aggregate Saving by Economic Agents in Chile," (in Spanish), in *Análisis Empírico del Ahorro en Chile*, ed. by Felipe Morandé and Rodrigo Vergara, Central Bank of Chile (Santiago: 2001).

Berg, Andrew, and Catherine Pattillo, "Are Currency Crises Predictable? A Test," *IMF Staff Papers*, 46 (June 1999), 107-38.

Berger, Helge, Jakob de Haan, and Sylvester C. Eijffinger, "Central Bank Independence: An Update of Theory and Evidence," *Journal of Economic Surveys*, 15 (February 2001), 3-40.

Bernanke, Ben S., and Mark Gertler, "Agency Costs, Net Worth, and Business Fluctuations," *American Economic Review*, 79 (March 1989), 14-31.

——, "Inside the Black Box: The Credit Channel of Monetary Policy Transmission," *Journal of Economic Perspectives*, 9 (September 1995), 27-48.

Bernanke, Ben S., Mark Gertler, and Simon Gilchrist, "The Financial Accelerator in a Quantitative Business Cycle Framework," in *Handbook of Macroeconomics*, ed. by John B. Taylor and Mark Woodford, North Holland (Amsterdam: 2000).

Bernanke, Ben S., and Refet S. Gurkaynak, "Is Growth Exogenous? Taking Mankiw, Romer, and Weil Seriously," Working Paper No. 8365, National Bureau of Economic Research (July 2001).

Bernard, Andrew B., and Steven N. Durlauf, "Interpreting Tests of the Convergence Hypothesis," *Journal of Econometrics*, 71 (March 1996), 161-73.

Berthélemy, Jean-Claude, and Sylvie Démurger, "Foreign Direct Investment and Economic Growth: Theory and Application to China," *Review of Development Economics*, 4 (June 2000), 140-55.

Bertola, Giuseppe, and Allan H. Drazen, "Trigger Points and Budget Cuts: Explaining the Effects of Fiscal Austerity," *American Economic Review*, 83 (March 1993), 11-26.

Besley, Timothy, and John McLaren, "Taxes and Bribery: The Role of Wage Incentives," *Economic Journal*, 103 (January 1993), 119-41.

Bester, Helmut, "Screening vs. Rationing in Credit Markets with Imperfect Information," *American Economic Review*, 75 (September 1985), 850-55.

Bevilaqua, Afonso S., and Márcio G. P. Garcia, "Debt Management in Brazil: Evaluation of the Real Plan and Challenges Ahead," Policy Research Working Paper No. 2402, World Bank (July 2000).

Bevilaqua, Afonso S., and Rogério L. Werneck, "Fiscal Impulse in the Brazilian Economy, 1989-96," Working Paper No. 379, Pontificia Universidade de Rio do Janeiro (October 1997).

Beyer, Harald, Patricio Rojas, and Rodrigo Vergara, "Trade Liberalization and Wage Inequality," *Journal of Development Economics*, 59 (June 1999), 103-23.

Bhagwati, Jagdish, and Arvind Panagariya, "Preferential Trading Areas and Multilateralism: Strangers, Friends or Foes?," in *The Economics of Preferential Trade Arrangements*, ed. by Jagdish Bhagwati and Arvind Panagariya, the American Enterprise Institute Press (Washington DC: 1996).

Bhagwati, Jagdish, Arvind Panagariya, and T. N. Srinivasan, *Lectures on International Trade*, 2nd ed., MIT Press (Cambridge, Mass.: 1998).

Bhattacharya, Amar, Peter J. Montiel, and Sunil Sharma, "Private Capital Inflows to Sub-Saharan Africa: An Overview of Trends and Determinants," in *External Finance for Low-Income Countries*, edited by Zubair Iqbal and Ravi Kanbur, World Bank (Washington, DC: 1997).

Bhattacharya, Prabir, "Rural-Urban Migration in Economic Development," *Journal of Economic Surveys*, 7 (September 1993), 243-81.

Bhattacharya, Sudipto, Arnoud W. Boot, and Anjan V. Thakor, "The Economics of Bank Regulation," *Journal of Money, Credit, and Banking*, 30 (November 1998), 745-70.

Bils, Mark, and Peter J. Klenow, "Does Schooling Cause Growth or the Other Way Around?," Working Paper No. 6393, National Bureau of Economic Research (February 1998).

Bird, Graham, "The Credibility and Signalling Effect of IMF Programmes," *Journal of Policy Modeling*, 24 (December 2002), 799-811.

Birdsall, Nancy, Stijn Claessens, and Ishac Diwan, "Policy Selectivity Foregone: Debt and Donor Behavior in Africa," *World Bank Economic Review*, 17 (September 2003), 409-35.

Blackburn, Keith, and Michael Christensen, "Monetary Policy and Policy Credibility: Theories and Evidence," *Journal of Economic Literature*, 27 (March 1989), 1-45.

Blanchard, Olivier-Jean, "Suggestions for a New Set of Fiscal Indicators," in *The Political Economy of Government Debt*, ed. by H. A. Verbon and F. A. van Winden, Elsevier (Amsterdam: 1993).

Blank, Rebecca M., and Richard B. Freeman, "Evaluating the Connection between Social Protection and Economic Flexibility," in *Social Protection versus Economic Flexibility: Is There a Trade-off?* ed. by Rebecca M. Blank, University of Chicago Press (Chicago, Il.: 1994).

Bleaney, Michael F., "Macroeconomic Stability, Investment and Growth in Developing Countries," *Journal of Development Economics*, 48 (March 1996), 461-77.

Bleaney Michael F., and David Greenaway, "Long-Run Trends in the Relative Price of Primary Commodities and in the Terms of Trade of Developing Countries,"

Oxford Economic Papers, 45 (July 1993), 349-63.

Blejer, Mario I., and Adrienne Cheasty, "The Measurement of Fiscal Deficits: Analytical and Methodological Issues," *Journal of Economic Literature*, 29 (December 1991), 1644-78.

Blejer, Mario I., and Ke-Young Chu, *Measurement of Fiscal Impact: Methodological Issues*, Occasional Paper No. 59, International Monetary Fund (Washington DC: 1988).

Blejer, Mario I., and Nissan Liviatan, "Fighting Hyperinflation: Stabilization Strategies in Argentina and Israel," *IMF Staff Papers*, 34 (September 1987), 409-38.

Bliss, Christopher, and Nicholas Stern, "Productivity, Wages, and Nutrition: Part I–The Theory," *Journal of Development Economics*, 5 (December 1978), 331-62.

Boone, Peter, "Politics and the Effectiveness of Foreign Aid," *European Economic Review*, 40 (February 1996), 289-329.

Boot, Arnoud W., and Anjan V. Thakor, "Self-Interested Bank Regulation," *American Economic Review*, 83 (May 1993), 206-12.

Boote, Anthony R., and Kamau Thugge, *Debt Relief for Low-Income Countries: The HIPC Initiative*, IMF Pamphlet Series, No. 51, revised (Washington DC: 1999).

Booth, David, "Introduction and Overview," *Development Policy Review*, 21 (March 2003), 131-59.

Borensztein, Eduardo, José De Gregorio, and Jong Wha Lee, "How Does Foreign Direct Investment Affect Economic Growth?," *Journal of International Economics* 45 (June 1998), 115–35.

Borio, Claudio E. V., "The Implementation of Monetary Policy in Industrial Countries: A Survey," Economic Paper No. 47, Bank for International Settlements (July 1997).

Borio, Claudio E. V., and Wilhelm Fritz, "The Response of Short-Term Bank Lending Rates to Policy Rates: A Cross-Country Perspectice," in *Financial Structure and the Monetary Policy Transmission Mechanism*, CB Document No. 394, Bank for International Settlements, Basel (March 1995).

Bosworth, Barry P., and Susan M. Collins, "Capital Flows to Developing Countries: Implications for Saving and Investment," *Brookings Papers on Economic Activity*, No. 1 (June 1999), 143-80.

——, "The Empirics of Growth: An Update," *Brookings Papers on Economic Activity*, No. 2 (December 2003), 113-206.

Bourguignon, François, Jaime de Melo, and Akiko Suwa, "Modeling the Effects of Adjustment Programs on Income Distribution," *World Development*, 19 (November 1991), 1527-44.

Bowe, Michael, and James W. Dean, *Has the Market Solved the Sovereign-Debt Crisis?*, Princeton Studies in International Finance, No. 83 (August 1997).

Boyd, John H., and Bruce D. Smith, "The Co-Evolution of the Real and Financial Sectors in the Growth Process," *World Bank Economic Review*, 10 (May 1996), 371-96.

Boyle, G. E., and T. G. McCarthy, "A Simple Measure of β-Convergence," *Oxford Bulletin of Economics and Statistics*, 59 (May 1997), 257-64.

Bravo, Ana B., and Antonio L. Silvestre, "Intertemporal Sustainability of Fiscal

Policies: Some Tests for European Countries," *European Journal of Political Economy*, 18 (September 2002), 517-28.

Brecher, Richard, and Carlos Díaz-Alejandro, "Tariffs, Foreign Capital, and Immiserizing Growth," *Journal of International Economics*, 7 (November 1977), 317-22.

Brock, William A., and Steven N. Durlauf, "Growth Empirics and Reality," *World Bank Economic Review*, 15 (May 2001), 229-72.

Broda, Christian, "Coping with Terms-of-Trade Shocks: Pegs versus Floats," *American Economic Review*, 91 (May 2001), 376-80.

Browning, Martin, and Anna Maria Lusardi, "Household Saving: Micro Theories and Micro Facts," *Journal of Economic Literature*, 34 (December 1996), 1797-855.

Brumm, Harold J., "Inflation and Central Bank Independence Revisited," *Economics Letters*, 77 (October 2002), 205-209.

Brunetti, Aymo, "Political Variables in Cross-Country Growth Analysis," *Journal of Economic Surveys*, 11 (June 1997), 163-90.

——, "Policy Volatility and Economic Growth: A Comparative, Empirical Analysis," *European Journal of Political Economy*, 14 (February 1998), 35-51.

Bruno, Michael, *High Inflation and the Nominal Anchors of an Open Economy*, Princeton Essay in International Finance, No. 183, Princeton University (Princeton, New Jersey: 1991).

Bruno, Michael, and William Easterly, "Inflation Crises and Long-Run Growth," *Journal of Monetary Economics*, 41 (February 1998), 3-26.

Bruno, Michael, and Stanley Fischer, "Seigniorage, Operating Rules, and the High Inflation Trap," *Quarterly Journal of Economics*, 105 (May 1990), 353-74.

Bruno, Michael, Martin Ravallion, and Lyn Squire, "Equity and Growth in Developing Countries: Old and New Perspectives on the Policy Issues," in *Income Distribution and High-Quality Growth*, ed. by Vito Tanzi and Ke-Young Chu, MIT Press (Cambridge, Mass.: 1998).

Bruton, Henry, "Import Substitution," in *Handbook of Development Economics*, II, ed. by Hollis B. Chenery and T. N. Srinivasan, North Holland (Amsterdam: 1989).

Bubula, Andrea, and Inci Otker-Robe, "The Evolution of Exchange Rate Regimes since 1990: Evidence from De Facto Policies," Working Paper No. 02/155, International Monetary Fund (September 2002).

Buffie, Edward F., "Devaluation, Investment and Growth in LDCs," *Journal of Development Economics*, 20 (March 1986), 361-79.

——, "Imported Inputs, Real Wage Rigidity and Devaluation in the Small Open Economy," *European Economic Review* 33 (September 1989), 1345-61.

Buiter, Willem H., "Structural and Stabilization Aspects of Fiscal and Financial Policy in the Dependent Economy," *Oxford Economic Papers*, 40 (June 1988), 220-45.

——, "Aspects of Fiscal Performance in Some Transition Economies Under Fund-Supported Programs," Working Paper No. 97/131, International Monetary Fund (April 1997).

Buiter, Willem H., and Urjit R. Patel, "Debt, Deficits and Inflation: An Application to the Public Finances of India," *Journal of Public Economics*, 47 (March 1992), 171-205.

Bulir, Ales, "Income Inequality: Does Inflation Matter?," *IMF Staff Papers*, 48 (December 2001), 139-59.

Bulir, Ales, and Javier Hamann, "Aid Volatility: An Empirical Assessment," *IMF Staff Papers*, 50 (March 2003), 64-89.

Burgess, Robin, and Nicholas Stern, "Taxation and Development," *Journal of Economic Literature*, 31 (June 1993), 762-830.

Burmeister, Edwin, and A. Rodney Dobell, *Mathematical Theories of Economic Growth*, Macmillan (New York: 1970).

Burnside, Craig, and David Dollar, "Aid, Policies, and Growth," *American Economic Review*, 90 (September 2000), 847-68.

Burnside, Craig, Martin Eichenbaum, and Sergio Rebelo, "Prospective Deficits and the Asian Currency Crisis," *Journal of Political Economy*, 109 (December 2001), 1155-97.

Bustos, Álvaro, Eduardo M. Engel, and Alexander Galetovic, "Could Higher Taxes Increase the Long-run Demand for Capital? Theory and Evidence for Chile," *Journal of Development Economics*, 73 (April 2004), 675-97.

Buttrick, J., "A Note on Professor Solow's Growth Model," *Quarterly Journal of Economics*, 72 (November 1958), 633–36.

Caballero, Ricardo J., "Consumption Puzzles and Precautionary Savings," *Journal of Monetary Economics*, 25 (January 1990), 113-36.

——, "On the Sign of the Investment-Uncertainty Relationship," *American Economic Review*, 81 (March 1991), 279-88.

Calderón, César, and Lin Liu, "The Direction of Causality between Financial Development and Economic Growth," *Journal of Development Economics*, 72 (October 2003), 321-34.

Calderón, César, and Klaus Schmidt-Hebbel, "Macroeconomic Policies and Performance in Latin America," *Journal of International Money and Finance*, 22 (December 2003), 895-923.

Calmfors, Lars, "Centralization of Wage Bargaining and Macroeconomic Performance: A Survey," *OECD Economic Studies*, 10 (Winter 1993), 161-91.

Calvo, Guillermo A., "Incredible Reforms," in *Debt, Stabilization and Development*, ed. by Guillermo A. Calvo, Ronald Findlay, Pentti Kouri, and Jorge Braga de Macedo, Basil Blackwell (Oxford: 1989).

——, "The Perils of Sterilization," *IMF Staff Papers*, 38 (December 1991), 921-26.

——, "Varieties of Capital-Market Crises," in *The Debt Burden and Its Consequences for Monetary Policy*, ed. by Guillermo A. Calvo and Mervyn King, Macmillan (London: 1998).

Calvo, Guillermo A., Leonardo Leiderman, and Carmen M. Reinhart, "Inflows of Capital to Developing Countries in the 1990s: Causes and Effects," *Journal of Economic Perspectives*, 10 (Spring 1996), 123-39.

Calvo, Guillermo A., and Enrique G. Mendoza, "Rational Contagion and the Globalization of Securities Markets," *Journal of International Economics*, 51 (June 2000), 79-113.

Calvo, Guillermo, and Frederic S. Mishkin, "The Mirage of Exchange Rate Regimes for Emerging Market Countries," Working Paper No. 9808, National Bureau of Economic Research (June 2003).

Calvo, Guillermo A., and Carmen M. Reinhart, "Fear of Floating," *Quarterly Journal of Economics*, 117 (May 2002), 379-408.

Calvo, Guillermo A., Carmen M. Reinhart, and Carlos A. Végh, "Targeting the Real Exchange Rate: Theory and Evidence," *Journal of Development Economics*, 47 (June 1995), 97-133.

Calvo, Guillermo A., and Carlos A. Végh, "Exchange Rate-Based Stabilization under Imperfect Credibility," in *Open Economy Macroeconomics*, ed. by Helmut Frisch and Andreas Worgotter, St. Martin's Press (New York: 1993).

——, "From Currency Substitution to Dollarization and Beyond: Analytical and Policy Issues," in Guillermo A. Calvo, *Money, Exchange Rates, and Output*, MIT Press (Cambridge, Mass.: 1996).

Calvo, Sara, and Carmen M. Reinhart, "Capital Flows to Latin America: Is There Evidence of Contagion Effects?" in *Private Capital Flows to Emerging Markets after the Mexican Crisis*, ed. by Guillermo A. Calvo, Morris Goldstein, and Eduard Hochreiter, Institute for International Economics (Washington DC: 1996).

Campbell White, Oliver, and Anita Bhatia, *Privatization in Africa*, World Bank (Washington D.C.: 1998).

Canavan, Chris, and Mariano Tommasi, "On the Credibility of Alternative Exchange Rate Regimes," *Journal of Development Economics*, 54 (October 1997), 101-22.

Caprio, Gerard, Jr., James A. Hanson, and Patrick Honohan, "The Case for Liberalization and Some Drawbacks," in *Financial Liberalization : How Far, How Fast?*, ed. by Gerard Caprio, Jr., Patrick Honohan, Joseph E. Stiglitz, Cambridge University Press (Cambridge: 2001).

Caprio, Gerard, Jr., and Daniela Klingebiel, "Bank Insolvencies: Cross Country Experience," Policy Research Working Paper No. 1620, World Bank (July 1996).

Cárdenas, Mauricio, and Felipe Barrrera, "On the Effectiveness of Capital Controls: The Experience of Colombia during the 1990s," *Journal of Development Economics*, 54 (October 1997), 27-58.

Cárdenas, Mauricio, and Andrés Escobar, "Saving Determinants in Colombia: 1925-1994," *Journal of Development Economics*, 57 (October 1998), 5-44.

Cardoso, Eliana, "Deficit Finance and Monetary Dynamics in Brazil and Mexico," *Journal of Development Economics*, 37 (November 1992), 173-97.

Cardoso, Eliana, and Ilan Goldfajn, "Capital Flows to Brazil: The Endogeneity of Capital Controls," *IMF Staff Papers*, 45 (March 1998), 161-202.

Cardoso, Eliana, R. Paes de Barro, and Andre Urani, "Inflation and Unemployment as Determinants of Income Inequality in Brazil: The 1980s," in *Reform, Recovery, and Growth: Latin America and the Middle East*, ed. by Rudiger Dornbusch and Sebastián Edwards, University of Chicago Press (Chicago, Il.: 1995).

Casella, Alessandra, and Barry Eichengreen, "Can Foreign Aid Accelerate Stabilisation?," *Economic Journal*, 106 (May 1996), 605-19.

Caselli, Francesco, Gerardo Esquivel, and Fernando Lefort, "Reopening the Convergence Debate: A New Look at Cross-Country Growth Empirics," *Journal of*

Economic Growth, 1 (September 1996), 363-90.

Cashin, Paul, "Government Spending, Taxes, and Economic Growth," *IMF Staff Papers*, 42 (June 1995), 237-69.

Cashin, Paul, and John McDermott, "Intertemporal Substitution and Terms-of-Trade Shocks," *Review of International Economics*, 11 (September 2003), 604-18.

Cashin, Paul, John McDermott, and Alasdair Scott, "Booms and Slumps in World Commodity Prices," *Journal of Development Economics*, 69 (October 2002), 277-96.

Catao, Luis, and Marco E. Terrones, "Fiscal Deficits and Inflation," Working Paper No. 03/65, International Monetary Fund (April 2003).

Cecchetti, Stephen G., Hans Genberg, John Lipsky, and Sushil Wadhwani, *Asset Prices and Central Bank Policy*, Centre for Economic Policy Research (London: 2000).

Chah, Eun Y., Valerie A. Ramey, and Ross M. Starr, "Liquidity Constraints and Intertemporal Consumer Optimization: Theory and Evidence from Durable Goods," *Journal of Money, Credit, and Banking*, 27 (February 1995), 272-87.

Chand, Sheetal K., "Fiscal Impulse Measures and Their Fiscal Impact," in *How to Measure the Fiscal Deficit*, ed. by Mario I. Blejer and Adrienne Cheasty, International Monetary Fund (Washington DC: 1993).

Chang, Roberto, "Political Party Negotiations, Income Distribution and Endogenous Growth," *Journal of Monetary Economics*, 41 (April 1998), 227-55.

Chang, Roberto, and Andrés Velasco, "Liquidity Crises in Emerging Markets: Theory and Policy," Working Paper No. 7272, National Bureau of Economic Research (July 1999).

——, "Dollarization: Analytical Issues," Working Paper No. 8838, National Bureau of Economic Research (March 2002).

Chenery, Hollis B., and Alan Strout, "Foreign Assistance and Economic Development," *American Economic Review* 56 (September 1966), 679-733.

Cheong, ChongCheul, "Regime Changes and Econometric Modeling of the Demand for Money in Korea," *Economic Modelling*, 20 (May 2003), 437-53.

Chiang, Alpha C., *Fundamental Methods of Mathematical Economics*, McGraw-Hill, 3rd edition (New York: 1984).

Chinn, Menzie D., "Before the Fall: Were East Asian Currencies Overvalued?," Working Paper No. 6491, National Bureau of Economic Research (April 1998).

Chinn, Menzie, and Eswar Prasad. "Medium-Term Determinants of Current Accounts in Industrial and Developing Countries: An Empirical Exploration," *Journal of International Economics*, 59 (January 2003), 47-76.

Choe, Jong Il, "Do Foreign Direct Investment and Gross Domestic Investment Promote Economic Growth?," *Review of Development Economics*, 7 (February 2003), 44-57.

Choudhry, Taufiq, "High Inflation Rates and the Long-Run Money Demand Function: Evidence from Cointegration Tests," *Journal of Macroeconomics*, 17 (Winter 1995), 77-91.

Christiano, Lawrence J., and Terry J. Fitzgerald, "The Band Pass Filter," *Interna-*

tional Economic Review, 44 (May 2003), 435-65.

Christopoulos, Dimitris K., and Efthymios G. Tsionas, "Financial Development and Economic Growth: Evidence from Panel Unit Root and Cointegration Tests," *Journal of Development Economics*, 73 (February 2004), 55-74.

Chuhan, Punam, Gabriel Perez-Quiros, and Helen Popper, "International Capital Flows: Do Short-Term Investment and Direct Investment Differ?," PRE Working Paper No. 1669, World Bank (October 1996).

Chui, Michael, Paul Levine, S. Mansoob Murshed, and Joseph Pearlman, "North-South Models of Growth and Trade," *Journal of Economic Surveys*, 16 (April 2002), 123-65.

Claessens, Stijn, "The Debt Laffer Curve: Some Estimates," *World Development*, 18 (December 1990), 1671-77.

Claessens, Stijn, Michael P. Dooley, and Andrew Warner, "Portfolio Capital Flows: Hot or Cold?," *World Bank Economic Review*, 9 (January 1995), 153-74.

Clarida, Richard, Jordi Galí, and Mark Gertler, "The Science of Monetary Policy: A New Keynesian Perspective," *Journal of Economic Literature*, 37 (December 1999), 1661-707.

Clarke, George R., "More Evidence on Income Distribution and Growth," *Journal of Development Economics*, 47 (August 1995), 403-27.

Cline, William R., *International Debt Reexamined*, Institute for International Economics (Washington DC: 1995).

Cnossen, Sijbren, "Design of the Value Added Tax: Lessons from Experience," in *Tax Policy in Developing Countries*, ed. by Javad Khalilzadeh-Shirazi and Anwar Shah, World Bank (Washington DC: 1991).

Coe, David T., Elhanan Helpman, and Alexander W. Hoffmaister, "North-South R&D Spillovers," *Economic Journal*, 107 (January 1997), 134-49.

Coe, David T., and Dennis J. Snower, "Policy Complementarities: The Case for Fundamental Labor Market Reform," *IMF Staff Papers*, 44 (March 1997), 1-35.

Cogley, Timothy, and James M. Nason, "Effects of the Hodrick-Prescott Filter on Trend and Difference Stationary Time Series: Implications for Business Cycle Research," *Journal of Economic Dynamics and Control*, 19 (January 1995), 253-78.

Cohen, Daniel, "Growth and External Debt," in *The Handbook of Internatioal Macroeconomics*, ed. by Frederick van der Ploeg, Basil Blackwell (Oxford: 1994).

——, "The Sustainability of African Debt," Policy Research Paper No. 1621, International Economics Department, World Bank (July 1996*a*).

——, "Tests of the Convergence Hypothesis: Some Further Results," *Journal of Economic Growth*, 1 (September 1996*b*), 351-61.

Coles, Melvyn, and Apostolis Philippopoulos, "Are Exchange Rate Bands Better than Fixed Exchange Rates? The Imported Credibility Approach," *Journal of International Economics*, 43 (August 1997), 133-53.

Collier, Paul, and Jan W. Gunning, "Policy toward Commodity Shocks in Developing Countries," Working Paper No. 96/84, International Monetary Fund (August 1996).

Collins, Susan M., "On Becoming More Flexible: Exchange Rate Regimes in Latin

America and the Caribbean," *Journal of Development Economics*, 51 (October 1996), 117-38.

Collins, Susan M., and Barry P. Bosworth, "Economic Growth in East Asia: Accumulation versus Assimilation," *Brookings Papers on Economic Activity*, No. 2 (December 1996), 135-203.

Conley, John C., and William F. Maloney, "Optimum Sequencing of Credible Reforms with Uncertain Outcomes," *Journal of Development Economics*, 48 (October 1995), 151-66.

Conlisk, John, "A Modified Neo-Classical Growth Model with Endogenous Technical Change," *Southern Economic Journal*, 34 (October 1967), 199-208.

Conway, Patrick, "IMF Lending Programs: Participation and Impact," *Journal of Development Economics*, 45 (December 1994), 365-91.

Cooper, Richard N., *Economic Stabilization in Developing Countries*, ICS Press (San Francisco, Cal.: 1991).

Corbo, Vittorio, and Leonardo Hernández, "Macroeconomic Adjustment to Capital Inflows: Lessons from Recent Latin American and East Asian Experience," *World Bank Research Observer*, 11 (February 1996), 61-85.

Corbo, Vittorio, Oscar Landerretche, and Klaus Schmidt-Hebbel, "Assessing Inflation Targeting after a Decade of World Experience," *International Journal of Finance and Economics*, 6 (October 2001), 343-68.

Corbo, Vittorio, and Klaus Schmidt-Hebbel, "Macroeconomic Effects of Pension Reform in Chile," in *Results and Challenges of Pension Reforms*, ed. by the Inter-American Federation of Pension fund Associations, CIEDESS (Santiago: 2003).

Corden, W. Max, "Booming Sector and Dutch Disease Economics: Survey and Consolidation," *Oxford Economic Papers*, 36 (November 1984), 359-80.

Cottarelli, Carlo, and Angeliki Kourelis, "Financial Structure, Bank Lending Rates, and the Transmission Mechanism of Monetary Policy," *IMF Staff Papers*, 41 (December 1994), 587-623.

Cowell, Frank A., *Cheating the Government: The Economics of Evasion*, MIT Press (Cambridge, Mass.: 1990).

Cuddington, John, "Long-Run Trends in 26 Primary Commodity Prices," *Journal of Development Economics*, 39 (October 1992), 207-27.

——, "Analyzing the Sustainability of Fiscal Deficits in Developing Countries," unpublished, Georgetown University (March 1997).

Cukierman, Alex, *Central Bank Strategy, Credibility, and Independence*, MIT Press (Cambridge, Mass.: 1992).

Cukierman, Alex, Miguel A. Kiguel, and Leonardo Leiderman, "Transparency and the Evolution of Exchange Rate Flexibility in the Aftermath of Disinflation," in *Financial Factors in Economic Stabilization and Growth*, ed. by Mario I. Blejer, Zvi Eckstein, Zvi Hercowitz, and Leonardo Leiderman, Cambridge University Press (Cambridge: 1996).

Cukierman, Alex, and Francesco Lippi, "Central Bank Independence, Centralization of Wage Bargaining, Inflation and Unemployment: Theory and Evidence," *European Economic Review*, 43 (June 1999), 1395-1434.

Cukierman, Alex, Yossi Spiegel, and Leonardo Leiderman, "The Choice of Exchange

Rate Bands: Balancing Credibility and Flexibility," *Journal of International Economics*, 62 (March 2004), 379-408.

Cumby, Robert E., and Maurice Obstfeld, "Capital Mobility and the Scope for Sterilization: Mexico in the 1970s," in *Financial Policies and the World Capital Market*, ed. by Pedro A. Armella, Rudiger Dornbusch and Maurice Obstfeld, University of Chicago Press (Chicago, Il.: 1983).

Currie, Janet, and Ann Harrison, "Sharing the Costs: The Impact of Trade Reform on Capital and Labor in Morocco," *Journal of Labor Economics*, 15 (July 1997), s44-s71.

Dalgaard, Carl-Johan, and Henrik Hansen, "On Aid, Growth, and Good Policies," *Journal of Development Studies*, 37 (August 2001), 17-41.

Dasgupta, Partha, "The Population Problem: Theory and Evidence," *Journal of Economic Literature*, 33 (December 1995), 1879-902.

Dayal-Gulati, Anuradha, and Christian Thimann, "Saving in Southeast Asia and Latin America Compared: Searching for Policy Lessons," in *Macroeconomic Issues Facing ASEAN Countries*, ed. by John Hicklin, David Robinson, and Anoop Singh, International Monetary Fund (Washington DC: 1997).

Deaton, Angus S., *Understanding Consumption*, Oxford University Press (Oxford: 1992).

——, "Saving and Growth," in *The Economics of Saving and Growth*, ed. by Klaus Schmidt-Hebbel and Luis Servén, Cambridge University Press (Cambridge: 1999*a*).

——, "Commodity Prices and Growth in Africa," *Journal of Economic Perspectives*, 13 (Summer 1999*b*), 23-40.

Deaton, Angus S., and Ronald I. Miller, *International Commodity Prices, Macroeconomic Performance, and Politics in Sub-Saharan Africa*, Princeton Essays in International Finance No. 79 (Princeton, New Jersey: 1995).

De Gregorio, José, "Economic Growth in Latin America," *Journal of Development Economics*, 39 (July 1992), 59-84.

——, "Inflation, Taxation, and Long-Run Growth," *Journal of Monetary Economics* 31 (June 1993), 271-98.

——, "Borrowing Constraints, Human Capital Accumulation, and Growth," *Journal of Monetary Economics*, 37 (February 1996), 49-72.

De Gregorio, José, Sebastian Edwards, and Rodrigo O. Valdés, "Capital Controls in Chile: An Assessment," unpublished, Central Bank of Chile (March 1999).

De Haan, Jakob, and Willem J. Kooi, "Does Central Bank Independence Really Matter?," *Journal of Banking and Finance*, 24 (April 2000), 643-64.

De Haan, Jakob, and Dick Zelhorst, "The Impact of Government Deficits on Money Growth in Developing Countries," *Journal of International Money and Finance*, 9 (December 1990), 455-69.

De la Fuente, Angel, "The Empirics of Growth and Convergence: A Selective Review," *Journal of Economic Dynamics and Control*, 21 (January 1997), 23-73.

De la Fuente, Angel, and Rafael Doménech, "Human Capital in Growth Regressions: How Much Difference Does Data Quality Make?," Working Paper No. 262, Organization for Economic Cooperation and Development (October 2000).

Dellas, Harris, and Alan C. Stockman, "Self-Fulfilling Expectations, Speculative

Attacks, and Capital Controls," *Journal of Money, Credit, and Banking*, 25 (November 1993), 721-30.

DeLoach, Stephen B., "More Evidence in Favor of the Balassa-Samuelson Hypothesis," *Review of International Economics*, 9 (May 2001), 336-42.

De Meza, David, and David C. Webb, "Too Much Investment: A Problem of Asymmetric Information," *Quarterly Journal of Economics*, 102 (May 1987), 281-92.

Demetriades, Panicos, and Michael P. Devereux, "Investment and Financial Restraints: Theory and Evidence," *International Journal of Finance and Economics*, 5 (October 2000), 285-96.

Demetriades, Panicos, and Khaled A. Hussein, "Does Financial Development Cause Economic Growth? Time-Series Evidence from 16 Countries," *Journal of Development Economics*, 51 (December 1996), 387-411.

Demetriades, Panicos, and Kul B. Luintel, "The Direct Costs of Financial Repression: Evidence from India," *Review of Economics and Statistics*, 79 (May 1997), 311-19.

Demirgüç-Kunt, Asli, and Enrica Detragiache, "The Determinants of Banking Crises in Developing Countries," *IMF Staff Papers*, 45 (March 1998), 81-109.

——, "Financial Liberalization and Financial Fragility," in *Financial Liberalization: How Far, How Fast?*, ed. by Gerard Caprio, Patrick Honohan, and Joseph E. Stiglitz, Cambridge University Press (Cambridge: 2001).

——, "Does Deposit Insurance Increase Banking System Stability? An Empirical Investigation," *Journal of Monetary Economics*, 49 (October 2002), 1373-406.

DeRosa, Dean A., "Regional Integration Arrangements: Static Economic Theory, Quantitative Findings, and Policy Guidelines," PRE Working Paper No. 2007, World Bank (November 1998).

Deshpande, Ashwini, "The Debt Overhang and the Disincentive to Invest," *Journal of Development Economics*, 52 (February 1997), 169-87.

Devarajan, Shantayanan, and Delfin S. Go, "The Simplest Dynamic General Equilibrium Model of an Open Economy," *Journal of Policy Modeling*, 20 (December 1998), 677-714.

Devarajan, Shantayanan, Delfin S. Go, Jeffrey D. Lewis, Sherman Robinson, and Pekka Sinko, "Simple General Equilibrium Modeling," in Joseph F. François and Kenneth A. Reinhert, *Applied Methods for Trade Policy Analysis*, Cambridge University Press (Cambridge: 1997).

Devarajan, Shantayanan, Jeffrey D. Lewis, and Sherman Robinson, "Policy Lessons from Trade-Focused, Two-Sector Models," *Journal of Policy Modeling*, 12 (Winter 1990), 625-57.

——, "External Shocks, Purchasing Power Parity and the Equilibrium Real Exchange Rate," *World Bank Economic Review*, 7 (January 1993), 45-63.

Devarajan, Shantarajan, and Dani Rodrik, "Do the Benefits of Fixed Exchange Rates Outweigh Their Costs? The Franc Zone in Africa," in *Open Economy Structural Adjustment and Agriculture*, ed. by I. Goldin and L. Alan Winters, Cambridge University Press (Cambridge: 1992).

Devarajan, Shantayanan, Vinaya Swaroop, and Heng-fu Zou, "The Composition of Public Expenditure and Economic Growth," *Journal of Monetary Economics*, 37 (April 1996), 313-44.

Devenow, Andrea, and Ivo Welch, "Rational Herding in Financial Economics," *European Economic Review*, 40 (April 1996), 603-15.

Devereux, Michael B., and Gregor W. Smith, "International Risk Sharing and Economic Growth," *International Economic Review*, 35 (August 1994), 535-50.

Dewatripont, Mathias, and Gilles Michel, "On Closure Rules, Homogeneity, and Dynamics in Applied General Equilibrium Models," *Journal of Development Economics*, 26 (June 1987), 65-76.

Dewatripont, Mathias, and Gérard Roland, "Economic Reform and Dynamic Political Constraints," *Review of Economic Studies*, 59 (October 1992*a*), 703-30.

——, "The Virtues of Gradualism and Legitimacy in the Transition to a Market Economy," *Economic Journal*, 102 (March 1992*b*), 291-300.

——, "The Design of Reform Packages under Uncertainty," *American Economic Review*, 85 (December 1995), 1207-23.

Diamond, Douglas W., and Philip H. Dybvig, "Bank Runs, Deposit Insurance, and Liquidity," *Journal of Political Economy*, 91 (June 1983), 401-19.

Díaz-Alejandro, Carlos, "Good-Bye Financial Repression, Hello Financial Crash," *Journal of Development Economics*, 19 (September 1985), 1-24.

Dinopoulos, Elias, and Peter Thompson, "Endogenous Growth in a Cross-Section of Countries," *Journal of International Economics*, 51 (August 2000), 335-62.

Disyatat, Piti, and Pinnarat Vongsinsirikul, "Monetary Policy and the Transmission Mechanism in Thailand," *Journal of Asian Economics*, 14 (June 2003), 389-418.

Dixit, Avinash, "Taxation in Open Economies," in *Handbook of Public Economics*, Vol. I, ed. by Alan J. Auerbach and Martin S. Feldstein, North Holland (Amsterdam: 1985).

——, "Hysterisis, Import Penetration, and Exchange Rate Pass-through," *Quarterly Journal of Economics*, 104 (May 1989), 205-28.

Dixit, Avinash, and Robert S. Pindyck, *Investment under Uncertainty*, Princeton University Press (Princeton, New Jersey: 1994).

Dobson, Stephen, and Carlyn Ramlogan, "Convergence and Divergence in Latin America, 1970-98," *Applied Economics*, 34 (March 2002), 465-70.

Dollar, David, "Outward-Oriented Developing Economies Really Do Grow More Rapidly: Evidence from 95 LDCs, 1976-1985," *Economic Development and Cultural Change*, 40 (April 1992), 523-44.

Dollar, David, and Jakob Svensson, "What Explains the Success or Failure of Structural Adjustment Programmes?," *Economic Journal*, 110 (October 2000), 894-917.

Dooley, Michael, "A Survey of the Literature on Controls over International Capital Transactions," *IMF Staff Papers* 43 (December 1996), 639-87.

Doppelhofer, Gernot, Ronald I. Miller, and Xavier Sala-i-Martin, "Determinants of Long-term Growth: A Bayesian Averaging of Classical Estimates (BACE) Approach," Working Paper No. 7750, National Bureau of Economic Research (June 2000).

Dornbusch, Rudiger, *Inflation, Exchange Rates, and Stabilization*. Princeton Essay in International Finance No. 165, Princeton University (Princeton, New Jersey: 1986).

Dornbusch, Rudiger, and Stanley Fischer, "Stopping Hyperinflations, Past and

Present," *Weltwirtschaftliches Archives*, 122 (March 1986), 1-47.

——, "Moderate Inflation," *World Bank Economic Review*, 7 (January 1993), 1-44.

Dornbusch, Rudiger, Federico Sturzenegger, and Holger Wolf, "Extreme Inflation: Dynamics and Stabilization," *Brookings Papers on Economic Activity*, No. 1 (March 1990), 1-84.

Doroodian, Khosrow, "Macroeconomic Performance and Adjustment under Policies Commonly Supported by the International Monetary Fund," *Economic Development and Cultural Change*, 41 (July 1993), 849-64.

Drazen, Allan H., "The Political Economy of Delayed Reform," *Journal of Policy Reform*, 1 (March 1996), 25-46.

Drazen, Allan H., and Leonardo Bartolini, "Capital Account Liberalization as a Signal," *American Economic Review*, 87 (March 1997), 138-54.

Drazen, Allan H., and Vittorio Grilli, "The Benefits of Crises for Economic Reforms," *American Economic Review*, 83 (June 1993), 598-607.

Drazen, Allan, and Paul R. Masson, "Credibility of Policies versus Credibility of Policymakers," *Quarterly Journal of Economics* 104 (August 1994), 735-54.

Driffill, John E., "Growth and Finance," *The Manchester School*, 71 (July 2003), 363-80.

Driffill, John E., Graham E. Mizon, and Alistair Ulph, "The Costs of Inflation," in *Handbook of Monetary Economics*, II, ed. by Benjamin H. Friedman and Frank H. Hahn, North Holland (Amsterdam: 1990).

Durlauf, Steven N., and Danny T. Quah, "The New Empirics of Economic Growth," in *Handbook of Macroeconomics*, ed. by John B. Taylor and Michael Woodford, Vol. 1A, North Holland (Amsterdam: 1999).

Easterly, William, "A Consistency Framework for Macroeconomic Analysis," Working Paper Series No. 234, World Bank (June 1989).

——, "Endogenous Growth in Developing Countries with Government-Induced Distortions," in *Adjustment Lending Revisited: Policies to Restore Growth*, ed. by Vittorio Corbo, Stanley Fischer, and Steven B. Webb, World Bank (Washington DC: 1992).

——, "When Are Stabilizations Expansionary? Evidence from High Inflation," *Economic Policy*, No. 22 (April 1995), 67-107.

——, "The Ghost of Financing Gap: Testing the Growth Model Used in the International Financial Institutions," *Journal of Development Economics*, 60 (December 1999), 423-38.

——, "Can Foreign Aid Buy Growth?," *Journal of Economic Perspectives*, 17 (Summer 2003), 23-48.

Easterly, William, and Ross Levine, "It's Not Factor Accumulation: Stylized Facts and Growth Models," *World Bank Economic Review*, 15 (May 2001), 177-220.

Easterly, William, Ross Levine, and David Roodman, "New Data, New Doubts: Revisiting Aid, Policies, and Growth," Working Paper No. 26, Center for Global Development (June 2003).

Easterly, William, Norman Loayza, and Peter J. Montiel, "Has Latin America's Post-Reform Growth Been Disappointing?," *Journal of International Economics*, 43 (November 1997), 287-311.

Easterly, William, and Sergio Rebelo, "Fiscal Policy and Economic Growth: An Empirical Investigation," *Journal of Monetary Economics*, 32 (December 1993),

417-58.

Easterly, William, and Klaus Schmidt-Hebbel, "The Macroeconomics of Public Sector Deficits: A Synthesis," in *Public Sector Deficits and Macroeconomic Performance*, ed. by William Easterly, Carlos A. Rodríguez, and Klaus Schmidt-Hebbel, Oxford University Press (Oxford: 1994).

Eaton, Jonathan, "Sovereign Debt: A Primer," *World Bank Economic Review*, 7 (May 1993), 137-72.

Ebrill, Liam, Janet Stotsky, and Reint Gropp, *Revenue Implications of Trade Liberalization*, Occasional Paper No. 180, International Monetary Fund (Washington DC: 1999).

Edison, Hali J., "Do Indicators of Financial Crises Work? An Evaluation of an Early Warning System," *International Journal of Finance and Economics*, 8 (January 2003), 11-53.

Edison, Hali J., Ross Levine, Luca Ricci, and Torsten Slok, "International Financial Integration and Economic Growth," *Journal of International Money and Finance*, 21 (November 2002), 749-76.

Edwards, Sebastián, *Real Exchange Rates, Devaluation and Adjustment: Exchange Rate Policies in Developing Countries*, MIT Press (Cambridge, Mass.: 1989).

——, "Exchange Rates, Inflation and Disinflation: Latin American Experiences," in *Capital Controls, Exchange Rates and Monetary Policy in the World Economy*, ed. by Sebastián Edwards, Cambridge University Press (New York: 1995).

——, "Public Sector Deficits and Macroeconomic Stability in Developing Eco- nomies," Working Paper No. 5407, National Bureau of Economic Research (January 1996*a*).

——, "The Determinants of the Choice between Fixed and Flexible Exchange Rate Regimes," Working Paper No. 5756, National Bureau of Economic Research (September 1996*b*).

——, "Why Are Latin America's Savings Rates So Low? An International Comparative Analysis," *Journal of Development Economics*, 51 (October 1996*c*), 5-44.

——, "Openness, Productivity and Growth: What Do We Really Know?," *Economic Journal*, 108 (March 1998), 383-98.

——, "How Effective Are Capital Controls?," *Journal of Economic Perspectives*, 13 (Fall 1999), 65-84.

Edwards, Sebastián, and Igal Magendzo, "Dollarization and Economic Performance: What Do We Really Know?," *International Journal of Finance and Economics*, 8 (October 2003), 351-63.

Edwards, Sebastián, and Sweder van Wijnbergen, "The Welfare Effects of Trade and Capital Market Liberalization," *International Economic Review*, 27 (February 1986), 141-48.

Eichengreen, Barry, "Does Mercosur Need a Single Currency?," Working Paper No. c98, University of California (October 1998).

Eichengreen, Barry, and Paul Masson, *Exit Strategies: Policy Options for Countries Seeking Greater Exchange Rate Flexibility*, Occasional Paper No. 168, International Monetary Fund (Washington DC: 1998).

Eichengreen, Barry, Andrew K. Rose, and Charles Wyplosz, "Contagious Currency Crises: First Test," *Scandinavian Journal of Economics*, 98 (December 1996),

463-84.

Eichengreen, Barry, James Tobin, and Charles Wyplosz, "Two Cases for Sand in the Wheels of International Finance," *Economic Journal*, 105 (January 1995), 162-72.

Elbadawi, Ibrahim A., Benno J. Ndulu, and Njuguna Ndung'u, "Debt Overhang and Economic Growth in sub-Saharan Africa," in *External Finance for Low-Income Countries*, edited by Zubair Iqbal and Ravi Kanbur, World Bank (Washington, DC: 1997).

Esaka, Taro, "Was It Really a Dollar Peg? The Exchange Rate Policies of East Asian Countries, 1980-1997," *Journal of Asian Economies*, 13 (January 2003), 787-809.

Evans, J. L., and George K. Yarrow, "Some Implications of Alternative Expectations Hypotheses in the Monetary Analysis of Hyperinflations," *Oxford Economic Papers* 33 (March 1981), 61-80.

Evans, Paul, "How Fast Do Economies Converge?," *Review of Economics and Statistics*, 79 (May 1997), 219-25.

Evans, Paul, and Georgios Karras, "Private and Government Consumption with Liquidity Constraints," *International Journal of Money and Finance*, 15 (April 1996), 255-66.

Evrensel, Aye Y., "Effectiveness of IMF-Supported Stabilization Programs in Developing Countries," *Journal of International Money and Finance*, 21 (October 2002), 565-87.

Fallon, Peter R., and Luis A. Riveros, "Adjustment and the Labor Market," PRE Working Paper No. 214, World Bank (June 1989).

Falvey, Rod, and Cha Dong Kim, "Timing and Sequencing Issues in Trade Liberalisation," *Economic Journal*, 102 (July 1992), 908-24.

Faria, Joao R., and Miguel León-Ledesma, "Testing the Balassa-Samuelson Effect: Implications for Growth and the PPP," *Journal of Macroeconomics*, 25 (March 2003), 241-53.

Faruqee, Hamid, "Dynamic Capital Mobility in Pacific Basin Developing Countries: Estimation and Policy Implications," *IMF Staff Papers*, 39 (September 1992), 706-17.

Favero, Carlo A., Francesco Giavazzi, and Luca Flabbi, "The Transmission Mechanism in Europe: Evidence from Banks' Balance Sheets," Working Paper No. 7231, National Bureau of Economic Research (July 1999).

Feldman, Robert A., and Rajnish Mehra, "Auctions," *IMF Staff Papers*, 40 (September 1993), 485-511.

Feliz, Raúl A., and John H. Welch, "Cointegration and Tests of a Classical Model of Inflation in Argentina, Bolivia, Brazil, Mexico, and Peru," *Journal of Development Economics*, 52 (February 1997), 189-219.

Fernández, Raquel, and Dani Rodrik, "Resistance to Reform: Status Quo Bias in the Presence of Individual Specific Uncertainty," *American Economic Review*, 81 (December 1991), 1146-55.

Fernández-Arias, Eduardo, "The New Wave of Private Capital Inflows: Push or Pull?," *Journal of Development Economics*, 48 (March 1996), 389-418.

Fernández-Arias, Eduardo, and Peter J. Montiel, "The Surge in Capital Inflows to Developing Countries: An Analytical Overview," *World Bank Economic Review*, 10 (March 1996), 51-77.

Fielding, David, "Money Demand in Four African Countries," *Journal of Economic Studies*, 21 (March 1994), 3-37.

——, "Investment under Credit Rationing and Uncertainty: Evidence from South Africa," *Journal of African Economies*, 9 (June 2000), 189-212.

Fielding, David, and Michael Bleaney, "Monetary Discipline and Inflation in Developing Countries: The Role of the Exchange Rate Regime," *Oxford Economic Papers*, 52 (July 2000), 521-38.

Fielding, David, and Kalvinder Shields, "Modelling Macroeconomic Shocks in the CFA Franc Zone," *Journal of Development Economics*, 66 (October 2001), 199-223.

Fields, Gary S., "Changing Labor Market Conditions and Economic Development in Hong Kong, the Republic of Korea, Singapore, and Taiwan," *World Bank Economic Review*, 8 (September 1994), 395-414.

Fields, Gary S., and Henry Wan, Jr., "Wage-Setting Institutions and Economic Growth," *World Development*, 17 (September 1989), 1471-83.

Fiess, Norbert, "Capital Flows, Country Risk, and Contagion," Policy Research Working Paper No. 2943, World Bank (January 2003).

Fischer, Stanley, "Exchange Rate versus Money Targets in Disinflation," in *Indexing, Inflation, and Economic Policy*, MIT Press (Cambridge, Mass.: 1986).

——, "The Role of Macroeconomic Factors in Growth," *Journal of Monetary Economics*, 32 (December 1993), 485-512.

Fischer, Stanley, and Jacob Frenkel, "Investment, the Two-Sector Model, and Trade in Debt and Capital Goods," *Journal of International Economics*, 2 (August 1972), 211-33.

——, "Economic Growth and the Stages of the Balance of Payments," in *Trade, Stability, and Macroeconomics*, ed. by G. Horwich and Paul Samuelson, Academic Press (New York: 1974).

Fischer, Stanley, Ratna Sahay, and Carlos A. Végh, "Moder Hyper- and High Inflations," *Journal of Economic Literature*, 40 (September 2002), 837-80.

Fishlow, Albert, "Inequality, Poverty and Growth: Where Do We Stand?," in *Annual World Bank Conference on Development Economics*, ed. by Michael Bruno and Boris Pleskovic, World Bank (Washington D.C.: 1995).

Flood, Robert P., and Peter M. Garber, "Collapsing Exchange Rate Regimes: Some Linear Examples," *Journal of International Economics*, 17 (August 1984), 1-13.

Flood, Robert P., Peter M. Garber, and Charles Kramer, "Collapsing Exchange Rate Regimes: Another Linear Example," *Journal of International Economics* 41 (November 1996), 223-34.

Flood, Robert P., and Nancy P. Marion, "Perspectives on the Recent Currency Crisis Literature," *International Journal of Finance and Economics*, 4 (January 1999), 1-26.

Forder, James, "Central Bank Independence: Conceptual Clarifications and Interim Assessment," *Oxford Economic Papers*, 50 (July 1998), 307-34.

Forteza, Alvaro, and Martín Rama, "Labor Market Rigidity and the Success of Economic Reform in More than 100 Countries," PRE Working Paper No. 2521, World Bank (January 2001).

Foster, James, Joel Greer, and Erik Thorbecke, "A Class of Decomposable Poverty Measures," *Econometrica*, 52 (May 1984), 761-766.

Fountas, Stilianos, and Agapitos Papagapitos, "The Monetary Transmission Mechanism: Evidence and Implications for European Monetary Union," *Economics Letters*, 70 (March 2001), 397-404.

Franco-Rodriguez, Susana, "Recent Advances in Fiscal Response Models with an Application to Costa Rica," *Journal of International Development*, 12 (April 2000), 429-42.

Frankel, Jeffrey A., and Chudozie Okongwu, "Liberalized Portfolio Capital Inflows in Emerging Markets: Sterilization, Expectations, and the Incompleteness of Interest Rate Convergence," *International Journal of Finance and Economics*, 1 (January 1996), 1-24.

Frankel, Jeffrey A., and David Romer, "Does Trade Cause Growth?," *American Economic Review*, 89 (June 1999), 379-99.

Freeman, Richard B., "Labor Market Institutions in Economic Development," *American Economic Review*, 83 (May 1993), 403-8.

Friedman, Milton, *A Theory of the Consumption Function*, Princeton University Press (Princeton, New Jersey: 1957).

Froot, Kenneth A., and Paul R. Krugman, "Market-Based Debt Reduction for Developing Countries: Principles and Prospects," in *Analytical Issues in Debt*, ed. by ed. by Jacob A. Frenkel, Michael Dooley, and Peter Wickham, International Monetary Fund (Washington DC: 1989).

Fry, Maxwell J., *Money, Interest and Banking in Economic Development*, Johns Hopkins University Press, 2nd ed. (Baltimore, Md.: 1995).

——, "In Favour of Financial Liberalisation," *Economic Journal*, 107 (May 1997), 754-70.

Fry, Maxwell J., Charles A. E. Goodhart, and A. Almeida, *Central Banking in Developing Countries*, Paul Routledge (London: 1996).

Fuhrer, Jeffrey C., and Geoffrey R. Moore, "Inflation Persistence," *Quarterly Journal of Economics*, 110 (February 1995), 127-59.

Fung, Ben S., "A VAR Analysis of the Effects of Monetary Policy in Asia," Working Paper No. 119, Bank for International Settlements (September 2002).

Furman, Jason, and Joseph E. Stiglitz, "Economic Crises: Evidence and Insights from East Asia," *Brookings Papers on Economic Activity*, No. 2 (June 1998), 1-135.

Furusawa, Taiji, and Edwin L. Lai, "Adjustment Costs and Gradual Trade Liberalization," *Journal of International Economics*, 49 (December 1999), 333-61.

Futagami, Koichi, Yuichi Morita, and Akihisa Shibata, "Dynamic Analysis of an Endogenous Growth Model with Public Capital," in *Endogenous Growth*, ed. by Torben M. Andersen and Karl O. Moene, Basil Blackwell (Oxford: 1993).

Gagnon, Joseph E., and Jane Ihrig, "Monetary Policy and Exchange Rate Pass-Through," unpublished, Board of Governors of the Federal Reserve System (March 2002).

Galindo, Arturo, and Fabio Schiantarelli, "Determinants and Consequences of Financial Constraints FacingFirms in Latin America: An Overview," in *Credit Constraints and Investment in Latin America*, ed. by Arturo Galindo and Fabio Schiantarelli, Inter-American Development Bank (Washington DC: 2003).

Galindo, Arturo, Fabio Schiantarelli, and Andrew Weiss, "Does Financial Liberalization Improve the Allocation of Investment?," unpublished, Boston University (June 2001).

Galor, Oded, and Daniel Tsiddon, "Income Distribution and Growth: The Kuznets Hypothesis Revisited," *Economica*, 63 (June 1996), s103-s17.

——, "The Distribution of Human Capital and Economic Growth," *Journal of Economic Growth*, 2 (March 1997), 93-124.

Galor, Oded, and Joseph Zeira, "Income Distribution and Macroeconomics," *Review of Economic Studies*, 60 (January 1993), 35-52.

Gandolfo, Giancarlo, *Economic Dynamics*, Springer Verlag (Berlin: 1996).

Garoupa, Nuno, "The Theory of Optimal Law Enforcement," *Journal of Economic Surveys*, 11 (September 1997), 267-96.

Garber, Peter, "Issues of Enforcement and Evasion in a Tobin Tax on Foreign Exchange Transactions," in *The Tobin Tax*, ed. by Mahbub Ul Haq, Oxford University Press (New York: 1996).

——, "Derivatives in International Capital Flows," Working Paper No. 6623, National Bureau of Economic Research (June 1998).

Garber, Peter M., and Subir Lall, "Derivative Products in Exchange Rate Crises," in *Managing Capital Flows and Exchange Rates*, ed. by Reuven Glick, Cambridge University Press (Cambridge: 1998).

Garber, Peter M., and Michael G. Spencer, "Dynamic Hedging and the Interest Rate Defense," in *The Microstructure of Foreign Exchange Markets*, ed. by Jeffrey A. Frankel, Giampaolo Galli, and Alberto Giovannini, University of Chicago Press (Chicago, Il.: 1996).

Garber, Peter, and Mark P. Taylor, "Sand in the Wheels of Foreign Exchange Markets: A Skeptical Note," *Economic Journal*, 105 (January 1995), 173-80.

Gatica, Jaime, Alejandra Mizala, and Pilar Romaguera, "Interindustry Wage Differentials in Brazil," *Economic Development and Cultural Change*, 43 (January 1995), 315-31.

Gauthier, Bernard, and Mark Gersovitz, "Revenue Erosion through Exemption and Evasion in Cameroon, 1993," *Journal of Public Economics*, 64 (June 1997), 407-24.

Gavin, Michael, "Unemployment and the Economics of Gradualist Policy Reform," *Journal of Policy Reform*, 1 (March 1996), 239-58.

Gelos, R. Gaston, and Alejandro M. Werner, "Financial Liberalization, Credit Constraints, and Collateral: Investment in the Mexican Manufacturing Sector," *Journal of Development Economics*, 67 (February 2002), 1-27.

Gersovitz, Mark, "Saving and Development," in *Handbook of Development Economics*, ed. by Hollis B. Chenery and T. N. Srinivasan, North Holland (Amsterdam: 1988).

Gertler, Mark, "Financial Capacity and Output Fluctuations in an Economy with Multi-Period Financial Relationships," *Review of Economic Studies*, 59 (July

1992), 455-72.

Gertler, Mark, and Simon Gilchrist, "Monetary Policy, Business Cycles, and the Behavior of Small Manufacturing Firms," *Quarterly Journal of Economics*, 109 (May 1994), 309-40.

Ghartey, Edward E., "Monetary Dynamics in Ghana: Evidence from Cointegration, Error Correction Modelling, and Exogeneity," *Journal of Development Economics*, 57 (October 1998), 473-86.

Ghosh, Atish R., Anne-Marie Gulde, Jonathan D. Ostry, and Holger C. Wolf, "Does the Nominal Exchange Rate Regime Matter?," Working Paper No. 5874, National Bureau of Economic Research (January 1997).

Ghosh, Atish R., Anne-Marie Gulde, and Holger C. Wolf, "Currency Boards—The Better Peg?," Working Paper No. G-97-04, Princeton University (November 1997).

Ghosh, Atish R., and Jonathan Ostry, "Export Instability and the External Balance in Developing Countries," *IMF Staff Papers*, 41 (June 1994), 214-35.

Ghura, Dhaneshwar, and Michael Hadjimichael, "Growth in sub-Saharan Africa," *IMF Staff Papers*, 43 (September 1996), 605-34.

Giavazzi, Francesco, Tullio Jappelli, and Marco Pagano, "Searching for Non-Linear Effects of Fiscal Policy: Evidence from Industrial and Developing Countries," *European Economic Review*, 44 (June 2000), 1259-89.

Gibson, Heather D., and Euclid Tsakalotos, "The Scope and Limits of Financial Liberalization in Developing Countries: A Critical Survey," *Journal of Development Studies*, 30 (April 1994), 578-628.

Gielen, A. M., and N. I. van Leeuwen, "A Note on Armington and the Law of One Price," *Economic Transition and the Greening of Policies*, ed. by J. François, T. Hertel, and M. Schmitz, Vauk (Kiel: 1998).

Giovannini, Alberto, and Martha De Melo, "Government Revenue from Financial Repression," *American Economic Review*, 83 (September 1993), 953-63.

Giovannini, Alberto, and Bart Turtelboom, "Currency Substitution," in *The Handbook of International Macroeconomics*, ed. by Frederick van der Ploeg, Basil Blackwell (Oxford: 1994).

Glick, Reuven, and Michael Hutchison, "Banking and Currency Crises: How Common Are the Twins?," Working Paper No. PB99-07, Federal Reserve Bank of San Francisco (December 1999).

Glick, Reuven, Michael Hutchison, and Ramon Moreno, "Is Pegging the Exchange Rate a Cure for Inflation? East Asian Experiences," in *International Trade and Finance: New Frontiers of Research*, ed. by Benjamin Cohen, Cambridge University Press (Cambridge: 1997).

Glomm, Gerhard, and B. Ravikumar, "Public Investment in Infrastructure in a Simple Growth Model," *Journal of Economic Dynamics and Control*, 18 (November 1994), 1173-88.

——, "Productive Govenment Expenditures and Long-Run Growth," *Journal of Economic Dynamics and Control*, 21 (January 1997), 183-204.

Goh, Ai-Ting, and Jacques Olivier, "Learning by Doing, Trade in Capital Goods and Growth," *Journal of International Economics*, 56 (March 2002), 411-44.

Goldfajn, Ilan, and Sergio R. Werlang, "The Pass-Through from Depreciation to Inflation: A Panel Study," Working Paper No. 5, Central Bank of Brazil (April 2000).

Goldstein, Morris, and Philip Turner, *Banking Crises in Emerging Economies: Origins and Policy Options*, Economic Paper No. 46, Bank for International Settlements (October 1996).

Gould, David M., "Does the Choice of Nominal Anchor Matter?," Working Paper No. 96-11, Federal Reserve Bank of Dallas (October 1996).

Green, John H., "Inflation Targeting: Theory and Policy Implications," *IMF Staff Papers*, 43 (December 1996), 779-95.

Greenaway, David, and Chris Milner, *Trade and Industrial Policy in Developing Countries*, University of Michigan Press (Ann Arbor, Michigan: 1994).

David Greenaway, Wyn Morgan, and Peter Wright, "Trade Liberalization and Growth in Developing Countries," *Journal of Development Economics*, 67 (February 2002), 229-44.

Greene, William H., *Econometric Analysis*, 4th edition, Prentice Hall (Upper Saddle River, New Jersey: 2000).

Greenwald, Bruce C., and Joseph E. Stiglitz, "Financial Market Imperfections and Business Cycles," *Quarterly Journal of Economics*, 108 (February 1993), 77-114.

Greenwood, Jeremy, and Boyan Jovanovich, "Financial Development, Growth, and the Distribution of Income," *Journal of Political Economy*, 98 (October 1990), 1076-107.

Greenwood, Jeremy, and Bruce D. Smith, "Financial Markets in Development, and the Development of Financial Markets," *Journal of Economic Dynamics and Control*, 21 (January 1997), 145-82.

Grisanti, Alejandro, Ernesto H. Stein, and Ernesto Talvi, "Institutional Arrangements and Fiscal Performance: The Latin American Experience," Working Paper No. 367, Inter-American Development Bank (January 1998).

Grobar, Lisa M., "Effect of Real Exchange Rate Uncertainty on LDC Manufactured Exports," *Journal of Development Economics*, 41 (August 1993), 367-76.

Grosse, Robert, "Jamaica's Foreign Exchange Black Market," *Journal of Development Studies*, 31 (October 1994), 17-43.

Grossman, Gene, and Elhanan Helpman, *Innovation and Growth in the Global Economy*, MIT Press (Cambridge, Mass.: 1991).

Gruben, William C., and Darryl McLeod, "Capital Account Liberalization and Inflation," *Economics Letters*, 77 (October 2002), 221-25.

Guidotti, Pablo E., and Carlos A. Rodríguez, "Dollarization in Latin America." *IMF Staff Papers* 39 (September 1992) 518-44.

Gundlach, Erich, "The Role of Human Capital in Economic Growth: New Results and Alternative Interpretations," *Weltwirtschaftliches Archives*, 131 (June 1995), 383-402.

Gunning, Jan Willem, and Taye Mengistae, "Determinants of African Manufacturing Investment: The Microeconomic Evidence," *Journal of African Economies*, 10 (September 2001), 48-80.

Gupta, Sanjeev, "Foreign Aid and Revenue Response: Does the Composition of Aid Matter?," Working Paper No. 03/176, International Monetary Fund (September

2003).

Gylfason, Thorvaldur, "Privatization, Efficiency and Economic Growth," Discussion Paper No. 1844, Center for Economic Policy Research (March 1998).

Gylfason, Thorvaldur, and Ole Risager, "Does Devaluation Improve the Current Account?," *European Economic Review*, 25 (February 1984), 37-64.

Gylfason, Thorvaldur, and Michael Schmid, "Does Devaluation Cause Stagflation?" *Canadian Journal of Economics*, 16 (November 1983), 641-54.

Haddad, Mona, and Ann Harrison, "Are there Positive Spillovers from Direct Foreign Investment?," *Journal of Development Economics*, 42 (October 1993), 51-74.

Hadjimichael, Michael, and Dhaneshwar Ghura, "Public Policies and Private Savings and Investment in Sub-Saharan Africa," Working Paper No. 95/19, International Monetary Fund (February 1995).

Hagemann, Robert P., "The Structural Budget Balance: The IMF's Methodology," in *Indicators of Structural Budget Balances*, ed. by Banca d'Italia (Rome: 1999).

Hall, Robert E., and Charles I. Jones, "Why Do Some Countries Produce So Much More Output per Worker than Others?" *Quarterly Journal of Economics*, 114 (February 1999), 83-116.

Handy, Howard, and others, *Egypt: Beyond Stabilization, Toward a Dynamic Market Economy*, Occasional Paper No. 163, International Monetary Fund (Washington DC: 1998).

Hanke, Steven H., and Kurt Schuler, *Currency Boards for Developing Countries*, International Center for Economic Growth, ICS Press (San Francisco, Cal.: 1994).

Hansen, Henrik, and Finn Tarp, "Aid and Growth Regressions," *Journal of Development Economics*, 64 (April 2001), 547-70.

Hanson, James A., "Opening the Capital Account: A Survey of Issues and Results." In *Capital Controls, Exchange Rates and Monetary Policy in the World Economy*, ed. by Sebastián Edwards, Cambridge University Press (New York: 1995).

Hanushek, Eric, and Dennis D. Kimko, "Schooling, Labor-Force Quality, and the Growth of Nations," *American Economic Review*, 90 (December 2000), 1184-208.

Harberger, Arnold C., "Currency Depreciation, Income and the Balance of Trade," *Journal of Political Economy*, 53 (February 1950), 47-60.

Harris, John, and Michael P. Todaro, "Migration, Unemployment and Development: A Two-Sector Analysis," *American Economic Review*, 60 (March 1970), 126-43.

Harrison, Ann, "Openness and Growth: A Time-Series, Cross-Country Analysis for Developing Countries," *Journal of Development Economics*, 48 (March 1996), 419-47.

Harrison, Ann, and Gordon Hanson, "Who Gains from Trade Reform? Some Remaining Puzzles," *Journal of Development Economics*, 59 (June 1999), 125-54.

Hayo, Bernd, and Carsten Hefeker, "Reconsidering Central Bank Independence," *European Journal of Political Economy*, 18 (November 2002), 653-74.

Heckman, James J., and Carmen Pagés, "The Cost of Job Security Regulation: Evidence from Latin American Labor Markets," Working Paper No. 7773, National

Bureau of Economic Research (June 2000).

Heller, Peter, Richard Haas, and Ahsan Mansur, "A Review of the Fiscal Impulse Measure," Occasional Paper No. 44, International Monetary Fund (Washington DC: 1986).

Helpman, Elhanan, "Voluntary Debt Reduction: Incentives and Welfare," *IMF Staff Papers*, 36 (September 1989), 580-611.

Helpman, Elhanan, and Paul R. Krugman, *Market Structure and Foreign Trade*, MIT Press (Cambridge, Mass.: 1985).

Helpman, Elhanan, Leonardo Leiderman, and Gil Bufman, "New Breed of Exchange Rate Bands: Chile, Israel and Mexico," *Economic Policy* 9 (October 1994), 260-306.

Hendricks, Lutz, "Equipment Investment and Growth in Developing Countries," *Journal of Development Economics*, 61 (April 2000), 335-64.

Hernández, Leonardo, and Klaus Schmidt-Hebbel, "Capital Controls in Chile: Effective? Efficient? Endurable?," unpublished, Central Bank of Chile (April 1999).

Herrendorf, Berthlod, "Importing Credibility through Exchange Rate Pegging," *Economic Journal*, 107 (May 1997), 687-94.

Ho, Corinne, and Robert N. McCauley, "Living with Flexible Exchange Rates: Issues and Recent Experience in Inflation Targeting Emerging Market Economies," Working Paper No. 130, Bank for International Settlements (February 2003).

Hodrick, Robert J., and Edward C. Prescott, "Postwar U.S. Business Cycles: An Empirical Investigation," *Journal of Money, Credit, and Banking*, 29 (February 1997), 1-16.

Hoeffler, Anke, "Openness, Investment, and Growth," *Journal of African Economies*, 10 (December 2001), 470-97.

——, "The Augmented Solow Model and the African Growth Debate," *Oxford Bulletin of Economics and Statistics*, 64 (May 2002), 135-58.

Hoffmaister, Alexander W., and Jorge E. Roldós, "The Sources of Macroeconomic Fluctuations in Developing Countries: Brazil and Korea," *Journal of Macroeconomics*, 23 (Spring 2001), 213-39.

Hoffmaister, Alexander W., Jorge E. Roldós, and Peter Wickham, "Macroeconomic Fluctuations in Sub-Saharan Africa," *IMF Staff Papers*, 45 (March 1998), 132-60.

Hoffman, Dennis L., and Chakib Tahiri, "Money Demand in Morocco: Estimating Long-Run Elasticities for a Developing Country," *Oxford Bulletin of Economics and Statistics*, 56 (August 1994), 305-24.

Holmes, Mark J., "The Inflationary Effects of Effective Exchange Rate Depreciation in Selected African Countries," *Journal of African Economies*, 11 (June 2002), 201-18.

Hopenhayn, Hugo A., and María E. Muniagurria, "Policy Variability and Economic Growth," *Review of Economic Studies*, 63 (October 1996), 611-25.

Hsieh, Chang-Tai, "Productivity Growth and Factor Prices in East Asia," *American Economic Review*, 89 (May 1999), 133-38.

Huang, Haizhou, and Chenggang Xu, "Financial Institutions and the Financial Crisis in East Asia," *European Economic Review*, 43 (April 1999), 903-14.

Huang, Zhangkai, "Evidence of a Bank Lending Channel in the UK," *Journal of Banking and Finance*, 27 (March 2003), 491-510.

Hulten, Charles R., "Total Factor Productivity: A Short Biography," in *New Developments in Productivity Analysis*, ed. by Charles R. Hulten, Edward R. Dean, and Michael Harper, University of Chicago Press (Chicago, Il.: 2001).

Husain, Aasim M., "Domestic Taxes and the Debt Laffer Curve," *Economica*, 64 (August 1997), 519-25.

International Finance Corporation, *Privatization: Principles and Practice*, IFC Lessons of Experience Series No. 1 (Washington DC: 1995).

International Monetary Fund, *Theoretical Aspects of the Design of Fund-Supported Programs*, Occasional Paper No. 55, International Monetary Fund (Washington DC: 1987).

——, *World Economic Outlook*, International Monetary Fund (Washington DC: October 1997*a*).

——, *International Capital Markets: Developments, Prospects, and Key Policy Issues*, International Monetary Fund (Washington DC: November 1997*b*).

Iqbal, Zafar, Jeffrey James, and Graham Pyatt, "Three-Gap Analysis of Structural Adjustment in Pakistan," *Journal of Policy Modeling*, 22 (January 2000), 117-38.

Irvine, Ian, and Susheng Wang, "Saving Behavior and Wealth Accumulation in a Pure Lifecycle Model with Income Uncertainty," *European Economic Review*, 45 (February 2001), 233-58.

Irwin, Douglas A., and Marko Tervio, "Does Trade Raise Income? Evidence from the Twentieth Century," *Journal of International Economics*, 58 (October 2002), 1-18.

Islam, Nazrul, "Growth Empirics: A Panel Data Approach," *Quarterly Journal of Economics*, 110 (November 1995), 1127-70.

——, "What Have We Learnt from the Convergence Debate?," *Journal of Economic Surveys*, 17 (July 2003), 309-62.

Jain, Arvind K., "Corruption: A Review," *Journal of Economic Surveys*, 15 (February 2001), 3-40.

Jansen, W. Jos, "What Do Capital Inflows Do? Dissecting the Transmission Mechanism for Thailand," *Journal of Macroeconomics*, 25 (December 2003), 457-80.

Jappelli, Tullio, and Marco Pagano, "Saving, Growth and Liquidity Constraints," *Quarterly Journal of Economics*, 109 (February 1994), 83-109.

Jaramillo, Fidel, Fabio Schiantarelli, and Andrew Weiss, "Capital Market Imperfections before and after Financial Liberalization," *Journal of Development Economics*, 51 (December 1996), 376-86.

Johnson, David R., "The Effect of Inflation Targeting on the Behavior of Expected Inflation: Evidence from an 11 Country Panel," *Journal of Monetary Economics*, 49 (November 2002), 1521-38.

Johnston, R. Barry, and Chris Ryan, "The Impact of Controls on Capital Movements on the Private Capital Accounts of Countries' Balance of Payments: Empirical Estimates and Policy Implications," Working Paper No. 94/78 (July 1994).

Jones, Charles I. "Time Series Tests of Endogenous Growth Models," *Quarterly Journal of Economics*, 110 (May 1995), 495-525.

Jones, Larry E., and Rodolfo E. Manuelli, "A Convex Model of Equilibrium Growth," *Journal of Political Economy*, 98 (October 1990), 1008-38.

——, "The Sources of Growth," *Journal of Economic Dynamics and Control*, 21 (January 1997), 75-114.

Jorgenson, Dale W., "Capital Theory and Investment Behavior," *American Economic Review*, 53 (May 1963), 247-59.

Kahkonen, Juha, "Liberalization Policies and Welfare in a Financially Repressed Economy," *IMF Staff Papers*, 34 (September 1987), 531-47.

Kamas, Linda, "External Disturbances and the Independence of Monetary Policy under the Crawling Peg in Colombia," *Journal of International Economics*, 19 (November 1985), 313-27.

Kamin, Steven B., "Devaluation, Exchange Controls, and Black Markets for Foreign Exchange in Developing Countries," *Journal of Development Economics*, 40 (February 1993), 151-69.

Kamin, Steven B., and Neil R. Ericsson, "Dollarization in Post-Hyperinflationary Argentina," *Journal of International Money and Finance*, 22 (April 2003), 185-211.

Kamin, Steven B., John W. Schindler, and Shawna L. Samuel, "The Contribution of Domestic and External Factors to Emerging Market Devaluation Crises: An Early Warning Systems Approach," International Finance Working Paper No. 711, Board of Governors of the Federal Reserve System (September 2001).

Kamin, Steven, Turner, Philip, and Van't dack, Jozef, "The Transmission Mechanism of Monetary Policy in Emerging Market Economies: An Overview," in *Financial Structure and the Monetary Policy Transmission Mechanism*, CB Document No. 394, Bank for International Settlements, Basel (March 1995).

Kaminsky, Graciela, Saul Lizondo, and Carmen M. Reinhart, "Leading Indicators of Currency Crises," *IMF Staff Papers*, 45 (March 1998), 1–48.

Kaminsky, Graciela, and Carmen M. Reinhart, "The Twin Crises: The Causes of Banking and Balance-of-Payments Problems," *American Economic Review*, 89 (June 1999), 473-500.

Kaplan, Ethan, and Dani Rodrik, "Did the Malaysian Capital Controls Work?," Working Paper No. 8142, National Bureau of Economic Research (February 2001).

Karras, Georgios, "Government Spending and Private Consumption: Some International Evidence," *Journal of Money, Credit, and Banking*, 26 (February 1994a), 9-22.

——, "Macroeconomic Effects of Budget Deficits: Further International Evidence," *Journal of International Money and Finance*, 13 (April 1994b), 190-210.

Kaufman, Martin D., "An Incursion into the Confidence Crisis-Credit Rationing, Real Activity Channel: Evidence from the Argentine 'Tequila' Crisis," unpublished, Central Bank of Argentina (February 1996).

Kawai, Masahiro, and Louis J. Maccini, "Fiscal Policy, Anticipated Switches in Methods of Finance, and the Effects on the Economy," *International Economic Review* 31 (November 1990), 913-34.

Kendall, Maurice G., and Alan Stuart, *The Advanced Theory of Statistics*, Griffin (London: 1967)

Khan, Mohsin S., and Manmohan S. Kumar, "Public and Private Investment and the Growth Process in Developing Countries," *Oxford Bulletin of Economics and Statistics* 59 (February 1997), 69-88.

Khan, Mohsin S., Peter J. Montiel, and Nadeem U. Haque, "Adjustment with Growth: Relating the Analytical Approaches of the IMF and World Bank," *Journal of Development Economics*, 32 (January 1990), 155-79.

Kiguel, Miguel A., and Leonardo Leiderman, "On the Consequences of Sterilized Intervention in Latin America: The Case of Colombia and Chile," unpublished, Tel-Aviv University (June 1993).

Kiguel, Miguel A., and Nissan Liviatan, "When Do Heterodox Stabilization Programs Work? Lessons from Experience," *World Bank Research Observer*, 7 (January 1992*a*), 35-57.

——, "The Business Cycle Associated with Exchange Rate Based Stabilization," *World Bank Economic Review*, 6 (May 1992*b*), 279-305.

Killick, Tony, *IMF Programmes in Developing Countries: Design and Impact*, Paul Routledge (Andover: 1995).

King, Robert G., and Ross Levine, "Finance, Entrepreneurship, and Growth: Theory and Evidence," *Journal of Monetary Economics*, 32 (December 1993), 513-42.

Kiyotaki, N., and J. Moore, "Credit Cycles," *Journal of Political Economy*, 105 (April 1997), 211-48.

Kletzer, Kenneth, "External Borrowing by LDCs: A Survey of Some Theoretical Issues," in *The State of Development Economics*, ed. by Gustav Ranis and Paul T. Schultz, Basil Blackwell (New York: 1988).

Klitgaard, Robert, *Controlling Corruption*, University of California Press (Berkeley, Cal.: 1988).

Knight, Malcolm, Norman Loayza, and Delano Villanueva, "Testing the Neoclassical Theory of Economic Growth," *IMF Staff Papers*, 40 (September 1993), 512-41.

Konan, Denise E., and Keith E. Maskus, "Joint Trade Liberalization and Tax Reform in a Small Open Economy: The Case of Egypt," *Journal of Development Economics*, 61 (April 2000), 365-92.

Koo, Chung M., "Fiscal Sustainability in the Wake of the Economic Crisis in Korea," *Journal of Asian Economies*, 13 (September-October 2002), 659-69.

Kopits, George, "Fiscal Rules: Useful Policy Framework or Unnecessary Ornament?," Working Paper No. 01/145 (September 2001).

Kose, M. Ayhan, and Raymond Riezman, "Trade Shocks and Macroeconomic Fluctuations in Africa," *Journal of Development Economics*, 65 (June 2001), 55-80.

Koskela, Erkki, "A Note on Progression, Penalty Schemes and Tax Evasion," *Journal of Public Economics*, 22 (October 1983), 127-33.

Kraay, Aart, "Do High Interest Rates Defend Currencies during Speculative Attacks?," *Journal of International Economics*, 59 (March 2003), 297-321.

Kraay, Aart, and Vikram Nehru, "When Is External Debt Sustainable?," unpublished, World Bank (October 2003).

Kreinin, Mordechai, and Lawrence H. Officer, *The Monetary Approach to the Balance of Payments: A Survey*, Essay in International Finance No. 43, Princeton

University (Princeton, New Jersey: 1978).

Kremer, Michael, Alexei Onatski, and James Stock, "Searching for Prosperity," Working Paper No. 8250, National Bureau of Economic Research (April 2001).

Krishna, Pravin, and Devashish Mitra, "Trade Liberalization, Market Discipline and Productivity Growth: New Evidence from India," *Journal of Development Economics*, 56 (August 1998), 447-62.

Krueger, Ann O., The Political Economy of the Rent-Seeking Society," *American Economic Review*, 64 (June 1974), 291-303.

——, *The Political Economy of Policy Reform in Developing Countries*, MIT Press (Cambridge, Mass.: 1993).

——, "East Asian Experience and Endogenous Growth Theory," in *Growth Theories in Light of the East Asian Experience*, ed. by Takatoshi Ito and Anne O. Krueger, University of Chicago Press (Chicago, Il.: 1995).

Krugman, Paul, "A Model of Balance of Payments Crises," *Journal of Money, Credit, and Banking*, 11 (August 1979), 311-25.

——, "Pricing to Market when the Exchange Rate Changes," in *Real-Financial Linkages among Open Economies*, ed. by Sven W. Arndt and John D. Richardson, MIT Press (Cambridge, Mass.: 1987).

——, "Financing versus Forgiving a Debt Overhang: Some Analytical Notes," *Journal of Development Economics*, 29 (December 1988), 253-68.

——, "Differences in Income Elasticities and Trends in Real Exchange Rates," *European Economic Review*, 33 (May 1989*a*), 1031-54.

——, "Market-Based Debt Reduction Schemes," in *Analytical Issues in Debt*, ed. by Jacob Frenkel, Michael Dooley, and Peter Wickham, International Monetary Fund (Washington DC: 1989*b*).

——, "Target Zones and Exchange Rate Dynamics," *Quarterly Journal of Economics*, 106 (November 1991), 669-82.

——, "Balance Sheets, the Transfer Problem, and Financial Crises," in *International Finance and International Crises*, ed. by Peter Isard, Assaf Razin, and Andrew K. Rose, International Monetary Fund (Washington DC: 1999).

Kuznets, Simon, "Economic Growth and Income Equality," *American Economic Review*, 45 (March 1955), 1-28.

Labán, Raúl, and Felipe B. Larraín, "Can a Liberalization of Capital Outflows Increase Net Capital Inflows?," *Journal of International Money and Finance*, 21 (June 1997), 415-31.

Larraín B., Felipe, M. Raúl Labán, and Rómulo A. Chumacero, "What Determines Capital Inflows? An Empirical Analysis for Chile," Harvard Institute for International Development, Discussion Paper No. 590 (June 1997).

Laursen, Svend, and Lloyd A. Metzler, "Flexible Exchange Rates and the Theory of Employment," *Review of Economics and Statistics*, 32 (November 1950), 281-99.

Lawrance, Emily C., "Consumer Default and the Life Cycle Model," *Journal of Money, Credit, and Banking*, 27 (November 1995), 939-54.

Lee, Jong-Wha, "International Trade, Distortions and Long-Run Economic Growth," *IMF Staff Papers*, 40 (June 1993), 299-328.

——, "Capital Goods Imports and Long-Run Growth," *Journal of Development Economics*, 48 (October 1995), 91-110.

Lee, Kevin, M. Hashem Pesaran, and Ron P. Smith, "Growth and Convergence in a Multi-Country Empirical Stochastic Solow Model," *Journal of Applied Econometrics*, 12 (July 1997), 357-97.

Lee, Kiseok, and Ronald A. Ratti, "On Seigniorage, Operating Rules, and Dual Equilibria," *Quarterly Journal of Economics*, 108 (May 1993), 543-50.

Leiderman, Leonardo, and Gil Bufman, "Searching for Nominal Anchors in Shock-Prone Economies in the 1990s: Inflation Targets and Exchange Rate Bands," in *Securing Stability and Growth in Latin America*, ed. by Ricardo Hausmann and Helmut Reisen, OECD (Paris: 1996).

Leland, Hayne E., "Saving and Uncertainty: The Precautionary Demand for Saving," *Quarterly Journal of Economics*, 82 (August 1968), 465-73.

Lensink, Robert, and Howard White, "Is there an Aid Laffer Curve?," *Journal of Development Studies*, 37 (August 2001), 17-41.

Levine, Ross, "Financial Development and Economic Growth: Views and Agenda," *Journal of Economic Literature*, 35 (June 1997), 688-726.

——, "Finance and Growth: Theory, Evidence, and Mechanisms," unpublished, University of Minnesota (March 2003).

Levine, Ross, Norman Loayza, and Thorsten Beck, "Financial Intermediation and Growth: Causality and Causes," *Journal of Monetary Economics*, 46 (August 2000), 31-77.

Levine, Ross, and David Renelt, "A Sensitivity Analysis of Cross-Country Growth Regressions," *American Economic Review*, 82 (September 1992), 942-63.

Lewer, Joshua J., and Hendrik Van den Berg, "How Large Is International Trade's Effect on Economic Growth?," *Journal of Economic Surveys*, 17 (July 2003), 363-96.

Li, Hongyi, Lyn Squire, and Heng-fu Zou, "Explaining International and Intertemporal Variations in Income Inequality," *Economic Journal*, 108 (January 1998), 26-43.

Li, Qing, "Convergence Clubs: Some Further Evidence," *Review of International Economics*, 7 (February 1999), 59-67.

Lienert, Ian, and Jitendra Modi, "A Decade of Civil Service Reform in sub-Saharan Africa," Working Paper No. 97/179, International Monetary Fund (December 1997).

Lindbeck, Assar, and Mats Persson, "The Gains from Pension Reform," *Journal of Economic Literature*, 41 (March 2003), 74-112.

Lindgren, Carl-Johan, Gillian Garcia, and Matthew I. Saal, *Bank Soundness and Macroeconomic Policy*, by International Monetary Fund (Washington D.C.: 1996).

Lipton, Michael, and Martin Ravallion, "Poverty and Policy," in *Handbook of Development Economics*, Vol. III, ed. by Jere Behrman and T. N. Srinivasan, North Holland (Amsterdam: 1995).

Lizondo, J. Saul, "Real Exchange Rate Targeting under Imperfect Asset Substitutability," *IMF Staff Papers*, 40 (December 1993), 829-51.

Loayza, Norman V., "The Economics of the Informal Sector: A Simple Model and Some Empirical Evidence from Latin America," Carnegie-Rochester Conference Series on Public Policy, Vol. 45 (June 1996).

Loayza, Norman V., Klaus Schmidt-Hebbel, and Luis Servén, "What Drives Private Saving across the World?," *Review of Economics and Statistics*, 82 (May 2000), 165-81.

Löfgren, Hans, Rebeccal Lee Harris, and Sherman Robinson, "A Standard Computable General Equilibrium (CGE) Model in GAMS," TMD Discussion Paper No. 75, International Food Policy Research Institute (May 2001).

Londoño, Juan Luis, and Miguel Székely, "Persistent Poverty and Excess Inequality: Latin America, 1970-1995," *Journal of Applied Economics*, 3 (May 2000), 93-134.

López-Mejía, Alejandro, and Juan R. Ortega, "Private Saving in Colombia," Working Paper No. 98/171 (December 1998).

Lora, Eduardo, and Felipe Barrera, "A Decade of Structural Reform in Latin America: Measurement and Growth Effects," Inter-American Development Bank, unpublished (July 1997).

Lora, Eduardo, and Mauricio Olivera, "Macro Policy and Employment Problems in Latin America," Working Paper No. 372, Inter-American Development Bank (March 1998).

Lucas, Robert E., "On the Mechanics of Economic Development," *Journal of Monetary Economics*, 22 (July 1988), 3-42.

——, "Why Doesn't Capital Flow from Rich to Poor Countries?," *American Economic Review*, 80 (May 1990), 92-96.

Ludvigson, Sydney, "Consumption and Credit: A Model of Time-Varying Liquidity Constraints," *Review of Economics and Statistics*, 81 (August 1999), 434-47.

Mackenzie, George A., Philip R. Gerson, and Alfredo Cuervas, *Pension Regimes and Saving*, Occasional Paper No. 153, International Monetary Fund (Washington DC: 1997).

Mackenzie, George A., David W. Orsmond, and Philip R. Gerson, *The Composition of Fiscal Adjustment and Growth*, Occasional Paper No. 149, International Monetary Fund (Washington DC: 1997).

Mackenzie, George A., and Peter Stella, *Quasi Fiscal Operations of Public Financial Institutions*, Occasional Paper No. 142, International Monetary Fund (Washington DC: 1996).

Maddala, G. S., and S. Wu, "Cross-Country Growth Regressions: Problems of Heterogeneity, Stability and Interpretation," *Applied Economics*, 32 (April 2000), 635-42.

Maddison, Angus, *Monitoring the World Economy, 1820-1992*, Development Centre Studies, Organisation for Economic Co-operation and Development (Paris: 1995).

Maloney, William F., "Testing Capital Account Liberalization without Forward Rates: Another Look at Chile, 1979-82," *Journal of Development Economics*, 52 (February 1997), 139-68.

Maloney, William, and F. Jairo Nunez Mendez, "Measuring the Impact of Minimum Wages: Evidence from Latin America," Working Paper No. 9800, National Bureau of Economic Research (June 2003).

Mankiw, N. Gregory, David Romer, and D. Weil, "A Contribution to the Empirics of Economic Growth," *Quarterly Journal of Economics*, 107 (May 1992), 407-37.

Manzocchi, Stefano, "Stages in the Balance of Payments: A Survey of the Neoclassical Theory," *Economic Notes* (September 1990), 397-416.

Markusen, James R., and Anthony J. Venables, "Foreign Direct Investment as a Catalyst for Industrial Development," *European Economic Review*, 43 (February 1999), 335-56.

Márquez, Gustavo, and Carmen Pagés-Serra, "Trade and Employment: Evidence from Latin America and the Caribbean," Working Paper No. 366, InterAmerican Development Bank (January 1998).

Marsh, Ian W., and Stephen P. Tokarick, "An Assessment of Three Measures of Competitiveness," *Weltwirtschaftliches Archives*, 132 (December 1996), 700-22.

Martinelli, Cesar, and Mariano Tommasi, "Sequencing of Economic Reforms in the Presence of Political Constraints," in *The Political Economy of Reform*, ed. by Federico Sturzenegger and Mariano Tommasi, MIT Press (Cambridge, Mass.: 1998).

Masson, Paul R., Tamim Bayoumi, and Hossein Samiei, "International Evidence on the Determinants of Private Savings," *World Bank Economic Review, 12* (September 1998), 483-502.

Mathieson, Donald J., and Liliana Rojas-Suárez, *Liberalization of the Capital Account: Experiences and Issues*, Occasional Paper No. 103, International Monetary Fund (Washington DC: 1993).

Matusz, Steven J., and David Tarr, "Adjusting to Trade Policy Reform," unpublished, World Bank (May 1999).

Mauro, Paolo, "The Effects of Corruption on Growth, Investment, and Government Expenditure: A Cross-Country Analysis," in *Corruption in the World Economy*, ed. by Fred Bergsten and Kimberly Elliott, Institute for International Economics (Washington DC: 1997).

Mayer-Foulkes, David, "Global Divergence," unpublished, Centro de Investigación y Docencia Económicas (September 2002).

Mazumdar, Joy, "Imported Machinery and Growth in LDCs," *Journal of Development Economics*, 65 (June 2001), 209-24.

McCallum, Bennett T., "Crucial Issues Concerning Central Bank Independence," *Journal of Monetary Economics*, 39 (June 1997), 99-112.

McCarthy, Jonathan, "Pass-Through of Exchange Rates and Import Prices to Domestic Inflation in Some Industrialised Economies," Working Paper No. 79, Bank for International Settlements (November 1999).

McCoskey, Suzanne K., "Convergence in sub-Saharan Africa: A Nonstationary Panel Data Approach," *Applied Economics*, 34 (May 2002), 819-29.

McDonald, Calvin A., and Yin-Fun Lum, "Operational Issues Related to the Functioning of Interbank Foreign Exchange Markets in Selected African Countries," Working Paper No. 94/48, International Monetary Fund (April 1994).

McGillivray, Mark, and Oliver Morrissey, "Aid Fungibility in Assessing Aid: Red Herring or True Concern?," *Journal of International Development*, 12 (April 2000), 413-28.

McKinnon, Ronald I., *Money and Capital in Economic Development*, Brookings Institution (Washington DC: 1973).

——, *The Order of Economic Liberalization*, 2nd ed., Johns Hopkins University Press (Baltimore, Md.: 1993).

McKinnon, Ronald I., and Huw Pill, "Credible Liberalizations and International Capital Flows: The Overborrowing Syndrome," in *Deregulation and Integration in East Asia*, ed. by Takatoshi Ito and Anne O. Krueger, University of Chicago Press (Chicago, Il.: 1996).

McNelis, Paul D., and Liliana Rojas-Suárez, "Currency Substitution as Behavior toward Risk: The Case of Bolivia and Peru," unpublished, Department of Economics, Georgetown University (November 1996).

Mehlum, Halvor, "Speed of Adjustment and Self-Fulfilling Failure of Economic Reform," *Journal of International Economics*, 53 (February 2001), 149-67.

Mehran, Hassanali, Piero Ugolini, Jean-Philippe Briffaux, George Iden, Tonny Lybek, Stephen Swaray, and Peter Hayward, *Financial Sector Developments in sub-Saharan African Countries*, Occasional Paper No. 169, International Monetary Fund (Washington DC: 1998).

Menon, Jayant, "Exchange Rate Pass-Through," *Journal of Economic Surveys*, 9 (June 1995), 197-231.

Mikić, Mia, *International Trade*, St. Martin's Press (New York: 1998).

Mikkelsen, Jan G., "A Model for Financial Programming," Working Paper No. 98/80, International Monetary Fund (June 1998).

Milbourne, Ross, G. Otto, and G. Voss, "Public Investment and Economic Growth," *Applied Economics*, 35 (March 2003), 527-40.

Miles, William, "Securitization, Liquidity, and the Brady Plan," *North American Journal of Economics and Finance*, 10 (June 1999), 423-42.

Milesi-Ferretti, Gian Maria, "Good, Bad or Ugly? On the Effects of Fiscal Rules with Creative Accounting," *Journal of Public Economics*, 88 (January 2004), 377-94.

Milesi-Ferretti, Gian Maria, and Assaf Razin, *Current-Account Sustainability*, Princeton Study In International Finance No. 81 (Princeton, New Jersey: 1996).

Milesi-Ferretti, Gian Maria, and Nouriel Roubini, "Growth Effects of Income and Consumption Taxes," *Journal of Money, Credit, and Banking*, 30 (November 1998), 721-44.

Miller, Marcus, Robery Skidelsky, and Paul Weller, "Fear of Deficit Financing: Is it Rational?," in *Public Debt Management: Theory and History*, ed. by Rudiger Dornbusch and Mario Draghi, Cambridge University Press (Cambridge: 1990).

Minford, Patrick, and David Peel, *Advanced Macroeconomics*, E. Elgar (Northampton, Mass.: 2002).

Mishkin, Frederic S., "The Channels of Monetary Transmission: Lessons for Monetary Policy," Working Paper No. 5464, National Bureau of Economic Research (February 1996).

——, *The Economics of Money, Banking, and Financial Markets*, Addison-Wesley (Reading, Mass.: 1998).

Modigliani, Franco, and Richard Brumberg, "Utility Analysis and the Consumption Function: An Interpretation of Cross-Section Data," in *Post-Keynesian Economics*, ed. by Kenneth Kurihara, Rutgers University Press (New Brunswick, New Jersey: 1954).

Mondino, Guillermo, Federico Sturzenegger, and Mariano Tommasi, "Recurrent High Inflation and Stabilization: A Dynamic Game," *International Economic Review*, 37 (November 1996), 981-96.

Montenegro, Claudio E., "Who Benefits from Labor Market Regulations?," Policy Research Working Paper No. 3143, World Bank (October 2003).

Montiel, Peter J., "Tight Money in a Post-Crisis Defense of the Exchange Rate : What Have We learned ?," *World Bank Research Observer*, 18 (Spring 2003), 1-23.

Montiel, Peter J., and Jonathan Ostry, "Macroeconomic Implications of Real Exchange Rate Targeting in Developing Countries," *IMF Staff Papers*, 38 (December 1991), 872-900.

——, "Real Exchange Rate Targeting under Capital Controls," *IMF Staff Papers*, 39 (March 1992), 58-78.

Montiel, Peter J., and Carmen M. Reinhart, "Do Capital Controls and Macroeconomic Policies Influence the Volume and Composition of Capital Flows? Evidence from the 1990s," *Journal of International Money and Finance*, 18 (August 1999), 619-35.

Morandé, Felipe G., and Matías Tapia, "Exchange Rate Policy in Chile: From the Band to Floating and Beyond," Working Paper No. 152, Central Bank of Chile (April 2002).

Moser, Gary G., "The Main Determinants of Inflation in Nigeria," *IMF Staff Papers*, 42 (June 1995), 270-89.

Muellbauer, John, and Ralph Lattimore, "The Consumption Function: A Theoretical and Empirical Overview," in *Handbook of Applied Econometrics*, ed. by M. Hashem Pesaran and Mike Wickens, Basil Blackwell (Oxford: 1995).

Mulligan, Casey B., and Xavier Sala-i-Martin, "Transitional Dynamics in Two-Sector Models of Endogenous Growth," *Quarterly Journal of Economics*, 108 (August 1993), 739-73.

Murphy, Kevin M., Andrei Shleifer, and Robert W. Vishny, "Industrialization and the Big Push," *Journal of Political Economy*, 97 (October 1989), 1003-26.

——, "The Allocation of Talents: Implications for Growth," *Quarterly Journal of Economics*, 106 (May 1991), 503-30.

Muscatelli, Vito A., and Andrew A. Stevenson, "Modeling Aggregate Manufactured Exports for Some Asian Newly Industrializing Economies," *Review of Economics and Statistics*, 77 (February 1995), 147-55.

Myles, Gareth D., *Public Economics*, Cambridge University Press (New York: 1996).

Nelson, Joan M., "Organized Labor, Politics, and Labor Market Flexibility in Developing Countries," in *Labor Markets in an Era of Adjustment*, Vol. I, ed. by Susan Horton, Ravi Kanbur, and Dipak Mazumdar, World Bank (Washington DC: 1994).

Nelson, Michael A., and Ram D. Singh, "The Deficit-Growth Connection: Some Recent Evidence from Developing Countries," *Economic Development and Cultural Change* 43 (October 1994), 167-91.

Nelson, Richard R., "A Theory of the Low-Level Trap in Underdeveloped Economies," *American Economic Review*, 46 (December 1956), 894–908.

Nelson, Richard R., and Howard Pack, "The Asian Miracle and Modern Growth Theory," *Economic Journal*, 109 (July 1999), 416-36.

Ng, Francis, and Alexander Yeats, "Open Economies Work Better! Did Africa's Protectionist Policies Cause Its Marginalization in World Trade?," *World Development*, 25 (June 1997), 889-904.

North, Douglas C., *Institutions, Institutional Change and Economic Performance*, Cambridge University Press (New York: 1990).

Nurkse, Ragnar, *Problems of Capital Formation in Underdeveloped Countries*, Oxford University Press (Oxford: 1953).

Obstfeld, Maurice, "Aggregate Spending and the Terms of Trade: Is There a Laursen-Metlzer Effect?," *Quarterly Journal of Economics*, 47 (May 1982), 251-70.

——, "Capital Flows, the Current Account, and the Real Exchange Rate: Consequences of Liberalization and Stabilization," in *Economic Adjustment and Exchange Rates in Developing Countries*, ed. by Liaqat Ahmed and Sebastián Edwards, University of Chicago Press (Chicago, Il.: 1986).

——, "Risk-Taking, Global Diversification and Growth," *American Economic Review*, 84 (November 1994), 1310-29.

——, "The Logic of Currency Crises," in *Monetary and Fiscal Policy in an Integrated Europe*, ed. by Barry Eichengreen, Jeffrey Frieden, and Jürgen von Hagen, Springer Verlag (London: 1995*a*).

——, "International Capital Mobility in the 1990s," in *Understanding Interdependence: The Macroeconomics of the Open Economy*, ed. by Peter B. Kenen, Princeton University Press (Princeton, New Jersey: 1995*b*).

——, "Models of Currency Crises with Self-Fulfilling Features," *European Economic Review*, 40 (April 1996), 1037-47.

——, "The Global Capital Market: Benefactor or Menace?," *Journal of Economic Perspectives*, 12 (Fall 1998), 9-30.

Obstfeld, Maurice, and Kenneth Rogoff, "The Mirage of Fixed Exchange Rates," *Journal of Economic Perspectives*, 9 (Fall 1995), 73–96.

Ogaki, Masao, Jonathan Ostry, and Carmen M. Reinhart, "Saving Behavior in Low- and Middle-Income Developing Countries: A Comparison," *IMF Staff Papers*, 43 (March 1996), 38-71.

Olivera, Julio H., "Money, Prices and Fiscal Lags: A Note on the Dynamics of Inflation," *Banca Nazionale del Laboro Quarterly Review*, 20 (September 1967), 258-67.

Olson, Mancur, "Big Bills Left on the Sidewalk: Why Some Nations Are Rich, and Others Poor," *Journal of Economic Perspectives*, 10 (Spring 1996), 3-24.

Önis, Ziya, and Süleyman Ozmucur, "Exchange Rates, Inflation and Money Supply in Turkey: Testing the Vicious Circle Hypothesis," *Journal of Development Economics*, 32 (January 1990), 133-54.

Orphanides, Athanasios, "The Timing of Stabilizations," *Journal of Economic Dynamics and Control* 20 (January 1996), 257–79.

Ortigueira, Salvador, and Manuel S. Santos, "On the Speed of Convergence in Endogenous Growth Models," *American Economic Review*, 87 (June 1997), 383-99.

Oshikoya, Temitope W., "Macroeconomic Determinants of Domestic Private Investment in Africa," *Economic Development and Cultural Change*, 42 (April 1994),

573-96.

Ostry, Jonathan D., and Carmen M. Reinhart, "Private Saving and Terms-of-Trade Shocks," *IMF Staff Papers*, 39 (September 1992), 495-517.

Otto, G., "Terms of Trade Shocks and the Balance of Trade: There Is a Harberger-Laursen-Metzler Effect," *Journal of International Money and Finance*, 22 (April 2003), 155-84.

Ozkan, F. Gulcin, and Alan Sutherland, "Policy Measures to Avoid a Currency Crisis," *Economic Journal*, 105 (March 1995), 510-19.

Ozler, Sule, and Guido E. Tabellini, "External Debt and Political Instability," Working Paper No. 3772, National Bureau of Economic Research (July 1991).

Pack, Howard, and John M. Page, "Accumulation, Exports, and Growth in the High-Performing Asian Economies," Carnegie-Rochester Conference Series on Public Policy, 40 (June 1994), 199-250.

Pagano, Marco, "Financial Markets and Growth: An Overview," *European Economic Review*, 37 (April 1993), 613-22.

Palokangas, Tapio, "Inflation and Growth in an Open Economy," *Economica*, 64 (August 1997), 509-18.

Panagides, Alexis, and Harry A. Patrinos, "Union-Nonunion Wage Differentiuals in the Developing World: A case Study of Mexico, PRE Working Paper No. 1269, World Bank (March 1994).

Papageorgiou, Demetris, Armeane M. Choksi, and Michael Michaely, *Liberalizing Foreign Trade in Developing Countries*, World Bank (Washington, DC: 1990).

Park, Yung Chul, "Financial Repression and Liberalization," in *Liberalization in the Process of Economic Development*, ed. by Lawrence B. Krause and Kim Kihwan, University of California Press (Berkeley, Cal.: 1991).

Parker, Karen, and Steffen Kastner, "A Framework for Assessing Fiscal Sustainability and External Viability, with an Application to India," IMF Working Paper, No. 93/78 (October 1993).

Pattillo, Catherine, "Investment, Uncertainty, and Irreversibility in Ghana," *IMF Staff Papers*, 45 (September 1998), 522-53.

Pattillo, Catherine, Hélène Poirson, and Luca Ricci, "External Debt and Growth," Working Paper No. 02/69, International Monetary Fund (April 2002).

Pedersen, Karl R., "Aid, Investment and Incentives," *Scandinavian Journal of Economics*, 98 (September 1996), 423-38.

Pericoli, Marcello, and Massimo Sbracia, "A Primer on Financial Contagion," *Journal of Economic Surveys*, 17 (September 2003), 571-608.

Perotti, Roberto, "Political Equilibrium, Income Distribution, and Growth," *Review of Economic Studies*, 60 (October 1993), 755-76.

——, "Fiscal Policy in Good Times and Bad," *Quarterly Journal of Economics*, 114 (November 1999), 1399-436.

Perry, Guillermo, and Luis Servén, "The Anatomy of a Multiple Crisis: Why Was Argentina Special and What Can We Learn from It?," Policy Research Working Paper No. 3081, World Bank (June 2003).

Persson, Torsten, and Guido Tabellini, "Is Inequality Harmful for Growth?," *American Economic Review*, 84 (June 1994), 600-21.

Persson, Torsten, and Sweder van Wijnbergen, "Signalling, Wage Controls, and Monetary Disinflation Policy," *Economic Journal*, 103 (January 1993), 79-97.

Pesaran, M. Hashem, and Ron Smith, "Estimating Long-Run Relationships from Dynamic Heterogeneous Panels," *Journal of Econometrics*, 68 (July 1995), 79-113.

Phylaktis, Kate, and Mark P. Taylor, "Money Demand, the Cagan Model, and the Inflation Tax: Some Latin American Evidence," *Review of Economics and Statistics*, 75 (February 1993), 32-37.

Pill, Huw, and Mahmood Pradhan, "Financial Indicators and Financial Change in Africa and Asia," *Savings and Development*, 21 (March 1997), 123-50.

Polackova, Hana, "Government Contingent Liabilities: A Hidden Risk to Fiscal Stability," Policy Research Working Paper No. 1989, World Bank (October 1998).

Polackova, Hana, and Ashoka Mody, "Dealing with Government Fiscal Risks: An Overview," in *Government at Risk*, ed. by Hana Polackova and Allen Schick, World Bank (Washington DC: 2002).

Polak, Jacques J., "Monetary Analysis of Income Formation and Payments Problems," *IMF Staff Papers*, 6 (November 1957), 1-50.

Pradhan, Basanta K., and A. Subramanian, "On the Stability of Demand for Money in a Developing Economy," *Journal of Development Economics*, 72 (October 2003), 335-51.

Premchand, A., *Public Expenditure Management*, International Monetary Fund (Washington DC: 1993).

Price, Simon, "Demand for Indonesian Narrow Money: Long-Run Equilbrium, Error Correction and Forward-Looking Behaviour," *Journal of International Trade and Economic Development*, 3 (July 1994), 147-63.

Prisker, Matthew, "The Channels for Financial Contagion," in *International Financial Contagion*, ed. by Stijn Claessens and Kristin J. Forbes, Kluwer Academic Publishers (Boston: 2001).

Pritchett, Lant, "Divergence, Big Time," *Journal of Economic Perspectives*, 11 (Summer 1997), 3-18.

Prock, Jerry, Gökçe A. Soydemir, and Benjamin A. Abugri, "Currency Substitution: Evidence from Latin America," *Journal of Policy Modeling*, 25 (June 2003), 415-30.

Przeworski, Adam, and James R. Vreeland, "The Effect of IMF Programs on Economic Growth," *Journal of Development Economics*, 62 (August 2000), 385-421.

Psacharopoulos, George, and others, "Poverty and Income Inequality in Latin America during the 1980s," *Review of Income and Wealth*, 41 (September 1995), 245-64.

Pyatt, Graham, Chau-Nan Chen, and John Fei, "The Distribution of Income by Factor Components," *Quarterly Journal of Economics*, 95 (May 1980), 451-73.

Pyle, D. J., "The Economics of Taxpayer Compliance," *Journal of Economic Surveys*, 5 (June 1991), 163-98.

Quah, Danny T., "Empirics for Economic Growth and Convergence," *European Economic Review*, 40 (June 1996a), 1353-75.

——, "Twin Peaks: Growth and Convergence in Models of Distribution Dynamics," *Economic Journal*, 106 (July 1996*b*), 1045-55.

——, "Empirics for Growth and Distribution: Stratification, Polarization and Convergence Clubs," Discussion Paper No. 324, London School of Economics (January 1997).

Radelet, Steven, and Jeffrey D. Sachs, "The East Asian Crisis: Diagnosis, Remedies, Prospects," *Brookings Papers on Economic Activity*, No. 1 (June 1998), 1-90.

Rama, Martín, "Empirical Investment Equations in Developing Countries," in *Striving for Growth after Adjustment*, ed. by Luis Servén and Andrés Solimano, World Bank (Washington DC: 1993).

——, "The Labor Market and Trade Reform in Manufacturing," in *The Effects of Protectionism on a Small Country: The Case of Uruguay*, ed. by Michael Connolly and Jaime de Melo, World Bank (Washington DC: 1994).

——, "Do Labor Market Policies and Institutions Matter? The Adjustment Experience in Latin America and the Caribbean," unpublished, World Bank (June 1995).

——, "Organized Labor and the Political Economy of Product Market Distortions," *World Bank Economic Review*, 11 (May 1997*a*), 327-55.

——, "Efficient Public Sector Downsizing," Policy Research Working Paper No. 1840 (November 1997*b*).

Ratti, Ronald A., and Jeonghee Seo, "Multiple Equilibria and Currency Crisis: Evidence for Korea," *Journal of International Money and Finance*, 22 (October 2003), 681-96.

Ravallion, Martin, *Poverty Comparisons*, Harwood Academic Press (Chur: 1994).

Razin, Assaf, and Efraim Sadka, "Efficient Investment Incentives in the Presence of Capital Flight," *Journal of International Economics*, 31 (August 1991), 171-81.

Rebelo, Sergio, "Long-Run Policy Analysis and Long-Run Growth," *Journal of Political Economy*, 99 (June 1991), 500-21.

Rebelo, Sergio, and Carlos A. Végh, "Real Effects of Exchange-Rate Based Stabilization: An Analysis of Competing Theories," *NBER Macroeconomics Annual 1996*, ed. by Ben S. Bernanke and Julio J. Rotemberg, MIT Press (Cambridge, Mass.: 1997).

Reinert, Kenneth A., and David W. Roland-Holst, "Social Accounting Matrices," in *Applied Methods for Trade Policy Analysis*, ed. by Joseph F. François and Kenneth A. Reinert, Cambridge University Press (Cambridge: 1997).

Reinhart, Carmen M., "Devaluation, Relative Prices, and International Trade: Evidence from Developing Countries," *IMF Staff Papers*, 42 (June 1995), 290-312.

Reinhart, Carmen M., and Carlos A. Végh, "Nominal Interest Rates, Consumption Booms, and Lack of Credibility," *Journal of Development Economics*, 46 (April 1995), 357-78.

Revenga, Ana, "Employment and Wage Effects of Trade Liberalization: The Case of Mexican Manufacturing," *Journal of Labor Economics*, 15 (July 1997), s20-s43.

Risager, Ole, "Devaluation, Profitability and Investment," *Scandinavian Journal of Economics*, 90 (June 1988), 125-40.

Rivera-Batiz, Francisco L., "Democracy, Governance, and Economic Growth: Theory and Evidence," *Review of Development Economics*, 6 (June 2002), 225-47.

Rivera-Batiz, Luis, and Paul Romer, "Economic Integration and Endogenous Growth," *Quarterly Journal of Economics*, 106 (May 1991), 531-56.

Robbins, Donald J., "Trade, Trade Liberalization and Inequality in Latin America and East Asia—Synthesis of Seven Country Studies," unpublished, Harvard Institute for International Development (March 1996).

Roberts, John M., "New Keynesian Economics and the Phillips Curve," *Journal of Money, Credit, and Banking*, 27 (November 1995), 975-84.

Robinson, David J., and Peter Stella, "Amalgamating Central Bank and Fiscal Deficits," in *How to Measure the Fiscal Deficit: Analytical and Methodological Issues*, ed. by Mario I. Blejer and Adrienne Cheasty, International Monetary Fund (Washington DC: 1993).

Robinson, Sherman, "Macroeconomics, Financial Variables, and Computable General Equilibrium Models," *World Development*, 19 (November 1991), 1509-25.

Rochet, Jean-Charles, "Capital Requirements and the Behavior of Commercial Banks," *European Economic Review*, 36 (June 1992), 1137-70.

Rodriguez, Francisco, and Dani Rodrik, "Trade Policy and Economic Growth: A Sceptic's Guide to the Cross-National Evidence," Working Paper No. 2143, Centre for Economic Policy Research (May 1999).

Rodrik, Dani, "Imperfect Competition, Scale Economies, and Trade Policy in Developing Countries," in *Trade Policy Issues and Empirical Analysis*, ed. by Robert E. Baldwin, University of Chicago Press (Chicago, Il.: 1988).

——, "Credibility of Trade Reforms—A Policymaker's Guide," *World Economy*, 12 (March 1989), 1-16.

——, "Limits of Trade Policy Reform in Developing Countries," *Journal of Economic Perspectives*, 6 (Winter 1992), 87-105.

——, "Trade and Industrial Policy Reform," in *Handbook of Development Economics*, III, ed. by Jere Behrman and T. N. Srinivasan, North Holland (Amsterdam: 1995*a*).

——, "Political Economy of Trade Policy," in *Handbook of International Economics*, Vol. III, ed. by Gene M. Grossman and Kenneth Rogoff, North Holland (Amsterdam: 1995*b*).

——, "Understanding Economic Policy Reform," *Journal of Economic Literature*, 34 (March 1996), 9-41.

——, "Trade Policy and Economic Performance in sub-Saharan Africa," Working Paper No. 6562, National Bureau of Economic Research (May 1998*a*).

——, "Why Do More Open Economies Have Bigger Governments?," *Journal of Political Economy*, 106 (October 1998*b*), 997-1032.

Rogers, John H., and Ping Wang, "Output, Inflation, and Stabilization in a Small Open Economy: Evidence from Mexico," *Journal of Development Economics*, 46 (April 1995), 271-93.

Rogoff, Kenneth S., and Carmen M. Reinhart, "The Modern History of Exchange Rate Arrangements: A Reinterpretation," Working Paper No. 8963, National Bureau of Economic Research (June 2002).

Rojas-Suárez, Liliana, and Steven Weisbrod, *Financial Fragilities in Latin America: The 1980s and 1990s*, Occasional Paper No. 132, International Monetary Fund (Washington DC: 1995).

Roldós, Jorge, "Supply-Side Effects of Disinflation Programs," *IMF Staff Papers*, 42 (March 1995), 158-83.

——, "On Gradual Disinflation, the Real Exchange Rate, and the Current Account," *Journal of International Money and Finance,* 16 (February 1997*a*), 37-54.

——, "Potential Output Growth in Emerging Market Countries: The Case of Chile," Working Paper No. 97/194 (September 1997*b*).

Romer, David, *Advanced Macroeconomics,* McGraw-Hill (New York: 1995).

Romer, Paul, "Increasing Returns and Long-Run Growth," *Journal of Political Economy,* 94 (October 1986), 1002-37.

——, "Capital Accumulation in the Theory of Long-Run Growth," in *Modern Business Cycle Theory,* ed. by Robert Barro, Harvard University Press (Cambridge, Mass.: 1989).

——, "Endogenous Technological Change," *Journal of Political Economy,* 98 (October 1990), s71-s102.

——, "Two Strategies for Economic Development: Using Ideas vs. Producing Ideas," in *World Bank Conference on Development Economics,* World Bank (Washington DC: 1992).

——, "New Goods, Old Theory, and the Welfare Costs of Trade Restrictions," *Journal of Development Economics,* 43 (February 1994), 5-38.

Rosenstein-Rodan, Paul N., "Notes on the Theory of the 'Big Push'," in *Economic Development for Latin America,* ed. by Howard S. Ellis and Henry C. Wallich, St. Martin's Press (New York: 1961).

Rossi, Nicola, "Government Spending, the Real Interest Rate, and the Behavior of Liquidity-Constrained Consumers in Developing Countries," *IMF Staff Papers,* 35 (March 1988), 104-40.

——, "Dependency Rates and Private Savings Behavior in Developing Countries," *IMF Staff Papers,* 36 (March 1989), 166-81.

Rostow, William W., *The Stages of Economic Growth,* Cambridge University Press (Cambridge: 1960).

Roubini, Nouriel, and Xavier Sala-i-Martin, "A Growth Model of Inflation, Tax Evasion and Financial Repression," *Journal of Monetary Economics,* 35 (April 1995), 275-301.

Saavedra, Jaime, "Labor Markets during the 1990s," in *After the Washington Consensus: Restarting Growth and Reform in Latin America,* ed. by Pedro-Pablo Kuczynski and John Williamson, Institute of International Economics (Washington DC: 2003).

Sachs, Jeffrey, "The Debt Overhang of Developing Countries," in *Debt, Stabilization and Development,* ed. by Ronald Findlay, Guillermo Calvo, Pentti J. Kouri, and Jorge Braga de Macedo, Basil Blackwell (Oxford: 1989).

——, "Resolving the Debt Crisis of Low-Income Countries," *Brookings Papers on Economic Activity,* No. 1 (June 2002), 257-86.

Sachs, Jeffrey, Aarón Tornell, and Andrés Velasco, "What Have We Learned from the Mexican Peso Crisis?," *Economic Policy,* No. 22 (April 1996*a*), 15-63.

——, "Financial Crises in Emerging Markets: The Lessons from 1995," *Brookings Papers in Economic Activity,* No. 1 (June 1996*b*), 147-98.

Sachs, Jeffrey, and Andrew M. Warner, "Fundamental Sources of Long-Run Growth," *American Economic Review*, 87 (May 1997a), 184-88.

——, "Sources of Slow Growth in African Economies," *Journal of African Economies* (October 1997b), 335-76.

Sah, Raaj K., and Joseph E. Stiglitz, *Peasants versus City-Dwellers*, Clarendon Press (Oxford: 1992).

Sandmo, Agnar, "The Effect of Uncertainty on Saving Decisions," *Review of Economic Studies*, 37 (July 1970), 353-60.

Sarantis, Nicholas, and Chris Stewart, "Liquidity Constraints, Precautionary Saving and Aggregate Consumption: An International Comparison," *Economic Modelling*, 20 (December 2003), 1151-73.

Sarel, Michael, "Nonlinear Effects of Inflation on Economic Growth," *IMF Staff Papers*, 43 (March 1996), 199-215.

——, "Growth and Productivity in ASEAN Countries," in *Macroeconomic Issues Facing ASEAN Countries*, ed. by John Hicklin, David Robinson, and Anoop Singh, International Monetary Fund (Washington DC: 1997).

Sato, Ryuzo, "Fiscal Policy in a Neoclassical Growth Model: An Analysis of Time Required for Equilibrating Adjustment," *Review of Economic Studies*, 30 (February 1963), 16-23.

Savastano, Miguel A., "Dollarization in Latin America: Recent Evidence and Some Policy Issues," in *The Macroeconomics of International Currencies*, ed. by Paul D. Mizen and Eric J. Pentecost, E. Elgar (Aldershot: 1996).

Sawada, Yasuyuki, "Are the Heavily Indebted Countries Solvent? Tests of Intertemporal Borrowing Constraints," *Journal of Development Economics*, 45 (December 1994), 325-37.

Sekkat, Khalid, and Aristomene Varoudakis, "Exchange Rate Management and Manufactured Exports in sub-Saharan Africa," *Journal of Development Economics*, 61 (February 2000), 237-53.

Schiff, Maurice, and Alberto Valdés, "Agriculture and the Macroeconomy," in *Handbook of Agricultural Economics*, ed. by Bruce L. Gardner and Gordon C. Rausser, Elsevier (Amsterdam: 2001).

Schmidt-Hebbel, Klaus, "Does Pension Reform Really Spur Productivity, Saving, and Growth?," unpublished, Central Bank of Chile (January 1999).

Schmidt-Hebbel, Klaus, Luis Servén, and Andrés Solimano, "Saving and Investment: Paradigms, Puzzles, Policies," *World Bank Research Observer*, 11 (February 1996), 87-117.

Schmidt-Hebbel, Klaus, and Matias Tapia, "Monetary Policy Implementation and Results in Twenty Inflation-Targeting Countries," Working Paper No. 166, Central Bank of Chile (June 2002).

Schmidt-Hebbel, Klaus, and Alejandro Werner, "Inflation Targeting in Brazil, Chile, and Mexico: Performance, Credibility, and the Exchange Rate," Working Paper No. 171, Central Bank of Chile (July 2002).

Scott, Andrew, "Consumption, 'Credit Crunches' and Financial Deregulation," Discussion Paper No. 1389, CEPR (May 1996).

Seater, John, "Ricardian Equivalence," *Journal of Economic Literature*, 31 (March 1993), 142-90.

Senhadji, Abdelhak, "Time-Series Estimation of Structural Import Demand Equations: A Cross-Country Analysis," *IMF Staff Papers*, 45 (June 1998), 236-68.

Sepehri, A., S. Moshiri, and M. Doudongee, "The Foreign Exchange Constraints to Economic Adjustment: The Case of Iran," *International Review of Applied Economics*, 14 (May 2000), 235-51.

Servén, Luis, "Uncertainty, Instability, and Irreversible Investment : Theory, Evidence, and Lessons for Africa," PRE Working Paper No. 1722, World Bank (February 1997).

——, "Macroeconomic Uncertainty and Private Investment in Developing Countries," PRE Working Paper No. 2035, World Bank (December 1998).

Shapiro, Carl, and Joseph E. Stiglitz, "Equilibrium Unemployment as a Worker Discipline Device," *American Economic Review*, 74 (June 1984), 433-44.

Sharer, Robert L., Hema R. De Zoysa, and Calvin A. McDonald, *Uganda: Adjustment with Growth*, Occasional Paper No. 121, International Monetary Fund (Washington DC: 1995).

Shleifer, Andrei, and Robert W. Vishny, "Corruption," *Quarterly Journal of Economics*, 108 (August 1993), 599-618.

Shome, Parthasarathi, and Janet G. Stotsky, "Financial Transactions Taxes," *Tax Notes International*, 12 (January 1996), 47-56.

Sikken, Bernd Jan, and Jakob De Haan, "Budget Deficits, Monetization, and Central Bank Independence in Developing Countries," *Oxford Economic Papers*, 50 (July 1998), 493-511.

Skinner, Jonathan, "Risky Income, Life Cycle Consumption, and Precautionary Savings," *Journal of Monetary Economics*, 22 (September 1988), 237-55.

Södersten, Bo, *International Economics*, 2nd ed., St. Martin's Press (New York: 1980).

Solow, Robert M., "A Contribution to the Theory of Economic Growth," *Quarterly Journal of Economics*, 50 (February 1956), 65-94.

——, "Perspectives on Growth Theory," *Journal of Economic Perspectives*, 8 (Winter 1994), 45-54.

Soto, Marcelo, " Taxing Capital Flows: An Empirical Comparative Analysis," *Journal of Development Economics*, 72 (October 2003), 203-21.

Spahn, Paul B., "International Financial Flows and Transactions Taxes: Survey and Options," Working Paper No. 95/60, International Monetary Fund (June 1995).

Spaventa, Luigi, "The Growth of Public Debt," *IMF Staff Papers*, 34 (June 1987), 374-99.

Spilimbergo, Antonio, Juan Luis Londoño, and Miguel Székely, "Income Distribution, Factor Endowments, and Trade Openness," *Journal of Development Economics*, 59 (June 1999), 77-101.

Srinivasan, T. N., "Tax Evasion: A Model," *Journal of Public Economics*, 2 (November 1973), 339-46.

Standing, Guy, "Structural Adjustment and Labour Market Policies: Towards Social Adjustment?," in *Towards Social Adjustment: Labour Market Issues in Structural Adjustment*, ed. by Guy Standing and Victor Tokman, International Labor Organization (Geneva: 1991).

Stasavage, David, "The CFA Franc Zone and Fiscal Discipline," *Journal of African Economies*, 6 (March 1997), 132-67.

Stein, Ernesto, "Fiscal Decentralization and Government Size in Latin America," unpublished, Inter-American Development Bank (October 1997).

Stern, Nicholas H., "The Economics of Development: A Survey," *European Economic Review*, 99 (September 1989), 597-685.

Stiglitz, Joseph E., "Alternative Theories of Wage Determination and Unemployment in LDCs: The Labor Turnover Model," *Quarterly Journal of Economics*, 98 (May 1974), 194-227.

——, "Alternative Theories of Wage Determination and Unemployment: The Efficiency Wage Model," in *The Theory and Experience of Economic Development*, ed. by Mark Gersovitz et al., Allen and Unwin (London: 1982).

Stiglitz, Joseph E., and Andrew Weiss, "Credit Rationing in Markets with Imperfect Information," *American Economic Review*, 53 (June 1981), 393-410.

——, "Asymmetric Information in Credit Markets and Its Implications for Macroeconomics," *Oxford Economic Papers*, 44 (October 1992), 694-724.

Stotsky, Janet G., "Summary of IMF Tax Policy Advice," in *Tax Policy Handbook*, ed. by Parthasarathi Shome, International Monetary Fund (Washington, DC: 1995).

Stotsky, Janet G., and Asegedech WoldeMariam, "Tax Effort in Sub-Saharan Africa," Working Paper No. 97/107, International Monetary Fund (September 1997).

Subramanian, Arvind, "The Egyptian Stabilization Experience: An Analytical Retrospective," Working Paper No. 97./105, International Monetary Fund (September 1997).

Suyker, Wim, "Structural Budget Balances: The Method Applied by the OECD," in *Indicators of Structural Budget Balances*, ed. by Banca d'Italia (Rome: 1999).

Svensson, Jakob, "Investment, Property Rights, and Political Instability: Theory and Evidence," *European Economic Review*, 42 (July 1998), 1317-41.

——, "When Is Foreign Aid Policy Credible? Aid Dependence and Conditionality," *Journal of Development Economics*, 61 (February 2000), 61-84.

Svensson, Lars, "Fixed Exchange Rates as a Means to Price Stability: What Have We Learned?," *European Economic Review*, 38 (April 1994), 447-68.

——, "Inflation Forecast Targeting: Implementing and Monitoring Inflation Targets," *European Economic Review*, 41 (June 1997), 1111-46.

——, "Price Level Targeting vs. Inflation Targeting: A Free Lunch?," *Journal of Money, Credit, and Banking*, 31 (August 1999), 277-95.

——, "What Is Wrong with Taylor Rules? Using Judgment in Monetary Policy through Targeting Rules," *Journal of Economic Literature*, 41 (June 2003), 426-77.

Svensson, Lars, and Assaf Razin, "The Terms of Trade and the Current Account: The Harberger-Laursen-Metzler Effect," *Journal of Political Economy*, 91 (February 1983), 97-125.

Swan, Trevor W., "Economic Growth and Capital Accumulation," *Economic Record*, 32 (November 1956), 334-61.

Talvi, Ernesto, "Exchange Rate-Based Stabilization with Endogenous Fiscal Response," *Journal of Development Economics*, 54 (October 1997), 59-75.

Tanner, Evan, "Intertemporal Solvency and Indexed Debt: Evidence from Brazil," *Journal of International Money and Finance*, 14 (August 1995), 549-73.

Tanzi, Vito, "Inflation, Real Tax Revenue, and the Case for Inflationary Finance: Theory with an Application to Argentina," *IMF Staff Papers*, 25 (September 1978), 417-51.

Tanzi, Vito, Mario I. Blejer, and Mario O. Teijeiro, "Effects of Inflation on Measurement of Fiscal Deficits: Conventional versus Operational Measures," in *How to Measure the Fiscal Deficit: Analytical and Methodological Issues*, ed. by Mario I. Blejer and Adrienne Cheasty, International Monetary Fund (Washington DC: 1993).

Tanzi, Vito, and Howell H. Zee, "Fiscal Policy and Long-Run Growth," *IMF Staff Papers*, 44 (June 1997), 179-209.

Tavares, José, and Romain Wacziarg, "How Democracy Affects Growth," *European Economic Review*, 45, (August 2001), 1341-78

Taylor, John B., "Aggregate Dynamics and Staggered Contracts," *Journal of Political Economy*, 88 (February 1980), 1-23.

Taylor, Lance, *Income Distribution, Inflation and Growth*, MIT Press (Cambridge, Mass.: 1991).

——, "Gap Models," *Journal of Development Economics*, 45 (October 1994), 17-34.

Temple, Jonathan, "Equipment Investment and the Solow Model," *Oxford Economic Papers*, 50 (January 1998), 39-62.

——, "The New Growth Evidence," *Journal of Economic Literature*, 37 (March 1999), 112-56.

Ter-Minassian, Teresa, "Decentralizing Government," *Finance and Development*, 34 (September 1997), 36-39.

Ter-Minassian, Teresa, and Gerd Schwartz, "The Role of Fiscal Policy in Sustainable Stabilization: Evidence from Latin America," Working Paper No. 97/94, International Monetary Fund (August 1997).

Thanoon, Marwan, and Ahmad Z. Baharumshah, "The Road to Recovery in Malaysia: A Three-Gap Analysis," *Journal of Policy Modeling*, 25 (November 2003), 857-61.

Thirsk, Wayne, "Overview: The Substance and Process of the Reform in Eight Developing Countries," in *Tax Reform in Developing Countries*, ed. by Wayne Thirsk, World Bank (Washington DC: 1997).

Thornton, John, "Cointegration, Error Correction, and the Demand for Money in Mexico," *Weltwirtschaftliches Archives*, 132 (December 1996), 690-99.

Tobin, James, "A Proposal for International Monetary Reform," Cowles Foundation Discussion Paper No. 506, Yale University (October 1978).

Tokman, Victor, "Policies for a Heterogeneous Informal Sector in Latin America," in *Beyond Regulation: The Informal Economy in Latin America*, L. Rienner (Boulder, Col.: 1992).

Tommasi, Mariano, and Andrés Velasco, "Where Are We in the Political Economy of Reform?," *Journal of Policy Reform*, 1 (June 1996), 187-238.

Tornell, Aaron, and Andrés Velasco, "The Tragedy of the Commons and Economic Growth: Why Does Capital Flow from Poor to Rich Countries?," *Journal of Political Economy*, 100 (December 1992), 1208-31.

——, "Fiscal Discipline and the Choice of a Nominal Anchor in Stabilization," *Journal of Development Economics*, 46 (October 1998), 1-30.

——, "Fixed versus Flexible Exchange Rates: Which Provides More Fiscal Discipline?," *Journal of Monetary Economics*, 45 (April 2000), 399-436.

Torvik, Ragnar, "Learning by Doing and the Dutch Disease," *European Economic Review*, 45 (February 2001), 285-306.

Towe, Christopher, "Government Contingent Liabilities and the Measurement of Fiscal Impact," in *The Measurement of Fiscal Deficits*, ed. by Mario I. Blejer and Adrienne Cheasty, International Monetary Fund (Washington DC: 1990).

Uctum, Merih, and Michael Wickens, "Debt and Deficit Ceilings, and Sustainability of Fiscal Policies: An Intertemporal Analysis," *Oxford Bulletin of Economics and Statistics*, 62 (May 2000), 197-222.

United Nations, *Agricultural Taxation in Developing Countries*, Food and Agriculture Organization (Rome: 1993).

Upadhyay, Mukti P., "Accumulation of Human Capital in LDCs in the Presence of Unemployment," *Economica*, 61 (August 1994), 355-78.

Uribe, Martín, "Exchange-Rate-Based Inflation Stabilization: The Initial Real Effects of Credible Plans," *Journal of Monetary Economics*, 39 (July 1997a), 197-221.

——, "Hysteresis in a Simple Model of Currency Substitution," *Journal of Monetary Economics*, 39 (July 1997b), 197–221.

Valdés-Prieto, Salvador, "Financial Liberalization and the Capital Account: Chile, 1974-84," in *Financial Reform: Theory and Experience*, ed. by Gerard Caprio, Jr., Izak Atiyas, and James A. Hanson, Cambridge University Press (Cambridge: 1994).

van Gompel, J., "Stabilization with Wage Indexation and Exchange Rate Flexibility," *Journal of Economic Surveys*, 8 (September 1994), 252-81.

van Wijnbergen, Sweder, "Exchange Rate Management and Stabilization Policies in Developing Countries," *Journal of Development Economics*, 23 (October 1986), 227-47.

——, "Aid, Export Promotion and the Real Exchange Rate: An African Dilemma?," Discussion Paper No. 199, World Bank (Washington DC: 1996).

Varian, Hal R., *Microeconomic Analysis*, W. W. Norton and Co. (New York: 1992).

Végh, Carlos A., "Government Spending and Inflationary Finance," *IMF Staff Papers*, 46 (September 1989), 657-77.

——, "Stopping High Inflation: An Analytical Overview," *IMF Staff Papers*, 39 (September 1992), 626-95.

Veidyanathan, Geetha, "Consumption, Liquidity Constraints and Economic Development," *Journal of Macroeconomics*, 15 (Summer 1993), 591-610.

Veiga, Francisco J., "What Causes the Failure of Inflation Stabilization Plans?," *Journal of International Money and Finance*, 18 (April 1999), 169-94.

Velasco, Andrés, "When are Fixed Exchange Rates Really Fixed?," *Journal of Development Economics*, 54 (October 1997a), 5-25.

——, "A Model of Endogenous Fiscal Deficits and Delayed Fiscal Reforms," Working Paper No. 6336, National Bureau of Economic Research (December 1997b).

Villanueva, Delano, "Openness, Human Development, and Fiscal Policies: Effects on Economic Growth and Speed of Adjustment," *IMF Staff Papers*, 41 (March 1994), 1-29.

Viner, Jacob, *The Customs Union Issue*, Cargenie Endowment for International Peace (New York: 1950).

Vousden, Neil, *The Economics of Trade Protection*, Cambridge University Press (Cambridge: 1990).

Warner, Andrew, "Did the Debt Crisis Cause the Investment Crisis?," *Quarterly Journal of Economics*, 98 (June 1993), 1161-86.

Wei, Shang-Jin, "Gradualism versus Big Bang: Speed and Sustainability of Reforms," in *The Political Economy of Reform*, ed. by Federico Sturzenegger and Mariano Tommasi, MIT Press (Cambridge, Mass.: 1998).

Welch, John H., and Darryl McLeod, "The Costs and Benefits of Fixed Dollar Exchange Rates in Latin America," *Economic Review*, Federal Reserve Bank of Dallas, No. 1 (March 1993), 31-44.

Wette, Hildegard, "Collateral in Credit Rationing in Markets with Imperfect Information," *American Economic Review*, 73 (June 1983), 442-45.

White, Howard, "The Macroeconomic Impact of Development Aid: A Critical Survey," *Journal of Development Studies*, 28 (January 1992), 163-240.

Williamson, John, and Stephan Haggard, "The Political Conditions for Economic Reform," in *The Political Economy of Economic Reform*, ed. by John Williamson, Institute for International Economics (Washington DC: 1994).

Williamson, John, and Molly Mahar, *A Survey of Financial Liberalization*, Essay in International Finance No. 211, Princeton University (November 1998).

Williamson, Stephen D., "Costly Monitoring, Financial Intermediation, and Equilibrium Credit Rationing," *Journal of Monetary Economics*, 18 (September 1986), 159-79.

Willman, Alpo, "The Collapse of the Fixed Exchange Rate Regime with Sticky Wages and Imperfect Substitutability between Domestic and Foreign Bonds," *European Economic Review* 32 (November 1988), 1817-38.

Wilson, Peter, "Exchange Rates and the Trade Balance for Dynamic Asian Economies: Does the J-Curve Exist for Singapore, Malaysia, and Korea?," *Open Economies Reviews*, 12 (June 2001), 389-413.

Winters, L. Alan, "Trade Liberalisation and Economic Peformance: An Overview," *Economic Journal*, 114 (February 2004), 4-21.

Wirjanto, Tony S., "Aggregate Consumption Behavior and Liquidity Constraints: The Canadian Evidence," *Canadian Journal of Economics*, 28 (November 1995), 1135-52.

Wolfson, Michael, "Diverging Inequalities," *American Economic Review*, 84 (May 1994), 353-58.

World Bank, *The East Asian Miracle*, Oxford University Press (Oxford: 1993).

——, *Adjustment in Africa: Reforms, Results, and the Road Ahead*, Ocford University Press (Oxford: 1994).

——, *Private Capital Flows to Developing Countries: The Road to Financial Integration*, Oxford University Press (New York: 1997a).

——, "RMSM-X: User's Guide," unpublished, Development Data Group, World Bank (July 1997*b*).

——, *Assessing Aid: What Works, What Doesn't, and Why*, Oxford University Press (New York: 1998).

——, *MENA's Employment Challenge in the 21st Century: From Labor Force Growth to Job Creation*, World Bank (Washington DC: 2003).

Wynne, Mark A., "Core Inflation: A Review of Some Conceptual Issues," in *Measures of Underlying Inflation and Their Role in the Conduct of Monetary Policy*, Bank for International Settlements (Basel: 1999).

Wyplosz, Charles, "After the Honeymoon: On the Economics and the Politics of Economic Transformation," *European Economic Review*, 37 (April 1993), 379-86.

——, "Fiscal Policy: Institutions versus Rules," Discussion Paper No. 3238, Centre for Economic Policy Research (March 2002).

Yanikkaya, Halit, "Trade Openness and Economic Growth: A Cross-Country Empirical Investigation," *Journal of Development Economics*, 72 (October 2003), 57-89.

Yano, Makoto, and Jeffrey B. Nugent, "Aid, Nontraded Goods, and the Transfer Paradox in Small Economies," *American Economic Review*, 89 (June 1999), 431-44.

Yeats, Alexander J., "Does Mercosur's Trade Performance Raise Concerns about the Effects of Regional Trade Arrangements?," PRE Working Paper No. 1729, World Bank (February 1997).

——, "What Can Be Expected from African Regional Trade Arrangements? Some Empirical Evidence," PRE Working Paper No. 2004, World Bank (November 1998).

Yilmaz, Akyuz, and Korkut Boratav, "The Making of the Turkish Financial Crisis," *World Development*, 31 (September 2003), 1549-66.

Yitzhaki, Shlomo, "A Note on Income Tax Evasion: A Theoretical Analysis," *Journal of Public Economics*, 3 (May 1974), 201-02.

Young, Alwyn, "The Tyranny of Numbers: Confronting the Statistical Realities of the East Asian Growth Experience," *Quarterly Journal of Economics*, 110 (August 1995), 641–80.

Zagler, Martin, and Georg Durnecker, "Fiscal Policy and Economic Growth," *Journal of Economic Surveys*, 17 (July 2003), 397-418.

Zee, Howell, "Sustainability and Optimality of Government Debt," *IMF Staff Papers*, 35 (December 1988), 658-85.

——, "Taxation and Efficiency," in *Tax Policy Handbook*, ed. by Parthasarathi Shome, International Monetary Fund (Washington, DC: 1995).

Zeira, Joseph, "Cost Uncertainty and the Rate of Investment," *Journal of Economic Dynamics and Control*, 14 (February 1990), 53-63.

Zhang, Jie, "Optimal Public Investments in Education and Endogenous Growth," *Scandinavian Journal of Economics*, 98 (September 1996), 387-404.

Figure Credits

2.2   Adapted with the permission of Cambridge University Press from Angus Deaton, "Saving and Growth," in *The Economics of Saving and Growth,* ed. Klaus Schmidt-Hebbel, Luis Servén, and Joseph Stiglitz (Cambridge, 1999), 42.

4.4   Adapted with the permission of the American Economic Association from Joseph E. Stiglitz and Andrew Weiss, "Credit Rationing in Markets with Imperfect Economics," *American Economic Review,* 53 (June 1981), 397.

8.2   Adapted with the permission of Springer-Verlag from Maurice Obstfeld, "The Logic of Currency Crises," in *Monetary and Fiscal Policy in an Integrated Europe,* ed. Barry Eichengreen, Jeffrey Frieden, and Jürgen von Hagen, copyright 1995.

9.1   Adapted with the permission of Elsevier from the *Journal of Development Economics,* vol. 32, no. 1, Mohsin S. Khan, Peter J. Montiel, and Nadeem U. Haque, "Adjustment with Growth: Relating the Analytical Approaches of the IMF and World Bank," 161, copyright 1990.

9.5   Adapted with the permission of Elsevier from the *Journal of Development Economics,* vol. 32, no. 2, Edmar L. Bacha, "A Three-Gap Model of Foreign Transfers and the GDP Growth Rate in Developing Countries," 291, copyright 1990.

9.6 and 9.7   Adapted with the permission of Cambridge University Press from Shantayanan Devarajan, Delfin S. Go, Jeffrey D. Lewis, Sherman Robinson, and Pekka Sinko, "Simple General Equilibrium Modeling," in *Applied Methods for Trade Policy Analysis: A Handbook,* ed. Joseph F. Françoise and Kenneth A. Reinert (Cambridge, 1997), 164, 167.

11.4   Adapted from E. Burmeister and A. Dobell, *Mathematical Theories of Economic Growth* (New York: Macmillan, 1970), 37.

12.1 and 12.2 Adapted with the permission of the International Monetary Fund from Delano Villanueva, "Openness, Human Development, and Fiscal Policies: Effects on Economic Growth and Speed of Adjustment," *IMF Staff Papers,* 41 (March 1994), 8, 11, 13.

16.1–16.4 Adapted with the permission of Blackwell Publishing from Karl R. Pedersen, "Aid, Investment, and Incentives," *Scandinavian Journal of Economics,* 98 (September 1996), 428, 431.

17.2 Reprinted with the permission of Elsevier from the *European Economic Review,* vol. 37, nos. 2–3, Charles Wyplosz, "After the Honeymoon: On the Economics and the Politics of Economic Transformation," 383, copyright 1993.

Index

Abel, A. B., 59

Abraham, K., 575

Absorption, 18–19; 1–2–3 model and, 399; RMSM-X model and, 380–389

Abugri, B. A., 157

Accountability, 152

Accounts, activity, 23

Accounts, aggregate, 2, 88, 124; absorption and, 18–19; accounting matrices for, 10–14, 23–27; balance sheet and, 21; budget constraints and, 18–22; capital inflows and, 253, 279 (*see also* Capital inflows); deficit rules and, 92; Diamond-Dybvig model and, 328–330; dollarization and, 155–157; exchange rate effects and, 136–137; feedback effects and, 132; financial crises and, 293–312 (*see also* Financial crises); fiscal imbalance and, 93; GDP and, 18–19; government and, 14–15, 17, 19–20; growth accounting and, 511–515, 541, 545–546; human capital and, 503 (*see also* Capital, human); inflation targeting and, 141–154; interest rate effects and, 135–136; investment and, 62 (*see also* Investment); Marshall-Lerner condition and, 193–194; Obstfeld model and, 301–312; 1–2–3 model and, 394–405; policy transmission effects and, 130–141; savings and, 15–16, 22

Accounts, commodity, 23

Accounts, factor, 25

Accounts, production, 23

Accounts, rest-of-the-world, 25–26

Adam, C., 79, 405n27, 622n2

Ades, A., 515n3

Adjustment, 1–2, 4, 8–9; asymmetric costs and, 59; capital inflows and, 278; civil service reform and, 592–594; constant of integration and, 455–456; decentralization and, 594–595; expenditure control and, 591–592; financial intermediation and, 118–121; foreign debt and, 632–637; gradualism and, 229; half-life and, 454; incentives structure and, 654–655; lags and, 405–406; learning by doing and, 464–471, 633–634; Obstfeld model and, 301–312; political economy and, 653–654, 665–677; prices and, 218 (*see also* Prices); ratio of, 471; Solow-Swan model and, 453–456; specification bias and, 64; speed of, 453–456, 460–462; spurious correlation and, 64; stabilization and, 654–655; taxes and, 89, 583–591; Taylor series for, 461; trade balance and, 188–196

Ad valorem tariffs, 549, 551, 553

Adverse incentive effect, 126

Africa, 8, 29, 569; capital inflows and, 248; commodity prices and, 106–107; inflation and, 153; investment and, 64; monetary policy and, 124; regression coefficients and, 65–67; savings and, 50

Age, 50, 67; life-cycle model and, 33–40

Agell, J., 188

Agénor, P.-R., 431; analysis tools and, 361n1, 362; capital inflows and, 255, 282, 290n36; consumption and, 46, 49; debt and, 86;